Antarctica is both a continent and an ocean. The continent is inextricably linked to the vast extent of the Southern Ocean surrounding it, an ocean which supports a teaming array of life, ranging from microscopic plants which form part of the phytoplankton responsible for primary production, to the mighty whales, our largest marine mammals. Whilst our knowledge of the biology of these waters has been accumulating since the first voyages of discovery in the eighteenth century, there is yet to be a comprehensive, single-author synthesis of the current state of that knowledge. This book sets out to correct that deficiency.

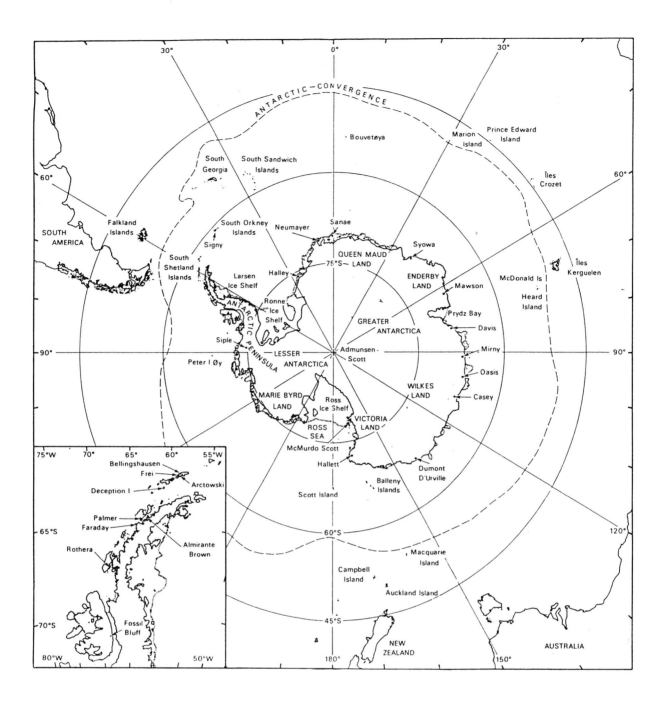

The biology of the Southern Ocean

The biology of the Southern Ocean

GEORGE A. KNOX

Zoology Department, University of Canterbury, Christchurch, New Zealand

Published by the Press Syndicate of the University of Cambridge
The Pitt Building, Trumpington Street, Cambridge CB2 1RP
40 West 20th Street, New York, NY 10011–4211, USA
10 Stamford Road, Oakleigh, Melbourne 3166, Australia

First published 1994

Printed in Great Britain at the University Press, Cambridge

A catalogue record for this book is available from the British Library

Library of Congress cataloguing in publication data

Knox, G. A.
The biology of the Southern Ocean/George A. Knox.
p. cm.—(Studies in polar research)
Includes bibliographical references.
ISBN 0 521 32211 1
1.   Marine ecology – Antarctic Ocean. 2.   Biotic communities –
Antarctic Ocean. 3.   Ecosystem management – Antarctic Ocean.
I. Title.   II. Series
QH95.58.K58 1994
574.92'4—dc20 93-28273 CIP

ISBN 0 521 32211 1 hardback

TAG

To my Antarctic students and associates.

Contents

Preface

Our knowledge of the biology of the seas surrounding Antarctica began with the descriptions and specimens brought back by the early naturalists on voyages of discovery to the Southern Ocean. Prominent among these were the early French navigators such as Bouvet de Lozier who discovered Bouvet Island in 1739, and Yves Joseph de Kerguelen-Tremarez who discovered the island which bears his name some 30 years later. These were followed by the voyages of Captain Cook, who in 1772 reached 71° 10′ S in the Bellingshausen Sea. In 1819 the Russian explorer Admiral Bellingshausen was the first to tow a net at the stern of his ship and found that it collected more organisms at night than during the day. He probably was the first to collect the Antarctic krill, *Euphausia superba*. The first serious scientific marine research was carried out by James Eights who sailed in 1829 with the American sealing captains Palmer and Pendleton. Eights described the natural history of the South Shetland Islands and his best known discovery was that of a ten-legged pycnogonid. Soon after there followed a series of national expeditions led by Durmont d'Urville of France (1837–40), Charles Wilkes of the United States (1838–42) and Sir James Clark Ross of Britain (1839–43). Among the naturalists who accompanied these expeditions the most notable were J. D. Dana on the Wilke's Expedition and J. D. Hooker on the Ross Expedition. These expeditions all made extensive collections of marine organisms.

There was a renewal of Antarctic exploration at the end of the nineteenth century beginning with the voyages in 1872–76. Major expeditions included the British (1899–1900), the Belgian (1898), the Swedish National Expedition (1902–04), the Scottish National Antarctic Expedition (1902–04), the German expedition (1901–03) in the *Gauss*, and the French expeditions in the *Français* (1903–05) and the *Pourquoi Pas* (1908–10). All these expeditions resulted in taxonomic studies which laid the foundation for later studies of the marine flora and fauna.

Ecological studies in the Southern Ocean began with the work of the naturalists attached to land-based over-wintering parties, such as those of Sir Ernest Shackleton's 1907–9 expedition and Captain Scott's two polar expeditions. Antarctic studies received a tremendous impetus from the investigations which began in 1925 with the study of whale carcasses at the whaling station at Grytviken in South Georgia. The work of the scientists expanded to include not only studies on whale demography and ecology, but of the physical, chemical and biological oceanography of the Southern Ocean in order to gain an understanding of the factors influencing the distribution, reproduction and growth of whale stocks. These investigations contributed the first long-term studies of the Antarctic pelagic ecosystem, and they were the first which extended right round the Antarctic continent. The voluminous reports which resulted laid an indispensable foundation for subsequent studies.

Southern Ocean marine research entered a new phase following the establishment in 1957 of the Special (later the Scientific) Committee on Antarctic Research (SCAR). This initiated the modern era of Southern Ocean research in which national programmes were initiated by many countries, notably the Soviet Antarctic Expeditions in the *Vitez* and the *Ob* and the United States *Eltanin* cruises. Other countries, especially, Great Britain, France, South Africa, Chile, Argentina and Japan were also very active during this period. In 1972 a coordinated international research programme was initiated with the establishment of the BIOMASS (Biological Investigation of Antarctic Systems and Stocks) Programme.

My own involvement with Antarctic research began with a visit to McMurdo Sound in 1960 where one of my staff in the Department of Zoology, University of Canterbury, Dr. Bernard Stonehouse, was initiating a research programme on Adélie Penguins and McCormick Skuas. This led to the establishment of the University of Canterbury Antarctic Research Unit (Knox, 1986, 1988) which carried out continuous summer research in the McMurdo Sound region over the period 1960–83, and over the last 12 years I was director of the unit. In the summer of 1969–70 I initiated an inshore marine research programme which continued until the 1982–83 season. Throughout the operation of the unit some 60 research students participated in the research programme. Interaction with these enthusiastic young minds had a significant influence on many of the concepts developed in this book. I also have had the good fortune to become involved in international Antarctic science activities, firstly as a member and secretary of the SCAR Working Group on Biology and as a member of SCAR since 1969. I was also a member of the Group of Specialists on the Living Resources of the Southern Ocean from its inception and I attended the first two meeting of CCAMLR as the SCAR observer. These activities brought me into contact with a wide range of Antarctic scientists from all SCAR countries.

The book commences with a description of the physico-chemical environment and then follows a logical sequence covering phytoplankton and primary production, the sea ice microbial community and the secondary consumers, the zooplankton. There is an extended chapter on the biology and ecology of Antarctic krill in view of its central position in the Southern Ocean food web. In addition krill have been the subject of intensive research programmes over the past two decades, especially during the BIO-MASS Programme. A series of chapters considers the higher consumers, nekton (with an emphasis on cephalopods), fish, seals, whales and seabirds. Then follows a series of chapters on selected ecosystems: the benthic communities, life beneath the fast ice and ice shelves, marginal ice edge processes, recent advances in understanding decomposition process and the roles of bacteria and protozoa. These are followed by an attempt at a synthesis of ecosystem dynamics with an emphasis on the pelagic ecosystem. The following three chapters deal with resource exploitation, the impact of such exploitation on the marine ecosystem of the Southern Ocean, and the problems involved in the management of the living resources.

The suggestion for this book was made by Dr. Bernard Stonehouse and without his encouragement it would not have been written. Discussions with Antarctic colleagues throughout the SCAR community have had a profound influence on the concepts developed in this book. Amongst these I would particularly wish to thank Professor S. Z. El-Sayed, the late Sir George Deacon, Professor A. L. DeVries, Dr. M. Fukuchi, Dr. M. Holdgate, Professor T. Hoshiai, Dr. J. C. Hureau, Dr. K. R. Kerry, Dr. J. K. Lowry, Dr. Y. Naito, the late Dr. T.

Nemoto, Dr. B. Oliver, Dr. B. Stonehouse, Dr. J. Warham, Dr. Watanabe, and Professor E.C. Young. Access to literature was greatly facilitated by periods spent in the libraries of the British Antarctic Survey and the National Institute of Polar Research, Tokyo. I am indebted to the directors of these institutes, Dr. R. M. Laws, Dr. D. Drewry and Professor T. Hoshiai and their librarians for the assistance provided. A number of people have reviewed or made helpful comments on various chapter drafts, in particular Professor S. Z. El-Sayed. Dr. L. Greenfield, and Professor C. Sullivan. Dr. D. W. H. Walton reviewed all of the chapters in various drafts and I am very grateful for his assistance and encouragement throughout the writing of this book. I would also like to thank Dr. Maria Murphy and the staff of Cambridge University Press for their patience and support during the preparation of this volume and for seeing the project through to completion. Any errors which remain are the author's responsibility and I would appreciate it if any reader cares to point them out.

As it can be seen by the reference list at the end of this book, there is a considerable body of recent literature on the ecology of the Southern Ocean. Because of this growing volume of published research I have had to be selective in the material which has been included. Examples have been carefully chosen from the pool of published research to illustrate the concepts discussed. There are doubtless others which could have been used and I apologise to authors whose work has not been included.

This book is an attempt to synthesize the available information into a coherent account on one of the most fascinating systems on the globe. Its preparation has been greatly facilitated by the published volumes of the five symposia which have been held on Antarctic biology, Volume Two of *Antarctic Ecology* edited by R. M. Laws, and the reviews of Southern Ocean fish and krill in the BIOMASS Scientific Series.

I hope that this book will prove useful to advanced undergraduates, graduate students and to professionals engaged in Antarctic marine research, as well as to all those interested in, or involved in, Antarctic conservation and management. It will also have been worthwhile if it stimulates others to work on some of the fascinating aspects of Antarctic marine research which have been discussed.

1

The Southern Ocean

1.1 Introduction

Over the past two decades in particular there has been an increasing emphasis on integrated studies of the Southern Ocean (Fig. 1.1) aimed at understanding what has been called 'the Antarctic or Southern Ocean ecosystem'. While the Southern Ocean can be considered a system, in reality it is a series of interconnected ecosystems. These will be discussed in subsequent chapters. Descriptions of the Southern Ocean system have been given by several workers over the years (Hart, 1942; Baker, 1954; Currie, 1964; Holdgate, 1967, 1970; Knox, 1970, 1983; Hedgpeth, 1977; Everson, 1977a, 1984c; Bengtson, 1978, 1984; Tranter, 1982; G. Hempel, 1985a,b, 1987).

The living resources of the of the Southern Ocean and their past and future exploitation were reviewed by the SCAR/SCOR Group of Specialists on the Living Resources of the Southern Ocean (El-Sayed, 1977, 1981); they have been the subject of numerous reviews: Everson (1977b), Bengston (1978, 1985), Knox (1983, 1984), Anon. (USSR) (1984a,b). The physical structure of the system has been described by Deacon (1937, 1982, 1984b), Brodie (1965), Gordon & Goldberg (1970), Gordon (1967, 1983), Gordon et al. (1978), Amos (1984), Forster (1981, 1984), Gordon & Molinelli (1982), Gordon & Owens (1987) and Squire (1987) and Foldvik & Gammelsrød (1988). Environmental data for the Southern Ocean is available from a variety of sources. Some of the most valuable are the *Discovery Reports*. The Soviet *Atlas of Antarctica* (Maksimov, 1966), the U.S. Navy Hydrographic Office *Oceanographic Atlas of the Polar Seas*, the U.S. National Center for Atmospheric Research *Climate of the Upper Air: Southern Hemisphere* , Taljaard et al. (1969, 1971) and the *American Geophysical Union Antarctic Research Series* (1964–) are useful sources. The interlinking of the biological and physical components of the system have recently been discussed by Lubimova et al. (1973, 1980), Deacon (1982), Tranter (1982) and Lubimova (1982, 1983).

Hedgpeth (1977) points out that the Southern Ocean is 'a rich, apparently high productive plankton–pelagic system supporting (at least in the past) great populations of whales and millions of penguins, fishes and seals, and abundant intermediate populations of fishes and cephalopods, depending on the near surface productivity'. Amongst the characteristics of the Southern Ocean are:

1. It is a large system; indeed probably the largest marine ecosystem on the globe.
2. It is semi-enclosed, especially in the overlying water masses, and the Antarctic Convergence forms a distinct northern boundary.
3. It is an old system with a long evolutionary history (Knox & Lowry, 1977). The main circulation patterns and water mass distributions were established at least 20 million years ago (Knox, 1980).
4. Most of the major taxonomic components are circumpolar in distribution. The principal variation is that of productivity which is greater in certain regions than in others.
5. The quantitative and qualitative features of the basic processes of the Southern Ocean system are obviously different from those of other oceanic systems, as demonstrated by the distribution of the dominant herbivore and key species of the system, *Euphausia superba*.

1.2 The evolution of the Southern Ocean

The unique characteristics of the Southern Ocean are the result of a long evolutionary history that can only be understood within a palaeo-geographic framework of continental drift, plate tectonics and polar wandering (Norton & Slater, 1979; Kennett, 1983; Knox, 1979, 1980; Elliot, 1985). Kennett (1977) has provided a detailed synthesis of the information concerning the evolution and palaeooceanography of the Southern Ocean, while Kemp (1978) has discussed the broad trends in climate since the Palaeocene.

A summary of the major events in this evolution follows. During the Cretaceous period equatorial seas extended almost uninterrupted throughout the globe (Frakes & Kemp, 1972). In the Southern Hemisphere, Antarctica, then a part of Gondwanaland, was very close to its present position near the rotational pole, but with

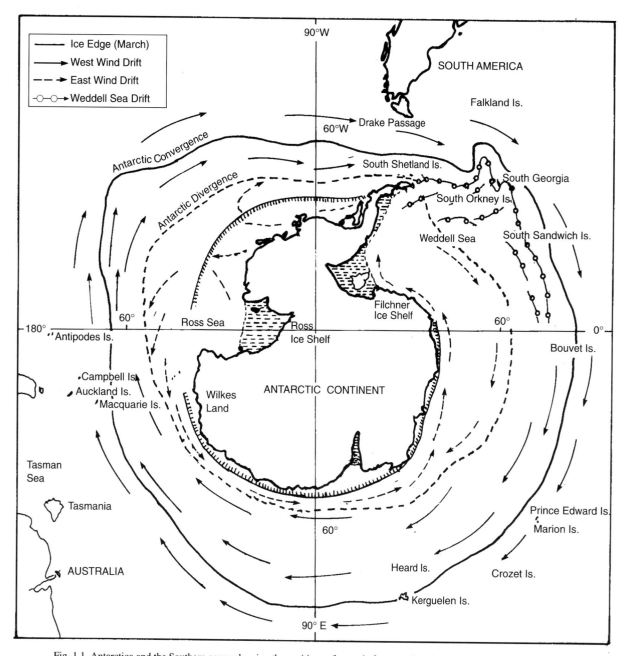

Fig. 1.1. Antarctica and the Southern ocean showing the positions of oceanic fronts and surface currents. Redrawn from Knox (1983).

South America, New Zealand and Australia attached (Fig. 1.2). New Zealand separated from Australia and Antarctica in the Cretaceous, 60 to 80 million years before present (my BP). By the late Palaeocene (53 my BP) the Tasman Sea had formed and Australia had begun to separate from Antarctica. However, the South Tasman Rise, which is of continental origin, was still part of Victoria Land, and because of this no major current system could develop between Australia and Antarctica. Frakes & Kemp (1972) postulated that during the Eocene large oceanic gyres extended from the equator to high latitudes and brought warm water to the Antarctic coastline. Their reconstructed palaeotemperatures at 60° latitude are 24 °C

for the Queen Maude Coast, 17 °C for the shallow sea between Australia and Antarctica, and 7 °C for the attached South America–Antarctic Peninsula coastline.

In the Late Eocene–Early Oligocene (39 my BP) major changes began to occur which transformed the global warm climate into the modern climate regime of today. At that time there was a dramatic lowering of austral temperatures. This resulted in near-freezing surface coastal waters along the Antarctic coastline, which probably caused sealevel glaciation around the continent, and the formation of cold Antarctic Bottom Water. Associated with the development of the thermoclinal circulation system was an increase in the calcium carbonate compensa-

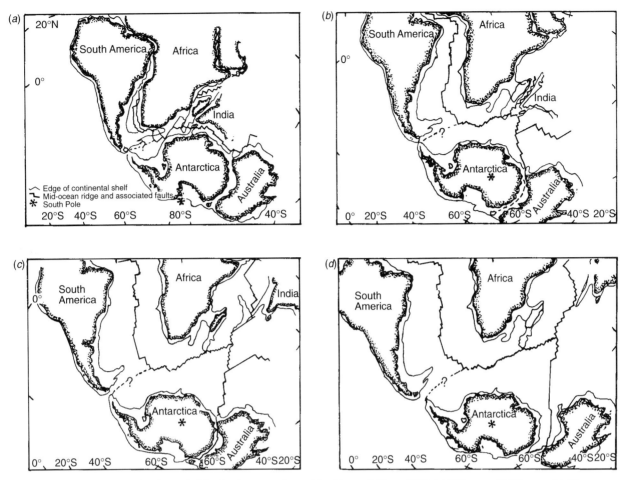

Fig. 1.2. Stages in the dispersal of the Gondwana continents (after Norton & Slater, 1979). (*a*) 115 my BP, (*b*) 80 my BP, (*c*) 53 my BP, (*d*) 39 my BP. No account is taken of the possibility of rearrangement of West Antarctica. Note that only a very limited separation of Australia and Antarctica had occurred by 53 my BP, and also that South America and the Antarctic Peninsula were most likely still abutting each other at 39 my BP. The position of the South Pole is that inferred for the time given in each diagram. Redrawn from Elliot (1985).

tion depth (CCD) (Heath, 1969; Van Andel & Moore, 1974). Evidence from sediment microfossils (foraminiferans, diatoms and radiolarians) indicated a marked change to a cold water biota (Margolis & Kennett, 1970; Jenkins, 1974).

In the Late Oligocene (25–28 my BP) the South Tasman Rise finally separated from Victoria Land sufficient to allow the formation of the Antarctic Circumpolar Current (West Wind Drift) (Fig. 1.1). The Drake Passage had formed some time between the initial separation of Australia from Antarctica and the final separation of the Tasman Rise (Kennett *et al.*, 1975). In the Early Miocene (22 my bp) the Antarctic Convergence formed, producing a major biological barrier which is still operating today. Large ice sheets developed rapidly in the East Antarctic during the middle Miocene. Dell & Fleming (1975), using fossil molluscan evidence, suggested that the sheltered rocky coastlines of the Ross Sea were, at that time, probably ice-free and kelp-fringed, not unlike Tierra del Fuego today. By the Late Miocene–Early Pliocene the West

Antarctic ice sheet had formed and was much thicker than it is today (Shackleton & Kennett, 1975). During this time the production of siliceous phytoplankton steadily increased. Hays (1969) observed two intervals of distinct cooling at 2.5 and 0.7 my BP, and climatic oscillations during the last 3.5 million years, with a steadily increasing coolness up to the present time.

1.3 Bathymetry

The bathymetry of the Southern Ocean is shown in Fig. 1.3. Three deep-water basins (4000–6500 m deep) surround the Antarctic continent: the Atlantic–Indian Basin, the Indian–Antarctic Basin and the Pacific–Antarctic Basin. These basins are partially bounded on the north by a series of ridges or rises: the Scotia Ridge and the Atlantic Indian Ridge, the Southeast Indian Ridge and the Pacific Atlantic Ridge respectively. These ridges and the Kerguelen Plateau tend to restrict the free flow of bottom water and in some areas they even deflect surface currents. The Drake Passage between South America and the

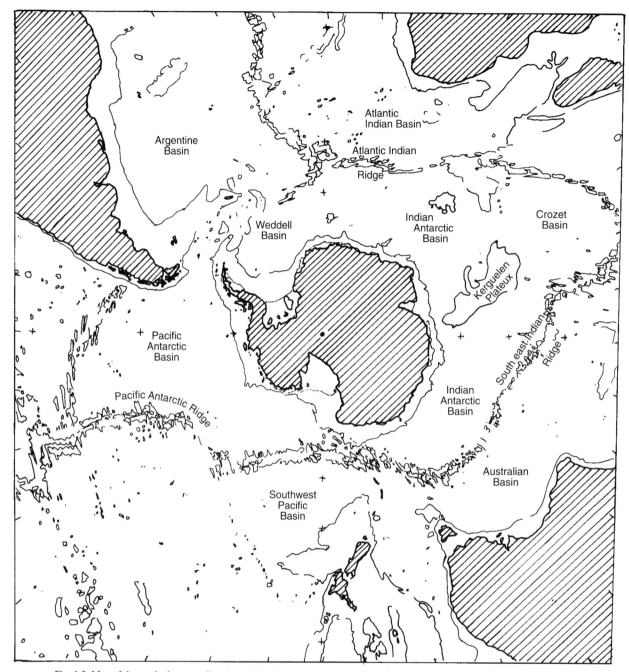

Fig. 1.3. Map of the sea bed surrounding Antarctica showing the principal deep-water basins and submarine ridges. Redrawn from Squire (1987).

Antarctic Peninsula restricts the circulation of the water masses and, as discussed later, it has a profound effect on the circulation in the Southern Ocean.

The continental shelf that surrounds Antarctica differs from that surrounding other continents in that it is unusually deep, with the 'shelf-break' (the transition between the continental shelf and the continental slope) lying two to four times deeper than in other oceanic regions. This is partly due to the isostatic equilibrium adjustment of the continent to the large mass of the Antarctic ice sheets. Both the Weddell Sea and the Ross Sea are characterized by broad ice shelves, the Filchner and Ronne Ice Shelves and the Ross Ice Shelf respectively. These shelves as we shall see profoundly influence the nearshore circulation and water properties.

1.4 Climate

1.4.1 Wind

A ring of low pressure surrounds the high Antarctic continental plateau, while a belt of tropical anti-cyclones lies to the north. Winds in the Southern Ocean blow towards the trough of low pressure, but they are directed to the left by the earth's rotation (Coriolis effect). As a result the Southern Ocean between about 38° S in the winter and 38–39° S in the summer, and the trough experience a regime of strong easterly winds. The westerlies within this circumpolar belt are quite strong, with maximum intensity in the region of the Antarctic Circumpolar Current (ACC) (see Fig. 1.6). It is this wind field that drives the Southern Ocean circulation. Superimposed on this westerly circulation are northwest–southeast moving depressions.

Over the Antarctic continent itself katabatic winds dominate the weather system. These winds, driven by very cold and dense air flowing down the glaciers and ice streams of the ice cap, can often reach very high velocities, and they are responsible for the strong southeast–northwest winds extending many kilometres from the coast out to sea. Near the peri-Antarctic trough of low pressure there is a belt of easterly winds.

To summarize, the prevailing wind system of the Southern Ocean comprises three main elements: a southeasterly component near the coast, a zone of easterly flow encircling the continent and extending north to about 65° S, and a wide zone of westerlies reaching as far north as 35° S (Squire, 1987). This zonal circulation pattern is more intense and constant than in any other region of the globe.

1.4.2 Temperature

The Southern Ocean is a cold ocean. Across the Antarctic convergence zone the temperature range in the summer is from 4 to 8 °C, and in the winter from 1 to 3 °C. Surface water immediately south of the Convergence have an average temperature of about 1 to 2 °C in the winter and 3 to 5 °C in the summer, while further south near the continent temperatures range from only about –1.0 to –1.9 °C. Temperature differences between cold surface and bottom layers and intermediate warmer layers is less than 5 °C; thus the total annual range throughout does not exceed 4–5 °C and is considerably less for the greater part of the area, e.g. in McMurdo Sound temperatures range seasonally only from –1.7 to –1.9 °C.

1.4.3 Solar radiation

In the far south near the continent the alternation between total darkness for half of the year and continuous daylight for the other half imposes a seasonal light regime in contrast to the diurnal cycles of lower latitudes. In addition, the amount of light penetrating the surface waters of the ocean is determined not only by its intensity, angle of incidence, surface reflection (up to 50% according to data given by El-Sayed (1967) for Marguerite Bay in February, 1965), and absorption by suspended particles, but also by the presence of sea ice and snow cover (see

section 2.7.5). It is also influenced by the transparency of the atmosphere. Anti-cyclonic conditions near the coast result in skies that are often lightly cloudy or clear. In the region of the ACC there is a continuous passage of low pressure systems and a predominance of cloudy weather resulting in insolation lower in this region relative to areas close to the continent (Holm-Hansen *et al.*, 1977).

Oceanic waters round Antarctica are typically blue and highly transparent with a maximum Secchi depth (the depth at which a standard Secchi disc becomes invisible) of about 40 m (Slawyk, 1979). The 1% light level is relatively deep at about 100 m. Tilzer *et al.* (1985) attribute the low concentrations of dissolved organic compounds and the low abiotic turbidity to the very low terrestrial input, of sediment and organic matter.

1.5 Ice cover

1.5.1 Seasonal variation

One of the salient characteristics of the Southern Ocean is the dramatic changes which occur in sea ice cover, from about 20×10^6 km^2 in late winter to about 4×10^6 km^2 in late summer (Zwally *et al.*, 1983a; Comiso & Zwally, 1984). The ways in which the sea ice forms and decays and the characteristics of the different types of sea ice are considered in section 3.2. While the general distribution of the sea ice has been known for many years from scattered ship observations, it is only comparatively recently that continuous year-round observations have been available from satellite imagery, thus enabling the detailed changes over the year and year-to-year variations to be documented.

Fig. 1.4 illustrates the growth and decay of the sea ice in the Southern Ocean. The months of minimum extent are February and March while those of maximum extent are September and October. The northern limit of the ice changes by no more than a few degrees from year to year. May and June are the months of the most rapid advance of the ice edge, when it moves northwards at a rate of 4.2 million km^2 per month; November and December are the months of the most rapid retreat when the ice edge recedes at 6.9 million km^2 per month (Squire, 1987). The average rates of advance and retreat are respectively 2.4 and 3.3 million km^2 per month. At the minimum extent scattered areas along the Antarctic coast retain some ice coverage. Most of this ice is found in the eastern Weddell Sea and the Bellingshausen–Amundsen Sea sector. No ice is found north of the Ross Ice Shelf at this time. Round the margins of the continent areas of unbroken fast ice (ice attached to the shore) may persist for two or more years forming thick multi-year ice. This is in contrast to the pack ice (drifting ice floes) zone of annual sea ice, which is 1–2 m in thickness. The distribution of ice in the pack

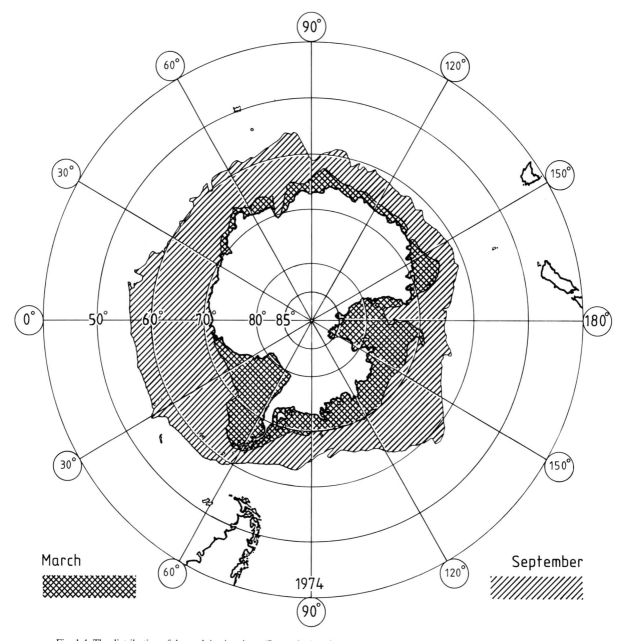

Fig. 1.4. The distribution of the pack ice in winter (September) and summer (March). Redrawn from Knox (1984); after Tranter (1982).

ice zone is highly variable as the ice cover is frequently broken-up by storms and the resulting floes drift considerable distances driven by surface currents and wind. Leads of open water (open channels in the ice) within the pack ice are highly variable.

Polynas: Satellite imagery has shown that large areas of open water (polynas) may occur and persist throughout the winter. Some of these polynas form from floe leads along the coast of Antarctica when offshore katabatic winds (downflowing air cooled by radiation) are sufficiently strong and persistent. The best known polyna is a large ice-free region in the area of the Maud Rise in the Weddell Sea, referred to as the Weddell Polyna (Carsey,

1980; Comiso & Sullivan, 1986). This polyna is maintained by deep-ocean convection (Gordon, 1982) and is regarded as a sensible heat polyna. Shorter-lived recurring polynas have been observed by microwave satellite data in the Maud Rise region and at the Cosmonaut Sea (near 65° S and 45° S; Comiso & Gordon, 1987).

Along the Antarctic coast there are frequent ice-free belts. These are believed to be due to offshore winds which remove ice as fast as it is formed. One such polyna, referred to as a latent heat polyna (Gordon, 1988), is that which occurs in Terra Nova Bay just north of the Drygakshi Ice Tongue.

The melting of the sea ice during the summer results in

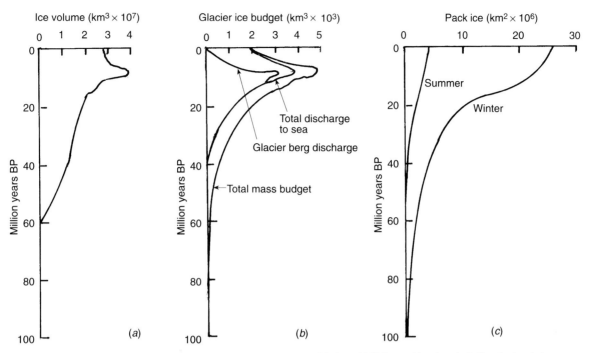

Fig. 1.5. Estimated variation of the Antarctic ice sheet parameters with time. (*a*) Volume of ice sheet including the ice shelves. (*b*) Annual (total) mass budget of the Antarctic ice sheet, together with annual ice discharge to sea across the flotation line, and the annual volume discharged by glaciers directly to open water but not to ice shelves (glacier berg discharge). (*c*) The aereal extent of pack ice. Redrawn from Robin (1988).

the introduction of a large amount of low-salinity melt water into the surface layer of the seasonal sea ice region. This has a profound effect on the trophic dynamics of the region as the presence of the meltwater is a key factor leading to phytoplankton blooms in the marginal ice zone (see Chapter 13; W. O. Smith & Nelson, 1986; W. O. Smith, 1987; Comiso *et al.*, 1990). Meltwater provides vertical stability in the water column and allows phytoplankton to grow in a high-light, high-nutrient environment. Furthermore, high concentrations of sea ice microalgae grow in association with the pack ice, and over the course of the austral summer large amounts of biogenic particulate material are introduced into the ocean when the ice melts (Ackley *et al.*, 1979; Palmisano & Sullivan, 1983a).

1.5.2 Ice shelves and icebergs

The Antarctic continent is largely covered with ice and round the margins the extensive ice sheets extrude from the continent into the sea. In the Ross and Weddell Seas these ice sheets float on the ocean forming the extensive Ross, Filchner and Ronne Ice Shelves. The layer of water under the Ross Ice Shelf varies from a few metres to several hundred metres thick. The ice layer varies from 200 m thick at the seaward edge to over 800 m thick at the grounded edge. The ice shelves are continually moving seaward at about 1 m a day due to the accumulation of snow on the continent. As they extend into the open ocean they are exposed to the action of long period waves and eventually they crack and calve icebergs. The large tabular icebergs so produced can range from a few hundred metres up to 100 km in horizontal extent and usually are about 200–300 m thick. It has been estimated (Radok *et al.*, 1975) that the total mass of icebergs is about one third of the mass of sea ice at maximum extent. The average life of icebergs is about four years, but large ones have been tracked for much longer periods (Swithinbank *et al.*, 1977).

Fig. 1.5 gives estimates of the variation of Antarctic ice sheet parameters with time. It can be seen that a rapid change in the mass budget of the Antarctic ice sheet occurred around 10 my bp when the total budget was two to three times its present level (Robin, 1988). The curve 'total discharge to sea' is ice lost by basal melting beneath the ice shelves and ice tongues and by the calving of icebergs. Both of these have decreased markedly since that period. The extent of the pack ice (Fig. 1.5c) shows the large increase in extent, especially during winter, since the opening of the Drake Passage resulted in Antarctic waters becoming thermally isolated as the circumpolar current developed (Robin, 1988).

1.6 Circulation patterns and water masses

1.6.1 Introduction

The basic feature of the circulation patterns and hydrographic processes of the Southern Ocean were first

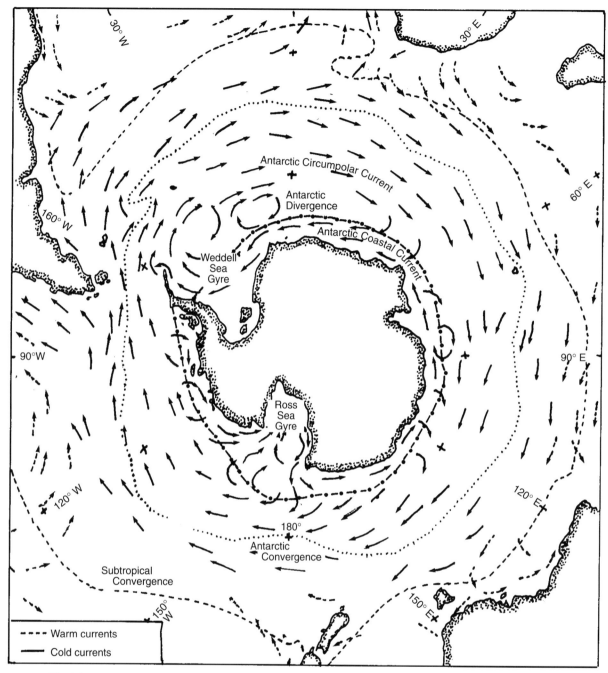

Fig. 1.6. Surface currents in the Southern Ocean and the mean positions of the principal frontal zones. After Tchernia (1980) and Knox (1983).

described by Deacon (1937, 1963, 1964a,b, 1977). Since then there have been a number of reviews including those of Gordon *et al.*, (1977a,b), Gordon & Owens (1987), Forster, (1981, 1984), Gordon & Molinelli (1982), Gordon (1983, 1988), Amos (1984), Deacon (1984b), and Squire (1987). The Southern Ocean–atmosphere–ice coupled system is extremely complex. Processes within the Southern Ocean are responsible for the production of water characteristics below the main thermocline of the world's oceans. Associated with this is significant heat flux across the ACC.

While the summary of circulation patterns given below represents a generalized picture of the dynamics of the system, it should be emphasised that superimposed upon this is a great amount of temporal, seasonal and year-to-year variability (see Chapter 15). The Southern Ocean is not radially symmetric and many of the circulation and water mass features vary markedly with longitude. The cryosphere complicates water mass properties in two ways: the highly spatially and temporarily variable sea ice cover strongly influences the coupling of the ocean and atmosphere in regard to momentum, heat, water and gas exchanges; and ocean interaction with glacial ice has a marked influence on the characteristics of the water masses (Gordon, 1988).

1.6.2 Driving forces

1.6.2.1 Wind
In general, the principle driving force for the Southern Ocean circulation is the wind field. The westerlies within the circumpolar belt are quite strong with the maximum westerlies situated in close proximity to the ACC. The wind field produces Ekman divergence (upwelling) south of the ACC and convergence (sinking) to the north. The upwelling poleward of the ACC carries about 45 Sv (1 Sv = 1×10^6 m^3 s^{-1}) into the mixed layer, two-thirds of which is directed to the north, with the rest towards the continent, where coastal sinking occurs (Gordon, 1988).

Along the margins of the continent, south of about 60° S, the wind field results in westerly flowing water, the Antarctic Coastal Current (East Wind Drift). Between the two well-defined current systems there is a series of eddies. Fig. 1.6 shows the general pattern of surface currents in the Southern Ocean. Since the water column is weakly stratified south of the Antarctic Convergence, the ocean currents generally extend to the bottom resulting in the deep circulation being similar to that of the surface circulation, although the former is more strongly influenced by bottom topography.

1.6.2.2 Ocean–atmosphere heat and freshwater flux
Within the region of the Southern Ocean there is a slight excess of precipitation over evaporation (Gordon, 1981). The annual freezing and thawing of the sea ice is a significant factor in the redistribution of freshwater. In addition, the waters of the Southern Ocean play a primary role in the wastage of glacial ice, mainly by direct melting of ice along the underside of the shelf ice (Jacobs et al., 1985; Schlosser, 1986).

As Gordon (1988) points out, estimates of ocean-atmosphere flux are subject to large errors due to the lack of meterological and sea ice (concentration, thickness) data, and especially the paucity of data from the winter period. The strong seasonal variability of the sea ice cover, coupled with approximately 10–20% inter-annual variability in maximum winter sea ice cover (Zwally et al., 1983b), further complicates estimates of the mean ocean–atmosphere energy exchange. South of 60° S, the northern limit of sea ice cover, heat loss is large (an annual average of 30 W m^{-2}; Gordon, 1981), but is highly dependent on ice cover. Heat flux across the ACC and Antarctic Convergence (average 53° S) is 3.1×10^4 W, while that across 60° S is larger, amounting to 5.4×10^4 W

(Gordon & Owens, 1987). In order to maintain a steady state condition the net poleward heat flux must involve the poleward transport of a large volume of water.

1.6.3 Oceanic circulation (Fig. 1.6)

1.6.3.1 Antarctic Circumpolar Current (West Wind Drift)
The Antarctic Circumpolar Current (ACC) is unique in that it is the only zonal current encircling the globe, and it is almost unobstructed by land masses, being constricted only in the region of the Drake Passage. It displays significant variations with longitude, principally related to bottom topography, being deflected where it passes over submarine ridges with a strong northerly component after it passes through the Drake Passage. Its width varies from less than 200 km wide south of Australia to over 1000 km wide in the Atlantic. Mean current speeds within the ACC are relatively low (0.04–0.25 m s^{-1}, some 2 to 3% of the wind velocity. Although the predominant movement is to the east, there is a strong northerly component. There is also some evidence that there are meanders and even loops within the current (Tchernia, 1974, 1980; Joyce & Patterson, 1977). The ACC joins the great current gyres of the South Atlantic, South Indian and South Pacific Oceans.

1.6.3.2 Antarctic Coastal Current (East Wind Drift)
In the vicinity of the Antarctic continent south of about 65° S, where winds from the east and southeast blow off the ice sheet, there is a surface current which flows westward. This Antarctic Coastal Current generally follows the coastline with two important indentations in the Ross and Weddell Seas. Its flow is estimated at 10 million m^3 s^{-1}, while its speed is variable between 0.1 and 1 m s^{-1}, with the largest values near the Ross Ice Shelf (Squire, 1987). The current may not be continuous but rather broken up by a series of gyres (Fig. 1.6).

1.6.3.3 Circumpolar frontal zones
There are a number of fronts within the Southern Ocean (Deacon, 1982). While some are circumpolar, such as the Antarctic Convergence (Polar Front), they display much variability in characteristics with longitude. The most significant of these fronts is the Antarctic Convergence which divides the Southern Ocean into two distinct regions: sub-Antarctic to the north and Antarctic to the south. It is a zone of variable width characterized by steep gradients in sea-surface temperature, abrupt changes in phytoplankton abundance, zooplankton distribution, pelagic bird species, weather conditions, and sometimes by a salinity maximum at the surface. A circumpolar

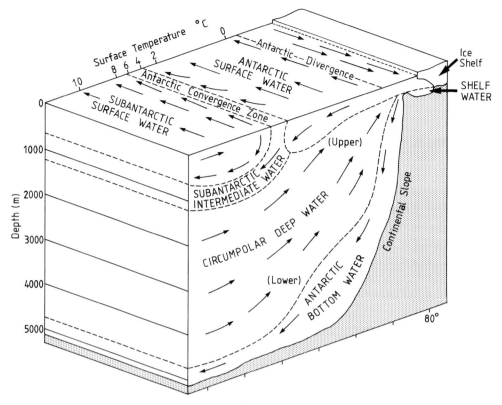

Fig. 1.7. Schematic diagram of the meridional and zonal flow and water masses of the Southern Ocean. The diagram represents average summer conditions and applies particularly to the Atlantic sector. Redrawn from Knox (1983); after Brodie (1965), adapted from Sverdrup *et al.* (1942).

subsurface salinity minimum closely follows the surface position of the convergence (Gordon *et al.*, 1977a,b; Joyce *et al.*, 1978; Sciermammano, 1989).

To the north of the convergence lies the Sub-Antarctic Front, while to the south lies the Antarctic Divergence. This divergence is caused partly by the northward component associated with the ACC and the southward component of the Antarctic Coastal Current, and partly by circulatory and thermohaline factors of the southern density gradient and the distribution of pressure and winds. In the region of the divergence deep water upwells to reach the surface. The classical schematic diagram of the horizontal and vertical movements of the Antarctic circumpolar waters is presented in Fig. 1.7.

1.6.3.4 Gyres, eddies and rings
A characteristic of the zonation of the circumpolar currents is the development of eddies of variable size and duration. This eddy variability is due to a combination of factors (Gordon, 1988). The current cores migrate laterally (Nowlin *et al.*, 1977) by as much as 100 km in 10 days. Meanders or waves form and propagate along the ACC fronts (Legechis, 1977; Sciermammano, 1989). These meanders sometimes develop into closed current rings (Joyce & Patterson, 1977). Cold and warm core rings have both been observed. The eddies are generally

30–100 km wide with surface velocities typically 30 cm s^{-1} or more and they are vertically coherent from the surface to the bottom. Numerous current rings and meanders have been reported from the Drake Passage.

In addition to the eddies there are three large permanent cyclonic flowing gyres. The largest and best-defined of these is the Weddell Gyre, extending east of the Antarctic Peninsula to about 20° W and from Antarctica near 70° S to 60° S (Deacon, 1979; Gordon *et al.*, 1981; Comiso & Gordon, 1987). The others are the Ross Sea Gyre, north and east of the Ross Sea (Tchernia & Jeannin, 1984), and a rather poorly defined gyre east of the Kerguelen Plateau (Deacon, 1977; Rodman & Gordon, 1982).

A review of the Weddell Gyre system is found in Deacon (1977). The easterly flow of the surface water of the ACC is intensified by the constriction of the Drake Passage. Some of this water flows into the Bransfield Strait but the bulk of the flow continues northeast past the Scotia Ridge where it meets the northern limits of the Weddell Gyre, forming the Weddell–Scotia Confluence (Gordon, 1967; Deacon & Moorey, 1975; Patterson & Sievers, 1980). This confluence varies in width from tens to hundreds kilometres scale and displays intense eddy activity (Forster & Middleton, 1984). The fronts marking the northern and southern edge of the confluence have been called the Scotia and Weddell Fronts respectively

(Gordon *et al.*, 1977b). The total transport in the Weddell Gyre is quite large and Carmack & Forster (1975) have estimated it to be in the order of 100×10^6 m^3 s^{-1}. The circulation of these gyres and eddies is of considerable importance to understanding sea ice build-up and decay and the distribution and production of the pelagic communities.

1.6.4 Water masses

Fig. 1.7 presents an idealized schematic diagram of the meridional and zonal flow in the Southern Ocean. There are three principal hydrographic realms: The area north of the Antarctic Convergence; the area south of the Antarctic Convergence; and the area on the continental shelf round Antarctica. Excluding the surface waters three water masses dominate the deep ocean: The sub-Antarctic Intermediate Water north of the Antarctic Convergence near the 1000 m level; the Antarctic Bottom Water near the bottom; and, the Antarctic Circumpolar Deep Water in between at various depths.

Warm Deep Water upwells at the Antarctic Divergence. Here the oxygen minimum and temperature maximum coincide and rise together with the the underlying salinity maximum. The cold, low-salinity, high-oxygen Antarctic surface waters move north to the Antarctic Convergence where they sink and contribute to the formation of the low salinity intermediate water. North of the Antarctic Convergence is the warmer sub-Antarctic Surface Water.

Near the bottom very cold Antarctic Bottom Water moves north from its primary site of generation round the continental margin, especially in the Weddell Sea. Sandwiched between the two Antarctic water masses is the broad compensatory flow of high-salinity Warm Deep Water. The south-flowing Deep Water mixes with the Antarctic waters above and contributes to the Circumpolar Deep Water which, in terms of volume, is the dominating water mass of the Southern Ocean. Mixing takes place across the boundaries between the water masses.

1.6.5 Bottom water formation

The problem of deep-water formation has long intrigued oceanographers. Brennecke (1921) first showed that the very cold bottom water in the Atlantic could be traced back to the Weddell Sea. Observations from the *Discovery* Expeditions (Deacon, 1937) confirmed the Weddell Sea as the main source of deep water. It probably accounts for about 80% of the total production. Other minor sources are in the Ross Sea and off the coast of Wilkes Land.

Water over the continental shelf is cold but displays a wide range of salinity and hence density. When the density of the shelf water is high enough it will sink, but the precise mechanisms involved in the sinking and the formation of bottom water is still not completely understood (Gordon, 1988). According to Gordon (1988) postulated processes and sources contributing to Weddell Sea Bottom Water formation have included haline convection by evaporation or freezing in open leads and polynas, cooling under the Filchner Ice Shelf, Ekman-layer effects, sinking along frontal zones, derivation from deeper oceanic areas, overflow of dense water from the Bransfield Strait, and double diffusive convection. Estimates of the circumpolar production rates of Bottom Water are in excess of 13 Sv (Jacobs *et al.*, 1985). The principal mechanism was believed to involve frontal zone mixing between water masses at the continental shelf break, with the dense water sinking down the slope (Gill, 1973; Forster & Carmack, 1976). Recent observations by Norwegian scientists (Foldvik & Gammelsrød, 1988) have shown that large volumes of Weddell Sea Bottom Water originate from Ice Shelf Water formed under floating ice shelves flowing down the continental slope as organized plumes and forming Weddell Sea Bottom Water through mixing with the overlying Weddell Deep Water.

1.7 Nutrients

In the Southern Ocean the concentration of nutrients is lowest in the surface waters and greatest in the Warm Deep Water for nitrate and phosphate, and usually near the bottom for silicate. In general the concentrations of nutrients in surface waters south of the Antarctic Convergence are much higher that those found in other oceanic waters (Knox, 1970; El-Sayed, 1978). Nutrient rich water upwells at the Antarctic Divergence spreading out to ultimately downwell at the Antarctic Convergence. On the basis of data from other upwelling regions one would expect to find almost complete stripping of plant nutrients with time in the upper 50–100 m due to the growth of phytoplankton (Andrews & Hutchings, 1980; Barlow, 1982). Holm-Hansen (1985) estimated that between 25 and 30 μmoles of nitrate per litre would have been consumed by the time the upwelled water reached the zone of the Antarctic Convergence (approximately 200 days in transit), and postulated that one would expect to find almost complete stripping of the nutrients in aged waters close to the Antarctic Convergence. However, data from studies by Kuramoto & Koyama (1987) and Watanabe & Nakajima (1982) from a transect along 45° E longitude reveals a completely different picture. Nitrate was 27 μM at 60° S, 22 μM at the Antarctic Convergence (52° S) and 20 μM a few degrees south of the Subtropical Convergence (41° S). Silica on the other hand was high (57 μM) at 67° S and it decreased sharply to 15 μM at 60° S, and dropped to low values (approximately 1 μM) just north of the Antarctic Convergence, reflecting its assimilation and polymerization by diatoms and silicoflagellates. The significance of these data and the degree to which nutrient depletion can occur in the waters of the Southern Ocean will be considered in detail in Chapter 2.

2

Phytoplankton and primary production

2.1 Introduction

Organisms in the plankton are generally assigned to one of three compartmental groups: bacterioplankton, phytoplankton and zooplankton. These groups are further subdivided into trophic levels on the basis of taxonomic categories well above the species level. Unfortunately this results in the grouping together of organisms with differing modes of nutrition, e.g. non-photosynthetic flagellates are grouped with the algae and are considered to be phytoplankton. In contrast, other protozoan groups, such as the ciliates and the sarcodinians, are assigned to the zooplankton as microzooplankton. In order to overcome these and other problems, Siebruth *et al.* (1978) proposed a scheme (Fig. 2.1) based on the level of organization (ultrastructure) and mode of nutrition.

The heterotrophic organisms fall into five major compartments: virioplankton (viruses), bacterioplankton (free-living bacteria), mycoplankton (fungi), protozooplankton (apochloritic flagellates, amoeboid forms and ciliates), and the metazooplankton (the multicellular ingesting forms). The metazooplankton span the size range from the mesoplankton through the macroplankton to the megaplankton. The mesoplankton consists mainly of copepods, while the macroplankton comprises mainly the larger crustaceans such as the mysids and euphausiids. Juvenile stages of the latter however fall within the mesoplankton size range. The megaplankton comprise the larger drifting forms such as the coelenterates and appendicularians.

The protozooplankton, mycoplankton, and the phytoplankton are unicellular eucaryotes and fall into three size groupings: picoplankton (<2.0 μm), nanoplankton (2.0–20 μm), and microplankton (20–200 μm). The bacterioplankton compartment consists of unattached unicellular bacteria; these can be selectively filtered with 0.1 and 1.0 μm porosity filters. In the scheme depicted in Fig. 2.1 the heterotrophic components of the plankton have been redefined into more discrete taxonomic groupings and in an expanded range of redefined size groups. The size groupings are indicative of the growth and metabolic rates of the organisms involved, generally a function of size (Ikeda, 1970; Sheldon *et al.*, 1972). Fig. 2.1 shows that there is little overlap between the size categories and compartmental groups of plankton organisms, apart from the phytoplankton and protozooplankton which occupy the same size categories. However they are distinguished by the presence or absence of chlorophyll, although it has now been shown that many chlorophyll-containing flagellates and ciliates are mixotrophic, being capable of ingesting phytoplankton (see Chapter 14).

In this chapter we will be concerned with the phytoplankton component; the other components will be dealt with in succeeding chapters.

2.2 Data base

The study of the marine phytoplankton of the Southern Ocean has had a long history that dates back nearly a century and a half, to when J.D. Hooker, the noted botanist-surgeon of the *Erebus* and *Terror* Expedition under James Clark Ross (1839–43), reported the ubiquitous presence of diatoms during the Antarctic summer: 'they occurred in such countless myriads, as to stain the Berg and the Pack-Ice . . . they imparted to the Brash and Pancake-Ice a pale ochreous colour' (Hooker, 1847). Hooker sent some of the samples collected between Cape Horn and the Ross sea to the German botanist Ehrenberg who published the first paper on Antarctic diatoms in 1844 (see Ehrenberg 1844, 1853).

The distribution, productivity and ecology of the phytoplankton of the Southern Ocean have been reviewed by El-Sayed (1968a,b,c, 1970a,b, 1971c, 1978, 1984, 1985, 1987, 1988a,b), El-Sayed *et al.* (1979), Heywood & Whitaker (1984), Sakshaug & Holm-Hansen, (1984), Priddle *et al.* (1986a,b), Medlin & Priddle (1990), and Jacques (1989). Despite the large amount of data that has been collected over the past decades, both the geographical and temporal coverage are sparse due to the vastness of the Southern Ocean. Observations of the standing crop and productivity have been dictated by logistics and the workload of research vessels rather than by sampling designed to answer questions pertaining to the ecology of the flora. Most of the expeditions have been limited to the austral spring and summer, and autumn and winter obser-

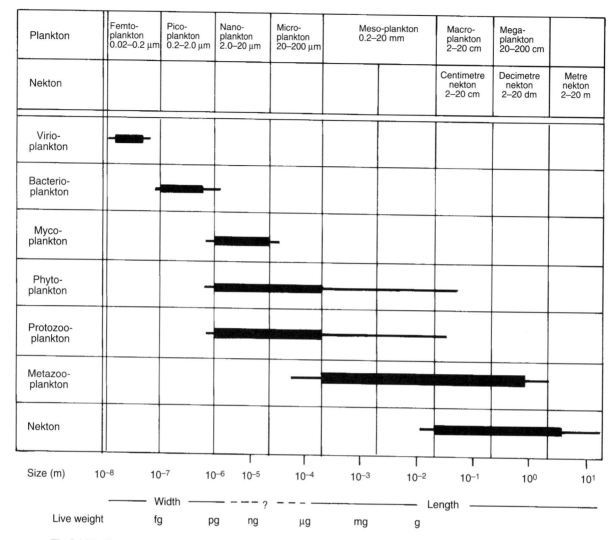

Plankton	Femto-plankton 0.02–0.2 μm	Pico-plankton 0.2–2.0 μm	Nano-plankton 2.0–20 μm	Micro-plankton 20–200 μm	Meso-plankton 0.2–20 mm		Macro-plankton 2–20 cm	Mega-plankton 20–200 cm	
Nekton							Centimetre nekton 2–20 cm	Decimetre nekton 2–20 dm	Metre nekton 2–20 m

Fig. 2.1 Distribution of different taxonomic–trophic compartments of plankton in a spectrum of size fractions, in comparison with a size range of nekton. Redrawn from Siebruth *et al.* (1978).

vations are few. As a consequence, we have an incomplete picture of seasonal variability. Inshore observations are also limited to a few locations. In addition, methods and techniques have changed, or have been modified, in the past two decades, making it difficult to compare more recent data with those of earlier decades. These limitations need to be borne in mind when discussing the phytoplankton of the Southern Ocean.

2.3 Species composition and distribution (Figs. 2.2 and 2.3)

2.3.1 Net phytoplankton (microplankton)

The net phytoplankton is generally dominated by diatoms. Diatom blooms commonly contain several species. Around South Georgia, for instance, these population maxima have comprised dense growth of *Thalassiosira scotia* and *Chaetoceros socialis*, or

Euchampia antarctica with *Odontella weissflogii*, *Rhizosolenia* and *Proboscia* spp., *Corethron* and *Thalassiosira* (Priddle, 1990). A very dense bloom of diatoms near King George Island (South Shetland Islands) contained *Odontella weissflogii*, *Proboscia 'alata'*, *Chaetoceros curvisetum* and *Thalassiosira tumida* (Heywood & Priddle, 1987). This predominance of colonial and chainforming taxa appears to be typical of many regions of the Southern Ocean, although other species may dominate under certain conditions.

Other important species are dinoflagellates and silicoflagellates. Over 100 species of diatoms and some 60 species of dinoflagellates have been found in Antarctic waters. While many of the diatom species are cosmopolitan, Hasle (1969) lists three species as having distributions limited to the Antarctic zone and 20 diatom taxa restricted to the southernmost part of the Antarctic zone. Endemism in the net phytoplankton appears to be high but

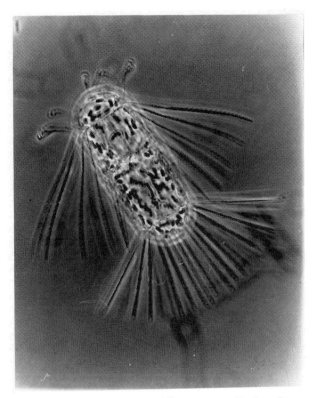

Fig. 2.2. *Corethron criophilum*, a common Southern Ocean diatom. Photograph provided by Dr. Greta Fryxell, Department of Oceanography, Texas A&M University, College Station, Texas.

early work by Hart (1934, 1942) indicated that most of the species are circumpolar in their distribution (Baker, 1954). Fryxell & Hasle (1979) came to similar conclusions for some *Thalassiosira* species.

There is a paucity of information on the distribution and abundance of dinoflagellates in the waters of the Southern Ocean and their contribution to phytoplankton biomass has probably been underestimated (El-Sayed, 1985). The most important species belong to a few thecate genera (those enclosed in cellulose plates), chiefly the genera *Protoperidium* and *Dinophysis*. The genus *Ceratium* which is widespread elsewhere in the world's oceans, is absent south of the Antarctic Convergence. Some 15 species of naked, or thin-walled, dinoflagellates have been recorded (Balech, 1975). but the assumption that they are rare is probably false, due to the fact that they do not preserve well. Endemism is higher (80–85%) than in any other oceanic region.

Of the other algal groups, *Phaeocystis pouchetii*, the unicellular motile and colonial brown-yellow prymnesiophyte belonging to the order Prymnesiales, can be exceedingly abundant. It is one of the few marine phytoplankton species which exhibit a life-cycle alternation between free-living flagellated zoospores and a gelatinous colonial aggregation of non-motile cells. It occurs prominently in the plankton in this latter stage, containing

hundreds of thousands of 3–8 μm cells in colonies which exceed 10 mm in diameter. In the colonial form it can produce very dense gelatinous blooms which are characteristic of the marginal ice edge zone and shelf waters. The dominance of *Phaeocystis* along the south east coast of the Weddell Sea prior to and during the ice melting has been noted by a number of investigators (Hayes *et al.*, 1984; v. Brockel, 1985; Boltovoskoy *et al.* 1989).

Silicoflagellates are unicellular chrysophycean algae with an internal skeleton with conspicuous siliceous tubes. Only one species, *Dictyota (Distephanus) speculum*, is common in Antarctic waters and sometimes it may outnumber any of the diatom species.

There have been numerous studies of the distribution patterns of the diatom flora in the open ocean and I do not propose to review them here. Few studies, however, have traced the seasonal changes which occur in species composition and dominance. One exception is that of Everitt & Thomas (1986), who studied the seasonal changes in the species composition and abundance of diatoms in inshore localities near Davis Station, East Antarctica. Highest numbers of species occurred during the months of ice cover from July to September, with the numbers dropping off in December to February when open water prevailed. Benthic assemblages (including epiphytic and ice algal species) were richer in species numbers than the planktonic assemblages.

2.3.2 Nanoplankton

It is only comparatively recently that attention has been paid to the role of the nanoplankton (greater than 2.0 μm and less than 20 μm) in the waters of the Southern Ocean. This is because most of the early investigations of phytoplankton were based on samples obtained with phytoplankton nets (usually about 35 μm mesh) and this led to the view that the flora was dominated by relatively large-volume diatoms (Hart, 1934, 1942; Hasle, 1969; Nemoto & Harrison, 1981). In water samples from the Scotia and Weddell Seas Holm-Hansen & Forster (1981) found that the nanoplankton generally accounted for between 25 and 75% of the total estimated phytoplankton carbon. This percentage is in agreement with data from other investigators; e.g. Fay (1973) 69–85%; El-Sayed (1971b) 38–87%; El-Sayed & Taguchi (1981) 64–80%; Koike *et al.* (1981) 97%; Yamaguchi & Shibata (1982) 54%; Rönner *et al.* (1983) 45%; Sasaki (1984) 43%; Weber (1984) 64%; Kosahi *et al.* (1985) 64%; Lipski (1985) 65%; Weber & El-Sayed (1985a,b) 52–92%; Weber & El-Sayed (1986a) 47%; Weber & El-Sayed (1986b) 64–78%. The average of all these studies for widely distributed localities is 66%. In Arthur Harbour, Anvers Island, Heinbokel & Coats (1985) found that in

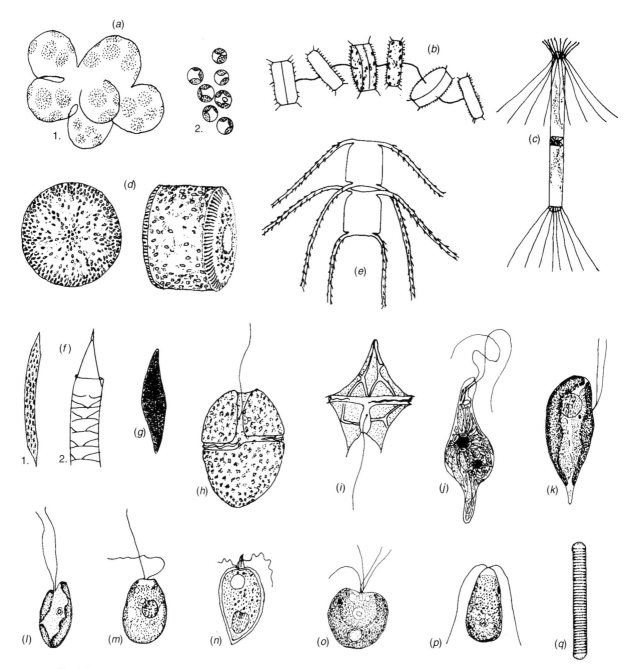

Fig. 2.3. Some characteristic phytoplankton species a–f microplankton species; j–g nanoplankton species. a. *Phaeocystis pouchetii* (Prymnesiophyte), (1) colony, (2) individual cells; b–g. diatoms; b. *Thalassiosira gravida*; c. *Corethron criophilum*; d. *Coscinodiscus* sp.; e. *Chaetoceros criophilum*; f. *Rhizosolenia curvata*, (1) whole cell. (2) cell apex; g. *Pleurosigma* sp.; h–i dinoflagellates; h. *Gymnodinium* sp.; i. *Peridinium* sp.; j–p. flagellates; j. *Eutreptia* sp. (Euglenophyceae); k. *Cryptomonas* sp. (Cryptophyceae); l. *Rhodomonas* sp. (Cryptophyceae); m. *Pleuromonas* sp.;' (Desmophyceae); n. *Procentron* sp. (Desmophyceae); o. *Pyranimonas* sp.; (Prasinophyceae); p. *Chlorella*-like flagellate (Chlorophyceae); q. *Nitzschia cylindrus* (diatom).

December and January between 47 and 75% of the total chlorophyll *a* passed through a 10 μm mesh and as much as 49% passed through a 5 μm nucleopore filter. At Elephant Island in the 1984–85 austral summer the contribution of the less than 20 μm size fraction to the total estimated chlorophyll *a* was 76% (the picoplankton component was not measured) (El-Sayed & Weber, 1986). The proportion was somewhat higher (83%) in the surface waters than in the deeper samples (68%). The *Africana* samples showed a lower mean contribution to the total chlorophyll *a* from cells less than 20 μm of 47% (range 29–84%). In contrast to the Elephant Island samples the contribution of the nanoplankton increased with depth, averaging 37% at the surface and 62% at 150 m depth. Gieskes & Elbrachter (1986), in samples taken during a cruise in the Antarctic Peninsula region, found

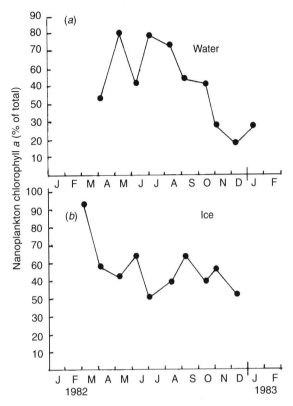

Fig. 2.4. Contribution of nanoplankton to total chlorophyll *a* (*a*) the seawater and (*b*) the sea ice 1 km offshore of Davis Station (68°35′ S; 77°50′ E). Redrawn from Perrin *et al.* (1987).

that between 8 and 80% of the chlorophyll *a* containing particles were smaller than 8 μm. In a study of the seasonal variation of phytoplankton and sea ice microalgae off Davis Station (Fig. 2.4) Perrin *et al.* (1987) found that for most of the year nanoplankton accounted for the major part of the chlorophyll in the water column, particularly in the winter, when sometimes it approached 100% of the total chlorophyll *a*. Only during blooms of *Phaeocystis pouchetii* and large diatoms did the relative nanoplankton decrease. In the sea ice the situation was similar with the nanoplankton contribution decreasing during diatom blooms in May and November–December.

The principal components of the nanophytoplankton are: (a) small diatoms (5 to 10 μm), e.g. *Chaetoceros neglectus*, *C. tortissimus* and *Nitzschia curta*, which at times can contribute up to 50% of the total phytoplankton cells (Brandini & Kutner, 1987) in oceanic areas; and (b) prymnesiophytes, cryptomonads and other green flagellates, which may dominate under certain conditions (Gieskes & Elbrachter, 1986; Jacques & Panouse, 1991).

According to Nishida (1986) the majority of the nanoplankton is composed of unicellular flagella-bearing organisms which have calcareous or siliceous skeletal elements. He identified four nanoplankton assemblages in the Southern Ocean between Australia and the Antarctic

Continent, namely subtropical, sub-Antarctic, Antarctic and circum-Antarctic pack ice assemblages. The first three were composed mainly of calcareous nanoplankton dominated by species of the Coccolithophyceae, while the last was dominated by dense population of siliceous species. This Antarctic assemblage was composed almost entirely of a single species, *Emiliana huxleyi*. The maximum number of individuals recorded was *c*. 226×10³ individuals l⁻¹ at 100 m depth in the circum-Antarctic pack ice zone.

Siliceous cysts in the size range of 2.0 to 5.5 μm are important components of the nanoplankton of the Southern Ocean. It had been suggested that these may be cysts in the life-cycle of choanoflagellates. However, Marchant & McEldowney (1986) have concluded from the study of living cells that they contain chlorophyll. This was confirmed by transmission electron microscope studies which showed the presence of chloroplasts.

2.3.3 Picoplankton

It is only recently that attention has been focused on the significance in the world's oceans of the phytoautotrophic picoplankton, chlorophyll-containing organisms which are less than 2.0 μm in size (see Li *et al.*, 1983; Platt *et al.*, 1983; Takahashi & Beinfang, 1983). There are, however, only a handful of studies on the role of picoplankton in the Southern Ocean (see Hewes *et al.*, 1983, 1985; Sasaki, 1984; Probyn & Painting, 1985; El-Sayed & Weber, 1986; Heinbokel & Coats, 1986; Brandini & Kutner, 1987; Weber & El-Sayed, 1987; Jacques & Panouse. 1991). In their study of the size fractionation of phytoplankton in the southwestern Drake Passage and Bransfield Strait, El-Sayed & Weber (1986) found that the picoplankton contribution to the phytoautotrophic biomass varied considerably from station to station, ranging from 3.0 to 70%, with a mean of 40%. Hosaka & Nemoto (1986) reported that chlorophyll *a* in the <1 μm size fraction accounted for 18% of the total in the sub-Antarctic Pacific. In contrast, in the western Indian Ocean sector of the Southern Ocean south of 60° S the picophytoplankton biomass was very much lower ranging from 7.0 to 43%, with a mean of 14%. According to Kosahi *et al.* (1985) the relative abundance of phytoplankton in the size range 0.2 to 1.0 μm in the Southern Ocean is low in comparison with tropical and subtropical seas.

Prominent among the picoplankton are phycoerythrin-rich chroococcoid cyanobacteria (0.8 to 1.4 μm in diameter), either in coastal (Marchant *et al.*, 1987) or oceanic areas, while the most commonly reported eucaryote is a *Chlorella*-like coccoid green flagellate. While representatives of other algal groups have been reported as members of the picoplankton assemblages their taxonomy has been little studied in Antarctic waters.

Different water masses have differing degrees of dominance of the various groups of phytoplankton. Suskin (1985) in a review of the phytoplankton communities of the Atlantic sector of the Southern Ocean noted that while the Antarctic Circumpolar Current was dominated by diatoms, in the Weddell Sea the predominant species were the peridinidae, coccolithophorids and silicoflagellates. In the southwest Indian Ocean between Africa and the Antarctic Continent Kopczynska *et al.* (1986) found that diatoms dominated in the net phytoplankton with numbers generally increasing southwards with peaks of abundance in the northern Antarctic zone and south of the Antarctic Convergence. Dinoflagellates, flagellates and 'monads' occurred in the highest concentration north of the Antarctic Convergence with their numbers somewhat reduced to the south.

The proportions of the various size categories not only vary geographically but also seasonally and with depth. For the Southern Ocean south of Australia Yamaguchi & Shibata (1982) found that the mean percentage contributions of the nano- (<10 µm), micro- (10–60 µm) and net-phytoplankton (>60 µm) to the total standing stock of chlorophyll *a* in the upper 200 m were 52.6, 25.1 and 22.3% respectively. Sasaki (1984) in the Indian Ocean sector found that the mean contributions of the microplankton (>10 µm) in the subtropical, sub-Antarctic and Antarctic zones in December were 24.1, 64.8 and 68.9% respectively.

It is thus clear that the nano- and picophytoplankton are important contributors to the biomass of phytoautotrophs in the Southern Ocean. Until recently their importance, especially that of the picoplankton, had been overlooked. Much more detailed research is needed in order to define their quantitative contribution to the phytoplankton biomass and production, both geographically and seasonally.

2.4 Phytoplankton biomass

In interpreting data on phytoplankton standing stock and primary production in the Southern Ocean the limitations of the data base must be born in mind. Relatively few observations have yet been made in this vast ocean and the methods and techniques now used make it difficult to compare the data obtained with those of earlier studies. Observations have often been made in isolation, both in space and time, as dictated by logistics and overall scientific workload of the research vessels, and not by the biology of the plants (Heywood & Whittaker, 1984). Anyone who has had experience in Antarctic waters can testify to the fact that phytoplankton blooms can develop very rapidly and can also be just as rapidly grazed down by

zooplankton or dispersed by storms. Apart from the observations made in coastal waters from shore stations, we lack year-round observations, especially in the pack ice zone. The vast majority of the observations have been carried out over a limited summer period only. Seasonal progression of maximum productivity with latitude as demonstrated by Hart (1934, 1942), modified by sea state and wind force, could help to explain the wide variation which has been found in phytoplankton biomass and productivity between areas within the same region of the Southern Ocean.

Early estimates of standing crop were made by counting phytoplankton (principally diatom) cell numbers. This does not take into account the contribution made by the nano- and picoplankton, which as we have seen is quite considerable. Estimates of phytoplankton standing crop are now usually made from chlorophyll *a* values by using standard chlorophyll *a* to carbon ratios. However, this ratio can vary by an order of magnitude between different physiological states of the same cell, or between species (Banse, 1977). In order to obtain more accurate information on phytoplankton biomass we need to know concurrent zooplankton grazing rates and the loss of cells through sinking, senescence and death; information that is generally not available. In a cruise off the Antarctic Peninsula, Gieskes & Elbrachter (1986) found that between 10 and 80% of the chlorophyll *a* containing particles were smaller than 8 µm. In many samples microscopic examination revealed that more than 50% of the nanoplankton-sized chlorophyll *a* containing particles were free-floating chloroplasts. Causes of the mechanical disruption of the cells include mechanical effects on the cells during storms and grazing by krill. However, in spite of these deficiencies comparative chlorophyll *a* levels are useful in overall comparisons both geographically and seasonally. Chlorophyll *a* concentrations are expressed either as values per cubic metre or the total amount in the water column beneath a square metre of the water surface.

2.4.1 Surface distribution of chlorophyll biomass

The bulk of the phytoplankton data shows chlorophyll *a* concentrations in the range of 0.1 to 1.0 mg m^{-3}, with a mean value of about 0.5 mg m^{-3} (Saijo & Kawashi, 1964; El-Sayed & Mandelli, 1965, El-Sayed, 1970a; Fukuchi, 1977, 1980). Within this low range of values there is a pronounced geographic variability. Typical of such variability are the observations reported by Priddle *et al.* (1986a) for the area round South Georgia, where the highest values for phytoplankton biomass were associated with stations off the southwest of the island and the lowest chlorophyll levels were located to the southeast.

Fukuchi (1980) analyzed data on chlorophyll stocks in the Indian Ocean sector of the Southern Ocean collected over the period 1965–1976. Surface chlorophyll *a* concentrations, measured at 631 stations in waters south of 35° S, ranged from 0.01 to 3.01 mg m^{-3}. At about half of the stations the values were less than 0.24 mg m^{-3} and at only 29 stations were values higher than 1.00 mg m^{-3} recorded. The mean surface chlorophyll *a* concentrations recorded in the literature from the oceanic waters of the Pacific, Atlantic and Indian Ocean sectors range from 0.12 to 0.42 mg m^{-3}. These values are much lower than those reported from upwelling areas but are higher than those in the North Equatorial Current and the central Indian Ocean.

In contrast to the generally low standing crop of phytoplankton in the oceanic waters of the Southern Ocean, elevated chlorophyll *a* levels have been reported from inshore waters, e.g. west of the Antarctic Peninsula in Gerlache Strait (El-Sayed, 1968a), near Kerguelen and Heard Islands (El-Sayed & Jitts, 1973), in the southern Ross Sea (El-Sayed *et al.*, 1983), and in the inshore waters of Signy Island (Horne *et al.*, 1969). Exceptionally high values (i.e., in excess of 25 mg m^{-3}) were reported by Mandelli & Burkholder (1966), during a phytoplankton bloom near Deception Island. In their studies of phytoplankton distribution and production in the southwestern Bransfield Strait in December–March Holm-Hansen & Mitchell (1991) found that all deep stations north of the continental shelf break were low in phytoplankton biomass (>41 mg chl *a* m^{-2}) while at some stations in shelf waters the biomass exceeded 700 mg chl *a* m^{-2}. The most extensive and richest phytoplankton bloom so far reported is one which occurred in the southwestern Weddell Sea (El-Sayed, 1978); this bloom, composed almost entirely of the diatom *Thalassiosira tumida*, covered an area of 15 000 km^{-2}, with chlorophyll *a* concentrations of up to 190 mg m^{-3}. High phytoplankton biomass at different latitudes in the Weddell Sea in March have been reported by a number of investigators (El-Sayed & Taguchi, 1981; Comiso *et al.*, 1990; Estrada & Delgado, 1990; Nothig *et al.*, 1991).

Blooms of the colonial flagellate *Phaeocystis pouchetii* are widespread, especially in coastal waters. In McMurdo Sound such blooms are an annual event occurring at approximately the same time of the year (Knox, 1986) (see Chapter 12).

High chlorophyll concentrations have frequently been associated with frontal structures such as the Antarctic Convergence (Allanson *et al.*, 1981; El-Sayed & Weber, 1982; Yamaguchi & Shibata, 1982; Lutjeharms *et al.*, 1985; Bidigare *et al.*, 1986), and the Weddell–Scotia Confluence (Bidigare *et al.*, 1986). El-Sayed (1987) has reproduced a satellite (Nimbus 7 Coastal Colour Scanner) image from the region of the Antarctic Convergence in the Weddell Sea which while showing generally low values in the Antarctic Convergence region (0.05 mg chl *a* m^{-2}) depicts a region of high pigment concentration squeezed between bands of low pigment concentration. In a study of the waters between 20° and 70° W Hayes *et al.* (1984) found that high concentrations of chlorophyll *a* were usually associated with hydrographic and bathymetric features.

There have been a number of recent studies of the distribution of phytoplankton biomass in regions of fast ice adjacent to the Antarctic Continent. Fukuchi *et al.* (1984) measured chlorophyll *a* concentrations in the water column under the fast ice at five stations (10–675 m depths) near Syowa Station for a period of 13 months in 1982–83. High chlorophyll *a* concentrations occurred between December and March, with other peaks in late January. The maximum concentration recorded was 11.3 mg chl *a* m^{-3}, while the average stock in the water column was 1.05–6.72 mg m^{-3}, at least one order of magnitude higher than that reported from open waters of the Southern Ocean. Satoh *et al.* (1986) subsequently also studied the seasonal changes in chlorophyll *a* concentrations off Syowa Station in 1983–84. A winter minimum of less than 0.1 mg chl *a* m^{-3} was recorded from June to October with a maximum concentration of 4.99 mg m^{-3} in mid-February. The standing stocks of chlorophyll *a* in mid-January 1984 were less than half of those recorded in 1983. This was probably due to the thicker snow cover on the sea ice resulting in reduced light penetration. Iwanami *et al.* (1986) investigated summer chlorophyll *a* levels at the same site in the mid-summer of 1984. At that time the ice was continuously melting, resulting in a low-salinity surface layer separated from the more saline water below by a well defined pycnocline (the plane of separation between two layers of water of differing density) at a depth of about 2 m. As a consequence a subsurface chlorophyll *a* maximum developed. Integrated chlorophyll *a* stocks increased rapidly from 20.5 to 103.8 mg chl *a* m^{-2} within two weeks. In Lutzow–Holm Bay Fukuda *et al.* (1985) recorded chlorophyll *a* levels of 0.54 to 0.73 mg m^{-3} under the fast ice on December 14 and 1.77–2.70 mg m^{-3} on January 3. The latter high values were probably correlated with the release of ice algae as the bottom ice melted; later concentrations in the open water after the ice breakout decreased rapidly. In Breid Bay on December 29–30 the following values were recorded: under the fast ice 2.49–4.48 mg m^{-3}; at the edge of the fast ice 4.62–4.99 mg m^{-3}; and in the open water 1.62–2.82 mg m^{-3}. In mid-February when the fast ice had disappeared the chlorophyll *a* levels were 0.76–2.54 mg m^{-3}.

Table 2.1. *Methods for estimating primary production in the ocean and the nominal time scales on which the results apply. The components P_g (gross primary production), P_n (net primary production) and P_c (P_n – respiration of all heterotrophs) refer to a scheme based on carbon; P_T (total production, P_r (regenerated production) and P_{new} (new production) to one based on nitrogen. Sedimentation rate refers to the gravitational flux of organic particles leaving the photic zone, not the (much smaller) flux arriving at the sediment surface.*

Method	Nominal component of production	Nominal time scale
In vitro		
^{14}C assimilation	P_T $(= P_n)$	Hours to 1 day
O_2 evolution	P_T	Hours to 1 day
$^{15}NO_3$ assimilation	P_{new}	Hours to 1 day
Bulk property		
Sedimentation rate below photic zone	P_{new} $(= P_c)$	Days to months (duration of trap deployment)
Oxygen utilization rate (OUR)	P_{new}	Seasonal to annual
Net O_2 accumulation in photic zone	P_{new}	Seasonal to annual
NO_3 flux to photic zone	P_{new}	Hours to days
Upper limit		
Optimal energy conversion of photons absorbed by phyto-plankton pigments	P_r	Instantaneous to annual
Lower limit		
Depletion of winter accumulation of NO_3 above seasonal thermocline	P_{new}	Seasonal

After Platt *et al.* (1909).

2.4.2 Vertical distribution of chlorophyll

The vertical distribution of phytoplankton biomass (in terms of chlorophyll *a*) generally exhibits maximum values at subsurface depths, with decreasing chlorophyll values to a depth of 200 m below which the chlorophyll concentration is generally negligible (El-Sayed, 1970b; El-Sayed & Turner, 1977; El-Sayed & Weber, 1982). However, it is not uncommon for substantial amounts of chlorophyll to be found below the euphotic zone.

Heywood & Whitaker (1984) and El-Sayed (1987) have discussed the relationship between surface chlorophyll *a* values and subsurface maximum values and integrated values over the water column. Some authors (e.g. Fukuchi *et al.*, 1984; Nast & Gieskes, 1986; Weber *et al.*, 1986) contend that the chlorphyll *a* measured near the surface is roughly indicative of the chlorophyll *a* distribu-

tion in the whole water column. However, El-Sayed (1970a) gave mean recorded chlorophyll *a* values for surface waters of the Atlantic and Pacific sectors of the Southern Ocean of 1.40 and 0.36 mg m^{-3} respectively while over the same time period the integrated values for the euphotic zone were 14.92 and 15.55 mg m^{-3} respectively.

2.5 Primary production

The absolute fixation rate of inorganic carbon into organic molecules is the gross primary production (P_g). When corrected for the respiration of the autotrophs (R), P_g reduces to net primary production (P_n):

$$P_g - R = P_n$$

A major complication is that the microheterotrophs coexist with and share the same size range as autotrophs, and in attempting to measure biomass or metabolism of one it is extremely difficult to discriminate the biomass or metabolism of the other (Li, 1986). If the respiration of all heterotrophs (both macroscopic and microscopic) is substracted from P_n, the residual is termed net community production (P_c).

Estimates of primary production are dependent on the measurement techniques employed (Eppley, 1980; Peterson, 1980; R. E. H. Smith *et al.*, 1984) (see Table 2.1). There are two kinds of index for primary production. Incubation in vitro (seawater containing natural phytoplankton assemblages, contained in bottles) provides one such index of photosynthetic rate. For example, the assimilation of carbon may be measured by the uptake of the tracer ^{14}C, the evolution of oxygen by direct titration. Changes in bulk properties of the water column give other indices of primary production. They include change in the dissolved oxygen content of the photic zone, the rate of sedimentation of organic particles, the consumption of oxygen below the photic zone by the decomposition of the sedimenting material (the oxygen utilization rate, OUR), and the vertical flux of nitrate into the photic zone (Platt *et al.*, 1983).

Primary production is generally estimated by the ^{14}C uptake method of Steeman-Nielsen (1952). While there has been much debate as to exactly what is measured by this method (Dring & Jewsen, 1979) it is currently the only technique sensitive enough to measure the low rates of production frequently encountered. However, the results of the ^{14}C experiments are often difficult to interpret and a number of workers consider that the method in general underestimates primary production (see Gieskes *et al.*, 1979). Bearing this in mind the next section discusses production values which have been determined by the ^{14}C method.

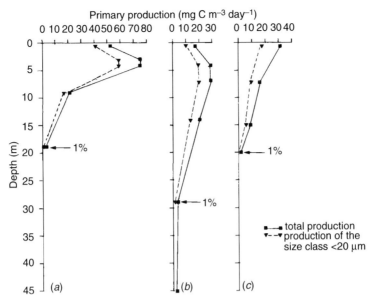

Fig. 2.5. Vertical distribution of primary production for two typical ice-free stations (*a* and *b*), and a station (*c*) covered to about 70% with ice-floes in the southeastern Weddell Sea. Redrawn from v. Brockel (1985).

2.5.1 Spatial distribution of primary production

Since the magnitude of primary production is a function of the phytoplankton biomass and growth rates it is not surprising that most of the primary productivity data show a good correlation with the distribution of the phytoplankton standing crop. For instance, low values of primary production rates reported from the Drake Passage, the Bellingshausen Sea and the oceanic waters of the Southern Ocean in general are typical of oligotrophic waters (<0.1 g C m^{-2} day^{-2}) (El-Sayed, 1985, 1987). On the other hand high values have been recorded in coastal regions in the vicinity of the Antarctic Continent and the off-lying islands, and in the ice-edge zone (see Chapter 13). El-Sayed (1967) recorded a value of 3.2 g C m^{-2} day^{-1} in the Gerlache Strait, Mandelli & Burkholder (1966) reported 3.6 g C m^{-2} day^{-1} near Deception Island, Horne *et al.* (1969) found a peak productivity of 2.8 g C m^{-2} day^{-1} in the inshore waters of Signy Island, while Jacques (1983) reported a maximum value of 5.2 g C m^{-2} day^{-1} from the Indian Ocean sector. In their Bransfield Strait studies Holm-Hansen & Mitchell (1991) found low rates of primary production (mean 0.34 g C m^{-2} day^{-1}) in oceanic waters in contrast to shelf waters in December where rates exceeded 3.0 g C m^{-2} day^{-1}. Such high values are comparable to those reported from upwelling areas off Peru, southeast Arabia, Somalia, and southwest Africa. It is these values that have contributed to the widespread idea that Antarctic waters are highly productive.

v. Bodungen *et al.* (1986) studied phytoplankton production during spring in the Antarctic Peninsula area. Three distinct and persistent zones were encountered: Zone I, low biomass comprising flagellates and diatoms in the Drake Passage and the Scotia Sea; Zone II, high to moderate biomass of *Phaeocystis* and diatoms in northern and central Bransfield Strait; and Zone III, moderate biomass (*Thalassiosira* spp. in the process of forming resting spores) in the vertically homogeneous water on the northern Antarctic Peninsula shelf. The rates of primary production for Zones I, II, and III averaged 230, 1660 and 830 mg C m^{-2} day^{-1}.

v. Brockel (1985) measured phytoplankton production for three size classes (<20 µm, 20–100 µm, >100 µm) in the southeastern Weddell Sea in February–March 1983. Total primary production ranged between 80 and 1670 mg C m^{-2} day^{-1}, with an average of 670 mg C m^{-2} day^{-1}, nearly 70% of which was contributed by the <200 µm size fraction. Production was in the range of higher values reported by other authors for the same region, e.g. a January to March range of 160–680 (El-Sayed & Mandelli, 1965), 350–1560 (El-Sayed, 1978) and 58–170 (v. Brockel, 1981). Fig. 2.5 depicts the vertical distribution of primary production for two ice-free stations and one covered with about 70% of ice floes. Around the Antarctic Peninsula and the northern Weddell Sea v. Brockel (1981) found that the very small phytoplankton (<20 µm) contributed between 60 and 90% of the total primary production.

It is clear that primary production is highly variable, especially in the pack ice zone. High values have been found where investigators encountered spring phytoplankton blooms. A number of authors have suggested that the interaction between hydrography and topography is the most important factor influencing the build-up of phytoplankton spring blooms in the Southern Ocean

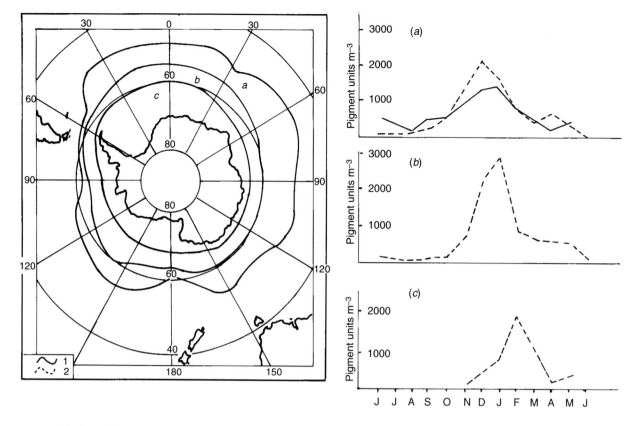

Fig. 2.6. Left. Phytoplankton zonation in the Southern Ocean (delineated by solid lines). (*a*) Northern Zone (ca 50° 00′–55° 50′ S); (*b*) Intermediate Zone (*c*. 55° 50′–66° 00′ S) (*c*) Southern Zone (Modified from Voronina, 1984). Right. Seasonal variation in plant pigment concentrations with latitude, (*a*) Northern Zone; (*b*) Intermediate Zone; (*c*) Southern Zone (After Hart's 1942 *Discovery* data). In (*a*) data from *Eltanin* cruises (El-Sayed, 1971a,b) are plotted for comparison. Redrawn from El-Sayed (1988b); modified from Voronina (1984).

(Hart, 1934; El-Sayed, 1984; Sakshaug & Holm-Hansen, 1984; v. Bodungen *et al.*, 1986). Jennings *et al.* (1984) emphasize the impact on phytoplankton production of brief, intense spring blooms which occur at the receding ice edge. This will be discussed further in Chapter 13. Jennings *et al.* (1984) derived productivity estimates for localities in the Weddell Sea from the seasonal depletion of phosphate and silicic acid. In the surface layer this gave production values 1.5 to 4 times higher than previously reported estimates of primary production in open areas of the Southern Ocean. It would appear that if blooms are not encountered the total primary production may be considerably underestimated.

2.5.2 *Vertical distribution of primary production*

Maximum photosynthetic activity generally occurs at depths corresponding to a photosynthetically available radiation (PAR) of between 500 and 100 μE m^{-2} s^{-1} (v. Bodungen, 1986). Carbon fixation, however, has been measured in samples well below the euphotic zone. For example, El-Sayed & Taguchi (1981) and El-Sayed *et al.* (1983) report that the primary production below the euphotic zone in the Ross and Weddell Seas was nearly one-fourth of the total water column production. However, in the Atlantic and Indian Ocean sectors carbon fixation below the euphotic zone did not exceed 5 to 10% of that in the euphotic zone (El-Sayed & Jitts, 1973; El-Sayed & Weber, 1982).

Based on *in situ* primary productivity experiments conducted by El-Sayed during *Eltanin* cruises 38, 46 and 51 in the Pacific and Atlantic sectors, a mean primary productivity value of 0.134 g C m^{-2} day^{-1} was calculated (El-Sayed & Turner, 1977). This mean value is considerably lower than those reported for phytoplankton blooms. The following conclusions can be drawn from the studies carried out to date on primary production in the Southern Ocean: (a) the productivity of these waters varies by at least one or two orders of magnitude; and (b) Antarctic waters, in general, exhibit high productivity levels mainly in coastal waters, especially at the receding ice edge. El-Sayed (1984) points out that given the fact that the ocean south of the Antarctic Convergence contains a circumpolar phytoplankton population living in a fairly uniform environment, with sufficient light for photosynthesis (at least during the spring and summer), a population that is more or less adapted to cold temperatures and with an abundant nutrient supply, it is somewhat surprising that the phytoplankton is not only patchily distributed, but very low in diversity, approaching that of an oligotrophic ocean over vast areas. According to Holm-Hansen & Huntley (1984) the nutrient levels should be able to support a phytoplankton biomass of at least 25 µg chl *a* l^{-1}, but it seldom attains this density except for the blooms referred to above.

2.6 Seasonal and geographic variation of phytoplankton biomass and primary production

At present there is a relative dearth of long-term phytoplankton data from the Southern Ocean and a further complication is that the information on seasonal cycles based on data from single stations, or from single depths, may not be representative (El-Sayed, 1987). For example, deep chlorophyll *a* maxima will be missed entirely if surface samples are used to reconstruct the seasonal cycle of phytoplankton biomass (Harris, 1980). Further, large-scale advection may also modify the seasonal cycle as observed at a single point if the seasonal cycle differs between water masses. These complications need to be borne in mind when examining the seasonal variability of the phytoplankton.

In spite of the methods that Hart (1934, 1942) used, his is still the most complete set of data on seasonal variability of Antarctic phytoplankton. He demonstrated that the onset of the period of maximum production changes from early spring to late summer or early winter with increasing latitude (Fig. 2.6). Further his data showed that the period of maximum production decreased in duration with increasing latitude and, further, that annual differences in hydrographic conditions could affect the timing and the magnitude of these peaks and the species that were active during the period. These early observations by Hart have been corroborated by many subsequent investigators. In Fig. 2.6 the marked resemblance between El-Sayed's (1971a,b) observations and those made by Hart in his 'Northern Zone' is clearly seen.

Holm-Hansen *et al.* (1989) in studies of phytoplankton blooms in the vicinity of Palmer Station, Anvers Island, in January have shown that the dynamics of such blooms are different from those of oceanic waters to the north. Large phytoplankton blooms in coastal waters appear to be predictable from year to year and to be of widespread geographical significance (Balech *et al.*, 1968; Krebs, 1983; Holm-Hansen *et al.* 1989; Knox, 1990). Holm-Hansen *et al.* (1989) found that in both 1985 and 1987 phytoplankton blooms in the vicinity of Palmer Station achieved concentrations of 20–30 µg chl *a* l^{-1}. Studies of phytoplankton growth in non-enriched seawater samples from the Antarctic have shown that the 'potential' for phytoplankton growth in waters of the Southern Ocean is generally in the range of 25–30 µg chl *a* l^{-1}, before nutrient limitations limit further increases in biomass (Sakshaug & Holm-Hansen, 1986; Spies, 1987). Holm-Hansen *et al.* (1989) found that in their studies the phytoplankton biomass had probably come close to depleting one or more essential elements, for example phosphate was below detectable levels (0.02 µM), and nitrate levels were as low as 1.0 µM. This is in contrast to nearly all previous studies in the Antarctic which have shown much higher nutrient concentrations, with nitrate, for instance, generally always above 10 µM and usually above 20 µM (Tilzer *et al.*, 1985; Nelson *et al.*, 1987; v. Bodungen, 1986).

As discussed previously nanoplankton sized cells tend to dominate Antarctic phytoplankton communities, especially in oceanic waters. In contrast, Holm-Hansen *et al.* (1989) found that not only was the microplankton a large and important component of the total phytoplankton biomass (approximately 42%), but that a significant proportion (about 20%) was retained on 202 µm Nitrix mesh netting. Size fractionation studies showed that nanoplankton accounted for only about 28% of the total phytoplankton biomass and that there was a near absence of heterotrophic protozoa. Larger cells (mainly diatoms) dominated and there was little active grazing during the early developmental stages of the bloom. Under such conditions of high phytoplankton biomass it appears that the cells are light-limited and hence dark-adapted resulting in high chl *a* :ATP ratios (average 7.6) and low assimilation values (0.49–1.64). These difference between coastal and oceanic waters will be discussed further in Chapter 15.

2.7 Factors influencing primary production

Forty-five years ago Hart (1934) reviewed the possible factors limiting the production of phytoplankton in the Southern Ocean. He concluded that of the major nutrients only silicate was likely to be limiting but then only in certain areas. Hart thought that it was the physical features of the environment (light intensity and duration, ice cover, surface water stability and currents) that exerted the 'strongest influence upon phytoplankton production in the far south'. Since then there has been considerable progress in our understanding of algal physiology and ecology and there has been an increasing number of physiological and ecological studies specifically dealing with Antarctic phytoplankton. In the last decade there have been a number of reviews of the factors governing the ecology and productivity of Antarctic phytoplankton (see Fogg, 1977; Holm-Hansen *et al.*, 1977; El-Sayed, 1978, 1984, 1985, 1987, 1988a,b; Jacques, 1983; Heywood & Whitaker, 1984; Priddle *et al.*, 1986a; Sakshaug &

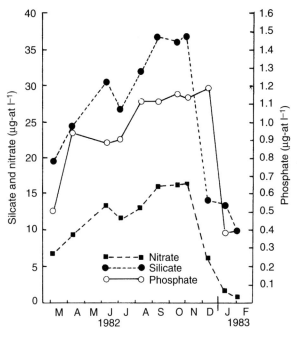

Fig. 2.7. Seasonal changes in the averaged concentrations of nitrate, silicate and phosphate in the water column 1 km off Davis Station (68° 35′ S; 77° 50′ E). Redrawn from Perrin *et al.* (1987).

Holm-Hansen, 1986, for reviews). Of the many physical and chemical and biological factors that might limit phytoplankton productivity in the Southern Ocean, the availability of macro- and micronutrients, temperature, solar radiation, water column stability and zooplankton grazing are considered to be the more important. Each of these factors will be considered in turn.

2.7.1 Macronutrients

Numerous observations of the concentrations of nitrate, phosphate and silicate have been made in the Southern Ocean commencing with the *Discovery* investigations (Hart, 1942; Deacon, 1937; Clowes, 1938), and they have shown that they are high in the surface waters and remain so throughout the year (Holm-Hansen *et al.*, 1977; Whitaker, 1982; Jacques, 1983; El-Sayed, 1984; Hayes *et al.*, 1984). The results of a series of enrichment and bioassay experiments in the Southern Ocean between 20° and 70° W carried out by Hayes *et al.* (1984) suggested that the availability of nitrate, phosphate, silicate, trace metals and vitamins exerted no control over phytoplankton production. Even at the peak of phytoplankton growth the concentration of nutrients generally remains well above limiting values. El-Sayed (1978b) measured 2.49 g-at l⁻¹ NO_2-N, 2.02 g-at l⁻¹ PO_4-P, and 18.00 g-at l⁻¹ SiO_2-Si, during a dense phytoplankton bloom in the Weddell Sea.

However, seasonal decreases of surface nutrient concentrations do occur in the summer and appear to be geographically widespread (Jennings *et al.* 1984). but even in

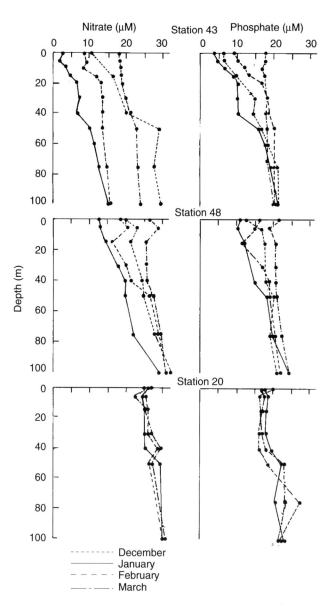

Fig. 2.8. Inorganic nitrogen (NO_3^- + NO_2^-) and phosphate concentrations in the southwestern Bransfield Strait and adjacent waters at stations with high biomass (Station 43), intermediate values for biomass (Station 48), and low biomass (Station 20). There were no data from Station 20 in December as it was covered by sea ice. Redrawn from Holm-Hansen & Mitchell (1991).

mid-summer the surface concentrations of nitrate, phosphate and silicate generally remain high enough (>25, >1.75, and 30 μM, respectively) to ensure that the phytoplankton are not nutrient limited. On the other hand, a number of studies have revealed that significant nutrient depletion can take place in certain circumstances. Satoh *et al.* (1986) found that in Pryds Bay, where there were high concentrations of chlorophyll *a* (>2.0 g l⁻¹) in the upper water layer, in the zone of the phytoplankton bloom nutrients were depressed; <1.0 g-at P l⁻¹ , < 10 g-at Si l⁻¹, and <16 g-at N l⁻¹. Off Davis Station Perrin et al. (1987) found that the concentrations of nitrate, phosphate and

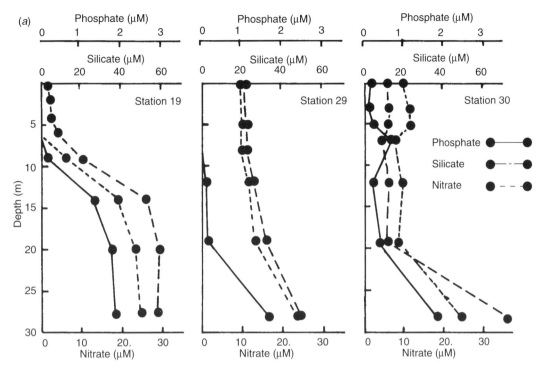

Fig. 2.9. (*a*). Vertical profiles of nitrate, phosphate, and silicic acid concentrations at 3 stations (Stations, 19, 29 and 30) in an ice edge phytoplankton bloom in the western Ross Sea. Stations 19 and 20 were the only ones at which nitrate and phosphate were depleted to undetectable concentrations within the surface layer. The profiles of Station 30 are more typical of the general condition within the bloom; there was clear depletion of nutrient concentrations within the surface layer, but the lowest concentrations observed were, well above analytical detection limits. Redrawn from Nelson & Smith (1986).

silicate increased throughout the year until December, when the concentration of silicate and nitrate fell sharply, followed a month later by reduction in phosphate concentration (Fig. 2.7). Inorganic nitrogen and phosphate concentrations in the upper 100 m of the water column at three stations in the southwestern Bransfield Strait, which are representative of stations with high, intermediate and low phytoplankton biomass (Stations 43, 48 and 20 respectively) are shown in Fig. 2.8 (Holm-Hansen & Mitchell, 1991). Nutrients were reduced to low levels (1.9 mmol m^{-3} inorganic nitrogen; 0.37 mmol m^{-3} phosphate) during January at Station 43 and increased during February and March to relatively high concentrations, while there was very little seasonal depletion at Station 20. Nutrients at Station 48 were intermediate between the other two stations.

However, during a *Phaeocystis pouchetii* bloom encountered by El-Sayed *et al.* (1983) nitrate concentrations were still high, with euphotic zone concentrations averaging 17 g-at l^{-1}. Within the high-biomass core of a very intensive ice edge phytoplankton bloom in the western Ross Sea (Nelson & Smith, 1986) uptake by phytoplankton depleted both nitrate and phosphate to analytically undetectable concentrations at some individual stations within the bloom (Fig. 2.9*a*). Apart from these exceptions the concentrations of nitrate, phosphate and

silicic acid generally exceeded 4, 0.1 and 10 μM, respectively, concentrations high enough to allow most planktonic algae to take up nutrients at their maximum experimental rates (Nelson *et al.*, 1981). It could therefore be concluded that nutrient availability is seldom, if ever, a significant limiting factor to the phytoplankton in the Southern Ocean.

There is, however, some evidence that under certain conditions nutrients could be limiting. Whitaker (1977a,b) in a series of experiments in Borge Bay, Signy Island found that the addition of phosphates and nitrates separately and in combination indicated that PO$_4$-P was rate limiting below 0.59 g-at l^{-1} for a natural mixed population of phytoplankton dominated by the diatom *Thalassiosira antarctica*. At that time the summer minimum of PO$_4$-P was 0.34 g-at l^{-1}. According to Walsh (1971) and Allanson *et al.* (1981) the pattern of silicate distribution indicates that silicates may be the most limiting of the major nutrients to phytoplankton growth.

However, it may not be the total quantity of nitrogen, phosphorus and silicon that is important but the uptake preferences for a particular molecular species of the inorganic nutrients in relation to the proportions of these species in the environment (Priddle *et al.*, 1986b). A recent analysis by Priddle *et al.* (1986b) has indicated the importance of silicon and its ratio to phosphorus in

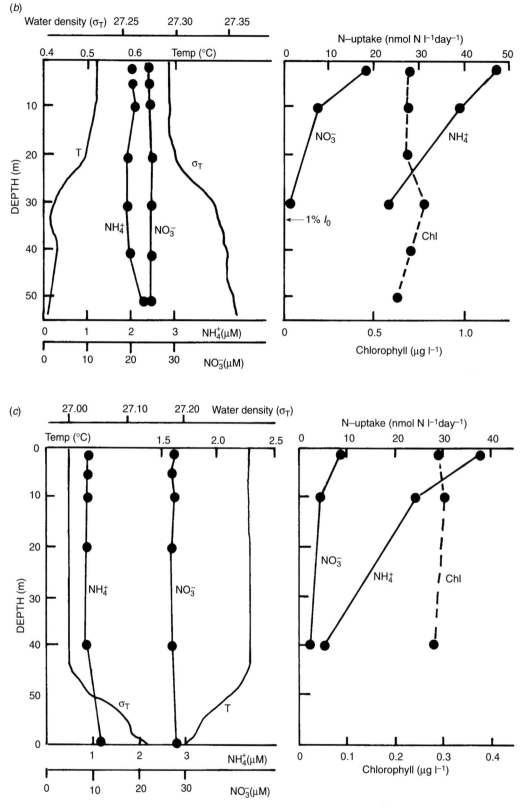

Fig. 2.9 (*b–c*). Depth profiles of physical, nutritional and biological properties at (*b*) a coastal station near Elephant Island in the southern Scotia Sea; and (*c*) an offshore station in the southern Scotia Sea. Depth of the euphotic zone (i.e. the depth at which the light is reduced to 1% of the incident surface value) in (*b*) and (*c*) indicated by the arrow. Redrawn from Koike *et al.* (1986).

interpreting phytoplankton dynamics near South Georgia. The very high measured concentrations of nitrogen are usually nitrate. However, N-uptake experiments with Antarctic phytoplankton have shown that ammonia, or occasionally urea (where measured), is the preferred nitrogen substrate, with between 50 and 80% of all the nitrogen assimilated by Antarctic phytoplankton being in the form of ammonium (Slawyk, 1979; Olson, 1980; Koike *et al.*, 1981, 1986; Biggs, 1982; Gilbert *et al.*, 1982; Rönner *et al.*, 1983; Probyn & Painting, 1985), and with the nanoplankton showing a higher uptake of ammonium than the microplankton. On the other hand, Colos & Slawyk (1986) concluded that nitrate could account for most of the primary production of the Southern Ocean south of the Antarctic Convergence.

Experiments by Koike *et al.* (1986) in the southern Scotia Sea in February 1981 determined that up to 93% of the phytoplankton nitrogen was at that time assimilated in the form of ammonium, with an overall mean of 78%. Time course experiments showed that the uptake of nitrate and ammonium during nighttime amounted to approximately 15 and 50% respectively of daytime values. Over the shallow waters of the Scotia shelf most of the ammonium uptake was associated with the nanoplankton. Profiles of nitrogen uptake rates, together with profiles of nutrients and water density are shown in Fig. 2.9*b* and *c*. It can be seen that the coastal waters (Fig. 2.9*b*) had more ammonium than offshore waters (Fig. 2.9*c*). Uptake rates decreased with depth. Probyn & Painting (1985) have found evidence of nitrogen resource partitioning between algae of different size classes. The average ammonium uptake as a percentage of total nitrogen uptake amounted to 62% for the nanoplankton and 75% for the picoplankton. In the eastern Scotia Sea Rönner *et al.* (1983) found that the summer phytoplankton production subsisted on ammonium (83%), with lower incorporation rates of nitrate (14%) and nitrite (1%).

In general ammonium represents only a small fraction (2–10%) of the inorganic nitrogen pool (Biggs *et al.*, 1983). It is possible that the phytoplankton switch to nitrate nutrition where ammonium levels are low, although Priddle *et al.* (1986a) found no evidence of this in their studies off South Georgia. However, Probyn and Painting (1985) using ^{15}N-labelled substrates to measure nutrient preferences of phytoplankton at five Southern Ocean stations found that high relative uptake of nitrate, particularly by cells >15 μm occurred at stations with low ammonium and urea concentrations.

2.7.2 Micronutrients

A range of mineral micronutrients (Mo, Mn, Co, Zn, Cu, V, B, Cl, Mg, Fe) have been shown to be important in plant growth. In addition a number of organic substrates, especially vitamins, are implicated. Volkovinskii (1966) found a positive correlation between phytoplankton production and levels of magnesium and molybdenum in the Weddell Sea. El-Sayed (1968b) concluded that cobalt zinc, copper and vanadium may be important, as may be iron (Fogg, 1977). Carlucci and Cuhel (1977), after studying the significance of vitamins, B_{12}, thiamine, and biotin in the Indian Ocean sector, concluded that most of the phytoplankton did not require vitamins. However, it is possible that availability of vitamins might alter the species composition of the phytoplankton without altering the overall rate of phytoplankton production. It is also possible that the availability of trace/micronutrients may be altered by pack-ice and iceberg meltwater, thus affecting the productivity or species composition of the waters in the vicinity of pack ice and icebergs. The role of trace elements and organic substances in the ecology of the Southern Ocean would appear to be a profitable future research area.

Iron is a particularly important macronutrient because it is instrumental in the biosynthesis of chlorophyll, and is a main component of ferrodoxin, which facilitates the intracellular transfer and storage of photosynthetically incorporated energy (Davies, 1990). Hart (1942) first suggested that the high productivity of Antarctic coastal waters relative to the open ocean was due to the presence of iron or manganese derived from the land. Martin *et al.*, (1990a) hypothesized that Antarctic phytoplankton suffer from iron deficiency which prevents them from blooming and using up the plentiful supply of nutrients that are present. They found that the highly productive inshore waters of the Gerlache Strait (3 g C m^{-2} day^{-1}) have an abundant supply of iron (7.4 nmol kg^{-1}) which facilitates phytoplankton blooming, whereas in the offshore Drake Passage waters (0.1 g C m^{-2} yr^{-1}) the dissolved iron levels are so low (0.16 nmol kg^{-1}) that the phytoplankton can use less than 10% of the available nutrients.

These conclusions have been challenged by other workers (e.g. Dugdale & Wilkerson, 1990; Broecker, 1990; Peng & Broecker, 1991). A. G. Davies (1990) questioned whether the 'dissolved' iron estimates of Martin *et al.* (1990a), based on the fraction of iron that passed through a 0.4 μm polycarbonate membrane filter, is truly in solution and thus available to the phytoplankton. de Baar *et al.* (1989, 1990) tested the iron hypothesis in a series of experiments in the Weddell and Scotia Seas encompassing different water masses and various phytoplankton communities, biomass and dynamic spring/summer conditions. Iron always stimulated chlorophyll *a* synthesis and nutrient assimilation. However, the controls also steadily outgrew typical chlorophyll *a* and particulate

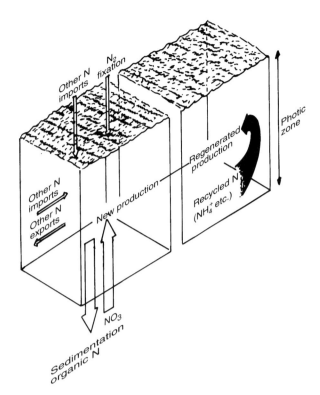

Fig. 2.10. Schematic diagram of the principal fluxes for new and regenerated primary production. The sole support for the regenerated production is reduced nitrogen supplied within the photic zone by the excretion of organisms. New production depends on nitrogen supplied from outside the photic zone, of which the dominant flux is the delivery of nitrate from below. In the steady state this vertical flux is balanced by the downward flux of nitrogen in sedimenting particles. Over a period of a year, current evidence is that in the open ocean, new production is very roughly from one third to one half of the regenerated production, but may deviate considerably from this figure over short time- and space-scales. Redrawn from Platt *et al.* (1989).

organic carbon (POC) levels in ambient waters. This strongly suggested that despite the enhancement of phytoplankton growth, iron was not the major factor controlling phytoplankton growth in the Weddell and Scotia Seas. Marginal sediments appeared to supply adequate dissolved iron for supporting at least the minimal growth of the phytoplankton. Banse (1990) points out that Fe limitation might apply not to the entire phytoplankton community but only to the larger diatoms. In the oligotrophic waters of the Southern Ocean as we have seen the phytoplankton is dominated by the smaller pico- and nano-phytoplankton. Thus it seems that the role of Fe in phytoplankton growth in the Southern Ocean is not yet resolved.

2.7.3 Nutrient cycling in the Southern Ocean

The limiting elemental resource for plant production in most oceanic regions is believed to be nitrogen (Carpenter & Capone, 1983), which is supplied in various chemical forms from a variety of sources. Thus primary production can be partitioned according to the source and oxidation state of the nitrogen substances utilized (Dugdale & Goering, 1967). This partition is based on whether the nitrogen is supplied by regeneration from organisms within the euphotic zone (regenerated production, P_r), or from outside the photic zone (new production, P_{new}). In the open ocean, the dominant contribution to the externally-supplied nitrogen is in the form of nitrate (Fogg, 1982), whereas regenerated production depends only on reduced nitrogen compounds, in particular ammonia. The sum of P_{new} and P_r is referred to as the total production, P_T. Total production is the nitrogen equivalent of gross primary production (P_g), in the sense that it represents the sum total of the nitrogen assimilation of the photoautotrophs. However, according to Platt *et al.* (1989) since there is no evidence that phytoplankton remineralize nitrogen, a case can be made for equating P_T with P_n. Fig 2.10 is a schematic diagram of the principal fluxes for new and regenerated production.

'Regenerated production' is intimately related to the rates of remineralization of organic matter by biological and chemical processes in the euphotic zone. The microbial processes which are involved in this process will be discussed further in Chapter 14. 'New production', on the other hand, is maintained by the supply of nitrogen by advection and turbulence from deeper waters. Studies assessing the roles of 'new' nitrogen (in the oxidized form as nitrate) and 'regenerated' nitrogen (in the form of ammonium) have given conflicting results depending on the type of system studied (e.g. open ocean, ice edge bloom, or coastal waters), and the time of year. Ammonium appears to play an important role in the nutrition of Antarctic phytoplankton in the open ocean and is generally present in substantial amounts throughout the euphotic zone. Concentrations have been found to increase from 0.1 µM in the late winter to early spring (Olson, 1980) to over 1.0 µM in late summer and autumn (Gilbert *et al.*, 1982; Rönner *et al.*, 1983). Investigations mostly in offshore waters (Slawyk, 1979; Olson, 1980; Gilbert *et al.*, 1982; Rönner *et al.*, 1983) have shown that Antarctic phytoplankton generally derive at least 50% of their nitrogen from ammonium. In an investigation of coastal waters in the Scotia Sea in February–March 1981 Koike *et al.* (1986) found that in spite of the high concentration of nitrate present (21 to 19 µM), up to 93% of the phytoplankton nitrogen was assimilated in the form of ammonium (Fig. 2.9). Over the shallow waters of the Scotia Arc close to Elephant Island, most of the ammonium was associated with nanoplankton, which actively assimilated both ammonium and nitrate, while the microplankton assimilated mostly nitrate.

On the other hand, in a study of phytoplankton bloom dynamics in the western Ross ice edge discussed above Nelson & Smith (1986) found that ammonium concentrations within the bloom were frequently below detection limits (<0.1 μM), and nearly always less than 0.25 μM. Rates of nitrate uptake were high enough to satisfy approximately 65% of the phytoplankton nitrogen demand estimated from C-primary productivity and particulate organic carbon:nitrogen ratios. The mean rate of biogenic silica production within the bloom was 38 mmol Si m^{-2} day^{-1}, which is an order of magnitude higher than previous estimates for the Southern Ocean remote from the ice edge (Nelson *et al.*, 1981). The significance of the observed high rates of nitrate uptake and biogenic silica production in the ice edge phytoplankton blooms will be discussed further in Chapter 13.

There are as yet comparatively few data for microbial remineralization of inorganic nutrients in the Southern Ocean, but it appears that nitrogen, and probably phosphorus, are recycled rapidly in the euphotic zone. Rönner *et al.* (1983) consider that nitrogen may be recycled approximately eight times before it is lost from the euphotic zone. Although a number of studies suggest rapid recycling of nutrients through the microbial community (Le Jehan & Treguer, 1985; Rönner *et al.*, 1983; Holm-Hansen, 1985), levels of ammonium ions remain low in the Southern Ocean indicating that it is rapidly used by the phytoplankton.

Holm-Hansen (1985) poses the question: 'What is the source of ammonia in Antarctic waters?' Since ammonium is not detectable in deep-water, upwelling could not be the source. Very small amounts originate from the atmosphere or the melting of ice. Thus it appears that nearly all of the ammonium must originate from *in situ* processes occurring in the euphotic zone. Data from Biggs (1982) suggest that a maximum of 2% of the ammonia flux could be accounted for by the grazing effects of net zooplankton (organisms greater than 200 μm) so it can be concluded that over 90% of the ammonium results from the activities of microbial organisms.

2.7.4 Temperature

Early workers (e.g. Gran, 1932 and Hart, 1934) thought that Antarctic marine plants were fully adapted to the prevailing low temperatures of the Southern Ocean. However, subsequently temperature has been commonly listed as one of the major factors influencing phytoplankton production (e.g. Saijo & Kawashi, 1964). The effects of temperature on photosynthetic carbon uptake have been investigated for a number of Antarctic phytoplankton species (Bunt, 1968b; Whitaker, 1977b; Neori & Holm-Hansen, 1982; Jacques, 1983; Hoepffner, 1984;

Tilzer *et al.*, 1985, 1986; Tilzer & Dubinsky, 1987). The species studied constantly showed maximum uptake of inorganic carbon at temperatures in the range of 7–12 °C, well above the ambient temperature range. Neori & Holm-Hansen (1982) in experiments conducted in the Scotia Sea/northern Weddell Sea concluded that temperature limited primary production rates at times when light intensity was saturating the photochemical apparatus of the cell. Since the phytoplankton are saturated by light intensities which are approximately 10–15% of that generally incident on the sea surface, it can be assumed that temperature will be a rate controlling factor in the upper 10–12 m of the water column (Fig. 2.11) (El-Sayed, 1988a). Fukuchi *et al.* (1986) observed variable positive or negative relationships between temperature and chlorophyll in the zones of the Subtropical Convergence, the Sub-Antarctic Front and the Antarctic Convergence. This variable relationship has also been noted by Hayes *et al.* (1984) and Taniguchi *et al.* (1986). Tilzer *et al.* (1986) studied carbon fixation rates of Southern Ocean phytoplankton incubated at various irradiances and temperatures. They found that the rates of both light-saturated- and light-induced-photosynthesis were temperature dependent in the range of –1.5 to 5.0 °C, with values for Q_{10} of 4.2 and 2.6 respectively. Above 5.0 °C no temperature enhancement could be detected. The authors concluded that Antarctic marine phytoplankton had not evolved mechanisms to overcome the inhibiting effects of low temperature on photosynthesis, although the temperature optimum for photosynthesis was low by comparison with phytoplankton from lower latitudes.

Temperature optima for growth (measured as the increase in cell numbers or biomass), as opposed to carbon fixation, may be closer to ambient temperatures, and growth rates at ambient temperatures may exceed predicted values such as those established by Eppley (1972). Recorded specific growth rates (μ) for Antarctic phytoplankton are of the order of 0.1 to 0.3 doublings per day in the Ross Sea (Holm-Hansen *et al.*, 1977), between 0.4 and 0.6 doublings per day in the southern Indian Ocean (Jacques & Minas, 1981), and 0.51 to 2.10 in the Indian Ocean sector south of Africa (Miller *et al.*, 1985). The maximum rate of 2.10 doublings per day was higher than the previously recorded maximum of 0.7 doublings per day (El-Sayed & Taguchi, 1981), and the mean of 1.23 doublings per day found by Miller *et al.* (1985) is also significantly higher than other recorded means. It also exceeds Eppley's (1972) theoretically predicted maximum growth rate for phytoplankton at 1.0 °C (0.91 doublings per day). There is thus a wide variation in recorded growth rates with evidence both in favour of and against the hypothesis that the low temperatures of

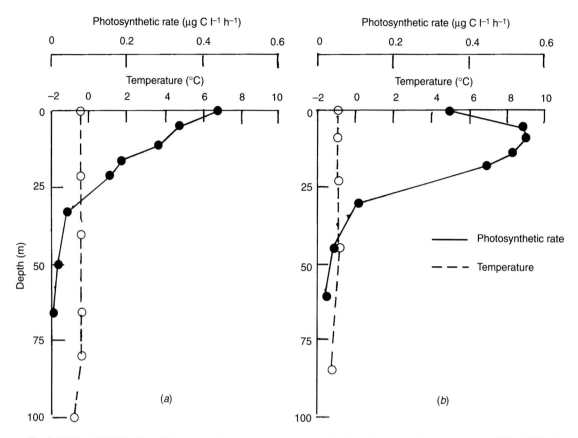

Fig. 2.11. Vertical distribution of photosynthetic rate and temperature in the Ross Sea during *Eltanin* cruise, Jan.–Feb., 1972: (*a*) Station 14 where PAR (photosynthetically available radiation) was 32 cal cm^{-2} (half-light-day)$^{-1}$; (*b*) Station 16 where PAR was 72 cal cm^{-2} (half-light day)$^{-1}$. Redrawn from Holm-Hansen *et al.* (1977).

Antarctic waters do limit algal growth rates. It would appear that under certain conditions growth rates are limited, while under others the low temperatures do not consistently limit phytoplankton biomass production, thus suggesting that phytoplankton photosynthesis in Antarctic waters may show *some* adaptive response to low ambient temperatures.

2.7.5 *Light*
Variations in available light intensity, duration and spectra are important factors in influencing phytoplankton growth in the Southern Ocean. Total incident radiation is a function of latitude, with higher latitudes experiencing more drastic variations (Fig. 2.12). Regions within the Antarctic Circle (66° S) will experience a period of complete darkness in winter (60 days at 75° S, 100 days at 75° S). This variation in light intensity is illustrated in Fig. 2.13 in which the mean values of radiant energy (with average cloudiness) are plotted, together with values of primary production and standing crop of phytoplankton collected in Antarctic waters. It is evident that phytoplankton biomass and primary production are directly related to the amount of energy received. During the austral summer months the total daily light flux can

exceed that of tropical latitudes (Holm-Hansen *et al.*, (1977).

Superimposed upon the annual pattern of incident radiation are a number of other factors influencing the availability of the light energy to the phytoplankton. Firstly the height of the sun above the horizon is relatively lower for a greater part of the year than in temperate and tropical latitudes. This low angle of incidence of the sun's rays increases the reflection from the sea surface. The period of effective submarine light per day is also reduced. Secondly, the Southern Ocean is particularly stormy affecting surface reflection, as well as producing bubbles which reduce transmission through the surface waters very considerably (Powell & Clarke, 1936). Light variation induced by turbulent mixing (Falkowski & Wirick, 1981) operates on a time scale which is highly variable (Falkowski, 1983). In experiments on Antarctic diatoms designed to study the effects of fluctuating light regimes it was found that cells grown under alternating periods of light and dark, which simulated the conditions of vertical mixing, revealed a higher rate of productivity than algae grown in continouus light. This increased efficiency of light utilization in a environment characterized by fluctuating light conditions is probably an adaptation enabling

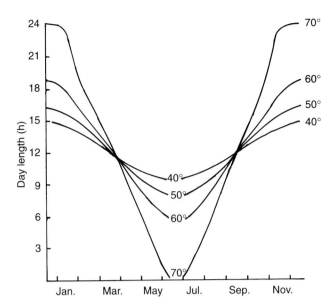

Fig. 2.12. Latitudinal variation in day length over the year and hence in the daily incident radiation in the Southern Ocean.

the algae to overcome such restraints and attain a higher productivity than expected. Thirdly, 56% of the Southern Ocean is covered with ice during the winter. Most of this breaks up, drifts north and melts during the summer, but approximately 17.5% of the sea ice remains as fast or pack ice. The ice, and especially the associated snow cover, reduces considerably the amount of radiation entering the water column and changes its spectral quality (Hoshiai, 1969; Whitaker, 1982; Palmisano & Sullivan, 1985b). This may amplify the annual variation in the amount of light that enters the water column 10 000-fold. The variation in the factors discussed above in combination is reflected in the extreme seasonality of phytoplankton growth in the Southern Ocean.

It is clear that the Antarctic phytoplankton are subjected to highly variable light regimes which can fluctuate on a variety of time scales. There is evidence that the phytoplankton of the pack ice zone are adapted to the low light levels caused by the presence of the ice. Holm-Hansen & Mitchell (1991) found that the summer populations in the southwestern Bransfield Strait were low-light adapted as they showed low P_{max} values (1.1 mg C (mg chl a)$^{-1}$ hr^{-1}), low saturating light values I_k = (18 µE m^{-2} s^{-1}), high initial slope of the fitted curve to plotted assimilation numbers, AN (0.06 (mg C (mg chl a)$^{-1}$ h^{-1} / µE m^{-2} s^{-1})), and a compensation point (see below) for net activated fixation of CO_2 of 1.0 µE m^{-2} s^{-1}. The P_{max} was higher than those reported by Tilzer *et al.* (1985), but similar to the mean value reported for the same region by Brightman & Smith (1989) and to those for Arctic waters (Harrison & Platt, 1986). The observed AN is higher and the I_k is lower than the values of Tilzer *et al.* (1985),

Sakshaug & Holm-Hansen (1986) and Brightman & Smith (1989). Holm-Hansen & Mitchell's (1991) AN value, however, was based on *in situ* observations and the algae in their study were low-light adapted.

In their study of the effect of radiant energy on the photosynthetic activity of Antarctic phytoplankton Holm-Hansen *et al.* (1977) found a high degree of correlation between the intensity of the solar radiation and the photosynthetic rates in the euphotic zone. When incident light was high, photosynthetic rates were low in the surface waters and these rates increased with depth. On the other hand, when incident light was low, photosynthetic rates remained constant in the upper waters of the euphotic zone, or were highest in the surface waters (Fig. 2.15). These results are most probably due to photoinhibition. The threshold for photoinhibition for Antarctic phytoplankton was calculated to be in the range of 40 to 50 cal m^{-2} (half light day)$^{-1}$. Sakshaug & Holm-Hansen (1986) have recently shown that the photochemical apparatus of Antarctic phytoplankton is 'saturated' at between 100–180 µE m^{-2} s^{-1}, depending on the depth from which the sample was taken. As the incident light flux (on a sunny day) is about 1500 µE m^{-2} s^{-1} it is evident that the phytoplankton in the surface waters will be either 'saturated' by the ambient flux, or will be photoinhibited. Jacques (1983) contends that during such times the phytoplankton are unable to use the available light optimally in the euphotic zone.

Particularly important is the effect of temperature on the compensation point light intensity (Heywood & Whitaker, 1984). The compensation point light intensity is that in which the production of carbon exactly balances carbon loss through other metabolic processes (as indicated by respiration). Cell growth occurs when light levels are above the compensation point light intensity. At the low temperatures of the Southern Ocean the rate of respiration (or carbon loss) is suppressed more than the photosynthetic rate (carbon gain). The result is a proportionate increase in net production for a given light intensity and the compensation point light intensity is correspondingly lowered. Based on their study of the effects of temperature and day length on Antarctic phytoplankton growth, Tilzer & Dubinsky (1987) suggested that under ample light energy supply during the long summer days in Antarctic waters, potential daily growth rates are not severely affected by the prevailing low temperatures. They also concluded that if the energy supply is restricted by short days and deep water column mixing, subsequently reduced respiration rates would allow the algae to survive.

Tilzer *et al.* (1985) in studies of phytoplankton photosynthesis in the Bransfield Strait and the Scotia Sea found

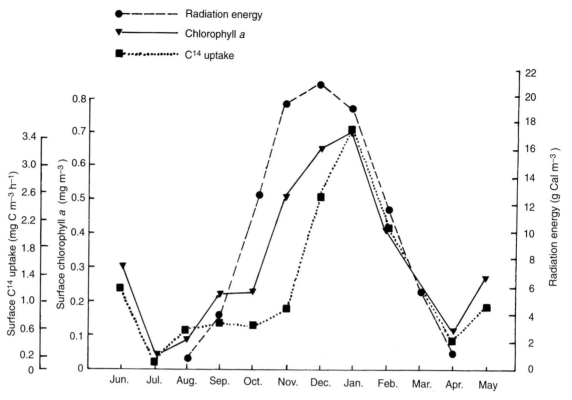

Fig. 2.13. Monthly variation of radiant energy (with average cloudiness) at Maudheim Station (71° 03′ S; 10° 56′ W) compared with monthly changes in surface chlorophyll *a* and C[14] uptake in Antarctic waters. Redrawn from El-Sayed (1971a).

that photosynthetic capacity (photosynthesis per unit of chlorophyll *a* at optimum light) and maximum quantum yield of photosynthesis (moles carbon dioxide assimilated per mole light quantum absorbed) on average were smaller by factors of seven and four respectively than in phytoplankton at lower latitudes. They concluded that because the utilization efficiency of incident radiation was reduced in the Antarctic by both reductions in the photosynthetic capacity and lower light-limited quantum yields the phytoplankton can utilize incident light only inefficiently even in situations where biomass accumulation is high.

The photosynthetic efficiencies measured by Tilzer *et al.* (1985, 1986) ranged from 0.001 to 0.011 mg C (mg chl)$^{-1}$ h^{-1} (μE m^{-2} s^{-1}) l . On the other hand Brightman & Smith (1989) in the Bransfield Strait during the austral winter when the photoperiod was 6.1 h ($\pm$0.28) and the mean integrated daily irradiance was 0.795 μE m^{-2} ($\pm$0.263), measured an average photosynthetic efficiency (α) for the surface population of 0.121 (range 0.01 to 0.06) mg C (mg chl)$^{-1}$ h^{-1} (μE m^{-2} s^{-1}) and mean maximum photosynthetic rates (P_m^b) of 1.19 mg C (mg chl)$^{-1}$ h^{-1}. They concluded that the winter phytoplankton assemblage was adapted to low light conditions. That the light intensity required to saturate photosynthesis was *c.* 45 μE m^{-2} s^{-1}, compared to near 100 μE m^{-2} s^{-1} during Tilzer *et al.*'s

(1985, 1986) summer study, supported this conclusion. Chlorophyll *a* concentrations were low, ranging from 0.01 to 0.33 μg l^{-1} in the mixed layer, and integrated production within the euphotic zone was also low, 1 to 7 mg C m^{-2} day^{-1}. Summer values measured in the same region (Burkholder & Mandelli, 1965; El-Sayed 1967) were nearly two orders of magnitude greater than the winter ones. This adaptation to low light irradiance enables the phytoplankton to remain in an active state throughout the winter and they are hence available as inocula to initiate growth in the water column early in the austral spring.

2.7.6 Vertical mixing and stability of the water column

A number of investigators (Baarud & Klem, 1931; Gran, 1932; Sverdrup, 1953; Pingnee, 1978) have drawn attention to the importance of stability of the water column in controlling primary production and, hence, phytoplankton biomass. The length of time that the phytoplankton cells remain within the euphotic zone depends on the extent of vertical mixing (Lewis *et al.*, 1984). Sverdrup (1953) demonstrated theoretically that phytoplankton blooms will occur only when the depth of the mixed layer is less than the critical depth (the depth at which surface waters can be mixed without stopping plant growth). The critical depth in the Southern Ocean is generally between 150 and 200 m (Jacques & Minas, 1981). The surface

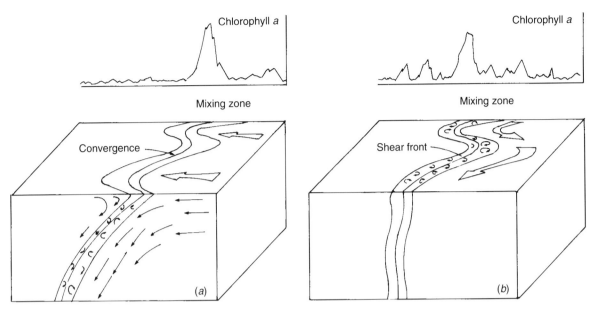

Fig. 2.14. Schematic illustration of the two types of dynamic ocean fronts found in the Southern Ocean, and the distribution of chlorophyll *a* concentrations at the sea surface across them: (*a*) a vertical convergence zone; (*b*) a horizontal shear front. Redrawn from Lutjeharms *et al.* (1985).

water of the Southern Ocean is characteristically well mixed with little vertical structure in the distribution of the inorganic nutrients. Mixed layer depths in the Southern Ocean are often difficult to define in the absence of a pycnocline but are usually >100 m. Euphotic depth (the depth to which 1% of the incident photosynthetic radiation penetrates) varies from 20 to 100 m over much of the Southern Ocean (Walsh, 1971; Gilbert *et al.*, 1982; Priddle *et al.*, 1986a,b). It would therefore seem that Sverdrup's critical depth hypothesis cannot explain low phytoplankton production in the Southern Ocean (Jacques, 1983). However, turbulence within the euphotic zone may play an insignificant role in preventing large increases in phytoplankton biomass (El-Sayed, 1987). Sakshaug & Holm-Hansen (1984) reported that for ten stations in the Scotia Sea when chlorophyll *a* was >2.0 mg m^{-3}, the pycnocline was located at 20–40 m. They speculated that 50 m may be the maximum pycnocline depth for a bloom to develop. Thus, the presence of a homogeneous (i.e. isothermal) water column reaching to depths of 50–100 m during most of the year hinders the development of blooms and contributes to the low primary production of Antarctic waters. It is of interest that the *Discovery* investigations found that the depth to which wind action was generally effective in overturning the water column in the open ocean (the depth of frictional resistance, Ekman, 1928) ranged from 60 to 80 m and the water was generally fairly uniform to a depth of 80 m, especially after storms (Deacon, 1937). Heywood observed a discontinuity layer at 112 m after a two-day storm at latitude 55° S (in the sector between 20° and 30°

E) (Heywood & Whitaker, 1984), and Nast & Gieskes (1986) reported a deep mixed layer (up to 200 m) north of Elephant Island as a result of high wind forces.

Priddle *et al.* (1986a) consider that the importance of energetic mixing and a deep mixed layer in diminishing phytoplankton production during the summer growing season has been overstated. They point out that few authors include measures of water column stability as environmental variables in descriptions of Antarctic marine phytoplankton ecology. Heywood & Priddle (quoted in Priddle *et al.*, 1986b) found that a region of very high phytoplankton biomass near King George Island, South Shetland Islands, coincided with local maxima of the coefficient of vertical stability, but attributed this, at least in part, to physical concentration of the cells rather than growth *in situ*. Weber & El-Sayed (1985a) found that water column stability was an important predictor variable for several attributes of the phytoplankton sampled at a series of stations between South Africa and the Antarctic continent (Dronning Maud Land). However, Priddle *et al.* (1986a) found that local phytoplankton biomass maxima which were found at a variety of locations from coastal to open sea could not be associated with increased vertical stability.

Bottom topography may, on a regional basis, play an important role in inducing vertical mixing. This was first suggested by Hart (1934) and corroborated by El-Sayed & Jitts (1973) at a station in close proximity to the Banzare Bank, which was notable for its extremely high standing stocks of phytoplankton and zooplankton. Lutjeharms *et al.* (1985) describe the occurrence of high levels of primary productivity and chlorophyll *a* concentrations, from a cruise between Africa and the Antarctic Continent, at sea surface fronts wherever such fronts have the characteristics of a convergence. Information gathered by the Coastal Zone Colour Scanner of the Nimbus-7 satellite off South Africa showed a clear relationship between the horizontal shear edges of currents and biological enhancement. Lutjeharms *et al.* (1985) recognized two types of fronts (Fig. 2.14), vertical convergence zones and horizontal shearing zones. In the former, conditions favourable to increased primary productivity may be created by an increase in density stratification in the upper layer enhancing vertical stability and causing retention of the phytoplankton in the euphotic zone. Higher than average values of chlorophyll *a* and primary production have been reported from the vicinity of the Antarctic Convergence (El-Sayed & Weber, 1982; Allanson *et al.*, 1981; Yamaguchi & Shibata, 1982). It is of interest that Kennett (1977) contends that the high rates of siliceous biogenic sedimentation at the Antarctic Convergence may be indicative of substantial primary production in the surface waters of this region. However, the continuous advection of phytoplankton into the frontal zone may be a mechanical means of increasing chlorophyll *a* concentrations without necessarily increasing primary production. A number of investigators (El-Sayed *et al.*, 1979; Grinley & Lane, 1979; Allanson *et al.*, 1985; Grinley & David, 1985) have reported enhanced chlorophyll *a* levels, primary production and zooplankton biomass in the lee of islands such as the Marion and Prince Edward Islands. Wind shear when coupled with island effects on the structure of the West Wind Drift causes vortex fields to be set up in the lee of the islands with consequent upwelling.

The vertical stability induced by meltwater has also been suggested as a significant process in initiating and sustaining near-ice phytoplankton blooms. B. G. Mitchell & Holm-Hansen (1991) in their multidisciplinary grid survey of the southwestern Bransfield Strait over the period December to March observed massive persistent mid-summer phytoplankton blooms (>10 mg chl *a* + phaeopigments m^{-2}) where there were shallow upper mixed layers (UMLs) of <20 m caused by meltwater stabilization. Stations with low phytoplankton biomass (<1.0 mg chl *a* + phaeo m^{-3}) had deep UMLs (>20 m) with small density gradients. The role of such melting and its impact on phytoplankton production will be considered in detail in Chapter 13.

2.7.7 *Grazing*

In the Southern Ocean euphausiids (particularly *Euphausia superba*) may constitute a substantial proportion of the zooplankton biomass and consequently their grazing potentially can have a significant impact on the phytoplankton. In areas where high concentrations of *E. superba* have been found low phytoplankton stocks have been encountered; this inverse relationship has been attributed to the effects of sustained grazing pressure (Uribe, 1982; El-Sayed, 1984; Whitaker, 1982). Weber & El-Sayed (1986a) concluded that while over the range of 4–20 km the variability in phytoplankton biomass was largely determined by physical processes, the steepness of the flourescence spectrum relative to the temperature spectra, together with consistent coherence between phytoplankton and krill profiles, suggested that predator–prey interactions were important in determining the distributional patterns of the phytoplankton on a smaller scale. In studies round Elephant Island in November 1983, Nast & Gieskes (1986) found a significant co-occurrence of high krill densities with low chlorophyll concentrations pointing to an inverse pytoplankton–zooplankton relationship. Price (1989) in mesocosm studies demonstrated that krill density within a phytoplankton bloom was higher by an order of magnitude than the control density within 0.5 hour after algal introduction. v. Bodungen *et al.* (1986) estimated the grazing loss of phytoplankton by krill at 45% of the primary production over a period of three weeks. However, large-scale surveys of phytoplankton standing stocks indicated that the build-up of blooms during the spring was not controlled by krill grazing. A distinct decline of large spring phytoplankton blooms prior to the occurrence of high krill densities has been noted by Witek *et al.* (1982b). v. Bodungen *et al.* (1986) have suggested that mass sedimentation of spring populations, triggered by deterioration of the physical environment, is the principal reason for the seasonal decline rather than grazing. This is in contrast to other regions where grazing has been reported as an important factor in controlling phytoplankton biomass build-up in the spring, e.g. for the sub-Arctic Pacific Ocean (Frost *et al.*, 1983) and the outer shelf regions of the Bering Sea (Dagg *et al.*, 1982).

The impact of krill grazing on phytoplankton community species composition and biomass will be considered in more detail in Chapter 5. However, in many areas of the Southern Ocean other grazing herbivores, especially copepods and salps, are dominant. Their impact on the phytoplankton will be evaluated in Chapter 4. Heavy selective grazing on phytoplankton by various herbivorous zooplankton (protozoans, copepods, salps and krill) can lead to a shift in species composition and a reduction in biomass of the larger, bloom-forming phytoplankters. While the overall proportion of the standing stock of phytoplankton that is consumed by the krill is low, *c.* 3% per day in two studies (Miller *et al.*, 1985; Priddle *et al.*, 1986a) the

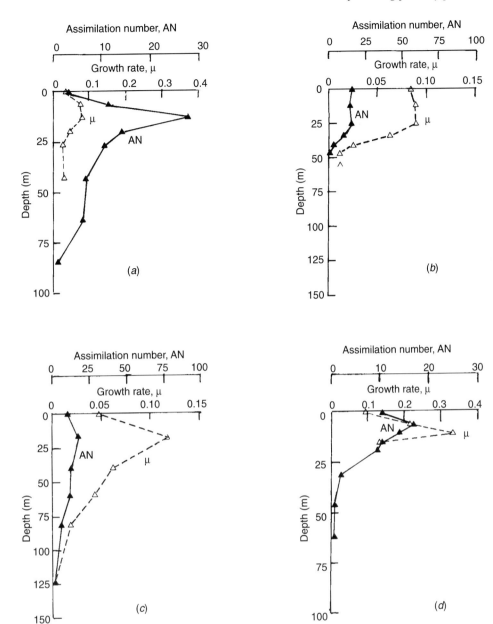

Fig. 2.15. Vertical distribution of assimilation number (AN, μg C l⁻¹ (μg chl *a* l⁻¹)⁻¹) and specific growth rate or doubling time (μ) from stations on *Eltanin* cruises 38, 46 and 51. (*a*). Station characteristic of sub-Antarctic waters. Euphotic zone, 43 m; photosynthetically active solar radiation 160 cal m⁻² (half-light-day)⁻¹. (*b*) Station characteristic of Antarctic Convergence waters. Euphotic zone 60 m; photosynthetically active solar raditation 62 cal m⁻² (half-light-day)⁻¹. (*c*). Station characteristic of Antarctic waters. Euphotic zone 145 m; photosynthetically active solar radiation 157 cal m⁻² (half-light-day)⁻¹. (*d*). Station characteristic of Antarctic (Ross Ice Shelf) waters. Euphotic zone 30 m; photosynthetically active solar radiation 72 cal m⁻² (half-light-day)⁻¹. Redrawn from Holm-Hansen *et al.* (1977).

local impact of krill swarms may be considerable (Rakusa-Suszczcewski, 1982; Uribe, 1982; Holm-Hansen & Huntley, 1984). Heywood *et al.* (1985) reported on a winter study from South Georgia when the standing stock of krill around the island was very much lower than expected. At that time the phytoplankton concentrations were concomitantly higher (Morris & Priddle, 1984) than found in previous studies (Hart, 1934, 1942; El-Sayed, 1967) and this suggested that the normal winter decline of phytoplankton could be attributed to removal by grazing exceeding replenishment by growth. It should however, be

pointed out that coincidence of high phytoplankton standing crop and high krill density has also been reported (Weber & El-Sayed, 1985a; Mujica & Asencio, 1983); but it is possible that the krill had only recently moved into an area of high phytoplankton density. Nast & Gieskes (1986) in discussing the relationship between krill and phytoplankton densities concluded that 'whereas the negative correlation between chlorophyll *a* and krill abundance seems to be valid on the mesoscale, a positive correlation between the high krill mass in the Scotia Sea and enhanced phytoplankton food sources may also exist'.

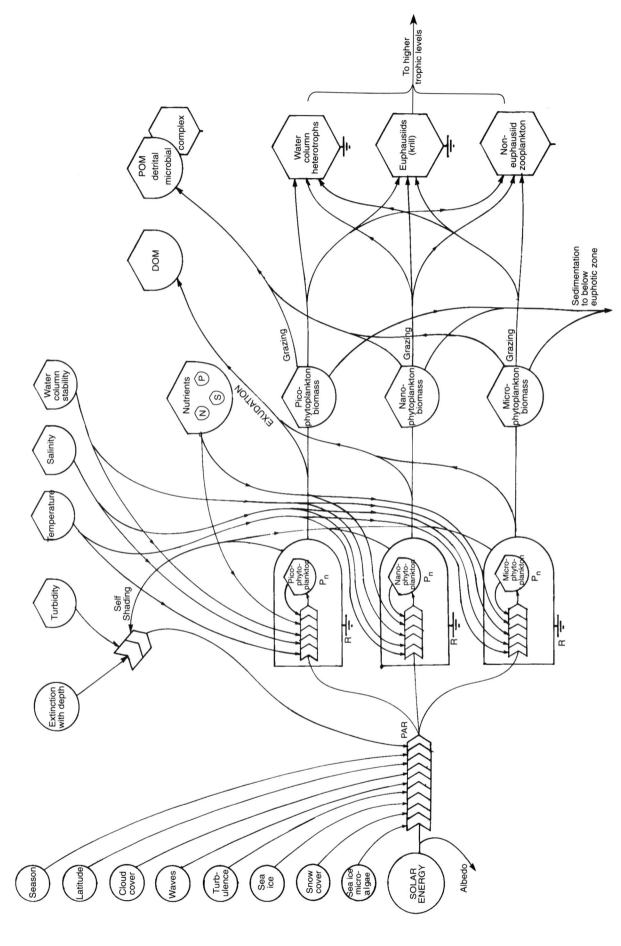

Fig. 2.16. Simplified model of the forcing functions and environmental variables influencing phytoplankton production and biomass in the Southern Ocean.

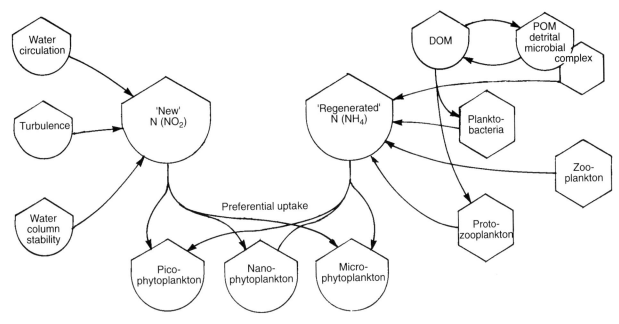

Fig. 2.17. Model of the variables influencing the concentration of nitrogen in the surface waters of the Southern Ocean.

2.8 Growth rates

Phytoplankton growth rates in the waters of the Southern Ocean have been considered to be low due to a combination of the effects from light (El-Sayed & Mandelli, 1965) and temperature (Neori & Holm-Hansen, 1982; Wilson *et al.*, 1986). Two indices are used in describing algal growth rates: assimilation number (AN), the number of micrograms of carbon fixed per litre per day divided by the number of micrograms of chlorophyll *a* per litre (μg C m^{-2} day^{-1} (μg chl *a* l)$^{-1}$); and the number of doublings per day (μ). Fig. 2.15 shows some typical profiles of AN and μ for stations in the Pacific sector (Holm-Hansen *et al.*, 1977). The observed growth rates in this study were low (0.05 to 0.33 doublings per day. Profiles of growth rates (Fig. 2.15) show low growth rates in surface waters, with increasing rates with depth until a maximum was reached at between 15 and 40 m, below which the values again decreased.

Sommer (1989) found that the maximal growth rates of 15 Antarctic phytoplankton species at 0 °C ranged from 0.32 to 0.72 day^{-1}, and showed only a weak dependence on cell size. These values are usually higher than those reported by Spies (1987) for congeric but unidentified species from the Weddell Sea. However, the light intensities used by Spies may not have been saturating. Thus, although the growth rates recorded are lower than those for phytoplankton from warmer waters, doubling in the range recorded by Sommer would lead to relatively rapid population increases.

2.9 Heterotrophic nutrition

While most microalgae satisfy their carbon requirements through the photochemical reactions of photosynthesis some are nutritionally opportunistic and can supplement their autotrophic metabolism by phagotrophy or osmotrophy (Droop, 1974; Hellebust & Lewin, 1977). Rivkin & Putt (1987) found that diatoms isolated from benthic, planktonic and sea ice microbial communities in McMurdo Sound assimilated ambient concentrations of dissolved amino acids and glucose both in the light and the dark. Amino acid uptake rates were up to 250 times greater than those of glucose. The amino acids were incorporated into proteins and other complex polymers at rates of assimilation and patterns of polymer synthesis similar to those of light-saturated photosynthetic incorporation of inorganic carbon. Thus, the diatoms are able to use exogenous amino acids to synthesize essential macromolecules. It is therefore probable that the assimilation of dissolved organic substrates could supplement light-limited growth during the austral spring and summer, and could potentially support heterotrophic growth through the aphotic polar winter.

2.10 A model of phytoplankton production

Fig. 2.16 is a simplified model illustrating the forcing functions and environmental variables that influence primary production and phytoplankton biomass. The photosynthetically available radiation (PAR) in the Southern Ocean at any one point in time or depth within the water column is determined by a complex of factors, including cloudiness, turbulence, wave action, season (day length), latitude (affecting the angle of incidence of the sun's rays), sea ice (thickness, percentage cover), depth of snow

Table 2.2. *Matrix of model forcing functions and environmental variables influencing water column primary production*

	Solar radiation	Season	Latitude	Cloud cover	Waves	Turbulence	Water circulation	Turbidity	Sea temperature	Salinity	Water column satbility	Sea ice formation	Sea ice melting and breakout	Sea ice snow cover	Sea ice microalgae	Nutrients	Grazing	Sedimentation
Solar radiation		x	x						x			x	x	x	x			
Season	x		x	x	x	x			x		x	x	x	x	x		x	x
Latitude	x	x		x				x	x			x	x	x	x	x	x	
Cloud cover	x	x	x															
Waves	x	x				x		x			x	x	x	x				
Turbulence	x	x			x		x				x					x		x
Water circulation		x	x			x			x	x	x				x	x	x	
Turbidity	x																	
Sea temperature		x	x			x				x	x	x	x					
Salinity		x				x			x		x	x	x					
Water column stability		x			x	x	x	x	x	x						x	x	x
Sea ice formation	x	x	x						x	x					x	x	x	x
Sea ice melting and breakout	x	x	x		x	x	x		x	x	x			x	x	x	x	x
Sea ice snow cover	x	x	x												x			
Sea ice microalgae	x	x	x													x	x	
Nutrients						x	x				x				x			
Grazing		x													x			x
Sedimentation		x													x		x	

After Knox (1990).

on the ice, the degree of development of the sea ice microalgae, and extinction with depth (influenced by the turbidity of the water, and self-shading, especially when dense blooms develop).

Net production (P_n) is determined by the interaction of PAR, the physiological state of the algae, including the degree of inhibition by high light intensity and the degree of adaptation to low light intensity, temperature, salinity, the stability of the water column and the kind and availability of nutrients. The major nutrients are nitrate, ammonium and silicate. Silicate may become limiting during dense diatom blooms. Availability of nitrate ('new' N) is determined by water circulation patterns (especially upwelling), turbulence and the stability of the water column (Fig. 2.17). On the other hand concentrations of ammonium ('regenerated' N), which is often the preferred nutrient, especially by the pico- and nanophytoplankton, is the result primarily of microbial processes in the euphotic zone (see Chapter 14) and excretion by zooplankton.

Table 2.2 give an interaction matrix of the model forcing functions and environmental variables that influence phytoplankton production. It can thus be seen that the primary production process is determined by a complex interaction of the variables listed in the matrix. Overall seasonality is the dominant influence with its impact on the light regime and weather, especially the wind strength and the prevalence and intensity of storms. While a number of studies have explored the impact of some of these variables the complexity of their interactions has yet to be elucidated.

Mitchell & Holm-Hansen (1991) developed a model of the Antarctic phytoplankton crop in relation to mixing depth. This model, based on mixing depth and pigment-specific light attenuation and *in situ* photosynthesis–irradiance relationships, indicated that the depth of the upper mixed layer (Z_{UML}) can be used to predict the upper limit of phytoplankton crop size. Assuming nutrients do not limit crop size, a best-fit of the model observations indicated that specific loss rates were approximately 0.3–0.35 day^{-1}, and that massive blooms occur only if Z_{UML} <25 m. They considered that in most studies grazing, particulary the contribution of protozooplankton, has been underestimated. Further such modelling studies are needed.

3

Sea ice microbial communities

3.1 Introduction

The geographical and seasonal distribution of the Antarctic sea ice, its zonal characteristics and pack ice movement have been described in Chapter 1. Here we are concerned with the microbial communities which develop in association with the sea ice and their relationships with the pelagic communities. Diatoms have been known from the sea ice for about 150 years. They were first described from the Arctic by Ehrenberg (1844, 1853) and from the Antarctic by Hooker (1847).

Early work on sea ice algae was principally of a taxonomic nature, although Vanhoeffen (1902) provided the earliest description of the seasonal cycle for ice diatoms. However it was not until the early 1960s that Bunt and his co-workers (Bunt & Wood, 1963; Bunt, 1963, 1964a,b, 1967, 1968a,b; Bunt & Lee, 1970; Bunt et al., 1968) carried out a detailed study of the community composition, primary productivity and physiology of the sea ice microalgae. Since then there have been a number of studies in various parts of the Southern Ocean, notably Hoshiai and his co-workers at Syowa Station (Hoshiai & Kato, 1961; Hoshiai, 1969, 1972, 1981a,b, 1985; Watanabe, 1988; Watanabe et al., 1990), Burkholder & Mandelli (1965) in the vicinity of the Palmer Peninsula, Whitaker (1977a) at Signy Island, Ackley et al. (1978a,b, 1979) in the Weddell Sea, and McConville and his co-workers in East Antarctica (McConville & Wetherbee, 1983; McConville et al., 1985). However, the most substantial recent contribution to our understanding of the ecology and physiology of the sea ice microbial community in Antarctica has been made by Sullivan and his co-workers working in McMurdo Sound (Sullivan & Palmisano. 1981, 1984; Palmisano & Sullivan, 1982, 1983a,b, 1985a,b,c; Sullivan, 1985; Sullivan et al., 1982; 1984, 1985; Grossi et al. 1984, 1987; Kottmeier et al., 1984, 1986, 1987a,b; Palmisano et al., 1984, 1985a,b, 1987a,b, 1988; Grossi, 1985; Grossi & Sullivan, 1985; Palmisano, 1986a; Kottmeier & Sullivan, 1987, 1988, 1990; Soohoo et al., 1987).

3.2 Sea ice as a habitat

Because of its extent and its seasonal pattern of formation, break-up and melting the sea ice is a dominant forcing function in the ecology of the Southern Ocean, strongly affecting the all the organisms living there. Ice effectively reduces the amount of light reaching the water column and reduces heat and gas exchange and vertical mixing. In addition, the upper surface provides a habitat for a number of sea birds and mammals, while at the same time, the ice itself, especially the lower part which is in contact with the water, constitutes a unique habitat for microalgae and bacteria, which provide a food resource for the associated microfauna and meiofauna, and the cryopelagic fauna of the surface water layer immediately below the ice (Fig. 3.1).

The sea ice itself as a habitat for microalgae, microfauna and meiofauna poses a number of problems. Ice formation is a rapid process accompanied by large changes in the light regime, carbon supply, nutrient concentrations, temperature and salinity. During the lifetime of the sea ice marked changes in these parameters occur, with the development of sharp vertical gradients.

3.2.1 Ice formation and structure

Once the surface layer of the sea reaches freezing point, additional heat loss produces slight supercooling of the water and ice formation. Initial ice formation occurs at or near the surface of the water in the form of small platelets and needles, termed *frazil* ice. Continued freezing results in the formation of *grease* ice, a soupy mixture of unconsolidated frazil crystals. Once the ice formation exceeds 30 to 40% the transition to a solid cover begins. In the presence of a wave field, the transition is marked by the formation of *pancakes*, rounded masses of semi-consolidated slush 0.3 to 3.0 m in diameter. These pancakes eventually consolidate and become welded together to form a composite ice sheet (Weeks & Ackley, 1982).

A second type of ice is *congelation* ice (sometimes called *columnar* ice), which grows at the ice–water interface in response to conductive heat losses along the tem-

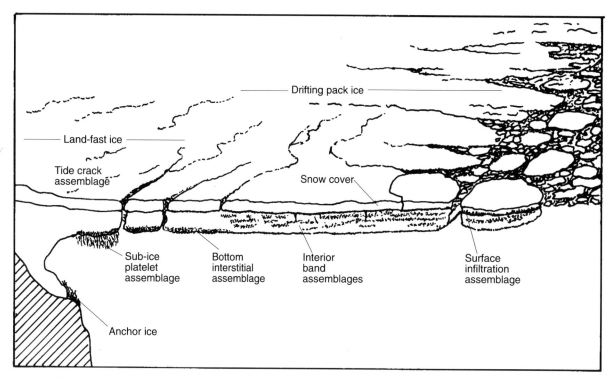

Fig. 3.1. Microalgal habitats associated with sea ice. Modified from Garrison *et al.* (1987); based on Whitaker (1977a) and other sources.

perature gradient in the ice. In this form of ice the crystals are orientated with their C-axis (the principal axis of symmetry) horizontal, and growth occurs perpendicular to this axis to produce interlocking columns about 1–2 cm in diameter (Lewis & Weeks, 1971). This forms a partly permeable columnar crystal structure with numerous small brine pockets and channels, many less than 100 μm in diameter (Palmisano & Sullivan, 1983b). Larger brine-containing chambers are formed during the early stages of freezing, but later these become filled with congelation ice (Lewis & Weeks, 1971). When large pockets of trapped brine drain down to the ice–water interface the resultant plume can produce an ice stalactite which may be up to 6 m in length (Dayton & Martin, 1971).

Frazil ice also forms in the water column, as well as at the surface. As has been documented for McMurdo Sound, two types of ice crystals are formed within the water column: extremely small crystals and large ice platelets 10 to 15 cm in diameter and 0.2 to 0.3 cm in thickness (Datyon *et al.* 1969). The platelets float up to the surface and accumulate on the undersurface of the sea ice, where they may attach to the ice and freeze together or, on occasions, especially in coastal fast ice areas, form billows of loose platelets 1 to 5 m thick (Dayton *et al.*, 1969; Barry, 1988, Knox, 1990).

The development of a bottom platelet layer varies from one part of the Southern Ocean to another. It has not been reported from the vicinity of Syowa Station (69° S; 39° E)

(Hoshiai, 1977), or from Casey (66° S, 100° E), Davis (68° S, 78° E) and Mawson (67° S, 62° E) (McConville & Wetherbee, 1983). In the Weddell Sea frazil ice layers are often sandwiched between congelation ice, indicating that frazil ice formation is episodic. The various types of ice formation comprise a highly variable percentage of the overall sea ice structure in various localities and in different years in the same locality. In the Weddell Sea ice core data indicate that congelation ice accounts for only about 20% of the multi-year ice and 47% of the first-year ice, with fine grained layers of frazil crystals making up most of the remainder. These variations in ice structure produce very different types of microenvironment for the development of microbial communities (see section 3.3.1).

The sea ice is commonly overlain by snow, which can vary considerably in depth. Regions near the coast that receive blowing snow from katabatic and other offshore winds may accumulate a layer of snow up to 6 m thick (Keys, 1984). Along leads in the pack ice and at the ice edge the snow–water interface may become flooded with sea water. Pools may also form on the surface of the sea ice either by thawing of the ice (McConville & Wetherbee, 1983), a combination of flooding and melting, or by flooding alone. These provide additional habitats for microbial growth.

Sea ice in the pack ice zone periodically breaks up under the influence of storms and can move considerable distances driven by wind and surface currents before refreezing into solid pack during calm periods. This contrasts with shore-fast ice which occurs along most of the coastline of the Antarctic continent. This forms early in the winter and either breaks up in the late summer, or remains for two or more years forming multi-year ice, which may be more than 10 m thick. At the shoreline it is anchored to the bottom. Although rigidly anchored it may move tens of metres in response to thermal and mechanical stress. Its extent is determined primarily by seabottom and shoreline topography and is highly variable. Where it adjoins the land or the ice sheets, tidal rise and fall create a series of parallel tide cracks through which seawater can often pass easily (Fig. 3.1). These cracks accumulate snow and often frazil crystals form, providing a nutrient-rich well-illuminated environment for microbial growth (Whitaker, 1977a; Rawlence *et al.*, 1987; Waghorn & Knox, 1989).

In contrast to the Arctic where surface melting is responsible for most of the disappearance of pack ice in the summer (Maykut, 1985), the disappearance of the Antarctic pack is due almost entirely to melting at the ice–water interface. Gordon (1981) estimates that no more than half of the necessary energy for this melting could be derived from the relatively warm deep water below the Southern Ocean pycnocline. The remainder must come from shortwave radiation absorbed by the upper ocean, either through leads in the pack ice or near the ice edge.

3.2.2 Sea ice chemistry

Nutrient concentrations and salinity within the sea ice are difficult to measure and techniques have yet to be developed for the *in situ* determination of these parameters within the brine channels. Early data collected by Bunt & Lee (1970) indicate that the McMurdo Sound frazil ice contains high levels of nutrients. The interstitial waters had 7.07 mmol m^{-3} of nitrate and 2.6 mmol m^{-3} of dissolved reactive phosphorus. These values, as well as salinity (31.89%), pH (8.03) and temperature ($-1.75\,^\circ$C) were comparable with the seawater below. However, higher in the ice column where there is less exchange with the underlying seawater the nutrient levels were lower, probably due to depletion by microbial growth. In the Weddell Sea (D. B. Clarke & Ackley, 1984) silicate and nitrate concentrations, particularly in the older ice, indicated nutrient depletion by the ice microbiota. On the other hand, high nitrite values suggested the presence of an active population of nitrifying bacteria.

Salinity profiles in McMurdo Sound revealed high salinity at the top, decreasing near the middle, and rising again towards the bottom (Weeks & Lee, 1962). This pattern is probably due to the rapid formation of near-surface ice trapping larger amounts of salt, the much slower rates

of freezing beneath this layer, and the gradual migration of brine as density currents down the ice column. Thus, the microbiota can be subjected to widely varying salinity concentrations. In the Weddell Sea, salinity was lower in the upper layers with a maximum in the middle, indicating only a partial migration of brine (Ackley *et al.*, 1979).

3.2.3 Physical properties

The major physical environmental factors influencing the development of the sea ice microbial communities are light and temperature, with the former usually considered to be the most important. Near-surface ice must experience winter air temperatures, which may fall below 0 °C. In contrast the temperature of the lower surface must be near that of the seawater (-1.5 to $-2.0\,^\circ$C).

Light changes in both quantity and quality down the sea ice column. Because ice is a translucent material, light penetrates into the interior where, at any given level, some is absorbed and some transmitted. Strong attenuation of the longer wavelengths causes the spectral composition of the light to undergo rapid changes as it passes through the ice. Measurements of downwelling irradiance beneath first-year ice show energy maxima occurring in the 470 to 480 nm wavelength band (Maykut & Grenfell, 1975). Red wavelengths are quickly absorbed in the surface layers of the ice so that the amount of energy reaching the water is negligible above 700 to 800 nm Once an ice algal layer is formed the transmission of light is further reduced.

Palmisano *et al.* (1987b) found that two metres of congelation ice reduced surface photosynthetically available radiation (PAR, light within the waveband available to plants, 400 to 700 nm) by about 90% with a peak transmission around 500 nm. The depth of snow cover also greatly influences the availability of light for ice algal photosynthesis. Palmisano *et al.* (1985a) found that the irradiance beneath a quadrat of sea ice artificially shaded with 70 cm of snow was less than 3% of the PAR beneath a control quadrat with 7 cm of natural snow. Sea ice microalgal assemblages can also strongly attenuate PAR. Palmisano *et al.* (1987b) found that they could reduce light levels to less than 0.5% of surface levels and shift the transmission peak by selectively absorbing blue and red wavelengths.

3.3 Sea ice microalgae

3.3.1 Community types, population structure and annual cycle

3.3.1.1 Community types

The sea ice provides a growth substratum and refugium for a complex microbial community (often termed the

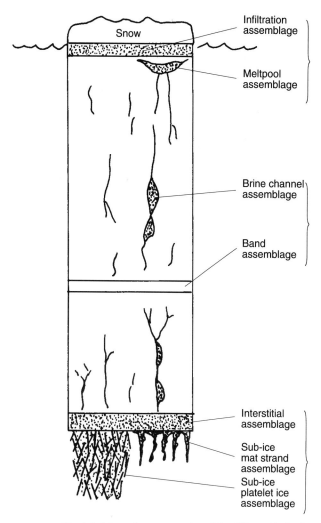

Fig. 3.2. Schematic representation of the different kinds of microalgal assemblages associated with Antarctic sea ice. Modified from Horner *et al.* (1988).

'epontic' community, or the 'sea ice microbial community' (SIMCO)) consisting primarily of microalgae, bacteria, protozoa and small metazoans. Horner (1985a) distinguished three main types of algal assemblages that develop in association with the sea ice, *bottom*, *surface* and *interior*, while more recently Horner *et al.* (1988) have proposed a uniform terminology for the variations that occur within these assemblages (see Fig. 3.2). Fig. 3.3 illustrates some of the regional variations in occurrence of the various assemblages that occur.

There are two main types of surface assemblage. *Infiltration assemblages* occur at the snow–ice interface when the snow nearest the ice surface is flooded with seawater (Fig. 3.3b and h). *Pool assemblages* develop in pools formed by the thawing of the ice (McConville & Wetherbee, 1983), or by a combination of flooding and melting, or by melting alone (Fig. 3.3d).

Two kinds of *interior assemblages* have been reported.

Band assemblages (Fig. 3.3a–c, e, and h) occur as algal zones of varying widths throughout the ice column. They are formed either by the accretation of new ice under a previously formed bottom ice layer (Hoshiai, 1977; Ackley *et al.*, 1979; Watanabe & Satoh, 1987), or by the incorporation of planktonic algae at the time of first freezing of surface waters. *Brine channel assemblages* occur in brine channels, cavities, and cracks within the ice (Fig. 3.3d). McConville & Wetherbee (1983) reported the development of a complex network of brine channels in the late summer in the sea ice off Davis Station in East Antarctica. The channels contained microalgae common to both the water column and the bottom ice assemblage.

Interstitial bottom assemblages occur in the bottom of the ice column and may be associated with a solid hard layer of bottom congelation ice (McMurdo Sound, Palmisano & Sullivan, 1983a; Grossi *et al.*, 1987; and Syowa Station, Watanabe, 1988), or with a platelet layer of varying thickness frozen to the underside of the ice (McMurdo Sound, Bunt, 1963; Bunt & Lee, 1970; Palmisano & Sullivan, 1985b; Grossi *et al.*, 1987). There is considerable variation both geographically and locally in the development of the bottom interstitial assemblage (Fig. 3.3a–d, f and g).

The *sub-ice mat strand assemblage* consists of algae floating directly beneath the ice, or attached to the underside of the ice forming strands that trail into the water column (the mat–strand community described by McConville & Wetherbee, 1983). This assemblage has been reported from Casey Station (McConville & Wetherbee, 1983), near Syowa Station (Sasaki & Watanabe, 1984; Watanabe, 1988), and from McMurdo Sound (Grossi *et al.*, 1987) (Fig. 3.3b and c). Watanabe (1988) reports that no strands were seen in mid-July, but strands 10–15 cm in length were observed hanging from the sea ice in early November and these had grown to 50–60 cm in length by early December. The strands were mainly composed of pennate diatoms, especially those that form long colonies. A second type of sub-ice assemblage, the *sub-ice platelet layer assemblage* is found in some localities, e.g. Syowa Station (Watanabe, 1988) and McMurdo Sound (SooHoo *et al.*, 1987) (Fig. 3.3b, and g). In contrast to the interstitial bottom assemblage, which may have platelet ice (frazil crystals) frozen to the bottom of the congelation ice, the platelets in this assemblage form a loose aggregation beneath the sea ice.

3.3.1.2 Population structure

Most of the studies on sea ice microbial communities have focused on the diatoms (Bacillariophyceae) which usually dominate the ice microalgal assemblages. Pennate species belonging to the *Fragilariopsis* group (e.g. *Nitzschia*

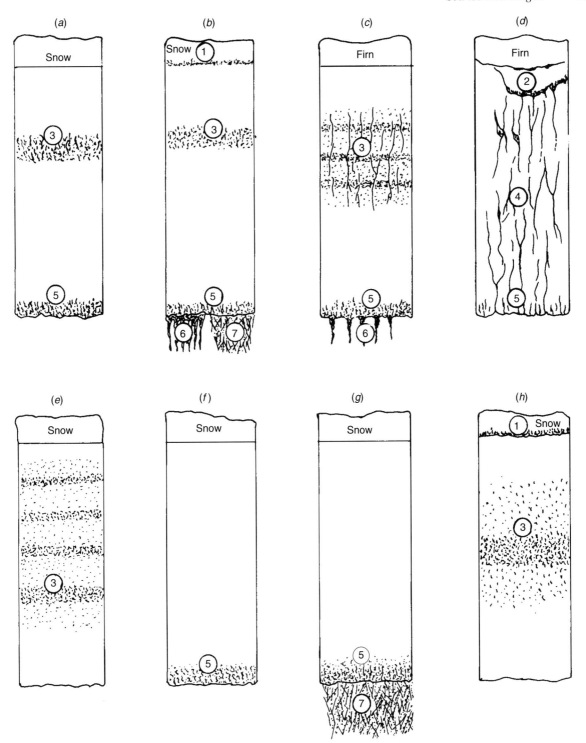

Fig. 3.3. Typical profiles through sea ice at different localities in Antarctica, showing the occurrence of the different microalgal assemblages. 1. Surface infiltration assemblege; 2. Surface meltpool assemblage; 3. Interior band assemblage; 4. Interior brine channel assemblage; 5. Bottom interstitial assemblage; 6. Bottom sub-ice mat strand assemblage; 7. Sub-ice platelet ice assemblage. (*a*) Syowa Station, Hoshiai (1977); (*b*) Syowa Station, Watanabe (1988); (*c*) and (*d*) Davis Station, McConville & Wetherbee (1983); (*e*) Antarctic Peninsula, Kottmeier & Sullivan (1987); (*f*) McMurdo Sound, Palmisano & Sullivan (1983a); (*g*) McMurdo Sound, SooHoo *et al.* (1987); (*h*) Weddell Sea, Ackley *et al.* (1979).

cylindrus and *N. curta*) often dominate, but several centric species may also be abundant (Watanabe, 1982; Horner, 1985a, 1990; Garrison *et al.*, 1987) (Fig. 3.4). Although a few diatom species form resting spores, the common species (e.g. *Nitzschia* spp.) do not have a distinctive resting stage (Garrison, 1984). A variety of small (nano) and large (micro) autotrophic flagellates occur in the ice assemblages and may sometimes predominate over

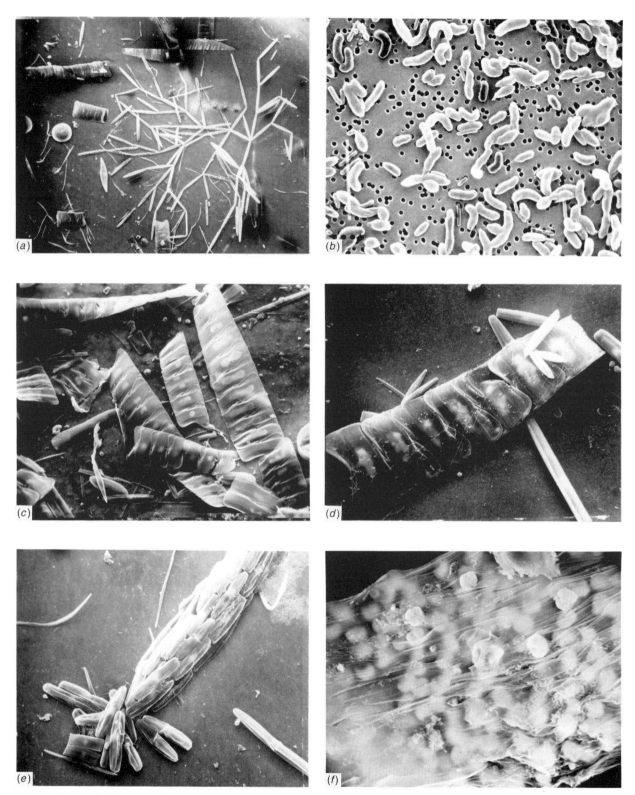

Fig. 3.4. (*a*) *Nitzschia stellata* colony, (*b*) bacteria, (*c*) *Amphiprora* 'ribbons', (*d*) *Amphiprora* with epibacteria and diatoms, (*e*) tube-dwelling diatoms, (*f*) *Phaeocystis* gelatinous colony. Photographs supplied by Professor C. Sullivan.

the diatoms (Garrison & Buck, 1985a, 1989a; Garrison, 1991). The relatively small number of flagellate species recorded is a consequence of the difficulty of species identification, and the fact that nano- and microflagellates, as well as other delicate forms, may have been missed because they can be easily destroyed during the melting of the ice (Garrison & Buck, 1986). Both solitary, motile cells and gelatinous colony lifestages of the prymnesiophyte *Phaeocystis pouchetii* are commonly found in the sea ice. Some nanoflagellates have resting spores. Cyst-like stages that Deflande (Deflande & Deflande-Rigand, 1970; J. G. Mitchell & Silver, 1982) called archaeomonads are very abundant in ice floes where they occur at densities of 10^4–10^7 l^{-1}. They are assumed to be the resting stages of chrysophytes and Takahashi (1987) has identified both siliceous cysts and vegetative stages of the chrysophyte *Paraphysomonas* in Antarctic fast ice. Autotrophic dinoflagellates belonging to the so-called unarmoured genera *Gymnodinium*, *Gyrodinium* and *Amphidinium* are sometimes abundant (Garrison, 1991).

In their pioneer studies of sea ice microalgal communities in McMurdo Sound Bunt & Wood (1963) listed two groups of diatoms: species attached to ice crystals, and non-attached forms that were living in close association with the ice. Of the 11 dominant species, five were centric diatoms, *Biddulphia weissflogii*, *Coccinodiscus subtilis*, *Euchampia balaustium*, *Rhizosolenia alata*, and *R. rostrata*, and six were pennate diatoms, *Amphiprora kjellmani*, *A. oestrupii*, *Fragilaria linearis*, *Nitzschia martiana*, *N. serrata*, and *Pleurosigma antarcticum*. More recent investigation in East McMurdo Sound has identified the chain-forming *Amphiprora kufferathii*, and a stellate colonial species *Nitzschia stellata* as the dominant species (Palmisano & Sullivan, 1983a; Grossi & Sullivan, 1985) in the interstitial bottom assemblage (congelation ice).

Burkholder & Mandelli (1965) listed the diatom species from ice habitats along the western coast of the Antarctic Peninsula. The ice contained the small diatoms *Fragilariopsis linearis* and *Nitzschia serrata*, plus small numbers of pennate diatoms, centric diatoms, a few dinoflagellates, small green flagellates and *Phaeocystis pouchetii*.

Species composition in the sea ice assemblages in the Weddell Sea were compared with the phytoplankton in the water column by Garrison & Buck (1985b). The ice algal populations comprised species usually characteristic of Antarctic phytoplankton assemblages. Of the species found in the ice, only a few were considered to be benthic or tycopelagic (e.g. *Nitzschia vanheurchii* and *N. sublineata*; Hasle, 1965), or generally have been reported to have distribution restricted to the ice edge (e.g. *N. subcarinata*, *N. obliquecostata*, and *N. castracanei*; Hasle, 1964, 1965). The most abundant species found in the ice

(e.g. *N. cylindrus* and *N. curta*) were planktonic species with wide distributions (Hasle, 1965, 1969; Steyeart, 1973; Guillard & Kilham, 1977). In addition to the pennate diatoms, which dominated the ice assemblages, they also found *Phaeocystis pouchetii* in densities up to 10^6 cells l^{-1} and centric diatoms such as *Coscinodiscus* and *Rhizosolenia*.

Sub-ice mat strand assemblages have been described in Western McMurdo Sound (Palmisano & Sullivan, 1983a), off Mawson, Davis and Casey Stations (McConville & Wetherbee, 1983), and off Syowa Station, East Antarctica (Watanabe, 1988). In McMurdo Sound the algal dominants were a chain-forming *Amphiprora* and a stellate colonial species, *Nitzschia stellata*. In the New Harbour region in West McMurdo Sound a tube-dwelling pennate diatom was common. This species produced mucilage-encased tubes up to 10 cm long, extending through the brine channels and hanging from the bottom of the congelation ice. McConville & Wetherbee (1983) reported a sub-ice community which developed in September and was largely suspended from the bottom surface of the annual sea ice, often extending into the underlying water as conspicuous strands up to 15 cm long. It was dominated by an unidentified tube-dwelling diatom belonging to the *Amphipleura/Berkeleya* group and chains of a species of *Entomoneis* (= *Amphiprora*). Associated with these colonial species were a number of epiphytic diatoms, particularly *Synedra* spp. During December several centric diatoms (e.g. *Stephanopyxis*) and phytoflagellates (*Chlamydomonas*) became common in the sub-ice assemblage. At Syowa Station Watanabe & Satoh (1987) did not observe sub-ice microalgal strands in mid-July but by early November strands 10–15 cm in length were hanging from the ice and by early December they had grown up to lengths of 50–60 cm. The strands were composed mainly of pennate diatoms, especially those forming long colonies, including *Amphiprora kufferathii*, *Berkeleya mitilans*, *Nitzschia lecointei*, *N. stellata*, *N. turgiduloides*, and several species of *Nitzschia* in the section *Fragilariopsis*, with smaller numbers of the single-celled species *Navicula glaciei*.

McConville & Wetherbee (1983) described several other types of ice microalgal assemblages from Casey Station. A bottom-ice interstitial assemblage colonized the microbrine cells that penetrated up to 5 cm into the congelation ice from the bottom surface (Fig. 3.3c). These brine channels were occupied by densely packed cells of *Nitzschia frigida* and *Entomoneis* spp. in concentrations of up to 3×10^8 cells l^{-1}. In mid- to late-summer a separate microalgal community developed in melt pools just beneath a 5–10 cm layer of consolidated snow (the firn layer) and was dominated by small diatoms

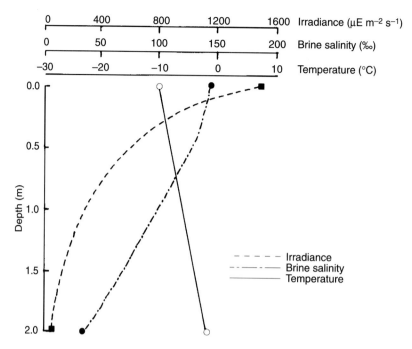

Fig. 3.5. Theoretical gradients for irradiance, temperature, and salinity for a 2 m ice column at McMurdo Sound, Antarctica in November. Redrawn from Grossi & Sullivan (1985).

(*Fragilariopsis linearis, F. obliquecostata, F. ritscheri*), flagellates (*Pyranimonas, Gymnodinium, Cryptomonas cryophila, Mantoniella squamata*) and colonies of *Phaeocystis*. The melt pools, which initially were patchy, spread rapidly, eventually developing a surface crust that was almost completely separated from the ice beneath. In January the brine channels throughout the ice became interconnected and contained algal species from both the melt pool and bottom interstitial assemblages. At the time of the ice breakup in mid-January the melt pools contained large aggregations of cells in densities of up to 2.8×10^6 cells l^{-1}. Areas of fast ice that formed during the previous autumn often contained a patchy visible coloured band up to 356 cm thick and 20–40 cm below the surface. The presence of empty diatom frustules indicated that it was a residual population from the autumn algal bloom, and significant primary production occurred in this layer in December.

Watanabe & Satoh (1987) working at Syowa Station, East Antarctica distinguished three types of microalgal assemblages, surface, interior and bottom. The bottom-ice microalgal assemblage was concentrated in a thin layer from 5 mm to a few centimetres in thickness, while the interior assemblage was found in an unconsolidated grease layer in the fast ice 20–70 cm in thickness from the beginning of ice formation in May. The surface assemblage was found in an unconsolidated snow layer on fast ice between October and December. The dominant species of the interior assemblage during its formation in

the autumn as a bottom assemblage were *Nitzschia* spp., *Fragilariopsis*, and several flagellates (Hoshiai, 1977). The bottom infiltration assemblage that developed in the spring was dominated by *Amphiprora, Pleurosigma, Stephanopyxis, Nitzschia* and *Navicula*.

Tide cracks may also provide a habitat for rich microalgal assemblages. Whitaker (1977a) described abundant, uni-algal populations of *Navicula glaciei* from the ice-slush in coastal tide cracks at Signy Island. *Nitzschia curta, N. lineata* and *Thalassiosira tumida* were found on the vertical walls of the tide cracks. At White Island, on the McMurdo Ice Shelf, McMurdo Sound Rawlence *et al.* (1987) described the standing crop and succession of microalgae in the surface water of the tide cracks. The tide cracks contained dense aggregations of platelet ice. The dominant species during late November was *Pyranimonas* sp. (Chlorophyta). Diatoms were dominant from early December until the end of the study in late January. The five most abundant species were *Nitzschia cylindrus, N. curta, N. obliquecostata, Fragilaria* sp. and *Synedra tabulata* (see Fig. 3.9*b*).

Vertical distribution patterns of the species in the various assemblages have been described from Lutzow-Holm Bay (Hoshiai & Kato, 1961), and McMurdo Sound (Grossi & Sullivan, 1985; Knox, 1986). At McMurdo Sound algal abundances in the ice decreased with increasing distance from the ice–seawater interface and with the depth of snow cover (Grossi &

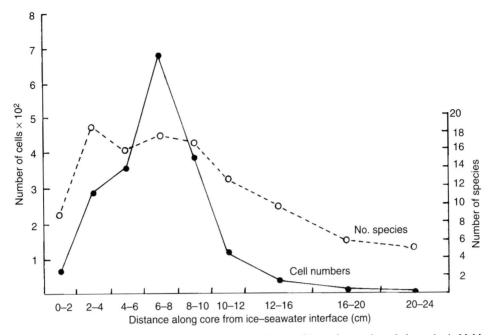

Fig. 3.6. Distribution of diatom species and total cell numbers in the bottom 24 cm of a core through the sea ice in McMurdo Sound. (The cell numbers are based on standard microscope counts of a small subsample from a 2 cm melted section.) Redrawn from Knox (1986).

Sullivan, 1985). Grossi & Sullivan hypothesized that microalgae, once incorporated into the sea ice matrix, exhibit differential growth along physico-chemical gradients within the ice column. Fig. 3.5 depicts the theoretical gradients for light, salinity and temperature over the depth of a snow-free, 2 m ice column. Once ice accretion has ceased competition amongst the algae for light, nutrients and space leads to a vertical zonation along these gradients. Diatoms may achieve this zonation either by active migration of motile species, or by differential growth rates dependent upon the physico-chemical milieu. *Nitzschia stellata*, the dominant diatom species, showed peak abundance in the bottom 5 cm of the ice. A second colonial alga, *Amphiprora kufferathii*, and an epiphytic diatom, *Fragilaria islandica* var. *adeliae* had peak abundance in the bottom 5–10 cm. Other algal species showed distribution patterns different from those of the dominants, e.g. two motile species, an *Auricula* Castracane sp. and *Navicula glaciei* , reached highest concentrations at depths of 10–20 cm above the ice–water interface.

In central McMurdo Sound Knox (1986) found a total of 30 diatom species in sea ice cores in the fast ice. Fig. 3.6 shows the vertical distribution of the diatom species and the total number of cells in a standardized subsample of melted 2 cm sections of the bottom 24 cm of an ice core. Cell numbers peaked at 6–8 cm from the ice–seawater interface and then declined rapidly up the column, with only small numbers being present at 12 cm. Species numbers peaked at 2–4 cm (20 species) and remained

high through to 8–10 cm, thereafter declining to a low of five species at 20–24 cm.

3.3.1.3 Annual cycle

Only a limited number of studies (e.g. Hoshiai, 1977; McConville & Wetherbee, 1983; Watanabe & Satoh, 1987) have followed the development of the sea ice microalgal assemblages over the full period from the initial ice formation to ice breakup and melting. Fig. 3.7 depicts the seasonal succession of the ice microalgal assemblages near Syowa Station (69° S, 39° E). Freezing of the seawater began in the middle of February and a brown algal layer had formed in the brine pockets in the bottom of the ice by the end of March, when the ice was about 30 cm thick. During the winter the sea ice grew downwards by the formation of congelation ice to form a hard ice column below the brown layer which now formed an interior assemblage. A second brown layer appeared at the bottom of the ice in spring (bottom infiltration assemblage). The species composition of these assemblages has been listed in section 3.3.1.2. Watanabe & Satoh (1987) have described the seasonal succession of the ice microalgal assemblages in the same area at four stations from March 1983 to January 1984. In addition they described a third assemblage (a surface melt pool assemblage). They confirmed the observations of Hoshiai on the initial development of what later became the interior assemblage in a grease ice layer at the initial stage of sea ice formation in May.

In the Weddell Sea Ackley *et al.* (1979) found that the

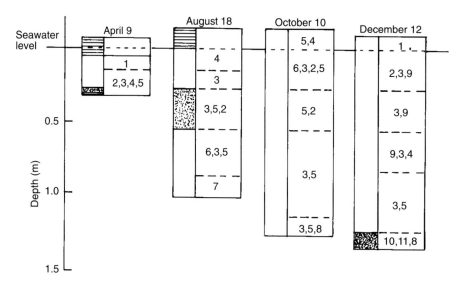

Fig. 3.7. Seasonal succession of microalgae in various strata of sea ice off Syowa Station. The left side of each ice profile shows the amount of snow cover (lined section), and light brown-stained ice (light shading) or dark brown-stained ice (dark shading). 1. *Biddulphia*, 2. *Nitzschia* a., 3. *Nitzschia* b., 4. Dinoflagellate a., 5. *Fragilariopsis*, 6. *N. frigida*, 7. *Peridinium*, 8. *Amphiprora*, 9. Dinoflagellate b., 10. *Navicula*,. 11. *Stephanopyxis*. Modified from Hoshiai (1977).

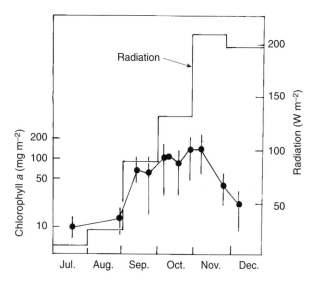

Fig. 3.8. The seasonal growth of a diatom population (as measured by chlorophyll *a*) in a tide crack at Signey Island. After Vincent (1988); redrawn from Whitaker (1977a); the radiation data are from Walton (1977).

below, freezing point to initiate, but not to complete, the brine drainage process.

Whitaker (1977a) has followed the seasonal growth of cycle of a diatom population (*Navicula glaciei*) in a tide crack at Signey Island (Fig. 3.8). Growth was slow until early September, then as irradiance increased the population grew rapidly to a peak in early November and then declined continuously until the breakup of the fast ice in the first week of December. In a tide crack at White Island on the McMurdo Ice Shelf the peak diatom biomass occurred in early December, but was preceded in early December by the development of a very large population of the flagellate *Pyranimonas* sp. (Rawlence *et al.*, 1987) (see Fig. 3.9*a*). The *Pyranimonas* population declined rapidly and by mid-December very low numbers were present. The *Pyranimonas* and the five dominant diatom species showed an interesting pattern of succession (see Fig. 3.9*b*) with *Nitzschia cylindrus* dominant in the early phase of the diatom bloom and *N. curta* in the declining phase.

3.3.2 Biomass structure

In any given locality the sea ice microbial biomass is dependent on a number of factors: the season, the relative development of surface interior, bottom and sub-ice assemblages, downwelling irradiance (dependent on latitude, ice depth, the nature of the ice and the degree of snow cover), availability of nutrients, temperature, salinity and grazing intensity.

In McMurdo Sound where the microalgal biomass was concentrated in the bottom interstitial assemblage the microalgal standing crop averaged 131(±121) mg chl *a*

greatest concentrations of chlorophyll *a* occurred in the interior assemblages. They proposed a model to account for the differences between the Weddell Sea ice microalga assemblages and those found in other parts of Antarctica. The specific structure of the assemblages depends on one or more physical factors. For the development of bottom assemblages the air temperatures must be high enough to promote complete brine migration to the bottom layers. Surface communities depend on heavy snowfall and temperatures high enough to induce melting, while interior communities such as those found in the Weddell Sea depend on air temperatures at, or slightly

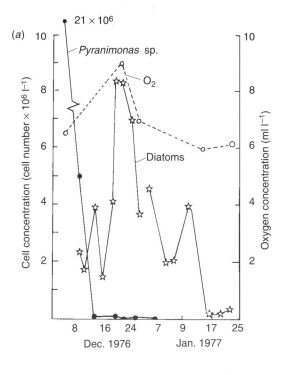
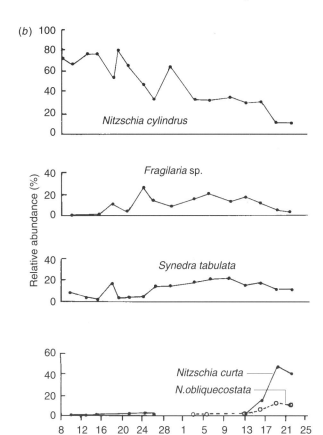

Fig. 3.9. (*a*) Dissolved oxygen concentration and concentration of diatoms and *Pyranimonas* sp. in a tide crack at White Island, McMurdo Sound, December 1976–January 1977. (*b*) The relative abundance of diatoms in the tide crack. Redrawn from Rawlence *et al.* (1987).

m^{-2} (Palmisano & Sullivan, 1983a). Chlorophyll *a* levels rose by more than four orders of magnitude from the top to the bottom of the ice column with a sharp maximum in the bottom 20 cm (Fig. 3.10) where concentrations averaged 656 mg m^{-3}, with similarly high phaeophytin (369 mg m^{-3}). These concentrations were more than two orders of magnitude higher than those in the underlying seawater. Particulate organic carbon (POC) also increased with depth to a lesser extent than chlorophyll *a* and a similar trend was also noted in bacterial carbon (Sullivan & Palmisano, 1984) (Fig. 3.11).

The seasonal variation in sea ice microalgal standing crop near Syowa Station has been studied by Hoshiai (1977) and Watanabe & Satoh (1987). Hoshiai (1977) found that the bottom infiltration assemblage demonstrated two biomass maxima over the year. Chlorophyll *a* concentrations were high in the autumn (up to 829 mg m^{-3}), decreased in the winter and then increased again in the spring when high concentrations >1000 mg m^{-3} were recorded. While peak chlorophyll *a* concentrations occurred in the bottom interstitial assemblage during the early spring the biomass maximum was in the interior assemblage higher in the ice column. Watanabe & Satoh

(1987) found that the chlorophyll *a* standing crop had peaks in April–June and October–November. The largest standing crop, 125 mg chl *a* m^{-2}, was recorded in mid-November under moderate snow cover with 95.1% of the chlorophyll *a* concentrated in the bottom 4 cm layer, where the chlorophyll *a* concentration was 2980 mg m^{-2}. In contrast to these high standing crops those measured by Ackley *et al.* (1979) in the Weddell pack ice were very much lower with a maximum of 4.5 mg m^{-3}.

Table 3.1 gives data for the maximum standing crop (mg chl *a* m^{-3}, or mg chl *a* m^{-2}) for a variety of sea ice microalgal assemblages from around the Antarctic continent. It can be seen that there are wide variations in the values from different localities and assemblages reflecting local environmental conditions. Standing crops in the vicinity of 300 mg chl *a* m^{-2} as found in McMurdo Sound in 1980 and 1981 (Sullivan *et al.*, 1982; Palmisano & Sullivan, 1983a) approach the theoretical maximum diatom standing crop of 400 mg chl *a* m^{-2} estimated by Steeman-Nielsen (1952) for natural waters.

3.3.3 Origin and fate of the sea ice microalgae

The origin of the sea ice microalgae has been the subject

Table 3.1. *Maximum standing crop of microalgae measured as chlorophyll* a *from different ice microalgal assemblages in the Antarctic*

Community and location	Chlorophyll *a*		Source
	mg m^{-2}	mg m^{-3}	
Surface melt pool			
Lutzow–Holm Bay	97	670	Meguro (1962)
Lutzow–Holm Bay	3.82	—	Watanabe & Satoh (1987)
Antarctic Peninsula	~122	407	Burkholder & Mandelli (1965)
South Orkneys	244		Whitaker (1977a)
Weddell Sea pack ice			
Late winter	—	43	D. B. Clarke & Ackley (1984)
Spring	—	54	Garrison *et al.* (1986)
Interior-band			
Lutzow–Holm Bay	16.4	—	Watanabe & Satoh (1987)
Weddell Sea pack ice			
Late summer	1.4	4.5	Ackley *et al.* (1979)
Late summer	9.6	9.8	Garrison & Buck (1982)
Spring	51.0	77.0	Garrison *et al.* (1986)
Late winter	0.6	3.8	D. B. Clarke & Ackley (1984)
Young ice			
Weddell Sea late summer	3.9	26.8	Garrison *et al.* (1983)
Bottom infiltration			
McMurdo Sound	309	>656	Palmisano & Sullivan (1983a)
McMurdo Sound	294	—	Sullivan *et al.* (1982)
Syowa Station, autumn	—	829	Hoshiai (1977)
Syowa Station, spring	—	>1000	Hoshiai (1977)
Syowa Station, autumn	30	944	Hoshiai (1981a)
Syowa Station, spring	35	5320	Hoshiai (1981a)
Davis Station	15	—	McConville *et al.* (1985)
Sub-ice			
Mat strand	1.58–32.92 h^{-1}		McConville & Wetherbee (1983)
Davis Station			
Platlet layer	~164	132	Bunt & Lee (1970)
McMurdo Sound			
	~125	250	Bunt (1963, 1968b)
Tide crack			
Signy Island	236	—	Whitaker (1977a)
White Island		30 µg l^{-1}	Rawlence *et al.* (1987)

~ integrated values not given but could be estimated from ice thickness data.
Modified from Garrison *et al.* (1986).

of much speculation (Horner, 1985a). The number of species common to both ice and water (Garrison & Buck, 1985b) suggests that the two populations constitute a closely coupled system. Garrison & Buck (1985b) consider that 'the striking similarity, both in species and relative abundance, may be maintained by a seasonal cycle where algal populations are regularly harvested from the water column and trapped in the ice, where cells persist in the ice, and where ice populations are again released into the water during melting'.

Phytoplankton cells in the surface waters may become incorporated in the ice when grease ice is formed by frazil crystal accumulation. This incorporation has been observed both by Hoshiai (1977) and Watanabe & Satoh (1987) near Syowa Station. Cells are accumulated in the

ice by a combination of scavenging and nucleation (Ackley, 1982). Scavenging occurs when ice crystals moving up the water column collide with and collect algal cells from the water. Nucleation occurs when a frazil ice crystal nucleates on an algal cell in seawater at its freezing point. The bottom ice assemblage may be formed when phytoplankton cells are scavenged by frazil platelets that attach and freeze to the underside of the ice (Ackley *et al.*, 1979). The sub-ice mat strand assemblages probably originate from the growth of cells originally incorporated in the bottom ice. Where platelets form an unconsolidated layer below the undersurface of the ice their associated microalgal assemblages may have originated from cells scavenged as the platelets floated up the water column, or from cells trapped within the platelet

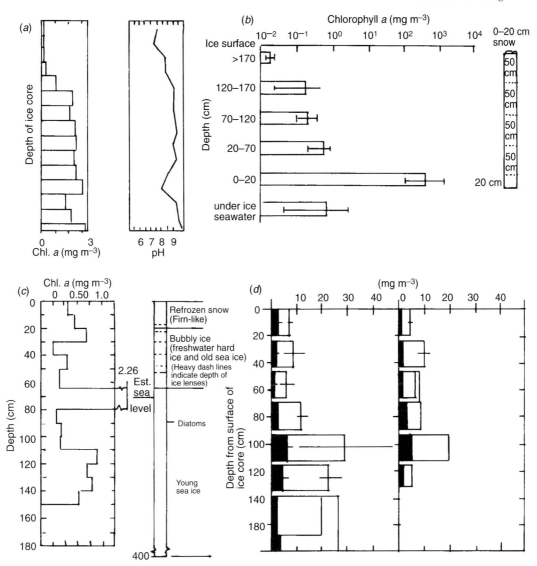

Fig. 3.10. Vertical distribution of chlorophyll *a*: (*a*) In the sea ice off Syowa Station, East Antarctica (left-hand diagram). The right-hand diagram is a vertical profile of the pH. Redrawn from Hoshiai (1977). (*b*) Means and ranges for five vertical sections of 15 sea ice cores and for the under-ice seawater from McMurdo Sound. Redrawn from Palmisano & Sullivan (1983a). (*c*) In the sea ice in the Weddell Sea pack ice (left-hand diagram). At the 60–80 cm level the chl *a* concentration was 2.26 mg m^{-3}. The right-hand diagram is a profile of the sea ice characteristics. Redrawn from Ackley *et al.* (1979). (*d*) In the sea ice cores off the Antarctic Peninsula. Phaeopigment concentrations (black areas) are shown in addition to chl *a* concentrations (white areas). The bars represent the ranges from duplicate cores. Redrawn from Kottmeier & Sullivan (1987).

layer as currents moved through the loose platelet aggregations.

Surface assemblages are formed when seawater containing algal cells floods the snow–ice interface (Meguro, 1962), or when cells are transported upwards through the brine channels in the ice to melt pools on the ice surface (McConville & Wetherbee, 1983). Freshwater algae also occur in these melt pools. They may have been blown from the land, or in areas close to glaciers and ice shelves transported in summer meltwater flowing out onto the fast ice.

In their examination of young ice Garrison & Buck (1985b) found that the assemblages in the water and the ice were essentially identical, except that the cells were more concentrated in the ice, indicating that the initial algal populations were non-selectively incorporated from the water column. However, the generally fewer species in ice cores, as compared with the water, may indicate that there is a selective survival of some species from the more diverse assemblages initially trapped in the ice.

There have been a number of conflicting views concerning the fate of the ice microalgae. The number of species abundant both in the ice and the water suggests that the pelagic populations may be derived from those within the ice, but as Garrison & Buck (1985a) point out this is difficult to establish directly. Hasle (1969) considered that the phytoplankton bloom in the pack ice region was due to the release of spores and vegetative cells from

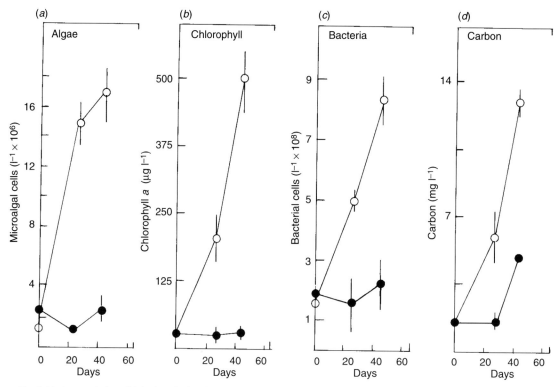

Fig. 3.11. Accumulation of (*a*) microalgal cell numbers; (*b*) chlorophyll *a*, (*c*) bacterial cell numbers; and (*d*) organic carbon in the bottom 20 cm of the annual sea ice in a light perturbation experiment conducted in McMurdo Sound. Open circles, data from control quadrat covered with 70–15 mm natural snow. Closed circles data from an experimental quadrat covered with 70 cm snow. Redrawn from Sullivan *et al.* (1985).

the ice. Krebs *et al.* (1987) in a study of the neritic diatoms of Arthur Harbour, Anvers Island, considered that the diatoms of the sea ice were an important inoculum for the phytoplankton bloom. However, as Horner (1985a) points out there is no quantitative information, and very little qualitative information, available on the survival and fate of microalgal cells in the water column. It is not known how long they survive and if they are able to grow. Once the ice algae enter the water column they will be subject to losses from grazing and sinking to the bottom. These loss mechanisms will be discussed in subsequent chapters.

3.3.4 Environmental factors and sea ice microalgal physiology

Microalgae living in sea ice are unique in their ability to photosynthesize under a set of extreme environmental conditions. Surface water temperatures in the pack ice zone are continually low (e.g. in McMurdo Sound they range from –1.81 °C to 0.08 °C (Littlepage, 1965)) and the bottom ice assemblages will be exposed to these temperatures. Algae trapped in the hypersaline brine pockets within the ice column may experience temperatures several degrees lower (Kottmeier *et al.*, 1986). The microalgae at the bottom of the congelation ice are subject to considerable salinity fluctuations. As the ice forms,

excluded salts are concentrated in microscopic (<1 mm) brine pockets. However, as snow and surface ice melts in the early summer, meltwater percolates through the porous sea ice, flushing the sea ice microalgae with low salinity water. The light regime to which the microalgae are subjected is highly variable and light is considered to be the most important environmental factor. Thus the environment in which the microalgae grow is an extreme one and their success reflects the metabolic adaptations to these extremes.

3.3.4.1 Growth

Relatively few estimates have been made of the growth rates in natural populations or laboratory cultures of sea ice microalgae. Estimates of annual production have usually been based upon the standing crop of chlorophyll *a* prior to the summer melt (Bunt, 1963; Sullivan *et al.*, 1985). Such estimates are based on the assumption that losses from the sea ice habitat (e.g. by grazing or sinking) are negligible due to the physical confinement of the cells within the ice (Bunt & Lee, 1970). *In situ* estimates of growth rates have been made by determining algal cell numbers in the ice at two different points in time during the spring bloom. However, increases in algal numbers may in large part be the result of algal accumulation rather than cell division (Palmisano & Sullivan, 1985b).

Table 3.2. *Growth rate estimates for the bottom microalgal assemblage in McMurdo Sound during a light perturbation experiment*

Basis for growth rate estimates	Control Quadrant (Snow depth 15–72 mm)		Perturbed Quadrant (Snow depth 670–700 mm)	
	Specific growth rate (μg day^{-1})	Generation time (days)	Specific growth rate (μg day^{-1})	Generation time (days)
Algal cell numbers	0.099	7	0	No net growth
Chlorophyll *a*	0.097	7	0	No net growth
Bacterial cell numbers	0.050	14	—	—
H^{14}CO$_3$ primary production	0.014–0.086	8–50	0–0.27	26

Data from Sullivan *et al.* (1985).

Growth of the sea ice itself can lead to the entrapment of algae from the water column (Ackley, 1982; Garrison *et al.*, 1983) and thus overestimation of algal growth. On the other hand, loss of algae due to ice ablation could lead to an underestimation of growth rates. Losses of algae due to grazing at the ice–seawater interface by sea ice community herbivores or cryopelagic grazers (Andriashev, 1968; Bradford, 1978; Knox, 1990) could also result in an underestimation of *in situ* growth rates.

In a study of the microalgae of the platelet ice and interstitial water Bunt (1963) found that they increased from 2.3×10^6 to 40.6×10^6 cells l^{-1} over an 18 day period. Assuming that this increase was solely due to cell division this represents a specific growth rate (μ) of 0.12 day^{-1}, or a doubling time of 6 days. From the data given in Bunt & Lee (1970) Palmisano & Sullivan (1985b) calculated a range of specific growth rates of 0.08 to 0.21 day^{-1} (doubling times 3 to 9 days) for the spring bloom. This compares with the maximum growth rate found for Antarctic phytoplankton by Holm-Hansen *et al.* (1977) of 0.33 day^{-1}; in most samples the maximum rates were closer to 0.1 day^{-1}.

In culture experiments Palmisano & Sullivan (1982) found an average doubling time of 2.5 days (μ=0.28 day^{-1}) for three sea ice diatoms, including two clones of *Nitzschia cylindrus* grown at 46 E m^{-2} s^{-1}, 0 °C and 20% in modified f/2 medium to mimic summer conditions under annual sea ice. Palmisano & Sullivan (1985b) point out that these growth rate estimates should not be considered maximal as the growth rate was light limited at the irradiance used.

3.3.4.2 Light and photosynthesis
Several studies in different geographic areas have proposed that light is the major factor limiting growth in sea ice microalgae (Bunt, 1964b; Horner & Schrader, 1982; Palmisano & Sullivan, 1982; Sullivan *et al.*, 1984, 1985;

Grossi *et al.*, 1987; SooHoo *et al.*, 1987). Downwelling irradiance is attenuated by snow cover, the sea ice itself and the development of various microalgal assemblages, so that the under-ice irradiance is typically less than 1% of that of the surface downwelling irradiance (Sullivan *et al.* 1982, 1984; Palmisano *et al.*, 1987a,b). Sullivan & Palmisano (1981) reported under-ice irradiances between 0.3 and 13.0 μE m^{-2} s^{-1} during the 1980 microalgal bloom in McMurdo Sound. In a light perturbation experiment in which 15–70 mm of snow was maintained on one quadrat and 700 mm on another Sullivan *et al.* (1985) found that the under-ice irradiance under the former quadrat ranged from 0.6 to 0.11 μE m^{-2} s^{-1} and 0.2 to 2.9 μE m^{-2} s^{-1} under the latter, while Palmisano & Sullivan (1985c) found that during the spring bloom the irradiance under annual sea ice with 50 mm of snow cover was low with a mean of 6 μE m^{-2} s^{-1}, representing only 0.4% of the surface downwelling irradiance.

Profiles of spectral irradiance through the ices column in McMurdo Sound (SooHoo *et al.*, 1987) have demonstrated that the irradiance environment of the sea ice is both vertically and horizontally heterogeneous (Fig. 3.15), changing from blue dominated to green dominated with depth in the ice column, and varying from site to site depending on the snow and ice microalgal patchiness. Changes in both total PAR and spectral irradiance that occur over tens of metres in an open water column are compressed within a vertical distance of only 2 to 3 metres within the sea ice column.

In spite of the reduced irradiance available to the bottom ice and platelet ice assemblages substantial standing stocks of microalgae are found and their productivity may be high (Palmisano & Sullivan, 1983a; Sullivan *et al*, 1985). Bunt & Lee (1970) were the first to establish that the size of the standing crop of the sea ice microalgae was a function of snow cover. In 1967 a site in McMurdo Sound with surface snow yielded 520 mg C m^{-2}, whereas

Table 3.3. *Productivity estimates for sea ice microalgal assemblages*

Locality	Assemblage	Productivity	
		mg C m^{-2} day^{-1}	mg C (mg chl *a*)$^{-1}$ h^{-1}
McMurdo Sound[1]	Platelet ice (interstitial water)	3.8[6]	0.4
McMurdo Sound[2]	Bottom congelation ice	—	0.6–7.5[7]
McMurdo Sound[3]	Platelet ice (snow-free)	1–2106	0.006–1.33
	Bottom congelation ice (snow-free)	0.07–240	0.20–1.95
	Platelet ice (5 cm snow)	1–334	0.04–0.24
	Bottom congelation ice (5 cm snow)	0.5–19	0.03–0.66
Casey Station[4]	Sub-ice mat strand	1.58–32.9[8]	—
Antartic Peninsula[5]	Interior band (late winter)	35.0±11.87	—

[1]Bunt & Lee (1970); [2]Palmisano & Sullivan (1983a); [3]Grossi *et al.* (1987); [4]McConville & Wetherbee (1983); [5]Kottmeier & Sullivan (1987). [6]mg C m^{-3} day^{-1}; [7]mg C (mg chl *a*)$^{-1}$; [8]mg C m^{-2} h^{-1}.

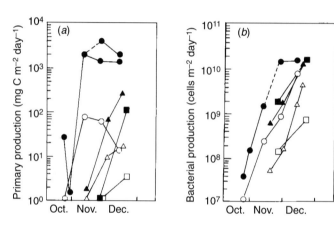

Fig. 3.12. (*a*) Microalgal primary production, and (*b*) bacterial cell production in sea ice cores from experimental quadrats with variable snow cover (0, 5, 25 cm) for bottom congelation ice (open symbols) and sub-ice platelet ice (closed symbols). Circles – 0 cm snow cover; triangles – 5 cm snow cover; squares – 254 cm snow cover. Redrawn from Kottmeier *et al.* (1987).

a snow-free site yielded 1076 g C m^{-2} (Bunt & Lee, 1970). Palmisano *et al.* (1985a) and Sullivan *et al.* (1982) conducted a light perturbation experiment in which snow cover over 1.5 m of congelation ice was manipulated to reduce the irradiance reaching the sea ice microalgae (Fig. 3.11). At the end of the growing season in 1981 a standing crop of 100 mg chl *a* m^{-2} was found under 1.5 cm of natural snow cover, while only 5.5 mg chl *a* m^{-2} was found under 100 cm of snow under a quadrat with an artificially increased amount of snow.

Subsequent studies have confirmed these results (Grossi *et al.*, 1987). Five quadrats were established in early October with 0, 5, 10, and 100 cm of snow cover. Under-ice irradiances ranged from <0.02 to 100 μE m^{-2} s^{-1}. Standing crop, growth rate and photosynthetic rate were greatest in the snow-free quadrat where the chlorophyll *a* concentration increased from 0.1 to 76 mg m^{-2} in the platelet ice layer (μ= 0.41 day^{-1}) and from 0.05 to 9.0

mg m^{-2} in the congelation ice layer (μ= 0.29 day^{-1}) over a 5-week period. Blooms occurred later in the snow-covered quadrats and growth rates were less than half of those in the snow-free quadrat (Table 3.2, Fig. 3.12).

Estimates of primary productivity of sea ice microalgae have been hindered by the difficulties of quantitative sampling of the sea ice and the contained microalgal assemblages and the carrying out of *in situ* incubations under the ice. In pioneering studies in McMurdo Sound Bunt *et al.* (Bunt, 1963; Bunt & Lee, 1970) estimated a peak fixation rate of 3.82 mg C m^{-3} h^{-1} for the interstitial water of the platelet ice assemblage, or a chlorophyll *a* specific photosynthesis of 0.4 mg C (mg chl *a*)$^{-1}$ h^{-1} at 1800 W cm^{-2} (about 100 μE m^{-2} s^{-1}) and 1.8 °C. This is an underestimate as the algae attached to the ice crystals were not included in the incubations. These and other estimates of primary production are given in Table 3.3. Palmisano & Sullivan (1983a) in incubations in a cham-

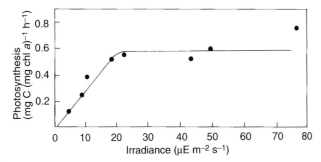

Fig. 3.13. Photosynthesis irradiance relationships of the microalgae of the sub-ice platelet ice assemblage in McMurdo Sound. Redrawn from Palmisano & Sullivan (1985).

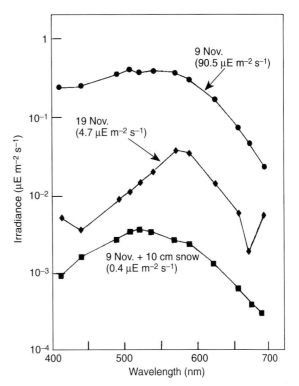

Fig. 3.14. Spectral distribution of irradiance beneath sea ice in McMurdo Sound. Snow reduces PAR penetration at all wavelengths. The bottom sea ice infiltration microalgal bloom strongly attenuates light at the blue and red ends of the spectrum. Redrawn from Palmisano *et al.* (1987b).

ber designed to mimic both the temperature and the quantity and quality of light available to the bottom congelation ice microalgal assemblage estimated the primary productivity to be 0.3 mg C (mg chl *a*)$^{-1}$ h^{-1} at 13 μE m^{-2} s^{-1}, an irradiance about one eighth that used by Bunt & Lee (1970). The most comprehensive set of productivity data is that which Grossi *et al.* (1987) obtained in their snow perturbation experiments (see above).

Ice algal assemblages are generally considered to be 'shade adapted'. Bunt (1967) found that photosynthesis by natural populations of sea ice microalgae in McMurdo Sound was light-saturated at 100 fc (about 22 μE m^{-2} s^{-1}) and photoinhibited at 1100 fc (about 240 μE m^{-2} s^{-1}). Assimilation numbers were found to be less than 1.5 mg C (mg chl *a*)$^{-1}$ h^{-1}. Bunt (1968b) later confirmed these observations in laboratory studies with the sea ice diatom *Fragilaria sublinearis* in which cells grown at –2.0 °C and 13 fc resulted in an assimilation number of only 0.37. Growing the cultures at 5.0 °C and 1000 fc increased the assimilation number to 1.2. Preliminary studies by Palmisano & Sullivan (1983b) indicated that the photosynthetic capacity (P_{max}) for natural populations of sea ice microalgae in McMurdo Sound was only 0.5 mg C (mg chl *a*)$^{-1}$ h^{-1}, a value less than one fourth that of temperate phytoplankton. The microalgae had an *I* (irradiance at which the photosynthesis is light-saturated) of only 19 μE m^{-2} s^{-1}, a value that compares with the lowest *I*s reported for microalgae (Fig. 3.13). Palmisano & Sullivan, in short-term experiments in McMurdo Sound in 1983, found that the bottom congelation ice microalgae were photo-inhibited at irradiances above 25 μE m^{-2} s^{-1}, a value about the same as that obtained by Palmisano *et al.* (1985b). These data serve to confirm Bunt's (1964b) observations that sea ice microalgae are very shade adapted. However, Grossi *et al.* (1987) in the snow perturbation experiments discussed above found that the microalgae grew fastest, reached highest standing crop, and demonstrated maximum assimilation numbers in the snow-free quadrat, where ambient irradiance was close to

100 μE m^{-2} s^{-1}. They concluded that several factors may have contributed to their divergent results. First, unlike previous investigators, they sampled the quadrats repetitively over a 3 month period, including the early phase of bloom development. Second, because snow manipulation was effected early in the season when algal biomass was low, the light gradient apparently selected for different species assemblages under the snow-cleared and snow-covered quadrats. Finally, extensive underwater observations allowed interpretation of disparities in production estimates derived from biomass and *in situ* photosynthetic rates in the light of physical changes.

Two other important aspects of light affecting primary production in bottom and sub-ice microalgal assemblages are the photoperiod and spectral composition of the light. Sullivan *et al.* (1982) found a pronounced diel change in under-ice irradiance during the spring bloom in McMurdo Sound, ranging from 2.9 μE m^{-2} s^{-1} at 1200 h to 0.5 μE m^{-2} s^{-1} at 2300 h on November 14, 1981, despite continuous surface downwelling irradiance of 1500 μE m^{-2} s^{-1}. Palmisano & Sullivan (1985b) suggest that diel rhthyms in photosynthesis may exist in sea ice diatoms similar to those reported for temperate phytoplankters (Preslin & Ley, 1980).

SooHoo *et al.* (1987) have measured the spectral irra-

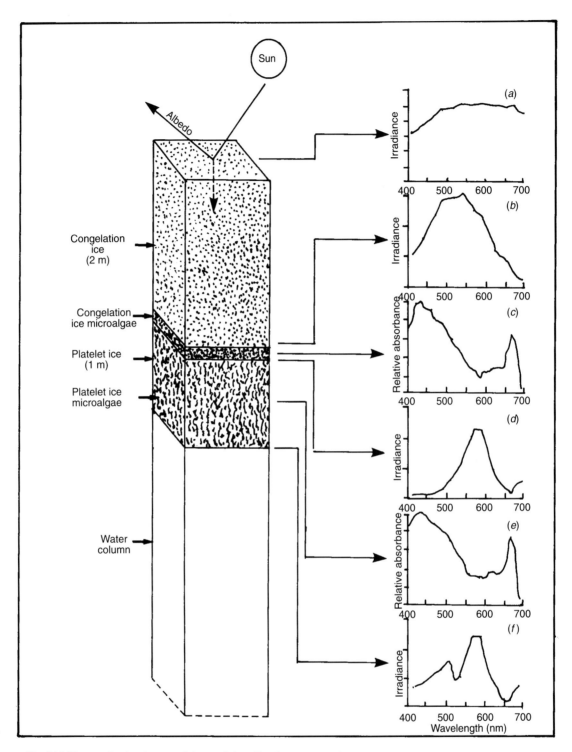

Fig. 3.15. Diagram showing the spectral characteristics of irradiance (in μE m⁻² s⁻¹) at different depths within the ice structure in McMurdo Sound and the *in vivo* spectral absorption characteristics of the microalgal assemblages. (*a*) Spectral irradiance incident on the surface of the ice. PAR = 1364 μE m⁻² s⁻¹. (*b*) Resulting irradiance spectrum after a 65% loss to albedo, and after passing through 1.8 m of first-year congelation sea ice. PAR = 46 μE m⁻² s⁻¹. (*c*) *In vivo* absorption spectrum for the bottom infiltration microalgal assemblage from the bottom 0.2 m of the ice column. (*d*) Spectral irradiance measured just underneath the congelation ice. PAR = 1.379 μE m⁻² s⁻¹. (*e*) *In vivo* absorption spectrum of the microalgae of the sub-ice platelet ice layer. (*f*) Spectral irradiance measured beneath the platelet ice layer. PAR = 0.656 μE m⁻² s⁻¹. Redrawn from SooHoo *et al.* (1987).

diance and *in vivo* absorption spectra for both the congelation ice and sub-ice platelet layer assemblages in McMurdo Sound, as well as the spectral irradiance throughout the ice column (Fig. 3.14). The bottom congelation ice and sub-ice platelet layer assemblages in gelation microalgae have available a spectrum with the quanta concentrated between 450 to 580 nm (Fig. 3.15*b*). A significant proportion of the quanta are available in the blue and blue-green regions of the spectrum where they can be absorbed by the photosynthetic pigments. Total PAR at this level in the ice column is about 46 μE m^{-2} s^{-1} or 3% of the value of PAR incident upon the surface. The absorption spectrum for the bottom congelation ice microalgae is shown in Fig. 3.15c. Blue and green light are selectively absorbed by the algal photosynthetic pigments further reducing the spectrum of the available light (Fig. 3.15d). Photosynthetically usable radiation (PUR) for the bottom congelation ice microalgae was calculated at 57$\pm$7% of their PAR. After passing through the 20 cm of this bottom assemblage, available quanta were reduced to less than 1.5 μE m^{-2} s^{-1}, or about 0.1% of the incident surface radiation, and were concentrated in a band from 540 to 620 nm (Fig. 3.15d), wavelengths where algal absorption is minimal. The microalgae of the platelet layer showed enhanced absorption in the blue-green region of the spectrum between 500 and 550 nm (Fig. 3.15e). This corresponds to the absorption region of the major carotenoid accessory pigment of the diatoms, the xanthophyll fucoxanthin. Consequently, the spectrum of irradiance available to the platelet ice microalgae was 31$\pm$2% of PAR as PUR. Platelet ice microalgae have consistently been found to show enhanced blue-green absorption relative to the bottom congelation ice microalgae (Sullivan *et al.*, 1984; SooHoo *et al.*, 1987). After passing through the platelet layer less than 1 μE m^{-2} s^{-1} (PAR = 10.05% incident surface PAR) is available at the top of the underlying water column for phytoplankton photosynthesis (Fig. 3.15f), and most of this is in the green spectrum where microalgae do not absorb light effectively. As a consequence PUR is only 25$\pm$2% of PAR. Absorption in the blue-green region of the spectrum (480–550 nm) for the platelet ice microalgae is enhanced relative to that for the congelation ice microalgae. Thus the rate and extent of development of the sea ice microalgal assemblages can have a dramatic effect on downwelling irradiance. Palmisano *et al.* (1987b) found that changes in the under-ice spectrum occurred in time scales as short as 10 days (Fig. 3.14).

While the interior, bottom and sub-ice assemblages are considered to be 'shade adapted', the microalgae of the surface melt pools can be considered to be 'sun adapted'. Burkholder & Mandelli (1965) found that the surface microalgal assemblages had a maximum photosynthetic rate at 18 klx (about 400 μE m^{-2} s^{-1}), with an assimilation number of 2.6 mg C (mg chl a)$^{-1}$ h^{-1}. Microalgae dominating the brash ice in blooms at the ice edge zone also appear to sun adapted (Palmisano & Sullivan, 1985b).

Most of the work on photosynthesis by sea ice microalgae in the Antarctic has been carried out on fast ice communities near land-based stations (see Horner, 1985a; Palmisano & Sullivan, 1985b; and Garrison *et al.*, 1986 for reviews). Pack ice on the other hand at its maximum extent covers eight to nine times the area of the fast ice, and includes a greater variety of microenvironments with different physico-chemical conditions (Ackley *et al.*, 1979; D. B. Clarke & Ackley, 1984), different microalgal species composition (Horner, 1985b; Garrison *et al.*, 1986, 1987), and different photosynthetic characteristics (Burkholder & Mandelli, 1965; Irwin, 1990; Lizotte & Sullivan, 1991a,b). Lizotte & Sullivan (1991a) in the western Weddell Sea found that the sea ice microalgae from the pack ice had higher photosynthetic capacities (higher P^b_m (g C (g chl a)$^{-1}$ h^{-1}); higher light saturation volume, I_k (μE m^{-2} s^{-1})) relative to fast ice microalgae. The pack ice microalgae had photosynthetic capabilities that were indistinguishable from Antarctic phytoplankton. They inhabit microenvironments with higher irradiances than those of the fast ice microalgae suggesting that they could have much higher rates of primary production than previously estimated on the basis of evidence from fast ice regions. These findings have been confirmed by Gleitz & Kirst (1991) in studies of ice algal assemblages in the northwestern part of the Weddell Sea. During the winter the ice cover, low sun angle (higher reflectance), short photoperiod, low incident radiation, and little stratification of the water column inhibits primary production by the phytoplankton. Thus, in the pack ice region the sea ice microalgae may be the most important primary producers in the winter and early spring and their contribution to the overall primary production has been underestimated.

3.3.4.3 Nutrient concentrations

Several researchers have concluded that nutrients probably do not limit the growth of sea ice microalgal assemblages (Meguro *et al.*, 1967; Bunt & Lee, 1970; Holm-Hansen *et al.*, 1977; Sullivan & Palmisano, 1981; D. B. Clarke & Ackley, 1984). Three processes are usually advanced to explain nutrient abundance in the sea ice habitat: 1. replenishment of nutrients by exchange between the lower part of the ice and the underlying water; 2. desalination; and 3. *in situ* bacterial regeneration (Meguro *et al.*, 1967; Sullivan & Palmisano, 1981). The rate of nutrient transport at the ice–water boundary depends on the downward flux by salt rejection, brine cell drainage from the ice and upward flux from the underlying water (Demers *et al.*, 1986). According to Legendre *et al.* (1981) active upward transport of nutrients from the water column is required for the growth of the bottom microalgal assemblages. This is supported by the findings of Gosselin *et al.* (1985) which indicated nutrient enrichment of the ice–water interface by tidal mixing. The upward flux of nutrients depends on the stability of the boundary layer beneath the ice. Stability varies from convectively unstable during brine rejection to very stable when meltwater forms a thin layer beneath the ice (Demers *et al.*, 1986). Thus, the rate of nutrient input to the sub-ice and bottom microalgal assemblages depends on the degree of destabilization of the boundary layer by factors such as brine rejection, tidal movement and current variability. Thus, under conditions where the boundary layer is stable upward nutrient exchange is reduced and the microalgae may deplete the available nutrients.

It has been suggested that enhanced assimilation of carbon into carbohydrates at the expense of proteins is indicative of nutrient-limited microalgal populations (Hitchcock, 1978; Konopka, 1983; Lancelot, 1984). Near Davis Station McConville *et al.* (1985) described a progressive decline of a sub-ice microalgal bloom – an algal sheet detached from the ice to form suspended strands prior to their release into the water column. The authors suggested that the pattern of carbon assimilation into these algal populations (high incorporation into carbohydrates but low into proteins) indicated nutrient limitation. In a study of a tide crack community dominated by *Phaeocystis pouchetii* in McMurdo Sound Palmisano & Sullivan (1985a) found that the end products of photosynthesis were primarily proteins and polysaccharides in contrast to the platelet ice microalgal assemblage in which the percentage of ^{14}C-CO_2 incorporated into small molecular weight metabolites was about twice that found in *P. pouchetii*. In a third assemblage, the bottom congelation ice assemblage, the percentage incorporation into polysaccharides was two to three times higher than for *P. pouchetii* and the platelet ice assemblage. These results suggest that the algae growing in the minute brine pockets in the congelation ice may exhaust their available nutrients and become nitrogen deficient.

3.3.4.4 Salinity
The salinity environment of the sea ice microalgae is highly variable. Salinities within the brine chambers have been observed to range from greater than 150‰ to 34‰. During the summer melt salinities at the ice–water interface may drop to 0‰ as the result of snow and ice melting and a fresh-water lens may form beneath the ice (Bunt, 1968b; Grossi *et al.*, 1984, 1987; Palmisano & Sullivan, 1985b).

Kottmeier & Sullivan (1988) have measured the rates of carbon fixation versus salinity. For congelation ice microalgae from Granite Harbour maximum carbon fixation occurred at 30‰, with a secondary peak from 10‰ to 20‰. A marked decline in carbon fixation occurred at salinities above 30‰. In a second sample from Hutt Point, maximum carbon fixation occurred at 5‰, with a

secondary peak at 40‰. There was a marked decline in carbon fixation in salinities above 50‰, with no net carbon fixation from 70‰ to 90‰. Thus, the sea ice microalgae are capable of substantial metabolism at the salinities which are characteristic of those encountered *in situ*. Before the onset of melting the congelation ice in McMurdo Sound (from as early as mid-November through to December) the maximum rate of carbon fixation occurred close to 34‰, the average salinity of surface seawater in McMurdo Sound (Littlepage, 1965). Following the onset of the melting of the congelation ice, maximum rates of carbon fixation occurred at lower salinities, close to those found by Bunt (1964) for platelet ice microalgae collected in McMurdo Sound in late December (7.5 to 10.0‰).

Palmisano *et al.* (1987a) found that the sea ice microalgae were actively photosynthetic at salinities ranging from 20 to 33‰ and that P^b_m (photosynthetic rate at optimal radiance) was slightly higher at the lower salinities. They were not able to detect photosynthetic activity at 60‰. Thus, high brine salinities may be a factor limiting the vertical distribution of microalgae in the ice column. Dilution of the high-salinity brine with seawater in the lower portion of the ice column (Reeburg, 1984) may be essential for algal growth, and this may be a partial explanation for why microalgal growth is primarily confined to the bottom 5–25 cm of the congelation ice in McMurdo Sound.

Gleitz & Kirst (1991) in their studies on the physiological ecology of ice micoalgal assemblages collected from the Weddell Sea pack ice found that while light-saturated production rates of three infiltration assemblages under hypersaline conditions (approximately 50 and 110‰) decreased by 15–55%, rates under hyposaline conditions (approximately 20‰) decreased only slightly (–9%), or were even stimulated (14–22%). This tolerance to reduced salinity coupled with high photosynthetic activity enables the pack ice microalgae to survive seasonal ice melt and to contribute to the open water phytoplankton.

3.3.4.5 Temperature
Metabolism and growth of microalgae are hypothesized to be limited in part by the low temperatures of the polar oceans (Holm-Hansen *et al.*, 1977; Neori & Holm-Hansen, 1982; Jacques, 1983; El-Sayed, 1984; Tilzer *et al.*, 1985, 1986). Sea ice microalgae in McMurdo Sound may be exposed to temperatures at the upper ice surface that may range from –42 °C in the winter to about 4 °C in the summer (Littlepage, 1965; Palmisano & Sullivan, 1982; Kottmeier *et al.*, 1987). The microalgae in the brine chambers at the bottom of the ice

Table 3.4. *Photosynthetic parameters for Antarctic sea ice microalgae*

a^h	Photosynthetic efficiency, the initial slope of the *P–I* curve	mg C (mg chl a)$^{-1}$ h^{-1} (μE m^{-2} s^{-1})$^{-1}$
P^h_m	Photosynthetic rate at optimal irradiance	mg C (mg chl a)$^{-1}$ h^{-1}
I^h_k	$P_m{}^h/I_a{}^h$, an index of photoadaptation	μE m^{-2} s^{-1}
I^h_m	Irradiance at which photosynthesis is maximal	μE m^{-2} s^{-1}

Adapted from Palmisano *et al.* (1987a).

column and those in the sub-ice assemblages may experience temperatures close to that of the underlying seawater (approaching –2.0 °C in the winter).

Palmisano *et al.* (1987a) in a series of experiments on short-term physiological responses of photosynthetic parameters to temperature (Table 3.4) found that the maximum photosynthetic rates (P^b_m) increased more than two-fold in bottom congelation ice microalgae, and three- to four-fold in sub-ice platelet ice microalgae between –2 °C and +6 °C. P^b_m decreased when both types of microalgae were incubated at +10 °C, indicating that the optimum temperature for light-saturated photosynthesis was around +6 °C. This falls at the low end of such estimates for sea ice microalgae and Antarctic phytoplankton; eg. 10–15 °C for platelet ice microalgae (Bunt, 1964), near 12 °C for Antarctic phytoplankton (Jacques, 1983), and 7 °C as the optimum temperature for phytoplankton (Holm-Hansen *et al.*, 1982). While the temperature optima were low they were about 8 °C higher than the ambient surface water temperatures. The I^b_k ($=P^b_m/I^b_a$ (photosynthetic efficiency)) which is an index of photoadaptation, inceased steadily with temperature from 7.4 (at –2 °C) to 14.8 μE m^{-2} s^{-1} in congelation ice microalgae, and from 11.7 to 54.3 μE m^{-2} s^{-1} in platelet ice microalgae. Even greater increases were found in I^b_m (irradiance at which photosynthesis is maximal) which changed from 31.4 to 88.4 μE m^{-2} s^{-1} in congelation ice microalgae and from 11.7 to 238 μE m^{-2} s^{-1} in platelet ice microalgae. Palmisano *et al.* (1987a) concluded that in the low-temperature-adapted sea ice microalgae, even relatively small changes in temperature could have a significant effect on photosynthesis–irradiance relationships.

Kottmeier & Sullivan (1988) in another series of experiments measured the rates of sea ice microalgal carbon fixation over a range of temperatures. Carbon fixation increased several-fold from –1.9 °C up to a maximum temperature ranging from 8 to 14 °C (Fig. 3.16). This maximum was followed by a marked decline in carbon fixation from 14 to 30 °C, with rates from 20 to 30 °C less than those at –1.9 °C. Thus, while substantial carbon fixation can occur at temperatures close to the –1.9 °C found *in situ* at the ice–seawater interface, maximum metabolic rates occur at temperatures considerably above –1.9 °C,

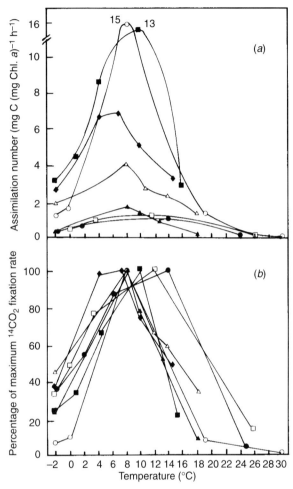

Fig. 3.16. Effect of temperature on carbon fixation by sea ice microalgae from a series of stations in McMurdo Sound from November to January expressed as (*a*) assimilation numbers, and (*b*) percent of maximum carbon fixed. ○=Hut Point, Nov. 16, 1983; ●=edge of fast ice, Nov. 18, 1983; □=Hut Point, Nov. 30, 1983; ■=edge of fast ice, Dec. 9, 1983; △=Cape Armitage, Dec. 27, 1983; ▲=Dunlop Island, Dec. 29, 1983; and ◆=Dunlop Island, Jan. 5, 1984. Redrawn from Kottmeier & Sullivan (1988).

but below 15 °C. The enhanced metabolic activity by sea ice microalgae up to a maximum temperature of 15 °C is probably due to the energetic cost of enzyme production and the thermodynamics of enzyme catalyzed reactions. The microalgae appear to be well adapted for growth at low temperatures, although they are not maximally active at the temperatures found in the sea ice.

Table 3.5 summarizes the results of a series of experi-

Table 3.5. *Range of temperatures where maximal
activities occurred in rates of nitrate uptake, ammonium
uptake, carbon dioxide uptake, and nitrate reductase
activity, and Q_{10} values for each process measured*

Activity	Temperature of maximum activity (°C)	$Q_{10}\pm$SD
Nitrate uptake	0.5–2.1	11.7±5.7
Ammonium uptake	2.1–3.8	15.4±0.1
Carbon uptake	2.1–3.8	16.3±0.1
Nitrate reductase activity	8.0–9.0	1.4±0.02

From Priscu *et al.* (1987).

ments designed to examine the influence of temperature on nitrate and ammonium uptake, and the activity of the enzyme nitrate reductase on natural assemblages of sea ice microalgae from McMurdo Sound (Priscu *et al.*, 1987). Nitrate, ammonium and carbon dioxide uptake had temperature maxima ranging from about 0.5 to 3.8 °C. These results clearly show that the metabolic pathways involved in these reactions characterize the microalgal assemblages as being psychrophilic. This is supported by the similarities in the Q_{10} values (Q_{10} represents the increase in metabolic rate for each 10 °C increase in temperature). Nitrate reductase showed a distinctly different activity versus temperature relationship. These results provide further evidence that low environmental temperatures have imposed selection pressures on sea ice microalgae resulting in physiological characteristics closely fitting habitat conditions.

3.3.4.6 Heterotrophy

Diatoms are nutritionally diverse; they may be obligate autotrophs, facultative heterotrophs (mixotrophs), or obligate heterotrophs. Facultative heterotrophy is not uncommon in pennate diatom species and the substances taken up include sugars, amino acids and organic acids (Hellebust & Lewin, 1977). Sea ice microalgae may use heterotrophic nutrition to supplement photosynthesis during the low light conditions of the spring bloom, or to support maintenance metabolism during the continuous darkness of the polar winter.

Palmisano & Sullivan (1982) found that the uptake of ^{14}C-glucose by three sea ice diatoms was enhanced by as much as 60% when incubated in the dark. However, the dark uptake of glucose provided less than 1% of the carbon needed for cell division, although it could be sufficient for maintenance metabolism. In another study Palmisano & Sullivan (1983b) demonstrated the dark incorporation and respiration of ^{14}C-serine by natural populations of sea ice microalgae. This was confirmed by

a subsequent study (Palmisano & Sullivan, 1985b) in which natural populations of platelet ice microalgae were found to take up ^{3}H-serine at natural substratum conditions under both dark and low light intensities (15 and 48 µE m^{-2} s^{-1}), but they found no significant differences in serine uptake among three different light treatments. Palmisano & Sullivan (1985a) concluded that some sea ice microalgae may use heterotrophic nutrition not only during the dark polar winter, but also during the spring bloom itself. Although microalgal heterotrophy does not provide new C for the microalgal assemblages, it could provide a means for more efficient utilization of the total carbon fixed. It is probable that some portion of the fixed carbon that is lost by extracellular release may be re-assimilated by certain species and used as a source of carbon and energy.

3.3.4.7 Dark survival

With the onset of the polar winter, sea ice microalgae are subject to a prolonged period of total darkness. There is ample evidence to demonstrate that the sea ice microalgae can survive this period. Both Hoshiai (1977, 1981a, 1985) and Watanabe & Satoh (1987) have followed the development of the microalgal assemblages in the sea ice near Syowa Station over a full year. From the results of these investigations it is clear that the microalgae survive the winter darkness as the chlorophyll *a* standing crops had peaks in both April–June and October–November.

In 1982 a pigmented band of microalgae was found 80 cm from the ice–seawater interface in two-year sea ice at New Harbour, McMurdo Sound (Palmisano & Sullivan, 1985b). This apparently was a remnant of the 1981 bottom congelation ice bloom to which an extra season's ice growth has been added. Samples stained with acridine orange and DAPI weakly fluoresced under epifluorescence microscopy, and a pennate diatom was cultured from the cells in the band thus confirming that some cells can maintain their viability over the winter.

Little is known of the physiological mechanisms of dark survival in sea ice diatoms. Bunt & Lee (1970) found that three of four sea ice microalgae remained viable after three months of dark incubation in the absence or organic supplements. Palmisano & Sullivan (1982) found that 1 to 100% of the populations of three sea ice diatom cultures were able to grow autotrophically after dark incubation for 5 months at –2 °C. Subsequently, Palmisano & Sullivan (1983b) subjected three anexic diatom cultures to a 30-day simulated summer–winter transition (gradually decreasing light and temperature, and increasing salinity). The diatoms responded to these changes by a reduction in cellular metabolism as demonstrated by: 1. a decline in growth rate and photosynthetic rate; 2. a decrease in cellular ATP; and 3. the storage and subsequent use of endogenous carbon reserves. In addition, the heterotrophic potential of the three clones increased as much as 60-fold. Palmisano & Sullivan (1983b) proposed three survival strategies enabling the diatoms to cope with the polar winter: facultative heterotrophy; storage and utilization of carbohydrates at a reduced rate; and resting spore formation. Ample evidence exist for the first two of these mechanisms but the formation of resting spores has yet to be established for Antarctic diatoms (Fryxell *et al.*, 1979).

3.4 Sea ice bacteria

The sea ice contains a diverse assemblage of bacteria. Most of our knowledge concerning these bacteria comes from recent studies by Sullivan & Palmisano (1981, 1984) and their co-workers (Grossi *et al.*, 1984; Sullivan, 1985; Sullivan *et al.*, 1984; Kottmeier *et al.*, 1987; Kottmeier & Sullivan, 1988) in the McMurdo Sound region.

3.4.1 Distribution and abundance

Sullivan & Palmisano (1984) found an abundant and diverse bacterial community in the brine channels of the annual sea ice and at the ice–seawater interface in McMurdo Sound. The mean bacterial standing crop was 1.4×10^{11} cells m^{-2} (9.8 g C m^{-2}) with bacterial concentrations as high as 1.02×10^{12} cells m^{-2} being found in the ice core meltwater. A study of the vertical distribution of the bacteria in sea ice cores 1.3 to 2.5 m in length showed that 47% of the bacterial numbers and 93% of the biomass was located in the bottom 20 cm of the ice column. The bacterial cells were much larger (average 80 femtograms (fg) C cell^{-1}) in this bottom section than those higher in the column (5 fg C cell^{-1}). Concentrations of bacterial carbon in the sea ice was more than ten times higher than that of the bacterioplankton in the water column below.

Scanning electron microscopy (Sullivan & Palmisano, 1984) showed a variety of morphologically distinct cell types, including coccoid, rod, fusiform, filamentous and prosthecate forms. Among the 155 bacterial strains isolated by Sullivan & Palmisano and their co-workers (Kottmeier *et al.*, 1987) 21% were psychrophylic (Morita, 1975), i.e. those capable of growth at 0 °C, but not above 18 °C (Kobori *et al.*, 1984). Free-living bacteria comprised 70% of the total numbers, with the remaining 30% being attached to either living microalgal cells or detritus. Epibacteria were primarily living in close physical association with healthy intact cells of one of the dominant diatoms *Amphiprora* sp., suggesting a symbiotic association. Sullivan & Palmisano (1984) advance two hypotheses to account for this association.

Amphiprora spp. may leak or excrete a large proportion of their photosynthate to the extracellular environment where it is taken up and utilized by the epibacteria, or *Amphiprora* spp. may fail to produce antibacterial substances by which other ice diatoms inhibit growth or attachment of bacteria (Siebruth, 1967).

Epibacteria were also found to be abundant in the sub-ice mat strand assemblage off Casey Station (McConville & Wetherbee, 1983). They were mostly Gram-negative rods, although Gram-negative cocci were also present, and they were attached to the mucilage sheaths of *Amphipleura* sp. (= *Berkeleya*) and the fustules of *Entomoneis*. Many other diatom species (e.g. *Nitzschia frigida*) were largely devoid of epibacteria. Bacterial densities ranged from 4×10^{11} to 2×10^{13} cells m^{-2}, up to ten times higher than those recorded from McMurdo Sound.

In sea ice core samples taken in the Weddell Sea (M.A. Miller *et al.*, 1984) the bacteria, unlike those in McMurdo Sound which were concentrated in the bottom 20 cm of the ice column, were distributed throughout the depth of the ice. The range of bacterial biomass present in the 1–2 m of sea ice was from 6.15 to 99.6 mg C m^{-2}, while that in 100 m of the water column below the ice was from 24 to 97.5 mg C m^{-2}.

3.4.2 Growth and production

Bacterial cells are likely to accumulate in the ice, especially where frazil ice formation dominates, by the same mechanisms as are operative for the microalgae (see section 3.3.3 above). Sullivan & Palmisano (1984) and Sullivan *et al.* (1985) found that the ice bacteria were robust compared with the bacterioplankton of the underlying waters. A high frequency of dividing cells were found and one morphologically distinct type was found to have a division frequency of >16%, a frequency indicative of high growth rates. Microautoradiographic evidence of ^{14}C-L-serine uptake by the ice bacteria under simulated *in situ* conditions provided additional evidence that the bacterial populations were capable of active metabolism at −1.8 °C. It is likely that selection takes place for those bacterioplankton whose growth is permitted or even favoured by the unique ice environment, i.e. high salinities, low temperatures, surfaces (ice crystals, organic detritus and microalgal cells) and high concentrations of micronutrients and dissolved and particulate organic matter.

Seasonal changes in the sea ice bacterial assemblage was followed by Grossi *et al.* (1984) and Sullivan *et al.* (1985). during a light perturbation experiment in McMurdo Sound in which a control quadrat with 7 cm of snow was left undisturbed while a second quadrat had the snow cover artificially increased to 70 cm. The bacteria in the control quadrat grew at a rate of 0.05 day[-1], whereas in the snow covered quadrat no growth occurred (Fig. 3.11*c*). Sullivan *et al.* (1985) determined a doubling time of 14 days. While this generation time is long it is within the range of values reported for other low-temperature systems. Over the six-week study period bacterial numbers increased six-fold to 1.8×10^{11} cells m[-2], whereas biomass increased ten-fold to 2.0 g C m[-2]. This disparity was due to the fact that the epiphytic bacteria grew at a rate twice that of the non-attached bacteria. In further support of the idea that bacteria undergo active growth in the sea ice microenvironment Sullivan *et al.* (1985) showed that the attached bacteria took up ^{3}H-serine, ^{3}H-glucose, and ^{3}H-thymidine, demonstrating that net DNA synthesis occurred by the incorporation of ^{3}H-thymidine. Net DNA synthesis is a prerequisite for growth.

In the late winter in the Weddell Sea Kottmeier & Sullivan (1987) found that bacterial production in the sea ice averaged 20.5 ± 11.0 (SE) $\times 10^{10}$ cells m[-2] day[-1], while the carbon production averaged 5.2 ± 2.8 (SE) mg C m[-2] day[-1]. The bacterial cell and carbon production in the seawater 3 m below the ice were much lower than in the sea ice, averaging 4.5 ± 3.5 (SE) $\times 10^{10}$ cells m[-2] day[-1], and 1.0 ± 0.7 (SE) mg C m[-2] day[-1].

The most comprehensive study of the growth and carbon production by sea ice bacteria is that of Kottmeier *et al.* (1987) during the 1982 austral spring and summer bloom of microalgae in McMurdo Sound. Bacterial cell numbers and biomass increased logarithmically during the prolonged microalgal bloom to less than 10-fold the initial values, reaching concentrations in the bottom congelation ice and sub-ice platelet ice layers ranging from 0.2 to 1.4×10^{12} cells m[-3] of ice meltwater. On the other hand, bacterial carbon production rate increased by three orders of magnitude. The final bacterial biomass was less than 1% of the microalgal biomass. This is much lower than the 8–75% reported for the bacterioplankton of the world's oceans (Ducklow, 1983). Bacterial carbon production was only 9% of that of the microalgal carbon production. Maximal growth rates ($\mu = -0.02$ to 0.2 day[-1]) were comparable to those reported for bacterioplankton in the Southern Ocean. Significant correlations were found between bacterial production (cell, biomass and thymidine incorporation per cell) and growth, and microalgal biomass, production and growth suggesting a potential coupling between bacterial growth and microalgal photosynthetic metabolism in the sea-ice microbial community (SIMCO). The significance of this will be discussed below.

3.4.3 Environmental factors

The principal environmental factors influencing the growth and development of the bacterial assemblages in

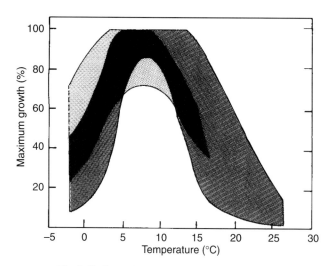

Fig. 3.17. Comparison of the relative growth rates of sea ice microalgae (autotrophs) and bacteria (heterotrophs) as a function of temperature. *Stippled areas* represent 'envelopes' which describe the relative growth rate versus temperature relationships for autotrophs (*dark stipling*) and heterotrophs (*light stipling*). Darkened areas represent region of overlap. Growth rate data is based on rates of fixation of CO_2 (autotrophs) and incorporation of ^{3}H-thymidine (heterotrophs). Redrawn from Kottmeier & Sullivan (1988).

the sea ice are salinity, temperature, and the available dissolved organic matter (DOM) and nutrient pools. Kottmeier & Sullivan (1988) have investigated the effects of salinity and temperature on the rates of metabolism and growth of the SIMCO bacteria. They found that autotrophs and heterotrophs exhibited two quite different patterns of metabolic rates in response to variations in salinity. Maximum rates of carbon fixation by the microalgae occurred at salinities which characterized the ice from which they were collected (see section 3.3.4). In contrast, the bacteria exhibited a more stenohaline response to variable salinity, with maximum incorporation of thymidine and uridine from 20‰ to 30‰. In addition, the bacteria may be better adapted for growth at higher salinities than the microalgae as significant incorporation of thymidine and uridine was found at salinities from 50‰ to 70‰.

The rate of incorporation of thymidine by the sea ice bacteria, like that of carbon fixation by the microalgae, increased several-fold at temperatures above ambient -1.9 °C (Kottmeier & Sullivan, 1988). Maximum incorporation of thymidine however occurred at lower temperatures (4–7 °C) than those found for carbon fixation (see section 3.3.4.5). Pomeroy & Deibel (1986) have recently suggested that the rate of phytoplankton photosynthesis declines more slowly at lower temperatures than does bacterial metabolism, leading to an uncoupling of primary production and bacterial production in cold waters. Kottmeier & Sullivan (1988) tested this hypothesis in relation to sea ice microalgae and bacteria. Their experiments can be defined by the envelopes in Fig. 3.17. These envelopes show similar responses of the microalgae and bacteria to low temperature with their maximum growth overlapping from 4 to 7 °C. This suggests that sea ice microalgae and bacteria from the same environment exhibit similar growth responses at low temperatures. Primary production and bacterial production are not uncoupled due to differential growth of microalgae and bacteria at low temperatures.

Kottmeier *et al.* (1987) have proposed that the timing and amount of bacterial production in sea ice are dependent on the phase and growth of the microalgae, the quality and quantity of the compounds in the DOM pool available for bacterial growth, and the rates of bactivory and herbivory. Grossi *et al.* (1984) considered that the sea ice microalgae may provide the bacteria with DOM, either dissolved photosynthate and/or extracellular polymeric substances, while the bacteria in turn may provide the microalgae with vitamins and/or recycled inorganic nutrients. The nature of the extracellular material produced by the microalgae is diverse, and includes actively secreted high molecular weight polysaccharides, as well as a number of low molecular weight metabolites (amino-acids, monosaccharides and frequently glycollate) (McConville, 1985). Recent studies of the release of extracellular organic carbon (EOC) have given varied results; 1% (Grossi *et al.*, 1984); 4% for the microalgae of the platelet ice layer (Palmisano & Sullivan, 1985a), 4 to 10% (Palmisano pers. commun., quoted in Kottmeier *et al.*, 1987). These amounts may not be sufficient to support more substantial bacterial production in the sea ice. Assuming a 50% efficiency of bacterial utilization of DOM (Fuhrman & Azam, 1982; Ducklow, 1983), and a maximum bacterial carbon production of 9% of primary production, bacteria would consume a maximum of 18% of the total fixed carbon in the sea ice, which is more than the estimated EOC provided by the microalgae. However, bactivory and herbivory by protozoans, death and lysis of diatom cells, and excretion and secretion by the meiofauna can also contribute to the DOM and mineral pool.

3.5 Sea ice micro- and meio-fauna

The micro- and meio-fauna of the SIMCOs have been little studied. However, recent work (Fenchel & Lee, 1972; Garrison *et al.*, 1984, 1986; Garrison, 1991) has shown that ciliates, dinoflagellates, small heterotrophic nanoflagellates, and amoebae are regular and sometimes abundant components of the ice biota.

The heterotrophic flagellates found in the pack ice include bodonids, choanoflagellates, euglenoids and

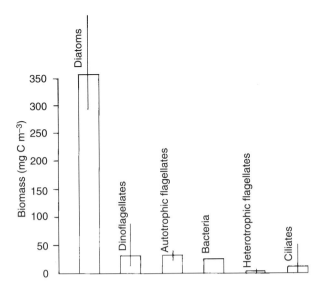

Fig. 3.18. Composition of the microbiota in sea ice in the Weddell Sea. Redrawn from Garrison *et al.* (1986).

dinoflagellates (Garrison, 1991). These heterotrophic nanoflagellates are phagotrophs that feed primarily on bacteria, while Marchant (1985) has reported that choanoflagellates may ingest small autotrophs and detritus. The largest heterotrophic flagellates in the sea ice are dinoflagellates. Species such as *Gyrodinium* and *Amphidinium* closely resemble the autotrophic forms. One large as yet unidentified species usually contains food vacuoles filled with large diatoms (Buck et al., 1990). Dinoflagellate cysts are also commonly found (Buck *et al.*, 1989).

Ciliated protozoa are also abundant in pack ice communities, and at times they comprise a major fraction of the heterotrophic biomass (Garrison & Buck, 1989a). Corless & Snyder (1986) found 26 separate taxa, including nine new species, in samples of sea ice from the Weddell Sea. The most abundant ciliates are the non-sheathed oligotrichs (e.g. *Strombidium* spp.), similar to the forms found in the plankton (Garrison & Buck, 1989a). The well-known symbiont-bearing ciliate *Myrionecta rubrum* is also frequently found in the ice at densities of up to 10^5 cells l^{-1} (Garrison & Buck, 1989a). The ciliates consume bacteria, diatoms and dinoflagellates, and some of the larger species (e.g. *Didinium*) are predators on other protozoa.

In addition, nauplii and other development stages of copepods, as well as adult copepods, mites and amphipods are also present, depending on the ice structure. As discussed in Chapter 12, larval and adult copepods in particular may be present in large numbers. Fig. 3.18 depicts the composition of the ice biota in the Weddell Sea (Garrison *et al.*, 1986). A much more diverse fauna comprising harpacticoid copepods,

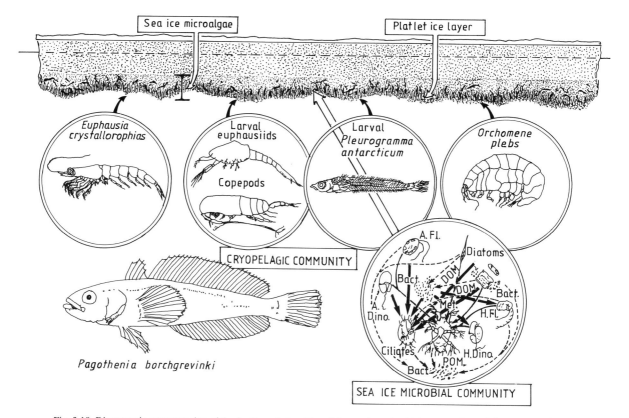

Fig. 3.19. Diagramatic representation of the feeding relationships of the sea ice microbial community and the cryopelagic community associated with the sea ice. A.Fl.=Autotrophic flagellate; H.Fl.=Heterotrophic flagellate; Dino.=Dinoflagellate; H.Dino.=Heterotrophic dinoflagellate; Bact.=Bacteria; DOM=Dissolved organic matter; POM=Particulate organic matter.

cyclopoid copepods, nematodes, and meroplanktonic larvae of benthic invertebrate species, has been reported from the Arctic sea ice (Carey, 1985). It is strange that nematodes which often dominate the Arctic sea ice meio-fauna have not been reported from the Antarctic sea ice. Much more work needs to be done to elucidate the roles played by the micro- and meio-fauna in the SIMCOs in Antarctica.

3.6 Dynamics of the sea ice microbial community

The lowermost circle in Fig. 3.19 depicts the food web of the SIMCO involving diatoms, autotrophic flagellates and dinoflagellates, heterotrophic flagellates and dinoflagellates, protozoa, small metazoans, POM, DOM and bacteria. Following Whitaker (1977a) and Carey (1985) this constitutes the sea ice *sympagic* community. Fig. 15.16 shows the primary producer component, the microalgae, with an attempt to show the ultimate fate of the carbon produced by photosynthesis. The figures and percentages given are highly speculative but probably are of the right order of magnitude. No data are available on the consumption of the sympagic consumers. On the basis of the various estimates for DOM production, cell death to form detritus, and consumption by the various consumers it is estimated that somewhere between 74 and 80% of the annual production of microalgae is released to the water column upon the melting of the ice.

Associated with the bottom ice and platelet ice SIMCOs is the *cryopelagic* community (Andriashev, 1968; Bradford, 1978) composed of the adult and larval stages of invertebrates and some fish species (Fig. 3.19). Some of these species feed directly on the ice microalgae, others feed them and on other species associated with the undersurface of the ice. Prominent among the algal grazers are the amphipods, *Paramoira walkeri, Orchomene plebs* and *Eusirus antarcticus*, adult and larval euphausiids, especially *Euphausia superba* (see Chapter 12) and *E. crystallorophias*, and copepods. Secondary consumers are dominated by larval fish, mainly *Pleuragramma antarcticum* (DeWitt & Hopkins, 1977) which feed mainly on the nauplii and the copepods.

A common species which is abundant in schools of varying size in the top few metres of the water beneath the ice is the small pelagic fish *Pagothenia borchgrevinki*. The feeding of this species has been studied by Bradfield (1980), Eastman & DeVries (1985) and Forster *et al.* (1987). The prey taken varied according to the season and locality and included species prominent in the cryopelagic community such as the polychaete

Harmothoe sp., the amphipods *Orchomene plebs* and *Eusirus antarcticus* and larval *Pleuragramma antarcticum*. Other zooplankton species eaten included copepods (*Calanoides acutus, Metridia gerlachi, Calanus propinquus* and *Euchaeta antarctica*), hyperiid amphipods (*Hyperiella dilata* and *Epimerella macronyx*), euphausiids and chaetognaths. The role of *P. borch-grevinki* in inshore ecosystems will be discussed further in Chapter 12.

4

Zooplankton

4.1 Introduction

In Chapter 2 we have seen that the annual primary production south of the Antarctic Convergence can be quite considerable although patchy in its distribution and strongly seasonal in its development. This phytoplankton production in turn serves to maintain large and diverse zooplankton communities. The herbivorous zooplankton consists largely of protozoans, the larval and juvenile stages of pelagic crustaceans, especially copepods and euphausiids, and appendicularians (doliolids and salps).

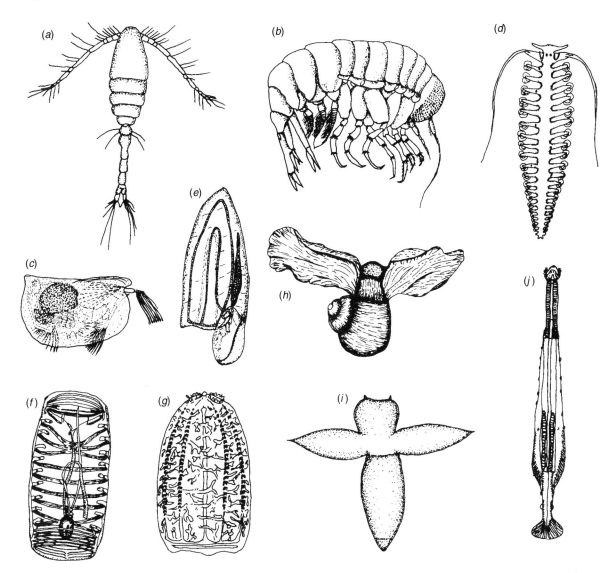

Fig. 4.1. Some representative zooplankton species. (*a*) *Oithona* sp. (Crustacea: Copepoda); (*b*) *Hyperia* sp. (Crustacea: Amphipoda); (*c*) *Conchoecia* sp. (Crustacea: Ostracoda); (*d*); *Tomopteris* sp. (Polychaeta); (*e*) *Dimophyes* sp. (Hydrozoa: Siphonophora); (*f*) *Salpa* sp. (Thaliacea: Salpida); (*g*) *Beroe* sp. (Ctenophora); (*h*) *Limacina* sp. (Mollusca: Thecosomata); (*i*) *Clione* sp. (Mollusca: Gymnosomata); (*j*) *Eukrohnia hamata* (Chaetognatha).

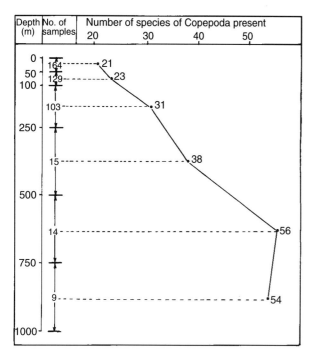

Fig. 4.2. Graph showing the number of species of Copepoda with increasing depth in Antarctic waters off South Georgia. Redrawn from Knox (1970); after A.C. Hardy (1967).

Other important groups are ostracods, pelagic amphipods (especially hyperiids) and pelagic molluscs (pteropods and heteropods). The carnivorous zooplankton is dominated by copepods, chaetognaths (arrowworms), pelagic polychaetes, medusae and siphonophores. Larval fishes can also comprise a significant component of the zooplankton.

As a result of the pioneer studies of the *Discovery* expeditions (e.g. Hardy & Gunther, 1936; David, 1958, 1965) and more recent Soviet studies we now have a relatively thorough knowledge of the taxonomy, general distribution and life-cycles of the dominant zooplankton species. However, the literature on the Southern Ocean zooplankton is dominated by studies on *Euphausia superba*, the Antarctic krill, because of its large biomass, ecological importance and resource potential. While the term 'krill' is generally taken as referring to *E. superba* it is also used in the sense of including all the other Southern Ocean euphausiid species. Euphausiids are generally considered to comprise at least 50% of the standing crop of zooplankton (El-Sayed, 1971c, 1977; Knox, 1983). However, there is evidence that other groups, especially the copepods, are significant in the pelagic ecosystem in terms of biomass and production, although they have in recent years received less attention than the euphausiids. In this chapter we will concentrate on the zooplankton groups other than the euphausiids, which will be dealt with in the next chapter.

There are a number of characteristics which serve to distinguish the Antarctic zooplankton (Fig. 4.1). These are:

1. The almost complete absence of the larval forms of bottom-living invertebrates, which seasonally form an important component of the zooplankton in temperate and tropical areas.
2. The surface layers tend to be poor in species but rich in individuals, with the number of species increasing with depth. This relationship is well illustrated in Fig. 4.2, which shows the increase in copepod species with depth off South Georgia.
3. In addition to diurnal vertical migration patterns exhibited by some species, the dominant zooplankton species perform an annual vertical migration (see section 4.4 below) (Mackintosh, 1970, 1972, 1973).
4. Reproduction in most species is timed to coincide with the extremely strong seasonal pulse of phytoplankton production, which occurs over a very restricted time period.

4.2 Species composition and distribution

Although the Antarctic Convergence marks the northern limit of many Antarctic zooplankton species it is a surface water phenomenon and as such does not represent a major boundary to some species. As a result the Southern Ocean planktonic fauna include some species that are found as far north as the Subtropical Convergence.

From an analysis of a large number of plankton samples taken by the *Discovery* expeditions in the Southern Ocean Baker (1954) concluded that the more important zooplankton species had a circumpolar distribution. The chaetognaths *Sagitta gazellae* and *Eukrohnia hamata* were found in almost all of the samples examined by David (1958) and the same was true for the copepods *Calanoides acutus, Calanus propinquus* and *Rhincalanus gigas* (Baker, 1954), as well as for the euphausiid *Thysanoessa*. Similar results have been reported in the Soviet studies of zooplankton distribution in the Southern Ocean (Voronina, 1968, 1969). Patchy distributions are general in those species which aggregate in swarms, especially the euphausiids and salps.

Nakamura *et al.* (1982) in a study of epipelagic calanoid copepods in the Indian Ocean sector of the Southern Ocean identified four groups of north to south distributions (Fig. 4.3): 1. distributed mainly in the southernmost region towards the Antarctic Continent; 2. distributed mainly in the northernmost region towards the Antarctic Convergence; 3. distributed mainly in the intermediate region; and 4. distributed widely from north to

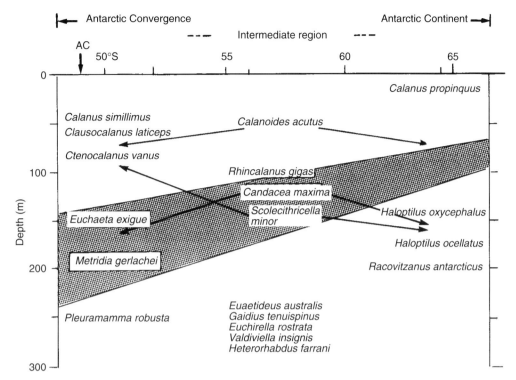

Fig. 4.3. Schematic diagram of the distribution of calanoid copepods in the surface waters of the Indian Ocean sector of the Southern Ocean. Arrows indicate that the species have a wide south to north distribution. The shaded area represents the south to north vertical distribution of the dominant copepod community. Redrawn from Nakamura *et al.* (1982).

south. The relative abundance was compared amongst ten depth ranges, and three groups were distinguished in relation to oceanographic conditions as follows: (a) occurring mainly in the surface layers above the temperature minimum layer; (b) occurring mainly in the temperature minimum layer; and (c) occurring mainly below the temperature minimum layer. A schematic representation of the horizontal and vertical distribution of the nineteen copepod species is shown in Fig. 4.3. From the viewpoint of feeding niche occupied, group (a) is composed of herbivorous species, group (b) mainly of omnivorous species and group (c) of both omnivorous and carnivorous species.

Chaetognaths are the dominant zooplankton predators in the waters of all oceans, including the Southern Ocean (David, 1958, Hagen, 1985). The chaetognath fauna of the Southern Ocean is made up of seven species, *Sagitta gazellae, S. marri, S. maxima, S. macrocephala, Eukrohnia hamata, E. bathyantarctica* and *Heterokrohnia mirabilis. S. marri, S. gazellae* and *E. bathyantarctica* are endemic forms (David, 1965). The basic pattern of distribution is circumpolar, with the Antarctic and Subtropical Convergences to a greater or lesser extent acting as geographical barriers. The most abundant species are *E. hamata* (often comprising 90 to 95% of all chaetognaths), *S. gazellae* and *S. marri.* In an investigation in the Australian sector Terazaki (1989)

found that the density of chaetognaths in the epipelagic layer of the Australian sector was 2.6–17.3 individuals m^{-3} with high values being found in the northern Antarctic region.

Hopkins (1987) carried out a detailed study of the zooplankton of McMurdo Sound in February after the breakup of the sea ice. The zooplankton was dominated by copepods and the pteropod *Limacina helicina.* Among the copepods the species *Calanoides acutus, Ctenocalanus citer, Euchaeta antarctica, Metridia gerlachei, Oithona similis* and *Oncaea curvata* contributed all but a small fraction of numbers and biomass. Other important taxa were *Euphausia crystallorophias* (furcilia), large radiolarians and the polychaete *Pelagobia longicirrata.* Zooplankton biomass was estimated at 1.5 to 3.4 g dry wt m^{-3}.

The most important macroplankton–micronekton species were: *Euphausia crystallorophias* (postlarval stages); the amphipods *Orchomene plebs, Epimeriella macronyx* and *Eusiris tridentatus*; the mysid shrimp *Antarctomysis ohlinii*; the chaetognaths *Sagitta gazellae* and *Eukrohnia hamata*; the pteropod *Clione antarctica*; the siphonophores *Diphyes arctica* and *Pyrostephos vanhoeffeni*; and larval and postlarval stages of the midwater nototheniid fish *Pleuragramma antarcticum.* The biomasses of the postlarval *E. crystallorophias* and *Pleuragramma antarcticum* on the basis of four sets of sweeps through the upper 800 m were estimated respectively at 0.21 (0.16–0.33) and 0.82 (0.18–3.68) g dry wt m^{-2} of McMurdo Sound sea surface.

Hopkins (1987) has compared the zooplankton communities of McMurdo Sound and Croker Passage, Antarctic Peninsula (Hopkins, 1985a,b). While the two areas have many species in common, the biomass composition is different. Croker Passage is a Southern Ocean high-biomass area dominated by krill, *Euphausia superba*, with a zooplankton–euphasiid–fish combined biomass of 58.0 g dry wt m^{-2} (Hopkins, 1985a). McMurdo Sound has much lower standing stocks, with a total zooplankton–euphausiid–fish biomass of only 3.5 g dry wt m^{-2} (Hopkins, 1987). Further, the ratios of these biomass components differ radically, with the zooplankton:euphausiid:fish ratios of Croker Passage and McMurdo Sound, respectively being 1.0:19.0:0.3 and 1.0:0.1:0.3. These ratios reflect the abundance and overwhelming dominance of krill in the vicinity of the Antarctic Peninsula (Marr, 1962; Amos, 1984) and the lesser importance of the ice krill (*E. crystallorophias*) in McMurdo Sound. This points to the reduction of the significance of the niche occupied by large-sized-particle grazers in McMurdo Sound. This is supported by the fact that salps, which were a major biomass component in Croker Passage, were absent from McMurdo Sound. Fish biomass was comparable in the two ecosystems, but while *Pleuragramma antarcticum* and the myctophid *Electrona antarctica* shared dominance in Croker Passage, myctophids were absent from McMurdo Sound. DeWitt (1970) attributed the absence of myctophids and other characteristic mid-water fishes to the cold temperature (<–1.5 °C) in the deeper waters over the shelf.

4.3 Life-history and growth

The marked seasonality of primary production (see Chapter 2) imposes a similar seasonality on the reproductive cycle of many zooplankton species. For example, the herbivores need to take in sufficient food to enable them to reproduce in time for the resulting larvae to get an adequate start before the winter.

In the Southern Ocean north of the seasonal pack ice the zooplankton biomass is usually dominated by copepods (Hopkins, 1971; Voronina, 1978; Hempel, 1985a,b). Numerically, small cyclopoids dominate, but the larger calanoids *Calanoides acutus* and *Rhincalanus gigas* have been shown by Hopkins (1971) and Chojancki & Wegelenska (1984) to comprise the larger proportion of the total biomass. The major events in the life-cycles of these species have been known since the work of Ottestad (1932), Ommaney (1936) and Mackintosh (1937), and are summarized by Vervoort (1957) and Andrews (1966).

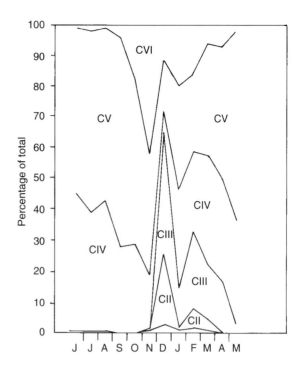

Fig. 4.4. Seasonal changes in the copepodite composition of the development stages CI to CVI of the copepods *Calanoides acutus* in the top 100 m of the water column. Redrawn from Everson (1984a); based on data from Andrews (1966).

More recent studies include those of Voronina (1978), Marin (1988a,b); Atkinson & Peck (1988). Atkinson (1991) and Huntley & Escritor (1991). The life-cycles can be summarized as follows. These copepods are seasonal migrants which overwinter at depth as late copepodites. Spawning is associated with their ascent in spring, and the new generation grows within the surface layers in summer. The later copepodites progressively and gradually descend later in the year, until overwintering depths are reached. Voronina (1970, 1978) noticed that the migration and spawning cycle of the dominant species was asynchronous and followed the order: *Calanoides acutus*, *Calanus propinquus*, *Rhincalanus gigas*. She postulated that this was a mechanism for reducing interspecific competition for food during the summer growing season. However, Marin (1988a,b) has challenged these conclusions.

The life-cycles of *Calanoides acutus*, *Calanus simillimus* and *Rhincalanus gigas* have recently been investigated by Atkinson (1991) in the Scotia Sea. The predominantly Antarctic species *C. acutus* mates below 250 m in middle to late winter and the summer generation develops rapidly to either Calyptopus CIV or CV (developmental stages between nauplius and adult) (Fig. 4.4). Its lifespan seems typically one year, but some of the CVs which fail to moult and spawn in the winter survive into the second summer. *C. simillimus* is a sub-Antarctic

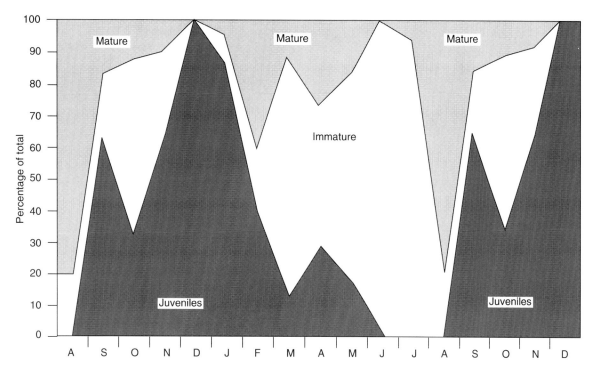

Fig. 4.5. *Parathemisto gaudichaudii*: percentage frequency of juvenile, immature and mature specimens in net hauls. Redrawn from Everson (1984a); based on data from Kane (1966).

species which mates in the top 250 m mainly in spring. The rapid development of the summer generation may allow a second mating period and a smaller second generation to appear in late summer. *C. simillimus* remains in the surface layers for a longer period than *Calanoides acutus* or *R. gigas*, and its depth distribution is bimodal throughout the winter. *R. gigas* is most abundant in sub-Antarctic waters to the north of the Polar Front (Antarctic Convergence Zone). It mates within the top 750 m later in spring than do the other two species, and its development seems less synchronized, with egg laying and the growth season being more protracted. Stages Calyptopus CIII and CIV are reached in the first autumn and further development resumes very early the following spring. It is not clear whether the majority then spawn or whether a further year may be needed to complete the life-cycle. A striking feature is the rapid growth attainable by these cold water species. Their geographic and vertical separation, together with their asynchronous life-cycles, support the concept of niche-partitioning developed by Vorinina (1970, 1978).

Contrasting growth patterns are shown in two of the dominant carnivorous zooplankton species, *Parathemisto gaudichaudii* and *Sagitta gazellae*. The amphipod *Parathemisto gaudichaudii* (Fig.4.5) exhibits a peak of growth during the summer period (Kane, 1966), but during the winter when food supplies are low there is practically no growth at all. Mating animals in the early spring

release large numbers of juvenile stages which feed on the early life-history stages of the herbivorous zooplankters when they appear at the commencement of the spring phytoplankton growth. Kane (1966) considered that in general *Parathemisto* has a life-cycle span of a year, but that a very small number of individuals survive to breed again in a second year.

On the other hand, the chaetognath *Sagitta gazellae* appears to be capable of breeding in most months of the year (David, 1955). Because of this, except at certain times when vertical migration separates the age classes, it is difficult to interpret the size classes. David, however, was able to follow the growth of one age group throughout the winter. He demonstrated that growth was more or less steady at about 5 mm per month from May to December. Since *S. gazellae* spawn when 75–80 mm long and growth in the summer is more rapid it was inferred that they reach sexual maturity in a year.

The life-history of one of the common salps *Salpa thompsoni* has been described in detail by Foxton (1966). During the winter months the population is composed almost entirely of solitary forms, which in the spring produce large numbers of asexually budded aggregate forms, and these in turn give rise to the solitary form at the end of the summer. There is thus a very clearly marked alternation of generations in this species. The production of aggregates begins in spring soon after the start of the phytoplankton bloom and is probably triggered by it. Since

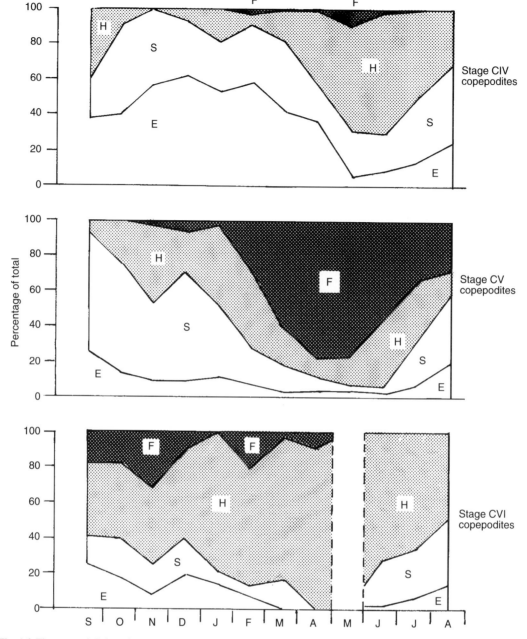

Fig. 4.6. The copepod *Calanoides acutus*: monthly variation in oil contained within the oil sac by four subjective categories; E = empty; S = very little; H = half full; F = full. Redrawn from Everson (1984a); based on data from Andrews (1966).

each solitary form is itself potentially capable of producing around 800 aggregates, even a moderate concentration of solitary forms during the winter could give rise to an enormous number of aggregates very quickly in the summer as a response to high phytoplankton densities. In this manner very dense swarms of salps can arise during the summer months.

For most species growth is limited to the summer months. *Salpa thompsoni* is an exception, for which Foxton (1966) estimated a growth rate of 6–8 mm per month over the winter. Of interest therefore is the mecha

nism whereby the animals survive over the winter when food resources are low. Observations on the development of the oil sacs of copepods and the storage of oil by euphausiids suggests that the animals accumulate lipids which may be used as a food reserve during the winter when food is scarce (Littlepage, 1964). This is shown for the copepod *Calanoides acutus* (Fig. 4.6) and the copepod *Paraeuchaeta antarctica* and the euphausiid *Euphausia crystallorophias* in Fig. 4.7. Fig. 4.6 depicts the variation in oil content contained in the oil sacs of copepodites CIV, CV and CVI of *C. acutus* (Andrews,

Table 4.1. *Comparative synopsis of main seasonal cycles in Southern Ocean zooplankton*

Cycle	Carnivorous	Herbivorous	Krill
Growth	Year-round except *Parathemisto*, which has strong peak in summer	Summer only, except salps, which also grow in winter	Summer
Reproduction	± independent of season, except *Parathemisto*, which is closely linked to season	Short period in summer	Two spawnings in summer
Feeding	Year-round	Summer only	Assumed summer only but possibly feeds year-round
Biochemical	No depot lipid, except *Paraeuchaeta*, which has large wax store, and *Parathemisto*, which has 'moderate' store	Establish wax rich depot lipids in summer	Effectively no depot lipid

From Everson (1984a)

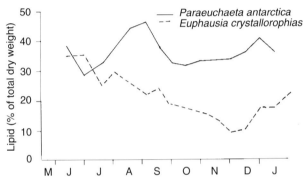

Fig. 4.7. Seasonal changes in the lipid content of two Antarctic crustaceans, the copepod *Paraeuchaeta antarctica* and the euphausiid *Euphausia crystallorophias*. Redrawn from Everson (1984a); based on data from Littlepage (1964).

1966). The overwintering stages of CVI and CV show some interesting differences. Relatively few Stage CVIs achieved a full oil sac before the onset of winter. This may be because they continued to divert energy to growth rather than to building-up maximum food reserves. In Stages IV and V the relatively high oil content remaining in the spring probably aids in the production of eggs coincident with the spring phytoplankton bloom.

The establishment of lipid stores during the summer has also been demonstrated for the copepods *Rhincalanus gigas* and *Paraeuchaeta antarctica*, and the euphausiid *Euphausia tricantha* . As *P. antarctica* is a carnivore it is capable of obtaining food year round and thus shows little fluctuation in its seasonal lipid content (Fig. 4.7). This difference between carnivorous and herbivorous zooplankton is also reflected in the type of lipid used as a energy store. Species capable of feeding year-round (such as *Paraeuchaeta*) tend to store triglycerides, whereas those which fast overwinter (such as *Calanoides acutus*) tend to store less readily mobilized lipids such as wax esters (see Benson & Lee, 1975; Sargent, 1976). It is

of interest that *Euphausia superba* has generally been found to contain very little, if any, wax esters and this may indicate that krill can feed year-round.

The carnivorous zooplankton, with the exception of the copepod *Paraeuchaeta* and the amphipod *Parathemisto*, do not tend to lay down lipid deposits because the biomass of small zooplankton in the upper 1000 m, which is more or less constant throughout the year (Foxton, 1956), ensures a constant food supply. Thus they do not need to rely on food reserves to live through periods of food shortage. The continuous feeding activity of such species throughout the winter results in the release of large quantities of detritus which may provide an alternative food source for other species (Everson, 1984a).

Everson (1984a) has given a comparative synopsis of the main annual cycles in herbivorous and carnivorous Antarctic zooplankton (Table 4.1). This confirms the close correlation of the annual cycle with food supply. However, what is particularly interesting is the degree to which *Euphausia superba* deviates from the typical herbivore seasonal cycle.

4.4 Vertical migration

Vertical migrations in zooplankton are well documented but rather poorly understood. The phenomenon may be considered under two broad headings dependent on the time scale: seasonal migrations, related to life-history patterns in which much of the summer season is spent in the surface waters; and a diurnal pattern in which the hours of darkness are spent near the surface and the daylight hours at deeper depths. Both types of migration pattern are found in Southern Ocean zooplankton.

As recorded elsewhere (Longhurst, 1976) Southern Ocean zooplankton species maintain their general oceanographic position by directed seasonal vertical

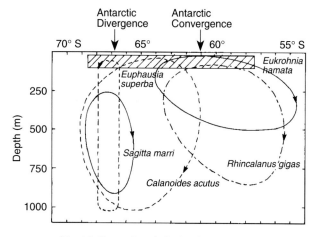

Fig. 4.8. Seasonal vertical migration patterns of the zooplankton in Antarctic waters based on data in Mackintosh (1937) and Marr (1962). Summer feeding zone is shaded. Redrawn from Nemoto & Harrison (1981).

migration related to differential water mass transport with increasing depth. They concentrate near the surface in the Antarctic summer where the general flow is towards the north, but descend into the deep water in the winter where the movement is southerly. They are thus maintained within the limits of their normal species distribution as shown in Fig. 4.8. The seasonal vertical movement of these species to depths between 500 and 1000 m results in horizontal displacements of many hundreds of metres (Mackintosh, 1937). Examples of species which spend the summer months in the surface layers and descent into the warm deep water in the winter are:

> Copepoda
> *Rhincalanus gigas* (Ommaney, 1936)
> *Calanoides acutus* (Andrews, 1966)
> *Calanus propinquus* (Voronina, 1972)
> Amphipoda
> *Parathemisto gaudichaudii* (Kane, 1966)
> Chaetognatha
> *Eukrohnia hamata* (David, 1958, 1965)
> *Sagitta gazellae* (David, 1958)
> *Sagitta marri* (Mackintosh, 1937)

The three copepods listed above are the three most abundant species in the water of the Southern Ocean. *Euphausia superba*, as discussed in the next chapter, releases its eggs in the upper 200 m; these subsequently sink to as much as 1000 m, and then progressively approach the surface again during development.

4.5 Swarming

The trophic importance of zooplankton in the Southern Ocean is enhanced by their habit of forming dense swarms. Swarming behaviour is particularly pronounced

in the euphausiids where *Euphausia crystallorophias, E. superba* and *Thysanoessa macrura* the principal swarming species are in Antarctic waters and *E. tricantha* in the sub-Antarctic. Swarming in euphausiids will be discussed in the next chapter.

Dense swarms of calanoid species are common, especially in sub-Antarctic waters. Kawamura (1974) has described such swarms of *Calanus tonsus* from waters where Sie and Right Whales feed on them. Such swarms or patches maintain their shape close beneath the surface, even in rough conditions, and they may be some hundreds of metres across. Density of *C. tonsus* in such swarms range from 330 to 23 860 individuals m^{-3}, with their biomass reaching 34 g m^{-3}. Other zooplankters that frequently occur in large swarms are the salp *Salpa thompsoni* and the amphipod *Parathemisto gaudichaudii*.

In the summer of 1983–84 *Salpa thompsoni* was a dominant member of the zooplankton community in waters near the Antarctic Peninsula, with biomasses in mid-March ranging from 49 to 671 mg C m^{-2} and 9.6 to 136 mg N m^{-2} (Huntley *et al.*, 1989). Direct measurements suggested that faecal production by 21 mm blastozoids was equivalent to 10.2% body C day^{-1} and 6.6% body N day^{-1}. Grazing by *S. thompsoni* removed the bulk of the daily primary production in March but only <1% in January at the peak of the phytoplankton bloom. It is clear that dense swarms of zooplankton can have a profound effect on the structure of plankton communities.

4.6 Feeding

While there have been many studies of the feeding ecology of *Euphausia superba* there have been few such studies on other Southern Ocean zooplankton. Exceptions are the studies of Schnack (1983a, 1985a,b) and Schnack *et al.* (1985) on copepods and Hopkins (1985a,b, 1987) on the total zooplankton community. Schnack (1985b) studied the feeding behaviour of the dominant copepod species (*Calanus propinquus, Calanoides acutus, Rhincalanus gigas, Metridia gerlachei* and *M. curticauda*) in comparison with that of *Euphausia superba* on two cruises in the Atlantic sector of the Southern Ocean. The phytoplankton differed markedly between the two cruises. In November–December 1980 *Thalassiosira* sp. dominated close to the ice edge, whereas *Corethron criophilum* was predominant in the Drake Passage. In February 1982, the diatoms *C. criophilum, Chaetoceros* spp. and *Biddulphia* sp., as well as nanoflagellates were most abundant.

Some interesting results were obtained in laboratory feeding experiments. It has often been stated that there is a relationship between the size of an animal and the size of its food: large animals feeding on large particles; small

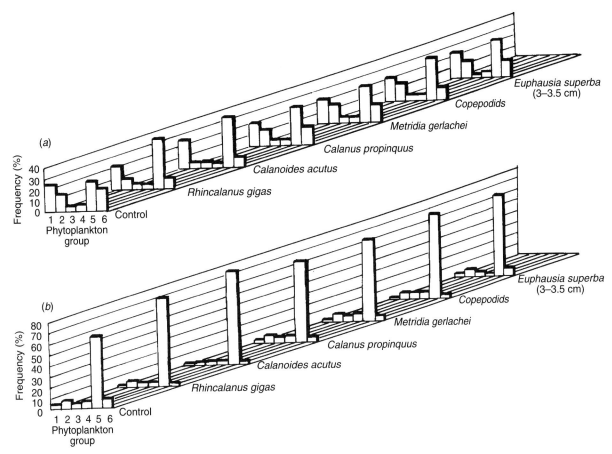

Fig. 4.9. Relative proportions of six different phytoplankton groups. (1, nanoflagellates; 2, pennate diatoms; 3, centric diatoms; 4, *Disteophamus speculum*; 5, *Corethron criophilum*; 6, remainder) in the diets of *Euphausia superba* and copepods, which fed either on an ambient food supply (72 µg C l⁻¹; (*a*)) on an enriched food supply (177 µg C l⁻¹; (*b*)). The control is the percentage composition of the food supply. Redrawn from Schnack (1985b).

animals feeding on small particles (e.g. Freyer, 1957; Parsons *et al.*, 1967). For marine environments Gamble (1978) and Harris (1982) have described rather similar particle-size feeding by copepods differing considerably in size (*c.* 10–20 times, in terms of body weight). In Schnack's feeding experiments, the differences in body weight between ecologically similar copepod species ranged between 89 and 505 µg C individual⁻¹ in November–December 1980 and between 59 and 392 µg C individual⁻¹ in February 1982. The ratios of these differences (5.7 and 6.6) are in between the values given by Gamble (1978) and Harris (1982). From Fig. 4.9*a* it can be seen that in spite of the considerable size differences between the zooplankton species (e.g. a mean dry wt of 185 µg for copepodites and 1102 µg for *Rhincalanus gigas*) the relative proportions of the different phytoplankton species consumed was the approximately the same at ambient food supply. In the enriched food supply experiment (Fig. 4.9*b*) the proprtion of the diatom *C. criophilum* was 67% compared to only 28% in the ambient food supply. All zooplankton species showed a positive selectivity index for *C. criophilum*, its proportion in

the diets of all species increasing considerably. There was no evidence for large copepod species feeding preferentially on large particles. All animals fed most efficiently when food was most abundant irrespective of the size and shape of the food particles (Fig. 4.9). This type of feeding behaviour has been described as opportunistic by Poulet & Chanut (1975) and Schnack's results agree with those of Poulet (1978) who reported opportunistic feeding by five small copepod species. Such feeding is to be expected in an environment where phytoplankton species composition, distribution and biomass is very patchy.

All copepod species, as well as krill, were found to feed efficiently on the most abundant food item and, on both cruises, they fed on the same food organisms. However, feeding rates differed between species, *Metridia gerlachei* showing higher feeding rates (in terms of food ingested on a weight-specific basis) than the other species studied. Thus, the most abundant, large, calanoid copepod species are trophically similar, and competition for food may be severe. *Rhincalanus gigas*, *Calanoides acutus* and *Calanus propinquus* are filter-feeding herbivores, whereas *Metridia gerlachei* and

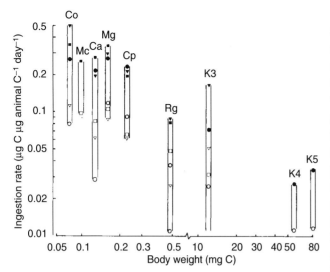

Fig. 4.10. Ingestion rates of food particles by *Euphausia superba* and copepods in relation to food supply and body weight. Open symbols: low food concentrations; closed symbols: high food concentrations. Co: Copepodids; Mc: *Metridia curticauda*; Ca: *Calanoides acutus*; Mg: *Metridia gerlachei*; Cp: *Calanus propinquus*; Rg: *Rhincalanus gigas*; K3: *Euphausia superba* (~3 cm); K4: *E. superba* (~4 cm); K5: *E. superba* (~5 cm). Redrawn from Schnack (1985b).

M.curticauda are omnivorous feeders. Thus, niche separation on feeding alone does not seem to apply, due to considerable overlap in feeding habits. Possible mechanisms through which zooplankton populations may avoid or reduce interspecific competition could include, besides differences in selective feeding, different spatial and temporal distributions connected with different overwintering strategies, e.g. there are obvious differences in vertical distribution, with *M. gerlachei* occurring mainly in deeper water and *C. propinquus* and *R. gigas* being more abundant in the upper layers (Schnack, 1985b).

Fig. 4.10 plots the weight-specific ingestion rate against body carbon for *E. superba* and various copepod species in the experiments carried out by Schnack (1985b). Each pair of experiments involved high and low food concentrations. In general ingestion rates were higher with higher food concentrations but the variation between ingestion rates with higher or lower food concentrations differed between the species. There was little difference between the feeding behaviour of the copepod species and the much larger *E. superba*. Schnack points out, however, that there is a great difference between the distributional patterns of copepods and krill. Adults and subadults of *E. superba* occur in large swarms and virtually no copepods were found in regions where large swarms of krill were found. Thus, niche separation on the basis of differences in distribution during the life-histories of krill and copepods could be a mechanism for reducing potential competition.

Schnack (1985b) has also compared the copepod biomass, species composition and feeding with the standing stock and production of phytoplankton in the upper 100 m of the water column off the Antarctic Peninsula. In the open waters of the Drake Passage, phytoplankton biomass was low (1–2 g C m^{-2}) and that of the copepods high (0.77 g C m^{-2}). Copepod ingestion was approximately 50% of the daily primary production (0.14 g C m^{-2} day^{-1}). In the region of the ice edge adjoining Joinville Island, phytoplankton biomass (10 g C m^{-2}) and production (1.1 g C m^{-2} day^{-1}) was high and biomass of zooplankton (0.02 g C m^{-2}) low. Daily ingestion was only 0.6% of primary production. Feeding activity by individual copepods in this locality was much higher than in the Drake Passage and, community ingestion was dominated by small copepods in contrast to large copepods in the open water region. Diatoms dominated phytoplankton in both these regions. In the Bransfield Strait *Phaeocystis* dominated the phytoplankton and its biomass and production levels were similar to those of the ice edge. The copepod biomass (0.07 g C m^{-2}) and feeding activity were low, possibly due to the unsuitability of *Phaeocystis* as copepod food. In the regions of high phytoplankton biomass, sinking of cells accounted for greater loss from the surface zone than grazing by copepods, which is similar to findings from spring blooms in shelf areas of the northern hemisphere (e.g. Taguchi & Fukuchi, 1975; Smetacek, 1980).

Hopkins (1987) examined the trophic structure of the mid-water pelagic ecosystem of McMurdo Sound in February through diet analysis of 35 species of zooplankton and micronekton. Ten feeding groups were suggested through cluster analysis. They can be grouped into three categories with respect to diet: small particle grazers, omnivores ingesting a variety of food types, and carnivores specializing on one or several types of metazoan prey. In McMurdo Sound the results of diet analyses can be summarized as follows:

Copepods. These were principally small-particle grazers. Some grazing species such as *Aetideopsis antarctica*, *Calanus propinquus*, *Metridia gerlachei*, *Oithona frigida* and *Oncaea antarctica* ingested metazoans in addition to phytoplankton. The principal phytoplankton in the copepod diets were species of the *Nitzschia* group (predominantly *N. curta*), species of coscinodiscoid diatoms, and peridinian dinoflagellates. Tintinnid ciliates, and to a lesser extent radiolarians, and the heliozoan *Stichlonche* sp. were also common in the diets. The three species of tintinnids abundant in the stomach contents were *Codonellopsis gausii*, *Laakmaniella naviculaefera* and *Cymatocylis antarctica* f. *vanhoeffeni*. The predatory copepods were *Euchaeta antarctica, E. erebi* and *E. similis*. Their diet was primarily copepods, the pelagic

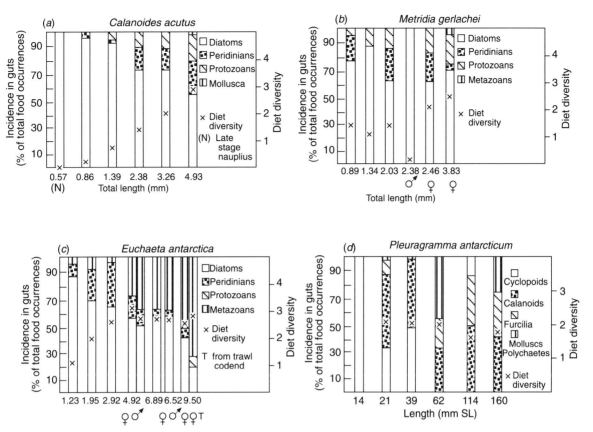

Fig. 4.11. Diet trends of three copepod species and the pelagic fish *Pleuragramma antarcticum* with respect to ontogeny in McMurdo Sound. (*a*) *Calanoides acutus*; (*b*) *Metridia gerlachei*; (*c*) *Euchaeta antarctica*; (*d*) *Pleuragramma antarcticum*. Diet diversity is indicated on a diversity scale of 0–4 by a cross for each size class. Redrawn from Hopkins (1987).

mollusc *Limacina helicina* and the pelagic polychaete *Pelagobia longicirrata*. Changes in diet with ontogeny were indicated for both the small particle grazers and the carnivores with the ingestion of an increasing proportion of protozoans and metazoans with age (Fig. 4.11).

Ostracods. The ostracods *Conchoecia belgicae* and *C. isocheira* were omnivorous. Their guts contained phytoplankton, protozoans and metazoans.

Euphausiids. Euphausia crystallorophias was abundant and *Thysanoessa macrura* were rare. The latter species was omnivorous, its diet being composed of phytoplankton, protozoans and metazoans. All three major food groups (phytoplankton, protozoans and metazoans) occurred in the diets of 5.5 to 7.5 mm furcilia and 28 to 33 mm postlarvae of *E. crystallorophias*. The incidence of phytoplankton was proportionately higher in the furcilia. Proportionately more tintinnids and metazoans occurred in the guts of the postlarvae.

Amphipods. While phytoplankton occurred in the diet of the three hyperiid species, *Hyperiella dilatata, H. macronyx* and *Hyperia macrocephala*, diet diversity was low and the principal food in terms of bulk was coelenterates. The gammarids had more diverse diets, which included more protozoans and an array of metazoans.

Phytoplankton was an important dietary component of the four gammarids *Epimeriella macronyx, Eusirus tridentatus, Orchomene plebs* and *O. rossi*. Coelenterates occurred in the diets of all the gammarids.

Mysids. The mysid *Antarctomysis ohlinii* was a generalist with its diet closely resembling that of the gammarids.

Chaetognaths. Eukrohnia hamata fed on copepods, most frequently on *Calanoides acutus*. Incidence of food in the gut of *Sagitta gazellae* was low with *C. acutus* the most frequently ingested copepod species. The polychaete *Pelagobia longicirrata* was also included in the diet.

Polychaetes; Molluscs. The polychaete *Pelagobia longicirrata* and the pteropod *Limacina helicina* both fed exclusively on phytoplankton. *Clione antarctica* fed on *L. helicina*.

Fishes. Larvae of *Artedidraco* and *Chionodraco* fed mostly on furcilia of *E. crystallorophias*, while the guts of macrourid larvae contained mostly ostracods. Larval *Pleurogramma antarcticum* fed on copepods, pelagic molluscs and polychaetes.

A comparison of the diets of the McMurdo Sound zooplankton (Hopkins, 1987) with those of the krill

Table 4.2. *Major components of the diet of species common to McMurdo Sound, Ross Sea and Croker Passage, Antarctic Peninsula. Comparisons are on groups of individuals of each species taken with the same type of net (i.e. plankton net or trawl)*

Diet composition	McMurdo Sound	Croker Passage
Phytoplankton >90%	*Ctenocalanus vanus (?)*	*Ctenocalanus vanus (?)*
	Microcalanus pygmaeus	*Metridia gerlachei*
	Oithona frigida	*Microcalanus pygmaeus*
	Oithona similis	*Oithona frigida*
	Oncaea curvata	*Oithona similis*
	Stephos longipes	*Oncaea curvata*
	Pelagobia longicirrata	*Oncaea antarctica*
		Stephos longipes
Phytoplankton + Protozoans >90%	*Aetideopsis antarctica*	*Calanus propinquus*
	Calanoides acutus	*Pelagobia longicirrata*
	Calanus propinquus	
	Metridia gerlachei	
Metazoans 20–40%	*Oncaea antarctica*	*Aetideopsis antarctica*
	Conchoecia isocheira	*Conchoecia isocheira*
	Thysanoessa macrura	
	Epimeriella macronyx	
	Orchomene plebs	
Metazoans 40–80%	*Conchoecia belgicae*	*Euchaeta similis*
	Antarctomysis ohlinii	*Conchoecia belgicae*
		Thysanoessa macrura
		Epimeriella macronyx
		Hyperiella macronyx
		Orchomene plebs
		Antarctomysis ohlinii
Coelenterates >40%	*Hyperiella dilatata*	*Hyperiella dilatata*
	Hyperiella macronyx	
	Orchomene rossi	
Metazoans >80%	*Euchaeta antarctica*	*Euchaeta antarctica*
	Euchaeta similis	*Eukrohnia hamata*
	Eukrohnia hamata	*Sagitta gazellae*
	Sagitta gazellae	
Not feeding	–	*Calanoides acutus*

From Hopkins (1987).

dominated Croker Passage (Antarctic Peninsula) (Hopkins, 1985a,b) indicated that species common to the two areas occupied approximately the same trophic position (Table 4.2). The major difference was that detritus in the form of moult debris was a major food resource in Croker Passage.

The impact of the small-particle grazers on the phytoplankton bloom dominated by *Nitzschia curta* in McMurdo Sound was considered by Hopkins (1987). The principal small-particle grazers among the zooplankton in McMurdo Sound are the copepods *Calanoides acutus*, *Metridia gerlachei*, *Ctenocalanus vanus*, *Oncaea curvata* and *Oithona similis*; the furcilia of *Euphausia crystallorophias*; the polychaete *Pelagobia longicirrata*; and the cosomatous pteropod *Limacina helicina*. Together these constituted over 80% of the biomass of net-caught zooplankton, with the small-particle grazing copepods alone

totalling 50%. These taxa have the greater impact on the phytoplankton. Average particulate concentration in the upper 150 m off Victoria Land 80 to 160 km northeast of McMurdo Sound in a bloom which covered considerable areas of the Ross Sea, was 191 µg C l^{-1} (=28.7 µg C m^{-2}) (W.O. Smith & Nelson, 1985a,b). At such carbon levels, the dominant Antarctic copepod particle grazers. e.g. *C. acutus*, *Calanus propinquus* and *M. gerlachei*, ingest up to 35% of body weight in terms of carbon per day (Schnack, 1985b). The biomass of the particle grazing copepods in McMurdo Sound was estimated at 50% of the standing crop, which using an average value for McMurdo Sound zooplankton tows of 2.45 g dry wt m^{-2} and a carbon fraction of 0.5×dry wt, converts to 0.6 g dry wt m^{-2} of grazer copepod carbon. Maximum possible impact would be obtained if copepods and other small grazers were concentrated in the upper 150 m, i.e. in the zone of primary production. On this basis then 0.6 g C m^{-2} of grazing copepods potentially could remove 0.6×0.35 or 0.21 g C m^{-2} of the particulate standing crop. This is 0.7% (0.21/28.7) of the particulate standing crop. If it is assumed that *L. helicina* and the remaining particle grazers remove a similar amount then total zooplankton consumption would be roughly 2% of the phytoplankton biomass per day. Thus, about 98% of the standing crop possibly remains uneaten by grazers. This removal estimate does not include daily phytoplankton growth which ranges from 0.1 to 0.6 doublings day^{-1} (Sakshaug & Holm-Hansen, 1986; Vargo *et al.*, 1986). In addition, the abundant protists and other heterotrophic organisms present in the water column could also have a considerable impact on the phytoplankton. Even taking this into account it is evident that at least 90% of the phytoplankton potentially is not consumed and is either mineralized within the water column or sediments to the bottom (see Chapter 14).

Oresland (1990) studied the feeding and predation impact of the chaetognath *Eukrohnia hamata*, which made up 94% of all chaetognaths by number and 2–7% of zooplankton wet weight in the Gerlache Strait in the 1986–87 summer. Gut content analysis showed that the copepods *Euchaeta* spp., *Calanoides acutus*, *Metridia gerlachei*, *Microcalanus pygmaeus*, *Oncaea* spp., and *Oithona* spp., and appendicularians were the main prey. Feeding rates for appendicularians were 0.8 individuals day^{-1} in January while that for copepods varied from 0.3 to 0.7 day^{-1}. *E. hamata* consumed between 5 and 11% of its dry weight in copepods day^{-1}.

4.7 Biomass and production

Due to the enormous difference in size, depth distribution, diurnal and seasonal migrations and absolute den-

Table 4.3. *Standing crop of zooplankton (in mg m⁻³) in the Southern Ocean.*

Depth (m)	Antarctic	Sub-Antarctic	Tropical	Subtropical
0–50	55.2	55.8	33.1	40.5
0–1000	25.6	20.9	9.8	9.0

After Foxton (1956).

sity of the considerable number of species that make up the zooplankton of the Southern Ocean there are enormous problems in making realistic estimates of the standing stock. For the most part the estimates which have been made exclude the physically large animals, such as medusae and salps, which generally are not caught by plankton nets. Since their biomass may be considerable their omission give an unrealistic picture of the total biomass. In addition, species which are known to be fast swimmers, such as krill, are certainly able to avoid plankton nets with efficiencies that vary with the type of net used and the conditions under which the samples were taken.

Foxton (1956) summarized the then available information on the zooplankton standing crop in various latitudinal zones of the Southern Hemisphere (Table 4.3). It can be seen that the Antarctic waters have a significantly higher standing crop than the tropical and temperate regions. He also showed that, although there was a clearly marked seasonal cycle in Antarctic seas, with a peak during the summer for zooplankton in the top 50 m, the biomass over the top 1000 m was more or less constant throughout the year due to the seasonal vertical migration and the fact that most of the species have a life span of one year. Voronina (1966) has given estimates of the standing crop based on the results of the first and second cruises of the Soviet Antarctic Expedition. In a profile along 20° E from 69° 46′ S to 36° 30′ S taken from February 21 to March 11 1957, it was found that the copepods constituted the greater part of the biomass in Antarctic waters. Below 100–200 m the mean biomass of the zooplankton was 10–50 mg wet wt m⁻³ along most of the length of the profile, with the exception of stations in the vicinity of the Antarctic Convergence (300 mg m⁻³) and the Antarctic Divergence (80 mg m⁻³). In the upper levels there were a number of clearly defined maxima with biomasses of more than 100 mg m⁻³. The three copepod species *Rhincalanus gigas, Calanus propinquus* and *Calanoides acutus* contributed 72.8% of the biomass. The averaged results from the profiles gave estimates of a similar order to those of Foxton (1956).

Boysen-Enney *et al.* (1991) have recently published data on zooplankton biomass in the ice-covered Weddell

Sea during the austral summer, and reviewed recent data on zooplankton biomass in the Southern Ocean. Mesoplankton (<14.5 mm) biomass in the Southern Ocean is generally between 0.8 and 3.6 g dry wt m⁻². High values have been measured in the Croker Passage near the Antarctic Peninsula (Hopkins, 1985b), and low values in the oceanic northern Weddell Sea (El-Sayed & Taguchi, 1981). Calanoid copepods clearly dominate the biomass. It is only in the high Antarctic shelf regions that copepods are partly replaced by smaller gastropods (*Limacina helicina*). The copepods *Calanoides acutus, Calanus propinquus* and *Metridia gerlachei* are responsible for a biomass peak in the 1 to 5 mm size range. A second biomass peak in the 7.0 to 8.5 mm range is sometimes caused by *Salpa thompsoni* (Everson, 1984a: Piakowski, 1985b; Boysen-Enney *et al.* 1991).

Published data on macroplankton biomass in the Southern Ocean are in the order of 0.2 to 2.4 g dry wt m⁻², excluding studies which are focused only on krill. Macroplankton biomass is lower than mesoplankton biomass at all latitudes and also decreases from lower to higher latitudes. Krill are often considered to be the most important zooplankton species in the Southern Ocean and on occasions in specific localities they can dominate the zooplankton biomass, e.g. in the Croker Passage krill biomass outnumbered that of other zooplankton by an order of magnitude (Hopkins, 1985a). However, the results of the intensive 'BIOMASS' investigations gave average densities of krill in its principal areas of distribution of 1 to 2 g dry wt m⁻² (Siegel, 1986a). This is the same order of magnitude as that of the mesoplankton biomass, even in the areas of main krill occurrence. It is clear that the overall contribution of krill to Southern Ocean zooplankton biomass has been overestimated in the past.

Taking into account the higher production:biomass ratio of copepods (4.5:1, Voronina *et al.*, 1981) over krill (1.0, Everson, 1977b), copepods contribute most to total zooplankton production in the Southern Ocean. Boysen-Enney *et al.* (1991) have listed estimates for mesoplankton production for the Atlantic sector of the Southern Ocean, and based on these estimates they concluded that in this sector mesoplankton production exceeds that of macroplankton production by a factor of 8 to 14. However, these copepods, with a few exceptions, do not constitute a major food resource for the large predators of the Southern Ocean. The main predators on these copepods are mesopelagic fishes such as the Myctophidae (Rowedder, 1979). These fishes are absent from the shallower waters over the high Antarctic shelf where the holopelagic fish *Pleuragramma antarcticum* dominates and feeds on copepods throughout its life-cycle (Eastman, 1985b; Hubold & Ekau, 1987).

To the copepod biomass must be added the production of the other herbivores, such as the euphausiids and salps, and the carnivorous zooplankton, which includes the carnivorous copepods, the pelagic amphipods, the chaetognaths, the pelagic polychaetes and the medusae and siphonophores. The data base is inadequate at present to estimate accurately the secondary production of these groups. However, from an ecological point of view, global estimates of annual secondary production are not of a great deal of value. In the Southern Ocean production is characterized by a great amount of variability, both geographically and seasonally, and in addition within any given locality it can be very patchy.

5

Krill

5.1 Introduction

As we have seen euphausiid crustaceans are conspicuous members of the Southern Ocean plankton communities. Collectively they are often referred to as 'krill', although the term is frequently reserved for the dominant species *Euphausia superba* (Fig. 5.1). This species, because of its widespread distribution and abundance, and its central position in the food web has attracted much attention. During the interwar period *E. superba* was studied intensively by several workers, especially the scientists of the *Discovery* Expeditions (e.g. Rudd, 1932; Fraser, 1936; Marr, 1962; Mackintosh, 1972), where the main interest was the importance of krill as food for baleen whales. In recent years an added dimension has been the commercial potential of krill as food for humans. *E. superba* has also been the focus of intensive research during the recently completed 10-year BIOMASS Programme. As a result there has been a considerable volume of publications on many aspects of krill biology, ecology, behaviour, physiology and biochemical adaptations (e.g. Schnack, 1983b; George, 1984a; Siegfried *et al.*, 1985; Sahrhage, 1988a; Miller & Hampton, 1989). Much of the recent work is as yet unpublished and when it is some of the unanswered questions raised below may be answered.

In comparison with other euphausiids *E. superba* has a number of unique characteristics (Kils, 1983). They are:

1. An unusually high body weight (e.g. 60 times that of *Euphausia pacifica*).
2. An unusually high metabolic rate for a euphausiid of its size living in a low-temperature environment (reflected in a respiration rate of 1 mg O_2 (g dry wt)$^{-1}$ h^{-1}, swimming speeds of 60 cm s^{-1} and a reaction time of 40 ms).
3. A large size ratio between krill and their food (e.g. the ratio between the length of a typical diatom (6 μm) and a 60 mm *E. superba* is 1:10000, while the weight ratios are 1:7 million).
4. An unusual relationship between energetics and size. Normally larger animals have a lower specific metabolism (energy per body unit and time unit) than smaller ones. However, in *E. superba* this does not vary with body size. The significance of this will be discussed below.

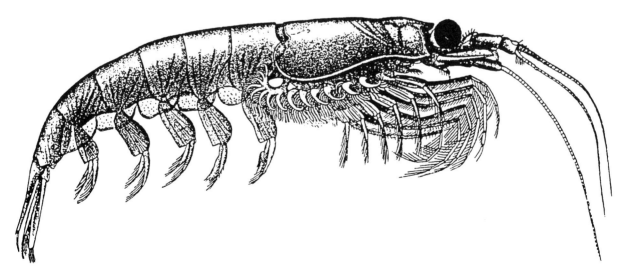

Fig. 5.1. *Euphausia superba*, the Antarctic krill.

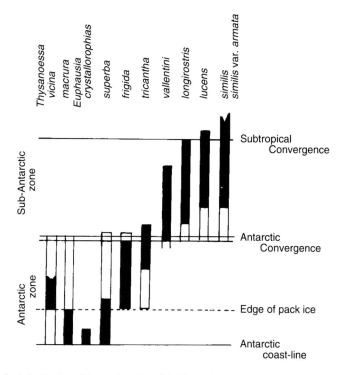

Fig. 5.2. Latitudinal distribution of Antarctic euphausiids. The dark areas represent the main distributional range of the species.

To these we can add the following (Quentin & Ross, (1991):

5. The ability to find concentrations of food in several types of habitat and efficiently exploit whatever food is available.
6. The close correspondence of life-cycle with seasonal cycles of food availability.
7. A combination of physiological and behavioural mechanisms which enable krill to survive the long winter period when often food resources are low.

5.2 Species of euphausiids

There are eleven species of euphausiids which occur in the waters of the Southern Ocean, but only six of these are important and endemic south of the Antarctic Convergence. All eleven species have circumpolar distributions. The latitudinal distributions of the species are shown in Fig. 5.2.

5.3 Life-history and growth

5.3.1 Introduction

As a result of early work on *E. superba*, particularly that of the *Discovery* Expeditions (Bargmann, 1945; Marr, 1962; Mackintosh, 1972), the broad outlines of the life-history and growth patterns of *E. superba* became known. However, a number of questions remained unanswered

and further uncertainties have arisen as a result of recent work. Recent research has been directed at finding answers to the following questions:

What are the factors influencing spawning in krill, where are the spawning grounds located and how many times may a female spawn in a season?

At what depth does spawning take place?

Do females spawn in one season only, or can they spawn in successive seasons?

What is the relationship between pressure and krill embryology and larval development?

What are the factors which are responsible for the distribution of krill larval stages?

What are the growth rates of larval and adult krill in relation to food supply and environmental factors?

What are the factors which are involved in krill swarming behaviour?

What is the feeding mechanism of krill and what kinds and quantities of food do krill consume?

What is the growth strategy of krill during the winter months, i.e. do they continue to feed and grow during the winter or do they cease feeding but continue to moult and decrease in size?

How long do krill live and as a corollary of this how can the age of krill be determined?

Information gathered in recent years goes some way towards answering the questions listed above but substantial gaps in our knowledge still remain. The missing information is vital to the development of strategies for the management of the krill resource.

5.3.2 Reproduction and fecundity

A species' reproductive potential is governed by two integral factors: the energy cost of reproduction and the energy transferred to successive generations (i.e. its fecundity) (Miller & Hampton, 1989). We need to consider the cost of producing eggs and the calorific losses incurred by spawning activities.

Ross & Quentin (1986) define fecundity as

$$F = E(T \cdot SF)$$

where F = fecundity, or total number of eggs released by an individual in a spawning episode, E = the total number of eggs per spawning episode, T = the length of the spawning season, and SF = the proportion of mature females releasing eggs per day. Krill fecundity has been determined in a variety of ways, including counts of all or part of the eggs present in the ovary, counts of the number of eggs spawned, measurement of the ratio of ovarian to body volume, and analysis of body lipid content. In spite of recent research there is no general agreement on the number of times a female spawns and the number of eggs released (Miller & Hampton, 1989).

Estimates of the number of eggs produced by a single female vary widely from a low of 310–800 (Mauchline & Fisher, 1969) to 20000 (Ross & Quentin, 1983b, 1986). The mean of these estimates falls within the range of 2200–8800 assessed by Denys & McWhinnie (1982). Estimates of the number of spawning episodes also vary considerably. El-Sayed & McWhinnie (1979) supported the view advanced by Makarov (1972, 1979b) that krill possibly spawn twice over a period of two seasons. However, Ettershank (1983) considered that spawning might extend over four or five seasons. Ross & Quentin (1983a,b) assumed that spawning took place nine to ten times per season with a mean interval of 6.7 days. However, recent experimental evidence does not support these assumptions (Siegel, 1985; Harrington & Ikeda, 1986). Siegel contended that the spawning season assumed by Ross & Quentin was too long. Spawning frequency also varies strongly not only over the season, but also amongst schools sampled simultaneously a short distance from one another.

It is essential from the viewpoint of future management of krill stocks that estimates of fecundity be refined, not only to determine precisely the total number of eggs produced, but also the number of spawning episodes

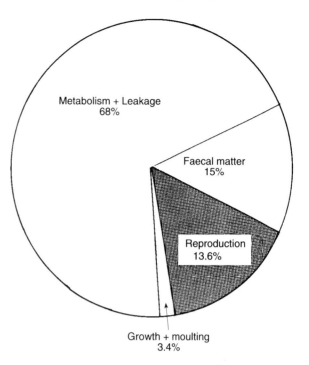

Fig. 5.3. Proportional allocation to metabolism plus leakage, faecal matter, reproduction and growth plus moulting of the total food ingested by a female, *Euphausia superba* based on the standard energy budget, where ingestion = faecal matter + metabolism + leakage + moulting + growth + reproduction. The following assumptions were made to derive the portion allocated to each activity: Assimilation efficiency = 85% (Ross, 1982); metabolism + leakage = 80% of assimilation (A. Clarke & Morris, 1983a; Ikeda, 1984b), and production (what remains after metabolism and leakage) = 20% of assimilation; reproduction = 80% of production. Redrawn from Ross & Quentin (1986).

and the number of seasons over which a female can spawn.

5.3.3 Energy costs of reproduction

The major energy cost of reproduction in krill is the accumulation of the large, lipid-rich yolk mass of the eggs (A. Clarke & Morris, 1983a,b). Since krill spawn in the summer or, at the earliest during the spring phytoplankton bloom (Hart, 1934; Bargmann, 1945; Marr, 1962), latitudinal variations in spawning time suggest that ovarian development is prompted by an increased availability of food rather than the lipid reserves laid down the previous summer (Clarke & Morris, 1983a,b).

At present it is only possible to determine roughly the energy cost of egg production in krill. Clarke & Morris (1983a) considered the minimum cost of egg production to be 46% of total production, based on the assumption that a female matures a single ovary. Ettershank (1983), however, presents some evidence that mature females may not grow, so that production would go primarily into eggs not tissue. Based on work with other euphausiids Ross & Quentin (1986) have considered the ratio of

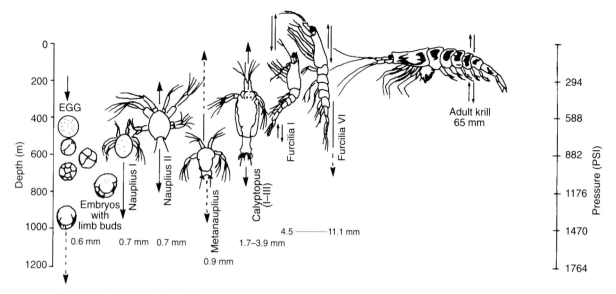

Fig. 5.4. Vertical distributions of the various ontogenetic stages of *Euphausia superba*, depicting the phenomenon of 'developmental descent' and 'developmental ascent'. Arrows indicate the depth distribution of the ontogenetic stages. Redrawn from George (1984b).

reproduction to growth and moulting to be 4:1 (Fig. 5.3). Under such assumptions Ross & Quentin estimated that a female would need to ingest more than 300 µg chlorophyll *a* day^{-1} to produce their predicted number of eggs. On this basis *E. superba* would require relatively high average concentrations of phytoplankton (c. 1.5 g chl *a* l^{-1}) to reproduce if all the energy for reproduction comes from feeding during the spawning season. Even if the estimate of the number of eggs produced were half of their estimate the phytoplankton concentration required would still be high. Such concentrations do not commonly occur in oceanic waters but do in bays around the Antarctic Peninsula and shallow areas near the Scotia Ridge (Bienati *et al.*, 1977; Holm-Hansen & Huntley, 1984), and in ice edge blooms (W.O. Smith & Nelson, 1986). Thus, patches of phytoplankton in high concentrations and/or food sources other than phytoplankton may be important for reproductive success.

5.3.4 Early life-history

Spawning is generally believed to take place in the upper 0–100 m layer (Fraser, 1936; Marr, 1962). According to Makarov (1983b) there is evidence for this occurring in *E. frigida* and *T. macrura* off South Georgia as at night most of the eggs are found in this layer. After spawning the eggs sink, undergoing development on the way. However, one of the problems encountered in studying the breeding patterns and development of euphausiids is the comparative rarity of eggs in plankton net hauls due to a combination of the patchy distribution of the spawning females, the vertical dispersion of the eggs and their

low catchability (I. Hempel, 1978; I. Hempel *et al.*, 1979; Marschall, 1983).

Euphausiids pass through a series of larval stages, as shown in Fig. 5.4, known as nauplius, metanauplius, calyptopus and furcilia. These larval types and their nomenclature have been discussed and defined in Mauchline & Fisher (1969). The early life-history has been described by Marr (1962) and the morphological structure of the larvae by Fraser (1936). Descriptions of the larval stages of other Southern Ocean euphausiids have been given by John (1936). After hatching at a depth of several hundred metres two stages of nauplius and one of metanauplius are passed through as the larvae ascend in the water column (Marr, 1962; George, 1984b; I. Hempel, 1983, 1985a,b; I. Hempel & G. Hempel, 1986) (Fig. 5.5). Feeding commences in the next phase, the calyptopus, when it enters the surface waters, about 30 days after spawning according to Kikuno (1981), or after 21–25 days according to Ross & Quentin (1983a). Recent investigations by Makarov (1978, 1979b, 1983b) have also shown that the sinking of the eggs and the developmental ascent of the larvae are characteristic for all species of Antarctic euphausiids except for *E. crystallorophias*, and not, as originally believed, for *E. superba* only. According to Makarov (1978, 1983b) there are species differences in the depths to which the eggs sink and in the ontogenetic migration. With increase in age the larvae of *E. superba* and *T. macrura* rise to the surface and concentrate in the subsurface layers, whereas those of *E. tricantha* and *E. frigida* tend to sink again after some time.

Growth rates of krill larvae, from calyptopus onward,

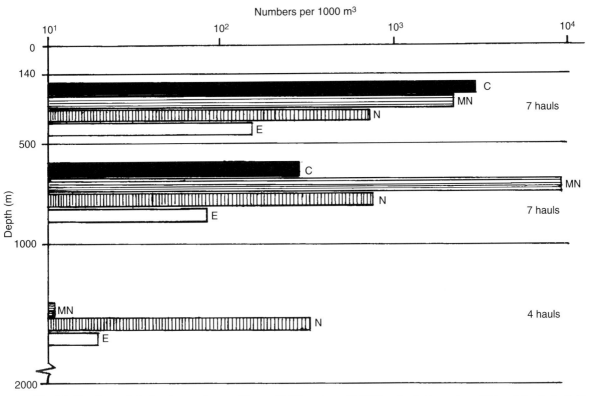

Fig. 5.5. Abundance of *Euphausia superba* eggs (E), nauplii (N), metanauplii (MN), and calyptopus stages (C) in relation to depth in the Bransfield Strait and the Scotia Sea, January 1981. Redrawn from I. Hempel (1985b).

are not well known. Witek *et al.* (1980) attempted an analysis using mid-points and limits of the varying periods during which the different developmental stages have been collected in the field. For example, they estimated 15–30 days from Calyptopus 1 to Calyptopus 2, and 135–240 days for the full duration of larval life. On the other hand, Brinton & Townsend (1984) found five larval stages in high abundance (>10 per 1000 m⁻³) north of the South Orkney Islands in March 1981 indicating that the spawning season must have been at least as long ago as five developmental stages. Based on their data Brinton & Townsend estimated a spawning period of 40 days with an average of eight days per developmental stage. This stage duration is shorter than that proposed by other investigators. Mauchline (1980a) gives 8.5–11.5 days (based on theoretical reasoning), Ross & Quentin (1983b) at least 15 days (laboratory rearing), and Ikeda (1984a) 9–14 days for calyptopus stages and 11–15 days for furcilia stages (laboratory rearing). Ikeda (1984a, 1985) estimated a total development time from egg to larval stage of 130 days.

5.3.5 General distribution of the larvae and breeding grounds

The occurrence of larval euphausiids generally follows the pattern of latitudinal distribution of the adults

(Lomakina, 1964). Larvae of *E. frigida* and *E. tricantha*, as a rule, have a more northerly distribution than those of the other euphausiid species. Larvae of *E. superba* and *E. crystallorophias* tend, to a large extent, to be distributed to the south, while those of *T. macrura* occur at almost all latitudes. This general pattern is substantially modified by the distribution of the water masses of different origin (Bogdanov *et al.*, 1980; Maslennikov, 1980). The situation becomes extremely complicated in the Atlantic Sector, in particular in the Scotia Sea, due to the convergence of the water masses of the Antarctic Circumpolar Current and the Weddell Drift.

E. frigida, E. tricantha and *T. macrura* breed over the whole of their habitat range whereas *E. crystallorophias* in general breeds in the shallow waters in the vicinity of the Antarctic Continent. The breeding sites of *E. superba* are unique among Southern Ocean euphausiids. Marr (1962) discussed the probable localities of spawning and concluded that the vicinity of the continental shelf was the most important factor in the location of the spawning areas. Mackintosh (1972) implied that spawning in oceanic areas as well as in the shelf area was of major importance. Makarov (1972, 1973) described a major spawning area in the frontal zone between the Weddell Sea and the Antarctic Circumpolar Current, thus confirming that spawning does take place in the open ocean.

Recent studies in the Scotia Sea, Bransfield Strait, and Drake Passage (Mujica & Asencio, 1983; I. Hempel, 1983; Guzman & Marin, 1983) have confirmed the importance of convergence zones as breeding locations for *E. superba*.

Evidence is accumulating that spawning in *E. superba* may be highly variable from year to year. I. Hempel (1983, 1985b) found striking differences in the overall abundances of krill larvae (mainly calyptopes) in the Scotia Sea and adjacent waters over the period January–March in 1976, 1978, and 1981. Larval abundance was highest in 1981, low generally in 1978 and intermediate in 1976. Maximum abundance varied by three orders of magnitude. It is thus clear that larval abundance in the western part of the Atlantic Sector of the Southern Ocean is subject to marked annual fluctuations.

5.3.6 Summary of the life-cycle of E. superba

Details of the life-cycle are best known from the Scotia Sea region. Based on studies carried out since the *Discovery* Expeditions (Fraser, 1936; Marr, 1962; Makarov, 1972, 1973; Mackintosh, 1972; Dolzhenkov, 1973; Voronina, 1974; Everson, 1976, 1977b, 1981; I. Hempel, 1978; I. Hempel & G. Hempel, 1978; Nast, 1978; Witek *et al.*, 1980) the life-cycle of *E. superba* can be summarized as follows:

1. Females spawn somewhere in the upper 200m, probably mostly below 80m.

2. Immediately after spawning the eggs sink at a rate of 150–250 m a day. The sinking rate of the eggs will be governed by their density and that of the surrounding water.

3. Spawning, as well as sinking, seems to occur over relatively short periods for individual swarms and egg batches.

4. As the eggs sink they undergo development, and hatch at variable depths, depending on the bathymetrical and hydrological conditions.

5. Although eggs under laboratory conditions will develop and hatch at atmospheric pressure, greater pressure may be necessary for normal development under natural conditions.

6. The sinking of the developing eggs culminates in the hatching of the short-lived Nauplius I. The depth of hatching is conditioned by the bottom water, where the upper boundary of which will become the lower boundary for egg sinking (according to Voronina, 1974), or will be the actual place of hatching (Marr, 1962).

7. After hatching the larvae ascend to the surface passing through a number of stages as they do so. This leads to the stratification of the larvae in oceanic samples, with nauplii generally below 150 m, metanauplii concentrated below 500 m, and calyptope stages towards the surface (see Fig. 5.5).

8. From the calyptope stages onward *E. superba* lives in surface waters exhibiting diel vertical migrations. Horizontal migrations of late larval stages and adults will be considered later.

5.3.7 Growth, moulting and longevity

Despite considerable efforts to elucidate the life cycle and ecology of krill there is as yet no general agreement as to its growth rates and longevity. The question of longevity is fundamental to the management of any commercial fishery; both the growth rate to maturity, and the number of eggs each adult can produce will directly affect estimates of production and hence safe harvesting rates. Growth can be estimated from the relationships between various body length measurements (e.g. Rudd, 1932; Bargmann, 1945; Marr, 1962; Ivanov, 1970; Siegel, 1982: Miller 1986a), or from laboratory experiments on growth rates (e.g. Mackintosh, 1967; Murano *et al.*, 1979; Ikeda & Dixon, 1982a,b; Poleck & Denys, 1982; Morris & Keck, 1984; Ikeda *et al.*, 1985), or from model studies (e.g. Asheimer *et al.*, 1985). From the viewpoint of production krill body length measurements need to be related to growth in terms of dry weight increase or energy fixed. Various authors have derived expressions for the relationships of krill body length to dry weight (A. Clarke, 1976; Kils, 1981), fresh wet weight (Heyerdahl, 1932; Lockyer, 1973; Jazdzewski *et al.*, 1978; Sahrhage, 1978; Stepnik, 1982; Miller, 1986a; Siegel, 1986b) and volume (Kils, 1979a, 1981); see review by Morris *et al.* (1988).

Growth in various euphausiid species has been reviewed by Mauchline & Fisher (1969), Mauchline (1980a) and more recently by Siegel (1987). Mauchline (1980a) points out that the growth rate, maturation and life span of euphausiid species is extremely difficult to determine, primarily due to the difficulty in validating field data through the maintenance of animals under laboratory conditions (cf. Baker, 1963; Komaki, 1966).

Ettershank (1983, 1984), Siegel (1986b, 1987) and S. Nicol (1990) have reviewed earlier work concerning growth and age determination in krill. Earlier opinions of a two-year life-cycle (Rudd, 1932; Mackintosh, 1972) conflicted with the conclusions of Bargmann (1945) and Marr (1962) that krill breed only in their third year of life spending the first two years as larvae and juveniles. Ivanov (1970) on the basis of modal size–class analysis concluded that there were five year classes. Other anal-

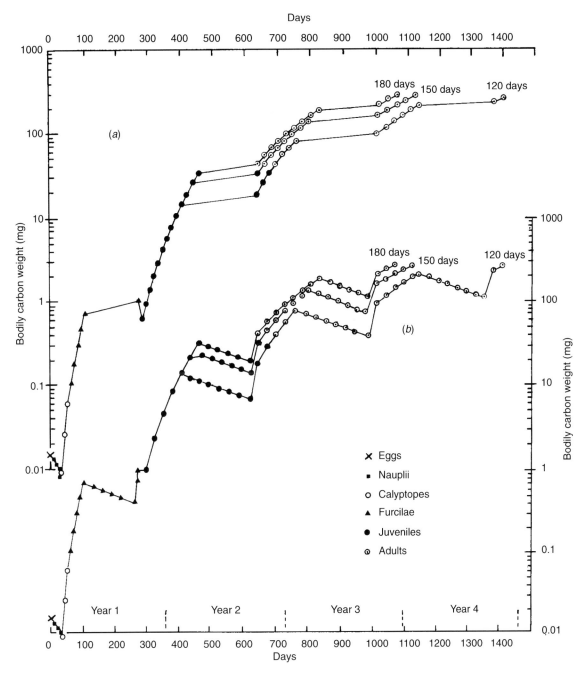

Fig. 5.6. Hypothetical growth curves for *Euphausia superba* in the Southern Ocean. (*a*) 'M-scheme': for 180, 150 and 120 days annual growth (=Antarctic summer), assuming little growth over winter (based on the scheme proposed by Mauchline, 1980a). In this scheme feeding is assumed to occur throughout the year, but moulting ceases over winter. This scheme also assumes a size-related intermoult period. (*b*). 'MS-scheme': considers the same annual periods of growth as the M-scheme, but assumes that (1) non-feeding and body shrinkage occurs over the winter, and (2) size-independent intermoult periods continue throughout the year. Redrawn from Ikeda (1985).

yses of modal length classes have given contradictory results, because of different interpretations of strongly overlapping size classes of the older age groups (Aseev, 1983). As noted above evidence has accumulated to show that krill may spawn in successive seasons (Makarov, 1975; Ross & Quentin, 1983b). This led Makarov (1979a), Kock & Stein (1978) and Fevolden (1979) to postulate that krill may live for three years or more.

Fevolden (1979) attributed much of the variation in observed growth rates to be the result of environmental effects causing animals from colder southern waters to grow more slowly than those from those to the north.

Mauchline (1980a) constructed a series of growth curves for euphausiids based on an earlier simulation (Mauchline, 1977), and on the results from experimental studies (Mackintosh, 1967; McWhinnie *et al.*, 1979) (Fig.

5.6). These suggested that given an annual growth period of 150–180 days (intermediate to northern populations), krill attain sexual maturity at a body length of between 40 and 50 mm and at an age of two years. Animals larger than 55 mm would be approaching three years of age. With a growth period of 120 days or less (southern populations) the majority of krill would mature at three years of age and the life span could extend to five years. Mauchline assumed that no moulting and little growth occurred during the rest of the year (i.e. during the Antarctic winter).

Much recent research has been directed towards resolving the impasse concerning growth rates and longevity. Such research has involved laboratory rearing experiments to determine moulting frequency and growth rates and the exploration of new methods of age determination.

Growth in euphausiids, as in other arthropods, is dependent on moulting, which continues in basically identical cycles during the greater part of the life span. Results of laboratory observations on moulting have been published by Mackintosh (1967), A. Clarke (1976), Murano *et al.* (1979), Ikeda & Dixon (1982a,b), Poleck & Denys (1982), Buchholz (1983, 1985), Segawa *et al.* (1983), Morris & Keck (1984) and Ikeda *et al.* (1985). The intermoult periods reported by these authors range from 13 to 30 days. These laboratory experiments required the maintenance of krill under controlled environmental conditions for prolonged periods. Such experiments are subject to considerable difficulty (Buchholz, 1983). Firstly, as pelagic animals, krill live in an environment without boundaries. Hence, they are maintained in a highly unnatural situation in maintenance chambers. Secondly, there are difficulties in providing the krill with the right amounts and kinds of phytoplankton as food.

Ikeda & Dixon (1982a,b) transported live krill from Australian Antarctic waters to Australia and maintained them under laboratory conditions. The mean intermoult period of specimens kept at 0.5 °C ranged from 22.0 to 27.5 days for females (mean 25.5±3.2), and from 25.7 to 29.8 for males (mean 27.6±3.9), with an overall mean of 26.6±4.1 days. Observed changes in body length included increase (positive growth), decrease (negative growth) and no change (zero growth). The largest increases in body length over a time of 4–5 months ranged from 0.025 to 0.007 mm day^{-1}. The maximum growth rates they recorded led Ikeda & Dixon to suggest that the overall exponential growth rate calculated for krill from the growth scheme proposed by Mauchline (1980a) is anomalous. If the maximum exponential growth rate obtained in laboratory experiments

approaches that which occurs in nature then it can be assumed that krill grow at half the rate of that postulated by Mauchline. Mauchline's (1980a) theoretical estimates of maximum growth rates for krill are about twice those observed experimentally by Ikeda *et al.* (1985) (negligible to 2.7%). Furthermore, Mauchline's figures are consistently higher than values for other euphausiid species (Ikeda *et al.*, 1985; Miller & Hampton, 1989). If the maximum growth rate obtained from laboratory experiments is more realistic than values obtained from Mauchline's simulations then this would put krill's life span at between two and seven years (Ikeda *et al.*, 1985), with the maximum figure applying to animals in colder waters, and the minimum figure to their faster-growing northern counterparts.

Ikeda & Dixon (1982a,b) maintained krill in the laboratory successfully for 211 days without food. During this time a significant reduction in body weight (32.1 to 56.1% of initial body weight) was observed. Ikeda & Dixon argued that body shrinkage might be a strategy for overwintering when the stock of phytoplankton is scarce, or nil, and the krill would need to burn up body tissue to fulfil energy needs.

Buchholz (1982, 1985) developed a more sophisticated flow-through system for keeping krill in the laboratory that reduced handling and furnished a constant supply of natural phytoplankton. The initial system was later modified by Morris & Keck (1984) who found a positive growth of 8.0% per moult and a mean intermoult period of 14.3 days, which is within the range obtained by other workers using similar maintenance temperatures. The average growth rate obtained by Buchholz was 0.132 mm day^{-1}; this agrees with the 0.142 mm day^{-1} reported by Morris & Keck (1984) and is higher than that recorded by Ikeda & Dixon (1982a). Both of the values using the flow-through technique fit the growth rate of 0.133 mm day^{-1} which can be derived from the theoretical growth curve of Mauchline (1980a).

The results obtained by Buchholz (1982, 1985) suggest that body shrinkage is not a universal phenomenon in euphausiids. This is supported by Siegel (1986b) who showed that young krill exhibit positive growth during the winter, and by Morris & Priddle (1984) who reported observing limited moult activity during winter. As we shall see below (section 5.6.6) evidence is accumulating that food is available to krill throughout the winter period. However, figures for growth of krill in the wild are lacking, and there have been no laboratory simulations of seasonal cycles. It is of interest that McClatchie (1988) recently showed that in Admiralty Bay, seasonal growth is closely associated with water column chlorophyll *a* concentration, providing some evidence that

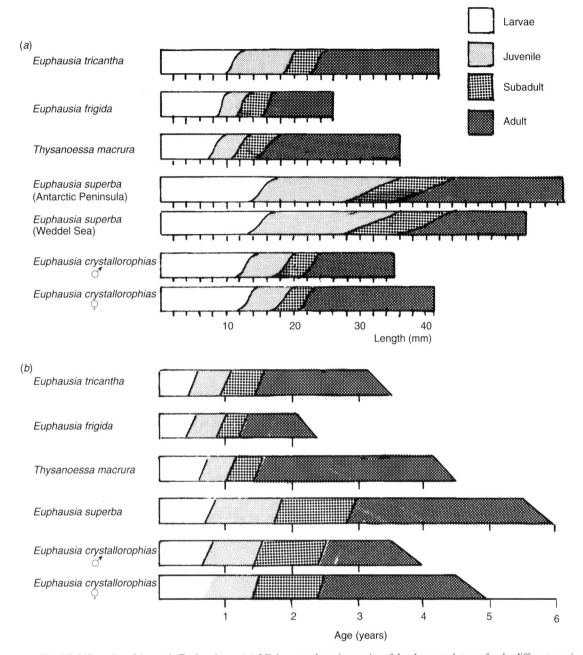

Fig. 5.7. Life-cycles of Antarctic Euphausiacea: (*a*). Minimum and maximum size of developmental stages for the different species. (*b*). Occurrence of the developmental stages at age of the species. Redrawn from Siegel (1987).

growth in wild krill in this locality is food limited for about six months of the year.

Buchholz (1991) measured positive growth in a large number of specimens of *E. superba* under controlled conditions using his sophisticated systems for their long-term maintenance. He considered that the often-reported 'abnormal' slow and predominantly negative growth was probably due to inadequate maintenance procedures. Moulting was found to be partly synchronous, and the moult frequency was temperature dependent. Moult frequency (14 to 29 days) and growth increment at moult

(−15 to 21%) varied together and were very sensitive to experimental variation in feeding. The apparent plasticity of growth parameters indicated that, in the wild, krill is able to adapt to the strong regional and seasonal changes in feeding conditions that are typical for Antarctic waters. Krill grow fast, and in spite of being predominantly planktonic attain a large size. This enables fast swimming, which facilitates the location of rich food sources. Favourable feeding conditions immediately initiate growth.

There are thus conflicting views on krill growth derived

from experiments. It appears that krill can adjust to the food situation by changing the frequency of moulting. Thus, krill can apparently adjust the growth rate very sensitively to the specific environmental situation by both altering the frequency of moulting and the growth increment between moultings. This sensitive adjustment pattern may result in moulting patterns in the experimental situation which are different from those under natural conditions.

Siegel (1987) has studied the age and growth of five species of euphausiids from the Antarctic Peninsula region and the south eastern Scotia Sea. Fig. 5.7 summarizes the minimum and maximum size of their developmental stages and the age of occurrence of each development stage for each species. Life spans range from two years for *E. frigida* to six years for *E. superba*. *E. superba* was calculated to develop from the larval phase (nauplii, metanauplii and calyptope stages) into the juvenile stage at a length of 15 mm, normally during the winter season in the first year of life. The juvenile stage covered the length classes of 14 to about 36 mm, while the smallest of the subadults already occurred at a length of 27 mm. The overlapping size distributions of the developmental stages were also found in the subadult and adult (reproductive) stages. The largest subadults measured 45mm, while the smallest adults were around 35 mm. Taking the seasonal growth curve into account, the juvenile stage is continued throughout the second year (age group 1+). At the end of age 1+ the krill develop into the subadult stage which then dominates the age group 2+. During this year only a few individuals mature. From age group 3+ onwards all krill are adults. Siegel considered that *E. superba* spawned three times during its life cycle. The Southern Weddell Sea krill showed the same pattern as those from the Antarctic Peninsula region.

5.3.7.1 Assessment of longevity

Although the data have given conflicting results concerning both growth rates and longevity in krill a consensus is emerging for the view that krill are long-lived, living for at least five or six years. Both Ettershank (1983, 1984) and Rosenberg *et al.* (1986) have estimated a maximum age of six to seven years for krill to approach 60 mm in length. The solution to the problem of krill longevity lies in the interpretation of the number of year classes in the adult krill group. Siegel (1987) points out that it is possible that his age group 5+, estimated as the oldest one, might possibly embrace one or two more cohorts of very low abundance which cannot be separated by distribution mixture analysis. However, he notes that the largest krill found in all of his samples taken in October/November were 55 mm in length, indicating that all krill larger than 55 mm had died off during the preceding winter season.

Ettershank (1982, 1983, 1984) has reviewed the extensive literature on the relationship between size and age in *E. superba*. He discusses the use of an age pigment, lipofuscin, which has been found in all aerobically respiring invertebrates. Lipofuscin accumulates as a result of metabolic activity (Ettershank *et al.*, 1982) and its assay by a fluorescence technique is thus a measure of the cumulative metabolism of an organism, or metabolic time. Ettershank (1984) analyzed the lipofuscin content of adult female krill from a sample taken in Prydz Bay in 1981. Seven age classes could be distinguished on the basis of this analysis. Recently, Berman *et al.* (1989) determined the ages of 252 mature female krill collected from Prydz Bay using length frequency analysis, combined with a computerized image analysis system, and the fluorescent age pigment technique. The results of both methods suggested six year classes for adult krill. Correspondence between ages determined by the two techniques was generally within one year. On the other hand, Nicol (1990) states that the lipofuscin technique as it was initially applied is now being questioned on a number of methodological and technical grounds (Eldred *et al.*, 1982; Nicol, 1987). Additionally, a number of recent studies of natural populations of crustaceans and fish have failed to show a clear relationship between fluorescence and age (Hill & Radthe, 1988; Mullin & Brooks, 1989). Hill & Womersley (1991) have recently reviewed the problems involved in fluorescent age pigment methodologies. They concluded that while the technique holds a great deal of promise, further investigation is necessary to define the importance of fluorescent age pigment content variation between the sexes and the effects of environmental factors (e.g. temperature, light, food ration, etc.) on tissue fluorescence, before it can be adopted as a standard for aging aquatic organisms. It is clear that further research is needed before the longevity of krill can be finally resolved.

5.4 Krill aggregations

5.4.1 Introduction

The salient characteristic of the distribution of euphausiids, especially *E. superba*, in the Southern Ocean is their patchiness. Throughout most of its life-cycle *E. superba* occurs near the surface of the sea in discrete swarms or schools (Marr, 1962; Mauchline, 1980b; Hamner *et al.*, 1983), and reddish patches of krill are often visible from aboard ship (Marr, 1962; Shust, 1969). Marr (1962) has plotted such observations up to that date. An understanding of the processes underlying the formation and persistence of such aggregations is essential for the management of krill fisheries, since they define the site of fishing

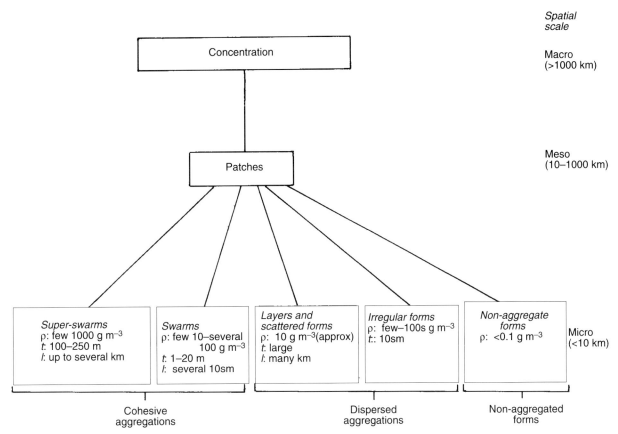

Fig. 5.8. A classification scheme for krill aggregations (modified from Kalinowski & Witek, 1985): ρ, density; *t*, thickness; *l*, length. Redrawn from Miller & Hampton (1989).

grounds, the major trophic relationships and energy flow within the system.

Past attempts to correlate krill aggregations with physical environmental factors have not been very conclusive. Hence recent research has focused on the biological and behavioural process involved in the formation and persistence of krill aggregations (e.g. Bidigare *et al.*, 1981; Antezana *et al.*, 1982; Hamner *et al.*, 1983; Antezana & Ray, 1983; Everson, 1984a). Increasingly, attention is being paid to the interrelationships between feeding, vertical migration, moulting, and predator–prey interactions in swarming behaviour.

5.4.2 Types of aggregation

The sizes and shapes of krill aggregations vary considerably. They vary in area, depth range, and in the sex ratios and age classes of the individuals in them (Marr, 1962). The diameter, or length, of krill swarms is generally in the range of 0.5 m to over 100 m, but is sometimes considerably greater. The area covered generally ranges from a few square metres to over 600 m² and exceptionally may cover many square kilometres. Most swarms appear to be laminar in shape, ranging from a few centimetres

to a few metres in thickness. They can also be ribbon-shaped through oval to circular.

Various terms ('swarm', 'patch', 'school', 'layer', 'super-swarm') have been used to describe the different observed types of krill aggregations. Classification schemes have been proposed by Mauchline (1980b), Kalinowski & Witek (1982, 1983, 1985) and Murphy *et al.* (1988). The scheme adopted here (Fig. 5.8) is the modified version of Kalinowski & Witek's (1985) scheme proposed by Miller & Hampton (1989). The three levels of organization shown in Fig. 5.8 correspond to three horizontal spatial scales (i.e., macro, >1000 km; meso, 10–100 km and micro, <10 km). As proposed by Murphy *et al.* (1988) they have a corresponding time scale: 'concentrations' at a scale of months, 'patches' from days to months, and 'aggregations' from hours to days.

5.4.3 Physical characteristics of aggregations

5.4.3.1 Swarms
Swarms are the commonest types of aggregation and they are characterized by relatively small dimensions and rela-

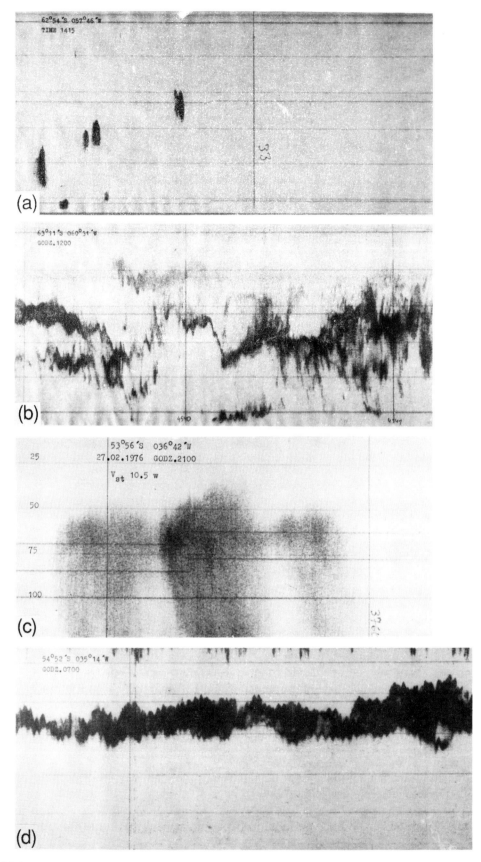

Fig. 5.9. Echo-recordings of different forms of krill aggregations: (a) swarms; (b) irregular forms; (c) scattered forms; (d) layers. From Kalinowski & Witek (1985).

Table 5.1. *Data on krill aggregation parameters as determined acoustically during FIBEX*

	Mean	SD mean	Range
Depth[1] (m)	44	0.3	152
Horizontal dimension[1] (m)	73	6	25682
Thickness[1] (m)	5	0.1	96
Spacing[1] (km)	2.2	0.01	366
Area[1] (m^2)	1021	124	513640
Density[2] (g m^{-3})[2]	59	3	5612

[1]N=7623; [2]N=2793.

Table 5.2. *Comparison of FIBEX krill aggregation data from the West Atlantic and the Indian Ocean*

	West Atlantic	Indian Ocean
Mean width (m)	84	12
Range of widths (m)	c. 6100	270
Mean swarm thickness (m)	5.6	4.0
Range of thicknesses (m)	94	32
Mean density (g m^{-2})	4.46	1.97
Area (km^2 x 10^6)	0.59	2.9
Biomass (t x 10^6)	2.65	4.51

Data from Miller & Hampton (1989).

tively uniform high density (Fig. 5.9) They are described by Kalinowski & Witek (1985) as 'being typically several tens of metres across, several metres to about 20 m thick, with densities generally between 100 and several 100 g m^{-3}'. Miller & Hampton (1989) have summarized information on krill aggregation parameters detected in 1976–77 and 1977–78 summer seasons (Kalinowski & Witek, 1982, 1985) and during the First International Biomass Experiment (FIBEX) (Tables 5.1 and 5.2). FIBEX data were consistent with those obtained by Kalinowski & Witek. Aggregations (mostly swarms) were estimated to have been on average 73 m wide (along the longest dimension) and 5 m thick, with a mean density of 2.49 g m^{-3}. The swarm biomass ranged from 90 kg to 407 tonnes. From the BIOMASS data (Table 5.2) it is clear that there are regional differences in krill swarm dimensions, density and biomass.

Acoustic work indicates that the distribution of swarm sizes tends to be highly positively skewed. Hampton (1985) studied acoustically the abundance, distribution and behaviour of *E. superba* between 15° E and 30° E and south of 60° S to the ice edge at about 69° S during February–March 1981. The krill were spread uniformly over the survey area, probably because of the absence of large-scale hydrodynamic features to concentrate them in any part of the region. The mean biomass and density of the 1304 swarms encountered were estimated by multi-channel echo location to be 0.139 tonnes and 31 g m^{-3} respectively. Ninety-eight percent of the swarms were estimated to have weighed less than 1 tonne. Most of the biomass was concentrated a few large swarms. This agrees with data from the Antarctic Peninsula and Scotia Sea regions between 1976 and 1979 (J. Kalinowski, pers. commun., quoted in Miller & Hampton, 1989) where 66% of all swarms detected had a biomass of less than 1 tonne.

In addition to acoustic estimates various estimates, of swarm density have been made directly either visually or photographically (Guzman & Marin, 1983), or indirectly

from catches in commercial trawls or various types of research nets. Underwater photographic estimates have given krill densities of 50000–60000 m^{-3} (Ragulin, 1969), and up to 550 individuals m^{-3} (Guzman & Marin, 1983). Density estimates from commercial catches and net-sampling of visible swarms exceed acoustically derived estimates by at least two orders of magnitude. Miller & Hampton (1989) consider that while no conclusive explanation of this discrepancy can be offered at present, it should be noted that non-acoustic estimates could be biased towards larger and denser swarms (cf. discussion in Hampton (1985) and Nicol *et al.* (1987)). It is possible that the true densities fall somewhere between the acoustically and indirectly derived estimates but exactly where has yet to be determined.

5.4.3.2 Super-swarms

Particular interest in krill aggregation behaviour in recent years has focused on the rare occurrence of ultra-large (over 1 km across) aggregations containing very large number of animals, which have been termed 'super-swarms' (Cram *et al.*, 1979). Super-swarm have been reported from the Gerlache Strait (Cram *et al.*, 1979), off South Georgia (Kalinowski & Witek, 1982), off Enderby Land (Kanda *et al.*, 1982), and near Elephant Island (Mathisen & Macaulay, 1983; Macaulay *et al.*, 1984). They have been reported as being up to several kilometres long and 100 to 200 m thick in places. Densities also tend to be high (in the order of a few hundred grams per cubic metre on average), according to Kalinowski & Witek (1982, 1983), Mathisen & Macaulay (1983) and Macaulay *et al.* (1984). They also appear to be able to sustain their integrity for several days at least (Kalinowski & Witek, 1982, 1983, 1985; Kanda *et al.*, 1982; Antezana & Ray, 1983; Macaulay *et al.*, 1984).

The biomass of krill in such super-swarms may be very high. For example Macaulay *et al.* (1984) estimated from acoustic measurements that the biomass of a super-swarm covering an area of about 450 km near

Elephant Island during FIBEX was 2.1 million tonnes. However, the BIOMASS Acoustic Working Party (Anon., 1986) substantially revised the acoustic target strength expression used for the estimate and the use of this revised expression would reduce the estimate to about 200 000 tonnes. Nevertheless, this would still be a very high biomass for a single krill aggregation.

5.4.3.3 Layers and other scattered forms
Layers and other scattered forms are diffuse aggregations which often may extend many kilometres at least in one direction, and which appear on echo-sounding recordings as thin layers (Fig. 5.9*d*), or at other times as clouds or diffuse smudges of far greater vertical extent (Fig. 5.9*c*). According to Kalinowski & Witek (1982, 1983) their density is generally low (in the order of 10 g m⁻³), which distinguishes them from the high-density super-swarms. Thin layers have been found by both day and night (Cram *et al.*, 1979; Kalinowski & Witek, 1982, 1983), whereas broad layers appear to be formed by the dispersal of day-time swarms (Everson, 1982; Kalinowski & Witek, 1982, 1983).

5.4.3.4 Irregular forms
Kalinowski & Witek (1982, 1985) distinguish between swarms with well-defined boundaries and larger irregular aggregations with poorly defined boundaries, and with variations in density (Fig. 5.9*b*). They reported that such aggregations are typically tens of metres thick, and vary in density between a few and several hundred grams per cubic metre. A distinguishing feature is that they are often multi-specific, containing other macroplankton species such as *Thermisto* sp., *Thysanoessa* sp. and salps (cf. Kalinowski & Witek, 1985; Schulenberger *et al.*, 1984).

The relative proportions of krill that are present in compact swarms or in dispersed form are debatable. However, it appears that the major proportion of the krill in any one area is concentrated in swarms (Miller, 1986a). Cram *et al.* (1979) found that in the Gerlache Strait 82% of the krill was concentrated in swarms (particularly in a few super-swarms), while in the Scotia Sea the proportion was 47%. The corresponding proportions in layers were 5.5 and 51.5% respectively.

5.4.4 Biological characteristics of aggregations

5.4.4.1 Homogeneity
From the available data from research and commercial catches it would appear that most krill aggregations are mono-specific (e.g. Marr, 1962; Everson, 1977b; Lubimova *et al.*, 1982), although as noted above this may

not be true for irregular aggregations. Schulenberger *et al.* (1984) have investigated the composition of a super-swarm of krill studied by Macaulay *et al.* (1984) and Brinton & Antezana (1984) near Elephant Island. They found that the large swarm was not composed entirely of euphausiids. Large fractions of many of the samples consisted of copepods, amphipods and salps. The euphausiid fraction of the super-swarm did not consist entirely of *E. superba*. In many samples *E. superba* were outnumbered by *E. crystallorophias* and/or *Thysanoessa* species. However, *E. superba* dominated in terms of biomass, because of its larger size. Larvae of *E. superba* and *Thysanoessa* spp. co-occurred. There was some evidence for separation of high concentrations of larvae from high concentrations of adults, with the separation occurring both vertically and horizontally.

The age and sex composition of krill swarm are variable. Swarms may consist exclusively of groups restricted in terms of size, age or sex (e.g. one or two successive larval stages, or of a single sex) in contrast to other swarms of mixed size and age groups and mixed sexes. Watkins (1986) found significant differences in the length distributions of krill taken from adjacent swarms, whereas length distributions in samples taken from the same swarm were not significantly different. In a subsequent study Watkins *et al.* (1986) found extensive heterogeneity in the length, sex ratio, moulting condition and gut fullness of krill taken in 28 discrete aggregations.

5.4.4.2 Swimming
Swimming activity is an integral part of aggregation behaviour. Hamner (1984) estimated that krill in orientated swarms could swim rapidly (with speeds of up to 20 cm s⁻¹) for considerable distances. He suggested that animals in such swarms maintained communication by rheotactic cues generated by the individuals above and ahead of them. This would ensure coordinated swimming in the dark. The swimming speeds in the wild were consistent with those measured in the laboratory.

Observations made by Kanda *et al.* (1982) off Enderby Land showed that moving swarms can stay together for long periods while covering considerable distances. They tracked one super-swarm for 18 days over a distance of 116 nautical miles, and another for a distance of 45 miles over 8 days. The average speeds were approximately 15 and 13 cm s⁻¹ respectively. Both swarms moved south against the prevailing current, as indicated by the drift of nearby icebergs. The swimming speeds are consistent with those recorded by Hamner (1984) and are close to the figure of 13 cm s⁻¹ for the maximum speed which krill can maintain without exceeding their 'standard' (i.e. hovering) metabolism.

5.4.4.3 Orientation

With a rare exception, swarming animals observed by Ragulin (1969) and Hamner *et al.* (1983) were orientated parallel to each other, even at night. Hamner *et al.* (1983) consider that parallel orientation of swarming krill is indicative of active foraging and is incompatible with intensive feeding, and this is supported by the observation that krill were feeding rapidly in the only non-orientated swarm which they observed. Underwater photography of swarming krill by Guzman & Marin (1983) showed predominantly parallel orientation, except in the early morning and at night when the orientation was more random. They suggested that the latter behaviour might be typical of nighttime feeding.

5.4.4.4 Feeding

While the connection between feeding and aggregating behaviour has been intensively studied the results are somewhat conflicting. Pavlov (1969) suggested that swarming is primarily related to foraging and considered, as did other investigators (e.g. Shust, 1969; Nakamura, 1973; Gubsch, 1979; Everson & Ward, 1980), that krill do not feed in swarms since food is likely to be limited. These authors therefore assumed that diel patterns in aggregation and dispersion were associated with diel patterns in feeding activity. However, recent evidence has accumulated to suggest that krill can, and do, feed actively in swarms (Miller & Hampton, 1989). This evidence will be considered further in section 5.6.5.

5.4.4.5 Moulting

Laboratory experiments by Mackintosh (1967), A. Clarke (1976) and Buchholz (1985) have established that krill may moult synchronously. Buchholz also found evidence of synchronous moulting in the wild. He concluded that synchronous moulting was a natural feature of krill swarms and also suggested that there may be a tendency for krill in a particular moult stage to aggregate, possibly as a result in differences in swimming speeds between moulting and non-moulting individuals. Hamner *et al.* (1983) observed individual krill leaving a swarm to moult and also observed synchronous moulting in a swarm disturbed by a diver. They speculated that the discarded moults could act as decoys for predators thus making it advantageous for moulting krill in the same state to swarm together.

5.4.4.6 Reproduction

As mentioned above krill swarms are often dominated by one sex, or one particular maturity stage (e.g. Marr, 1962; Everson, 1977b; Anon. 1981a). It has therefore been suggested that reproductive behaviour may influence aggregating behaviour or, alternatively, that close proximity of individuals in swarms may play an important role in mating and/or spawning (Miller & Hampton, 1989). While it has been postulated that certain krill swarms, especially those in specific areas associated with particular topographic features, constitute spawning or breeding aggregations (Marr, 1962; Naumov, 1962; Makarov, 1973, 1979a; Kock & Stein, 1978) the relationships between swarming and reproduction are not at all clear. Naito *et al.* (1986) observed mating in association with swarming and concluded that a single pair of mating krill can stimulate other animals in a swarm to mate. However, the male:female ratio in swarms can vary considerably, e.g. from 1:3 to 4:1 in one study (Watkins *et al.*, 1986) and 1:1.5 to 1.47:1 in another (Siegel, 1986a). Quentin & Ross (1984) found that while gravid females were present in most discrete swarms sampled they were dominant in only a few swarms and concluded that females do not have to dominate a swarm to produce eggs.

5.4.4.7 Interactions with predators

While there is much indirect evidence (based on records of diving patterns) to suggest that seals and some penguin species feed on krill swarms mainly at night (e.g. Croxall *et al.*, 1985; Doidge & Croxall, 1985; Kooyman *et al.*, 1986) there have been only a limited number of direct observations of predators feeding on krill in the field.

Some of the models outlined below are based on the assumption that the gregarious behaviour of krill confers greater defence against predators. They assume that predators have greater difficulty in locating patchy prey, that rapid satiation occurs once the patches are located (Brock & Riffenberg, 1960) and that they may be distracted or confused making the capture of prey more difficult (Cerri & Fraser, 1983). However, as Antezana & Ray (1983) point out this would not apply to whales as 'mass' predators. Much more information is needed on the strategies used by various predators (cephalopods, fishes, birds, seals, whales and some benthic invertebrates) and the behaviour of krill in avoiding predators.

5.4.5 Factors influencing aggregation

Factors which influence aggregation patterns include light, physiological stimuli, phytoplankton (i.e. food) concentration, and a range of hydrographic mechanisms. Mauchline (1980a) considers that aggregation is probably achieved by several or all of the following processes rather than by any one in isolation: (a) the innate drive towards aggregation, triggered in some populations by the attainment of a physiological condition, e.g. approaching sexual maturity; (b) the physical and chemical discontinuities and gradients in the environment in conjunction with

Table 5.3. *Vertical migration of some Southern Ocean euphausiids*

Species	Day depth range (m)	Night depth range (m)	Total vertical range (m)
Euphausia superba	100–10	70–0	900–0
Euphausia frigida	500–250	100–50	750–0
Euphausia tricantha	500–250	250–0	750–0

From Mauchline & Fisher (1969).

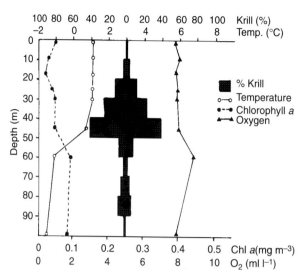

Fig. 5.10. Vertical profiles of krill abundance, temperature, chlorophyll *a* and dissolved oxygen at a typical station during the MVSA. *Agulhas* krill survey in the Southern Ocean between 15° E and 30° E. Krill abundance profiles were constructed from underway echo-sounder data interfaced with a digital echo integrator data 50 km on each side of the station position. Redrawn from Hampton (1985).

the physiology of the species population, resulting in the population having a restricted distribution (this situation produces populations in which the threshold densities that trigger the formation of shoals and swarms occur); (c) visual clues in the presence of threshold densities; (d) chemical cues in the presence of threshold densities which may be an order of magnitude less than the densities active for visual cues; and (e) mechano-reception by individuals, probably assuming greatest importance in maintaining and structuring shoals and swarms.

5.4.5.1 *Light and diurnal variations*

Euphausiids in general have well developed vision and it might be expected that they would respond actively to light (Mauchline & Fisher, 1969) and thus exhibit vertical migration patterns. Many observers (e.g. Marr, 1962; Witek *et al.*, 1981; Everson, 1982; Anon., 1986) have found changes in size, density, and depth of aggregations with time of day. The most common feature which emerges from these studies is the tendency for euphausiids to migrate towards the surface and disperse at night, although such behaviour is by no means consistent and regular (Table 5.3). Several species of Southern Ocean euphausiids have shown diurnal vertical migration patterns. Two species, *E. frigida* and *E. tricantha*, exhibit a definite migration pattern which would take them from the warm deep water in the daytime to the surface water at night. However, the situation for *E. superba* is less clear since although this species does migrate vertically it is only on rare occasions that a definite migration pattern has been detected (see Marr, 1962; Mohr, 1976; Fischer & Mohr, 1978).

5.4.5.2 *Physiological stimuli*

The question as to whether rhythmic changes in krill aggregation behaviour could be induced by physiological or other intrinsic rhythms, as distinct from behavioral responses to external factors, has yet to be resolved. Miller & Hampton (1989) point out that the results from field and laboratory studies are not consistent with strict physiological or intrinsic control over feeding and aggre-

gation since they do not show regular periodicity in either of these activities.

5.4.5.3 *Phytoplankton concentration*

There is little specific information on the influence of phytoplankton concentration and availability on krill aggregation behaviour. In laboratory studies Antezana *et al.* (1982) showed that krill can feed over a wide range of phytoplankton densities. While Weber (1984) and Weber & El-Sayed (1985a) found correlations between phytoplankton and swarm biomass the results were somewhat ambiguous because of the lack of suitable time-course information. Orientated swimming has been observed in both clear water and in the midst of a dense phytoplankton bloom (Hamner *et al.*, 1983) and this would perhaps indicate the absence of a causal link between aggregation and phytoplankton density.

5.4.5.4 *Hydrographic factors*

Rakusa-Suszczeswki (1978), Witek *et al.* (1981) and Weber & El-Sayed (1985a) have all investigated the influence of various physical and chemical factors (e.g. temperature, salinity, oxygen concentration, and concentrations of various nutrients) on krill horizontal distribution, but all failed to find any direct association between such factors and krill aggregation. There is, however, some evidence to indicate that vertical stratification of water properties (e.g. temperature and oxygen concentration) may influence aggregation by causing krill to concentrate at certain depths. Hampton (1985) found that krill tended to be most abundant near the top of the thermocline (Fig. 5.10). Since chlorophyll *a* concentrations were always greatest below the thermocline, it seems unlikely that this behaviour was directly related to food density.

5.4.6 Models of aggregation

5.4.6.1 Introduction
As detailed below (see section 5.6.5) euphausiids, especially *E. superba*, tend to disperse while feeding and to re-aggregate after feeding. Swarms also actively migrate horizontally in search of food. Dispersion and aggregation suggests that communication between individuals is maintained. From work carried out to date it is clear that the formation and dispersal of swarms in krill is a complex process brought about by patterns of vertical migration, responses to environmental gradients, responses to predation, and by hydrographic features. Most of the models that have been developed have concentrated on the interaction between feeding and aggregation/dispersal. In such models, feeding state is the proximate cause of aggregation or dispersal, while aggregation itself is thought to improve the feeding efficiency of the aggregation and ultimately the survival, growth and reproduction of the population.

5.4.6.2 Models
Pavlov (1969) was the first to advance a model linking feeding and aggregation. He stated that krill feed in dispersed aggregations near the surface where phytoplankton is abundant. When replete, the animals form into swarms and migrate downwards, remaining in swarms until they ascend to feed again.

Hamner and his co-workers (Hamner *et al.*, 1983; Hamner, 1984) proposed that krill actively search for food in compact orientated swarms (maintained by rheotactic cues). No feeding takes place during this search phase but when a patch of food is located the animals engage in bouts of rapid feeding during which the swarm structure is disrupted and a slow-moving aggregation develops. Hamner *et al.* (1983) suggested that this pattern of alternate foraging and intensive feeding when suitable food conditions are found promotes the efficient use of a patchily distributed food resource. This then is the ultimate beneficial effect of swarming. However, such a pattern is by no means universal.

Antezana & Ray (1983, 1984) combined laboratory-based information on feeding behaviour designed to test the hypothesis that feeding and swarming are mutually exclusive events (Antezana *et al.*, 1982; see also section 5.6.5) with field data to produce a model of

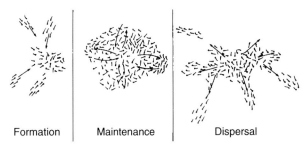

Formation   Maintenance   Dispersal

Fig. 5.11. Dynamics of feeding aggregations of *Euphausia superba*. *Formation*: 1. Detection and encounter of feeding grounds by small schools of solitary individuals; and 2. Horizontal migration and assemblage into larger feeding groups. *Maintenance*: Feeding in large semi-stationary swarms until the depletion of the resources. Individuals are randomly orientated to one another and moving to and from the periphery. *Dispersal*: 1. Disbandment of large feeding swarms into small foraging schools composed of individuals with parallel orientation and unidirectional motion; and 2. foraging is associated with horizontal and vertical diel migrations until they encounter of new feeding grounds. From Antezana & Ray (1983).

feeding and swarming based on the principles of optimal foraging theory (Pyke *et al.*, 1977). The widespread occurrence of swarming in zooplankton (Omori, 1978) suggests a variety of adaptive strategies for aggregation behaviour. By analogy with schooling fishes, these include minimized predator detection and rapid predator satiation once schools (or swarms) are encountered (Brock & Riffenberg, 1960).

Antezana & Ray (1983) hypothesized that small foraging schools locate feeding groups, and assemble into large-scale aggregations, where feeding occurs in semi-stationary swarms until the depletion of the food resource, whereupon the swarm disengages into small schools, where foraging is associated with horizontal migration and vertical diel migration. In Fig. 5.11 the dynamics of feeding aggregation in *E. superba* is subdivided into three stages, formation, maintenance and dispersal.

This is contrary to the model proposed by Pavlov (1969) and discussed above, where it was suggested that krill dispersed to feed and swarmed only on repletion. This has not been supported by recent laboratory experiments (Antezana *et al.*, 1982) and field observations (Antezana & Ray, 1983, 1984; Hamner, 1984). These authors showed that krill at aggregation densities similar to those encountered in the field (*c*. 2000–5000 individuals m^{-3}) fed at elevated rates in the laboratory, and had elevated stomach contents and rapid ingestion rates in swarms in the field.

In contrast to the models discussed above, Witek *et al.* (1982a, 1988) have proposed one that does not involve feeding (Fig. 5.12). They point out that there are numerous publications linking the formation of large krill con-

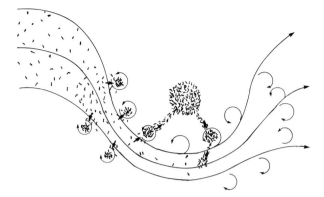

Fig. 5.12. Schematic representation of the processes whereby krill may accumulate in current meanders: long arrows represent the direction of the prevailing current flow; short arrows represent the direction of krill movement; short black lines show the position of individual krill. Redrawn from Witek *et al.* (1982a).

centrations and the circulation of water masses (e.g. Marr, 1962; Makarov *et al.*, 1970; Elizarov, 1971; Maslennikov, 1972). The connection between the occurrence of commercial krill concentrations and eddies and fronts has been pointed out by Wolnomeijski *et al.* (1978), and Witek *et al.* (1982a) suggested that water circulation patterns cause the inflow of krill into an area where specific reactions to turbulent water flow combined with social behaviour serve to maintain and concentrate the swarms. In large stabilized currents where the water flow is laminar krill are dispersed. Here, swarms are small and large quantities of krill are dispersed outside the swarms. In regions of meanders and eddies there is increased turbulence and high gradients of current velocity, and the krill react in such a way that they tend to concentrate in quiescent regions, which are most likely to exist in the centre of localized areas and current meanders, which develop on either side of the strong flow (Fig. 5.12).

5.5 Distribution and abundance

5.5.1 Introduction

In this section an attempt is made to summarize recent data on krill distribution and abundance, methods of estimating abundance, factors controlling krill distribution, and the question as to whether the Southern Ocean krill constitute a single stock or series of stocks. The starting point is Everson's (1977b) review of the living resources of the Southern Ocean. There have been several substantive reviews of krill distribution and behaviour (e.g. Mackintosh, 1972, 1973; Everson, 1977b; Lubimova *et al.*, 1984; Bengtson, 1984), the broad-scale oceanography of the krill's habitat (e.g. Deacon, 1937; Ostapoff,

1965; Treshnikov *et al.*, 1978; D. J. Baker, 1979; Forster, 1981, 1984; Amos, 1984; Hellmer *et al.*, 1985; Anon. 1985a), and correlations between the hydrography and biological productivity of Antarctic waters in general (e.g. Jaragov, 1969; Knox, 1970, 1983; Everson, 1977b; Tranter, 1982; Deacon, 1982, 1984a; Amos, 1984; Hempel, 1985a,b).

The determination of the distribution patterns and abundances of Antarctic euphausiids, and in particular krill, is extremely difficult. In the past there have been numerous attempts to estimate the overall biomass of krill in the Southern Ocean but such estimates have little relevance in an ecological sense. Abundance estimates are complicated by krill's aggregation behaviour (see section 5.4). As we have seen krill can on occasions form very large swarms or super-swarms, in which a large proportion of the local population may be concentrated. Swarms also vary enormously in size, shape and density of individuals. This makes it difficult to sample the krill using a series of stations along transect lines. The chance encounter of one or more large swarms may alter biomass estimates for an area by an order of magnitude or more.

While the broad-scale distribution patterns of Antarctic euphausiids are known as a result of the work of the *Discovery* Expeditions (Marr, 1962; Mackintosh, 1972) and that of Russian scientists (Lubimova *et al.*, 1984) we still have much to learn about the finer details of krill distribution, especially on a seasonal basis. The situation is further complicated by the year-to-year variations which can occur in krill distribution and abundance (see Chapter 15).

5.5.2 Standing stock estimation

5.5.2.1 Introduction

Various techniques have been used or proposed for estimating the abundance of krill. Attempts have been made to estimate krill total standing stocks indirectly from estimates of predator consumption, primary production, and the assumed surplus arising from the large decline in the large baleen whale stocks. Such estimates have been summarized in Knox (1970, 1983), Everson (1977b), Lubimova *et al.* (1984) and Lillo & Guzman (1982). Table 5.4 shows some of these estimates. There are large uncertainties surrounding these arising from major sources of errors in the various conversion factors used and the fact that the authors have made little attempt to place error limits on their estimates, or to examine the assumptions upon which they are based. While there is a wide range of figures for standing stock given in Table 5.4 even the more conservative estimates indicate that the

Table 5.4. *Some indirect estimates of total krill standing stock*

Estimate (t×10⁶)	Method	Source
750	Estimate of total secondary production: krill taken as 50% of total herbivorous zooplankton	Gulland (1970)
5000–7000	As above	Moiseev (1970)
305–1200	Primary production	Knox (1983)
953–1350	Primary production	Makarov & Shevtsov (1972)
(14–277)	From estimates (Gulland, 1970) of total annual production (109 tonnes) assuming phytoplankton/euphausiid conversion ratios of between 10:1 and 40:1, and that krill comprise between 10% and 50% of total herbivorous zooplankton	Everson (1977b)
(>111)	Total present-day predator consumption	Everson (1977b)
(>71)	Potential 'surplus' from whale decline (estimaed at 147 million tonnes)	Laws (1977b)
(>55)	As above (surplus estimated at 100 million tonnes)	Moiseev (1970)

After Miller & Hampton (1989).

standing stock is very large for a marine invertebrate species.

5.5.2.2 Net sampling

A variety of nets have been used for sampling krill. The desired qualities of these nets have been discussed in several BIOMASS documents (e.g. Mauchline, 1980b) and bongo nets and rectangular mid-water trawls (RMTs) have been recommended as standard krill sampling nets. Unfortunately, there are also certain problems, or disadvantages, associated with net sampling (Everson, 1983). There is firstly gear selectivity, the mesh size used introducing a bias into the size frequency distribution of the catch, and secondly net avoidance. Large krill being more powerful swimmers are more able to avoid sampling nets than small krill. The problem of avoidance is a complicated one dependent upon the effect of the towing wire and bridle in front of the net mouth, mesh size, colour of the net, towing speed and time of day. In addition to the bias resulting from the sampling nets used, net-based estimates of mean density can be expected to be very inexact because of the krill's contiguous distribution. Miller & Hampton (1989) concluded that: 'Given the potentially large biases, the high variances and the relatively small areas covered, we conclude that density estimates from plankton nets are of little real value in estimating global abundance.'

5.5.2.3 Acoustic surveys

Increased sophistication, coupled with reliability, has meant that hydroacoustics has become a recognized and standard method for estimating fish abundance. Hence, during the BIOMASS programme a concerted effort was made to test the suitability of hydroacoustic techniques for estimating krill abundance (Anon., 1980). The hydroacoustic method has several distinct advantages (Everson, 1983). Firstly, the time delay between the transmission pulse and the return echo can be measured very accurately thus giving a fine depth discrimination. Secondly, large areas can be surveyed in a comparatively short time compared to net sampling, which is very time consuming. Thirdly, because the pulse repetition frequency is quite high sampling along a transect is effectively complete. Unfortunately, there are also a number of difficulties. Firstly, the technique cannot discriminate between euphausiid species, or the life-history stages of krill. Hence, this must be determined by net hauls aimed at specific targets. Secondly, the effective depth range is limited to about 120 m, and due to the use of downward directed transducers there is an unsampled layer from the surface to about 10 m. Thirdly, in order to convert the acoustic data into abundance measures a scaling factor, the target strength (TS), is required (Anon., 1986). While in principle acoustic techniques can give rapid and direct estimates of density over a wide area, the accuracy of such estimates is determined by sampling variance, systematic errors (particularly from inaccurate calibration and errors in the expression used to estimate target strength from length), and bias arising from failure to detect part of the population (Miller & Hampton, 1989).

During the FIBEX (1981), SIBEX I (1983) and SIBEX II (1984) (First and Second International BIOMASS Experiments) phases of BIOMASS (Anon., 1980, 1981a, 1982, 1986) systematic echo-integrator surveys were made in selected areas of the Southern Ocean. The most

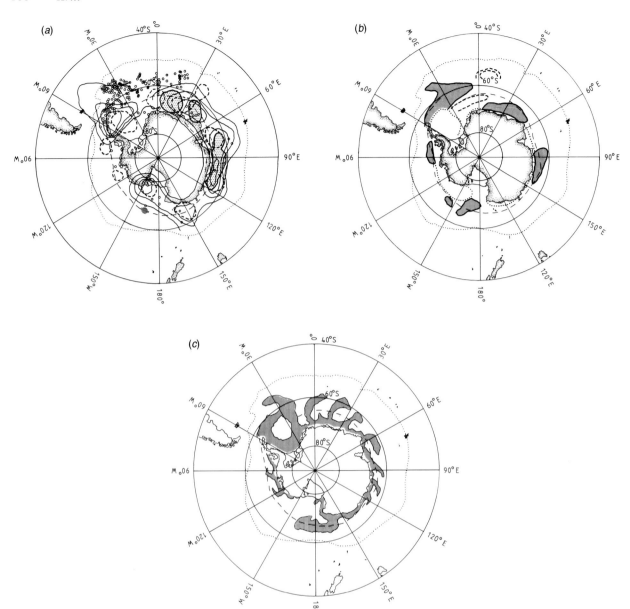

Fig. 5.13. Large scale concentrations of krill in the Southern Ocean. (*a*) Based on Amos (1985), after Jarogov (1969). Circles are Marr's (1962) major krill concentrations; stippled areas show krill concentrations, based on data from Canadian sources; small black areas are krill concentrations as found by Russian expeditions up to 1969; dotted and unbroken contours are overlying 'cyclonic activity' (contour values unknown). Location of the Antarctic Convergence (dotted line) and northern limit of the East Wind Drift (dashed line) are shown. (*b*) According to Mackintosh (1973). Dark areas are 'stocks' of krill; determined mainly from pre-1940 *Discovery* observations; heavy dashed lines (———) enclose low-density regions east of the Weddell Sea; heavy dotted line (•••) is the maximum (March) extent of the sea ice. Location of the Antarctic Convergence (light dotted line, ...) and the northern limit of the East Wind Drift (light dashed line, – – –) are shown. Redrawn after Amos (1985). (*c*) According to Maslennikov (1980). Dark areas are hypothetical patterns of krill and zooplankton concentrations from Soviet data. Location of the Antarctic Convergence (dotted line) and the northern limit of the East Wind Drift (dashed line) are shown. Redrawn from Amos (1985).

comprehensive of these was in FIBEX during which eleven ships from ten nations surveyed four sectors in the West Atlantic and Indian Oceans. From joint analyses of the integrator data (Anon., 1981a; Hampton, 1983; Anon., 1986) total krill biomass was assessed and the survey variance estimated (Table 5.1). While it is difficult to extrapolate the results to the Southern Ocean as a whole two such attempts have given figures of 41 million tonnes (Miller & Hampton, 1989) and 25 million tonnes, values

which are substantially lower than the most conservative indirect estimates from predator consumption rates (see section 5.7.4).

5.5.2.4 Conclusions

In a recent paper Everson (1988) posed the question: 'Can we satisfactorily estimate variation in krill abundance?', and concluded that the answer must be '*no*' because although we can estimate variation within each sampling method, there is no information to indicate how these estimates relate to total krill abundance over the Southern Ocean as a whole. However, despite all the uncertainties, attempts to estimate krill standing stock directly have narrowed the possible range of estimates that previously had been inferred (Miller & Hampton, 1989). It is unlikely that the mean summer standing stock is either as low as the lowest estimate in Table 5.4 or in excess of 1000 million tonnes. It can be concluded that typically the stock size in summer is probably in the order of hundreds of millions of tonnes – an exceptionally high biomass by global standards.

5.5.3 General distribution patterns
There are many papers which outline in general terms the distribution of krill in the Southern Ocean, in particular those arising from the *Discovery* Expeditions and from the studies of the numerous Russian expeditions. These have been summarized by Marr (1962), Makarov *et al.* (1970), Mackintosh (1972), Voronina (1972, 1974), Everson (1976, 1977b), Maslennikov (1980), Lubimova (1983), Makarov (1983a), Lubimova *et al.* (1984) and Amos (1984). Further information is to be found in the reports of the FIBEX acoustic surveys (Hampton, 1983; Anon. 1986) and in a recent account of Japanese commercial catches (Shimadzu, 1984a). However, because of the size of the area involved and the problems of sampling krill quantitatively, there is still a great deal of uncertainty about important details

Around the Antarctic continent krill postlarval forms are distributed between the Antarctic Continent and the Antarctic Convergence. There is universal agreement that they are most abundant in the East Wind Drift, the Scotia Sea, the Weddell Drift, round South Georgia, in the vicinity of the Kerguelen–Gaussberg Ridge and north of the Ross Sea (Marr, 1962; Nemoto, 1972; Mackintosh, 1973; Everson 1977b). Three views of krill distribution are given in Fig. 5.13: those of Amos (1985) (Fig. 5.13*a*), Mackintosh (1973) (Fig. 5.13*b*), and Maslennikov (1980) (Fig. 5.13*c*). All show a series of circular, elliptical or eddylike patches ringing the Antarctic Continent. Some coincide with major gyres known from hydrographic studies, the ones of most importance in krill distribution being the those in the Weddell Sea, the east Atlantic and the Ross Sea. In the Indian and Pacific Oceans, krill seem to be concentrated in the East Wind Drift, particularly in the vicinity of the Antarctic Divergence (Marr, 1962; Voronina, 1968; Nasu, 1983: Lubimova *et al.*, 1984, Amos, 1984). It would appear from Soviet and Japanese commercial catches (Lubimova *et al.*, 1984; Shimadzu, 1984a,b), plankton net samples (Marr, 1962) and whaling records (Mackintosh, 1973) that krill abundances in the

Pacific Sector is substantially less than in other areas. By far the greatest concentrations of krill occur in the Scotia Sea–Weddell Drift area, and this is the region that has been most intensively studied. In the Scotia Sea an important feature is the confluence between the Pacific Water of the West Wind Drift and the Weddell Sea Water in the Weddell Gyre. Bogdanov *et al.* (1980) described this and his conclusions have been supported by Gordon & Goldberg (1970) and Mackintosh (1972). Areas of divergence and eddy formation would be important mechanisms in maintaining the observed distribution patterns.

5.5.4 Factors affecting distribution
Many theories have been proposed to explain the observed distribution patterns of krill (see Marr, 1962; Mackintosh, 1972, 1973; Everson, 1977b; Amos, 1984) and some of these have been discussed in the previous section. Practically all of these attempt to explain large-scale distributional patterns in terms of water circulatory effects on the larvae and/or postlarvae. As we have seen the major circulatory features of the eastward-flowing West Wind Drift, or Antarctic Circumpolar Current, the East Wind Drift and the cyclonic Weddell Gyre to the west of the Antarctic Peninsula are the main features maintaining the observed asymmetrical circumpolar krill distribution (Marr, 1962; Mackintosh, 1972, 1973; Everson, 1977b; Deacon, 1979, 1983).

Recent studies have emphasized the importance of gyres and eddies in the region of the divergence zone between the East and West Wind Drifts. Such features, which vary considerably in size and life span, must result in the exchange of krill between the East and West Wind Drifts (Maslennikov, 1980; Lubimova *et al.*, 1984). Large-scale, topographically induced gyres have been identified in the surface waters north and east of the Ross Sea, east of the Kerguelen Plateau, north of Prydz Bay and in the Lasarev Sea (e.g. Trechnikov, 1964; Treshnikov *et al.*, 1978; Makarov & Solyankin, 1982; Amos, 1984; N. R. Smith *et al.*, 1984; Anon., 1984a). These gyres plus the Weddell Gyre coincide to a large degree with the distribution of Mackintosh's proposed krill stocks (see Fig. 5.13*b*), and with the general distribution of Soviet commercial krill catches (Lubimova *et al.*, 1984).

Fig. 5.14 depicts the distribution of water temperatures at 50 m off Enderby Land along with the Catch Per Unit Effort (CPUE) from Japanese commercial krill trawlers (Nasu, 1974). It is clear that the krill are concentrated in a area of about 15 miles N/S and 25 miles E/W, where a strong meandering isotherm and evidence of small eddy formation were observed. The location of these krill concentrations corresponds with the southern limit of the

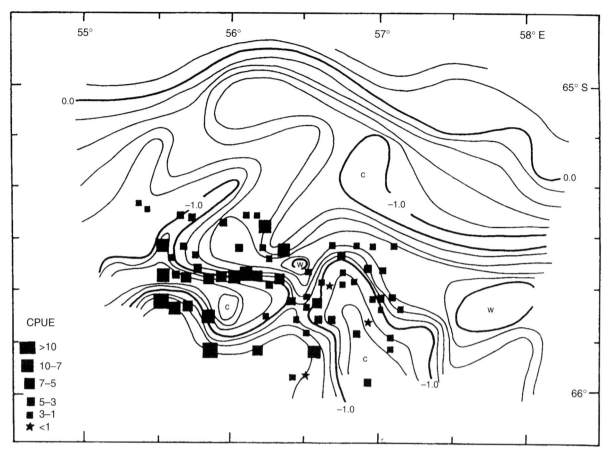

Fig. 5.14. Distribution of water temperatures at 50 m off Enderby and together with Catch Per Unit Effort (CPUE) from Japanese commercial trawlers c=cold, w=warm. Redrawn from Nasu (1974).

Warm Deep Water where the Antarctic Divergence occurs. Here upwelling deep water brings nutrient salts to the surface. According to Nasu (1974) the major krill concentrations are to be found in meandering oceanic fronts and cyclonic or anti-cyclonic circulation south of the Antarctic Convergence.

Sea ice cover appears to be an important factor influencing the distribution of krill (Marr, 1962; Mackintosh, 1972, 1973; Nast, 1982; Guzman, 1983). In their study of the abundance and distribution of krill in the ice edge zone of the Weddell Sea Daly & Macaulay (1988) found that the vertical depth distribution of *E. superba* under the pack ice was similar to that of the open water. Average krill biomass under the ice ranged from 1 to 68 g m^{-3} while in open water it ranged from 10 to 100 g m^{-3}. However the pack ice directly influenced the distribution of young krill. Juveniles were much more abundant under the ice than in the open water north of the ice edge. Numerous observations were made of juvenile krill feeding on the microalgae on the undersurfaces of the ice floes. Evidence collected during the Winter Weddell Sea Project 1986 (G. Hempel, 1988)

indicated that the bulk of the krill population was located in the pack ice zone during the winter. There is ample evidence (Marr, 1962; Mackintosh, 1972: Guzman, 1983; Heywood *et al.*, 1985; Siegel, 1989) to postulate that extensive seasonal horizontal migration of krill is a yearly occurrence.

5.5.5 Overwintering strategies

Until recently *E. superba*, unlike other euphausiids, which are characterized by versatile feeding behaviour, was widely regarded as being totally dependent upon phytoplanktonic food (Mauchline & Fisher, 1969). The generally accepted picture of *E. superba* as an active (Kils, 1981), swarm-forming (Hamner *et al.*, 1983), filter-feeding herbivore (Mauchline & Fisher, 1969; Boyd *et al.*, 1984), with a high respiration rate (Kils, 1981), restricted in its adult phase to the upper 200 m water layer (Mauchline & Fisher, 1969), is in reality true only in the summer in ice-free habitats (Smetacek *et al.*, 1990). There had been much speculation, without hard evidence, as to how *E. superba* survived during the winter when phytoplankton stocks were severely depleted.

Table 5.5. *Comparison of CPUE and independent survey estimates of krill abundance during the same months for CCAMLR sub-area 48.1*

Date	Location of study	Biomass (t)	Density published (g$(\times10^3$ m$)^{-3}$)	Density estimated[1] (g m^{-2})	CPUE (Japan)	Source
Acoustic surveys (FRG)						
Oct./Nov. 1983	SIBEX I	51 680	7.2	0.72	10.25, 13.75	Klindt (1986)
Nov./Dec. 1984	SIBEX II	379 750	54.8	5.48	— 1.06	Klindt (1986)
Mar./Apr. 1985	SIBEX II	16 490	2.59	0.26	(9.46 Feb.)	Klindt (1986)
Net haul surveys (FRG)						
Oct./Nov. 1983	SIBEX I	723 000	103.18	10.32	10.25, 13.75	Nast (1986)
Nov./Dec. 1984	SIBEX II	252 000	36.01	3.60	— 1.06	Nast (1986)
Mar./Apr.	SIBEX II	164 000	23.39	2.34	(9.46 Feb.)	Nast (1986)

Data from Miller & Hampton (1989).
[1]assumes 1 t per nautical square mile = 0.292 g m^{-2}. All values assume a depth range of 100 m.

Ikeda & Dixon (1982b) observed that krill shrank when starved and proposed that body shrinkage, as a result of a food-depleted environment, may aid in the survival of krill during the Antarctic winter. However, Ikeda (1985) has re-examined his earlier negative growth model, which predicted that body shrinkage should prohibit krill from attaining body lengths greater than 45 mm. Krill up to 60 mm in body length are regularly found indicating that food must be available during the winter period. Such food resources could include copepods or the cryopelagic invertebrates associated with the under-ice water layer, the sea ice microalgae, or, in shallow waters, the benthic microalgae.

As discussed in section 5.6.3 krill are omnivorous and potentially can feed on other zooplankton species, especially copepods. While Price *et al.* (1988) found in their experimental work that krill could feed very efficiently on copepods they concluded that such feeding would meet less than 10% of their minimum metabolic requirements at the 'typical' copepod concentrations reported for Antarctic waters. However, it is possible that the large concentrations of copepod developmental stages which have been reported associated with the bottom layer of the sea ice and the platelet ice layer where it occurs (Fukuchi & Tanimura, 1981; Fukuchi *et al.* 1985b; Hoshiai *et al.*, 1987; Waghorn & Knox, 1989) could provide a substantially greater potential prey resource.

Recent studies (Garrison *et al.*, 1986; Marschall, 1988; Stretch *et al.*, 1988) have documented widespread feeding by krill on sea ice microalgae. Marschall (1988) found that in winter in the Weddell Sea krill were scarce in the water column with densities of 2–4 individuals m^{-3}. This contrasted with remote operated vehicle surveys, which indicated densities under the ice of 40–400 individuals m^{-3}. It is now clear that krill undertake seasonal migrations to the north in the summer and to the south in the winter. During the winter when the water column phytoplankton stocks are low the sea ice microalgae are the only substantial source of nutrition, excluding carnivory, detritivory and cannibalism.

In an investigation of the marginal ice edge zone during the winter in the Scotia Sea–Weddell Sea Confluence area Daly (1990) found that krill larvae were abundant at the ice edge and on the undersurfaces of ice floes. Larval development and growth, which are dependent on food supply, progressed steadily from June to August. The krill larvae moulted about every 20 days and growth rates (0.7 mm day^{-1}) were similar to reported summer rates. Gut fullness indicated that 98% of the larvae were feeding both day and night. Examination of gut contents revealed that diatoms, such as *Nitzschia cylindrus*, *N. curta*, *N. pseudonana* and *Pinnularia* sp., as well as the archaeomonad *Archaeomonas aereolata*, were common. In addition to the diatoms dinoflagellate trichocysts, costal strips of choanoflagellates, scales of prasinophytes and chrysophytes were present. Thus, if this heterotrophic carbon (protozoans and possibly detritus) is taken into account larval krill feeding on sea ice biota could ingest enough carbon to support the observed growth.

Little is known about the predators of larval krill. Hamner *et al.* (1989) observed predation by a ctenophore and the ice amphipod *Eusirus antarcticus*. In the marginal ice zone in the autumn larval krill were found in the guts of two species of copepod *Euchirella rostromanga* and *Heterorhabdus austrinus*, the euphausiid *Thysanoessa macrura*, the ice amphipod *E. antarcticus*, the chaetognath *Sagitta marri*, the salp *Salpa thompsoni*, and the fishes *Bathylagus antarcticus, Electrona antarc-*

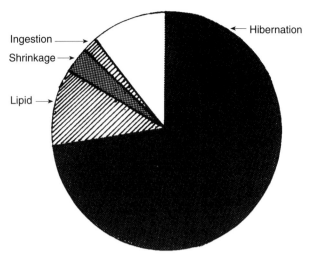

Fig. 5.15. Relative importance of the four major overwintering mechanisms proposed for a non-hibernating *Euphausia superba* in the waters west of the Antarctic Peninsula. The entire circle represents the energy requirement for the six months of low food availability as predicted from summer metabolic rates. The hibernation segment shows how much the energy requirement would be reduced by hibernation. The white segment is the proportion of the energy requirement that remains unexplained. Redrawn from Quentin & Ross (1991).

tica, Gymnoscopelus braueri, and *G. opisthopterus* (Hopkins & Torres, 1989). Also, furcilia are occasionally found in the guts of adult *E. superba*. During the winter most of these are predators, including ctenophores, salps, myctophids (especially *Electrona antarctica*), *Eusirus antarcticus*, the decapod *Pasiphaea scotiae* (Torres *et al.*, 1989). Refuge from these predators is provided by the undersurface of the pack ice with the rafting of ice floes with numerous caverns and crevices.

Quentin & Ross (1991) have discussed in detail possible overwintering mechanisms in krill. Four major hypotheses, shrinkage (discussed above), lipid utilization, switching of food sources, and 'hibernation' have been proposed to explain how krill survive the winter period of low food, low light and often extensive ice cover. In contrast to earlier work which suggested that krill do not utilize lipids as an energy source during the winter (Mauchline & Fisher, 1969; A. Clarke, 1984), Quentin & Ross (1991) found that in krill off the Antarctic Peninsula the lipid content of the combined sexes was 7.48% in autumn, dropping to 3.68% in late winter indicating that lipid reserves were used during the winter for energy production. In contrast to the studies in the Weddell Sea on winter feeding of krill discussed above Quentin & Ross (1991) found that the winter rates of phytoplankton ingestion by krill off the Antarctic Peninsula were less than 2% of the summer rates.

The final hypothesis is that krill hibernates or enters a state of severely reduced metabolism and only swims

enough to remain in the water column during winter. Evidence suggests that there is a reduction in respiration (Kawaguchi *et al.*, 1986) and digestive enzyme activity (Mumm, 1987) in the late autumn and early winter. In laboratory experiments Boyd *et al.* (1984) found that under winter environmental conditions the respiration rate of krill was half that of krill maintained under summer conditions, while Quentin & Ross (1991) found that the rates of oxygen consumption were only 33% of those in the summer. In the autumn a large proportion of the adult krill may migrate south and simultaneously reduce metabolism. Respiration rates increase again in the spring. Kawaguchi *et al.* (1986) found that they increased twofold from August to September. There is also evidence that growth rates derived from length frequency measurements start to increase again in the early spring well before the onset of phytoplankton primary production (Mackintosh, 1972).

Fig. 5.15 from Quentin & Ross (1991) depicts their evaluation of the relative importance of the four major overwintering mechanisms for krill west of the Antarctic Peninsula. It appears that in contrast to the multi-year pack ice of the Weddell Sea where the ice cover is predictable and extensive with complex undersurfaces providing hiding places and ample food, the ice cover west of the Antarctic Peninsula is unpredictable and the undersurface smooth providing the krill with little refuge from predation and the krill remain in the water column and feeding is reduced.

Marschall (1988) concluded that seasonal migration of a substantial part of the adult krill population, combined with a reduction in food requirements during the first half of the winter, has the advantage of spreading the population over a wider area. It separates the adult and juvenile stocks and hence reduces competition and possible cannibalism.

5.5.6 Stock separation

Over the years there has been much speculation as to whether local krill concentrations represent discrete krill stocks, or whether substantial intermixing occurs (Mackintosh, 1972; Makarov, 1973; Lubimova *et al.*, 1984). However, recent research has not been able to confirm the existence of separate stocks of krill.

Siegel (1986a,b) in an analysis of morphometric variability in krill populations around the Antarctic Peninsula was unable to distinguish any differences in krill from the northern Bellingshausen Sea, the Drake Passage, the Bransfield Strait, and the northern and southern Weddell Sea. Because of the inherent difficulties associated with morphometric studies an alternative approach, the electrophoretic analysis of variations in the structure of

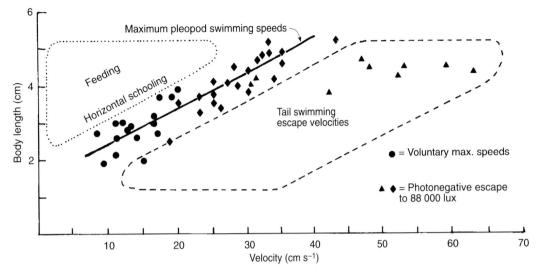

Fig. 5.16. Swimming speeds versus body lengths of *Euphausia superba*. Voluntary maximum pleopod swimming speeds of disturbed individuals in a 751 litre aquarium at Palmer Station were measured via a stop-frame analysis of video tapes. Dotted and dashed lines encompass the presumed ranges of feeding and schooling speeds maintained by pleopod swimming and of backward escape velocity generated by tail swimming. Redrawn from Hamner (1984).

enzymic proteins, has been developed. While early electrophoretic analyses (Ayala *et al.*, 1975; Fevolden & Ayala, 1981) suggested the existence of at least discrete krill populations in the Antarctic Peninsula region this has not been confirmed by subsequent studies. Analyses of krill samples from locations in the Weddell Sea, and the Scotia Sea, and around the Antarctic Peninsula and Prydz Bay (MacDonald & Schneppenheim, 1983; Schneppenheim & MacDonald, 1984; Fevolden, 1986; Kuhl & Scheppenheim, 1986; MacDonald *et al.*, 1986; Fevolden & Scheppenheim, 1988) have shown that all the samples were from a single population.

5.6 Feeding and energy expenditure

5.6.1 *Introduction*
Because of the abundance of *E. superba* and its pivotal position in the food web between the primary producers and secondary consumers its feeding activities have consequences of great importance to the structure, functioning and management of the Antarctic marine ecosystem (Quentin & Ross, 1985). The Peruvian anchovy is one of the few comparable examples of a single species whose abundance is so crucial to the structure of a large marine ecosystem (Idyll, 1973). Field studies have indicated that feeding in krill is one element of a complex interaction between nutritional requirements, swimming, swarming behaviour and vertical and horizontal migration (Pavlov, 1969; Nemoto, 1972; Gubsch, 1979; Kalinowski & Witek, 1980; Kils, 1981; Morris *et al.*, 1983, 1984; Boyd *et al.*, 1984; Morris & Priddle, 1984; Morris & Ricketts,

1984; Morris, 1984, 1985). Field and laboratory studies on the feeding of krill have provided much information on potential feeding mechanisms, filtration, ingestion and egestion, effects of chlorophyll levels and swarming behaviour in relation to feeding.

5.6.2 *Swimming behaviour*
Swimming behaviour, which is intimately related to feeding, has been investigated in detail by Kils (1979b, 1981, 1983) utilizing experimental aquaria and *in situ* underwater observations. Krill use two methods to produce propulsion for active forward movement: swimming by beating the abdominal pleopods (the normal method of forward propulsion) and tail swimming characterized by jerky driving of the tail (generally used as a flight reaction). Fig. 5.16 depicts the maximum swimming velocities of pleopod and tail swimming. Roughly it can be said that krill can reach eight times its body length per second with pleopod swimming and eleven times its body length per second with tail swimming. In Kils' experiments on swimming activity krill maintained swimming speeds of 1.5 to 3.5 body length s^{-1} for more than a week.

The density of krill at 1.070 g cm^{-3} is extraordinarily high for a pelagic animal. According to Aleyev (1977) most pelagic animals have densities similar to that of seawater; of 67 investigated pelagic species from different animal groups, all values were under 1.055 g cm^{-3}. Where the density of the body tissue exceeded this value the animals possessed other diverse buoyancy aids which are lacking in krill. Thus krill must constantly swim in order to maintain position in the water column, otherwise they would sink within three hours to a depth of 500 m.

5.6.3 The feeding mechanism

It is clear that in the summer when phytoplankton productivity is high *E. superba* feeds predominantly on phytoplankton (Barkley, 1940; Hart, 1942; Hustedt, 1958; Marr, 1962; Nemoto, 1972; A. Clarke, 1980a). Recent studies of feeding behaviour (Hamner *et al.* 1983; Kils, 1983; Morris, 1984; Boyd *et al.*, 1984; Quentin & Ross, 1985) have provided detailed descriptions of the feeding mechanism. Descriptions of the feeding apparatus have been provided by Berkes (1975), Kils (1979a, 1983), Alberti & Kils (1980), Antezana *et al.* (1982), A. Clarke & Morris (1983a), McClatchie & Boyd (1983) and Marschall (1985). A V-shaped filtering basket is formed by the six periopods (thoracic appendages or thoracopods). The first two segments of the periopods bear primary setae, each of which have two rows of secondary setae arranged along their length. Tertiary setae on the latter result in a filter net mesh size smaller than 1.0 μm. The terminal segments of the periopods bear comb setae which have a comb-like device at their ends. The two basic types of setal arrangements form two different kinds of filter nets: 1. a very fine net with a relatively large net area formed by the filter setae (mesh size 1–4 μm), and 2. a coarse net with a comparatively small net area formed by the basal parts of the comb setae (mesh size 25–40 μm) (Fig. 5.17).

When not feeding *E. superba* swims rapidly pressing its six pairs of thoracic legs (periopods) together to form a keel. Two principal feeding methods have been proposed (Kils, 1981, 1983). In the first, 'pump filtering', the filtering basket formed by the thoracopods is periodically opened and closed directing food towards the mouth. This type of feeding has been observed by several workers both in the laboratory (Antezana *et al.*, 1982; Kils, 1983; Boyd *et al.*, 1984) and in the field (Hamner, 1984).

The second feeding method is termed 'compression feeding'. In this method the periopods are extended to push a pocket of water through the feeding basket which is rapidly collapsed. Food particles are retained by the setae as the water is extruded (Antezana *et al.*, 1982; Hamner *et al.*, 1983). The feeding basket is filled and compressed with a frequency that varies from 1–5 Hz. The relationship between the filtering net and the potential food organisms is shown in Fig. 5.17. These filter-feeding mechanism can reject particles greater than 30 μm and potentially retain particles greater than 1 μm, including bacteria.

Kils (1983) notes that the dactylopodites (terminal segments) of the thoracopods (thoracic appendgaes) have rake-like structures which have a quite different morphology than the normal setae; they are much stronger and increase in diameter from tip to base. They are thus well suited to grazing diatoms from ice or other surfaces. As discussed in section 5.5.5 this has been confirmed by recent observations of krill actively feeding on sea ice microalgae and by laboratory experiments. In laboratory experiments Hamner *et al.* (1983) concentrated and refroze sea ice microalgae into small blocks which were than floated in an aquarium containing krill. As the blocks softened the *E. superba* located the food by area-intensive search. They then extruded the dactylopodites and raked the ice algae into the feeding basket, moving along the submerged surfaces of the blocks or holding themselves in place at sites of high algal concentration.

The observations of Hamner *et al.* (1983) have been confirmed by Spiridonov *et al.* (1985), O'Brien (1985, 1987), Stretch *et al.* (1988) and Marschall (1988). Stretch *et al.* (1988) found that when *E. superba* foraged near ice floes they exhibited two distinct behaviour patterns. When stimulated by algae released from melting ice they show area-intensive foraging behaviour. This behaviour is characterized by high speed swimming and rapid turning, accompanied by rapid opening and closing of the feeding basket. This behaviour is often followed by ice grazing behaviour during which the euphausiids orient themselves towards the undersurface of the ice to rake algal cells off the ice with their dactylopodites.

Observations by Marschall (1988) using a remotely operated vehicle enabled an assessment of krill abundance and behaviour in relation to ice conditions. The highest concentrations occurred in rugged ice caused by piled up floes of pressure ridges and/or melting. Individuals located close to the ice were mostly feeding, and had dark green guts. They moved along the ice at approximately 0.1 to 0.5 body length s[-1], continuously scraping the surface with the tips of their thoracopods and opening and closing their feeding baskets at a frequency of 2–3 Hz. These observations were confirmed by laboratory experiments in which krill left clearly visible feeding traces on glass plates coated with sea ice microalgae.

Krill are also capable of raptorially capturing and holding large particles, including moulted cuticles of crustaceans, in their feeding basket (Hamner *et al.*, 1983; Boyd *et al.*, 1984). Boyd *et al.* (1984) carried out a series of experiments in which furcilia larvae were fed to adult krill. Filtration rates and ingesting rates of these adults feeding on furcilia, when normalized to mg dry wt of adult predator, were surprisingly close to that obtained

Table 5.6. *Estimates of krill filtration rates*

Method	Filtration rate (ml h^{-1})	Source
Constant volume		
Chlorophyll *a*	20.3±15.2	Kato *et al.* (1979)
	21.2±14.8	Kato *et al.* (1982)
	257.6±50.5	Meyer (1981)
	43.6	Antezana *et al.* (1982)
	210.0	Boyd *et al.* (1984)
	1411**	Price *et al.* (1988)
Particle counter		
>3 μm particles	175.0	Boyd *et al.* (1984)
	24.6±9.5	Morris (1984)
F_{max}	210*	Antezana *et al.* (1982)
	754.7	Morris (1984)
	430*	Boyd *et al.* (1984)
	357	Quentin & Ross (1985)
Flagellate *Isochrysis galbana* (=4 μm sphere)	130	Quentin & Ross (1985)
Pennate diatom *Phaeodactylum tricornutum* (EDS=4 μm)	167	Quentin & Ross (1985)
Centric diatom *Ditylum brightwellii* (EDS=30 μm)	281	Quentin & Ross (1985)
Centric diatom *Thallasiosira eccentrica* (EDS=40 μm)	371	Quentin & Ross (1985)
Flow-through		
>3 μm particles	947±524.9	Morris (1984)
F_{max}	66 816	Morris (1984)
Extrapolations		
Filter basket	169–777	Antezana *et al.* (1982)
Chlorophyll *a* required	320–5 120	Morris (1984)
	700–13 400*	Morris (1984)
	1 000–20 000	Ikeda & Bruce (1986)
Energy equivalents	1 800–4 700	Kils (1979b, c)
Oxygen consumption	1 893	Rakusa-Suszczewski & Opalinski (1978)

After Morris (1984) and Miller & Hampton (1989).
Calculated for an animal of about 50 mg dry weight, except:* F_{max} and other values for animals of unknown weights; ** very large (50 litre) experimental container used.

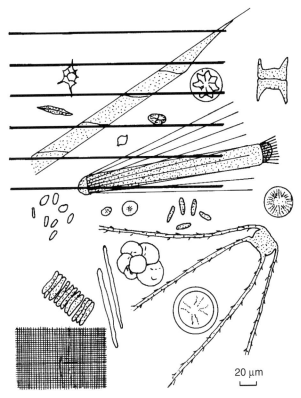

Fig. 5.17. Size relationship between ambient food organisms and the filtering nets of *Euphausia superba*. Top solid bars represent comb setae; lower left corner represents filter setae net. Redrawn from Kils (1983).

when adults were fed algal cells. McWhinnie & Denys (1978b) noted that in krill kept in aquaria cannibalism was relatively common and they were also observed to feed on other zooplankton. Thus, under certain circumstances krill may be carnivorous or cannibalistic (Miller, 1982).

5.6.4 Experimental studies on feeding and filtration rates

A number of feeding studies have investigated the clearance rate (filtration rate) and the apparent selectivity of food particles. Clearance rates have been determined in a variety of ways: from the rate of chlorophyll *a* depletion in closed vessels containing euphausiids and natural phytoplankton (Kato *et al.*, 1979; Meyer & El-Sayed, 1983); from the difference in chlorophyll *a* in the seawater from the inlet and outlet of an aquarium containing thousands of animals (Antezana *et al.*, 1982); and more recently from changes in cell numbers of natural phytoplankton consumed by krill in flow-through (Morris, 1984) or closed systems (Boyd *et al.*, 1984; Quentin & Ross, 1985). The clearance rates obtained with the flow-through systems used by Morris were several orders of magnitude higher than those reported by other investigators using closed vessels (see Table 5.6).

The apparent filtration rate derived from the particle size analysis in Morris's 1984 experiments is plotted for each size channel in Fig. 5.18. The shape of this curve indicates that not all particles are filtered with equal efficiency (Boyd *et al.*, 1984; Hamner, 1984; Kils, 1981). The maximum filtration rate occurred in the 24 μm size range and was 42.8 l h^{-1}. The highest rate measured in any experiment was 66.8 l h^{-1}. Kils (1981) estimated that the retention efficiency of *E. superba* at approximately 50%, while McClatchie & Boyd (1983) suggested a maximum efficiency of 30–40%. These estimates indicate that the actual filtration rates are in the range of 80–100 l h^{-1}. If, however, some degree of particle selection occurs then these high filtration rates will be over-estimates.

Table 5.7. *Percentage of cells retained by* Euphausia superba *feeding on four species of phytoplankton*

Species	CDS (μm)	A	B	C
Thalassiosira eccentrica	49.7	48	45	78
Ditylum brightwelli	40.9	38	35	58
Phaeodactylum tricornutum	7.5	18(22)	14(18)	35
Isochrysis galbana	5.3	18(14)	14(10)	17

A = estimates using the regression on the single highest clearance rate;
B = estimates using the regression on the average of the highest
clearance rates for each animal and C = estimates based on a 95%
retention efficiency for an 80 μm particle (McClatchie & Boyd, 1983)
and computed using the calculated spherical diameter (CDS) for each
phytoplankton species.
From Quentin & Ross (1985).

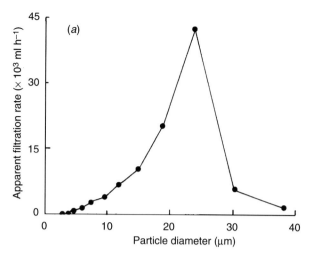

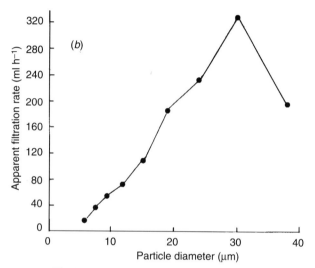

Fig. 5.18. (*a*) Apparent filtration rate (R_f) for *Euphausia superba* as a function of mean particle size from constant volume experiments; krill wet weight = 226.0 mg. (*b*) As for (*a*) but for flow-through experiments; krill wet weight = 255.5 mg. Redrawn from Morris (1984).

In a series of closed system experiments Quentin & Ross (1985) found that the maximum clearance rates were closely linked to the size, but not the species, of phytoplankton being ingested (Table 5.7). The physical dimensions, not the chemical composition, of the cells are probably the most important parameters affecting maximum clearance rates. Several other recent studies indicate that *E. superba* does not feed equally well on all sizes of phytoplankton (Meyer & El-Sayed, 1983; Clarke & Morris, 1983a; Morris, 1984; Boyd *et al.*, 1984). Morris (1984) found that particles of 30 μm size were maximally retained, and that particles >30 μm in diameter were apparently rejected (Fig. 5.18). Boyd *et al.* (1984) found that phytoplankton with diameters of >12 μm were retained maximally and that cells only 6 μm in diameter were retained with a 50% efficiency (Fig. 5.19). The maximum clearance rate of 357 ml h⁻¹ found by Quentin & Ross (1985) generally agrees with that found by Boyd *et al.* (1984) who obtained a clearance rate of 500 ml h⁻¹ for euphausiids of 45 mm total length, and the value of 210 ml h⁻¹ measured by Antezana *et al.* (1982). The differences between the three studies are probably due to the different sizes of the animals used. Morris (1984), on the other hand, reported a maximum clearance rate for *E. superba* of 66 816 ml h⁻¹, more than 130 times the maximum rate found by the other workers. Such a rate is considered on theoretical grounds to be much too high.

In their flow-through experiments on the omnivorous feeding behaviour of *E. superba* Price *et al.* (1988) found that the clearance rate for phytoplankton increased linearly with phytoplankton concentration. Clearance rates increased from approximately 300 ml krill⁻¹ h⁻¹ at an initial concentration of 0.1 μg chl *a* l⁻¹ to over 800 ml krill⁻¹ h⁻¹ at the highest concentration of 23 μg chl *a* h⁻¹. Other authors have reported conflicting results. The discrepancies may be due to differences in the types and sizes of

the cells and the range of concentrations used. However, it seems that krill do not become satiated under most field conditions, since algal concentrations, except under bloom conditions, seldom exceed 13 μg chl *a* l⁻¹ and generally are much lower, in the order of 0.6 μg chl *a* l⁻¹ (Holm-Hansen & Huntley, 1984).

The complex interaction of krill filtration mechanism, particle size distribution in the water and experimental conditions have produced varied data for the actual filtration rate. These are summarized for a 50 mg dry wt animal in Table 5.6. It can be seen that there is wide variation in the data. However, it is clear that the filtration rates are high, in the order of hundreds and in some cases thousands of ml h⁻¹. Flow-through particle size analysis data are more likely to be representative than data obtained from constant volume technique.

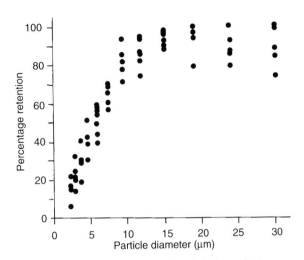

Fig. 5.19. Efficiency of retention of algal particles by *Euphausia superba*. Data based on filtration rates and normalized to allow the highest efficiency in each experiment to be 100%. Redrawn from Boyd *et al*. (1984).

5.6.5 Feeding and swarming

Early conceptual models of the relationship between feeding and swarming in *E. superba* (Pavlov, 1969, 1977; Nakamura, 1974; Mezykowski & Rakusa-Suszczewski, 1979; Everson & Ward, 1980) assumed that krill did not feed in swarms, particularly in dense swarms, because food was limiting. However, Antezana *et al*. (1982) challenged this model and suggested that feeding and swarming were co-occurring events. They list three lines of evidence suggesting that feeding and swarming may neither be exclusive nor diel events: 1. In their experiments *E. superba* fed at maximum rates at relatively high densities (2400–8900 individuals m⁻³) which fall within various estimated ranges for krill in swarming conditions (Mauchline, 1979; Nemoto *et al*., 1981; Brinton & Antezana, 1984; Macauley *et al*., 1984); 2. *E. superba* in laboratory swarm densities fed actively within a wide range of chlorophyll concentrations (0.6–11.5 µg chl *a* l⁻¹), which fall within those encountered in the Southern Ocean, including oceanic, coastal and blooming conditions (El-Sayed, 1967; Holm-Hansen *et al*., 1977; Holm-Hansen & Huntley, 1984); and 3. in the experiments ingestion and egestion rates were sustained throughout the day showing no significant diel rhythm.

5.6.6 Food resources and feeding requirements

Considerable evidence has accumulated to substantiate the view that krill are essentially herbivorous (Hart, 1932; Barkley, 1940; Marr 1962; Nemoto, 1972; Kawamura, 1981; Ligowski, 1982), especially during the austral spring and summer when phytoplankton blooms occur. Analysis of krill storage lipids (A. Clarke, 1980b, 1984) and high O:N ratios confirm the view that they feed predominately on phytoplankton during the summer.

Unlike other Antarctic zooplankton species krill are not known to lay down seasonal lipid reserves (A. Clarke, 1983, 1984; Hagen, 1988) as a food reserve for the winter when phytoplankton stocks are low. Tanoue (1985) found that the composition of the faecal lipid in small krill (mean body length 21–29 mm) suggested that diatoms constitute the main food consumed, whereas larger krill (mean length 51.2 mm) ingest a mixture of diatoms, choanoflagellates and other phytoplankton. Tanoue & Hara (1986) through an analysis of essential amino acids confirmed Tanoue's findings and suggested that choanoflagellates, which are abundant in Antarctic waters (Silver *et al*., 1980; Buck, 1981; Buck & Garrison, 1983; Marchant, 1985), could be an important dietary item.

There is increasing evidence that in addition to choanoflagellates krill are able to exploit food resources other than phytoplankton. Stomach analyses from field and laboratory studies (e.g. Barkley, 1940; Marr, 1962; Pavlov, 1969, 1977; Price *et al*., 1988) indicate ingestion of other zooplankton species, especially copepods (see section 5.6.3). In addition, as we have seen cannibalism has been observed in captive animals (e.g. McWhinnie *et al*., 1979; Miller, 1982), and digestive enzyme activity indicates a capacity to assimilate a variety of foods (Mayzand *et al*., 1985). Krill may also consume heteroflagellates and planktonic protozoa such as the tintinnids, which are often common but which are extremely difficult to detect in stomach contents.

In their study of krill and their food resources in the Scotia Sea Holm-Hansen & Huntley (1984) found an inverse relationship between phytoplankton biomass and zooplankton, which was first noted by Hardy & Gunther (1936). They also found a marked difference between the composition of the phytoplankton standing crops in January, when zooplankton biomass was low, and March, when krill furcilia were abundant (see Table 5.8). In March the relatively large diatoms were reduced in concentration (by 98%), as were the dinoflagellates (by 91%). However, the nanoplankton (monads and flagellates) were reduced only 50% in biomass. These data and laboratory feeding studies have demonstrated that krill swarms can change the size composition of the phytoplankton in the water column, shifting it towards the smaller sizes. The effect of selectively reducing the abundance of certain species could have a profound effect on the structure of the phytoplankton community.

Holm-Hansen & Huntley (1984) also assessed the food requirements of the krill in the above study area. The mean krill biomass in the upper 200m of the water column was estimated at 10.6 mg dry wt m⁻³ and this was calculated to require a food ration of 0.105–0.211 mg C

Table 5.8. *Apparent effect of grazing by krill (furcilia) on the composition of the phytoplankton crop. Data are from 5 m depths at a station north of Elephant Island sampled on 27–28 January and 16–18 March 1981. Plant carbon has been estimated by floristic analysis of preserved samples, in which all cells are counted, sized, and cellular organic carbon calculated by applying data equating cell size to organic carbon (Reid* et al., *1970).*

	Biomass (μg C l^{-1})	
	January	March
Diatoms		
Pennate	30	2.0
Centric	221	1.2
Dinoflagellates		
Thecate	12.1	0.1
Non-thecate	5.8	1.5
Monads and flagellates (>10 μm)	29.3	14.7

From Holm-Hansen & Huntley (1984).

m^{-3} day^{-1}. The corresponding value for the krill in a super-swarm off Elephant Island was 2.4–5.4 mg C m^{-3} day^{-1}. On the other hand the phytoplankton productivity for the upper 200m in the Scotia Sea and the super-swarm area was estimated to be 4.8 and 4.2 mg C m^{-3} day^{-1} respectively. On this basis it would appear that there was ample phytoplankton to provide for the food requirements of the krill. They estimated that the krill in the super-swarm were consuming between 58 and 81% of the daily production and that the mean *E. superba* populations in the Scotia Sea consumed only between 2.5 and 3.5% of the daily primary production. They point out that there are several reasons why the consumption of *E. superba* should be substantially lower than the total primary production. First, though *E. superba* may dominate the zooplankton, it makes up no more than half of the total zooplankton standing stock (Holdgate, 1967; Knox, 1970), and thus could be expected to consume about half of the total zooplankton consumption of phytoplankton. Second, a large proportion of the primary production occurs in the particle sizes <10 μm, which are filtered at relatively low efficiencies (McClatchie & Boyd, 1983; Morris, 1984; Quentin & Ross, 1985). If it is assumed that the production of particles large enough to be effectively filtered by *E. superba* is approximately 10% of the total primary production (v. Brockel, 1981) and that approximately half of this must be shared with the non-euphausiid zooplankton, then about 5% of the total primary production would be available for consumption by *E. superba*. This compares well with Holm-Hansen & Huntley's estimate of 2.5–3.5%.

Miller *et al.* (1985) used acoustic measurements of krill standing stock, together with concurrent primary productivity measurements and recently published data on krill energy requirements, to assess the importance of *E. superba* as a herbivore in a sector of the Indian Ocean surveyed during FIBEX. The mean phytoplankton production measured during the survey was 188 mg C m^{-3} day^{-1}, or 1.88 g (wet wt) phytoplankton m^{-3} day^{-1}, assuming a phytoplankton:C ratio of 10:1 (Holm-Hansen *et al.*, 1977; Sorokin & Mikleev, 1979). Expanding this over the survey area gave a daily phytoplankton production of approximately 1.2×10^6 tonnes. The acoustically derived estimate of krill density was 1.46 g m^{-3} (Hampton, 1985), giving a standing stock of 9.1×10^5 tonnes at the time of the survey. Miller estimated that the krill consumed 3.66×10^4 tonnes of phytoplankton per day, or 3.05% of the estimated daily phytoplankton production. This agrees well with the estimate arrived at by Holm-Hansen & Huntley (1984) for the Scotia Sea.

The question arises as to whether there is competition between krill and other consumers, especially the copepods, for the planktonic food resource. This has been investigated by Schnack (1985b). In constant volume feeding experiments he found no great difference between the feeding patterns of *E. superba* and five copepod species. Schnack points out that the very similar feeding behaviour implies that severe competition for food might occur. However, he notes that there is a great difference between the distributional patterns of copepods and krill with few copepods being found in regions where large swarms of krill occur. In addition, niche separation on the basis of differences in distribution during the life-histories of krill and copepods could be a mechanism for reducing potential competition.

5.6.7 Energy budgets

There have been a number of attempts to develop energy budgets for individual krill (e.g. Chekunova & Rynkova, 1974; A. Clarke & Morris, 1983a,b; Ikeda, 1984b). Data from these studies can be combined with information on population biomass and structure to produce a population energy budget (e.g. Everson, 1977b; Nemoto & Harrison, 1981) and thus estimate krill production. However, we are still a long way from being able to do this due to the scarcity of data on important parameters and the comparative lack of data on winter energy budgets. Because of the strong seasonality in primary production, the availability of food is likely to be the major ecological factor influencing krill's growth, reproduction and life-history (A. Clarke, 1980a, 1983), and hence population energy budgets. Thus, at present we do not have sufficient information to estimate accurately the annual energy consumption and expenditure for an individual krill.

5.6.7.1 Energy budgets for individual krill

In estimating energy budgets for the individuals of a species the frequently used equation (Ricker, 1968) is:

$$C - P + R + F + U$$

(where C = consumption; P = production, i.e. growth and gonad development; R = respiration, energy loss through metabolism; F = energy lost in faeces; and U = energy lost in urine; all in energetic units). However, as discussed by A. Clarke & Morris (1983a,b), this equation is inappropriate for krill since this species must expend significant amounts of energy merely maintaining its position in the water column. A. Clarke & Morris (1983a) partitioned respiration into three separate physiological processes–basal metabolism, metabolic cost of feeding, and metabolic cost of swimming.

Newell (1979) has developed the concept of the cost of feeding. He points out that the balanced energy budget can be reformulated by considering the assimilated energy (A), or the actual amount of energy consumed (C), which is utilized by the organism. Thus modifying his equation of krill:

A	$= C$	$-(F + U + M + R)$	$= P_g + P_r$
Net assimilated energy	Food consumed	Losses through faeces, dissolved organic matter, moulting and respiration	Energy available for growth

where M = energetic cost of moulting; R = total respiratory losses (R_b, basal metabolism + R_s, energetic cost of swimming + R_f, energetic cost of feeding); P_g = energy available for growth; and P_r = energy available for reproduction.

A. Clarke & Morris (1983a) have given an estimated energy budget for an adult male and female *E. superba* during a 190 day summer growing period (Table 5.9). It can be seen that information is not yet available for many items in the energy budget. Basal metabolism (R_b) cannot be determined directly and A. Clarke & Morris (1983b) made the assumption that the oxygen consumption of krill at $-1.0\,^\circ$C approximates the true basal metabolism. It is important that this be more accurately determined. The metabolic cost of swimming (R_s) is most likely to be a function of krill size but this is as yet not known. As we have seen swimming activity is intimately related to feeding, and the as yet undetermined metabolic cost of feeding (R_f) must be added to that of the metabolic basal rate. Feeding behaviour is complex and the proportion spent on filter-feeding, compression feeding and raking (grazing on

Table 5.9. *An estimated energy budget for adult male and female* Euphausia superba *during the summer at South Georgia*

	Total energy intake in 190 days (kJ)	
	Male	Female
Basal metabolic rate (R_b)	7.637	8.742
Metabolic cost of activity (R_s) (including swarming and vertical migration)	unknown	unknown
Metabolic cost of feeding (R_f)	unknown	unknown
Somatic growth (P_g)	6.754	6.754
Moults (M)	0.837	0.837
Testis (P_r)	unknown	—
Ovary (P_r)	—	6.390
Total	15.228	22.723
	37.955[1]	

[1]Assuming total respiratory losses (basal + swimming + feeding) are 80% of assimilated energy in males. If mean weight of a male krill in summer is taken to be 1.08 g (= 3.94 kJ), then daily energy intake is 0.0506 J J^{-1} day^{-1} (= 5.1% body weight per day). Daily energy intake for females is higher due to large amount of energy involved in reproduction.
From A. Clarke & Morris (1983a, b).

sea ice microalgae) will need to be taken into account. In their model A. Clarke & Morris (1983a,b) assumed that the total respiratory losses ($R_b + R_s + R_f$) were 80% of the assimilated energy in males. There does not appear to be any agreement as to the metabolic cost of moulting (M). A. Clarke & Morris (1983a,b) calculated this at 0.837 kJ for a male krill over the 190 days of the spring–summer period, i.e. 2.2% of the assimilated energy. *M* has been determined as 38% in a similar species, *E. pacifica* (Paranjape, 1967). Ikeda & Dixon (1982a) assumed *M* to be 40% of the daily O_2 uptake on the day of moulting. There is a need to determine more accurately not only the energy cost of the actual moulting process but also the energy loss in the discarded exoskeleton.

Using the relationships discussed above, A. Clarke & Morris (1983a) calculated that the total energy intake during the spring–summer season (~190 days) is about 5% (6% or more for females) of the body weight. This is very similar to the value calculated by Chekunova & Rynkova (1974) from estimates of oxygen consumption and food intake but ignoring swimming activity. Chekunova & Rynkova also calculated the metabolic carbon loss by an individual krill during its life from calorific equivalents. Their estimate of 74% is very similar to Ikeda's (1984b) range of 71.5 to 85% of the total carbon assimilated from egg to adult.

From laboratory data on the ingestion rates of chlorophyll *a* (Antezana *et al.*, 1982; Kato *et al.*, 1982; Ishii *et al.*, 1987) it has been calculated that krill's daily energy

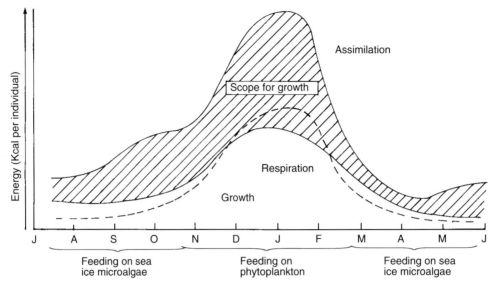

Fig. 5.20. Scope for growth in *Euphausia superba*.

requirements are equivalent to between 1.0 and 1.7% body carbon. The maximum clearance rates in the experiments of these authors were between 150–210 ml individual⁻¹ h⁻¹ for krill weighing approximately 250 mg, with maximum ingestion rates of 1.8 to 2.0 g chl *a* individual⁻¹ h⁻¹ being found at average concentrations of 8–12 μg chl *a* l⁻¹. On the other hand, experiments by Price *et al.* (1988) at similar average concentrations of chlorophyll *a* gave ingestion rates of 10 μg chl *a* individual⁻¹ h⁻¹. If these higher ingestion rates are used in calculations of energy intake a value of 8.5% of body carbon day⁻¹ is obtained, a value which compares favourably with estimated metabolic requirements.

The difference between the net energy gain from the assimilated energy and the energy losses from respiration can be regarded as the 'scope for growth' (Newell, 1979). An attempt has been made to depict this for *E. superba* in Fig. 5.20. In this diagram the halving of the respiration rate during winter and the two-fold increase that occurs in spring is depicted. The approximate proportions of assimilated energy from sea ice microalgae and phytoplankton are also shown. A hypothetical growth curve is also depicted. The proportion of assimilated energy from other sources (zooplankton, choanoflagellates, protozoa, detrital organic matter) cannot be estimated at present from the available data.

5.7 Krill production

5.7.1 Introduction

For an understanding of the ecological role of krill in the Southern Ocean pelagic ecosystem it is necessary to know the rate at which new krill biomass is being pro-

duced, i.e. the productivity or rate of krill production. This is a function of the growth rate of each individual krill, which varies according to the age of the individual. It is a dynamic function that rarely, if ever, can be measured directly, but it is essential if we are to understand the rates of the transfer of energy and materials through the large stocks of krill in the Southern Ocean, and if we are to be in a position to undertake sustained rational exploitation of these stocks.

The actual estimation of production requires information on the stock biomass at the beginning and end of some set period of time, usually one year. This will give the production per unit time, which is balanced against the losses resulting from catabolism, death from natural causes or predation (mortality), and emigration. However, mortality and emigration are difficult parameters to measure (Allen, 1971). Consequently, production has to estimated indirectly. Three indirect methods have been used: 1. estimates from animal size and number observed at a series of points over time (Allen, 1971); 2. estimates based on energy budgets (Omori & Ikeda, 1984), and; 3. estimates based on the amount and proportion of the population consumed by its principal predators (Miller & Hampton, 1989). An alternative approach developed below is to use predator consumption rates.

5.7.2 Production estimates from animal size and number

Growth rates and age of krill have been discussed in section 5.3.7. Such data forms the basis for the estimation of production over a given time span, taking into account mortality rates. However, growth and mortality vary throughout the animal's life span. Taking this into account, Allen (1971) has shown that the ratio of production to biomass (i.e. the standing stock) (*P/B* ratio) is equal to the ratio of the total production by any particular cohort to its total biomass over time. Assuming linear growth in length over four time periods with different rates in each, Allen estimated a *P/B* ratio for krill of between 1.8 and 2.3. Other investigators have obtained ratios much closer to unity (e.g. Gulland, 1970; Hempel, 1970; Horwood, 1981), indicating that krill's annual production is approximately equal to its biomass. Yamanaka (1983) using data from Kawakami & Doi (1979) calculated *P/B* ratios of 1.19 and 2.77 for krill surveyed in a sector of the Indian Ocean during FIBEX, while Siegel (1986b) found values of between 0.8 and 1.1 (mean 0.95, excluding 0-year olds) for animals from the Bransfield Strait.

A number of studies (e.g. Waters, 1969; Robertson, 1979) have shown that there is a general relationship between *P/B* ratios and the life span, the shorter the life span the higher the ratio. Animals with a life span of 4–6 years would be expected to have a *P/B* ratio of between 1.0 and 2.0. In order to obtain a reasonable estimate of *P/B* in krill we must have good data on growth and mortality. As Miller & Hampton (1989) point out there are three serious shortcomings that hinder the estimation of krill production from individual mass data. These are: 1. a lack of reliable mortality estimates; 2. inadequate knowledge of growth rates and functions; and 3. incomplete data on age, length-at-age and longevity. Estimates of mortality vary widely, e.g. 5.50, Kawakami & Doi (1979); 2.31 and 0.60 for 1–2 and 2–3 year old krill respectively, Brinton & Townsend (1984); and 1.0, Siegel (1986a). This would seem to imply significant variations in the composition of the population from different areas.

It is clear that we are still far from being able to estimate krill production with any degree of confidence from individual mass data alone. More accurate information is required on natural mortality at all ages, and on life span, growth, age structure and rematuration cycles. In addition, we as yet know little of the effect of the austral winter on these parameters.

5.7.3 *Production estimates from energy budgets*

Energy budgets for individual krill have been discussed in section 5.6.7.1 Various attempts have been made to use calculations of the metabolic requirements of individuals to develop energy budgets for populations with varying success (e.g. Holm-Hansen & Huntley, 1984; Miller *et al.*, 1985). Given the available information on krill population dynamics, size and age structure, and generation

times and the comparative lack of information on krill energetics during the winter the development of production estimates from energy budgets is no easy task.

5.7.4 *Production estimates from predator consumption*

Historically, krill production was largely estimated from assumed relationships between krill and primary production (e.g. Gulland, 1970; Hempel, 1970; Everson, 1977b; Knox, 1983). These calculations assessed the annual krill production at between 75 and 700 million tonnes (Gulland, 1970; Makarov, 1972; Lubimova, 1983) (Table 5.10). The calculation of these estimates assumed different levels of phytoplankton production, various efficiencies for the conversion of phytoplankton to krill (e.g 10% by Gulland, 1970, and 2.5% by Chekunova & Rynkova, 1974), and various values for the ratio of krill to other herbivorous zooplankton (usually 50%, Vinogradov & Naumov, 1958; Holdgate, 1967; Knox, 1970, 1983). Knox (1983) using a range of estimates for annual primary production and conversion efficiencies arrived at krill production estimates ranging from 450 to 1900 tonnes per annum. In view of the uncertainties of these estimates they are of little real value for estimating krill production. As a consequence, attention has focused on attempts to estimate production from data on predator consumption.

5.7.4.1 *Consumption by whales*

Southern Ocean whale stocks, once abundant and diverse, supported the world's largest whale fishery, eventually leading to their marked decline. There is a great deal known about the great whales because of their commercial importance and several reviews have been published (e.g. Mackintosh, 1942, 1965; Gambell, 1973, 1976a,b, 1985; Gaskin, 1976, 1982; Gulland, 1976; Laws, 1977a,b; Nishiwaki, 1977; Allen, 1980; S.G. Brown & Lockyer, 1984). The more recent data have been reviewed by Laws (1977a), Bengtson (1984), Miller & Hampton (1989), Armstrong & Siegfried (1991) and Ichii & Kato (1991) (see Table 5.10). Laws' (1977b) figures indicate that the Antarctic whales before exploitation removed about 190 million tonnes of krill annually, which gives an ecological efficiency (i.e. the ratio of energy absorbed by the predator to the food energy absorbed by the prey) of about 1%. This is a much lower efficiency than the 10% usually typical of conversions in natural fish populations (Everson, 1984c), but is probably due to the slow growth of whales older than four years (Everson, 1984c).

Armstrong & Siegfried (1991) and Ichii & Kato (1991) have recently estimated the consumption of krill by Minke Whales in the Southern Ocean. Ichii & Kato

Table 5.10. *Estimated annual consumption of krill by different species of whales*

Whale species	Whale stock size (×10³)		Krill consumption (×10⁶ t y⁻¹)	
	Bengtson[1]	Laws[2]	Bengtson[1]	Laws[2]
Blue	4.5	10	1.3	3.38
Pygmy	7.4	—	1.93	—
Fin	126	84	21.21	16.43
Sei	16	40.5	1.01	2.88
Humpback	3.5	3	0.41	0.32
Minke	258.5	200	8.42	19.82
Total	415.7	337.5	34.28	42.83

[1]Laws (1977b) assumed that minke whales feed all year round.
[2]Bengtson (1984) assumed feeding for only 120 days a year and considered only mature animals.
Based on data in Bengtson (1984) and compared with figures from Laws (1977b, 1985). From Miller & Hampton (1989).

Table 5.11. *Estimated annual consumption of krill by whales before and after exploitation*

Krill consumption (×10⁶ t y⁻¹)			
Before exploitation	After exploitation	'Surplus' (×10⁶ t)	Source
38	—	—	Marr (1962)
—	270	—	Studentsky (1967)
—	24–36 (Fin whale)	—	Kasahara (1967)
150	—	—	Zenkovich (1970)
120–70	10	100–150	Mackintosh (1970)
45–60	—	—	Hempel (1970)
>50	—	—	Gulland (1970)
77	—	—	Nemoto (1970)[1]
200	—	—	Doi (1973)[1]
800–5000	200	±1000	Lubimova (1983), Lubimova *et al.* (1973, 1984)
250	40	100–200	Omura (1973)
190	43	147	Laws (1977b) Everson (1984a)
188	40	148	Yamanaka (1983)
—	34	—	Bengtson (1984)
190	40	150	Laws (1985)

[1]Cited in Nemoto & Nasu (1975).
Modified after Everson (1977b). From Miller & Hampton (1989).

(1991) found that *E. superba* was the dominant food species, comprising 100% and 94% by weight in stomachs in the ice edge and offshore zones respectively. The total food consumption per day was estimated to be 1170 t and 596 t in the ice edge and offshore zones respectively. Armstrong & Siegfried (1991), based on estimates obtained from stomach capacity, ingestion rates and respiratory allometry methods, estimated that an 'average-sized' female Minke Whale consumed 56.2 t of krill during a 120-day stay in Antarctic waters. Their data suggested that the Minke Whale population (760 396±132 230, SHMIREP, 1990) in the Southern Ocean (60° and higher) consumes 35.5×10^6 t of krill annually. Previous estimates for Minke Whale krill consumption gave values between 8×10^6 and 20×10^6 for population estimates smaller by 67 to 75% than the SHMIREP estimate (Miller & Hampton, 1989).

Present consumption of the reduced whale stocks is in the order of 34–42 million tonnes (Bengtson, 1984; Laws, 1985; Armstrong & Siegfried, 1991), and the difference (*c.* 150 million tonnes) between this and the pre-exploitation estimate has often been referred to as the 'krill surplus' (Lubimova *et al.*, 1984) (Table 5.11). The fate of this so-called surplus which is no longer consumed by the whales has been the subject of much conjecture, especially the proportion utilized by other predator groups (see Chapter 9), and thus resulting in increases in their populations (Beddington & de la Mare, 1984; Bengtson & Laws, 1984).

5.7.4.2 Consumption by seals
Seal krill consumption is discussed in Chapter 8. The principal krill consumers are Crabeater Seals (*Lobodon*

carcinophagus) and Leopard Seals (*Hydrurga leptonyx*) with smaller amounts being consumed by Fur Seals (*Arctocephalus gazella*) and Ross Seals (*Ommatophoca rossii*) (see Table 5.12). The gross conversion efficiency of krill to Crabeater Seal has been estimated at 1%, the same (Everson, 1984c).

5.7.4.3 Consumption by squid
While it is known that several species of Antarctic squid feed on krill (Marr, 1962; Dell, 1965; Nemoto *et al.*, 1985), there is little available information either on the standing stocks of squid krill consumers, or on their krill consumption rates (Okutani & Clarke, 1985) (see Chapter 6). Everson (1984a) estimated that the annual consumption of krill by squid could be as high as 30–50 million tonnes. While there is a great deal of uncertainty concerning the actual consumption it is potentially important and cannot be ignored.

5.7.4.4 Consumption by fish
The importance of krill in the diet of fish is discussed in Chapter 7, and the available data indicate that while fish are substantial krill consumers it is not possible at present to determine the exact amount they consume. Everson (1977b, 1984b) estimated that the fish stocks of the Southern Ocean could potentially consume approximately 300 million tonnes of food and concluded that the

Table 5.12. *Estimated annual consumption of krill by seals*

Seal species	Seal stock size (×10⁶)		Krill consumption (×10⁶ t y⁻¹)	
	Bengtson	Laws	Bengtson	Laws
Crabeater	30	14.8	127.62	63.2
Leopard	0.4	0.22	1.15	0.52
Ross	0.22	0.73	0.04	—
Antarctic Fur	1.10	0.20	0.44	0.12
Total	32.45	16.17	129.33	63.92

Based on data in Bengtson (1984) and compared with figures from Laws (1977b, 1985).
From Miller & Hampton (1989).

total amount of krill consumed was in the order of several tens of million tonnes.

Nototheniid and channichthyid consumption of krill in the Scotia Arc region has been estimated at between 5.4 and 6.6 million tonnes annually (Lubimova & Shust, 1980). Kock (1985) calculated that, in the same region, the total annual consumption of krill by demersal fish prior to the very heavy recent exploitation of the fish stocks is in the order of 10 million tonnes. In addition to the krill consuming demersal species, pelagic species (notably *Pleuragramma antarcticum* and a number of Myctophid species) also consume significant quantities of krill (Rowedder, 1979; Lubimova *et al.*, 1984; Hopkins, 1985b, R. Williams, 1985a,b), and this added to the consumption by demersal fishes would support the view that a figure of between 10 and 20 million tonnes for the annual consumption of krill by fish is a reasonable estimate.

5.7.4.5 Consumption by birds

Birds, especially the penguins, and in particular the Adélie Penguin (*Pygoscelis adeliae*), are major euphausiid consumers (see Chapter 10). From a detailed study of food consumption of some 22 bird species in the Scotia Sea Croxall *et al.* (1984b, 1985) estimated that they consumed 11 million tonnes of krill per year. Croxall (1984a) estimated that the total sum of direct and indirect (via fish and squid) predation of krill by seabirds at 115 million tonnes per year. Everson's (1977b) estimate of direct consumption was 25 million tonnes per year and a figure of 50 million tonnes for the annual direct consumption of krill by seabirds seems not unreasonable.

6

Nekton

6.1 Introduction

There is no sharp dividing line between pelagic animals that are regarded as plankton and those that constitute the nekton. Most free-swimming invertebrates are usually regarded as part of the zooplankton, even though many of them, such as some crustaceans, chaetognaths and others, may have considerable swimming speeds, equal to those of some species that are usually treated as part of the nekton. In the previous chapter, for example, we have seen that krill have the ability to swim for considerable distances. Many members of the nekton, e.g. larval fishes, also exist as plankton during the early stages of their life-cycle. There is also a considerable size overlap between the zooplankton and the nekton. Some species that are regarded as megazooplankton, e.g. siphonophores, scyphozoans (jellyfishes) and colonial salps, can be very large, greatly exceeding in size many nektonic species. Such species, however, generally drift with the currents and do not actively swim.

6.2 Species composition and distribution

Two groups of animals – the cephalopod molluscs and the fishes – have evolved numerous, large, actively swimming species which constitute the bulk of the nekton as generally understood. The fishes will be considered in the next chapter, while in this chapter an account will be given of the cephalopods.

Generally, apart from taxonomic accounts, there is a paucity of information available on the Southern Ocean invertebrate nekton fauna, especially that which inhabits the mesopelagic zone (100–1000 m). In most areas of the world's oceans a substantial fraction of the mesopelagic fauna migrates from 200 to 500 m daytime depths to, or near, the surface at dusk and returns to depth at dawn. At night these vertical migrants can make up greater than 70% of the micronektonic biomass in the top 100 m (Foxton & Roe, 1974; Hopkins & Lancraft, 1984). In the Antarctic the diel light–dark regimes differ markedly between winter and summer and this could have a profound influence on vertical migration patterns. In addition, the shading of the ocean by pack ice could further complicate the vertical migration patterns.

In their study of Antarctic mesopelagic micronekton in the austral spring of 1983 Ainley *et al.* (1985) found that representatives of the classical mid-water crustacean fauna (e.g. Pasiphaeidae, Oplophoridae, Mysidacea, Penaeidae, Ostracoda) which are common in boreal, temperate and tropical regions, were not captured with any regularity until north of 58^0 S. The myctophid fishes *Electrona antarctica* and *Gymnoscopelus braueri* were the main nektonic prey of seabirds in open water. However, deep into the pack ice crustacea of the genera *Pasiphaea* and *Eurythenes* replaced myctophids in the seabird (principally Snow and Antarctic Petrels) diet. The presence of these species at the surface indicated that the under-ice environment was strongly reminiscent of that of the mesopelagic zone, influencing such species to remain at the surface.

Abundance and biomass data on macrozooplankton and micronekton species in the Southern Ocean, apart from krill and other euphausiids, are fragmentary. While *Euphausia superba* may dominate in the upper 200 m other species, particularly *Salpa thompsoni*, squid and mesopelagic fish, can be very important, especially when depths down to 1000 m are considered. *S. thompsoni* (Piakowski, 1985a,b) can exceed *E. superba* in numerical abundance, and stocks of mesopelagic fishes (Rowedder, 1979; Asencio & Moreno, 1984; Hopkins, 1985a; R. Williams, 1985a,b) are also considerable. Lancraft *et al.* (1989) have sampled the micronekton and macrozooplankton assemblages in the vicinity of the marginal ice edge zone in the southern Scotia and the western Weddell Seas. Forty-nine species, including 17 fish and 19 crustaceans were collected. Decapod shrimps, which are typically abundant in other oceanic systems, were uncommon, being represented by only three rare species. Most species exhibited broad vertical ranges with no distinct pattern of vertical migration. However, many mesopelagic fishes and *Salpa thompsoni* undertook diel vertical migrations.

Biomass was high (2.4 to 3.1 g dry wt m^{-2}), four to five times more than that found by Hopkins & Lancraft (1984) in the Gulf of Mexico (0.573 g dry wt m^{-2}), but was similar to that found by Pearcy (1976) in the sub-Arctic waters off Oregon. In terms of biomass, euphausiids were the most important group at shallow depths (0–200 m) but were surpassed by salps in the Scotia Sea and by mesopelagic fishes in the Weddell Sea. Mesopelagic fish biomass for the entire Southern Ocean was computed at 133–191×10^6 tonnes, a value very close to that estimated by Russian surveys (140–190×10^6 tonnes; Kock, 1987). It is also ten times that calculated for all Antarctic bottom fish (Kock, 1987). The estimates of mesopelagic fish biomass (3.3 to 4.4 g wet wt m^{-2}) greatly exceeds that for Antarctic birds (0.025–0.070 g wet wt m^{-2}), seals (0.068–0.089 g wet wt m^{-2}) and whales (0.167–0.339 g wet wt m^{-2}) as estimated by Ainley *et al.* (1985) and Laws (1977b). Thus, on the basis of biomass alone mesopelagic fish are probably the most prevalent predators on krill in the Southern Ocean.

6.3 Cephalopods

6.3.1 Introduction

The principal group of cephalopods found in the waters of the Southern Ocean is the squids, with their shell reduced to thin, non-buoyant chitinous stiffening 'pens'. Their role in the Antarctic marine pelagic ecosystem is not clear due to the lack of data on their abundance and relationships. Potentially they represent one of the most important components of the ecosystem. They are probably major predators on krill and are themselves important prey of a range of vertebrate predators, including fishes, birds, seals and toothed whales. Squid are fast-swimming predators with well-developed nervous systems and are thus able to avoid being caught in ordinary nets. According to M. R. Clarke (1977), no net currently available can effectively sample any of the species of squid forming the main food of Sperm Whales. Fig. 6.1 makes a comparison between squids caught in research net hauls, commercial trawl nets and those eaten by predators (M. R. Clarke, 1977, 1983). Whereas squids in the family Histioteuthidae are dominant in the whale samples, enoploteuthids are dominant in trawl hauls and various other families are important in 9 m^2 nets.

The sizes of squids caught in research nets is also very different from those eaten by Sperm Whales and there is little overlap in the size distributions (M. R. Clarke, 1985). Nemoto *et al.* (1985) have compared the size distribution of the squid *Kondakovia longimana* collected by trawling operations with those found in the stomach contents of Sperm Whales (M. R. Clarke, 1980b). The size range (dorsal mantle length) of the former sample was

100–360 mm, whereas that of the latter sample was 340–820 mm.

6.3.2 Species composition, distribution and abundance

Approximately 72 cephalopod species are known, or thought to occur, south of the Antarctic Convergence. Of these, 55% are considered endemic to that area (Filipova, 1972). There are certainly a number of new species to be described (Roper, 1969, 1981; SCAR/SCOR, 1983c).

Most species of Antarctic squid are thought to be circumpolar, although a few species appear to be restricted to certain localities (Everson, 1977b). There is some indication that they may undertake seasonal migrations similar to those exhibited by northern cephalopods (Squires, 1957). M. R. Clarke (1983) noted that some species of squid descend in the water column as they mature. The differences in the sizes of squid captured by trawls and those taken by Sperm Whales may be partly due to the fact that trawls often operate in the upper water column only and thus sample the smaller sized stage found there; the Sperm Whales on the other hand take the larger mature squid in deeper water.

Because of the sampling problems it is difficult to estimate the abundances of the various species. The most abundant cephalopods as estimated from beaks present in Sperm Whale stomachs from Antarctica are Onychteuthids and Cranchiids, representing 53% and 23% respectively (M. R. Clarke, 1983). Estimates of the biomass eaten by predators using a known relationship between body size and beak size can be made (M. R. Clarke, 1983).

6.2.3 Reproduction and growth

Very little is known about reproductive activity, growth rates and longevity of Antarctic cephalopods. It seems that many species lay egg masses on continental slopes deeper than 1000 m (M. R. Clarke, 1985). McSweeny (1978) speculated that in *Galiteuthis glacialis*, large numbers of eggs are produced, followed by rapid growth, spawning, deterioration and death. Voss (1973) considered that many squid are short-lived, maturing at one year of age and dying after a single spawning. Some, however, may live for several years (Kristensen, 1980).

6.3.4 Food and feeding

Although it is known that several species of squid feed on krill (Marr, 1962; Dell, 1965; Nemoto *et al.*, 1985) the feeding behaviour is poorly known. Filipova (1972) has noted that some species such as *Kondakovia longimana* have not been found outside areas where krill are present and suggested that it and many similar species are specialist predators on krill. Everson (1981) estimated that

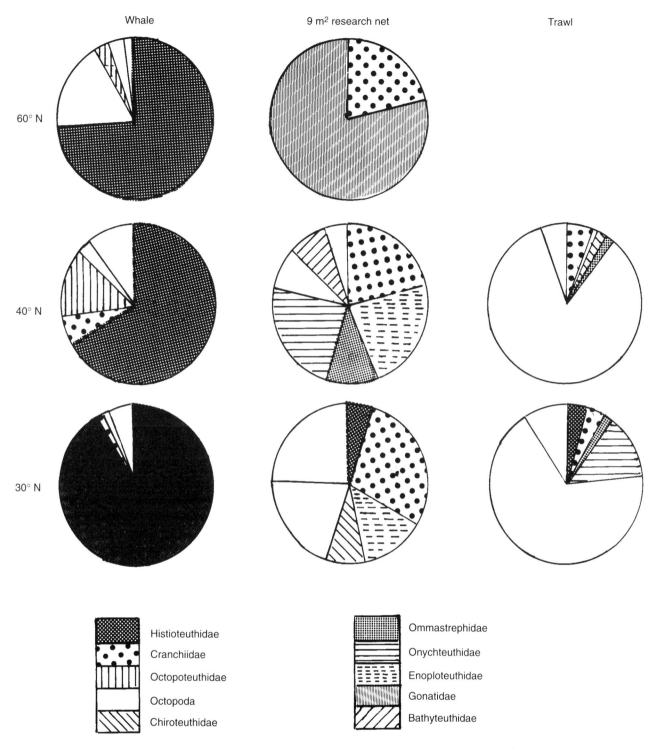

Fig. 6.1. The families of oceanic cephalopods (mainly squid) caught by Sperm Whales, research nets (9 m² mouth) and commercial trawls in three areas of the North Atlantic. The whales eat mainly histoteuthids, cranchiids and octopoteuthids, while nets catch mainly squids from other families. Redrawn from M. R. Clarke (1983).

the annual consumption of krill by cephalopods may be as high as 100 million tonnes per annum.

Nemoto *et al.* (1985) have examined the food contents of the stomachs of squid caught by mid-water trawling in depths between 10 and 200 m north of the South Shetland Islands. The species collected were all considered to be young juveniles distributed at shallower depths than adults. Two species *Kondakovia longimana* and *Moroteuthis knipovitchi* were dominant; other species included in the collections were *Pholidoteuthis boschmai*,

Brachioteuthis picta and *Galiteuthis glacialis*. These squid were found to consume various kinds of food, predominantly macrozooplankton and micronekton. The amphipod *Parathemisto gaudichaudii* was also a major component of the food of *K. longimana*, which also preyed on small euphausiids (*Thysanoessa macrura*), the large chaetognath *Sagitta gazellae*, fish and other squid. Fish together with krill were the predominant food of *M. knipovitchi*. Nemoto *et al.* (1985) concluded that *K. longimana* was predominantly a fish feeder which took myctophid and other fishes in the mesopelagic layer. In contrast to the findings of this study M. R. Clarke (1980a,b) found the remains of teleost fish, crustaceans, squid and sponges in the stomachs and caecae of specimens of *K. longimana* taken by Sperm Whales; teleosts were the most common. The larger adult specimens examined by Clarke would have been feeding in deeper water.

The work of Karpov & Cailliet (1978), studying *Loligo opalescens* in California can provide information on some of the factors which could influence the feeding behaviour of squid in the Southern Ocean. They found that in California prey composition: 1. is dependent on squid size, large squid feed mainly on euphausiids, cephalopods and fish; small squid feed mainly on crustacea such as megalops larvae, mysids and cumaceans; 2. is dependent on the depth of feeding; 3. is largely independent of predator sex; and 4. differs between spawning grounds and shallow water areas.

6.3.5 Ecological relationships

The impact of cephalopods as predators in the Southern Ocean ecosystem is unquantified. It depends not only on their feeding habits but their depth distribution and abundance. Most of the commercial fisheries for squid are carried out on continental shelves for species which either live near the land, such as the cuttlefishes and loligos, or move inshore seasonally, such as the ommastrephids, especially on spawning migrations. In the Southern Ocean cuttlefishes, loligos, and with one exception the ommastrephids, are absent from or unimportant (M. R. Clarke, 1985). The cephalopods that are abundant and important are the oceanic squids.

Squid constitute a significant proportion of the diets of many Antarctic vertebrate predators such as Sperm Whales, Commerson's Dolphin, Killer Whales, Weddell Seals, Ross Seals, Elephant Seals, penguins and albatrosses, and larger cephalopods are also reported to prey on squid (M. R. Clarke, 1983). Some of these predators at times feed entirely on krill and others include krill as a substantial component of their diets (SCAR/SCOR, 1983a).

If the stomachs of Sperm Whales caught by commercial

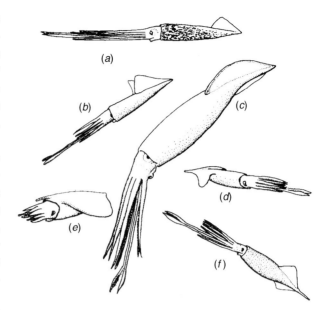

Fig. 6.2. The three squids of greatest importance in the diets of Southern Ocean squid predators, (*a*). *Kondakovia longimana* (mean length ML >80 cm), (*b*). *Moroteuthis knipovitchi* (ML >40 cm), (*c*). *Mesonychoteuthis hamiltoni* (ML >200 cm); and three squids which extend into the Southern Ocean from the north, (*d*). *Todarodes* sp. (ML <75 cm), (*e*). *Taningia danae* (ML >140 cm), F. *Moroteuthis robsoni* (ML <9 cm). Redrawn from M. R. Clarke (1983).

activities in the Southern Ocean are examined, large numbers of squid beaks are found and as many as 18 000 have been collected from a single stomach (M. R. Clarke, 1985). These Sperm Whales catch many species of squid which have rarely or never been caught in nets. The predominant species in the Sperm Whale's diet (75%) is the cranchiid squid *Mesonychoteuthis hamiltoni* which grows to a length of 10 m. This species has been caught in nets only once (M. R. Clarke, 1983). Second in importance are the oncyhoteuthids *Kondakovia longimana* and *Moroteuthis knipovitchi*. These species are illustrated in Fig. 6.2.

Goodall & Galeazzi (1985) have reviewed the food habits of small cetaceans in the Antarctic. From the scanty information that is available the beaked whales (Ziphidae), especially the Southern Bottlenosed Whale (*Hyperioodon planifrons*), all include squid in their diets. Squid appear to form a minor component of the diet of Killer Whales (*Orcinus orca*) (Shevchenco, 1976). Other delphinids known to feed on squid include the Pilot Whale (*Globicephala obscurus*), the Dusky Dolphin (*Lagenorhynchus obscurus*), the Bottlenosed Dolphin (*Tursiops truncatus*), and Commerson's Dolphin (*Cephalorhynchus commersonii*). The quantitative importance of squid in the diet of these species is unknown.

Cephalopods are also an important prey item for Elephant Seals which feed on fish and squid almost

Table 6.1. *The percentages by number of the species of Antarctic cephalopods in the diet of some predators in the Southern Ocean*

	Sperm Whales		Seals				Albatrosses		
	Antarctic	South Georgia	Elephant	Weddell	Fur	Leopard	Wandering	Grey-headed	Black-browed
Cranchiidae									
Mesonychoteuthis hamiltoni	16	30							
Galiteuthis glacialis			2		44		4	8	25
Taonius							17		
Onychoteuthidae									
Kondokovia longimana	18	28	4	<1	14	4	40	<1	1
Moroteuthis knipovitchi ⎫ *Moroteuthis robsoni* ⎭	51	23	14	31	14	92	2		
Gonatidae									
Gonatus	4	<1	42	1			6		1
Octopoteuthidae									
Taningia danae	—	14					1		
Ommastrephidae									
Todarodes ? sagittatus	—	3			28			88	68
Brachioteuthidae									
Brachioteuthis picta				1					
Histioteuthidae									
Histioteuthis spp.	11	2				15	<1		
Mastigoteuthidae									
Mastigoteuthis							3	<1	
Psychroteuthidae									
Psychroteuthis glacialis			6	29					
Neoteuthidae									
Alluroteuthis sp.			2	2			4		
Octopoda			10	35			2		1

From M. R. Clarke (1985).

exclusively (Laws, 1960a, 1977b; King, 1964; McCann, 1981b; M. R. Clarke & MacLoed, 1982a). M. R. Clarke & MacLoed (1982a) have reported on the stomach contents of Elephant Seals at Signey Island. Eight species of cephalopods from four to five families were identified. By number a gonatid, *Gonatus antarcticus*, an unidentified teuthoid, an onychoteuthid, *Moroteuthis knipovitchi*, and an octopod comprised 42%, 20%, 14% and 10% respectively of the total prey taken. By weight the octopod, *G. antarcticus*, and *M. knipovitchi* comprised 60%, 15% and 10% of the cephalopods present.

Ross Seals also feed on squid (King, 1969; Øritzland, 1977). Siniff & Stone (1985) found that in the Antarctic Peninsula area cephalopods were taken in small quantities (10–20%) throughout the year by Leopard Seals, but that in January squid comprised over 40% of the diet as determined by frequency of occurrence (percentage of food items in the stomachs).

Doidge & Croxall (1985) found that at South Georgia in the summer squid comprised 3% by weight of the food

taken by adult female, juvenile and weaner Fur Seals and 10% of that taken by males. For juvenile and adult males in the winter they estimated that squid comprised 30% by weight of food consumption. Four taxa of squid were identified from beaks present in the stomachs: *K. longimana*, *M. knipovitchi*, ? *G. glacialis* and an unidentified ommastephid, with *K. longimana* estimated to form nearly half the squid diet by weight and the ommastrephid one-third. Further north on Gough Island the related Fur Seal, *Arctocephalus tropicalis*, was found to consume mainly pelagic squid (Bester & Laycock, 1985). A surprising find was the presence of the Antarctic species *M. knipovitchi*.

Many species of bird take cephalopods in their diet. Abrams (1985a,b) record the following species from the African sector of the Southern Ocean as having squid as their principal food: Wandering Albatross, Black-browed Albatross, Grey-headed Albatross, Sooty Albatross, Light-mantled Sooty Albatross, Antarctic Fulmar, Pintado Petel, Great-winged, Petrel, White-headed

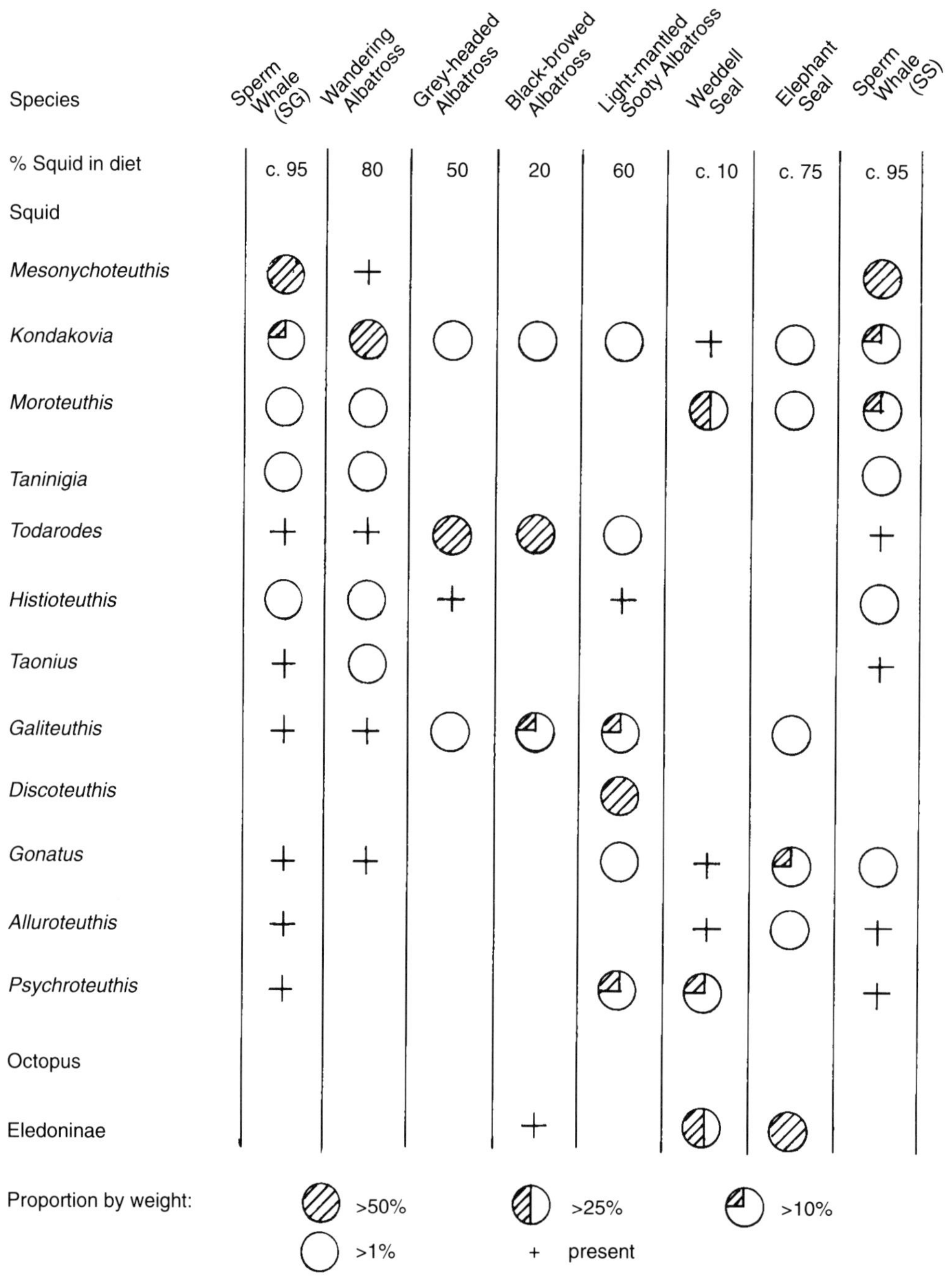

Species	Sperm Whale (SG)	Wandering Albatross	Grey-headed Albatross	Black-browed Albatross	Light-mantled Sooty Albatross	Weddell Seal	Elephant Seal	Sperm Whale (SS)
% Squid in diet	c. 95	80	50	20	60	c. 10	c. 75	c. 95
Squid								
Mesonychoteuthis	>50%	+						>50%
Kondakovia	>10%	>50%	>1%	>1%	>1%	+	>1%	>10%
Moroteuthis	>1%	>1%				>50%	>1%	>10%
Taninigia	>1%	>1%						>1%
Todarodes	+	+	>50%	>50%	>1%			+
Histioteuthis	>1%	>1%	+		+			>1%
Taonius	+	>1%						+
Galiteuthis	+	+	>1%	>25%	>25%		>1%	
Discoteuthis					>50%			
Gonatus	+	+			>1%	+	>25%	>1%
Alluroteuthis	+					+	>1%	+
Psychroteuthis	+				>25%	>25%		+
Octopus								
Eledoninae				+		>25%	>50%	

Proportion by weight: >50%; >25%; >10%; >1%; + present

Fig. 6.3. Composition by weight of squid in the diet of albatrosses, seals and Sperm Whales in the Scotia Sea. Only squid comprising more than 1% by weight of the diet of any species are included. SS=Scotia Sea; SG=South Georgia. Redrawn from Croxall *et al.* (1985).

Petrel, Atlantic Petrel, White-chinned Petrel, Grey Petrel and Great Shearwater. Prince (1980a,b, 1985) has examined the feeding ecology of the Black-browed and Grey-headed Albatrosses at South Georgia. He found that 50% of the diet of the Grey-headed Albatross was squid. Of the squid taken, two species *Todarodes sagittatus* and *Mesonychoteuthis* sp. comprised 88% and 8% by number and 91% and 4% by weight respectively. The Black-browed Albatross on the other hand took a lesser quantity of squid (21%). Wandering Albatrosses at South Georgia

are known to feed on larger squid than they would normally have access to. These larger squid, such as *Taninigia* sp. and *Kondakovia* sp. are probably obtained by feeding on the vomit of Sperm Whales.

M. R. Clarke (1985) has summarized the available data on the consumption of squid by predators in the Southern Ocean (Table 6.1). He suggests that this could perhaps be answered by estimating the weight, or 'biomass', of cephalopod stocks which must be consumed to sustain the populations of their predators. Croxall *et al.* (1985) have recently estimated cephalopod consumption for the Scotia Sea. Of the estimated 3.7 million tonnes of squid taken by seabird and seal predation in the Scotia Sea, 76% is consumed by Elephant Seals largely round South Georgia. Other species which take more than 1% of all squid eaten are White-chinned Petrels (10%), Antarctic Fulmars and Crabeater Seals (2.5% each), and King Penguins (1%). Sperm Whales are considered not to be important in this sector, and are estimated to take 162 000 tonnes of squid, or about 4% of the consumption of the seabirds and seals. About 94% of all squid consumed are taken by species breeding at South Georgia, with seals accounting for 88% and seabirds only 12%. In the rest of the Scotia Sea Crabeater Seals and Weddell Seals account for 48% and seabirds (mainly Antarctic Fulmars) 52%.

Fig. 6.3 depicts the composition by weight of the principal species (by analysis of beak collections, and estimation of squid mass from standard relationships; M. R. Clarke; 1980b) by the seven predator species that have so far been studied quantitatively (Croxall *et al.*, 1985). Although most species of squid are taken by several predators, the main prey of each (apart from the Grey-headed and Black-browed Albatrosses) is usually different.

An estimate of the total consumption of cephalopods in the Southern Ocean can only be extremely rough and of necessity is a minimum estimate. One such estimate is that of M. R. Clarke (1985), who suggested that the total consumption of cephalopods by whales, seals and birds is in the order of 30 million tonnes per annum. Clarke also estimated that the stock of squid necessary to support predation is in excess of 30 million tonnes a year and it may well be over 100 million tonnes, which is a very large biomass.

6.3.6 Commercial exploitation

Rodhouse (1990) has reviewed the cephalopod fauna of the Scotia Sea and the South Georgia area and their potential for commercial exploitation. Although no cephalopod fishery exists in the Scotia Sea, or elsewhere in Antarctica, the potential for their commercial exploitation has long been recognized (Voss, 1973; Everson, 1977a), and major cephalopod fisheries already exist in adjacent cool temperate seas around the Falkland Islands

(Csirke, 1987) and in the New Zealand region (Sato & Hatanaka, 1983). It has been suggested that the Antarctic stocks of cephalopods have increased this century as a direct result of the decrease in the numbers of their principal consumer, the Sperm Whale, through overexploitation, and as an indirect result of the overexploitation of baleen whales, resulting in the presumed greater availability of their common food resource *Euphausia superba* (Laws, 1985).

Of the 12 common species of squid in the seas around South Georgia, the ommastrephid *Martialia hyadesi* appears to have the most potential for exploitation. In 1986, 22 000 tonnes of this species from the Patagonian shelf were landed in Japan and in February 1989 two Japanese squid jigging vessels caught commercial quantities at the Sub-Antarctic Front near South Georgia (Rodhouse, 1990). Other candidates for commercial exploitation are the onychoteuthids, *Kondakovia longimana, Moroteuthis ingens, M. knipovitchi* and *M. robsoni*, and the gonatid *Gonatus antarcticus*. All are members of families which are the subject of directed fisheries elsewhere, or are caught as a by-catch and have commercial value.

Cephalopods that are fished commercially are fast-growing, short-lived and semelparous. Most species live for approximately one year, spawn once and die soon after (Boyle, 1983). This life-history differs from that of most exploited fish species and poses special problems for stock management (Amaratunga, 1987). Because cephalopods are generally semelparous and have a short generation time they are prone to extreme fluctuations in population size and are particularly susceptible to overfishing, because recruitment is dependent on the breeding success of a single exploited generation. Populations are also liable to expand rapidly under favourable conditions and cephalopods may have increased to fill the vacant niches created by overfishing in fish stocks.

Since a number of predators, especially in the Scotia Sea–South Georgia area, rely on the cephalopod stocks for a major proportion of their breeding season diet they would be severely affected by any overexploitation of the cephalopod populations. Adverse impacts on seabird populations by fisheries for their prey species are well documented (Furness, 1982; Nettleship *et al.*, 1984).

7

Fish

7.1 Introduction

In most of the world's seas the fish have been the subject of special study because of their economic importance. However, the lack of an indigenous population, the harsh climate and the opportunity to exploit stocks closer to the markets of the world delayed the exploitation of the fish resources of the Southern Ocean. As fish stocks declined in other parts of the world's oceans the possibility of the existence of substantial exploitable stocks in the Southern Ocean attracted the attention of fishing nations. Exploratory fishing commenced in the early 1960s and developed into large-scale fishing round South Georgia in the late 1960s. From there it spread to other parts of the Southern Ocean.

Increasing interest in Antarctic fish biology and stock estimation accompanied the exploitation of the stocks. Because of their physiological adaptations to extreme cold Antarctic fishes have been of considerable interest to physiologists (DeVries, 1974, 1977, 1978, 1983, 1988; A. Clarke, 1983; MacDonald *et al.*, 1987). Major reviews of the recent body of literature on Antarctic fishes and fisheries include those of Marshall (1964), Andriashev (1965), DeWitt (1971), Kock (1975, 1984), Permitin (1977), Everson (1978, 1984b) and Bengtson (1984).

7.2 Species composition and distribution (Fig. 7.1; Table 7.1)

Of the 20000 or so modern fish species only 120 are found south of the Antarctic Convergence. This frontal zone has had a marked effect on the evolution and composition of the shallow-water or coastal living species. In general, as discussed in Chapter 1, the depth of water over the continental shelf is much greater than for other oceans (Adie, 1964) and there is no shallow-water connection from this shelf to the continents to the north. Because of this many of the shelf species have the aspect of deep-water fishes. A direct consequence of this isolation is the high degree of endemism in the shelf species. The deep-water fauna, on the other hand, does not show the same endemism, with only half the species being restricted to the Antarctic (Table 7.1). The two faunas appear to overlap about the continent proper on the edge and upper part of the continental shelf.

The coastal bottom or demersal fishes form a diverse group including representatives from fifteen families. The dominant group is the suborder Notothenioidei, whose four families, the Nototheniidae (Antarctic cod), Harpagiferidae (plunder fish), Bathydraconidae (dragon fish) and Channichthyidae (ice or white fish), include more than 60% of the species and over 90% of the individuals. The Notothenioidei form a group of about 127 species (Balushkin, 1988) with a wide variety of eco-morphological types adapted to nearly all habitats from shallow tidal pools to the upper continental slope down to 2000 m (Kock, 1985). With relatively few non-notothenioid fishes in Antarctic waters, notothenioids fill ecological roles normally occupied by taxonomically diverse fishes in temperate waters (Eastman, 1991). The Nototheniidae and the Channichthyidae include the major Antarctic fish species currently or potentially of commercial importance (Table 7.2).

In contrast to the other oceans of the world the Southern Ocean does not contain obligate, shoaling, pelagic species. Except for the opah *Lampris guttatus* and the pork-beagle *Lamma nasus* which are occasional invaders from the north (Kock *et al.*, 1980; Prutkto, 1979; Svetlov, 1978), there are no true epipelagic families (i.e. families which are more or less confined to surface waters throughout their life-cycle). The pelagic families which occur in Antarctic waters are descendants from faunal groups of different origins: bathypelagic species, mesopelagic species and species originating from demersal families which are secondarily adapted to permanent or temporary mid-water life.

The mesopelagic fauna, living in waters below the euphotic zone down to a depth of 1000 m, comprises two groups of species. One group, apparently adapted for a long time to cold water, gave rise to a number of sub-Antarctic–Antarctic species (Kock, 1984). By far the most numerous group is the myctophids (*Electrona antarctica, Gymnoscephalus braueri, Bathylagus antarcticus, Cyclothone microdon, Protomyctophum* and

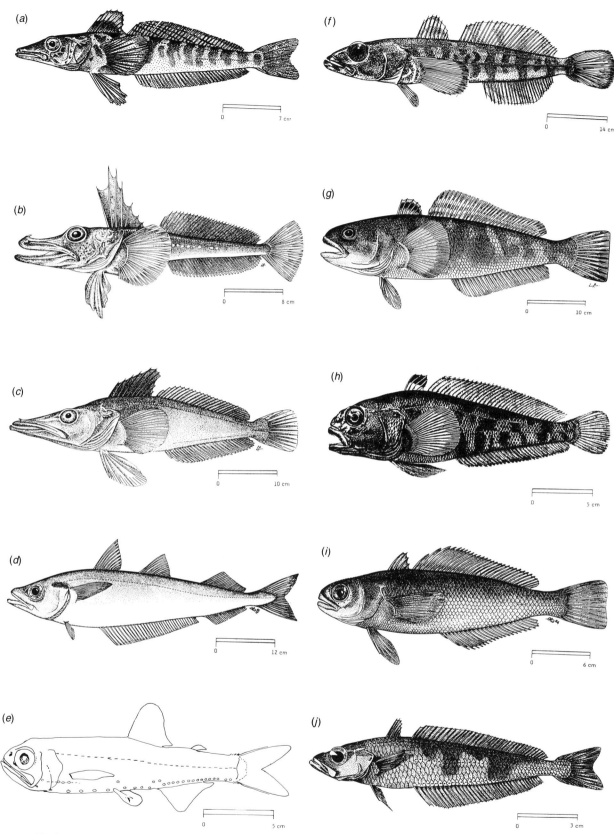

Fig. 7.1. Some common Antarctic fishes. (*a*) *Champsocephalus gunnari* (Fam. Channichthyidae), (*b*) *Channichthys rhinoceratus* (Fam. Channichthyidae), (*c*) *Pseudochaenichthys georgianus* (Fam. Channichthyidae), (*d*) *Micromesistius australis* (Fam. Gadidae), (*e*) *Kreffichys* (Fam. Myctophidae), (*f*) *Dissostichus eleginoides* (Fam. Nototheniidae), (*g*) *Notothenia (Notothenia) rossii* (Fam. Nototheniidae), (*h*) *Pagothenia bernacchii* (Fam. Nototheniidae), (*i*) *Pagonotothenia magellanica* (Fam. Nototheniidae), (*j*) *Pleuragramma antarcticum* (Fam. Nototheniidae). From FAO (1985).

Table 7.1. *The number of genera and species of each family found in the Antarctic, showing the number restricted to the Antarctic and the number also found farther north*

Family	Antarctic only		Antarctic and farther north		Totals	
	Genera	Species	Genera	Species	Genera	Species
Geotriidae (lampreys)	0	0	1	1	1	1
Myxinidae (hag fish)	0	0	1	1	1	1
Rajidae (skates)	0	3	2	1	2	4
Synaphobranchidae[1]	0	0	1	1	1	1
Halosauridae[1]	0	0	1	1	1	1
Muraenolepidae (eel cod)	0	2	1	1	1	3
Moridae	0	0	2	2	2	2
Gadidae (true cod)	0	0	1	1	1	1
Macrouridae[1]	0	4	5	3	5	7
Brotulidae[1]	0	1	1	0	1	1
Zoarcidae (eel pouts)	3	8	3	3	6	11
Nototheniidae (Antarctic cod)	4	31	2	3	6	34
Harpagiferidae (plunder fish)	4	14	1	1	5	15
Bathydraconidae (dragon fish)	8	15	0	0	8	15
Channichthyidae (icefish)	9	15	1	0	10	15
Congiopodidae (horse fish)	1	1	0	0	1	1
Liparidae (snail fish)	0	5	3	0	3	5
Bothidae (flounders)	0	1	1	1	1	2
Totals						
All families	29	100	27	20	56	120
All but abyssal families	29	95	19	15	48	110

[1]Denotes a bathyal or abyssal family (DeWitt, 1971).
From Everson (1984b).

Table 7.2. *Some of the common fishes of the Southern Ocean*

Group	Species	Common name
Rajidae	*Raja georgiana*	
	Raja murrayi	Rays
	Raja eatoni	
Gadidae	*Micromesistius australis*	Southern poutassou or blue whiting
Nototheniidae	*Notothenia gibberifrons*	Bumphead notothenia
	Notothenia rossii rossii	
	Notothenia rossii marmorata	Marbled notothenia
	Notothenia squamifrons	Scaled notothenia
	Paranotothenia magellanica	
	Notothenia coriiceps coriiceps	
	Notothenia coriiceps neglecta	
	Notothenia kempi	
	Notothenia angustifrons	
	Nototheniops larseni	
	Pagothenia bernacchii	
	Pagothenia borchgrevinki	
	Patagonotothen brevicauda guntheri	Gunther's notothenia
	Dissostichus mawsoni	Antarctic toothfish
	Dissostichus eleginoides	Patagonian toothfish
	Pleuragramma antarcticum	Antarctic sidestripe or Antarctic silverfish
Channichthyidae	*Champsocephalus gunnari*	Antarctic icefish
	Channichthys rhinoceratus	Longsnouted icefish
	Pseudochaenichthys georgianus	South Georgia icefish
	Chionodraco rastrospinosus	Kathleen's icefish
	Chaenodraco wilsoni	

Kreffichys) and the lepids or ionah fishes *Notolepis coatsi* and *N. annualta*. The second group consists of fishes with a more northerly distribution which regularly undertake feeding migrations to the peripheral waters of the Southern Ocean: Notosuridae, Trichiuridae (hairtails), Oreosomatidae (dories), Anotopteridae (daggertooths) and some of the Myctophidae and Paraleoidae.

The secondarily pelagic fishes comprise members of the families Nototheniidae, Channichthyidae, Bathydraconidae and even Harpagiferidae, which either spend the first year, or years, in mid-water and are often associated with drifting or fast ice, or krill aggregations, or are temporary or pelagic species during most of their life. Included in the latter group are the widespread and abundant Antarctic herring *Pleuragramma antarcticum* and the epipelagic *Pagothenia borchgrevinki*, which is associated with the underside of the sea ice in inshore waters (DeVries, 1978).

7.3. Morphological and physiological adaptations

Two important characteristics of the Antarctic marine environment are the narrow annual temperature range and, especially in deeper water and close to the continent, a water temperature that is near or at the freezing point of seawater. Because of this stability of the environment Antarctic fishes have evolved to be most efficient at low temperatures. However, in the near-freezing water they have needed to evolve systems to prevent freezing. The physiology and morphology of Antarctic fishes covering aspects such as buoyancy adaptations, cold adaptations, freezing resistance, metabolic adaptation, white bloodedness in channichthyids, and buoyancy adaptations have been extensively studied in recent years (see MacDonald *et al.*, 1987 for a recent review).

7.3.1 Metabolic adaptation

Temperate water fishes are able to adjust to quite large changes in their environmental temperature, i.e. they can 'acclimate' to higher or lower temperatures, with such acclimation being achieved usually over an extended period of several weeks. Higher latitude Antarctic fish, however, are only able to survive over a narrow range of temperatures and cannot tolerate temperatures beyond $+4$ to $+6\,°C$, and these limits do not change even after long periods of acclimation.

The consistently low temperatures present in the Southern Ocean means that rates of biochemical reactions will be much slower than they would be in temperate regions. Yet Antarctic fish function efficiently at the low temperatures of their habitat. Wohlschlag (1964) found that the basal oxygen consumption of polar fish (Arctic as well as Antarctic) was five to ten times higher

than expected and considered that this elevated rate, which he termed 'cold adaptation', to be an evolutionary adaptation to overcome the rate-depressing effects of temperature. Holeton (1974), however, considered that Wohlschlag's results were an artefact of the experimental technique used and thus did not indicate true metabolic rates. Everson (1977a) examined growth rates of Antarctic fishes in relation to their warm-water relatives and found that growth rates were slow, indicating little in the way of adaptation. It would therefore appear that Wohlschlag's original concept of 'cold adaptation' needs to be abandoned or at least modified.

On the other hand, compensation for decreasing temperatures in biochemical systems at the tissue level has been demonstrated for several species (Somero *et al.*, 1968; Lin *et al.*, 1976) and also in terms of direct enzyme activities (Johnston & Walesby, 1977; Somero, 1969). These results show that at the low environmental temperatures found in Antarctic waters the enzymes of Antarctic fishes are more efficient catalysts than those of temperate fishes living at higher temperatures. M. A. K. Smith & Haschemeyer (1980) found that in Antarctic fishes the protein synthesis rate in the liver was twice, and in white muscle three times, that predicted from theoretical temperature dependency relationships. However, the low protein synthesis rate of 6% liver protein per day compared with values of about 20% measured in tropical fish (M. A. K. Smith *et al.*, 1980), nevertheless indicated a reduced metabolic rate. Thus, the enzyme systems of Antarctic fish exhibit features which seem to be related to their operation at low temperatures. These features (Macdonald & Montgomery, 1990) are: 1. most enzymes function best at $20–40\,°C$, but those of Antarctic fish are most active near $0\,°C$; 2. many Antarctic fish enzymes do not increase activity markedly at higher temperatures, which indicates that relatively little energy is needed to activate the enzymatic reactions; and, 3. enzymes and other proteins of Antarctic fishes tend to be less stable than those of warm-water fishes, and are easily denatured by both chemical agents and high temperatures. Under the assumption that the energetic costs of feeding and activity are comparable to those for temperate water species, the evidence of reduced basal metabolism, reduced growth and reduced reproductive effort leads to a new concept of cold adaptation (A. Clarke, 1980b).

7.3.2 Freezing resistance

Seawater has a freezing point of about $-1.8\,°C$, depending on the salinity – the higher the salinity, the lower the freezing point. While most marine invertebrates have body fluids which contain as much, if not more, salts than the surrounding water fishes have much more dilute body fluids, which result in a salt concentration which will depress their freezing point by only about –0.7 °C. Since the temperatures in the inshore regions of Antarctica are below this for most of the time the fishes must have some mechanism to avoid freezing. They are able to do this because they have evolved macromolecules which have unique antifreeze properties. In Antarctic notothenioids there are glycoproteins composed of the amino-acids threonine and alanine and the sugars galactose and galactosamine. In the nototheniid *Pagothenia borchgrevinki* eight glycoproteins of different sized molecules have been identified (DeVries, 1978). The antifreezes depress the freezing point of water by via a non-colligative mechanism termed absorption-inhibition (DeVries, 1988). Ice enters Antarctic fish in their natural habitat. However, the antifreezes keep the ice crystals small so that they have no detrimental effect on the fish.

7.3.3 White bloodedness

The respiratory physiology of Antarctic fish has attracted a great deal of attention ever since Matthews (1931) and Rudd (1954, 1965) established that the Channichthyidae (icefish) had no haemoglobin or respiratory pigment in their blood. Several other workers who have examined the blood of a range of Antarctic fishes have drawn attention to the lowered concentration of haemoglobin and the reduced number of erythrocytes present in comparison with temperate and tropical fishes. In general haemoglobin concentrations of Antarctic fishes fall within the range of 4–6 g (100 ml)$^{-1}$ of blood as compared to 7–12 g (100 ml)$^{-1}$ for other teleosts, while the erythrocyte counts generally fall within the range of $0.5–1.0 \times 10^6$ mm^{-3} of blood as compared with 1.2×10^6 mm^{-3} for most other teleosts (Tyler, 1960; Kooyman, 1963; Hureau, 1966; Everson & Ralph, 1970).

In the icefish the oxygen is transported by simple physical solution in the blood plasma and consequently the oxygen carrying capacity is only about 10% that of the nototheniids living in the same environment. In spite of this the white blooded fish are not sluggish sedentary species but reach sizes of 60–75 cm, and occupy a range of ecological niches, including active swimmers hunting for prey in the pelagic zone, such as the South Georgian icefish *Pseudochaenichthys georgianus*. They have developed a number of adaptations which largely compensate for their presumed physiological 'disadvantage'. The blood passages in the secondary gill lamellae are larger than those of any other teleost (Steen & Berg, 1966; Jakubowski & Byczkowska-Smyk, 1970) so that they may act more efficiently. It has been suggested that cutaneous respiration may be a significant process. However, recent research (Hemmingsen & Douglas,

1970; Holeton, 1970) indicated that it probably only accounts for between 2.8 and 3% of the total oxygen uptake. The blood volume (8–9% of the total volume) is much higher than in other nototheniids (Hemmingsen & Douglas, 1970; Twelves, 1972) and the size of the heart and the thickness of the cardiac muscle are much larger than in other teleosts (Everson & Ralph, 1970; Holeton, 1974). Everson & Ralph (1970) estimated that the cardiac output of *Chaenocephalus aceratus* was about ten times that of an equivalent cod and Holeton (1970) found a several-fold difference between this species and red-blooded fish from the same locality. Thus, the increase in cardiac output and stroke volume and reduction in vascular resistance brought about by an increase in the bore of the blood vessels results in a large-volume system operating at low pressure, with a higher blood to tissue oxygen gradient than that found in other fishes. Although the blood has a low oxygen capacity this is not a problem in the cold Antarctic waters where the percentage oxygen saturation is high.

7.3.4 Buoyancy adaptations

The notothenioids are primarily bottom dwellers lacking swim bladders. Some nototheniids and channichthyids, however, show a trend towards the evolution of neutrally buoyant species (Nybelin, 1947), which have become permanent members of the mid-water community. The absence of competition from other mid-water species and the abundant food supply (especially krill) have probably been responsible for this trend (Eastman, 1980, 1985a). *Pleuragramma antarcticum, Aethotaxis mitopteryx* and *Dissostichus mawsoni* are all neutrally buoyant. *D. mawsoni* is the largest predatory fish in the mid-waters of the Southern Ocean. In McMurdo Sound, *D. mawsoni* feeds predominantly on fish and mysid shrimps (Eastman, 1985a). Evolutionary adaptations for buoyancy are reflected as morphological specializations such as reduced mineralization of the skeleton, reduced scale mineralization and lipid storage (DeVries & Eastman, 1978; Eastman, 1985a, 1988; Eastman & DeVries, 1978, 1981, 1982, 1985, 1986). *P. antarcticum* is unique among vertebrates in storing lipids in large subcutaneous and intermuscular sacs. Lipid in *Dissosticus* is contained in adipose cells in subcutaneous and muscular deposits, accounting for 4.7% and 4.8% of the body weight respectively. In both species the lipids consist primarily of triacylglycerols.

In the neutrally buoyant nototheniids the skeleton is weakly calcified with a considerable amount of cartilage and consequently a considerable reduction in weight. The scales are also incompletely mineralized. A subcutaneous lipid layer in *D. mawsoni* and subcutaneous lipid sacs in *P. antarcticum*, together with the high lipid content of the

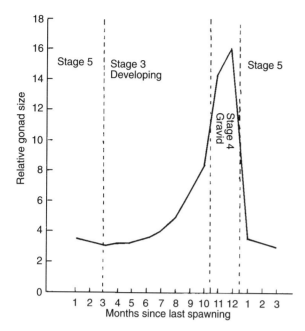

Fig. 7.2. Probable seasonal pattern of relative female gonad size (gonad weight/total weight)×100. Morphological characteristics of stages: 1. immature – ovary small, firm, no ova visible to the naked eye, (not shown); 2. maturing virgin – ovary 1/4 length body cavity, firm, full of eggs, (not shown); 3. developing ovary – ovary large, contains eggs of two sizes; 4. gravid – ovary large, when opened large ova spill out; 5. Spent – ovary flaccid, contains few large and small ova. Redrawn from Everson (1984b).

white muscles provide buoyancy (Eastman & DeVries, 1982). The liver of *D. mawsoni* is unique in that it contains large amounts of lipids (Eastman & DeVries, 1981). The lack of a swim bladder and the development of large pectoral fins in the nototheniids may allow vertical migration over several hundred metres in a short time.

7.4 Reproduction and growth

7.4.1 Size and growth

Most Antarctic fish are relatively small, with fewer than half reaching 25 cm in length and only about 12 species growing to more than 50 cm in length (Andriashev, 1965). There are, however, large species such as *Dissostichus mawsoni*, which attains a length of 165 cm, a weight of 77 kg (Raymond, 1975), and an age of 31 years (Burchett *et al.*, 1984). *D. elegenoides* reaches a length of 186 cm, a weight of 52 kg, and an age of 22 years (Zacharov & Frolkina, 1976; Kock, 1980).

In general Antarctic fish have slow, seasonal growth patterns (Everson, 1970a, 1984b; Burchett, 1983b), and low metabolic rates (A. Clarke, 1983). Everson (1977a) has compared growth rates of Antarctic fishes with other cold water species and confirmed that they have slower growth rates.

7.4.2 Age at sexual maturity

As a consequence of their slow growth rates, slow metabolic rates, and relatively long life spans, many Antarctic fish do not reach sexual maturity until three to eight years. Length at first spawning may be from 55% of the maximum length (L_{max}) onwards, but in many species it is not attained until 70–80% of L_{max}. The only exception is *Champsocephalus gunnari* at South Georgia which may begin spawning at about 40% of L_{max} (Kock & Kellerman, 1991). Male *Notothenia neglecta* (Everson, 1970b), *N. rossii marmorata* (Olsen, 1954; Shust, 1978), *N. rossii rossii* (Hureau, 1970) and *Chaenocephalus aceratus* (Kock, 1981) mature approximately one year earlier than females. However, in other species, such as *N. kempi* (Shust, 1978), *N. squamifrons* (Duhamel & Hureau, 1981), *C. gunnari* and *Pseudochaenichthys georgianus* (Kock, 1981), both sexes mature at the same age.

7.4.3 Gonad maturation and development

The development and maturation of the gonads of several species of Antarctic fish have been described by Dearborn (1965a), Everson (1970b) and Hureau (1970). Both the development and maturation proceed synchronously in individuals of the same species so that the spawning season is generally of limited duration. In *Notothenia neglecta* the ovary starts to increase in size during November, after being more or less constant at 3% of the total body weight for the preceding six months (Fig. 7.2). The increase is gradual over the period six to eight months after spawning, followed by a rapid two-month increase (March–April) so that the gonad is nearly twice its March size when spawning takes place in May. The final maturation of the testis begins in December when there is a steady increase in size until spawning in May. There is then a steady reduction in size dues to release and resorption of sperm (Fig. 7.3).

7.4.4 Ova development and fecundity

Early studies by Marshall (1953) concluded that Antarctic fish produce relatively few, large, yolky eggs and larvae which hatch at an advanced stage. Eggs range in size from 0.7 mm for *Muraenolepis microps* to 4.8 mm for *Notothenia rossii marmorata*, with an average egg size of 2.8 mm. There is a general trend in nototheniids of increasing egg size and decreasing relative fecundity towards higher latitudes (Kellerman, 1990a). Recent studies on *Notothenia neglecta* indicate that due to the large size of the ova yolk deposition may take more than one year (Everson, 1970b), so that there are two distinct classes of yolky oocytes present in a mature ovary. A biennial process of maturation has also been reported in

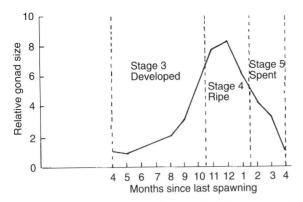

Fig. 7.3. Probable seasonal pattern of relative male gonad size. Morphological characteristics of the stages: 1. immature – testis small, translucent; 2. developing – testis small, white, convoluted; 3. developed – testis large, white, convoluted, no milt produced when cut; 4. ripe – testis large, opalescent, white, milt produced when cut; 5. Spent – testis smaller, dirty white in colour. Redrawn form Everson (1984b).

other species such as *Pagothenia borchgrevinki* (Andriashev *et al.*, 1979) and *Champsocephalus gunnari* and *Pseudochaenichthys georgianus* (Koch, 1979).

A consequence of the production of large yolky eggs is that fecundity is generally quite low. Overall fecundity ranges from about 100 eggs in *Paraliparis antarcticus* (Lisovenko & Svetlov, 1980) to more than 50 0000 in *Dissostichus eleginoides*. Relative fecundity (i.e. the number of eggs per gram body weight) is in general 4–30 for all channichthyids, most nototheniids, *Pseudochaenichthys georgianus* and *Harpagifer* spp. A higher relative fecundity of about 50–150 eggs is found in several late winter and spring spawning species of *Notothenia*, in the dragon fish *Psilodraco breviceps* and in the eel cod *Muraenolepis microps*. Fecundity in different populations of the one species, as well as in different genera of one family (e.g. *Champsocephalus gunnari*, *Notothenia* and *Trematomus*), normally decreases with higher latitudes (Permitin & Sil'yanova, 1971; Kock, 1981).

7.4.5 Spawning

Spawning dates are now fairly well known for a good number of species (Hureau, 1966, 1970; Everson, 1970b; Permitin, 1973; Keysner *et al.*, 1974; Permitin & Sil'yanova, 1971; Bengtson, 1984). Of the 24 species for which data are available 30% of all individuals spawn in the summer, 43% in the autumn, 17% in the winter and 10% in the spring. Approximately 71% of species spawn in the late summer and autumn (March to June), with peak spawning occurring around May–June (54%). Only 28% of the species spawn during the eight months of the year between July and February. Those species spawning in the summer (January to April), especially in the early

summer (February), have a longer spawning period than fish spawning in autumn and winter. Species spawning between January and April have an average spawning period of over 61 days, while those spawning from May to December have an average spawning period of 48 days.

Spawning migrations have been described for several species. The marbled notothenia, *Notothenia rossii*, undertakes regular migrations from the feeding grounds in the northeast to the spawning area in the southeast of the Kerguelen Plateau, probably assisted by a prevailing southward flowing current (Meissner *et al.*, 1974). South Georgian icefish in spawning condition are found only in inshore waters, whereas those caught offshore are less advanced in their maturation, indicating an onshore migration movement. Males generally start spawning migrations earlier than females (Kock, 1981).

Based on the lack of oil droplets the eggs of most species are considered to be deposited on the bottom (demersal), or to float loosely on the sea floor (benthopelagic), where they are protected against the lower salinity surface water and damage by drifting or freezing ice. M. G. White *et al.* (1982) found that the developing eggs of *Notothenia neglecta* at Signy Island are free-floating, but become negatively buoyant after 14 days when they sink to the bottom, whereas those from South Georgia floated throughout the whole period of their embryonic development. Protection by nest guarding has been described in *Harpagifer bispinis* and *Pagothenia bernacchii* (Daniels, 1979; Moreno, 1980).

7.4.6 Hatching period and larval development

Although the spawning season for most Antarctic fishes is relatively short there is a considerable time lapse between spawning and hatching (Burchett *et al.*, 1983). Burchett *et al.* found that the time between spawning and first hatching varied from 60 days in *Notothenia squamifrons* to 270 days in *Chionodraco* sp. However, hatching primarily occurs in the late winter and spring (August to October) regardless of the spawning timing. Fish spawning in the spring and early summer have a short embryonic period, hatching at the end of summer. Marshall (1953), Everson (1970b), North & White (1982), Burchett (1983b) and Efremenko (1983) all found that the larvae of Antarctic fish species were hatched at a large size and with an average length of 10 mm.

The large size of the larvae is a consequence of the large eggs with ample food reserves. The larger larvae have a smaller food requirement per unit weight, and are capable of swimming more actively in search of food than smaller larvae (Marshall, 1953). Even though rela-

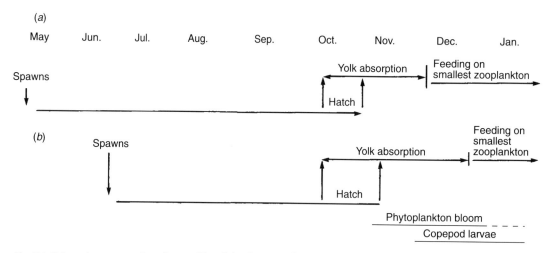

Fig. 7.4. Schematic representation of egg and larval development of two Antarctic fish; (*a*) *Notothenia neglecta*, and (*b*) *Harpagifer bispinis*. Redrawn from Everson (1984b).

tively large, the early postlarvae are able to feed on only the smallest zooplankton (Daniels, 1979; Hoshiai & Tanimura, 1981; Burchett, 1983b). Because these food items, especially larval copepods, are most abundant immediately following the summer phytoplankton bloom, the development of the fish larvae needs to be synchronized in such a way that yolk reserves are used up as copepod larvae become available at peak abundance. Fig. 7.4 gives a calendar of events in the early life-history of two species, *Harpagifer bispinis* and *Notothenia neglecta*, which fit well with the cycle of primary production and thus the production of copepod larvae as food.

During the first few weeks after hatching, the larvae do not migrate far away from the spawning area, but remain over the shelves (Efremenko, 1983). Once they develop into fingerlings they may disperse away from the continental shelves to over deep water. This dispersal has been recorded in species such as *Notothenia neglecta* (M. G. White *et al.*, 1982) and *N. rossii marmorata* (Burchett, 1982, 1983a) in the Scotia Sea, where the young fish may be carried by currents into lower latitudes from the South Orkneys and the South Shetland Island to South Georgia and the South Sandwich Islands.

7.4.7 Reproductive strategies

Reproductive strategies of Antarctic notothenioids have recently been reviewed by North & White (1987) and Kock & Kellerman (1991). Two groups of notothenioids can be distinguished with respect to egg size. The first group comprises species with a moderatively high fecundity which spawn numerous smaller eggs resulting in a large number of larvae. This strategy is common among late winter/spring spawners in the Seasonal Pack Ice Zone, e.g. *Nototheniops larseni*, *Notothenia gibberifrons*, *N. squamifrons* and *N. kempi*, and *Pleuragramma*

antarcticum in the High Antarctic Zone. Their larvae are small particle feeders which utilize mainly copepod eggs, nauplii and copepodite stages as well as pelagic molluscs such as *Limacina* sp. (Balbontin *et al.*, 1986; Hubold, 1985a; Kellerman, 1987, 1990a,b). The second group produces fewer, larger eggs which release correspondingly large larvae, e.g. icefishes, *Trematomus* and some larger-sized *Notothenia*. Most of these are large particle feeders. Icefish, for example, commence feeding on larval stages of euphausiids and fish larvae (Kellerman, 1986).

The majority of species hatch in the spring and early summer when zooplankton production increases following the onset of the spring phytoplankton bloom. Spring hatching larvae originate from eggs spawned from early autumn and exhibit a wide range of lengths at hatching (5–17 mm), indicating that different food size spectra are utilized by the feeding larvae (R. Williams, 1985b; Balbontin *et al.*, 1986; Kellerman, 1986), thus allowing for size-dependent resource partitioning by the abundant co-occurring larvae (Kellerman, 1987; Hubold & Ekau, 1990). A number of species hatch during the winter. They all have large larvae emerging from large and yolky eggs of 4–5 mm in diameter. These larvae have lower relative food requirements and large search volumes so that they can cope with food scarcity under the winter ice cover. However, the larvae of some species form part of the cryopelagic community feeding on the ice algal communities or on the copepod larvae associated with the ice (Knox, 1986, 1990). Besides the trophic niche segregation by larval size variation in spring there exists a temporal sequence of hatching periods by species throughout the summer. This is thought to be related to the sequential occurrence of reproductive peaks of calanoid copepods (Kellerman, 1986, 1987).

7.5 Feeding ecology

In the last 20 years feeding behaviour has been investigated in many Antarctic fishes. Notable among the studies are those of Hureau (1970), Permitin (1970), Yukhov (1971), Permitin & Tarverdiyera (1972, 1978), Tarverdiyera (1982), Richardson (1975), DeWitt & Hopkins (1977), Moreno & Osorio (1977), Hoshiai (1979), Kompowski (1980a,b), Moreno & Zamorano (1980), Tarverdiyera & Pinskaya (1980), Duhamel (1982), Kock (1981, 1984, 1985), Targett (1981), Wyanski & Targett (1981), Daniels (1982), Burchett (1982, 1983a), Chekunova & Naumov (1982), Linkowski *et al.* (1983), Takahashi (1983), Duhamel & Hureau (1985), Takahashi & Nemoto (1984), Durante & Moreno (1985), Hubold (1985b), Kellerman (1987) Kozlov & Tarverdiera (1989), North & Ward (1989) and Casaux *et al.* 1990). Knowledge of the feeding ecology of Antarctic fishes is becoming increasingly important in the light of the increase which has occurred in the exploitation of Antarctic fish stocks and the krill upon which many of the species depend for food.

7.5.1 Feeding niches and food availability

As mentioned previously, although notothenioids are primarily bottom dwelling species they have nevertheless occupied a wide range of ecological niches. Although the feeding niche of a fish is determined by a complex set of dimensions (habitat, prey species, prey size, etc.), there is a broad vertical distribution of the niches. Antarctic fishes can be grouped into: 1. demersal species (bottom living) feeding on sedentary and motile benthic animals; 2. demerso-pelagic species (above the bottom) feeding on motile benthic animals and nekton swimming above the bottom; and 3. pelagic (free-swimming) species feeding on zooplankton and pelagic larval and adult fishes. Pelagic fishes may inhabit the first 200 m of surface water (epipelagic), or deeper waters between 200 and 1000 m (mesopelagic). Equivalent demersal and demerso-pelagic fish may be encountered in the shallow sublittoral (0–50 m), or bathydemersal zone (1000 m+). Table 7.3 lists selected common Antarctic fish species according to their feeding niches.

The bulk of the food available to pelagic feeders is copepods, euphausiids, salps and fish larvae, with cnidarians and pteropods important in some areas (Everson, 1984b). Zooplankton available to the fish include grazers (herbivores) and predators (carnivores). Grazers which are frequently found in fish stomachs include calanoid copepods, small euphausiids, medusae, and ctenophores, while the carnivores include euchaeted copepods, chaetognaths, amphipods and pteropods (Everson, 1984a).

As discussed above the development of yolky eggs developing over the winter allows the larval fish to hatch at an advanced stage coinciding with the phytoplankton bloom and abundant zooplankton grazers, especially copepods. Many of the zooplankton species that the pelagic fishes feed on spend their summer months in the epipelagic zone (0–200 m) and the winter period (May to August) in deeper water or under the ice (David, 1955, 1958, 1965; Hopkins, 1971). Both demersal and pelagic fish benefit from the vertical migration and swarming behaviour of the invertebrate zooplankton. In the winter the deeper depth distribution of the zooplankton brings them near the seabottom in shallow areas on the continental shelves. This allows both the demersal and demerso-pelagic fish to prey on the zooplankton not available to them at other times of the year (Kompowski, 1980a; Naito & Iwami, 1982).

In the summer zooplankton abundance in the surface waters increases as a consequence of vertical migration (Foxton, 1956) and reproductive and growth cycles. Many pelagic fish, especially in their larval and juvenile stages, feed on the concentrated zooplankton at this time. For example, juvenile *Champsocephalus gunnari* is often a by-catch species in krill harvesting (Kompowski, 1980b). Krill, salps, gammarid amphipods, and hyperiids are often found in the stomachs of demersal and demerso-pelagic fish such as *Notothenia kempi, N. gibberifrons, N. rossii, Chaenocephalus aceratus* and *Chionodraco* species (Permitin & Tarverdiyera, 1972. 1978). When the epipelagic concentrations of summer zooplankton (especially in the top 50 m) extend into the nearshore sublittoral zone they become available to demersal species present in that zone. Pelagic zooplankton have been identified in the stomach contents of *N. rossii* juveniles in the nearshore waters of South Georgia (Hoshiai, 1979) and krill are a common item in the diet of *N. gibberifrons* from the shallows at the South Shetland Islands (Takahashi, 1983).

Demersal fish, as well as some of the demerso-pelagic species, feed principally on benthic invertebrates (Targett, 1981; Burchett *et al.*, 1983). The species composition of the benthic community varies with depth, substrate, and to a lesser extent, with season (Daniels, 1982), and this is reflected in the diets of the fishes. Many infaunal species are unavailable to the fishes, with the possible exception of *N. gibberifrons* (Moreno & Osorio, 1977). The epifaunal invertebrates are important prey items for most of the benthic fishes and are available year round (Burchett, 1983a).

7.5.2 Niche changes over the life-cycle

Most species change their feeding niche at least once

Table 7.3. *Ecotypes of selected species of Antarctic fish based on body morphology, diet and depth of capture*

Demersal fish species	Zone[1]	Demerso-pelagic fish species	Zone[1]	Pelagic fish species	Zone[1]
Raja georgiana	3	*Nototheniops larseni*	2, 3	*Pleuragramma antarcticum*	5, 6
R. murrayi	2	*N. rossii marmorata* (adult)	2, 3	*Dissostichus mawsoni*	5, 6
R. eatoni	2	*N. rossii rossii* (adult)	2, 3	*D. eleginoides*	3
Notothenia giberrifrons	2, 3	*P. magellanica*	2, 3	*Micromesistius australis*	3
N. rossii marmorata (juv)	2	*Pagothenia hansoni*	2, 3	*Electrona antarctica*	6
N. rossii rossii (juv.)	2	*T. newnesi*	2, 3	*Gymnoscopelus nicholsi*	6
N. coriiceps neglecta	2	*Champsocephalus spp.*	2, 3	*Notolepis coatsi*	6
N. angustifrons	1, 2	*Chaenocephalus aceratus*	2, 3	Larvae and postlarvae of many	
N. kempi	2, 3	*Pseudochaenichthys georgianus*	2, 3	fish species and young of	
N. cyanobrancha	2			*Champsocephalus gunnari* and	
N. squamifrons	2, 3			Myctophidae	
Paranothenia magellanica	1, 2				
Trematomus spp.	2, 3				
Harpagifer spp.	1, 2				
Artedidraco spp.	2, 3				
Pogonophyrne spp.	3, 4				
Muraenolepis microps	2, 3				
Psilodraco breviceps	2				
Pseudochaenichthys spp.	2				
Channichthys rhinoceratus	2				
Chionodraco spp.	2, 3				

[1]Zone 1, littoral, 0–3m depth; Zone 2, sublittoral, 3–200 m depth; Zone 3, archidemersal, 200–1000 m depth; Zone 4, abyssodemersal, 1000+ m depth; Zone 5, epipelagic, 0–200 m depth; Zone 6, mesopelagic, 200–1000 m depth.
From Bengston (1984).

during their life-cycle. For example, *Notothenia rossii mamorata* spend the first year after hatching in subsurface waters far from the coast feeding on krill and copepods. They then migrate towards the coasts and live for the next five to six years close to the bottom in nearshore kelp beds where they feed primarily on amphipods. Hoshiai (1979) found that at South Georgia juvenile *N. rossii marmorata* feed on hyperid amphipods, gammarid amphipods, a shrimp (*Chorismus antarcticus*), an epitokous nereid polychaete (*Neanthes kerguelensis*), and the fry of two species of fish, *N. rossii marmorata* and Bathydraedonidae sp., algae and ctenophores. After attaining maturity they leave the inshore waters for the offshore feeding grounds at 150–300 m depth from where they ascend to the mid-water zone to feed on krill, fish and salps.

7.5.3 Feeding behaviour
The demersal and demerso-pelagic fishes show a great diversity in feeding behaviour and the type of prey consumed (M. G. Richardson, 1975; Targett, 1981; Daniels, 1982; Takahashi, 1983). Diversity in diet and feeding behaviour is greatest among the demersal and demerso-pelagic nototheniids, especially in nearshore communities under 90 m deep (Burchett, 1982; Burchett *et al.*, 1983). Demersal nototheniids prey primarily on amphipods, isopods, fish (mostly larvae, postlarvae and young fish), polychaetes, decapods, gastropods and

bivalves (Targett, 1981; Daniels, 1982; Takahashi, 1983; Linkowski *et al.*, 1983). Studies on channichthyids by Permatin & Tarverdiyera (1972, 1978) and Daniels (1982) have demonstrated that they are specialized feeders. Most channichthyids are planktivorous feeders, with the exception of *Chaenocephalus aceratus* and *Channichthys rhinoceratus*, which consume a high proportion of fish (Hureau, 1970; R. Williams,1983).

The most extensive studies of the feeding behaviour of Antarctic fishes have been carried out in nearshore waters in depths of 0–70 m. Around islands such as South Georgia and Kerguelen the shallow, nearshore areas with depths of 0–30 m are often dominated by large brown algae such as *Macrocystis pyrifera*, *Himanothallus grandifolius* and *Durvillaea antarctica* (Burchett, 1982; Duhamel, 1982), which provide a specialized habitat, not only for the fishes, but also for their prey. Burchett (1983c) and Burchett *et al.* (1983) working at South Georgia found that much of the benthos upon which the fish feed were nocturnally active and SCUBA diving observations and net hauls confirmed that the fish were also active only at night.

Linkowski *et al.* (1983) have studied the food habits of five species of Nototheniidae (*Notothenia neglecta, N. rossii marmorata, Nototheniops nudifrons, Trematomus newnesi* and *Pleuragramma antarcticum*). The diets of the first three species were benthic organisms with amphipods (especially representatives of the families

Lysianassidae and Eusiridae) predominating, 79–82.9% for *N. coriiceps neglecta* and 62.1–75.6% for *N. rossii marmorata*. While the diet included polychaete worms, amphipods, isopods and gastropods, pelagic salps made up 41.9% of the total number of stomach components and 70.7% by weight. *T. newnesi* fed principally on *Euphausia superba,* which in the summer comprised 94.5% of the stomach contents by weight.

Around Kerguelen and South Georgia *N. negelecta* actively graze on the macroalgae which appear to be an important dietary component at certain times of the year (Burchett, 1983c; Burchett *et al.,* 1983). Algal consumption has also been observed by Everson (1970a), Hureau (1970), Daniels (1982) and Linkowski *et al.* (1983) for equivalent subspecies at the South Orkney islands, South Shetland Islands and the Antarctic Peninsula.

Diets for individuals of the same species vary between localities (Rowedder, 1979; Naito & Iwami, 1982; Linkowski *et al.,* 1983). For example, for *Notothenia gibberifrons, Nototheniops larseni, Trematomus scotti* and *Harpagifer bispinis,* individuals of similar size caught at the same time of the year but at different localities have significant differences in prey taken and the amount of food eaten (Daniels, 1982). Richardson (1975) at the South Orkney Islands studied the feeding habits of *N. neglecta* in shallow water (1–20 m) and found that the diet consisted of benthic animals (amphipods, gastropods, bivalves) and did not record any pelagic species. On the other hand, Permitin & Tarverdiyera (1978) studied samples from deeper water (down to a depth of 170+ m) and noted a predominance of pelagic animals (*E. superba,* fish, hyperiid amphipods) in the diet.

Differences in the diets of fish of different sizes have also been noted by a number of authors for many species including *Pleuragramma antarcticum* (DeWitt and Hopkins, 1977), *Pogonophyrne* sp. (Wyanski & Targett, 1981), *Notothenia gibberifrons, Paranotothenia magellanica* and *Champsocephalus gunnari* (Takahashi, 1983), *P. magellanica* (Blankley, 1982), *N. neglecta* (Showers *et al.,* 1977) and *Dissostichus eleginoides* (Duhamel & Pletikowsic, 1983). In all these species, prey size, prey quantity consumed, and numbers of different prey types taken increased with fish size.

Seasonal changes have been reported in the diets of many demersal and demerso-pelagic fishes. Burchett (1983c) found that juvenile *Notothenia rossii* have a more varied diet in the summer months. There were definite seasonal variations in the numbers of amphipods, bivalves and polychaetes consumed. Daniels (1982) found differences in the composition of the diet and the amount of food consumed in similar sized individuals of *Notothenia gibberifrons, Nototheniops nudifrons,*

Nototheniops larseni and *Trematomus scotti* collected at the same time at different times of the year.

Eastman (1985b) examined the stomach contents of nine species of notothenioid fishes near the southern limit of their range in ice-covered McMurdo Sound (Fig. 7.5). Pelagic species with reduced or neutral buoyancy fed exclusively on nektonic organisms. *Pagothenia borchgrevinki* fed in the platelet ice on the underside of the sea ice and in the water beneath the ice predominantly on small (2–3 mm) copepods and amphipods. *Dissostichus mawsoni,* the largest Antarctic fish, was a neutrally buoyant mid-water predator which ate primarily fishes and mysids. *Pleuragramma antarcticum* was a shoaling mid-water species that ate copepods, mysids and other fishes. *Gymnodraco acuticeps* was predominantly piscivorous, with amphipods and fish eggs being the only other significant food items in the diet.

The other six species were trophic generalists confined primarily to benthic habitats. *Pagothenia bernacchii, T. centronotus* and *Pagothenia hansoni,* for example, were typical benthic species that fed primarily on errant polychaetes. *T. nicolai* was a shallow-water benthic species that preyed actively on moving organisms (copepods, amphipods, small fishes, molluscs and errant polychaetes), some of which may have been captured in the water column. *T. loennbergi* fed predominantly on amphipods and errant polychaetes.

One of the most interesting findings of this study was that fishes, especially *Pleuragramma,* were of wide occurrence in the diets of McMurdo fishes. Fishes were a dietary item in eight of the nine species, and two of these eight species, *Dissostichus* and *Gymnodraco,* were predominantly piscivorous. *Pleuragramma* was the most common prey species consumed, being present in four of the eight species, including *Pleuragramma.* In the Ross Sea *Pleuragramma* eat copepods and adult euphausiids, with copepods dominant by number and euphausiids by weight (DeWitt & Hopkins, 1977). Near the Antarctic Peninsula euphausiids are most important in the diet both by number and volume (Daniels, 1982). In the northern part of the Weddell Sea small *Pleuragramma* consume copepods, polychaetes and chaetognaths (Kellermann & Kock, 1984). In the southern and eastern Weddell Sea the most abundant food items in the diet by number are copepods, gastropods and euphausiids, with euphausiids dominant by weight (Hubold, 1985b) (Fig. 7.6). In Prydz Bay, East Antarctica, copepods and larval euphausiids are the most important dietary items by weight (Table 7.4) (R. Williams, 1985b). Fishes are in general present in the diet of *Pleuragramma* only as incidental items (Hubold, 1985b; R. Williams, 1985b). In contrast, Eastman (1985b) found that in the inner McMurdo Sound fishes constituted

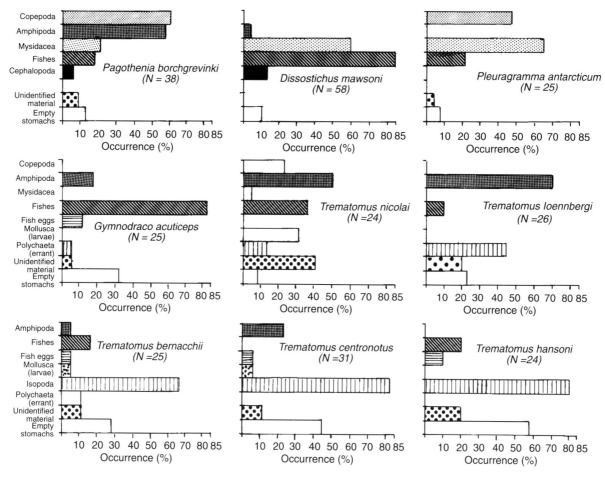

Fig. 7.5. Diets for nine species of notothenioid fishes from McMurdo Sound. Redrawn from Eastman (1985a).

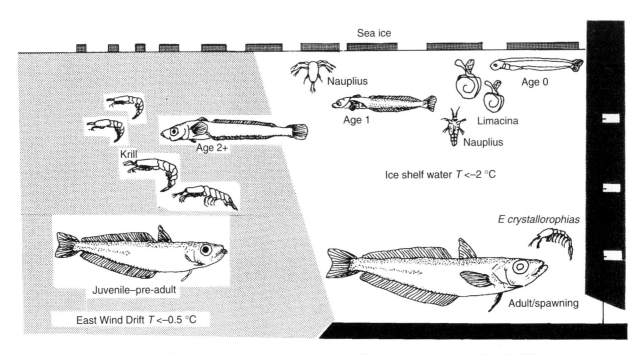

Fig. 7.6. Schematic life-cycle of *Pleuragramma antarcticum* in the Weddell Sea. Redrawn from Hubold (1985a).

Table 7.4. *Stomach contents of pelagic fishes in the region of Prydz Bay. Data for food items are given as percentage by number and pecentage by weight (eg. 18.31; 0.22)*

	Gymnoscopelus nicholsi	*Gymnoscopelus braueri*	*Notolepis coatsi*	*Cryodraco antarcticus*	*Pagetopsis macropterus*	*Chaenodraco wilsoni*	*Electrona antarctica*	*Krefftichys anderssoni*	*Pleuragramma antarcticum*	*Trematomus scotti*	*Trematomus sp.*
Polychaetes	—	—	18.31; 0.22	—	—	—	1.49; 0.14	—	0.08; 1.23	—	—
Chaetognaths	—	—	36.52; 0.50	—	—	—	0.83; 0.15	—	—	—	—
Ostracods	—	—	—	—	—	—	2.81; 0.33	—	—	—	—
Copepods	40.91; 2.87	—	12.68; 0.72	—	—	—	47.85; 12.02	76.22; 64.58	64.21; 48.28	48.81; 76.78	98.11; 90.08
Amphipods	18.19; 5.75	—	—	—	—	—	7.45; 27.24	1.11; 4.58	—	—	—
Euphausiids											
Euphausia superba	27.27; 89.98	—	28.17; 96.24	50.0; 97.92	—	—	0.99; 12.26	—	9.16; 4.45	—	—
E. crystallorophias	—	—	—	—	60.0; 22.53	37.5; 73.68	—	—	20.97; 17.83	—	—
E. frigida	—	—	—	—	—	—	0.99; 2.80	—	—	—	—
Thysanoessa macroura	13.64; 2.40	—	12.68; 0.72	—	—	—	5.13; 7.80	22.20; 23.76	—	—	—
Unidentified euphausiids	—	—	—	—	20.0; 68.0	62.5; 26.32	4.80; 5.66	—	—	51.19; 23.21	
Total euphausiids	40.91; 92.38	—	40.85; 96.96	50.0; 97.92	80.0; 90.53	100.00; 100.0	11.91; 28.52	22.20; 23.76	30.13; 22.28	51.19; 23.21	
Decapods	—	—	1.41; 3.27	—	—	—	5.46; 1.01	—	—	—	—
Crustaceans unidentified	—	—	—	50.0; 2.08	—	—	8.11; 6.79	0.048; 0.05	0.17; 0.70	—	—
Molluscs	—	—	—	—	—	—	6.29; 18.19	—	0.18; 2.46	—	1.26; 6.11
Fish	—	—	—	—	20.0; 9.6	—	0.33; 0.47	—	0.60; 20.88	—	—
Unidentified remains	—	—	—	—	—	—	7.45; 3.10	4.36; 7.64	—	—	0.63; 3.82

Data from R. Williams (1950b).

22% of the diet by occurrence, including 13% cannibalism. The heavy cover of ice and the reduction in euphausiid abundance are probably the reasons for this difference.

The Antarctic silverfish, *Pleuragramma antarcticum*, is the only true pelagic species among the Notothenioidea (Andriashev, 1965, 1966). In the Ross Sea, the pelagic fish fauna is dominated by this species (92% in numbers and 96.7% in biomass), and northern mid-water fish, such as myctophids, are excluded from the area by the steep temperature gradient over the edge of the outer shelf (DeWitt, 1970). In the Weddell Sea in 1979–80 95% of the larval fish taken in bongo nets were *P. antarcticum* (Hubold, 1985a). The importance of this species as food for predatory vertebrates is reflected in its occurrence in its diet. It is present in the diet of all McMurdo Sound fishes that either live in the water column or rise from the bottom to feed in the water (Eastman, 1985b). It is the main food of the Antarctic cod (*Dissostichus mawsoni*) (Eastman & DeVries, 1981), and is also an important component of the diet of Weddell Seals (*Leptonychotes weddelli*) (DeWitt & Tyler, 1960; Dearborn, 1965b; Testa *et al.*, 1985), of whales (Andriashev, 1965), of Gentoo (*Pygoscelis papua*), Adélie (*P. adeliae*) and Emperor (*Aptenodytes forsteri*) Penguins (Norman, 1937; Emison, 1968; Volkman, *et al.*, 1980), of South Polar Skuas (*Catharacta maccormicki*) (Young, 1963b) and of Antarctic Petrels (*Thalassoica antarctica*) (Hubold, 1985b). Emison (1968) noted that Adélie Penguins can

live successfully and rear chicks in areas nearly devoid of euphausiids if the water is rich in *Pleuragramma*.

Sabourenkov (1990) has recently reviewed Soviet research on the feeding of myctophids. Their diet in open waters in both winter and summer consists primarily of certain species of copepods. Myctophids of the 5–11 cm length group feed exclusively on small planktonic organisms. Larger myctophids such as *Electrona antarctica* and *Gymnoscephalus nicholsi* also take macroplanktonic organisms, including *Euphausia superba*.

7.5.4 Krill consumption by Antarctic fishes

A number of studies (e.g. Latogurskij, 1972; Tarveridiyera, 1972, 1982; Permitin & Tarveridiyera, 1972; Naumov & Permitin, 1973; Rowedder, 1979; Kompowski, 1980a; Lubimova & Shust, 1980; Tarveridiyera & Pinskaya, 1980; Kock, 1981, 1985; Chekunova & Naumov, 1982; Takahashi, 1983; R. Williams, 1985b) have shown that krill are an important component of the diets of the Notothenioidea, especially of those nototheniids and channichthyids which are adapted for temporary or permanent pelagic life. Kock (1985) studied the feeding ecology and food intake of four species of channichthyid fishes (*Champsocephalus gunnari, Chaenocephalus aceratus, Pseudochaenichthys georgianus, Chionodraco rastrospinosus*) and three nototheniids (*Notothenia rossii marmorata, N. gibberifrons, Nototheniops larseni*) in western Antarctic waters

Table 7.5. *Consumption of krill by six notothenoids round South Georgia*

Species	Krill consumption (t×10³)		
	1975–76	1977–78	1980–81
Notothenia rossii	160.8	42.0	9.3
N. gibberifrons	18.0	9.0	5.5
Nototheniopsis larseni	1.0	0.9	—
Champsocephalus gunnari	630.0	156.2	354.0
Chaenocephalus aceratus	33.7	33.1	12.4
Pseudochaenichthys georgianus	131.0	11.8	27.9
Totals	974.5	253.0	409.1

Data from Kock (1985).

and off South Georgia. Data from South Georgia are summarized in Table 7.5. While *C. rastrospinosus* consumed krill in other localities it did not do so at South Georgia. The proportions of krill found in the diets of these species ranges up to 100%. For the purposes of calculating the amounts of krill consumed Kock (1985) estimated the weight percentages at 50% for *N. rossii. C. gunnari* and *N. larseni*, 10% for *Ch. aceratus* and 60% for *C. rastrospinosus* and *P. georgianus*. Before the onset of commercial exploitation the total consumption of krill by the seven species off South Georgia was probably $5×10^6$ t y⁻¹. *N. rossii* and *C. gunnari* probably accounted for more than 80% of this annual krill consumption. Due to the substantial reduction in the stock sizes of fishes due to commercial harvesting the consumption of krill by fishes has declined markedly (Table 7.6) (e.g. for *N. rossii* from an estimated $160.8×10^3$ t before exploitation to $9.3×10^3$ t in 1980–81).

Consumption of euphausiids (mainly *Euphuasia superba* and *E. crystallorophias*) by fish inhabiting Antarctic shelf waters has been estimated at $24–28×10^6$ t y⁻¹ (Lubimova & Shust, 1980). Consumption by the icefish *Champsocephalus gunnari* in western Antarctic waters has been assessed at $3–4×10^6$ t in 1975–76 (Kock, 1981).

The relationship between euphausiids and pelagic fishes has been less intensively studied. There is general information on the diets of *Notolepis coatsi* (Solyanik, 1965), *Electrona antarctica* (Solyanik, 1967) and various species caught in the Scotia Sea area (Rembiszewski *et al.*, 1978). More information is available on the diet of *Pleuragramma antarcticum* (DeWitt & Hopkins, 1977; Rowedder, 1979; Gorelova & Gerasimchuk, 1981; Eastman, 1985b; Hubold, 1985b). The most comprehensive study of the feeding habits of pelagic fishes is that of R. Williams (1985b) in the Prydz Bay region, East

Antarctica. Ten of the eleven species studied had euphausiids as a significant component of their diet (Table 7.4). Only *Trematomus* sp. juveniles had no euphausiids in their stomachs. The ten species fell into three groups on the basis of the contributions of euphausiids to their diets. In the first group, which included *Notolepis coatsi*, *Gymnoscopelus* spp. and the juveniles of *Crydraco antarcticus, Pagetopsis macropterus* and *Chaenodraco wilsoni* euphausiids were the dominant part of the diet (30–100% by number and 90–100% by weight), with other prey being definitely secondary. The second group contains general plankton feeders in which euphausiids formed a major part (12–52% by number and 23–26% by weight), but are secondary to copepods (35–76% by number and 48–79% by weight) (*P. antarcticum, Krefftichthys anderssoni* and *Trematomus scotti*), or codominant with copepods and amphipods (*E. antarctica*). The last group comprises *Chionodraco* sp. in which fish predominated in the diet (55%). Thus the commonly encountered fish in the Prydz Bay region depended heavily on euphausiids, and in some areas specifically on *E. superba*, for their food. While the large fish take adult krill, there is a significant predation by juvenile fish on the younger stages of krill. Estimates of the importance of krill in the diets of seven Antarctic fish species are given in Table 7.6. It can be seen that krill consumption differed between the regions, ranging from 3.7 to 100%. In general, consumption is highest in the mid-Antarctic region, ranging from 38.5 to 100%

7.5.5 Feeding communities

It is clear from the above discussion that a number of different pelagic and benthic feeding communities can be distinguished (Kock, 1984).

1. A *cryopelagic community* closely associated with drifting or fast ice in Antarctic high latitudes formed mainly by juvenile and adult *Trematomus* spp. which feed on ice-dwelling amphipods and copepods. The fish cling to the undersurface of the ice when resting and hide in ice crevices and holes when disturbed. Other fishes that feed on the ice-associated organisms and in the top few metres of the water column include the pelagic nototheniids *Pagothenia borchgrevinki* and juveniles of *Pleuragramma antarcticum* (Bradfield, 1980; Eastman, 1985b; Hubold, 1985b; Knox, 1986).

2. A specific *epipelagic krill–fish community* has been suggested by several authors (e.g. Rembiszewski *et al.*, 1978), since about 40 notothenioid and mesopelagic species have been

Table 7.6. *Estimates of the importance of krill in the diets of Antarctic fishes*

Species	Locality	Percentage of krill		Source
Notothenia rossii	W.A.	F	90–100	3, 4, 6, 8, 14, 19
	S.G.	F	15.2–90.4	5, 10, 11, 12, 13
	S.G.	B	40.2–56.2	1, 5, 9, 15
Champsocephalus gunnari	W.A.	F	90–100	3, 5, 6, 8, 14, 19
	W.A.	B	95	5, 16, 18
	S.G.	F	18.1–94	5, 10, 11, 12, 13
	S.G.	B	42–90	1, 5, 9, 15
Nototheniopsis larseni	S.A.	F	20.6–95	2, 13, 14, 16, 19
	W.A.	B	38.5–92	15, 16, 17
Notothenia gibberifrons	W.A.	F	22.2–97.6	11, 13, 14, 16
	S.A.	B	3.7–5.7	15
	S.G. (winter)	B	18	1
Chionodraco rastrospinosus	W.A.	F	98.1	19
Chaenocephalus aceratus	W.A.	B	10–90	7
Pseudochaenichthys georgianus	S.G.	F	25–87.4	7
	S.A.	F	38.5–100	7
	W.A.	B	>60%	5, 11, 14, 19

1, Chekunova & Naumov (1982); 2, Daniels (1982); 3, Freytag (1977); 4, Gubsch (1979); 5, Kock (1981); 6, Kock (1982); 7, Kock (1985); 8, Kock *et al.* (1985); 9, Kompowski (1980a); 10, Latogurskij (1972); 11, Linkowski & Rembiszewski (1978); 12, Naumov & Permitin (1973); 13, Permitin & Tarverdiyera (1972); 14, Permitin & Tarverdiyera (1978); 15, Rowedder (1979); 16, Takahashi (1983); 17, Targett (1981); 18, Tarverdiyera (1982); 19, Tarverdiyera & Pinskaya (1980).
W.A. = West Antarctica; S.G. = South Georgia; S.A. = Scotia Arc. F = frequency of occurrence. B = biomass.
Based on data in Kock (1985).

encountered in association with krill swarms. This community is composed mainly of juvenile notothenioids living at the border of krill swarms, and of various icefish, Antarctic cod and mesopelagic species that undertake temporary and regular migrations from the bottom or deeper layers to subsurface waters to feed on krill (Efremenko, 1983; R. Williams, 1985b). This vertical migration has been confirmed by echo sounder and visual observations (Olsen, 1955; Basalaev & Petuchov, 1969). Efremenko (1983) reports that the most frequently encountered mesopelagic species in the Scotia Sea were eight species of the families Myctophidae (*Electrona antarctica, Krefftichthys anderssoni, Protomyctophum bolini, Gymnoscopelus baureri, G. nicholsi, G. opisthopterus*), Bathylagididae (*Bathylagus antarcticus*) and Paralepidae (*Notolepis coatsi*). These fishes spawn at a depth below 200 m and all their eggs and prelarvae have been collected between 200 and 1000 m. The vertical distribution of the larvae and prelarvae depends on the season. At the end of autumn and during the winter they are present in the warmer waters below 200 m; but in the spring and summer they are also found in the surface waters (0–100 m). The larval stages of 27 notothenioid species have been found over the continental shelf between 0 and 200 m.

These larval notothenioids all feed on zooplankton, including the larval stages of euphausiids.

3. Various *nearshore and offshore benthic and bentho-pelagic communities* have been distinguished by several authors (Richardson, 1975; Targett, 1981; Takahashi, 1983). The dominant species in each community partition the prey resources by vertical separation. Prey overlap is low in some of the nearshore communities but may be high in offshore communities where krill is at least temporarily abundant, forming the staple food of most species. In these situations krill is a non-limiting resource and thus interspecific competition is reduced to a minimum (Takahasi, 1983). Off South Georgia, for example, where krill is only temporarily abundant, the icefish *Champsocephalus gunnari* and *Pseudochaenichthys georgianus* feed almost exclusively on krill when it is available. When a shortage of krill occurs as it did in 1977–78 *C. gunnari* substituted part of their diet with hyperiids and mysids and *P. georgianus* increased the proportion of fish in their diet (Kock, 1981).

Many benthic feeding species, such as the plunder fishes and some of the Antarctic cod generally take the same prey species so it appears that there could be competition for the same food resource. However, interspecific competition is reduced as the various species take different proportions of the same prey groups. For example, in the morphologically similar *Notothenia gibberifrons* and *Nototheniops nudifrons* the former primarily exploits sedentary polychaetes while the latter feeds on errant polychaetes (Targett, 1981).

In addition to the resident species preying on krill a considerable number of species migrate from north of the Antarctic Convergence into Antarctic waters in the summer to feed on krill. Various mesopelagic species such as the daggertooth *Anotopterus pharao*, the paralepid *Notolepis rissoi*, the nototheniid *Paranotothenia magellanica* and part of the population of the southern blue whiting *Micromesistius australis* undertake such migrations from the Patagonian shelf.

8

Seals

8.1 Introduction

Because of their effective thermal insulation in the form of dense fur and a layer of blubber beneath the skin seals are well able to exploit the cold waters of polar seas. These insulating layers are effective in air as well as in water and consequently they suffer little heat loss in air, even at the low temperatures which occur in the Southern Ocean.

The order Pinnipedia, to which the Antarctic seals belong, evolved in the Northern Hemisphere, probably from two separate stocks. One stock, arising from a dog-like ancestor in the North Pacific, gave rise to the walruses and the related eared seals, the Otariidae. Another stock, derived from a otter-like ancestor in the North Atlantic, radiated to produce the true seals, the Phocidae. Early in the radiation of the phocid seals during the Miocene, the subfamily Monachinae originated in the Mediterranean region and spread across the Atlantic, with one group, the Lobodontini, colonizing the Antarctic during the Miocene or early Pliocene, at a time when the region was much warmer than it is today, and radiating to produce four very distinct and successful Antarctic seals. They are the Crabeater Seal *Lobodon carcinophagus* (Fig. 8.1), the Leopard Seal *Hydrurga leptonyx* (Fig. 8.2), the Ross Seal *Ommatophoca rossii* (Fig. 8.3), and the Weddell Seal *Leptonychotes weddelli* (Fig. 8.4). The Crabeater Seal comprises at least half the total world stock of pinnipeds (Laws, 1984a). The four species listed above have been estimated to amount to about 56% of the world's seal stocks, and because individuals of those species tend to be larger than other seals they comprise about 79% of the biomass (Laws, 1977a). However, Laws (1984a) considers that the population increases which have occurred in recent years suggest that they may amount to considerably more than this.

The Elephant Seals were another group of monachine seals which invaded the Southern Hemisphere. They developed no special adaptations for the Antarctic ice environment and the main distribution of the Southern Elephant Seal *Mirounga leonina* (Fig. 8.5) is north of the Antarctic Convergence. Otariid seals originated in the Northeast Pacific and early in their radiation crossed the equator and radiated to give rise to eight species of Southern Fur Seal (genus *Arctocephalus*) (Repenning *et al.*, 1971). The Southern Fur Seal, *Arctocephalus australis*, probably gave rise to a number of closely related species, one of the most numerous of which is the Antarctic Fur Seal, *Arctocephalus gazella* (Fig. 8.6), which is found on the islands south of the Antarctic Convergence but generally on those that are not regularly surrounded by sea ice.

The ecology of Antarctic seals has been the subject of a number of reviews (Turbott, 1952; Scheffer, 1958; Bonner & Laws, 1964; Carrick, 1964; King, 1964; Laws, 1964, 1977a, 1977b, 1984a,b; Øritzland, 1970a; Ray, 1970; Erickson & Hofman, 1974; Stirling, 1975; Gilbert & Erickson, 1977; Bonner, 1985a; Siniff, 1991). Studies of Antarctic seals have added much to the development of pinniped and mammalian studies in general, for example age determination, reproduction, population dynamics, energetics, behaviour and diving physiology.

8.2 Species composition and distribution

8.2.1 General

Although seals feed exclusiveiy at sea, their pups are born on land, or on ice, and remain at their birth site until weaned. In most parts of the world seals must return to land, at least during the breeding season, so that their distribution is discontinuous and limited to areas where suitable islands or reefs occur. In polar regions, however, some species breed on the drifting pack ice and this has allowed them to colonize a much larger geographic area and enabled their breeding system to closely match their prey distribution. However, the pack ice is an unstable environment where the pups may crawl into the sea and be crushed between the floes.

Habitat has greatly influenced our state of knowledge of the species concerned. Best known are the Weddell Seals, which breed on fast ice, and the beach-breeding Elephant and Fur Seals. Least known are the Crabeater, Leopard and Ross Seals, which inhabit the pack ice.

Crabeater Seal (Fig. 8.1): The Crabeater Seal is one of

Fig. 8.1. Crabeater Seal (*Lobodon carcinophagus*).

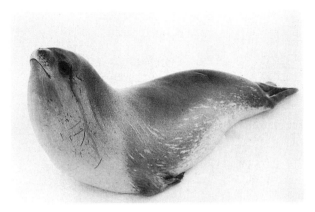

Fig. 8.3. Ross Seal (*Ommatophoca rossii*)

Fig. 8.2. Leopard Seal (*Hydrurga leptonyx*).

Fig. 8.4. Weddell Seal (*Leptonychotes weddelli*).

the most remarkable, but least known, of the marine mammals of the world. Its population probably numbers between 15 and 40 million, making it one of the most abundant large mammals in the world. More than one in every two seals in the world is a Crabeater Seal and the population biomass of the Crabeaters is about four times that of all other pinnipeds put together.

Crabeater Seals are large seals, although slender in comparison with their length, and they are very active creatures. Female adults are 230–260 cm in length and 200–227 kg in weight. Males are slightly smaller (Bertram, 1940). When freshly moulted in January or February the coat is mainly dark brown above and fawn below. The pattern becomes slightly mottled, particularly in young animals, with patches of darker colour on a lighter ground. The pattern is more conspicuous on the flanks behind the flippers and around the posterior end of the body.

Leopard Seal (Fig. 8.2): The Leopard Seal is one of the largest and most mobile of the phocids (Kooyman, 1981b). As in other lobodontine seals the female is slightly longer than the male. While the largest recorded

specimen was 358 cm long (Hamilton, 1939), females generally average 291 cm and males 179 cm in length. Average weights are 367 kg for females and 324 kg for males, but some large female Leopard Seals estimated to weigh 500 kg have been seen hauled out at South Georgia (Kooyman, 1981a). Despite their size Leopard Seals have a slender appearance and they are lithe and graceful in the water and on the ice. The fore-flippers are long and tapered, the neck sinuous and the head is large with a huge gape. Unlike most seals they move rapidly when on the ice and land and are not to be approached too closely.

The coloration on the back is dark grey to black, changing on the flanks to steely grey while the underparts are silver. On the ventral surface there is a scattering of dark spots while on the dorsal surface the pattern is reversed and the spots there are lighter. New-born pups have a pattern similar to that of the adults.

Ross Seal (Fig. 8.3): Mystery surrounds the Ross Seal. It may be the least abundant of the Antarctic seals, although Gilbert & Erickson (1977) consider that it could be as numerous as the Leopard Seal. It frequents the heavy pack ice, which even modern ice-breakers can pen-

Fig. 8.5. Southern Elephant Seal (*Mirounga leonina*).

Fig. 8.6. Antarctic Fur Seal (*Arctocephalus gazella*).

etrate only with difficulty; hence it is not often seen.

Ross Seals are the smallest of the Antarctic phocids. Of the few which have been measured the largest female was 256 cm long and weighed 204 kg, and the largest male 208 cm and 216 kg (Ray, 1981). They are stout thickset animals, with short necks, and an extraordinarily long snout set on a wide head. The eyes are large, up to 7 cm in diameter, although the eye openings are no larger than those in comparable phocids. The anterior flippers, which reach nearly 22% of the standard body length, are proportionately the largest of any phocid (Ray, 1981).

Weddell Seal (Fig. 8.4): The Weddell Seal has the most southerly distribution of any mammal. It is another very large phocid. As with other ice-breeding seals, females are larger than males. In early spring, when the seals are fat, both males and females may commonly weigh around 400–500 kg (Kooyman *et al.*, 1973). Adults grow up to 3 m in length. In contrast to the Leopard Seal the snout is short and the head seems small for its body.

Weddell Seals are strongly spotted with irregularly shaped patches. The background colour is blue-black with silver grey spotting, the underside being paler in colour. As the hair ages it fades to a yellowish hue with darker areas of the back becoming rusty brown. The coat of the new-born pup is a very light or silvery grey with no traces of the spotting that is characteristic of the adult until the moult begins at about nine to 21 days after birth.

Southern Elephant Seal (Fig. 8.5): The Southern Elephant Seal is the largest of all the pinnepeds and one of the largest mammals excluding the whales. There is a striking sexual dimorphism, which is opposite to that shown in the lobodontine seals. Fully grown males may reach a length of 4.5 m and weigh about 4000 kg. The female is very much smaller reaching a length of 2.8 m and a weight of about 900 kg.

Adult males are recognizable by their inflatable proboscis, which plays an important part in agonistic behav-

iour during the breeding season. The coat of the Elephant Seal is composed of rather sparsely distributed short, very stiff recurved hairs. The colour is generally a uniform brownish colour though there is considerable variation from a very dark chocolate to a pale sandy colour. Adults of both sexes are much scarred, especially the males, as a result of wounds on the neck and chest received during the breeding season. The young are born with a coat of jet black woolly hair which is shed at about three to four weeks, to expose a coat that is steely-black above and silvery below.

Antarctic Fur Seal (Fig. 8.6): The Antarctic Fur Seal is the only eared seal (Family Otariidae) which lives in polar waters. As an otariid it is very much more mobile on land than the phocids. It is a medium-sized seal with adult males reaching a length of 200 cm and a weight of around 125–200 kg. As in the Elephant Seal the female is smaller than the male, up to 140 cm long and weighing about 50 kg. The fur is composed of two layers, an outer coarser layer of guard hairs, and an inner layer of very fine under-fur fibres. It is this latter layer which provides the Fur Seal fur for commerce after the removal of the guard hairs. The layer of air trapped in the fur provides thermal insulation as the Fur Seals do not have such a well developed blubber layer as is found in the phocid seals.

The colour is grey to brownish on the back and sides while the throat and breasts are creamy and the belly is a dark brown. In adult males a heavy mane is developed around the neck and shoulders. The new-born pup is clad in a black coat.

8.2.2 Distribution and migrations

The Antarctic seals are essentially distributed in circumpolar latitudinal zones, except where the Antarctic Peninsula and Scotia Arc intervene, extending the breeding distribution of some high latitude species northwards (e.g. Weddell and Leopard Seals), and some lower

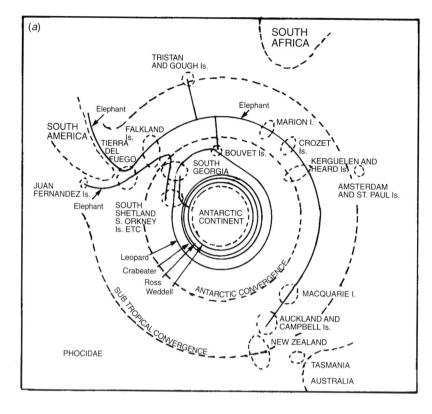

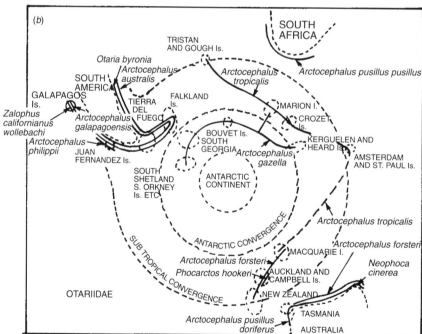

Fig. 8.7. Diagram of the geographical distribution of southern seals. The thick lines are drawn to join the breeding localities of (*a*) Phocidae, and (*b*) Otariidae. Redrawn from Laws (1984a).

latitude species southwards (Fig. 8.7). Climate and substrate are the main factors limiting breeding distributions. The distribution of food organisms may also be important. Important physical barriers affecting overall distributions are the Antarctic and Subtropical Convergences. The breeding distribution of three species is strictly lim-

ited to the south of the Antarctic Convergence (Crabeater, Ross and Weddell Seals). Of those breeding on sea ice, pupping is restricted to fast ice in the Weddell Seal (and in the Elephant Seal in a few localities).

Breeding distribution: As all seals must give birth to their pups on land or ice, their distributions during the breeding season are determined by the availability of suitable habitats. Fur Seals and Elephant Seals breed on ice-free beaches, and in the Antarctic region these only occur on islands in the Scotia Arc and other isolated islands close to the Antarctic Convergence (Bonner, 1981). Competition for breeding sites between Fur and Elephant Seals is slight since the former breed mainly on rocky shores and the latter on sandy beaches. The breeding stock of the Fur Seal is concentrated at Bird Island, Willis Island, and the neighbouring coast of South Georgia. Smaller colonies are present on the South Orkney Islands, South Shetland Islands, Elephant and Clarence Islands, South Sandwich Islands, Bouvetya, Heard and MacDonald Islands, and Isles Kerguelen (Fig. 8.7*b*).

Elephant Seals are circumpolar, but they appear to subdivided into three main breeding stocks (Laws, 1960b; Fig. 8.7*a*). The first is centred on South Georgia and includes breeding populations in South America, Falkland Islands, South Orkney Islands, and possibly Bouvetya (Laws, 1984a). The second group breeds at Isles Kerguelen, Heard Island, Marion and Prince Edward Islands, Crozet Island, and Amsterdan and St. Paul Islands. The third stock is found at Macquarie Island and the New Zealand sub-Antarctic Islands. Although branding and tagging experiments have demonstrated movements within the three geographic areas covered by the three groups, no interchange between them has been observed (Dickinson, 1967; Ingham, 1967; Scolaro, 1976; Hunt, 1973).

Weddell Seal breeding colonies have been recorded from fast ice areas adjacent the Antarctic Continent and the off-lying islands in every region that has been visited during the breeding season. Suitable habitat occurs wherever tidal or glacial action forms cracks large enough to be used as breathing or exit holes (Stirling, 1969a). The long-term tagging programmes at McMurdo Sound (Stirling, 1971a; Siniff, 1982; Siniff *et al.*, 1977b) and Signy Island (Croxall & Hiby, 1983) have shown a general fidelity to the general area of the colony of birth with no evidence for long-range movements.

The remaining three species have severed their attachment to the land and spend the whole of their lives in the drifting pack ice which surrounds the continent. Due to logistic difficulties observations on their breeding have been limited and have been confined to the Antarctic Peninsula (Siniff *et al.*, 1979; Bengston & Siniff, 1981) and in the vicinity of the South Orkney Islands (Øritzland, 1970b). Unconsolidated pack ice, covering 30–70% of the water surface, is the preferred summer habitat of Crabeater Seals (Siniff *et al.*, 1970; Erickson *et al.*, 1971). Gilbert & Erickson (1977) found that

Crabeater Seals were predominantly distributed relatively close to the edge of the pack ice in cake and brash ice where there was access to open water and food. As the ice edge recedes during the summer the Crabeater Seals move southwards (Bonner & Laws, 1964; Solyanik, 1964).

The breeding distribution of the Leopard Seal is similar to that of Crabeater Seals, perhaps due to the importance of krill and Crabeater Seals in its diet (Gilbert & Erickson, 1977). They are often found in the sea round penguin colonies, and are frequently seen hauled out ashore, or on fast ice off the coast or offshore islands.

Very little is known about the breeding of the Ross Seal and only a few pups have been seen (Tikhomirov, 1975; Øritzland, 1970b). From the limited data which is available it appears that the breeding distribution is circumpolar but there is evidence that they are very much more abundant in some areas than others. One such area is in the King Haaken VII Sea (Condy, 1976), and they may be more abundant near Cape Adare than further south in the Ross Sea (Ray, 1981).

Non-breeding distribution: In contrast to the breeding distribution, the non-breeding distribution is less well known for the Fur, Elephant and Weddell Seals than for the pack ice species.

Almost nothing is known about the pelagic distribution of the Fur Seal, adults of which are absent from the breeding grounds between May and October. Antarctic Fur Seals tagged at South Georgia have been sighted at the South Orkney Islands, the South Shetland Islands, and Tierra del Fuego (Hunt, 1973; Payne, 1979). Payne (1979) suggested that the Antarctic Fur Seals may undertake a seasonal migration similar to that exhibited by Northern Fur Seals in the North Pacific.

In the case of the Elephant Seal sightings of marked seals reported by Laws (1984a,b) indicate that these seals disperse widely up to 2000 km from their breeding grounds (Ingham, 1967; Dickinson, 1967; Hunt, 1973; Laws, 1960b; Scolaro, 1976; van Aarde & Pascel, 1980). They have been recorded from the Antarctic Continent and as far north as South Africa, Tasmania, New Zealand, Mauritius and the Rodriguez Islands.

Non-breeding Weddell Seals range into the pack ice during the winter. While the winter distribution of Crabeater Seals is unknown it is likely to be in the pack ice zone, since in some years large numbers of Crabeater Seals have been recorded at Signy Island and South Orkney Islands, which are near the pack ice edge (Mansfield, unpublished report, quoted in Laws, 1984a). During the non-breeding season Leopard Seals range widely, many migrating northwards (most of the sightings at the sub-Antarctic islands occur at this time), and occasionally individuals are reported from the coasts of Patagonia, South Africa, Southern Australia, Tasmania and New Zealand (Bonner, 1985). The most northerly record is from Rarotonga in the Cook Islands at 21° S (Berry, 1961). Possible seasonal movements of Ross Seals are completely unknown. The only sighting north of 55° S has been made at Heard Island (Ingham, 1960).

8.2.3 Habitat preferences

On land in the breeding season the Antarctic Fur Seal shows a preference for rocky shores and small beaches in sheltered coves (Bonner, 1968), while at other times of the year it is more widely dispersed in more open areas, and, at South Georgia, in tussock grassland behind the beaches. Elephant Seals tend to occupy the more open beaches in the breeding season, and at South Georgia they are found in muddly wallows in low-lying tussock grass (Laws, 1960b).

Weddell Seals form pupping colonies on the fast ice in the spring, along the shorelines, associated with broken ice, tide cracks and hummocking (Stirling, 1971a; Siniff *et al.*, 1977b; Kooyman, 1981c). They enlarge existing cracks with their canine teeth to form holes for hauling out (Stirling, 1969b), but are unable to make new holes. Although females usually return to the same colony, or a neighbouring colony, year after year, they will pup at other sites should cracks not open at the colony site used in the previous year (Stirling, 1969c).

The most detailed studies of Weddell Seal distribution and movements have been made in McMurdo Sound (Stirling, 1969c, 1971b; Siniff *et al.*, 1971, 1977b; M. S. R. Smith, 1965). Most of the seals remain in McMurdo Sound throughout the year but local movements occur as the distribution of the breathing holes changes. By mid-December the pups have been weaned and many seals move south to occupy cracks near Cape Armitage and Scott Base which form as the seaice breaks up. Others disperse north, some to Cape Bird where in the late summer they haul out on stony beaches, bared as the beach push ice retreats. Subadults tend to move to more peripheral areas than the adults. During the winter the seals move back to the breeding areas as the sea ice re-forms. An unusual habitat found at White Island on the McMurdo Ice Shelf is a land-locked colony of some 20–30 Weddell Seals which overwinter beneath the ice (Stirling, 1972; Kooyman, 1981c).

The habitat of the pack ice species is very different in that they show preferences for particular ice types (Gilbert & Erickson, 1977). Highest densities of Crabeater Seals have been recorded in the summer within 120 km of the ice edge. Densities are most closely corre-

lated with dominant flow size, not ice cover, and in the summer they are most abundant in cake and brash ice with a cover of about 7–8 oktas (a measure of the percentage ice cover, maximum 8, minimum 1); densities are lowest in areas with larger floes (Gilbert & Erickson, 1977) (Fig. 8.8). Peak haul-out periods for Crabeaters are around midday, with some regional year-to-year variability (Condy, 1977b). In spring their family groups are associated with the larger hummocked floes, and the immatures can be found in large concentrations of several thousands, associated with the fast ice remaining in the bays (Bengtson & Siniff, 1981).

In the summer Leopard Seals generally occur as solitary animals and like the Crabeater Seals they show higher densities near the pack ice edge. Although their predatory activities in the vicinity of penguin colonies have attracted a lot of attention, relatively few are seen in inshore waters (Laws, 1981). Their daytime haul-out patterns and distribution in relation to floe size are similar to those of the Crabeater Seals (Fig. 8.8).

Ross Seals are usually seen as solitary individuals and their highest densities are associated with larger floes than is the case for other species, typically where the ice cover is about 6–8 oktas (Gilbert & Erickson, 1977).

8.3 Abundance

Different methods have been used to assess the abundances of different species of Antarctic seals (Laws, 1981; SCAR/SCOR, 1983b). For the colonial breeding species (Fur, Elephant, and Weddell Seals) counts of pups raised by a factor related to the age structure of the population is the method generally used. For the pack ice species, estimates are calculated from stratified random strip census counts supported by surveys from ships or aircraft.

Prior to exploitation in the nineteenth century Antarctic Fur Seals were estimated to number from 1–2 million individuals (Bonner, 1976). Following the slaughter of these seals, their reduction to some hundreds of individuals and the collapse of sealing (Bonner, 1964, 1968, 1981), the stocks began to recover (see Chapter 16). This recovery has been reviewed by Bonner (1976), Laws (1973, 1977a) and Payne (1977, 1978). Bonner (1981) estimated that the annual pup production in 1978 was 138 000, corresponding to a total population of about 554 000 and by 1982 it was estimated that there were probably over 900 000 (Laws, 1985). The current population is probably over one million.

Laws (1960b), on the basis of the information then available, concluded that the total mid-year population of the Southern Elephant seal was 600 000±100 000. This estimate has been updated by McCann (1980a) to *c*.

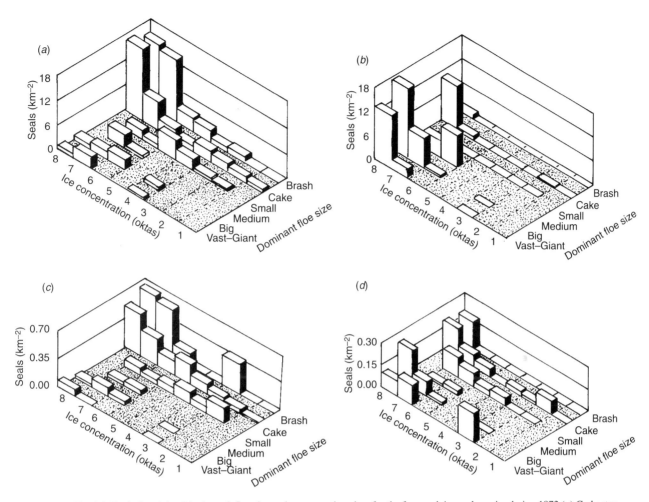

Fig. 8.8. Typical seal densities in each floe size and concentration class for the four pack ice seal species during 1972 (*a*) Crabeater Seal, (*b*) Weddell Seal, (*c*) Leopard Seal, (*d*) Ross Seal. Redrawn from J. R. Gilbert & Erickson (1977)

750 000, with the South Georgia stock comprising 350 000, Macquarie Island 136 000, Isles Kerguelen 157 000 and Heard island 80 000. Elephant Seals are increasing in some areas and declining in others. Condy (1977a) estimated a decline of approximately 69.5% at Marion Island between 1951 and 1976. A more recent evaluation (SCAR/SCOR, 1983c) indicates that Elephant Seals throughout the Antarctic and sub-Antarctic might be declining at a rate as high as 8–11% per annum. Counts of Elephant Seals at the Vestfold Hills from 1858 to 1988 indicate that the population had declined by a half to two-thirds, similar to the reported decline of breeding populations on Kerguelen.

The most carefully planned and executed estimates of the four Antarctic pack ice seals are those described by Erickson *et al.* (1971), Siniff *et al.* (1970) and by Gilbert & Erickson (1977) based on investigations made from icebreakers in 1968, 1979, 1972 and 1973. A variety of parameters affects these estimates, including activity patterns, haul-out rates, transect width, weather, light conditions and the ability to spot seals behind drift ice. Gilbert

& Erickson (1977) concluded that there were six residual pack ice regions and estimated their overall seal densities in February to March, within the range 1.86 to 6.56 individuals km^{-2}, to give a conservative population estimate of 14 858 000 Crabeater Seals. However, as they point out, juveniles are probably under-represented in the estimates, and the recorded densities are likely to be low. In 1984 (Laws, 1984a) considered that a estimated population of 15 million could well be conservative and that a population of 30–40 million or more was not unlikely, as the species appeared to have been increasing at a comparatively rapid rate.

Leopard Seals are estimated to total between 220 and 400 thousand, with the population on the increase, while the Weddell Seal population is estimated at 800 000 (Laws, 1984a). The least reliable estimate is that of 220 000 for the Ross Seal. In percentage terms the estimated populations associated with the residual pack ice regions represent 92.36% Crabeater, 1.35% Leopard, 1.35% Ross and 4.93% Weddell Seals (Laws, 1984a). While the species composition of seals within the

Table 8.1. *Abundance estimates for the Antarctic seal populations.*

Species	Population size 1982 (×10³)	Status
Fur	930	Increasing
Elephant	750	Stable, some decreasing
Crabeater	30000	Increasing
Leopard	220–440	Increasing
Ross	220	Not known
Weddell	800	Stable, some colonies decreasing
Total	33140	Increasing

After Laws (1984a).

pack ice remains remarkably constant, the inshore ratios change. For example, Ray (1970) found 43% Weddell Seals in counts on the western side of the Ross Sea. Estimates of the total populations of all six species are given in Table 8.1. From this table it can be seen that the total population, estimated at some 18 million in the early 1970s had risen to possibly some 33 million in 1982.

8.4 Social organization and reproductive behaviour
The social and reproductive behaviour of the six Antarctic seals varies widely and is, in part, associated with breeding habitat and predatory pressure. Crabeater, Leopard and Ross Seals inhabit an unstable area of constantly shifting pack ice which varies from place to place and day to day. Floe size, surface features and the proportion of sea covered also vary. Weddell Seals breed in areas of predictable fast ice, permitting association with specific sites. Elephant and Fur Seals have developed social systems adapted to female aggregation, terrestrial parturition, and seasonal breeding at specific sites.

8.4.1 Ice-breeding species
We know very little of the social organization of the pack ice-breeding species. Aspects of the social organization and reproductive behaviour of Crabeater Seals have been described by King (1957), Øritzland (1970a), Corner (1972), Siniff & Bengtson, (1977) and Siniff *et al.* (1977a, 1979). Crabeater Seal overall mean densities in the pack ice range from about 4.83 individuals km⁻² in the summer to about 0.5 individuals km⁻² in the winter and spring. During the breeding season the seals form pairs when a pregnant female hauls out to give birth on a suitable floe and is joined by a male either before or after parturition. Pups are born in September and October, with most births occurring in early to middle October (Fig. 8.9a). Lactation lasts for about four weeks during which

time the pup increases in weight from about 20 to 113 kg, while the mother loses about 50% of her weight. During this period the male defends an area of about 50 m round the family group from other adult males and Leopard Seals. Competition for mates must occur as the males frequently bear wounds characteristic of interspecific encounters. After the pup is weaned the male maintains close contact with the female preventing her from leaving the floe and often biting her on the upper back and neck. This is probably precopulatory behaviour as the female returns the male aggression. Copulation probably occurs on the ice, unlike that of most ice-breeding species where it occurs in the water (Stirling, 1975). Perhaps this is because copulating seals would be vulnerable to predators (Killer Whales and Leopard Seals) in the water.

The social organization and mating strategies of the Leopard and Ross Seals are less well known than that of the Crabeater. Ross Seals are almost invariably solitary, although groups of up to 13 have been recorded (Laws, 1964). During the summer their closest observed spacing was 1 km and the average overall density was about 0.09 individuals km⁻² in the summer and probably about 0.02 individuals km⁻² in the spring (Gilbert & Erickson, 1977). Very few Ross Seal pups have ever been recorded. The greatest number is eight recorded near the Balleney Islands (Tikhomirov, 1975). Pups are probably born in November, later than those of the Crabeater Seal. Males do not appear to accompany the females as in the Crabeater Seal, and perhaps this may be because copulation occurs in the water.

Leopard Seals are mostly solitary inhabitants of the pack ice zone (Laws, 1964; Marlow, 1967; Øritzland, 1970a; Siniff *et al.*, 1970; Erickson *et al.*, 1971; Hofman *et al.*, 1973). They are not known to form aggregations except for occasional small groups on the ice floes (Hofman *et al.*, 1977). Along the Antarctic Peninsula females haul out alone in November and December, deliver their pups, and remain with them to weaning (Fig. 8.9b). The breeding behaviour of the males and females is practically unknown, and copulation is presumed to take place under water after the pups have been weaned (Harrison *et al.*, 1952; Harrison, 1969; Siniff *et al.*, 1980).

The Weddell Seal is quite different in its social organization and reproductive behaviour from the other ice-breeding species and this has been described by Mansfield (1958), Stirling, 1969c, 1971b), Kaufman *et al.* (1975); Siniff *et al.* (1977b) and Siniff (1982). In the summer, outside the breeding season, Weddell Seals probably move to the outer edge of the fast ice and the inner zones of the pack ice, although dispersal may be limited in some areas. They are nearly always single when found in the pack ice in the summer. The main den-

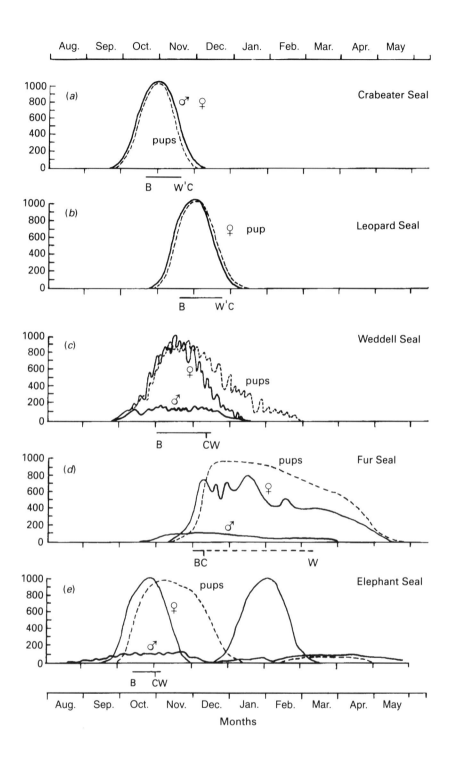

Fig. 8.9. Breeding season activities of Antarctic seals. Pups are shown by dashed lines. Average dates of birth (B), conception (C), and weaning (W) are indicated. (*a*) Crabeater Seal, Antarctic Peninsula, family groups and mated pairs in pack ice. (*b*) Leopard Seal, Antarctic Peninsula, female and pup pairs on ice. (*c*) Weddell Seal, McMurdo Sound, haul-out of mature males, females and pups on fast ice for breeding; fluctuating curves reflect aquatic activity (data from Kaufman *et al.*, 1975). (*d*) Fur Seal, Bird Island, haul-out of mature males and females for parturition, lactation and mating. Note the suckling period is broken by feeding trips to sea. Data to early March from Bonner (1968), extrapolated to May from other reports. (*e*) Elephant Seal, South Georgia. Adult haul-out for moult in January–May is also shown (data from Laws, 1956 and McCann, 1980a). Hypothetical curve inferred from very limited observations. Redrawn from Laws (1984a).

sity in the pack ice at this time is about 0.14 individuals km^{-2}, while in the winter it may be about 0.002 individuals km^{-2}, assuming an even distribution as the pack ice spreads (Gilbert & Erickson, 1977).

In spring pupping colonies form on the nearshore fast ice. Several females may share a single breathing hole, giving birth (in September to November, depending on latitude) to the pup on the sea ice surrounding it (Fig. 8.9c). Pups are suckled until weaning at about six weeks. They weigh about 15 kg at birth, and by 10 days they have about doubled this, being weaned at about 110 kg around six to seven weeks.

During the winter and spring there is intraspecific competition for space, and non-breeding seals and subadults are excluded from the preferred breeding areas. In the breeding season the males spend most of the time in the water beneath the cracks, where they defend aquatic territories against other males (Siniff *et al.*, 1977b). This enables them to have exclusive access to all females using the same breathing hole or length of crack. The mature female ovulates just before the pup is weaned in late November–December and underwater mating occurs then; it has been observed only once (Kaufman *et al.*, 1975). Unlike the pack ice seals, lactating female Weddell seals leave the pups periodically to feed, this occurring more frequently as the pups grow. The pups first enter the water at two to three weeks (Stirling, 1969a).

8.4.2 Land-breeding species

In contrast to the ice-breeding species, the two land-breeding species, the Fur Seal and the Elephant Seal, are highly polygynous and gregarious in their breeding behaviour, and they may also form large aggregations at other times.

The breeding grounds of the Fur Seal tend to be rocky or shingle sites, and the seals return to their breeding grounds year after year, showing very strong fidelity. The males come ashore and establish territories averaging 60 m^{-2} in late October two to three weeks before the females haul out (Fig. 8.9d). Territory size declines to about 22 m^{-2} later in the season when the beaches are fully occupied. Bulls defend their territories with displays, vocal threats and fighting encounters, often resulting in severe wounds. Successful fighting and territory maintenance means that the bull is on site to mate with the oestrous cows on his territory. Territories are held from late October to late December for an average period of 34 days during which the bulls do not feed (McCann, 1980b).

A cow produces a pup about two days after coming ashore. For about eight days she remains with her pup,

suckling it at about six-hourly intervals. At the end of this period she comes into oestrous and is mated by the bull in whose territory she occurs. After mating the females goes to sea to feed. She is away for three to six days and then returns to suckle her pup for two to five days. This pattern is repeated for the whole of the lactation period which lasts for 110–115 days until April (Bonner, 1968; Doidge & Croxall, 1983). The pups grow rapidly; males gain weight at an average of 98 g day^{-1} from a birth weight of 5.9 kg, while females born at 5.4 kg grow more slowly at about 84 g day^{-1} (Payne, 1979).

Elephant Seals also form harems but they are of a different kind to those of Fur Seals. In September the bulls arrive to take up positions on the preferred beaches which are generally sand or shingle, and shortly afterwards the cows haul out to give birth (Fig. 8.9e). The cows are gregarious and form groups which quickly attract the larger bulls to join them. These territorial bulls drive off intruding bulls usually by threat alone and very exceptionally by fighting. Pups are born about eight days after haul-out and unlike the Fur Seals the cows do not go to sea until the pups are weaned. Both cows and bulls go without food on the breeding beaches, living on their reserves of blubber, the female for over three weeks and some of the males for up to three months. As the season advances the groups of cows increase in size and may coalesce, reaching a maximum in October. The larger groups may have several bulls among them but of these one is usually clearly dominant. Subordinate bulls lower in the dominance hierarchy are found around the groups of cows and in the water just offshore (Laws, 1956).

At birth the pups weigh about 46 kg. The weight is doubled in about 11 days and quadrupled at the end of lactation, which lasts for about three weeks. The cows come into oestrous about 19 days after they give birth and are mated over a receptive period of about four days by the dominant bulls (McCann, 1980a). Adult male Elephant Seals reach sexual maturity at about four years, but do not achieve physical maturity or breeding status until at least seven years. The dominant bulls, the beachmasters, probably only have one or two seasons of dominance, but during this time they pass their genes to a large number of offspring as they achieve the great majority of matings (McCann, 1981a).

8.5 Feeding ecology

8.5.1 Food consumption

Understanding the feeding ecology of Antarctic pinnipeds is essential to our elucidating the role of this important group of animals in the Southern Ocean ecosystem. As Laws (1984a) points out there are many

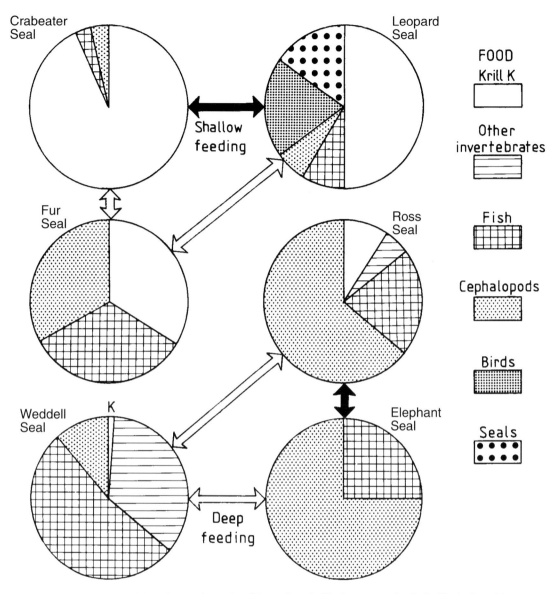

Fig. 8.10. Percentage composition of stomach samples of Antarctic seals. Black arrows, major similarities in diet; white arrows, minor similarities in diet. Redrawn from Laws (1984a).

difficulties in establishing the qualitative and quantitative aspects of their feeding due to the vast areas they occupy, the inaccessibility of the pack ice and fast ice regions, and the lack of opportunity of observing feeding directly except on rare occasions. Nevertheless, some generalizations can be made, mainly on the basis of the records of stomach contents of collected animals (Fig. 8.10). Recent reviews of food consumption include those of Øritzland (1977) and Laws (1977b, 1984a). Table 8.2 updates their calculations with recent estimates of stock sizes and prey selection.

The Crabeater Seal is a specialist feeder with over 90% of its diet made up of krill, with small amounts of fish, squid and other invertebrates. The Crabeater's dentition is very complex with each cheek tooth having a main backwardly directed cusp, flanked by one anterior and two posterior cusps (Fig. 8.11). When the teeth occlude they leave a small gap forming a strainer which enables the retention of the krill while expelling the water taken in with the prey. King (1961) described the straining mechanism of the Crabeater, including a bony projection on the mandible which closes the gap between the last, upper cheek tooth and the scoop-like lower jaw. Racovitza (1900) described the Crabeater as swimming with the mouth open in krill swarms, while Wilson (in Kooyman, 1981a) reports it as catching invertebrates one by one.

Little is known about the feeding of the Ross Seal. Cephalopods appear to be an important component of the diet (about 57%), although fish (about 37%) have also

Table 8.2. *Rough estimates of food consumption of Antarctic seals. Feeding rate estimated at 7% of body weight for all seals except Elephant Seals, which were assumed to consume 6% of body weight daily. Elephant seals were assumed to feed 290 days/year, all others 335 days/year*

Species	Crabeater	Leopard	Ross	Weddell	Elephant	Fur	Total
Stock size ($\times 10^3$)	30000[1]	400[1]	220[2]	730[2]	741[1]	1108[1]	33199
Mean wt (t)	0.193	0.272	0.173	0.246	0.500	0.500	—
Antarctic biomass ($\times 10^3$ t)	5790.0	108.8	38.1	179.6	370.5	55.4	6542.4
Individual consumption							
kg d^{-1}	14	19	12	17	30	3	—
t y^{-1}	4.53	6.38	4.05	5.77	8.70	1.17	—
Annual consumption of stock ($t \times 10^6$) and average food item frequencies (%s in brackets)[3]							
Euphausiids	127.4 (94)	1.15 (45)	0.08 (9)	0.04 (1)	—	0.44 (34)	129.11
Cephalopods	2.72 (2)	0.13 (5)	0.57 (64)	0.46 (11)	4.48 (75)	0.43 (33)	8.79
Other inventebrates	1.36 (1)	—	0.04 (5)	1.48 (35)	—	—	2.88
Fish	4.08 (3)	0.13 (5)	0.20 (22)	2.23 (53)	1.61 (25)	0.43 (33)	8.68
Birds	—	0.25 (10)	—	—	—	—	0.25
Seals	—	0.89 (35)	—	—	—	—	0.89
Total	135.56	2.55	0.89	4.21	6.09	1.30	151.06

[1]Stock estimates from SCAR/SCOR (1983)
[2]Stock estimates from Gilbert & Erickson (1977)
[3]Percentages for Leopard Seals from Siniff & Stone (1985), for Leopard Seals, from Øritzland (1977) for Crabeater, Ross and Weddell Seals; and from Laws (1977b) for Elephant and Antarctic Fur Seals.
Modified from Øritzland (1977) & Laws (1977b) with data from SCAR/SCOR (1983c) and Siniff & Stone (1985).
From Bengtson (1985).

been found (Barrett-Hamilton, 1901; Wilson, 1907; R. N. R. Brown, 1913). King (1969) suggested that Ross Seals may take larger cephalopods (up to 7 kg in size) than do other seals. However, Øritzland (1977) states that of the cephalopods he found in Ross Seal stomachs 92% were small.

In contrast to the above two species the Leopard Seal is an opportunistic predator, taking a variety of prey, including krill, squid, fish, penguins and seals. Leopard Seals are perhaps best known for their predation on penguins. At the landing place of most Antarctic penguin rookeries one or more Leopard Seals lie in wait to take toll of the birds as they arrive and depart. This predatory behaviour has been described by Muller-Schwarze & Muller-Schwarze (1975), Penny & Lowry (1967) and Hunt (1973). They pursue, catch and kill penguins in the water, dismembering them by powerful jerks of the head. Penguins, however, are a temporary food resource when the birds are concentrated on the breeding colonies. Where it has been possible to identify the sex of the predatory seals they have all been males.

Another important food for Leopard Seals is the flesh of other seal species. While five other species of seal have been identified as being preyed upon by Leopard Seals (Wilson, 1907; Bertram, 1940; Laws, 1964; Gilbert & Erickson, 1977; Erickson & Hofman, 1974; Siniff & Bengtson, 1977; Siniff et al., 1979; Bengtson, 1982; and Stone & Siniff, 1983), by far and away the most impor-

tant species is the Crabeater. The importance of Crabeater Seals in the diet of Leopard Seals is supported by the observations of Condy (1976), Siniff & Bengtson (1977), Siniff et al. (1979), Siniff (1982) and Siniff & Stone (1985) who all emphasized the high rate of scarring of Crabeater Seals. The spacing of the scars on the flanks of the majority of these seals is consistent with Leopard Seal attacks. Up to 93% of seals encountered during census surveys had such scars. Crabeater Seals older than one year old are seldom attacked and fresh wounds on adults are rare (Laws, 1977a).

In view of their predatory behaviour it is surprising that Leopard Seals take substantial quantities of krill. Like those of the Crabeater the teeth of the Leopard Seal are intricately cusped and when the jaws are closed they interlock to form an efficient strainer (Fig. 8.11). Øritzland (1977) concluded that overall the Leopard Seal takes 37% krill in its diet, but Hofman et al. (1977) at Palmer Station on the Antarctic Peninsula found a much higher proportion of 87%. The latter sample was biased towards the younger age classes which may take krill more frequently than the older ones.

Øritzland's (1977) stomach samples from the pack ice comprised 58% krill, 16% penguin, 12% fish, 9% cephalopods and 3% seal. Siniff & Stone (1985) have broadly confirmed Øritzland's conclusions. From samples taken along the west coast of the Antarctic Peninsula during November–March, they found 45% krill, 10%

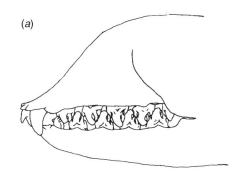

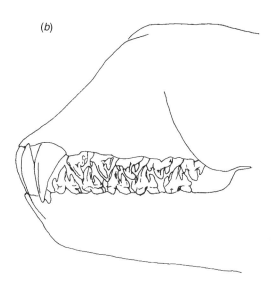

Fig. 8.11. (*a*) Cheek teeth of the Crabeater Seal. The lobed teeth fit together to form strainer to separate water from its krill prey. (*b*) Cheek teeth of the Leopard Seal. Though Leopard Seals are more versatile feeders than Crabeaters, their pointed teeth, like the lobed teeth of the Crabeater form an efficient sieve when feeding on krill. Redrawn from Bonner (1985a).

penguin, mainly Adélie, 35% seal, mostly Crabeater, and 10% fish and squid. On the basis of all published information Laws (1984a) suggested that the overall relative proportions are 50% krill, 20% penguins, 14% seals, 9% fish and 6% cephalopods.

Siniff & Stone (1985) have shown that in the Antarctic Peninsula area the diet of Leopard Seals changes over the year (Fig. 8.12). They found that the consumption of Crabeater Seals rose sharply in November, when the newly weaned Crabeater pups became available (Siniff *et al.*, 1979). After November, the proportion of Crabeater Seals continued to rise until early February, after which there was a sharp decline in Crabeater consumption accompanied by an increase in krill consumption. This decline in Crabeater Seals in the diet coincides with an increase in the ability of growing young animals to escape predation. Krill probably remain an important component of the diet over the winter as a high level of

krill consumption (60%) was recorded in late September. Penguins were an important item in mid-February when young penguins were fledging and entering the sea. Cephalopods were a major food item in January but some were taken throughout the year. These finding confirmed the view that Leopard Seals are very catholic in their choice of food. Peaks in the incidence of the various groups of prey in the diet apparently occur when the prey is most available and vulnerable, or when opportunities to take other prey items are few.

Analysis of the stomach contents of Weddell Seals indicates that a variety of prey is taken including fish (Dearborn, 1965b; Calhaem & Christoffel, 1969), squid (M. R. Clarke & MacLoed, 1982b) and crustaceans, including krill (Lindsay, 1937; Bertram, 1940). A study by M. R. Clarke & MacLoed (1982b) analyzed the contents of eight stomachs of seals taken at Deception Island. The majority contained fish, as well as crustaceans, isopods, amphipods and krill. All of the stomachs contained stones, as is common in Leopard and Crabeater Seals (Bengtson, 1982). From 336 lower beaks of cephalopods found in the stomachs they were able to estimate the frequency and biomass of eight species, six squid and two octopuses. Cephalopods were the predominant food taken in contrast to Weddell Seals in the McMurdo Sound area where fish were the main prey occurring in 97% of the stomachs sampled (Kooyman, 1981c). In McMurdo Sound Testa *et al.* (1985) found that the diet of Weddell Seals during November–February consisted of small nototheniid fish (*Pleuragramma* and *Trematomus*), decapod and amphipod crustaceans and cephalopods. Over a limited period in December the large Antarctic cod *Dissostichus mawsoni* is an important prey species in McMurdo Sound.

There is essentially no information available on the pelagic food habits of Elephant Seals and most food consumption studies have been conducted during the moult period when Elephant Seals are ashore fasting (Laws, 1977a). Laws (1956) noted that young Elephant Seals may feed on amphipods for a short time after weaning. Only 35 of the 139 stomachs he examined contained food; of these 83% had cephalopods remains and 26% fish. On the basis of these results and evidence from other studies (Matthews, 1929; Murphy, 1914) Laws concluded that the Elephant Seal's year round diet probably includes 75% cephalopods and 25% fish (Laws, 1977b; McCann, 1983). M. R. Clarke & MacLoed (1982a) identified eight species of cephalopods from five to six families in the stomachs from Elephant Seals at Signy Island; four of these species were in the size range eaten by Sperm Whales.

As with the Elephant Seals there is little information on

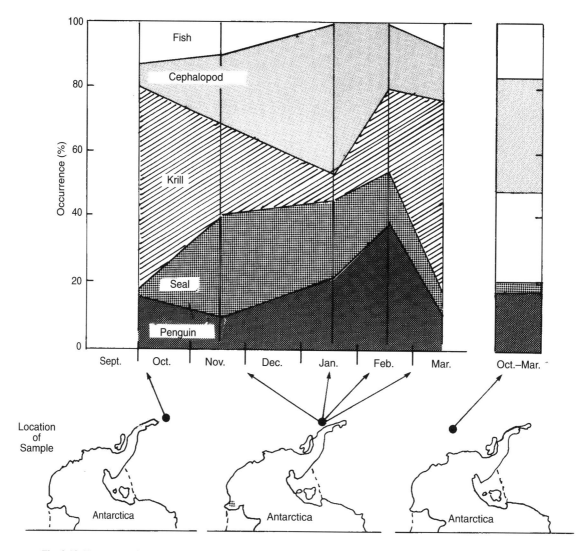

Fig. 8.12. Frequency of occurrence (%) of food items in the stomachs of Leopard Seals in relation to time of the year. Sample size and date as follows: Sep.–Oct., $n = 38$ specimens with food in stomachs (data from Øritzland, 1977); pooled data for Oct.–Mar., $n = 39$ specimens with food (data from Tikhomirov, 1975) not broken down by month; Nov.–Mar., n = 66 specimens with food (from Siniff & Stone, 1985). Redrawn from Siniff & Stone (1985).

feeding of Fur Seals during the pelagic phase. However, it is clear that in the Peninsula region during the breeding season krill are a staple food for lactating females (Doidge & Croxall, 1985). Fish and squid are taken by juvenile and non-breeding adults (Bonner, 1968; North *et al.*, 1983). The most comprehensive study is that of Doidge & Croxall who examined 79 stomachs collected at Schlieper Bay, South Georgia and 238 collected at Bird Island. On the basis of all the available data they estimated that in the summer krill consumption varied from 75 to 92% by weight, but that in the winter the males consumed only 20% krill, with 30% squid and 50% fish. At Heard Island Green *et al.* (1989) found that Fur Seals during the breeding season fed mainly on fish in contrast to those in the Peninsula region. An average of 95.2% of the scats in monthly collections contained fish remains. Pelagic myctophids constituted more than 50% of the fish

taken by the seals at the beginning of summer and at the end of the season when there was an influx of non-breeding males. From October to December fish from the surrounding shelf area (various benthic nototheniid species, the bentho-pelagic ice fish *Champsocephalus gunnari*, and skate *Bathyraja* spp.) comprised the bulk of the catch. Laws (1977b) concluded that the overall diet of the Fur Seal was approximately 34% krill, 33% cephalopods and 33% fish.

8.5.2 *Feeding and diving behaviour*

The depth of feeding dives and the timing of feeding activity differ among the various species of Antarctic seals. Ross, Weddell and Elephant Seals appear to feed at great depths, up to several hundred metres, with diurnal feeding patterns that may vary seasonally (Laws, 1984a). Crabeater, Fur and Leopard seals, on the other hand, are

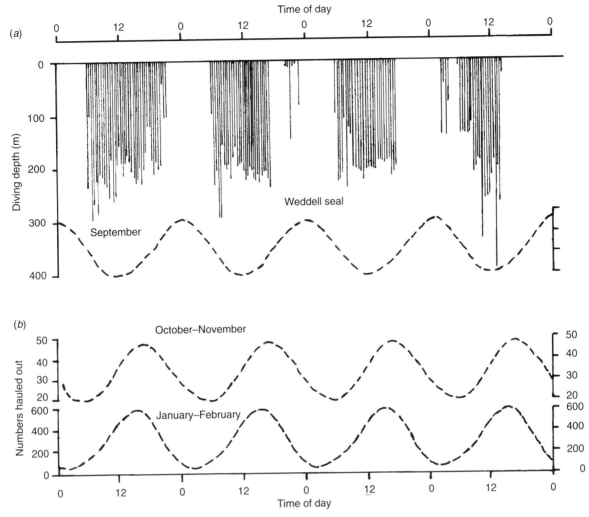

Fig. 8.13. (*a*) Diagrammatical representation of typical Weddell Seal time/depth diving pattern over four days in September (after Kooyman, 1981d), described haul-out pattern for September. (*b*) Actual haul-out cycle for McMurdo Sound Weddell Seals during October–November and January–February, reported over four days, for comparison with the diving pattern of the experimental animal (data from Kaufmann *et al.*, 1975; Stirling, 1969c). Redrawn from Laws (1984a).

shallow feeders generally utilizing the upper portions of the water column, usually feeding to depths of about 60–80 m in summer, mainly feeding at night and being hauled out on land or ice, or swimming at the surface during the day.

Virtually nothing is known of the feeding behaviour of the Elephant Seal. Laws (1984a) has suggested three reasons why Elephant Seals probably feed at depth in the water column. Firstly, the very similar Northern Elephant Seal, *M. angustirostris*, takes prey species usually found between 100–300 m (Huey, 1930); secondly, Southern Elephant Seals take prey similar to that of Sperm Whales which feed at great depths; and, thirdly, their eyes have a visual pigment – 'a deep-sea rhodopsin' – similar to that found in deep-water fishes and which has been suggested as an adaptation for detecting bioluminescence of deep-sea squids (Lythgoe & Dartnall, 1970).

Ross Seals are also thought to be deep divers, although

only very limited information is available. Their over-sized eyes, as well as the presence of very large squid remains in their stomachs (King, 1969), suggest that they may be adapted for feeding at great depths. There appears to be a peak haul-out in the middle of the day indicating nocturnal feeding (Gilbert & Erickson, 1977; Condy, 1977b). The diving pattern of the Weddell Seal is better known than that of any other marine mammal. It has been extensively studied by Kooyman (1981c, d) by using time–depth recorders attached to free-diving seals. Dives of 200–400 m are common and one dive was measured at 600 m. As the latter dive was to the sea floor they may be capable of even deeper dives. The usual duration of such dives was 15 minutes or less. A typical pattern based on the record of diving behaviour in one individual over four days in September is depicted diagrammatically in Fig. 8.13. At McMurdo Sound where the diving behaviour was studied fish were found in 97% of the stomachs that contained any food (Dearborn, 1965b). Kooyman (1981d) identified two types of dives: deep dives and exploratory dives. Exploratory dives were shallow and of longer duration. Daytime dives were to a maximum depth of 600 m and averaged about 120 m, whereas at night the maximum depth was 270 m, and the average depth 40 m. There were also more exploratory dives during the day.

The diurnal haul-out pattern for Weddell Seals on the fast ice has been studied by several authors (Stirling, 1969c; Erickson *et al.*, 1971; Kaufman *et al.*, 1975; Gilbert & Erickson, 1977; Thomas & DeMaster, 1983). In spring there is a diurnal pattern of night activity which changes during the summer so that in the October–November breeding season there is a peak haul-out on the ice at about 16.00–18.00 h (Kaufman *et al.*, 1975). In January–February the peak haul-out is at 13.00–14.00 h (Erickson *et al.*, 1971) and Gilbert & Erickson (1977) reported a similar Weddell Seal haul-out in the pack ice. These haul-out patterns are shown in Fig. 8.13

Recently Kooyman & Davis (1980) and Kooyman *et al* (1982) have investigated Fur Seal diving behaviour at Bird Island, South Georgia. In Fig. 8.14 a typical diving pattern of a female feeding on krill off South Georgia is depicted. Like the Weddell Seal, there is a diurnal pattern but with most of the diving activity taking place at night. Diving depths are shallower than in the Weddell Seal, most being between 20–50 m in depth, with a maximum depth of 100 m, and with dives to shallower depths at night. In Fig. 8.14 a comparison of the diurnal patterns is made with that of the diurnal variation in the depth of the krill. It can be seen that there is a clear correlation between prey availability and diving depth.

8.5.3 *Amounts of food consumed*

Laws (1984a) and Bengston (1984) have analyzed the available data and estimated the amount of food consumed by the Antarctic seals (Table 8.1). They concluded that Elephant Seals feed for some 255–315 days annually, varying according to age and sex, Fur Seals for 315–336 days, and the pack ice seals for about 335 days. However the quantities of food consumed are somewhat difficult to estimate. Øritzland (1977) estimated the average meal size as follows: Weddell Seal, 23 kg; Leopard Seal, 16 kg; Crabeater Seal, 8 kg; and Ross Seal, 6 kg. Data on captive seals can give some estimate of daily feeding rates: 6–10% of body weights; less for Elephant Seals (Keyes, 1968); 4–7% (Geraci, 1975); adults 6%, young 19% (Ray in Sergeant, 1973); 5% (Samuelson, in

Øritzland, 1977; Sergeant, 1973); 5% (Blix *et al.*, 1973). These estimates of 4–10% are for captive animals under different conditions and at higher temperatures than wild Antarctic seals.

Laws (1977b) accepted Øritzland's (1977) tentative estimates of an average daily food intake of 7% of body weight for pack ice seals, a similar rate for Fur Seals and 6% for Elephant Seals when not fasting. He applied these percentages to the feeding periods listed above to arrive at the following suggested daily food intake averaged over the year: 55 g food kg^{-1} for the Elephant Seal; 62m g kg^{-1} for the Fur Seal; and, 64 g kg^{-1} for the pack ice seals. Thus, the average annual food consumption would be about 20 times mean body weight for Elephant Seals; 23 times for Fur Seals, and about the same for the pack ice seals.

8.5.4 *Energy requirements*

The energetic values of different foods consumed varies (Laws, 1984a): for krill it is about 4.2–4.5 kJ (g wet wt)$^{-1}$ (A. Clarke & Prince, 1980); for lipid-rich myctophid fish 5.6–8.0 kJ g^{-1}; and for nototheniid fishes about 4.1 kJ g^{-1}; compared with 3.5 kJ g^{-1} (range 2.9–4.5) for squid (Croxall & Prince, 1982). Thus the ratio of energy content of krill:fish:squid eaten by seals is probably about 1.00:0.94:0.80. The energetic value of seal prey is about 20.5 kJ g^{-1}, that is about four to five times the energy value of krill. That of penguins is probably similar.

Pinniped energetics have been reviewed by Lavigne *et al.* (1982, 1986). Naumov and Chekunova (1980) calculated energy expenditure and needs for Crabeater Seals from generally accepted equations for mammalian energy balances. A total metabolic energy expenditure of 16 867 kcal day^{-1} (70 672 kJ day^{-1}) was calculated for a 190 kg female. Growth energy requirements were calculated at 782 kcal day^{-1} (3277 kJ day^{-1}). They further estimated that a female spends over 51% of its energy resource on reproductive metabolism. They calculated that their 190 kg seal must consume 10.4% of its body weight (20 kg) daily to satisfy energy requirements of 22 062 kcal day^{-1} (92 440 kJ day^{-1}), but estimated that it would feed intensively for only about 120 days a year, and for 200 days would only eat enough (15 kg) to maintain its resting metabolism. Averaged over the year this represents 14.8 kg day^{-1} or 7.8% of body weight.

Doidge & Croxall (1985) have analyzed energy requirements and food consumption of the Fur Seal population at South Georgia. They estimated that krill accounted for 69% of the food biomass taken by the herd, fish 19% and squid 12%. In summer the population could consume about 23% of its biomass daily, assuming an assimilation rate of 75%. If there was a higher assimilation rate (say 90%, as has been estimated by Lavigne *et*

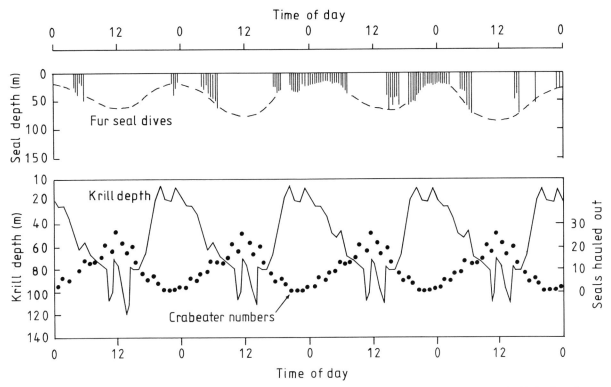

Fig. 8.14. Diagrammatic representation of typical Fur Seal diving patterns over four days in January compared with the diurnal variation in mean depth of krill in the Scotia Sea in summer (data from Everson, 1984a), and diurnal variation in Crabeater Seal numbers hauled out in pack ice on 21, 23 and 15 January at about 69° 40′ E (data from Condy, 1977b). Redrawn from Laws (1984a).

al., 1982, 1986) then 19% of the body weight would be required each day. For the northern Fur Seal *Callorhinus ursinus* it has been estimated that juveniles need to consume 14% of their body weight in order to meet existence requirements. A higher rate of 16% (Costa & Gentry, to be published, quoted in Doidge & Croxall, 1985) has recently been calculated. These estimates indicate that Fur Seals have higher energy demands than those (e.g. 7% of body weight daily) previously assumed (McAlister *et al.*, 1976; Laws, 1977b; Payne, 1979).

8.6 Reproduction, growth and development

8.6.1 Annual reproductive cycle
Antarctic seals produce their pups in spring during a short synchronized period which varies according to species and latitude. The timing of pupping season of all species is shown in Fig. 8.9. This timing seems to be remarkably constant for any one colony, from year to year (E. A. Smith & Burton, 1970; McCann, 1980a,b). The latitudinal changes which occur in this timing are illustrated by the Weddell Seal where the peak birth date varies with latitude from 7 September at Signey Island (61° S) to 23 October at McMurdo Sound (78° S) (Mansfield, 1958; Stirling, 1969a). Within a population age classes tend to pup or mate at different times, e.g. young Elephant Seal

females pup earlier than old females (Laws, 1956; McCann, 1980a,b).

Table 8.3 gives details of the approximate duration of the female reproductive cycle. From this table it can be seen that the lactation period ranges from about 23 days in the Elephant Seal to 110–115 days in the Fur Seal; these periods are all much longer than in Arctic seals. The growth of the seal pups is rapid due to the quantity and quality of the milk produced by the females. In the Elephant Seal the fat content of the milk increases from about 12% at birth to over 40% in the second week. The percentage fat then ranges from 12 to 40%. In the Fur Seal, which has a much longer period of lactation, the mean percentage fat is 26.4%.

Pinnipeds as a group exhibit delayed implantation. The blastocyst arrives in the uterus about six days after successful mating and the subsequent period until implantation varies from five weeks in the Leopard Seal and Weddell Seal to four months in the Fur Seal and Elephant Seal. From Table 8.3 it can be seen that the period from parturition to conception is inversely proportional to the period from conception to implantation, or parturition to implantation, and directly proportional to the period from implantation to parturition (Laws, 1984a). Delayed implantation can be seen as a mechanism which compensates for the varying period from parturition to conception.

Table 8.3. *Approximate duration (days) of the stages in the annual cycle of the Antarctic female seals*

Species	Lactation period	Parturition to conception	Conception to implantation	Parturition to implantation	Implantation to parturition
Fur	110	8	125	133	232
Elephant	23	19	120	139	226
Crabeater	28	30	80	110	225
Weddell	50	48	48	96	269
Leopard	30?	48	48	96	269
Mean	(48)	31	84	115	245
Range	(87)	40	77	43	43
Range as % of mean	(181)	129	92	37	17

From Laws (1984a).

8.6.2 *Comparisons of mating systems*

As Laws (1984a) points out the feeding behaviour and breeding behaviour of seals occur in completely different habitats; they are adapted, anatomically and physiologically to exploit marine food resources, but give birth to their young on land. The gregarious behaviour of the land-breeding species has made it possible for them to become concentrated in closely-packed breeding colonies. In the polygynous species, such as the Elephant Seal and the Fur Seal, the males holding territories for the longest periods have opportunities to fertilize more females than other males. Thus in these species the males have evolved to be much larger than the females. Fat stored in the blubber serves as an energy source during fasting and larger animals can go for longer periods without food than smaller ones, because of the more favourable ratio of surface area to metabolic rate. There is also strong selection for male aggressiveness, larger canines, protective shields of skin or fur, structures used in visual or oral threats and the capacity for prolonged fasting – all characters which contribute to territory maintenance.

In contrast to the land-breeding species the ice-breeding species have a reversed sexual dimorphism, with the males smaller than the females. In the pack-ice-breeding species the spacing of the females is strongly influenced by the distances between floes and floe size. The unpredictability of floe size, and the predominance of floes that will hold only one female group has selected against the development of colonial breeding. Siniff (1982) suggests that predators may have played an important role in the evolution of Crabeater reproductive behaviour since underwater copulation would probably attract large predators and increase vulnerability. The Leopard Seal, on the other hand, appears to copulate under water and presumably is able to cope with the only other large predator, the Killer Whale *Orcinus orca*. Where mating is under water (Leopard, Ross and Weddell Seals), the

advantage may lie, not in male size, but in agility under water where smaller size may be an advantage. The Weddell Seal is of special interest in that in its breeding areas on the fast ice it is not subject to predation. The predictable annual tide cracks along which the pupping colonies form can be considered a resource required by the females for reproduction. Siniff (1982) suggested that: 'Rather than defending the female directly, it is advantageous (for the individual males) to defend sections of the tide crack, since their mating success is thus increased.' In addition there may be advantages to the male in remaining in the water where energy expenditure may be less than on the surface and opportunities for feeding may occur. If he were defending females on the surface he would have to fast, like the Elephant and Fur Seals.

8.7 Population dynamics

In common with other large mammals the Antarctic seals have certain characteristics which make them unique but difficult to study (Fowler & Smith, 1981). The most commom characteristic is their lengthy life span, an attribute which makes it difficult to understand their population dynamics. Since individuals live to 25 to 30 years long-term population studies are needed, and of these there are all too few, the exceptions being studies on Weddell Seals (Croxall & Hiby, 1983; Testa *et al.*, 1985: Testa, 1987; Testa & Siniff, 1987) and those on the Fur Seals at Bird Island (Croxall *et al*, 1988b).

Estimation of a number of population parameters is needed for each species if we wish to understand the factors influencing survival, and population trends, i.e. whether the population is increasing or decreasing, and at what rate. These include reproductive parameters such as age at maturity, percentage pregnant and secondary sex-ratio, age structure, longevity, population density, both during the breeding season and non-breeding season, and how these may vary with population density and

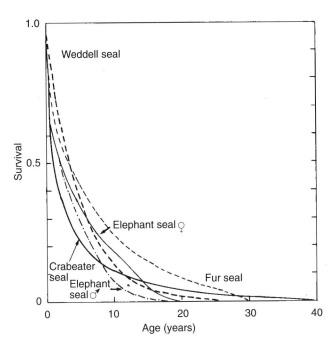

Fig. 8.15. Equilibrium survival curves for female Antarctic Seals and male Elephant Seals, Redrawn from Laws (1984a).

food supply. Changes in population size are probably due to concurrent changes in several parameters.

8.7.1 Age structure, fecundity and survival

Laws (1960b) constructed what was probably the first life table for a pinniped, the Elephant Seal, for South Georgia females, exposed only to natural mortality, for males exposed only to natural mortality, and for males exposed to both natural and hunting mortality. These data were used to formulate new management regulations for the Elephant sealing industry (see Chapter 16). Since then commercial sealing operations have stopped (in 1964) and subsequently McCann (1980a) developed revised life tables incorporating additional information, including sightings of known-age branded animals (Carrick & Ingham, 1962). The current data indicate higher survival but they are approximately fairly close to Law's values. McCann (1980a) recalculated Law's (1960b) 82.5% pregnancy rate as 88%, and for the life table construction assumed pregnancy rates of 2% at three years, 79% at four years, and 85% for five years and over. Sex ratio at birth was estimated at 53% males.

Bonner (1968) estimated Fur Seal survival to age at first pupping at three years as 19–56%, while Payne (1977) estimated the same parameter at 52%. Payne's survival curve for the Bird Island population is plotted in Fig. 8.15. Doidge & Croxall (1983) investigated density-dependent effects by comparing a high-density breeding site (Bird Island; 170 pups at 1.5 individuals m⁻²) and a low, but increasing density site (Schlieper

Bay; 415 pups at 0.2 individuals m⁻²). Pup mortality at Schlieper Bay was only 5% compared with 15–30% at Bird Island.

Bengtson & Laws (1984) aged a sample of 1304 Crabeater Seals. The foetal sex ratio was 55% male:45% female, while the sex ratio at birth was 51% male:49% female. The observed later (tertiary) sex ratio of 42% male:58% female indicated a substantially higher male mortality after weaning, and as the population aged there was an increasing proportion of females, reaching 63% of the animals older than 20 years. The survival curve for females is shown in Fig. 8.15. The data for the construction of this curve included an estimated first-year survival of 56% and an overall survival to first pupping at four years of 25%. The average pregnancy rate for all mature females was 90%; for ages 3–25 it was 94%, and 97% for the most fertile years, declining at higher ages.

Much more research has been carried out on Weddell Seal populations, both in space and time (Stirling, 1969a, 1971b; Siniff *et al.*, 1977b; Croxall & Hiby, 1983). Human interference, especially the taking of seals for dog food, has affected a number of study populations. For the Signy Island population Croxall & Hiby (1983) estimated that the annual female survival rate from 1970 to 1977 was constant at 0.80. This is in close agreement with rates for McMurdo Sound populations of 0.77 (Siniff *et al.*, 1977b) and the reanalysis of Stirling's (1971a) data which gave rates of 0.84 and 0.87. Male survival rates were 0.72, 0.75 and 0.88, depending on the analytical method (Siniff *et al.*, 1977b).

In Fig. 8.15 a survival curve for an equilibrium population of Weddell Seal females is plotted, based on a survival rate from birth of 0.815. Stirling (1971b) calculated an overall pregnancy rate of 80.5% to age 17 years. However, Siniff *et al.* (1977b) obtained a fecundity rate of only 62% from 7 to 18 years for 1970–1974; the comparable rate for the same population in 1966–1968 was 83% (Stirling, 1971b) and for the Signy Island population it was 90%.

Data on Leopard and Ross Seal population dynamics are lacking, apart from some published pregnancy rates. For Leopard Seals the pregnancy rates are 85% (K. G. Brown, 1957), 93% (Tikhomirov, 1975), and as low as 61% (Øritzland, 1970a, 1970b). For Ross Seals rates of 88% (Øritzland, 1970a,b) and 90% (Tikhomirov, 1975) have been recorded.

The survival curves in Fig. 8.15 are for females, apart from the curve for the Elephant Seal male. The lower survival of the male in this species is probably paralleled, to a greater or lesser extent, in the other Antarctic seal species. Laws (1977a) drew attention to the different shape of the survival curve of Crabeater and Weddell

Seals. The Crabeater Seal is a solitary breeder in an unstable habitat and it clearly suffers from significant predation, especially from Leopard Seals, in the first year of life; subsequently it probably faces fewer hazards and has a higher adult survival rate than the Weddell Seal. In contrast predation is insignificant in the southerly breeding Weddell Seal where breeding take place on fast ice; as an adult, however, the Weddell Seal is subject to mechanical senescence due to the wear of teeth in maintaining breathing holes (Bertram, 1940; Stirling, 1969b).

Population studies have revealed conspicuous variations in year class strength of Antarctic Peninsula Crabeater Seals, with peak year classes at mean intervals of 4.67 years (range four to five years) (Laws, 1984a). Strikingly similar fluctuations in the abundance of juvenile Leopard Seals occur at Macquarie Island (Rounsevell & Eberhard, 1980) with peaks occurring every four to five years (mean 4.67). Laws (1984a) lists some possible explanation for these fluctuations.

1. In Crabeater or Leopard Seals, or both, recruitment may be directly correlated with krill abundance, pack ice extent and type, or weather.

2. Year-to-year Crabeater recruitment may be dependent on Leopard Seal predation pressures, perhaps influenced by conditions in the pack ice (e.g. packing of floes).

3. Successful Leopard Seal conceptions and therefore births may be related to abundance or availability of Crabeater pups promoting improved nutritive status of mating Leopard Seals.

A similar fluctuation might also exist in the krill-eating Fur Seal at South Georgia. Payne (1977) analyzed population data which suggested peak year classes at a mean interval of 4.25 years. Moreover in 1978, a year when krill availability at South Georgia was low, there was the highest ever recorded pup mortality (30%) at Bird Island (Doidge & Croxall, 1983); 1978 was also a year in which Crabeater recruitment would have been particularly low.

Population trends, i.e. whether seal populations are increasing or decreasing, will be discussed further in Chapter 16.

9

Whales

9.1 Introduction

There is probably no conservation issue which has aroused as much heated debate and controversy as the question of the exploitation of whales. Apart from the ethical question as to whether it is right to kill these highly intelligent animals there are also the questions to whether any of the species of whales are sufficiently abundant to withstand exploitation, and whether our state of knowledge of their ecology and population dynamics is sound enough to ensure that their exploitation could take place without endangering their survival and causing irreversible changes in the ecosystem of which they are an integral part.

Prior to commercial exploitation during this century, the Antarctic whales comprised, at least in biomass, one of the largest mammalian stocks ever to have existed on earth. Within a short span of time these abundant whale stocks were decimated with consequent changes in the composition and structure of the Southern Ocean ecosystem. General accounts of the attributes of whales are given by Slijper (1962) and Mackintosh (1965). Recent reviews of their ecology include those of H. T. Anderson (1969), Gaskin (1976, 1982), Allen (1980) and FAO (1981). Reviews of the state of knowledge of Antarctic whales include those of S. G. Brown & Lockyer (1984), Bengtson (1984), Gambell (1985), and Chapman (1988).

9.2 Species composition

Seven species or subspecies of Mysticete (baleen) whales and twelve species of Odontocete (toothed) whales occur in the waters of the Southern Ocean south of the Antarctic Convergence. Five of the baleen whale species (the Blue, Fin, Sei, Minke and Humpback Whales) belong to the family Balaenopteridae (rorquals). All of the six baleen whales and two toothed whales, the Sperm and Killer Whales are, or were, abundant in Antarctic waters. All of the baleen whales and the Sperm Whale have been caught in large numbers by the Antarctic whaling industry. Of the toothed whales the Killer Whale, the two beaked whales and the Pilot Whale have also been caught in smaller numbers.

Baleen Whales: The baleen or whalebone whales can be recognized by the triangular plates of horny baleen which grow from the upper jaws and form an efficient mechanism for sieving small food particles from the water. Their bodies are more or less streamlined in shape and they have a relatively large head with a pair of blowholes on the top.

The Blue Whale (*Balaenoptera musculus*) (Fig. 9.1) is the largest of all species of whales and is probably the largest animal that has ever existed. Lengths of up to 30 m and weights exceeding 150 tonnes can be attained. The Fin Whale (*B. physalus*) (Fig. 9.2) grows to 15 m and a weight of 90 tonnes, the Sei Whale (*B. borealis*) (Fig. 9.3) up to 18 m and 30 tonnes, while the smaller Minke Whale (*B. acutirostrata*) (Fig. 9.4) seldom exceeds 11 m in length and 19 tonnes in weight. The Humpback Whale (*Megaptera novaeangeliae*) (Fig. 9.5) is placed in the same family, the rorquals, as those belonging to the genus *Balaenoptera* but it is rather plumper in form and has extraordinarily large flippers, up to a third of its total length, which may reach 16 m, with a maximum weight of 60 tonnes (Matthews, 1937). The Right Whale (*Eubalaena australis* also known as *Balaena glacialis*) (Fig. 9.6) is also a plump animal, reaching a weight of 90 tonnes for an 18 m specimen. It is distinguished from the rorquals in that it lacks a dorsal fin and throat grooves.

Toothed Whales: The Sperm Whale (*Physeter macrocephalus* also known as *P. catadon*) (Fig. 9.7) is the largest of the toothed whales and it shows marked sexual dimorphism. Only the larger males which grow to 18 m and 70 tonnes, penetrate Antarctic waters. The females, which are less than 11.5 m in length and weigh less than 17 tonnes, juveniles and the smaller males remain in temperate and tropical waters. Killer Whales (*Orcinus orca*) (Fig. 9.8) show a smaller difference in the size between the sexes, the males reaching 9 m and the females 8 m, with weights of up to 7 or 8 tonnes. The dorsal fin of the adult males can measure up to 1.8 m in length and is twice the size of that found in the females.

Toothed whales differ from all other mammals in having only one nostril, normally set in the midline, although

162   *Whales*

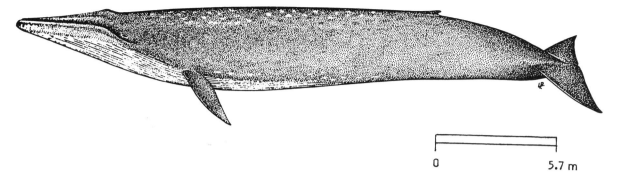

Fig. 9.1. The Blue Whale (*Balaenoptera musculus*). From FAO (1985).

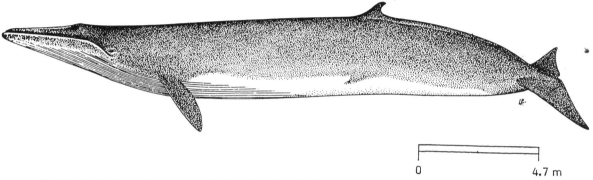

Fig. 9.2. The Fin Whale (*Balaenoptera physalus*). From FAO (1985).

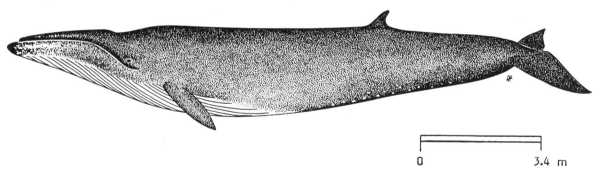

Fig. 9.3. The Sei Whale (*Balaenoptera borealis*). From FAO (1985).

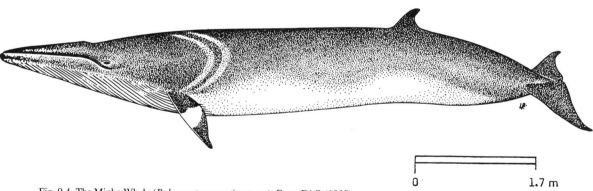

Fig. 9.4. The Minke Whale (*Balaenoptera acutirostrata*). From FAO (1985).

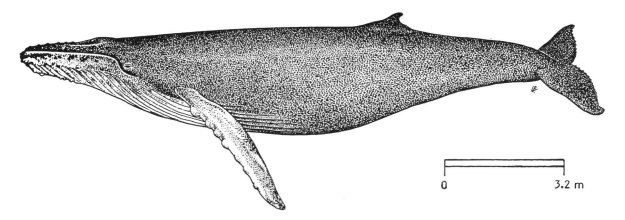

Fig. 9.5. The Humpback Whale (*Megaptera novaeangeliae*). From FAO (1985).

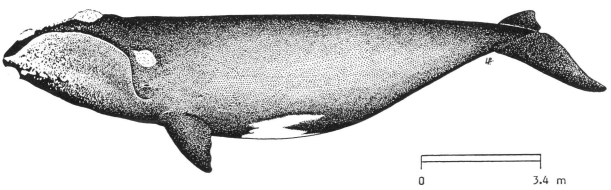

Fig. 9.6. The Right Whale (*Balaena glacialis*). From FAO (1985).

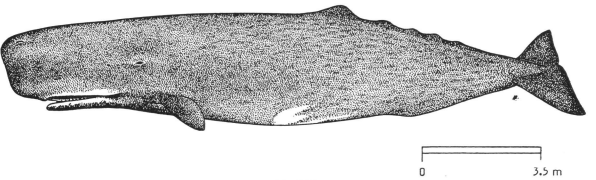

Fig. 9.7. The Sperm Whale (*Physeter catadon*). From FAO (1985).

two nasal passages are present internally. The blowhole of the Sperm Whale is sigmoid in shape and is asymmetrically located on the left side of the dorsal surface of the head. The right naris (tubular part of the nostril) forms a wax-filled 'case' set on the top of the skull, giving the Sperm Whale its characteristic blunt head which makes up to a third of the total length of the body. It is thought that the spermaceti wax may have roles both in buoyancy and in sound transmission.

Many of the smaller toothed whales are comparatively rare and poorly known (see Goodall & Galeazzi, 1985 for a recent review of their distribution and ecology). Most are under 5 m in length. The two largest are the Southern Bottlenose Whale (*Hyperoodon planifrons*), which reaches a length of 7 m and a weight of 3–4 tonnes, and Arnoux's Beaked Whale (*Berardius arnuxii*), which attains a maximum length of 10 m and weights of 7–8 tonnes.

9.3 Distribution, general life-histories and migrations

There is no exclusively Antarctic cetacean and all the species occurring south of the Antarctic Convergence are more widely distributed. The five balaenopterid species are found in both southern and northern hemispheres, and although they undertake extensive latitudinal migrations,

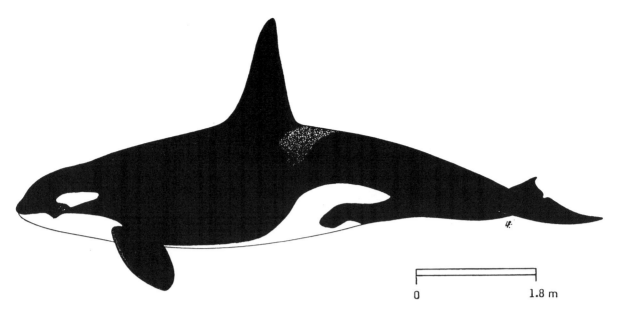

0   1.8 m

Fig. 9.8. The Killer Whale (*Orcinus orca*). From FAO (1985).

the populations of the two hemispheres remain separate, a gap between the two stocks being maintained at all times. Migration patterns have been determined by seasonal trends in abundance, direct observation of migration, or tagging studies (Mackintosh, 1965; Dawbin, 1966; Lockyer & Brown, 1981). The adult whales migrate from their winter breeding grounds in subtropical and temperate waters to Antarctic waters for the summer where intensive feeding takes place for periods of up to 6.5 months (Dawbin, 1966). Many whales, however, remain in Antarctic waters for a lesser period of up to 4 months. Juvenile whales also migrate but their timing is slightly different from that of the adults and their penetration into higher latitudes is not as great (Mackintosh & Wheeler, 1929; Kawamura, 1974; Lockyer, 1981a; Lockyer & Brown, 1981). Whereas the Sperm Whales also undertake annual feeding migrations, the migratory patterns of the other Southern Ocean odontocetes is poorly known.

Breeding of the large baleen whales takes place in warm tropical and subtropical waters to the north of the summer feeding grounds and their lifecycle is very closely related to the pattern of seasonal migrations between breeding and feeding areas. In the Humpback, Blue, Fin and Sei Whales mating takes place during the winter resulting in conception in many of the females. In the spring the whales migrate southwards towards the polar feeding grounds, and as the ice retreats they penetrate further into Antarctic waters to feed on the rich planktonic organisms that comprise their diet. After a period of three or four months of intensive feeding the whales migrate once more in the autumn to temperate or subtropical waters. Gestation takes nearly a year and the

pregnant females give birth in these temperate waters approximately a year after mating. Rather little feeding appears to take place in the warmer waters since Blue, Fin, Humpback and Sei Whales examined at subtropical whaling stations in winter usually have little or no food in their stomachs compared with animals examined on the Antarctic whaling grounds (Macintosh & Wheeler, 1929; Chittleborough, 1965; Bannister & Baker, 1967; Best, 1967). Thus, during the winter the whales live largely on reserves of food laid down in the blubber and body tissues during the intensive summer feeding period.

The newborn calves accompany their mothers on the following spring migration towards the waters of the Southern Ocean, living on their mothers milk. Six months after birth they are weaned and can follow the migration cycles independently; Humpback calves, however, may be dependent on their mothers for up to a year. The migration of Minke Whales follows a somewhat different pattern to that of the larger rorquals, since some Minke Whales are present in temperate waters throughout the year, for example in the Indian Ocean (Best, 1982).

Distribution patterns in the Southern Ocean and other areas are as follows:

Blue Whale: Blue Whales have a circumpolar distribution. The distance covered on a round trip migration between 20° S and 65° S may be 9000–10000 km (Lockyer, 1981a). Their arrival in Antarctic waters commences in early November, before that of Fin, Sei and Minke Whales. Adults arrive first, followed by juveniles about a month later. Pregnant females are frequently the first to arrive and the last to leave. Lactating cows with calves are usually the latest arrivals (Mackintosh &

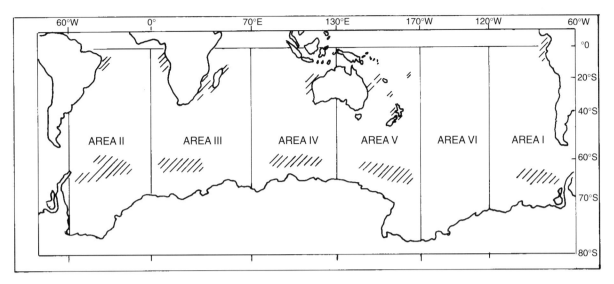

Fig. 9.9. Blue Whale feeding areas in the Antarctic. After Mackintosh (1942).

Wheeler, 1929; Lockyer, 1981a). The whales depart in the same order as they arrived, except for pregnant females. Their average stay in Antarctic waters is about four months, so that most of the Blue Whales will have left by March–April.

Based mainly on evidence from the concentrations of whales reflected in commercial catches and sightings in the Antarctic, Mackintosh (1942) proposed that the distribution of Blue Whales could be divided into six areas extending through some 60–70 degrees of latitude (shown in Fig. 9.9). These feeding concentrations were considered as stocks at least for management purposes and were believed to correspond to biological stocks.

Pygmy Blue Whale: Pygmy Blue Whales are found mainly around Marion Island, Isles Crozet and Isles Kerguelen (Ichihara, 1966b). Their distribution is mostly sub-Antarctic, occurring in a restricted zone between 45° S and 55° S and 0–80° W (Mackintosh, 1965; Ichihara, 1966a).

Fin Whale: Gunther (1949) described a uniform circumpolar distribution of Fin Whales throughout their feeding grounds. The densest concentrations are found where Antarctic krill are abundant (Mackintosh, 1965, 1973; Lockyer & Brown, 1981). Their annual migration pattern is thought to be similar to that of the Blue Whales (Lockyer & Brown, 1981; S.G. Brown & Lockyer, 1984). Whale marking has shown that most Blue and Fin Whales return to the same region of Antarctica after their winter sojourn in warmer waters (S.G. Brown, 1962b) and many may travel hundreds of kilometres east or west of the feeding grounds within one summer season (S.G. Brown, 1962a). Fin Whales are considered to have similar stock divisions to those of Blue Whales, with the addition of the subdivision of the Fin Whales in the Atlantic

and western Indian Ocean sectors into eastern and western groupings, to give a total of eight stocks (Gambell, 1985).

On the basis of catches made in Antarctic waters it appears that the Fin Whale migrations into the feeding areas are headed by the males while the females tend to migrate later (Gambell, 1985). Older animals precede the younger, and Laws (1961) concluded that the older animals and pregnant females migrated first with sexually immature individuals at the rear of the migration. Although the first Fin Whales migrants penetrate the Antarctic from October–November onwards, the peak presence of this species probably occurs two to three weeks later than that of the Blue Whales (Lockyer, 1981a). Most adult Fin Whales arrive in Antarctic waters about three weeks before the juveniles.

Sei Whale: Omura (1973) and Budylenko (1978) suggested that there were up to six southern hemisphere populations of Sei Whales, two (east and west) in each of the Atlantic, Indian and Pacific Oceans, with possibly additional populations in the central Indian and central Pacific Oceans. The general pattern of migration is similar to that of Blue and Fin Whales, although the timing is a little later and they do not penetrate into such high latitudes (Gambell, 1968; S.G. Brown, 1977; Budylenko, 1978). Doi *et al.* (1967) suggested that most Sei Whales remain north of 50° S year-round. Peak animal numbers occur in January and departures in April (Gambell, 1968).

Minke Whale: Minke Whales have a circumpolar distribution and they are concentrated in high latitudes close to the ice edge. (Ohsumi, 1976). Doroshenko (1979) suggests that there are at least four population units – 'Brazilian', 'Indian', 'New Zealand' and 'Chile-Peruvian'. The occurrence of Minke Whales in subtropical waters in the winter and spring (Best, 1974a; Williamson, 1975) suggests that they migrate into these waters, although Laws (1977a) believes that the Antarctic stocks may have a more southerly year-round distribution.

Minke Whale catch data have demonstrated that there is a considerable temporal and spatial segregation of the sexes on the high latitude feeding grounds (Kasamatsu & Ohsumi, 1981). Females predominate nearest the ice edge, while males are more abundant away from the edge of the pack ice even though they arrive earlier and stay longer on the feeding grounds than the females. School composition of Minke Whales is highly variable; groups of 10–25 are not uncommon, and aggregations of up to 90 have been observed (Bengtson, 1985).

Humpback Whale : More is known about the seasonal distribution and migrations of the Humpback Whales (Dawbin, 1966) than for any other species. This is because they characteristically stay close to coastlines during their migrations between summer and winter grounds (Chittleborough, 1965). They breed in tropical coastal waters with a temperature of about 25 °C and at least six southern hemisphere stocks have been identified. These concentrate in the winter in breeding areas on the east and west coasts of South America, Africa and Australia, and among the island groups of the southwest Pacific Ocean. Each stock migrates southwards in the spring to form five areas of concentration in the southeast Pacific, south Atlantic, to the south of South Africa, in the southeast Indian Ocean, and to the south of New Zealand. Although there may be some overlap on the feeding grounds there is good evidence that there is little interchange of individuals between the stocks (Mackintosh, 1942).

The speed of migration is about 15° of latitude per month and there is a very clear segregation of the different classes or categories of Humpback Whales throughout the seasonal cycle. In the vanguard of the migration and arriving first on the Antarctic feeding grounds are a mixture of females in a sexually resting condition and others in early pregnancy. Following these whales at intervals of several days are successive groups of immature males, the mature males, and females in early lactation accompanied by their young calves. On the Antarctic feeding grounds the various groups become randomly mixed, but on the northward migration they become segregated once again. Females at the end of lactation accompanied by weaning yearling calves depart northward first, followed in succession by immature animals, mature males with resting females, and finally females in late pregnancy. Pregnant females therefore spend the greatest amount of time on the feeding grounds south of 60° S (about 6.5 months. late November–May), and lac-

tating females accompanied by their calves least (about 4.5 months, late December–April).

Right Whale: Much of the information on the distribution of the Southern Right Whale comes from the records of nineteenth century whaling, during which the species was very much reduced in numbers (Townsend, 1935), but recent recovery of the species is providing additional information (Best, 1970b, 1974a; .Cawthron, 1978; Omura *et al.*, 1969). The Antarctic distribution is virtually circumpolar (Kawamura, 1978), with the densest concentration near land masses. Most of the whaling for Right Whales occurred between 30° and 50° S, north of the Antarctic Convergence, and while Right Whales have been taken off South Georgia, the South Shetland Islands and the Antarctic Peninsula it is probable that today most remain outside Antarctic waters (Hinton, 1925). The migrations of this species are less extensive than in the balaenopterids.

Sperm Whale: Sperm Whales have a world-wide distribution but only the larger males penetrate Antarctic waters south of the Antarctic Convergence (Best, 1974b; Lockyer & Brown, 1981). The region of the Subtropical Convergence (*c.* 40° S) generally marks the southern limit of the distribution of females and young males, though this limit extends to 45–50° S in the Indian Ocean and the southwest Pacific (Ohsumi & Nasu, 1970). Whale marking has provided direct evidence of some extensive north–south movements, and the occurrence of the Antarctic diatom *Cocconereis ceticata*, which forms a yellowish film on the skin of medium-sized and large males in south temperate waters (Best, 1969, 1974b; Bannister, 1969), is indicative of northward movements from Antarctic waters, as does the presence of the beaks of Antarctic cephalopods in the stomachs of whales killed off Durban (M. R. Clarke, 1972). Evidence for separation of the Sperm Whales in the southern hemisphere into separate stocks is sparse, although it is clear that the females occupying the oceanic basins and separated by major continental land masses must constitute independent breeding units (Gambell, 1985).

Other odontocetes: Brownell (1974) reviewed the state of knowledge of the biology of the smaller odontocetes found in Antarctic waters and plotted records of their occurrence in detail, while Nishiwaki (1977) and Goodall & Galeazzi (1985) have recently added information on their distribution and reviewed their food habits.

The southern Bottlenosed Whale and Arnoux's Beaked Whale both range south to the edge of the pack ice. Killer Whales are abundant in Antarctic waters where their distribution is circumpolar (IWC, 1982), and seasonally related to potential prey such as seals and penguins (Voisin, 1972, 1976; Condy *et al.*, 1978). Dense seasonal concentrations are found in Antarctic coastal waters and along the shores of the off-lying islands such as South Georgia.

The Longfinned Pilot Whale appears to be generally distributed throughout the Southern Ocean (J. L. Davies, 1960), while the Hourglass Dolphin has a circumpolar distribution in temperate and Antarctic waters. Commerson's Dolphin occurs commonly in coastal waters off Argentina and Tierra del Fuego, and around the Falkland Islands (Brownell, 1974; Goodall, 1978). In Antarctic waters it is recorded from South Georgia and Isles Kerguelen, and these may be separate populations (Brown & Lockyer, 1984). Information on the distribution of other species is sparse. They are probably more abundant than the occasional stranding records would indicate. Overall, the importance of the smaller cetaceans in the southern hemisphere food webs has been underestimated.

9.4 Segregation

Changes in the composition of whale catches in Antarctica and at lower latitude shore stations indicate that the migrations of the different species are staggered (Dawbin, 1966). Peak numbers of baleen whales are present in Antarctic waters in January to April (Mackintosh & Brown, 1953) but the various species arrive at different times – Blue whales arrive before Fin Whales, the former being more abundant in the catches from November to December, while the Fin Whales are more numerous in the latter part of the season from January to March. Humpback Whales are most frequent in December and January while Sei Whales are the latest arrivals with their highest densities occurring in the period January to March (Gambell, 1968). Not only do the species vary in the time of their arrival, but also in the extent of their penetration into the colder waters of high latitudes, and this penetration is correlated with body size. The small Minke Whale is an exception to this rule and it has a more southerly year-round distribution. It penetrates the coldest Antarctic waters and may even winter there (R. J. F. Taylor, 1957; Ohsumi *et al.*, 1970). According to Ohsumi *et al.*, the highest densities of Sei Whales are found in the zone 40° S to 50° S, Fin Whales 50° S to 60° S, and Minke and Blue Whales 60° S to 70° S.

Within a particular species, the migration of the different sexes and age classes is also staggered in relation to size and feeding (energy) requirements (Laws, 1977a). Larger and older whales tend to penetrate to higher latitudes than smaller and younger animals; pregnant females arrive early and lactating females late (Laws, 1960a, 1961; Mackintosh, 1965; Dawbin 1966). Laws (1960a) has noted that, in addition to the latitudinal segre-

gation, there is also a longitudinal segregation by size. The larger and older whales arrive first and tend to occupy the preferred feeding grounds, and later animals seem to be displaced to the periphery to the east or west. This suggests some form of competition for food.

9.5 Reproduction

As discussed earlier the breeding season in the baleen whales is well defined with the majority of the conceptions occurring during the time spent in warm water. Of the toothed whales the Sperm Whale is the only species for which there is a good knowledge of the reproductive cycle. Strictly speaking the Sperm Whale is not a true Antarctic species as only large, sexually mature bulls penetrate south of the Antarctic Convergence. Little can be reported on the timing of the breeding season in other toothed whales. Table 9.1 give details of the phenology of reproduction in the larger baleen whales and the Sperm Whale.

9.5.1 Reproductive cycles

Baleen whales: A two-year reproductive cycle is common for most of the baleen whales and is closely tied to the annual migration and feeding cycle (Laws, 1961; Chittleborough, 1965; Gambell, 1968; Donnelly, 1969). Birth, which occurs on the warmer winter grounds, is not normally followed by another pregnancy even if there has been a post-partum ovulation. With the exception of the Minke Whale one ovulation occurs approximately every 1.5 years. Gestation is approximately one year and normally a single calf is born. Right Whales differ from other species in that they may breed only once every three years (Lockyer, 1981a).

The Minke Whale has an ovulation rate of approximately once per 1.15 years (Ohsumi & Masaki, 1975). According to S. G. Brown & Lockyer (1984) there is uncertainty as to whether or not the reproductive cycle is one or two years. The pregnancy rate has been shown to be higher than that of other species and may reach 86% (IWC, 1979). It is likely that the Minke Whale reproduces annually (Masaki, 1979), with annual calving in most seasons. Because the Minke Whales have a shorter calving interval than the other baleen whales (annual versus biannual calving), their populations may be able to respond to changes in the environment quicker than other whales.

Age-specific reproductive rates: Age-specific reproductive rates are an important source of information for the analysis of population dynamics. For this reliable methods of age determination are necessary. The most reliable and widely used method of age determination for baleen whales is that of counting growth layers in the ear

Table 9.1. *Reproductive cycle of baleen whales*

Species	Month of conception	Gestation period (months)	Month and length at birth (m)	Suckling period (months)	Length at weaning (m)	References
Blue	Jun.–Jul.	11	May 7.0	7	12.8	Mackintosh & Wheeler (1929)
Fin	Jun.–Jul.	11	May 6.4	7	11.5	Laws (1959) Lockyer (1981a)
Sei	Jul.	11–11.5	Jun. 4.5	65	8.0	Gambell (1968), Lockyer (1977a)
Minke	Aug.–Sep.	10	May–Jun. 2.8	4	4.5	Williamson (1975), Ivashin & Mikhalev (1978), IWC (1979)
Humpback	Aug.	11.5	Jul. Aug.	16.5–11.0	8.8	Chittleborough (1958), Dawbin (1966), Matthews (1937)
Southern Right	Aug.–Oct.	10	May–Jul.	—	—	Donnelly (1969)

From S. G. Brown & Lockyer (1984).

plug (Purves, 1955; Laws & Purves, 1956; Nishiwaki, 1957; Nishiwaki *et al.*, 1958; Ohsumi, 1964; Ichihara, 1966b). For Southern Fin and Sei Whales there is evidence that one growth layer forms annually (Roe, 1967; Lockyer, 1972, 1974). In Blue and Minke Whales it has been assumed that one growth layer forms annually. In the Humpback Whale, however, two growth layers may form annually Chittleborough (1959, 1960, 1962). Physical maturity occurs at an age of about 25–30 years in most baleen whales (Lockyer, 1981a). Life spans of some species may extend to 90 years (Lockyer, pers. commun. in Bengtson, 1984).

Various methods have been used to estimate the age of sexual maturity. In general it is determined from (a) mean age of whales just mature, (b) age at which 50% of the catch is mature, and (c) the transition phase between juvenile widely spaced and/or irregular growth layers and more compact and regular ones (Lockyer, 1972, 1974). The age of attainment of sexual maturity has been estimated as approximately 5 years for Blue Whales (Lockyer, 1981a), 5–6 years for the Pygmy Blue Whale (Ichihara, 1966b), 6–12 years for Fin Whales (Lockyer, 1972), 8–11 in Sei Whales (Lockyer, 1974), and approximately 7–14 years in Minke Whales (Kato, 1983), depending on the area and season. Pregnancy rates (the proportion of females in the catch that are pregnant, excluding lactating females) may have fluctuated in relation to exploitation. Evidence for this will be discussed later.

Toothed whales: The Sperm Whale is polygynous (Best, 1979) breeding from August to March, with a mid-summer peak in temperate waters (Best, 1968; Gambell, 1972). Births occur in February or later, gestation being 14.5 months (Best, 1968; Gambell, 1972).

Calves are suckled for approximately two years (Gambell, 1972; Best, 1974a). This gives a reproductive cycle of four years. Females become sexually mature at about 9 years , males at about 19 years (Bannister, 1969; Best, 1970a, 1974b; Gambell, 1972; Lockyer, 1981b).

Little is known of the reproductive cycles of the other odontocetes in Antarctic waters. They are likely to be similar to those of their counterparts in the northern hemisphere.

9.5.2 Social structure
As discussed earlier rorquals and Humpback Whales show segregation of both sexes, sexual classes and ages of whales at different times, especially during migration.

The number of whales commonly found together on the feeding grounds in Antarctic waters varies considerably; they tend to mingle freely or associate in small groups (Gambell, 1968). However, these groupings may reflect more the abundance and distribution of the prey species, rather than the social tendencies of the whales themselves (Gambell, 1975). Blue, Fin, Sei, Minke and Humpback Whales are commonly found in groups of three to five, although solitary whales and much larger concentrations are not infrequent. Aggregations of up to 100 Minke Whales have been observed on the feeding grounds, and similarly large groups of Fin Whales have been reported. Little is known of the groupings of Right, Bottlenosed and beaked whales in Antarctic waters.

Sperm Whales in the Antarctic consist of only large mature bulls, which tend to be solitary and evenly distributed, but north of the Antarctic Convergence many kinds of school are found, sometimes being up to several hundreds in number. The composition of such schools is variable. Ohsumi (1971) has described at least six categories of school: nursery, harem, juvenile, bachelor and bull schools as well as lone bulls.

Killer, Pilot, Bottlenosed and Baird's Beaked Whales are all known to swim in schools, and in the case of Pilot Whales these can be large, sometimes containing several hundred animals. Killer Whales exhibit a high degree of group cooperative activities, usually in an extended family pod of five to twenty animals, but sometimes combining into larger groups of 100 or more animals (Tomlin, 1967).

9.6 Feeding ecology
The baleen whales are the terminal predators on a very short food chain (diatoms → krill and other zooplankton → whales), and therefore have a major impact on planktonic secondary production. As filter feeders on planktonic crustacea their morphology and behaviour are functionally adapted for feeding on small particles. The toothed whales are predators on fish, squid and other larger animals and are thus terminal predators at the end of longer food chain.

9.6.1 Methods of feeding
Baleen whales: Nemoto (1959, 1966, 1970) arbitrarily described three types of feeding category in baleen whales. These were skimming, swallowing, swallowing and skimming. The various species can be classified as follows:

1. Skimming	Right Whale
2. Swallowing	Blue Whale
	Pygmy Blue Whale
	Fin Whale
	Minke Whale
	Humpback Whale
3. Swallowing and skimming	Sei Whale

Swallowing type feeding occurs when the whale engulfs a mouthful of food and water which is then sieved through the baleen plates by contraction of the previously distended ventral grooves beneath the chin and throat, and by raising the tongue in the mouth. The food organisms are retained on the baleen filter and subsequently swallowed (Gaskin, 1976). As Mackintosh (1965) pointed out, smaller food organisms necessitate a finer filter; for larger food items a coarser filter can be used, with more rapid filtration and a relatively smaller filtration area. The Right Whale, which feeds on small copepods, has very fine long baleen, so long that the mouth is enlarged to accommodate it, while the baleen of Sei, Minke, Humpback, Fin and Blue Whales is increasingly coarse (Nemoto, 1959).

Humpback Whales have been observed to carry out some interesting feeding behaviours. One of these involves circling a swarm of krill then diving under the surface and coming up vertically with the mouth open to engulf the concentrated food organisms. Another method is for the whale to swim in a circle below the surface of the water releasing a trail of air bubbles that rise in a whorl to the surface. The whale then swims up through the centre of this bubble net to engulf the food organisms entrapped in the centre.

The jaw shape and feeding apparatus are very different in the skimmer, the Right Whale, and the rostral areas of the head are also very different, being very high, arched and narrow. The actual method of feeding is to swim slowly forward with the jaws agape and usually with the head raised partly out of the water. The water and food are filtered through the baleen plates, and when a quantity of food is accumulated on them the mouth is closed and the food swallowed. The Sei Whale feeds by a method somewhere between the two methods described above, according to Nemoto's study of its anatomy.

Toothed whales: Toothed whales very probably use echo-location to detect their food (Gaskin, 1976); this is especially true of Sperm Whales. A number of observations point to this. Sperm Whales are known to make dives to a depth of at least 1200 m (Lockyer, 1977b); here they may remain for periods of up to one hour. Even at 200 m the light is negligible so that the prey cannot be detected by sight; thus the Sperm Whale must feed in total darkness. Recently a sound-stunning behaviour has been proposed (Norris & Mohl, 1981), in which the Sperm Whale is thought to project a beam of sound onto its prey to render it immobile. Although male Sperm Whales have homodont teeth the maxillary teeth may be unerupted. Juvenile males and females have unerupted teeth yet their diet is similar to that of toothed individuals. Because they feed at depth no one has yet observed a Sperm Whale feeding.

Teeth are probably not used directly in feeding by the bottlenosed and beaked whales, which like the Sperm Whale are known to dive very deeply and for similarly long periods (Tomlin, 1967). As their diet is very similar to that of the Sperm Whales (Gaskin, 1976), it is likely that they employ similar echo-location feeding methods. Delphinids, on the other hand, are known actively to chase their prey and to use their sharp teeth for seizing and grasping (Gaskin, 1982). Killer Whales use their powerful teeth for grasping, biting and tearing. Unlike other odontocetes they will attack large prey such as seals, penguins and even other cetaceans, including some of the large rorquals (Tomlin, 1967; Gaskin, 1976). They hunt in large packs or schools (Condy *et al.*, 1978) and appear to coordinate group attacks on large prey (Tarpy,

1979). Killer Whales are neither deep nor lengthy divers and most of their prey are taken at the sea surface or even off ice floes (Condy *et al.*, 1978).

9.6.2 *Food quantities and preferences*

Baleen Whales: The chief food of all rorquals and the Humpback Whale when feeding south of the Antarctic Convergence is *Euphausia superba* (Nemoto, 1959; Marr, 1962; Mackintosh, 1965; Gaskin, 1976; Kawamura 1978). The Blue Whale tends to feed at high latitudes on first-year krill (20–30 mm), the Minke Whale feeds on even smaller krill (10–20 mm), thus not competing with the Blue Whale. The Fin Whale feeds mainly on second-year krill (30–40 mm), while the chief diet of the Sei Whale shows a latitudinal succession from north to south of *Calanus tonsus, C. simillimus, Depranopus pectinatus, Euphausia vallentini, Parathemisto gaudichaudii* and *Euphausia superba.* Mackintosh (1974) concluded that whales take the bulk of their food from krill between 27 and 50 mm in length and impose the heaviest mortality on krill in the 15–40 mm range. Blue and Minke Whales also take the small euphausiid *Euphausia crystallorophias* over the continental shelf, while the finer baleen of the Minke Whale also enables it to take copepods. Other organisms taken occasionally include fish, especially larvae, of many species, predominantly myctophids.

Thus, the baleen whales, especially Blue, Fin, Humpback, Sei and Minke Whales, appear to be in competition for the same food resource. krill, when feeding south of the Antarctic Convergence. However, they tend to have, as discussed above, staggered peaks of arrival in Antarctic waters, so that neither different species nor age classes of the same species are in direct competition all of the time. The extent of penetration into polar waters is also an important factor in reducing interspecies competition.

For Blue Whales a daily food intake of 30–40 g (kg body wt)$^{-1}$ was estimated for a 120 day stay in Antarctic waters (Lockyer, 1981a). The first stomach (which is three-chambered) reportedly holds 1000 kg (Zenkovich, 1969), and a daily intake of about 4000 kg for a fully adult Blue Whale has been estimated (Lockyer, 1981a). The quantities of prey consumed by Fin Whales are somewhat less than those consumed by Blue Whales and a daily intake of 2000–2500 kg day^{-1} was estimated by Lockyer (1981a) for adult Fin Whales. Ohsumi (1979) assumed a feeding rate of about 4% of body weight daily for Minke Whales in Antarctic waters. He observed that stomachs full of krill weighed on average 136.4 kg. On that basis Minke Whales would need to consume two meals daily to meet their energy deeds. Zenkovich (1969) estimated that adult Humpback Whales consumed 2200

kg of krill daily. However, Sergeant (1969) estimated for northern Humpback Whale populations that a 3–4% body weight consumption per day was required to satisfy their energy requirements. On this basis a daily food intake of 1000 kg is more likely.

Toothed whales: Squid form the greater part of the diet of Sperm Whales (Berzin, 1972; M. R. Clarke, 1980a,b), and they are also known to be the preferred food of many other odontocetes such as Pilot Whales (Sergeant, 1962). Bottlenosed and beaked whales feed almost exclusively on cephalopods (Tomlin, 1967).

Many bathypelagic squid are known to exist only from their presence in Sperm Whale stomachs. M. R. Clarke (1956), Tomlin (1967), Berzin (1972) and M. R. Clarke (1980a,b, 1983) all give accounts of the species of squid and other supplementary items in the diet of Sperm Whales. Squid and fish are taken in the approximate ratio of 9:1. Some Sperm Whales taken off Durban, South Africa (30° S), had the beaks of Antarctic squid species in their stomachs (the majority were *Moroteuthis ingens, Mesorynchoteuthis hamiltoni, Gonatus antarcticus,* and an unidentified species of *Moroteuthis*). There was a sudden increase in the incidence of Antarctic squid in the stomachs of whales above 18 years old, and the proportion with stomachs containing Antarctic squid beaks continued to increase with the size and age of the whale to over 80%. Fish are apparently taken opportunistically. Large nototheniid fish *Dissostichus mawsoni* and *D. eleginoides*, up to 170 cm in length and 74 kg in weight have been reported in the stomachs of Sperm Whales from Antarctic waters (Koraolbel'nikov, 1956; Zemsky, 1962; Solyanik, 1963; Berzin, 1972). Additional fish taken include *Micromestistius australis* and *Ceratus holbochi* and large rays and bottom living sharks (M. R. Clarke, 1972). Feeding rates have been calculated at approximately 3% of body weight daily in whales under 15 000 kg and up to 3.5% of body weight daily in whales of 40 000–50 000 kg (Lockyer, 1981b). The first stomach would need to be filled three times daily for normal energy intake, while a nursing female might need to fill her stomach four to five times daily (Lockyer, 1981b).

Our knowledge of the diet of Killer Whales in Antarctic waters is biased, because it is based on two sources; observations of attacks on other animals (usually near the surface), and on specimens caught by whalers, who concentrate on adult males for higher yields, thus leading to a bias towards relatively large food items. The diet of Killer Whales is very catholic. Squid, fish, cephalopods, birds, seals, and other cetaceans are all attacked and taken. Shevchenko (1976) examined 49 stomachs of specimens caught between 50° S and the pack ice. Five were empty while 84% of the others contained remains of Minke Whales, 45% contained seals, 7% fish and only 2% squid. Delphinids and phocoeinids both prefer fish but also take squid (Gaskin, 1976).

9.7 Bioenergetics

9.7.1 Introduction

In the preceding section the quantities of food consumed by whales in Antarctic waters were considered. The feeding season lasts for about four months during the austral summer, when krill and or copepods and cephalopods are consumed in Antarctic waters. In this section we shall consider the role of the consumed food in the bioenergetics of the various species.

9.7.2 Seasonal fattening

Since most whales feed intensively only for about one-third of the year and at a reduced rate (and sometimes taking no food for extended periods) for the rest of the year, food energy needs to be stored in the body to meet metabolic needs during periods of reduced feeding or no feeding at all. This energy is generally stored as fat in the tissues of the blubber, muscle, viscera and bone (Brodie, 1975; Lockyer, 1981a). Lockyer (1981a) has estimated that the total increase in body weight during the summer feeding season is from 30 to 100% of the lean body weight for rorquals such as Fin, Blue and Humpback Whales.

9.7.3 Metabolic energy expenditure

Direct measurement of metabolic energy output is extremely difficult in cetaceans. Theoretical estimates of metabolism energy requirements for Fin and Blue Whales (Brodie, 1975; Kawamura, 1975; Lockyer 1981a) give values in the range of 3–8 kcal (kg body wt)$^{-1}$ day^{-1}. For Sperm Whales Lockyer (1981a,b) estimated the resting metabolic rate at 5–8.5 kcal (kg body wt)$^{-1}$ day^{-1}. Lockyer (1981a) has also calculated the relative amounts of energy required for growth and maintenance at various ages. In the Mysticete whilst the suckling calf was estimated to utilize about 68% of the consumed energy for metabolism, by puberty 94% is used for this purpose, and near physical maturity nearly all is required for metabolism.

There is evidence that in their annual migrations whales swim continuously not slowing or ceasing swimming at night (Kawamura, 1975). A Sei Whale marked in the Antarctic was was found 10 days later some 335 km distant, having averaged 14.5 km h^{-1} (S. G. Brown, 1971). Kawamura (1975) considered that a sustained swimming speed equivalent to 18.5 km h^{-1} was possible, and Lockyer (1981a) was of the opinion that for the largest rorquals, such as the Blue and Fin Whales, a speed of 24 km h^{-1} was possible.

A major difference between the Mysticetes and Odontocetes (especially the Sperm Whale) is that the latter undertake deep, prolonged dives. While this activity must require energy expenditure which is well above the resting level, the increase which is needed is unknown.

Reproduction places extra metabolic demands on female whales. Lockyer (1981a) notes that the blubber fat of pregnant female Blue and Fin Whales has been recorded as being about 25% thicker than that of non-pregnant females. In order to accumulate this extra fat pregnant females must remain longer on the southern feeding grounds to consume more food. Nearly all of the extra fat is used in lactation. Lockyer (1978) calculated that the energy cost of lactation was about 12–15 times the cost of foetal development. The energy demands of pregnancy and lactation are less stressful on the female Sperm Whale than on female baleen whales. Lockyer (1981b) has calculated that in Sperm Whales the energy cost of pregnancy is negligible until the fifth or sixth month and that this would be met by an increase in daily food consumption of only about 5–10%. However, the greater energy demands of lactation would require an increased daily food intake of 32–63%.

9.7.4 Energy budgets

Since whales in the past, and possibly also in the future, have consumed a major proportion of the annual krill production and also large quantities of fish and squid, their impact on energy flow through the Southern Ocean ecosystem is of considerable interest. An energetics approach to the role of whales in the ecosystem enables the evaluation of this impact in quantitative terms and provides an insight into our understanding of ecosystem stability. The aim of the bioenergetics approach is the preparation of a 'balance sheet' to account for the energy inputs and outputs of 'typical' individuals at all the critical stages of the life-cycle in relation to variations in the environment. The data may then be used to calculate an energy budget for a species population.

In compiling a budget the following need to be estimated:

1. The calorific value of the food.
2. Food intake and feeding rates.
3. Metabolism and activity.
4. Heat loss.
5. Energetic cost of locomotion.
6. Energetic cost of growth.
7. Energetic costs of reproduction.

Lockyer (1975, 1976) has provided separate estimates

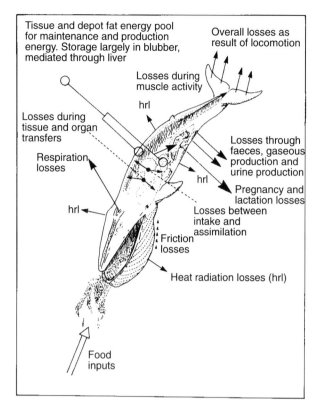

Fig. 9.10. Schematic diagram to illustrate the balance of energy inputs, outputs and storage for a whale. White arrows indicate food inputs, which in baleen whales are usually seasonal. Open circles indicate storage, generally in the form of lipids, in depot fat and the liver. Mobilization of food stores is generally mediated through the liver. Energy losses are indicated by black arrows. These losses occur before the assimilation of food, during transfers from organ to organ and tissue to tissue, through heat radiation, respiration, and through faeces and urine; in the adult female, there is a major loss as a result of pregnancy. Hrl represents heat radiation losses from the body surface. Redrawn from Gaskin (1982).

of projected energy budgets for Blue, Fin, Sei and Sperm Whales according to sex and maturity stages. The components of the energy budget for a large cetacean (the Sperm Whale) based on Lockyer's data has been summarized by Gaskin (1982) (Fig. 9.10).

The body weight of a Sperm Whale at physical maturity may be as much as 50 tonnes in the case of the male, but much less, about 10–12 tonnes, in the case of the female. The stomach capacity of the adult male approaches 2000 litres. Current data suggest that food consumption could equal 3% of the body weight per day : about 1500 kg for the male and only 420 kg for the female.

Lockyer calculated that the annual food intake of the male might be as much as 550 000 kg, but only slightly more than 150 000 kg in the female. The calorific yields of these weights of squid are 43.9×10^7 kcal (183.8×10^7 kJ), and 12.2×10^7 kcal (51.1×10^7 kJ) respectively. For the purpose of calculating the energy outputs, growth in

physically mature adults can be neglected as the annual increment is negligible. To maintain the theoretical resting metabolic rate the male needs about 2.52×10^5 kcal (10.5×10^5 kJ) and the female 1.02×10^5 kcal (4.3×10^5 kJ) per year. For active metabolism the equivalent value is 2.02×10^6 kcal (8.5×10^5 kJ) and 8.2×10^5 kcal (34.3×10^5 kJ) respectively. The yearly total expenditures for maintenance and normal activity amount to 31.79×10^7 kcal (133.1×10^7 kJ) for the male and 8.97×10^7 kcal (37.4×10^5 kJ) for the female. The cost of lactation in the female is high, probably adding another 2.8×10^7 kcal (11.7×10^7 kJ). Fig. 9.10 illustrates the balance of energy inputs, outputs and storage for the mature Sperm Whale.

9.8 Population Dynamics

9.8.1 Introduction

For commercially exploited populations it is important to have accurate estimates of the population sizes of the stocks. Considerable effort has gone into research on the population dynamics of whales by the scientists associated with the International Whaling Commission. A number of computer models have been developed to provide information for decision-making in conservation and management. These models have been used to obtain a description of the current characteristics, including size, of a population of whales, or to compare its current characteristics with those of the past, or to forecast its characteristics in the future. The characteristics of such models have been discussed by Allen (1980).

9.8.2 Estimation of population size

Allen (1980) and S. G. Brown & Lockyer (1984) have reviewed the various methods which have been used to determine the population sizes of the various species of whales. These are:

1. *Direct counts* (sightings). Here the number of whales sighted within a given area is extrapolated to cover the much larger areas occupied by the population.
2. *Mark and recapture*. The proportion of marks (numbered metal darts) recovered provides a factor which relates the associated catch to the total population being exploited.
3. *Methods based on catch and effort*. These methods rely on accurate catch and effort data from the whale fishery. Essentially, they compare the changes in an observed relation between catch and effort with the changes which would occur in a population model. Allowances must be made for natural mortality and recruitment,

particularly if they are changing during the period under investigation (Chapman, 1970).

4. *Mortality coefficient method.* If in addition to catch and coefficient statistics, the age composition of the catch is known, then mortality coefficients can be calculated from linear logarithmic regression of catch on age class after the initial age at full recruitment. Calculation of the natural mortality coefficient at the beginning of the period of fishing enables the fishing mortality to be derived by its subtraction from the total mortality. The ratio between the catch and fishing mortality coefficient gives an estimate of population size.

5. *Least squares method.* The method (Allen, 1966, 1968) utilizes catch and age composition data to derive the proportion of new recruits in all catches, which can then be used to calculate the population size.

6. *Recruitment curve method.* This method depends on the relationship between population size, catch and recruitment, which is a theoretical value based on estimates of reproductive parameters.

7. *Cohort analysis.* This method requires data on age composition of each season's catch, natural mortality coefficient and estimated annual rate of exploitation. The value for exploitation rate is used to calculate population size in each year class.

9.8.3 *Estimating mortality and recruitment rates*

In order to construct realistic models of the dynamics of whale populations good data on mortality and recruitment rates are needed. Mortality is of two basic kinds, that arising from natural causes and that due to catching. Both kinds of mortality vary with age. Most methods of measuring mortality rates require observations of changes in abundance, either with absolute time or with age, and for this purpose it is generally necessary to be able to age the animals.

Age determination. For baleen whales three structures have been used in age determination. Baleen plates show ridges which are probably formed annually but as they wear with age they are only useful for aging quite young animals. Counts of corpora albicanta in the ovaries provide a record of the number of ovulations. The rate of ovulation must be known in order to convert the number of ovulations into years. Since the rate of ovulation varies between species of whales, and moreover it is not constant within a species, or even individual animals, this method has been little used in recent years. The most reli-

able and widely used method is based on counting the growth layers (light and dark bands) in the waxy plugs found in the ears. For southern Fin and Sei Whales there is evidence that each pair of light and dark bands forms annually (Roe, 1967; Lockyer, 1972, 1974). It is assumed that this is also true for Minke and Blue Whales.

In Odontocetes age determination is mostly based on tooth structure. The teeth are bisected and the cut surface is etched with 10% formic acid so that the growth layers appear as alternating ridges and troughs. Current evidence (Best, 1970a; Gambell, 1977) suggest that a ridge and a trough together constitute an annual growth layer.

Mortality. Three main methods are used for estimating mortality rates. They are based on marking techniques, on changes in the abundance of age groups over time, and on the age structure of the population. However, mortality estimations are complicated by the fact that no good techniques currently exist for separating accurately the fishing mortality component in the total mortality rate.

Recruitment. The rate of recruitment can be expressed in two ways: either as a proportion of the total present population, or as a proportion of the current recruited population (IWC, 1978). Estimates of the age at recruitment, or the age at maturity (i.e. when the individuals become sexually mature) and pregnancy rates are needed for the models used in stock management. In the management of commercially exploited stocks the concept of maximum sustainable yield (MSY) is generally used. In theory, the net recruitment rate (recruitment rate less mortality rate) of an exploited population is believed to increase as the population is reduced. This is brought about by changes in parameters associated with fecundity, growth and mortality so that there is effectively a surplus of recruits in order to return the population to maximum size. The surplus or replacement yield can be harvested as a sustainable yield, so that after the catch has been taken, the net recruitment rate remains at zero, so maintaining the population at that size. As we shall see in Chapter 16 there have been problems in applying these concepts to commercially exploited whale populations.

9.8.4 *Growth*

In baleen whales growth in the first years is very rapid. As puberty is reached the growth rate slows down and then continues at a decreasing rate until physical maturity is reached when the vertebral epiphyses become fused, and further linear growth is not possible (Laws, 1961). This stage is generally not reached until an age of 25 years or more in rorquals. In Fig. 9.11 simplified average growth curves are shown for the Humpback and Minke Whales. However, there is much variability in growth patterns within whale populations and also between populations

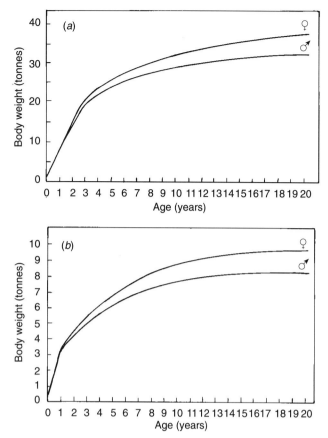

Fig. 9.11. Average curves of body length at age based on catch data corrected for length bias. (*a*) Humpback Whales. (*b*) Minke Whales. Redrawn from S.G. Brown & Lockyer (1984).

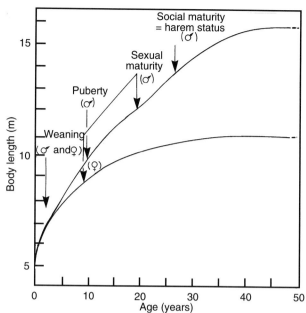

Fig. 9.12. Predicted average curves of body length at a given age for Sperm Whales; based mainly on catch data. Redrawn from S.G. Brown & Lockyer (1984).

(Ichihara, 1966b; Lockyer, 1977b, 1979, 1981a).

The predicted average growth in body length for the Sperm Whale is shown in Fig. 9.12. It can be seen that there is marked sexual dimorphism, with the male attaining a much larger size than the female. The female attains sexual maturity at about 7–12 years when the body length is about 80% of maximum. Physical maturity is reached after about 30 years. Puberty in males is a prolonged process. It commences at about 9–11 years, with sexual maturity being attained at about 18–19 years at a length of about 12 m. Functional maturity, or social maturity, is attained later corresponding to the attainment of harem bull status at a length of about 13.7 m and an age of about 26 years.

9.9 Role in the ecosystem

Whales have played a dominant role in the Southern Ocean ecosystem, in determining the relative abundances of both their dominant prey species, *Euphausia superba*, and the co-occurring krill consumers. Prior to their exploitation they were the major consumers of krill. Now that the stocks of the larger baleen whales have been reduced to low levels the smaller whale species, the seals, the birds and the fish have had the opportunity of consuming a large amount of krill that formerly was taken by the whales. The degree to which this has occurred and the consequent changes in the demographic parameters of these other krill consumers will be considered in detail in Chapter 17.

The baleen whales, by consuming large concentrations of krill, would have had an impact on the abundance and composition of the phytoplankton populations. As we will see in Chapter 15 krill grazing on phytoplankton blooms can rapidly alter the biomass and species composition of the phytoplankton community, changing it from one dominated by microplankton (diatoms) to one dominated by smaller nano- and picophytoplanktpn.

Odontocetes, particularly Sperm Whales, must have consumed overall much greater quantities of cephalopods than they now consume. However, the changes which may have occurred in squid population densities can only be guessed at as there are no quantitative data available.

10

Birds

10.1 Introduction

Because they are obvious components of the Southern Ocean the seabirds have attracted considerable attention. Due to this and the large colonies of penguins that are found round the margins of the continent and on the surrounding islands there is the popular view that the Southern Ocean supports extraordinarily abundant and dense populations of a great variety of seabirds. Certainly in the summer large numbers of seabirds congregate in certain areas for breeding. However, in the winter few birds are to be seen round the continent and in the pack ice zone, and even in the summer in parts of the open ocean few birds are encountered. Nevertheless, the seabirds are an important component of the Southern Ocean ecosystem and locally have a significant impact as predators on krill, other zooplankton and larval fishes.

There are three essential features of the Antarctic region that are critical to an understanding of Antarctic ornithology. They are the position of the Antarctic continent almost exactly centred on the South Pole, with most of its land mass below latitude 70° S; the permanent cover of ice and snow on the continent with most of its periphery at sea level girdled with glaciers and fast ice with little exposure of rock; and, its great isolation from other substantial land masses by the wide expanse of the Southern Ocean with its pronounced circumpolar air and water currents (Young, 1980). As a consequence the birds are almost exclusively marine species.

The birds which breed on the Antarctic continent and the associated islands, including the penguins which constitute about 90% of the avian biomass, prey largely on animals whose populations build up rapidly during a short period of concentrated reproduction and growth. The strong summer 'pulse' of solar energy is rapidly converted into phytoplankton which provides abundant food for the zooplankton and larval fishes upon which the birds feed. This is available in the summer after the breakup of the pack ice but is not accessible over the winter when a large proportion of the sea is frozen over. Consequently, those species breeding on the continent have a short breeding season after which they disperse northwards.

10.2 Species composition and distribution

A seabird is one which habitually obtains its food either directly or indirectly, as is the case in certain scavengers and predators, from the sea. There are approximately 250 seabird species in the world of which some 62, including seven penguins, breed south of a line corresponding roughly to 50° S latitude, but including the Tristan–Gough group of temperate islands. If those species occurring only north of the Antarctic Convergence, i.e. those species breeding on one or more of Tristan da Cuhna, Gough Island, Marion and Prince Edward Islands, Isles Kerguelen, Macquarie Island and the New Zealand sub-Antarctic Islands, are excluded then the number falls to 36 (Croxall, 1984).

The majority of the Southern Ocean's flying seabirds consists of albatrosses and petrels (Procellariiformes), and skuas, gulls and terns (Charadriiformes). The albatrosses and petrels account for some 40 species (21 south of the Antarctic Convergence), of which most are truly oceanic, avoiding land except when breeding. The order Procellariiformes is represented by members of all four of its families: six species of albatrosses (Diomedeidae), 26 typical petrels, prions and shearwaters (Procellariidae), four storm petrels (Oceanitidae), and three diving petrels (Pelecanoidae). The balance of the flying birds consists of two species of gull and three terns (Laridae), two skuas (Stercoriidae), two sheathbills (Chionididae), which are almost exclusively land based, and four cormorants (Phalacrocoracidae), often now regarded as subspecies. Further detailed information on the classification and breeding habits of these birds are to be found in Watson *et al.* (1971, 1975) and Croxall (1984).

Penguins, which belong to the order Sphenisciformes, with its single family Spheniscidae, are almost entirely restricted to the Southern Hemisphere (Stonehouse, 1985). Of the 18 species of these flightless birds ten breed in the area south of 50° S as defined above. Of these, seven breed south of the Antarctic Convergence. These species with their breeding distributions, are listed in Table 10.1. Figs 10.1 and 10.2 summarize the distribution of penguins south of the Antarctic Convergence. Of the

Table 10.1. *Weights, body lengths, and breeding localities of polar penguins*

	Antarctic			Sub-Antarctic	
	Continental	Maritime	Peripheral	Cold Temperate	Warm Temperate
Emperor *Aptenodytes forsteri*	+	–	–	–	–
King *Aptenodytes patagonicus*	–	–	+	+	–
Adélie *Pygoscelis adeliae*	+	+	–	–	–
Chinstrap *Pygoscelis antarctica*	–	+	+	–	–
Northern Gentoo *Pygoscelis papua papua*	–	–	+	+	–
Southern Gentoo *Pygoscelis papua ellsworthii*	–	+	–	–	–
Macaroni *Eudyptes chrysolophus*	–	+	+	+	–
Rockhopper *Eudyptes crestatus*	–	–	+	+	+

Breeding localities are defined as follows: *Continental Antarctic* – Continent and offshore islands to 65° S, Peter I, Oy and Balleney Islands. *Maritime Antarctic* – Peninsula south to 65° S, and islands within the pack ice zone. *Peripheral Islands* – South Georgia, Heard and MacDonald Islands and Archipel de Kerguelen. *Sub-Antarctic Islands* – lie north of the Antarctic Convergence and within the Subtropical Convergence, separated by the 10 °C summer isotherm (Stonehouse, 1967, 1970, 1982). After Stonehouse (1985).

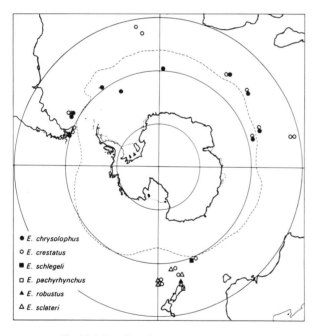

Fig. 10.1. Breeding distribution of *Eudyptes* species. Redrawn from Croxall (1984).

- ● *E. chrysolophus*
- ○ *E. crestatus*
- ■ *E. schlegeli*
- □ *E. pachyrhynchus*
- ▲ *E. robustus*
- △ *E. sclateri*

seven species only four, the Emperor, Adélie, Chinstrap and Gentoo breed on the Antarctic Continent proper, and the two latter species are found only on the more northerly parts of the Antarctic Peninsula.

One salient characteristic of the Antarctic avifauna is the uniformity of each species across a very large geographic area. Only four species have differentiated into subspecies within the region. The Snow Petrel is considered to have two forms, with the smaller subspecies *Pagodroma nivea nivea* over most of the continent and a much larger form *P. n. major*, with the habit of nesting on more open ground, being found in Adélie Land. The Blue-eyed Shag is considered to have three subspecies, *Phalacrocorax ateiceps gaini* on the Antarctic Peninsula and the Scotia Arc islands, *P. a. nivalis* on Heard Island, and *P. a. georgianus* on South Georgia. Wilson's Storm Petrel has one subspecies *Oceanites oceanicus oceanicus* on Kerguelen and other northern islands and another, *O. o. exasperatus*, to the south. The penguin *Eudyptes chrysolophus* has two distinct subspecies, *E. c. chrysolophus*, the Macaroni Penguin, widespread throughout the region, and *E. c. shlegeli*, the Royal Penguin, on Macquarie Island. Apart from these four species all the others are monotypic throughout.

In 1970 Carrick & Ingham summarized the then available information on the distribution of Antarctic seabirds. Important sources of distributional data that have appeared since are Watson *et al.* (1971), Prévost & Mougin (1970), Prévost (1981), Barrat & Mougin (1974), Prince & Payne (1979), G. J. Wilson (1983), Ainley *et al.* (1983b), Harper *et al.* (1984), Jouventin *et al.* (1984), A. J. Williams (1984) and Croxall *et al.* (1984a).

The pelagic marine fauna of the Southern Ocean, as we have seen (Chapter 4), is zonally distributed round the Antarctic continent. These zones tend to be less well

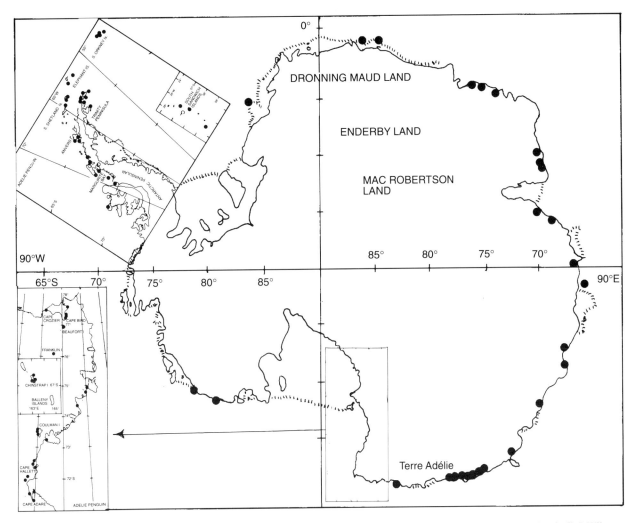

Fig. 10.2. Breeding distribution of Adélie Penguins on the Antarctic Continent and the offlying islands. Based on data in G. J. Wilson (1983).

defined for seabirds, which are frequently constrained by the shortage of available breeding areas but are able to compensate by often being wide-ranging at sea. Two well-defined zonal boundaries are the Antarctic Convergence and the northern limit of the permanent pack ice zone, defining the limit of the cold Antarctic sub-zone (see Chapter 13 for a discussion of bird distribution in relation to fronts and ice edge processes). Only one breeding bird species, the Antarctic Petrel, is entirely restricted to the latter sub-zone but a number of others, e.g. the Emperor Penguin, Antarctic Skua, Adélie Penguin and Snow Petrel have their greatest concentration here, although they also occur on the Antarctic Peninsula. The latter area, with its associated island groups, comprises the maritime Antarctic sub-zone, providing a bridge facilitating the intermingling, along an essentially north–south axis, of Antarctic species and those more typical of sub-Antarctic islands.

Local conditions, climatic, oceanographic and topographical, all influence the composition of the avifauna of the islands in the vicinity of the Antarctic Convergence. South Georgia, Heard Island and Bouvetoya are the only islands well south of the Convergence. Of these South Georgia, being larger with a more varied topography and closer to a continental land mass, has several additional species more typical of islands at or north of the Convergence, such as Macquarie or Kerguelen. Both of the latter, especially Kerguelen, have species derived from islands to their north (Rounsevell & Brothers, 1984; Jouventin *et al.* 1984).

The seabirds of Prince Edward and Crozet, which lie just north of the Convergence and close enough for cold Antarctic water to upwell in the lee of the islands (Grinley & David, 1985), are essentially similar to those of Kerguelen (A. J. Williams, 1984). Other islands lying further north of the Antarctic Convergence are the Auckland, Campbell, Antipodes, Bounty and Falkland Islands. These islands have some species whose presence reflects the islands' proximity to New Zealand and South America respectively, but in general they lack some of

Table 10.2. *Population estimates (number of breeding pairs) of penguins in the Southern Ocean*

Species	Antarctic Peninsula Scotia Arc	African Sector	French sub-Antarctic Is. Adélie Land	Ross Sea	Total sector
Emperor *Aptenodytes forsteri*	31 500	—	*c.* 2 500	*c.* 40 000	*c.* 135–200 000
King *Aptenodytes patagonicus*	34 000	*c.* 228 600	*c.* 485 000	—	*c.* 700 000+
Adélie *Pygoscelis adeliae*	746 219	—	25 000	*c.* 750 000	2 million+
Chinstrap *Pygoscelis antarctica*	6 435 000	—	—	10	6.5 million
Gentoo *Pygoscelis papua*	132 200	—	*c.* 14–21 000	—	*c.* 180 000
Macaroni *Eudyptes chrysolophus*	5 410 295	1 457 000	*c.* 3–4 million	–	*c.* 10–11 million
Rockhopper *Eudyptes crestatus*	10	128 000+	*c.* 50–100 000	—	*c.* 178 000–229 000
Totals	12 788 216	*c.* 1 813 600	*c.* 3.5–4.5 million	*c.* 790 000	*c.* 19 693 000–20 809 000

Data from G. J. Wilson (1983), Croxall *et al.* (1984a), Harper *et al.* (1984), A. J. Williams (1984).

the colder water species and also some of the warmer water species widespread in the Indian Ocean.

10.3 Abundance

In recent years under the impetus of the SCAR sponsored International Survey of Antarctic Seabirds (ISAS) (Siegfried & Croxall, 1983) considerable progress has been made in answering the question: How many seabirds are there in the Southern Ocean? Although precise figures have yet to be determined it has been established that the actual abundance is well short of some of the earlier gross over-estimates.

Apart from the penguins, our best current information is for the six species of albatross: Wandering Albatross *Diomedea exulans*, Black-browed Albatross *D. melanophris*, Grey-headed Albatross *D. chrysostoma*, Yellow-nosed Albatross *D. chlororhynchus*, Sooty Albatross *Phoebetria fusca* and Light-mantled Sooty Albatross *P. palpebrata*. Since these large surface-nesting birds tend to congregate in colonies at relatively few breeding sites that are easier to census than many other species. The Wandering Albatross' breeding population is about 20 000 pairs. Taken together, the breeding population of all six species probably amounts to about 759 000 pairs (Siegfried, 1985).

Population estimates for the balance of the surface nesting flying species are far less comprehensive and complete, although fair estimates are available for the Giant Petrels *Macronectes* spp., cormorants, skuas, kelp gulls and terns. It is unlikely that their populations, in combination, account for more than 500 000 birds. Considerably less is known about the numbers of the

Southern Fulmar *Fulmarus glacialoides*, Antarctic Petrel *Thalassoica antarctica*, Cape Pigeon *Daption capense* and Snow Petrel *Pagodroma nivea*, which according to a recent report (Mougin & Prevost, 1980) might total between four and five million birds.

Omitting the two Sheathbills, the remaining flying birds include the prions (five species), gadfly petrels (six species), shearwaters (four species), and diving petrels (two species). Since these birds tend to nest in burrows, or in crevices and under boulders, and normally visit land only at night, censusing their populations is difficult. Improved field techniques are enabling more accurate estimates to be made but it will be some time before definite pronouncements can be made on the total abundances of these species. Nevertheless, one recent series of estimates (Mougin & Prévost, 1980) yields a grand total of a little short of 150 million birds of these species.

More accurate information is available on the numbers of penguins since they are concentrated in dense colonies during the breeding season. Population estimates for the region have been summarized by G. J. Wilson (1983) and data for specific areas by Croxall *et al.* (1984a), Harper *et al.* (1984), Jouventin *et al.* (1984) and A. J. Williams (1984). These population estimates (Table 10.2) are for the number of breeding pairs and do not include juveniles and non-breeding adults. Depending on the species the population estimates would need to be increased by a variable percentage to give estimates of the total population. The total number of breeding pairs in the Southern Ocean (excluding Macquarie Island and the African sub-Antarctic Islands) is in the order of 20–21 million. The greatest number occur in the Antarctic Peninsula–Scotia Arc region (about 13 million). Of the seven species of penguin the most abundant is the Macaroni Penguin (*c.* 10–11 million), with the Chinstrap Penguin being the second most abundant (6.5 million). Contrary to popular opinion the Adélie Penguin, which is found right round the fringes of the Antarctic continent, is not as numerous with an estimated population of somewhat over 2 million breeding pairs. The two rarest species are the Emperor Penguin (*c.* 135–200 000 breeding pairs) and the Gentoo Penguin (*c.* 180 000 breeding pairs). Somewhat more than 1.2 million pairs of penguins breed on Macquarie island, including King, Gentoo, Southern Rockhopper and Royal Penguins. The latter has a population of over a million.

10.4 Breeding biology

10.4.1 Breeding location and habitat
Reviews of breeding dispersion, colony size and preferred habitat by Carrick & Ingham (1967) for Antarctic seabirds generally and by Croxall & Prince (1980a) for South Georgia have revealed some species characteristic patterns. In general seabirds are colonial and the only exceptions are the Light-mantled Sooty Albatross and the charadriform species (skuas, gulls and terns). These latter species defend isolated nest territories and in the case of some skuas feeding territories based on parts of penguin colonies (Young, 1963a,b; Muller-Schwarze & Muller-Schwarze, 1977; Trillmich, 1978; Trivelpiece *et al.*, 1980). Sheathbills, which also scavenge on colonies, are similar in this respect (Burger, 1979), and nest in isolated colonies.

The burrow-dwelling habit, which is confined to the smaller and medium sized petrels, is best developed on the sub-Antarctic islands, where large areas of peaty grassland are found. Other habitats suitable for burrow excavation include screes, moraine debris and mossbanks and these are used principally by storm and diving petrels. Crevice nesters include storm petrels, prions and the Snow Petrel, Cape Pigeon, Antarctic Fulmar and Antarctic Petrel. The latter, with their preference for nesting on sheltered ledges, provide a link between the crevice nesting Snow Petrel one the one hand and the Giant Petrel, which prefers sheltered open sites.

The colonial surface nesting habit is virtually restricted to the larger seabirds such as the albatrosses and penguins. Most albatrosses tend to nest in compact colonies on tussock slopes and cliffs, although the Wandering Albatross is usually found in dispersed groups on flatter areas. Penguins generally breed on flattish sites of exposed rock, beaches, moraines or tussock. The Emperor Penguin is unique in that it breeds on fast sea ice. While distinct habitats are often attributed to pygoscelid penguins (e.g. White & Conroy, 1975) it has

been shown that they are by no means consistent between sites (Volkman & Trivelpiece, 1981), and it is likely that Adélie and Chinstrap Penguins have broadly overlapping requirements. The Gentoo Penguin, while preferring flat sites, has catholic tastes, being found on beaches, tussock and even boulder areas.

There has been speculation that the availability of suitable terrain has the potential to influence the number and distribution of breeding Antarctic seabirds. However, as Croxall (1984) points out it is unlikely that its role in limiting breeding numbers is of overriding importance since, for most species in most parts of the Antarctic, adequate breeding sites would appear to be superabundant. On a broader basis, however, the nature of available habitat, e.g. suitable terrain for burrowing, presence of grassland, availability of crevices, etc., does limit the number of breeding birds in specific localities. Climate, however, is perhaps a more significant factor in determining distributions and breeding success.

10.4.2 Timing of the breeding season
The duration of the breeding season from egg laying to chick fledging, for species for which adequate data are available, is shown in Fig. 10.3. Croxall (1984) has synthesized the available information on the breeding cycles of Antarctic seabirds and the following account relies heavily on that review.

A number of points arise from a consideration of the overall patterns. Firstly, there are differences in the time of the onset of breeding activities at various sites. Characteristically, the more northerly populations of most species breed two or three weeks earlier than the more southerly ones (Stonehouse, 1964, 1967, 1970; Watson *et al.*, 1971). This is particularly evident between sub-Antarctic islands and the Antarctic Continent and Peninsula. In some species there is also a difference in timing between sites at the same latitude, e.g. the Royal Penguin breeds two weeks earlier at Macquarie than at Heard Island (Carrick & Ingham, 1967). Gentoo Penguins show the greatest variation in timing.

Secondly, even in a single general area, a few species exhibit poor synchrony of breeding, with eggs being laid over two or more months. This is in contrast to most species, in which the breeding is highly synchronized with the eggs being laid over a period of generally less than three weeks. This is attributable to the relatively short period of favourable conditions and to the predominantly colonial breeding habit. Exceptions are some medium-sized petrels in lower latitudes (Barrat, 1974; Mougin, 1975), storm petrels (*O. oceanicus* and *Fregetta tropica*) at some sites on Signy Island (Beck, 1970), the Brown Skua, the Southern Black-backed Gull (*Larus*

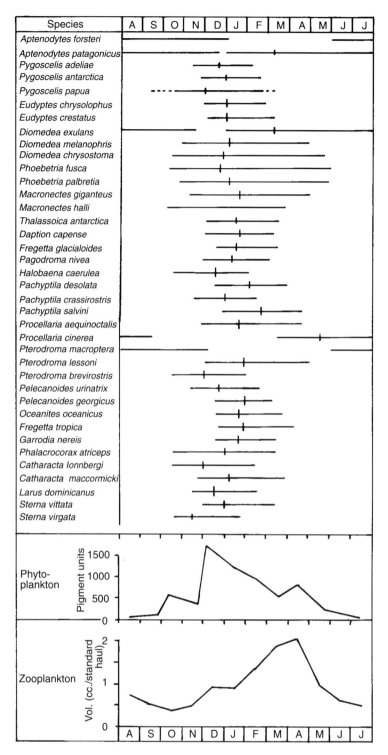

Fig. 10.3. Timing of the breeding season in Antarctic seabirds. Vertical bars represent hatching dates. Phytoplankton data from Hart (1942) and Foxton (1956) respectively. Redrawn from Croxall (1984).

dominicanus) and the Antarctic Tern (*Sterna vittata*), which are essentially solitary species, and the King and Gentoo Penguins. King Penguins have an unusual breeding cycle involving maintaining chicks in winter and late breeding by parents which have successfully fledged a chick in spring. While the reasons for the well-docu-

mented lack of synchrony in Gentoo Penguins are less clear, Croxall & Prince (1980a) have suggested that as an inshore feeding species with a relatively small foraging range, this may be an adaptation to reduce interspecific competition, especially during chick rearing and adult premoult fattening periods.

Thirdly, there are season-to-season variations in laying dates at a single site or colony. These are often caused by climatic factors such as the late breakout of sea ice, or snow and ice blocking burrows. However, the variation is seldom more than a week or two and for some species, colony or population mean laying dates are relatively consistent over long periods of time.

It appears that most species begin breeding as early in the season as practicable so that the principal demand for food (during rapid chick growth and once the chick has fledged) can coincide with the availability of food. There are, however, a number of species which are winter breeders. The most celebrated of these is the Emperor Penguin. Winter breeding in the Wandering Albatross and certain petrels (Grey Petrel and Great-winged Petrel) is probably an adaptation to take advantage of the reduced competition in the winter for food resources where climatic conditions are suitable, e.g. in the sub-Antarctic islands. Such a strategy seems possible only for large species adapted for catching squid, and possibly fishes, as crustaceans are usually not available in sufficient quantities in winter.

10.4.3 Breeding cycles

The basic pattern of events during the breeding season is very similar for most procellariformes and penguins. Potential breeding birds arrive at the colonies some weeks before egg laying (males often before females), and a period of courtship behaviour, pair bond formation (or re-establishment) and burrow prospecting (or modification of the burrow/nest of the previous season) ensues. The duration of this period is usually about 20–30% of the time from egg laying to chick fledging (Mougin, 1975). After copulation the female generally departs for the sea for a period often lasting two to three weeks and returns immediately before egg laying. Egg laying quickly follows the female's return and she departs after a short incubation shift.

Large birds lay heavier eggs but the eggs of smaller birds are proportionately larger in relation to body weight. All procellariform species lay one egg. Most penguins (except *Aptenodytes* spp.), however, lay more than one egg, usually two. Incubation duties are shared between the parents until the chick hatches and (except for *Eudyptes* spp.) they can often rear more than one chick. Chicks hatch asynchronously and often only the older one survives.

Incubation duties are shared between the parents until the chick hatches, with a tendency for the shift, or shifts, prior to hatching being shorter, ensuring that on hatching the chick receives a meal quickly. This tendency is most marked in large birds with long incubation shifts (e.g. alba-

trosses), where shift length decreases from about the mid point of incubation. In penguins the pattern of incubation is extremely variable ranging from the usual daily changeovers in the Gentoo Penguin to stints of over a month in eudyptid species. Fig. 10.4 gives a simplified diagram of the duration of periods ashore and at sea for both sexes throughout the breeding season for selected species. Of the pygoscelid species the Gentoo is not illustrated as once incubation commences it has a pattern of daily changeovers. Desperin (1972), however, recorded mean shifts of 2.8 days for females and 3.3 days for males at Isles Crozet. Gentoos maintain a similar pattern throughout the chick rearing period. There is insufficient information to construct a diagram for the Chinstrap Penguin, although it has been suggested (Conroy *et al.*, 1975) that its incubation shifts are shorter (mean 2–8 days), and visits to the chicks more frequent than in the Adélie Penguin. In the Adélie the females sometimes takes the first shift which is then short (6 days), but this is followed by a normal length (15 days) male shift (Spurr, 1975).

In the procellariformes the chick is brooded after hatching for a varying period in alternating shifts by one parent while the other feeds the chick. Subsequently both parents feed the chick, which gains weight rapidly, accumulating substantial fat reserves, to reach a peak weight normally substantially in excess of adult weight. Thereafter it continues to be fed, often with gradually decreasing frequency while the body tissue, muscles, feathers, etc. grow. Weight decreases until fledging as the reserves are used up. Penguins follow a similar pattern but in most species chicks do not fledge until the moult is completed. In penguins the mean fledging period varies from 50 days in the Adélie Penguin to 350 days in the King Penguin; in the Chinstrap the period is 54 days and in the other species the period ranges from 62–90 days. In albatrosses the period is generally in the order of 120–140 days with the exception of the Wandering Albatross where it is 278 days. In the petrels the fledging periods range from 42 (Antarctic Petrel) to 125 (Grey-faced Petrel).

The Emperor Penguin as a winter breeder breeds under the most extreme environmental conditions of any bird. If it were to lay eggs in the spring the chicks would be unable to fledge before winter; consequently laying takes place in late summer with the adults in peak condition and the chick is reared throughout the winter. It fledges in mid-summer at only 60% of the adult body weight (Prévost, 1961), the lowest proportion of any penguin, the adults having lost up to 40% of their body mass to cope with the problems of incubation and brooding fasts In temperatures that may drop as low as –49 °C, the Emperor shows a number of adaptations: its ambient critical

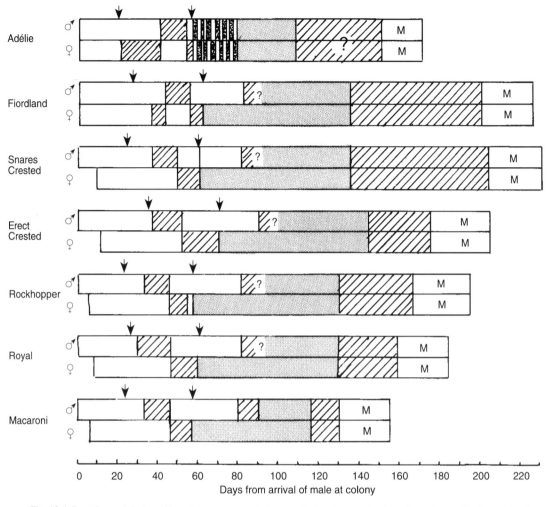

Fig. 10.4. Duration and timing of breeding season events in some Antarctic penguins (data from, in turn: Taylor, 1962; Spurr, 1975; Warham, 1963, 1971, 1972, 1974; Croxall, 1984). First arrow, mean laying of second egg; second arrow, mean hatching date; cross-hatched, at sea; stippled, feeding chicks; blank, in colony; M, moult. Periods of unknown duration indicated by ? Redrawn from Croxall (1984).

temperature (below which metabolic rate must be increased to maintain body temperature at a constant level) is –10 °C (Le Maho *et al.*, 1976); its appendages (flipper, bill) are about 25% smaller in proportion than in other penguins (Stonehouse, 1967); its flippers and feet have extremely well developed vascular counter current heat exchangers (for reducing heat expenditure in cold air); heat loss is minimized in the nasal passages (Murrish, 1973); and, it has a behavioural adaptation of huddling, which may involve up to 5000 birds at 19 per m^{-2} (this has been calculated to reduce the theoretical heat loss of body weight by 25–50%, Prévost, 1961).

10.4.4 Breeding success

Data on the proportion of eggs hatched and chicks fledged (summarized by Mougin, 1975; Berruti, 1979; Croxall & Prince, 1979) suggest that it is rare for chicks to fledge from more than half of the eggs laid. Albatrosses

and petrels normally have greater (and more consistent) breeding success than penguins. While direct natural predation is rare, skuas and giant petrels, sheathbills and gulls take eggs and more rarely chicks. Environmental conditions affect breeding success, especially in penguins. Jouventin (1975) and Yeates (1968, 1975) found a direct relationship between the severity of environmental conditions and egg and chick loss in the Emperor and Adélie Penguins. The importance of the timing of the sea ice break-out, which influences the distance that the birds have to travel for food has been demonstrated for the latter species; early break-out is correlated with high breeding success at Cape Crozier (Ainley & LeResche, 1973) and Cape Royds (Stonehouse, 1963; Yeates, 1968).

Pack ice conditions, ice-blanketed burrows or snow-covered nest sites may delay the onset of breeding and may result in chicks fledging at less than optimum weights and time. The relationship between breeding success and colony size (better in larger colonies; Oelke, 1975) and nest position (better in central than peripheral birds; Spurr, 1975; Tenaza, 1971) has been studied in Adélie penguins. This reflects the tendency for the younger birds which lay fewer (Tenaza, 1971) and smaller (Yeates, 1968) eggs, to breed at the periphery of the colony. Age affects laying date, clutch size, incubation routine (but not incubation period), egg fertilization and hatching and fledging success (Ainley *et al* 1983a). The older birds are the most successful breeders.

10.5 Non-breeding biology

10.5.1 Moult

Apart from the penguins, information is sparse on the timing and duration of moult in Antarctic seabirds. In petrels moult usually begins during the incubation period but primary feather moult takes place after the chicks have fledged. In the Cape Pigeon (Beck, 1969) and possibly the Snow Petrel (Maher, 1962), however, the primary moult commences shortly before the chicks fledge, and, as it lasts about 85 days in the Cape Pigeon, it is completed in May before the start of winter. An early start to the moult appears to be a characteristic of the larger petrels in high latitudes. Penguins come ashore for a complete moult during a relatively brief and well-defined period (see Fig. 10.4). Prior to this they accumulate considerable fat reserves which are lost during the moultfast.

10.5.2 Dispersion and migrations

In recent years there have been numerous papers summarizing the results of the recordings of bird sightings at sea. Under the stimulus of the BIOMASS Bird Ecology Working Group the making of such observations has been standardized so that data from various regions of the Southern Ocean can be compared. Typical of the information that can be obtained from such studies is that of Ainley and his co-workers in the Ross Sea region (Ainley & Jacobs, 1981; Ainley *et al.*, 1983b; Ainley, 1985). During December and January they recorded a total 9 733 000 birds at an average density of 16.3 birds km^{-2} and a biomass of 0.04 g m^{-2}. Nine species were recorded during the census period with the dominant species by numbers being the Antarctic Petrel (55%) and by biomass the Emperor Penguin and Adélie Penguin (42.8 and 39.3% respectively). Bird biomass was concentrated over the Antarctic Slope Front and in the pack ice of the southwestern Ross Sea. The Antarctic Slope Front described by Ainley & Jacobs (1981), lies over the Ross Sea continental slope and is characterized by steep gradients in physical properties. Biggs (1982) reported peaks in zooplankton biomass over this slope front.

In a similar manner, Abrams (1985a,b) has studied the pelagic distribution of seabirds, excluding penguins, in the African Sector of the Southern Ocean over the period 1979–81. Seabird density estimates were calculated for four frontal zones and five zones between the fronts and South Africa and the Antarctic Continent. During the non-breeding season the procellariiform birds disperse widely. The larger albatrosses, especially the Wandering Albatross, follow the air currents of the westerly winds and may circumnavigate the Southern Ocean. Wilson's Storm Petrels (B. B. Roberts, 1940) and some Antarctic Skuas (Voous, 1965) travel as far north as Greenland (Parmelee, 1976), and several sub-Antarctic species such as the Sooty Shearwater (Richdale, 1963), Great Shearwater and Mottled Petrel (Seventy, 1957) are transequatorial migrants. Most other Antarctic seabirds also tend to move northwards in the winter. Those which breed at high latitudes, except the Emperor Penguin, need to move at least to the pack ice edge in order to feed.

Related species often show different degrees of winter movement. For example, while Snow and Antarctic Petrels maintain a high Antarctic distribution, the other fulmarine petrels range much further north, even into the Humbolt and Benguela cold surface-water currents off South America and South Africa respectively. Black-browed Albatross populations move well to the north in the winter whereas Grey-headed Albatrosses remain in high latitudes (Tickell, 1967; Prince, 1980b). Amongst the penguins the Gentoo is much more sedentary than the other species.

10.6 Food and feeding ecology

10.6.1 Food

Most of the early studies of the nature of the food of Antarctic seabirds was chiefly based on observed stomach contents analyzed on the basis of the frequency of occurrence of the main food types (see Carrick & Ingham, 1967 and Mougin, 1975 for reviews). Such studies can be misleading as they emphasize the presence of indigestible remains (especially squid beaks) (Ashmole & Ashmole, 1967). More recent work (e.g. Emison, 1968; Croxall & Furse, 1980; Croxall & Prince, 1980a,b; Prince, 1980a,b; Thomas, 1982; Hunter, 1983; Croxall *et al.*, 1984b, 1985; Offredo *et al.*, 1985; Montague, 1984; Lishman, 1985; Klages, 1989; Arnould & Whitehead, 1991) has provided information on the number of individuals and total weight of each prey class and this has enabled estimates of total consumption to be made.

Croxall (1984) has proposed, on the basis of the preferred dietary items, the following greatly simplified clas-

Table 10.3. *Percentage composition by weight of the diet of Antarctic penguins*

Species	Main prey classes			Crustacean prey			Locality	Source
	Squid	Fish	Crustacea	Euphausiids	Amphipods	Copepods		
Adélie	+	39	61	98[1]	2	+	Cape Crozier	Emison (1968)
Adélie		+	100	100	+		S. Shetland Is.	Volkman *et al.* (1980)
Chinstrap		4	96	100	+		S. Shetland Is.	Croxall & Furse (1980)
Chinstrap		+	100	100	+		S. Shetland Is.	Volkman *et al.* (1980)
Gentoo		15	85	100	+		S. Shetland Is.	Volkman *et al.* (1980)
Gentoo		32	68	100	+		South Georgia	Croxall & Prince (1980a)
Macaroni		2	98	100	+		South Georgia	Croxall & Prince (1980a)
Macaroni		25	75	75[2]	+		S. Shetland Is.	Croxall & Furse (1980)

Euphausiids all *Euphausia superba* except [1]*E. crystallorophias*, [2]50% *Thysanoessa macrura*.
+ = present in small quantities.

sification of Antarctic seabirds' principal natural dietary preferences:

Crustacea: *Eudyptes* spp., *Pygoscelis* spp., *D. melanophris*, *Phoebetria* spp., *Daption*, *Pagodroma*, *Thallassoica*, *Fulmarus*, *Halobaena*, *Pachyptila* spp., Pelecanoides, storm petrels.

Squid: *Aptenodytes* spp., *Diomedia* spp. (except *D. melanophris*), *Phoebetria* spp., *Macronectes* spp. (at some localities), *Fulmarus*, *Procellaria* spp., *Pterodroma* spp., *Puffinus* spp.

Fish: *Aptenodytes fosteri*, *Pygoscelis papua*, *P. adeliae* (continent), some *Diomedea* spp., *Halobaena*, *Phalacrocorax* spp. (some squid), *Sterna vittata* (and crustacea?).

Other: *Macronectes* spp. (carrion), *Catharacta* spp. (eggs, chicks, small petrels, also fish and crustacea in *C. maccormicki*), *Larus* (beach invertebrates), *Sterna virgata* (insects, etc.).

In his study of seabird distribution and feeding in the African sector Abrams (1985a) found that the proportions of plankton, fish and squid eaters changed from north to south (Fig. 10.5). Squid was predominant in the diets in the subtropical zone, north of the Subtropical Convergence, in the sub-Antarctic Front and in the sub-Antarctic zone. The percentage of plankton in the diet increased at the Antarctic Convergence reaching a maximum in the Antarctic Water Zone.

Plankton-feeding species account for approximately 55% of the total abundance of pelagic seabirds (excluding penguins). Most are prions and petrels, which feed on the surface of the sea on crustaceans, e.g. the Antarctic Petrels at Prydz Bay, which feed exclusively on *Euphausia superba* (Montague, 1984). Arnould & Whitehead (1991) studied the breeding season diet of the three surface-nesting petrel species (the Cape Pigeon, the

Antarctic Petrel and the Southern Fulmar) at Prydz Bay. The pelagic fish *Pleuragramma antarcticum* and krill dominated the diets of all species. By mass they constituted 78% and 22% respectively of the Antarctic Petrel diet, 63% and 36% of the Southern Fulmar diet and 14% and 85% of the Cape Pigeon diet. This group of birds tends to be most abundant south of the Antarctic Convergence. Squid-eating species, comprising approximately 20% of the pelagic avifauna, dominate north of the Antarctic Convergence (Siegfried, 1985). These are the larger birds, including the albatrosses and the larger petrels. At South Georgia squid constituted 49% of the diet by weight of the Grey-headed Albatross (Prince, 1980b) and 47% in the Light-mantled Sooty Albatross (Thomas, 1982). The third group consists of fish-eating species. Except in the vicinity of land and the Antarctic ice shelves, these birds account for an almost negligible proportion of the avian abundance, probably reflecting the comparative rarity of pelagic fishes in the Southern Ocean. Fish, however, do constitute a substantial percentage of the diets of some species, e.g. 35% by weight in the Grey-headed Albatross and 37% in the Black-browed Albatross at South Georgia (Prince, 1980b, 1985), and 24% in the White-chinned Petrel at the same locality. Few species, except some of the plankton feeders, feed exclusively on one category of prey. Most have a mixed diet with one of the main diet categories being predominant. Some species, the mixed-diet group, have a more varied diet. Such species constitute about 20% of the avian abundance.

While the plankton-eaters predominate in the total avian numbers of the Southern Ocean, they probably account for less than 25% of the total avian biomass. The larger albatrosses, in contrast, help to boost the squid-eating group to approximately 50% of the total avian biomass (excluding penguins) (Siegfried, 1985). As a consequence the southern part of the Southern Ocean

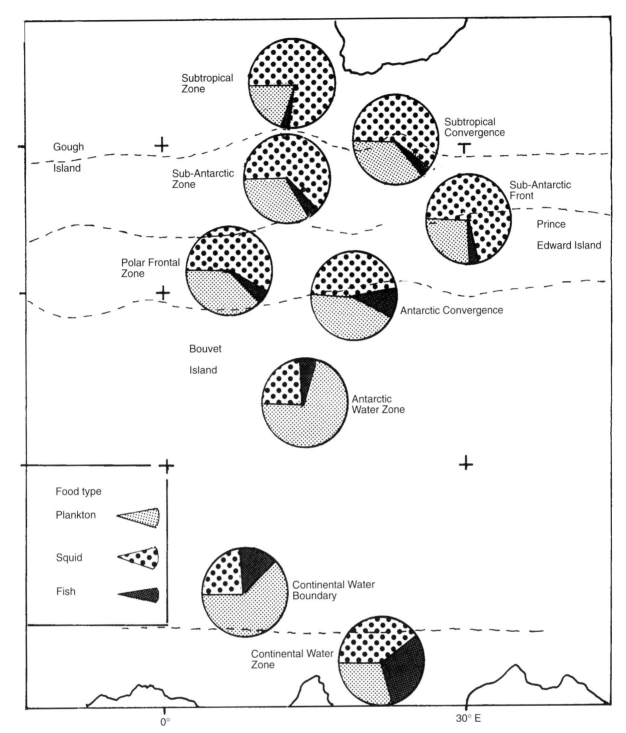

Fig. 10.5. Proportions of seabird food types based on diet and carbon requirements for seabird populations in different zones of the African Sector of the Southern Ocean. Redrawn from Abrams (1985a).

supports many more relatively small-bodied birds than the northern part.

The percentage composition by weight of the diet of those Antarctic penguins for which adequate data are available is given in Table 10.3. Crustacea are the predominant item in the diets, ranging from 61 to 100% by weight. At the South Shetland Islands Adélie and Chinstrap Penguins feed almost exclusively on *Euphausia superba*. At Cape Crozier *E. superba* is replaced in the diet of Adélie Penguins by the smaller *E. crystallorophias* (Emison, 1968). Penguins take other crustaceans, occasionally, especially hyperiid amphipods. Depending on the location fish, especially larvae, may be an important secondary component of the diet, e.g. at Cape Crozier where they constituted 39% by weight of the diet of Adélie Penguins. The fishes consumed are mostly larval or juvenile specimens, especially those of the pelagic species *Pleuragramma antarcticum*. Information on the food of Emperor Penguins (*Aptenodytes forsteri*) is rather sparse. Offredo & Ridoux (1986) studied the diet of Emperors in Adélie Land and found that the birds were largely fish-eaters, fish constituting 65% of the stomach contents by weight. The diet of Emperor Penguins in the Weddell Sea in October and November was mainly krill, the Antarctic Silverfish, *Pleuragramma antarcticum*, and the squid *Psychroteuthis glacialis* (Klages, 1989).

The majority of the dietary studies discussed above do not break down the major dietary categories into species, apart from the crustaceans. Such a breakdown is impossible with fish, which are usually highly digested. However, with an increasing ability to identify squid species on the basis of beaks alone M. R. Clarke, 1972, 1980a,b) it has been possible to determine species as well as the sizes of squid taken, e.g. for the four albatrosses breeding at South Georgia (Croxall & Prince, 1980a; A. Clarke & Prince, 1980; Prince, 1980b).

The bulk of the crustaceans consumed by Antarctic seabirds are krill, except near the continent where krill are replaced by *E. crystallorophias*. Other groups of crustaceans may be important, e.g. copepods in the diet of the Broad-billed and Dove Prions (and possibly *Pachyptila salvini*), diving petrels and possibly storm petrels. Amphipods, especially the hyperiid *Parathemisto gaudichaudii* may be important to *Pachyptila belcheri* (Harper, 1972; Strange, 1980), and significant differences have been noted in the proportions taken by Blue Petrels and Dove Prions of amphipod species common to the diets of both (Prince, 1980a).

Very little is known about the winter diets of most of the bird species of the Southern Ocean. Krill may not be as accessible to the birds due to the extensive ice cover and alternative species may be taken. Those species which feed on fish and squid in the summer would doubtless continue to do so.

10.6.2 Feeding methods

The main feeding methods of Antarctic seabirds are shown in Table 10.4. There are two principal feeding techniques, pursuit diving and surface feeding (Croxall & Prince, 1980a; Croxall, 1984). The former technique is particularly characteristic of penguins, which are pre-eminently adapted for life as aquatic pursuit divers. Diving depth is one aspects of penguin feeding behaviour which

has been investigated recently in some detail (Croxall *et al.*, 1988b; Croxall & Davis, 1990). Multiple depth recorders, logging the number of dives within set depth ranges have been deployed on King (Kooyman *et al.*, 1982), Adélie (R. P. Wilson, 1989; R. P. Wilson *et al.*, 1991) Chinstrap (Lishman & Croxall, 1983) and Gentoo Penguins (R. P. Wilson, 1989). The large *Aptenodytes* spp. (feeding on fish and squid) dive to depths of 236–265 m (Kooyman *et al.*, 1971, 1982) whereas the krill-eating Chinstrap Penguins' dives do not exceed 70 m, and 40% of the dives have found to be shallower than 10 m (Lishman & Croxall, 1983). A Gentoo Penguin has been caught in a net at 100 m (Conroy & Twelves, 1972). A Blue-eyed Shag has been caught in a net at 25 m (Conroy & Twelves, 1972), and although diving times of up to 2.5 minutes have been recorded (Kooyman, 1975), comparable with those of the smaller penguins, it is doubtful if they have the capacity for controlled diving. The diving petrels are also specialized for diving and swimming underwater, chiefly by a reduction in wing length so that a 'paddle-like' condition for underwater propulsion has been attained (Kurodo, 1967). However, they are certainly not deep divers and they feed in the top few metres.

Nearly all the albatrosses and petrels take prey at the surface. Following Ashmole (1971) the surface-feeding methods can be subdivided into several categories. There are a few species which mainly detect prey while in flight and either execute a shallow plunge to catch it (Antarctic Tern), or stop to secure it during flight. Plunging is occasionally recorded in albatrosses but is more common in some petrels. Dipping is characteristic of the storm petrels, which patter near the surface, and the gadfly petrels (*Pterodroma* spp.) and the Blue Petrel which swoop down from a height. Surface diving is most prevalent amongst the petrels, especially *Puffinis* and *Procellaria* species, but is also used by albatrosses and diving petrels. The most specialized technique is that of certain prions (*Pachyptila desolata*, *P. salvini* and *P. vittata*) which have broad deep bills with a comb-like lamella forming a fringe on the inside of the upper mandible through which they expel water and filter out small prey organisms.

Most seabirds are opportunistic scavengers but some species obtain most of their food in this way either at sea or on land. Pre-eminent carrion feeders are the Giant Petrels (Johnstone, 1977, 1979; Hunter, 1983, 1985). Hunter (1985) estimated that a total world breeding population of *c.* 8600 pairs for *Macronectes halli* and *c.* 38 000 pairs for *M. giganteus*, with a total non-breeding population of *c.* 26 000 and 113 000 respectively. He calculated that annually they consumed 1328.4 tonnes of seals, 12 947.5 tonnes of penguins and 1200 tonnes of small birds. They also take other prey including

Table 10.4. *Feeding methods and foraging range of South Georgia seabirds*

Species	Pursuit	Plunge	Dive	Surface seize	Dip	Filter	Scavenge	Max. foraging range (km)
King Penguin	XXX							*c.* 500
Chinstrap Penguin	XXX							
Gentoo Penguin	XXX							31.5
Macaroni Penguin	XXX							115
Wandering Albatross				XXX			XX	2650
Black-browed Albatross		X	X	XXX			XX	925
Grey-headed Albatross		X	X	XXX			X	950
Light-mantled Sooty Albatross		X	?	XXX			X	1250
Southern Giant Petrel				XXX			XXX	*c.* 330
Northern Giant Petrel				XXX			XXX	*c.* 350
Cape Pigeon				XXX			XX	
Snow Petrel				XXX			X	
Dove Prion				XX			XXX	300
Blue Petrel			XX	XX	XX			600
White-chinned Petrel			XXX	XXX				1650
Common Diving Petrel	XXX	XX	XX	XX				360
South Georgia Diving Petrel	XXX	XX	XX	XX				330
Wilson's Storm Petrel		X			XXX		X	250
Black-bellied Storm Petrel		XX			XXX		X	
Grey-backed Storm Petrel		XX			XXX			
Blue-eyed Shag	XXX							
Brown Shua							XXX	
Southern Black-backed Gull				XXX			XX	
Antarctic Tern		XXX			XXX			

XXX: Common, XX: Occasional, X: Rare.

Foraging range estimate based on (a) interval between successive feeds to chick by the same parent and (b) calculated flight and swimming speeds.

After Croxall & Prince, (1980a).

an estimated 3049 tonnes of crustaceans (principally euphausiids), 661.6 tonnes of squid and 253.9 tonnes of fish. Skuas, particularly the Brown Skua, (and the Southern Black-backed Gull, also scavenge. Detailed studies of the role of skuas and their effect on penguin colonies have been made by Young (1963a), Muller-Schwarze & Muller-Schwarze (1977), Trivelpiece *et al.* (1980) and Trivelpiece & Volkman (1982). Young (1963a) showed that some Antarctic skuas, particularly those which do not have territories which include portions of penguin colonies, sustain themselves by catching fish (mainly *Pleuragramma antarcticum*) and even crustaceans at sea.

10.6.3 Foraging range

Species with similar breeding seasons, diets and foraging methods may still be ecologically separated if there are sufficient differences in their feeding zones and feeding depths. For breeding birds the length of the incubation shifts, and particularly the time between successive visits to feed a chick, are an indication of the potential foraging range. Using information from a variety of sources Croxall & Prince (1980a,b) provided estimates of the times between successive feeds by the same parent for South Georgia penguins and petrels. These varied between at least twice daily (Giant Petrel) to every five to six days (Wandering Albatross). Imber (1976) gives a parental absence period of eight days for Grey-faced Petrels. Such information was used by Croxall (1984) to classify birds into inshore (at least one feed by each parent per day), offshore (each parent visits at about two-day intervals) and pelagic (interval of at least three days) (Table 10.5).

The maximum distance travelled by birds on their foraging trips can be calculated from estimates of reasonable swimming and flight speeds (see Croxall & Prince, 1980a, Table 10.4 and Fig. 10.6 for details). It should be emphasized that these estimates are far from accurate, especially for inshore species, since they assume a straight direct path and no stops for feeding (A. J. Williams & Siegfried, 1980).

Table 10.5. *Feeding zones of Antarctic seabirds*

	Inshore	Intermediate	Offshore	Intermediate	Pelagic
Diving	Gentoo Penguin Shags Diving petrels	Chinstrap penguin	Macaroni Penguin Adélie Penguin	King Penguin	
Surface feeding	Storm petrels Diving petrels Giant petrels Antarctic Skua Antarctic Tern	Prions	Black-browed Albatross Grey-headed Albatross Snow Petrel Antarctic Fulmar Cape Pigeon	Blue Petrel Antarctic Petrel	Wandering Albatross Sooty Albatross White-chinned Petrel Grey-faced Petrel Grey Petrel Kerguelen Petrel White-headed Petrel

From Croxall (1984).

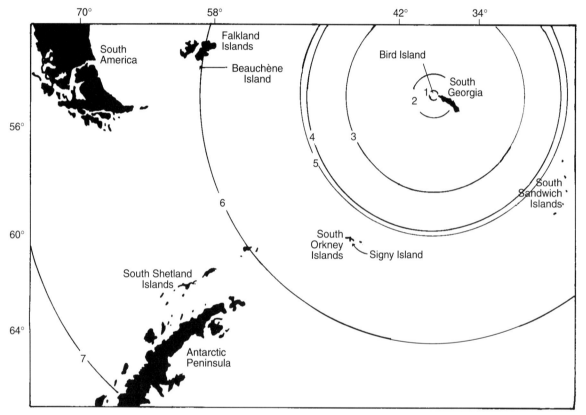

Fig. 10.6. The maximum estimated foraging range of seven species of South Georgia birds during chick rearing. Estimated from swimming/flying speeds and duration of feeding trips at sea. 1. Gentoo Penguin, 2. Macaroni Penguin, 3. King Penguin, 4. Black-browed Albatross, 5. Grey-headed Albatross, 6. Light-mantled Sooty Albatross, 7. Wandering Albatross. Redrawn from Croxall & Prince (1983).

The development of new radiotelemetry techniques in which radio transmitters are attached to penguins to monitor their behaviour at sea can now provide more accurate information on foraging behaviour. Penguin swim speeds measured with autoradiography range from 1.6 to 2.4 m s[-1] (average 2.1 m s[-1]), while transit speeds estimated from radiotelemetry are in the range 1.2 to 1.3 m s[-1] (Croxall & Davis, 1990). Using this technique with Gentoo and Chinstrap Penguins Trivelpiece *et al.* (1986) were able to distinguish five foraging behaviours: porpoising, under-water swimming, horizontal diving, vertical diving and resting or bathing. Gentoo Penguins spent a significantly greater proportion of their foraging trips engaged in feeding behaviours than Chinstraps, which spent significantly more time travelling. The study provided new insights into the feeding ecology of the two species. Gentoos had significantly longer feeding dives than Chinstraps (128 seconds versus 91 seconds) and significantly higher dive–pause ratios (3.4 versus 2.6 seconds). Trivelpiece *et al.* (1986) concluded from their observations that travelling speeds of penguins at sea may be considerably lower than the 7.2 km h⁻¹ speeds reported for Adélie Penguins (Kooyman, 1975), and that penguin foraging ranges based on swimming speeds (see Table 10.5) may have been over-estimated (Croxall & Prince, 1980b; Croxall *et al.*, 1984b). They estimated maximum overall swimming speeds of 5.5 km h⁻¹. Gentoo Penguins require significantly more krill to rear their chicks to fledging than do Chinstraps (118 kg versus 73 kg per breeding pair; Trivelpiece *et al.*, 1986), and have significantly shorter nest relief intervals during chick rearing (12.5 hours versus 16.7 hours; Volkman *et al.*, 1986). Foraging ranges based on nest relief intervals, feeding times and travelling times were estimated as within 17 km of the rookery for Gentoos and within 27 km for Chinstraps (Trivelpiece *et al*, 1980). Thus, gentoos, which require more krill per day, can acquire this food from a more restricted foraging range because of their greater diving ability. There is thus less overlap in the feeding niches of the two species than would appear at first sight.

At Esperanza on the Antarctic Peninsula R. P. Wilson *et al.* (1991) found that foraging Adélie Penguins with eggs and with brooded and creching chicks spent mean periods away from the nest of 96, 36 and 21 hours respectively, during which time means of 29.0 h (30%), 11.2 h (31%) and 2.7 h (13%) respectively, were spent under water at depths of >5 m. Maximum depth reached was 170 m but overall the birds spent most time at shallow depths. The principal prey was krill, caught at a mean rate of 7.2 g min⁻¹ spent under water.

The breeding success of penguins is dictated by the distribution, abundance and availability of prey. However, there is a dearth of information on the location of feeding areas relative to penguin breeding sites, apart from the pioneering studies of Trivelpiece *et al.* (1986) discussed above and Sadlier & Lay (1990) using radiotelemetry. In their study Sadlier & Lay (1990) found that Adélie Penguins at Cape Bird, McMurdo Sound generally foraged close inshore and within 15 km of the rookery.

Stahl *et al.* (1985) have studied the foraging ranges of the birds which breed on Crozet in the southwestern Indian Ocean. They found that four species were restricted to the immediate vicinity of the islands: the Imperial Cormorant (*Phalacrocorax atriceps*), the Southern Black-backed Gull (*Larus dominicanus*), and the terns *Sterna vittata* and *S. virgata*. A second group, typified by the King Penguin (*Aptenodytes patagonicus*), the Macaroni Penguin (*Eudyptes chrysolophus*) and the Black-browed Albatross (*Diomedea melanophris*), foraged principally over the shelf and slope areas. The remaining species such as the Blue Petrel, Thin-billed Prion, White-chinned Petrel, Yellow-nosed Albatross, White-headed Petrel, and Kerguelen Petrel foraged regularly over pelagic waters. In general the birds were concentrated over the productive shelf areas and frontal zones.

Obst (1985) has examined the relationships between krill and seabirds off the Antarctic Peninsula. Mean avian density was 2.6 times greater in waters where krill schools were present than in waters without krill schools. While seabird density was a good predictor of the presence of krill it did not correlate with krill density or krill school depth. However, two species, the Southern Fulmar (*Fulmaris glacialoides*) and Wilson's Storm Petrel (*Oceanites oceanicus*) were associated with krill significantly more often than expected by chance alone. Where penguin densities were high (>30 penguins km⁻²) krill schools were always present.

It is clear that the differing abilities of species to feed at different distances from a breeding colony is important in reducing direct competition (Croxall & Prince, 1980a). This, combined with dietary and feeding method differences, and differences in the timing of the breeding season may, as has been emphasized by Croxall & Prince (1979) for South Georgia, will provide adequate ecological isolating mechanisms to ensure that in normal circumstances direct competition for food is avoided, at least in the summer.

10.6.4 Quantities of food eaten

Various estimates have been made of the overall food consumption of seabirds in the Southern Ocean. Such global figures, however, while they indicate the order of magnitude of consumption, are subject to considerable uncertainty due to the inadequacy of the information on the populations of many species, and their food intake and energetics.

The most reliable data on the levels of food consumption by seabirds are for the Scotia Arc region which has been the site of the most detailed quantitative studies on diets (e.g., Croxall & Prince, 1980a) and studies of bioenergetics (e.g., Croxall, 1982a, 1984). In a series of papers Croxall and his co-workers (Croxall & Prince, 1980a, 1982; Croxall *et al.*, 1984a,b, 1985) have summarized the available information on seabird population estimates, sex-specific weights, the nature and timing of the activities for each sex throughout the annual cycle, mortality rates, calorific contents of prey and bioenergetics. The seabirds breeding at South Georgia and the Scotia Arc were estimated to consume 6720×10³ tonnes of krill, 600×10³ tonnes of squid, 400×10³ tonnes of fish, 1010×10³ tonnes of copepods and 262×10³ tonnes of amphipods annually. It is thus clear that they have a major impact on the food resources, especially krill.

Estimates of the overall consumption of food by the seabirds of the Southern Ocean are given in Table 10.6.

Table 10.6. *Biomass and energy consumption of Antarctic seabirds*

	Sub-Antarctic		Antarctic		Total	
	Biomass (t×10⁶)	Energy consumption (kcal×10¹² y⁻¹)	Biomass (t×10⁶)	Energy consumption (kcal×10¹² y⁻¹)	Biomass (t×10⁶)	Energy consumption (kcal×10¹² y⁻¹)
Penguins	410	22.3	198	14.1	608	36.4
Other species	53	5.1	3	0.5	56	5.6
Total	463	27.4	201	14.6	664	42.0

From Croxall (1984).

10.7 Energetics

10.7.1 Species requirements

Croxall (1984) has reviewed the available information on metabolic rates in birds with special reference to the seabirds of the Southern Ocean. He points out that the relationship between basal metabolic (BMR) and resting and active metabolic rates is imperfectly understood, e.g., flapping flight has been assessed at six times the resting metabolic rate. Kooyman *et al.* (1976) showed that for Adélie Penguins immersed (but not swimming) in water at 5 °C the metabolic rate was 3.6 times that of resting in air. This response to cold ambient temperatures is probably an additional energy cost to Antarctic seabirds.

The energy budgets of active adult birds are difficult to assess. The use of labelled isotopes to estimate total energy costs over a known period shows promise (e.g. Hails & Bryant, 1979). However, it is difficult to obtain a breakdown of activity (e.g., the time spent flapping, gliding resting, feeding, etc.) over time. Preliminary information for King, Macaroni and Gentoo Penguins suggests that the daily costs of foraging during chick rearing are about 2.5 to 3.5 times the BMR (Kooyman *et al.*, 1982; Davis *et al.*, 1983; Davis & Kooyman, 1984).

During the breeding season most birds spend long periods ashore and, in the case of penguins, also during the moult. At these times they suffer considerable weight loss. It had been assumed that the bulk of the loss comprised fat but Groscolas & Clement (1976) for fishing Emperor Penguins obtained results of 55.5% fat, 9.2% protein and 35.3% water. A. J. Williams *et al.* (1977) for moulting, fasting Rockhopper and Macaroni Penguins determined that the weight loss comprised 38.0% fat, and 12.0% protein and 50% water. Croxall (1982a) in reviewing available data on fasting weight loss and energy requirements in petrels and penguins concluded that fat is unlikely to comprise more than 50% of weight loss. Average daily costs of incubation in petrels were assessed as 1.3 times BMR (range 0.8–2.0), of incubation in penguins as 1.4 times BMR (range 1.0–1.6)

and of moulting in penguins as 2.0 times BMR (range 1.6–2.4).

10.7.2 Population requirements

Estimates of the overall energy consumption of Antarctic seabirds vary widely (e.g., Mougin & Prévost, 1980; A. J. Williams *et al.*, 1979). Croxall (1984) has modified the estimates of Mougin & Prevost (1980) on the basis of data in Croxall & Kirkwood (1979), Croxall & Prince (1979, 1980a), the references cited in A. J. Williams *et al.* (1979), and some unpublished information, and has come up with some very approximate figures for Southern Ocean bird biomass and energy requirements (Table 10.6). The data in this table emphasize the pre-eminent role of penguins. In terms of biomass and consumption almost all the seabirds of the Antarctic region are effectively penguins, and two-thirds of these are Adélie Penguins; in the sub-Antarctic region 80% of the birds are penguins and of these 50% are Macaroni Penguins.

According to Green & Gales (1990) the energy budgets which have been formulated to date can only be regarded as approximate, and without more extensive data from isotope turnover studies, reliable calculations of population energy and food requirements will not be forthcoming.

10.8 Population structure and dynamics

Seabirds are known to be long-lived (i.e., having low annual mortality, especially as adults) and to delay breeding until they are several years old (Carrick, 1972; Ainley & DeMaster, 1980). The age of onset of breeding is variable, from two years in the Common Diving Petrel to ten years in the Sooty Albatross. For most species it takes several years from the time when breeding is first recorded for half that year-group to be breeding.

Annual survival may reach 95% per annum. However, diving petrels seem to be a notable exception and penguins, apart from Emperor Penguins, have a lower adult survival rate of 82–87%. As adults many species do not have important natural predators. Skuas take numerous storm petrels, diving petrels and prions at night when they arrive on their nesting sites to feed their chicks, while some Leopard and Fur Seals take penguins as they come and go from their nesting sites; giant petrels and skuas take penguin chicks and recently-fledged individuals.

In terms of mean life expectancy the smaller petrels may reach 10–15 years of age and the albatrosses and giant petrels at least 25 years. Many of the larger birds live longer; Wandering Petrels and Snow Petrels aged over 35 years were still breeding at South Georgia and Signy Island in 1984 (Croxall, 1984). There is a field record of a 16-year-old Adélie Penguin (Ainley & DeMaster, 1980).

The bulk of mortality probably occurs in the first year after fledging and it has been estimated that perhaps only one third of the birds fledged survive this period (Croxall, 1984). Subsequently the survival of pre-breeding birds is high until they commence breeding, when mortality become high again until the survivors become established. Mean annual survival rates vary from 96% in the Wandering Albatross (Tickell, 1968; Croxall, 1982b; Barrat, 1976), and 95% in the Snow Petrel (Hudson, 1966), the Sooty Albatross (Weimerskirch, 1982), the Grey-headed Albatross (Croxall, 1984) and the Emperor Penguin, to 82% for the King Penguin (Barrat, 1976; Jouventin & Mougin, 1981) and to 61–70% for the Adélie Penguin (Ainley & DeMaster, 1980). Adélie Penguins have the poorest survival both as juveniles and adults of any of the penguin species (Ainley & DeMaster, 1980).

10.9 Role in the ecosystem

The seabirds of the Southern Ocean have an important role in the marine ecosystem. Although our knowledge of their distribution, abundance, biomass and energetics is far from complete, even rough estimates of their biomass and prey consumption indicate that especially in the vicinity of breeding colonies their impact as predators is important in structuring the pelagic communities. As we have seen annual krill consumption by seabirds in the Scotia Arc region may be in excess of 16 million tonnes per annum while the total consumption throughout the Southern Ocean may be as much as 115 million tonnes per annum. This is considerably more than the annual amount consumed by present whale stocks and nearly two-thirds of the estimated annual krill consumption by seals.

The birds also have a considerable impact on the terrestrial ecosystems of their breeding areas. As a consequence the relatively long-lasting incubation and chick-rearing phase of many procellariiformes, these birds play an important role in the functioning of the terrestrial ecosystems of the islands of the Southern Ocean, especially in the sub-Antarctic. As Siegfried (1985) points out, their land-based activities have three important consequences: first, the birds are on land for long enough to support populations of avian scavengers, such as Black-backed Gulls and Sheathbills, and predators, such as skuas; second, the birds deposit considerable amounts of organic products in the form of excreta, eggs, carcasses and feathers; and, finally, they modify the physical nature of the terrain, chiefly by burrowing into the ground and by trampling the vegetation. Considerable progress has been made by South African scientists in quantifying these impacts (V. R. Smith, 1977; Siegfried, 1985).

The amounts of avian products deposited annually by the surface-nesting birds on Marion Island in the 100 km of coastal lowland are impressive: 32 000 tonnes of fresh guano (Burger *et al.*, 1978), 500 tonnes of feathers (A. J. Williams *et al.*, 1978) and 200 tonnes of eggs (Siegfried *et al.*, 1978). Moreover, these figures take no account of the contributions of thousands of burrow-nesting petrels. The egg shells contain predominantly calcium, which is duly returned to the ecosystem to be taken up by the plants. Calcium is an important element limiting primary production on the island. The Marion Island soils are essentially deficient in nitrogen and the contribution of the birds via their guano could be essential for the growth of the vegetation. Much of the avian-derived guano is penguin guano, which is washed straight into the sea fertilizing the inshore waters and enhancing the production. Similar enrichment occurs off penguin colonies on the continent. However, at least 100 tonnes, representing 90% of all the nitrogen introduced annually into the Marion Island terrestrial ecosystem reaches the plants (V. R. Smith, 1978).

The seabirds thus transport considerable quantities of nutrients from the sea to the land, a process that is crucial to the production of the terrestrial vegetation. Little of the vegetation if consumed by herbivores and it essentially is recycled through the detritus pathway. Populations of macroinvertebrates, such as earthworms, snails and mites are enhanced and they are important food for sheathbills and Black-backed Gulls (Burger, 1985).

11

Benthic communities

11.1 Introduction

Since the Belgian Antarctic Expedition by the *Belgica* (1897–1899) to the South Shetland Islands and the Antarctic Peninsula made the first systematic collection of benthic animals the unique fauna of the Southern Ocean has had a continuing fascination for naturalists and others on numerous Antarctic expeditions. The early expeditions used remote sampling methods, a variety of grabs, dredges, trawls, etc., to sample the benthos and consequently they provided limited information on the quantitative composition and biomass of the fauna. It was not until the establishment of permanently occupied research stations during and following the International Geophysical Year that progress was made in understanding the dynamics of the inshore benthic communities in particular, and the life-history strategies and physiology of the component species. At the same time more quantitative techniques were being used to study the benthic faunas of the continental shelf and deeper waters.

In addition to the benthic studies around the Antarctic Continent and in deeper waters of the Southern Ocean there has been considerable research on the ecology of the intertidal and shallow littoral benthos of the sub-Antarctic islands, commencing with the pioneer work of Skottsberg (1907, 1941) on the marine algae of the sub-Antarctic islands, especially the Falklands and South Georgia. Contributions to our understanding of the benthic ecology of these islands have been made by Kenny & Haysom (1962) and Simpson (1976a,b, 1977) on Macquarie Island, J. M. B. Smith & Simpson (1985) on Heard Island, Delepine & Hureau (1968), Desbruyeres & Guille (1973), Arnaud (1974), Desbruyeres (1977) and Bellido (1982) on Isles Kerguelen, De Villiers (1976) on Marion and Prince Edward Islands and Knox (1960, 1963, 1975, 1979) and Hay *et al.* (1985) on the New Zealand sub-Antarctic islands.

The history of research on the Antarctic benthos is summarized and the bulk of the early literature cited in Dell's (1972) comprehensive review of Antarctic benthos. In addition the reviews of Hedgpeth (1969, 1970, 1971), Arnaud (1970, 1974, 1977), Picken (1980,

1985a,b), M. G. White (1977, 1984), Knox & Lowry (1977), A. Clarke (1979, 1983) and Dayton (1990) provide much information on the principal characteristics of the Antarctic benthos.

11.2 The Antarctic benthic environment

The Antarctic continental shelf is generally narrow, varying in width from 64 to 240 km. Ice moving off the continent carries a large quantity of debris gouged from the underlying land surface, and this is deposited on the seabed when icebergs break up and melt. An estimated 500 million tonnes of material are transported out to sea every year, the equivalent of depositing 135 tonnes on each square kilometre. Hough (1956) found that the northern limit of the glacial deposits coincided with the average maximum northern extension of pack ice. The northern boundary of these glacial deposits is a junction with a wide belt (100–2000 km) of diatom ooze, consisting mainly of diatom frustules that have settled out from the surface waters.

Thus, the sedimentary history of the Antarctic shelf and slope is similar right round the continent. As Brodie (1965) points out, the glacial deposits on these areas are derived from a continent on which subaerial chemical weathering of the rocks is effectively non-existent, and where the total seaward transport of rock fragments is by ice. There are thus no river- or wind-borne organic or inorganic deposits added to the shelf sediments. The marine sediments that result are poorly sorted and include muds, fine and coarse sands, pebbles and large and small rocks. Large areas of the shelf are covered with coarse, poorly sorted deposits, interspersed with boulders of various sizes and gravel transported by icebergs (Uschakov, 1963).

Ice is a major factor influencing the distribution of Antarctic benthos and its direct effect may extend to a depth of 33 m. In its various forms ice affects water temperature, levels of transmitted light, ocean currents, salinity, and the composition and stability of benthic sediments and of littoral and sublittoral communities (Picken, 1985a). Shorelines, both rock and gravel, or sand, are abraded by fast ice, pack ice, brash ice and push ice (floes driven ashore and piled upon each other by storms). The impact of such ice may scour the littoral and sublittoral areas to a depth of 15 m. Icebergs, which float with about 80% of their bulk submerged can have a considerable impact on the benthos. A berg with a height of 30 m will therefore ground in a water depth of 150 m. When driven by ocean currents bergs can plough furrows in the bottom thus disturbing benthic communities. In inshore areas platelet ice forming on the bottom is another factor influencing benthic communities (Dayton *et al.*, 1974; see section 3.3.4).

The benthic environment is characterized by low stable temperatures. The greatest seasonal variation occurs in surface waters, especially in the more northern localities, but even here the extreme range is only from −1.9 to 4.0 °C. Near the seabed at a depth of 10 m off Signy Island the temperature range is from −1.8 to 0.4 °C (Picken, 1985a). Further south and in deeper waters the annual temperature range is even smaller; at 585 m in McMurdo sound the range is only 0.07 °C around an average of −1.89 °C (Littlepage, 1965). Generally oxygen levels and salinities are high, although in shallow areas salinity may be reduced by ice melting in the summer. Superimposed on this very equitable environment are seasonally fluctuating levels of light intensity and food availability. Picken (1985a) has characterized the Antarctic benthic environment as follows: 'Conditions in the antarctic benthos are therefore unique. A deep shelf and abyssal plain are littered with hard substrates. Water temperature is constantly low, and the impact of primary production is large, short-lived and generally regular every year. Ice constantly invades the littoral and shallow sublittoral regions. Despite the apparent harshness of the environment many invertebrate taxa thrive here although their communities are very different from those found in other continental shelf assemblages.'

11.3 Littoral communities
Agietos de Castellanos & Perez (1963) have given an account of the animals in a series of tide pools at Cape Spring on the Antarctic Peninsula, Delepine & Hureau (1968) have discussed the zonation of marine plants down to 50 m at Isles Petrels and on the coast of Terre Adélie, while Arnaud (1965) has briefly discussed the zonation of plants and animals on the same coast and Delepine *et al.* (1966) have reported on the vegetation of the Melchoir Peninsula. More recently Arnaud (1974) has compared in greater detail the Antarctic littoral communities of Adélie Land with those of sub-Antarctic Kerguelen, while Castilla & Rozbaczylo (1985) have described the rocky intertidal assemblages of the South

Shetland Islands. The sub-Antarctic islands are much better known, beginning with the pioneer study by Kenny & Haysom (1962) on the littoral ecology of Macquarie Island, which was followed by further studies by Simpson (1976a,b, 1977). Grua (1971), Arnaud (1974) and Bellido (1982) have described aspects of the littoral ecology of Isles Kerguelen. More recently J. M. B. Smith & Simpson (1985) have described biotic zonation patterns on the littoral shores of Heard Island while De Villiers (1976) has given an account of the littoral ecology of Marion and Prince Edwards Islands. In a series of papers Knox (1960, 1963, 1975) has reviewed information on the littoral ecology of the sub-Antarctic region.

11.3.1 Distribution patterns of the biota
Ice abrasion and snow cover severely limit the extent and composition of the intertidal communities of the shores of the Antarctic Continent and the off-lying islands. The zonation pattern described by Castilla & Rozbaczylo (1985) at Robert Island, South Shetland Islands, where ice action is not as severe as on the continental mainland further south, will be used as a starting point to describe the distribution patterns of the biota. The upper eulittoral is characterized by a belt of the red alga *Porphyra endiviifolium*, the greens *Urospora penicilliformis* (mixed with *Ulothrix* sp.) and *Enteromorpha bulbosa* and a yellow lichen. In the mid-eulittoral there is a well developed belt of the red alga *Iridaea obvata* and a less conspicuous belt of the brown *Adenocystis utricularis*. Lithothamnioid algae cover the bottom of tidal pools and patches of the dark encrusting red alga *Hildenbrandia* and black lichens are relatively abundant. The small gastropod *Laevlitorina antarctica* is present throughout this zone. The lower eulittoral has dense concentrations of the limpet *Nacella concinna*, and abundant rusts of lithothamnioid alga. Along the upper fringe of the sublittoral large algae such as *Desmarestia ligulata* and *Ascoseira mirabilis* are abundant.

Table 11.1 shows the zonation pattern on the shores of the Antarctic Continent. This basic zonation pattern shows regional variations influenced to a large extent by the amount of ice and snow that is present. The littoral fringe is characterized by seasonal growths of the dark green alga *Prasiola crispa* and a number of lichen species. The upper eulittoral has seasonal growths of the filamentous greens *Ulothrix australis* and *Urospora penicilliformis*. A 'bare zone' is characteristic of the mid eulittoral which, however, is colonized in the summer by a dense felt of diatoms. In the lower eulittoral annual algae such as the reds *Monostroma hariotii*, *Leptosomia simplex* and the green *Chaetomorpha* develop. These species also extend into the sublittoral. The fringe of the

Table 11.1. *Zonation patterns on Antarctic coasts*

	Basic pattern	Iles des Pétrels[1]	South Shetland Islands[2]
Upper littoral fringe	Lichens *Verrucaria*	Lichens	
Lower littoral fringe	Lichens *Verrucaria*	Lichens	
Eulittoral	?Lichens Seasonal growths of diatoms and filamentous green algae	↑ *Ulothrix* 1 m *australis* ↓ ↑ 1.5 m Diatoms ↓	Tide pools with crustose corallines *Phyllophora appendiculata* *Plocamium secundatum*
Sublittoral fringe	Red algae esp. *Leptosomia* spp. *Patinigera*	↑ *Monostroma hariotii* 2–3 m *Leptosomia* ↓ *simplex*	*Leptosomia* *Patinigera* *Odonaster*
Upper sub-littoral zone	*Desmarestia* spp. *Phyllogigas grandifolius* *Ascosiera mirabilis* *Cystosphaera jacquinotii* *Patinigera* *Odonaster* Red algae	*Desmarestia menziesii* *Phyllogigas grandifolius*	*Desmarestia* spp. *Phyllogigas grandifolius* *Ascosiera mirabilis* *Cystosphaera jacquinotii* *Adenocystis utricularis*

[1]Delepine & Hureau (1968), [2]Neushul (1968).

upper sublittoral is marked by encrusting growths of the coralline algae *Lithophyllum aequable* and *Lithothamnion granuliferum*. These species extend up into the lower and mid littoral zones where rock crevices and pools are present. In the lower eulittoral the black obligate marine lichen *Verrucaria serpuloides* is usually present extending down to 9 m below mean low water. Seasonal growths of the brown alga *Adenocystis utricularis* may occur in the lower part of the eulittoral. Other algae that have been recorded from the lower eulittoral, especially in rock pools, include *Porphyra* sp., *Iridaea obvata*, *Phaerus antarcticus*, *Curdiea racovitzae*, *Monostroma hariotii*, and *Phyllophora antarctica*. In the summer the bottom of many of the rock pools is covered with a thick diatom felt.

The dominant animal is the 3–4 cm long Antarctic limpet *Nacella concinna*, which grazes freely on the diatom felt and encrusting algae when submerged. The extent of the penetration of this species into the intertidal varies considerably from locality to locality. In general the dominant populations are found in the sublittoral. In many localities, especially on the Antarctic Peninsula area and the Scotia Arc Islands, the small byssate bivalve *Kidderia subquantrulatum* forms dense populations at the bases of the algae in the lower half of the eulittoral

zone (Agietos de Castellanos & Perez, 1963; Stout & Shabica, 1970; Castilla & Rozbaczylo, 1985). Associated species reported by Castellanos at Melchor Island include the bivalves *Lassarca miliaris*, *Philobrya olstadi*, and *Lasaea consanguinea*, the chiton *Tonicina zschaui*, the gastropods *Eatoniella caliginosa*, *E. kerguelensis*, *Laevlitorina coriacea*, *L. elongata.*, *L. umbilicata* and *Laevilacunaria bransfieldensis*, the amphipods *Pontogenia antarctica* (dominant), *P. magellanica*, *Eurymera monticulosa*, *Bovallia gigantea* and *Pariphimedia integricaudata*, the isopod *Cymodocella tubicauda*, the nemertine *Amphiphoxus michaelseni* and the turbellarians *Procerade gerlachi* and *P. wondeli*.

Away from the impact of ice the littoral flora and fauna become more varied. J. M. B. Smith & Simpson (1985) have recently described zonation patterns on the rocky shores of Heard Island (73° 30' E, 53° 05' S) which lies to the south of the Antarctic Convergence (Table 11.2, Fig. 11.1). The littoral fringe is characterized by a covering of a black lichen colonized by arthropods, especially the beetle *Mesembriorhinus brevis*. The upper and mid littoral zones are covered by filmy and filamentous algae, predominantly reds (especially *Porphyra columbina* and *Iridaea cordata*) lower down and green algae (especially *Enteromorpha* spp.) higher up. The littorinid

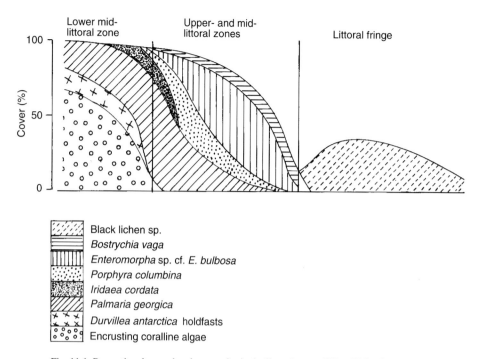

Fig. 11.1. Proportional cover by plant species in the littoral zone of Heard Island rocky shores. Redrawn from J. M. B. Smith & Simpson (1985).

Table 11.2. *Heard Island rocky shore littoral zonation pattern*

Universal scheme zone	Heard Island zones
Littoral fringe	Lichen zone
Eulittoral zone	Mixed algal zone – comprisong mainly *Porphyra* and *Palmaria*
Sublittoral fringe	Kelp zone
Sublittoral zone	Encrusting corallines

Based on data in J. M. B. Smith & Simpson (1985).

Laevlitorina heardensis and the small bivalve *Kidderia bicolor* occur in crevices and in sheltered situations. Where the algae forms a spongy mat abundant oligochaetes occurs. The lower eulittoral is dominated by the bull kelp *Durvillaea antarctica*, between the holdfasts of which encrusting pink coralline algae forms an almost complete cover. Other small red algae also grow there, including *Ballia callitricha*, *Iridaea cordata* and *Palmaria georgica*. The limpet *Nacella kerguelensis* is abundant and the chiton *Hemiarthrum setulosum* common. The fringe of the upper sublittoral is dominated by encrusting corallines.

11.4 Shallow sublittoral communities

Sampling through tide cracks, seal breathing holes and holes dug through the fast ice by members of the early expeditions to Antarctica revealed a rich and abundant fauna, especially of epibenthic invertebrates. With the establishment of permanent stations the pace of work on benthic ecology increased. The quality of this work was enhanced and the output considerably increased from the mid-1960s by the introduction of SCUBA diving at a number of stations, notably Grytvikin on South Georgia, McMurdo in the Ross Sea, Mirny, Moldezhnaya, Palmer on Anvers Island, Signy on the South Orkneys, and Syowa. More recently remotely controlled vehicles with TV cameras and still cameras enabling stereophotographs to be taken have extended the possibilities of estimating the distribution of the benthos, especially in deeper water (Hamada *et al.*, 1986).

11.4.1 Benthic microalgae

Two groups of microscopic algae are included within the benthic microalgae, the sediment microalgae in the top few millimetres of the sediments and the epiphytic algae growing on rock surfaces or attached to macroalgae and the epibenthos. There have been only a limited numbers of studies of the benthic microalgae in Antarctic coastal waters. Palmisano *et al.* (1985d) and Dayton *et al.* (1986) have studied the ecology of benthic diatoms in McMurdo Sound, N. S. Gilbert (1991a,b) investigated benthic microalgal biomass and production in shallow waters at Signy Island, and Everitt & Thomas (1986) and Thomas & Jiang (1986) have studied the seasonal changes of epiphytic diatoms near Davis Station.

Table 11.3 presents data from Dayton *et al.* (1986) for the standing stock of chlorophyll *a* and phaeopigments for the east McMurdo Sound (from north to south, Cape

Table 11.3. *Station location, depth, annual ice thickness, snow cover, percentage surface downwelling irradiance, benthic substrate; mean (±95% confidence interval) chlorophyll* a *and phaeopigments for benthic microalgae in McMurdo Sound during the austral summer 1975–1976 and winter 1977. (See Fig. 12.1 for locations.)*

Location	Season	Annual ice thickness (m)	Snow cover (m)	Depth (m)	Substrate	Chl a (mg m^{-2})	Phaeopigments (mg m^{-2})	Chl a/ phaeo.	%surface down-dwelling irradiance
Cape Royds	Summer	—	—	25	mud and gravel	273±109	253±38.0	1.06±0.33	2.78
Cape Evans	Summer	0.1–0.2	0	19	sand	293±93.2	110±71.1	2.86±1.13	—
					mud and sand	913±185	499±119	1.87±0.14	—
Turtle Rock	Summer	—	—	25	mud and gravel	139±24.2	127±30.1	1.11±0.22	—
				40	mud and gravel	60.8±28.1	146±42.0	0.43	—
Cinder Cones	Summer	—	—	19	mud and gravel	241±157	308±131	0.81±0.46	
				25	mud and gravel	325±73.3	283±147	1.21±0.38	
				40	sponge spicule	360±146	86.4±51.7	4.33±1.19	
Hutt Point	Summer	2.6	0.02	25	mud and gravel	156±106	310±98.3	0.50±0.26	0.31
				40	sponge spicule	515±399	99.7±43.8	5.38±4.30	
				40	sponge spicule	610±255	192±43.4	3.43±2.28	
				31	sponge spicule	611±230	175±52.2	3.56±1.18	
				43	sponge spicule	561±468	99.4±9.8	5.66±0.69	
Cape Armitage	Summer	2.0–2.5	0.05–0.3	6	mud and gravel	269±84 to 457±128	50.5±14.3 to 349±262	1.08±0.67 to 7.12±0.92	ND – 0.05
	Winter			6	mud and gravel	96±55	110±89.6	0.89±0.19	
	Summer			18	mud	265±80.2 to 533±206	78.2±36.5 to 316±30.5	0.97±0.30 to 6.90±0.64	
	Winter			18	mud	47.3±14.4 to 76.2±24.7	90.1±27.8 to 179±36.8	0.43±0.14 to 0.54±0.14	
	Summer			24	sponge spicule	736±253 to 960±220	94.5±63.2 to 186±225	5.58±4.38 to 15.90±4.3	
	Winter			24	sponge spicule	227±76 to 374±177	62.2±15.1 to 118±62.8	3.18±0.67 to 3.63±0.69	
	Summer			42	sponge spicule	317±91 to 518±261	30.8±11.2 to 128±44	4.14±1.41 to 10.50±2.99	

Data from Dayton *et al.* (1986).

Royds to Cape Armitage) and west McMurdo Sound (New Harbour) (see Fig. 12.1 for localities). From this table it can be seen that there are seasonal (summer–winter), substrate and depth differences, as well as differences due to the amount of light that penetrates through the fast ice and snow cover. Off Cape Armitage where the snow cover was removed from the ice above a sponge spicule mat at a depth of 6 m the chlorophyll *a* concentration increased in a little over two weeks from 756 to 960 mg chl *a* m^{-2} and the chlorophyll *a*/phaeopigment ratio doubled from 7.4 to 15.9. The effect of season on chlorophyll *a* and phaeopigment can be seen in Table 11.3. At the Cape Armitage 6 m site the chlorophyll *a* concentration fell from 457 to 96 mg chl *a* m^{-2} between December and June. The chlorophyll *a* concentration at the 18 m site fell from 310 to 95 mg chl *a* m^{-2} between 22 November and 25 March. By 18 August the chlorophyll *a* was as low as 47 mg m^{-2}. Similar differences between winter and summer values can be seen at other sites.

Standing stock estimates for West Sound New Harbour sites were much lower than in the East Sound sites. Two comparable sites on the east and west sides of the Sound are Cinder Cones and New Harbour with chlorophyll *a* concentrations of 241 and 326 mg chl *a* m^{-2} at Cinder Cones compared with 145 and 45 mg chl *a* m^{-2} at New Harbour at 19 and 25 m respectively. Values of 18 to 60 mg chl *a* m^{-2} are typical of the deeper New Harbour areas; for similar substrates, depths and seasons the comparable values in the East Sound are 300–900 mg chl *a* m^{-2}.

Some of the standing stock data recorded by Dayton *et al.* (1986) are extremely high. Most of the high readings occur in sponge spicule mats and there are a number of reasons for this. Firstly, the sponge spicules form a complex lattice. Each spicule provides a substratum for diatoms, thus providing a tremendous increase in surface area which is covered with diatoms. In addition, this structure affords benthic microalgae protection from grazers. It also allows ice algae and phytoplankton settling out from the water column to accumulate in the interstices between the spicules. The shift in the ratio of

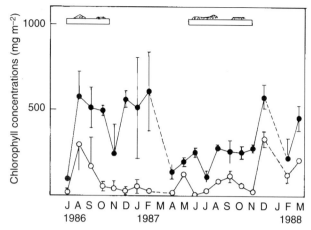

Fig. 11.2. Seasonal variation of benthic total chlorophyll concentration (●) and chlorophyll *a* (○) in the top 5 cm of the sediment at a nearshore site (12 m) on the east coast of Signy Island, South Orkney Islands. The blocks at the top of the graph represent sea ice and snow cover (stippled) up to a maximum depth of 10 cm. Redrawn from Gilbert (1991a).

chlorophyll *a*/phaeopigments which decreases markedly in the winter give a preliminary estimate of the degradation of the microalgae.

Palmisano *et al.* (1985d) have studied the photosynthesis–irradiance relationship of a dense community of shade-adapted benthic microalgae dominated by the diatom *Trachyneis aspersa* in the sponge spicule mat in depths of 20 to 30 m off Cape Armitage. Ambient irradiance was less than 0.6 μE m^{-2} s^{-1} due to light attenuation by surface snow, sea ice, ice microalgae and the phytoplankton in the water column. Photosynthesis–irradiance relationships determined by the ^{14}C method revealed that the benthic diatoms were light-saturated at only 11 μE m^{-2} s^{-1}, putting them among the most shade adapted microalgae reported. Unlike most shade–adapted microalgae, however, they were not photoinhibited by irradiances even as high as 300 μE m^{-2} s^{-1}. This contrasts with sea ice algae at the same site, which may be photoinhibited by irradiances above 25 μE m^{-2} s^{-1} (Palmisano *et al.*, 1985b).

The seasonal pattern of benthic microalgal biomass (as measured by chlorophyll concentrations) at a nearshore site (12 m depth) on the east coast of Signy Island, South Orkney Islands is shown in Fig. 11.2 (N. S. Gilbert, 1991a). Seasonal chlorophyll levels showed distinct seasonal variation related to the photon flux density reaching the benthos. The benthic microalgae responded rapidly to higher light intensities following the breakout of the sea ice. Low rates of sedimentation of material from the water column during the benthic bloom indicated that the benthic microalgae were mostly responsible for the increase in sediment chlorophyll concentrations. In December at the peak of the benthic microalgal bloom a

primary productivity rate of 700.9 mg C m^{-2} day^{-1} was measured (N. S. Gilbert, 1991b). However, in January at the peak of the phytoplankton bloom when light intensities reaching the benthos were greatly reduced a rate of 313.4 mg C m^{-2} day^{-1}, about half of that in January, was measured. In March, when the phytoplankton bloom died, off benthic light intensities had increased and production was 391.4 mg C m^{-2} day^{-1}.

Measurements of the productivity of the benthic microalgae prior to the development of the dense growth of the ice algae in October are required before estimates of their production can be made. It is probable that the benthic microalgae play an important role in providing carbon and energy to the abundant benthic macrofauna in McMurdo Sound, especially prior to the release of algae from the sea ice in January and the onset of the water column phytoplankton bloom. It is clear that in inshore waters benthic microalgal production plays an important role in the seasonal primary production cycle.

11.4.2 *Benthic macroalgae*

About 700 species of benthic macroalgae belonging to 300 genera have been recorded from the Southern Ocean. In addition to the classical overviews of Southern Ocean marine algae by Gain (1912) and Skottsberg (1941, 1964) more recent accounts include those of Zinova (1958), Papenfuss (1964), Delepine (1966), Delepine *et al.* (1966), Zaneveld (1966a,b, 1968), South (1979) and Heywood & Whitaker (1984). Neushul (1968) estimated that about 35% of the algae were endemic. However, many records are fragmentary, often identifications are suspect and there is an urgent need for critical reviews of many of the genera (South, 1979; Heywood & Whitaker, 1984). Most of the species appear to have a circumpolar distribution and many also occur in the warmer sub-Antarctic waters. Skottsberg (1964) distinguishes a sub-Antarctic flora using the 0 °C surface isotherm as a rough guide. Many algal genera in the sub-Antarctic zone are not found in the Antarctic zone and vice versa; South Georgia appears to be situated on the boundary having representatives from both zones (Skottsberg, 1964; Neushul, 1968).

The distribution of the littoral algae has been described above. Here the shallow sublittoral communities will be dealt with. Below extreme low water there is a zone (0–5 m) where algae are sparse due to the abrasive action of ice. Where this is severe the only species on exposed rock surfaces are encrusting calcareous red algae *Lithophyllum aequable* and *Lithothamnion granuliferum*. The obligate submerged marine lichen *Verrucaria serpuloides* grows here down to a depth of 9 m. Sheltered crevices support small clumps of mostly annual species such as the brown

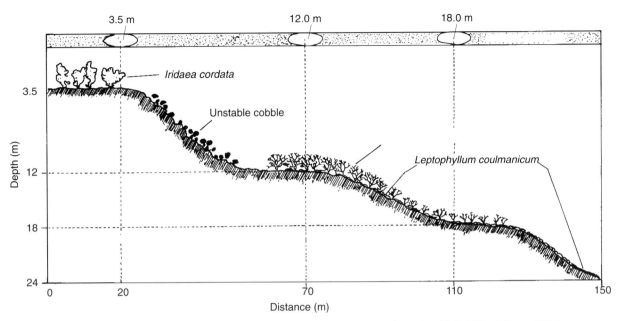

Fig. 11.3. Macroalgal zonation at Cape Evans, Ross Island, McMurdo Sound. Redrawn from K. A. Miller & Pearse (1991).

alga *Adenocystis utricularis* and green algae of the genera *Enteromorpha, Ulothrix* and *Cladophora*. Further north on the islands of the Scotia Arc where ice action is less severe more luxuriant algal growths occur. On Signy Island parts of the upper sublittoral have dense algal growths (Picken, 1985a). Red seaweeds, *Leptosarca simplex* and *Gigartina apoda*, and the brown *Adenocystis utricularis* are common in the 2–5 m range. Below 5 m large browns dominate, *Ascoseira mirabilis*, dense thickets of *Desmarestia menziesii* and *D. anceps* up to 1 m high, and *Himanothallus grandifolius*. Of these the perennial brown alga *Himanothallus* becomes dominant below 9 m. Beneath the canopy formed by these four large species there is often a rich 'understory' of reds, *Iridaea obvata, Myriogramme magini, Plocamium secundatum, Porphyra umbilicalis* and species of *Gigartina*. However, the algal biomass at these depths on Antarctic shores is significantly lower than that at comparable sites on temperate shores because of the effects of ice abrasion, unstable hard substrates in the shallow sublittoral zone, and short periods of available light for primary production (Richardson, 1979).

K. A. Miller & Pearse (1991) studied the distribution of the dominant species of macroalgae at several sites in McMurdo Sound. The depth-related distribution pattern of the three dominants off Cape Evans is shown in Fig. 11.3, with *Iridaea cordata* in shallow water, *Phyllophora antarctica* abundant and fertile at intermediate depths and *Leptophyllum coulmanicum* dominant below 20 m. The vertical distribution of the species is correlated with irradiance levels. At sites with thinner annual ice and less

snow accumulation vertical distributions are shifted downwards relative to sites which remain covered most of the year with thick or snow-covered fast ice.

Throughout those regions of the Antarctic in which algal zonations have been explored the vegetation becomes richer with depth. Shallow-water species such as *Curdiea, Leptosomia, Iridaea, Ascoseira mirabilis* and *Gigartina papillosa* appear increasingly in the more exposed situations. *Desmarestia ligulata, D. anceps*, and *D. menziesii* often dominate down to a depth of 10–25 m, often extending to greater depths. Below about 25 m the largest Antarctic brown alga *Himanothallus grandifolius* tends to be dominant and it has been reported well below 50 m.

11.4.3 Epifaunal communities

Because of the availability of hard substrates, rock, boulders, pebbles and coarse sediments, extensive growths of macroalgae and sessile particle-feeding invertebrates are a feature of the benthos below the region of ice scour. The composition of these communities varies with latitude. The most profuse algal growths are found in the northern part of the Antarctic region, particularly on the islands of the Scotia Arc, while dense multistoried growths of suspension-feeding invertebrates are to be found under the fast ice around the margins of the continent.

The best documented shallow sublittoral benthic epifaunal communities are those found in McMurdo Sound (Dayton *et al.*, 1970, 1974; Dayton, 1972). Here, three vertical zones have been described (Fig. 11.4): Zone I (upper), or the 'bare zone', from 0–15 m; Zone II (inter-

Zone I 0–15 m

Zone II 15–30 m

Zone III below 33 m

Fig. 11.4. Vertical zonation of the benthos off the east coast of Ross Island, McMurdo Sound. A few motile animals forage into Zone I, which is otherwise bare of sessile animals. The sessile animals of Zone II are almost exclusively coelenterates, while those of Zone III are predominantly sponges. Redrawn from Dayton *et al.* (1970).

Table 11.4. *Abundance of sponges at 30–60 m depth, Cape Armitage, McMurdo Sound, in terms of percentage cover of benthic surface and percentage of total biomass*

Sponge species	Percentage cover	Percentage of sponge biomass
Rosella racovitzae	41.8	70.9
'Volcano' sponge	3.8	18.3
Tetilla leptoderma	3.2	6.7
Cinachyra antarctica	1.2	0.6
Haliclona dancoi	1.1	0.2
Myacale acerata	1.1	2.4
Polymastia invaginata	1.0	0.5
Dendrilla membranosa	0.8	0.08
Gellius tenella	0.6	—
Sphaerotylus antarcticus	0.5	0.3
Leacetta leptorhapsis	0.2	0.04
Gellius benedeni	0.08	—
Calyx arcuarius	0.03	[1]
Isodictya setifera	0.02	[1]
Kirkpatrickia variolosa	0.02	[1]
Kirkpatrickia coulmani	0.01	[1]
Isodictya erinacea	0.01	[1]
Pachychalina pedunculata	0.01	[1]

[1]Less than 0.01.

Total percentage cover of sponges = 55%; byozoans, actinarians, hydroids etc. = 5.4%; free space = 29.1%. Total area surveyed = 410 m². From Dayton *et al.* (1974).

mediate), the 'coelenterate-hydroid zone', from 15–33 m; and, Zone III (lower), the 'sponge zone', from 33 to 100+ m. The upper zone is essentially devoid of sessile animals because of the annual certainty of ice scour by drifting ice and disturbance through anchor ice formation. The intermediate zone is below the limit of ice scour but is still influenced by anchor ice formation. Below 33 m anchor ice does not form, and scouring and other physical disturbances rarely occur. Littlepage (1965) found that at 75 m in McMurdo Sound the mean annual temperature was −1.87 °C (SD = 0.11), the mean annual salinity 43.7% (SD = 0.19), and the dissolved mean annual oxygen concentration 6.79 ml l⁻¹ (SD = 0.38). Thus the physical environment is a very uniform one.

The substratum in Zone I consists of rock, pebbles and volcanic debris. Zone II has a cobble rocky bottom with coarse sediment between. The substratum below 33 m is a mat of siliceous sponge spicules, which varies in thickness from a few centimetres to more than 2 m thick. Below the sponge spicule mat there is usually a layer of bivalve shells (mostly *Limatula hodgsoni*).

The bare zone is briefly colonized during ice-free periods by the detritus-feeding echinoid *Sterechinus neumayeri* and starfish *Odonaster validus*, as well as the nemertine *Parborlasia corrugatus*, the large isopod *Glyptonotus antarcticus*, a few pycnogonids and fish. In

contrast Zone II is colonized by an abundant fauna of soft corals, anemones, hydroids and ascidians. The alcyonarian, *Alcyonium paessleri*, and the anemones, *Artemidactis victrix*, *Isotealia antarctica*, *Urticinopsis antarcticus* and *Hormathia lacunifera* are the largest and most conspicuous sessile components of this zone. The stoloniferan, *Clavularia frankliniana*, and the hydroids, *Tubularia hodgsoni* and *Lampra parvula* grow in discrete patches. There are a few scattered individuals of the hydroid *Halecium arboreum*, and a few clumps of sponges in the lower part of the zone. In most areas the large ascidian, *Cnemidocarpa verrucosa*, is also present. The most conspicuous motile animals in this zone again are *Odonaster*, *Sterechinus*, *Parborlasia*, and the fishes *Pagothenia bernachii* and *T. centronotus*. The pycogonids *Thavmastopygnor striata*, *Colossendeis robusta* and *C. megalonyx* are also common.

Zone III begins abruptly at 33 m and continues down to at least 180 m. Sponges are the most conspicuous sessile species covering almost 55% of the surface area. These sponges, some of which resemble staghorn corals, large fans, bushes, volcanoes, sheaves, etc., contribute most of the remarkable vertical structure of the community and provide refuges for motile species and attachment sites for a range of sessile animals. Prominent among the 18 species of sponges identified by Dayton *et al.* (1974) are *Rosella nuda* and *Scolymastra joubini* (white volcano sponges up to 2 m tall and 1.5 m wide), *Rosella racovitzae* (light grey), *Myacale acerata* (slimy, white), *Polymastia invaginata* (grey cone sponge), *Cinachyra antarctica* (grey spiky sponge), *Tetilla leptoderma* (white basketball sponge) and *Haliclona dancoi* (white finger sponge). Table 11.4 lists the abundance of the sponges in terms of percentage cover of the benthic surface and percentage biomass.

In addition to the sponges the most conspicuous epibenthic sessile species are the anemones *Stompia selaginella*, *Artemidactis victrix*, *Isotealia antarctica*, *Hormantha lacunifera* and a few individuals of *Urticinopsis antarcticus*, the alcyonarium *Alcyonium paessleri*, the hydroids *Lampra paevula*, *L. microrhiza*, *Halecium arboreum*, *Tubularia hogsoni* and many other unidentified hydroids, a few sabellid polychaetes, some bryozoans, especially *Hippadenella carsonae*, *Terepora frigida*, and *Caberea darwinii*, some ascidians, especially *Cnemidocarpa verrucosa*, the pterobranch *Cephalodiscus antarcticus*, and many molluscs. The most abundant mollusc is the bivalve *Limatula hodgsoni*. Within the sponge spicule mat there is a rich infauna for which Dearborn (1967) recorded more than 12 500 individuals representing an unspecified number of species per cubic decimetre.

Table 11.5. *Estimated annual effects of predators on their sponge prey in the McMurdo Sound epibenthic community standing crop (biomass) of sponges in terms of kcal 100 m^{-2} and year's supply of the sponge species to predators*

Predator species	Density (no. 100 m^{-2})	Rosella racovitzae	'Volcano' sponge	Tetilla leptoderma	Haliclona dancoi	Mycale acerta	Polymastia invaginata	Gellius tenella	Calyx acurarius	Isodictya setifera	Kirkpatrickia variolosa	Pachychalina pedunculata
Odonaster meridionalis	12.8	4.39	2.55		0.23	2.07	5.55	0.46	0.93	1.16		0.23
Odonaster validus	267	75.14	42.25	134.91								
Acodonaster conspicuus	5.6	96.51	344.53	358.06	75.76	20.74					7.22	
Acodonaster hodgsoni	0.3	0.88			1.74			0.83	1.74			
Perknaster fuscus antarcticus (adult)	1.0		1.21	1.21		48.01						
Perknaster fuscus antarcticus (juvenile)	±10			1.24	1.24	3.72	1.24			1.24		
Austrodoris mcmurdensis	3.3	23.22	19.81	1.03	2.44		0.70	2.11	4.49	0.32		
Total		200.14	410.35	496.45	81.41	74.54	7.49	3.4	7.16	1.48	8.46	0.23
kcal 100 m^{-2}		277398	128629	80698	1667	6141[1]	5532	Not known	15	12	66	12
No. of year's supply to predators		1286	311	163	20	82[2]	739	Not known	2	8	9	30

[1]kcal useful to predators; this figure is 51.8% of the kcal m^{-2} as determined by bomb calorimetry since 48.2% of the dry weight of *Mycale acerata* is spongin, which is not consumed by the predators but which contributes to the calorific value as determined by bomb calorimetry.
[2]Also corrected for the presence of spongin.
From Dayton *et al.* (1974).

The asteriods *Perknaster fuscus antarcticus, Acodonaster conspicuus, A. hodgsoni, Odonaster meridionalis,* and *O. validus* and the dorid nudibranch *Austrodoris mcmurdensis* are the most conspicuous predators on sponges. Several other nudibranchs prey on stoloniferans and hydroids. Hydroids and actinians are also eaten by pycogonids. The bivalve *Limatula hodgsoni* is consumed by the asteroids *Diplasteras brucei* and *O. validus,* and the gastropod *Trophon langstaffi.* The sea urchin *Sterechinus neumayeri,* and *O. validus,* are conspicuous detritus feeders, and *O. validus* and the nemertine *Parborlasia corrugatus* are efficient scavengers. The actinian *Urticinopsis antarcticus* is an efficient predator of echinoderms and medusae.

Faunal distributions similar to those outlined above have been described by Gruzov & Pushkin (1970) and Gruzov (1977) in the Davis Sea and the South Shetland Islands and by Watanabe *et al.* (1982) and Hamada *et al.* (1986) from the coast off Syowa Station. Propp (1970) has described the shallow-water benthos at the Halswell Islands in East Antarctica. He described an upper zone (2–10 m) with a community of diatoms, the dominant species belonging to the genera *Pleurosigma,* *Fragilariopsis, Amphiprora, Achanthes* and *Nitzschia,* the asteroid *Odonaster validus* and the hydroid *Tubularia ralphy.* A second zone (6–25 m) was dominated by the red alga *Phyllophora antarctica,* calcareous algae, and the sea urchin *Sterechinus neumayeri.* Both of the above zones were subject to anchor ice formation. From 25–30 m a third zone dominated by the alcyonarian *Eurephthya* sp. had a varied fauna of some 70 to 80 species. Below 30 m sponges, *Rosella racovitzae* and *Stolymastra joubini,* the hydroid *Oswaldella antarctica* and ascidians dominated the community. It would appear that with some regional variation the shallow-water benthic communities are similar right round the Antarctic Continent.

11.4.4 Epifaunal community dynamics
There are only a limited number of studies of the dynamics of the shallow-water epifaunal communities. The most comprehensive and detailed study is that of Dayton and his co-workers (Dayton *et al.*, 1970, 1974; Dayton & Oliver, 1977; Dayton, 1979; Oliver & Slattery, 1985) on the biological interactions in the complex epifaunal community along the coast of Ross Island, McMurdo Sound. In their investigations they concentrated on the role

played by competition and predation in this community living in a physically constant environment. The composition of the community has been described above.

Dayton (1979) studied the relative growth rates of the dominant sponges and the feeding rates of their predators, using cages to exclude predators and observing the predator's feeding rates by SCUBA diving. Field experiments demonstrated that, with the exception of *Myacale acerata*, the growth rates of the sponges were too low to measure in one year. *Myacale*, however, was observed to increase its mass by as much as 67%. Because of its rapid growth rates, *Myacale* appears to be the potential dominant in competition for substratum space, the resource potentially limiting to sessile species. This conclusion was supported by observations of *Myacale* growing over and, in some cases, apparently having smothered other sessile species representing at least three phyla (other sponges, such as 'Volcano' sponge, *Rosella racovitzae*, *Haliclona dancoi*, *Polymastia invaginata*, *Kirkpatrickia variolosa*, and *Calyx acuarius*; the anemones *Hormathia lucinifera* and *Artemidactis vitrix*; and the solitary ascidian *Cnemidocarpa verrucosa*).

The densities, percentage feeding, dietary composition and energy consumption were determined for the sponge predators. The predator populations tended to be characterized by low densities and broad diets. Table 11.5 list the annual effects of the predators on their sponge prey. Of the predators listed *Odonaster validus* spent less than 30% of its feeding time consuming sponges, and the balance of its diet consisted of molluscs, hydroids, bryozoans and detritus. The data from the field survey and the energetics studies suggested that *Myacale* is prevented from dominating the space resource by the predation of two asteroid species, *Perknaster fuscus fuscus* and *Acandaster inconspicuous*. Adult *Perknaster* specialize on *Myacale*, and the sponge provides a small proportion of the diet of *A. inconspicuous*. The latter species and the dorid nudibranch *Austrodoris mcmurdensis* were the most important predators on three species of rosellid sponges (*Rosella racovitzae*, *R. nuda*, and *Scolymastra joubini*). Despite the relatively high consumption of sponges by their predators and despite the fact that none of the sponges has a refuge during growth from potential mortality from *A. inconspicuous* very large standing crops of the rosellid sponges accumulate.

Dayton *et al.* (1974) consider that the McMurdo Sound epibenthic community, in common with other marine epibenthic communities, is structured by biological interactions, especially predator–prey interactions. Selective predation tends to counter the more effective growth and greater competitive abilities of *Myacale acerata*. Thus this community of organisms in a physically stable environment can be considered to be 'biologically accommodated' in a similar manner to deep-sea communities where the physical environment is stable, and in which there is an increasingly significant role for interspecific competition along a gradient of decreasing physical stress (Sanders, 1969, 1979).

11.4.5 Infaunal communities

It is only comparatively recently that the community structure of Antarctic soft bottom communities have received attention. There are now a number of quantitative studies of the soft bottom macrobenthos at a range of localities round the continent, including Arthur Harbour, Anvers Island (Lowry, 1969, 1975, 1976; M. D. Richardson, 1972; M. D. Richardson & Hedgpeth, 1977), Admiralty Bay, King George Island, South Orkney Islands (Jazdzewski *et al.*, 1986), Chile Bay and Foster Bay, South Shetland Islands (Gallardo & Castilla, 1968, 1969, 1970; Gallardo *et al.* 1977; Larrain, 1981, Retamal *et al.*, 1982), Signy Island, South Orkney Islands (P. Hardy, 1972; M. G. White & Robins, 1972), King Edward Cove, South Georgia (Platt, 1980), McMurdo Sound (Dayton & Oliver, 1977), and Moubry Bay, Cape Hallett and Cape Bird, Ross Island (Lowry, 1976). These studies have shown that the soft substrates are generally characterized by a high density, diversity and biomass of polychaetes, molluscs and crustaceans.

Table 11.6 compares the data on species diversity, density and faunal composition from three studies, in Arthur Harbour, Cape Hallet and Cape Bird, discussed below, with other benthic studies. At depths of 26 to 40 m in Arthur Harbour (68° 48′ S, 64° 06′ W) Lowry (1969, 1976) recorded 64 species with a mean density of 7502 individuals m^{-2}. The dominant species were the tube building peracarid crustaceans *Ampelisca baureri* and *Gammaropsis* (*Megamohorus*) sp., and the burrowing polychaete *Aspitobranchus*. Other important species were the peracarids *Eudorella* sp. and *Harpina* sp., the oligochaete *Torodrilus lowryi* (11% of the individuals in the yearly population), and the polychaetes *Haploscoloplos kerguelensis*, *Paraonis gracilis*, and *Capitella peramata*. The dominant groups were the peracarids and the polychaetes which together made up 88% of the population (Table 11.6). Although bivalves made up 10% of the species they constitute only 2% of the individuals, most of which represented the conspicuous protobranch *Yoldia eightsi*.

In a more wide-ranging survey in Arthur Harbour, sampling in depths from 5 to 700 m, Richardson & Hedgpeth (1977) recorded 282 taxa with densities (retained on a 0.5 mm screen) ranging from 2891 to 86 514 individuals m^{-2}, with an overall mean of 35 668

Table 11.6. *Species diversity, density and the percentage composition of the crustacean, polycheate, and bivalve components of the benthic infaunal communities from various Antarctic localities compared with selected sub-Antarctic and temperate localities*

Locality	Latitude (°S)	Number of species	Mean density (no. m^{-2})	Composition of population (% of total)		
				Crustacean	Polychaeta	Mollusca
Stewart Island (Lowry, 1976)	43°	107	2965	9.0	41.0	45 0
Auckland Islands (Lowry, 1976)	50°	83	47122	20.0	51.0	27.0
Port Foster (Larrain, 1981)	62°	43	9074	83.7	13.4	1.4
Chile Bay (Larrian, 1981)	62°	65	996	10.0	66.0	8.0
Arthur Harbour (Lowry, 1976)	64°	64	7502	53.0	35.0	2.0
Cape Hallett (Lowry, 1976)	72°18′	147	7755	25.0	50.0	5.0
Cape Bird (Lowry, 1976)	77°13′	72	34024	39.0	39.0	0.5
McMurdo Sound, West (Dayton and Oliver, 1977)	77°45′	—	4087	17.2	68.8	4.4
McMurdo Sound, East (Dayton and Oliver, 1977)	77°45′	—	140021	17.7	16.5	1.9

m^{-2}. The numbers retained on a 1.0 mm screen ranged from 1317 to 43 267 individuals m^{-2}, with an overall mean of 16 426 m^{-2}. The latter values are four times greater than those reported by Wigley & McIntyre (1964) for the inner continental shelf off New England, and five time greater than those reported by Gallardo *et al.* (1977) for Discovery Bay, Greenwich Island. Richardson & Hedgpeth attributed the high macrofaunal densities to high productivity, physical stability, and increasing organic input with depth.

In Moubry Bay, Cape Hallett (72° 18′ S, 170° 12′ E) in depths of 104 to 250 m Lowry (1976) recorded 147 species with a mean density of 7755 individuals m^{-2} (similar to that in Arthur Harbour). The most important species were the sedentary polychaetes *Spiophanes tcherniai* and *Potamilla antarctica*. Other important species were the eulamellibranch *Thyasira bongraini*, the sedentary polychaetes *Leonice cirrata, Neosabellides elongatus* and *Maldane sarsi*, the tubificid oligochaete *Torodrillus lowryi*, and the foraminiferan *Pelosina* sp. In the shallower samples (104 and 134 m) the most common species, along with *S. tcherniai* and *P. antarctica*, were the polychaetes *N. elongatus* and *Myxicola* sp., and the peracarids *Leaun antarctica, Orchomene franklini, Metaphoxus* sp., *Leptognathia antarctica,* and *Neoxenodice cryophile*. In the deeper samples (208 and 250 m) The eulamellibranch *T. bongraini* and the oligochaete *T. lowryi* became more conspicuous. Polychaetes and peracarids dominated the community,

with peracarids making up 42% of the total number of species and one quarter of the individuals. Polychaetes made up another third of the species and half the population. Bivalves were relatively insignificant.

Although there were less than half the number of species (72) in the Cape Bird (77° 13′ S, 166° 26′ E) samples (35 to 54 m depth) as in the samples from Cape Hallett, the sampled population was over ten times larger (34 024 individuals m^{-2}). The dominant species were the myodocopid ostracod *Philomedes heptathrix*, the burrowing anemone *Edwardsia* sp., and the tube building polychaete *Spiophanes tcherniai*. These three species together made up 70% of the population sampled. The peracarid *Nototanais dimorphus* and an Archianellid species were also well distributed and abundant. Other relatively abundant species occurring in all samples included the isopods *Austrosignum glaciale* and *A. grande*, the cumacean *Eudorella splendida*, and the amphipods *Heterophoxus videns* and *Orchomene franklini*. Aside from *S. tcherniai* and the Archianellid species, other annelids well represented in the samples included the sedentary polychaetes *Tharyx* sp. and *Haploscoloplos kerguelensis* and the oligochaete *Torodrilus lowryi*. At Cape Bird the structure of the major component groups differed from that of the other areas studied by Lowry (1976). Peracarids and myodocopids formed a crustacean component that together accounted for 39% of the population. Together with the polychaete component they comprised 78% of the individuals. If the burrowing anemone is included then the

Table 11.7. *Number of organisms per square metre of different taxa from various localities in the Ross Sea and McMurdo Sound (depths of the various studies are given in brackets).*
Numbers, with percentages in brackets.

Taxon	Ross Sea (74°58' S, 170°48' E) (500 m)	McMurdo Sound — West Sound				McMurdo Sound — East Sound		
		Garwood Valley (30 m)	Ferrar Glacier (30 m)	New Harbour (30–40 m)	Marble Point (30 m)	McMurdo Station Jetty (20 m)	Cape Armitage soft bottom (20 m)	Cape Armitage sponge spicule mat (30 m)
Ostracoda	70	18	110	132	6586	948	55	4354
Cumacea	40	55	367	885	2150	31548	12950	937
Tanaidacea	25	73	239	282	579	19932	53512	69596
Isopoda	43	18	110	132	1185	23392	19339	33285
Amphipoda	56	184	294	207	3059	11728	9975	8432
Total Crustacea	214 (10.9)	348 (15.9)	1120 (18.5)	1638 (16.3)	13559 (29.9)	87548 (73.7)	95891 (61.6)	116604 (79.9)
Other Arthropoda	16	55	37	55	55	0	496	6282
Total Arthropoda	230 (11.7)	403 (18.4)	1157 (19.2)	1693 (16.8)	13614 (30.0)	87548 (73.7)	96387 (61.9)	122886 (84.3)
Mollusca	560 (28.5)	128 (5.8)	184 (3.0)	1102 (10.9)	184 (0.4)	136 (0.1)	770 (0.5)	7660 (5.2)
Polychaeta	1070 (54.6)	1598 (73.1)	3896 (64.6)	4718 (47.0)	27142 (59.9)	11276 (9.5)	52143 (33.5)	9500 (6.5)
Other Vermes[1]	70	55	147	2060	3913	19752	6281	5735
Total Vermes	1140 (58.1)	1653 (75.6)	4043 (67.0)	6778 (67.5)	31055 (68.5)	31028 (26.1)	58415 (37.5)	15235
Echinodermata	8 (0.4)	0	0	0	0	0	0	0
Miscellaneous	2	0	643	463	441	0	0	0
Total	1960	2184	6027	10036	45294	118712	155572	145781

[1]The category 'other vermes' refers to all other soft-bodies worms such as Memertea, *Edwardsia*, Phoronidae and Oligochaeta.
After Dayton & Oliver (1977).

total is 97% of the individuals. Bivalves were an insignificant component, and together with the nematodes, sipunculids, gastropods and asteroid and ophiuroid echinoderms, they made up the remaining 3% of the population.

Dayton & Oliver (1977) have shown that the soft bottom benthos of the east and west sides of McMurdo Sound are characterized by diagrammatically different assemblages (see Chapter 12 for a discussion of the reasons for these differences). Data from this study are given in Table 11.7. A deep-water station in the Ross Sea is included for comparison. The most obvious trend in the table is the difference of an order of magnitude in the faunal densities between the east and west sides of the Sound, a difference which is particularly evident in the crustacean densities. Molluscs are poorly represented in the samples and almost all of the bivalves recorded were recently settled and metamorphosed pectens, *Adamussium colbecki*. Another trend is the south-to-north gradient along the coast of the West Sound. The standing crops of the benthic organisms at the southerly sites in the West sound are similar to those of the deep shelf and bathyal habitats. Due to the small size of the sampler used, species living on the surface of the sediments, such as adult pectens and ophiuroids (*Ophionereis victoriae*) were not sampled. Dayton & Oliver (1977) note that at New Harbour the latter species occurs at a relatively constant density of 1.7 individuals m^{-2}. In the East Sound the recorded densities are among the highest recorded in the world's oceans.

11.4.6 Infaunal community dynamics

From the data given in Table 11.6 and discussed in the previous section a number of trends can be detected. Infaunal densities appear to be related to latitude, in general increasing with higher latitudes. Such increases appear to be related to the input of microalgal production to the benthos. Dayton *et al.* (1986) have shown that in the shallow waters of McMurdo Sound the benthic microalgal production is important in such inputs, and may be important in explaining the differences in infaunal biomasses between the east and west sides of the Sound. There are also significant differences in the community composition of Antarctic shallow water soft bottom communities when compared with those of temperate and tropical waters.

Lowry (1976) has compared species diversity, trophic structure and species composition of the soft bottom benthos in a latitudinal transect between 47° S and 77° S (Fig. 11.5). A comparison of the species diversity of the macrobenthic communities along the latitudinal gradient showed no correlation between diversity of the mac-

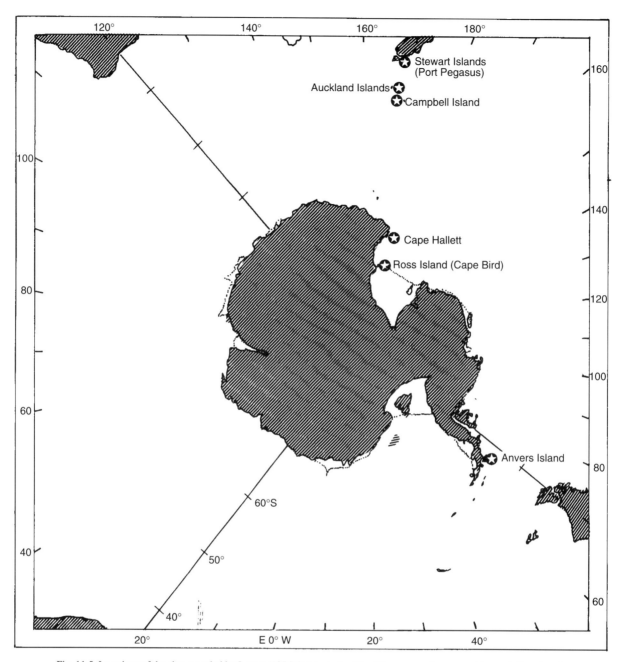

Fig. 11.5. Locations of the sites sampled by Lowry (1976) in his study of benthic community composition and diversity along a latitudinal gradient.

robenthos and latitude. Macrobenthic communities with the highest species diversity occurred at Cape Hallett (72° S), Port Pegasus, and Stewart Island (47° S). These communities have very similar mixed suspension, deposit-feeding structure. They occur on silty-sand to sandy-silt bottoms. The macrobenthic communities with intermediate density are found in Arthur Harbour (64° S) and Perseverence Harbour, Campbell Islands (52° S), and both occur on sandy-mud bottoms and have a deposit-feeding structure. The macrobenthic communities with the lowest diversity occur at the Auckland

Islands (50° S), and at Cape Bird (77° S), and both are found on predominantly sandy bottoms.

The proportion of suspension-feeding and deposit-feeding animals at Cape Hallett was 41% and 50% respectively (Fig. 11.6b). These mixed suspension–deposit-feeding communities have high species diversity due in part to the fact that communities with mixed trophic structure provide more niches, and thereby support more different kinds of benthic animals, than other macrobenthic communities. In contrast to similar communities in temperate waters, e.g. Port Pegasus,

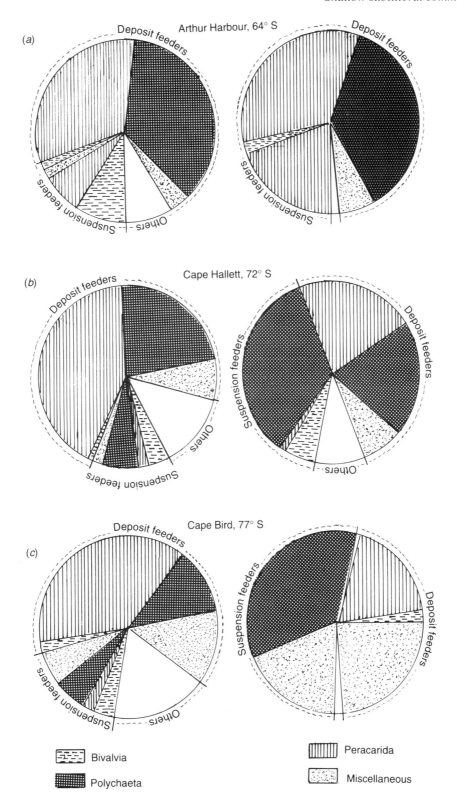

Fig. 11.6. Trophic structure of (*a*) the deposit-feeding community in Arthur Harbour, Anvers Island; (*b*) the mixed suspension–deposit-feeding community in Moubry Bay, Cape Hallett, Ross Sea; (*c*) the suspension-feeding community at Cape Bird, Ross Island. Left – species; right – individuals. After Lowry (1976).

Stewart Island where bivalves constitute some 45% of the individuals, bivalves make up only 5% of the population. Polychaetes made up 32% of the species and 50% of the individuals. Sabellid and spionid polychaetes are the dominant suspension feeders. Peracarids are a significant proportion of the deposit-feeding component.

In Arthur Harbour the proportions of suspension- and deposit-feeders in the population were 22% and 74%

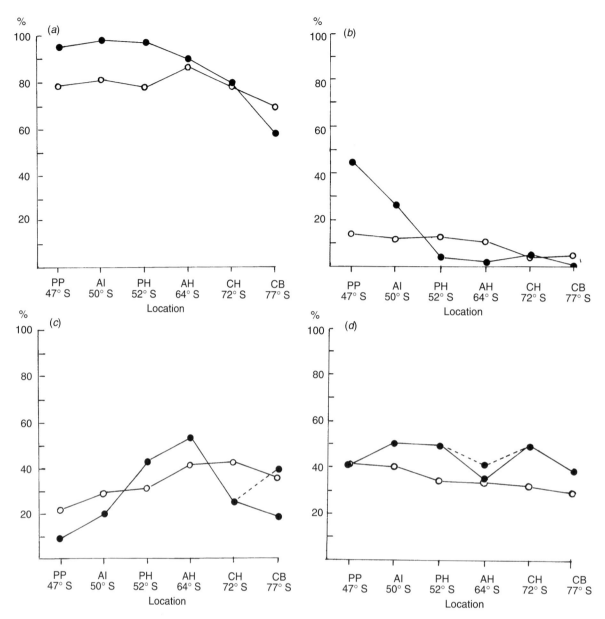

Fig. 11.7. Percentage of the various faunal components in a latitudinal transect from Stewart Island, New Zealand to the Antarctic Continent: for species (○) and individuals (●); (*a*) the bivalves, peracarids and polychaetes combined; (*b*) the bivalves; (*c*) of the peracarids; and (*d*) the polychaetes. For the Anvers Island sample the upper point connected by the dashed line represents the polychaete plus oligochaete numbers. PP, Port Pegasus, Stewart Island; AI, Waterfall Inlet and Sandy Bay, Auckland Islands; PH, Perseverence harbour, Campbell Island; AH, Arthur Harbour, Anvers Island; CH, Moubry Bay, Cape Hallett; CB, Cape Bird, Ross Island. Redrawn from Lowry (1976)

respectively (Fig. 11.6*a*). Bivalves were an insignificant component comprising 11% of the species and only 2% of the individuals. The suspension-feeding component is dominated by the ampeliscid amphipod (*Gammaropsis* (*Megamphopsis*) sp.). Among the peracarids, the amphipods were the most diverse group.

The community with the lowest diversity was that at Cape Bird in which suspension-feeders comprised 54% of the individuals (Fig. 11.6*c*). Bivalves represented 22% of the species but only 1% of the population. Polychaetes comprised 33% of the suspension-feeding species and

64% of the individuals. The dominant species was the spionid *Spiophanes tcherniai*. The densely packed tubes of *Spiophanes* trap and stabilize the sediment providing a substrate for surface deposit-feeders. The most abundant suspension-feeder is the very abundant actinarian *Edwardsia*, which makes up 35% of the suspension-feeding individuals. Amongst the polychaetes the only actively burrowing polychaete is *Haploscoloplos kerguelensis*, while the most abundant species were the surface deposit-feeding maldanids and cirratulids. Peracarids make up a significant proportion of the deposit feeders, while ostracods, particularly *Philomedes heptathrix*, are the most abundant deposit-feeders, making up over 50% of the deposit-feeding population. Deposit-feeding peracarids include the tanaidacean *Nototanais dimorphus*, and the cumaceans *Diastylis helleri* and *Eudorella splendida*, the isopod *Austrosignum glaciale* and the amphipods *Heterophoxus videns*, *Orchomene franklini* and *Gammaropsis longicornis*.

Fig. 11.7 shows that in the shallow coastal waters between southern New Zealand and McMurdo Sound the major components are the Bivalvia, Peracarida, and Polychaeta. The percentage composition of the bivalve molluscan species on the Campbell Plateau remains fairly constant between 11% and 14% from southern Stewart Island to Campbell Island. South of the Antarctic Convergence the percentage composition decreases from 10% of the infaunal benthos at Anvers Island to about 5% along the Victoria land coast. Peracarid crustaceans form a mirror image of the bivalve distribution, and always make up a larger proportion of the shallow water benthos than the bivalves. The percentage composition of the peracarid species is fairly constant from 14% of the benthos at Stewart Island to 31% at Campbell Island. There is an increase in the percentage composition of peracarids south of the Antarctic Convergence. At Anvers Island the peracarid component comprises 41% of the benthos and along the Victoria Land coast the range is 35% to 41%. The polychaetes show a slightly decreasing percentage composition from 41% of the benthos at Port Pegasus, Stewart Island to 31% in McMurdo Sound, Ross Sea. There is no significant change across the Antarctic Convergence.

Oliver *et al.* (1982) and Oliver & Slattery (1985) have drawn attention to the effects of small crustacean predators on the species composition and population structure of soft-bodied infauna in the shallow waters of McMurdo Sound. The macrofaunal density at their study site (20 m) varied from 90 000 to 150 000 individuals m⁻². The assemblage was dominated by eleven species, which maintained populations of over 2000 individuals m⁻² (Table 11.8). Most of the larger species were tube dwellers with 30–50% of the sediment volume and weight being composed of their tubes. The dense assemblage was divided into three faunal guilds with similar ecological characteristics: canopy species (the suspension feeders *Edwardsia* and *Spiophanes*); understory species, motile species living in the top 0 to 1 cm of the sediment (deposit-feeders and predators, including the crustaceans *Heterophoxus*, *Monoculodes*, *Nototanais*, *Austrosignum* and *Eudorella*, and the protozoan *Gromia*); and subsurface species (mainly polychaetes, *Tharyx*, *Haploscoloplos*, *Axiothella*, and *Maldane*).

Oliver & Slattery (1985) postulated that the tanaid

Table 11.8. *Abundant members of the benthic infaunal assemblage near McMurdo Station Jetty, Cape Armitage, McMurdo Sound. Means and standard deviations in 12 cores*

Organism	Functional group	Number 0.018 m⁻²	Number m⁻²
Polychaetes			
Myriochele cf. *herri*	t	379±208	21224
Spiophanes tcherniai	t	64±48	3584
Tharyx sp.	m	40±19	2240
Axiothella sp.	t	14±9	784
Maldane sp.	t	15±14	840
Haploscoloplos kerguelensis	m	8±4	448
Crustaceans			
Austrosignum grandis I	m	519±191	29064
Nototanais dimorphus T	t	310±114	17360
Heterophoxus videns A	m	114±32	6367
Eudorella splendida C	m	95±49	5342
Monoculodes scabriculosus A	m	65±41	3627
Others			
Edwardsia meridionalis	sb	268±84	15012
Gromia sp.	m	87±30	4877
Oligochaeta	m	86±89	4826
Total individuals		2064±978	115595

I = isopod, A = amphipod, T = tanaid, C = cumacean, t = tube, sb = sedentary burrow, m = mobile.
From Oliver & Slattery (1985).

(*Nototanais*), and the phoxocephalid amphipod (*Heterophoxus*), regulated the species composition and population-size of the soft-bodied infauna (primarily the polychaetes) by preying on small species and small individuals of large species. Small individuals of these larger species were rare in the community. Evidence for their regulatory role came from: the gut contents; from laboratory experiments where the crustaceans consumed spionid larvae or juveniles, and small polychaete species; from field experiments where the abundances of crustaceans and small polychaetes were negatively correlated after the colonization of defaunated sediments; from experiments demonstrating that depth in the sediment provided a refuge from predation; and from community patterns along a gradient in water depth where the abundance of the crustaceans was negatively correlated with the abundance of small species and individuals of the larger polychaete species. Because most of the soft-bodied species have a size refuge from the crustaceans, the dense assemblage was dominated by large and long-lived forms.

Interspecific competition is thought to be the major biological process which structures benthic communities in physically constant environments (Sanders, 1969,

1979; Grassle & Sanders, 1973). Even when predators are ascribed an important community role, it is by virtue of preying on competitive dominants and, thus, mediating the effects of interspecific competition (Dayton & Hessler, 1972; Dayton *et al.* 1974). However, the results of the study by Oliver & Slattery (1985) strongly support the primary role of predators which prey on the young of many species. The dense infaunal communities in the shallow waters of Antarctica have evolved in the absence of bottom-feeding mammals comparable to the walrus and Grey Whale (Ridgeway & Harrison, 1981; Gaskin, 1982; Oliver *et al.*, 1983) and, of flatfish, skates, rays, or other disruptive demersal fish (DeWitt, 1971). Their persistence is due to the absence of such disruptive species.

The population densities of the three dominant groups (molluscs, polychaetes and crustaceans) show similar trends to the species composition, but in a more pronounced manner. Bivalves drop from the most abundant group in the benthos of southern New Zealand, with 39% of the population, to an insignificant group, making up only 4% of the population at Campbell Island. Below the Antarctic Convergence they never make up more than 6% of the benthos, and in McMurdo Sound they make up only 1% of the population.

Peracarid populations show the largest fluctuations among the three groups. From only 16% in Port Pegasus they increase to make up 21% of the Auckland Islands population, and 43% of that at Campbell Island. Even though the peracarids maintain the highest proportion on the macrobenthic species on the Antarctic shelf their proportion of the population decreases sharply from a high of 50% in Arthur Harbour to a low of 16% at Cape Bird. At Cape Bird the peracarids appear to be in direct competition with the equally successful, though less diverse, ostracods. If the ostracods are included along with the peracarids then the crustacean and polychaetes are equally abundant at Cape Bird, each with 40% of the macrobenthos. Polychaetes generally are the most abundant animals over the entire latitudinal range.

Bivalve molluscs do not appear to be a very important or successful part of the Antarctic shelf benthos. In the Antarctic benthic fauna families, genera, and species of bivalves are all depauperate (Table 11.9), and compare favourably only with the Arctic cold water fauna. On the other hand, peracarid crustaceans increase in number of species, and have higher population densities, with increasing latitude, while polychaetes remain basically unchanged with regard to numbers of species and population densities along the latitudinal transect. The obvious differences in these groups along the latitudinal gradient are due to the different responses to selective pressures operating along the gradient. The cold water Antarctic

Table 11.9. *Families, genera, and species of bivalves*

Geographic area	Families	Genera	Species
Antarctic (Nicol, 1967)	19	32	68
Arctic (Nicol, 1967)	23	37	66
New Zealand (Dell, 1964)	44	142	400
Panamic Province (Keen, 1958)	46	147	555

After Nicol (1967).

environment selects for slow growing, long-lived animals which brood their young. They may be large or small, but if they require large amounts of calcium they are usually small. The depauperate nature of the Antarctic bivalve molluscan fauna appears to be due to an inability to adapt to these requirements.

Kennett (1968) has discussed the question of the calcium carbonate compensation depth (CCD) in the Ross Sea. Using the depth distribution of calcareous and arenaceous benthic foraminifera he determined the CCD to be at 550 m, which is very shallow compared with other areas of the world's oceans. He attributed this shallow solution boundary to the very low temperatures and high salinities of the Ross Sea. The unsaturated nature of the water as far as calcium is concerned means that extracting calcium carbonate for shell building and maintenance requires relatively more energy than in warmer waters. Nicol (1967) and Kennett (1968) have remarked on the thin and chalky appearance of Antarctic bivalve shells, and Arnaud (1974) has commented on the exceedingly fragile nature of the Mollusca, Echinodermata, and Bryozoa living on the Antarctic shelf. Nicol (1964a,b) has demonstrated that the Antarctic bivalve fauna is the smallest fauna known.

In contrast, the Peracarida are a very successful group in the Antarctic macrobenthos. Peracarids are brooders, a strong requirement for success in cold waters. They are mainly generalized deposit-feeders, which means that they have a continuous food supply and do not have to adapt their reproductive behaviour to a short summer plankton cycle. In addition, peracarids are not reliant on large amounts of calcium carbonate for exoskeleton production. It is interesting to note that large reptant decapod crustaceans with heavily calcified shells and pelagic larvae are absent from the Antarctic shelf fauna. In adjusting to a cold water environment the polychaetes were at an advantage because of their generalized feeding habits. Their major change has been the suppression of the pelagic trochophore larvae into a form which develops demersally, either in the tubes of sedentary forms or on the body of errant forms (Hartman, 1967; Arnaud, 1974).

Table 11.10. *Degree of endemism in selected Antarctic benthic groups*

Group	Endemic genera (% of total)	Endemic species (% of total)	Source
Fishes	70	95	Andriashev (1965)
Isopoda and Tanaidacea	10	66	Kussakin (1967)
Pycnogonida	14	>90	Fry (1964)
Echinodermata	27	73	Ekman (1953)
Echinoidea	25	77	Pawson (1969b)
Holothuroidea	5	58	Pawson (1969a)
Bryozoa	—	58	Bullivant (1969)
Polychaeta	5	57	Knox & Lowry (1977)
Amphipoda	39	90	Knox & Lowry (1977)
Chlorophyta			
Sub-Antarctic	—	16	Heywood & Whitaker (1984)
Low Antarctic	—	33	Heywood & Whitaker (1984)
High Antarctic	—	67	Heywood & Whitaker (1984)
Phaeophyta			
Sub-Antarctic	—	41	Heywood & Whitaker (1984)
LowAntarctic	—	73	Heywood & Whitaker (1984)
High Antarctic	—	83	Heywood & Whitaker (1984)
Rhodophyta			
Sub-Antarctic	—	70	Heywood & Whitaker (1984)
Low Antarctic	—	92	Heywood & Whitaker (1984)
High Antarctic	—	100	Heywood & Whitaker (1984)

After Knox & Lowry (1977), Heywood & Whitaker (1984), and Dayton (1990)

11.5 Biogeography and origin of the benthic biota

The Antarctic Continent is the most isolated of all the continents. Its shores are 960 km from South America, 4020 km from South Africa, and 3380 km from New Zealand, the nearest land masses. While the shelf and slope connect with the deep ocean basins in the Atlantic, Indian and Pacific Oceans, there are three comparatively shallow-water connections to the north. These are the Scotia Arc, the island chain from South America through the Falkland Islands, South Georgia, South Sandwich and South Orkney Islands to the Antarctic Peninsula, and the Macquarie–Balleney and the Kerguelen–Gausberg Ridges which rise within 1800 and 200 m of the surface respectively.

A number of authors have discussed the origin and relationships of the Antarctic fauna. Pertinent general reviews include those of Ekman (1953), Hedgpeth (1969, 1970), Dell (1972) and Knox & Lowry (1977). Various aspects of the biogeography of the Southern Ocean with special reference to the Pacific sector have been dealt with by Knox (1960, 1963, 1970, 1975, 1979, 1980) in a series of papers. Others have presented accounts based on the distribution and affinities of particular groups: for example fish (Andriashev, 1965), polychaetes (Knox, 1979), polychaetes and amphipods (Knox & Lowry, 1977), isopods (Kussakin, 1967), amphipods (Thurston, 1972), molluscs (Powell, 1965), echinoderms (Fell & Dawsey, 1969; Fell *et al.*, 1969), ascidians (Kott, 1969a,b, 1971), sponges (Koltun, 1969) and benthic

macroalgae (Delepine, 1966; South, 1979).

When one examines the distribution patterns detailed in the papers listed at the beginning of this section, a number of major distribution patterns are seen to occur in all groups. These can be summarized as follows (modified from Knox & Lowry, 1977):

1. Circumpolar, throughout the Antarctic and including the Magellanic area and the sub-Antarctic islands.
2. Circum-Antarctic, throughout the Antarctic and the Scotia Arc.
3. Circum-sub-Antarctic, throughout the sub-Antarctic islands and the Magellanic area, and sometimes extending into the Scotia Arc.

The affinities of these faunal components suggest that they originated from (Fig. 11.8):

1. A relict autochthonous fauna.
2. Eurybathic species derived from the adjacent deep-water basins of the South Atlantic, the South Pacific and the South Indian Ocean.
3. Abyssal species often endemic at the generic level.
4. Species of Magellanic origin which have migrated to Antarctica via the Scotia Arc, and subsequently spread to a greater or lesser extent round the continent.

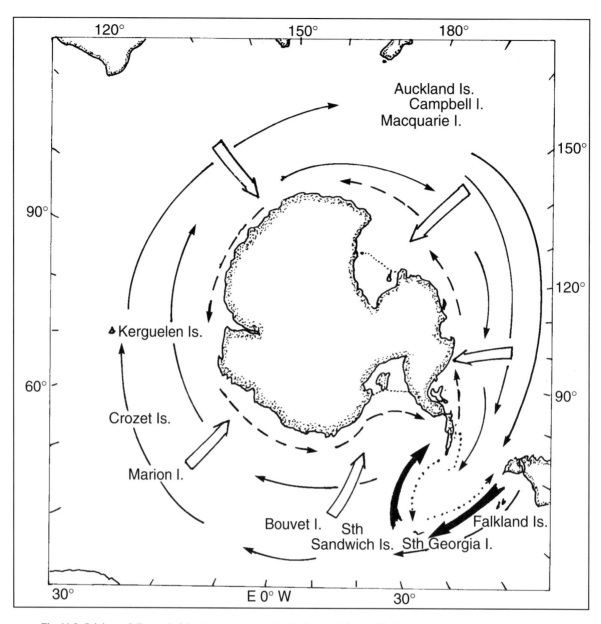

Fig. 11.8. Origins and dispersal of the Antarctic marine benthic fauna: 1. dispersal by the Antarctic Coastal Current (dashed arrows); 2. dispersal by the Antarctic Circumpolar Current (narrow solid arrows); 3. migration of abyssal forms onto the Antarctic shelf (large open arrow); 4. northward migration along the Scotia Arc (thick solid arrow); and, 5. southward migration along the Scotia Arc (dotted arrow). Redrawn for Knox & Lowry (1977).

5. Species of Antarctic origin which have migrated in the opposite direction northwards along the Scotia Arc.
6. Sub-Antarctic species of predominantly northern origin.

Many workers have commented on the distinctiveness of the Antarctic fauna, which is especially notable for the high degree of endemism at the specific level. For the groups listed in Table 11.10, this varies from 57% to as high as 95%. There is, however, much greater variation in endemism at the generic level, varying from as low as 5% to as high as 70%. This presumably is related to the evo-

lutionary history of the groups concerned. The high degree of endemism is indicative of the long isolation of Antarctica from other land areas and their associated shelf and slope regions, and the active speciation that has occurred during this isolation.

11.6 Biogeographical schemes for the Antarctic region.
Ideally, biogeographic syntheses should be based on the analysis of distribution patterns of whole communities of organisms. So far this has not been attempted for the benthic flora and fauna of the Antarctic and sub-Antarctic,

apart from the analysis of the zonation patterns of the littoral zone by Knox (1960). The early work on Antarctic biogeography was carried out by ichthyologists (Regan, 1914; Nybelin, 1947). Andriashev (1965) revised their work and proposed a scheme, based on coastal fishes, which integrated their work with more recent findings.

The results of the polychaete study indicated an old homogeneous fauna with a slow evolutionary rate. Many of the species are widespread, vertically (eurybathic) and laterally (circumpolar). This type of distribution supports the theory of a fauna able to advance and recede from deep to shallow water, as glaciation receded and advanced. At the same time its age, cosmopolitan nature, and slow rate of evolution would allow it to advance laterally around the continent forming the type of fauna which occurs there today. This fauna is characterized by a moderately high endemism at the species level (*c.* 60%), a very low endemism at the generic level (*c.* 5%) and many widespread eurybathic species.

Of the various biogeographical schemes that have been advanced, that of Hedgpeth (1969) with various minor modifications has been most generally accepted (Fig. 11.9). In this scheme the Antarctic Region, covering the whole of the area south of the Antarctic Convergence, is divided into two sub-regions, the Western Antarctic (composed of the Antarctic Peninsula, and the Scotia Arc) and the Continental Antarctic. The Sub-Antarctic region includes the area between the Antarctic Convergence and the Sub-tropical Convergence. New Zealand is not included in the Sub-Antarctic Region, but southern South America is included. Heard Island is included as an extension of Continental Antarctic, and South Georgia District is recognized.

11.7 Diversity, abundance and biomass

11.7.1 Diversity
Lowry (1976) has compared the species diversity of macrobenthic communities at Arthur Harbour, Anvers Island, and Moubry Bay, Cape Hallett and Cape Bird, Ross Island. At Arthur Harbour species richness was not particularly high (69 species only being present). On the other hand, equitability (the proportional distribution of individuals among species in the population) was high reflecting the even distribution of individuals among species. Heterogeneity (a measure of the community diversity relating the number of species and the numerical distribution of individuals among the species) was lowered by the number of species present. Richardson & Hedgpeth (1977) sampled a much wider range of habitats in Arthur Harbour in which the number of species present ranged from 43 to 117 species. Species richness values

were higher than those recorded by Lowry. They compared the values derived for the Arthur Harbour, benthos with similar observations by Boesch (1972) for the North Carolina shelf. The diversity values were similar in both localities but species richness values were much higher and equitability values much lower at Arthur Harbour. At Moubry Bay species richness and heterogeneity values were higher due to the higher number of species in the samples (147), the relatively low number of individuals and the even distribution of individuals among the species. Species diversity statistics for the Cape Bird macrobenthos characterize an extreme suspension-feeding community with low heterogeneity, richness and equitability. The samples contained only 73 species and of these three represented 71% of the total sampled population.

Lowry (1976) compared the diversity of the macrobenthic communities at the localities that he studied in the Antarctic with that of a latitudinal range of studies from tropical, temperate and Arctic habitats, including both shelf and deep-sea communities. Heterogeneity, species richness and species equitability showed no correlation between macrobenthic diversity and latitude in the shallow shelf communities. However, heterogeneity and species richness correlated well with trophic structure, with suspension-feeding communities having the lowest equitability. Mixed suspension–deposit-feeding communities, such as those in Moubry Bay and Port Pegasus, Stewart Island, are more diverse than deposit-feeding communities such as those at Arthur Harbour and Perseverence Harbour, Campbell Island, which in turn are more diverse than the suspension feeding communities, such as those at Cape Bird and the Auckland Islands. Arctic communities are characterized by a low heterogeneity, due probably to insufficient food input.

The deep sea (except for the Arctic) and the Antarctic shelf have similar heterogeneity, tending to support the conclusion of Sanders (1969) that species diversity is enhanced in physically stable environments. They also have a similar percentage composition in the major groups (polychaetes, peracarids, bivalves), but the Antarctic benthos is up to at least 23 times more densely populated.

11.7.2 Abundance
In section 11.4.5 the high densities of some Antarctic benthic infaunal communities were highlighted. These high densities in general occur in shallow shelf areas in depths not exceeding 100 m. The studies in Arthur Harbour by Richardson & Hedgpeth (1977) demonstrated a reduction of about one order of magnitude for sites below 300 m when compared with shallow sites

214   *Benthic communities*

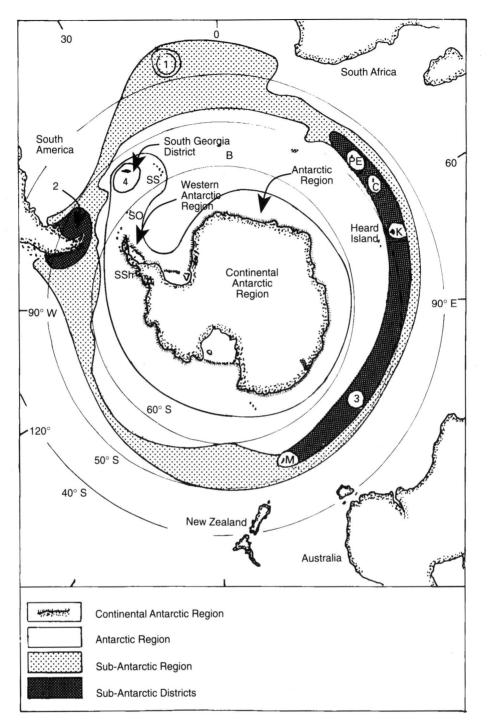

Fig. 11.9. Biogeographical regions for the benthos of the Southern Ocean. Numbered sub-Antarctic districts or sub-regions are: 1. Tristan da Cuhna District; 2.Magellanic Sub-region or Province; 3. Kerguelen Sub-region or Province. Numbered Antarctic District is: 4. South Georgia District. Islands identified by letters are: B. Bouvetoya; C. Crozet; F. Falklands; K. Kerguelen; M. Macquarie; PE. Prince Edward and Marion; SO. South Orkney; SSa. South Sandwich; SSh. South Shetland.

under 75 m. While their maximum recorded density was 86 514 individuals m⁻², Dayton & Oliver (1977) recorded higher densities in eastern McMurdo Sound of up to 155 000 m⁻² (these are among the highest densities recorded anywhere).

It is probable that these high densities are attributable to the high (but seasonal) primary production and to the diverse substrate characteristics (e.g. the sponge spicule mat provides a wide range of microhabitats thus enhancing both density and diversity). As noted in Chapter 3 a high proportion of the summer pulse of phytoplankton production sediments to the bottom to provide energy

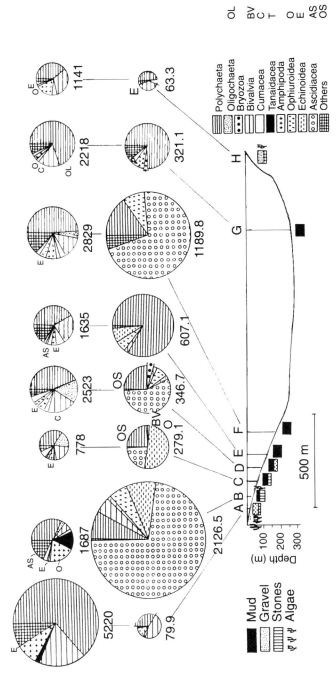

Fig. 11.10 Abundance (no. individuals m^{-2}) (top) and biomass (g m^{-2}) (bottom) estimates for the benthic fauna in a transect across the entrance to Ezcurra Inlet, Admiralty Bay, King George Island. Redrawn from Jazdzewski *et al.* (1986).

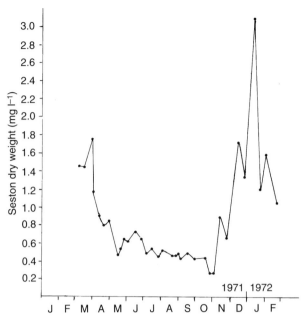

Fig. 11.11. Changes in the quantity (dry weight) of seston throughout the year at a shallow water station off Zykov Island, Halswell Islands. Redrawn from Gruzov (1977).

input to the benthos. In addition, as Dayton *et al.* (1986) have documented for the shallow areas of McMurdo Sound, benthic microalgal standing stocks reach very high levels in the summer months. The stability of the physical environment, along with the slow growth rates and life-cycles attuned to the summer pulse of primary production, tend to lead to the evolution of an efficient stable community structure with low annual turnover rates.

11.7.3 Biomass

While general observations of the shallow-water benthos of the Antarctic gave rise to the view that the Antarctic shelf supported a high biomass of benthic macroinvertebrates, especially sessile epifaunal suspension-feeders, there have been only a few quantitative studies to support this view. However, a number of generalizations can be made on the basis of the reported data. Values for epifaunal biomass are very much greater than those for infaunal biomass, up to 4200 g m^{-2} for the former and up to 700 g m^{-2} for the latter. On hard substrates the epifaunal biomass in shallow depths (1–5 m) is low (20–25 g m^{-2}), but high (450–4200 g m^{-2}) in intermediate depths (8–50 m). Below 200 m there is a rapid decrease in biomass, e.g. off the Sabrina Coast the biomasses at 200, 300, 2000, and 3500 m were 1363, 183–483, 28 and 1.4 g m^{-2} respectively.

The most comprehensive quantitative study of the Antarctic benthic fauna is that of Jazdzweski *et al.* (1986) in Admiralty Bay, King George Island, South Shetland

Islands, in which three transects of 18 stations each were sampled at depths of between 15 and 250 m. Fig. 11.10 depicts one of these transects. The most abundant groups were bivalves, polychaetes and amphipods, whereas the largest part of the biomass was due to ascidians, ophiuroids, echinoids, polychaetes and bivalves. In the transect shown in Fig. 11.10 polychaetes were the dominant group at all stations and usually constituted over 59% of the non-colonial benthic species. Bivalves and amphipods were the second most abundant groups. Oligochaetes were numerous at Stations C (60 m) and D (90 m). Ascidians contributed the largest proportion of the biomass at depths of 30, 90 and 170 m. Polychaetes also made up a considerable proportion of the biomass at all depths except 30 m. At 120 and 150 m, the proportions were 83 and 75% respectively. The total biomasses ranged from 63 to 2127 g m^{-2}.

11.8 Food and feeding

As Arnaud (1974) points out trophic processes in the Antarctic are determined principally by: 1. the seasonal discontinuity of phytoproduction (phytoplankton, ice algae, and benthic microalgae); and 2. the relatively small amounts of terrigenous sedimentation. Three types of diet are considered to be adaptive to these conditions: suspension-feeding, necrophagy, and omnivory, or opportunistic feeding.

Suspension-feeding: The extraordinary development of assemblages of suspension feeders on the Antarctic shelf, as first described by Belyaev & Usachov (1957), has been described above. Such assemblages are dominated by hexactinellid sponges, demosponges, hydroids, gorgonians and bryozoans, and contain a high proportion of polychaetes, actinarians, scleractinian corals, stylasterine corals, brachiopods, and many motile animals, especially holothurians, crinoids, asteroids, crustaceans and pycnogonids. Bottom currents transport an abundance of organic detritus (diatoms, protozoans, faecal pellets, exuvia and the remains of planktonic metazoans), as well as living plankton, larvae and eggs, to the waiting filtration mechanisms of the sessile suspension-feeders. This input of suspended particulate organic matter (seston) is largely limited to the short summer period in which the growth of phytoplankton occurs. Fig. 11.11 shows the changes which occurred in this input in the shallow waters off Zykov Island, Halswell Islands (66° 32′ S, 93° 00′ E). The seston peaked in mid-January, with a secondary peak in March, declined to a low level in May, and remained low until it began to increase again in November.

Necrophagy: Arnaud (1970) was the first to draw attention to the fact that numerous Antarctic invertebrates are potential carrion eaters, or scavengers, and that others adopt this method of feeding seasonally in winter. Arnaud used the term necrophagy for this type of nutrition. In subsequent papers Arnaud (1974, 1977) explored the concept further and more recently Presler (1986) has examined the species composition and seasonal changes in the assemblage of necrophagous invertebrates in Admiralty Bay. As Arnaud (1977) points out scavengers are present in every marine ecosystem, but the numbers are higher in Antarctic benthic communities than elsewhere. Presler (1986) identified 23 species as necrophagous in Admiralty Bay with a further 10 being suspected of necrophagy.

Omnivorous and opportunistic diet: Many Antarctic benthic invertebrates are omnivorous and feed on a wide variety of prey. For example, Dearborn (1967) found that the diet of the giant isopod *Glyptonotus antarcticus* was surprisingly varied: ophiuroids (52.3%), gastropods (19.3%), isopods (17.4%), echinoids (14.7%), ectoprocts (6.4%), but also pycnogonids, sponges, crinoids, brachiopods, algae, amphipods (especially *Orchomene*), and carrion.

11.9 Ecological strategies

Antarctic poikilotherms exhibit a number of features such as slow seasonal growth, delayed maturation, longevity, large size, low fecundity, large egg size, non-pelagic larval development, seasonal reproduction and low metabolic rate, that appears to be associated with a suite of mechanisms by which the organisms respond to cold, highly seasonal environments where primary production is confined to a brief period during the summer. (White, 1984).

11.9.1 Reproduction and development

A salient characteristic of the Antarctic zooplankton is the paucity of pelagic larvae of benthic animals. On the other hand, invertebrate groups which reproduce by brooding, such as the Amphipoda and Isopoda, are well represented in the Antarctic fauna, whereas the benthic crustacean groups which are the dominant components elsewhere, such as the Decapoda and Cirripedia, are poorly represented. White (1977) and Picken (1980) have provided comprehensive reviews of the reproductive adaptations of Antarctic benthic invertebrates.

In marine invertebrates four reproductive patterns are generally recognized (Mileikovsky, 1971), two of which can be called 'free development' and two 'protected development'. Species with free development characteristically discharge large numbers of small eggs into the sea where they develop through intermediate pelagic or non-pelagic stages. There is no free larval stage in species with protected development. A small number of large yolky eggs are produced, and to ensure a high level of survival they are generally protected during development. Maximum protection is obtained when the developing eggs are brooded by the adult, either inside, or outside the parent's body, and by either sex (Arnaud, 1974). The majority of Antarctic species whose reproduction is known have no pelagic larval stage, and there is a strong tendency towards protected development. In sponges more than 80% of the species exhibit brood protection (Arnaud, 1974). Brood protection is the principal adaptation of the lamellibranchs (Soot-Ryen, 1951; Dell, 1965, 1972), and brood protection and viviparity are common among the echinoderms and widespread in the isopods and amphipods (Arnaud, 1974). More than 59% of the Antarctic ophiuroids whose reproduction is known exhibit brood protection, and this is a much higher proportion than is found in other parts of the oceans, including the Arctic (Mortensen, 1936). In the echinoids, two of the three Antarctic families are dominated by species which brood (Arnaud, 1974), while the third family is represented by a single species which produces demersal larvae (Pearse & Giese, 1966). Seventeen species of Antarctic holothurians exhibit brood protection (Arnaud, 1974), while eleven species of crinoids are known to brood in the Antarctic (John, 1938, 1939) compared with only three species known to brood elsewhere. This high incidence of non-pelagic development contrasts with the scarcity of pelagic larvae. Only the larvae of two asteroids, one echinoid, one holothurian and several polychaetes are known from the Antarctic plankton (Mackintosh, 1934; Thorson, 1950).

Several theories have been advanced to explain the tendency towards non-pelagic and protected development among high latitude marine invertebrates. The most satisfactory explanation is that of Thorson (1950) who proposed that in the polar oceans a combination of a short period of phytoplankton production, and low water temperatures, which would slow the rate of development, increase the difficulty of completing pelagic development before food becomes scarce in surface waters. Under such conditions non-pelagic development, either by large yolky eggs, brood protection or viviparity, is an adaptation which ensures the survival of the offspring to the juvenile state. Non-pelagic development by demersal larvae is a similar development, since food will be present on the sea floor long after the phytoplankton bloom is over.

The timing and pattern of reproduction varies. (M. G. White (1977) suggested that the timing of reproduction is largely controlled by the degree to which adults or juve-

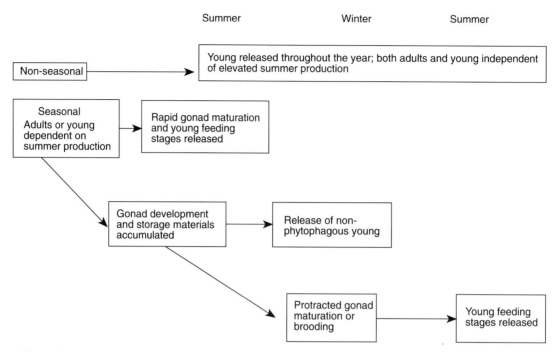

Fig. 11.12. Model of Antarctic benthic invertebrate breeding cycles. Redrawn from M.G. White (1977).

niles are dependent on the summer production. The onset of summer production is predictable in offshore waters, but in shallow inshore waters the presence of sea ice can drastically affect the timing (M. G. White, 1977). Reproductive activities, such as gametogenesis, spawning and liberation of ova may either be synchronized with the annual production cycle or may be independent of it. M. G. White (1977) proposed a model which includes the various breeding cycles found in Antarctic invertebrates (Fig. 11.12).

The various species can be grouped as follows:

Group 1: Species with a non-seasonal breeding cycle where the young stages are released throughout the year, and both adults and young are independent of the elevated summer production level. Most species are predator–scavengers with highly adaptable diets. One example is the giant isopod *Glyptonotus antarcticus* which has prolonged development rates and breeds continuously (Dearborn, 1967; M. G. White, 1975).

Group 2: These are species which have seasonal breeding cycles in which the adults, or young, or both are dependent on the summer pulse of primary production. Cyclic growth rates are typical. Sub-group 2a, which includes many planktonic herbivores, have life-histories which are completed in one year. Sub-group 2b, which included the echinoderms *Odonaster validus* and *Sterechinus neumayeri*, and the polychaete *Scoloplos marginatus mcleani*, have prolonged breeding cycles and protracted gonad development. They accumulate energy

reserves during the summer, in some cases over more than a year, and release young non-phytophagous stages during the winter. Sub-group 2c species have similar prolonged life-cycles and protracted gonad development, and the young may be brooded, with young feeding stages being released during the subsequent summer season. Typical species are amphipods such as *Cherimedon femoratus*, *Bovallia gigantea*, and *Paramoera walkeri*.

11.9.2 Growth

While it is generally accepted that polar marine invertebrates grow slowly Antarctic invertebrates show a wide range of growth rates (M. G. White, 1975; Everson, 1977a; A. Clarke, 1980b). Everson (1977a) found that three species of bivalves (*Laternula elliptica*, *Adamussium colbecki*, and *Gaimardia trapesina*) had faster, and three species (*Yoldia eightsi*, *Kidderia bicolor*, and *Lassarca miliaris*) slower growth rates than the temperate species *Venus striatula*. However, when species with similar maximum size and ecology are compared (Ralph & Maxwell, 1977a,b,c) the polar species have been found to grow more slowly than their temperate counterparts. Similar relationships have been demonstrated for fish (Everson, 1977a; Arnaud, 1977), echinoderms (Pearse, 1965), and crustaceans (Luxmore, 1982). Associated with this slow growth rate is a slowing of embryonic development, with a prolonged period of larval development, e.g. the brooding incubation period for Antarctic crustacea is five to eight months, compared

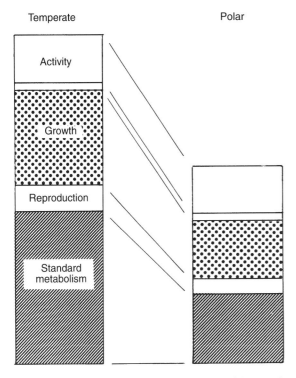

Fig. 11.13. A diagrammatic representation of the annual energy intake of a typical temperate-water marine invertebrate, and a typical polar marine invertebrate showing the effect of adaptation to cold water as proposed by A. Clarke (1980b). The relative sizes of the boxes representing the metabolism, reproduction, growth and moulting (unlabelled) in the polar rectangle are based on data for the Antarctic isopod *Serolis polita* (Luxmore 1982). The sizes of these boxes in the temperate-water species have been obtained from the literature for temperate-water species. The size of the box representing activity is arbitrary, and is the same for both temperate and polar species. Redrawn from A. Clarke (1985).

with temperate species, which generally have periods of eight days to two months (Bregazzi, 1972; M. G. White, 1984).

A. Clarke (1980b) concluded that low environmental temperatures were no bar to fast absolute growth but, nevertheless, polar species grew more slowly than the related species of similar ecology and potential maximum size from warmer waters. He noted, as others have done, that growth was often markedly seasonal, and since temperatures fluctuate very little at high latitudes, concluded that food was a major regulating factor.

11.9.3 Large size

'Gigantism' is frequently mentioned as a characteristic of Antarctic benthic invertebrates and it has been noted in pycnogonids, sponges, isopods, amphipods and free-living nematodes (Arnaud, 1974, 1977; De Broyer, 1977). It is postulated that slow growth, delayed maturation, prolonged gametogenesis and embryonic development result in enhanced longevity and large size in Antarctic invertebrates. Arnaud (1974) tested this hypothesis in

various groups of Antarctic invertebrates and concluded that while the phenomenon was real in some groups, it was lacking in others which were of 'normal' size, or showed a tendency towards 'dwarfism'. He found that the only Antarctic invertebrates which reached a large size were those which were not hampered by calcium problems, that is invertebrates requiring only small amounts of calcium (arenaceous foraminiferans, crustaceans and tubiculous polychaetes), or no calcium (hydroids, nudibranchs, ascidians, and many polychaetes). According to Arnaud (1977) species which are not limited by this factor reach a large size as a consequence of three favourable factors: 1. slow rates of development and growth; 2. low predation pressure on certain species; and 3. high availability of silica to siliceous organisms (e.g. radiolarians and hexactinellid sponges). When predation and interspecific competition is weak, organisms grow to an old age and large size. For example, the asteroid *Odonaster validus* may live for more than 100 years according to Pearse (1969), and the large rosellid hexactinellid sponges in McMurdo Sound may live much longer than this.

11.9.4 Metabolic adaptations

The concept of metabolic cold adaptation (i.e. that polar poikilotherms are characterized by an elevated metabolic rate) has already been discussed with reference to Antarctic fishes (see section 7.3). Experiments on amphipods by Armitage (1962) and Rakusa-Suszczewski & Klekowski (1973), on euphausiids by McWhinnie (1964) and on isopods by George (1979) seemed to support the idea of cold adaptation in Antarctic invertebrates. The concept of cold adaptation was attractive because it conveniently explained the frequently observed phenomena of slow growth, delayed maturation and prolonged gametogenesis. However, this concept has been challenged in the light of a growing body of biochemical and physiological data. Well-controlled experiments on polar marine invertebrates (M. G. White, 1975; Maxwell, 1977; Ralph & Maxwell, 1977b,c; Maxwell & Ralph 1985) have demonstrated low, not elevated, metabolic rates at ambient temperatures. Everson (1977a) concluded that in Antarctic invertebrates there is no detectable elevation of routine, and by inference basal, metabolic rate. Thus, the concept that an elevated basal metabolic rate in cold water invertebrates resulting in less energy being available for growth and reproduction cannot explain the slow growth rates which have been observed.

A. Clarke (1980b) in a reappraisal of the concept of cold adaptation in polar marine invertebrates on the basis of a reduced basal metabolism, reduced growth, reduced reproductive effort, and on the assumption that the energetic costs of feeding, movement and other activities are comparable between different environments, advanced the view that polar adaptations tend towards an overall reduction in energy utilization (Fig. 11.13). In comparing crustacean species living at temperate (10 °C) and polar (0 °C) environmental temperatures it was found that the basal metabolism of polar species was reduced by 55%, growth by 40%, and reproductive effort by 30% in comparison with temperate species (A. Clarke, 1979; A. Clarke & Lakhani, 1979).

A. Clarke (1980b) points out that many of the features of the Antarctic marine benthos can be interpreted as the result of the evolution of typical *K*-adapted qualities, that is slow growth, protracted development, reduced effort, low basal metabolic rate, large yolky eggs, advanced newly-hatched juvenile stages, seasonal breeding, deferred maturity, increased longevity and large size. These qualities act together so as to adapt the species to cold temperatures and seasonal availability of primary production. Those organisms which have been selected for reduced annual energy intake will have been the most successful in colonizing the Antarctic benthos.

12

The fast ice and ice shelves

12.1 Introduction

Round the margin of the Antarctic Continent lies the fast ice region. This is sea ice that either breaks out very late in the season or remains for two or more years forming multi-year ice which may reach a thickness of several metres. It lies within the coastal area of the permanent pack ice zone as defined in Chapter 15. In addition there are the floating ice shelves formed by glacial ice outflowing from the ice-covered Antarctic Continent. While such ice shelves extend to varying degrees at locations right round the continent the most extensive are the Ross Ice Shelf in the Ross Sea and the Filchner and Ronne Ice Shelves in the Weddell Sea.

12.2 The coastal fast ice environment

12.2.1 Sea ice

The formation of the sea ice and its characteristics have already been discussed in Chapter 3. There it was noted that there are two main types of sea ice, *columnar* or *congelation* ice and *frazil* ice. The proportions of columnar and frazil ice can vary widely, although the former dominates the sea ice of the fast ice zone. However, in the inner Weddell Sea ice core data indicate that congelation ice accounts for only about 20% of the multi-year ice and 47% of the first-year ice, with fine grained layers of frazil crystals making up most of the remainder.

12.2.2 Anchor ice and platelet ice

Anchor ice and platelet ice have been discussed in section 3.2.1. Where they are especially well developed (e.g. in inner McMurdo Sound and under the McMurdo Ice Shelf, Knox, 1986; Barry, 1988) they occur where the seawater becomes supercooled (temperatures below the *in situ* freezing point). Nucleation leading to frazil or platelet ice formation can occur when deep water cooled below freezing point is upwelled. In McMurdo Sound such conditions occur where water cooled by contact with the bottom of the shelf flows northward from underneath the McMurdo Ice Shelf (Barry & Dayton, 1988) (Fig. 12.1). Ice platelets can range from 10–20 cm in diameter and

0.2–0.2 cm in thickness. Dayton *et al.* (1969) have observed aggregations of platelets frozen to each other on the bottom in depths shallower than 33 m.

There is considerable variation throughout the McMurdo Sound region in the development of the platelet ice layer beneath the fast sea ice. In the early 1980s in the middle of McMurdo Sound near the edge of the McMurdo Ice Shelf the layer formed by small platelets was only 10–20 cm thick, while at White Island the layer of larger platelets was up to 5 m in thickness (personal observations). In some areas the tide cracks which develop along the margin of the land are filled with platelet ice to a considerable depth. There is also considerable variation in the occurrence of platelet ice round the Antarctic Continent. In many areas it has not been reported. However, the winter expedition of the *Polarstern* found extensive areas of platelet ice under the pack ice in the southern Weddell Sea (see section 12.3).

Dayton *et al.* (1969) consider that the anchor ice has considerable biological significance. When the anchor ice becomes detached due to currents, inherent buoyancy or a disturbance, it floats to the underside of the sub-ice platelet layer carrying with it portions of the substratum, which in one instance was observed to weigh at least 12 kg. Epibenthic organisms such as asteroids, nemerteans, isopods, pycogonids, fishes and algae entrapped within the anchor ice can thus be transported to the underside of the ice. This may act as an important distribution mechanism (Knox & Lowry, 1977) when the sea ice breaks up to form pack ice which may drift a considerable distance before melting.

12.2.3 Thermohaline characteristics

The most extensively studied fast ice area is that investigated by Japanese scientists off Syowa Station (Hoshiai, 1969, 1977, 1981a,b, 1985; Fukuchi & Tanimura, 1981; Fukuchi *et al.*, 1984, 1985a,b; Wakatsuchi, 1982; Fukui *et al.*, 1986; Hoshiai *et al.*, 1987). Fukuchi *et al.* (1985a) reported on data from five oceanographic stations in Lutzow–Holm Bay (1–5) in depths of 10, 25, 50, 160 and

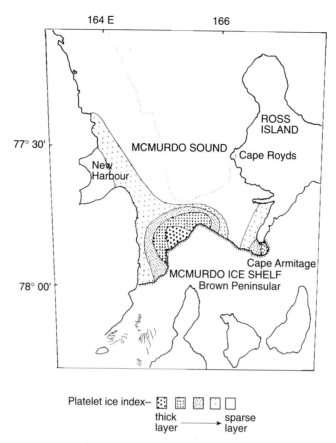

Fig. 12.1. Platelet ice abundance index distribution during November 1984 in McMurdo Sound. Heavier dot pattern indicates greater platelet ice thickness indicative of cold water outflow from under the McMurdo Ice Shelf. Redrawn from Barry (1988).

675 m respectively. Temperatures varied from a maximum of −1.19 °C to a minimum of −1.89 °C while salinities varied from a maximum of 34.425‰ to a minimum of 33.525‰ . Littlepage (1965) occupied a station on the fast ice over 290 m of water in McMurdo Sound during 1961. Values of temperature and salinity ranged from −1.4 to −2.5 °C and 33.96 ‰ to 34.99‰. This temperature range was about 0.3° lower than those recorded in Lutzow–Holm Bay, while the salinity range was about 0.5‰ higher. In contrast to the distinct seasonal variation observed for physical properties the levels of nutrient salts did not show clear seasonal trends. Phosphate-P, silicate-Si, and nitrite-N remained high throughout the studies in Lutzow–Holm Bay while levels of ammonium-N and nitrate-N generally were low.

In McMurdo Sound, Barry (1988) has made an extensive study of the hydrographic patterns under the fast ice (Fig. 12.2). During spring water temperature was nearly homogenous apart from some surface variations and very cold water near the bottom in the central Sound. Temperatures below freezing point were observed at several sites, particularly where currents flowed northward from under the McMurdo Ice Shelf (see Fig. 12.1), indicative of cooling by contact with the bottom of the shelf. Although summer temperatures near the bottom were near spring values (−1.9 °C), the upper 100 m became highly stratified with relatively warm water near surface temperatures (−0.8 to −1.3 °C), and a few values above zero in some isolated localities (Fig. 12.2b).

In spring the highest salinities were in the northern and eastern Sound (34.86–34.89‰). Western Sound waters were slightly less saline (34.73–34.77‰) due to dilution by meltwater input from beneath the shelf and/or glacial meltwater from the Koettlitz Glacier region. Salinity was strongly heterogeneous during the summer with a substantial halocline near the surface. In addition to dilution from sea ice meltwater, terrestrial and especially McMurdo Ice Shelf surface meltwater diluted the surface waters, especially in the western Sound. During late January 1984 a 6 m surface layer of freshwater (0.2–0.9‰) was present at an isolated station in the western Sound under permanent ice.

A number of studies of the fast ice environment have recorded the presence of a low-salinity surface layer beneath the ice in late summer due to the melting of the ice (Hoshiai, 1969; Watanabe et al., 1982; Iwanami et al., 1986; Matsuda et al., 1990). Often this layer is less than a metre thick and it may be concentrated in hollows on the

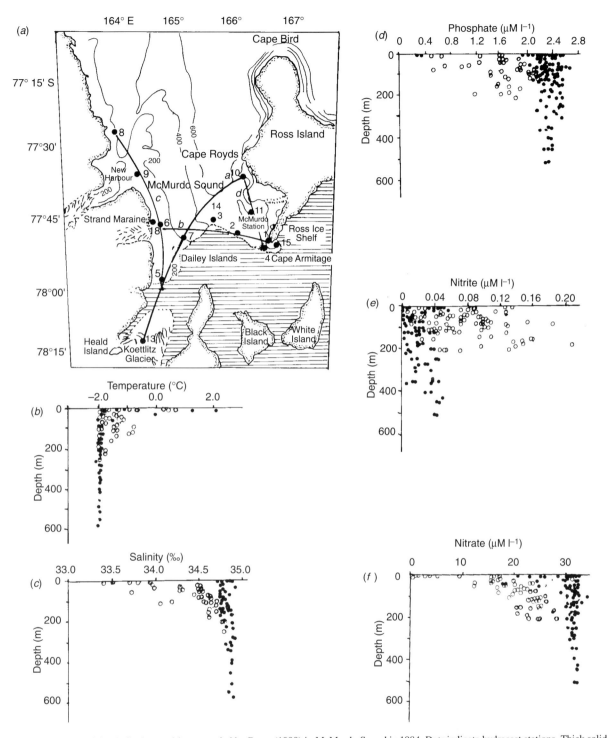

Fig. 12.2. (*a*). Station positions sampled by Barry (1988) in McMurdo Sound in 1984. Dots indicate hydrocast stations. Thick solid lines indicate transect lines. Dashed line indicates the approximate position of the sea ice edge during November. (*b*)–(*f*) spring (closed circles), and summer (open circles) values for (*b*) temperature, (*c*) salinity, (*d*) phosphate, (*e*) nitrite, and (*f*) nitrate. Redrawn from Barry (1988).

underside of ridges in the ice and consequently may be missed in sampling through hole in the ice.

On the third winter cruise of the *Polarstern* a survey of the hydrographic conditions under the sea ice was carried out in November 1987 (Eicken *et al.*, 1987). At that time most profiles showed a slight decrease in salinity close to

the surface indicating that some melting had taken place (see Fig. 12.8). At Station 587 a temperature drop of 0.06 °C occurred within 40 to 50 cm below the ice. At Station 620 there was a layer of platelets some 60 cm thick below the solid ice. Within this platelet layer there was only a slight decrease in salinity (0.2‰). Nutrient levels in the upper low salinity layer were much reduced with both nitrate and phosphate levels at the water surface under the ice near the limit of detection.

12.2.4 Nutrients

There have been a limited number of studies of nutrient distributions in the waters of the fast ice zone. In the spring the McMurdo Sound nutrient (NO_3, NO_2, PO_4) distributions reflected the post-winter pattern before the onset of the seasonal summer phytoplankton bloom (Barry, 1988) (Fig. 12.2 *d–f*). There were relatively homogeneous and high nutrient levels throughout the Sound as a consequence of low productivity and winter replenishment by regeneration and mixing. Nitrate (30 μM) and phosphate (2.3 μM) concentrations were high while nitrite was usually low (<0.01 μM). On the other hand, in contrast to results obtained at Syowa Station nutrients (NO_2, PO_4) were low following the seasonal phytoplankton bloom and were near zero at isolated localities. Depletion was greatest near the surface where the water column stability was high. Nitrate levels were about 15% of the pre-bloom levels under the sea ice near McMurdo Station (3.9–5.4 μM) and were lower (0.1–1.6 μM) in the western Sound. In contrast nitrite concentrations were highest during the summer. Nutrient depression was probably due to a combination of phytoplankton utilization and dilution from low nutrient levels in glacial and sea ice meltwater.

12.2.5 Currents

Inshore current systems have been extensively studied in inner McMurdo Sound. Mean currents in McMurdo Sound are the result of the additive effects of various driving forces including local and large scale wind driven circulation, tidal rectification, and pressure gradient forces arising from variations in density. Barry & Dayton (1988) contrast their 1984 results with those of Lewis & Perkin (1985) in 1982 when northerly input from beneath the shelf dominated the southern Sound. They speculate that the differences were due to changes in the driving force of the Antarctic Coastal Current which flows west along the Ross Ice Shelf barrier and contributes strongly to net transport into McMurdo Sound through the southern extension (Cape Bird Current) sweeping into McMurdo Sound. It is probable that global atmospheric anomalies such as ENSO (El Niño Southern Oscillation) is linked to these differences, as they have been linked by numerous authors to global scale variability in atmospheric pressure and associated zonal winds (Rogers & VanLoon, 1979).

12.2.6 The light regime

The light regime under the sea ice has been discussed in Chapter 3. Since the fast ice environment is located round the margins of the Antarctic continent at high latitudes the incident light regime has a very strong seasonal component, with a varying period of complete darkness depending on the latitude. Light penetration into the water column as discussed in section 3.3.4.2 is determined by ice thickness, snow cover and the degree of shading by the sea ice microalgal community. The most important variable, however, is the depth of the snow cover on the ice (Satoh *et al.*, 1986; Grossi *et al.*, 1987).

12.3 Primary production

In this section we will be concerned primarily with water column phytoplankton production. Sea ice microalgal and benthic microalgal production are considered in Chapters 3 and 11 respectively. An ecosystem model for the fast ice zone will be considered in Chapter 15.

Because of the thick layer of ice, which is often covered with snow drifts of varying thickness, light penetration in the water column is very low in the coastal fast ice region. Littlepage (1965) reported that up to 0.5% of the incident light on the surface of the snow reached the surface of the water. However, with the development of the ice algal community the amount of light is further reduced. Fig 12.3 illustrates this with data from McMurdo Sound. Total photosynthetically available radiation (PAR) was reduced to 10% of the surface downwelling irradiance in passage through the ice, and to less than 1% under the platelet ice layer. Absorption of light by the ice algae also affected the spectral composition of the light by strong absorption at 670 nm and between 400–500 nm (Sullivan *et al.*, 1984). In September–October the light penetration was between 4 and 6%, while in early November as the ice algal community developed, the light transmission declined, to some hundreds of one per cent. As the ice algal layer disintegrated in late December–January the light penetration increased to one per cent.

Bunt (1964a,b) was the first to investigate in detail the water column phytoplankton under the fast ice. He recognized at least three distinct communities of algae in the waters of McMurdo Sound. The first appeared to be composed entirely of a limited range of planktonic diatoms, with *Nitzschia serrata* as the numerically dominant species. In 1961 this community was evident in early December until it was overwhelmed suddenly by a second assemblage composed of diatoms and high concentrations of *Phaeocystis*. In the following summer, when the fast ice was thicker and more extensive, *Phaeocystis* did not make its appearance until the first week in January. The *Phaeocystis* bloom, which may persist for several weeks (personal observations at Cape Bird and in inner McMurdo Sound over several seasons), is replaced

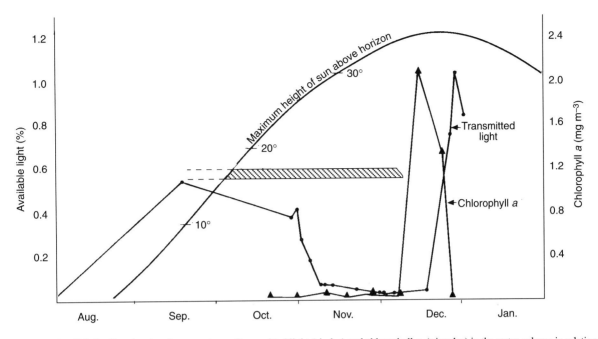

Fig. 12.3. Profiles showing the percentage of transmitted light (circles) and chlorophyll *a* (triangles) in the water column in relation to the maximum height of the sun above the horizon, the presence of sea ice (Aug. to Nov.–early Dec.) and the development of the sea ice microalgae (shaded area). Adapted from Bunt (1964a).

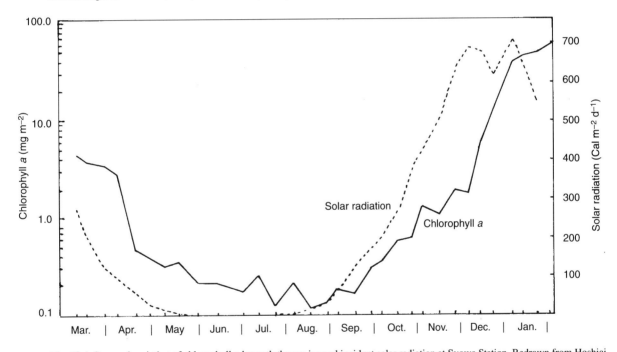

Fig. 12.4. Seasonal variation of chlorophyll *a* beneath the sea ice and incident solar radiation at Syowa Station. Redrawn from Hoshiai (1969).

by a diverse assemblage of species typical of more northern Antarctic waters such as *Thalassiosira antarctica* and *Synedra pelagica*.

At Mawson Station in late December Bunt (1960) recorded a maximum surface chlorophyll *a* concentration of 3.9 mg m^{-3} at 5 m, with a value of 152 mg m^{-2} (0–100 m). At a deeper station on 28 January the maximum chlorophyll *a* concentration of 2.15 mg m^{-3} at a depth of 75 m was recorded, with an integrated stock (0–100 m) of

152 mg m^{-2}. Off Cape Armitage in inner McMurdo Sound Bunt (1964a,b) studied the standing crop of phytoplankton beneath the fast ice. The peak chlorophyll *a* level recorded in early January at 5 m was 16 mg m^{-3}. On 13 December 1962, water from 5 m contained approximately 0.01×10^6 diatom cells l^{-1}. By 16 January 1963, this value had increased 36 times to 0.36×10^6 cells l^{-1}. Between 2 January 1983, when *Phaeocystis* first appeared, and 6 January, the numbers of this species rose

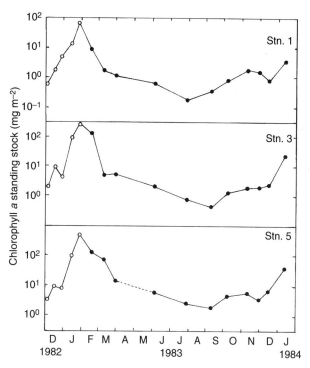

Fig. 12.5. Seasonal variation of integrated chlorophyll *a* stocks from the water column under the sea ice at three stations (Station 1, 12 m; Station 3, 38 m; Station 5, 700+ m) off Syowa Station. Station 1, was sampled from 2 to 11 m; Station 3 from 2.5 to 35 m; and Station 5 from 2.5 to 150 m. Redrawn from Satoh *et al.* (1986).

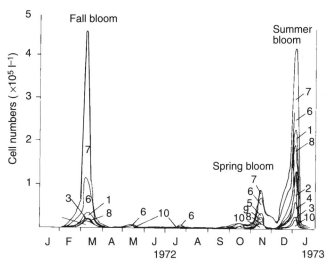

Fig. 12.6. Phytoplankton species composition and cell concentrations at a depth of 6.1 m in Arthur Harbour, Anvers Island. 1. *Chaetoceros* spp., 2. *Charcotia actinochilus*, 3. *Corethron criophylum*, 4. *Euchampia antarctica*, 5. *Navicula glaciei*, 6. *Nitzschia* spp., 7. *Porosira glacialis*, 8. *Rhizosolenia* spp., 9. *Thalassiosira* spp., and 10. Others. Redrawn from Krebs (1983).

sharply to more than 10^6 l^{-1} cells (the numbers refer to individual unicells and not to colonies) and reached a peak of almost 3×10^6 l^{-1} in a sample from 20 m on January. Fig. 12.4 shows that at Syowa Station in the summer of 1967–68 chlorophyll *a* levels closely followed the solar curve with low levels (<1.0 mg m^{-2}) over the winter months and a peak (over 70 mg m^{-2}) in late December to January (Hoshiai, 1969a). Surface chlorophyll *a* increased in early December to reach a peak on 22 December of 6.13 mg chl *a* m^{-3} after which the levels declined to a low of 0.42 on 20 January. A second peak of 2.64 mg chl *a* m^{-3} occurred on 1 April. Chlorophyll *a* levels in deeper water increased later with single peaks of 4.8 mg chl *a* m^{-3} on 4 January at 2 m, 7.62 mg m^{-3} on 11 January at 4 m, 11.93 mg m^{-3} on 29 January at 6 m and 10.99 mg m^{-3} on 29 January at 8 m.

Fukuchi *et al.* (1984, 1985a) measured chlorophyll *a* concentrations in the water column under the fast ice at Syowa Station at five stations (10–675 m depths) for a period of 13 months from January 1982 to January 1983. High chlorophyll *a* concentrations were recorded between December and March with peak values in late January: Station 1 (10 m) 7.01 mg m^{-3} at 6 m; Station 2 (25 m) 9.74 mg m^{-3} at 5 m; Station 3 (50 m) 11.3 mg m^{-3} at 5 m; Station 4 (160 m) 9.91 mg m^{-3} at 0 m. The maximum concentration recorded was 11.3 mg chl *a* m^{-3}. The

peak levels were apparently caused by a slight decrease in the water temperature (> –1.73 °C) and a slight decrease in salinity (< 34.5‰). The average chlorophyll stock in the water column was 1.05–25 mg chl *a* m^{-3}, at least an order of magnitude higher than those reported from Antarctic open waters, such as 0.39 mg m^{-3} by El-Sayed & Jitts (1973), 0.22 mg m^{-3} by Holm-Hansen *et al.* (1977) and 0.52 mg m^{-3} by Kundo & Fukuchi (1982).

Satoh *et al.* (1986) repeated Fukuchi *et al's* (1984) observations over the period February 1983 to January 1984. Fig. 12.5 depicts the seasonal variation in integrated chlorophyll *a* stocks over this period at Stations 1, 3 and 5. At all three stations there was a clear single annual peak of phytoplankton biomass over the period mid-January to mid-February. These peak biomass levels, however, were less than half of those occurring in 1983. Satoh *et al.* (1986) attributed this difference to less light penetrating into the water column due to the increased snow cover on the sea ice. This single phytoplankton bloom, which is characteristic of high latitude fast ice locations contrasts to the three blooms (autumn, spring and summer) that occurred during the period November 1972 to March 1973 in Arthur Harbour (64° 46′ S, 64° 06′ W) on Anvers Island (Krebs, 1983) (Fig. 12.6). While there are differences in the species composition of the three blooms, the two dominant species *Porosira glacialis* and *Nitzschia* spp. were the same. The differences between the two locations can be attributed to the fact that the Arthur Harbour waters are ice-free from spring to autumn and to the longer daylight hours.

Table 12.1. *Daily production by bacterioplankton and phytoplankton in McMurdo Sound*[1]

Date	Production (mg C m^{-2} day^{-1})		Ratio of phyto.:bact. production
	Bacterial	Phytoplankton	
Early Sep.	30–40	1.2–1.5	0.033–0.045
Mid-Sep.	40–60	1.6–1.5	0.030–0.045
Mid-Oct.	70–90	2.3–2.8	0.028–0.035
Mid-Nov.	0.9–2.4	5.0–120	50–125
	0.4[4]		
Early Dec.	2.6–18.7	200–500	30–75
Mid-Dec.	2.5[4]	250–800	90–190
	1.3–8.9[3]		
Late Dec.	11[2]	1000–1500	50–90
	13–83[2]		
Early Jan.	10[4]	2000–2500	10–20
	23–240[3]		

[1]Rivkin (1991); [2]Bunt (1964b); [3]Fuhrman & Azam (1980); [4]Kottmeier *et al.* (1987).
After Rivkin (1991).

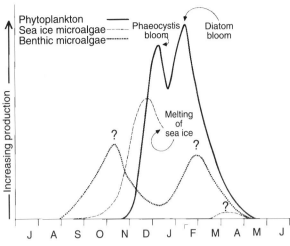

Fig. 12.7. The seasonal cycle of microalgal production in inner McMurdo Sound. Redrawn from Knox (1990).

Fig. 12.7 illustrates an attempt to depict the annual microalgal production in inner McMurdo Sound (Knox, 1990). The phytoplankton cycle is now well established with diatoms dominating early in the season (mid-November to mid-December), followed by the *Phaeocystis* bloom from mid-December to early January, and the subsequent diatom bloom in late January–February. The sea ice microalgal production commences in spring, reaching a peak in mid-December and from mid-January the production is released into the water column with the melting of the sea ice. There may be a further smaller sea ice microalgal production in the autumn after the sea ice has reformed. The production curve for the benthic microalgae is somewhat speculative. It is hypothesized that a spring peak of production occurs in early November before the growth of the sea ice microalgae reduces the light available to the algae. A second peak is hypothesized after the breakout and melting of the sea ice in February–March.

In his study of the patterns of phytoplankton production in McMurdo Sound over the months of September to January Rivkin (1991) found that the biomass, size distribution and production of the phytoplankton and bacterioplankton undergo distinct seasonal cycles (Table 12.1). As detailed by Knox (1990, see above) the peak phytoplankton biomass in mid- to late-December was largely due to the advection of phytoplankton from the Ross Sea. The size distribution of the phytoplankton was highly seasonal; nano- and picophytoplankton were dominant from August through November, while net phytoplankton were more abundant in December and January.

During September and mid-October bacterioplankton production was up to 35 times greater than concurrent autochthonous phytoplankton production. However, by mid-November autochthonous phytoplankton production was *c.* 10 to 200 times greater than the bacterioplankton production. The late austral winter and spring situation contrasts with most temperate and tropical environments where bacteria typically 'bloom' with or after the phytoplankton bloom. It is therefore clear that the bacterioplankton in McMurdo Sound were utilizing organic material from sources other than autochthonous phytoplankton production. As detailed by Knox (1990) there is considerable input of phytoplankton and organic matter into McMurdo Sound from the Ross Sea during the late spring and early summer. Only a small proportion of the phytoplankton is consumed, and the rest sinks to the bottom where that which is not immediately consumed by the benthic herbivores is decomposed, releasing DOM back into the water column where it would be utilized by the bacteria, thus supporting the late austral winter and early spring bacterioplankton production.

In October–November 1987 during the third winter cruise of the *Polarstern* brown discolouration of the water immediately below the pack ice was observed over an extensive area south of 70° S in the Weddell Sea. Examination of the water revealed that the brown colour was due to a dense diatom crop dominated by the genus *Thalassiosira* which is an important constituent of Antarctic spring phytoplankton blooms. It was found that the brown water was invariably associated with masses of platelets of 1–20 cm diameter and 0.1 cm thick. The *Thalassiosira* populations were suspended in the interstitial water between the platelets. Brown water was also encountered under ice in the absence of a layer of loose

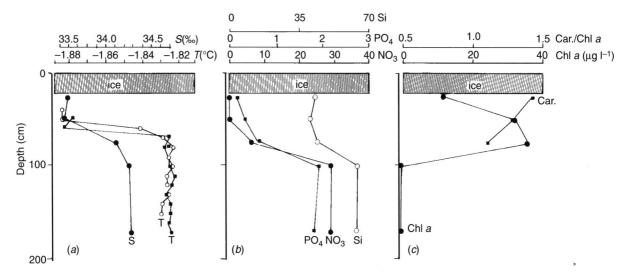

Fig. 12.8. Profiles recorded from the under ice water layer from Station 587 (76° 06′ S, 28° 27′ W) on 12 November 1986 in the Weddell Sea. (*a*) Temperature (*T*) and salinity (*S*). (*b*) Nutrient concentrations: Notice that nitrate had been reduced to the limit of detection in the uppermost water layer. (*c*) Chlorophyll *a* (μg l⁻¹) depth distribution and carotenoid/chlorophyll (Car./chl. *a*) ratios. Redrawn from Eiken *et al.* (1987).

platelets. In such cases the brown water was maintained in position by what appeared to be a layer of loosely intermeshed ice crystals. The strong gradients shown in Fig. 12.8 confirm the presence of a stabilized layer about 50 m thick beneath the ice layer. The relationship between the chlorophyll gradient and low nutrient levels in this upper layer bears a striking resemblance to the situation observed in the open ocean in a 'normal' water column during a declining diatom bloom: following nutrient depletion in the upper layer, in particular nitrogen depletion, the diatom population sinks out and the highest chlorophyll concentrations linger for some time at the pycnocline. Diatom populations suffering nitrogen depletion have a higher carbon to chlorophyll ratio than rapidly growing populations, and the carotinid:chlorophyll ratio rises accordingly as can be seen in Fig. 12.8.

Bunt (1964a) has studied primary production in the water column under the fast ice in McMurdo Sound, both by laboratory incubation of samples taken on the eastern and western sides of the sound and by *in situ* measurements under the ice off Cape Armitage. In early December the values for the eastern McMurdo Sound samples lay between 0.3 and 0.4 mg C m⁻³ h⁻¹. With the appearance of increasing concentrations of microalgae, this figure rose sharply to a maximum mean of 1.78 mg C m⁻³ h⁻¹ on 22 December 1961 and then began to decline. On the western side of the sound lower values were recorded and the peak was later in occurrence. Rates of carbon fixation varied between 0.010 and 0.056 mg C m⁻³ h⁻¹ and represented only 1.6 to 6.8% of the values recorded in parallel samples incubated in the laboratory.

This illustrates the effect of the ice cover in reducing light penetration to the water column below.

12.4 Sedimentation and resuspension

There have been a limited number of studies of sedimentation of particulate organic matter in the water column under the fast ice. Fukuchi *et al.* (1988) deployed a sequential, multiple-sampling sediment trap, set at depths of 5, 57 and 120 m respectively in Breid Bay off Syowa Station (70° 11.54′ S, 24° 18.68′ E) over the period 28 December 1985 to 13 February 1986. Over this period the approximate chlorophyll concentrations (5 to 6 mg m⁻³) and standing stocks (300 to 400 mg m⁻², 0–200 m) were high. Other recent studies in Breid Bay (Fukuda *et al.*, 1985; Taniguchi *et al.*, 1986; Ohno *et al.*, 1987) have found that the summer phytoplankton bloom differs greatly in timing and magnitude from summer to summer. In the summer of 1985 to 1986 the bloom had already started on 28 December 1985 and had not yet terminated when the deployment terminated in mid-February 1986. Fig. 12.9 is a schematic representation of the bloom and sedimentation process. Results from the moored chlorophyll buoy and sampling in its vicinity indicated a patchy phytoplankton distribution and advective water movements. A single diatom species, the widespread *Thalassiosira antarctica*, dominated the sediment trap samples. The similarity in pigment flux and cell volume flux (Fig.12.9*c*) suggests that the pigment flux was largely due to the sinking of cells of this species. Fukuchi *et al.* (1988) estimated sinking rates for *T. antarctica* of 6.5 to 19.4 m day⁻¹. Evidence from this study and those in other localities (e.g. v. Bodungen *et al.*, 1986 in

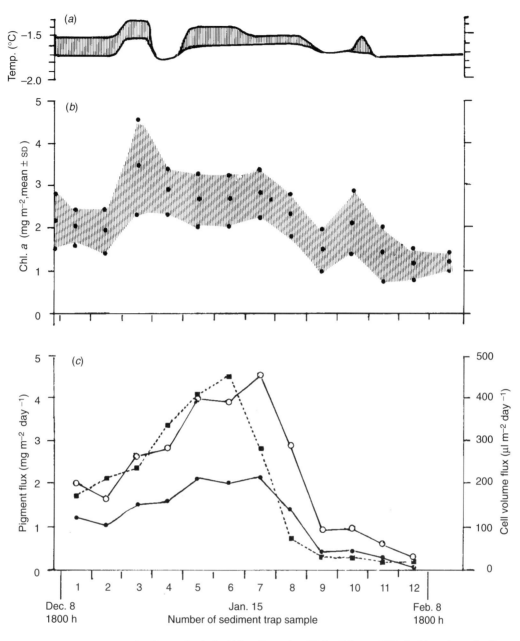

Fig. 12.9. The bloom process and sedimentation in Breid Bay, December 1985 to February 1986. Serial numbers of sediment trap samples (1 to 12) correspond to 3.5 day intervals. Temperature (*a*), and chlorophyll *a* ; (*b*) at 52 m depth; (*c*) pigment (chl *a* + phaeo. ○—○; chl *a* ●—●) and cell volume flux (■---■) at 120 m. Redrawn from Fukuchi *et al.* (1988).

Bransfield Strait) suggests that this species is not subject to heavy grazing pressure and that it may form a more important source of food for benthic than for planktonic animals.

Matsuda *et al.* (1987) studied the seasonal variation in downward flux of particulate matter under the fast ice in Kita-no-ura Cove (69° 00′ S, 39° 35′ E) in Lutzow–Holm Bay. A marked seasonal variation in the particulate organic carbon (POC) flux was observed (Fig. 12.10), with larger fluxes in the summer (max.: 136 mg C m^{-2} day^{-1}) and smaller ones in the winter (min.: 1.5 mg C m^{-2}

day^{-1}). Chlorophyll *a* flux varied much more than that of POC (max.: 4500 μg m^{-2} day^{-1} in the summer, min.: 3 μg m^{-2} day^{-1}) suggesting direct input of sea ice microalgae and/or phytoplankton to the benthic community in the summer.

A complicating factor in the flux of particulate organic matter to the sediments is sediment resuspension. Such resuspension has been studied by Berkman *et al.* (1986) during the period March to July 1981 in McMurdo Sound. The sedimentation pattern during this period is shown in Fig. 12.11*a*. Throughout the period there was suspended

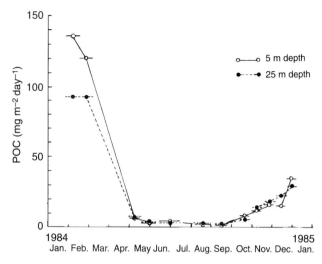

Fig. 12.10. Seasonal variation of particulate organic carbon (POC) under the fast ice in Lutzow–Holm Bay. Redrawn from Matsuda *et al.* (1987).

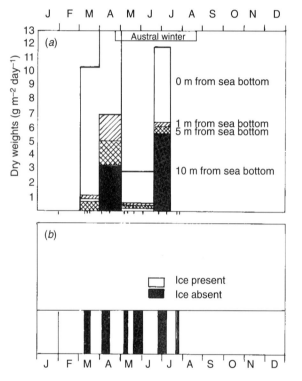

Fig. 12.11. (*a*) Dry weights of suspended matter collected in cones placed at 0, 1, 5 and 10 m from the sea bottom in inner McMurdo Sound during the austral winter. (*b*) The periods when sediment resuspension was influenced by wind-generated waves (ice absent), or by anchor ice and currents (ice present). Redrawn from Berkman *et al.* (1986).

matter in the water column and material from the sediments (sponge spicules, benthic foraminiferans, diatom frustules, and gastropods) in the 10 m from bottom collecting cone suggested a benthic origin for much of this suspended matter. The presence or absence of sea ice may affect the magnitude of the resuspension (Fig. 12.11*b*),

e.g. the bulk of the sedimentation in late June coincided with intense wind activity (up to 35 m s^{-1}). When sea ice was present, anchor ice and currents caused less extreme peaks of resuspension. Viable phytoplankton cells were present in the resuspended sediments during the winter. The resuspended detrital material may provide a viable food resource for plankton herbivores and epifaunal suspension feeders during the austral winter.

12.5 Zooplankton

There have been a limited number of studies of the zooplankton under the fast ice near the Antarctic coast (e.g. Bunt, 1960; Hicks, 1974; Zvereva, 1975; Fukuchi & Sasaki, 1981; Fukuchi & Tanimura, 1981; Krebs, 1983; Fukuchi *et al.*, 1985b; Knox, 1986; Tanimura *et al.*, 1986; B. A. Forster, 1987; Tucker & Burton, 1990; Knox *et al.*, in press). These studies have been carried out in the vicinity of shore stations in McMurdo Sound and near Mawson, Syowa, Molodezhnaya and Mirny. The most detailed study is that of Tanimura *et al.* (1986) of the zooplankton under the fast ice near Syowa Station in a water depth of 10 m. Thirteen groups of zooplankton were recorded. In order of abundance they were Copepoda, Polychaeta, eggs, the larvae of benthic animals other than Polychaeta, Appendicularia, Foraminifera, Siphonophora, Ostracoda, Euphausiacea, Chaetognatha, Mollusca, Amphipoda and Isopoda. The seasonal change in the total numbers is shown in Fig. 12.12*a*. In January 1982 the number of zooplankters was 3×10^3 individuals m^{-3}, but by late March it had decreased to 0.7×10^3 individuals m^{-3}. A peak number of 5.0×10^3 individuals m^{-3} was recorded in June. Numbers decreased gradually over the ensuing months but remained above 1×10^3 individuals m^{-3}. In the early December the number began to increase and again reached 3×10^3 individuals m^{-3} in the following January.

Among the 13 zooplankton groups five constituted more than 99% of the total numbers. The copepods, including nauplii, were by far the most dominant, contributing 84.5% of the total numbers. Polychaetes, including the larvae of benthic species, were ranked next in abundance (5.2%). The larvae of benthic animals other than polychaetes and eggs contributed 2.9 and 5.1% respectively. The final group in order of abundance was the Appendicularia (1.5%). Fig. 12.12*b* depicts the seasonal change in these five groups. The polychaetes, mainly the pelagic species *Pelagobia longicirrata* and spionid larvae, occurred throughout the year and were abundant between September and February. *Fritillaria borealis* was the dominant appendicularian with the greatest abundance between September and February. The various larvae of benthic animals other than polychaetes, consisting mainly of lamellibranch veligers, gas-

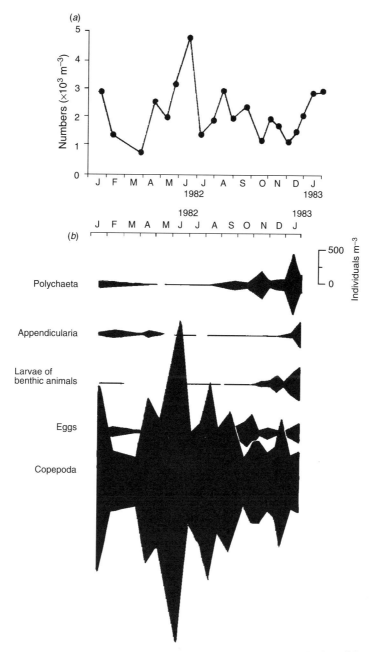

Fig. 12.12. Seasonal change in (*a*) the total numbers of zooplankton collected beneath the fast ice off Syowa Station, and (*b*) the abundance of the major groups of zooplankton collected beneath the fast ice off Syowa Station. Redrawn from Tanimura *et al.* (1986).

tropod veligers, echinoderm larvae, bryozoan larvae and ascidian larvae, were numerous between November and January. Eggs, which largely could not be identified, were present in considerable numbers from mid-October to early December. Total copepod numbers decreased during the late summer of 1982, but thereafter numbers increased abruptly from March to June and declined gradually from June to October. They remained low from late October 1982 to January 1983.

A total of 11 species of copepods excluding harpacticoids were identified: *Calanus propinquus, Ctenocalanus vanus, Microcalanus pygmaeus, Stephus longipes, Euchaeta* sp., *Scolecithricella glacialis, Metridia gerlachei, Paralabidocera antarctica, Oithona frigida, Oithona similis* and *Oncaea curvata.* The seasonal change in the abundance of these 11 species and the harpacticoids and nauplii (as a whole) is shown in Fig. 12.13. Of the three cyclopoid copepods, the dominant species throughout the year were *Oithona similis* and *Oncaea curvata*, except in the summer months when *Paralabidocera antarctica* was dominant. The latter species was not present during the rest of the year. The

Table 12.2. *Different phases of the zooplankton community under the antarctic fast ice*

Phase	I	II	III	IV
Month	May–Jun.	Jul.–Sep.	Oct.–Dec.	Jan.–Apr.
Season	autumn–winter	winter–spring	spring–summer	summer–autumn
Biomass	increasing	large	decreasing	increasing–decreasing
(g wet wt 1000 m^{-3})	(1.5–7.5)	(25.5–15.3)	(15.2–8.7)	(?8.7–15.0–7.5)
Numbers				
(no. 1000 m^{-3})	increasing	large	decreasing	increasing–decreasing
% Copepods	98	77–83	75–50	?50–80–50

After Funuchi *et al.* (1985b).

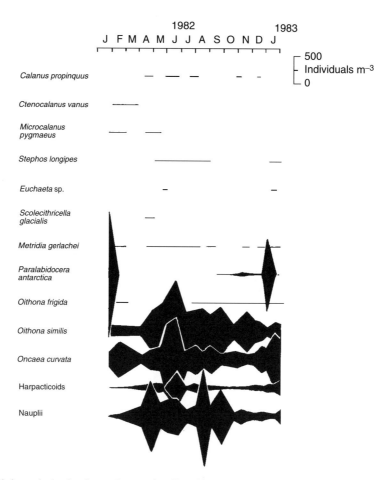

Fig. 12.13. Seasonal change in the abundance of copepods collected beneath the fast ice off Syowa Station. Redrawn from Tanimura *et al.* (1986).

harpacticoids were present throughout the year and were most abundant in mid-June. Copepods, in contrast to those in Antarctic oceanic waters where numbers increase in the summer and decline in the late autumn (Mackintosh, 1934; A. C. Hardy & Gunther, 1936; Foxton, 1956, 1966), have their peak of abundance in the winter season with a maximum in mid-June.

Fukuchi *et al.* (1985b) studied the seasonal changes in the biomass and composition of the zooplankton community under the fast ice near Syowa Station over the period May to December 1982. Average biomass was 13.5 g wet wt (1000 m)$^{-3}$, with a maximum of 25.5 g (1000 m)$^{-3}$ in August. Fig. 12.14 shows the seasonal changes in the numbers of total zooplankton and of the three dominant groups, copepods, ostracods and chaetognaths. Copepods were the dominant group with their numbers varying from a high of 97.7% of the total numbers in June to a low of 50.3% in early December. Amongst the copepods calanoids were the most numerous comprising as much as 85–99% of total copepods. Chaetognaths, principally *Eukrohnia* spp. (82–100%) were scarce in May, but increased to more than 1000 individuals (1000 m)$^{-3}$ in

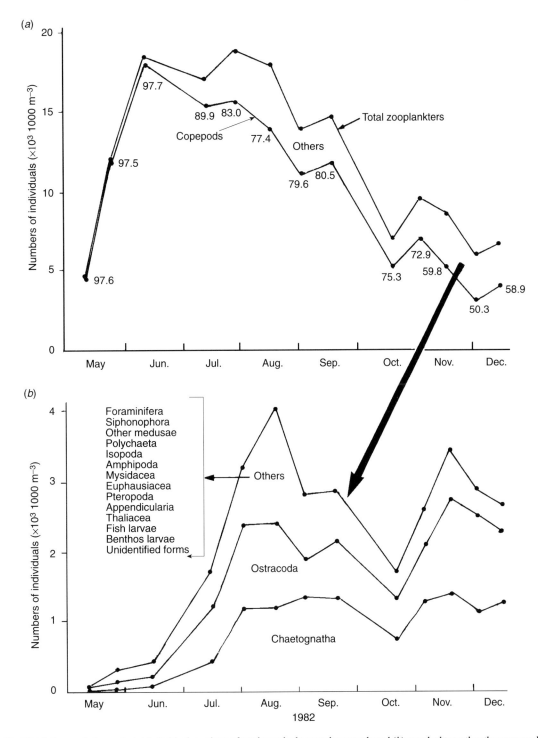

Fig. 12.14. Seasonal change in (*a*) individual numbers of total zooplankton and copepods and (*b*) zooplankton other than copepods in a 0–660 m water column beneath the fast ice off Syowa Station. Numerals in the upper figure indicate the percentage of copepods. Redrawn from Fukuchi *et al.* (1985b).

July–September and November–December. Ostracods showed a similar pattern. The seasonal changes in the zooplankton community are summarized in Table 12.2. It is of interest that the maximum biomass and numbers occurred during the July–September period. There were some major differences in the species composition at

Tanimura *et al.*'s shallow-water station (10 m) and Fukuchi *et al.*'s deeper-water station (660 m). While the peak of copepod numbers occurred during the winter at both sites, ostracods and chaetognaths were numerically more abundant at the deeper-water station.

I have studied the summer distribution of the zooplankton beneath the fast ice at a station (water depth 540 m) on the edge of the McMurdo Ice Shelf some 17 km from McMurdo Station (Knox, 1986, Knox *et al.*, unpublished). The zooplankton samples were numerically dominated by Copepoda with the numbers generally being higher in January than in December. The small euphausiid *Euphausia crystallorophias* was common with higher numbers in January. A second euphausiid, *Thysanoessa macrura*, was sparsely present. Cnidaria, especially the siphonophoran, *Pyrostephos vanhofferii*, were abundant in all samples. Pteropods were present on all occasions, the most common species being *Limacina helicina*. Larval fish, especially *Pleuragramma antarcticum*, were recorded from all samples after, and including, 4 January. Less abundant members of the zooplankton included a large mysid, amphipods, isopods, ostracods, chaetognaths, pelagic polychaetes and polychaete larvae. The zooplankton community differed from that found at Syowa Station in the absence of appendicularians and in the abundance of siphonophorans, pteropods, euphausiids and larval fishes; the first two of the last four groups were present only in low numbers at Syowa Station, while the latter two groups were absent. The reason for this difference was probably due to the advection of water from the open water to the north in the Ross Sea under the fast ice and ultimately under the McMurdo Ice Shelf.

Bunt (1960) reported nine species of copepods, excluding harpacticoids, at Mawson Station; seven out of these nine species occurred at Syowa Station and in McMurdo Sound. Zvereva (1975) reported 15 species from Mirny Station and 19 species from Molodezhnaya Station, excluding harpacticoids. All of the species were present at Syowa Station. Tucker & Burton (1990) recorded 12 copepod species from shallow-water sites adjacent to Davis Station, seven of which were also found off Syowa Station. It would appear that there is a common copepod fauna in inshore coastal waters under the fast ice round the Antarctic Continent. Dominant species in all localities are *Oithona similis*, *Oncaea curvata* and *Paralabidocera antarctica*. While some of the species are found in the adjacent ocean many of the species are known to be associated with ice. It would appear that the sea ice algae form an important food source for these species, especially for nauplii and copepodite stages during the winter. Hoshiai *et al.* (1987) found large numbers of the development stages of *P. antarctica* and harpacticoids in the lower platelet ice layer of the sea ice during the winter at Syowa Station.

The benthos under the fast ice will not be dealt with here but has been included in the chapter on the benthos (Chapter 11).

12.6 The role of the cryopelagic community

In Chapter 3 an account was given of the cryopelagic community associated with the bottom-ice microalgal assemblages. The dominant members of this community were copepods, amphipods, adult and larval euphausiids (principally *Euphausia crystallorophias*), some fishes (especially *Pagothenia borchgrevinki*), larval and juvenile fishes (*Pleuragramma antarcticum* and some benthic species), and the larvae of some benthic invertebrates.

Tanimura *et al.* (1984) collected the zooplankton at the sea ice–water interface off Syowa Station in January 1982. A dense monospecific swarm of the calanoid copepod *Paralabidocera antarctica* (primarily adults with a density of $2–6\times10^4$ individuals m^{-3}) was observed during the day. At night the swarm disappeared from the whole of the water column and the zooplankton community in the 0 m layer consisted of *P. antarctica* (13.1–39.5%), the calanoid copepods *Oithona similis* (14.1–39.5%) and *Oncaea curvata* (11.4–34.2%), harpacticoid copepods (1.1–3.3%), copepod nauplii (2.7–34.2%), polychaete larvae and chaetognaths. It was postulated that the disappearance of the swarm at night was due to its entering the interstitial water of the loose lower layer of the sea ice. In their study of the meiofauna of the sea ice in the fast ice zone off Syowa Station Hoshiai & Tanimura (1986) found that in addition to the copepods *Ctenocalanus vanus, O. similis* and *O. curvata*, which were temporary members of the meiofauna, the copepod *P. antarctica* and harpacticoids (three species) were present continuously throughout the winter in the bottom layer of the sea ice with a maximum abundance of 21.8×10^4 m^{-2} in September. Nauplii of *P. antarctica* appeared in the sea ice in late March and reached a maximum density of 7.1×10^4 m^{-2} in July. Copepodites appeared in late September and at the stage of copepodite IV they migrated into the water column (Hoshiai *et al.*, 1987). It therefore appears that the nauplii feed and grow in the sea ice habitat. Hoshiai *et al.* (1989) investigated the gut contents of the nauplius, copepodite and adult stages of *P. antarctica* from the sea ice and found diatom frustules and/or their fragments in the guts of the nauplius stages IV, V and VI, and copepodite stages I, II and III. Common species found in the guts were *Amphiprora kufferathii, Navicula glaciei, Pinnularia quadratanea, Gomphonema* sp., and *Nitzschia cylindrus*, all members of the sea ice microalgal assemblage. The tube-forming *Berkeleya rutilians* although one of the dominant ice algal species was not found in the guts of the copepodites. After *P. antarctica* shifted to the water column its gut contents reflected the species composition of the water column diatoms, which was very similar to that of the sea ice.

The largest member of the cryopelagic community is

Table 12.3. *List of items from the stomach contents of*
Pagothenia borchgrevinki *from inner McMurdo Sound
during the summer*

	Size (mm)		Size (mm)
Invertebrates		Amphipods	
Polychaetes		*Hyperiella macronyx*	6
Harmothoe sp.	10	*Orchomene plebs*	12
		Eusirus antarcticus	10
Molluscs			
Clione antarctica	9	Euphausiids	
Limacina helicina	1.5	*Euphausia crystallorophias*	20
Crustaceans		Vertebrates	
Small copepods		Fish	
Calanoides arcutus		*Pleuragramma antarcticum* (larva)	50
Metridia gerlachei	4		
Calanus propinquus			
Large copepods		Eggs	1.5
Euchaeta antarctica	8		
E. eribi			

From Bradfield (1980).

the small fish *Pagothenia borchgrevinki*, which occurs singly or in schools in the surface layers beneath the ice. Studies of the diet of this species have given varying results depending on the locality and the season. Eastman & DeVries (1985) analyzed 38 specimens caught in November 1978 in McMurdo Sound and found low diet diversity with copepods and amphipods the most frequent prey. The prey items identified by Eastman & DeVries were as follows; copepods (in 61% of fish), the amphipod *Orchomene plebs* (58%), hyperid amphipods (21%), mysids (21%), fish (18%) and cephalopods (6%). Bradfield (1980) determined the dietary composition from the examination of the stomach contents of 156 *P. borchgrevinki* collected at the edge of the McMurdo Ice Shelf in the centre of McMurdo Sound. A list of the food items is given in Table 12.3. *Pleuragramma antarcticum* larvae and the amphipod *Hyperiella dilatata* occurred in half the stomachs, with the latter occurring in the largest numbers. The most important food items in terms of biomass were larval *P. antarcticum*, *Euphausia crystallorophias*, *O. plebs* and *H. dilatata*. Prey-size distribution and prey diversity suggested an opportunistic feeding strategy and it was concluded that *P. borchgrevinki* obtained its food from the ice algal community or in the top few metres of the water column below the ice.

B. A. Forster *et al.* (1987) collected specimens of *P. borchgrevinki* from below the sea ice 1.5 km off Pram Point, McMurdo Sound over the period 8 November to 6 December, 1985. Numerically, the dominant prey was

the pteropod *Limacina helicina* (83%), followed by the hyperid amphipod *Hyperiella dilatata* (5%). Other prey species in decreasing order of occurrence were *E. crystallorophias*, *Euchaeta antarctica*, other copepods, a decapod crustacean larva, chaetognaths, the amphipods *O. plebs* and *Epimeriella macronyx*, and unidentified juvenile fish. In volumetric terms, the dominant diet contributors were *O. plebs* (38%), *L. helicina* (17%) and chaetognaths (15%) (Fig. 12.15). This contrasts with Bradfield's results in which the dominant food items were larval *P. antarcticum*, *E. crystallorophias*, and the amphipods *O. plebs* and *Eusirus antarcticus*.

In contrast Hoshiai *et al.* (1989) found that the stomachs of *P. borchgrevinki* from under the fast ice near Syowa Station contained copepods, appendicularians, tintinnids, polychaetes and unidentified items. More than 90% of the food items were copepods, including nauplii. Species present were *Ctenocalanus vanus*, *Stephos longipes*, *Oithona similis*, *Oithona frigida*, *Oncaea curvata* and *Paralabidocera antarctica*, as well as a few harpacticoids. Most of the nauplii were *P. antarctica*. Since *P. antarctica* nauplii live and feed in the bottom sea ice layer this is evidence that *P. borchgrevinki* feed on the sea ice community meiofauna.

The McMurdo Sound fast ice ecosystem will be further considered in Chapter 15.

12.7 The Ross and McMurdo Ice Shelves

The Southern Ross Sea is overlain by the world's largest floating ice sheet (540 000 km^{-2}, Zumberge & Swithinbank, 1962), the Ross Ice Shelf or Ross Ice Barrier (see Fig. 12.16). Ice thickness varies from about 200 m near the barrier edge to 700 m in the southeastern area of the shelf. Along the clifflike barrier edge an average of 35 m rises from the surface of the water and about 165 m are submerged. The average depth of the water along the barrier is 567 m. The width of the shelf in places exceeds 1300 km. A number of banks shallower than 500 m exist beneath the Ross Ice Shelf (Fig. 12.16) while depressions exceeding 800 m are found along the ice shelf periphery, with a maximum sounding of about 1400 m near 165° E, 79° S.

The McMurdo Ice Shelf is that part of the Ross Ice Shelf opening into the McMurdo Sound (see Fig. 12.16). It has a maximum width of about 40 km. To the south it is bounded by White Island, Black Island and the Brown Peninsula. The Koettlitz Glacier descends onto the shelf in the southwestern corner. On the eastern side of the shelf, ice thickness varies from approximately 5 m at the seaward edge of in McMurdo Sound to 70 m to the east of White Island (Littlepage & Pearse, 1962). A narrow band of multi-year sea ice extends along the northwestern

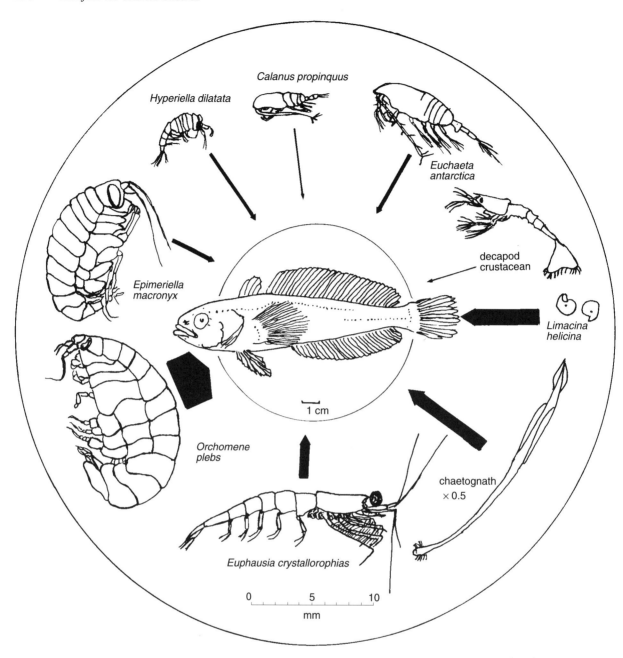

Fig. 12.15. The dominant prey of the cryopelagic fish *Pagothenia borchgrevinki* collected from under the fast ice in inner McMurdo Sound in November–December. The arrows represent estimated proportionate volumetric contribution of each prey species. The prey are drawn to the same scale except for the chaetognath. Redrawn from Forster *et al.* (1987).

coast of White Island where a tide crack has developed along the coast. Extensive crack systems in the shelf occur off the northern end of White Island and in the Koettlitz Glacier Region. Along the southern coast of White Island there are large ice billows and domes.

12.7.1 Circulation patterns beneath the shelf

12.7.1.1 Ross Ice Shelf
Jacobs *et al.* (1970, 1979) suggest a possible circulation pattern beneath the Ross Ice Shelf. Modified Circumpolar

Deep Water reaches the Ice Shelf primarily over the broad central channel between 170° W and 180°, with a warm core centred around 300 m. This warm core flows beneath the Ice Shelf and undergoes cooling, dilution and lateral mixing. As the water flows beneath Ice Shelf it would be divided by the shallow bank lying to the southwest of Roosevelt Island. One branch would then turn east round Roosevelt Island to emerge with lowered salinity and temperature near freezing point. The other branch would travel in a large cyclonic gyre beneath the Ice Shelf. As the ice shelf thickens this water moves to

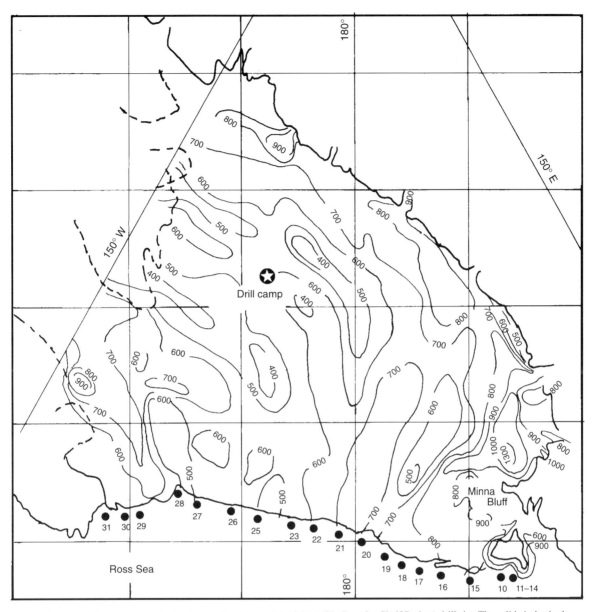

Fig. 12.16. Map of the Ross Ice Shelf showing the location of the RISP (Ross Ice Shelf Project) drill site. The solid circles in the open Ross Sea are the oceanographic stations described by Jacobs *et al.* (1979). The contour lines are the depths (in metres) of the sea bottom beneath the shelf. The dashed lines represent the approximate contours of the land. Redrawn from Clough & Hansen (1979).

deeper levels and melting near the Barrir edge would lower the temperature to near freezing point, after which any transfer of heat to the cold shelf ice would be accompanied by freezing, releasing salt to the Ross Sea Shelf Water. Inceaase in salinity and density due to freezing would reinforce the cyclonic circulation.

In the summer the prevailing wind blows from the east parallel to the ice barrier. The wind-induced currents transports the low-salinity (*c.* 50 m) layer towards the ice shelf where it must descend. Directly off the shelf low salinities are found to a depth of 150 m. Because of the sinking of this low-salinity layer near the barrier, diatoms live in abundance at sub-compensation depths. Off Cape

Crozier the diatom *Trigonium arcticum* has been found in abundance on the sea bed at 300 m.

12.7.1.2 McMurdo Ice Shelf

Because of its possible biological significance, there has been considerable interest in the circulation and hydrology under the sea ice of McMurdo Sound and the McMurdo Ice Shelf. Circulation patterns are complex and variable (see reviews by R. A. Heath, 1971, 1977; Raytheon, 1983; Lewis & Perkin, 1985). Based on observations carried out up to 1975 (Gilmour *et al.*, 1960, 1962; Gilmour, 1975; Tressler & Ommundsen, 1962; Littlepage, 1965; R. A. Heath, 1971, 1977). R. A. Heath

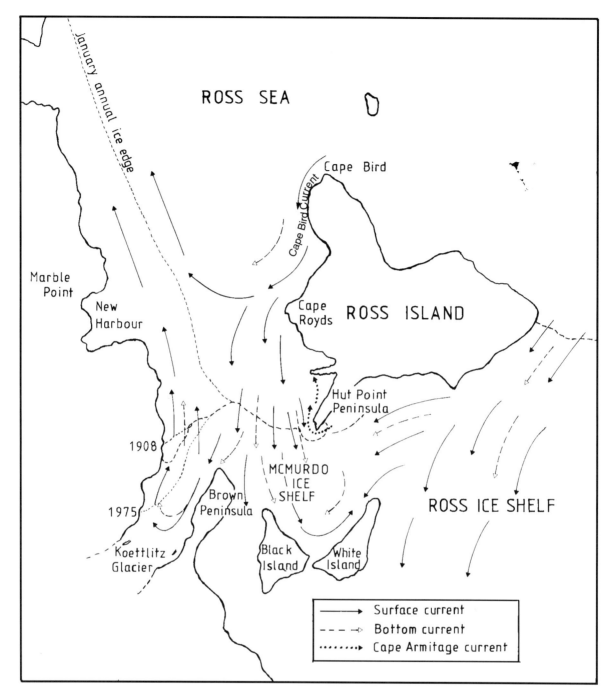

Fig.12.17. Water circulation patterns in inner McMurdo Sound and beneath the McMurdo Ice Shelf. Redrawn from Knox (1986).

(1977) proposed a circulation pattern that has in large part been confirmed by subsequent studies (see Fig. 12.17). All of these studies identified a strong tidal influence on the current patterns, with the currents being strongest when the tidal range is greatest.

In the outer Sound a strong southerly current, the Cape Bird Current, passes round Cape Bird towards Cape Royds where it swings across the Sound to join a north-ward flowing current on the west side of the Sound. Estimates of the net movement of surface currents in the

East Sound from north to south vary from 2.5 km day^{-1} (Barry & Dayton, 1988), to 6.5 (Gilmour *et al.*, 1962), 10.3 (Littlepage, 1965), and 4–12 km day^{-1} (Palmisano *et al.*, 1988), with a mean of 6.8 km day^{-1}. These currents show considerable variation indicative of either seasonal or year-to-year variations. The majority of the studies have confirmed a northerly flow from under the shelf on the west side of the Sound. Further north this flow from under the shelf joins the northward flow of the water that originated from the Cape Bird Current.

The most controversial aspect of the current flows is a northward flowing surface current on the east side of the Sound, the Cape Armitage Current, which has been identified by a number of investigators (Littlepage, 1965; Evans, 1965; Car & Codspoti, 1968; R. A. Heath, 1971). Measurements made closer than about 2 km from the coast near Cape Armitage at the end of Hut Point Peninsula indicated a flow out from under the shelf. Barry & Dayton (1988), on the other hand, consider that the flow along Cape Armitage is to the south. Heath (1971), on the basis of hydrological measurements, considered that the northerly outflow near Ross Island probably originated from water flowing under the Ross Ice Shelf from the Ross Sea to the west of Ross Island.

12.7.2 Water characteristics under the Ross Ice Shelf
Measurements of water characteristics at the Ross Ice Shelf Project site (82° 22.5′ S, 168° 37.5′ W) have been made by a number of workers (e.g. Jackson *et al.*, 1978; Gilmour, 1979; Jacobs *et al.*, 1979; Michel *et al.*, 1989). At this site, the ice thickness is 370 m thick and the water column under the ice measures 237 m. Within the water column, temperature and salinity increased from –2.16 °C (the freezing point *in situ*) and a salinity of 34.39‰ at the ice-sea water interface to –1.86 °C and 34.83‰ (Fig. 13.14). (Gilmour, 1979; Jacobs *et al.*,1979). Mixed layers beneath the ice and near the bottom were separated by an inverse thermocline but the stratification was stabilized by a halocline. Temperature and salinity characteristics of the bottom boundary layer indicate that it is part of the high-salinity shelf water from the western Ross Sea. T. D. Forster (1978) advances the following tentative interpretation of the temperature and salinity fields found under the Ross Ice Shelf but at the same time points out that more data are needed. Water from the open ocean is found under the ice shelf as a bottom layer near the sea floor. The water is subsequently modified by net melting at the bottom of the ice shelf. This water then returns to the open ocean in the top layer just beneath the ice.

From the biological point of view there is considerable interest in the age of the water beneath the Ross Ice Shelf and the period of interchange with the open sea. Estimates based on tritium and carbon-14 concentrations in sea water have been made by Jackson *et al.* (1978) and Michel *et al.* (1989). The tritium concentrations in the upper 100 m of water at the RISP site are similar to a surface concentration of 0.5 TU reported by Jacobs (1977). The presence of a tritium concentration of 0.5 TU under the shelf indicates that this water has been renewed within the period since nuclear weapons testing (1957 through 1962) in the atmosphere.

Measurements of $\Delta^{14}C$ ml^{-1} made in the surface waters of the Ross Sea in 1971 were of the order of –100 ml^{-1} while krill collected at 77° 44′ E in 1972 was found to have a $\Delta^{14}C$ ml^{-1} of –107 ml^{-1}. Therefore, the value for the Ross Sea in the early 1970s was less than –100 ml^{-1} The most recent measurements were made in McMurdo Sound. The sample from the east side of the Sound had a $\Delta^{14}C$ value of –69 ml^{-1}, whereas the other samples had values of –106 to –1145 ml^{-1}. Tritium measurements showed similar trends. The water on the east side of the Sound is derived from water from the Ross Sea to the east of Ross Island, whereas on the west side of the Sound (Heald Island and Cape Chocolate) the water flows out from under the McMurdo Ice Shelf. The sample collected at the RISP site had a $\Delta^{14}C$ ml^{-1} value of –74 ml^{-1}. Since this value is much higher than found in 1972, the water at a depth of 22 m at the RISP site must have been in the open Ross Sea within the past six years.

12.7.3 The McMurdo Ice Shelf tide crack communities
Tidal rise and fall and the northward movement of the McMurdo Ice Shelf form tide cracks along the coast. Such tide cracks are particularly well developed along the west coast of White Island. The phytoplankton of the White Island tide cracks has been discussed in Chapter 3. Three species of copepod (a calanoid, *Paralabidocera grandispina*, a cyclopoid *Pseudocyclopina belgica*, and an harpacticoid, *Tisbe prolata*) were associated with the tide crack (Knox, 1986; Waghorn & Knox, 1989). Two of these were described as new species (Waghorn, 1979). Each species had marked peaks of abundance; from late November until mid-December *P. belgica* and *T. prolata* were most abundant while from mid-December till early January *P. grandispina* dominated (Fig. 12.18). The species appeared to use different life-history strategies to utilize the short spring–summer food abundance. *P. grandispina* probably overwinters as non-adults (possibly as eggs as do other Arctiidae) which develop through the adult stage during spring and summer. *P. belgica* probably overwinters as late copepodites or adults. It appears to lay its eggs and complete some of its development during spring and summer. *T. prolata* probably overwinters as late larval or adult stages and lays eggs in the summer which probably do not hatch until late summer. It seems that the tide crack is an important nursery for *P. grandispina* and *P. belgica* and that it is a habitat for the older stages of *T. prolata*.

12.7.4 The plankton beneath the McMurdo Ice Shelf
The plankton in the water column at White Island (78° 10′ S, 167° 30′ E), McMurdo Sound have been studied over two summers (Knox, 1986; Knox *et al.*, in press).

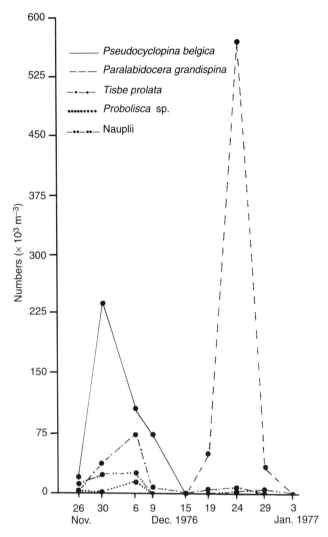

Fig.12.18. The succession of copepod species in a tide crack at White Island on the McMurdo Ice Shelf. Redrawn from Waghorn & Knox (1989).

Since 1960, the University of Canterbury (Christchurch, New Zealand) Antarctic Research Unit had been observing and tagging an apparently isolated Weddell Seal population along the northwestern coast of White Island (Stirling, 1965, 1972; R. Davis *et al.*, 1982; Kooyman, 1981c). This population was first recorded in the austral summer of 1958–59 by Heine (1960) and since then there has been considerable speculation as to its origin, permanence and regulation of numbers (Littlepage, 1965; Stirling 1972). Most observers believe that the population of some 20 individuals has no contact with other Weddell Seal populations in McMurdo Sound, and that they are unable to migrate the distance of about 20 km beneath the permanent ice to cracks in the sea ice at the edge of the ice shelf. They overwinter by maintaining breathing holes in the tide cracks or pressure ridges. The good condition of the animals indicate that they have access to an

abundant food supply. The research carried out aimed at identifying the nature of the energy input to the ecosystem beneath the ice shelf.

Movement of the ice sheet away from the northwestern coast of White Island gives rise to an area of thinner ice which is probably only a few years old and averages about 3 m in thickness. Water column processes under the ice shelf (temperature, salinity, current speed and direction, light penetration and dissolved oxygen) were measured at weekly intervals over the summer of 1976–77 through a hole in the thinner ice over a water depth of 67 m (Knox, 1986; Knox *et al.*, in press). Seawater temperatures ranged from –1.91 to –1.96 °C. Dissolved oxygen levels varied from 5.0 to 6.05 ml l^{-1} in early December to 4.65 to 4.8 ml l^{-1} in late January. Water current speeds of up to 0.13 m s^{-1} were recorded at a depth of 50 m and a predominantly northward flow was detected. Light levels under the ice were low with less than 1% of the incident light being transmitted to a depth of 3 m. No chlorophyll *a* was detected in the water column when measured by processing one litre of seawater.

Zooplankton were sampled using a WP2 free-fall net. Zooplankton biomass values in the water column ranged from 12 to 447 mg wet wt m^{-3} and were similar to values recorded elsewhere from Antarctic coastal waters. Hicks (1974) measured zooplankton biomass at a series of stations in the seasonal sea ice off Pram Point near Scott Base on Ross Island. His stations were some 20 km north of the White Island station. His biomass values for 100 m sectional hauls ranged between 0.073 and 3.309 mg m^{-3}. These values are about two orders of magnitude lower than the values recorded at White Island and probably indicate that he was sampling either a different water mass or that the zooplankton production is highly variable from year to year depending on ice conditions.

Thirty-two zooplankton species were recorded: an ostracod, 21 copepods (10 calanoids, 3 cyclopoids and 8 harpacticoids), 4 amphipods, 2 euphausiids (*Euphausia crystallorophias* and *Thysanoessa macrura*), a chaetognath, and 3 pteropods. Larvae of polychaetes and fish (*Prionodraco evansii* and *Pleuragramma antarcticum*) were found on some occasions. The species composition of the zooplankton was similar to that found in the inner Ross Sea (Hicks, 1974). Amongst the Copepoda, however, there were a number of species which have previously not been recorded from the region, but which are known to be associated with ice in other localities in Antarctica. Copepods were the most abundant animals but other common species were the pteropods, *Clione antarctica* and *Limacina helicina* and the ostracod, all of which have a circumpolar distribution (Baker, 1954). The amphipods, *Orchomene plebs* and *O. rossi*, and the euphausiid *E. crystallorophias* were occasionally caught in large numbers. The dominant copepods were *Calanoides acutus, Calanus propinquus, Ctenocalanus citer, Euchaeta* sp., *Metridia gerlachei, Paralabidicera grandispina, Oithona similis, Oncaea curvata* and *Tisbe prolata*.

The absence of chlorophyll *a* in the water column at White Island during the study was puzzling, as it had been expected that phytoplankton from the blooms which occur in McMurdo sound following the breakup of the sea ice would have been carried under the McMurdo Ice Shelf towards White Island. The decreasing concentrations of dissolved oxygen over the summer, the low water temperature and the absence of detectable chlorophyll *a* in the water column at White Island support the hypothesis that during the 1976–77 summer the water under the shelf at White Island had not originated directly from the southward flow of water under the shelf past Ross Island, but was water from a northward flow from under the shelf. This water was probably derived from water moving south in the middle of the Sound, which then turned north as it encountered grounded ice in the vicinity of Black Island (Knox, 1986). The stock of phytoplankton in this water mass could have been consumed by the abundant zooplankton or sedimented to the bottom before it reached the vicinity of White Island.

The research at White Island was continued during the 1978–79 summer through a hole in the ice over 75 m of water. The zooplankton was similar to that recorded during the 1976–77 season but was more varied and more abundant in the early part of the season. This difference can be attributed to the earlier breakout of the sea ice in McMurdo Sound in the 1978–79 summer season with earlier and enhanced plankton production in the Sound. ATP levels reached a marked peak in early January following the peak in phytoplankton production which occurred in the Sound (Fig. 12.19). In this season greater volumes of water were processed for chlorophyll *a* determinations. In order to obtain a reading 16 litres of water had to be filtered during November but later in the season this volume was reduced to 4 litres. Nevertheless, the amount of phytoplankton in the water column was very low.

12.7.5 The benthos beneath the McMurdo Ice Shelf

Littlepage & Pearse (1962) were the first to report the presence of animal life under the permanent ice shelves in McMurdo Sound. They collected benthic invertebrates belonging to 16 major taxonomic groups from 43 to 75 m at White Island (22 km from the ice edge) and from the Koettlitz Glacier (28 km from the ice edge). They reported that a number of the extremely common, shal-

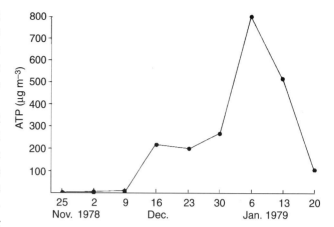

Fig. 12.19. Summer distribution of ATP in the water column beneath the McMurdo Ice Shelf at White Island. Redrawn from Knox (1986).

low-water invertebrates found at McMurdo Sound were absent from White Island. Dayton & Oliver (1977) dived through a tide crack at White Island and reported a range of epifaunal plankton-feeding species which were also common at Cape Armitage, such as the sponges *Polymastia invagitata* and *Latrunculia apicalis*, the alcyonarian *Alcyonium paessleri*, the actinarians *Artemidactis victrix, Isotelia antarctica* and *Urticinopsis antarctica*, the stoloniferan *Clavularia frankliniana*, the hydroids *Lampra* spp. and *Halecium arboreum*, and the large bivalve *Laternula elliptica*. Bruchhausen *et al.* (1979) captured a single cryopelagic fish *Pagothenia borchgrovinki* in a trap lowered through a crevasse near Minna Bluff, 80 km from the shelf edge. The thicknesses of the ice layer and the water layer at this point were approximately 175 m and 500 m respectively. It is also of interest that Heywood & Light (1975) caught four specimens of the same species in a large periglacial lake, lying in Ablation Valley in King George Sound (70° 49′ S; 68° 25′ W). King George Sound is covered by shelf ice 100 to 500 m thick.

During the two seasons that the University of Canterbury Antarctic Research Unit worked at White Island benthic collections were made through the ice holes with an orange peel grab. Analysis of the samples has revealed a rich benthic fauna (Knox, 1986; Knox & Ensor, unpublished). A total of over 300 species has been recorded from this somewhat limited sampling. The species composition is similar to that found at similar depths near the northern edge of the McMurdo Ice Shelf. However, some differences are apparent. The thick layer of sponge spicules, mollusc shells and debris that is characteristic of much of the benthic area in eastern McMurdo Sound was not found at White Island. The bottom was composed of pebbles and cobbles with relatively coarse sediment between them. The most common epifaunal species were particle feeding sponges, alcyonarians, bryozoans and hydroids, suggesting that the major food source was plankton and detritus. Detrital feeding amphipods were abundant.

In addition to the benthic invertebrates collections of benthic fishes were made (Zurr, 1977). Two nototheniod fishes *Trematomus centronotus* and *Pagothenia bernacchii* were common. *T. centronotus* was caught early in the season, while more *P. bernacchii* were caught later. The *P. bernacchii* were significantly larger than the *T. centronotus* and were predominantly old females. Castellini *et al.* (1984) caught fish at White Island throughout 1981. Between March and August four species of fish were captured: *T. centronotus* (37 specimens), *P. bernacchii* (10), *T. loenbergii* (2) and *T. hansoni* (1).

12.7.6 Circulation and production beneath the McMurdo Ice Shelf

Circulation patterns have briefly been touched upon in section 12.7.1. Here we will attempt to relate the circulation patterns to the production of the under-ice benthic communities. The benthic area off White Island, as we have seen, has a substantial biomass of benthic invertebrates and fish, the latter being sufficiently abundant to support year round the resident Weddell Seal population. White Island is ice locked and the marine community there represents a unique ecosystem, since there is little or no primary production in its vicinity due to the thick ice and low light levels. Consequently, the ecosystem must be supported by energy flux from the open sea. As little or no phytoplankton has been found in the water column during the period of summer phytoplankton bloom in the open waters of McMurdo Sound, the energy input must be through detrital material, bacteria and the abundant zooplankton in the water which moves past the island.

There is still debate as to the exact pattern of water movement under the shelf. Based on an examination of the available data on current flows within McMurdo Sound Knox (1986) has hypothesized the circulation pattern depicted in Fig. 12.17. This proposed pattern is supported by the available information on the distribution of the phytoplankton, zooplankton and benthic invertebrate communities in the inner Sound. Dayton & Oliver (1977) have drawn attention to the contrasts between the soft-bottom benthic assemblages on the east and west sides of McMurdo Sound. In their studies Dayton & Oliver recorded 37 species and 2828 individuals in a core (with an area of 0.018 m^{-2}) in 20 m of water off Cape Armitage on the east side of the Sound and 50 species and 176 individuals in a similar core taken in 40 m of water on the west side of the Sound. The infaunal assemblages of the East Sound have higher densities than almost any

other area in the world's oceans, whereas those in the West Sound have very low densities, similar to deep-sea habitats. In addition, there is a decreasing north–south infaunal gradient along the West Sound (Dayton & Oliver, 1977). One obvious hypothesis to explain such patterns is that there are differences in the amount of primary production available to the benthic communities.

However, phytoplankton pigment concentrations do not show consistent East–West Sound differences. Dayton *et al.* (1986) sampled a range of sites in the East and West Sounds and found no consistent differences; within site and between site differences reflected advection and local differences in ice and snow cover. Advection of phytoplankton from the open water is especially important in the East Sound (Palmisano *et al.*, 1986). In contrast to the chlorophyll data of Knox (1986) and Knox *et al.* (in press), Dayton *et al.* (1986) recorded chlorophyll *a* values of 0.15 to 0.62 mg m^{-3} at White Island and postulated that this was due to advection of phytoplankton from the north. However, since the samples were taken in the vicinity of the tide cracks it was possible that it was the tide crack phytoplankton that was being sampled. Southerly sites sampled in the West Sound by Dayton *et al.* (1986) at Marshall Valley, Garwood Valley and Heald Island have either extremely low values or no chlorophyll in the water column. The other possible contributors to the primary production base are the ice algae and the benthic microalgae. Palmisano & Sullivan (1983a) found no consistent differences in the biomass and productivity of the ice algae in the East and West Sounds. In contrast, the benthic microalgal biomass and production showed considerable differences, with high values in the East Sound and low values in the West Sound (Dayton *et al.*, 1986; see section 11.4.1). In the 1982–83 summer I sampled water column production processes at three sites across the Sound: Station A, 1.5 km south of Scott Base (water depth 340 m); Station B, approximately 1.0 km north of the edge of the McMurdo Ice Shelf and 22 km from Cape Armitage (water depth 350 m); and Station C, approximately 2.0 km north of the Dailey Islands on the west side of the Sound (water depth 210 m). Station A was sampled five times from mid-November to late February, while Stations B and C were sampled in early December and early January.

At Station A there was no chlorophyll present in the water column on the first and second samplings on 29 November and 6 December. Significant chlorophyll levels were recorded on 23 December, coincident with a *Phaeocystis* bloom being advected under the ice. Very high chlorophyll levels were recorded at Station B on January 5 1983 following the breakout of the sea ice in the outer part of the inner Sound. As expected low chlorophyll levels were recorded on both occasions at Station C. Zooplankton samples were dominated by copepods with numbers increasing over the season. The first two samplings at Station A (29 November and 6 December) revealed a very sparse fauna. Juveniles of the euphausiid *Euphausia crystallorophias* were present throughout the sampling period with adults occurring late in the season. Numbers increased as the season progressed. Amphipods and ostracods were generally present and were most numerous in the later samples. Pteropods were present in all samples and on several occasions occurred in large numbers. Larval fish were present in the latter part of the season. There were some significant differences between the three stations. Station B in the middle part of the Sound had the richest fauna, both in terms of species and numbers, on all occasions. Station C on the west side of the Sound had the sparsest fauna.

Thus the circulation pattern depicted in Fig. 12.17 is supported by the biological data. The inshore surface current moving round Cape Armitage and up the coast of Ross Island is derived from Ross Sea water advected under the Ross Ice Shelf, with the addition of water advected under the McMurdo Ice Shelf in the centre of the Sound returning northward along the coast of White Island. Some of this water which advects under the McMurdo Ice Shelf returns as the northward flowing current along the coast of the West Sound.

Castellini *et al.* (1984) have made some preliminary calculations of the minimum energy flow to White Island necessary to support the seal populations found there. An adult Weddell Seal consumes about 15 kg of fish per day (Kooyman, 1981c). Of the 25 to 30 resident seals, about 10 are young animals and it is assumed that they consume half an adult's amount of food. This yields a total of 2×10^5 kg fish per year taken in the immediate area. While the fish population density may vary, the seals have been at White Island for over 25 years, which indicates a fairly consistent food supply. Assuming the fish population to be relatively stable, the maximum sustainable yield equations (E. O. Wilson & Bossert, 1971) predict that the seals are not removing more than 50% of the fish. This suggests that the fish biomass is at least 4×10^6 kg. If the fish population requires about eight to ten times its biomass to survive (Gulland, 1970), then at least 3.6×10^6 kg of zooplankton are brought into the area from the open sea via undershelf currents. However, a primary component of the fish diet is detrital feeding, scavenging amphipods, which occur in large numbers at White Island. In addition other benthic invertebrates are consumed. Part of the energy input therefore passes through other consumers before being consumed by the fish. Thus, the energy

influx must support the benthic invertebrates, which as we have seen occur in considerable numbers off White Island, although not as abundantly as further north off Cape Armitage.

Castallini *et al.* (1984) also calculated from data in Holm-Hansen *et al.* (1977) that a section of open water in the Ross Sea equivalent to the area fished by the Weddell Seals at White island (20 km shoreline, 4 km offshore) would yield 3.9×10^7 phytoplankton each year. Using a 10% estimate (Gulland, 1970; Knox, 1970) for the biomass for each successive consumer level this primary production would result in about 3.9×10^6 zooplankton and 3.9×10^5 fish in the area each year. This is the same stable fish biomass figure arrived at above by using estimates of the food consumption patterns of seals. Castellini *et al.* calculated that the primary productivity which could maximally be produced in the White Island tide crack (a 20 km crack by 1 m wide) would produce only 20–25 kg of fish – a minimal amount relative to the 2.0×10^5 kg necessary to support the seals. The calculations by Castellini *et al.* (1984) for the White Island area predict that the seals are removing 0.5% of the energy flowing into the area each year.

12.7.7 Life beneath the Ross Ice Shelf
From the water below the Ross Ice Shelf at the RISP site, Lipps *et al.* (1977, 1978, 1979) and Bruchhausen *et al.* (1979) observed a number of invertebrates and fishes. Large numbers of amphipods (*Orchomene plebs*, *O. rossi* and *Orchomene* sp.) were trapped and observed by television and one large isopod (*Serolis trilobitoides*) was captured. Two fish species (*Trematomus* cf. *T. loennbergi* and *?Gymnodraco acuticeps*) and two large crustaceans were seen on the television screens. The sediments showed no signs of animal activity, no bioturbation, and no faecal pellets (Ronan *et al.*, 1978). Meiofaunal bivalve, gastropod, ostracod and foraminiferan skeletons were found but no living infauna was detected. These findings indicated that a significant biological community, apparently without unique forms, exists as far south as 450 km from the open sea.

Azam *et al.* (1979) studied the microbial life beneath the Ross Ice Shelf at the RISP site. Bacterial numbers as estimated by epiflourescence microscopy were 1.2×10^6 l^{-1} in the 66 m sample and somewhat lower in the deeper samples (8.7×10^6 to 9.5×10^6 l^{-1}). These bacterial densities are similar to those reported from the deep sea. The total microbial biomass in the water samples from 20 to 200 m, as estimated from the measurement of ATP, was between 0.14 and 0.5 ng ATP l^{-1}. These values are two to three orders of magnitude lower than those from sea water in the Ross Sea (Holm-Hansen *et al.*, 1977). Microbial heterotrophic activity was measured as rates of assimilation and respiration of several isotopically labelled substrates and also by micro-autoradiography. D-glucose assimilation and respiration of samples incubated at 0 °C yielded turnover times of the order of 5×10^5 hours, 10^3 to 10^4 times less activity than in the Ross Sea around McMurdo Sound (Holm-Hansen *et al.* 1978). These studies and auto-radiographic observations confirmed that the bacteria were metabolically active. Assimilation of thymidine, uridine and adenosine triphosphate occurred at extremely low rates similar to those in deep-sea populations. Occurrence and metabolic activity of bacteria were also examined in the sediments. Epiflourescence microscopy revealed the presence of 8.7×10^7 and 1.6×10^8 bacteria (gm sediment)$^{-1}$ (dry weight) in the top 2 cm of the two samples examined. In one case 3.9×10^7 bacteria were found per gm (dry weight) at 8–10 cm depth in a core.

Water samples were examined for small microplankters. Many small unidentified organisms were seen, with the largest numbers, 1.1×10^4 cells l^{-1} being found in the 200 m sample. A few naked dinoflagellates were seen. Larger phytoplankters occurred at between 10 and 200 cells ml^{-1}, with the greatest abundance at 20 m; abundances were more than one order of magnitude lower at 100 and 200 m. The phytopkankton consisted mainly of pennate diatoms together with a few centric forms. While no protozoans were seen in the sample at 20 m, the skeletal remains of simple nassellarian radiolarians were found in the deeper samples. Metazoan forms observed included naupliar and post-naupliar copepods of the family Oithonidae. Two specimens of another segmented metazoan, probably a polychaete larva, were found in the sample at 20 m.

Thus, albiet in low abundance, several components of what might constitute a planktonic food chain were found in the waters under the Ross Ice Shelf. With the data available, it cannot be determined whether the microbial organisms represent an indigenous population, or if they represent remnants of populations from the Ross Sea.

13

Ice edge processes

13.1 Introduction

In 1971 El-Sayed (1971a) reviewed the biological aspects of the pack ice ecosystem. He concluded that 'despite the valuable information we now have concerning the taxonomy, distribution and abundance of marine organisms in the pack ice zone, there are still enormous gaps in our knowledge of the biomass and relative abundance of these organisms. . . . Further our data is poor with regard to the relationships between the trophic levels and the flow of energy through the Antarctic pack ice.' Apart from isolated observations, particularly of phytoplankton blooms (Burkholder & Mandelli, 1965; El-Sayed, 1971b; El-Sayed & Taguchi, 1981) it was not until recently that multidisciplinary research programmes have been directed at understanding the quantitative relationships of the flora and fauna and energy flow in the pack ice ecosystem. The Group of Specialists on Southern Ocean Ecosystems and Their Living Resources early in their deliberations stressed the importance of pack ice zone studies, and particularly of studies of processes occurring at the edge of the retreating ice, recommending that such investigations be included in the BIOMASS Programme.

The marginal ice edge zone is an oceanographic front in which a transition from dense pack ice (water completely covered with ice) to water completely free of ice occurs (W. O. Smith, 1987). It is a dynamic zone, responding rapidly to physical forcing such that the transition from complete ice cover to open water may be abrupt or occur over hundreds of kilometres. The position of the ice edge can vary widely, with mesoscale changes occurring over a period of days and large-scale changes occurring seasonally. Furthermore, significant interannual variations occur (Niebauer, 1980; Zwally *et al.*, 1983b) which are related to global variations in air–sea interactions.

The U.S. National Academy of Sciences Committee to Evaluate Antarctic Marine Ecosystem Research recommended that an intensive study of the marginal ice zone be undertaken (National Academy of Sciences, 1981). A workshop was held in Woods Hole in April 1981 at which proposals for such a study were discussed. Further meetings resulted in the development of a project called Antarctic Marine Ecosystem Research at the Ice Edge Zone (AMERIEZ). Two major hypotheses provided the focus for the studies recommended:

1. The pack ice edge is associated with an oceanographic front which enhances biomass and productivity. This kind of enhanced productivity is similar to that found in association with other ocean fronts, such as upwelling along continental shelves and divergences. A combination of physical and chemical factors, including vertical water column stability, enhanced light levels, and the physical presence of ice as a substrate, interact to control the enhanced productivity.
2. The seasonal ice margin constitutes an ecological interface between two biological communities – one associated with the open ocean, the other with the pack ice – and the advance/retreat of the ice edge is a factor reflected in the life-history of associated organisms. The ice and associated open-water communities differ with respect to species composition, life-history patterns and rates of organic matter transfer.

Work carried out to date in both the Arctic and Antarctic seas has demonstrated that rapid gradients in ice, water properties and atmospheric states, as well as in the composition of the biological communities, take place at the ice edge (e.g. Alexander, 1980; Stirling, 1980; Ainley & Jacobs, 1981; D. B. Clarke & Ackley, 1981a,b; Dunbar, 1981; Stirling & Cleator, 1981; Buck & Garrison, 1983; Johannsen *et al.*, 1983; Muench, 1983; Ainley & Sullivan, 1984; Garrison *et al.*, 1984; Miller *et al.*, 1984; W. O. Smith & Nelson, 1985a,b, 1986, 1990; Comiso & Sullivan, 1986; Fraser & Ainley, 1986, Wilson *et al.*, 1986; Buck *et al.*, 1987; W. O. Smith, 1987; W. O. Smith *et al.*, 1987, 1988; Sullivan *et al.*, 1988, 1990; Sakshaug & Skjoldal, 1989; Cota *et al.*, 1990; Kottmeier & Sullivan, 1990; W. O. Smith & Sakshaug, 1990). The ice edge zone has frequently been reported to be a region of increased phytoplankton biomass and productivity, both in the Southern Ocean (e.g. Hart, 1934; Ivanov, 1964; El-Sayed & Taguchi, 1981; Nelson & Gordon, 1982; W. O. Smith & Nelson, 1985b, 1986; Fryxell & Kendrick, 1988; W. O. Smith *et al.*, 1988; Fryxell, 1989; Sullivan *et al.*, 1990), and in northern polar seas (e.g. McRoy & Goering, 1974; Alexander, 1980; Alexander & Niebauer, 1981). In addition the marginal ice edge zone has been noted as being associated with elevated abundances of marine birds and mammals in the Bering Sea and other parts of the Canadian Arctic (McRoy & Goering, 1974; Dunbar, 1981; Stirling & Cleator, 1981), and in the Southern Ocean (Siniff *et al.*, 1970; Zenkovitch, 1970; Laws, 1977a,b; Ainley & Jacobs, 1981). There is thus a growing body of evidence that ice edge phenomena may be of great importance in the overall biomass, production and nutrient and sedimentation cycles of the Southern Ocean (Nelson & Gordon, 1982; Jennings *et al.*, 1984; Fraser & Ainley, 1986; Johnson & W. O. Smith, 1986; W. O. Smith & Nelson, 1986; Ainley *et al.*, 1988; Nelson, 1989; Nelson *et al.*, 1989).

13.2 The ice edge habitat

The location of the ice edge is controlled by the combined effects of the upper ocean circulation and local winds which advect ice from one location to another, and by thermodynamic processes such as freezing and thawing which create or destroy ice *in situ*. The nature of the ice edge varies greatly. Often there is a sharply delineated boundary between complete ice cover and open water over a very short distance (often less than one kilometre), while at other times a considerable area of loose pack (often many tens of kilometres) separates the consolidated pack from the open ocean. The ice edge itself can be extremely complex with features on a range of scales varying from bands 1–10 km across (Muench & Charnell, 1977; D. Martin *et al.*, 1983; Wadhams, 1983; Muench *et al.*, 1983), through mesoscale features (10–100 km) possibly connected with ocean eddies (LeBlond, 1982; Johannessen *et al.*, 1983; Wadhams & Squire, 1983), up to basin scale features. Associated with the ice edges are complex oceanographic structures with a wide range of temporal and spatial scales which have been described in both the the Arctic and Antarctic (e.g. Gordon & Huber, 1982; Johanssen *et al.*, 1983; Muench, 1983).

Significant regional variations in the character of the Antarctic ice edge have been reported. In regions where the underlying currents are northward flowing the sea ice is advected into lower latitudes as ice 'promontories'. With summer melting this ice injects significant quantities of meltwater to the north. Because of its low salinity this meltwater is confined to a surface layer which over-

lies a denser layer. The best developed of these ice 'promontories' occurs in the western Weddell Sea where a strong western boundary current transports water from the coast of the Antarctic Peninsula towards Bransfield Strait and the eastern Scotia Sea (Gordon *et al.*, 1981).

The boundary region between the Weddell Sea cyclonic and the eastward circumpolar flow of the West Wind Drift is an extremely dynamic region marking the boundary between the two current regimes and zones of temperature–salinity properties. This boundary is a frontal zone corresponding to the maximum northern extent of the Weddell Sea pack ice. The front can be sharp and well-defined with evidence of mesoscale features such as eddies. In addition to the role of frontal zones in influencing the position and nature of the ice edge, vertical transfer processes with the redistribution of heat and salt are also important to the thermodynamic balance which ultimately determines the ice edge position.

The ice floes at the ice edge undergo three distinct structural stages (AMERIEZ, 1981): Stage 1. a 'formation' stage where the ice initially grows and agglomerates into floes; Stage 2. a 'metamorphic' stage characterized by temperature changes, snow deposition and removal, ice ridging, and rafting; and Stage 3. a 'decay' stage where wave action and top, bottom and lateral melting all contribute to erode the floes and distribute both organic (algae, bacteria, protozoa, invertebrates, detritus) and inorganic (freshwater, nutrients, etc.) substances into the ocean. Each of these three physical phases is also characterized by the kinds and diversity of species and the amount of biological activity present.

In the formation stage several types of sea ice algal communities (see section 3.3.1) have been observed which have roughly been categorized into *bottom* communities and *interior* communities (Ackley *et al.*, 1979; Garrison *et al.*, 1986; Garrison & Buck, 1985b; Horner, 1985a; Horner *et al.*, 1988). Sea ice bottom communities are of two types; those associated with congelation or columnar ice and those in structurally weak ice which may be attached to the undersurface of the floes as platelets and frazil billows beneath the intact ice cover. Interior communities are those formed by incorporation into the sea ice (both frazil and congelation or columnar ice) and which are somewhat removed from contact with the ocean water. Such communities develop somewhat in isolation under unique temperature, salinity, light and nutritional conditions.

During the 'metamorphic' or second stage of ice floe development, the ice floe island community develops further. As pressure ridges form in the ice cover, they act as snow fences. The loading of ice blocks can depress the floes so that local flooding saturates the snow cover at the

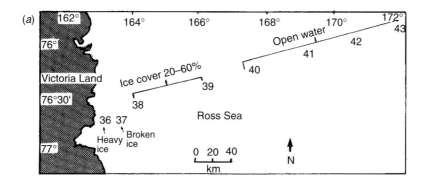

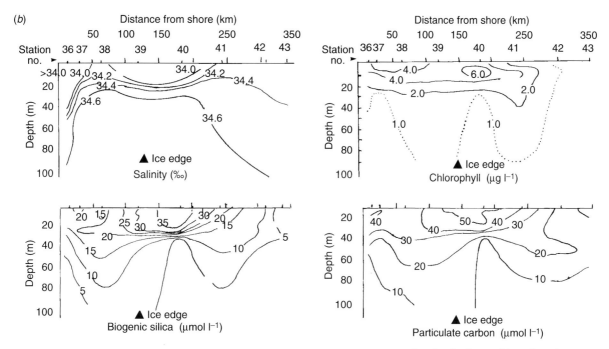

Fig. 13.1. (*a*). The location of the transect study across a receding ice edge in the Ross Sea, showing ice conditions along the transect. Redrawn from W. O. Smith & Nelson (1985b). (*b*) Vertical sections of salinity, chlorophyll *a*, particulate carbon and biogenic silica along the transect depicted in (*a*). Redrawn from Smith & Nelson (1985b).

base of the ridges. Such conditions produce an additional habitat, the *snow–ice surface* communities. Such communities are again characterized by a different set of temperature, salinity, light and nutrient conditions. Flooding caused by wave action can also produce a similar habitat. Temperature fluctuations can also create additional habitats by melting the snow cover and leading to melt accumulation on low spots under the snow cover.

Finally, in the decay phase, the ice warms, increasing its water content by internal melting, and developing an interconnected pore space throughout the floe and eventually a semi-open connection with the water below. The 'pore water' develops a rich algal, bacterial and protozoan community. In the latter stages of this structural development zooplankton may enter the labyrinth system and graze on the rich communities found there. Floe breakup leads to local isostatic imbalances and the devel-

opment of lagoons and pools at the bases of the ridges, some of which may be periodically flushed by wave action. These form another habitat which is particularly rich in algae and associated microbial populations.

13.3 Ice edge phytoplankton biomass and primary production

As discussed in Chapter 3 the Southern Ocean as a whole is considered, based on sampling to date, to be a region of low productivity. However, it is also well known that Antarctic waters may exhibit occasional, periodic phytoplankton blooms. The conclusion that the Southern Ocean is somewhat oligotrophic seems paradoxical since there are large concentrations of phytoplankton consumers, especially krill, and since the primary production supports large stocks of birds, seals and whales. In addition there are substantial deposits of diatoms on the

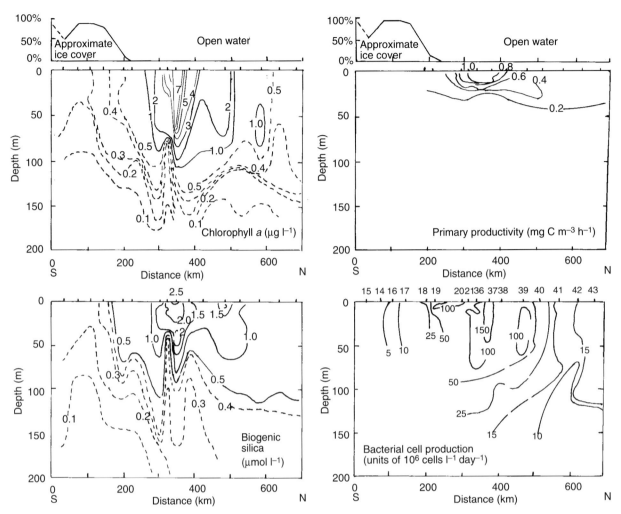

Fig. 13.2. Vertical sections of chlorophyll *a*, primary production, biogenic silica and bacterial cell production along a north–south transects across the ice edge in the Weddell Sea in November 1983. Redrawn from AMERIEZ (1983).

Antarctic continental shelf (DeMaster, 1981) indicating high surface productivity. This suggests that a large source of primary production has been missed in most previous investigations of the Southern Ocean; it is highly probable that the missing link is the occurrence of ice edge phytoplankton blooms which can often produce massive amounts of phytoplankton over very short periods (reviewed by W. O. Smith, 1987). Examples of some recent studies of ice edge phytoplankton biomass and production are given below.

The first of these is the study carried out in the western Ross Sea off the Victoria Land coast (W. O. Smith & Nelson, 1985a,b) (Fig. 13.1*a*). Ice conditions along the transect were variable. Heavy ice (virtually 100%) was encountered near the coast (Station 36), while Station 37 was at a distinct boundary between heavy ice and broken ice. Ice cover in the middle part of the transect (Stations 38 and 39) ranged from 20 to 60%, while Stations 40 to 43 were in open water. Sections of temperature, salinity

and density clearly showed the influence of the melting pack ice (Fig. 13.1*b*). A layer of low-salinity water was present on the surface and it extended about 250 km from the dense ice pack at Station 37, with a sharp halocline and pycnocline at a depth of 20 to 30 m. Further offshore from this feature surface salinity and the depth of the mixed layer increased markedly.

Phytoplankton biomass, as measured by chlorophyll *a*, particulate carbon and biogenic silica distributions was tightly coupled to the region of meltwater influence, being embedded in the meltwater lens. Dominant species in the bloom were the pennate diatom *Nitzschia curta* (generally considered to be an ice algal species), which constituted up to 85% of the total cell numbers, and the congeneric species *N. closterium*. While the phytoplankton biomass was substantially greater in the bloom (Stations 36 to 41) than seaward of it (Stations 42 and 43), the major compositional ratios of the surface phytoplankton did not change appreciably, indicating that the bloom was dissipated by

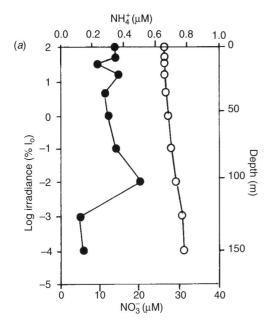

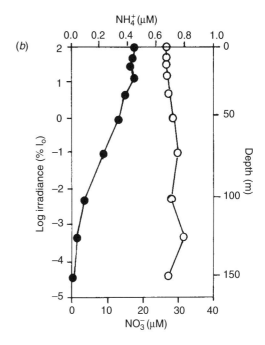

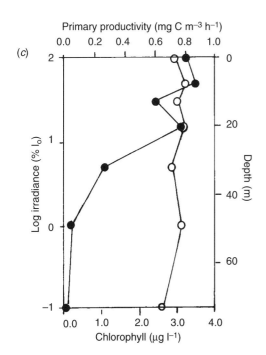

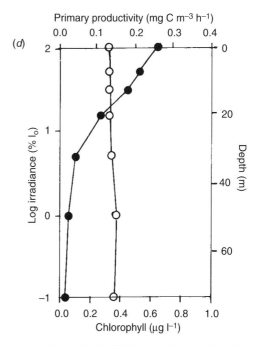

Fig. 13.3. Measurements of nutrients, chlorophyll *a* and productivity in the upper 150 m in the Weddell Sea ice edge zone. Sampling depths were based on penetration of radiation. The depth axis represents the mean depth associated with the light depths. (*a*), (*b*) Mean NH$_4$ (●) and NO$_3$ (○) in (*a*) spring 1983 and (*b*) autumn 1986. (*c*), (*d*) Mean chlorophyll *a* concentrations ○) and primary productivity rates in (●) (*c*) spring 1983 and (*d*) autumn 1986. Redrawn from W. O. Smith & Nelson (1990).

both vertical and lateral processes. The decrease in stratification away from the meltwater input allowed for more active vertical mixing. The two zones were sharply discontinuous and separated by an abrupt change in water colour. Concentrations of particulate organic matter within the bloom's euphotic zone were much greater than outside the bloom. The particulate carbon values were extremely high, resembling the concentrations found in

hyperproductive upwelling areas such as those off the coast of Peru (Hobson *et al.*, 1973). Concentrations of biogenic silica in this bloom were the highest yet reported from the world's oceans; they averaged approximately three times higher than concentrations reported off the coast of northwest Africa (Krebs, 1983). The data suggested that the bloom was initiated by seeding of the water column by the release of ice algae.

Table 13.1. *Summary of mean f-ratios and mean total primary productivity from studies from polar regions that reported f-ratios*

	Season	f-ratio	Primary productivity (mg C m⁻² day⁻¹)	Source
Pelagic studies				
Scotia Sea	Spring	0.54	520	Olson (1980); El-Sayed & Weber (1982)
Ross Sea	Summer	0.42	515	Olson (1980); El-Sayed et al. (1983)
Scotia Sea	Summer	0.37	149	Gilbert et al. (1982); El-Sayed & Weber (1982)
Baffin Bay	Summer	0.53	227	Harrison et al. (1982)
Scotia Sea	Summer	0.22	—	Rönner et al. (1983)
Antarctic Peninsula	Autumn	0.42	—	Probyn & Painting (1985)
Scotia Sea	Summer	0.22	—	Koike et al. (1986)
Mean[1]		0.39	353	
Ice-edge studies				
Scotia Sea	Summer	0.48	114	Gilbert et al. (1982) El-Sayed & Weber (1982)
Ross Sea	Summer	0.65	962	Nelson & Smith (1986); D. L. Wilson et al. (1986)
Bering Sea	Spring	0.74	—	Muller-Karger & Alexander (1987)
Fram Strait	Summer	0.62	426	W. O. Smith & Kettner (1989); W. O. Smith et al. (1987)
Weddell Sea	Spring	0.52	489	W. O. Smith & Nelson (1990)
Weddell Sea	Autumn	0.72	126	W. O. Smith & Nelson (1990)
Mean[1]		0.62	423	

[1]Means are simple arithmetic means and are presented to show trends rather than absolute values of the two regions.
From W. O. Smith & Nelson (1990).

The second example is the November 1983 AMERIEZ cruise to the Weddell Sea. This cruise undertook several approximately north–south transects through the marginal ice zone (W. O. Smith & Nelson, 1986). Selected results from one such transect are shown on Fig. 13.2. All transects through the open water at the ice edge showed a pronounced phytoplankton bloom. Phytoplankton biomass, as measured by chlorophyll *a*, increased from background levels (>0.1 µg l⁻¹) in areas of virtually complete ice cover to >9.0 µg l⁻¹ in open water. The distribution of biogenic silica (a measure of diatom biomass) showed a similar pattern with the region of high concentration (>1.0 µmol SiO_2 l⁻¹) coinciding almost exactly with the high chlorophyll region. This relationship strongly suggested that the phytoplankton biomass in the bloom area was dominated by diatoms, of which *Thalassiosira gravida* was the dominant species, in spite of the high numerical abundance of very small *Phaeocystis* cells. The phytoplankton biomass was strongly influenced by water mass characteristics and physical fronts, which are distinguished by large changes in surface salinity and dissolved silicic acid concentrations. The region of enhanced phytoplankton biomass was limited to a region that had a salinity less than 34.2‰, and the seaward extent of the bloom was limited by a hydrographic front which was best defined by silicic acid distribution. Primary productivity as measured by photosynthetic ¹⁴C incorporation was centered in the high bio-

mass region where the vertically integrated primary productivity was *c*. 750 mg C m⁻² day⁻¹. Bacterioplankton cell production coincided closely with the distribution of chlorophyll *a* and primary production rates.

More recently W. O. Smith & Nelson (1990) have summarized rates of primary production, nitrate uptake, and ammonium uptake by phytoplankton in the marginal ice edge zone of the Weddell Sea in the austral spring of 1983 and autumn 1986 (Fig. 13.3). In spring chlorophyll *a* concentrations averaged 3 µg l⁻¹, primary productivity 490 mg C m⁻² day⁻¹, and surface phytoplankton growth rates 0.30 doublings day⁻¹. In autumn these were all much lower, averaging 0.14 µg l⁻¹, 126 mg C m⁻² day⁻¹, and 0.14 doublings day⁻¹. During both seasons ammonium was consistently the preferred source of nitrogen, but because of the much greater availability of nitrate in the euphotic zone (21–26 µM NO_3^- versus 0.4 µM NH_4^+ during both seasons), nitrate uptake rates generally equalled or exceed those of ammonium. Vertically integrated ratios (the ratio of nitrate uptake to the total uptake of nitrate and ammonium) averaged 0.52 (range 0.35 to 0.70) in spring and 0.72 (range 0.60 to 0.84) in autumn.

W. O. Smith & Nelson (1990) have tabulated the available information on nitrogen uptake by phytoplankton in high latitudes (Table 13.1). The data indicate that marginal ice edge zones may be characterized by *f*-ratios higher than those elsewhere in polar regions, indicating that nitrate-N ('new'-N) is the dominant source of nitrogen in these zones. W. O. Smith & Nelson (1990) note that in 1983 they observed sharply elevated relative preference indices for ammonium whenever ambient ammonium concentration was <0.3 μM, and they interpreted this as evidence that Antarctic phytoplankton growing at ammonium concentrations less than 0.3 μM have an ability to increase their rate of ammonium uptake in response to increased availability.

The overall spatial extent of the Weddell Sea ice edge bloom was about 250 km, remarkably similar to that of the bloom in the Ross Sea. However, although the average chlorophyll *a* concentrations were similar in the two studies (3.1 for the Weddell Sea versus 3.7 μg l^{-1} for the Ross Sea), the concentrations of particulate carbon, nitrogen and biogenic silica were much lower in the Weddell Sea. The two areas also differed in that the extraordinarily high carbon to chlorophyll and biogenic silica to carbon ratios found in the Ross Sea were not present in the Weddell Sea, where the ratios were more typical of oceanic phytoplankton (Parsons *et al.*, 1977). The differences may be due to the fact that the Ross Sea study took place in late January when the ice cover was near a minimum while the Weddell Sea study took place in November when ice cover was near maximum.

Japanese scientists (e.g. Tanimura, 1981; Fukuchi & Tanimura, 1982; Watanabe *et al.*, 1982; Watanabe & Nakajima, 1982; Fukuchi *et al.*, 1984, 1985a; Fukuda *et al.*, 1986; Fukui *et al.*, 1986; Taniguchi *et al.*, 1986; Ohno *et al.*, 1987) have reported high values of surface and integrated chlorophyll *a* concentrations in the pack ice and fast ice regions of the Indian Ocean sector. In a study of the distribution of chlorophyll *a* along 45° E in the Southern Ocean in February–March Watanabe & Nakajima (1982) recorded the highest levels of chlorophyll *a* close to the edge of the fast ice and in a polyna (0.69 mg chl *a* m^{-2}). Low surface salinities (<33.9‰) were associated with the high phytoplankton standing stocks. Fukuchi *et al.* (1984) recorded very large integrated chlorophyll *a* stocks (466.5 mg chl *a* m^{-2}, 0–150 m) from the fast ice region of the eastern part of Lutzholm Bay.

In a study of the distribution of water column physical properties, chlorophyll *a* and nutrients off MacRobertson Land (65–70° E, 61–69° S) in December Fukui *et al.* (1986) recorded high chlorophyll *a* levels near the edge of the pack ice (Fig. 13.4). From Fig. 13.4*a* it can be seen that the edge of the pack ice had retreated towards the coast from 63–64° S in mid-December to 67–69° S in January–February. The ice edge zone was characterized by low surface salinities, 33.6–33.8‰ in December and 33.4–34.2‰ in January–February (Fig. 13.4*a*). A maximum integrated chlorophyll *a* value of 200 mg chl *a* m^{-2} (0–200 m) was recorded in a bloom at the ice edge in Prydz Bay in January (Fig. 13.4*b*). In the upper layers of this bloom (0–30 m) inorganic nutrients were depressed; <1.0 μg-at P l^{-1}, <20 μg-at Si l^{-1}, and <16 μg-at N l^{-1}. Tanimura (1981), Fukui *et al.* (1986) and Watanabe & Satoh (1987) have all suggested that these high chlorophyll concentrations were associated with the release of ice algae to the water column in spring and summer.

Comiso *et al.* (1990) using CZCS satellite data in the Weddell Sea marginal ice edge zone and adjacent areas during the austral summer–autumn transition detected large areas of elevated phytoplankton pigment concentrations. Phytoplankton blooms, about 200 km wide and extending several hundred kilometres along the ice edge, were observed. Analysis of the data indicated that phytoplankton blooms are not simply a spring/summer phenomenon since large areas of elevated pigment concentrations were observed through the middle of March, a period in which the ice was generally advancing. In general, blooms were in relatively shallow waters (less than 500 m), which may in some manner enhance residence time, stratification, and/or micronutrient flux. Phytoplankton growth occurred as far south as 77° S indicating that even in the middle of March surface irradiance levels were sufficient to promote phytoplankton growth. Thus estimates of ice edge phytoplankton production will need to be revised upwards to take into account phytoplankton production in the late summer–early autumn.

13.4 Potential causes of phytoplankton blooms

According to W. O. Smith & Nelson (1986) the following sequence takes place during the initiation, development and decay of an ice edge phytoplankton bloom:

1. Meltwater produces a stable environment with light levels favourable to phytoplankton growth.
2. A bloom begins and, since the water column biomass is low, the phytoplankton comprises mainly those species released from the ice.
3. Ice melt continues, further increasing water column stability.
4. Some species grow in the stable surface layer, and their contribution to the overall phytoplankton assemblage increases with time. Although they may be considered as ice algal species, most of their growth occurs in the water column.
5. As the low-density meltwater is degraded by vertical and lateral flow, vertical mixing increases, and the phytoplankton bloom is dissipated by physical processes. Thus, the production and degradation of the vertical stability produced by melting sets the dimensions of the bloom.

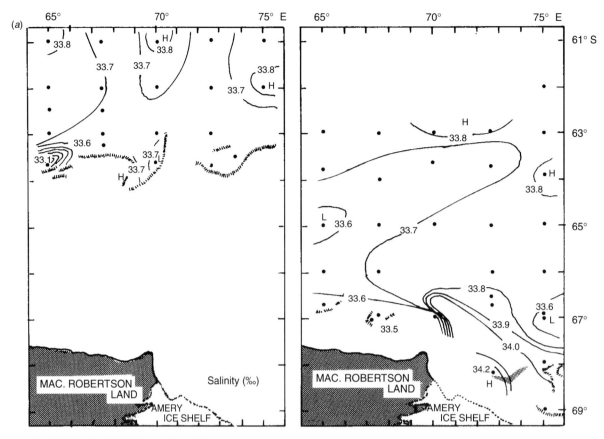

Fig. 13.4. Surface distributions of (*a*) salinity, and (*b*) chlorophyll *a* MacRobertson Land in mid-December 1983 (on the left) and January–February 1986 (on the right). The hatching represents the edge of the pack ice. Redrawn from Fukui *et al.* (1986).

The possible mechanisms involved in the above sequence will now be examined in more detail.

13.4.1 Water column stability

The primary mechanism proposed for the initiation and development of a bloom is the stable layer of low salinity (hence low density) water produced at the surface by the melting of the pack ice. Seasonal sea ice typically has a salinity of 5–10 ‰ in contrast to the 30–35‰ in the surface waters. Because storms are infrequent and thermal stratification rarely, if ever, occurs in the water column, the Southern Ocean usually has a deep mixed layer. The introduction of relatively fresh water from the melting ice greatly reduces surface density and causes vertical stability. A low density layer is formed above the high-salinity water with the two layers separated by a discontinuity layer, through which mixing is negligible. The discontinuity layer is usually formed at between 10 and 50 m in depth, thus ensuring that the surface phytoplankton would not be transported to greater depths. This in turn allows the phytoplankton to grow in a well-illuminated environment. If the water were deeply mixed the average light intensity encountered by the phytoplankton cells would be low. In all of the investigations of phytoplank-

ton blooms to date a stable surface layer of low salinity water has been implicated and it would appear to be a major factor.

13.4.2 Ice edge upwelling

A second potential mechanism is ice edge upwelling, which can occur as a result of complex interactions between atmosphere, ocean and ice (Røed & O'Brien, 1983). However, while such ice edge upwelling has been observed in the Arctic (Johannsen *et al.*, 1983) it has not been identified so far in the Antarctic. In temperate and tropical systems the upwelling of nutrient-rich water supports rapid phytoplankton growth in the euphotic zone. In the Arctic such upwelling replenishes nutrients depleted by phytoplankton growth (Alexander & Niebauer, 1981; W.O. Smith, 1987). In the Antarctic, however, nutrients are generally well above the concentrations needed for plant growth (El-Sayed, 1970a; Gilbert *et al.*, 1982) so that any nutrients brought to the surface by upwelling would not increase phytoplankton production. Thus, it would appear that in the Antarctic upwelling is not a mechanism contributing to the formation of ice edge phytoplankton blooms.

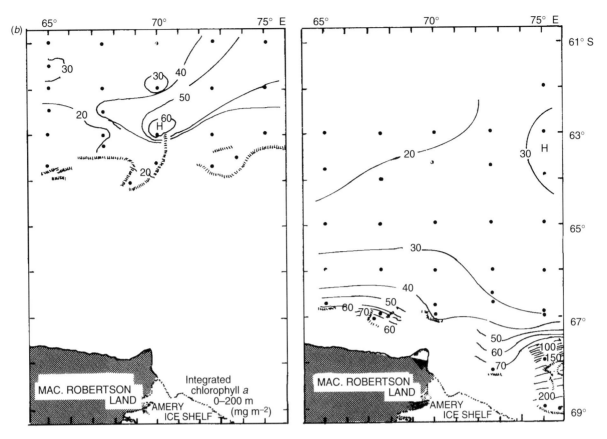

Fig. 13.4. For legend see opposite.

13.4.3 Decrease in turbulence

A third possible mechanism contributing to bloom formation is a decrease in turbulence within the mixed layer caused by reduced wind stress due to the presence of ice. The decreased wind stress enhances primary production in nutrient-rich waters by decreasing turbulence within the mixed layer depth (Nelson *et al.*, 1981), so that the phytoplankton cells are not mixed rapidly between euphotic and subphotic depths. Because the ice's effects on wind drag reaches tens of kilometres from the ice edge (Overland *et al.*, 1983), a bloom caused by reduced wind stress would be less extensive than one initiated by ice melt, which may extend some 250 km (W. O. Smith & Nelson, 1985a, 1986).

13.4.4 Release of ice microalgae

A further potential mechanism for initiating ice edge phytoplankton blooms is the release of ice microalgae into the surface waters from the melting ice floes. As we have seen in Chapter 3 the algal biomass in sea ice can be extremely high (Whitaker, 1977a; Ackley *et al.*, 1979; Palmisano & Sullivan, 1983a; Garrison *et al.*, 1986). However, the ice algal concentrations, in spite of their abundance, are of a magnitude that could not account for the chlorophyll *a* concentrations typical of ice edge phytoplankton blooms. Furthermore, some of the ice algal species may sink very rapidly and thus have a short residence time in the euphotic zone. Johnson & Smith (1986) have examined the sinking rates of phytoplankton assemblages in the Weddell Sea marginal ice zone. Sinking rates, as determined by chlorophyll *a* levels, ranged from 0 to 2.73 m day^{-1} (mean = 0.89) and were similar to those reported from tropical (Bienfang, 1985), temperate (Bienfang & Harrison, 1984), and subpolar regions (Bienfang, 1984). Despite apparently low sinking rates, passive sinking of phytoplankton has been shown to have a large impact on the composition of phytoplankton communities (Trimble & Harris, 1984). Diatoms make up the overwhelming proportion of the biogenic material in sediments beneath the bloom in the Ross Sea discussed above (section 13.3) (W. O. Smith & Nelson, 1985a,b), and sediment accumulation rates indicated that a large proportion (*c.* 80%) of the surface siliceous production was being delivered to the sediments (Nelson *et al.*, unpubl., quoted in Johnson & Smith, 1986). Material collected by sediment traps in the region of the Ross Sea bloom consisted primarily of single phytoplankton cells that apparently had not been ingested by herbivores (Dunbar *et al.*, 1985). Furthermore, there is a strong taxonomic correlation between species found in the ice edge

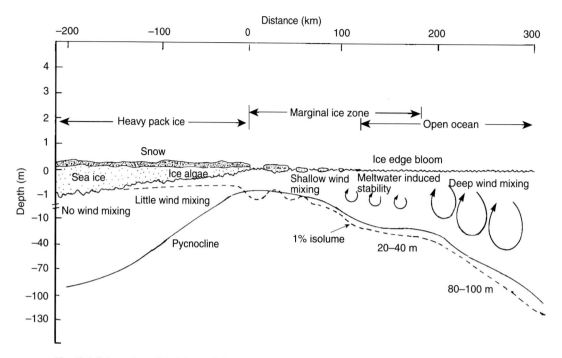

Fig. 13.5. Schematic model of the conditions necessary for the development of an ice edge phytoplankton bloom. Redrawn from Sullivan *et al.* (1988).

bloom (W. O. Smith & Nelson, 1985a) and those in the sediments (Truesdale & Kellog, 1979). Johnson & Smith (1986) estimated that from 8 to 12% of the daily production was lost from the euphotic zone by passive sinking, a percentage similar to Bienfang's (1984) estimate for a sub-Arctic system.

A number of workers (e.g. Sasaki & Watanabe, 1984; Fukuchi *et al.*, 1984; Sasaki & Hoshiai, 1986) have noted the increase which occurs in chlorophyll *a* concentration in the summer due to the release of ice algae from the melting ice at the bottom of the sea ice. As Sasaki & Hoshiai (1986) point out there are three possible fates for the ice algae once they are released into the water column: 1. as discussed above they may sink through the water column to be deposited on the bottom; 2. they may be consumed by animals living in the water column and their digested faeces sink to the bottom; and, 3. the released ice algae may actively grow within the water column and contribute to phytoplankton blooms. The relationships between the ice algal species and those of the water column phytoplankton community have been discussed in Chapter 3. The phytoplankton bloom in the Ross Sea (Smith & Nelson, 1985a) was dominated by a single diatom species *Nitzschia curta* which is considered to be an ice algal species. The dense bloom in the Weddell Sea, off the Ronne Ice Shelf, reported by El-Sayed (1971b) was dominated at the surface by the diatom *Thalassiosira tumida*, a widespread dominant of Antarctic phytoplankton communities. In the Weddell Sea the phytoplankton

blooms at the ice edge (W. O. Smith & Nelson, 1986; Nelson *et al.*, 1987) consisted of chain-forming species such as *Euchampia antarctica*, *Corethron criophilum*, *Rhizosolenia hebetata* and *Thalassiosira tumida*, while beyond the ice edge, the early spring bloom was dominated by the gelatinous colony formers *Thalassiosira gravida* and the prymnesiophyte *Phaeocystis pouchetii* (Fryxell *et al.*, 1984; Fryxell & Kendrick, 1988).

13.5 A model of ice edge bloom dynamics

Fig. 13.5 from Sullivan *et al.* (1988) schematically illustrates the relationships among light, ice distribution and vertical stability. Phytoplankton growth under the ice is extremely low because of low *in situ* light levels and a deep mixed layer, whereas in the vertically stable area immediately seaward of the ice edge, phytoplankton growth can approach the maximum possible for the prevailing temperatures (~0.8 doublings day^{-1}, Eppley, 1972). With distance from the ice edge the vertical stability is degraded by lateral flow and increased vertical mixing and as a consequence phytoplankton growth again becomes limited by light in the deep mixed layer.

Sullivan *et al.* (1988) point out that ice edge 'bloom' dynamics have two major components, each with different time scales and fundamentally different forcing functions. The first component involves active growth and decay of the phytoplankton population at the ice edge; it occurs over weeks and is controlled by factors which influence growth (light and vertical stability) and losses

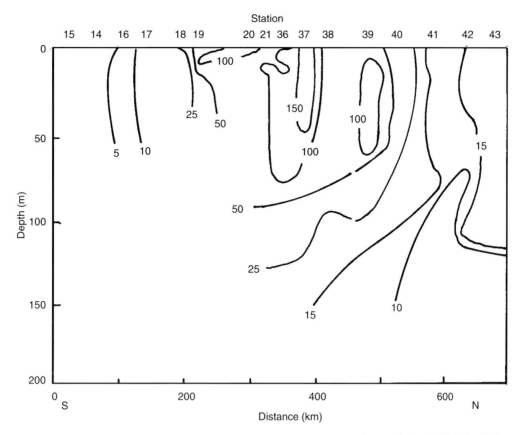

Fig. 13.6. Bacterial cell production rates in units of 10^6 cells l^{-1} day^{-1} across an ice edge zone in the Weddell Sea. Redrawn from M. A. Miller *et al.* (1984).

(grazing, sinking, vertical mixing, and advective processes). The second involves the movement of the bloom over large geographic areas with the receding ice edge; it occurs over months and is in large part controlled by ice dynamics, which in turn are largely a function of atmospheric effects. As a result, the temporal and spatial extent of the bloom is controlled by the relative rates of these processes.

13.6 Bacterioplankton

M. A. Miller *et al.* (1984) investigated the vertical and horizontal distribution, activity and growth rates (μ) of bacteria during the November–December 1983 AMEREIZ cruise (Fig. 13.6). Data on growth rates of the bacteria in the water column are from a transect extending from 120 nautical miles into the pack to 160 miles north of the ice edge. There was a fourfold increase both in bacterial numbers and cell biomass over the transect. Bacterial cell numbers and biomass integrated throughout the water column to a depth of 150 m ranged from an average of 7×10^{12} cells m^{-2} (100 mg C m^{-2}) at the southernmost stations to an average of 33×10^{12} cells m^{-2} (400 mg C m^{-2}) to the north. The maximum bacterial growth rates (measured by 3 trimethylated thymidine incorpora-

tion) occurred in the upper 50 m of the water column in the region most recently uncovered by the receding ice (Fig. 13.6). These were located in the low-salinity surface layer. The growth rates steadily declined by two orders of magnitude to the south and by one magnitude to the north. Growth rates ranged from 0.02 doublings day^{-1} deep within the pack ice to 0.4 doublings day^{-1} just north of the ice edge zone, declining to 0.03 doublings day^{-1} further north. These growth rates fit within the range calculated for other Southern Ocean regions (Fuhrman & Azam, 1980; Hanson *et al.*, 1983a,b). Ice edge bacterioplankton will be considered further in Chapter 14.

13.7 Ice edge microheterotrophs

It is only comparatively recently that the abundance and role of microheterotrophs has been studied in the ice edge zone (Buck & Garrison, 1983; Heinbokel & Coats, 1984, 1986; Garrison *et al.* 1984; Garrison & Buck, 1985a, 1989a,b; Garrison & Van Scoy, 1985). Table 13.2 presents a summary of the occurrence and numerical abundance of the major planktonic forms encountered in the Weddell Sea ice edge zone (Buck & Garrison, 1983). Heterotrophic flagellates were the dominant component of the protozooplankton comprising 24–75% of the total

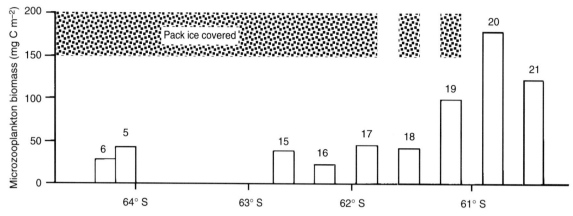

Fig. 13.7. Microheterotroph biomass in the upper 50 m of the water column in the Weddell Sea in November 1983. Stations 5 and 6 were under heavy ice cover while stations 15–21 were along the transect across the ice edge zone. Redrawn from Garrison & Buck (1985a).

Table 13.2 *A summary of the occurrence and numerical abundance of the major protist forms in the ice edge zone of the Weddell Sea*

Taxon	Abundance (cells l⁻¹)	
	Mean	Range
Pyrmnesiophyceae		
(*Phaeocystis pouchetti*)	1×10^6	3×10^3–4×10^6
(Motile cells)	2×10^4	1×10^3–9×10^4
Bacillariophyceae (diatoms)	5×10^5	1×10^4–1×10^6
Prasinophyceae	1×10^4	~0–3×10^4
Misc. flagellates	8×10^4	3×10^3–2×10^5
Cryptophyceae	5×10^4	1×10^4–1×10^5
Dinophyceae (dinoflagellates)	2×10^4	5×10^3–6×10^4
Archaeomonads Chrysophyceae	2×10^4	2×10^3–7×10^4
(*Distephanus speculum*)	3×10^4	~0–5×10^3
Choanoflagellata (choanoflagellates)	2×10^4	1×10^3–2×10^6
Siliceous cysts	9×10^5	–
Ciliata		
(Ciliates)	5×10^3	1×10^3–9×10^3
(tintinnids)	3×10^3	3×10^3–3×10^3

A lower range ~0 means that the organisms were recognizable in a qualitative examination of the sample but were too rare to detect in quantitative counts; in such cases an abundance of 0 was used in calculating the group mean.
From Buck & Garrison (1983).

protozoan biomass during AMERIEZ 83 and 62–67% of the biomass during AMERIEZ 86. Naked (non-loricate) flagellates were usually dominant among the heterotrophic flagellates, followed by dinoflagellates and choanoflagellates. Heterotrophic flagellates, principally *Gyrodinium* spp., *Amphidinium* spp., and *Gymnodinium* spp., are considerably larger than the naked or loricate flagellates. Although a variety of ciliates were present,

non-sheathed oligothrichs (i.e. *Strombidium* spp.) dominated the ciliate biomass both during the 1983 (spring) and 1986 (autumn) AMERIEZ cruises. Tintinnids were rare in the spring cruise but made up a significant fraction of the ciliate biomass during the autumn cruise.

During both AMERIEZ cruises protozooplankton biomass increased with increasing phytoplankton and bacterioplankton biomass and productivity and bacterioplankton biomass and production in transects across the ice edge (Table 13.3). In the spring 1983 cruise the protozooplankton biomass in the area of the ice edge to open water was almost five times that of the ice covered waters, while in the autumn 1986 cruise the open water biomass was over three times that of the ice covered stations.

The abundance of microheterotrophs in the upper water column for stations under heavy ice cover (Stations 5 and 6) and along a transect across the ice edge zone (Stations 15–21) is shown in Fig. 13.7 (Garrison *et al.*, 1984, 1986). The abundance of microheterotroph biomass was concentrated in the upper 50 m; abundance dropped rapidly below approximately 50 to 60 m. Garrison *et al.* (1984) have tabulated data on the abundance and biomass of heterotrophs in the ice edge zone in comparison with those in the sea ice (see Table 13.4). While the concentrations of heterotrophic flagellates and choanoflagellates were greater in the sea ice than in the water, heterotrophic dinoflagellates and tintinids were not found in the sea ice and the abundance of ciliates was very much greater in the water.

13.8 Ice edge zooplankton and nekton

There have been limited investigations of the ice edge zooplankton. Brinton (1984) carried out zooplankton sampling along two transects across the ice edge in the southern Scotia Sea in November–December 1983 using

Table 13.3. *Summary of mean phytoplankton and bacterial production and protozooplankton and macrozooplankton biomass during AMERIEZ 83 and AMERIEZ 86*

Cruise	Values integrated over upper 100 m.					
	Production (mg C m⁻² day⁻¹)		Biomass (mg C m⁻²)			
	PHYTO	BACT	PHYTO	BACT	PZOO	ZOO
AMERIEZ 83						
Ice covered	284.8	24.95	947	147.1	88.33	—
Ice edge to open water	516.8	138	4372.3	384.1	426.77	—
AMERIEZ 86						
Ice covered	161.13	11.53	816.67	228.93	165.8	45.8
Open water	206.25	111.15	4989.5	394.95	551.85	213.6

BACT, bacterio-plankton; PHYTO, phytoplankton; PZOO, protozooplankton; ZOO, macrozooplankton.
Data from Garrison & Buck (1989a).

Table 13.4. *Average concentrations of the major groups of protists in cells ml⁻¹ in the water column in relation to the Weddell Sea ice edge*

Taxa	Under-ice stations						Ice-edge stations			
	2	5	31	61	64	65	84	1	71	73
Choanoflagellata	246	21	15	39	215	151	818	155	80	1
Prymnesiophyceae	29	71	36	188	107	148	3107	2140	115	35
Bacillariophyceae	73	215	35	67	611	742	480	1245	1437	485

From Garrison *et al.* (1984).

Bongo nets. Predominant organisms collected were pelagic tunicates, salps (*Salpa thompsoni*) and euphausiid crustaceans. Amphipod crustaceans, the large gammarids *Cyphocaris* and *Parandania*, and the smaller hyperiids *Vibalia* and *Cyllopus* commonly associated with salps, occurred at varying abundances occurred throughout the upper water zone. During 10–20 November the highest densities of salps were at the northernmost stations, 58–59° S, remote from the ice edge within the maximum surface temperature gradient, 0.25 to 0.1 °C. Torres *et al.* (1984) reported a mean salp biomass of 0.239 g m⁻² for the upper 600 m. During sampling carried out from November 21 to December 2 the highest densities extended further south.

Franz *et al.* (1987) have provided a preliminary report on an investigation of the ice edge zooplankton carried out on the winter expedition of the *Polarstern* in early October and early December. The October crossing went from open water through the marginal ice zone into solid pack and then through a zone of ice floes into the coastal polynya. The total plankton biomass decreased with increasing percentage of ice cover and ice thickness but increased again slightly near the polynya. In the northern part of the crossing larvae of the euphausiids *Euphausia*

frigida and *E. superba* occurred in fair numbers, up to 200 larvae (100 m)⁻³, but were absent in the south. Ostracods and polychaetes were more evenly distributed along the crossing. Fish larvae and appendicularians were virtually absent in early October. Chaetognaths and the copepods *Calanoides acutus* and *Rhincalanus gigas* (copepodids IV–V and adults) were prominent features of the open water sample in the north. When entering the marginal ice zone the abundance of chaetognaths dropped by an order of magnitude and the two copepod species were replaced by another copepod, *Metridia gerlachei*, and juvenile *Calanus propinquus*. In the zone of heavy pack ice even those species were virtually absent. In all the copepods the ratio of adults to juveniles varied considerably. Also the numerous small copepod species *Oithona similis* and *Ctenocalanus citer*, as well as the eggs and nauplii of *Calanus propinquus*, decreased in density when entering the heavy pack ice.

In their investigation of the abundance and distribution of krill in the ice edge zone of the Weddell Sea Daly & Macaulay (1988) found that in the austral spring of 1983 the vertical distribution of krill under the pack ice was similar to that of the open water. Average krill biomass under the ice ranged from 1 to 68 g m⁻², and in the open water 10 to 100 g m^{-2}. However, the pack ice directly influenced the distribution and abundance of young krill. Juvenile *E. superba* were much more abundant under the ice than in the open water north of the ice edge. Numerous observations were made of juvenile krill feeding on the sea ice microalgae on the undersides of the ice floes. In contrast to species at other trophic levels, krill did not increase in biomass at the ice edge. Krill, however, may have been grazing phytoplankton which developed to the north of the ice edge in an earlier stage of the ice retreat, which was rapid at the time of sampling. The krill distribution may also have been part of a mesoscale patchiness, as krill are strong swimmers and swarms can move considerable distances when foraging for food (see section 5.4).

Torres *et al.* (1984) investigated the distribution of fishes and salps in relation to the ice edge in the southern Scotia Sea. The dominant fishes in the upper 500 m were *Electrona antarctica* and *Gymnoscopelus braueri* (Myctophidae) and *Notolepis coatsi* (Paralepididae). Dominant fishes in the lower 500 m of the water column were *Bathylagus antarcticus* (Bathylagidae) and *Cyclothone microdon* (Gonostomatidae). Mean fish biomass for the upper 1000 m of the water column was 327 g (100 m)$^{-2}$, a figure somewhat lower than that found by Frost & McCrone (1979) for the sub-Arctic-transitional waters off Washington (450 g (100 m)$^{-2}$ for myctophids only) but considerably higher than that found in tropical-subtropical systems studied by Maynard *et al.* (1973; 214 g (100 m)$^{-2}$, Gulf of Mexico). Piscivorous fishes were extremely rare in the study area.

There was a clear trend of increasing biomass moving from south to north away from the marginal ice zone, followed by a sharp drop in biomass north of 58° S. The biomass peak corresponded to the pronounced phytoplankton bloom found in the vicinity of 59° S. There was a marked increase with time in both fish and salp biomass in the southern part of the study area. The increase corresponded to an intensifying phytoplankton bloom at the retreating ice edge. This suggested a gradual southward displacement of mobile micronektonic species in response to the increased production of ice edge blooms and its associated increases in prey species. In the case of salps it suggested an increased population size through reproduction.

As a consequence of the research carried out through AMERIEZ new information on the impact of pack ice cover on the deeper-living (100–1000 m) mesopelagic micronekton community has been provided (Ainley *et al.*, 1985). In ice-free waters throughout the world's oceans, a substantial fraction of the mesopelagic community migrates from 200–500 m daytime depths to, or near,

the surface at dusk and return to depth at dawn. Such organisms orient to a constant light level or isolume, which moves up and down in the water column with the setting and rising of the sun (Kampa & Boden, 1954). In the Antarctic, where the diel light regimes differ markedly between winter and summer it would be expected that such vertical migration patterns would have radically different patterns through the austral seasons. Shading of the water column by pack ice would further complicate such patterns during periods of increasing day length through the contrasting light levels of open water and consolidated pack ice.

Moving northwards from the pack ice there is a clear trend of increasing biomass and diversity of the ichthyofauna (Torres *et al.*, 1984), as well as a change in the seabird fauna (Fraser & Ainley, 1986) At 58° S (the Weddell–Scotia confluence) there was a sharp drop in fish biomass and seabird composition. The dominant diel distribution pattern of the fishes was a vertical migration pattern (Torres *et al.*, 1984).

Amphipods and crustacea dominated the crustacean component in open waters south of 59° S. Representatives of classical mid-water crustacean faunas (for example Pasiphaeidae, Opolaridae, Mysidacea, Panaeidae, Ostracoda) common in boreal, temperate and tropical waters, were not taken north of 59° S. No decapods, mysids or ostracods were captured in trawls reaching less than 310 m anywhere in the open-water transects, by day or night.

The myctophids, *E. antarctica* and *G. braueri*, and krill were the main prey of seabirds in open waters, while the amphipods *Vibalia* and *Cyllopus* were most prevalent in seabird diets north of 58° S. Most of the prey were captured when they moved upwards into the surface waters at night as part of their diel migration cycle (Ainley *et al.*, 1983b; Ainley & Boekelheide, 1983). Dietary changes occurred in the pack ice region. The above prey were captured with less regularity, and deep into the pack ice region crustacea of the genera *Pasiphaea* and *Eurythenes* replaced myctophids as dominant items in the diet. The dominance of *Pasiphaea longispina* in the diets of the few seabirds that frequent consolidated pack ice, which were principally Snow Petrels, was unexpected as it had not been captured in trawls shallower than 310 m. The fact that two other deep-water species, the large amphipod *Eurythenes gyrllus* and the ostracod *Gygantocypris mulleri*, were also eaten by the pack ice seabirds indicated that an upward seasonal displacement of these mesopelagic crustacea had occurred. Thus, these species which were unavailable to birds in areas of open water became available at the surface in the pack ice. In the open water primary production extended to a depth of

110 m, but southward in the more concentrated ice phyto-plankton chlorophyll became increasingly constricted to the surface until it was eventually confined to the ice itself, with extremely low concentrations in the water beneath. The reduction in light (the cue associated with vertical movement) encouraged mesopelagic species to reside at the surface.

13.9 Ice edge vertebrates

Beginning with the whalers, Antarctic voyagers have noted an increase in the abundance of vertebrates at the pack ice edge (Marr, 1962; Ainley & Jacobs, 1981; Stirling & Cleator, 1981). According to the authors of the AMERIEZ Research Plan (AMERIEZ, 1981) the basis for this pattern could be due to (a) increased productivity due to upwelling at the ice edge (Buckley *et al.*, 1979); (b) enhanced productivity resulting from processes in the water column (Ainley & Jacobs, 1981); (c) the release of ice algae and bacteria to seed the water column; (d) the rich community of prey organisms closely associated with or within the ice; (e) increased productivity and food web interactions as a retreating ice edge exposes enriched water to sunlight (A. C. Hardy, 1967); (f) an artifact forced on shipboard observers not capable of proceeding into the ice (Marr, 1962); or (g) to an accumulation of organisms when they reach the sharp boundary of their preferred habitat (Ainley *et al.*, 1988).

The vertebrate ice edge community has rather low species diversity and includes six major species of birds, including Adélie Penguin (*Pygoscelis adeliae*) and Snow Petrel (*Pagodroma nivea*), and several species of mammals, including Crabeater Seal (*Lobodon carcinophagus*), Leopard Seal (*Hydrurga leptonyx*), Ross Seal (*Ommatophoca rossii*), and the Minke Whale (*Balaenoptera acutirostrata*). The open-water community is much more diverse, has strong ties with the sub-Antarctic regions, and includes several species of birds, including Macaroni Penguin (*Eudyptes chrysolophus*) and Cape Pigeon (*Daption capense*), Southern Fur Seal (*Arctocephalus gazella*), Southern Elephant Seal (*Mirounga leonina bonina*), and the great whales.

13.9.1 Seabirds

Fraser & Ainley (1986) have recently reviewed the relationships of seabirds to the pack ice edge. They point out that it is only comparatively recently that it had been recognized that most species of seabirds are constrained by specific oceanic characteristics, including temperature and salinity, water clarity, depth to bottom, depth of the mixed layer, and the presence or absence of ice, as well as feeding and flight characteristics (e.g. R. G. B. Brown *et al.*, 1975; Pocklington, 1979; R. G. B. Brown, 1980; Zink,

1981; Ainley & Boekelheide, 1983; Kinder *et al.*, 1983; Ainley *et al.*, 1983b). Other studies (e.g. Zink, 1981; Ainley *et al.*, 1983b) have shown that the ice edge is a region of overlap between two distinct seabird communities, one associated with the pack ice and the other with waters generally free of ice but still under its influence (cold temperatures and icebergs) (Fraser & Ainley, 1986). These two communities are each composed of four to five dominant species and up to five minor ones. The pack ice community comprises Emperor (*Aptenodytes forsteri*) and Adélie Penguins, and Snow and Antarctic (*Thalassoica antarctica*) Petrels. Penguins generally dominate in terms of biomass although Snow and Antarctic Petrels are more abundant. North of the ice edge the Southern Fulmar (*Fulmarus glacialoides*), the Cape Pigeon, Wilson's Storm Petrel (*Oceanites oceanicus*) and the Mottled Petrel (*Pterodroma inexpectata*) are the primary (Ainley *et al.*, 1983b) components. In the Ross Sea Southern Fulmars and Cape Pigeons dominate the community, both in terms of biomass and abundance. Except for the Antarctic Petrel most of the species in the community north of the ice edge tend to be associated with ice-free water (less than 20% ice coverage). This is especially evident among the major components, the Light-mantled Sooty (*Phoebetria palpebrata*) and the Black-browed (*Diomedea melanophris*) Albatrosses. Most of the open water species have specialized foraging behaviours relying on dynamic soaring – taking advantage of air movement above the waves for support – which is difficult over the pack ice because the ice dampens sea swells (Ainley *et al.*, 1983b).

The presence of two distinct seabird associations in the pack ice and ice-free habitats is consistent with the hypotheses that seabirds are strongly tied by morphological and behavioural adaptations to specific water types or marine habitats. Fraser & Ainley (1986) discuss the factors which specifically determine the distribution patterns. One common explanation is that the increased abundance of seabirds at the ice edge (Fig. 13.8a) is due to greater access to the ocean and its resources (Divorky, 1977; Stirling, 1980). This idea was developed from studies in the Arctic where the major seabird concentrations were associated with recurring polynas (R. G. B. Brown & Nettleship, 1981). However, in the Antarctic, in contrast to the Arctic where the pack ice has few internal leads and little open water (Zwally *et al.*, 1983a), the pack ice has numerous leads and polynas (Ainley & Jacobs, 1981; Zwally *et al.*, 1983a). During the 1983 AMERIEZ cruise vast polynas were found in the Weddell Sea near 63° S yet the seabird densities were low. Fraser & Ainley (1986) pose the question: 'If open water is so important to the seabirds and is available within the ice, why are they still concentrated at the ice edge?'

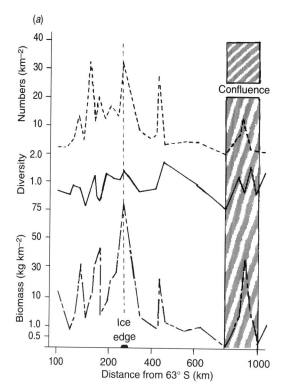

Fig. 13.8. (*a*) A transect in the Weddell sea illustrating changes in the density, species diversity (Shannon–Weaver diversity index), and biomass of the seabirds at the ice edge and other locations. Note changes in scale to illustrate the patterns at the confluence (shaded area) of the Scotia and Weddell Seas (900 km north of 63° S). (*b*). Seabird abundance and chl *a* concentrations in the pack ice in the western Weddell Sea during the AMERIEZ cruise in November–December 1983 relative to the ice edge (shown by vertical dashed lines). Stations 6 and 15 represent the southernmost stations; north is plotted relative to these stations. No data was available for Stn 1 in the Eastern Sector and Stns 11, 12 and 13 in the Western Sector. (*c*). Transects from the Weddell and Scotia Seas illustrating the positions of peaks in biomass, species diversity and density of seabirds early in the season (thin lines) and two weeks later (thick lines). All distances are measured from 63° S. Redrawn from Fraser & Ainley (1986).

Therefore, the alternative hypothesis, the idea that ice edge zones are biologically more productive, thus offering seabirds superior prey availability, would appear to be more soundly based. Fig. 13.8*b*, which is based on data from the Weddell Sea, illustrates how low seabird numbers increased at each of four ice edge stations (Stations 3, 10, 12, and 20). Seabird numbers closely paralleled chlorophyll concentrations throughout much of the study area, including stations 10 and 20 at the ice edge. At Stations 3 and 12, where chlorophyll values were low, features of the water column suggested frontal discontinuities. There is a time lag between the ice disintegration with the release of ice algae to seed the water column and the surge in the productivity of the water previously covered by ice (Ackley *et al.*, 1979; Alexander, 1980). This suggests that seabirds should actually

concentrate north of the retreating ice edge. Fig. 13.8*c* illustrates how seabirds respond to the retreating ice edge in the Weddell Sea. Peaks in their density, diversity and biomass were first recorded about 500 km north of the ice edge at 63° S, but two weeks later they occurred 100 km south, a shift in tandem with the latitudinal displacement of the ice edge, suggesting that seabirds were following the ice retreat. Pack ice surveys of seabird distributions (e.g. Zink, 1981; Ainley *et al.*, 1984, and others) have shown that seabird numbers peaked over intrusions of extremely thick, densely concentrated multi-year ice which were laced with floes showing extraordinarily abundant algal and bacterial communities and being in advanced stages of decomposition. They were also the only sites within the pack ice where euphausiids, decapod crustaceans and other prey regularly occurred. Fraser & Ainley (1986) suggest that the birds were responding to the physical features of the ice, not to prey availability.

13.9.2 *Mammals*

A number of authors (e.g. Marr, 1962; Laws, 1977b; Mizroch *et al.*, 1986) have noted that some species of baleen whales concentrate in the marginal ice edge zone and follow the southward retreat of the ice, thus gaining access to their principal food, the krill. Seals are also attracted to the ice edge (Ribec *et al.*, 1991).

Erickson (1984) has reported on studies of mammal distribution patterns in the pack ice during the 1983 AMERIEZ cruise. The overall composition of the seals observed was 77% Crabeater, 18% Leopard, 4% Weddell and 0.4% Ross. The 18% observed for Leopard Seals was several time greater than the normal abundance of this species in most censuses (Erickson *et al.*, 1971; Condy, 1976; J. R. Gilbert & Erickson, 1977). The apparent explanation was that the AMERIEZ census coincided with the whelping period of the Leopard Seal when large numbers of females were hauled out on the ice tending their young. Leopard Seals were also distributed deeper into the pack ice than has been observed in other censuses taken later in the season (Gilbert & Erickson, 1977). Crabeater Seal densities ranged from four seals per nautical mile at the ice edge (60.5° S) to less than one seal per nautical mile at 100 nautical miles into the pack ice. The general pattern which emerges is one of increasing numbers of seals from deep within the pack ice to the ice edge.

While only four Minke Whales were seen by Erickson (1984), concentrations of Minke Whales have frequently been observed at the ice edge. In the McMurdo Sound region in late January I personally have observed groups of up to eight individuals at the ice edge.

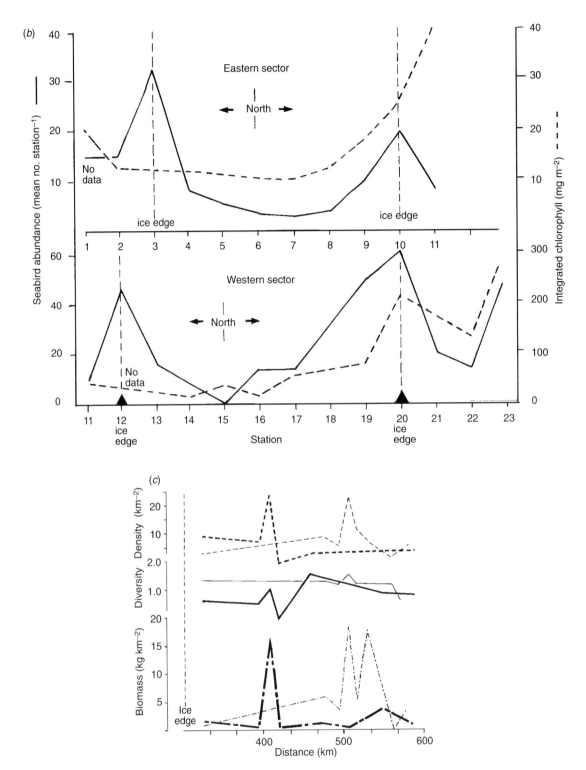

Fig. 13.8. For legend see opposite.

13.10 The importance of the ice edge in the ecology of the Southern Ocean

It is clear that in the past the importance of ice edge blooms in the overall primary productivity of the Southern Ocean has been underestimated. W. O. Smith & Nelson (1986) have attempted to estimate the role of ice edge blooms in the overall phytoplankton production in the Southern Ocean based on information from the Weddell Sea on the bloom's spatial extent, its measured productivity, and its duration based on rates of ice retreat. Productivity was greatest within the bloom averaging 571 mg C m^{-2} day^{-1}. If the region's background production

Table 13.5. *Predicted monthly ice edge production in the Southern Ocean, the Ross Sea, and the Weddell Sea*

	Southern Ocean		Weddell Sea		Ross Sea	
	Ice cover[1] ($\times 10^6$ km^{-2})	Production ($\times 10^{12}$ g C day^{-1})	Ice cover ($\times 10^6$ km^{-2})	Production ($\times 10^{12}$ g C day^{-1})	Ice cover ($\times 10^6$ km^{-2})	Production ($\times 10^{12}$ g C day^{-1})
January	6.54	103.1	1.82	27.4	1.96	37.6
February	4.17	56.3	1.26	9.0	0.86	29.6
March	5.50		1.61		1.71	
April	8.00		2.32		2.90	
May	12.36		3.72		3.57	
June	15.81		5.47		3.95	
July	17.54		6.39		4.16	
August	19.82		6.60		4.41	
September	20.53		7.09		4.30	3.2
October	20.00	12.2	6.74	5.8	4.41	
November	17.72	54.2	6.21	9.1	4.20	6.1
December	10.88	157.3	3.37	50.2	3.22	29.2
Total		383.1		101.5		105.7

[1]Represents period ending on 15th of each month.
Area of ice cover estimated from Zwally *et al.* (1983). Aerial ice edge production for the Weddell Sea calculated from W. O. Smith & Nelson (1985a) and for the Ross Sea from Wilson *et al.* (1986); Southern Ocean production is calculated using the average of these two values.
After W. O. Smith & Nelson (1985b).

(i.e. that not influenced by the ice) is taken to be 134 mg C m^{-2} day^{-1} (Holm-Hansen *et al.*, 1977), then the ice edge bloom would supply approximately 3.4 times the daily production occurring before and after the bloom. The bloom follows the retreat of the ice, which in the Weddell Sea (60° S. 24° W) is approximately 130 km per month from September through December (Zwally *et al.*, 1983a). Since the bloom's spatial extent was estimated to be 250 km, the bloom would last 1.9 months or 58 days at any given point in the area. By multiplying the bloom's duration by the mean productivity it was estimated that the ice edge productivity was 32.9 g C m^{-2} y^{-1}. Annual production in the Southern Ocean has been calculated to be 16 g C m^{-2} (Holm-Hansen *et al.*, 1977); thus the ice edge bloom may produce an amount up to two times the production over the rest of the growing season. This figure is similar to that calculated by Jennings *et al.* (1984) (556 mg C m^{-2} day^{-1}), which was based on apparent seasonal rates of nutrient depletion. Jennings *et al.* (1984) concluded that previous researchers had under-estimated production by 25–67% because ice edge production was not included.

W. O. Smith & Nelson (1986) made a similar calculation based on data from the Ross Sea study discussed above (W. O. Smith & Nelson, 1985a,b). In this case the mean productivity was 962 mg C m^{-2} day^{-1} (D. L. Wilson *et al.*, 1986), more than seven times the productivity of the open water of the Southern Ocean. From data in Zwally *et al.* (1983a) the average rate of ice retreat at 76° S, 166° E during November and December, when the ice edge retreats most of its distance, is approximately

160 km per month. Therefore the bloom, would last approximately 1.6 months or 48 days at any given point. From the available data, the W. O. Smith & Nelson bloom would produce 45.6 g C m^{-2}, or nearly three times more than the non-bloom production.

W. O. Smith & Nelson further attempted to assess the impact of the ice edge blooms on the total primary production of the Southern Ocean. Since the ice edge blooms begin in regions with substantial ice cover they used the progression of 15% ice cover as a convenient measure of the area uncovered by the ice retreat. Table 13.5 lists the mean monthly variations in area covered in the entire Southern Ocean, the Weddell Sea and the Ross Sea. It was calculated that the total annual production associated with ice edge blooms in the Southern Ocean is approximately 380×10^{12} g C. Of that the Weddell and Ross Seas produce approximately equal amounts (each producing approximately 25% of the Southern Ocean total). This can be compared with El-Sayed's 1978 estimate of 619×10^{12} g C for the Southern Ocean as a whole. This value is based on a productive area of 38.1×10^6 km^{-2}, whereas W. O. Smith & Nelson (1986) assumed that the ice retreats over 38.1×10^6 km^{-2}. Thus their calculations suggest that including the ice edge production from this smaller area the estimate of annual production from the Southern Ocean is 990×10^{12} g C, an increase of more than 60%.

W. O. Smith & Nelson point out that the above calculations involve numerous assumptions, and therefore, some uncertainty. They note that we know little of the productivity of a reducing bloom, and that we have no information on the extent to which productivity within a bloom changes seasonally, or whether the spatial extent of the bloom varies. Furthermore, the contribution of the ice algae was not included in the calculations. Clearly a great deal more research is needed. Nevertheless, it is apparent that the ice edge system potentially plays a major role in the ecological and biogeochemical cycles of the Southern Ocean. Because production at the ice edge is potentially a large source of energy for herbivores, and is restricted both in space and time, grazers may have developed life-history strategies for exploiting the resources efficiently. Secondary consumers likewise are likely to have their migrations and reproductive cycles keyed into the availability of prey as a consequence of grazer activity.

14

Decomposition and the roles of bacteria and protozoa

14.1 Introduction

The most important generality to emerge from the last two decades of intensive research on aquatic ecosystem energy flux is the conclusion that a large proportion of the energy moves through the detritus food web rather than through the more conspicuous grazer food web (Pomeroy, 1980). The organisms involved in this detritus food web comprise bacteria, heterotrophic microflagellates and heterotrophic ciliates. There has been an increasing appreciation of their role not only in the breakdown of organic matter and the regeneration of nutrients but also as a potential food resource for larger consumer organisms. As a result of this work it has been established that the standing stocks of planktonic microorganisms are far greater than originally inferred from early investigations, and that they may be comparable to the combined biomass of all other heterotrophs (Sorokin, 1981).

In this chapter we shall consider the quantities and sources of organic matter (both dissolved and particulate) in both the water column and the sediments of the Southern Ocean. Information on the fate of this organic matter, including its remineralization to regenerate nutrients, is summarized. An account is given of the distribution, abundance, growth and production of both bacteria and heterotrophic protozoa, and recent information on their roles in what is now referred to as the 'microbial loop' in the pelagic food web is critically examined. Bacteria and protozoa in ice edge systems and in the sea ice have been considered in Chapters 13 and 3 respectively.

14.2 Quantities and sources of organic matter

14.2.1 Introduction

One of the generalizations to emerge from research on oceanic ecosystems is that there is a large pool, of non-living organic matter (detritus) present at all depths of the water column, and that its organic carbon content may exceed that of the living microbial (primarily phytoplankton, bacteria and microprotozoa) and zooplankton components combined. While it is convenient to classify the

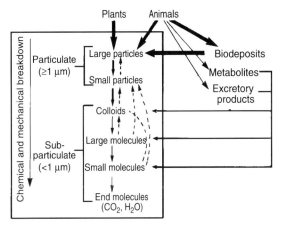

Fig. 14.1. Schematic view of detritus formation and decomposition. Modified from Darnell (1967b).

organic matter in the ocean into two categories, particulate organic matter (POM) and dissolved organic matter (DOM), it in reality constitutes a continuum from organic matter in true solution, through macromolecules, colloids to small particles and finally to large particles (Darnell, 1967b; Fig. 14.1). The differentiation between particulate and dissolved organic matter is purely operational, depending on the size of the filter used. In the world's oceans the dissolved organic carbon (DOC) is considered to average about 700 µg l^{-1} (P. J. Le B. Williams, 1975). The biomass of POM in oceanic waters ranges from 100–2000 µg l^{-1} (P. J. Le B. Williams, 1975).

Darnell (1967a) defines organic detritus broadly as 'all types of biogenic material in various stages of decomposition which represent potential energy sources for consumer species'. Thus defined organic detritus includes all dead organisms as well as secretions, regurgitations and egestions of living organisms, together with all the subsequent products decomposition which still represent potential sources of energy, such as proteins or amino acids. It is sometimes convenient to distinguish coarse POM (that material retained by filters with apertures of 1 µm in diameter) and fine or subparticulate (sometimes called nanodetritus) POM (material that passes through such filters).

14.2.2 Particulate organic matter (POM)

There have been a limited number of studies of POM in the waters of the Southern Ocean. The bulk of such studies have analyzed the filtrate from standard water samples for particulate organic carbon (POC). Such samples would include both living and dead plants and animals. Tanoue *et al.* (1986) determined POC concentrations in water samples from the surface to deep water along three transects in the Pacific sector of the Southern Ocean between 50° S and 65° S, and one in the Indian Ocean from 45° S to 62° S. In the Pacific sector average POC concentrations ranged from 55.6–82.0 µg C l^{-1} in the surface water layer (0–100 m), with the concentration decreasing with depth to 24.5–47.5 and 19.2–40.4 µg C l^{-1} in the intermediate (125–300 m) and deep (300–1500 m) water layers respectively. These values are lower than those reported in most productive oceanic areas, but higher that those reported from other high latitude seas, and comparable to those reported from the middle latitudes of the Pacific and Atlantic Oceans.

POM within the water column comes in a multiplicity of sizes and from a great variety of sources (Table 14.1). Dead phytoplankton cells, fragments from attached macroalgae, dead bacteria, dead protozoa, dead micro- and macrozooplankton, crustacea exuvia, and faecal pellets, especially those from copepods, euphausiids and salps. Microscopic examination of organic particles in the open ocean has revealed two main types: amorphous particles typically with maximum dimensions >100 m which clearly show remnants of previous cellular structure; and smaller amorphous particles which are clearly organic precipitates (Bowen, 1984; Goldman, 1984b; Biddanda, 1985). There are a variety of mechanisms which bring about the conversion of DOM to particulate form, all of them involving the collection of surface-active material at a gas–liquid interface and compression of the interface. The surface of bubbles and the surface of the seas are sites of aggregation of surface-active molecules. Wave action is an important agent in the conversion process. In addition inorganic particles frequently act as a focus for the condensation of DOM to POM.

In addition to the smaller aggregates referred above larger particles, which have variously been referred to as marine snow, faecal matter, agglomerates, conglomerates, macroflocs or large amorphous aggregates are frequently encountered. Such large marine amorphous aggregates, (generally referred to as 'marine snow') have been reported as a ubiquitous component of pelagic marine waters (Knauer *et al.*, 1982; Fowler & Knauer, 1986; Herndl & Peduzzi, 1988) and I have found them to be abundant in water samples from McMurdo Sound. Such marine snow aggregations are a microhabitat for a

Table 14.1. *Principal sources of dissolved organic matter (DOM) and particulate organic matter (POM)*

Sources of DOM	Sources of POM
Phytoplankton exudation	Phytoplankton
Sea ice microalgal exudation	Bacteria
Benthic microalgal exudation	Protozoa
Benthic macroalgal exudation	Zooplankton
Autolysis of photoautotrophs	Crustacean exuvia
Release of DOM by	Thalacian houses
microflagellates and ciliates	Faecal pellets
Excretion by zooplankton	(especially those of
Sloppy feeding by zooplankton	copepods, euphausiids
	and salps)
	Macroalgal detritus
	Organic precipitates
	from DOM

rich detrital community of living phytoplankton (Beers *et al.*, 1986), cyanobacteria, bacteria and protozoans (Caron *et al.*, 1982; Goldman, 1984b; Silver *et al.*, 1984). Compared with the mean abundance of these groups of organisms in an equivalent volume of water, macroaggregates are 5–1500 times more concentrated (Preslin & Aldridge, 1983; Beers *et al.*, 1986). The high population density of heterotrophic bacteria and Protozoa suggest that these macroaggregates may be major sites of remineralization of organic matter (Silver & Aldridge, 1981).

Bacteria often form large quantities of extracellular POM, which often brings about the adhesion of bacteria into clumps (Massalaski & Leppard, 1979; Paerl, 1974). Similar clumping can occur in some species of phytoplankton. Blooms of *Phaeocystis pouchetii* in the Southern Ocean add large quantities of extracellular organic slime to the water column. As the *Phaeocystis* bloom decays particulate matter in the water column adheres to the slime aggregates. Zooplankton contributions to the macroaggregates include copepod, euphausiid and salp faecal pellets and the exuvia of the crustaceans. To date the role of detrital aggregates in the pelagic waters of the Southern Ocean has received little attention. This should be a fruitful area for future research.

14.2.3 Faecal pellets

Faecal pellets may play an important role in the vertical transport of organic matter (Tanoue & Handa, 1980) from the surface to the bottom sediments (Turner, 1977; Honjo & Roman, 1978). The principal producers of large faecal pellets in the Southern Ocean are the copepods, euphausiids and salps. It had been assumed that the bulk of the organic carbon and opal vertical flux with the Antarctic euphotic zone and to the deep ocean was contributed by the faecal pellets of these organisms (v. Bodungen *et al.*, 1988; Fischer *et al.*, 1988). However, a significant proportion of the faecal pellets in the Southern Ocean has been found to be composed of small pellets (30 to 150 μm) (Sasaki & Hoshiai, 1986; Nothig & v. Bodungen, 1989). The specific sources of these small faecal pellets are not known, although several small metazoans (Sasaki & Hoshiai, 1986), and protists (Nothig & v. Bodungen, 1989) have been suggested as potential producers. Radiolarians and hydromedusae have also been reported as potential producers of small faecal pellets in temperate regions (Gowing & Silver, 1985) and both of these groups are abundant in the waters of the Southern Ocean. Recent studies in the southeastern Weddell Sea indicate that dinoflagellates are capable of ingesting large particles (Nothig & v. Bodungen, 1989) and producing consolidated faecal pellets.

Buck *et al.* (1990) in studies in the Weddell Sea ice edge zone during autumn 1986 found that a phagotrophic athecate dinoflagellate was common in the sea ice and the underlying water column. The single large vacuole of this dinoflagellate contained a variety of protistan prey but the predominant item was the pennate diatom *Nitzschia cylindricus*. Membrane bound faecal pellets were produced from the vacuoles. Fifteen per cent of the faecal pellet was identifiable protoplasm. Dinoflagellate concentrations in the sea ice brine ranged from 1.2×10^2 to 1.0×10^5 individuals l^{-1}. Faecal pellet concentrations within the sea ice ranged from 3.6×10^2 to 1.8×10^5 pellets l^{-1}, while those in the water column ranged from 6.4×10^0 to 8.9×10^1 pellets l^{-1}. Release of the faecal pellets into the underlying water column from the sea ice upon melting may account for a significant proportion of the POC in the water column at the ice edge.

Studies of organic particle flux beneath coastal sea ice at Lutzow-Holm Bay (Fukuchi & Sasaki, 1981; Sasaki & Hoshiai, 1986) have identified copepod faecal pellets as a major component of the flux. Because of their large and often concentrated populations Southern Ocean euphausiids, particularly *Euphausia superba*, are major producers of faecal pellets. In contrast to the compact faecal pellets of the copepods those of *E. superba* are string-shaped, up to several hundred μm long and about 150 μm wide (Wefer *et al.*, 1988). Tanoue *et al.* (1982) and Tanoue & Hara (1986) have examined the chemical composition and identified the remains of phytoplankton and other species present in *E. superba* faecal pellets.

The contribution of euphausiid faecal pellets to the flux of organic matter in the water column of the Southern Ocean must be considerable. They have been shown to dominate the vertical particulate flux in a number of areas

(Wefer *et al.*, 1988). *E. superba* faecal pellets have sinking rates of between 100 and 525 m day^{-1} (Ross *et al.*, 1985). A. Clarke *et al.* (1988b) measured faecal pellet production rates for this species of between 0.54 and 1.66 mg dry wt of faeces h^{-1} (for a 600 mg fresh wt animal). Organic matter loss was shown to be constant and was estimated at 0.13 mg h^{-1}. On the assumption that egestion remains constant, then a 120 mg dry wt animal would produce between 4730 and 4542 mg dry wt of faeces and 11.39 mg of organic matter per year (A. Clarke *et al.*, 1988b).

14.2.4 Crustacean exuvia

Copepods and euphausiids undergo rhythmic moulting cycles. In *Euphausia superba* this cycle ranges from 12 to 30 days. The cast exoskeletons result in the input of a significant quantity of organic matter to the water column. The residence time of this POM input to the water column is a function of the sinking rate and the rate of decomposition by heterotrophs.

Nicol & Stolf (1989) have studied the sinking rates of cast exoskeletons of *E. superba* and their role in the vertical flux of particulate matter from specimens collected at the ice edge south of Australia. They found that the cast exoskeletons represented 7.5% of the dry body weight. This compares with A. Clarke's (1976) estimate of 2.3 to 3.1%, and Ikeda & Dixon's (1982a) figures of 2.36 to 4.25%. Values for other species of euphausiids in the literature range from 5 to 12.7%. The sinking rates of the cast exoskeletons ranged from 0.06 to 1.28 cm s^{-1} (mean 0.78 cm s^{-1}, SD >0.183). This is similar to that measured for other euphausiids. Freshly moulted exoskeletons had a C:N ratio of 5.6:1 and a mean organic content of 73.3% (Table 14.11).

Ikeda & Dixon (1982a) examined the contribution of moulting by *E. superba* to organic detritus in the Southern Ocean. Calculations assuming 13 moults per year and a biomass production estimate of 1.08 g dry wt m^{-2} y^{-1} yielded values for moult production of 0.45 g dry wt m^{-2} y^{-1}, or 0.11 g C m^{-2} y^{-1}. Using similar calculations Nicol & Stolf (1989) obtained a slightly higher estimate for moult production of 1.053 g dry wt m^{-2} y^{-1}, and 0.18 g C m^{-2} y^{-1}. These estimates are similar to those obtained for other euphausiid species (e.g. Lasker, 1966).

14.2.5 Macroalgal debris

Most parts of the world's coastal areas receive a considerable input of organic matter of terrestrial origin. However, such sources are very much reduced or lacking in Antarctica due to the paucity of ice-free land and the lack of rivers. However, dense growths of macroalgae are a conspicuous feature of shallow rocky substrates round the Antarctic coast (see Chapter 11). In the Bransfield Strait macroalgal production has been estimated at about 2000 g C m^{-2} y^{-1}, compared to 60 g C m^{-2} y^{-1} for the phytoplankton (Liebezeit & v. Bodungen, 1987). These dense algal beds are the subject of ice scour, storms and grazing by invertebrates and fishes. As a consequence considerable quantities of algal debris ranging from whole plants to fine fragments collect in cracks and depressions and are sedimented to deeper waters. In their sediment trap experiments in Bransfield Strait Leibezeit & v. Bodungen (1987) found that material of macroalgal origin was a major contributor to the particle flux, increasing from 37% at 539 m to 71% at 1833 m.

Reichardt (1987) investigated the fate of macroalgal debris and its potential participation in deep-sea benthic food chains in the Weddell Sea area and the Bransfield Strait. He found that in two sediment samples at 2280 and 1570 m the upper 8–10 cm contained considerable amounts of macroalgal fragments larger than 1 mm (22.9 and 20.9 g m^{-2} of ash-free dry weight respectively) derived from red and brown algae. The thallus fragments served as a matrix for epiphytic bacteria and thus they would form a potential food source for the polychaete-dominated infauna.

14.2.6 Dissolved organic matter (DOM)

Within oceanic waters there is a large reservoir of DOM. According to Bada & Lee (1977) oceanic waters in general contain 0.5 to 1.5 mg l^{-1} of DOC. The chemical composition of this DOM pool, however, is poorly known. The vast majority of the pool is composed of complex refractory materials (Bada & Lee, 1977), while a small, but significant, proportion is composed of biologically active organic compounds. Of the biologically active dissolved compounds amino acids, peptides, proteins, mono- and polysaccharides, fatty acids, organic acids and nucleotides have been detected in seawater (see review by P. J. Le B. Williams, 1975). The DOC:POC ratio in the ocean is on average 10:1 (Wetzel, 1984).

While various sources of DOM are well known there is only limited information available on the importance of the various sources and the mechanisms of utilizable DOM production The most important sources are (Table 14.1):

1. *Phytoplankton exudation*: Excretion of a proportion of the photoassimilated carbon from phytoplankton is now generally accepted, although the quantities and rates of excretion are still debated (Fogg *et al.*, 1965; Fogg, 1966; Hellebust, 1974; Mague *et al.*, 1979; Sondergaard, 1989). A variety of molecular species is released. However, exudation as a percentage of the total assimi-

lated carbon is highly variable, not only between species but for individual species depending on the specific environmental conditions. Release amounts in experimental studies range from 0 to 70% (Fogg *et al.*, 1965; Choi, 1972; Berman & Holm-Hansen, 1974; Sondergaard, 1989). Hellebust (1974) estimated that on average approximately 10% of the photosynthate of phytoplankton is excreted as DOC, and this figure is often used in calculating carbon budgets.

2. *'Sloppy feeding'*: There is evidence that there is a significant loss of algal cell contents during handling and grazing by herbivores (Copping & Lorenzen, 1980; Eppley *et al.*, 1981). The quantitative significance of such 'sloppy feeding' in the Southern Ocean is unknown.

3. *Autolysis*: Stress may cause the death and autolysis of photoautotrophs, particulary in the senescent stage of a phytoplankton bloom. The *Phaeocystis* blooms which are a common feature of phytoplankton dynamics in the Southern Ocean produce large amounts of extracellular carbon. Unusually high concentrations of DOC have frequently been reported as a general characteristic associated with *Phaeocystis* blooms (e.g. Bolter & Dawson, 1982 in the Bransfield Strait and Eberlein *et al.*, 1985 in the North Sea). As the bloom decays bacteria may attach to the autolysing algae or remain in close proximity in order to take up the released nutrients.

4. *Sea ice microalgae*: The release of DOM by sea ice microalgae has already been discussed in Chapter 3. Any DOM that has not been utilized by the sea ice bacteria will be released into the water column upon the melting of the ice. It is also probable that DOM is released into the water column from the sea ice microalgal bottom assemblages, the sub-ice mat strand assemblages.

5. *Release of DOM by microflagellates and ciliates*: Andersson *et al.* (1985) have recently demonstrated that during the consumption of bacteria heterotrophic microflagellates released 13% of the ingested nitrogen as ammonia and 30% of the ingested phosphorus as phosphate. They also showed that the concentration of dissolved free amino acids (DFAA) increased when flagellates fed on bacteria and concluded that they played a small but significant role as a source of DFAAs in the sea. Further studies by G. T. Taylor *et al.* (1985) suggested that the bactivore grazing by ciliates altered the DOM pool both quantitatively and qualitatively. The presence of bactivores appeared to enhance the DOM pool by contributing organic compounds with <5×10^2 to 5×10^4 nominal molecular weight (NMW). As suggested by Fenchel & Harrison (1976) herbivorous ciliates and microzooplankton stimulate bacterial growth by reducing growth-inhibiting bacterial competition through grazing and by supplying DOM through excretion and through

stimulation of bacterial exudation. It is therefore likely that the abundant ciliate and microflagellate populations of the Southern Ocean play a role in carbon cycling along the lines discussed above.

6. *Zooplankton secretion and excretion*: Zooplankton secretions and excretion contribute an as yet unqualified percentage to the DOM pool.

7. *Benthic microalgal exudation*: Diatom films on rocky substrates and the benthic microalgae in the surface layers of inshore sediments are another potential source of DOM. The excretion of the sediment microalgae has proved difficult to measure since the abundant sediment bacteria would be expected to assimilate any labile organic material as fast as it is released (Pomeroy *et al.*, 1981). It is probable that the rate of release of extracellular carbon by the benthic microalgae is comparable to that of the phytoplankton.

8. *Benthic macroalgae*: As mentioned above dense growth of benthic macroalgae occurs in inshore Antarctic waters and as we have seen in Chapter 11, they grow to considerable depths. Siebruth (1969), Moebus & Johnson (1974) and Khailov & Burkalova (1976) have reported that between 23 and 40% of the photoassimilated carbon is excreted by various macroalgae. Thus, the macroalgae may contribute considerable quantities of DOM to Antarctic inshore waters.

14.3 Sedimentation of POM

Almost all non-living particulate organic matter tends to sink, and unless consumed, continues to do so until it reaches the sediment. It has been demonstrated that there is a relationship between primary production in the water column and the flux of carbon to the sediment surface (Hargraves, 1975). However, the relationship is not a simple one. The greater the depth of the water column the greater the proportion of the organic matter that is decomposed before it reaches the bottom. Furthermore, the greater the depth of the mixed layer the greater the amount of mineralization occurring in the water column. Sedimentation of phytoplankton and larger particles such as faecal pellets is primarily responsible for the vertical flux of organic matter in the oceans. In recent years the development of automatic sediment traps which can be moored at different depths has added much to our understanding of this flux.

Recently, techniques have been developed to measure the sinking rate of particulate matter in the field (Bienfang, 1981). Results from a wide range of geographic regions, including the Antarctic and sub-Antarctic, have revealed a dependency of sinking rate on phytoplankton cell size (Bienfang, 1984; Jacques & Hoepffner, 1984), and ambient light intensity (Johnson &

Table 14.2. *Sinking rates of different particle types*

Particle types	Sinking rate (m day^{-1})	Source
Salp faecal pellets		
Two different species	450–1210 (836) 600–2700 (1080)	Bruland & Silver (1981)
Three different species	320–1987 (1060)	Madin (1982)
Copepod faecal pellets		
Acartia tonsa	80–150	Honjo & Roman
Calanus finmarchicus	180–200	(1978)
Different species		
various ages	19.5–100.7	Small *et al.* (1979)
adults	12–225	
Larvacean houses		
Oikopleura dioica	64.9* at 5 °C 57.0* at 16 °C	Silver & Aldridge (1981)
Diatom cells		
small-celled phytoplankton (tropical waters)	0.06	Bienfang (1985)
Large-celled, long chained species (temperate waters)	0.96	Bienfang & Harrison (1984)
Large-celled and pennate species		
Sub-Arctic ecosystem	0.43	Bienfang (1984)
Sub-Antarctic waters	0.1–0.52	v. Bodungen *et al.* (1981)
Different species	0.10–2.10*	Smayda & Boleyn (1965)
Fragilaria crotonensis	0.27*	Burns & Rosa (1980)
Natural community		
0–20μm	0.34–0.83*	Bienfang (1980)
20–102μm	0.95–1.65*	
Natural community	0.32–1.69 (0.64)	Bienfang (1981)
Natural community	0.21*	Smyada & Bienfang (1983)

Average sinking rates are in brackets or designated by an asterisk.
Based on Anderson & Nival (1988).

Smith, 1986; Riebesell, 1989) with increased sinking rates on overcast days. Sinking rates are also dependent on nutrient concentrations (Bienfang, 1981; Bienfang & Harrison, 1984), the density and viscosity of the water, and local water movements. The overall sinking rate of phytoplankton is largely a function of cell size and chain length, with the larger cells sinking more rapidly (Burns & Rosa, 1980; Riebesell, 1989). Increases in sinking rates can also be caused by the formation of cell aggregates, which increase in abundance during the decline of a phytoplankton bloom (v. Bodungen *et al.*, 1981). Widely different sinking rates have been reported in the literature (Table 14.2).

Phytoplankton dynamics during an ice edge bloom in the Ross Sea revealed depletion of dissolved silicic acid from the water column which was closely matched by the appearance of biogenic particulate silica (Nelson & Smith, 1986). The results of the study revealed low loss rate of biogenic silica, i.e. the loss of diatomaceous material via passive sinking or grazing and subsequent downward flux of faecal material. However, diatoms made up an overwhelming proportion of the biogenic material in the sediments beneath the bloom, and sediment accumulation rates indicated that a large proportion (*c.* 80%) of the surface siliceous production was being delivered to the sediment (Johnson & Smith, 1986). Furthermore, there was a strong taxonomic correlation between the species found in the ice edge bloom (W. O. Smith & Nelson, 1985a) and those in the sediments (Truesdale & Kellog, 1979). In order to resolve the question as to the proportion of the diatom production which is eventually deposited on the sea floor recent research has been directed at determining the sinking rates of particulate material and estimating the consumption rates of phytoplankton and the fate of the unconsumed material.

Johnson & Smith (1986) have studied the sinking rates of phytoplankton assemblages in the Weddell Sea marginal ice zone in November–December 1983 (Table 14.3). Parameters measured included chlorophyll *a*, phaeophytin, biogenic silica, particulate carbon, particulate nitrogen and diatom cell numbers. Sinking rate varied with each measurement but exhibited the following trends: phaeophytin >biogenic silica >particulate carbon >diatom cell numbers >particulate nitrogen >chlorophyll *a*. Sinking rates as determined by chlorophyll *a* ranged from 0 to 2.73 m day^{-1} (mean = 0.89), which were similar to those reported for temperate (Bienfang & Harrison, 1984), and sub-Arctic (Bienfang, 1984) regions of the ocean. It was estimated that 8 to 12% of the daily production was lost from the euphotic zone, a percentage similar to Bienfang's (1984) estimate for a sub-Arctic ecosystem.

Diatom production within the photic zone is the dominant mechanism for the uptake of dissolved silica from the water column (G. R. Heath, 1974). Annual silica production on the Antarctic shelf ranges between 100 and 500 g SiO$_2$ m^{-2} y^{-1}, with diatoms accounting for >99% (by weight) of the total (Lisitzin, 1972). This is much higher than at lower latitudes where annual silica production is only about 100 g SiO$_2$ m^{-2} y^{-1}, with diatoms accounting for 35% of the total (Lisitzin, 1972). Leford-Hoffman *et al.* (1986) have estimated that as much as one-third of the dissolved silica supplied to the oceans is ultimately deposited on the Antarctic shelf. Processes influencing the composition of the sedimentary microfossil assemblage include production in the sea ice or water column, release of microalgae from the sea ice, settling, dissolution, winnowing, resuspension and deposition.

Table 14.3. *Sinking ranges and means of particulate matter parameters measured in the marginal ice zone of the Weddell sea*

Parameter	Range (m day^{-1})	Average (m day^{-1})
Phaeopigment	0–5.47	1.17
Biogenic silica	0–3.44	1.11
Particulate carbon	0–4.93	1.08
Diatom cell numbers	0–2.88	0.91
Particulate nitrogen	0–3.30	0.89
Chlorophyll *a*	0–2.73	0.89

From Johnson & Smith (1986).

Table 14.4. *Concentration of particulate organic carbon (POC) and the vertical flux of POC at 50, 100 and 150 m depth under the ice-covered Lutzow-Holm Bay*

Depth	Concentration of POC (mg C m^{-3})	Vertical flux of POC (mg C m^{-2} day^{-1})
50	56	21
100	24	103
150	30	27

From Fukuchi & Sasaki (1981).

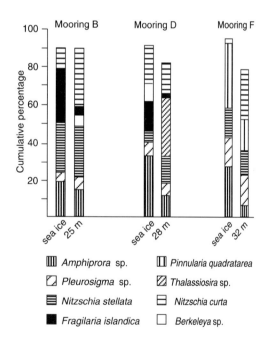

Fig. 14.2. Cumulative percentage of dominant species of diatoms for sea ice and corresponding shallow sediment traps in McMurdo Sound. Mooring B, at the tip of Erebus Ice Tongue; Mooring D, 5 km west of McMurdo Station; Mooring F, in New Harbour. Redrawn from Leventer & Dunbar (1987).

In McMurdo Sound Leventer & Dunbar (1987) found that although diatom abundances in the sea ice reach 10^8–10^9 cells m^{-2} during the period October–December, diatom fluxes measured by sediment trap samples were

Table 14.5. *Compound fluxes in the Bransfield Strait. All values are in mg m^{-2} day^{-1}*

Compound	Depth (m)				
	18	323	539	963	1410
Total flux	558	3170.8	3289.7	3462.4	4923.4
Particulate organic carbon	8	131.9	120.3	80.3	94.3
Particulate organic nitrogen	—	14.5	13.2	7.3	9.6
Total particulate phosphate	—	0.9	1.3	2.4	4.0
Amino acid carbon	2	28.2	21.0	21.5	27.0
Amino sugar carbon	—	0.6	1.2	1.2	2.2
Monosaccharide carbon	—	5.5	10.8	9.3	17.0
Chlorphyll	—	3.5	2.9	1.7	1.4
Phytoplankton carbon	>0[1]	1.4	1.4	>0[1]	>0[1]

[1]Degraded plasma.
From Liebezeit & v. Bodungen (1987).

only 10^5–10^7 individuals m^{-2} day^{-1}. However, it would expected that this flux would increase dramatically when the sea ice melted and released the particles trapped in the ice. Fukuchi & Sasaki (1981) measured the vertical flux of POC under the sea ice in Lutzow-Holm Bay (Table 14.4). The depth of the maximum flux occurred at 100 m depth, which is comparable to that reported from other seas. Faecal material was the major contributor to the vertical flux and of this copepod faeces were the dominant component. Ice algal species were common in the faecal material. This was similar to that of the McMurdo Sound study where the sediment trap assemblage closely resembled that found in the sea ice (Leventer & Dunbar, 1987) (Fig. 14.2). Here, five species dominated the sea ice assemblage: *Amphiprora* sp., *Pleurosigma* sp., *Nitzschia stellata, Pinnularia quadratarea*, and *Nitzschia curta*. These species were also common within the water column, along with *Thalassiosira* spp., a genus that was quite rare in the sea ice. Within the upper 250 m of the water column, at a site in Granite Harbour, diatom flux decreased from between 47–79% from 34 to 20 m. Opal flux, however, decreased by only 13–40% over the same depths, indicating that the dissolution of thinly silicified diatom frustules occurred. Species common in the sea ice, especially *Fragilaria islandica* var. *adeliae* and *Berkeleya* sp., appeared to be disproportionately dissolved in the water column. Lateral advection in the water column can also modify the composition of the diatom assemblage reaching the sea floor. At all sites it was found that the greatest increase in diatom flux occurred just above the sea floor. Resuspension of diatom tests and/or lateral advection, combined with the preferential dissolution of species dominating the sea ice assemblage, are responsible for the production of a sediment assemblage composed of *Thalassiosira* spp., *Nitzschia curta*, and other robust forms of *Nitzschia*.

14.4 Biogenic fluxes in the water column

Liebezeit & v. Bodungen (1987) determined the fluxes of organic carbon and nitrogen, total phosphorus, chlorophyll pigments, carbohydrates, amino acids and amino sugars for a depth-series sediment trap in November–December 1983 in the Bransfield Strait. Table 14.5 and Fig. 14.3 show the relative contribution of the various categories to the total carbon flux. Total mass flux was relatively constant in the upper traps and increased with depth. The observed amino acid depth distribution was very uncommon. Generally as a result of heterotrophic degradation, contribution of amino acids to both POC and POM decreases with depth both in the water column particulates (Liebezeit & Bolter, 1986) and sediment trap material (Liebezeit, 1985). In deeper traps sugar fluxes were significantly higher than in the upper ones. Absolute and/or relative increases of phosphorus, glucose and chlorophyll *b* fluxes and decreases of the β-aline flux with depth suggested a second source of organic plant material besides phytoplankton. Liebezeit & v. Bodungen (1987) identified this as originating from shallow-water macroalgae which are abundant in the shallow waters of the Bransfield Strait (Dieckmann *et al.*, 1985).

Fischer *et al.* (1988) deployed a multi-year sediment trap in the Weddell Sea (62° 26′ S; 34° 45.5′ W) at 835 m depth in a water depth of 3880 m. This station is covered by sea ice for about 70% of the year (Zwally *et al.*, 1983a,b). Fig. 14.4 depicts the total particle flux from the various sampling periods. The annual particle flux was extremely low 1.37 g m^{-2} y^{-1}, and highly variable, very much lower than that recorded for the Bransfield Strait (107 g m^{-2} y^{-1}). Faecal pellets played an important role in the sedimentation process, although krill pellets were extremely rare. The particle fluxes shown in Fig. 14.4 demonstrate that a large increase occurred following the

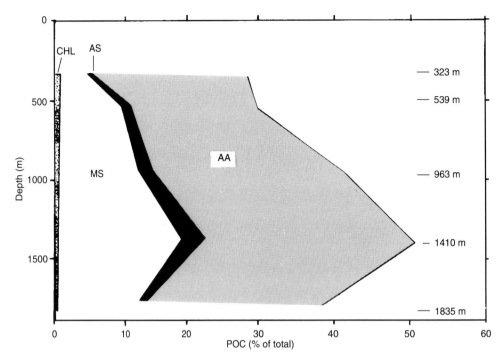

Fig. 14.3. Relative contributions of chlorophyll (CHL), monosaccharides (MS), amino sugars (AS) and amino acids (AA) to total particulate organic carbon flux (POC) in Bransfield Strait in November–December 1983. The depths of the sediment traps are shown on the right. Redrawn from Liebezeit & v. Bodungen (1987).

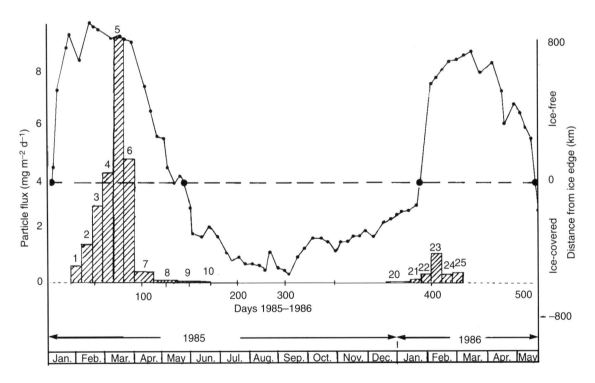

Fig. 14.4. Total flux of particulate matter for each sediment trap sampling period for a station in the Weddell Sea (see text for details). Sample numbers are on the top of the bars. The horizontal dashed line represents the ice edge with the superimposed solid line representing the shortest distance (in kilometres) from the approximate ice edge to the sediment trap site. Redrawn from Fischer *et al.* (1988).

Table 14.6. *Particle flux from the northern Weddell Sea, compared to that from other studies. The data were obtained during roughly the same time period using one year time series experiments from the Arctic, Northern Pacific and Antarctica*

	Weddell Sea 62° 26' S 34° 45' W Jan. 1985–Dec. 1985 ($g\ m^{-2}\ y^{-1}$)	Bransfield Strait 62° 15' S 57° 31' W Dec. 1983–Nov. 1984 ($g\ m^{-2}\ y^{-1}$)	Greenland Basin 74° 35' N 06° 43' W Aug. 1985–Jul. 1986 ($g\ m^{-2}\ y^{-1}$)	C. Fram Strait 78° 32' N 01° 22' E Aug. 1984–Aug. 1985 ($g\ m^{-2}\ y^{-1}$)	Station P 50° 00' N 144° 59' W Nov. 1985–Oct. 1986 ($g\ m^{-2}\ y^{-1}$)
Total	0.371	107.7	10.8	6.6	45
Biogenic	0.367	53.7	7.1	2.9	44.7
Carbonate	0.011	5.2	3.3	1.4	21.9
Opal	0.293	38.8	2.6	0.6	19.0
Combustible	0.063	9.7	1.2	0.9	3.8
Lithogenic	0.004	53.5	3.1	4.0	0.3
POC	0.02	3.0	0.4	0.4	3.7

From Fischer *et al.* (1988).

spring thaw of the sea ice. Table 14.6 compares data from Fischer *et al.*'s (1988) study in the Weddell Sea with those from the Bransfield Strait where the flux was very much higher (total POC flux several times that of the Weddell Sea). Fluxes in the Bransfield Strait were much higher than those recorded at Arctic stations and were compar-able to those measured at a station at 55° N.

Sedimentation off Vestkapp in the Weddell Sea was studied by v. Bodungen *et al.* (1988) in the summer of 1985. The material collected in the traps was dominated by faecal material from several species: string-shaped krill faeces, copepod faecal pellets (in low numbers), and oval, or triangle-shaped, pellets of various sizes (50–300 µm) of unknown origin filled with diatom frustules. Sedimentation over the study period amounted to 2–4 g C m^{-2}. It was estimated that the daily flux of POC was equivalent to between 43 and 65% of the daily primary production, but only between 1 and 15% for the other stations.

Wefer *et al.* (1988) deployed time-series sediment traps at 494 and 1588 m in the Bransfield Strait from 1 December 1983 to 25 November 1984. During the austral summer (December and January) the total flux was more than 1.5 g m^{-2} day^{-1} at both depths, while during all the other months the flux was between 10 and 1000 times lower, with the flux for the most productive months being 97% of the total (Fig. 14.5). The annual total flux to the deeper trap was 110 g m^{-2}. Biogenic materials (carbo-hydrate, POM, and opaline silica) accounted for about 67% in the upper trap and 50% in the lower one. On an annual average the fluxes were comparable to world averages (Angel, 1984), although the bulk occurred in one-sixth of the year. Peak daily fluxes during this period were very high. Similar high fluxes have been reported for short-term sediment trap

deployments elsewhere in Antarctic waters during the austral summer months (Fukuchi & Sasaki, 1981; Wefer *et al.*, 1982; Dunbar, 1983; Schnack, 1985a; v. Bodungen, 1986; Gersonde & Wefer, 1987). The bulk of the material in the traps consisted of krill faecal pellets resulting from krill swarms feeding on phytoplankton blooms.

Karl *et al.* (1991b) carried out simultaneous measurements of the seasonal depletion of dissolved inorganic carbon (CO_2), nitrogen ($NO_3 + NO_2$) and phosphate (HPO_4) and concentrations of C, N and P at five representative sites in the western Bransfield Strait over a period of 4 months. During the spring bloom period (December to January) there was a substantial removal of dissolved inorganic carbon, nitrogen and phosphate, corresponding to a net upper water column (0–50 m) seasonal production of 8410 mmol C m^{-2}, 825 mmol N m^{-2}, and 53.1 mmol P m^{-2}. This study confirmed the results obtained in the investigations discussed above documenting the phenomenon of a relatively short (2–3 months) downward flux of particulate organic matter. Karl *et al.* (1991b) have tabulated the data from all previous studies of particle flux in the Southern Ocean. These show short-term fluxes of 10^2 to 10^3 mg C m^{-2} day^{-1}, which are equivalent to values previously measured in upwelling conditions off central California and along the coasts of Peru (Martin *et al.*, 1987).

Karl *et al.* (1991b) and Leventer (1991) found that diatom resting cell formation was an important mechanism for removing intact, viable phytoplankton cells from the Antarctic coastal ecosystem. In addition to diatom resting spores and vegetative phytoplankton cells the sediment traps contained substantial concentrations of marine snow, faecal pellets (mostly from krill), unidentified eggs and mineral particles.

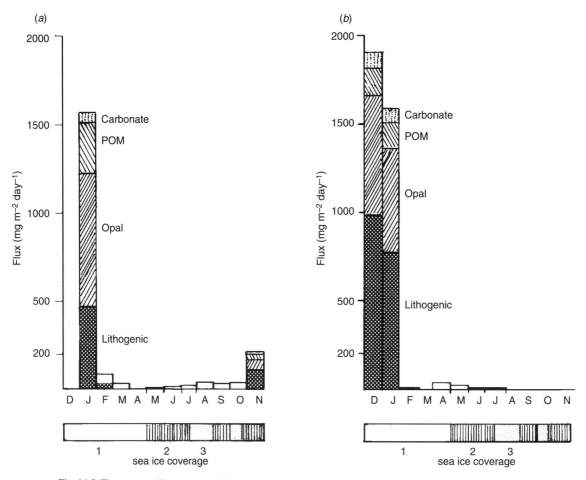

Fig. 14.5. Flux rates at 494 m (*a*) and 1588 m (*b*) water depth in the Bransfield Strait (62° 15.4′ S; 57° 31.7′ W) between 1 December 1983 and 25 November 1984. Total dry mass flux is partitioned into total carbonate (acid-leaching) flux, combustible flux (POM), opal (NaOH-leaching) flux, lithogenic (residue after combustion and NaOH-leaching) flux and carbonate (acid-leaching) flux. Sea ice coverage: 1. free of sea ice; 2. ice edge shifting in Bransfield Strait, 3. Bransfield Strait ice covered. Redrawn from Wefer *et al.* (1988).

A number of processes appear to be important in vertical particle flux in the Southern Ocean:

1. Water mass exchange (e.g. vertical water currents, Bathmann et al., 1991).
2. Mass sedimentation of phytoplankton triggered by a reduction in light supply (v. Bodungen, 1986).
3. Sinking of zooplankton faecal material, especially krill faecal strings following extensive grazing on phytoplankton blooms (Bruland & Silver, 1981; v. Bodungen, 1986; v. Bodungen et al., 1987; Cadee *et al.*, 1992).
4. Sedimentation of sea ice microalgae following the melting of the sea ice (Bathmann *et al.*, 1991).
5. Selective sedimentation of small faecal pellets probably of protozoan origin (Gowing, 1989; Nothig & v. Bodungen, 1989; Buck *et al.*, 1990; Bathmann *et al.*, 1991).
6. Sinking of aggregations of organic matter (marine snow).

14.5 Bacteria

14.5.1 Water column bacteria

Until the late 1970s most investigators (e.g. Mitskevich & Kriss, 1973; Kriss, 1973) considered that the bacterioplankton of the water column in Antarctic waters was present in low concentrations and that heterotrophic activity was temperature limited. Sorokin (1971) hypothesized that the oxidation of DOM in Antarctic waters was slow due to low rates of microbial activity. However, contrary to this hypothesis Gillespie *et al.* (1976) found high microbial heterotrophic potential for the assimilation of organic substrates from Antarctic seawater at low temperatures. The data from the early investigations were critically reviewed by Sorokin & Federov (1978) who demonstrated that the early counts of bacterial numbers were too low due to the loss of bacteria in the process of concentration on membrane filters. Subsequent investigations have shown that the numbers and production of bacteria in the Southern Ocean, especially in the more

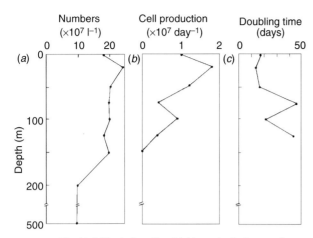

Fig. 14.6. Vertical profile of (*a*) bacterioplankon numbers, (*b*) production rate and (*c*) doubling times at a station (approximately 62° S) in the Australian sector during the austral summer. Redrawn from Kogure *et al.* (1986).

productive areas, are quite considerable (Hodgson *et al.*, 1981; Holm-Hanson, 1981; Hanson *et al.*, 1983a,b; Hansen & Lowery, 1985; Samyshev, 1986; Mullins & Priddle, 1987; Cota *et al.*, 1990; Sullivan *et al.*, 1990). Measurements of the activity of heterotrophic bacteria at various localities and depths in the Southern Ocean (e.g. Morita *et al.*, 1977; Kogure *et al.*, 1986) have indicated that they are also uniquely adapted to the prevailing low temperatures.

Hodgson *et al.* (1981) examined the distribution and activity of the bacterioplankton and the turnover of DOM in McMurdo Sound. They found that on the eastern side of the Sound bacteria averaged 6.5×10^8 l^{-1}, and the turnover rates of dissolved adenosine triphosphate (DADP), D-glucose and 1-leucine averaged 16, 116 and 124 hours respectively. These molecules, as well as thymidine, were taken up maximally from -1.5 to 0 °C, indicating bacterial adaptation to rapid turnover of DOM at ambient temperatures. An average of 84% of the turnover was attributable to unattached bacteria. Since such cells comprised only 10% of the total microbial biomass, it was concluded that, per unit biomass, free-living bacteria were approximately 50- to 100-fold more active than larger organisms and/or attached bacteria in the turnover of DOM.

The results obtained by Hodgson *et al.* (1981) have been confirmed by subsequent investigators. Studies in the Scotia Sea and Bransfield Strait by Bolter & Dawson (1982) gave a mean carbon value for bacterial biomass production (based on the uptake of glucose) of 0.6 µg l^{-1} h^{-1}, with all values down to 100 m yielding a mean value of 0.25 µg l^{-1} h^{-1}. This was comparable to values in the range of 0.01 to 10 µg l^{-1} h^{-1} for Kiel Fjord (Bolter, 1981). Epiflourescence counts of bacteria in the Drake Passage

during January varied from 1×10^7 to 2×10^8 cells l^{-1}, concentrations that were approximately a factor of ten lower than those found in the Scotia Sea and coastal Antarctic waters (Hanson *et al.*, 1983a).

Kogure *et al.* (1986) studied the abundance and production rate of bacterioplankton in the Australian sector of the Southern Ocean from December 1983 to February 1984. Total bacterial counts in Antarctic waters ranged from $7.1–78 \times 10^7$ cells l^{-1}. Fig. 14.6 gives bacterial parameters measured at a station near the Antarctic continent. The production rate (estimated by the incorporation of thymidine) in the upper water layer ranged from $0.45–5.2 \times 10^7$ cells l^{-1} day^{-1}, corresponding to 0.688–0.79 µg C l^{-1} day^{-1}. The apparent doubling time in the upper euphotic zone was about 10 days and ranged from 10 to 40 days below that zone. At one station the doubling time was 2–3 days, comparable the that of subtropical waters near the Subtropical Convergence.

Twenty-seven stations were sampled in the Bransfield Strait and Drake Passage in January–February by Mullins & Priddle (1987), and they found that the bacterial biomass ranged from 3.16×10^{13} to 6.23×10^{13} cells m^{-2}. Bacterial numbers were relatively constant over the top 50 m, decreasing rapidly to half the surface values at 150 m, and more slowly to 250 m (Fig. 14.7). The ratio of bacterial:phytoplankton carbon increased with depth, with a mean value of 9.32 (range 0.19 to 53.03) for samples from the top 50 m of the water column, and was usually less than 50 at depths exceeding 100 m.

Satoh *et al.* (1989) investigated seasonal changes in the numbers of heterotrophic bacteria under the fast ice near Syowa Station (60° 00′ S; 39° 35′ E) from May to January. At three stations (water depths 12, 38 and 700 m) the numbers of heterotrophic bacteria began to increase in October, with the maximum number (2.4×10^2 colony-forming units ml^{-1}) being found in late December (Fig. 14.8) The changes in bacterial numbers corresponded well with those of POC, suggesting that the growth of the heterotrophic bacteria depends on the supply of POC from the sea ice microalgal assemblages which developed rapidly in the bottom layer of the sea ice in the austral spring.

Gibson *et al.* (1990) studied the seasonal fluctuation of bacterial numbers at a site 10 km off Davis Station. Bacterial numbers from May to September were constant and low (*c*. 1.1×10^5 cells ml^{-1}) suggesting that little growth of the bacteria was occurring beneath the sea ice. The combination of low light levels, low temperatures, and little DOM available for heterotrophic activity (none was detected in the water column during this period) would result in the maintenance of low bacterial populations with little or no growth. An increase in bacterial

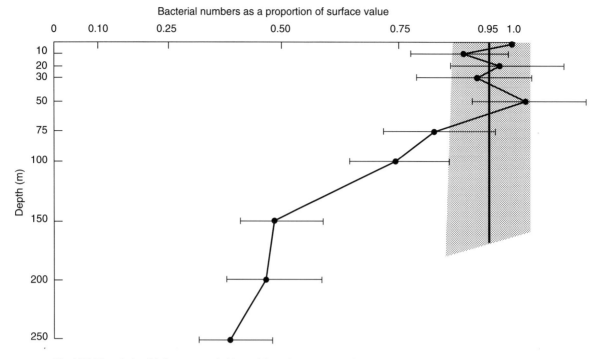

Fig. 14.7. The relationship between pooled bacterial numbers, averaged for appropriate stations in the Bransfield Strait and expressed as a percentage of the surface value, and depth in the water column. Estimates are based on a log-linear model and horizontal bars denote 95% confidence intervals. A mean proportion of the surface count derived from the depth layer 10–50 m is also indicated (shading indicates 95% confidence intervals for this mean of 0.86–1.04) to show the great similarity of counts in shallow depths. Redrawn from Mullins & Priddle (1987).

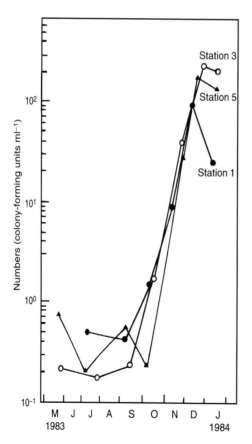

Fig. 14.8. Seasonal variation in bacterial numbers at a depth of 2 m under the fast ice near Syowa Station (60° S; 39° 35′ E). Redrawn from Satoh *et al.* (1989).

numbers occurred in October, coinciding with the appearance of a considerable amount of mucilaginous material which probably originated from the sea ice microalgae. This increase in numbers was followed by a dramatic decrease to a minimum on 2 December. The decrease could have resulted from grazing by heterotrophic protozoa. This minimum was followed by another sharp increase which continued to the end of January. It coincided with a similar increase in the density of *Phaeocystis pouchetii*, a species which gives rise to considerable quantities of DOM.

It is evident that despite the low temperatures of the waters surrounding the Antarctic continent the microbial populations maintain a high energy status indicative of active metabolism. Hanson *et al.*, 1983a found that rates of bacterial DNA synthesis (measured by tritiated thymidine uptake and incorporation) were lower in the Drake Passage (0.005–5.4 pmol l^{-1} day^{-1}) than in temperate coastal waters (2.4–502 pmol l^{-1} day^{-1}). However, the specific rates of synthesis (about 10^{-21} mols of thymidine cell^{-1} h^{-1}) were comparable with those of other marine areas.

Sullivan *et al.* (1990) and Cota *et al.* (1990) have investigated the bacterioplankton of the marginal ice zone in the Weddell Sea in spring and autumn respectively. These studies have enabled comparisons to be made between processes occurring in open and ice-covered water at different times. Both studies revealed a

Table 14.7. *Regional means for microbial parameters observed in ice-covered versus open waters of the marginal ice edge zone during AMERIEZ cruises during austral spring (Sullivan* et al.*, 1990) and autumn (Cota* et al.*, 1990). All aereal estimates were integrated over the euphotic zone (i.e. depths $\leq 0.1\%$ optical depth), or to a depth of 100 m if optical depths were not sampled. Values are means $\pm$ SD*

	Spring 1983		Autumn 1986	
Parameter	Ice-covered waters	Open waters near ice edge	Ice-covered waters	Open waters near ice edge
Chlorophyll *a*				
(mg m^{-3})	0.25±0.16	2.9±2.6	0.08±0.03	0.28±0.24
(mg m^{-2})	21±10	142±81	9±2	29±18
Particulate organic carbon				
(mg C m^{-3})	48±30	115±100	29±20	46±47
(mg C m^{-2})	4838±1302	5844±2839	2933±1178	4354±2048
Bacterial biomass				
(mg C m^{-3})	1.8±2.1	3.7±1.9	2.9±1.7	3.1±2.0
(mg C m^{-2})	154±119	258±89	229±59	382±172
Primary production				
(mg C m^{-3} d^{-1})	3.8±3.0[1]	14.8±15.8	2.1±1.8[1]	2.8±3.4
(mg C m^{-2} d^{-1})	269±87[1]	521±226	137±58[1]	126±81
Bacterial production				
(mg C m^{-3} d^{-1})	0.3±0.4	1.2±1.5	0.2±0.2	1.3±1.0
(mg C m^{-2} d^{-1})	20±18	70±65	19±10	96±69
Production : biomass (P:B)				
Phytoplankton[2]	0.45±0.14	0.13±0.07	0.15±0.05	0.06±0.04
Bacteria	0.17±0.09	0.35±0.27	0.07±0.03	0.40±0.19
Bacteria : phytoplankton (2°:1°)				
Biomass[2]	0.23±0.18	0.07±0.05	0.34±0.17	0.12±0.05
Production	0.07±0.07	0.14±0.09	0.14±0.13	0.76±0.45
Algal growth rate[3] doublings (d^{-1})	0.08±0.06[1]	0.11±0.08	0.07±0.06[1]	0.06±0.06
Bacterial growth rate doublings (d^{-1})	0.34±0.31	0.42±0.29	0.15±0.15	0.59±0.32
Amino acid turnover times[4] (d)	83	13	45	18

[1]Values are not corrected for ambient light regime in pack ice.
[2]Assumes a C:Chl. ratio of 32 in 1983 and 100 in 1986 for all phytoplankton.
[3]Values are not corrected for non-algal components of particulate carbon.
[4]Substrates: amino acid mixture in 1983 and leucine in 1986.
From Cota *et al.* (1990).

considerable degree of coherence between the distributions of phytoplankton and bacterial biomass. In Table 14.7 microbial parameters for the ice-covered and open waters are compared. In the austral spring chlorophyll *a* concentrations were seven times higher in the open water than in the ice-covered water. In contrast the bacterial biomass in the open water was less than double that of the ice-covered water. Bacterial biomass represented only about 3% of the total POC, with little variation between ice-covered and open-water regions.

Secondary production by bacterioplankton displayed a trend similar to that of primary production, with higher values in the open water. Bacterial production averaged 0.3 mg C m^{-3} day^{-1} beneath the pack ice and 1.2 mg C m^{-3} day^{-1} in the centre of a dense algal bloom. Previous estimates of production rates for bacterioplankton range from about 2 to 15 mg C m^{-3} day^{-1} in coastal regions, and from 0.6 to 2 mg C m^{-3} day^{-1} in oligotrophic, open-ocean regions (Ducklow, 1983). Rates of bacterial production during the austral spring were generally between 2 and

25% those of the primary production, and averaged 7 and 14% in ice-covered and open water respectively. Fuhrman & Azam (1980) suggested that a large fraction (25 to 29%) of the primary production may be utilized by the bacterioplankton in McMurdo Sound, and that bacterial production may often be more than 10% of the primary production. Hanson *et al.* (1983b) compared their estimates of bacterial production in Antarctic waters with previous literature values for primary productivity and speculated that bacterial production might be of the order of 15 to 45% of the primary production. Kottmeier & Sullivan (1987) reported data for the late austral winter in the Bransfield Strait which suggested that bacterial productivity ranged from less than 1% to well over 174% of primary production. In the Weddell Sea in the austral autumn Cota *et al.* (1990) estimated that bacterial production in the euphotic zone of ice-covered and open waters, respectively averaged 14 and 76% of primary production. The reasons for these widely varying values will be discussed below.

In the austral autumn bacterial production averaged 19 ± 10 mg C m^{-2} day^{-1} in regions partially covered with ice, and in open waters mean rates were 96 ± 69 mg C m^{-2} day^{-1}. Unlike the primary productivity values these production rates were similar to those found in the spring, whereas the primary production was very much lower in the autumn than in the spring. Ratios of production per unit biomass (P:B ratios) provide an indication of the relative activities from different environments. Bacteria exhibited P:B ratios two to six times higher in open waters (Table 14.7) even though their abundance and biomass were also higher there. Comparing integrated biomass units in carbon, bacterial biomass averaged 23–34% of phytoplankton biomass under ice cover but only 7–12% in open waters.

Estimates of the turnover times for small organic molecules provided indirect indication of the role that bacteria play in remineralization. Primary bacterial parameters such as the incorporation of thymidine, uridine, mixed amino acids, and bacterial abundance were found by Sullivan *et al.* (1990) to be often more strongly correlated with POC or chlorophyll *a* concentrations than with the rate of primary productivity. Metabolic rates comparable to rates in temperate waters have been demonstrated for Antarctic waters during the *Eltanin* Cruise 51 in the Pacific sector (Morita *et al.*, 1977), in McMurdo Sound (Hodgson *et al.*, 1981) and between the Falkland Islands and the ice edge in the Weddell Sea (Bolter & Dawson, 1982).

Studies of bacterial growth rates and doubling times have given conflicting results ranging from a doubling time of two to four days in the Scotia Sea (Azam *et al.*,

1981) to 18 days in Prydz Bay (Painting *et al.*, 1985). These estimates can be compared with those of 15–33 hours for northern temperate waters (Newell & Linley, 1984). Production estimates likewise vary from 0.022–1.309 mg C m^{-2} day^{-1} for Prydz Bay (Painting *et al.*, 1985) to 49–180 mg C m^{-2} day^{-1} for Sodruzhestro Sea (Samyshev, 1986). As Painting *et al.* (1985) point out estimates of bacterial production by H-thymidine incorporation into DNA give a wide range of values, depending, as the method does, on numerous factors required to convert thymidine into cellular carbon (see Fuhrman & Azam, 1982, and for a critical review Pollard & Moriarty, 1984). According to Painting *et al.* (1985) bacterial production in the Antarctic is up to two or three orders of magnitude less than in temperate waters. This is in contrast to the conclusions of other workers (e.g. Kogue *et al.*, 1986) who consider that the production rates are comparable.

Table 14.8 compares estimates of bacterial abundance, biomass, production, bacterial production to biomass ratio, bacterial production as a percentage of phytoplankton production and bacterial growth rate in Antarctic waters to 100 m deep south of the Antarctic Convergence. As Cota *et al.* (1990) point out: 'Given large spatial and seasonal differences and the wide variety of techniques employed in comparable studies of bacterioplankton in the southern ocean the degree of similarity in bacterial abundance, biomass and growth rates is striking.' Most of the variation in abundance and biomass is within an order of magnitude; but the rate processes such as productivity and growth exhibit more variance (at least two orders of magnitude), ranging from values near detection limits to around 17 mg C m^{-3} day^{-1}. These differences can be attributed to the phase of the phytoplankton bloom and the time of the year during the sampling period. In their studies in the Weddell Sea Sullivan *et al.* (1990) and Cota *et al.* (1990) found that in the autumn, bacteria were consuming about three quarters of the primary production in open water compared with only 14% in spring when algal biomass and primary productivity were several times higher.

As emphasized by Hodgson *et al.* (1981) the results of investigations of bacterioplankton in the Southern Ocean have led to the following conclusions: 1. the bacterial assemblages have temperature optima for the assimilation of organic substrates that are near the ambient sea water temperatures; 2. the abundance of bacteria in the seawater is not atypically low, but is rather comparable to that of temperate oceans; and the turnover times of amino acids and other DOM constituents are highly variable ranging from several days to several weeks.

Table 14.8. *Estimates of bacterial abundance, biomass, production, bacterial production to biomass ratio (P:B), bacterial production as a percentage of phytoplankton production (%PP) and bacterial growth rate in Antarctic waters of less than 100 m depth south of the Antarctic Convergence. Values are ranges of observations for depths <100 m from all appropriate stations. In the Weddell Sea studies P:B and %PP are based upon values integrated over the euphotic zone or 100 m*

Site	Abundance (10^{12} cells m^{-3})	Biomass (mg C m^{-3})	Production (mg C m^{-3} d^{-1})	P:B	%PP	Growth rate	Source
Ross Sea							
Nov.–Dec.	0.02–0.3	0.6–4.7	0.005–0.1	—	0.08–0.2	0.002–0.05	1
Dec.–Jan.	0.07–1.0	0.5–8.3	0.004–2.9	—	≈20–25	0.001–0.4	2
Drake Passage							
Sep.–Oct.	0.1–0.5	0.8–4.2	2.6–17.1	—	15–45	0.9–2.1	3
Bransfield Strait							
Sep.	—	—	0.1–0.6	—	1–174	—	4
Indian Ocean Sector							
Dec.–Jan.	0.2–1.8	<5.0–40.0	0.07–3.5	0.02–0.31	≈111	—	5
Dec.–Feb.	0.1–0.5	0.1–0.8	0.07–0.8	—	≤22	0.08–0.3	6
Scotia Sea							
Feb.–Mar.	0.5	—	—	—	—	0.2–0.4	7
Weddell Sea							
Nov.–Dec.							8
Open water	0.06–0.3	0.2–17.3	0.001–9.0	0.05–1.0	1–32	0.002–1.2	
Ice-covered water	0.01–0.2	0.2–5.1	0.002–2.4	0.01–0.32	2–32	0.004–0.9	
Mar.							9
Open water	0.01–0.6	0.3–15.2	0.05–6.7	0.18–0.88	18–151	0.04–1.8	
Ice-covered water	0.03–0.4	0.5–8.6	0.002–1.0	0.01–0.16	2–44	0.007–1.1	

1, Kottmeier *et al.* (1987); 2, Fuhrman & Azam (1980); 3, Hanson *et al.* (1983b); 4, Kottmeier & Sullivan (1987); 5, Samyshev (1986); 6, Kogue *et al.* (1986); 7, Azam *et al.* (1981); 8, Sullivan *et al.* (1990); 9, Cota *et al.* (1990).
From Cota *et al.* (1990).

14.5.2 Sediment bacteria

To date there have been only a limited number of studies of the bacteria of sediments in Antarctic waters. Recent research efforts on the ecology of sediments have established that bacteria are abundant, with typical population densities of 1×10^7 to 3×10^9 cells g^{-1} (dry wt) of bulk sediment (Novitsky, 1987; Karl & Novitsky, 1988), irrespective of habitat type, latitude or water depth. Consequently, it appears that continental shelf sediments support many times as many bacteria per unit volume than are typically found in the overlying surface seawater. The percentage of metabolically active cells has been found to range from 1% to greater than 95% of the total population (data summarized in Douglas *et al.*, 1987). Greater activity occurs in the top 5 cm and decreases rapidly with depth.

It has been shown that bacterial populations in Antarctic sediments can reach very high levels. White, Smith and their co-workers (D. C. White *et al.*, 1984, 1985; G. A. Smith *et al.*, 1986, 1988), have studied the community structure and metabolic activity of nearshore sediments in McMurdo Sound and Arthur Harbour, Anvers Island. These investigations have shown that the bacterial populations can achieve very high biomass levels. Phospholipid analyses of the sediments off Cape Armitage, McMurdo Sound, revealed concentrations of microbial biomass equivalent to that of a subtropical Florida estuary (D. C. White *et al.*, 1985). However, the bacterial rate of synthesis of DNA from thymidine was some 300-fold slower than in the Florida estuary sediments. The Antarctic sediments contained 10 times the biomass of a deep-sea area subject to abyssal storms, and 100 times that of a relatively undisturbed deep-sea bottom off Venezuela. Sponge spicule mats in particular contained very rich and diverse algal and bacterial assemblages.

G. A. Smith *et al.* (1989) have described the benthic microbial communities of Arthur Harbour by analyses of their cell membrane phospholipid ester-linked fatty acids and metabolic rates. Biomass averaged 6 nM (phospholipid) or 3.5×10^8 cells g^{-1} (dry wt). These biomasses were lower than those which were found in McMurdo Sound, where they averaged 2.1×10^9 cells g^{-1} (dry wt). The difference between the two localities is probably due to the greater input of POM from the annual *Phaeocystis* bloom (Palmisano *et al.*, 1985c), from the dense sea ice microalgal community upon the melting of the sea ice in the summer and possibly from the rich benthic microalgal communities which have been identified in the shallow waters of the Sound (Dayton *et al.*, 1986).

It is thus clear that Antarctic sediments, especially in shallow waters, have populations of bacteria which are comparable to those of marine sediments elsewhere in the world's oceans, but that their metabolic activity proceeds at slower rates. These sediments receive large quantities of organic detritus which is eventually broken down with the release of nutrients. Much more research is needed to quantify the rates of mineralization and the role of the sediment microbial communities in energy cycling in Antarctic marine ecosystems.

14.6 Protozoa

Protozoa dominate the nano- (2–20 µm) and microzooplankton (20–200 µm) assemblages in pelagic waters and collectively they comprise what has been termed the protozooplankton (Siebruth *et al.*, 1978). Heterotrophic protozoa are now recognized as the major consumers of microbial production. They function as predators of bacteria and small phytoplankton, as prey of larger zooplankton and as agents for remineralization and recycling of elements essential for phytoplankton and microbial growth (Sherr & Sherr, 1984; Porter *et al.*, 1985). They can be classified according to size classes (see Table 14.9 and Fig. 14.9) as follows:

Picoheterotrophs: 0.2–2.0 µm. These are small heterotrophic flagellates (Johannes, 1965) and have been postulated to be important grazers of bacteria (Fuhrman & McManus, 1984).

Nanoheterotrophs: 2.0–20 µm. These comprise two groups, microflagellates and naked ciliates. The heterotrophic microflagellates have been identified as major consumers of bacteria in many marine pelagic food webs (Sherr & Sherr, 1984; Caron, 1987) and they may also be important grazers of autotrophic picoplankton. Heterotrophic flagellates fall taxonomically into both Phytomastigophora and Zoomastigophora. Frequently observed microflagellates include monads, bodonids, kinetoplastids, non-pigmented euglenoids, choanoflagellates, cryptomonads, chrysomonads, dinoflagellates and biocoeids (Fig. 14.9) (Fenchel, 1982a; Siebruth *et al.*, 1978). There are often pigmented and unpigmented forms that are closely related taxonomically and structurally, and there is increasing evidence that some pigmented forms may be able to utilize particulate food sources (bacteria, picoheterotrophs and picoautotrophs) (Porter *et al.*, 1985). Thus, algal mixotrophy, the utilization of energy as particulate matter by photosynthetic forms, is another component of the food web.

Ciliates smaller than 20 µm have been observed in many parts of the world's oceans and they may form an important component of the nanoplankton (Porter *et al.*, 1985). Besides bacteria such ciliates may feed on procaryote and eucaryote autotrophs in both the picoplanktonic and nanoplanktonic size ranges (Sherr *et al.*, 1986).

Microheterotrophs: 20–200 µm. Spirotrichous ciliates are the dominant group with most species falling into the suborders Oligotrichina and Tintinnina. The most studied group is the tintinnids. Tintinnids feed mostly on small flagellated phytoplankton (Heinbokel & Beers, 1979). Naked oligotrichous ciliates are ubiquitous in marine pelagic ecosystems (Burkhill, 1982). Other types of ciliates, including scuticociliates, didinids, halotrichs and hypotrichs are also present, especially in the more eutrophic waters, or associated with detrital particles (Siebruth *et al.*, 1978; Siebruth, 1979; Caron *et al.*, 1982). Photosynthetic ciliates in the genus *Mesodinium* are also common members of the microzooplankton. Up to 40% of the microplankton ciliate fauna has been found to contain chloroplasts (Stoeckner *et al.*, 1987).

A second group of protozoa of importance in the microzooplankton are the large unpigmented dinoflagellates. About half of the dinoflagellate species lack chloroplasts and are obligate heterotrophs. Naked (non-thecate) dinoflagellates, such as species of the genera *Oxyrrhis* and *Noctiluca*, are voracious phagotrophs consuming large amounts of phytoplankton. Heterotrophic dinoflagellates with thecae, such as species of the genera *Dinopsalis, Protoperidinium* and *Dinophysis*, do not ingest particles but may be saprophagic. Pigmented dinoflagellates, like the pigmented ciliates, may be mixotrophic (Porter *et al.*, 1985).

Amoeboid protozoa may be transiently abundant in pelagic ecosystems (Sorokin & Kogelschatz, 1979). Common marine taxa include naked amoebae (order Amoebidae), Acantharia, heliozoans, foraminiferans and

Table 14.9. *Composition of the microbial community by size class*

Size class	Heterotrophs	Autotrophs
Picoplankton 0.2–2.0µm	Bacteria Microflagellates	Cyanobacteria Chemolithotrophic bacteria Eucaryote algae
Nanoplankton 2–20µm	Microflagellates Naked ciliates	Phytoflagellates Non-flagellate algae Smaller diatoms
Microplankton 20–200µm	Naked ciliates Tintinnids Larger dinoflagellates Amoeboid protozoa Rotifers Other metazoa	Larger diatoms Larger dinoflagellates

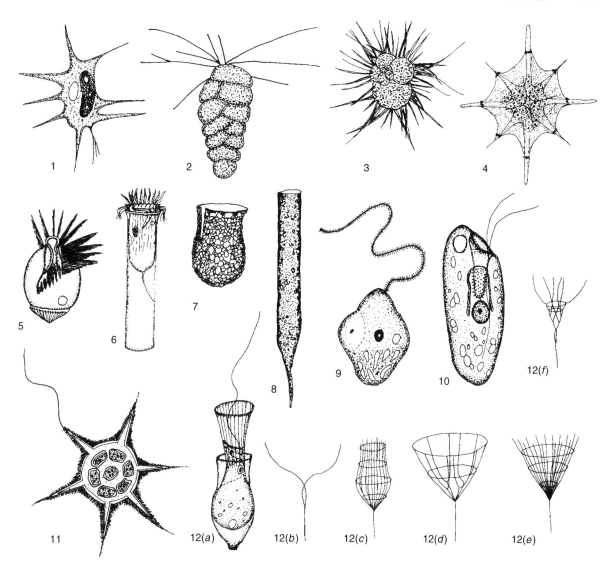

Fig. 14.9. Some representative planktonic Protozoa. 1. *Chrysamoeba* sp. (Chrysamoebidales); 2. *Textularia* sp. (Foraminifera); *Globigerina* sp. (Foraminifera); 4. *Acanthostaurus* sp. (Radiolarian); 5. *Strombidium* sp. (Oligotrich ciliate); 6. *Eutintinnus* sp. (Tintinnid with naked lorica); 7. *Tintinnopsis* sp. (Tintinnid lorica covered by sand grains); 8. *Tintinnopsis* sp. (Tintinnid with lorica covered by fine sediment); 9. *Oikomonas* sp. (Chrysophycean flagellate); 10. *Cryptomonas* sp. (Cryptomonad flagellate); 11. *Distephanus* sp. (Salicoflagellate); 12 (*a–f*) Choanoflagellates; (*a*) *Salpingoecia* sp. (showing the structure of the living animal); (*b*) *Bicosta spinifera* (this and the succeeding illustrations show the siliceous costal strip pattern of the lorica); (*c*) *Diaphanoeca multiannulata*; (*d*) *Parvicorbicula socialis*; (*e*) *Acanthoecopsis spiculifera*; (*f*) *Callicantha multispina*.

radiolarians (Siebruth, 1979). Very little is known about the ecology of these organisms in the Southern Ocean.

Although only a small number of studies have been carried out on the protozoan communities of the Southern Ocean the available data suggest that protozoa are as abundant as in other oceans (Silver *et al*., 1980; Buck & Garrison, 1983; Hewes *et al*., 1983, 1985; Heinbokel & Coats, 1985; Garrison & Buck, 1989a,b), and the abundance and productivity of their prey (e.g. Hasle, 1969; Fay, 1973; Fuhrman & Azam, 1980; Hodgson *et al*., 1981; Azam *et al*., 1981, 1983) are as high in Antarctic waters as in other oceans. For 15 stations in the Antarctic Coastal Current the average biomass of the heterotrophic nanoflagellates was 14 µg C l^{-1} (range 7–60 µg C l^{-1}),

about one half of that of the autotrophic nanoplankton (avergae 48 µg C l^{-1}; range 10–303 µg C l^{-1}) (Hewes *et al*., 1985). At five stations in the Scotia Sea tintinnid biomass ranged from 0.24 to 3.54 µg C l^{-1} (mean 1.2±1.3), and total ciliate biomass from 1.9 to 7.3 µg C l^{-1} (mean 3.6±2.4). This can be compared to >20 µm diatom biomass of 0.7–42.6 µg C l^{-1} (mean 13.9±17.8). Tintinnid and total ciliate biomass was found to be proportional to that of the flagellates, consistent with the view that nanoflagellates are food for ciliates (Hewes *et al*., 1985). In two geographically separated areas (deep Weddell Sea and shallow Scotia Ridge) it was found that ciliates could effectively control population growth of the dominant phytoplankton species and that the less fed upon phytoplankton species had much higher measured growth rates.

The relative proportions of autotrophic and heterotrophic biomass reported by Hewes *et al.* (1985) are consistent with other data from the Southern Ocean. v. Brockel (1981) found that the 'protozooplankton' biomass ranged from 8–110 mg C m^{-2} in the northern part of the Weddell Sea, to 325 mg C m^{-2} near South Georgia, and averaged 16% of the total 'phytoplankton' biomass. Choanoflagellates appeared to be an especially abundant and conspicuous component of the Southern Ocean pelagic ecosystem. They have been reported from the waters of Terre Adélie (Deflande, 1960), the Weddell Sea (Silver *et al.*, 1980; Buck, 1981; Buck & Garrison, 1983; Marchant, 1985), Lutzow-Holm Bay (Takahashi, 1981), Prydz Bay (Marchant, 1985), and from the pack ice (65° 50′ S; 155° 16′ E) (Tanoue & Hara, 1986). In the Weddell Sea choanoflagellates have been reported to average 3.6×10^5 cells l^{-1} (approximately 5 µg C m^{-2}) (Silver *et al.*, 1980; Buck, 1981; Buck & Garrison, 1983; Marchant, 1985) which compares with a total phytoplankton biomass of 1.9–3.3 g C m^{-2} (Hewes *et al.*, 1985). Hara *et al.* (1986) in their study of heterotrophic protists along 75° E in the Indian Ocean sector in the summer of 1983–84 found that naked amoebae and choanoflagellates were dominant and that most groups were represented. In the Prydz Bay region Marchant (1985) found that choanoflagellates comprised 10–40% of the total nanoplankton. The recorded genera in open ocean samples were *Acanthoecopsis, Bicosta, Callicantha, Crinolina, Diaphanoeca, Parvicorbicula* and *Pleurasiga*. The overall mean abundance averaged 2.7±1.7×10^4 cells l^{-1} for the oceanic sites, but at the inshore stations in the summer ten-fold higher cell concentrations were recorded. Marchant found that in addition to bacteria the food of the choanoflagellates included nanoplanktonic autotrophs, particulate extracellular products and cellular debris from larger phytoplankton. Tanoue & Hara (1986) in a study of the faecal pellets of *Euphausia superba* found that they contained abundant remains of choanoflagellates and estimated that they occupied 10% of the total plasma volume of the pellets.

The most comprehensive investigation to date of pelagic Protozoa in the Southern Ocean is that of Garrison & Buck (1989a,b) who sampled the protozooplankton from the open water across the ice edge zone into the pack ice in the Weddell Sea during the austral spring of 1983 and the austral autumn of 1986. The biomass and production of the organisms they found are summarized in Table 14.10. Protozooplankton biomass in the upper 100 m of the water column ranged from 55 to >650 mg C m^{-2}. Heterotrophic flagellates were the domi-

nant component of the protozooplankton comprising 24–75% of the protozoan biomass during the austral spring and 62–79% of the biomass during the austral autumn. Naked (non-loricate) flagellates were usually dominant, followed by dinoflagellates and choanoflagellates. Although a variety of ciliates were present, non-sheathed oligotrichs (i.e. *Strombidium* spp.) dominated the ciliate biomass on both occasions. Tintinnids were rare during the spring cruise but they made up a significant fraction of the ciliate biomass during the autumn cruise. Other protozoans (e.g., radiolarians and foraminiferans) were rare.

During the spring cruise (Garrison & Buck, 1989b) integrated protozoan biomass in the upper 100 m ranged from 7–12% of the autotrophic biomass, while during the autumn it was slightly higher relative to the phytoplankton biomass ranging from 15–23% of the autotrophic biomass at ice-covered stations and 9–24% in the open water (see Table 14.10). Bacterial biomass predominated over that of the protozoans at ice-covered stations in both cruises, but the protozooplankton biomass reached up to twice that of the bacteria at some open-water stations during the 1976 autumn cruise.

The biomass of the different protozoan groups was positively correlated with primary production, chlorophyll *a* concentrations and bacterial biomass and production. It appears that it was largely controlled by prey availability and production. Garrison & Buck (1989b) estimated the potential importance of the protozoa as consumers using clearance rates in the literature. They used the lower of Davis & Siebruth's (1984) range of clearance rates for flagellates feeding on bacteria (0.04–0.6 l h^{-1} individual^{-1}), and the lower rates measured by Lessard *et al.* (1987) for heterotrophic dinoflagellates (0.4–6.0), naked ciliates (0.8–2.0) and tintinnids (0.4–1.0 l h^{-1} individual^{-1}) feeding on ^{3}H-thymidine labelled cells in McMurdo Sound. They calculated that daily population clearance rates within the upper 50 m of the water column ranged from 11% of the water column (or prey biomass) at ice-covered stations up to 55% at open-water stations. Thymidine uptake measurements (Krempin, 1985) indicated bacterial generation times of 5 to >10 days at ice-covered stations and 2.5 days in open-water stations, and Garrison & Buck (1989b) concluded that it was not unreasonable to consider the protozoans as capable of utilizing most of the daily production.

In studies in McMurdo Sound Lessard *et al.* (1987) concluded that the protozoa were primarily consuming bacteria. However, other studies (Heinbockel & Beers, 1979; Smetacek, 1981; Jacobsen & Anderson, 1986; Buck *et al.*, 1987) have shown that ciliates, especially tintinnids, are capable of preying on larger diatoms.

Table 14.10. *Summary of phytoplankton and bacterial production and biomass and protozooplankton and macrozooplankton in the Weddell Sea during the austral spring 1983 and the austral autumn 1986. Values integrated over upper 100 m. Means are given in brackets*

Cruise	Production (mg C m^{-2} day^{-1})		Biomass (mg C m^{-2})			
	Phytoplankton	Bacteria	Phytoplankton	Bacteria	Protozooplankton	Zooplankton
Austral spring 83						
Ice covered	225.6–345.6 (284.8)	11.8–42.6 (24.9)	566–1320 (944.5)	60.4–247.2 (172.1)	55.3–130.5 (88.3)	—
Ice edge to open water	242–758.4 (516.8)	105.7–154.3 (138.0)	1508–6449 (4372.3)	351.2–512.6 (384.1)	199.5–494.9 (426.8)	—
Austral autumn 86						
Ice covered	99.6–201.6 (161.1)	2.8–16.6 (11.5)	656–1076 (819.7)	197.4–272.7 (228.9)	101.7–252.6 (165.8)	45.8
Open water	80.8–274.6 (207.3)	83.2–126.6 (111.2)	4121–7149 (4989.5)	249.4–582.0 (394.9)	485.5–651.6 (551.9)	175.2–304.80

Modified from Garrison & Buck (1989a).

Lessard & Swift (1985) measured grazing rates of microalgae by protozoa in low latitudes of 1.0–200 l h^{-1} individual^{-1}. Using the lower ranges of clearance (1–2 l h^{-1} individual^{-1}) Garrison & Buck (1989b) estimated protozoan clearance rates in the Weddell Sea of 14 and 20% of the water column day^{-1} at ice-covered stations and open-water stations respectively. They concluded that if the phytoplankton stock doubling times were 3 to >8 days then the protozoan grazing rates could be sufficient to maintain the phytoplankton stocks at the low levels that they observed.

Bjornsen & Kuparinen (1991) studied the growth and herbivory of heterotrophic dinoflagellates (*Gymnodinium* sp.) from the Weddell Sea and the Weddell–Scotia Confluence in 100 l microcosms. In microcosms exposed to 'dim' light phytoplankton production was almost balanced by dinoflagellate grazing. They concluded that heterotrophic dinoflagellates may contribute significantly to the maintenance of the low levels of phytoplankton biomass found in oceanic waters of the Southern Ocean.

14.7 Bacteria–protozoa–POM interactions

In oceanic water POM is generally five times that of the phytoplankton biomass and ten times that of the DOM on a carbon basis (Cauwet, 1981). The mineralizaton of this enormous quantity of organic matter is achieved by the activity of the heterotrophic bacteria (e.g. P. J. Le B. Williams, 1975; Joint & Morris, 1982). Since the bacterial biomass is kept at relatively low and constant levels (Anderson & Fenchel, 1985) the importance of microprotozoan predator control of bacterial biomass has been emphasized (Sorokin, 1981; Fenchel, 1982c; Siebruth & Davis, 1982). In the following sections we will examine the microbial processes associated with the degradation of various categories of detritus such as phytoplankton derived detritus, amorphous aggregates, copepod, euphausiid and salp faecal pellets, and microbial expolymer secretions.

14.7.1 Phytoplankton derived detritus

Fukami *et al.*, (1985a,b) and Biddanda & Pomeroy (1988) have examined the pattern of microbial succession in the decomposition of detritus derived from phytoplankton. Biddanda (1985) and Biddanda & Pomeroy (1988) observed that during the early stages of decomposition of particulate detritus derived from phytoplankton (the 1 to 8 day period, when bacterial numbers colonizing the detritus increased rapidly), aggregation and formation of macroaggregates occurred (here termed detrital–microbial complexes), identical to those described by Hobbie *et al.* (1972), Wiebe & Pomeroy (1972), Pomeroy & Deibel (1980) and others. During the first few days of the incubation of the detrital material in seawater there appeared an increasing proportion of rod-shaped bacteria. These were then replaced by a mixed assemblage of cocci, spirilla, rods and filamentous forms (Biddanda, 1985). Biddanda (1986) has shown that the aggregate formation which occurs is microbially mediated through the production of sticky extracellular mucopolysaccharides by the bacteria. These are sometimes referred to as microbial exopolymer secretions (Decho, 1990) (see section 14.7.4). Subsequently, mixed assemblages of bactivorous protozoa such as flagellates, ciliates, choanoflagellates and amoeboid forms colonize the aggregate and keep the bacterial numbers in check. The bacteria rapidly convert the POM in the detritus into DOM by mean of exoenzymes and assimilate, as well as respire, it (Hoppe, 1984). The combined activities of the bacteria and protozoa disrupt the

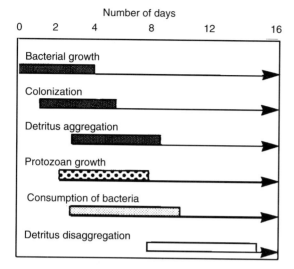

Fig. 14.10. Schematic diagram of microbial succession during phytoplankton decomposition in sea water. Redrawn from Biddanda & Pomeroy (1988).

Table 14.11. *Comparisons of characteristics of* Euphausia superba *faecal pellets and cast ecoskeletons*

	Cast exoskeletons		Faecal pellets[1]	
	Minimum	Maximum	Minimum	Maximum
Daily production (mg dry wt day^{-1})[2]	0.25[3]	0.63[4]	13.0	39.8
Sinking rates (m day^{-1})	52	1019	100	525
Organic matter (% of dry wt)	64.9	81.3	~8	~27
Carbon (% of dry wt)	12.3	22.9	5.0	13.7
Nitrogen (% of dry wt)	1.9	4.2	0.4	1.9
C:N ratio	5.1	8.0	8.4	14.6

[1]Data from Ross *et al.* (1985) and A. Clarke *et al.* (1988b).
[2]Based on 120 mg dry wt animal.
[3]12 moults per year.
[4]30 moults per year.
From Nicol & Stolf (1989).

structure of the aggregate and result in disaggregation. Fig. 14.10 is a schematic diagram of this process of microbial succession.

14.7.2 Amorphous aggregates

In a study of amorphous aggregates ('marine snow') Herndl & Peduzzi (1988) found dense assemblages of both autotrophic and heterotrophic microorganisms associated with the aggregates. The autotrophic component was enriched on the aggregates by a factor of up to 1000. Both diatoms (mostly living) and dinoflagellates (mainly empty frustules) were found. Coccolithophorids were enriched on the aggregations with a mean enrichment factor of about 500. Heterotrophic bacterial density ranged from 1.94–64.95×10^8 cells g^{-1} (marine snow dry weight). Heterotrophic microflagellates reached densities only one order of magnitude lower than those of the bacteria. In terms of biomass, expressed in carbon equivalents, bacteria reached 3–95% of the heterotrophic microflagellate biomass. In terms of cell concentration, heterotrophic microflagellates comprised between 32 and 71% of the total microflagellate (autotrophic and heterotrophic) community. On occasions large cyanobacteria populations (2.72×10^8 cells g^{-1} marine snow dry wt) were found. Since microbial processes in the Southern Ocean have been shown to be similar to those elsewhere in the world's oceans it is likely that the same process of microbial succession of marine snow aggregates occurs in Antarctic waters.

14.7.3 Faecal pellets and cast exoskeletons

Faecal pellets generally constitute the bulk of the material collected in sediment traps in the oceans. Although they may often account for only a small percentage of the suspended organic particles they often constitute the bulk (over 90% in many instances) of the total vertical mass flux. Adult copepods can defecate from 25 to 200 pellets individual^{-1} day^{-1} (Marshall & Orr, 1955; Smetacek, 1980). The contents of such faecal pellets comprise three general categories: fragments of living organisms, pigments and miscellaneous compounds. Fragments include diatoms, radiolarians, coccoliths, silicoflagellates, foraminiferans, whole cells and cell organelles and parts of prey such as copepods (Silver & Alldredge, 1981). Pigments are generally degradation products of photosynthetic pigments.

Jacobsen & Azam (1984) found that freshly egested faecal pellets from the copepod *Calanus pacificus* were rapidly colonized by free-living bacteria. In 24 hours the bacteria covered 27% of the available area of the pellets. Bacterial concentrations reached 1×10^5 cells (faecal pellet)$^{-1}$ (average volume of pellet 3×10^6 µm^3) after 14 hours of incubation. The number of bacteria associated with the faecal pellets then steadily declined to 1×10^4 cells (faecal pellet)$^{-1}$ in four days. The sinking of the faecal pellets through a column of seawater increased the rate of initial colonization.

Euphausiid faecal pellets and cast exoskeletons, especially those of *Euphausia superba*, form a significant proportion of the POM in the waters of the Southern Ocean (A. Clarke *et al.*, 1988b; Nicol & Stolf, 1989) Nicol & Stolf (1989) have quantified the daily production of both cast exoskeletons and faecal pellets (Table 14.11). While the sinking rates are comparable, the daily production of faecal pellet POM is up to 50 times greater than that of exoskeleton POM, although the latter has higher organic matter, carbon and nitrogen as a percentage of dry weight. However, their quantitative occurrence and microbial colonization have not been studied. Tanoue *et al.* (1982) and Tanoue & Hara (1986) have examined the species composition of the food particles in *E. superba* faecal pellets and have compared their chemical composition with that of their prey species. In a transect from the Scotia Sea to the Weddell Sea Cadee *et al.* (1992) found that free-floating sediment traps collected larger, more-degraded krill faecal strings in the deeper (150 m) than in the 50 or 75 m traps. The smallest faecal strings were only present in the shallower traps. Sinking velocity of the smaller faecal strings was, as expected, much lower than for the larger ones, with a total range of 50 to 500 m day^{-1} for faecal strings with volumes of 0.007 to 0.53 mm^3. Krill feeding on diatoms produced larger strings with higher settling velocities than those feeding on non-diatom phytoplankton. Small faecal strings did not settle out of the upper mixed layer. In the uppermost layer (0–50 m) krill faeces contributed an average of 130 g dry wt m^{-3} (Gonzales, 1992). There was an exponential decrease with depth, with a minimum of 0.6 g dry wt m^{-3} in the 500–1000 m stratum. Thus, it appears that krill faecal strings are largely retained and recycled in the upper 150 m of the water column. A factor in their breakdown could be their consumption by macrozooplankton (Lampitt *et al.*, 1990; Noji *et al.*, 1991) leading to their disintegration. The roles of the macrozooplankton and that of bacterial and protozoan activity in the breakdown process need to be elucidated.

Studies of salp faecal pellets have shown a similar pattern of utilization by bacteria and protozoans to that of copepod faecal pellets and amorphous aggregations. Salps which frequently occur in the waters of the Southern Ocean in dense swarms have high filtration and defecation rates (Madin, 1982; Pomeroy *et al.*, 1984; Andersen, 1985). They filter water at very high rates (relative to other planktonic organisms) removing minute particles (<5 μm) with high efficiency by means of a mucous feeding net (Alldredge & Madin, 1982). The daily defecation rate of these pelagic organisms constitutes a large proportion of their body weight, and they produce large (>1 mm) faecal pellets which sink rapidly (Madin, 1982). Because of these characteristics, grazing by salps can be an important mechanism for the rapid vertical flux of particulate matter in the oceans (Madin, 1982; Pomeroy *et al.*, 1984; Andersen, 1985).

The sinking rate of salp faecal pellets depends on the amount and kind of particulates collected and ingested. When food is abundant salps produce compact faeces which sink rapidly (Madin, 1982; Pomeroy *et al.*, 1984).

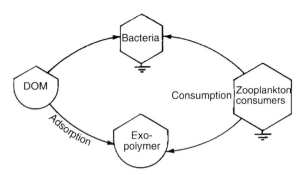

Fig. 14.11. Diagram showing the conceptual role of microbial exopolymers in pelagic food webs. DOM is absorbed and concentrated on the exopolymers and can then be directly transferred to consumer animals via ingestion of the exopolymers thus by-passing microbial metabolism of DOM. Modified from Decho (1990).

Small salps produce a faecal ribbon which breaks into segments and smaller fragments after release (Pomeroy & Deibel, 1980). Caron *et al.* (1989) found that in large pellets little microbial degradation occurred due to their cohesive nature and rapid sinking rate.

14.7.4 Microbial exopolymer secretions

Microbial expolymers are high molecular weight mucous secretions of bacteria and microalgae (Geesey, 1982; Decho, 1990). They range from tight capsules which closely surround cells to the loose-slime matrix associated with aggregates, sediment, detritus and other surfaces. They are largely polysaccharide in composition and can exist in dissolved and particulate form. Due to their physical properties, exopolymers are highly absorptive and rapidly sequester DOM. The ingestion of this exopolymer-bound DOM could represent a means whereby DOM could reach higher trophic levels directly (Fig. 14.11).

14.8 Interactions of bactivorous grazers and heterotrophic bacteria

As discussed above biodegradable organic material in the sea is supplied from a variety of sources, with the bulk being mostly supplied by excretion and lysis of phytoplankton in the form of macromolecular polymers (Billen, 1984). These cannot be directly taken up by bacteria and have first to be hydrolysed through the action of coenzymes and converted to monomeric substances. Exoenzymatic hydrolysis therefore constitutes the limiting step in the whole process of organic matter utilization (Sommerville & Billen, 1983). On the other hand, the uptake of 'direct' monomeric substrates is very rapid, so that their concentration is maintained at a steady low value (Billen *et al.*, 1980; Billen, 1984; Linley & Newell, 1984). Once taken up by the bacteria, direct substrates

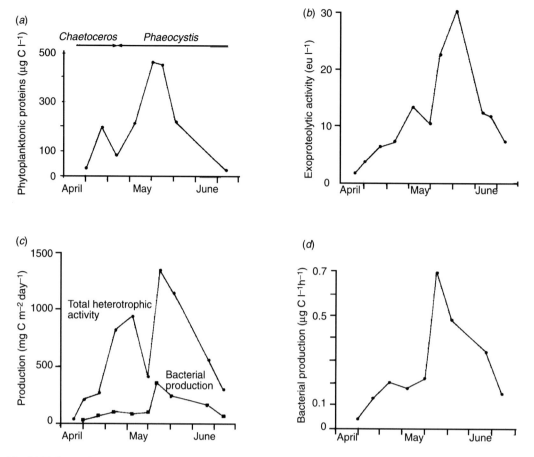

Fig. 14.12. Seasonal variation in (*a*) proteolytic phytoplankton biomass; (*b*) exoproteolytic activity; (*c*) direct substrate utilization (monosaccharides+amino acids+glycolate utilization) and, (*d*) bacterial production, showing the close coupling between phytoplankton production and bacterial activity during a *Phaeocystis* bloom. Redrawn from Billen & Fontigny (1987).

can either be catabolized and respired or used for biosynthesis. The bacterial biomass which is formed is subject to mortality, caused either by grazing or virus-induced lysis (Servais *et al.*, 1985).

Fig. 14.12 illustrates the close coupling which occurs between phytoplankton production during a *Phaeocystis* bloom and bacterial activity and production (Billen & Fontigny, 1987). Three measures of bacterial activity – exoproteolytic activity (Fig. 14.12*b*), direct substrate utilization (Fig. 14.12*c*) and bacterial production (Fig. 14.12*d*) – show a distinct two-peak pattern which corresponds to the two peaks of the phytoplankton biomass (Fig. 14.12*a*). The data demonstrate a rapid response of the bacterioplankton to the production of organic matter by the phytoplankton. Fuhrman (1987) confirmed this in a study of the release and uptake of dissolved free amino acids. He found that the release and uptake of dissolved free amino acids were tightly coupled, as evidenced by direct measurements, as well as by rapid turnover.

P. J. Le B. Williams (1981) on the basis of the rather limited data available at that time, suggested that bacter-

ial production averaged about 20% of primary production. Cole *et al.* (1988) have reviewed the available data since then. For all plankton systems analyzed, bacterial production ranged from 0.4 to 150 µg C l⁻¹ day⁻¹ and averaged 20% (median 16%) of planktonic primary production. On an aerial basis for the entire water column, bacterial production ranged from 118 to 2439 mg C m⁻² day⁻¹ and averaged 30% (median 27%) of the water column primary production. Cole *et al.* (1988) concluded that: 1. bacterial production both in the water column and in the sediments is broadly predictable; and 2. bacterial production is a large component of total secondary production in planktonic ecosystems, and is roughly twice that of the macrozooplankton.

Recent information, reviewed in Azam *et al.* (1983), Ducklow (1983), Siebruth (1984) and Taylor *et al.* (1985) suggests that bactivory (ingestion of bacteria) by microzooplankton (20 to 200 µm in diameter, primarily ciliated protozoa and micrometazoa) and nanozooplankton(2 to 20 µm in diameter, primarily heterotrophic mastigophora and ciliated protozoa), may regulate standing stocks, species composition and metabolic activity of bacterioplankton. Planktonic protozoa as we have seen represent a diverse and ubiquitous component of the water column biota, contributing a biomass of 1 to 16 000 µg C l^{-1} (Taylor, 1982). A number of investigators (e.g. Sorokin, 1981; Fenchel, 1982c; Siebruth, 1984; Azam *et al.*, 1983) have shown that heterotrophic microflagellates in the size range of 3 to 10 µm are effective bactivores, capable of filtering 12 to 67% of the water column per day. These are principally choanoflagellates and colourless chrysomonads. However, while these microflagellates are conspicuous grazers on bacteria most are omnivorous, grazing also on a wide assortment of phytoplankton, especially the smaller pico- and nanophytoplankton (Goldman & Caron, 1985). The densities of heterotrophic microflagellates on microscopic detrital aggregates can exceed their densities in the surrounding water by as much as four orders of magnitude (Caron *et al.*, 1982, 1986). Thus, protists, with and without chloroplasts (Stoeckner *et al.*, 1988), can occupy overlapping roles and the two groups need to be studied together to give true estimates of predation on bacteria (Estep *et al.*, 1986a).

The grazing of >20 µm ciliates, particularly tinitinnids, on nanoplankton (2–20 µm) phytoplankton has been established as a significant pathway in the marine planktonic food web (Verity, 1986). Recent studies also suggest that pelagic ciliates can consume and grow on picoplankton (<2 µm) cells, i.e. tiny eucaryote algae, cyanobacteria and bacteria (Sherr & Sherr, 1987; Rassoulzadegan *et al.*, 1988; Sherr *et al.*, 1989). Sherr *et al.* (1989) estimated that it would be possible for a choreotrich (<15 µm in size) to grow at a rate of about 0.5 day^{-1} on an exclusive diet of bacteria at a concentration of 10^6 bacteria ml^{-1}, but that larger ciliates would obtain less than 15% of their food rations as bacteria.

14.9 The microbial loop

The classical paradigm concerning marine planktonic food webs, which persisted until the mid-1970s, has been summarized by Steele (1974) in his book *The Structure of Marine Ecosystems*: 'The phytoplankton of the open sea is eaten nearly as fast as it is produced so that effectively all plant production goes through herbivores'. Coincidentally, at the same time, Pomeroy (1974) proposed a new paradigm which included an alternative energy-flow pathway, the 'microbial loop'. This emerging evidence that much of the organic matter synthesized by the primary producers entered an extracellular pool as algal exudates and losses during feeding and excretion by metzoans and was utilized by heterotrophic microorganisms, principally bacteria. As discussed above, other organisms, such as microflagellates and ciliates,

also contribute to this extracellular organic pool (see Table 14.1).

14.9.1 The elaboration of the 'microbial loop' concept

In a landmark review P. J. Le B. Williams (1981) attempted to reconcile the classical view of a herbivore dominated food chain with the observations of high growth yields (50–80%) for bacteria based on glucose and amino acid substrates (Crawford *et al.*, 1974; P. J. Le B. Williams *et al.*, 1976), and concluded that at least 50–60% of the primary production should pass through the planktonic heterotrophs before it is mineralized. However, he stressed that calculations on the proportion of the primary production entering the bacterioplankton are very sensitive to estimates of the proportion of primary production exuded as DOC, as it has been shown that while the net growth yield on labile soluble substrates may be high (up to 85%), the net growth yields on particulate matter is much lower (19–15%) (Linley & Newell, 1984).

Azam *et al.* (1983) further elaborated the concept of the 'microbial loop'. Their hypothesis envisaged primarily phytoplankton derived DOM supporting bacterioplankton production, a part of which may be transferred to the traditional grazing food chain via bacterioplankton, nanoflagellate and ciliate links. Bacteria (0.3 to 1 µm) utilize the DOM. When sufficient DOM is available for bacterial growth their populations generally do not exceed about 3×10^{-3} cells ml^{-1} as they are preyed upon primarily by heterotrophic nanoflagellates and small ciliates (Wright & Coffin, 1984; Rassoulzadegan & Sheldon, 1986). The heterotrophic microflagellates may reach densities of 5×10^6 cells ml^{-1}. Fig. 14.13 presents a schematic model which illustrates the roles of bacteria and other microbes in the water column. Azam *et al.*'s (1983) model was based on the Sheldon *et al.* (1972) particle size model, the main feature of which is that organisms tend to utilize particles one order of magnitude smaller than themselves. However, this may not be strictly true. Goldman & Caron (1985) found that the phagotrophic marine microflagellate *Paraphysomonas imperfecta* grazed on a wide assortment of phytoplankton species as well as on bacteria, and that it also resorted to canabalism when food was in short supply. Cell sizes of acceptable prey varied 400-fold from 0.5 µm^3 bacterial cells to 200 µm^3 cells of the chlorophyte *Dunaliella*. Goldman & Caron (1985) concluded that omnivory may be a common feeding strategy amongst heterotrophic protozoa and that the size ratios between predator and prey at the microbial level may not be rigid, and may in fact approach one.

The situation is further complicated by the fact that

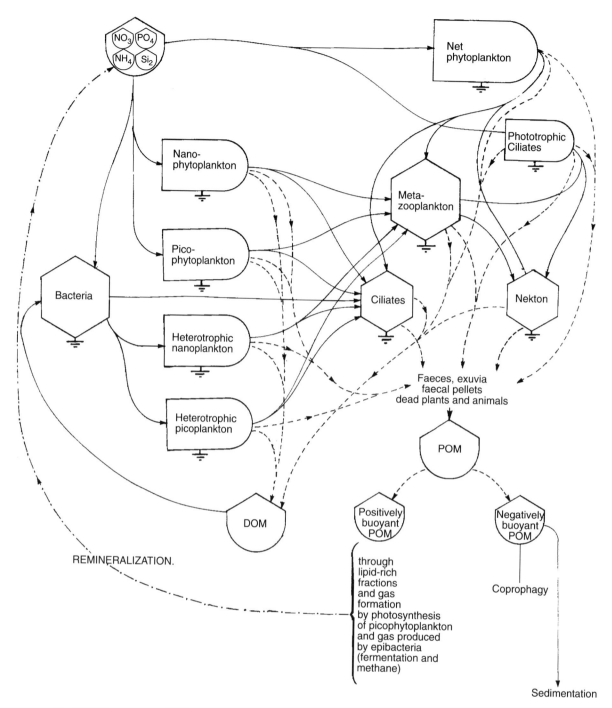

Fig. 14.13. Conceptual model illustrating the pathways of energy flow from photoautotrophs and bacteria to consumers in the pelagic food web.

chloroplast-containing nanoflagellates and ciliates have been observed to prey on bacteria. Estep *et al.* (1986a) found that nanoflagellate chrysophytes could be maintained for extended periods on bacteria. Current *in situ* estimates of nanoflagellate predation on bacteria assume that only flagellates without chloroplasts are predacious (Fenchel, 1982c; Sherr & Sherr, 1983; Davis & Siebruth, 1984). However, it is clear that protists with and without chloroplasts can occupy overlapping roles. Thus, if

chloroplast-containing nanoflagellates consume bacteria then the transfer of material from bacteria to protists may be greater than currently estimated.

14.9.2 *The role of detrital aggregates*
As discussed in section 14.2.2 the importance of the role of aggregates of various sizes in marine planktonic ecosystems is increasingly being recognized (Newell *et al.*, 1981; Goldman, 1984a,b; Biddanda, 1985, 1986;

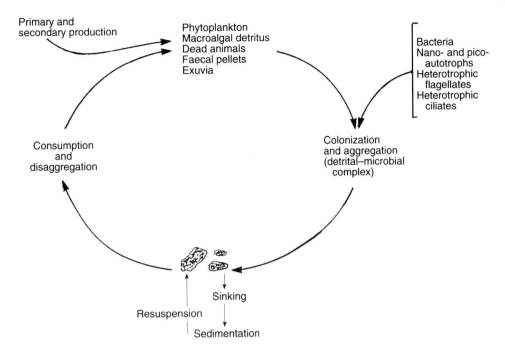

Fig. 14.14. Schematic diagram of microbial succession during phytoplankton decomposition in sea water. Redrawn from Biddanda & Pomeroy (1988).

Biddanda & Pomeroy, 1988). The rapid turnover of microbial populations in oligotrophic waters has inspired several authors to consider whether microbial populations occur in some sort of structured nutrient environment (Azam & Ammerman, 1984), or in macroaggregates (Goldman, 1984b). It has also been hypothesized that bacteria and microzooplankton may even establish a zone of enriched nutrients around the aggregates (Hoppe, 1981), and that the microorganisms maximize their position within such nutrient fields leading to the formation of 'microbial clusters' in the vicinity of such aggregates (Azam & Ammerman, 1984). Biddanda & Pomeroy (1988) have called this microenvironment the 'detritosphere', similar to the phycosphere concept used by Bell & Mitchell (1972) to describe the environment of bacteria associated with live phytoplankton cells exuding soluble organic materials.

Biddanda & Pomeroy (1988) have demonstrated that regardless of its source, organic detritus suspended in sea water develops a remarkably similar and well defined sequence of microbial succession. They proposed that there is a regular process of aggregation of organic matter, microbial colonization and utilization, followed by a process of aggregate disaggregation (Fig. 14.14). Depending on their density and the vertical density structure of the water column the aggregates sink at varying rates. Some will be lost from the photic zone and some will sediment to the bottom. Turbidity currents and upwelling, and in shallow water wave action, will result

in resuspension of the aggregates. This model is driven by inputs from primary and secondary production. The loss of detritus and biomass by respiration and sinking is compensated through new primary and secondary production inputs as well by resuspension. Thus, the fate of detritus in the water column is seen as aggregation–disaggregation sequences in time and space.

In his experiments on phytoplankton (diatom) derived detritus Biddanda (1986) found that about 30 to 35% of the carbon in the detritus is mineralized (34 to 39% is utilized) by the microbial community in 4 days, whereas 63% is mineralized within 16 days. The period of rapid detritus utilization coincides with the period of detritus aggradation (Biddanda & Pomeroy, 1988). The rate of utilization decreases steadily as the more refractive compounds in the particulate and dissolved pools are gradually mineralized or incorporated by the microbial community. Heterotrophic bacteria can actually only utilize dissolved compounds, and therefore must colonize particles and convert them into dissolved substances. It is thus difficult to distinguish between particle-attached and free-living bacteria.

In the Southern Ocean pelagic ecosystem episodic events such as the collapse of phytoplankton blooms, the production of large quantities of faeces by feeding swarms of krill, and the release of the sea ice microalgae and detritus upon the melting of the ice present sudden and large available detrital resources to the heterotrophic microbial communities. In their study of the factors influ-

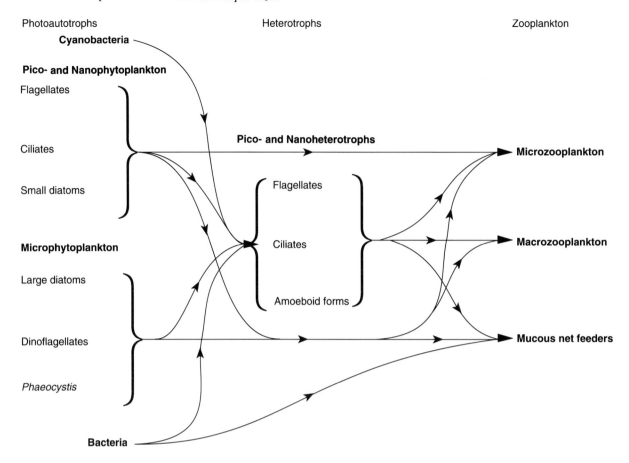

Fig. 14.15 Conceptual model illustrating the consumption of photoautotrophs and bacteria in the pelagic food chain. Possible food chains involving bacteria, protozoans and zooplankton are:
Cyanobacteria→Flagellates→Zooplankton
Cyanobacteria→Flagellates→Ciliates→Zooplankton
Bacteria→Flagellates→Zooplankton
Bacteria→Ciliates→Zooplankton
Bacteria→Flagellates→Ciliates→Zooplankton
Bacteria→Amoeboid forms→Zooplankton

encing the fate of sea ice microalgae released from melting sea ice in the northern Weddell Sea, Riebesell *et al.* (1991) found that they had a high propensity to form aggregates, the sinking rates of which were three orders of magnitude higher than those of dispersed sea ice microalgae. They suggested that the sea ice microalgae released from the melting ice were subject to rapid sedimentation. If an average residence time in the mixed layer of 30 days is assumed (Lande & Wood, 1987) the results of Biddanda's (1986) studies indicate that since 25, 32 and 63% of the organic matter in the detritus is mineralized by 2, 4 and 16 days respectively there is ample opportunity for a rapid recycling of detritus-bound carbon.

Aggregates, as we have seen, become rapidly colonized by bacteria, microalgae and heterotrophic flagellates and ciliates. Small flagellates have high swimming speeds relative to their size (Throndsen, 1973; Fenchel 1982a), and hence have the potential to migrate among

the aggregates even though the density of such aggregates may be low. Motility in marine bacteria is common and swimming speeds of up to 20–40 μm s⁻¹ have been observed (Azam & Ammerman, 1984). In addition, chemotaxis may be a characteristic of the bacteria. Thus, although the percentage of particle-bound microbes has been used in the past as an indicator of the degree to which aggregates contribute to microbial interactions in the pelagic environment, Azam & Hodgson (1981) suggest that this may give a false picture of particle–microbe dynamics.

14.9.3 Consumption of bacteria, detritus and protozoa by marine zooplankton

As we have seen detritus dominates the suspended organic particulate matter in the sea. This greater abundance of detritus compared with estimates of phytoplankton standing stocks has promoted speculation on the importance of detritus and its associated microbial community as a food source for pelagic zooplankton (Marshall & Orr, 1955; Heinle & Flemer, 1975; Roman, 1984a,b). Also the importance of bacterioplankton (comprising 10–40% of the phytoplankton carbon biomass) has been the subject of much controversy. Marine larvaceans (P. J. Le B. Williams, 1981; Ducklow, 1983), salps (Harbison & McAllister, 1979; Mullin, 1983), calanoid copepods (*Eurytemora* sp.; Boak & Gulder, 1983, and *Euclanus* and *Eucalanus*; Sorokin, 1981) have been found to ingest free-living bacteria, but with less efficiency than larger (>3.0 µm) particles.

In a study of the carbon budget of the copepod *Eurytemora affinis* (Heinle & Flemer, 1975; Heinle *et al.*, 1977) it was concluded that detritus must be a food supply for the copepods. The hypothesis was tested by rearing copepods on standardized diets of detritus, with and without microorganisms, using copepods grown on algal diets as controls. The conclusion was that copepods could grow and produce eggs on a diet of detritus when microorganisms were present, or on a mixed diet of microalgae and detritus, but that they did not thrive on a diet of detritus which had been autoclaved to control the microorganisms. The results also suggested that they could also do very well on a diet of ciliates. When fed on a protozoan infusion egg production was as high, if not higher, than for copepods fed on algal cultures. Sorokin's work on the consumption of bacteria by zooplankton supports the above conclusions. He found that the appendicularian *Oikpleura* could take up to 100% of its body weight a day

from bacteria, and that the cladoceran *Penilla* could take about 50% at an assimilation efficiency of about 35%. He also found a small but significant uptake of bacterial biomass by the copepods *Euclalnus* and *Paracalanus*, and suggested that they were able to filter from the water 20–30% of the bacteria present in aggregates.

One of the problems in determining the extent to which protozoa provide energy for zooplankton is that they are predominantly soft-bodied and readily digestible so that they do not leave recognizable remains in the stomach contents and faecal pellets. Tanoue & Hara (1986) found many costal strips of the choanoflagellate *Parvicorbicula socialis* in *Euphausia superba* faecal pellets. Because of their high abundance of choanoflagellates in the pelagic waters of the Southern Ocean and their known feeding habits (bacteria, picoplankton such as cyanobacteria) Tanoue & Hara (1986) postulated a food chain: non-living particulate matter and dissolved organics bacteria choanoflagellates krill vertebrate krill consumers.

The possible pathways which may be involved in the consumption of bacteria are shown in Fig. 14.15. The consumption by zooplankton of bacterial aggregates may be of greater importance than of single bacterial cells since coarse filterers such as copepods are not efficient at ingesting very small particles. The relative importance of the various possible routes are unknown at this time for the Southern Ocean. However, the combination of alternative pathways may have an important stabilizing effect on the pelagic food webs.

15

Ecosystem dynamics

15.1 Introduction

In this chapter an attempt will be made to undertake an holistic approach to the Southern Ocean ecosystem. The principal environmental features of this system are listed in Table 15.1. Whether the Southern Ocean can be considered a single ecosystem, or a series of interconnected ecosystems, is a moot point. It is purely a matter of choice. For the purpose of this analysis one can consider the sea ice, the pelagic waters and the benthic sediments as separate ecosystems, and these can be further subdivided on geographic and depth criteria. However, it must be borne in mind that they are all interconnected to a greater or lesser degree. In previous chapters submodels of component populations or trophic levels have been discussed. Models of whole systems, or ecosystems, focus on the ways in which the individual components of the ecosystem are linked to each other, and the ways in which the state variables (components, or compartments within the system, e.g. trophic levels) are linked together, and how they interact with the ecosystem-forcing functions (inputs, e.g. energy) which drive the system. A systems model provides a conceptual hypothesis within which different sets of data can be explored. It can identify which critical observations have not been made, and it suggests laboratory and environmental experiments which might be performed (Knox, 1986).

Early models assumed linear food chains of the Lindeman (1942) type, consisting of phytoplankton, zooplankton, benthos and fish (G. L. Clarke, 1946; Riley, 1963). The compartments of such models were equated with trophic levels, and ecological transfer efficiencies were applied to evaluate energy flux. Ryther (1969) attempted to show how fish production was limited by the number of transfers of energy. Steele (1974) developed a bifurcated compartmental model with one pathway involving phytoplankton, zooplankton herbivores, zooplankton carnivores, and pelagic fish, and the other pathway involving faecal pellets, bacteria, benthic meiofauna, benthic macrofauna, epibenthos and demersal fishes. In a landmark paper Pomeroy (1979) presented a compartmental model of energy flow through a continental shelf

Table 15.1. *Environmental features of the Southern Ocean*

A.   Epipelagic Zone
1. An oceanic ring surrounding a central land mass.
2. Free connection with the world's major oceans, the Atlantic, Pacific and Indian Oceans.
3. Zonal transport by circumpolar currents (Antarctic Circumpolar Current and Antarctic Coastal Current) dominates over meridional transport.
4. Temperature between 3–4 °C (summer) 2 °C (winter) at the Antarctic Convergence and approaching –2 °C at the ice shelves.
5. No dilution of inshore waters by freshwater inflow but surface dilution in summer due to sea ice melting.
6. No pronounced stratification or vertical stability except at the ice edge during the retreat of the sea ice. Considerable sinking of high salinity water (greater than 34.5%) and low temperature (less than 0.5 °C) near the continent, and up welling of high salinity (34.7%) and high temperature (1–2 °C) in the region of the Antarctic Divergence.
7. Continuous high nutrient levels in the euphotic zone.
8. Variable sea ice cover.
9. Light intensity providing ample Photosynthetically Available Radiation (PAR) in the summer but very low in the winter and under ice cover.
10. High degree of stability of the marine climate over the past 3 million years.

B.   Benthic Shelf habitats
1. Continental shelf narrow in most places, partly under ice shelves. Shelf mostly deeper than in other world oceans, 300–800 m deep.
2. Mozaic of glacial marine sediments, including muds, fine and coarse sands and large and small boulders. Sediments generally poorly sorted. No river-borne sediments.
3. Depths down to 300–400 m subject to iceberg scour.
4. Intertidal and near-shore zone abraded by sea ice and anchor-ice.
5. Meridional transport by Antarctic Bottom Water, zonal transport by circumpolar currents.
6. Temperature low and stable, ranging from *c.* 2–3 °C near the Antarctic Convergence to –2 °C at the continent.
7. Water well-mixed and oxygen levels high.
8. Rich supply of phytoplankton and detritus (POM) during the short summer production period.
9. Light intensity low in most places due to water depth and ice cover.

ecosystem examining the potential for substantial energy flow through dissolved organic matter (DOM), detritus (POM) and microorganisms to terminal consumers. This model was further developed by Pace *et al*. (1984). These models involved the abandonment of the classic idea of trophic levels and instead regarded food webs as anastomosing structures which defy classification into trophic levels. Pomeroy demonstrated that it was possible for energy to flow either through the grazer, or alternative pathways, to support all major trophic groups at a reasonable level, and to maintain fish production at about the levels that commonly occur.

In previous chapters we have seen that the Southern Ocean sustains large populations of krill, seabirds and seals, and in the past it was the world's most productive whaling ground (Laws, 1985). It is also the site of 75–85% of the biogenic siliceous sedimentation of the world's oceans (DeMaster, 1981; Leford-Hoffman *et al*., 1986). While these indirect lines of evidence indicate high primary production, estimates using ^{14}C incorporation rate measurements in the Southern Ocean indicate production rates typical of oligotrophic oceans elsewhere (Holm-Hansen *et al*., 1977; El-Sayed, 1978, 1984; Jacques & Treguer, 1986; Priddle *et al*., 1986a). However, recent work on ice edge phytoplankton blooms (W. O. Smith & Nelson, 1985a,b; Garrison *et al*., 1986; W. O. Smith, 1987; Fryxell & Kendrick, 1988; Sullivan *et al*., 1988) has provided some answers to this paradox. In the following sections of this chapter we shall see the degree to which our understanding of productive processes and their magnitude in the Southern Ocean has undergone dramatic changes in the last decade.

15.2 Pelagic zonation

The productivity of the Southern Ocean is to a large extent determined by its unique environmental features. These are listed in Table 15.1. The circulation system, coupled with the seasonal changes in the light regime and sea ice cover have imposed on the Southern Ocean a north–south pattern in bioproductivity, species composition, distribution of biological resources, the pattern of food webs and the trophic relationships of marine organisms (Lubimova, 1983). Hart (1942) for phytoplankton and Voronina (1966), Lubimova (1982) and Lubimova *et al*. (1984) for the zooplankton distinguish similar latitudinal zones (Fig. 15.1). Descriptions of these zones are given by Lubimova (1982) and I. Hempel (1985a,b).

15.2.1 Ice-free zone or zone of open Antarctic water (I in Fig. 15.1)

This zone covering an area of some 27 million km^{-2} is free of ice all year round and occupies the area of the Antarctic

Circumpolar Current. It is rich in nutrients but relatively poor in primary production. Two peaks of phytoplankton production occur each year. Nanoplankton dominate the phytoplankton biomass while herbivorous copepods, salps and small euphausiids dominate the zooplankton, with high biomasses being recorded to a depth of 700–1000 m for most of the year (Hart, 1942; Foxton, 1956; Vorinina, 1966, 1971; Vorinina *et al*., 1980a,b). According to Voronina *et al*. (1980) secondary production of the copepods in the productive mesopelagic layer equals 70 g m^{-2} y^{-1}. Krill are not a significant feature of this zone.

The highly productive mesopelagic layer is inhabited by mesopelagic fish belonging to the family Myctophidae (Lubimova *et al*., 1984). Both the meso- and bathypelagic waters of this zone are inhabited by a number of species of southern and Antarctic cephalopods which eat mainly mesopelagic plankton-eating fishes. They include species such as *Monoteuthis ingens*, *M. knipovitchi*, *Gonatus antarcticus*, *Galiteuthis aspersa*, *Batoteuthis scopolis*, *Mesonychoteuthis hamiltoni*, and some other species known primarily from the analysis of the stomach contents of sperm whales (Fillipova, 1972).

15.2.2 Seasonal pack ice zone (II in Fig. 15.1)

The seasonal pack ice zone covering an area of some 19 million km^2 is covered by ice in the winter and spring but is mainly ice-free in the summer and autumn. It occupies most of the Antarctic Coastal Current and its large eddies along the Antarctic Divergence, and includes the northern branch of the Weddell Gyre and the waters off the Antarctic Peninsula. Stabilization of the euphotic zone at the ice edge following the melting of the sea ice and the seeding of the water column by the release of the sea ice microalgae make this zone the most productive over the entire year. With the breakup and retreat of the pack ice in the spring and summer, a series of phytoplankton blooms proceed from north to south. In contrast to the ice-free zone there is a single peak of phytoplankton production.

The food web is a complex one with copepods, salps, euphausiids, fish larvae and chaetognaths (Hopkins, 1985b). Krill, because of their large total biomass and swarming behaviour, provide the food base for large populations of baleen whales, Crabeater and Fur Seals, and Penguins.

Krill are largely restricted to the south of approximately 60° S, which corresponds to the mean northern boundary of the drifting ice (Maslennikov, 1980; Lubimova *et al*., 1984). Krill and other euphausiid species are most available to baleen whales and seals which are widely distributed in the epipelagic zone of the drifting ice in the summer. They are most available to the permanent inhabitants of the zone such as the Minke

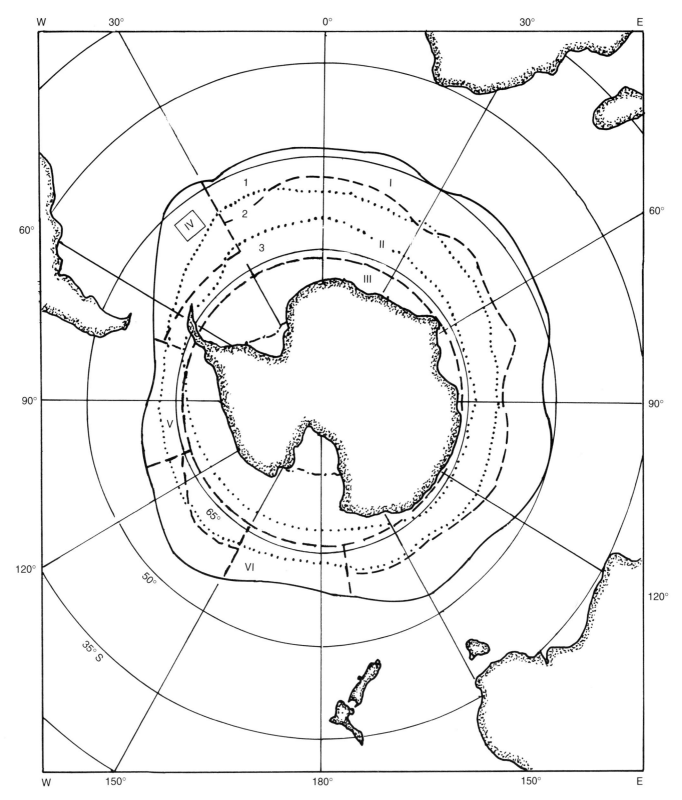

Fig. 15.1. Zonation of phytoplankton (*Roman numerals* and *dashed lines*; after Hart, 1942) and zooplankton (*Arabic numerals* and *dotted lines*; after Voronina, 1971) in the Southern Ocean. I Ice free zone or zone of open waters; II Seasonal pack ice zone; III Permanent pack ice or fast ice zone; IV South Georgia zone. Redrawn from Hempel (1985b).

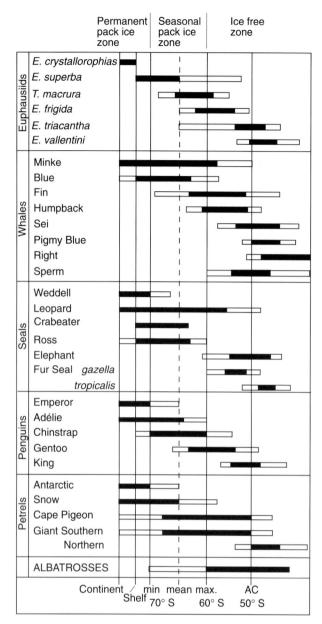

Fig. 15.2. Comparison of the zones occupied by selected species of euphausiids, marine mammals and birds from the Antarctic Continent northwards. The relative area of the shelf, the minimum, mean and maximum area of pack ice and the area south of the Antarctic Convergence (AC) are indicated, as is the pelagic zonation (ice-free, seasonal pack ice and fast ice zones). Each species has a circumpolar distribution, and the range indicated is the approximate average latitudinal range, with the shaded areas indicating higher densities. Redrawn from Laws (1977b).

Whale and the Crabeater, Leopard, and Ross Seals, or those bird species which spend the summer on breeding colonies round the continent such as Adélie and Chinstrap Penguins and the Antarctic and Snow Petrels (Fig. 15.2), but they are less available to some of the migratory species of baleen whales, e.g. the Sei Whale, which does not penetrate into this zone.

15.2.3 Permanent pack ice or fast ice zone (III in Fig. 15.1)

The permanent pack ice zone, including the fast ice zone, is that nearshore zone which is covered by ice for most of the year. The fast ice comprises the sheets of sea ice which are attached to the shore and which only break out in the late summer (February–March). In some areas the ice does not break out each year, if it does not multi-year ice results. This permanent pack ice zone roughly coincides with the area covered by the pack ice at the time of the maximum retreat towards the Antarctic Continent. Within this area polynas of various sizes and duration are conspicuous features. It extends over the area of very cold nearshore water masses (ice-shelf water) which are partly separated from the Antarctic Coastal Current by the Continental Divergence. Such water masses are particularly well developed in the shallow parts of the inner Weddell Sea and the Ross Sea. A characteristic feature of parts of this zone is the extensive development of platelet ice, which often forms a band of loosely aggregated platelets up to several metres thick on the lower surface of the sea ice.

Phytoplankton production is restricted to a brief, intense summer period. Zooplankton diversity and biomass are not as high as in the seasonal pack ice zone. Krill are largely replaced by the smaller *Euphausia crystallorophias*, and krill-eating mammals are less abundant than in waters to the north. Pelagic fish, especially *Pleurogramma antarcticum,* are particularly abundant. The bulk of the primary production is not consumed, but sediments to the bottom where it is incorporated in the sediments or consumed by the extremely rich epibenthic fauna of suspension feeders.

15.3 Phytoplankton and primary production

15.3.1 Introduction

Early studies using net plankton hauls gave the impression that large diatoms dominated the Antarctic phytoplankton community. However, although they often dominate the cell numbers south of the Antarctic Convergence, many are small, 10 μm in size (of nanoplankton dimensions; (Weber & El-Sayed, 1986a). The diatom species *Nitzschia cylindricus* and *N. pseudonana*, which are only 3–6 μm in length, often constitute the bulk of the diatom species present. It is now well established that the size distribution of the primary producers plays an important role in the overall community structure and trophic organization of marine pelagic ecosystems (Pomeroy, 1974; Siebruth *et al.,* 1978; P. J. Le B. Williams, 1981; Siebruth & Davis, 1982; Stockner & Anita, 1986; Stockner, 1988). As discussed in

Chapter 2 it is now recognized that phototrophic nanoplankton (generally considered to be phytoplankton 2–20 µm in size) account for a high proportion of the biomass and production of most marine phytoplankton communities (see Pomeroy, 1974; Malone, 1980; Hallegraeff, 1981; Hannah & Boney, 1983; and Reid, 1983 for examples and reviews of the literature). More recently, phytoplankton investigators have become aware of a subpopulation of even smaller cells (<2 µm), the pico-phytoplankton (see Glover *et al.*, 1985, Probyn & Painting, 1985; W. G. Harrison, 1986; Stockner & Anita 1986; Stockner, 1988). The waters of the Southern Ocean have now been shown to resemble those of other oceans with respect to the roles played by pico- and nanophytoplankton.

15.3.2 *Importance of pico- and nanophytoplankton*

It is only comparatively recently, starting with the paper by v. Brockel (1981), that the relative important of pico-(<2 µm) and nano- (2–20 µm) phytoplankton has been recognized (Hewes *et al.*, 1985; Weber & El-Sayed, 1986a; Brandini & Kutner, 1987). Kosahi *et al.* (1985) concluded that picophytoplankton was negligible in Antarctic waters, but that nanophytoplankton constituted as much as 55% of the chlorophyll biomass. On the other hand, Hewes *et al.* (1985) and Brandini & Kutner (1987) found that >50% of the total chlorophyll found in Antarctic waters was contained in the pico- and nanophytoplankton size fractions, although they did not determine their relative proportions. In a like manner many investigators have not separated their relative contributions to biomass and production and have included the pico- and nanophytoplankton together.

The most recent review of the contributions of net, nano- and picophytoplankton to the phytoplankton standing of crop and primary production in the Southern Ocean is that of Weber & El-Sayed (1986a). They reported that the relative contributions of nano- and picoplankton are highly variable both in space and time. In the vicinity of Elephant Island, Drake Passage and the Bransfield Strait (western Altantic sector) the contribution of nanoplankton to integrated water column chlorophyll was 39–98% (mean = 40% for 26 stations). In the western Indian sector of the Southern Ocean 31–92% (mean = 64% for 69 stations) of the chlorophyll was in the nanoplankton size fraction. Picoplankton accounted for 5–74% (mean = 40% for 6 stations) and 7–42% (mean = 15% for 14 stations) in the Drake Passage–Bransfield Strait region and the Indian sector respectively. Size-fractionated measurements of carbon uptake in the Indian Ocean sector revealed the nanoplankton account for 16–92% (mean = 53% for 26 stations), and picoplankton for 0–32% (mean

= 53% for stations) of the primary production. Thus, it seems that a considerable proportion of the primary productivity is dominated by cells in the nano- and picoplankton size ranges. For 166 stations south of the Antarctic Convergence, nanoplankton contributed a mean (and median) of 66% to the total integrated water column chlorophyll *a*. In contrast to conclusions drawn from studies in temperate to tropical waters (Malone, 1980) the relative contribution of nanoplankton to total chlorophyll *a* does not appear to be a function of the total phytoplankton standing stock (the correlation coefficient between percentage contributions of the nanoplankton was only –0.21). Many studies have revealed that the concentration of chlorophyll *a* in the net size fraction is subject to large fluctuations (e.g. Malone, 1980; Hallegraeff, 1981; Kosahi *et al.*, 1985).

The limited data on Antarctic picoplankton suggested that cells which pass through a 2.0 µm filter often constitute only a small percentage of the Antarctic phytoplankton community (Reid, 1983; Kosahi *et al.*, 1985; Probyn & Painting, 1985; Hosaka & Nemoto, 1986), ranging in different areas from 2–22% (mean = 7–18%). However, in the studies carried out by Weber & El-Sayed (1988) in the Bransfield Strait and the waters of the Indian Ocean picophytoplankton accounted for up to 74% and 42% of the integrated chlorophyll *a* respectively. It is therefore probable that picophytoplankton is of greater importance than hitherto considered. Apart from the blooms dominated by net phytoplankton most of the standing stock and primary production of Southern Ocean phytoplankton can be attributed to cells which pass through a 20 µm (and in some cases a 2.0 µm) filter. This has important implications for the overall community structure and trophic organization of Antarctic marine pelagic ecosystems.

15.3.3 *Phytoplankton succession*

In those regions where ice edge or coastal phytoplankton blooms occur there is a well defined pattern of phytoplankton succession. This was first described by Bunt (1964a,b) for McMurdo Sound. In early November to mid-December a limited range of diatoms was found with *Nitzschia serrata* as the dominant species. Mid-December to early January was characterized by a *Phaeocystis pouchetii* bloom, which in late January was replaced by a diverse assemblage of diatoms more typical of northern Antarctic waters, such as *Thalassiosira antarctica* and *Synedra pelagica*. On December 13 diatom cell concentrations were only 0.01×10^6 l^{-1}, while at the height of the *Phaeocystis* bloom they reached 3×10^6 l^{-1}. During the latter stages of the succession in late January diatom concentrations were 0.36×10^6 l^{-1}, and during the latter stages of the succession in late January diatom concentrations were 0.36×10^6 l^{-1}. Perrin *et al.* (1987) reported a similar process of succession in Prydz Bay, with *Phaeocystis* being the most abundant alga at the time of the fast ice breakout in late December and early January. Following *Phaeocystis* the diatom *Nitzschia lanceolata* became numerically dominant in the water column reaching a concentration of 5.8×10^7 cells l^{-1} in February and dominating until just after sea ice formed in early March. The contribution of the nanoplankton chlorophyll was at a minimum at the time of the phytoplankton blooms in late November to early January (< 20%). In May the proportion was 80%, decreasing to 50% in October and 30% in early November.

As discussed in the previous section the marginal ice edge zone is characterized by both *Phaeocystis* and diatom blooms. In the early spring the melting of the sea ice at the retreating ice edge introduces sea ice microalgae into the water column. This results in cholorophyll *a* concentrations up to 0.4 µg l^{-1} and phytoplankton blooms in which chlorophyll can reach as high as 10 µg l^{-1} grow in the stabilized less saline surface layer (Bennekom *et al.*, 1989). It is during these blooms that the vertical flux of phytoplankton-derived detritus is high, resulting in the sedimentation of large quantities of organic matter towards deeper water and the sediments. However, bloom senescence and zooplankton grazing, especially by krill, can rapidly reduce the volume of the blooms. Heterotrophic protozoa increase rapidly in abundance and the phytoplankton community shifts towards one dominated by nano- and picophytoplankton. Table 15.2 lists the main trends in this succession process and the concomitant changes in other indices of pelagic ecosystem structures.

Recent studies in widely spread geographic locations have shown that the 'macro' pathway (net phytoplankton) is preponderant wherever the total primary production is high (blooms), and the 'micro' pathway (pico- and nanophytoplankton) is dominant in situations where phytoplankton biomass is low (Jacques & Panouse, 1991). The latter is the usual situation in the Ice Free Zone south of the Antarctic Convergence, and post-bloom conditions in the Seasonal Pack Ice Zone. As Platt & Harrison (1985) have predicted, we should expect that each province of the Southern Ocean can occupy, at a given time, in a given place, and at a given depth, any position in the total spectrum from extreme oligotrophy to extreme eutrophy. Jacques & Panouse (1991) stress that this is a more realistic view than the one which definitively classifies a given oceanic region as either oligotrophic or eutrophic.

Table 15.2. *Phytoplankton succession and associated indices of pelagic ecosystem structure*

	Winter	Spring	Summer
Phytoplankton biomass	Low	Increasing rapidly	Decreasing
Diatoms	Low	High	Decreasing
Nano- and picophyto-plankton	Moderate	Low	Increasing rapidly
Nitrate	High	Reduced	Increasing
Ammonia	Low	Increasing	High
Silicate	High	Decreasing	Increasing
Bacteria	Low	Increasing	High
Heterotrophic proto-zoans	Low	Increasing	High
Sedimentation	Low	High	Decreasing

15.3.4 Sea ice microalgal production

As outlined in Chapter 3 the sea ice microalgal production is a significant component of the overall productivity of the Southern Ocean. Its contribution to Southern Ocean food webs can be summarized as follows:

1. There is now evidence that significant microalgal production and increase in biomass occurs after the formation of the sea ice in late March before the onset of winter, thus providing the conditions for the growth of sea ice bacterial and heterotrophic protozoa. The algal biomass thus produced is available to consumers during the austral winter.

2. Release of DOM by the sea ice microalgae provides the organic material for an increase in the numbers of the water column bacteria in the early spring before the melting of the ice occurs (Gibson *et al.*, 1990).

3. It is now clear that the development of the various kinds of bottom microalgal assemblages provides a significant food resource for larval and adult copepods (Hoshiai & Tanimura, 1981; Hoshiai *et al.*, 1987), larval and adult krill (Smetacek *et al.*, 1990), larval fishes and other members of the cryopelagic community (Knox, 1990), especially in the winter and early spring when phytoplankton stocks in the water column are low.

4. Copepod larval stages, especially in the fast ice zone, live and grow in the bottom sea ice microbial assemblages where there is an abundant food supply throughout the austral winter and early spring (Hoshiai *et al.*, 1987).

5. The release of DOM by the sea ice microalgae provides the organic substrate for the growth of the sea ice bacteria, which in turn provides a food resources for the sea ice heterotrophic protozoa.

6. When the sea ice melts in the late spring and early summer the sea ice microalgae are released into the water column. A proportion of these microalgae may be sedimented to deeper water where it becomes available to the zooplankton, especially the copepods which are characteristic of such waters. They also provide a food resource for the zooplankton in the surface waters before the onset of the spring phytoplankton blooms.

7. Most of the species of the sea ice microalgal assemblages are identical to those found in the water column. When they are shed into the water column on the melting of the ice they probably 'seed' the water and some species grow rapidly forming ice edge blooms in the favourable conditions of ample light and nutrients and water column stability resulting from the release of freshwater by the melting ice.

8. When the sea ice melts the sea ice bacteria and heterotrophic protozoa are also released to 'seed' the water column.

15.3.5 The importance of ice edge blooms

As discussed in Chapter 13 ice edge (or marginal ice) phytoplankton blooms have clearly been shown to be consistent features of the marginal ice zone (Hart, 1942; Marshall, 1957; El-Sayed, 1971b; El-Sayed & Taguchi 1981; W. O. Smith & Nelson, 1985a,b, 1990; Garrison *et al.*, 1986; W. O. Smith, 1987; Fryxell & Kendrick, 1988; Sullivan *et al.*, 1988; W. O. Smith & Sakshaug, 1990). Oceanographic processes operating within ice edge region stimulate primary production, and this increased production through assimilation by herbivorous zooplankton supports elevated standing stocks of higher trophic levels. The extent of the sea ice and its production and meltback influence the productivity and release of the sea ice microalgae into the water column. According to Sullivan *et al.* (1988) if it is assumed that there is a relatively uniform content of photosynthetic pigments of 10 mg m^{-2} (Kottmeier & Sullivan, 1987) contained in the melted ice of the Southern Ocean between 30° W and 45° W in the Weddell Sea, then 5.5×10^5 tonnes of pigment would be released with the meltwater. This would seed the actively growing algal cells at 0.2 mg chl *a* m^{-3}, which is equal to or greater than the pigment concentrations derived from the sparse phytoplankton found in the water

column under the ice. These algal cells would provide an inoculum for the observed ice edge blooms. If the model that Sullivan *et al.* (1988) have proposed is correct then it would be expected that enhanced biological productivity would occur along the entire circumpolar ice edge.

Sullivan *et al.* (1988) point out that the interannual variability in the ice extent can potentially induce large variations in predicted primary productivity at the ice edge. The magnitude of such variations can be as much as 50% from one year to the next and is highly dependent on the dynamics of the seasonal ice. Thus it would be expected that there would be considerable mesoscale spatial and temporal variability in the aerial extent and intensity of the ice edge blooms, as well as biological variability related to local ice dynamics in a particular region. The dynamics of the ice edge blooms could also be highly variable from one location to another depending on weather conditions, water column stability, local hydrology, and the intensity of grazing by herbivorous zooplankton, especially krill. W.O. Smith & Nelson (1986) estimated, for a receding ice edge in the Ross Sea, that the bloom could persist for about two months (rate of ice retreat c. 5.2 km day^{-1}; Nelson *et al.*, 1987). Fryxell & Kendrick (1988) estimated that in the summer in the Weddell Sea the spatial extent of the blooms at the ice edge and northwards was in the order of 250 km.

15.3.6 Role of Phaeocystis

Phaeocystis pouchetii, a prymnesiophyte, is one of the few phytoplankton species which exhibit a life-cycle alternation between free-living flagellated zoospore and a gelatinous colonial aggregation of non-motile cells. It occurs most prominently in the plankton in this later stage and enormous blooms of colonial *Phaeocystis* have been documented over the past 100 years in many oceans including the Southern Ocean (see Chapter 2). It is also common as a member of the sea ice microalgal communities in many parts of the seasonal pack ice zone and the fast ice zone, and is released into the water column on the melting of the ice. Colonies can be formed by two mechanisms, the formation of colonies from solitary cells and the cleavage of large colonies into daughter colonies. As discussed in Chapter 14 the production of DOC and mucilage is an integral part of the physiology of *Phaeocystis* (Chang, 1984), and this requires substantial fractions of the photosynthate (Lancelot & Mathut, 1985). Studies of its carbon metabolism have suggested that *Phaeocystis* produces exopolymeric substances in the light which are stored in the gelatinous matrix and used in the dark to meet the energetic need of the cells (Lancelot & Mathut, 1985; Veldhius & Admiraal, 1985). Physiologically, *Phaeocystis* is a remarkably complex species as evidenced by the degree to which it became adapted to low light levels following advection under the fast ice in McMurdo Sound (Palmisano *et al.*, 1985c).

Bunt (1964a) was the first to draw attention to the occurrence of *Phaeocystis* blooms in Antarctic coastal waters. During the seasons of 1961–62 and 1962–63 phytoplankton rich in *Phaeocystis* appeared quite suddenly, coinciding with widespread deterioration of the sea ice to the north of McMurdo Sound. Since then *Phaeocystis* blooms have been shown to be a regular annual occurrence (Knox, 1990). The development of a *Phaeocystis* bloom is a complex process which is as yet poorly understood. *Phaeocystis pouchetii* is widely distributed in Antarctic waters (as mapped from Kashkin in Parke *et al.*, 1971; Fryxell & Kendrick, 1988). Blooms have been reported from the Weddell Sea (El-Sayed, 1971b; Buck & Garrison, 1983; Garrison & Buck, 1985b; Fryxell & Kendrick, 1988), and from McMurdo Sound (Bunt, 1964a; Palmisano *et al.*, 1988; Knox, 1990). El-Sayed (1971b) found *Phaeocystis* in large numbers (1.7×10^6 cells l^{-1}) in the Weddell Sea, while Garrison & Buck (1985b) in their Weddell Sea studies found that *Phaeocystis* made up >35% of the cells in net samples, 53% of the cells in just-forming ice samples, but only 1% in melted ice samples. *Phaeocystis* is also common in other inshore areas around Antarctica, and it has been reported in extensive blooms extending deep into the water column along the barrier edge of the Ross Ice Shelf in the austral summer of 1978 (El-Sayed *et al.*, 1983).

The fate of the *Phaeocystis* blooms and their contribution to the planktonic food webs and energy flow is of interest. It has been considered that the colonial forms are not consumed by herbivores due to their production of biochemical substances that prevent their consumption. Schnack *et al.* (1985) found no evidence of predation by copepods on *Phaeocystis*. On the other hand, culture experiments have shown that *Phaeocystis* can be excellent prey for various copepod species (Huntley *et al.*, 1987; Tande & Bamstedt, 1987). In studies in the Arctic Estep *et al.* (1990) found that predation on *Phaeocystis* colonies was a function of the physiological state of the colonies. Healthy colonies were not consumed, possibly as a result of the production of anti-predator compounds. They speculated that without this anti-predator ability *Phaeocystis* would have great difficulty in maintaining itself for prolonged periods as a bloom species, since the colonies would represent easily captured parcels of food for copepod species. They found that unhealthy colonies found during the latter stages of a bloom were consumed by zooplankton at higher rates than were co-occurring diatom species. The ability of *Phaeocystis* to avoid predation pressure has important implications for differential predation pressure and the species composition of Antarctic food chains.

The slimy colonies of *Phaeocystis* have not been thought to contribute significantly to the vertical flux of phytoplankton-derived detritus due to their buoyancy. However, Wassman *et al.* (1990) reported sedimentation rates of POC, PON and especially pigments from a *Phaeocystis* bloom in the Barents Sea which were among the highest rates recorded from northern cold temperate waters. They concluded that *Phaeocystis* is a significant contributor to marine snow (Alldredge & Silver, 1988) in polar and boreal oceans, enhancing the removal of particulate and dissolved matter from the surface waters. The extracellular polymeric material of aged *Phaeocystis* colonies gives rise to adhesive and sticky capsular secretions which are readily colonized by bacteria, pennate diatoms, and heterotrophic protozoans (Estep *et al.*, 1990). These aggregates sink and also remove other particles (e.g. algae, faecal pellets, detritus) from the upper layers. It is highly probable that a similar process takes place in the Southern Ocean. Autolysis, production of exudates, bacterial colonization of sinking colonies and amorphous material during *Phaeocystis* blooms (Davidson & Marchant, 1987; Vaqué *et al.*, 1989) and ingestion of bacteria-rich aggregates by copepods (Estep *et al.*, 1990) suggest that the particulate and dissolved organic matter derived from *Phaeocystis* blooms effectively recycle in the upper layers of the aphotic zone (Fig. 15.3).

It would appear that *Phaeocystis* plays a dual role in ice edge and coastal phytoplankton dynamics. The release of living cells from melting ice may provide 'seed' for the bloom which follows. In addition large amounts of extracelluar DOM and mucilage provide a ready substrate for bacterial growth and subsequent development of heterotrophic protozoa. The activities of both the bacteria and the heterotrophic protozoa result in the remineralization of organic matter producing large amounts of ammonia, which is the preferred form of nitrogen for subsequent diatom blooms. One aspect of phytoplankton succession which has had little attention in the Southern Ocean is the question of the 'conditioning' of the water by the bloom of one species of microalgal leading to a milieu that favours the development of another species.

15.4 Nutrient cycling

Waters south of the Antarctic Convergence are characterized by relatively high nutrient concentrations, which are maintained by large-scale upwelling and turbulent mixing in the upper water column. The relative instability of the water column often results in deep 'mixed layers' which enhance the supply of nutrients to the surface

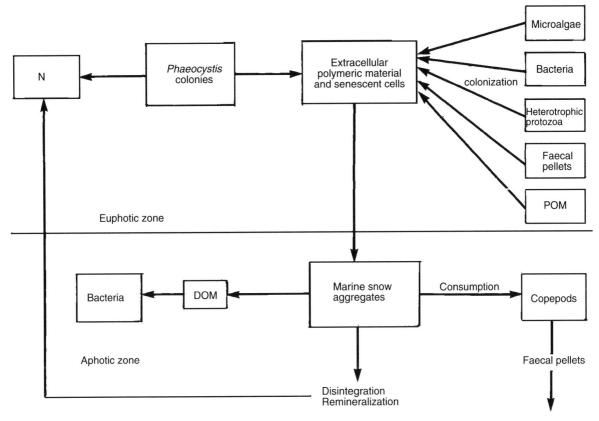

Fig. 15.3. Fate of organic matter produced during a *Phaeocystis* bloom.

waters. This is in contrast to the Arctic where there is generally depletion of nutrients in surface waters (Nemoto & Harrision, 1981). Thus, the waters of the Southern Ocean have some similarities with upwelling systems off the west coasts of South America and Africa.

In Chapters 2 and 14 the relative roles of 'new' (nitrate-N derived primarily from upwelling) and 'regenerated' nitrogen (principally ammonium, derived from microbial remineralization within the euphotic zone) nitrogen were discussed in detail. Spring phytoplankton blooms are composed mainly of *Phaeocystis* and diatoms which assimilate both nitrate and ammonium. Much of the production is fuelled by 'new' nitrogen in the form of nitrate from upwelling at the Antarctic Divergence and this dominates the particulate nitrogen pool. This forms the basis of the 'classic' food web (Fig 15.4) in which a large proportion of the organic matter produced by the microplankton is exported from the eutrophic zone to deeper water and the sediments through the rapid sinking of large diatoms and faecal pellets. As the spring advances localized nitrogen depletion occurs but the levels do not fall to those which can severely limit phytoplankton growth as is often the case in temperate waters. Stabilization of the water column limits the supply of 'new' nitrogen from deeper waters and the particulate

nitrogen pool becomes more and more based on ammonium ('regenerated' nitrogen) derived via microbial decomposition and grazing. This 'microbial loop' cycle proceeds principally in the euphotic layer with rapid recycling through the excretion of microheterotrophs and bacterial remineralization. This system is a weak exporter of organic matter to the deeper layers as it is dominated by highly buoyant microorganism (Jacques, 1989). If, at the same time local ammonium production becomes greater than ammonium consumption by phytoplankton, which will be the case in the declining phase of a bloom, accumulation of ammonium will occur in the water column. Thus, a shift in nitrogen consumption towards ammonium occurs, and by the summer about 80% of primary production is supported by ammonium and the composition of the phytoplankton community shifts from one which is diatom dominated to one dominated by nano- and picophytoplankton. Over the autumn and winter the ammonium in the water column is gradually dissipated, either by advective or oxidative processes. In the following spring the 'cycle' of ammonium production and utilization begins anew.

Preferential uptake of ammonium over oxidized forms of inorganic nitrogen by phytoplankton has been reported in many marine environments (Dugdale & Goering,

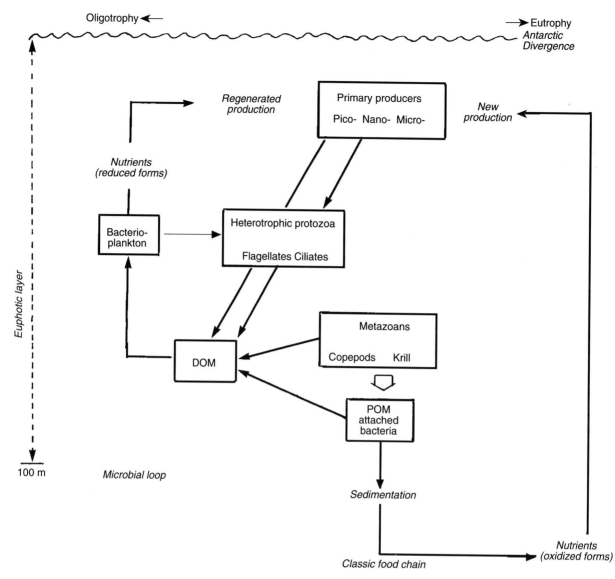

Fig. 15.4. The relationship between the 'classical food web' and the 'microbial loop' and nutrient supply in the euphotic zone. DOM = dissolved organic matter; POM = particulate organic matter. Modified from Jacques (1989).

1967; McCarthy & Goldman, 1979), and the Southern Ocean is no exception. Even in the early spring, when the ammonium concentration in the surface waters was low (0.1 to 0.4 µM) phytoplankton in the Scotia Sea assimilated approximately half of their nitrogen as nitrate and half as ammonium (Olson, 1980). In the late summer when ammonium concentrations in the same area had increased to approximately 1.0 µM , the phytoplankton obtained more than 60% of their nitrogen as ammonium (Gilbert *et al.*, 1982). Other studies by Rönner *et al.* (1983) and Koike *et al.* (1986) showed that ammonium uptake averaged 78% in oceanic areas of the Scotia Sea in the early austral summer, and from 65% to 93% in an area of the Scotia Arc in the late summer.

Koike *et al.* (1986) have estimated standing stocks of nitrogen in the euphotic zone of Antarctic waters near

Elephant Island in the summer (Table 15.3). The partitioning of the nitrogen stocks in Antarctic waters has several interesting features compared to other oceanic regions. According to Koike *et al.* (1986) the total nitrogen in the water was about 5.5 times higher than the global average for surface waters. About 73% of this total was in the form of nitrate. Particulate organic nitrogen, of which about 84% occurs in living organisms, represented less than 4% of the total nitrogen. Bacterial biomass represented about 27% of the total microbial biomass, which falls into the upper range of estimates for coastal waters (3 to 25%; Ferguson & Rublee, 1976: Fuhrman & Azam, 1980). Microzooplankton-N was 6% of the total microbial biomass-N (9% of the phytoplankton-N). This is somewhat lower than previous estimates by v. Brockel (1981) who reported that the microzooplankton biomass averaged 16% of the phytoplankton biomass in the same area at the same time of the year. The large amounts of inorganic nitrogen, including ammonia, were sufficient to support over four generations of exponential phytoplankton growth.

Table 15.4 summarizes estimates of the rates of ammonium production and consumption associated with various components of the food web in the coastal waters near Elephant Island. It should be noted that the 'microzooplankton' data do not include heterotrophic nanoplankton (mostly flagellates), which are known to be major ammonium producers (Hewes *et al.*, 1985). Thus, heterotrophic eucaryote organisms in the pico- and nanoplankton are probably a major source of ammonium. The significance of bacterioplankton for ammonium concentrations in Antarctic waters is not known, as they can both compete with phytoplankton for assimilation of ammonium (Azam *et al.*, 1983) and also produce ammonium from nitrogenous substrates. In periods of nutrient limitation phytoplankton release extracelluar organic carbon thus making reduced carbon available for bacterial utilization. Since both the phytoplankton and bacteria compete for the same inorganic nutrients it seem paradoxical that phytoplankton should stimulate bacteria in this way (Bratbak & Thingstad, 1985). However, heterotrophic protozoa keep populations in check, but also recycle nutrients, thus indirectly alleviating the competitive pressure of bacteria on the phytoplankton by providing a supply of nutrients.

In most oceans nitrate exhaustion by a preceding phytoplankton bloom is assumed to be the triggering factor leading to the establishment of a regenerating system in which autotrophs are dependent on the release of reduced nitrogen by the heterotrophs. In open Antarctic waters, however, the regenerating community establishes itself in the presence of abundant nitrate. While ammonium provides the bulk of the microbial nitrogen requirements (Olson, 1980; Koike *et al.*, 1986) nitrate can also be utilized (supplying between 20 and 50% of requirements according to Holm-Hansen, 1985). Thus nitrate exhaustion by a spring bloom is not necessary for the establishment of a regenerating community in Antarctic waters.

In the Weddell Sea in the winter the plankton consisted of an active regenerating community functioning at very great dilution (Smetacek *et al.*, 1990). Such communities are flagellate dominated. However, the autotrophs in these communities utilize both ammonium and nitrate and they cannot be categorized exclusively as either 'new' or 'regenerating' systems as they combine characteristics of both. Smetacek *et al.* (1990) have suggested that the term 'retention' system is more appropriate. The 'regenerating' system is then the characteristic system of

Table 15.3. *Estimates of standing stock of fixed nitrogen by major food-web components in the euphotic zone of Antarctic coastal waters*

	Standing stock (mg N l⁻¹)
Particulate nitrogen	
Phytoplankton	7.6
Bacteria	3.1
Detritus	2.8
Krill	2.0
Net zooplankton	1.4
Microzooplankton	0.7
Sub total	17.6
Dissolved nitrogen	
Nitrate (incuding nitrite)	350
Ammonium	29
Dissolved organic-N	77
Sub total	456
Total	474

From Koike *et al.* (1986).

Table 15.4. *Ammonium consumption and production (nmol N l⁻¹ day⁻¹) by major food web components in the euphotic zone of Antarctic coastal waters*

	Amount (nmol N l⁻¹) day⁻¹
Consumption	
Phytoplankton	30–40
Nitrifying bacteria	?
Production	
Microzooplankton	20
Net zooplankton	~3
Krill	~1
Bacteria	?

From Koike *et al.* (1986).

the Southern Ocean pelagic zone with blooms representing transitory events superimposed on the basal state (Fig. 15.5).

15.5 Food webs

The transfer of food energy from its source in phytoplankton through a series of organisms is referred to as a food chain. At each transfer a large proportion, 80 to 90% of the potential energy is lost as heat. Therefore the number of 'links' in the chain is limited. Food chains have been considered to be of two basic types: the *grazing food chain*, which starts with phytoplankton which is eaten by grazing herbivores (primary consumers), and which in

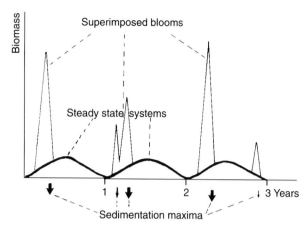

Fig. 15.5. A hypothetical scheme illustrating the relationship between seasonality of the microbial network regenerating system (thick line) with superimposed 'blooms' (thin lines). The latter exhibit more variability as they are induced by weather conditions operating on a scale of weeks. They are followed by a correspondingly variable sedimentation pulse. Redrawn from Smetacek *et al.* (1990). Based on Pace *et al.* (1984).

turn are eaten by carnivores (secondary consumers), and the *detritus food chain,* which starts with particulate organic matter which is consumed by bacteria and heterotrophic protozoa, thus forming the detrital–microbial complex which is consumed by detritus-feeding organisms which in turn are consumed by predators. However, in the marine pelagic ecosystem these food chains are often not clearly separated, and as detailed in the previous chapter primary consumers such as the euphausiids and copepods may consume bacteria, heterotrophic protozoa, phytoplankton, small metazoans and detrital aggregates with their associated microbial community. Food chains thus are not isolated sequences but are interconnected with each other to form an interlocking pattern, the *food web.*

Our view of the functioning of pelagic ecosystems has changed dramatically in the last 15 years (P. J. Le B. Williams, 1981; Fenchel, 1988). It is now recognized that phototrophic and heterotrophic protozoa play a substantial and sometimes dominating role in the cycling of matter in the sea, that plankton food chains include a higher number of trophic levels than previously believed, and that a large proportion of the primary production is not consumed directly by primary consumers but is channelled through a pool of dead organic matter before it becomes available – via bacterial degradation – to phagotrophic organisms (Fenchel, 1988). It has frequently been stated that the Southern Ocean pelagic ecosystem is characterized by short food chains – the classic phytoplankton—>krill—>baleen whale food chain. However, it appears that only a maximum of 3% of phytoplankton primary production is consumed by krill and that something in excess of 90% is not consumed

directly by herbivores. It is now clear that food webs in the Southern Ocean are not radically different from those of other oceans.

Fig 15.6 is a compartmental model based on the elaboration of Pomeroy's (1979) model by Pace *et al.* (1984), in which some of the complexity of the Southern Ocean pelagic food web is depicted. Implicit in this model is the recognition of: 1. the complementary roles of pico-, nano- and net phytoplankton; 2. the central role of DOM produced from a great variety of sources; 3. the utilization of this pool of DOM by bacteria and their consumption by heterotrophic protozoa (the *microbial loop*); 4. the diversity of food items consumed by the herbivores or primary consumers; and 5. the role of sedimentation of POM (primarily microplankton and faecal pellets). In the following sections we will explore the roles of selected groups of organisms in the Southern Ocean pelagic food web.

15.5.1 Role of bacteria

It is now generally accepted that the abundance of bacteria in the Southern Ocean is similar to that of other oceans. Bacterial production has been found to average 5 to 20% of the net primary production in many locations in coastal areas and the open oceans implying that about 10 to 50% of the primary production is cycled through the bacteria if one assumes their growth efficiency is 50% (Ducklow, 1983). Studies by Cota *et al* (1990) and Sullivan *et al.* (1990) have suggested that the bacterioplankton contribute about 11% of the net primary productivity in the marginal ice zone in the austral spring, with lower values in ice-covered waters and slightly higher ones in open waters. In their studies of the marginal ice zone of the Weddell Sea Cota *et al.* (1990) and Sullivan *et al.* (1990) found that while the spring phytoplankton biomass (as measured by chlorophyll *a*) was 10 times more abundant in the open water of the ice edge than within the pack ice, the difference in the autumn was only threefold. In contrast, there was usually less that a two-fold difference, regionally or seasonally, in the bacterial biomass.

Ratios of production per unit biomass (P:B ratios) provide an indication of the relative activities of populations in different environments. In contrast to phytoplankton where P:B ratios were several times higher under the pack ice than in the open waters, as a result of the low biomass levels under the ice, bacteria exhibited P:B ratios two to six times higher in open waters even though their abundance and biomass were also higher there. Bacterial carbon biomass averaged 23–24% of phytoplankton biomass under ice cover but only 7–12% in open waters. The portion of the primary production which is consumed by

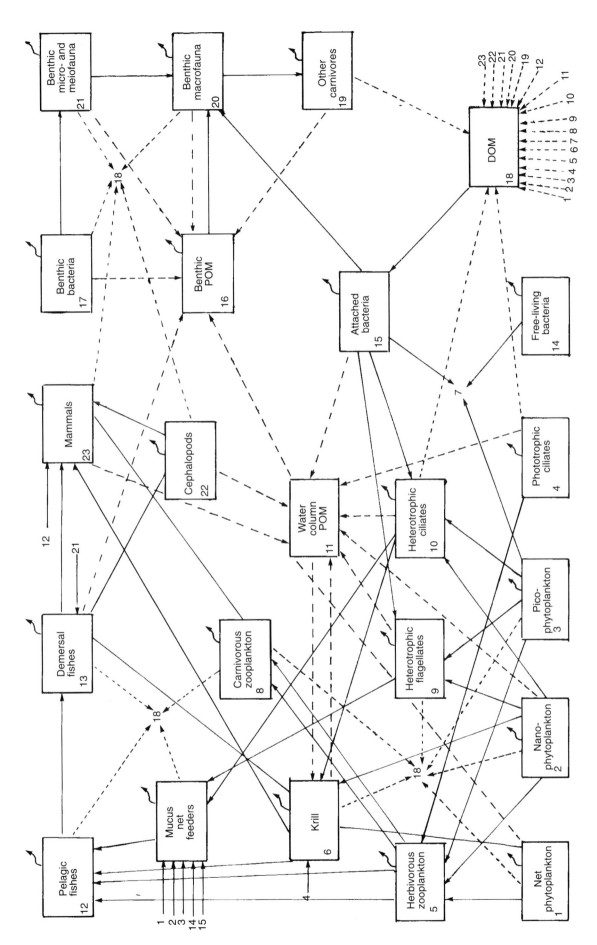

Fig. 15.6. A compartmental model of the Southern Ocean euphotic zone food web. Each compartment is numbered and the numbered inputs to some of the compartments refer to the input from the corresponding numbered compartment.

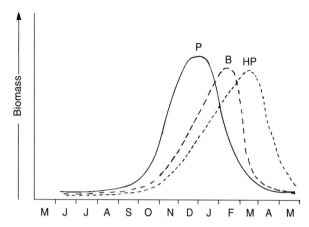

Fig. 15.7. The inter-relationship between a phytoplankton bloom (P) in the marginal ice edge zone and the growth of bacteria (B) and heterotrophic protozoa (HP).

Table 15.5. *Microbial and micrometazoan biomass (mg C m⁻²) in two cores of consolidated ice from different floes during spring 1983 in the Weddell Sea. From Kottmeier & Sullivan (1990).*

	Core J	Core K
Microalgal biomass[1] (diatoms, autotrophic dinoflagellates and other flagellates)	24.1	200
Bacterial biomass	25.6	217
Heterotrophic biomass (flagellates, ciliates, amoebae and micrometazoans)	3.09	17.2
Total biomass	52.8	434.2
Bacterial: microalgal biomass (%)	106	108
Microheterotrophic: microalgal biomass	12.80	8.60
Microheterotrophic: bacterial biomass	12.10	7.93
Microheterotrohic: microalgal + bacterial biomass	6.22	4.12

[1]Chlorophyll $a \times 38$ (Sullivan *et al.*, 1985).
From Kottmeier & Sullivan (1990).

bacteria depends upon numerous physiological and environmental factors, but the most important appears to be the growth phase of the phytoplankton bloom (Cota *et al.*, 1990). In the autumn, bacteria were consuming about three quarters of the primary production in the open water compared with only 14% in the spring when algal biomass and productivity were several times higher. The sequence of events appears to be as follows. In spring bloom conditions the bacteria do not increase rapidly enough to consume the available DOM released by the microalgae. As the bloom progresses and decays in the late summer bacterial biomass has built up to higher levels, and with algal senescence and autoylsis greater amounts of POM and labile DOM become available to the bacteria. However, the build-up of the heterotrophic protozoan populations results in higher levels of grazing on the bacteria and this results in the decline of their populations to winter levels (Fig 15.7). Thus the bacteria play a dual role in the marginal ice edge zone, as mineralizers making 'regenerated' nitrogen available to primary producers and as secondary producers which are eaten by other organisms in the pelagic food webs, especially the heterotrophic flagellates.

Bacteria have been shown to be abundant in the sea ice of the fast ice zone (Sullivan & Palmisano, 1981, 1984; McConville & Wetherbee, 1983; Grossi *et al.*, 1984; Kottmeier *et al.*, 1987). The sea ice bacteria are more abundant and of 5–10 times greater volume than the bacterioplankton and are frequently found in long chains, typical of bacteria from organic-rich environments. Bacteria in the pack ice are similarly more abundant and larger than the bacterioplankton and are associated with high concentration of microalgae (Marra 1980; Miller *et al.*, 1985; Sullivan, 1985; Garrison *et al.*, 1986).

Kottmeier *et al.* (1987) estimated that bacterial production in the fast ice was as high as 9% of primary production, with growth rates up to 0.2 day⁻¹ during the austral spring microalgal bloom.

Kottmeier & Sullivan (1990) have studied bacterial biomass and production in the pack ice during the spring, autumn and late winter. They hypothesize that bacteria accumulate in the pack ice as a result of both physical and biological processes. During the formation and growth of the ice physical processes act to concentrate and accumulate bacteria within the ice matrix. This is followed by growth along the physico-chemical gradients which are found in several sea ice microhabitats. Bacterial biomass and production were much greater than in the underlying seawater (Table 15.6) and equal to that in several metres of water. Among microhabitats, highest bacterial production and most rapid growth rates (>1 doublings day⁻¹) were found in saline ponds on the surface of the floes and in the pore water in the interior on the floes. Bacterial carbon production ranged from 2% of primary production in surface brash ice to 45–221% of primary production in surface ponds and porewater. The bacterial production within the sea ice supports subsequent populations of microheterotrophs of the 'microbial loop', which in turn may support organisms at higher trophic levels. The sea ice bacteria may provide remineralized inorganic nutrients for the continued microalgal growth in localized microhabitats within the ice, or, on the other hand, they

Table 15.6. *Enrichment of bacterial characteristics in sea ice. Estimated by determining the ratio of bacterial characteristics in various sea ice microhabitats to the underlying water during spring 1983 and autumn 1986 in the Weddell Sea and during winter 1985 in the Bellingshausen Sea. Values are the ratio sea ice : underlying water for each characteristic*

| Characteristic | Spring ice | Autumn | | | | Winter ice |
		Ice	Slush	Surface pond	Pore-water	
Bacteria	10.2	5.11	16.6	19.2	1.86	—
Bacterial biomass	28.4	14.9	45.6	80.3	4.44	—
Average cell biomass	2.80	3.98	2.73	4.16	2.38	1.20
Bacterial cell production	—	0.466	0.607	12.4	7.31	15.3
Bacterial carbon production	—	17.8	16.5	4840	208	18.3
Bacterial growth rate	—	0.737	0.199	8.78	6.47	—

From Kottmeier & Sullivan (1990).

may compete with the algae for nutrients. Upon the melting of the ice the actively growing bacteria are released into the water column where they contribute to the microbial biomass in the seawater.

15.5.2 Comparative roles of krill and other zooplankton

In Chapter 4 a general account of the zooplankton of the Southern Ocean was given. Here we shall consider their role in the pelagic ecosystem with special reference to the seasonal pack ice zone, and the role of krill in relation to other zooplankton species. It has generally been considered that krill contribute 50% of the biomass of the zooplankton as a whole. However, in spite of the intensive decade of the BIOMASS programme directed at understanding the biology, distribution and standing stock of krill we do not know with any certainty how many krill there are. The situation is further complicated by a number of factors. Firstly, due to their aggregating and swimming behaviour krill are discontinuously distributed both in space and time. Variability in krill distributions will be discussed in detail in section 15.7.4. Secondly, there are other zooplankton species. Apart from the early life-history stages, krill are largely found in the euphotic zone, whereas the copepods, which along with the eupohausiids are the dominant zooplankton, are distributed from the euphotic zone to depths of 1000m plus. Thirdly, mucus feeders (predominately salps) can on occasions form dense swarms, but their role in relation to other zooplankton species is not well understood.

A remarkable feature of the Antarctic meso- and macrozooplankton is that the biomass in the upper 1000 m is more or less constant throughout the year (Foxton, 1956, 1966; Hopkins, 1971; Atkinson & Peck, 1988). The bulk of the stock is contributed by a few large copepod species which overwinter in the deeper layers in a dormant state. These copepods form an integral part of the microbial network, not only feeding on it as top predators, but also helping to maintain it by adding detritus in the form of faecal pellets and exuvia, as well as ammonia and microzooplankton in the form of nauplii.

Protozoan herbivores such as large dinoflagellates, many ciliates, heliozoans, radiolarians and foraminiferans are common in Antarctic waters (v. Brockel, 1981; Hewes *et al.*, 1983; Spindler & Dieckmann, 1986; Brandini & Kutner, 1987; Nothig, 1988). These herbivores, must exert considerable grazing pressure on the phytoplankton. They in turn, however, are grazed by the copepods, which have been shown to feed collectively on them in the presence of low phytoplankton biomass (Nothig & v. Bodungen, 1989). Hence, the copepod biomass in any given region is largely geared to the microbial network and is not dependent on transient phytoplankton blooms.

There is considerable variability in the relative proportions of krill and other zooplankton species in the Southern Ocean (K. A. Green, 1977) (Table 15.7). As would be expected compact krill swarms have a low percentage of other zooplankton species. In more diffuse swarms the proportion of these other species would be expected to be higher. In Chapter 5, where the swimming and feeding behaviour of krill were discussed in detail, it was noted that krill can swim for considerable distances as foraging swarms, and that when they locate a dense

Table 15.7. *Krill biomass as a proportion of total zoo-plankton biomass*

Locality	Period	Biomass (% of total)
Scotia Sea	24 Jan.–14 Feb.	
Total zooplankton		25
Excluding two swarms		
Western sector		6
Eastern sector		4
North of Elephant Island		
Total zooplankton	4–7 Mar.	70
	20–23 Mar.	72
Excluding large swarm	4–7 Mar.	40
	20–23 Mar.	24
Bransfield Strait	10–11 Mar.	
Total zooplankton		69
Excluding large swarm		40
South of Elephant Island	14–10 Mar.	25
East of Elephant Island		29
North of South Orkney Islands	14–19 Mar.	61
West of South Orkney Islands		4

Data from Brinton & Antezana (1984).

supply of phytoplankton they can graze it down and reduce the biomass of the preferentially grazed species (usually larger diatoms) to low levels. In this process they can change the species composition of the phytoplankton community and shift it towards one dominated by nanoplankton.

Although the total standing stock of krill is not known with any degree of certainty it clearly is in excess of 100 million tonnes. By any standard this is an exceptionally large biomass for a single species. It is a species that is the product of a long evolutionary history of being in isolation and becoming adapted to the strong seasonality and variability of the pack ice zone. Because of its swarming and foraging behaviour it can seek out pelagic food in an environment where phytoplankton blooms can be very patchy in their distribution. In section 5.5.5 accounts were given of recent research which established that, contrary to earlier opinions, krill have an ample food supply available in the winter in the form of the sea ice microalgae at a time when phytoplankton stocks in water column are low. This feeding behaviour is especially important to the furcilia stages which are particularly abundant within the pack ice.

Fig. 15.8 depicts the energy flow through a krill stock to its consumers. The filtering basket and mouth parts of krill can cope with a food spectrum of ten orders of magnitude in weight, ranging from nanoplankton to adult krill. Adult krill are very large in relation to other pelagic herbivorous zooplankton and the energy demands for

metabolism are very high. When feeding in the euphotic zone the principal food is phytoplankton, but in the process of filtering they certainly also consume heterotrophic flagellates and ciliates and probably other zooplankton. However, in spite of their large biomass it has been estimated that in the areas where they occur krill consume at most 5% of the spring phytoplankton blooms, and often much less (see Chapter 5). The extent to which they also consume POM aggregates with their associated microbial community (the detrital–microbial complex) is unknown. In the process of 'sloppy' feeding they add to the POM and DOM pools within the water column. Excretion adds to the DOM pool and also N and P to the euphotic zone. As detailed in Chapter 14, krill exuvia and faecal pellets are a significant component of the vertical flux of organic material.

Krill support either directly or indirectly large populations of vertebrate consumers as depicted in Fig. 15.9 (Everson, 1984c). Krill also compete for the primary production of the euphotic zone with other zooplankton species, especially the copepods and the salps. The salps as mucus-net feeders are able to feed on much smaller-sized particles, such as bacteria and picoplankton, and thus may not directly compete for the larger diatoms. However, it is significant that dense swarms of salps and krill do not coincide, and areas where krill may have dominated in one season may be dominated by salps in the next.

15.5.3 *The role of vertebrates*
The apex predators in the Southern Ocean include fishes of several families (predominantly the Nototheniidae), the Fur Seals (Otariidae), the Sea Elephants (Phocidae), the baleen whales (Mysticetes), toothed whales (Odontocetes), and seabirds of various families, the most important ones being the penguins (Spheniscidae) and petrels (Procellariidae). Only a handful of warm-blooded vertebrates overwinter round the margins of the continent, the most well-known being the Emperor Penguins, which breed during the austral winter. The warm-blooded vertebrate communities of the Southern Ocean can be subdivided into two groups, shelf residents and slope and oceanic water residents.

Permanently resident, high-trophic-level predators in the pack ice over the shelves include the Minke Whale, four seals (Crabeater, Weddell, Ross and Leopard) and five birds (Emperor and Adélie Penguins, Snow and Antarctic Petrels and the South Polar Skua) (Fig.15.9). Key prey species at the intermediate levels of the food web are the small euphausiid (*Euphausia crystallorophias*) the pelagic silverfish (*Pleuragramma antarcticum*), some pagotheniid fishes and a squid

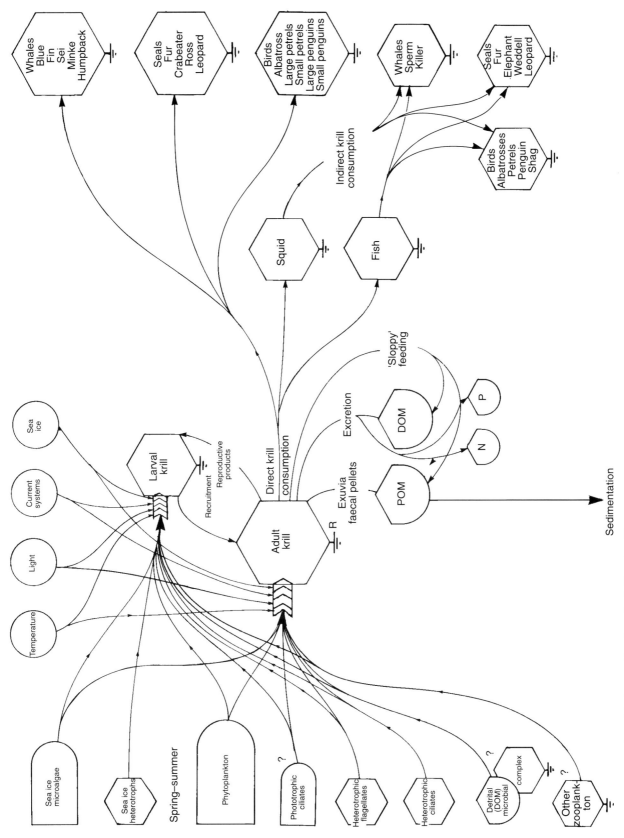

Fig. 15.8. Model of energy flow through a krill stock and its consumers.

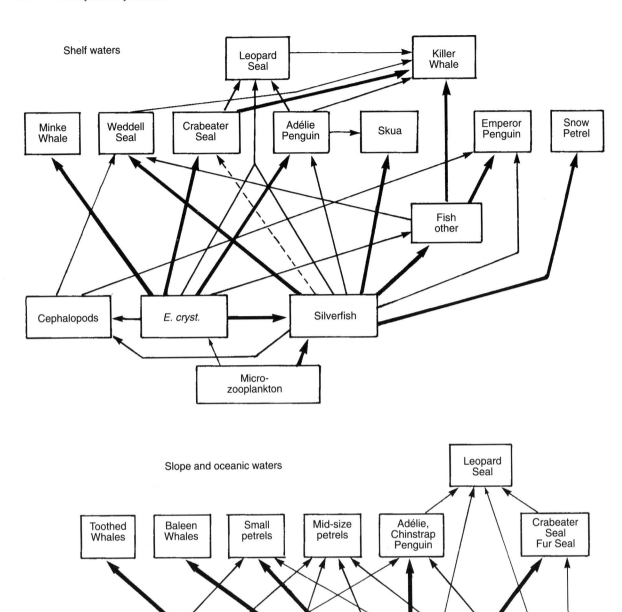

Fig. 15.9. Summary of the major energy flows in the upper trophic levels of the ice-influenced, shelf and slope/oceanic waters in the Antarctic. Data from Ainley *et al.* (1984), Ainley & Fraser (unpublished), DeWitt & Hopkins (1977), Nemoto *et al.* (1985), Siniff & Stone (1985), Williams (1985a), and Offredo & Ridoux (1986). Redrawn from Ainley & DeMaster (1990).

(*Psychroteuthis glacialis*) (Plotz, 1986; Hopkins, 1987; Thomas & Green, 1988; Ridoux & Offredo, 1989). During the winter at the pack ice edge the predators characteristic of the shelf are present, as well as the beaked whales (Ziphiidae), Antarctic Fur Seals, Elephant Seals, Chinstrap Penguins and several species of petrels (Procellariidae). Here *E. superba*, myctophid fishes, pasiphaeid shrimps, and two squid species (*Gonatus antarcticus* and *Galiteuthis glacialis*) are important prey (Ainley *et al.*, 1985, 1988; Laws, 1984a). Mesoplagic fish, which are important consumers of krill, are ecologically very important in this food web (Lancraft *et al.*, 1989).

As the pack ice retreats in the summer the surface waters of the Southern Ocean are invaded by a range of predators which feed on the abundant macrozooplankton and microplankton. In addition to many species which resided at the ice edge during the winter, the ecologically important species include several large baleen whales (Balaenopteridae and Balaenidae), male Sperm Whales (*Physeter catadon*), which feed in the mesopelagic zone, Killer Whales (*Orcinus orca*) and about ten seabird species, mostly belonging to the order Procellariiformes (Laws, 1977b; Ainley & Jacobs, 1981). While *E. superba* is the dominant food item in the summer some species such as the Right Whale (*Balaena glacialis*), prions (*Pachyptila* spp.) and diving petrels (*Pelecanoides* spp.) also feed on small copepods (S. G. Brown & Lockyer, 1984; Ainley & DeMaster, 1990).

Ainley & DeMaster (1990) have discussed the factors which concentrate these predators and their prey in specific locations. These concentrations occur at the marginal ice edge zone (Fraser & Ainley, 1986), in association with polynas, at continental shelf-break fronts (Ainley *et al.*, 1985; Veit & Braun, 1984), and at insular fronts.

15.6 Ecosystem models

In order to obtain a coherent picture of the functioning of a marine ecosystem we need to summarize the available information quantitatively and in a systematic manner. Over the past two decades systems analysis and simulation models have become increasingly important analytical tools to complement field and laboratory techniques in an attempt to understand the dynamic behaviour of aquatic ecosystems. Early models of the Antarctic marine ecosystem, or rather of components thereof, were directed at assessing the abundance of marine resources, their behaviour and their distribution, and at ascertaining the responses of these resources to exploitation and possible environmental change. Notable among these were the models developed for the International Whaling Commission on the stocks of

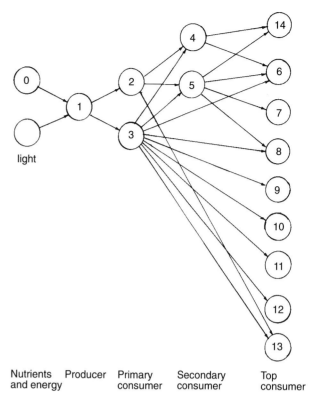

Fig. 15.10. Doi's trophic network model for the Antarctic pelagic ecosystem. 0 Nutrients; 1. Phytoplankton; 2. Zooplankton other than krill; 3. Krill (*Euphausia superba*); 4. Squid; 5. Fishes; 6. Seals; 7. Penguins; 8. Sea birds; 9. Minke Whales; 10. Blue Whales; 11. Fin Whales; 12. Humpback Whales; 13. Sei Whales; 14. Toothed whales. Redrawn from Shimadzu (1984b), after Doi (1979).

whales and the impact of different levels of exploitation. For example, Beddington & Cooke (1981) and Cooke and Beddington (1982) developed a model for assessing Sperm Whale abundance based on length composition. Other models (e.g. Kirkwood, 1981) investigated the relationship between whale catch per unit effort and true abundance.

Modelling of Southern Ocean ecosystems, apart from K. A. Green's (1975, 1977; Green-Hammond, 1981b) model of the Ross Sea pelagic ecosystem, has been a much neglected aspect of research into the functioning of the Antarctic ecosystem. However, with the establishment of the Convention on the Conservation of Antarctic Marine Living Resources (CCAMLR) there has been an increasing interest in model development as an aid to decision making.

15.6.1 Some current models

Nearly all of the models which have been developed to date have focused on fisheries aspects of the Southern Ocean ecosystem. Examples of such models are given in May (1979), who used heuristic models to investigate the

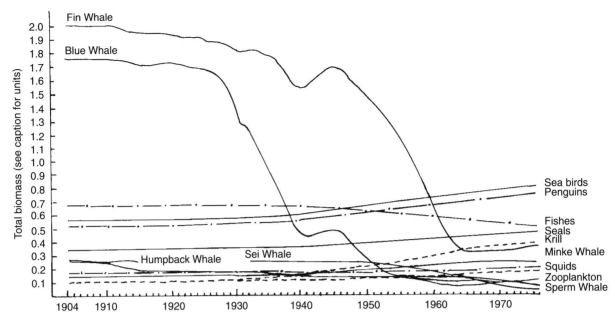

Fig. 15.11. Estimated historical trends for nine species groups based on the output from the simulation of the model depicted in Fig. 15.10. Biomass units: Zooplankton ($\times 10^{10}$t); Krill ($\times 10^{10}$t); Squid ($\times 10^9$t); Fishes ($\times 10^8$t); Seals ($\times 10^7$t); Penguins ($\times 10^6$t); Sea birds ($\times 10^5$t); Whales ($\times 10^7$t). Redrawn from Shimadzu (1984b), after Doi (1979).

behaviour of biological systems exploited simultaneously at two or more trophic levels (e.g. krill and baleen whales; krill, whales and seals; and krill, cephalopods and sperm whales). The conclusions for these models will be discussed in the next section.

Shimadzu (1984b) reviewed some published work on krill biomass estimates and ecosystem models developed by Japanese scientists. The latter included Lotka–Volterra type models (Yamanaka, 1983) and a network model (Doi, 1979). Doi selected 13 species, or components, for his model connected in the manner shown in Fig. 15.10. Energy flows from producer to consumer through predation. For example, the energy balance for component 2 in Fig. 15.10 (zooplankton other than krill) is expressed as:

$$\underset{\text{(food intake)}}{C1,2Q(2)} - \underset{\text{(predation)}}{C2,4Q(4)} - \underset{\text{(dissimilation)}}{C1,2Q(2)RC(2)}$$

$$- \underset{\text{(egestion)}}{C1,2Q(2)EC(2)} - \underset{\text{(natural death)}}{DC(2)Q(2)} - \underset{\text{(catch)}}{FQ(2)} = 0$$

where C1,2 = energy transformation coefficient from species 1 to 2 through the process of predation; C2,4 is similar to C1,2, but for species 2 and 4; Q(2) = standing stock of species 2; Q(3) = standing stock of species 3; RC(2) = dissimilation rate; EC(2) = egestion rate; DC = death rate; FQ(2) = catch rate.

Historical catches of whales were utilized to estimate historical projection of the 15 components in the network. As shown in Fig 15.11 a reduction of whale biomass over

a 70-year period resulted in a growth of krill biomass (3.7 times), while that of seals, penguins and other seabirds also increased, but to a lesser extent. Krill biomass in 1976 was estimated at 3700 million tonnes and it is of interest that about 70% of the predation on krill was by squid. Simulations of different levels of whale and krill populations gave various population estimates after 30-year runs. Doi noted that only 17% of the primary production (an estimated 30 billion imperial tons) was consumed within the ecosystem. One of the shortcomings of Doi's modal analysis was the difficulty in assigning values for many of the parameters due to inadequate information. For example, the estimate of 173 million tonnes of squid in the pre-whaling period has an important influence on the analysis. The squid were estimated to have been consuming 543 million tons of krill, 58% of the total predation on krill, during the pre-whaling period. If their biomass was lower (and currently there is no basis for estimating their biomass) then the projections would be very different. Much more reliable estimates of stock sizes and energy consumption for some species, especially squid, are needed before models such as that of Doi's can be useful.

Apart from Doi's model that of K. A. Green (1975) and Green-Hammond (1981b) for the Ross Sea is the only other comprehensive model with a whole-ecosystem perspective. The main objectives of Green's model were:

1. To express a hypothesis on the structure of the food web within the Ross Sea ecosystem

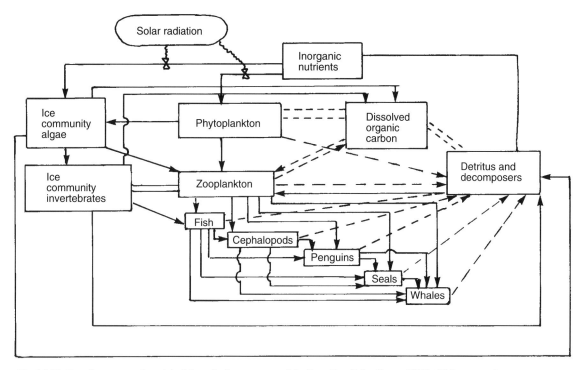

Fig. 15.12. Green's conceptual model of the pelagic ecosystem of the Ross Sea (After Green, 1975). thick arrows ───▶ represent trophic flows; dashed arrows - ─▶ represent mortality; ─ ─ ─ represent DOC uptake and release. Exchanges between the system and its environment are not shown. Redrawn from Green-Hammond (1981b).

2. To simulate standings stocks of the major species groups for one year on a weekly basis.
3. To keep track of carbon flow in the food web on a weekly basis and on an annual total basis.

The conceptual model had 12 compartments (Fig. 15.12). Both ice and water column communities were included in the model. Benthic communities were considered only as a sink while krill and other zooplankton were lumped in a single compartment. A matrix of transfer coefficients (flows) for the 12 system components was drawn up. Differential equations were then derived so as to describe rates of change of biomass. The simulation model has a series of simultaneous equations of the form:

$$\frac{d}{dt} \text{biomass} = (\text{income rate}) - (\text{loss rate})$$

Weekly values for the total biomass of the 12 compartments in the Ross Sea model are shown in Fig. 15.13.

It should be noted that the model applies to data from the Ross Sea and is not directly applicable to other areas of the Southern Ocean. Green did not claim that the Ross Sea model was realistic but regarded it as a necessary first step towards providing a greater insight into ecosystem functioning. It would be necessary to increase the complexity of the model by incorporating additional data.

Insights from chemical and physical oceanographic models for the Antarctic, and feedback between modelling efforts and field studies would all help to improve the model. It is a great pity that Green's pioneering efforts have not been capitalized on and her model further developed and refined and applied to other geographic areas of the Southern Ocean.

15.6.2 Conceptual models of Antarctic marine ecosystems

15.6.2.1 A coastal fast ice ecosystem

Some aspects of the coastal fast ice ecosystem have already been discussed in Chapters 3 and 12. Here we will be concerned with an overall ecosystem model. Fig. 15.14 is a model of the carbon flow in McMurdo Sound to the mouth of the edge of the McMurdo Ice Shelf. This model uses the energy circuit language developed by H. T. Odum and the basic symbols used in the model are explained in the Appendix. The various components and flows in the model are expressed in terms of carbon equivalents. By the use of appropriate conversion factors they can be converted into energy units (kcal or kJ).

This carbon flow model is divided into five levels : 1. primary producers; 2. dissolved organic matter (DOM); 3. the detrital–microbial complex (particulate organic

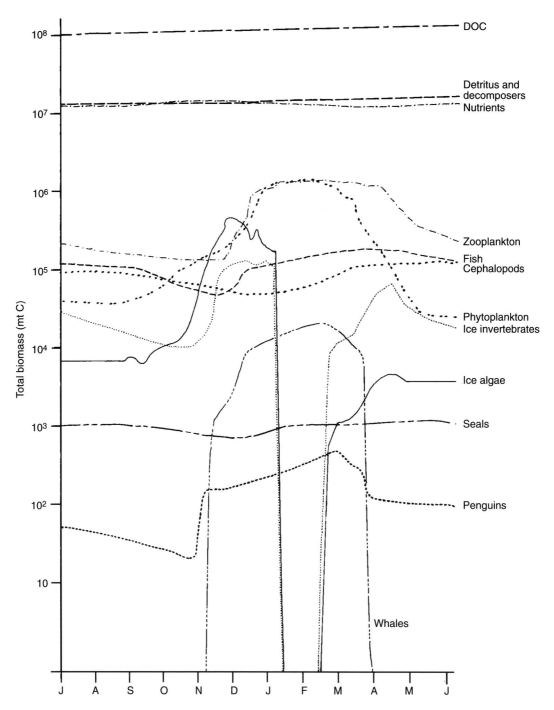

Fig. 15.13. Graph of the state variables of the compartments from a simulation of the model depicted in Fig. 15.12. Redrawn from Green-Hammond (1981b).

matter (POM)) plus its microbial community; 4. invertebrate consumers; and 5. vertebrate consumers. The horizontal line separates sediment processes from those occurring in the water column. Four major and two minor producer units are shown. The detrital–microbial complex compartment includes detritus of plant and animal origin and the organisms associated with it (unicellular algae, bacteria, yeasts, fungi, protozoa and microscopic invertebrates). The invertebrate consumers include the planktonic heterotrophs, zooplankton, cephalopods, benthic epifauna, and benthic fauna, while the vertebrate consumers include fishes, birds, seals and whales.

A number of minor pathways have not been included in order to simplify the model. In addition, it does not portray predation within compartments. For example, within the benthic invertebrate compartment considerable predation occurs, such as that by several species of asteroids on the abundant sponges (Dayton *et al.*, 1974).

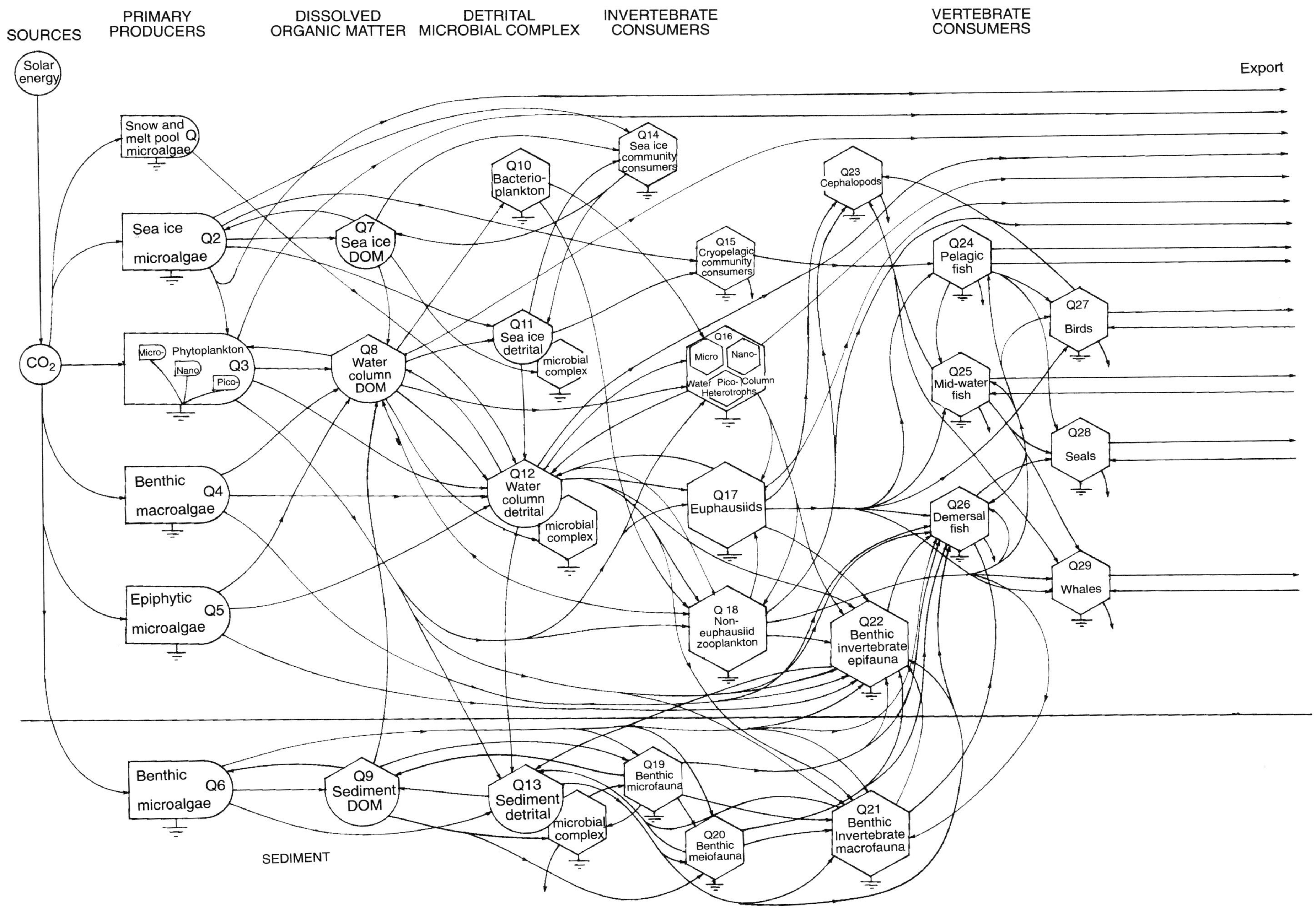

Fig. 15.14. Energy flow in the coastal fast ice ecosystem of McMurdo Sound.

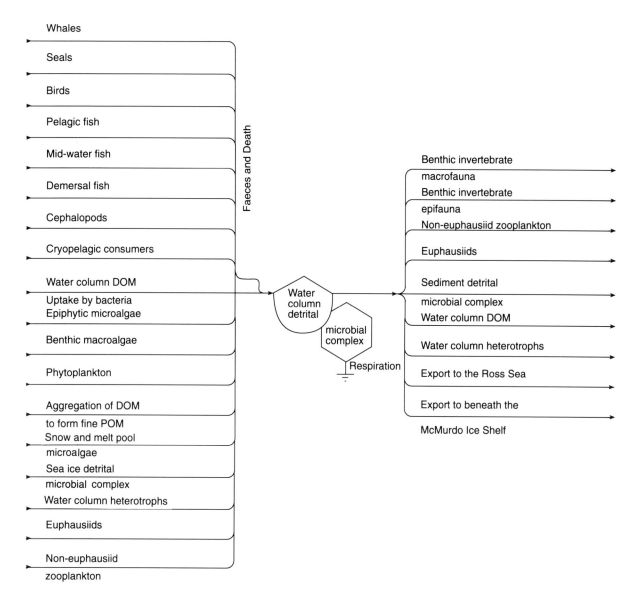

Fig. 15.15. Energy flow through the detrital–microbial complex compartment in the energy flow model depicted in Fig. 15.14.

In spite of this the model is complex, but it could be further simplified by combining compartments and omitting some of the smaller flows to produce a model suitable for simulation. Submodels of this model could also be developed. As it stands, in spite of the shortcomings discussed below, it is a realistic model of the McMurdo Sound marine ecosystem. The value of such a model from the conservation/management point of view is that the relative importance of the various flows are clearly evident, and simulation could be used to predict changes which might occur following alterations to producer inputs, or declines or increases in consumer populations.

Estimates of the biomass values for the carbon storages and for the flows between compartments have where possible been derived from data obtained by various investigators working in the McMurdo Sound region. Where

data were not available estimates are based on studies carried out elsewhere in the Antarctic, or on data in the general literature on marine ecosystems.

Phytoplankton succession in McMurdo Sound has been described in section 12.3. Estimates for primary production for eastern McMurdo Sound and for the whole Sound are given in Table 15.8. For the purposes of calculating the total phytoplankton production, the January–February diatom bloom is estimated at half the value given by W.O. Smith & Nelson (1985a) for the ice edge bloom in the waters to the north of McMurdo Sound. The total annual phytoplankton production for McMurdo Sound has been calculated by Knox (1990), as 16.1 g C m^{-2} for the *Phaeocystis* bloom, plus 22.8 g C m^{-2} for the later diatom bloom, plus 5 g C m^{-2} at other times, making total of 43.9 g C m^{-2}, which is more than three

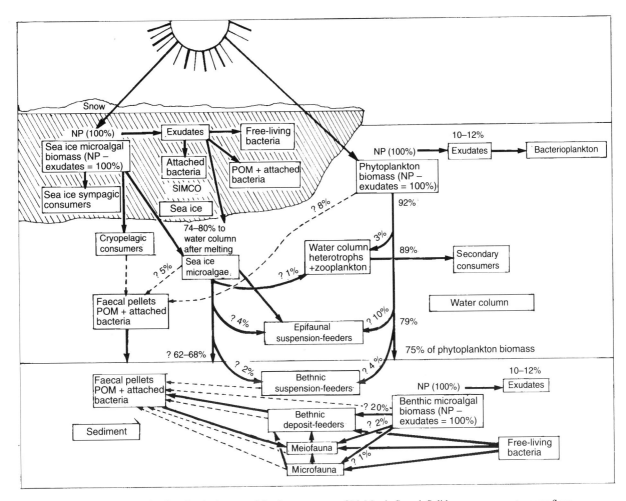

Fig. 15.16. Microalgal carbon flux in the coastal fast ice ecosystem of McMurdo Sound. Solid arrows represent energy flow (comsumption) and sedimentation. Dashed arrows represent POM production. The percentages are the percentage of the microbial biomass (NP–exudates) that is either consumed or sedimented. NP=net production of the microalgae.

Table 15.8. *Primary production in McMurdo Sound[1]*

Compartment	Annual net production (g C m⁻¹ y⁻¹) (Eastern Sound)	Total annual production (t C y⁻¹) (for the whole sound)
Snow and meltpool microalgae	Not known	Not known
Sea ice microalgae	11.83	500–700000
Phytoplankton		
Phaeocystis	16.10	
Other species	27.8	
Total	43.9	1.5–2.25 million
Benthic macroalgae	Not known	Not known
Epiphytic microalgae	Not known	Not known
Benthic microalgae		
East Sound	26.0	25–30000
West Sound	3.0	2–3500

[1]Assuming that phytoplankton production in the Western Sound is half of that in the Eastern Sound.
From Knox (1990).

times that calculated by Holm-Hansen *et al.* (1977) for the open waters of the Southern Ocean.

There are three pools of DOM, the sea ice pool, the water column pool and the sediment pool. The major sources of the water column organic matter is the release of extracelluar organic carbon by the sea ice microalgae, the phytoplankton and the benthic microalgae. In shallow water the benthic macroalgae can contribute substantial amounts of DOM. Fig. 15.15 depicts the water column detrital–microbial complex. As can be seen the water column POM is derived from a great variety of sources: from the sea ice microbial community after the melting of the sea ice; from the phytoplankton, epiphytic microalgae and the benthic microalgae; and from contributions from all the other water compartments. Faecal pellets from the zooplankton and faeces from the higher consumers are a major input. Crustacea exuvia, the unconsumed remains of zooplankton and the dead bodies of the consumers also contribute to the water column POM. Berkman *et al.* (1986) have postulated that sediment resuspension by wind-generated waves during periods of open water, and by anchor ice or current when there is ice cover is an important mechanism for introducing organic matter into the water column in the shallow waters of McMurdo Sound. All of this POM is colonized by a rich community. In addition to the bacteria attached to the POM there are the free-living bacteria of the bacterioplankton.

Microalgal carbon flux. Fig. 15.16 is an attempt to illustrate the microalgal carbon flux in McMurdo Sound. Some of the estimates are speculative and these are prefaced by question marks. Nevertheless, they are probably of the right order of magnitude. Of the sea ice macroalgal net production (NP) some 20% is released as extracelluar organic carbon (DOM). This extracelluar carbon is either released to the water column, or utilized by bacteria attached to the diatoms or POM or utilized by free-living bacteria. Of the sea ice microalgal biomass produced (NP–exudates) it is estimated that 7% becomes POM after death of the cells, 2% is consumed by the sea ice sympagic community, and 11–16% is consumed by the cryopelagic consumers. Thus, of the microalgal biomass something of the order of 74–80% is released into the water column on the melting of the ice. Some of the microalgae which are released from the ice survive and grow in the phytoplankton community, but it has now been shown that the bulk may form aggregates which sediment through the water column (Riebesell *et al.*, 1991).

The phytoplankton production and its fate are depicted in Fig. 15.17. The phytoplankton on average release 10–12% of their net production into the water column as DOM (exudates). Of the phytoplankton biomass produced (NP–exudates) 3% only is estimated to be consumed by the zooplankton and the water column heterotrophs, while some 8% after cell death is estimated to contribute to the water column POM and by lysis to the water column DOM. The remaining 89% sediments through the water column to the sea bottom. Depending on the depth of the water column a percentage of this will be remineralized as it sinks to the sediments. In the shallower depths it is estimated that about 10% of the biomass is consumed by the epifaunal suspension feeders. Thus, in order of 75% of the original phytoplankton biomass, at least in the shallow water, reaches the surface of the sediments.

Invertebrate consumers. The food web of the sea ice microbial community and the associated cryopelagic community has been discussed in Chapters 3 and 12. Water column heterotropic protozoa have as yet not been studied in McMurdo Sound but are likely to be similar to those of other fast ice regions. It is probable that the total heterotropic protozoan biomass is in the order of 50–300 mg C m^{-2}, and they form an important link in the transfer of carbon from the extracelluar carbon secreted by the phytoplankton via the bacteria that they consume to higher trophic levels (Hewes *et al.*, 1985, 1990).

The zooplankton of McMurdo Sound has been considered in Chapter 12. The zooplankton is dominated by copepods and pteropods; other species include ostracods, euphausiids, mysids, amphipods, chaetognaths, pelagic polychaetes, the larvae of benthic polychaetognaths, and larval and postlarval stages of the mid-water fish *Pleuragramma antarcticum*. *E. superba* is not present, and while *Thysanoessa macrura* occurs sparsely in the early spring the principal euphausiid present throughout the summer is the small *E. crystallorophias*. Hicks (1974) estimated zooplankton wet weights of 0.073–3.309 mg m^{-2} during January and early February in the vicinity of Cape Armitage. B. A. Forster (1987) in the same area in early November to early December recorded biomass values ranging from under 1 mg m^{-2} to 5.0 mg m^{-2} wet weight, with a mean of 2.5 mg m^{-2}. Further north in McMurdo Sound in February Hopkins (1987) recorded higher densities and estimated the zooplankton biomass at 1.5 to 3.5 g dry wt m^{-2}. The biomasses of postlarval *E. crystallorophias* and *P. antarcticum* were estimated at 0.21 (10.16 to 0.33) (5.63% of the zooplankton biomass) and 0.82 (3.69 to 0.18) g dry wt m^{-2}, respectively. Euphausiid biomass in McMurdo Sound is much lower than that recorded from other parts of Antarctic coastal waters (Hopkins, 1985a). In addition, salps and myctophid fishes, which are prominent elsewhere, are virtually absent.

The diets of the McMurdo Sound zooplankton have been discussed in section 4.6, where it was noted that the total zooplankton consumption was only about 2% of the phytoplankton biomass. While ciliates and other heterotrophic microorganisms consume an as yet undetermined amount of phytoplankton, the total phytoplankton consumption is not likely to exceed 3%. Thus, at least 97% of the standing crop remains unconsumed by the grazers. Fig. 15.18 depicts the non-euphausiid zooplankton compartment.

Much more research needs to be done before carbon flow through the benthic epifauna and infauna can be quantified. In shallow water the benthic microalgae are important producers at the base of the food web. The epifaunal filter-feeders obtain their food from the sedimenting phytoplankton or from resuspension from the sediments. Feeding is largely restricted to the short summer phytoplankton blooms during which food reserves are laid down to enable the species to survive for the rest of the year. While benthic filter-feeders also feed in a similar manner, detrital feeders have food available to them throughout the year.

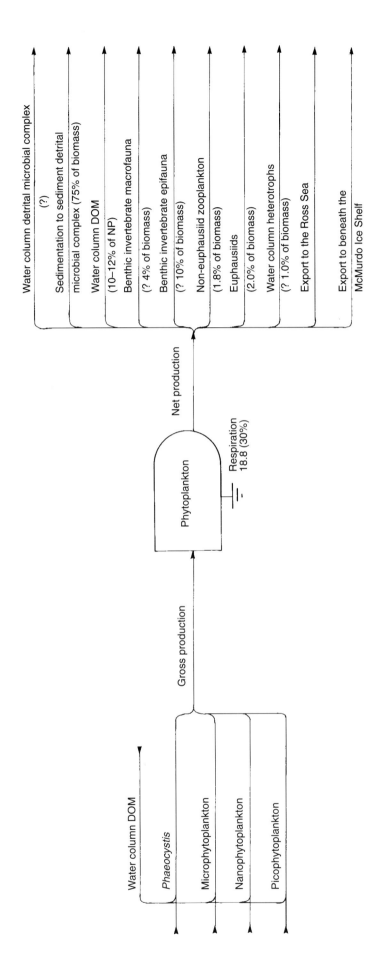

Fig. 15.17. Energy flow through the phytoplankton compartment in the energy flow model depicted in Fig. 15.14.

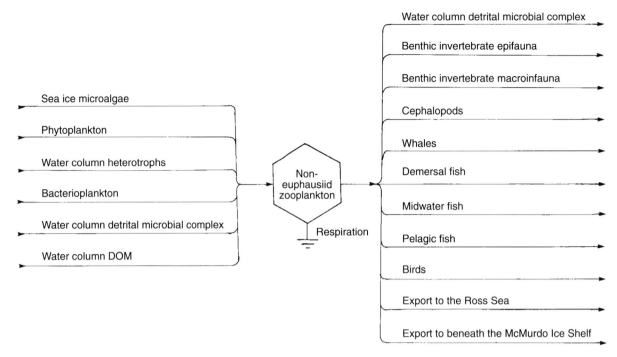

Fig. 15.18. Energy flow through the non-euphausiid zooplankton compartment in the energy flow model depicted in Fig. 15.14.

Higher consumers. Nothing is known at present concerning the distribution and abundance of cephalopods in McMurdo Sound. The diets of many of the fish species are reasonably well known but there is little information available on the population densities of the fishes so that it is not possible to quantify carbon flow through their stocks. Only a single species of seal, the Weddell Seal, occurs in McMurdo Sound and while it would be possible to estimate their food consumption the scanty data on the fish stocks make it impossible to evaluate their impact. While Killer and Minke whales penetrate into McMurdo Sound in the late summer after the ice breakout their impact is not likely to be large. Of the birds McCormick Skuas and Adélie Penguins feed in the sound when there is open water but they do so in relatively small numbers.

15.6.2.2 The marginal ice edge zone

In Fig. 15.19 an attempt has been made to construct a carbon flow model of a marginal ice edge zone ecosystem in the seasonal pack ice Zone during a phytoplankton bloom. Although the model is complex it nevertheless does not completely represent the complexity of the system. Nevertheless, the major energy flow pathways are depicted. The model is divided into levels (from left to right): 1. primary producers; 2. organic matter and bacterioplankton; 3. first level (primary) consumers, including invertebrates and heterotrophic protozoans; and 4. higher level consumers.

When the sea ice melts the sea ice microalgae, bacteria,

protozoans, and micrometazoans, as well as the sea ice DOM and POM, are released into the water column. With the seeding of the euphotic zone by the sea ice microalgae and the resulting stability of the surface layer due to the freshwater input, coupled with the increase that occurs in PAR, an ice edge phytoplankton bloom develops rapidly. This bloom is dominated by diatoms, and/or *Phaeocystis pouchetii*, and is supported in the first instance primarily by 'new'-N, although 'regenerated'-N is often preferentially used if it is available. The dominant diatoms require large amounts of silica, and although the stocks of silica, along with those of nitrate-N, may be considerably reduced they do not become limiting to phytoplankton growth. The release of large amounts of extracellular carbon by the microalgae results in an increase in the DOM pool. The bacterioplankton and the attached bacteria of the water column detrital–microbial complex utilize this DOM but their growth is kept in check by the grazing of the heterotrophic flagellates and ciliates.

The major consumers of the diatoms are krill. Although the krill swarms can rapidly graze down patches of phytoplankton, the overall proportion of the primary production consumed does not exceed 5%. Other grazers on the phytoplankton include the protozoa, and the zooplankton other than euphausiids, especially the copepods and salps. Their consumption, however, does not exceed that of the krill. Consequently a large proportion of the phytoplankton production sediments out of the euphotic zone, and either contributes to the mesopelagic

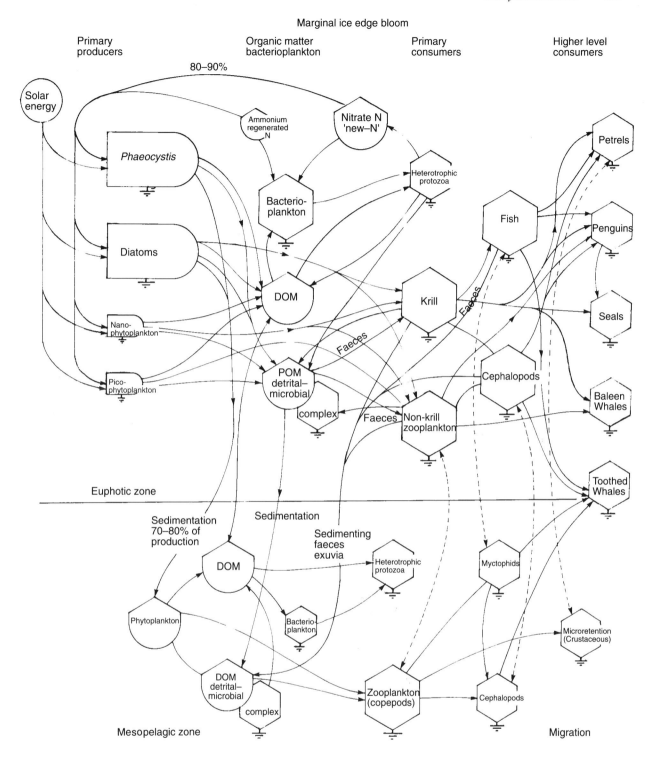

Fig. 15.19. Energy flow in the marginal ice edge zone ecosystem during a phytoplankton bloom. Dashed arrows show vertical migration.

detrital–microbial complex or, via senescence and autolysis, to the mesopelagic DOM pool which supports the growth of the mesopelagic bacteria. Some of the sedimenting phytoplankton cells will be consumed by the mesoplankton zooplankton (principally copepods and salps). The detrital–microbial complex (with its associated bacteria, microalgae, fungi, flagellates and ciliates) is a complex of detrital aggregates of varying sizes derived from a multiplicity of sources (phytoplankton, regurgitations, faecal pellets, crustacean exuvia, and dead animals, etc.). Where *Phaeocystis* blooms occur they contribute to these aggregations in the manner outlined above.

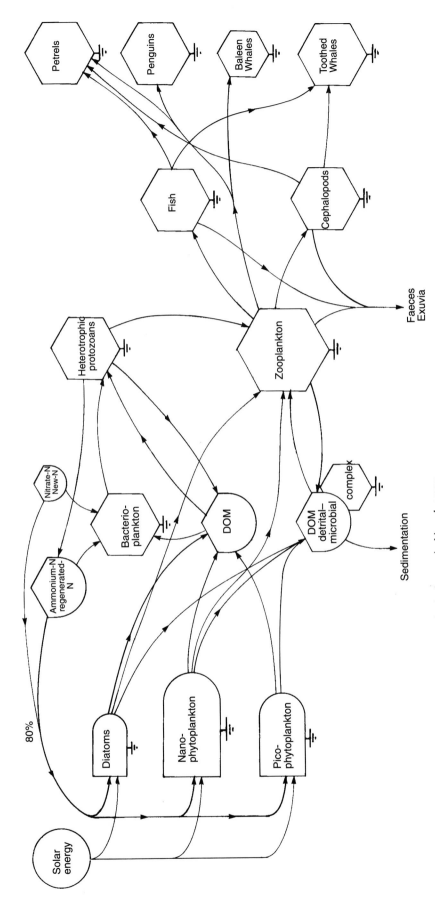

Fig. 15.20. Energy flow in the 'post-bloom' situation in the marginal ice edge zone.

The principal consumers of the krill are cephalopods, fish, petrels, penguins, Leopard and Crabeater Seals, and baleen whales. The cephalopods, myctophid fishes and some of the copepod species regularly undergo vertical migrations between the euphotic and mesopelagic zones. Toothed whales feed on fish and cephalopods in both the euphotic and the mesopelagic zones. The vertically migrating cephalopods and the micronekton are consumed in the surface waters by the petrels and penguins.

Fig. 15.20 depicts a model of the euphotic zone in the 'post-bloom' situation. Diatoms are now a minor component of the phytoplankton community, which is dominated by nano- and picophytoplankton (mainly flagellates). Primary production is now largely supported by 'regenerated'-N (ammonium). Krill are largely absent and the zooplankton is dominated by copepods. Krill and many of the higher consumers have migrated southwards following the retreating ice edge blooms.

15.6.2.3 The pack ice zone ecosystem

Fig. 15.21 is a model of carbon flow in the upper water column of the pack ice in the winter–early spring before the melting of the ice floes. The sea ice microbial community (SIMCO) is represented at the top left. This community has been discussed in detail in Chapters 3 and 12. The sea ice microalgae and associated organisms (bacteria, sea ice heterotrophic protozoa and small metazoans) are consumed by members of the cryopelagic community (fishes, especially larval forms and amphipods; see Fig. 15.16). As we have seen in Chapter 5, furcilia and adult krill graze extensively on the SIMCO when the phytoplankton in the water column is low.

In the water column beneath the ice the sparse phytoplankton community is dominated by nano- and picophytoplankton which is fueled by both nitrate-N ('new'-N) and ammonium-N ('regenerated'-N), the latter derived from the metabolism of the water column microbial community. The higher consumers are dominated by fishes, principally myctophids, cephalopods, some penguins and petrels and the ice seals, principally Crabeater and Leopard Seals.

15.7 Southern Ocean environmental variability and its impact on the pelagic ecosystem

15.7.1 Introduction

In 1987 CCAMLR and the International Oceanographic Commission (IOC) jointly sponsored a seminar on 'Antarctic Ocean and resources variability', (Sahrhage, 1988a), with the support of SCAR and SCOR. The Seminar discussed the following questions:

- What is known on the variability of the Antarctic Ocean circulatory system?
- What are the possible causes for such variations?
- To what extent and how does the ocean variability influence primary productivity, zooplankton and other organisms?
- To what extent and how does this variability influence krill distribution and abundance?
- What are the effects on krill predators (seals, penguins, fishes, etc.)?

Significant interannual variability occurs in ecosystems which are coupled tightly to local physical processes (W.O. Smith *et al.*, 1988). Examples from marine systems include upwelling systems (Barber & Smith, 1981), intertidal communities (Dungan *et al.*, 1982), the Bering Sea (Niebauer, 1980), the Fram Strait (W.O. Smith *et al.*, 1987) and coral reefs (Woodley *et al.*, 1991).

The seminar focused on meso- and large-scale variability and identified future research needs.

15.7.2 Meso/large-scale variability in the Southern Ocean

As Sahrhage (1988a) points out meteorologists and oceanographers tend to use average values of parameters in their investigations to describe the structure and processes of the atmosphere and ocean. However, it is the interannual change and seasonal abnormality in the weather, ice and hydrographic conditions which have the greatest influence on distribution, growth, reproduction and mortality of living organisms. Thus, biologists are mainly interested in the environmental conditions during a specific year, or season, and the environmental extremes.

15.7.2.1 Variations and trends in temperatures

Unfortunately there are few long time series of observations available for the Antarctic and most of these are from a few localities, mostly at or close to the Antarctic Peninsula. Records from the South Orkney Islands (Jaka *et al.*, 1984) show that from 1908 until 1949 the ten-year annual running means of annual air temperature were below the overall long-term average (–4.3 °C), with a particularly cold period between 1922 and 1935. On the other hand, temperatures well above the long-term average were measured from 1950 to the present. Evidence of increases in sea surface temperatures are inconclusive. While particularly cold and warm periods can be identified in the Antarctic Peninsula area these do not coincide with such years in other parts of Antarctica (Jaka *et al.*,

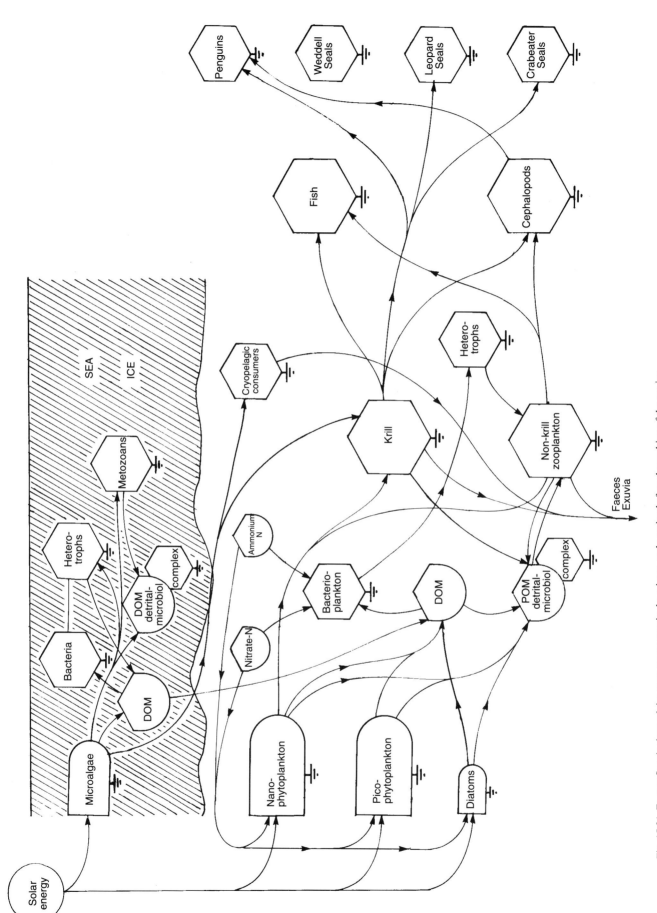

Fig. 15.21. Energy flow in the pack ice zone ecosystem in the winter–early spring before the melting of the sea ice.

1985). Data from 22 years of observations in the Indian Ocean Sector have revealed interannual variations in the position of the Antarctic Polar Front Zone and the position of the northernmost edge of the 0 °C isotherm (Nagata *et al.*, 1988).

15.7.2.2 Circulation patterns

Reviews of spatial and temporal variation in the Southern Ocean circulation patterns, water mass distributions and frontal positions (Gordon, 1988), and for specific areas such as the Drake Passage (Sievers & Nowlin, 1988), the Antarctic Peninsula and Southwest Scotia Sea (Stein, 1988), and the Indian Ocean Sector (Nagata *et al.*, 1988) have provided evidence of large variability between seasons and from year to year, long-term trends, and also differences from one region to another.

The Southern Ocean is not radially symmetrical and many circulation and water mass features vary markedly with latitude, as well as being influenced by topographic features (ridges, islands). The Antarctic Circumpolar Current displays significant temporal variation ranging from mesoscale features such as meanders and eddies to broad regional low frequency variations (Klinch & Hofman, 1986; Gordon, 1988). The importance of wind-induced variations in the circulation patterns was stressed by contributors to the seminar. Such wind-induced variations, perhaps coupled to changes in the freshwater balance, would also influence the vertical stability of the water column, the vertical heat flux, and the extent of sea ice cover.

15.7.2.3 The Southern Oscillation

One phenomenon which influences the air pressure distribution over the Southern Hemisphere, and which impacts on the oceanic circulation patterns is the irregular Southern Oscillation (ENSO), resulting in the El Nino off Peru (van Loon & Shea, 1987). While the influence of El Niño/Southern Oscillation (ENSO) events on the Southern Ocean are likely to be significant the precise influence is not yet firmly established. W. O. Smith *et al.* (1988) have discussed the possible effects on primary production at the ice edge while Croxall *et al.* (1988a) and Priddle *et al.* (1988) point out that the seasons 1977–78 and 1983–84, when krill was scarce around South Georgia and land-based predators experienced poor breeding success, both followed years with strong ENSO events. Barry & Dayton (1988) have drawn attention to the correlation between ENSO events and the extent of fast ice off McMurdo Sound.

15.7.2.4 Variation in the extent and timing of the advance and retreat of sea ice cover

As we have seen in Chapters 2 and 3 the sea ice is a major environmental variable influencing the distribution and production of the biota in the Southern Ocean. Mackintosh (1972) evaluated information on ice limits in the Southwest Atlantic Sector over the periods 1926–39 and 1950–51. He found that there was an anomalous northward extension of the ice edge during the cold season of 1930–31, and a decrease in ice cover during the relatively warm seasons of 1929–30, 1932–33, and 1936–37. Variations in the latitude of the northward extent of drift ice in the Scotia Sea which were identified in the study were probably related to the outflow of water from the Weddell Sea.

Carleton (unpublished) found that the substantial annual variations in the rate of ice advance and retreat, and the timing of the maximum and minimum extent were linked with large-scale variations in atmospheric circulation, particularly cyclonic activity. During the period 1973 to 1977, the mean positions of the ice edge in the Southwest Atlantic Sector were found increasingly further south, while during the following years they were shifting back north, and they remained on average, rather stable, latitudes during the 1980s (Sahrhage, 1988b) (Fig. 15.22). Variations in the annual position of the fast ice edge in McMurdo Sound have been documented by Barry (1988).

15.7.3 Meso/large-scale variability in the Southern Ocean biota (related to the environment)

Many publications have discussed the relationships between water mass circulation and the distribution of krill and other living organisms in the Southern Ocean (e.g. Maslennikov, 1980; Amos, 1984; Lubimova *et al.*, 1982). The conclusions of the seminar participants on variations in primary production in relation to environmental variability are summarized in the next two sections.

15.7.3.1 Phytoplankton

El-Sayed (1988a) has analyzed information collected during the past 25 years on spatial and temporal variabilities in the distribution and abundance of phytoplankton in the Drake Passage/Scotia Sea, the Bransfield Strait/Elephant Island, and Ross Sea areas of the Southern Ocean. The general picture which emerged was one of great variability in phytoplankton biomass and primary production. This spatial variability (up to two orders of magnitude) tends to overshadow that of seasonal differences. The timing of the peak phytoplankton abundance also varied from year to year. El-Sayed concluded that seasonal variability was much more pronounced than interannual variability.

15.7.3.2 Primary production in the marginal ice zone

As detailed in Chapter 13 large accumulations of phyto-

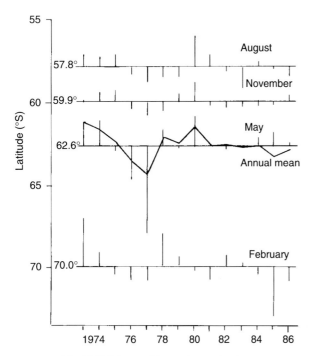

Fig. 15.22. Mean positions and annual variations of the ice edge in the Southern Ocean between 0° and 60° W at the end of the months February, May, August and November, 1973–86. Data source: weekly ice charts of the Navy/NOOA Joint Ice Center, USA. Redrawn from Sahrhage (1988b).

plankton (W. O. Smith & Nelson, 1985), zooplankton (Marr, 1962), seabirds (Ainley & Jacobs, 1981; Fraser & Ainley, 1986), and marine mammals (Laws, 1985) are associated with the marginal ice edge zone. W. O. Smith *et al.* (1988) have considered the interannual variability of the estimated primary productivity of the Antarctic marginal ice edge zone. This was considered to be substantial, with the maximum productivity being 50% greater than the minimum. While it appears that there is a significant potential for interannual variability in the primary productivity in the marginal ice edge zone, it does not appear to be as great as that observed in some pelagic ecosystems, e.g. the Peruvian upwelling ecosystem (Chavez & Barker, 1987). The variability which does occur is directly related to the advance and retreat of the seasonal pack ice, which can be highly variable from year to year (Zwally *et al.*, 1983a,b).

15.7.4 Krill variability in relation to the environment

Investigations of the patterns of the distribution and abundance of krill have been discussed in Chapter 5. As we have seen, krill form an important component of the Southern Ocean pelagic food web. They account for a substantial proportion of the diet of many predators, some of which rely exclusively on krill for food during their breeding period. Recent studies summarized by Priddle *et al.* (1988) have provided direct evidence of substantial

interannual changes in the abundance of krill in certain parts of the Southern Ocean, particularly in the Southwest Atlantic Sector. Parallel data on the breeding success of land-based krill predators (breeding seabirds and seals) have provided additional evidence over a longer time scale (see below).

15.7.4.1 Large-scale fluctuations in the distribution and abundance of krill

Studies by British Antarctic Survey scientists revealed that the stocks of krill around South Georgia in August 1983 were very much lower (3%) than expected from a comparison with those found in December 1981 (Heywood *et al.*, 1985). In contrast, the stocks of other zooplankton approximated to anticipated levels, after allowing for seasonal change. Krill biomass in September 1983 was also much lower than in February 1982 along three transects across the Scoria Sea.

The SIBEX cruises in the following summer (1983–84) in the Bransfield Strait area also showed very greatly reduced krill biomass (Mujica & Asensio, 1985; Witek *et al.*, 1985). Both studies also noted the predominance of salps in their samples. Wormuth (1987) in comparing samples taken near Elephant Island in 1981 and 1984 found that the four dominant copepod specis (*Calanus propinquus*, *Calanoides acutus*, *Metridia gerlachei*, and *Rhincalanus gigas*) were more abundant by factors of 101. 807, 20 and 1000 respectively, while the salp *Salpa thompsoni* was 10.5 times more abundant in 1984 than in 1981. In contrast, the biomass of krill in the Southern Scotia Sea appears to have been normal during the 1983–84 season (Everson, 1988). The Prydz Bay region also had a lower than expected krill biomass during the same period (D. G. M. Miller, 1985, 1986; Terazaki & Wada, 1986). Krill biomass in the Bransfield Strait returned to the expected levels in the second year (1985–86) of the BIOMASS SIBEX survey after the low biomass of the 1984–85 season. Two larger data sets on krill predators suggest that low krill biomass episodes in the Bransfield Strait–South Georgia region may occur two or three times in a decade (Priddle *et al.*, 1988; Croxall *et al.*, 1988a).

According to Priddle *et al.* (1988) it seems most unlikely that the changes described above could be ascribed to features of krill biology. Simple models of recruitment failure or mortality could not explain the observed changes, and alterations in small-scale distribution patterns were not indicated from the available data. They considered that the more probable mechanisms must involve large-scale changes in the distribution of krill brought about by ocean–atmosphere processes. They postulated that a breakdown of the hydrographic structure

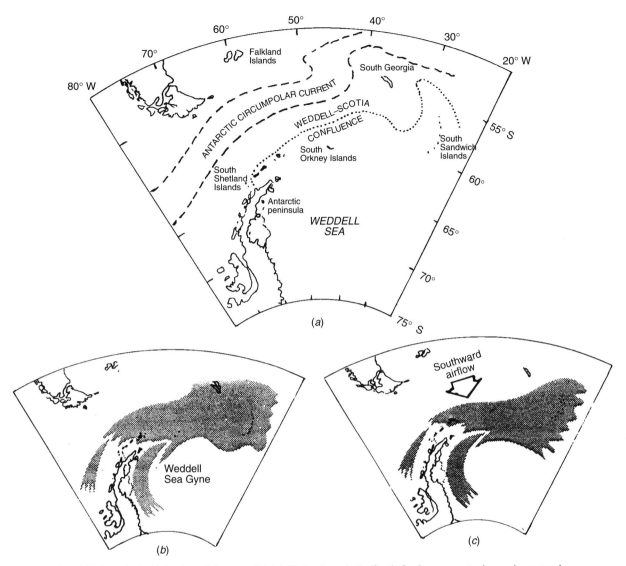

Fig. 15.23. Hypothetical behaviour of the area of high krill abundance in the Scotia Sea in response to changes in mesoscale hydrography. (*a*) Mean position of fronts within the Scotia Sea (After Gordon, 1967). (*b*) Normal situation in which krill derived from the Weddell Sea Gyre and from the Bransfield Strait are entrained within the Antarctic Circumpolar Current, reaching parts of the northern Scotia Sea, including South Georgia. (*c*) Extreme conditions in which a southward airflow displaces frontal zones and breakdown of surface structure of eddies releases krill into the main current flow. A conjectured deflection of the influx of krill from the Weddell Sea is also indicated. Redrawn from Priddle *et al*. (1988).

in the surface waters over a large area would drastically reduce the residence time of krill and that it would take some time to reestablish the former high krill density.

15.7.4.2 Mesoscale changes in the distribution of krill
The presence of krill in the open ocean, such as the seas around South Georgia, is dependent largely on the transport of animals to the area by ocean currents. Mesoscale hydrographic features impinging on krill distribution in this region (Fig. 15.23) are the Antarctic Circumpolar Current and the Weddell Sea Gyre. Bottom topography of the submarine ridges and the associated islands of the Scotia Arc deflect these currents northwards in the vicinity of South Georgia. Meridional transport in this region

of the Southern Ocean is therefore slowed down (Baker *et al.*, 1977), and this, combined with the numerous eddies which are formed in the Drake Passage and the western edge of the Scotia Sea, would provide conditions which may retain or concentrate planktonic organisms including krill (Angel & Fasham, 1983).

Influx of krill to the Scotia Sea is a second factor of major importance in determining the distribution and abundance of krill in the region. Animals are brought into the Scotia Sea from two main sources: in water from the Weddell Sea Gyre, and in water from the Southwest Pacific Basin, carried through the Drake Passage in the Antarctic Circumpolar Current.

One process which could redistribute krill in the region

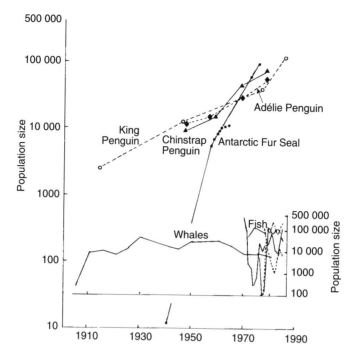

Fig. 15.24. Changes in population size of Adélie and Chinstrap Penguins (breeding pairs: Signy Island, South Orkney Islands), King Penguins (adults: South Georgia) and Antarctic Fur seals (pups: South Georgia), in relation to *(inset)* commercial harvests of Antarctic whales (individuals; from Bonner, 1984), fish and krill (tonnes; CCAMLR, 1986) on the South Georgia (○–○) and South Orkney Islands (●––●). Note the log scale. Redrawn from Croxall *et al.* (1988a).

and give rise to low abundances near South Georgia, is a southward shift of the Polar Frontal Zone under the influence of wind-forcing produced by atmospheric depressions which track across the region (Fig.15.23). Priddle *et al.* (1988) note that synoptic charts of sea-surface temperatures derived from satellite remote sensing data (NOAA), show that the Polar Frontal Zone (and hence the Antarctic Circumpolar Current) is a highly mobile feature of the Scotia Sea. The tracks of mesoscale eddies must be similarly affected. Southward displacement of the Polar Frontal Zone could be sufficient to remove krill beyond the foraging ranges of seals and seabirds breeding at Bird Island, South Georgia. Breakdown of the eddy system would release krill into the main current flow to be dispersed downstream. While these mesoscale processes provide mechanisms by which krill may be distributed in the Scotia Sea region their impact would be for only a comparatively short time and do not explain the six to nine month period of krill paucity noted in 1983–84.

However, if the changes outlined above acted together with the eddy structure breaking down when the polar frontal system moved south to the southern limit of its range, krill would then be both displaced from the South Georgia region and released from the eddies to pass downcurrent and to the east of the Scotia Sea (Fig. 15.23c). When the frontal zones returned to more northerly positions, replenishment of the Scotia Sea krill biomass would depend on the influx of animals carried by

the Weddell Sea surface water and the surface water in the Antarctic Circumpolar Current derived from the Southeast Pacific Basin. Such 'reseeding' of the area would clearly take longer than the original loss of animals form the area.

Maslennikov & Solyankin (1988) have analyzed data on the hydrometeorlogical conditions in the Atlantic Sector of the Southern Ocean over the period 1903–1975. 'Cold' and 'warm' epochs were identified. Sea surface isotherms during the cold period (1911–1937) and the warm period (1959–1979) were compared (Maslennikov, 1986). These comparisons revealed a northward extension of water from the Weddell Sea during the cold period. This would have increased the concentrations of krill in the vicinity of South Georgia. The reverse would have occurred during the warm period.

15.7.4.3 Krill variability detected from predator studies
Measuring the reproductive effort of seabirds which during their breeding season feed predominately on krill has been suggested as a means of providing good indices of the state of the local marine system and of the local krill biomass (Everson, 1977a; Croxall & Prince, 1979). Recent relevant studies undertaken at South Georgia and Signy Island over the period 1976–1987 have been analyzed by Croxall *et al.* (1988a). Changes in reproductive success need to be considered in relation to human exploitation of the marine resources, especially of seals,

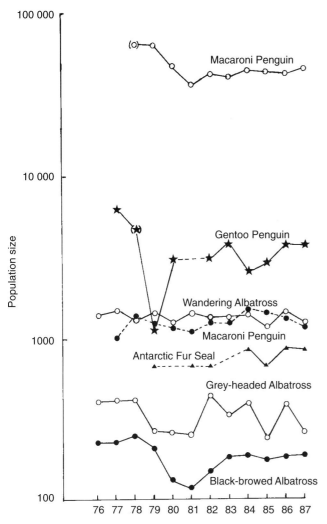

Fig. 15.25. Changes in population size of seabirds
(breeding pairs) and Antarctic Fur seals (pups born) at Bird
Island, South Georgia, 1976–1987. Note the log scale.
Redrawn from Croxall *et al.* (1988a).

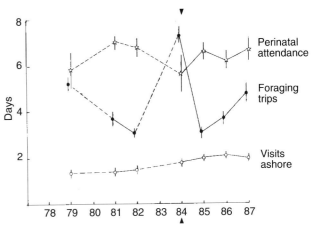

Fig. 15.26. Duration of attendance periods ashore and
foraging trips to sea in Antarctic Fur Seals at Bird Island,
South Georgia, 1979–1987. Values are means ±2 SE.
Arrowheads indicate an anomalous year. Redrawn from
Croxall *et al.* (1988a).

whales, fish and krill. The changes in the magnitude of
the catches of whales, fish and krill, and the changes
which occurred in penguin species and Antarctic Fur
Seals at Signy Island and South Georgia over this period
are shown in Figs. 15.24 and 15.25. Here, however, we
are concerned with the interannual variations in reproductive success over the period for which data is available.

15.7.4.3.1 Birds
The data presented by Croxall *et al.* (1988a) show that not
all seabird populations are currently increasing. The pattern at South Georgia (Figs. 15.24 and 15.25) over the
past decade has been one of substantial fluctuation. A
common feature was an abrupt decline in breeding numbers after 1978, which persisted for several years and
which was succeeded either by a gradual increase or by

further fluctuations. Another notable decrease occurred
after 1984, although that of the Gentoo Penguin actually
started in 1984. Fluctuations at Signy Island have not followed a similar pattern. Over the period 1979–87 Adélie
Penguins at Signy have increased, by an average of 4%
per annum, whereas Chinstrap Penguin numbers did not
change significantly. Breeding numbers of both species
decreased abruptly in 1981 and, after a rapid recovery,
Chinstraps decreased again in 1983–85. Breeding success
of the Wandering Albatross, which breeds in the winter
and eats fish and squid, has remained constant, while the
population size has declined gradually but significantly.
The other species which breed at South Georgia in the
summer and which feed extensively on krill have shown
major fluctuations in some, or all, of the following parameters: breeding population size, foraging trip duration,
and offspring growth rate.

15.7.4.3.2 Seals
The reproductive behaviour of seals at South Georgia
have been studied at Bird Island by Croxall & Prince
(1979), Croxall *et al.* (1985), Doidge & Croxall (1985)
and Doidge *et al.* (1986). Variability in attendance patterns of the breeding females has been identified in these
studies. These patterns comprise three elements;

1. The period between the birth of the pup and the
   mother's departure to sea (perinatal attendance).
2. The foraging trips at sea.
3. The interval between these trips when the pups
   are suckled.

Data for these elements over the period 1979–87 are
summarized in Fig. 15.26. A number of points can be identified from this figure. First, the duration of the shore visits

varies little between the years, and although the visits were somewhat longer from 1984 onwards than in other years; this is not matched by variations in other parameters. Second, perinatal attendance was significantly shorter, and much more variable, in 1979 and 1984 than in other years, which show no obvious pattern. Third, foraging trips to sea were very long in 1979 and 1984, and were exceptionally so in the latter. Bengtson (1988) has examined the foraging patterns of seals at Bird Island over the period 1962–81 by analyzing the growth layers in the canine teeth. He found that over the 20-year period the number of feeding trips made by the females varied markedly. His analysis confirmed 1979 as a year in which there was a significant decrease in the number of foraging trips.

15.7.4.3.3 Possible explanations for the variation in reproductive performance

From the data discussed above it is clear that 1984 in particular was an anomalous year with reduced breeding success in Antarctic Fur Seals, Grey-headed Albatrosses, Black-browed Albatrosses, Macaroni Penguins, and Gentoo Penguins. The breeding populations of albatrosses, Fur Seals, and Macaroni Penguins were depressed in the following year but generally seemed to have recovered by 1986 and 1987. While the data for the earlier years are not complete it is evident that in 1978 seabird breeding success was very poor and that the Antarctic Fur Seal growth rates were low. The fact that in these years several species with different ecologies were affected is indicative of some environmental change that impacted on them.

Croxall *et al.* (1988a) note that there is evidence of medium- to large-scale environmental anomalies in both 1978 and 1984. In 1978 a variety of fishing and research vessels failed to locate krill concentrations around South Georgia (Bonner *et al.*, 1978), with the only abundant planktonic crustacean being the amphipod *Parathemisto gaudichaudii*. Krill were, however, present around the South Shetland and South Orkney Islands. Events leading up to the 1984 summer season are well known (Heywood *et al.*, 1985, Priddle *et al.*, 1988), with evidence of substantial oceanographic anomalies and very low numbers of krill over a wide area, and possibly for a long time. Krill predators would need to stay away foraging for a longer time than usual until they had met their own requirements and collected enough extra food to make the return to their offspring energetically worthwhile (Chernov *et al.*, 1976) Because the food shortage persisted for a long period it resulted in major offspring mortality and, eventually, adult mortality judging by the reduction in the breeding population size in the following year.

Croxall *et al.* (1988a) drew attention to the fact that the two years in which there was evidence of food shortages and diminished breeding success were both one year after strong (massive in 1983) ENSO events. If in the future such phenomena are consistently detectable one year after an ENSO event, then this will have profound effects on resource management.

16

Resource exploitation

16.1 Introduction

The total world fish catch (including shellfish) reached a plateau in the early 1970s at about 70 million tonnes per annum, and since then has remained steady or declined. Estimates of total world potential of marine living resources of the conventional kind indicate that the total sustainable catch is probably of the order of about 100 million tonnes per annum (Gulland, 1976). With the rapid increase which has occurred in the world's population in the past few decades, and the increased demand for protein, attention has been focused on the remaining unexploited resources, and in particular on the harvesting of unconventional resources. Of the latter many consider that Antarctic krill is the most promising. Additional stimuli for the exploitation of the living resources of the Southern Ocean have come from the fishing restrictions which have been placed on many fishing nations by the establishment of 200 mile Exclusive Economic Zones (EEZs), and the declines which have occurred in the stocks of some major fisheries in the Northern Hemisphere. This has resulted in many countries having under-utilized or surplus fishing capacity.

The magnitude and distribution of the living resources of the Southern Ocean and their potential for exploitation have been the subject of a number of recent reviews (Gulland, 1970, 1983a,b, 1986; Moiseev, 1970; Lubimova et al., 1973, 1980; Nemoto & Nasu, 1975; El-Sayed, 1977; Everson, 1977b, 1978, 1981; Bengtson, 1978, 1984; Knox, 1978, 1984; McWhinnie & Denys, 1978b; Lubimova, 1983; Budzinski et al., 1985). However, in spite of the comparatively large body of information which is available, the magnitude of the resources and the possibilities of their sustained exploitation are still subject to considerable speculation.

The exploitation of the living resources of the Southern Ocean started with sealing in the nineteenth century. Drastic though the effects were on the stocks of Antarctic Fur Seals in particular, the impact on the ecosystem as a whole was not great. In contrast, whaling has had considerable impact, with the depletion of the stocks of the larger baleen whales, resulting in increases in the popula-tions of some of the competing species. These interactions will be discussed further in the next chapter. Exploitation is now concentrated on krill and demersal (bottom-living) fishes. While several fish stocks have already been greatly reduced from their original level, the stocks of krill have so far probably been little altered.

16.2 Krill

Recently an article appeared in a New Zealand newspaper entitled 'Soviet scientists argue the case for krill harvest'. An extract from this article follows:

> Soviet scholars have achieved major success in evaluation of the reserves of Antarctic krill . . . . The area of krill domination has been set at 13–17 million square kilometres, with the total area of the Antarctic standing at 45 million square kilometres. It has also been established by modelling the life-cycle of the krill population that their average annual output in the domination zone ranges from 24 to 17 grams per sq. m, while the annual aggregate krill mass is estimated at up to a billion tons.
>
> According to the latest Soviet and foreign experts, the volume of krill consumption by the principal consumers (whales, seals, fishes, birds and squid) stands at 200 to 300 million tons a year. It is obvious that in the ecological system where krill is the dominant species its annual growth exceeds the volume of consumption by other species.
>
> . . . This means that a certain part of the krill mass can be used by man for obtaining valuable food products without damage to the ecological system. Soviet experts evaluate the potential krill catch on the basis of the results of many years of direct mature krill stock surveys in the individual areas of krill domination at 15 to 30 million tons a year, which is a safe minimum that cannot cause any damage to the optimal reproduction of krill and to the adequate food supply of its consumers.

In this and the succeeding chapter we will evaluate the accuracy of the conclusions arrived at in the above statement, and assess the likelihood of the development of large-scale sustainable exploitation of krill.

16.2.1 The development of the Antarctic krill fishery

The krill fishery was the most recent one to develop in the Southern Ocean, and the one that appeared to be potentially the largest, as well as the one that has attracted the greatest attention. The earliest reports of krill fishing are for the 1962–63 season when 3 imperial tons were caught by the USSR (Budkoviskiy & Yaragov, 1967). Further USSR exploratory expeditions took place in 1963–64, 1964–65 (Nemoto & Nasu, 1975), and in 1967–68 (Ivanov, 1970). For the first ten years of the fishery the USSR was the only country involved. It was joined in the 1972–73 season by Japan, which undertook exploratory trawling in that season (Nemoto & Nasu, 1975), and subsequently in the 1973–74, 1974–75, and 1976–77 seasons. Catches by Japanese ships in these seasons amounted to 59, 656, 2600 and 500 tonnes respectively. Other countries which carried out exploratory fishing in these early years were Chile (1974–75, 1975–76), the Federal Republic of Germany (1975–76, 1977–78), Poland (1975–76) and Norway (1976–77). More recently these countries have been joined by the German Democratic Republic, Bulgaria, South Korea and Taiwan.

The fishery was slow to develop although the USSR began marketing 'Coral' brand krill-butter and cheese spreads and 'Ocean' brand krill paste in 1970. It was not until the 1976–77 season that the total catch exceeded 100 000 tonnes.

16.2.2 Catch statistics

It was not until 1973 that krill was reported separately in the FAO statistics (Fig. 16.1). Prior to this the catches were reported as 'Marine Crustacea unspecified' taken in the areas adjacent to Antarctica. The recorded catches over the seasons 1969–70 to 1974–75 were 100, 1300, 2100, 7459, 5476 and 8867 tonnes respectively (Table 16.1). Commercial catching on a larger scale commenced in the 1976–77 season when the catch reached 135 000 tonnes, and subsequently the catches increased rapidly to a peak of 528 000 tonnes in 1982–83. Since then the catches have declined to a low of 130 875 in the 1984–85 season, but they recovered to 445 673 tonnes in the 1986–87 season. Subsequently they have remained at around 370 000 tonnes.

16.2.3 Problems in the exploitation of krill

There are a number of problems associated with the harvesting and processing of krill. Ice in areas where krill

Table 16.1. *Annual krill catches prior to 1973/74*

Season	Catch (t)	Comments	Source
1961–62	4	krill	Budkoviskiy & Yaragov (1967)
1963–64	70	krill	Stasenko (1967)
1964–65	306	krill	Nemoto & Nasu (1975)
1966–67	?	krill	Nemoto & Nasu (1975)
1967–68	>140	krill	Ivanov (1970)
1969–70	100	UMC[1]	FAO (1976)
1970–71	1300	UMC	FAO (1976)
1971–72	2100	UMC	FAO (1976)
1972–73	7459	krill	FAO (1976) Nemoto & Nasu (1975)

[1]Unspecified crustacea.
From Everson (1978) and Bengston (1984).

concentrations are found is the main obstacle to fishing operations. It determines the length of the fishing season, which on average lasts five months from mid-November to mid-April. The season, however, may extend to seven months, or longer, in the more northerly areas of the Southern Ocean when weather conditions are favourable.

Problems also arise when the catch rate, or quantities of krill per haul, exceeds the processing capacity on board the ships. Any surplus can only be used for the production of animal feed because of the spoilage of the raw material. This is caused by the very active system of proteolytic enzymes in the krill. Such activity is particularly high in immature krill, due to the intensive metabolism associated with their growth (Mitskevitch & Mosolov, 1981). Immediately after death, interrelated biochemical changes take place reducing the quality of krill for processing. These include autolysis, which results in drip and unpleasant odour, as well as changes in colour and texture. After 12–16 hours bacterial decomposition of the tissues begins. After three to four hours of storage at air temperatures the intensity of changes in taste, odour and texture reaches such a level that the raw material is no longer fit for processing into food (Andreev *et al.*, 1981). During cold storage, proteolytic activity increases due to the diffusion of enzymes from the intestines to the muscle tissue. The shelf life of frozen krill at −18 °C is only three months (Bidenko *et al.*, 1981).

Other processing problems are caused by the phytoplankton upon which krill feed. Intensively feeding 'green' krill are unfit for processing into mince-type products (Bykova & Radakova, 1981) and produce canned products of inferior quality. Krill processing is also made more difficult by the presence of by-catch species (salps, jellyfish, juvenile fish and fish larvae), which often constitute over 20% of the catch.

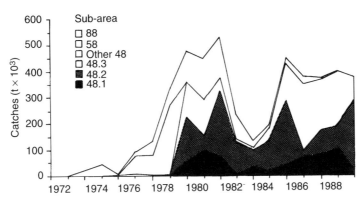

Fig. 16.1. The total krill catch by sub-area (see Fig. 16.3) since 1973. Redrawn from SC-CCAMLR (1990a).

A paper by Soevik & Braekhan in 1979 on the presence of fluoride in krill has had a considerable impact on the optimistic views on the potential of krill for human consumption and animal feed. High levels found in whole krill (up to 2440 ppm) led these authors to state: 'This would make krill in any form, even peeled, fail to comply with the requirements for human consumption.' Numerous publications have confirmed these high levels of fluoride in krill (e.g. Schneppenheim, 1980; G. Hempel & Manthey, 1981; Boone & Manthey, 1983; Adelung *et al.*, 1987), even when compared with other Antarctic animals (Scheneppenheim, 1980; Oelenschlager & Manthey, 1982; Culik, 1987). However, it has been found that in living krill most of the fluoride is concentrated in the exoskeleton and it has been shown that the fluoride migrates from the shell to the muscle tissue in frozen krill (Christians & Leinemann, 1980; Christians *et al.*, 1981). Lowering the temperature to -40°C stops the migration process. By previously separating the body fluids the migration of the fluoride during the frozen storage period is reduced. Similarly, boiling the raw material arrests the migration. Techniques have also been developed for the production of meat with reduced shell content. The adoption of such procedures can result in the production of an acceptable product. The US Food and Drug Administration has concluded that the 14 ppm of fluoride contained in krill meat does not constitute a health hazard. However, care will need to be taken to prepare and market krill products which are acceptable and meet stringent health standards.

16.2.4 Catching and processing krill

There have been a number of recent reviews of the development of the krill fishery, dealing with the catching of krill, the technology of krill utilization, the mechanization of the processing and the problems of the economics of the industry and the marketing of the products (Grantham, 1977; McElroy, 1980a,b,c: Budzinski *et al.*, 1985).

Krill fishing techniques. As we have seen in Chapter 5 krill concentrations are readily located by hydroacoustic techniques which enable the fishermen to distinguish such concentrations from those of other organisms such as salps and jellyfish. The fishing techniques are generally similar to those used for pelagic fishes. Since krill are characterized by low resistance to mechanical damage, large single trawls are of little value as the raw material is badly crushed when the trawl is brought aboard. Experience has shown that single hauls should not exceed 5–6 tonnes so that the processing can proceed smoothly. Polish factory trawlers have found that 70–89% of the krill are caught in the daytime.

Daily catch rates. Many factors influence catch rates, including type of krill concentration, size of vessel and type of fishing gear, ice and weather conditions, processing capacity of the vessel, etc. In early publications the daily catch rate was estimated on the basis of the potentially obtainable catch in tonnes per hour. As a consequence there were over-optimistic estimates of the daily catch rates. The maximum catch rate achieved by a Federal Republic of Germany experimental trawling expedition was 35 tonnes in eight minutes, with an overall catch rate of 8–12 tonnes h^{-1}. USSR catches have been quoted at 139–272 tonnes day^{-1}, and it has been estimated that daily catch rates of 200–300 tonnes day^{-1} should be practicable, and that under favourable conditions 500 tonnes day^{-1} should be possible.

These optimistic forecasts have not been realized in practice. Results from three Polish factory trawlers over the 1977–78 season show that the vessels caught 8003 tonnes of krill in 139 days of fishing at a daily rate of 57.8 tonnes per vessel (Russek *et al.*, 1981). This is similar to the catch rates reported for a large Japanese factory trawler (104.5 m in length) which in the 1982–82 and 1982–83 fishing seasons fished for 115 days and 118 days respectively with an average catch of 51.5 tonnes day^{-1}.

Krill as a raw material. The chemical composition of

krill is well balanced in terms of a potential food material. The nitrogenous substances in krill vary around 13% of wet weight, made up of 8% true protein and 2.5% true amino acids (Grantham, 1977). The amino acid fraction is characterized by its relatively high content (46%) of essential amino acids. It is thus a highly nutritious food for human consumption.

Possibilities of krill processing. There are a number of products which can be processed from krill. They include:

1. Frozen, boiled-frozen and dried krill. With the exception of the Asian markets, the prospects for the sale of these products is not promising. In some countries (Japan, South Korea, Taiwan), where euphausiids are a traditional food more attention is being paid to the production of products from frozen and dried krill.

2. Coagulated and minced krill. In the USSR, Poland, the Federal Republic of Germany, and South Korea the interest in krill products has concentrated on products such as coagulated pastes and minces. Coagulated pastes are produced by pressing out the protein from the krill by means of a screw press, thermal coagulation of the juice, separating coagulated protein from the liquid, cooling of the paste, freezing and packaging. The biological and nutritive value of the coagulated paste is high and comparable to fish. In the USSR there is wide experience in the marketing of coagulated pastes as a variety of canned products, including pastes, shrimp butter, cheese with paste, etc. However, problems of consumer acceptance have not been solved. Krill mince is produced from pre-cooked raw material. It is a dense pink paste which appears to have limited use except as a additive to other food products.

3. Whole tail meat. It is considered that tail meat is the most valuable krill food product but it is the most difficult to obtain satisfactorily (Grantham, 1977). Research on the production of whole tail meat in Denmark, Chile, Japan, the Federal Republic of Germany, the United States and the USSR has resulted in three main methods for its production; roller peeling, attrition of boiled-frozen krill and flotation of the shells from boiled krill. Tail meat can be used for a variety of products with krill meat added such as casseroles, stews, sausages, pates, krill sticks and other products.

4. De-proteinized shells of krill contain 30–40% chitin. By deacetylation of chitin a valuable product chitosan is obtained. Considerable research has been carried out in the past few years on the production technology and possible industrial application of chitin/chitosan and their derivatives. Present applications of chitosan on a commercial scale is in waste water treatment as a protein coagulant. It can also be used for the removal of heavy metals, including plutonium and uranium. Promising results have also been obtained using chitosan as a haemostatic agent (Fradet, 1985), Chitin and its derivatives are biodegradable and so do not introduce any disturbances into the human body. This makes chitosan an appealing substance for the controlled release of drugs, nutrients, agricultural chemicals, etc. (Muzzarelli, 1977).

16.2.5 Future prospects

The worldwide interest in krill resources during the years 1980–87 was much lower than during the 1974–79 period, when many studies published by international, governmental and private institutions had prophesied that the exploitation of krill resources would reduce the world deficit of animal protein, and make the problem of under-nutrition in some countries less severe. While it has been demonstrated that krill could be caught in quantity and processed into products which were nutritive and acceptable for human consumption, many problems remain to be solved before the krill fishing industry can be placed on a firm basis.

In the past few years the expected gradual rise in krill catches has not materialized. This may in part be due to the fact that the marketing of krill products did not turn out to be commercially viable. Budzinski *et al.* (1985) have carried out a detailed study of the production costs, prices and demand for krill products. Their study is an advance on earlier ones by authors such as Eddie (1977), McElroy (1980a) and B. Mitchell & Sandbrook (1980). Budzinski *et al.*'s (1985) estimate of production costs was based mainly on the actual costs incurred by Polish vessels fishing for export to other countries in FAO Major Fishing Areas 48.1 and 48.2 (see Fig. 16.3). On this basis the cost of catching and manufacturing 1 kg of tail meat delivered in frozen blocks and treated as a semi-finished product by inland processors would most likely amount to US$3.60. This might be expected as efficiency improved to drop to US$2.20. Unit cost for meal production were estimated at US$2035 tonne^{-1} for a vessel with a daily catch rate of 55 tonnes, and $1999 with a daily catch rate of 65 tonnes. These unit costs considerably exceed fish meal prices on the world market and the authors concluded that the production of meal for animal food from krill would not be viable.

More serious problems are, however, encountered in the marketing of krill products. There is a great need for extensive, systematic and impartial processing and marketing research. A demand for krill products has yet to be established at a price which would be profitable to the producers. With the current available technology it is possible to produce krill on factory trawlers as tail meat, and canned and minced products. It is considered that the techniques developed in Japan, Poland and the USSR for

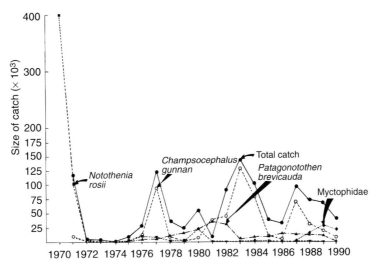

Fig. 16.2. Catches of various fish species FAO fishing from sub-Area 48.3 (South Georgia sub-Area) (see Fig. 16.3) by year. The total catch (●—●), and that of the three major species, *Notothenia rossii* (●---●), *Champsocephalus gunnari* (○---○), and *Patagonotothen brevicauda* (▲–··–▲). Other minor species contributing to the total catch include *Chaenocephalus aceratus, Pseudochaenichthys georgianus, Notothenia squamifrons, Dissostichus eleginoides* and Myctophid species (♦···♦). Based on data in SC-CCAMLR (1990b).

the production of tail meat have the best prospect for the profitable exploitation of the krill resource. However, for this to happen two main conditions must be met (Budzinski *et al.*, 1985). First krill tail meat would need to be accepted in the market as an analogue or substitute for small shrimp. In 1984 the average prices for the lowest grade, frozen headless and shipped from India, Pakistan and Sri Lanka, was US$3.75 to $4.00 per kg to US ports and US$3.30 to $3.80 to Japanese ports. Grantham (1977) thought it unlikely that the price of krill tail meat could be higher than 70% of the locally prevailing price for small shrimp. On this basis the anticipated price for krill tail meat would have been US$2.50 to $2.90 per kg. A more optimistic view by some experts would put the price on US and Japanese markets at US$3.00 to $4.00 per kg. This would result in a return to the industry of a minimum of US$2500 tonne⁻¹, in the first case and US$3000 tonne⁻¹ in the second. However, the profitability threshold for commercial fishing operations could be higher.

The above exploitation model was based on the assumption that the factory trawler would catch fish and squid in the remaining six months after the krill season, and that the vessels would be based at a close port. When fishing operations start in faraway ports in Europe, the United States and Japan the number of days at sea would increase and output would drop making the unit cost of production of tail meat much higher. It is for this reason that Japanese fishing companies have entered into joint fishing agreements with Chilean companies. In addition, any further substantial rise in fuel costs could substantially affect the economics.

It is thus clear that the considerable difficulties still

encountered in the utilization of Antarctic krill for human food, animal meal and other products are greater than those found in the production and marketing of other products of marine origin. In addition to the processing problems mentioned above, the high fluoride content of the raw material imposes some constraints. However, technological solutions can be found to overcome the latter problem, but they will add to the cost of production. The best prospects for the future exploitation of krill appear to lie in high-quality, low-volume products for human consumption. Supplies of frozen fresh and boiled krill to some Far East countries could be an exception to this. There are, however, serious economic constraints to the development of mass production aimed at increasing the supply of highly processed protein products to developing countries. Thus, the original hopes that had been held of alleviating problems of protein shortage in developing countries are unlikely to be realized.

In addition, there is the question as to whether krill exploitation could have an impact on the dependent predators, in particular whether it could prevent the recovery of the whale stocks. In relation to the total stocks the present level of exploitation is small. However, the potential for the overexploitation of localized stocks still exists. Everson & Goss (1991) have analyzed fine-scale catch data reported in recent years on the krill fishery in the Atlantic sector. Their analyses indicate that the krill fishery is concentrated on the continental shelf or close to it. Seasonal changes in the location of the fishery are in the main associated with the northern limit of the pack ice. During the summer months the fishery is operating in areas where key krill predators are likely to be active. It is therefore likely that krill catches in such areas, although minor in the context of the total krill resource, could deplete the krill available to the predators.

16.3 Fishes

As commercial exploitation of Antarctic fish stocks is comparatively recent the detailed information available on their biology, age and growth, stock sizes, stock discreteness, natural mortality and recruitment is limited in comparison to that available for Northern Hemisphere fish stocks. It is only comparatively recently that reliable information has been collected on aspects such as catch statistics, fishing effort, impact of fishing on the stocks and catch per unit effort (CPUE). The available information has been summarized by Kock (1975), Everson (1977b, 1978, 1981), Anon (USSR) (1984a,b), and Kock *et al.* (1985) and Kock & Koster (1990).

The Southern Ocean is divided into three major fishing areas (Nos 48, 58, and 88) with each divided into sub-areas as proposed by Everson (1977b), and subsequently modified by the 1984 meeting of the Scientific Committee of the Commission on the Conservation of Antarctic Marine Living Resources (see Fig. 18.1). Due to the lack of major exploitable pelagic stocks, trawling is primarily directed on demersal (bottom-living) fish of the suborder Notothenioidei at depths down to 500 m. The most important fishing grounds are:

1. In the Atlantic Ocean Sector (FAO Area 48), along the Scotia Arc (Shag Rocks, South Georgia, South Sandwich Islands, South Orkney Islands, Elephant Island, South Shetland Islands and Joineville Island).

2. In the Indian Ocean Sector (FAO Area 58) (Ob and Lena Seamounts, Crozet Island, Shiff Bank, Kerguelen Islands, Kerguelen–Heard Ridge and MacDonald Islands).

16.3.1 The development of the Antarctic fisheries

Attempts to exploit Antarctic fish stocks commercially date back to the beginning of this century. E. Vanhoeffen, the biologist of the German *Gauss* Expedition, hoped to find commercially utilizable fish in the Southern Ocean. He also proposed to increase the fish harvest from Kerguelen waters by the introduction of new species from the islands of St Paul and New Amsterdam (Vanhoeffen, 1902). His suggestion was not acted upon, but more recently trout and salmon were introduced into the rivers of the Kerguelen Islands, and proposals have been advanced for the seeding of South Chilean waters with Pacific salmon from where they could undertake feeding migrations into Antarctic waters (Joyner *et al.*, 1974).

At the same time as Vanhoeffen was putting forward his ideas, whalers discovered large concentrations of mar-

bled Notothenia (*Notothenia rossii*) off South Georgia. A considerable number of barrels of salted fish were sold to Buenos Aires and the Norwegian biologist Sorling raised the possibility of establishing an important fishery off the island. Due to the abundance of the more profitable whales and the distance from the market this suggestion was not followed up. Repeated fishing trials by Argentinian, Norwegian and Japanese companies in the 1930s, 1950s, and 1960s with purse seiners and small bottom trawlers all failed (Olsen, 1954).

Exploratory fishing by the Soviet Union in the Scotia Sea commencing at the beginning of the 1960s developed into large-scale fishing around South Georgia in the late 60s. The main target species was the Marbled Notothenia (*Notothenia rossii*) and catches soon reached a maximum of more than 400 000 tonnes in the 1969–70 season, followed by rapid decline to a few thousand tonnes over the next two seasons (Fig. 16.2) (Everson, 1978). This decline can be attributed to a lower fishing effort (e.g. fewer vessels), and a sharp decline in the CPUE (Everson, 1977b). The fishing effort subsequently increased from 1975–76 onwards with the entry of Poland, the German Democratic Republic and Bulgaria into the fishery, and its extension to the South Orkney Islands in 1977–78 (Sosinski & Sikora, 1977; Sosinski & Kuranty, 1979). This led to another rapid buildup of the catches to between 150 000 and 200 000 tonnes. Much of this increase was due to catches of the Icefish (*Champsocephalus gunnari*), in 1976–77 and 1977–78 (FAO, 1981). From 1978–79 onwards, fishing was extended to the South Shetland Islands and Joineville Island (Sosinski & Sikora, 1977; Bech, 1982). In the 1978–79 season catches declined to 130 000 tonnes, and until 1981–82 they oscillated around 100 000 tonnes. The catches consisted mainly of *N. rossii* and *C. gunnari* and *N. guentheri* in subsequent years. In 1982–83 catches rose again (mostly *C. gunnari*) to more than 160 000 tonnes, nearly all of which was caught by the USSR. The change from early dominance by *N. rossii* to later dominance by *C. gunnari* was probably due to heavy fishing aimed at *N. rossii* in the early years reducing the standing stock, thus causing effort to be transferred to other species. The pattern of catches is typical of the situation when a virgin stock is exploited – initial high catches followed by a sharp decline (see Fig. 16.2).

Kock & Koster (1990) have recently analyzed the status of the exploited fish stocks in the Atlantic sector. Of the exploited stocks *N. rossii* is the species most adversely affected by the fishery. The present stock size is less than 5% of that before the fishery started. Recruitment has fallen since the second half of the 1970s and even if catch levels were zero or less than 1000 tonnes y^{-1} an increase in

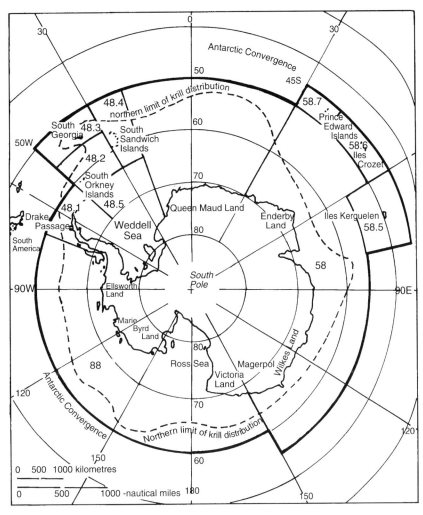

Fig. 16.3 The boundaries of the Convention on the Conservation of Antarctic Marine Living Resources and the FAO Southern Ocean Fishing Areas zone. The numbered areas are the areas established by FAO for the reporting of statistical data on fish catches.

stock size to only about 40 000 tonnes could be expected at the turn of the century. This is still less than 10% of the unexploited stock size. Kock & Koster (1990) consider that the stocks of *C. gunnari* around South Georgia and the Antarctic Peninsula are in urgent need of conservation measures. Some of these have already been established (SC-CCAMLR, 1990a,b). It is to be hoped that the findings documented by Kock & Koster (1990), as well as those of the CCAMLR Working Group on Fish Stock Assessment, will bring about a change from the purely 'reactive management', which CCAMLR adhered to in the first years, to more predictive (i.e. active) management measures more in tune with the objectives of Article II of the Convention on the Conservation of Antarctic Marine Living Resources (see Chapter 18).

Exploitation of fishes in the Indian Ocean Sector began around Kerguelen after several exploratory cruises by the USSR in 1958–59 to 1960–61. Commercial exploitation, which started in 1970, was preceded by three years of semi-commercial fishing. The progress of the fishery was similar to that which occurred in the Atlantic Sector, a rapid build-up of catches in 1971–72 to 229 500 tonnes (about 65% *N. rossii*) was followed by low catches of 12–13 000 tonnes in the next two years (Duhamel & Hureau, 1990). This was followed by a second and third maximum with 101 000 and 90 000 tonnes respectively in 1974–75 and 1977–78, followed by several years of low catches. Main target species were the Icefish (*C. gunnari*) and the Grey Notothenia (*N. squamifrons*), which together made up 75–85% of the catches. In 1978 the French Government established a 200 Mile Exclusive Economic Zone around Kerguelen. Since then the fishery has been strictly controlled by the French authorities and the Crozet Islands have been closed to fishing. Both the number and allowable catch of the Soviet vessels were limited, and in 1981 three French deep-sea trawlers joined the Soviet vessels (a maximum of seven vessels for the area was set by the French authorities).

Heard Island waters were fished by Soviet ships during 1977 and 1978, but this terminated when Australia created a 200 Mile EEZ around the Island. There have been no fisheries established around Macquarie Island or round the Antarctic Continent. However, the USSR has reported catches of pelagic *Pleurogramma antarcticum* four times between 1977 and 1983. In addition to catches of Nototheniids and Channichthyids small catches of Southern Blue Whiting (*Micromesistius australis*) and Patagonian Hake (*Merluccius hubbsii*) have been made in the Atlantic Sector.

16.3.2 Impact of the fishing on the stocks

The deficiency of the data on catch-per-unit-effort (CPUE) in the Atlantic Ocean sector, the lack of long-term series of age length keys, and of length–frequency data from the most recent years in the Atlantic Ocean sector, make an assessment of the present status of the exploited Antarctic fish stocks very difficulty and speculative. (Kock *et al.*, 1985).

Thus, the hard data are not currently available to make predictions of what effects the levels of exploitation have had, and will have in the future, on the stocks. Nevertheless, the indications are that in some areas the impact has been severe.

Standing stock biomass of demersal fishes has been estimated at about 500 000 tonnes for South Georgia (Everson, 1977b), and about 130 000 tonnes for Kerguelen (Hureau, 1979). Corresponding values for maximum sustainable yield (MSY) have been estimated at 50 000 and 20 000 tonnes respectively, although both projections may be under-estimates. Catches in many years have exceeded these MSY estimates by considerable amounts.

Due to their relatively high age at first sexual maturity and the low growth rates, at least of mature individuals, Antarctic fishes are very vulnerable to overfishing, even at low levels of fishing activity. The Green Notothenia (*Notothenia gibberifrons*), for example, off South Georgia is a typical by-catch species. Catches rarely exceed 10 000 tonnes. This species reaches a maximum size of 52 cm when about 20 years old. Most of the individuals become sexually mature at about 32–35 cm (six to eight years old) (Boronin & Frolkina, 1976). Length composition of the catches in four successive seasons showed a rapid decline of large (i.e. old) individuals from 1975–76 onwards when the stock was obviously in a quasi virgin state. Mean lengths of the fish in the catch declined from 41 cm in 1975–76 to about 30 cm in 1978–79, which is about the length at first sexual matu-

rity. Kock (1981) arrived at similar conclusions for the Icefish (*C. gunnari*) off South Georgia by comparing research vessel data from 1975–76 and 1977–78. Kock *et al.* (1985) provide additional data on a range of species. For *N. rossii marmorata* off South Georgia the mean length and average age in Soviet catches declined from 68.1 cm and 9.3 years in 1969 to 59.1 cm and 6.8 years in 1973. From 1976–77 to 1980–81 the mean length of Polish commercial catches declined year-by-year from 59.1 cm to 43.0 cm. The average age declined from 6.5 to 5.3 years.

Until recently the lack of any mesh-size regulations, combined with the availability of both adults and juveniles of several species on the fishing grounds made the species vulnerable to recruitment overfishing, i.e. exploitation of the part of the stock prior to the onset of sexual maturity. This is indicated by the growing proportion of juveniles in the catches of the Green Notothenia. Catches of the Patagonian Toothfish (*Dissostichus eleginoides*), for example, consisted of more than 90% juveniles.

The abundance of krill appears to be an important factor governing the distribution of the larval and juvenile stages of a number of notothenioids. Rembiszewski *et al.* (1978), Slosarczyk & Rembiszewski (1982) and Slosarczyk (1983) noted that juvenile Icefish were a frequent by-catch of the krill fisheries in areas of the Scotia Arc, the Bransfield Strait and west of the Antarctic Peninsula. Juvenile *C. gunnari* and *Chaenocephalus aceratus* have also been reported to be abundant in krill swarms around South Georgia (Kompowski, 1980a,b). Slosarczyk & Rembiszewski (1982) and Slosarczyk (1983) calculated that up to several hundred juvenile nototenioids per 100 kg of krill were present in the krill catches, particularly around South Georgia. Off the Balleney islands, juvenile *Trematomus bernacchii* have been observed in concentrations of several thousands per 100 kg of krill, together with the rather less abundant *Patagonia brychysoma* (Slorsarczyk, 1983).

There is thus ample evidence that intensive krill fishing in FAO Area 48, where nototenioids are abundant in, or close to, krill swarms could endanger the recruitment of a number of nototenioids, as most species are characterized by low absolute fecundity.

16.3.3 Biomass and production

There are limited data available on the biomass and production of Antarctic fish stocks. At Signy Island Everson (1970a) estimated that the biomass of *Notothenia neglecta*, the dominant species in shallow water, to be 194 kg ha^{-1}, and the annual production to be 0.34 kg ha^{-1}. Hureau (1979) estimated the standing stock of fishes on the shelf area around Kerguelen to be about 120 000 tonnes, or about 24 kg ha^{-1}. This is probably an underestimate due to the small beam trawl that was used in the sampling.

Estimates of fish production have also been made by summing the estimates of total fish consumption by major predators. This gives an estimate of 15 554×10^3 tonnes, or 66 kg ha^{-1}, which includes all species of fish and the total production of species of potential commercial importance must be assumed to be less, although by what proportion is not known. Production of the sexually mature fish has been estimated at about one third of the total, i.e. about 5 million tonnes (Kock *et al.*, 1985).

The demersal fish are for the most part restricted to the continental and island shelf areas which together cover an area of approximately 2.2 million km^2 (excluding the ice shelves) (Everson, 1978). Thus, the total predator consumption of fish if averaged over the whole shelf area would be about 7.75 tonnes km^{-2}. Extrapolation from Croxall's 1984 figures for fish consumption by predators would indicate that the production, at least in the Scotia Sea and around South Georgia, might be higher.

However, it should be borne in mind that the above estimates are subject to considerable error, and the figures should only be taken as an indication that they are in the correct order of magnitude. Bearing this in mind, the estimated production for the South Georgia continental shelf area (of *c.* 36 000 km^2) would be between 230 000 and 280 000 tonnes for the whole of the demersal life span. As only a third of this would be due to sexually mature fish the production of interest to the fishery would be about 77 000 tonnes y^{-1}. The catchable stock, however, would be lower than this. On the basis of the commercial catch statistics Everson (1977b) estimated that the standing stock around South Georgia prior to exploitation was about 500 000 tonnes and that the annual production was about 90 000 tonnes. By erring on the side of caution, and taking the lowest possible estimate, the South Georgia area would appear to have been capable of a MSY of 50 000 tonnes y^{-1}. This figure, as we have seen, has been exceeded in a number of seasons since the fishery commenced in the mid-1970s.

16.4 Seals

16.4.1 The history of Antarctic Sealing

The first of the Southern Ocean's living resources to be exploited was the Antarctic Fur Seal. When Captain Cook returned from his voyage of discovery in 1775 he reported that the beaches of South Georgia were swarming with Fur Seals. It was not long before fur sealers descended on these beaches to slaughter the seals. By 1822 James

Weddell, the Scottish sealer, calculated that no fewer than 1 200 000 skins had been taken from the islands and that the species was virtually extinct there. Another rich stock of seals was discovered on the South Shetland Islands in 1819 and by 1822 some 320 000 skins had been taken and the population virtually exterminated. Other populations on the South Orkney islands, the South Sandwich Islands and Bouvetova suffered a similar fate, and the sealing soon declined due to a lack of seals. There were minor revivals of the industry in the 1950s and 1970s but the seals were not given a chance to recover. This was largely due to the fact that the sealers had turned to taking Elephant Seals for their blubber, an operation which was less profitable than that of taking the skins of Fur Seals, so that they killed Fur Seals whenever they came across them. By the beginning of this century the old fashioned fur sealer had virtually disappeared from the Southern Ocean.

The lobodontine Antarctic seals, especially the Crabeater Seal, constitute a very considerable resource which has been virtually untapped. The only occasions on which any substantial harvest appears to have been taken were in 1982–83 and 1983–84 when four Dundee whalers and a Norwegian vessel, prospecting for Right Whales and failing to find them, took 32 588 skins and a great quantity of blubber in the pack ice zone. It is not known which species was taken, but the numbers involved make it likely that they were Crabeaters. The only other commercial venture was in 1984 when the Norwegian sealer *Polarhay* took 861 Crabeater Seals in an exploratory cruise between the South Orkneys and Elephant Island.

16.4.2 Recovery of the Antarctic Fur Seal stocks

In recent years the Antarctic Fur Seal has undergone one of the most spectacular population increases recorded for any marine mammal (Payne, 1977; Laws, 1977a,b). The most recent account, based mainly on Payne's (1977, 1978) studies, is that of Bonner (1981). After the early exploitation on South Georgia the Fur Seal was thought to be extinct and no seals were seen until 1919, when a young male was shot at the eastern end of the island. In the 1930s a small breeding population with 12 pups was found on Bird Island at the northwest end of South Georgia. It was not until 1956 that studies were initiated on this population and counts were made between 1956 and 1968, and from 1972 to 1975 (Laws, 1973, 1979). Bonner visited Bird Island in 1958 and found a flourishing population there with an annual pup production estimated at 3500 (Bonner, 1958). Between 1958 and 1972 the annual rate of increase was shown to be 16.8% and from 1972 to 1975, 14.5%. The annual pup production in 1975 was carefully assessed by Payne (1977, 1978) at

90 000. Further studies by the British Antarctic Survey indicate that the rate of increase at Bird Island had decreased, but satellite colonies on the main island continued to increase rapidly. By 1975–76 over half the number of pups were born on the mainland beaches and the population has continued to rise since then. However, the Fur Seals are very much concentrated at the northwest end of the island, and many important former breeding sites have no breeding seals, or only negligible numbers.

Small breeding groups, which most certainly have been derived from South Georgia, have been established at the South Shetland, South Orkney and South Sandwich Islands. The reported rates of increase on the latter two island groups range from 2 to 6% (Laws, 1973, 1981; Bonner, 1981). On the other hand, Aguaya (1978) has reported that the seals on the South Shetlands have been increasing at 34% per year, a rate of increase which is impossible unless their numbers were being reinforced by immigration from elsewhere. Bonner (1981) estimated that the total annual pup production of the Antarctic Fur Seal in 1978 was 135 000, corresponding to a total population of 554 000, and that by 1982 it was estimated that there were probably over 9 million seals.

While the recovery of a nearly exterminated population of a marine mammal is generally looked upon as a desirable event there have nevertheless been some undesirable side effects, especially on Bird Island. Bird Island is some 5.5 km long by 1.5 km wide with less than 5 km of shoreline accessible to the seals. Some 150 000 Fur Seals now come ashore annually during the breeding season from November to April, a period that coincides with the growing season of terrestrial plants and the breeding season of a number of ground-nesting bird species.

Profound changes have taken place in the vegetation of Bird Island since 1966 (Bonner, 1985b). Fur Seals destroy tussock grass (*Poa flabellata*), which is the dominant plant cover, by trampling and lying on the tops of the tussocks. Meadows of one of the two flowering plants (*Deschampsia antarctica)* and cryptograms (mosses and lichens) are also destroyed by trampling and this can lead to local erosion. Destruction of the tussock deprives birds of habitat. The endemic pipit (*Anthus antarcticus*), and the Pintail (*Anus georgica*) are deprived of breeding habitat and protected nest sites, and foraging habitat for the pipit; the Dove Prion (*Pachyptila desolata*), the Blue Petrel (*Halobaena caerulea*), the Common Diving Petrel (*Procellaria aequinoctalis)*, and several burrowing petrels are deprived of burrowing sites. Trampling can cause burrows to collapse, destroying the nests, and the destruction of cover exposes the smaller birds to predation by Brown Skuas (*Catharacta lonnbergi*) when on the

ground. The destruction of the tussock grassland also profoundly alters the habitat of many invertebrates.

The question may be posed as to whether this is a return to the pre-exploitation conditions of the late eighteenth century when the Fur Seal populations were in a pristine state, or whether it represents a new development. From the accounts of the early sealers and the occurrence of Fur Seal hairs in peat it appears that the breeding colonies were more widely distributed round South Georgia, and while the population was larger the high densities now seen at Bird Island were not present. Another piece of evidence strongly suggesting that the conditions at Bird Island are more extreme than in the past is the destruction of the lowest raised beach at Freshwater Inlet, a feature which had persisted throughout the pre-exploitation period, but which was rapidly eroded in the span of 15 years after 1960.

It appears that the Fur Seals are bringing about substantial changes to the terrestrial ecosystems with destruction of the vegetation and serious consequences for some birds (including two species which are much less abundant than the Fur Seals). There have been many examples where the local abundance of a protected species can cause considerable damage to the environment (Jewell & Holt, 1981). A common response to this in conservation management is interventive management. As Bonner (1985b) points out it would be possible to devise management policies for the Fur Seal at South Georgia which would control the environmental damage. This would involve fencing off vulnerable areas, or culling the Fur Seals, or both.

Elephant Seals were quicker to recover than the Fur Seals as their populations were never reduced to a low level. By 1910 there was a good stock of Elephant Seals at South Georgia and the British administrator of the area permitted licensed exploitation; only adult bulls were allowed to be taken and the island was divided into four sealing divisions, only three of which were worked in any one year. In addition sealing reserves and closed seasons were instituted, and a quota of no more than 6000 bulls per year was set. Under these control measures sealing was profitably pursued at South Georgia for three decades.

In the 1940s the quota was raised with adverse effects on the stock. R. M. Laws, a British biologist who worked with Elephant Seals on Signy Island, was asked to propose a management plan for sealing at South Georgia. The plan resulted in the quota being reduced to that which could be properly sustained and its allocation between the various colonies in proportion to the stocks present. Law's discovery that the ages of the seals could be determined by the growth increments on their teeth made it possible to monitor the age structure of the catch and adjust it accordingly. Under this new management scheme the Elephant Seal population recovered and the rate of the catch and oil production per seal increased. It was found that the average age at sexual maturity of the females during exploitation was about two years, compared with more than three years in 1977 when the seals had not been harvested for 13 years. During exploitation the growth of the females was faster due to less competition for food from the much larger males. The South Georgia sealing industry finally ceased in 1964 due to the collapse of the whaling round South Georgia of which sealing was an adjunct.

16.4.3 The Convention on the Conservation of Antarctic Seals

When the prospect of a resumption of Antarctic sealing arose with the Norwegian exploratory cruise for pelagic seals in 1964, the SCAR Working Group on Biology proposed to SCAR that measures be instituted to control such activities if they eventuated (they did not in fact materialize). These proposals were conveyed to the Antarctic Treaty leading eventually to the signing in London in 1972 of the Convention on the Conservation of Antarctic Seals. This convention is unique in that it was the first international agreement to make provision for the management and protection of species *before* an industry to exploit them had actually developed. The convention came into force in March 1978 after it had been ratified by 10 countries.

The convention applies to the area south of 60° S, though provision is made for the reporting of catches in the areas of floating sea ice north of 60° S. It recognizes the importance of Antarctic seals as a resource and the need to regulate their harvesting. It covers all the six species of seals which occur within the Convention area, and catch limits are set for the Crabeater (175 000), the Leopard (1200) and the Weddell (5000) Seals. The taking of Ross Seals (*Omatophoca rossii*), Elephant Seals (*Mirounga* spp.), and Fur Seals (*Arctocephalus* spp.) is completely banned, and the adult stock of Weddell Seals is completely protected in the breeding colonies on the fast ice. The Southern Ocean is divided into six zones and in the event of sealing taking place one of these would be closed each year in rotation. Three sealing reserves have been established – around the South Orkney Islands, the southwestern Ross Sea, and Edisto Inlet. Provision is made for special permits, exchange of information, future meeting of the consultative parties, review of operations at regular intervals and for amendments to the convention. Scientific advice is provided by the SCAR Group of Specialist on Seals. This group also has the responsibility of coordinating data on the number of seals killed in the treaty area for scientific purposes and for dog food (this latter practice is being phased out) as required under the 'Agreed Measures for the Conservation of Flora and Fauna'. Should a sealing industry develop at any time in the future then the convention provides adequate means of its regulation and monitoring.

16.4.2 Possible future exploitation

While the seals of the Southern Ocean represent a considerable natural resource Bonner (1985a) considers that it is unlikely that their harvesting will ever be commercially viable. Such harvesting would be labour intensive, and this combined with the distance from the market and a product that would be likely to be inferior to that obtained from seals in the Northern Hemisphere would inhibit development. Fur Seals would be relatively simple to exploit and could be managed in such a way that would not deplete the stocks. However, as Bonner points out, there is a major impediment to the redevelopment of a southern sealing industry. A very considerable body of public opinion opposed to the killing of seals has been fostered under the umbrella of the conservation lobby and countries which could mount sealing ventures would probably be reluctant to expose themselves to the opposition which would result, even if the conduct of the industry could be guaranteed to be irreproachable.

16.5 Whales

16.5.1 The history of Antarctic whaling

The earliest European whaling of which we have any record appears to have been carried out by the Norsemen of northwestern Europe between about 800 and 1000 AD. Other nations, especially the Basques, joined the hunt for whales and by the end of the fifteenth century whaling had become a major commercial operation. While Right Whales were initially exploited, the whalers soon turned their attention to the Bowhead as they penetrated toward Arctic waters. The stocks of this species became commercially extinct within 50 years. American whaling commenced shortly after the settlement of North America, and in 1772 a major advance took place when the whalers turned their attention to the Sperm Whales. While the hunt for this species was slow to develop it eventually ushered in the era of the great Yankee whalers of New England. These New England whalers, joined later by whalers from other countries, particularly the British, gradually spread their activities, first of all southwards in the Atlantic and then round Cape Horn (1789) into the Pacific.

Sperm whaling flourished until around 1850 and subsequently declined rapidly until it reached a low level by

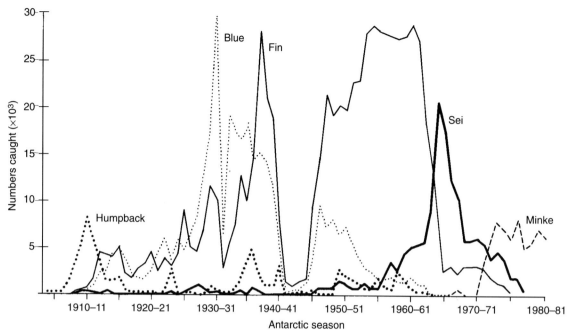

Fig. 16.4. Catches of whales 1904–1905 to 1980–1981 (including land stations, moored factory ships and pelagic whaling).

1860. While Sperm Whales were the main target species the whalers turned their attention to Right Whales when they were found in large numbers in the cooler waters of the Southern Hemisphere. Important fisheries for this species developed, particularly off New Zealand, Australia and the Kerguelen Islands, from about 1800 to 1850. From 1840 onwards Right Whales were found in the cooler waters of the North Pacific and still later Bowheads were found in the Bering Sea, and subsequently in the Chukchi and Beaufort Seas. In 1853 a Captain Charles Scammon discovered calving grounds of the Grey Whale in Baja California. The exploitation of this species, like that of the Bowhead, lasted less than 50 years when the population was reduced to a very low level.

Throughout this period the whaling techniques had hardly changed from the early days of European whaling, and the whalers still hunted from rowing boats with hand harpoons and processed their whales at sea alongside their ships. All this was to change when in 1868 the Norwegian Svend Foyn developed the harpoon gun fired from a cannon. The harpoon was fitted with hinged barbs which opened out in the body of the whale and the tip consisted of a grenade which detonated in the body of the whale. The steam-powered whale chaser was developed to take advantage of this new weapon, and this enabled the whalers to catch the faster swimming species which it had not been possible to catch from rowing boats with hand harpoons.

From Norway this second wave of whaling spread throughout the world following a similar route to earlier whaling, but expanding more rapidly than did the earlier whaling. This modern whaling operation reached Newfoundland by 1898 and penetrated the Pacific by 1900. The scene was now set for the last great whale gold-rush, the exploitation of the Antarctic whale stocks. This dates from 1904 when the Norwegian whaler C. A. Larsen opened a whaling station at Grytviken in Cumberland Bay, South Georgia. The success of this operation encouraged other whalers to move into the Antarctic to exploit the large stocks of Blue and Fin Whales found there. Stations were set up, not only on South Georgia where a British company operated at Leith Harbour, but also in the South Orkney, South Shetland and Deception Islands. The Southern Ocean rapidly became the centre of whaling in the world, and between 1910 and 1925 50% of the world's annual catch was taken from these waters.

Because all of this early whaling was carried out in the Falklands Island Dependency, it occurred within the territorial waters controlled by the Government of the United Kingdom. By 1908 the British had instituted the first practical controls on harvesting. They imposed a licensing system and protection of females with calves. All parts of the whale were to be used, not just the valuable blubber, and a tax was levied on every barrel of whale oil produced. In order to avoid these restrictions attempts were made to develop a factory ship which could operate at sea. The breakthrough came in 1925 when the factory ship *Lancing*, fitted with a stern slipway, operated successfully for the first time in Antarctic waters. With this development the whalers were freed from the restriction to areas where they could take their whales ashore.

Consequently, whaling in Antarctic waters began to build up rapidly; in 1925–26 there were two floating factory ships at work with nine catchers, while in the 1930–31 season 41 factory ships operated with 205 catchers and they caught sone 37 500 whales. In the 1936–37 season catches peaked at 46 000 whales. There was a hiatus during World War II, and the catches never again reached their pre-war levels, although from 1947–48 to 1964–65 catches were maintained in the vicinity of 30 000 whales a year. After this the catches fell off very rapidly as a result of both depletion of the stocks and the adoption of more conservative management measures.

The history of whaling catches in the Southern Ocean is shown in Fig. 16.4. Initially, the shore-based stations were able to take numbers of Humpback Whales which were close to the land around the island bases. As the numbers of this species were reduced the catchers tended to go further afield taking the largest whales which they came across, the Blue and Fin Whales. The Blue Whale grows to the largest size (30 m long and 160 tonnes total weight), and was the most valuable to the industry. As the catches of this species declined the whalers increasingly turned their attention to the Fin Whale, which originally was the most abundant whale in the Southern Ocean. Fin Whales formed much the largest part of the catch from the middle 1930s until the early 1960s, after which their numbers collapsed very rapidly.

Sei Whales were almost entirely ignored by the whalers as long as the larger species were available in sufficient numbers. However, as the numbers of the larger whales declined the industry attempted to maintain its profitability by increasing the amount of meat produced from the carcasses with a lesser emphasis on oil production. This resulted in the catching of greater numbers of Sei Whales, but their stocks were reduced rather rapidly when more than 60 000 Sei Whales were caught in four seasons in the mid-1960s. Since 1972 the catches of Sei Whales have been limited by quotas. The relatively small Minke Whales were ignored until 1971–72, but since that time they formed numerically the largest component of the southern baleen whale catch. From about this time on the catch regulated by quotas remained fairly steady at about 5000 to 7000 whales.

While the catches of Sperm Whales in Antarctic waters have always been of secondary importance to the industry they have nevertheless formed a significant component of the total operation. In the ten seasons before the 1979–80 season the catch of Sperm Whales averaged 3211. This compares with average annual catches of 4393 and 4622 Sperm Whales in the two preceding decades respectively. Catches of Killer Whales in the Antarctic have generally been small. The USSR took 110 in the 1958–59 season,

Table 16.2. *Population estimates of Antarctic baleen whale stocks (original and recent), with total Antarctic catches from 1920 to end of commercial whaling*

Species	Original stock size	Recent stock size estimate	Date to which estimate applies	Total catch since 1920
Blue	150 000	8000 (total)	1965–78	307 638
Fin	750 000	70 000 (total)	1965–78	664 248
Sei	?250 000	15 000 (exploitable)	1979	177 811
Right	?not known	3000 (total)	1965–78	Not known
Minke	?not known	436 000	1978–84	106 188
Humpback	90–100 000	40 000 (total)	1965–78	36 504

Modified from Chapman (1988).

while from 1969 to 1978 the average was 24 per season. However, when the catch of Sperm Whales was reduced to zero in the 1979–80 season, the USSR caught 916 Killer Whales.

Table 16.2 gives the original and present estimates of the stocks of whales in the Southern Ocean. A century ago the initial numbers of baleen whales feeding in the Antarctic waters during the summer totalled about one million with a biomass of about 43 million tonnes. By the 1930's the population had been reduced to about 340 000. The current biomass is about one sixth of the initial stock, about 7 million tonnes. In 1932 the average weight of all species of whale caught was about 66 tonnes; in 1936, 56 tonnes; in 1950, 46 tonnes; in 1970, 23 tonnes; and in 1978 about 20 tonnes. The one inescapable fact which emerges from the above account of whaling is that in every case it has caused a severe decline of the exploited stocks. In the next section we shall explore the attempts which were made to regulate the industry, and the reasons for the failure to prevent the overexploitation of most of the whale stocks.

16.5.2 The International Whaling Commission and the regulation of the Antarctic whaling industry

The reduction which occurred in the Blue Whale population, and the past history of the depletion of whales in the Northern Hemisphere led to serious consideration of methods for conserving Antarctic whales. In 1931 the First International Convention for the Regulation of Whaling was negotiated. While this provided for the protection of Right Whales, the protection of females with calves, the licensing of whaling vessels, and the collection of statistics it was only partially successful. The next important step was taken in 1937, when the first so-called International Whaling Convention was agreed to by most of the countries actively involved in whaling. This added the Grey Whale to the protected list, established a defined season for whaling in the Southern Hemisphere, and introduced size limits for several species. This convention, which had a life of only one season, was renewed for 1938, and was extended to include the protection of the Southern Hemisphere Humpback Whales from pelagic, but not from coastal whaling and the establishment of a so-called sanctuary area in the Pacific sector of the Southern Ocean. In addition, the industry itself set up working agreements between most of the countries concerned to limit the number of whales taken and the level of oil production.

After a series of conferences held between 1945 and 1946 the International Convention for the Regulation of Whaling was signed in Washington, USA by 15 countries. The convention recognized in its preamble 'the interest of the nations of the world in safe-guarding for future generations the great natural resources represented by the whale stocks'. It also stated that the purpose of the convention was to provide for the proper conservation of whale stocks, and thus make possible the orderly development of the whaling industry. The convention set up the International Whaling Commission as an executive body to formulate regulatory measures and with the responsibility for their implementation. The commission met for the first time in 1949, and the membership has now expanded to over 40 member governments. A scientific committee was established to advise the commission. Since 1960 the scientific committee has been heavily involved in stock assessment and this has been reflected in the notable increase in the part played in the work of the committee by scientists specializing in population dynamics.

The history of the commission and the problems which it has encountered have been documented by Mackintosh (1965), Chapman (1973), McHugh, (1974), Gulland (1976), and Allen (1980). In spite of its good intentions the Commission was unable to prevent the decreases which occurred in the exploited stocks of Antarctic whales. Although an over-all limit to the pelagic catch was established, there were three short-comings in the methods used (Gulland, 1976): 1. it was expressed as a total quota without separate quotas for the different stocks; 2. the quota was slightly too high but there were no provisions for an easy revision; and, 3. no arrangements were made for the allocation of quotas to the individual whaling countries. The quota was set in terms of Blue Whale Units (BWUs), one Blue Whale being equivalent to two Fin Whales, six Sei Whales, and two-and-a-

half Humpback Whales. Thus, the whalers were free to pursue whichever whales were the most profitable regardless of the state of the stocks. Whalers which came across one of the few remaining Blue Whales would pursue and capture it, because Blue Whales were the most cost-effective species. Thus, while the whalers increased their catch of the smaller and more abundant Fin and Sei Whales they at the same time continued to inflict further damage on the already depleted stocks of Blue Whales. As a result the Blue Whales were being caught long after the majority of the scientists had demanded their protection. In face of the declining numbers of Blue and Humpback Whales the commission took additional measures to protect them, mainly through reducing the length of the open season for these species. Ultimately, both species were so reduced in numbers that they were given complete protection.

The lack of any division of the total quota between countries soon led to economic difficulties. Initially the open season was four months long, but as the various countries attempted to increase their quotas by increasing their fleets, the quota was reached increasingly earlier, and the open season was reduced to 64 days. This state of affairs could not continue, and in 1961, the whaling countries met outside the auspices of the IWC to divide the spoils. Japan got 33%, Norway 32%, the Soviet Union 20%, Great Britain 9%, and the Netherlands 6%.

In addition to the fatal errors made by the commission in not adopting both species quotas and national quotas, the commission was deprived of real 'teeth' for most of its existence by the provision which enabled any country to enter an objection to proposed amendments to the conservation measures within a 90-day period following the annual meeting. A nation doing this was then not bound by the amendment. This built-in veto made it almost impossible to implement any serious conservation measures during the 1950s. As Chapman (1973) has pointed out the combination of the Blue Whale quota system, together with the lack of national quotas and the requirement for unanimous decisions rendered the commission virtually impotent during ten crucial years.

Management of whale stocks, as with most other marine resources, is based on the concept that each stock has a natural rate of increase through births and a rate of natural mortality which balance to reach an equilibrium level. Reduction of the number of whales in a particular stock leads to compensating changes in the recruitment rate through earlier maturity and increased pregnancy rates, so that the stock can rebuild to its previous level. Once the carrying capacity of the habitat niche occupied by the stock is reached, recruitment declines through factors such as food limitation so that the stock numbers stabilize once again.

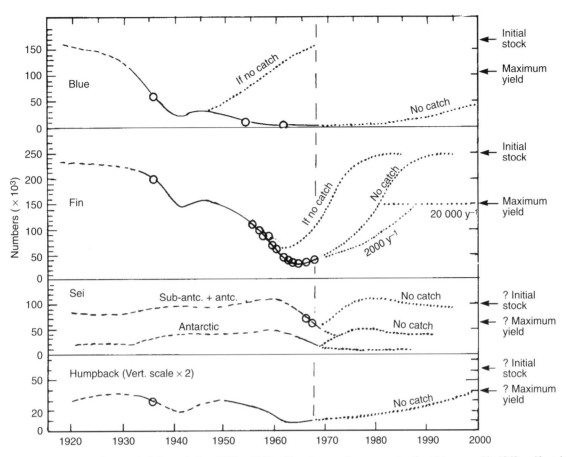

Fig. 16.5. Estimates of whale stock sizes 1920 to 1968, with estimates of recovery rates if catching ceased in 1968, or if catching had ceased at an earlier date. Based on Mackintosh (1970)

In 1974 the International Whaling Commission adopted in principle the so-called 'new management procedure', which consisted of formalized rules to be applied by the commission on the basis of advice by the scientific committee, and what the catch limits should be for those stocks whose exploitation would be permitted.

These rules divided the stocks into three categories:

1. Initial management stocks, which may be reduced in a controlled manner to the maximum sustainable yield (MSY) level, or some optimum which is determined;.
2. Sustainable management stocks, which are to be maintained at or near the MSY level (or optimum as this is defined);
3. Protection stocks, which are below the maximum sustained management level and which should be fully protected.

This strategy, based on the theory of maximum sustainable yield, was not entirely successful for many reasons. Firstly, the scientific knowledge of the stocks has been inadequate, and secondly, the models which were developed have been less precise than has proved necessary to

operate the policy. The whole approach presupposed that the number of animals in each whale stock was the direct and only cause of changes in their vital parameters, through density-dependent responses to food availability. As we shall discuss later this approach is inadequate due to interspecies interactions where the whales share a common food resource, and other ecosystem variables, such as the responses of other krill consumers such as seals, birds, fish and cephalopods. One positive result of the new approach was that more and more stocks were found to be below the theoretical MSY level, so that they were given total protection.

16.5.3 The economics of the whaling industry
The question arises as to why did the whalers kill the goose that laid the golden egg? Why were they not interested in conserving the whale stocks so that a sustainable yield of whales could be maintained into the indefinite future? Fig. 16.5. illustrates what might have happened to the stocks if conservation measures has been implemented early enough, and what the sustainable catch might have been. The answers to the above questions are to be found in the economics of the whale fisheries and its

influence on industry policy, and the fact that the whalers were exploiting a common resource which nobody owned Chapman (1980). The demise of pelagic whaling to some degree parallels the collapse of other marine resources such as that of the anchoveta fishery in Peru in the early 1970s.

Fishing, like any other industry, is a function of cost–benefit balance. With a freely competitive and completely unregulated fishery, a balance will eventually be struck between the biological productivity of the fishery and the rate of harvesting. At first when the stocks are abundant and fishermen few, the profits are very high. These high profits attract further fishermen, who deplete the stocks and cause the prices to fall. At the balance, when the stocks are at the so-called bionomic equilibrium, there will be zero profits, and no incentive either for further fishermen to join or for greater effort by those already involved. This was the situation which was reached for many of the fisheries for the whale stocks.

One of the major reasons why this happened and why the whaling nations bitterly resisted demands to cut back on the catch quotas, or for a moratorium, relates to the high-risk and high-discount rate of the industry. Maintenance costs in the industry are very high and deterioration of the equipment in the Antarctic environment is severe. As in any business the whalers' investment decisions would be based on the desire to maximize the present value of the profits that they would obtain. There would be a minimum expected rate of return, usually based on the 'opportunity cost' which could be obtained by putting the money into some equally risky alternative investment, and the owner would discount any future profit by the expected rate of return. The discount rate takes into account such things as the cost of borrowing money and the likely inflation, as well as the risks of the business, and this becomes particularly important in investment decisions to exploit natural resources.

The whaling industry never was, is not, and never would be really interested in sustainable-yield exploitation, simply because it makes no economic sense. When considering the exploitation of a stock of whales the industry could choose between milking and mining, between conserving the asset for ever and harvesting only the sustainable yield, or selling off the whole resource for an early profit which could be invested in some other venture. The crucial point is the relationship between the rate of return on whales versus the rate of return on money. If whale multiplied more rapidly than money then milking would be better than mining. Whale stocks, however, reproduce slowly, certainly less than 4% per annum, while monetary investments often provide considerably in excess of 10%. As long as this is true conservation will not pay.

16.5.4 Current status of the Antarctic whale stocks.

Most assessments of whale population sizes until recently have relied on information obtained from commercial whale fisheries, and in particular, catch per unit-effort (CPUE). However there have been difficulties in relating changes in CPUE to changes in whale abundance (Gambell, 1989) and the situation has been further complicated by the cessation of commercial whaling in Antarctic waters in 1988. Thus in recent years emphasis has been placed on dedicated sighting surveys. At the 1989 meeting of the International Whaling Commission the scientific committee presented estimates for the various whale stocks, including a series of new estimates of abundance for the large whales in the Antarctic (south of 60° S) from eight years of the International Decade of Cetacean Research sighting cruises. These estimates in comparison with the 1970 estimates are shown in Table 16.3.

Table 16.3 *Estimates of whale stocks south of 60° S by the International Whaling Commission in comparison with 1970 estimates*

	1970	1989
Blue Whales	8000	453
Humpback Whales	3000	4047
Fin Whales	100000	2096
Sei Whales	37000	1498
Sperm Whales	950000	3059

From IWC (1990)

These figures were substantially lower than previously thought. In addition Minke Whale Antarctic populations (95% confidence limits) have been estimated at being 760 396 (±132 220) (IWC, 1990).

From the data listed above it is clear that the populations of Humpback and particularly Minke Whales have been increasing at a higher rate than those of other species. Surveys of migrating Humpack Whales have been conducted off the Australian east coast since 1981 (Bryden *et al.*, 1990). These whales are from the Area V stock which was formerly heavily exploited. The estimated number of migrating whales over May to August in 1981, 1982, 1986 and 1987 were 356, 396, 778 and 790 respectively, representing an increase of 130 to 140% over five years, or an annual net increase of approximately 14%. The total numbers are underestimated, as recent evidence has shown that the migration continued beyond the period of observation (Paterson & Paterson, 1989). Estimates collected by the International Whaling Commission (1990) for the annual rate of increase of whale stocks which have been protected for at least 20 years include five for Humpback Whale stocks, which ranged from 4.8 to 13.8%. Bryden *et al*'s estimate is at the higher end of this range and it is clear that the Area V population is increasing rapidly

16.5.5 The future of Antarctic whales

Currently there is a moratorium on whaling. The question then arises as to whether at some time in the future whaling could be resumed, and if so what controls would be applied to the fishery. Much will depend on the future of the International Whaling Commission. Despite all the criticisms that have been levelled at it the IWC still provides the one organization which would be in a position to develop the necessary models and mechanisms for the rational exploitation of the stocks. The best thing which could happen would be for the nations which were formerly involved in Antarctic whaling to maintain a strong and indefinite commitment to the commission, or some renegotiated international body, and for all the current non-signatory whaling nations to be brought into the orbit of the commisssion.

While, taken as a whole, the post-war history of whaling conservation in Antarctica has been a failure, Gulland (1976) points out that in spite of the disasters which befell the IWC it did have some real achievements. While some species did become commercially extinct, the Right, Blue and Humpback Whales have been protected and do appear to be increasing. The Fin Whale was rescued from commercial extinction, and maintained at a level where a small sustainable harvest was maintained for a period, while the Sei Whale stocks were kept at a level giving a maximum sustainable yield.

With the current moratorium and the possibility of its extension the populations will recover to some extent. However, at present we can only guess as to what the level of recovery will be and it is fairly certain that the species ratio will never be the same as it was before exploitation. In addition, if an intensive krill fishery were to develop the recovery plateau could be much lower than anticipated. The question then arises as to whether the preservationist ideal of totally protected populations for the indefinite future will be realized. Given human history this is doubtful. The pressures of human population increase, climatic changes and uncertainties of food crops as a result of such changes, will probably dictate that some form of whaling will occur in the future. One of the problems which would be faced by any regulatory body is that the cessation of whaling will have had an effect on the acquisition of data, and in particular of information concerning the manner in which the stocks may be changing in relation under universal protection. The relationship of whale management to that of managing the Southern Ocean living resources as a whole will be discussed in Chapter 18.

17

Ecosystem changes resulting from resource exploitation

17.1 Introduction

In the previous chapter the impact of exploitation of the stocks of the living resource of krill, fish, seals, and whales was considered. Here, we will consider changes in species attributes such as nutritional condition, growth rates, reproductive parameters and ecosystem dynamics which have resulted from the changed relationships between predators and their prey. As we have seen in the previous chapters ecosystems are dynamic entities with complex relationships between their component parts. In the Southern Ocean ecosystem krill is a dominant prey species at the base of the food web, intimately affecting species groups such as whales, seals, birds, fish and squid. From the data discussed previously on krill consumption by predators it is evident that krill are fundamental to the functioning of the Southern Ocean ecosystem.

Food webs are dynamic with the various components interacting through competition and predation within the constraints imposed by the physical environment and the processes of primary production and decomposition. It is into this dynamic system that humans have entered as a commercial predator (Fig. 17.1). Before the exploitation of baleen whales, there would have been significant competition between krill-eating species and it can be assumed that reduced whale populations would allow greater use of the krill resource by their competitors. This potentially could lead to increased populations of seals, seabirds, squid and those baleen whale populations which had not been exploited. Evidence for this will be discussed below.

17.2 Ecosystem changes following the decline in whale stocks

The current hypotheses concerning the present status of the Antarctic marine ecosystem include three main assumptions:

1. As a result of reduced baleen whale stocks, krill availability increased.
2. Non-exploited krill predators responded functionally and numerically to the increase in krill availability.

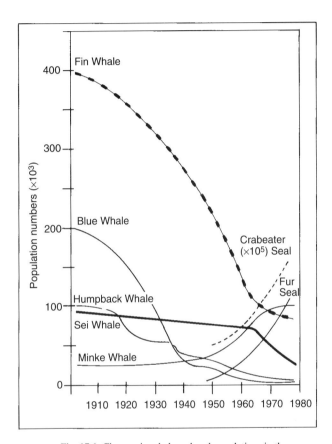

Fig. 17.1. Changes in whale and seal populations in the Southern Ocean from 1900 to 1980. Based on information in the Southern Ocean Convention Workshop on the Management of Antarctic Marine Living Organisms (1980).

3. A new carrying capacity and community composition developed.

Before the advent of humans, a balance would have been achieved between the competing species of consumers (and their predators) within the undisturbed ecosystem, such that each population remained at or near its asymptote for the natural environmental pressures and restraints to which it was exposed. In such a situation the recruitment coefficient (r) would approximate the natural mortality coefficient (M) so that the population fluctuated about a stable level (Anon., 1985a).

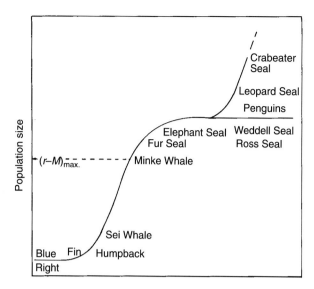

Fig. 17.2. Present relative positions of major consumers in the Antarctic marine ecosystem on a population growth curve. Redrawn from Anon (1985a).

If there were a long-term trend changing the environmental pressures and constraints, those populations which were subject to greater pressures and restraints would be exposed to higher mortality and/or lower recruitment such that r–M being negative would bring about a decline in the population, while a population under reduced pressure or restraints would have a positive value for r–M, resulting in an increase in the population. This would result in adjustments between the competing species such that a fresh balance, possibly in different proportions to that existing previously, would result.

The removal this century of nearly 84% of Antarctic baleen whale biomass (Laws, 1977b) may have temporarily reduced competition among krill predators. As the populations of baleen whales were reduced, competition for food between the remaining whales and other krill consumers was eased and the resulting improved nutrition would result in faster growth, earlier maturity, higher reproductive rates (Laws, 1977b), and the potential for better survival of the young. In such a situation the difference between recruitment (r) and natural mortality (M) would become positive enabling the populations not being hunted to increase exponentially in the form

$$N = N\, e^{(r-M)T}$$

An estimate of the current relative positions of the major consumers on the sigmoid population growth curve are indicated in Fig. 17.2 (Anon., 1985*a*). In absolute terms the vertical scale will be different for each species, but the figure nevertheless illustrates the relative conditions of the populations at the present time. Evidence in support

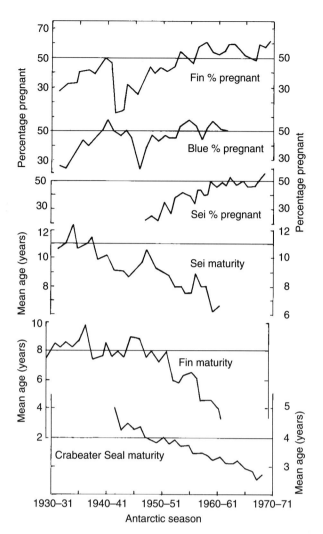

Fig. 17.3. Collective evidence for changes in pregnancy rates and age at sexual maturity in female Fin, Blue, and Sei Whales and decreasing age at sexual maturity in Crabeater Seals (after Laws, 1977a, incorporating data from Lockyer, 1972, 1974; Gambell, 1973: Laws, 1977b).

of the assumptions upon which the figure was based and for increased growth rates and pregnancy rates will now be considered.

17.2.1 Whales

Mackintosh (1942), Laws (1960a, 1961, 1977a,b) Lockyer (1972, 1974) and Gambell (1973, 1975, 1976b) all noted that shifts in growth rates, pregnancy rates and age of sexual maturity in seals and in Blue and Sei Whales have a high correlation with whaling activities in the Southern Ocean. They considered that these changes implied that the whale stocks before exploitation were food-limited and perhaps close to maximum population levels. Under such conditions growth may have slowed down and sexual maturity delayed. With the decline in whale stocks, more krill would presumably have been available to the remaining whales, allowing for faster

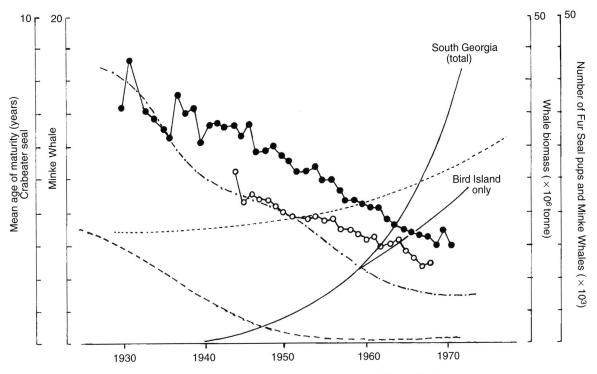

Fig. 17.4. Interspecific correlations between krill feeding animals and baleen whale biomass in the Antarctic marine ecosystem. ●—● mean age of Minke Whale sexual maturity (Kato, 1983); ○—○ mean age Crabeater Seal sexual maturity (Laws, 1977a); –•–•– total baleen whale biomass (Gambell, 1975); ——— Blue Whale biomass (Gambell, 1975); —— number of Fur Seal pups (Laws, 1977a) ---- number of Minke Whales. Redrawn from Bengtson (1985); after Kato (1983).

growth, higher pregnancy rates and earlier sexual maturity (Fig. 17.3).

Mackintosh (1942) was the first to suggest that pregnancy rates of female baleen whales in the Southern Hemisphere were increasing. His figures showed that pregnancy rates in Blue Whales increased from about 48% in the period 1935–31 to about 66% during the 1932–41 period. He also observed an increase in Fin Whale pregnancy rates from 65% to 80% in the same period. Similar percentages were given by Laws (1961) who calculated that the Fin Whale pregnancy rates rose from 46% to 76% between the years 1925 and 1930. Later analyses by Gambell (1973, 1975, 1976b) confirmed these results and gave data for other species. However, Mizroch (1980, 1981a, 1981b, 1983) has argued that the data may be suspect because of the high natural variability of pregnancy rates and the pooling of data across months.

Age at the attainment of sexual maturity is another indicator parameter which has been examined in the baleen whales of the Southern Ocean. On the basis of several analyses, including the transition phase in the ear plugs, counts of *corpora albicanta*, and the percentage of mature individuals within age classes, a decline in the age at sexual maturity has been suggested for several baleen whale species (Lockyer, 1972, 1974; Laws, 1977a,b;

Masaki, 1979). Both Gambell (1973) and Masaki (1977) found evidence of decreases in the age of sexual maturity in Sei Whales from about 12 years to six years over the period from 1930–31 to 1960–61. Direct study of the reproductive status of Fin Whales compiled in the mid-1960s indicated an age of sexual maturity of six to seven years for both sexes (Ohsumi, 1972). Kato (1983) evaluated trends in the age at sexual maturity of Minke Whales using all three methods. He found a similar decrease in the age of sexual maturity, which he attributed to reduced competition with harvested whales and a higher availability of krill (Fig. 17.4). Again, like the pregnancy rate increase, these results have been questioned (Cooke & de la Mare, 1983). This controversy as to whether the observed trends reflect true population conditions or artifacts of sampling, analysis and interpretation is as yet unresolved, although the weight of evidence would appear to support the hypothesis that the changes are real.

Such dramatic increases in growth rates must involve considerably increased feeding following the depletion of Blue and Fin Whale stocks. This illustrates a density dependent response by the remaining whales. Surprisingly, in spite of the evidence for an increase in pregnancy rates and a decline in the age of sexual maturity the expected corresponding increase in recruitment rates has not been confirmed by direct estimates. In fact some analyses suggest a decline in recruitment. Nevertheless, normal population theory would suggest that the density dependent responses discussed above would occur, since a species would otherwise very quickly be driven to extinction by any random decline in its numbers. However in the case of the southern Minke Whales there has been an increase in abundance prior to the onset of its exploitation. This is reinforced by evidence from the age distribution of the initial stocks, which suggest enhanced recruitment rates substantially exceeding the estimated natural mortality (IWC, 1979). It has been estimated that the Minke Whale population which lay between 172 000 and 225 000 in 1960 had risen to about 323 000 in 1976 (S. G. Brown & Lockyer, 1984). On the other hand, although the Australian populations of the Sperm Whale were reduced to such an extent that complete protection was imposed, there is little direct evidence of any changes having occurred in their reproductive characteristics compared with those found in baleen whales (Gambell, 1985).

E. Mitchell (1975) has speculated that following the reduction of Southern Right Whales in southern waters, Sei Whales extended their range to utilize food resources previously unavailable to them due to competition from Right Whales. There is also evidence that Minke Whales have also extended their range.

17.2.2 Seals
Seals which utilize krill may have also responded to declining whale stocks (see Fig. 17.4). The rapid growth in the populations of Antarctic Fur Seals discussed in Chapter 8 may have been due in part to an increased availability of krill (Laws, 1977a,b; Payne, 1977; Croxall & Prince, 1979). However, it is difficult to separate the effects of potentially increased krill availability from the recovery of the Fur Seal populations from over-exploitation in the early 1800s. On the other hand, increases in the populations of Crabeater and Leopard Seals may be more directly related to the decline in whale populations. Based on Law's (1977a) data on Crabeater Seal survival and pregnancy rates Beddington & Grenfell (1980) modelled Crabeater Seal populations and concluded that the average annual increase between 1947 and 1979 was about 3% per annum. On the basis of the larger data set then available they concluded that both the pregnancy rate and the annual survival rate were both higher than originally assumed and considered that a maximal annual rate of increase in recent years of 7.5% was not unlikely. Data suggest that the Crabeater Seal population was *c.* 5 million up to 1950, with maximal rates of increase in the 1970s, deceleration in the 1980s, which would result in a

population of *c.* 50 million by the end of the century. The Fur Seal, which has been increasing at a rate of 15–17%, is projected to reach a level of four million. Laws (1984a) assumes a similar rate of increase (7.5%) for the Leopard Seal as for the Crabeater. Projected backwards and forwards from 1972 this suggests that the total population may have been about 60 000 up to 1955, 440 000 in 1982, and would reach about 600 000 by the year 2000.

Laws (1977b) used tooth back-calculation (back-calculating age at maturity evidenced by the transition in rates of cementum deposition) in Crabeater Seals to demonstrate a decrease in the age at sexual maturity from approximately 4.5 years in 1945 to 2.5 years in the late 1960s (Fig. 17.3). However, Bengston & Siniff (1981) who examined a small sample of seals taken in 1977 near the South Shetland Islands could find no clear evidence of a decrease in the age of sexual maturity. Bengtson & Laws (1984) further examined larger samples of Crabeater Seals of both sexes and all age classes collected in 13 seasons from 1964 to 1982, in order to test the hypothesis that the presumed increase in seal, fish and seabird populations in the early 1970s which followed the decline in whale stocks should have resulted in a reversal of the declining age of sexual maturity. They demonstrated that the tooth back-calculation technique used in earlier studies produced trends that were artifacts of sampling. However direct evaluation of ovarian *corpora* did show an increasing trend in the age of sexual maturity as predicted (Bengtson & Laws, 1984). Crabeater Seal age at sexual maturity was found to have increased steadily from about 2.5 years in 1962 to over four years in 1976. Hence it appears that the age of sexual maturity in Crabeater Seals fell and rose in response to the presumed availability of krill.

17.2.3 Birds
Evidence of increases in bird populations in response to changes in krill availability is somewhat inconclusive. While Prévost (1981) doubts that seabird populations have increased in response to the reduction in whale numbers Conroy & White (1973) and Conroy (1975) presented information which suggested that populations of King, Macaroni, Adélie, Chinstrap and Gentoo Penguins have increased in the Scotia Arc area during the period of commercial whaling. Data on more recent population counts and breeding success of birds on South Georgia, Signy and Bird Islands indicate increases in King, Emperor, Macaroni, Adélie, Chinstrap and Gentoo Penguins in the Scotia Arc region (Croxall, 1984) indicating that the trend noted in the early 1979s has continued.

Changes in food availability and competition have presumably led to a new balance in the biomass composition of the community. Tables 5.10 and 5.12 in Chapter 5 give

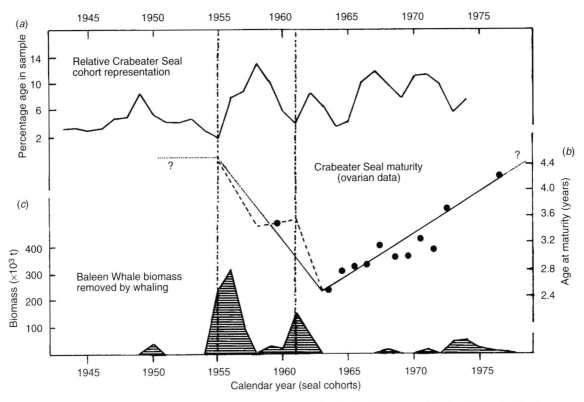

Fig. 17.5. (*a*) Relative representation of seal cohorts. The percentage distribution of 7–21 year olds plotted for each collection year. Means of these values were calculated for each calendar year, yielding the curve shown. (*b*) Age at maturity as estimated from ovarian material. Mean values for 2–7 year olds from each collection year plotted by mean cohort year (4.5 years prior to collection year). Dotted line shows presumed trend of maturity, and dashed line shows alternative trend of decline. (*c*) Baleen whale biomass removed from Area I annually. The following average body size (tonnes) is assumed: Blue, 88; Fin, 50; Humpback, 27; Sei, 18.5; and Minke, 7. Redrawn from Bengtson (1985); after Bengtson & Laws (1984).

estimates of the consumption of krill by the major consumers. As discussed in Chapter 5 while the data for whales, seals and birds are reasonably good, we do not have reliable estimates for fish consumption and no data at all for squid consumption which is probably large. What is certain is that shifts in krill consumption and in the biomass composition of krill consumers have occurred. As some populations have increased there is evidence that in some areas a reversal in the declining age at sexual maturity is taking place, as for example in the Crabeater Seals (Bengtson & Laws, 1984), and that in these areas the populations are stabilizing at a new level. Increases in the populations of competing species (seal and birds, and perhaps some fish and squid populations) may inhibit the recovery of the protected whale stocks (Tranter, 1982). What is clear is that the present community composition of the Southern Ocean marine ecosystem is substantially different from that prior to sealing and whaling. What is less clear is whether this situation can be reversed.

17.3 Potential ecosystem changes which might result from future resource exploitation

For the purposes of considering potential impacts and

conservation strategies Edwards & Heap (1981) believe that it is useful to think of the living resources of the Southern Ocean in terms of three broad levels of population : 1. species in the *low trophic levels*, which form the food base for species in the higher trophic levels (e.g., zooplankton, particularly krill); 2. species at *intermediate trophic levels*, which prey on low trophic levels but are themselves subject to significant predation by the top trophic level (e.g., squid and fish); and 3. species at the *top trophic level*, which prey on levels 1 and 2 but are not themselves subject to significant natural predation (e.g., whales, seals and birds).

It is suggested that the effect of harvesting species which make up the final stages of the food chain (level 3) and are not themselves preyed upon (e.g., whales) is to increase the productivity of other species at the same trophic level (e.g., seals and birds). But the effect on the ecosystem of harvesting species on which predators depend (e.g., krill, level 1, and, possibly to a lesser extent, level 2) is increased competition between the predators for a reduced quantity of prey.

With the current state of knowledge, it is difficult to predict with any certainty the impact that substantial krill harvest would have on the Southern Ocean ecosystem. It could result in: (a) increases in the abundance of competing species, i.e., a shift in trophic relationships from a phytoplankton–krill–marine mammal food chain to a phytoplankton–copepod–fish food chain; (b) interference with the recovery of depleted whale stocks; (c) depletion of dependent populations of seals, birds, fish and squid; and (d) depletion of krill populations.

In the Southern Ocean ecosystem, krill occupy a role identified by Paine (1966) as that of a 'keystone predator' (one which has a dominant influence in structuring the community). Dayton (1972) coined the term 'foundation species' for non-predators, those species at low levels in the food web which contribute in a major way to community structure and function. Species such as krill, through which a significant proportion of the energy and nutrients of an ecosystem flow, represent such a fundamental unit of the system. If they are stressed, the effects on the ecosystem can be more dramatic than when species at higher levels are stressed.

It is unclear as to what level of commercial krill harvesting would significantly affect krill and other species. One possibility is that competition for food among zooplankton would be reduced. However, as detailed in Chapter 5 krill consume only a small proportion of the total phytoplankton production and it would appear that the zooplankton is not food limited. On the other hand, current data are insufficient to judge whether, or at what level, vital parameters of krill, such as recruitment, survival or growth would be affected by an overall reduction in their biomass caused by commercial harvesting. In addition, our lack of understanding of the discreteness of krill stocks (see Chapter 5) does not enable predictions to be made as to how different fishing strategies might affect the stocks. Everson (1981) postulated that significant differences in the potential impacts of commercial fisheries depend on whether krill stocks are continuous or discrete (Table 17.1).

However, it is clear that a substantial reduction in krill biomass is likely to have a direct effect on krill predators. A large-scale commercial harvest of krill would result in a reduction of krill availability and an increase in competition between the various krill consumers. This has occurred in other large-scale commercial pelagic fisheries (e.g., the Californian sardine, *Sardinops sagux*, the peruvian anchovey, *Engraulis ringeus*, and the South African pilchard, *Sardinops ocellatus*, fisheries). Reduced krill availability would probably result in lower growth rates and reproductive rates, and consequently recruitment, of the krill consumers. In a simple model of the joint exploitation of krill and whales Horwood (1981) demonstrated that harvesting of krill decreased whale abun-

Table 17.1. *Postulated effects of an intensive krill fishery in one limited area*

	Krill stock	
	One continuous	Several discrete
On krill (stock parameters)		
(a) Growth	Small	Probably small
(b) Mortality	No change (male)	May change (male) Small (female) Large (female)
(c) Biomass	Small	Significant reduction after start of fishing
On natural consumers		
(a) species linked closely to fishing area (e.g. breeding birds)		
(i) Intensive fishing prior to critical predator period each season	Significant in fishing area elsewhere minimal	Significant: increasing with time to level off eventually
(ii) Intensive fishing during and after critical predator period	Small	Significant in subsequent years
(b) Species not tied to fishing area (e.g. whales)		
(i) Intensive fishing before predator normally present in fishing area	Small overall	Reduced density (i.e. feeding elsewhere)
(ii) Intensive fishing before and after predator present in fishing area	None or slight reduction in density	Slight reduction in short term reduction in long term

From Everson (1981).

dance. Ultimately, significantly lowered krill biomass would result in steady, or even declining, populations of whales, seals, seabirds and other groups.

The degree to which the various krill consumers would be affected by krill fishing would depend upon the species and its ecology (Bengtson, 1984). For example, Gulland (1983a) noted that while all Antarctic baleen whales consume krill, the proportion of krill in the diet of each species varies considerably. Consequently, the degree to which krill availability will affect each species will also vary. Krill predominate in the diet of Blue and Minke Whales, for example, whereas copepods are the principal food of Sei Whales. Sei Whales therefore could be expected to benefit from a change to copepod dominance in the pelagic food chain.

Commercial fisheries also have the potential to change the behaviour and distribution, as well as the density, of krill. Gulland (1983a) has raised the question as to whether dispersion of krill swarms by commercial harvesting might affect the availability of krill to predators to a greater or lesser extent than change in the absolute abundance of krill itself. Longhurst (1981) has discussed the important role of patchy distribution of plankton within marine ecosystems. Lasker (1975, 1980) has demonstrated the inability of larval fish to survive if they cannot locate phytoplankton above a certain threshold density. If euphausiids were dispersed rather than concentrated in layers or swarms, the energetic costs to baleen whales searching for food would be higher than the calorific value of the prey themselves. Nemoto & Harrison (1981) have stressed the importance of dense swarms of euphausiids for baleen whales, noting that although *Euphausia trican-tha* is distributed in high latitudes throughout the Southern Ocean, it is not found in the stomachs of baleen whales presumably because it not accessible to whales in the energy efficient form of dense swarms (Baker, 1959). Similarly, although the copepod *Calanoides acutus* is abundant in Antarctic waters, it is not a prey species for many of the large predators presumably due to its lack of swarming behaviour (Andrews, 1966). However, the likelihood of krill swarms being dispersed, or their behaviour being affected, by fishing activity, and the consequent effect on predators, is not known.

Probably the most important potential impact of krill harvests would be the shifts which might occur in the ecosystem species composition and abundance and the abundance of the predominant species. The impact of removing species from the food web has been examined by several investigators. For example, Menge & Sutherland (1976) and Peterson (1979) have outlined the effects of removing predators from benthic and littoral systems. Well-known documented examples of previous shifts in dominant species include: the collapse of the sardine stocks off the Californian coasts in the 1930s and their replacement by anchovies (Gulland, 1983a); the crash of anchovetta stocks off Peru in 1972 to be replaced by sardines (Idyll, 1973; G. I. Murphy, 1977; Walsh, 1978); declines in herring and mackerel stocks in the North Sea leading to increase in cod, haddock and plaice (Holden, 1978); and the ecological replacement of depleted herring and mackerel stocks in the eastern north Atlantic by the sand lance (*Ammodytes* sp.) (Sherman *et al.*, 1981). As we have seen the perturbation induced by commercial whaling has resulted in a change in the composition of the dominant mammal species. However, the degree to which it may again be approaching a steady state is not known.

18

Management of the living resources

18.1 Introduction

The past history of the exploitation of the living resources of the Southern Ocean has led to the severe depletion of the stocks of Fur Seals, many of the whale species and some of the fish stocks. Although the stocks of the Fur Seals have made a remarkable recovery, the extent to which the exploited whale and fish stocks will recover is uncertain. It is unlikely that the seal stocks will be exploited in the foreseeable future and currently a moratorium is in effect on the further harvesting of whales. However, exploitation of both fish and krill is continuing. The fish resources are not large and their exploitation will need to be strictly controlled and limited. Although the krill catches have exceeded 500 000 tonnes on one occasion only there is the potential for considerable expansion, which could well have serious consequences for the Southern Ocean marine ecosystem as a whole.

Traditionally, the management of marine living resources has been conducted with reference to the harvested species alone, being built around the concept of 'unit stock' (Edwards & Hennemuth, 1975). However, it is clear that this single-species approach is not adequate for the ecosystem protection envisaged under the Convention for the Conservation of Antarctic Marine Living Resources. This protection must take into account the interrelations of the biotic components as well as their physical environment. The type of integrated comprehensive plan which makes provision for rationally controlled harvesting of the component species cannot be achieved by the conventional single-species maximum sustainable yield (MSY) approach (Laevastu & Favourite, 1981). In the succeeding sections in this chapter we shall consider what is involved in the ecosystem approach to the management of the living resources of the Southern Ocean.

18.2 The Convention on the Conservation of Antarctic Marine Living Resources

The fisheries Convention on the Conservation of Antarctic Marine Living Resources which entered into force on 7 April 1982 was in many ways the outcome of the work of the SCAR Group of Specialists on the Living Resources of the Southern Ocean and the BIOMASS Programme (Knox, 1984). As is usual in such international fisheries agreements the convention established two main institutions: a commission charged with carrying out its objectives and a scientific committee charged with providing advice to the commission. The convention is unique in that in the preamble to the convention recognizes 'the importance of safeguarding . . . the integrity of the ecosystem and the seas surrounding Antarctica'. The objectives recognize the need to ensure the continued health of individual species of Antarctic marine organisms and defines the rational use of the living resources as actions that will not disturb the ecosystem's balance. The area covered by the Convention is shown in Fig. 16.3; it covers approximately 8% of the world ocean and the northern boundary is the approximate position of the Antarctic Convergence. The structure of the convention and its subsidiary bodies is depicted in Fig. 18.1.

Because there were limited data available on the status of Antarctic stocks and species interactions the scientific committee initially set out to develop a programme of commercial fisheries data collection and analysis, as well as directed ecological research, to obtain the necessary information. A number of working groups were established:

- Informal Group on the Long-term Programme of the Work of the Scientific Committee
- Working Group on Fish Stock Assessment
- Working Group on Krill
- Working Group on the CCAMLR Ecosystem Monitoring Programme

The Working Group on Fish Stock Assessment regularly reviews the catch and effort statistics and the size and age composition of the commercial and research catches. One of the major problems encountered has been that attempts to provide such advice 'were being regularly and substantially undermined by the failure to provide data in a timely manner' (SC-CCAMLR, 1990a). This is a situation which must be rectified. The commission has acted in many instances on the recommendations of the scientific committee but in others it has not acted

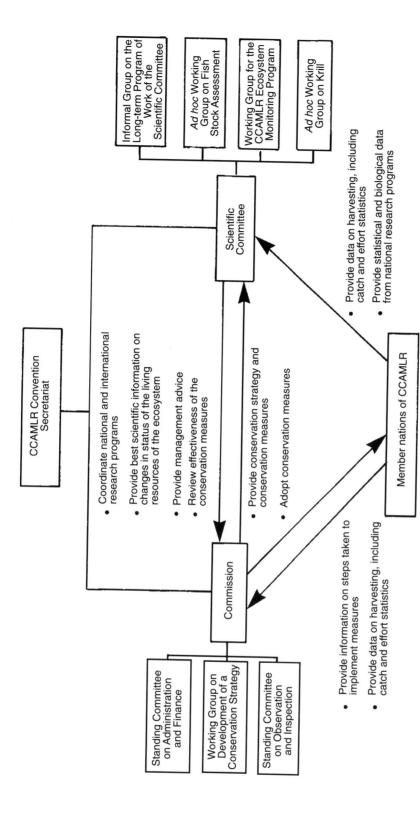

Fig. 18.1. Organizational structure of the Convention on the Conservation of Antarctic Marine Living Resources. After Sherman & Ryan (1988).

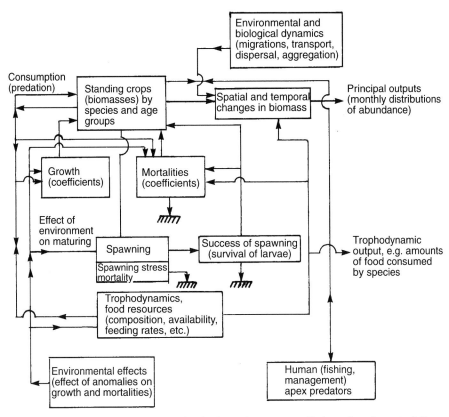

Fig. 18.2. Scheme of principal processes and interactions in the marine ecosystem. Redrawn from Laevastu & Favourite (1981).

on them or delayed their implementation. This is partly due to the fact that the commission's decisions are arrived at by consensus not by a majority decision. The third meeting of the commission in 1984 provided the first conservation measures for the depleted stocks of finfish. The fourth meeting in 1985 followed initial mesh-regulation measures for aiding the recovery of fish stocks with the adoption of more stringent regulations prohibiting all directed fishing for the bottom-living species of Antarctic cod, *Notothenia rossii*, in the waters of South Georgia, the South Orkneys and the Antarctic Peninsula. The fifth meeting in 1986 adopted conservation measures to protect for the severely depleted Antarctic cod, and permitting the commission to set catch limitations as a management technique. The sixth meeting in 1987 established new conservation measures to address the serious depletion of fish stocks. Three measures of significance were taken for the first time – an overall total allowable catch for each species (TACs which have been set annually since then), a reporting system and a closed season.

The CCAMLR represents a significant milestone in the evolution of a more holistic approach to the conservation and management of marine living resources (Southern Ocean Convention Workshop, 1980; Sherman & Ryan, 1988). It is a young convention, which is still in the process of coming to grips with this task, but the indications are that it has been operating more smoothly and efficiently each year. The conservation measures instituted so far are proof that it is able to reach important and difficult decisions. It is clear that the difficulties involved in implementing the ecosystem approach will require more and new research. In view of the history of marine living resource depletion in most seas CCAMLR in its development represents a new approach to management which will be followed with great interest.

18.3 Ecosystem approach to the management of the living resources of the Southern Ocean.

While the single-species approach can have some validity for species in the top trophic level, such as whales and seals, even then there are several risks and problems associated with such an approach (Edwards & Hennemuth, 1975). These have been listed in The Southern Ocean Convention Workshop on the Management of Antarctic Marine Living Resources (1980):

1. There are often problems associated with the data being noisy, inadequate, or simply not available.
2. As the harvested population changes to new densities, its various life-history parameters

change, affecting its ability to recover from environmental disturbance.

3. The interplay between the dynamic behaviour of the population and the level of harvesting will depend on the details of the population's recruitment curve, which in turn depends on the life-history strategy of the species. Seal recruitment curves vary widely and are, for example, very different from those for whales and krill. Furthermore, the recruitment curve for krill is as yet little understood.

4. Compounding the above problems is the fact that many populations (such as krill swarms) are distributed patchily, so that yields cannot be assumed to be simply linearly proportional to fishing effort and stock density. Studies of herring populations harvesting curves which incorporate the effects of patchiness are likely to generate systems with more than one equilibrium point as well as exhibiting the potential for sudden collapse under harvesting.

5. The recruitment of new cohorts into adult, sexually mature populations involves substantial lag times, which add an extra complication to population dynamics.

All the difficulties and problems outlined above also apply to multi-species/multi-trophic-level fisheries, but in addition the system interactions introduce further complications (Dickie, 1975, 1979).

There are several problems in dealing with static concepts such as MSY when several species are involved. MSY for top-trophic-level species is typically attained by not harvesting the lower levels; MSY for the lower levels is typically achieved by minimizing their natural death rate by eliminating all their predators. Therefore, it is not possible to simultaneously exploit both top and bottom levels for MSY.

There are also considerable problems associated with the trajectories, the change in numbers against time, which the system components are likely to take towards any specified equilibrium point. Predator–prey systems are well known for their cyclic behaviour, especially when the prey populations change on a slower time scale than the predator populations (as is the case with krill).

In addition, many multi-species systems possess several equilibrium or stable states. As a consequence, a disturbed or harvested system can move irreversibly to some new equilibrium state. There are many instances of this in the literature.

The essential feature of the ecosystem approach to be adopted by CCAMLR as detailed in Article II of the convention are:

1. The ecosystem is to be managed in a manner which maintains the ecological relationships between harvested, dependent and competing populations.
2. Management will include the restoration of depleted populations (to a level defined in 3).
3. Management should prevent any harvested populations from falling below a level close to the greatest net annual increment.
4. Management should take into account the indirect impact of harvesting and prevent (or minimize the risk of) changes in the marine ecosystem which are not potentially reversible over one or two decades.

As Gulland (1986) points out the direct implementation of the objectives detailed above will not be easy. For example, item 3 above involves management for stable recruitment, but as we know more about fish populations it has become apparent that it is clear that stable recruitment is comparatively rare in nature. Data on recruitment range from the apparently random (or at least with little discernable patterns) year to year fluctuations over some three orders of magnitude in the North Sea haddock, to the long-term (over many decades) changes between periods of high and low abundance in many clupeoid stocks (Scandanavian herring, Californian sardine). As Gulland (1986) points out, the history of some clupeoid stocks also show that changes can occur, sometimes possibly triggered by over-exploitation, but sometimes due solely to natural events, which are not reversible in 'two or three decades', and that it would be surprising if some elements at least of the Southern Ocean marine ecosystem did not exhibit similar instability and changes which are, in the short term, irreversible.

Gulland (1986) further points out that the objectives, as expressed in the convention, are not intended to be an exposition of scientific realities and the complexities of the Southern Ocean ecosystem, but are largely the result of the difficult negotiations leading up to the agreement on the text of the convention when there were very different views regarding approaches to managing and conserving the Southern Ocean ecosystem, both within and between countries. Consequently, there are a number of problems facing the scientific committee and the commission of CCAMLR in interpreting the precise scientific meaning of portions of the text of the convention.

An ability to manage rationally, and to take into account the indirect impacts of harvesting, implies an ability to predict the effect of perturbing the system. Inevitably this implies *quantitative* prediction. Such quantitative predictions require the construction of a model in which 'species–species', as well as 'human–species' interactions are taken into account explicitly rather than implicity (i.e. a multi-species model). Such a model is dependent upon adequate information for parameters such as the population sizes of the interacting species and the manner in which these sizes have changed and are now changing with time.

The ecosystem approach outlined above requires:

1. An adequate information base.
2. The development of multi-species models.
3. Directed ecological studies.
4. Ecological monitoring.

18.3.1 Information needs

At its 1985 meeting the scientific committee of CCAMLR decided on a long-term programme of work for the committee. It identified a major task as being that of providing information and management advice about a complex ecosystem. In order to accomplish this task the committee must oversee the collection, analysis and reporting of a broad spectrum of data, which would include 'fisheries statistics, biological attributes and status of target and non-target species, characteristics of the physical environment, and ecological relations among living resources and their environment' (CCAMLR, 1985).

18.3.2 Fisheries assessment

A major problem which has faced the scientific committee has been the deficiencies on both access to and the reporting of data on the activities of commercial fishing. Modern fisheries assessment techniques require detailed data on fishing activities and catch characteristics, including data on fishing methods (e.g. trawl characteristics and mesh sizes), fishing locations, catch level, by-catch composition, age and length composition of the catches, etc. For many species and areas of the Southern Ocean such comprehensive data is not available and much of the effort of the scientific committee at its early meetings has gone into the drafting of better procedures for obtaining such information. In particular the lack of information on net selectivity for all Antarctic fish species was emphasized and research on this topic was recommended for high priority.

Another critical area addressed by the Scientific Committee was that of the relationships between krill density and catch per unit effort (CPUE). Recommendations have been made for detailed reporting on krill fishing to include data on the type of vessel, gear used (with detailed information on items such as the effective mouth opening of the trawl, mesh sizes, etc.), tow information (duration, depth, towing speed etc.) and detailed catch records (total catch, approximate species composition, average sizes, etc.).

Gulland (1985) has assessed the current state of knowledge of the population dynamics of the species groups in the Southern Ocean which either have been exploited in the past, are currently being exploited, or have potential for future exploitation. This assessment is summarized below.

18.3.2.1 Whales
Abundance: Good estimates of past abundance, fair estimates of current levels; little chance of estimating trends except over long periods.

Population parameters: Good estimates of past age, growth, mortality, age at maturity, reproductive rate, and fair estimates of natural mortality and of how these other parameters have changed with changes in whale density. Little chance of getting further estimates in the absence of whaling.

18.3.2.2 Seals
Abundance: Fair to good estimates (good locally), and possibility of good estimates of local trends in abundance.

Population parameters: Fair to good estimates of age, growth, reproductive rate, etc. Good chances of reliable monitoring of these parameters in some localities.

18.3.2.3 Birds
Similar to seals.

18.3.2.4 Fish (commercially exploited)
Abundance: Moderate estimates of absolute abundance from surveys, and of relative abundance and of trends from catch per unit effort of commercial trawlers. Moderate to poor estimates of annual recruitment.

Population parameters: Moderate to good estimates of growth and total mortality. Probably sufficiently good estimates of division of total mortality between fishing and natural causes (e.g. by analogy with other species) to construct reasonable yield-per-recruit curves.

18.3.2.5 Fish (others)
Very little information.

18.3.2.6 Squid
Virtually no information other than deduction from consumption by predators.

18.3.2.7 Krill
Abundance: Poor estimates of total abundance; moderate

to good estimates of current abundance in some areas, at least of that part of the population which is in swarms. Moderate to poor chance of studying trends in abundance from commercial catch and effort data (cf. problems with pelagic fish). Estimation from special surveys possible, but likely to be expensive, and with high variance.

Population parameters: Fair estimates of most parameters, though with doubts about aging. Good chances of monitoring future changes except to the extent that commercial fisheries or scientific nets are selective.

18.3.3 Ecosystem dynamics

The convention requires that the fisheries in the convention area be conducted so as to: 1. maintain the ecological relationships between harvested, dependent, and related populations of the Antarctic marine fauna; 2. take into account the indirect impacts of harvesting; 3. ensure that depleted populations are restored to a level close to that which ensures the greatest annual increment; and 4. prevent changes, or minimize the risk of changes, in the marine ecosystem which are not potentially reversible over two or three decades. This presupposes that there is a good understanding of the dynamics of the Southern Ocean ecosystem.

One of the key questions which will need to be addressed is whether the rate of recovery of the whale stocks, or the level which would be reached by such recovery, would be affected by different levels of krill harvesting. In order to provide answers to the above, two sets of questions need to be addressed (Gulland, 1985).

First, we need to know what parameters (age at sexual maturity, percentage of females pregnant, juvenile mortality, etc.) of which whale stocks are affected by which changes in krill stocks (abundance, density at particular times and in particular areas), and whether changes are simple (e.g. linear with krill density), or occur at critical levels. There is evidence from some of the more realistic models of the dynamics of large mammal populations (Fowler & Smith, 1987) that the relations between parameter values and population density may be non-linear and that the onset of density-dependent factors may be abrupt at high populations densities and may lead to a substantial and sustained drop in carrying capacity. We also need to know whether such changes in whale parameters are the same as those caused by changes in whale abundance, e.g. socially dependent factors within the whale stocks which are not, or only partly associated with krill availability.

Second, we need to be able to measure changes in abundance and any other characteristics of the krill stocks which can be shown to be important for the population dynamics of whales, and determine the extent to which

these changes have been due to fishing for krill, and to predict the impact of such characteristics on the future development or modifications of that fishery. Given the current deficiencies in the data base (e.g. the wide range of variance in krill abundance estimates, the unresolved questions of krill longevity and fecundity, and the need for improvement in CPUE data) this is a very tall order.

A second key question which needs to be addressed is the degree of stability and reversibility of the Southern Ocean ecosystem. There is a large volume of literature on the stability of ecosystems as a function of the number and abundances of the component species and their interrelationships (see Cushing, 1981 for a recent review). From this information it is clear that there can be more than one stable equilibrium position. Thus, if the exploitation of krill, whales, or other species components displaces the ecosystem across the boundary between the areas of attraction of two stable points, the system may not return to its original position even if all exploitation ceased.

We do not know whether there is a real danger of non-reversible changes in the Southern Ocean ecosystem, and in particular whether the larger baleen whales will ever recover to their former population levels. The drastic reduction in the Fur Seal population has been reversed and the population is approaching its pre-exploitation level, although the breeding distribution is not the same as it used to be. It may well be that following the depletion of the large whales, the smaller 'r-selected' species would have, by virtue of their reproductive strategy, expanded more rapidly, but it might be expected that in the long-run (and the long-run may be very long indeed) the larger 'k-selected' species would have, by virtue of their reproductive strategy, the competitive advantage and would recover to their initial level, provided that they have maintained a foothold in the system (Gulland, 1985). Information is therefore needed on both past changes in the system and on the changes which are currently taking place.

18.3.4 Directed ecological studies

It is clear that an understanding of the structure and function of the Southern Ocean marine ecosystem is fundamental to the management of the living resources. Such an understanding can only come from extensive ecological studies directed at both system-wide studies as well as ones which address specific data needs targeted by management questions.

18.4 The role of modelling studies

The ecosystem approach to management as required under Article II of the convention necessitates the availability of an acceptable multi-species model of the Southern Ocean ecosystem. In Chapter 15 modelling of the ecosystem and its subsystems were discussed. Such models were concerned with the dynamics of the ecosystem, especially directed at quantifying energy flow and the circulation of materials through the system, and were not specifically developed to answer management questions. In the final section of this chapter we will discuss the reasons why an acceptable multi-species model with predictive capacity is not possible at this point in time. However, more simplified theoretical models can play a useful role in interpreting the likely behaviour of the system under different types and levels of perturbation (Beddington *et al.*, 1985).

In a series of papers (e.g. May *et al.*, 1979; Beddington & Cooke, 1982; Beddington & May, 1980, 1982; Yamanaka, 1983; Sissenwine, 1985; Shimadzu, 1984b; Beddington & de la Mare, 1984) various authors have discussed simple models of the components of the Southern Ocean ecosystem. It is not possible to review these here and readers can refer to the original works for details. Beddington & de la Mare (1984) point out that the text of the Convention on the Conservation of Antarctic Marine Living Resources raises a variety of complex problems which can only be illuminated by the use of models. One whole set of problems is concerned with the interpretation of the behaviour of the system under different types of perturbation, e.g. different levels of krill harvest.

Most of the simple models aimed at elucidating the behaviour of the system employ simple predator–prey models (e.g. May *et al.*, 1979; Beddington & May, 1980, 1982; Beddington & Cooke, 1981; Yamanaka, 1983; Shimadzu, 1984b) framed in differential equations based on density dependent processes and assuming that the unexploited system is in equilibrium. Most of the models use the maximum sustainable yield (MSY) concept, not because it is likely to be a practically achievable objective but, because of its familiarity, it is a useful concept around which to develop discussion. In addition, for all practical purposes the MSY level can be equated with the level of maximum net productivity referred to in the convention. Beddington & de la Mare (1984) discuss the implications of models of krill–whales, krill–whales–seals and krill–cephalopods–Sperm Whales. In general the predictions derived from the krill–whales and krill–whales–seals models have been realized.

The models developed to date are relatively simple models which consider at most three interacting species. However, in order to provide general management guidance, and especially to assess the effects of exploitation in a complex ecosystem holistic ecosystem models with

an emphasis on the role of exploited species need to be developed. The models described in Chapter 15 started with tropho-dynamics computations at the base of the food web, i.e. basic organic production. Such models do not always lead to reliable quantitative results because the pathways of basic organic production to secondary and tertiary production are very variable in space and time, and not fully known quantitatively.

P. E. Smith (1978) and Cushing (1981) have recently discussed the scales of temporal variability in marine ecosystems. Long-term series for phytoplankton, zooplankton and fish production are available for the North Atlantic, the North Sea and off California. These all show considerable fluctuations in abundance and there is strong evidence of a cyclic periodicity. Such periodicities have been shown to be linked with climatic events, e.g. the periodicity of the Norwegian herring has been correlated with the amount of ice cover north of Iceland (Beverton & Lee, 1965), and fluctuations in zooplankton and fish stocks (sardines, anchovies, hake, mackerel and saury) off California with upwelling (Soutar & Isaacs, 1974). These studies have shown that primary production is variable in response to oceanographic conditions. Recent research in the Southern Ocean has demonstrated that production is variable both spatially and from year to year (see Chapters 2, 5, 13 and 15). However, evidence for cyclic phenomena requires long-term series of data of the order of several decades. For the Southern Ocean long-term series are not available.

Various authors (e.g. Beddington & de la Mare, 1984; Butterworth, 1986; Sissenwine, 1985) have recognized that in order to achieve the objectives of CCAMLR Article II it will be necessary to develop a suite of multi-species models for the Southern Ocean marine ecosystem as a whole (or at least for some geographically isolated parts of the system). D. G. M. Miller (1986b) points out that to date such models have appeared to have been used less, or have been less useful, in decision making associated with the management of renewable fish resources. So far the models developed for the Southern Ocean are inadequate to address the range of problems which the managers are faced with in interpreting Article II of the convention. The managers are primarily concerned with demersal fin fisheries and the krill system with its important predators (including whales, seals, penguins and various seabird species). Article II requires the managers to ensure that fishing activity is reasonably stable over a long period of time, while at the same time ensuring the restoration of depleted species.

Levin *et al.* (1988) have listed the important questions being addressed in scientific studies of the living marine resources in the Southern Ocean as:

1. How important are physical processes, such as the movement of fronts and sea-surface contiguous zones, in determining the distribution and dynamics of krill and fish?
2. How important are biological factors such as predation and food availability?
3. What is the interaction between spatial patterns and fishing behaviour?
4. How can theoretical approaches to stock assessment and prediction facilitate the estimation of the size of the resource, and aid in the development of optimal harvesting strategies?

Physical and biological factors interact to produce patterns of multiple spatial and temporal scales, and the development of predictive models must involve an examination of such scales (Denham & Powell, 1984; Levin *et al.*, 1988). Spectral analysis and other statistical procedures allow comparisons of observed distributions of physical factors, primary producers and consumers (e.g. Weber, 1984; Weber *et al.*, 1986a); mechanistic investigations provide complementary information on natural time and space scales for biological and physical processes underlying patterns. Levin *et al.* (1988) in their modelling approaches assume that phytoplankton abundance is determined by physical processes. On the other hand Weber *et al.* (1986a) believe that grazing is an important factor in the small-scale distribution of phytoplankton.

Miller (1986b) recommends that a suite of models with different model outputs will be required to meet the objectives of Article II. Eight attributes (purpose, description, variables, driving forces, time horizons, time steps, constraints and data) were identified as the essential elements in the development of suitable simulations of important Antarctic marine system interactions, and the facilitation of the formation of a suitable decision-making protocol for management purposes. The *purpose* of a model refers to the specific reason for the model's use. The *description* encompasses the type of model (e.g. speculative simulation model or predictive model) being used. The outputs of the model are the quantitative or qualitative changes in values of dependent *variables* in response to *driving forces*, which are the independent variables or parameters which force the behaviour of the modelled system. The *time horizon* is the period over which the behaviour of the variables is assessed, and the *time step* is the incremental period within the model. The *constraints* are the boundaries imposed on the behaviour or interpretation of the model (e.g. limitations of data), and the *data* are the items of information upon which the model is structured.

An example of such a model is given in Table 18.1 as

Table 18.1 *An example of attributes required for a model exploring management decisions in the context of predators*

Purpose	To explore possible mechanisms influencing the abundance of predators in the system
Description	Speculative multi-species predator simulation model
Variables	Predator biomass
Driving forces	Prey biomass and harvesting
Time horizon	5 years
Time steps	1 year unless there is a seasonal influence on the population
Constraints	Data limited
Data	Predator population sizes and dynamics, consumption rates, diet analysis

From Miller (1986b).

an illustration of the kinds of model which need to be developed. Such models might be used when exploring decisions in the context of predators (e.g. Crabeater Seals) and their prey (i.e. krill). The model would explore causal factors, determining the relative abundance of predators within the system. Such a multi-species model would be directly relevant to the performance of the joint exploitation of several co-existing predators (e.g. seals and whales), the abundance of which may be influenced directly by exploitation or by competition for resources which are themselves harvested (e.g. krill).

Laevastu & Favourite (1981) have outlined modelling developments leading up to holistic ecosystem simulation directed towards management needs. In particular they describe a biomass-based (DYNUMES) model with spatial resolution which was developed for the eastern Bering Sea (Laevastu & Favourite, 1981). Fig. 18.2 presents a simplified view of the principal processes emphasized in the DYNUMES simulation. In the simulation a complex series of computations are carried out at each point on a grid covering the area of study for each time step (e.g., monthly). The numerous species-specific coefficients (such as growth coefficients, food requirements, and fishing mortality coefficients) are influenced by a number of factors at each grid point and at each time step. Growth of biomass, fishery yields, mortalities, consumptions (predation), and migrations are also computed in each time step. The simulations also include most of the pronounced environment–biota interactions (e.g., depth, temperature, nature of the bottom, currents, etc.). The DYNUMES model is a bulk biomass model which is heavily dependent on good reliable estimates of the quantitative composition of the food of species and/or ecological groups. While such information is available on some species in the Southern Ocean there are large gaps which

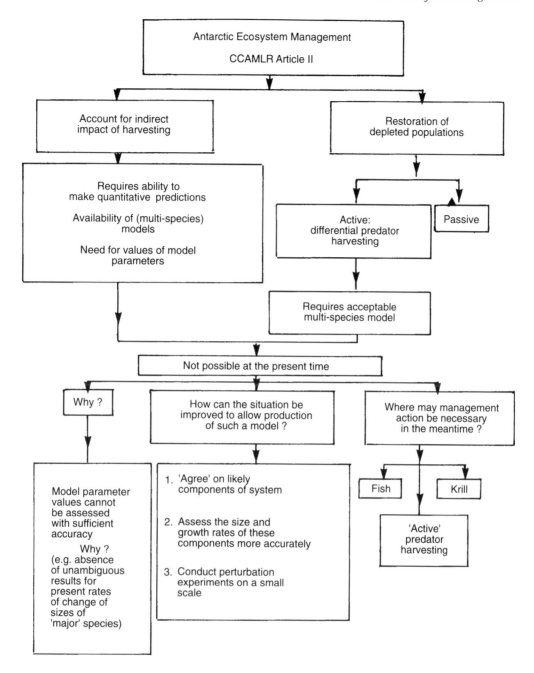

Fig. 18.3. Plan of Antarctic ecosystem management. Redrawn from Butterworth (1984).

would make it difficult at this time to develop a model similar to that of Laevastu & Favourite.

The DYNUMES model, run over several year spans, shows that marine ecosystems are unstable and sensitive to changes in growth rates, relative distributions, abundance of predators/prey, and changes in the composition of food. Due to the multiple interactions in the ecosystem, the abundance and distribution of most species show quasi-cyclic variations (Laevastu & Favourite, 1981).

An outcome of this new ecosystem approach to fisheries is the realization of the shortcomings of the single species approaches, which lack trophodynamic interactions between species. Another is the realization of the necessity to deal with age/size dependent mortalities, and to ascertain predation mortalities as well as spawning stress mortalities in ecosystem models.

Quantitative numerical ecosystem simulation models can bring out processes and resulting changes in the ecosystem which have not been easily observed in the past, and permit ecological experiments which would be impossible to conduct in nature. Such simulations with emphasis on exploited populations can provide new powerful tools for fisheries management. They not only allow the determination of the magnitude of the resources and their distributions, but also the simulation of variable space and time responses to any desired/or any prescribed fishery, as well as indirectly on other species via interspecies interactions. Such simulations have shown the importance of the determination of the magnitudes and periods of large-scale 'natural fluctuations' in the marine ecosystem which can occur without the influence of the fishery.

Gulland (1983a) stressed the importance of understanding species interactions, changes in behaviour, and fluctuations in vital rates due to density-dependent factors. Changes in any of these parameters may be non-linear. For example, how does the abundance of Blue or Minke Whales affect the population dynamics of Sei Whales? Is it the total abundance of krill or the abundance of dense krill swarms which is more critical to predators? To what extent might the dispersion of krill swarms by commercial harvesting affect prey accessibility for various predators? These and other questions regarding interactions in the Southern Ocean ecosystem stress the need for the development of multi-species ecosystem models which incorporate the species interactions outlined above.

To date there has been no attempt to apply the kind of ecosystem analysis outlined above to the Southern Ocean. While it is recognized that there are deficiencies in the data base as far as the Southern Ocean is concerned, there is an urgent need for work to commence on the development of models of this type to help in the resolution of some of the issues in resource management faced by the Commission on the Conservation of Antarctic Marine Living Resources. While it would not be possible to develop such a model for the Southern Ocean as a whole, models could be developed on a regional basis. In the first instance a model of the South Georgia–Antarctic Peninsula area would be feasible as the data base is more complete for this region than for other parts of the Southern Ocean.

18.5 Monitoring indicators of possible ecological changes in the Antarctic marine ecosystem

One of the central problems in the management of the Southern Ocean 'ecosystem' is the assessment of actual and potential impacts on the system by various harvest regimes (species and quantities to be harvested). This question can be approached in three different ways:

1. assessment of target species directly;
2. evaluating target competitors and by-catch species; and
3. monitoring predators.

At its third annual meeting, held in Hobart in September 1984, the scientific committee of CCAMLR established an *ad hoc* working group to formulate and recommend actions for planning, implementing, and coordinating the multi-national research programmes necessary for effective assessment and monitoring key components of the Southern Ocean marine ecosystem. This group first met in Seattle, Washington, in May 1985 and, following consideration of its report at the September 1985 meeting of the scientific committee, a formal working group was constituted for the CCAMLR Ecosystem Monitoring Programme. This working group met in July 1986 to develop definitive proposals for a monitoring programme, and in 1988 (CCAMLR, 1988) published a handbook on standard methods for monitoring parameters.

18.5.1 Target species

As we have seen there are considerable problems in simulating the stocks of krill in particular and in evaluating population changes which might be due to harvesting. Gulland (1983a) has pointed out that the patchy distribution of krill swarms, plus the uncertainty of how much krill are present outside the swarms, makes it difficult to interpret the relationship between catch and effort data. Furthermore, the fishery statistics for krill may reflect processing capacity and temporary abundance of krill at fishing sites rather than regional population densities.

Krill biomass is likely to be a function of the time of the year and it may be sensitive to large recruitment fluctuations as is typical of many relatively short-lived marine species. A large variance is likely in any index of the size of krill populations (see Chapter 5). In addition krill behaviour markedly affects catchability (the ratio of CPUE to biomass), and hence indices of catch rate. The Scientific Committee of CCAMLR has set up an ad hoc workshop on krill CPUE.

18.5.2 Target competitors and by-catch species

Competitors of krill include other herbivorous zooplankton such as salps, copepods and juvenile fish. If the abundance of krill were affected by harvesting then these competitors might be expected to manifest compensatory responses resulting from altered competition. However, past research has shown that the populations of such competitors are subject to the same spatial and seasonal variation as those of the krill (Longhurst, 1981). Salp populations are well known for their cyclic population fluctuations. By-catch species include some of the competitors, especially larval fishes. While the monitoring of by-catch species would help in evaluating whether non-target zooplankton and juvenile fishes manifest responses to krill fishing pressure (e.g., competitive displacement), it is unlikely to provide any reliable quantitative measures.

18.5.3 Predators

Fluctuations in food availability as discussed in Chapter 5 may be reflected in the responses of the primary and secondary predators of krill. Many species variables such as growth, reproduction, and behaviour are flexible parameters which change in response to factors such as prey availability. A number of recent papers (e.g. Eberhart, 1977; Eberhart & Siniff, 1977; Fowler, 1980; Hanks, 1981) have explored the use of various indices to assess the status of large mammal populations, while Green-Hammond *et al.* (1983) and Bengtson (1985) have discussed the general principles of indicator species monitoring and the criteria for their selection.

The CCAMLR Ecosystem Monitoring Programme (CEMP) mentioned above aims 'to detect and record significant changes in critical components of the ecosystem, to serve as the basis for the conservation of Antarctic marine living resources. The monitoring system should be designed to distinguish between changes due to the harvesting of commercial species and changes due to environmental variability, both physical and biological' (SC-CCAMLR, 1985). The choice of predatory species to monitor has been based on criteria whose definition has evolved over several years. Croxall *et al.* (1988a) summarized these criteria, stating that species to be monitored have the following characteristics:

> (a) important components (in terms of prey consumption of the Southern Ocean system);
>
> (b) specialist predators on harvestable prey, especially krill;
>
> (c) have broad geographical breeding ranges including sites near and far from areas likely to be subject to intensive fishing;
>
> (d) readily accessible to breeding sites and tolerable of human presence and activity.

A number of species of penguins and seals have been designated as CEMP species and several locations have been selected as CEMP Network Sites for monitoring programmes.

According to Croxall (1989) the possible aims of the CEMP might include any or all of the following:

> (i) To detect changes in indices of the status in either demographic or physiological (e.g. condition) aspects and/or reproductive performance of seabirds and seals.
>
> (ii) To relate these changes to indices of prey (at present krill) abundance and availability (to the predators).
>
> (iv) To use predator indices, on the basis of the relationships between predators and prey developed above, as a measure of (a) prey availability (to the predators) and (b) prey stock abundance.
>
> (vi) To use the predator indices to detect changes in food availability that result from commercial harvesting as distinct from changes due to natural fluctuations in the biological and physical environment.

The parameters currently recommended for penguin monitoring studies are: breeding population size, breeding success, incubation shift duration, chick fledging weight, adult arrival weight, and demographic parameters (CCAMLR, 1988). Trivelpiece *et al.* (1990) have examined data on these parameters from studies carried out over several years in Admiralty Bay, King George Island on Adélie and Chinstrap Penguins. The parameters showed considerable variability. However, interpretation of the variability was greatly enhanced when several parameters were considered simultaneously.

One of the major problems involved in these ecosystem monitoring studies is to distinguish natural fluctuations in population density and breeding success from those due to reduced food supply caused by commercial harvesting. Some of the short-term and long-term variability in the Southern Ocean marine system has been discussed in Chapter 15. Variability in Antarctic seabird population densities and breeding success is well documented; e.g. Whitehead *et al.* (1990) for Adélie Penguins, Southern Fulmars and Antarctic Petrels in Prydz Bay; Ainley & LeResche (1973) and K. J. Wilson (1990) for Adélie penguins on Ross Island; Taylor *et al.* (1990) for Adélie Penguins in the Ross Sea region; and Lishman (1985) for Adélie Penguins at Signy Island. Reduced breeding success and decline in population numbers in nearly all of these studies have been attributed either to the increased energetic costs of travelling over sea ice in years of persistent ice and/or the scarcity of food resources. Taylor *et al.* (1990) in their surveys of Adélie Penguins in the Ross Sea region where there are 38 rookeries with a total of 1 082 000 breeding pairs – about half the world population – have shown that nearly all the rookeries have increased in size over the last 10–20 years. Possible reasons for the increase and annual fluctuations in numbers include seasonal variations in sea ice and weather conditions, and longer-term climatic change. It is of interest that the diets of the southernmost rookeries at Cape Bird and Cape Crozier are different from those of the more northerly rookeries. Krill which does not figure in the diets of the southern rookeries, is the predominant food item taken by the birds in the more northern rookeries. These results stress the need for caution when using trends in bird populations to detect the impact of human-induced changes such as those brought about by krill harvesting.

It is clear that the influence of naturally varying environmental parameters is of sufficient magnitude to obscure the effects of human-induced changes over the short term. This points for the need for long-term integrated studies of avian population parameters, prey distribution and abundance, weather conditions and fluctuations in oceanographic conditions.

18.6 Experimental fishing as a management tool

In 1984 Australia presented as a basis for discussion a proposal to undertake a coordinated fishing and research experiment at selected sites in the Southern Ocean (Anon., 1985b). A number of sites were proposed, including areas adjacent to the Scotia Arc, around South Georgia, and regions of the South Indian Ocean. For the Prydz Bay Gyre (55–110° E) an experiment in two phases, each of five year's duration, was proposed. During the first phase the level and type of fishing effort would be held constant while the ecology of the site would be documented, population levels and trends of target and key consumer species would be assessed, and complementary research would be undertaken to refine further a conceptual and quantitative ecological model of the experimental site. In the second phase of the experiment the system would be manipulated through planned variations in the level and type of fishing effort and, possibly, by the co-harvesting of selected consumer species. The effects of this manipulation would be studied and the results used to develop a plan for the management of the Prydz Bay subsystem.

The aim of this experimental approach would be to enable management guidelines for Southern Ocean fisheries to be based on the best possible scientific advice derived from experience and the results of scientific research. In discussing the ways in which the development of a multi-species model for the Southern Ocean ecosystem could be facilitated Butterworth (1986) considered that without carefully regulated experimental programmes to reduce certain predator populations in a few selected areas, the dynamic parameters required for workable multi-species models could be determined only with great difficulty and after considerable time.

18.7 Alternative management strategies

It is abundantly clear that traditional fisheries management programmes are inappropriate for the management of the living resources of the Southern Ocean and that the management issues are complex. Consequently new management approaches are necessary. In discussing the limitations of the mean sustainable yield approach to the management of fish resources Holt (1978) lists a series of principles which should be used as the basis for the reformulation of management objectives:

1. Ecosystems should be maintained in such a state that both their consumptive and non-consumptive values to humanity can be realized on a continuing basis.
2. Options for different uses by present and succeeding human generations should be ensured.
3. Risk of irreversible changes or long-term adverse effects of exploitation should be minimized.
4. Decisions should include a safety factor to allow for limitations of knowledge and the inevitable imperfections of management institutions.
5. Measures to conserve one resource should not be wasted to another.
6. Survey or monitoring, analysis, and assessment should precede planned use and accompany actual use of a resource, and the results should be made available promptly for critical public review.

These are the principles which should underpin the management of the living resources of the Southern Ocean.

Throughout this chapter reference has frequently been made to Article II of the Convention on the Conservation of Antarctic Marine Living Resources. The two key objectives enunciated in this article are: 'accounting for the indirect impacts of harvesting' and 'the restoration of depleted populations'. Butterworth (1986) has discussed the practical implications of these objectives and these are set out in Fig. 18.3. The requirements for the construction of multi-species models and the difficulties in developing an acceptable multi-species model at this time have been outlined previously in this chapter.

There are two possible approaches towards achieving the second objective, the restoration of depleted populations. The 'passive' approach would be to curtail all harvesting (of any species) on the assumption that, after a time (and probably a long time, of the order of centuries, rather than decades) the various species would return to a new population equilibrium, hopefully approaching that of the pre-exploitation levels. An alternative hypothesis would be that more than one stable state exists for the unexploited system, and that the system would not necessarily return to its original unexploited state if undisturbed in the future. The other possible approach then is an 'active' one, where other species (in some cases competitors of the exploited species)are harvested to reduce their size and prevent their further growth. Again this implies the availability of a multi-species model in order to predict quantitatively the effect on some species of changing the stock sizes of others. Butterworth (1986) discusses how the situation might be improved so as to allow the production of such a model. He considers that three lines of investigation are needed:

1. Selection of the major components of the system to be incorporated in the model.
2. Assessing the size and growth rates of the component populations more adequately.
3. Conducting carefully regulated perturbation experiments.

However, in the absence of an acceptable multi-species model 'active' predator harvesting is not a viable option for the Southern Ocean ecosystem *as a whole* at this stage. Nevertheless, this could be an option if positive evidence for the existence of more than one stable state for the system were forthcoming.

Since it is clear that many species in the Southern Ocean are predominantly dependent (directly or indirectly) on krill as a food source, it can reasonably be concluded that any substantial depletion of the krill standing stock would have widespread deleterious effects upon at least some of the predator species. In the light of this avoidance of any substantial reduction in the krill stock should be a particular priority. It is also essential that the monitoring programmes discussed in section 18.5 be put into operation without delay. Butterworth (1986) suggests that the primary objective of krill management might be expressed as follows: 'the standing stock of krill in each management area must not be permitted to fall to less than an agreed proportion of its current level'.

There are, however, a number of problems associated with the above objective. Firstly, there is no definitive evidence for the existence of separate genetic stocks of krill (see section 5.5.6). In spite of this, 'management areas' could be provisionally established on the basis of available biological and oceanographic information, together with historic whaling and other records (e.g. Mackintosh, 1972). Secondly, as we have seen, there are considerable problems in estimating the biomass and distribution of krill. Thirdly, if krill predator stocks are still increasing in response to the depletion of baleen whale populations, then the krill standing stock could be expected to decrease from its present level.

An important aspect in the management of short-lived species subject to recruitment fluctuations (as appears to be likely in the case of krill) is the requirement quickly to detect and react to poor recruitment periods by decreasing the TAC (total allowable catch) for each management area, or whatever other major limitation to the catch effort, as may be adopted. There is a need therefore to place a ceiling on the rate at which fishing effort (or corresponding TACs) is allowed to increase in the early stages of the development of the fishery in order to prevent the over-capitalization which has been involved in the decline of many fisheries. In the first instance a conservative empirical ceiling should be set.

Fish stocks have already been heavily exploited in some areas, with past catches representing mainly the depletion of accumulated stocks rather than the harvesting of surplus production (Gulland, 1983a; Kock *et al.*, 1985). Urgent management measures are necessary in order to prevent further depletion of the stock. Butterworth (1986) has suggested that an interim operational objective for the exploited (or potentially exploitable) fish stocks might be: 'The stock-size of the species concerned must not be permitted to fall below, or must be allowed to recover to, an agreed fraction of its estimated pre-exploitation level in each designated management area'. He suggests that because surplus production to biomass ratios for Antarctic demersal stocks are low (Gulland, 1983a,b), 'pulse fishing' may prove to be the only economically viable long-term harvesting strategy (i.e. rather than fishing every year, fishing should be carried out intensively over a short period once every number of years). The pulse-fishing strategy assumes that the population can always increase after harvesting. Therefore, it is important that the stock size be not allowed to fall below the agreed level, especially when there are insufficient data to enable surplus production to be estimated accurately.

As Holt (1978) points out, it will not be easy to put the principles outlined in this chapter into operation, and herein lies the challenge to CCAMLR. The scientific committee is composed of dedicated scientists, the majority of whom are, or have been, active in Antarctic marine research. With the cooperation of the SCAR BIO-MASS community I am confident that soundly based scientific advice, based on the best available data, will be provided. In the past, this kind of advice has not always been heeded by fisheries commissions, as the history of the International Whaling Commission testifies. Some of the early experiences in the operation of the CCAMLR Commission have not been encouraging. It will be up to the members of the commission to resist political and other pressures and to heed and act upon the scientists' recommendations.

Epilogue

From the accounts given in the various chapters of this book the extent to which our understanding of the functioning of the Antarctic marine ecosystem has changed is evident. Prior to research of the last three decades the prevailing view of the Southern Ocean pelagic ecosystem could be summarized as follows:

1. High diatom dominated primary production flourishing in an environment where nutrients were never limiting.

2. A system dominated by short food chains (e.g. diatoms → krill → baleen whales).

3. Little information available on the roles of heterotrophic Protozoa. It was believed that they did not play as prominent a role as in temperate and tropical waters.

4. A view that Antarctic marine bacteria were temperature limited in their activity, and that their populations were much lower than those of temperate and tropical seas.

5. There was practically no information on the vertical flux of particulate organic matter and its remineralization.

6. It was believed that krill (*Euphausia superba*) had a life span of two, or a maximum three years, that they spawned only once, and that they did not feed during the long Antarctic winter.

7. Although the existence of the sea ice microbial community had been known for 150 years there was practically no information available on its dynamics and role in the pelagic ecosystem.

8. Although enhanced diatom production at the ice edge had been known for some time there was little appreciation of the importance of ice edge processes.

9. There was little information available on the impact that the decline in baleen whale stocks had on the system.

10. There was a prevailing view that the system was largely predictable and that it was fragile.

11. While the taxonomy of the species of the benthic communities is reasonably well known, there was little information on the biomass of the benthos, the ecology of individual species, including their adaption to low temperatures (near the freezing point of sea water), the synchronization of life cycles to the brief input of organic matter during the spring–summer phytoplankton blooms, and of community dynamics.

In contrast the current view can be summarized as follows:

1. We now know that much of the phytoplankton production, especially in the open water zone and the seasonal pack ice zone, following the ice edge diatom and *Phaeocystis* blooms, is dominated by small nano- and picophytoplankton which can account for up to over 70% of the total net primary production. Although temporary reduction in nutrient levels occurs during the blooms they are seldom reduced to levels where they become limiting.

2. While the diatom→krill→vertebrate consumer food chain is an important component of the Antarctic pelagic food web we now know that krill consume only something in the order of 2–5% of the phytoplankton primary production. However, locally they can have a major impact on the phytoplankton community composition by their intensive grazing activity in which they contribute to the pool of 'regenerated' nutrients (ammonium), and bring about a change to a system dominated by autotrophic microflagellates and heterotrophic microflagellates and ciliates. The pelagic food web is now known to a very complex one that is similar to that of other oceans. Rather than categorizing areas of the Southern Ocean as eutrophic or oligotrophic it is now considered that at different times any particular area can occupy the total spectrum from oligotrophic to eutrophic.

3. As a result of recent research we now known that the heterotrophic protozoa are as abundant as those of other oceans and that they play a similar role in the pelagic ecosystem.

4. Our views on the role of bacteria have changed dramatically. They are as abundant as in other oceans and, although their activity may approach that found in temperate seas, their metabolic rates are to some degree limited by the prevailing low temperatures.

5. Recent research has shown that the vertical flux of particulate organic matter from the euphotic zone to deeper water and the sediments occurs mainly during the intense diatom blooms, and that at other times such flux is

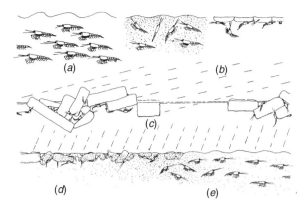

Fig. E.1. Postulated annual cycle of krill (see text for explanation). Redrawn from Smetacek *et al.* (1990).

negligible or low. When the pelagic primary production is dominated by the small nano- and picophytoplankton organic matter is recycled within the euphotic zone with remineralization resulting in the production of 'regenerated'-N (ammonium).

6. There has been a dramatic change in our view of krill and its roles in the Southern Ocean ecosystem. We now know that krill may live for at least up to seven years (not to three) and that they may spawn at least over three seasons. In contrast to the idea that krill did not feed during the Antarctic winter research carried out in the last decade has established that in the pack ice during the winter they have an abundant food supply, and that they feed on the sea ice microalgae (Fig. E.1). The under pack ice habitat is of considerable importance to the furcilia larval stages.

7. A considerable body of information has now accumulated on the sea ice microbial community. The development, growth rates and physiological ecology of the sea ice microalgae is now reasonably well known and estimates of the right order of magnitude can be made of the sea ice microbial contribution to the overall primary productivity of the Southern Ocean. We now have a better understanding of the composition and ecological role of the sea ice heterotrophic protozoa. It is now clear that the release of the sea ice microalgae upon the melting of the pack ice 'seeds' the water column and gives rise to the marginal ice edge phytoplankton blooms. The role of the sea ice community as a nursery for the development stages of some copepod species has been established and the role of the cryopelagic community is now better known.

8. As a result of research in the last decade in particular the importance of the marginal ice edge primary production and its role in supporting primary consumers and higher trophic levels is now clear. If this ice edge production is taken into account then the apparent anomaly of

overall low primary production in the Southern Ocean (derived primarily from determinations in the ice free zone) and the large populations of vertebrate consumers and high rates of biogenic sedimentation can be resolved.

9. We now know that the decline in baleen whale stocks has resulted in changes in the demographic parameters of other krill consumers (birds, seals and Minke Whales), although we do not yet know what new equilibrium will be reached.

10. Far from being stable and predictable the Southern Ocean system has been shown to be highly variable on a range of scales. This is particularly evident in the distribution and abundance of krill which we now know can fluctuate widely from year to year in any given locality. It is subject to natural perturbations of varying intensity and duration and this results in a system that is resilient and not fragile.

11. Research over the past few decades has established that the Antarctic benthos, especially on the shelf, is characterized by very high biomass levels, several times that of the benthic communities at comparable depths in the Arctic, with infaunal invertebrate densities equal to the highest densities recorded anywhere in the world's oceans. More information is now available on the adaption of the species to the prevailing low temperatures.

In spite of the considerable advances that have been made, there are still many gaps in our understanding of the functioning of the Southern Ocean ecosystem. Considerable uncertainty still remains concerning the primary production processes. To what extent the recently investigated phenomena of marginal ice edge blooms in a few locations can be extrapolated to the Southern Ocean as a whole remains to be determined. If substantiated this could substantially revise estimates of total primary production. What is needed is continuous year round observations. While satellite observations of chlorophyll concentrations can help (Sullivan *et al.*, 1988), moored sensor buoys such as that developed by Fukuchi *et al.* (1988) should be developed, around the continent at selected locations. We still have a long way to go before we have reliable estimates of krill stocks and krill production and a good understanding of the dynamics of krill swarming behaviour. As discussed in Chapter 15 the system is characterized by considerable variability, not only in the physical features of the environment, but also in its biological components. This variability which occurs on a variety of scales (interannual, meso- and large-scale, etc.) needs to be fully understood both as a basis for the management of the Southern Ocean's living resources and for the assessment and predication of possible climate change.

While some progress has been made in the elucidation of the changes which have occurred in the Southern Ocean pelagic ecosystem following the decimation of the stocks of baleen whales we are still a long way from being able to predict if, and when, a new position of stability will be reached and to what extent it will differ from pre-whaling days. Another critical gap in our understanding concerns the role of cephalopods in the ecosystem. We know that they are an important food resource for certain seabirds, elephant seals and toothed whales. However, we have virtually no data on their population densities, life cycles and the food that they consume. They are potentially major krill consumers but we can only guess as to what extent.

As detailed in Chapter 14 we now know that the Southern Ocean pelagic ecosystem resembles that of other oceanic areas in the roles played by bacteria and heterotrophic protozoans in the 'microbial network', and in the remineralization of organic detritus. However, much more research is needed on the rates of formation of particulate and dissolved of detrital particles, the rates of their decomposition in the water column, and the rates and quantities of particulate vertical flux to the sediments. There is also a paucity of information on the role of benthic communities in the process of remineralization. Shelf benthic communities have densities and biomass comparable to the most productive elsewhere in the world's oceans. Only a handful of studies have been carried out in the dynamics of such communities.

Against the background of the past history of the exploitation of the living marine resources of the Southern Ocean, and recognition of the fact that in recent years man's activities have acquired the capability of greatly accelerating changes in ecosystems leading to their deterioration and loss of species diversity, there has developed a world-wide concern for the future of the Antarctic continent and the surrounding areas. In recent years the focus of concern about exploitation of Antarctic resources has shifted to the potential for extracting marketable quantities of minerals, especially oil. In anticipation of this the Antarctic Treaty negotiated the 'Convention on the Regulation of Antarctic Mineral Resources' which incorporated strict guidelines for the regulation of mineral exploration and exploitation. However, in face of growing opposition to any mineral exploitation the future of the Minerals Convention is uncertain and it is unlikely to come into force. The nations of the Antarctic Treaty are currently negotiating a comprehensive conservation regime for the Antarctic which may extend the current temporary ban on mineral exploration and exploitation for a further 50 years and which would require unanimous agreement to terminate.

The view has been expressed that the Antarctic is the world's last great remaining wilderness and that it should be preserved as such. However, while many view the Antarctic region as a pristine one it has suffered destructive exploitation of its living resources, whales, seals and fish, over 200 years. In addition there has been an increasing human presence in the form of logistic bases for scientific research and Antarctic tourism is on the increase. While logistic bases in the past have had localized negative impacts considerable advances have been made in recent year's in minimizing such impacts.

Exploitation of the living resources as discussed in Chapter is controlled by the CCAMLR. This provides a framework for the regulation of fisheries for krill, fish, squid and any other marine living resources, apart from seals and whales. As we have seen the Convention is unusual in its ecological emphasis requiring that exploitation should not be allowed to progress to the point at which non-target species are at risk. While the current level of exploitation of krill probably does not have a significant impact on dependent species it is a fact that 'virtually every commercially attractive fish stock has been allowed to decline below it most productive level: (Gulland, 1986). CCAMLR has been moving, at a pace which has been criticized as too slow, to conserve heavily depleted stocks and ensure their recovery. However, uncertainty regarding the dynamics of Antarctic marine ecosystems, and in particular the magnitude of krill stocks and their production rate, has made practical management difficult. In such a situation of uncertainty it is essential that allowable catches be set at very conservative levels. It can be said that as far as CCAMLR is concerned the jury still has not rendered a verdict and every encouragement should be given to it in its endeavours to develop sound sustainable management for the living resources of the Southern Ocean. We cannot allow this world's first ecologically-based living resources management regime to fail. Currently there is a moratorium on whaling, apart from the killing of Minke Whales for 'scientific purposes'. World opinion strongly supports the continuation of the moratorium and the cessation of scientific whaling. Any future exploitation of Antarctic seals is controlled by the Convention on the Conservation of Antarctic Seals (CCAS). However, in view of the current world attitudes regarding sealing and the unfavourable economics of any Antarctic sealing operation it is highly improbable that exploitation of seals will occur in the foreseeable future.

The Scientific Committee on Antarctic Research (SCAR) has played a lead role in Antarctic conservation in its roles of coordinating scientific research programmes, and in providing scientific advice to the

Antarctic Treaty and the Scientific Committee of CCAMLR. Through its Working on Biology it has been involved in the drawing up of the Agreed Measurers for the Conservation of Antarctic Flora and Fauna and the initiation of the proposal for a Convention on the Conservation of Antarctic Seals, as well as the development of the concept of Sites of Special Scientific Interest. The work of the Group of Specialists on the Living Resources of the Southern Ocean provided stimulus for the development of the Convention on the Conservation of Antarctic Marine Living Resources. A new Group of Specialists on Environmental Affairs and Conservation (GOSEAC) was constituted by SCAR in 1988 as recognition of the increasing need for scientific advice in these areas. The permanent Working Groups, Groups of Specialists and Groups of Experts have prepared a number of reports on the initiative of SCAR or following requests from the Antarctic Treaty System. These include *Conservation Areas in Antarctic* (Bonner & Lewis Smith, 1985), *Man's Impact on the Antarctic Environment* (Benninghoff & Bonner, 1985) and *Waste Disposal in Antarctica* (SCAR, 1989). Reviews of the current status of knowledge on fish (Kock *et al.*, 1985) and krill (Miller & Hampton, 1989) have been provided at the request of the Scientific Committee of CCAMLR. Over the years SCAR has provided scientific input to the advantage of the Antarctic Treaty System at virtually no cost to that system.

'Fragile' is a term that is often applied to Antarctic ecosystem, often without scientific justification. I would suggest that marine ecosystems in the Southern Ocean are actually rather robust. In Chapter 15 the high degree of natural variability of the system was documented. There is a high degree of natural perturbation within the system, e.g. current and water mass changes, changes in annual sea ice cover, intensive grazing activity by dense swarms of krill and benthic scour by drifting ice bergs to mention only a few. The system as a whole recovers from such perturbations on varying time scales. It was also subject to an enormous perturbation due to commercial sealing and whaling activity, but other predator groups have increased as a response to the increased availability of krill.

Effects of increases in the level of ultra-violet radiation

Stratosphere ozone shields the earth from much of the solar middle ultra-violet radiation (UV-B, 240–320 nm wave band), which is the most biologically injurious component of sunlight (Catkins & Thordardottiv, 1980; Jagger, 1985). The reduction that has occurred in the ozone layer over the Antarctic, popularly referred to as the 'ozone hole' by human pollution (Bowman, 1988) has

raised the question as to how this might impact on Southern Ocean ecology (Roberts, 1989; Karentz, 1990, 1991a,b; Voytek, 1990) . A number of studies (e.g. Worrest *et al.*, 1978, 1981; R. C. Smith *et al.*, 1980; R. C. Smith & Baker, 1982) have shown that increased levels of UV-B exposure results in reduced primary production as measured by the ^{14}C uptake method and are likely to alter community diversity, as well as phytoplankton size distribution (Fig. E.2). Voytek (1990) and Karentz (1991) have recently reviewed the ecological consequences of Antarctic ozone depletion.

Since Southern Ocean phytoplankton are the basis of the food web, decreases in their growth rate and/or changes in species composition resulting from enhanced UV-B radiation could 'indirectly reduce the standing stocks of higher trophic levels' (Worrest *et al.*, 1978; R. C. Smith & Baker, 1982; Worrest, 1983). The deleterious effects of UV radiation on phytoplankton, macroalgae and zooplankton have been known for some time (for a review see Worrest, 1982). Exposure of phytoplankton to UV radiation produces significant reductions in growth, photosynthesis, cellular proteins and photosynthetic pigments. Macroalgae exposed to UV radiation exhibit selective loss of photopigments and depressed rates of photosynthesis (Wood, 1987). For *Acartia clausii*, a marine copepod, exposure to UV-B produced significant decreases in survival rate and fecundity (Karanas *et al.*, 1979).

There have been a number of studies on the impact of UV radiation on Antarctic phytoplankton and currently a number of research groups have ongoing research programmes. During November–December 1987 El-Sayed *et al.* (1990a,b) conducted a series of experiments designed to study the effects of UV radiation on phytoplankton and sea ice microalgae. The results showed an enhancement of production rates in tanks where UV-A and UV-B were excluded, with much lower production rates under ambient and enhanced UV conditions. Significant decreases in phytoplankton pigmentation samples exposed to enhanced UV radiation. These tentative conclusions have been confirmed by Vosjan *et al.* (1990) who found that after 5 hours of irradiation with UV-B (290–320 nm) of 1.35 W m there was a 75% decrease in the ATP content of the phytoplankton microogranisms in the upper 30 m water layer of the Weddell Sea.

Bigidare (1989) carried out a series of experiments at Palmer Station in the austral summer. Long-term (24–48 h) exposure of phytoplankton to UV radiation under ambient light conditions produced drastic changes in phytoplankton pigments. In contrast to these results, short-term (4 h) exposure of sea ice microalgae to UV

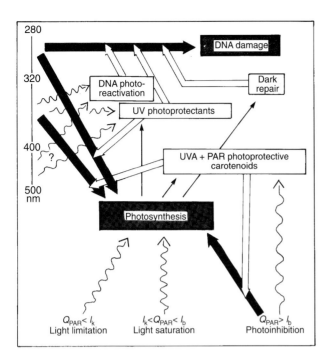

Fig. E.2. A working model of the photoregulatory interactions of Q_{UVB}, Q_{UVA} and Q_{PAR} productivity and DNA integrity for phytoplankton communities in the Antarctic Marginal Ice Zone. I_k is the saturation parameter for photosynthesis, and I_b is the photoinhibition onset parameter. Shaded arrow, known direct photoinhibitory effects on phytoplankton vitality by high fluxes of Q_{UVB}, Q_{UVA} and Q_{PAR}. Open arrow , known processes that diminish the photoinhibitory effects of Q_{UVB}, Q_{UVA}, and Q_{PAR}. Wavy arrow, known light-mediated processes that regulate biosynthetic rates. Straight arrow, known biosynthetic processes that regulate photoprotective processes. Question mark, hypothesized pathways of photoregulation consistent with the database of the cruise in the Bellingshausen Sea in the austral spring of 1990. Redrawn from R. C. Smith *et al.* (1992).

radiation produced no significant changes in the concentrations of chl *a*, chl *c* and fucxoanthin.

A primary hazard of UV exposure is absorption by DNA leading to direct mutagenic and lethal effects (Harm, 1980; Zolzer & Kiefer, 1989; Karentz *et al.*, 1991a). Karentz *et al.* (1991a) studied 12 species of Antarctic diatoms to assess their sensitivity in relation to cellular and molecular aspects of DNA damage and repair. The species studied showed a wide range of UV resistance, induction of photopigments and rates of dark- and light-mediated repair. Thus diatom species within a phytoplankton community exposed to the same UV levels will respond in different ways as a result of variations in damage reduction and repair capability. The results of this study suggested that the primary effect of increased UV-B and shifts in ratios to higher wavelengths would be to initiate changes in cell size and in the taxonomic structure of Antarctic phytoplankton communities.

Marine organisms can reduce their susceptibility to UV damage by any of the following strategies; avoidance, nocturnal cell division, repair of UV-damaged

DNA and biosynthesis of photo-protective compounds (Bidigare, 1989). These protective features are species specific. A recent survey of Antarctic invertebrates and algae (Karentz *et al.*, 1991b) has shown that these organisms contain UV-absorbing mycosporine amino acids (MMAs) similar to those of tropical and temperate marine species (Dunlop *et al.*, 1989). UV-absorbing pigments have also been observed in Antarctic marine phytoplankton (B. G. Mitchell *et al.*, 1989, 1990; Vernet *et al.*, 1989). These compounds act as natural sunscreens, protecting internal organs and/or organelles from excessive doses of UV.

Recently Marchant *et al.* (1991) have investigated the UV-B protecting compounds in the marine prymesiophyte *Phaeocystis pouchetii*. Colourless, water-soluble compounds produced by the Antarctic colonial stage in the life cycle absorb strongly between 271 and 323 nm. However, cultures from near Tasmania, from the north Sea and in the English Channel had substantially less of the 323 nm absorbing material per g of chl *a* than the Antarctic strain. Sublethal irradiance of the Antarctic colonial strain with UV-B significantly increased the absorbence per cell at 323 nm. It would appear that Antarctic *P. pouchetii* are more resistant to UV-B than diatoms which contain little or no UV-B absorbing pigments (Yentsch & Yentsch, 1982; Davidson & Marchant unpublished data quoted in Marchant *et al.*, 1991). There is therefore the possibility that with increased UV-B radiation *P. pouchetti* could replace diatoms in some of the spring phytoplankton blooms. This could have a considerable impact on the food web as *P. pouchetii* is largely unconsumed by herbivorous zooplankton.

In spite of the recent research on UV-B radiation effects on Antarctic phytoplankton and the large body of literature on such effects elsewhere, extremely little is known about the adaptive responses of marine organisms in the field. Nor do we know how much damage can be sustained and how much can be repaired under Antarctic conditions of ozone depletion, short day lengths, and freezing ambient temperatures (Karentz, 1991). The large degree of interspecies variation in the efficiency of DNA repair, dose responses, and occurrence of UV-B-absorbing substances has been observed in the response and protective mechanisms of only a few Antarctic species. Interspecies differences in the ability to cope with UV are perhaps the most crucial factor in assessing the ecological implication of ozone depletion (Karentz, 1991).

Voytek (1990) points out the need to study the impact of UV radiation, not only on the total phytoplankton community but on the pico-, nano- and microphytoplankton components. In addition it has been shown that bacterial production and growth in temperate surface waters is limited by UV-B radiation (Sicrachi & Siebruth, 1986). The possible impact on the heterotrophic flagellates and ciliates is unknown, but they would contribute to the ATP content of the plankton microorganisms studied by Vosjan *et al.* (1990). Thus a reduction in the overall production of the planktonic microorganisms could impact on the micro- and macrozooplankton and higher consumers. It is therefore essential that the reaction of various components of the Antarctic pelagic ecosystem to increased UV-B radiation be studied both in the field and in laboratory and mesocosm experiments.

The studies outlined above highlight the need for integrated Southern Ocean studies of the potential impact of UV radiation. El-Sayed *et al.* (1990) point out that a host of very complex interrelated factors influences the level of UV radiation to which planktonic organisms will be exposed in the 'real world' and these need to also be studied. They include, the diffuse attenuation coefficient for UV radiation (influenced by the often extreme clarity of Antarctic surface waters), depth of the mixed layer, residence time of the cells in the euphotic zone, seasonality of exposure, behavioural responses of the impacted organisms, their tolerance to and avoidance of UV radiation, and their capabilities of producing UV-absorbing substances and repairing UV-impaired DNA molecules.

The Southern Ocean, bounded on the north by the Antarctic Convergence, is a key component, approximately 10% of the total global ocean area, and by virtue of its uninterrupted circumpolar flow and water masses it acts as a link in the exchange of energy and matter. In addition much of the world's oceanic deep water originates along the margins of the Antarctic continent. Within this ocean one key environmental factor dominates the system – the sea ice which covers over half the ocean at its maximum extent. This sea ice has a dramatic effect on all aspects of environmental variation (SCAR/SCOR, 1988, 1990). Thus it:

- affects the magnitude of fluxes of heat, gases and matter to and from the atmosphere;
- plays a key role on CO_2 fluxes;
- has a dominant influence on water column structure, nutrient supply, primary production and sedimentation rates; and
- supports a unique and tightly coupled biological community.

The structure and functioning of the sea ice ecosystems (including the krill-dominated pelagic food web) and their reactions to possible changes in world climate is of considerable importance to the Southern Ocean as a whole. Modelling of world climate in relation to projected increases in 'greenhouse gases' in the atmosphere indicate that global warming would produce mist marked effects in polar regions. This could result in drastic changes in the distribution, character and thickness of the sea ice and crucial alterations in Southern Ocean dynamics, with consequent changes to current energy and matter fluxes. This could interrupt the contribution of the sea ice microbial communities to dependent food chains. A drastic reduction in the sea ice extent could have dramatic flow-on effects, especially on krill which as noted in Chapters 5 and 15 depend on the sea ice microalgae for winter food. Any reduction in krill could impact on the other components of the krill food web such as birds, seals and whales.

As an integral component of the Antarctic contribution to the ICSU Geosphere–Biosphere Programme SCAR is developing a integrated multidisciplinary research programme on the Antarctic sea ice zone. A Group of Specialists on Antarctic Sea Ice was established and it has produced a 'Proposal for a SCAR Multidisciplinary Programme for the Antarctic Sea Ice Zone (ASIZ)' (SCAR, 1989). The SCAR/SCOR Group of Specialists on Southern Ocean Living Resources) has been developing the ecological contribution to the proposed integrated programme. This work culminated in the report of the 'SCAR/SCOR Workshop on the Ecology of the Antarctic Sea Ice' held in Trondheim, Norway in May 1990. This workshop developed proposals for research programmes on sea-ice formation and colonization processes, sea-ice community organization, sea-ice community production, adaptations of the sea-ice biota, water column processes, including primary production, primary consumption, and secondary (and higher) production, the role of the benthos and fluxes and interactions. While the flux of biogenic particles out of the photic zone is a central process in the oceanic carbon cycle and the Southern Ocean is believed to play an important role in the flux of opaline silica and calcium carbonate, few direct measures of carbon and other elemental fluxes have to date been made in the Southern Ocean.

This programme needs to be urgently developed in an integrated manner by those nations involved in Southern Ocean research. In essence it is the logical successor to the highly successful BIOMASS (Biological Investigation of Marine Antarctic Systems and Stocks) (El-Sayed. 1988b). The primary goal of this ten-year programme (1978–1980) was to build a sound scientific foundation on which to base future management decisions concerning the Southern Ocean living resources. Because of the pivotal role of krill in the Southern Ocean pelagic ecosystem krill studies played a key role in the BIOMASS programme, although studies on other organisms at higher levels in the food web such as fish, seals and birds were also included. The First International BIOMASS Experiment (FIBEX), in which 13 ships from 11 countries participated was the largest biological expedition ever mounted in the Southern Ocean. The BIOMASS Programme marked a new era in international research collaboration in the Southern Ocean. One of the major achievements of BIOMASS was the establishment of the BIOMASS Data Centre in Cambridge, England. This was the first international data centre established to receive biological oceanographic data and it ushered in a new phase of data analysis and data interpretation. A series of data analysis workshops have been held at the Data Centre where scientists from varied backgrounds agreed to pool their unpublished data for communal analysis and joint publication of the results. The continuation of this process with the development of additional specialized data centres will be neces-

sary for the successful carrying out of the international sea ice research programme.

It is clear from the information analyzed in this book that a great deal of progress has been made in the last few decades in our understanding of the functioning of the Southern Ocean ecosystem. However, as is the nature of scientific research, it has raised many questions and provided directions for future research. While the challenges are great the community of Antarctic marine scientists are better organized and better equipped to meet such challenges than in the past. While individual researchers still have a role to play there will be increasing emphasis in the future on multidisciplinary team research. A significant trend in recent years has been the internationalization of Antarctic research and this is a trend that will accelerate. It has been my good fortune to participate in and contribute in some small way to these developments.

Appendix: Approaches to systems modelling

Organizing and understanding the complexity of marine ecosystems can best be carried out by the construction of models which have the potential for stimulation. The two approaches adopted in this book are compartmental approaches and the energy analysis approach.

A. Compartmental systems approach

Investigators using this approach are usually interested in the gross dynamics of whole ecosystems as energy processing or nutrient cycling units. Ecosystems are seen as consisting of compartments (or pools) of energy or nutrients. Each pool represents a species population or trophic level comprising the aggregated species populations at that level. For the purposes of the model, the complicated processes associated with populations making up each pool are assumed to counterbalance one another, resulting in simple behaviour of the pool as a whole. Figures 15.6, 15.12 and 15.16 are examples of such compartmental models.

B. Energy analysis approach

The principal approach adopted in this book to constructing models is Odum's (1983) energy analysis. Energy circuit diagramming is a visual mathematics which uses models of chemical, physical, biologic and geologic subsystems. The first step in energy analysis is the construction of an overview of the system being studied using energy language diagrams. Symbols representing units and processes within the system are connected by pathways representing flows of energy (or materials) from sources outside the system, through the web of the system, and finally out as degraded energy. Fig. A.1 presents the symbols that are used with a little explanation.

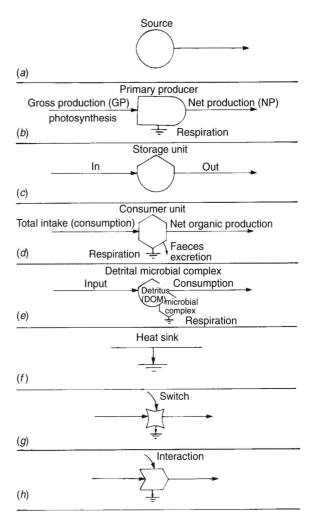

Fig. A.1 Basic energy symbols. (a) *Source*. Outside energy source delivering forces according to a programme controlled from outside; a forcing function. (b) *Producer*. Units that collect and transform low-quality solar energy. (c) *Storage*. A compartment of energy storage within the system that stores a quantity of energy as the balance of inflows and outflows; a state variable. (d) *Consumer*. Unit that transforms energy, stores it and feeds it back autocatalytically to improve inflow. (e) *Detrital–microbial complex*. A particulate organic matter (POM) storage unit with its associated microbial community. (f) *Heat sink*. Dispersion of potential energy into heat; loss of potential energy from further use by the system. (g) *Switch*. A symbol that indicates one or more switching actions. (h) *Interaction*. Interactive intersection of two pathways coupled to produce an outflow in proportion to a function of both; a work gate.

References

Abrams, R. W. (1985a) Energy and food requirements of pelagic aerial seabirds in different regions of the African sector of the Indian Ocean. In *Antarctic Nutrient Cycles and Food Webs*, ed. W. R. Siegfried, P. R. Condy & R. M. Laws, pp. 466–472. Berlin Heidelberg: Springer-Verlag.

Abrams, R. W. (1985b). Environmental determinants of pelagic seabird distribution in the African sector of the Southern Ocean. *Journal of Biogeography*, **12**, 173–492.

Ackley, S. F. (1982). Ice-scavenging and nucleation: two mechanism for incorporation of algae into newly-forming sea ice. *EOS Transactions American Geophysical Union*, **63**, 54–55.

Ackley, S. F., Taguchi, S. & Buck, K. R. (1978a). Sea ice algal relationships in the Weddell Sea. *Antarctic Journal of the United States*, **13**, 70.

Ackley, S. F., Taguchi, S. & Buck, K. R. (1978b). Primary productivity in sea ice of the Weddell Region. *Report 78–19 Cold Regions Research and Engineering Laboratory, Hanover, N.H.*

Ackley, S. F., Buck, K. R. & Taguchi, S. (1979). Standing crop of algae in the sea ice of the Weddell Sea region. *Deep-Sea Research*, **26**, 269–281.

ACMRR (FAO) (1977). *Report on the Scientific Consultation on the Conservation and Management of Marine Mammals and Their Environment and ACMRR Working Party on Marine Mammals*, Bergen, Norway, 31 August–9 September, 1976.

Adelung, D., Buchholz, F., Calik, B. & Keck, A. (1987). Fluoride in the tissues of krill *Euphausia superba* Dana and *Meganyctiphanes norvegica* M. Sars in relation to the moult cycle. *Polar Biology*, **7**, 43–50.

Adie, R. J. (1964). Geological history. In *Antarctic Research. A Review of British Scientific Achievement in Antarctica*, ed. R. Priestley, R. J. Adie & G. de Q Robin, pp. 118–162. London: Butterworths.

Aguaya, A. (1978). The present status of the Antarctic fur seal *Arctocephalus gazella* at the South Shetland Islands. *Polar Record*, **19**, 167–176.

Ainley, D. G. (1985). Biomass of birds and mammals in the Ross Sea. In *Antarctic Nutrient Cycles and Food Webs*, ed. W. R. Siegfried, W. R. Condy & R. M. Laws, pp. 498–515. Berlin & Heidelberg: Springer-Verlag.

Ainley, D. G. & Boekelheide, R. J. (1983). An ecological comparison of oceanic seabird communities in the South Pacific Ocean. *Studies in Avian Biology*, **8**, 2–13.

Ainley, D. G. & DeMaster, D. P. (1980) Survival and mortality in a population of penguins. *Ecology*, **61**, 522–530.

Ainley, D. G. & DeMaster, D. P. (1990). Upper trophic levels in polar marine ecosystems. In *Polar Oceanography. Part B. Chemistry, Biology and Geology*, ed. W. O. Smith Jr., pp. 599–630. San Diego: Academic Press.

Ainley, D. G. & Jacobs, S.S. (1981). Seabird affinities for ocean and ice boundaries in the Antarctic. *Deep-Sea Research*, **28A**, 1173–1185.

Ainley, D. G. & LeResche, R. E. (1973). The effects of weather and ice conditions on breeding Adélie penguins. *Condor*, **75**, 235–239.

Ainley, D. G. & Sullivan, C. W. (1984). AMERIEZ 1983: A summary of activities on board RV *Melville* and USGS *Westwind*. *Antarctic Journal of the United States*, **19**, 100–102.

Ainley, D. G., LeResche, R. E. & Sladen,.W. J. L. (1983a). *Breeding Biology of Adélie Penguins*. Berkeley: University of California Press. 240 pp.

Ainley, D. G., O'Connor, E. F. & Boekelheide, R. J. (1983b). *The Marine Ecology of the Birds in the Ross Sea*. American Ornithological Union Monograph No. 32. Washington, DC. 97 pp.

Ainley, D. G., Fraser, W. R., Sullivan, C. W., Torres, J. J., Hopkins, T. L. & Smith, W.O. (1985). Antarctic mesopelagic micronekton: Evidence from seabirds that pack ice affects community structure. *Science*, **232**, 847–849.

Ainley, D. G, Fraser, W. R. & Daley, K. L. (1988). Effects of pack ice on the composition of micronekton communities in the Weddell Sea. In *Antarctic Ocean and Resources Variability*, ed. D. Sahrhage, pp. 140–146. Berlin & Heidelberg: Springer-Verlag.

Alberti, G. & Kils, U. (1980). The filtering basket of *Euphausia superba*. *ICES CM 1980/L*, 54.

Alexander, V. (1980). Interrelationships between seasonal sea ice zone and biological regimes. *Cold Regions Science and Technology*, **2**, 157–178.

Alexander, V. & Niebauer, J. H. (1981). Oceanography of the eastern Bering Sea ice-edge zone in spring. *Limnology & Oceanography*, **26**, 1111–1125.

Aleyev, Y. (1977). *Nekton*. The Hague: Dr.W. Junk Publishers.

Allanson, B. R., Hart, R. C. & Lutjeharms, J. R. (1981). Observations on the nutrients, chlorophyll and primary production of the Southern Ocean south of Africa. *South African Journal of Antarctic Research*, 10, 3–14.

Allanson, B. R., Boden, B., Parker, L. & Duncombe, R. (1985). A contribution to the oceanology of the Prince Edward Islands. In *Antarctic Nutrient Cycles and Food Webs*, ed. W. R. Siegfried, P. R. Condy & R. M. Laws, pp. 38–45. Berlin & Heidelberg: Springer-Verlag.

Alldredge, A. L. & Madin, L. P. (1982). Pelagic tunicates: unique herbivores in marine plankton. *Bioscience*, **32**, 655–663.

Alldredge, A. L. & Silver, M. W. (1988). Characteristics, dynamics and significance of marine snow. *Progress in Oceanography*, **20**, 41–82.

Allen, K. R. (1966). Some methods for estimating exploited populations. *Journal of the Fisheries Research Board of Canada*, **32**, 1123–1143.

Allen, K. R. (1968). Simplification of a method for estimating exploited populations. *Journal of the Fisheries Research Board of Canada*, **25**, 2701–2702.

Allen, K. R. (1971). Relation between production and biomass. *Journal of the Fisheries Research Board of Canada*, **28**, : 1573–1581.

Allen, K. R. (1980). *Conservation and Management of Whales*. Seattle: University of Washington Press.

Amaratunga, T. (1987). Population biology. In *Cephalopod Life Cycles*, vol. 2, ed. P. R. Boyle, pp. 239–252. London: Academic Press.

AMERIEZ (1983). *A Research Plan for: Antarctic Marine Ecosysten Research at the Ice Edge Zone (AMERIEZ)*. Washington, DC: AMERIEZ Steering Committee. 38 pp. (mimeo).

Ammerman, J. W., Fuhrman, J. A., Hagstrom, A. & Azam, F. (1984). Bacterioplankton growth in seawater: I. Growth kinetics and cellular characteristics in seawater cultures. *Marine Ecology Progress Series*, **18**, 31–39.

Amos, A. F. (1984). Distribution of krill (*Euphausia superba*) and the hydrography of the Southern Ocean: large-scale processes. *Journal of Crustacean Biology*, **4** (Special Issue No. 1), 306–329.

Andersen, V. (1985). Filtration and ingestion rates of *Salpa fusiformis* Cuvier (Tunicata: Thaliacea): effects of size, individual weight and algal concentration. *Journal of Experimental Marine Biology and Ecology*, **87**, 13–27.

Anderson, H. T. (ed.) (1969). *The Biology of Marine Mammals*. New York: Academic Press.

Anderson, P. & Fenchel, T. (1985). Bacterivory by microheterotroph flagellates in sea water samples. *Limnology and Oceanography*, 30, 198–202.

Anderson, V. & Nival, P. (1988). A pelagic ecosystem model simulating production and sedimentation of biogenic particles: role of salps and copepods. *Marine Ecology Progress Series*, **44**, 37–50.

Andersson, A., Lee, C., Azam, F. & Hagstrom, A. (1985). Release of aminoacids and inorganic nutrients by heterotrophic marine microflagellates. *Marine Ecology Progress Series*, **23**, 99–106.

Andreev, M. P., Bykov, V. P. & Smirnov, V. M. (1981). Investigation of the influence of post-modern in krill on the quality of processed flesh. In *Krill Processing Technology*, ed. V. P. Bykov, pp. 68–72. Moscow: VIRNO. (in Russian with English summary.)

Andrews, K. J. H. (1966). The distribution and life-history of *Calanoides acutus* (Giesbrecht). *Discovery Reports*, **34**, 117–162.

Andrews, W. R. H. & Hutchings, L. (1980). Upwelling in the Southern Benguela Current. *Progress in Oceanography*, **9**, 1–81.

Andriashev, A. P. (1965). A general review of the Antarctic fish fauna. In *Biogeography and Ecology of Antarctica*. ed. P. van Oye & J. van Meigham, pp. 491–550. The Hague: Dr. W. Junk Publishers.

Andriashev, A. P. (1968). The problem of the life community associated with the lower layer of the Antarctic fast ice. In *SCAR/SCOR/IABO/IUBS Symposium on Antarctic Oceanography, Santiago, Chile, 13–16 September, 1966*, ed. R. I. Currie, pp. 147–155.

Andriashev, A. P., Butskaya, N. A. & Faleeva, T. I. (1979). Polovye tsikly antarkticheskih ryb *Trematomus bernachii* i *Pagothenia borchgrevinki* (Notheniidae) v sviazi s adaptatsiei k usloviian obitaniia. *Dolklady Akademii Nauk SSSR*, **248**, 400–502.

Angel, M. V. (1984). Detrital organic fluxes through pelagic ecosystems. In *Flows of Energy and Materials in Marine Ecosystems: Theory and Practice*, ed. M. J. Fasham, pp. 175–516. New York: Plenum Press.

Angel, M. V. & Fasham, M. J. R. (1983). Eddies and biological processes. In *Eddies in Marine Science*, ed. A.R. Robinson, pp. 492–524. Berlin & Heidelberg: Springer-Verlag.

Anon. (1980). FIBEX acoustic survey design. *Biomass Report Series*, **20**, 1–14.

Anon. (1981a). Post FIBEX data interpretation workshop. *BIOMASS Report Series*, **20**. 27.

Anon. (1981b). Convention on the conservation of Antarctic marine living resources. *SCAR Bulletin*, **67**, 383–395.

Anon. (1982). Technical group on programme implementation and coordination. Third meeting. *Biomass Report Series*, **29**, 1–28.

Anon., USSR (1984a). Results of research into distribution and status of stocks of target species in the Convention area–Atlantic, Indian and Pacific Ocean Sectors of Antarctica. In *Selected Papers Presented to the Scientific Committee of CCAMLR 1982–84. Part I*, pp. 227–328. Hobart: Commission for the Conservation of Antarctic Marine Living Resources.

Anon., USSR (1984b). General circulation of the Southern Ocean: status and recommendations for research. (A report by SCOR Working Group 74). *World Climate Programme Series*, No. 108. 50 pp.

Anon (1984c). Soviet fishery investigations conducted in the Southern Ocean. In *Selected Papers Presented to the Scientific Committee of CCAMLR 1982–84. Part I.*, pp. 329–352. Hobart: Commission for the Conservation of Antarctic Marine Living Resources.

Anon. (1985a). An approach to a management strategy for the Antarctic marine ecosystem. In *Selected Papers Presented to the Scientific Committee of CCAMLR. Part II.*, pp. 1–14. Hobart: Commission for the Conservation of Antarctic Marine Living Resources.

Anon. (1985b). Ecosystem management: proposal for undertaking a coordinated fishing and research experiment at selected sites round Antarctica. In *Selected Papers Presented to the Scientific Meeting of CCAMLR, Part II.*, pp. 285–294. Hobart: Commission on the Conservation for Antarctic Marine Living Resources.

Anon. (1986). Post FIBEX acoustic workshop, Frankfort, Federal Republic of Germany, September, 1984. *Biomass Report Series*, **40**, 1–106 pp.

Antezana, T. & Ray, K. (1983). Aggregation of *Euphausia superba* as an adaptive group strategy to the Antarctic ecosystem. *Berichte zur Polarforschung*, **4**, 199–215.

Antezana, T. & Ray, K. (1984) Active feeding of *Euphausia superba* in a swarm north of Elephant Island. *Journal of Crustacean Biology*, **4** (Special Issue No. 1), 142–155.

Antezana, T., Ray, K. & Melo, C. (1982). Trophic behaviour of *Euphausia superba* in laboratory conditions. *Polar Biology*, **1**, 77–82.

Armitage, K. B. (1962). Temperature and oxygen consumption of *Orchomenella chilensis* (Heller) (Amphipoda: Gammeroidea). *Biological Bulletin*, **123**, 225–232.

Armstrong, A. J. & Siegfried, W. R. (1991). Consumption of Antarctic krill by Minke Whales. *Antarctic Science*, **3**, 13–18.

Arnaud, P. M (1965). Nature de L'entagement du benthos algal et animal dans l'Antarctique. *Comptes rendus de l'Academie des Sciences, Paris*, **26**, 256–266.

Arnaud, P. M. (1970). Frequency and ecological significance of necrophagy among benthic species in Antarctic coastal waters. In *Antarctic Ecology*, Vol. I, ed. M. W. Holdgate, pp. 259–267. London: Academic Press.

Arnaud, P. M. (1974). Contribution à la bionomie marine benthique des régions antarctiques et subantarctiques. *Téthys*, **6**, 465–656.

Arnaud, P. M. (1977). Adaptations within the Antarctic marine benthic ecosystem. In *Adaptations Within Antarctic Ecosystems*, ed, G. Llano, pp.135–157. Washington, DC: Smithsonian Institution.

Arnould, J. P. V. & Whitehead, M. D. (1991). Diet of Antarctic petrels, cape pigeons and southern fulmars rearing chicks at Prydz Bay. *Antarctic Science*, **3**, 19–27.

Aseev, Y. P. (1983). Size structure and longevity of krill population from the Indian Ocean sector of Antarctica. In *Antarctic Krill: Distribution Pattern and Environment*, ed. T.G. Lubimova. *Sbornik Nauk Trudy Vses Nauchno-issled Rybnogoz Khoziaistra Okeanografii*, pp. 103–110. Moscow: Trusy VIRNO. (In Russian.)

Asencio, G. & Moreno, C. A. (1984). Dieta y selectividad alimentaria de *Protomyctophum bolini* Fraser-Brunner (Pisces; Myctophidae) en el paso Drake (Antarctica). *Series Cientifica INACH*, **31**, 85–96.

Asheimer, H., Hrause, H. & Rakusa-Suszcewski, S. (1985). Modelling individual growth of the Antarctic krill, *Euphausia superba*. *Polar Biology*, **4**, 65–73.

Ashmole, N. P. (1971). Seabird ecology and the marine environment. In *Avian Biology*, Vol. I, ed. D. S. Farner & J. R. King, pp.192–304. New York: Academic Press.

Ashmole, N. P. & Ashmole, M. J. (1967). Comparative feeding ecology of sea birds of a tropical oceanic island. *Bulletin of the Peabody Museum of Natural History*, **24**, 1–131.

Atkinson, A. (1991). Life cycles of *Calanoides acutus, Calanus simillimus* and *Rhincalanus gigas* (Copepoda; Calanoidea) within the Scotia Sea. *Marine Biology*, 109, 79–91.

Atkinson, A. & Peck, J. M. (1988). A summer–winter comparison of the zooplankton in the oceanic area around South Georgia. *Polar Biology*, **8**, 463–473.

Ayala, F. J., Valentine, J. W. & Zumwalt, G. S. (1975). An electrophoretic study of the zooplankter *Euphausia superba*. *Limnology & Oceanography*, **20**, 635–640.

Azam, F. & Ammerman, J. W. (1984). Cycling of organic material by bacterioplankton in pelagic marine ecosystems: environmental considerations. In *Flows of Energy and Materials in Marine Ecosystems*, ed, M. J. R. Fasham, pp. 345–360. New York: Plenum Press.

Azam, F. & Hodgson, R. E. (1981). Multiphasic kinetics for D-glucose uptake by assemblages of natural marine bacteria. *Marine Ecology Progress Series*, **6**, 213–222.

Azam, F., Beers, R. J, Campbell, L., Carlucci, A. F., Holm-Hansen, O. & Reid, F. M. H. (1979). Occurrence and metabolic activity of organisms under the Ross Ice Shelf, Antarctica, at Station J9. *Science*, **203**, 451–453.

Azam, F, Ammerman, J. W. & Cooper, N. (1981). Bacterioplankton distributional patterns and metabolic activities in the Scotia Sea. *Antarctic Journal of the United States*, **16**, 164–165.

Azam, F., Fenchel, T., Field, J. G., Gray, J. S., Meyer-Reil, L. A. & Thingstad, F. (1983) The ecological role of water-column microbes in the sea. *Marine Ecology Progress Series*, **10**, 257–263.

Baarud, T. & Klem, A. (1931). Hydrological and chemical investigations in the coastal waters off More in the Romsdatfjord. *Hvalrådets Skrifter*, **1**, 1–88.

Bada, J. L. & Lee, C. (1977). Decomposition and alteration of organic compounds dissolved in seawater. *Marine Chemistry*, **5**, 523–534.

Baker, A. de C. (1954). The circumpolar continuity of Antarctic plankton species. *Discovery Reports*, **29**, 201–218.

Baker, A. de C. (1959). The distribution and life history of *Euphausia tricantha* Holt and Tattersall. *Discovery Reports*, **29**, 309–340.

Baker, A. de C. (1963). The problems of keeping animals alive in the laboratory. *Journal of the Marine Biological Association, UK*, **43**, 291–294.

Baker, D. J. (1979). Polar oceanography II: South Ocean. *Reviews of Geophysics and Space Physics*, **17**, 1578–1585.

Baker, D. J., Nolin, W. P., Pillsburg, R. D. & Bryden, H. L. (1977). Antarctic Circumpolar Current; space and time fluctuations in the Drake Passage. *Nature* (London), **268**, 696–699.

Balbontin, F., Garreton, M. & Newling, J. (1986). Composicion del alimento y tarnano de las presas en larvas de peces del estrecho Bransfield (SIBEX Fase II-Chile). *Serie Cientifica Instituto Antarctico Chileno*, **35**, 125–144.

Balech, E. (1975). *Clave Ilustrada de Dinoflagelados Antarcticos*. Buenos Aires: Instituto Antarctico Argentino Direction Nacional del Antarctico, Publ. IAA No. 11. 99 pp.

Balech, E., El-Sayed, S. Z., Hasle, G., Neushel, M. & Zaneveld, J. S. (1968). Primary productivity and benthic marine algae of the Antarctic and SubAntarctic. *Antarctic Map Folio Series, Folio 10.*, 12 pp. Washington, DC: American Geographical Society.

Balushkin, A. V. (1988). Suborder Notothenioidae. In *Working List of Fishes of the World*, ed. D. E. McAllister, pp. 1118–1126. Ottawa: National Museum of Canada.

Bannister, J. L. (1969). The biology and status of the sperm whale off Western Australia – an extended summary of results of recent work. *Report of the International Whaling Commission*, **19**, 70–76.

Bannister, J. L. & Baker, A. de C. (1967). Observations on food and feeding of baleen whales off Durban. *Norwegian Whaling Gazette*, **56**, 78–82.

Banse, K. (1977). Determining the carbon to chlorophyll ratios of natural phytoplankton. *Marine Biology*, **41**, 199–212.

Banse, K. (1990). Does iron really limit phytoplankton production in offshore subarctic Pacific. *Limnology & Oceanography*, **35**, 772–775.

Barber, R. T. & Smith, R. L. (1981). Coastal upwelling systems. In *Analysis of Marine Ecosystems*, ed. A. R. Longhurst, pp. 31–68. London, New York: Academic Press.

Bargmann, H. E. (1945). The development and life history of adolescent and adult krill *Euphausia superba*. *Discovery Reports*, **23**, 105–141.

Barkley, E. (1940). Nahrung und Filterapparat des Walkrebschens *Euphausia superba* Dana. *Zeitschrift für Fischeri und deren Hilfswissenschaften*, **1**, 65–156.

Barlow, R. G. (1982) Phytoplankton ecology in the Southern Benguela Current III: Dynamics of a bloom. *Journal of Experimental Marine Biology and Ecology*, 63, 239–248.

Barrat, A. (1974). Note sur le pétrel gris *Procellaria cinerea*. *Comité National Français des Recherches Antarctiques*, **33**, 19–24.

Barrat, A. (1976). Quelques aspects de la biologie et de l'ecologie du manchant royal (*Aptenodytes patagonicus*) de îles Crozet. *Comité National Français des Recherches Antarctiques*, **40**, 9–52.

Barrat, A. & Mougin, J. L. (1974). Donnés numériques sur le zoogéographie de l'avifauna antarctique et sub-antarctique. *Comité National Français des Recherches Antarctiques*, **33**, 1–18.

Barrett-Hamilton, G. E. K. (1901). Seals. Expedition Antarkies Belgique. Results Voyage 'Belgica' 1897–1899. *Rapport Scientific Zoologie*, 1–19.

Barry, J. P. (1988). Hydrographic patterns in McMurdo Sound and their relationships to local biotic communities. *Polar Biology*, **8**, 377–391.

Barry, J. P. & Dayton, P. K. (1988). Current patterns in McMurdo Sound, Antarctica and their relationships to local biotic communities. *Polar Biology*, **8**, 367–376.

Basalaev, V. M. & Petuchov, A. G. (1969). Experimental poutassou fishing in the Scotia Sea from the research factory ship *Academik Kripovich*. *Trudy VIRNO*, **66**, 307–310. (In Russian.)

Bathmann, U., Fischer, G., Muller, P. J. & Gerdes, D. (1991). Short-term variations in particulate matter sedimentation off Kapp Norvegia, Weddell Sea, Antarctica: relation to water mass advection, ice cover, plankton biomass and feeding activity. *Polar Biology*, **11**, 185–195.

Bech, E. (1982). Der Frangplatz Antarkis: seine Rhstoffbasis und Fangbedingungen. *Siewirtschungen*, **14**, 443–445.

Beck, J. R. (1969). Food, moult and age of first breeding in the cape pigeon *Daption capensis* Linneaus. *British Antarctic Survey Bulletin*, **21**, 33–44.

Beck, J. R. (1970). Breeding seasons and moult in some smaller Antarctic petrels. In *Antarctic Ecology* vol. 1, ed. M. W. Holdgate, pp. 542–550. London: Academic Press.

Beddington, J. R. & Cooke, J. G. (1981). Development of an assessment technique for male sperm whales based on length data in catches, with special reference to the North-West Pacific stock. *Report of the International Whaling Commission*, **31**, 741–760.

Beddington, J. R. & Cooke, J. G. (1982). Harvesting from a predator prey complex. *Ecological Modelling*, **14**, 155–177.

Beddington, J. R. & de la Mare, W. K. (1984). Marine mammal fishery interactions. In *Selected Papers Presented to the Scientific Committee of CCAMLR 1982–1984. Part II*, pp. 155–178. Hobart: Commission for the Conservation of Antarctic Marine Living Resources.

Beddington, J. R. & Grenfell, B. (1980). *The Status of Major Zoological Groups in the Southern Ocean*. International Union of the Conservation of Nature. 85 pp.

Beddington, J. R. & May, R. M. (1980). Maximum sustainable yields in systems subject to harvesting at more than one trophic level. *Mathematical Bioscience*, **51**, 261–281.

Beddington, J. R. & May, R. M. (1982). The harvesting of interacting species in a natural ecosystem. *Scientific American*, **247**, 62–69.

Beddington, J. R., Beverton, R. J. H. & Lavigne, D. M. (1985). *Marine Mammals and Fisheries*. London: George Allen & Unwin.

Beers, J. R., Trent, J. D., Reid, F. M. H. & Shanks, A. L. (1986) Macroaggregates and their phytoplankton components in the Southern California Bight. *Journal of Plankton Research*, **8**, 475–487.

Bell, W. & Mitchell, R. (1972). Chemotactic and growth responses of marine bacteria to algal extracellular products. *Bulletin Marine Biological Laboratory, Woods Hole*, **143**, 265–277.

Bellido, A. (1982). Les biocenoses du littoral rocheux aux Isles Kerguelen. *Colloque sur les Ecosystèmes Subantarctiques, 1981. CNFRA*, **51**, 81–92.

Belyaev, G. M. (1958). Some characteristics of the quantitative distribution of the bottom fauna in the Antarctic. *Soviet Antarctic Information Bulletin*, **3**, 119–121.

Belyaev, G. M. & Usachov, P. V. (1957). Certain regularities in the quantitative distribution of the benthic fauna in Antarctic waters. *Dolkady Akademii Nauk SSSR*, 12, 137–140.

Bengtson, J. L. (1978). *Review of Information Regarding the Conservation of Living Resources of the Antarctic Marine Ecosystem.* Report prepared for the U.S. Mammal Marine Commission, Washington, DC Marine Mammal Commission. 148 pp.

Bengtson, J. L. (1982). Reproductive ecology of crabeater and leopard seals along the Antarctic Peninsula. *Antarctic Journal of the United States*, **17**, 185.

Bengtson, J. L. (1985). Review of Antarctic marine fauna. In *Selected Papers Presented to the Scientific Committee of CCAMLR 1982–1984. Part I*, pp. 1–226. Hobart: Commission for the Conservation of Antarctic Marine Living Resources.

Bengtson, J. L. (1985). Monitoring indicators of possible ecological changes in the Antarctic marine ecosystem. In *Selected Papers Presented to the Scientific Committee of CCAMLR 1982–1984, Part II*, pp. 43–154. Hobart: Commission for the Conservation of Antarctic Marine Living Resources.

Bengtson, J. L. (1988). Long-term trends in the foraging patterns of female Antarctic fur seals at South Georgia. In *Antarctic Ocean and Resources Variability*, ed. D. Sahrhage, pp. 286–291. Berlin & Heidelberg: Springer-Verlag.

Bengtson, J. L. & Laws, R. M. (1984). Trends in crabeater seal age at maturity: an insight into Antarctic marine interactions. In *Selected Papers Presented to the Scientific Committee of CCAMLR 1982–1984. Part II*, pp. 341–368. Hobart: Commission for the Conservation of Antarctic Marine Living Resources.

Bengtson, J. L. & Laws, R. M. (1985). Trends in crabeater seal age at maturity: an insight into Antarctic marine ecosystem interactions. In *Antarctic Nutrient Cycles and Food Webs*, ed. W. R. Siegfried, P. R. Condy & R. M. Laws, pp. 669–675. Berlin & Heidelberg: Springer-Verlag.

Bengtson, J. L. & Siniff, D. B. (1981). Reproductive aspects of female crabeater seals (*Lobodon carcinophagus*) along the Antarctic Peninsula. *Canadian Journal of Zoology,* **59**, 92–102.

Bennekom, J. von, Burma, A., Geoyens, L., Linder, L., Morvan, J., Nothig, R., Panouse, M. Sorensson, F. & Treguer, P. (1989). Uptake and regeneration of nitrogen, silica and phosphorus. *Berichte zur Polarforschung*, **65**, 56.

Benninghoff, W. S. & Bonner, W. N. (1985). *Man's Impact on the Antarctic Environment: A Procedure for Evaluating Impacts from Scientific and Logistic Activities.* Cambridge: Scientific Committee on Antarctic Research. 56 pp.

Benson, A. A. & Lee, R. F. (1975). The role of wax in oceanic food chains. *Scientific American*, **232**, 77–86.

Berkes, F. (1975). Some aspects of the feeding mechanisms of euphausiid crustaceans. *Crustaceana*, **29**, 266–269.

Berkman, P. A., Marks, D. S. & Shreve, G. P. (1986). Winter sediment resuspension in McMurdo Sound, and its ecological implications. *Polar Biology*, **6**, 1–3.

Berman, T. & Holm-Hansen, O. (1974). Release of photoassimilated carbon as dissolved organic matter by marine phytoplankton.

Marine Biology, **28**, 305.

Berman, M. S., McVey, A. L. & Ettertshank, G. (1989). Age determination of Antarctic krill using fluorescence and image analysis of size. *Polar Biology*, **9**, 267–271.

Berruti, A. (1979). The breeding biologies of the sooty albatross *Phoebetria fusca* and *P. palpebrata* at Marion Island. *South African Journal of Antarctic Research*, **8**, 99–108.

Berry, A. J. (1961). The occurrence of a leopard seal (*Hydrurga leptonyx*) in the tropics. *Annals Magazine Natural History, 13th ser., 1960 (1961)*, 591.

Bertram, G. C. L. (1940). The biology of the Weddell and crabeater seals, with a study of the comparative behaviour of the Pinnipedia. *British Grahamland Expedition 1934–37. Scientific Report*, **1**, 1–139.

Berzin, A. A. (1972). *The Sperm Whale.* (Israel Program for Scientific Translations, Jerusalem.) 394 pp.

Best, P. B. (1967). Distribution and feeding habits of baleen whales off the Cape Province. *Division of Sea Fisheries Investigational Report South Africa*, **57**, 1–44.

Best, P. B. (1968). The sperm whale (*Physeter catadon*) off the west coast of South Africa. 2. Reproduction in the female. *Division of Sea Fisheries Investigational Report South Africa*, **66**, 1–32.

Best, P. B. (1969). The sperm whale (*Physeter catadon*) off the west coast of South Africa. 3. Reproduction in the male. *Division of Sea Fisheries Investigational Report South Africa*, **72**, 1–20.

Best, P. B. (1970a). The sperm whale (*Physeter catadon*) off the west coast of South Africa. 5. Age, growth and maturity. *Division of Sea Fisheries Investigational Report South Africa*, **79**, 1–27.

Best, P. B. (1970b). Exploitation and recovery of right whale *Eubalaena australis* off the Cape Province. *Division of Sea Fisheries Investigational Report South Africa*, **80**, 1–20.

Best, P. B. (1974a). Status of the whale population off the west coast of South Africa and current research. In *The Whale Problem. A Status Report*, ed. W. E. Schevill, pp. 53–81. Cambridge, Massachusetts: Harvard University Press.

Best, P. B. (1974b). The biology of the sperm whale as it relates to stock management. In *The Whale Problem. A Status Report*, ed. W. E. Schevill, pp. 257–293. Cambridge, Massachusetts: Harvard University Press.

Best, P. B. (1979). Social organization in sperm whales *Physeter macrocephalus*. In *Behaviour of Marine Mammals Vol 3*, ed. H. E. Winn & B. L. Olla, pp. 227–289. New York: Plenum Press.

Best, P. B. (1982). Seasonal abundance, feeding, reproduction, age and growth in minke whales off Durban (with incidental observations from Antarctica). *Report of the International Whaling Commission*, 32, 755–786.

Bester, M. N. & Laycock, P. A. (1985). Cephalopod prey of the sub-Antarctic fur seal *Arctocephalus tropicalis* at Gough Island. In *Antarctic Nutrient Cycles and Food Webs*, ed. W. R. Siegfried, P. R. Condy & R. M. Laws, pp. 550–554. Berlin & Heidelberg: Springer-Verlag.

Beverton, R. J. H. & Lee, A. J. (1965). Hydrographic fluctuations in the North Atlantic Ocean and some biological consequences. In *The Ecological Significance of Biological Change in Britain*, pp. 79–107. London: Institute of Biology Symposium 14.

Biddanda, B. A. (1985). Microbial synthesis of macroparticulate matter. *Marine Ecology Progress Series*, 20, 241–251.

Biddanda, B. A. (1986). Structure and function of microbial aggregates. *Oceanologica Acta*, **9**, 209–221.

Biddanda, B. A. & Pomeroy, L. R. (1988). Microbial aggregation and degradation of phytoplankton derived detritus in sea water. I. Microbial succession. *Marine Ecology Progress Series*, **42**, 79–88.

Bidenko, M. S., Rasulova, T. A. & Odintsor, A. B. (1981). On the activity of proteolytic ferments in Antarctic krill. In *Research in Technological Characterization and Processing of Krill*, ed. M. S. Bidenko, pp. 15–18. Kalingrad: Atlant-VIRNO. (In Russian with English summary.)

Bidigare, R. R. (1989). Potential effects of UV-B radiation on marine organisms of the Southern Ocean: distribution of phytoplankton and krill during austral spring. *Photochemistry & Photobiology*, **50**, 469–477.

Bidigare, R. R., Johnson, M. A., Duffy, J. D. & Biggs, D. C. (1981). Nutrient chemistry of ammonium in Antarctic surface waters. *Antarctic Journal of the United States*, **16**, 168–170.

Bidigare, R. R., Frank, T. J., Zastraw, C. & Brooka, J. M. (1986). The distribution of algal chlorophylls and their degradation products in the Southern Ocean. *Deep-Sea Research*, **33**, 923–937.

Bienati, N. L., Comes, R. A. & Spiedo, H. (1977). Primary production in Antarctic waters: seasonal variation and production in fertilized samples during the summer cycle. in *Polar Oceans*, ed. M. J. Dunbar, pp. 377–390. Calgary: Arctic Institute of North America.

Bienfang, P. K. (1980). Phytoplankton sinking rates in oligotrophic water off Hawaii. *Marine Biology*, **61**, 69–77.

Bienfang, P. K. (1981). Sinking rates of heterogeneous temperate phytoplankton populations. *Journal of Plankton Research*, **3**, 235–253.

Bienfang, P. K. (1984). Size structure and sedimentation of biogenic microparticulates in a subarctic ecosystem. *Journal of Plankton Research*, **6**, 958–995.

Bienfang, P. K. (1985). Size structure and sinking rates of various microparticulate constituents in oligotrophic Hawaiian waters. *Marine Ecology Progress Series*, **23**, 143–151.

Bienfang, P. K. & Harrison, P. J. (1984). Sinking rate response of natural assemblages of temperate and subtropical phytoplankton to nutrient depletion. *Marine Biology*, **83**, 295–302.

Biggs, D. C. (1982). Zooplankton excretion and NH_4 cycling in near surface waters of the Southern Ocean. I. Ross Sea, austral summer 1977–1978. *Polar Biology*, **1**, 55–67.

Biggs, D. C., Johnson, M. A., Bidigare, R. R., Duffy, J. D. & Holm-Hansen, O. (1983) Shipboard autoanalyzer studies of nutrient chemistry, 0–200 m, in the eastern Scotia Sea during FIBEX. *Technical Report 82–11-T*. Department of Oceanography, Texas A&M University, College Station, Texas.

Billen, G. (1984). Heterotrophic utilization and regeneration of nitrogen. In *Heterotrophic Activity in the Sea*, ed. J. E. Hobbie & P. J. LeB. Williams, pp. 313–356. New York: Plenum Press.

Billen, G. & Fontigny, A. (1987). Dynamics of a *Phaeocystis*-dominated spring bloom in Belgian coastal waters. II. bacterioplankton dynamics. *Marine Ecology Progress Series*, **37**, 249–257.

Billen, G., Joiris, C., Wijnant, J. & Gillain, G. (1980). Concentration and microbial utilization of small organic molecules in the Scheldt Estuary, the Belgian coastal zone of the North Sea and the English Channel. *Estuarine Coastal Marine Science*, **11**, 279–294.

Bjornsen, P. K. & Kuparinen, J. (1991). Growth and herbivory by heterotrophic dinoflagellates in the Southern Ocean, studied by microcosm experiments. *Marine Biology*, **109**, 397–405.

Blankley, W. O. (1982). Feeding ecology of three inshore fish species at Marion Island (Southern Ocean). *South African Journal of Zoology*, **17**, 164–170.

Blix, A. S., Iversen, J. A. & Paske, A. (1973). On feeding and health of young hooded seals (*Cystophora cristata*) and harp seal (*Pagophilus groenlandica*) in captivity. *Norwegian Journal of Zoology*, **21**, 55–58.

Boak, A. C. & Goulder, R. (1983). Bacterioplankton in the diet of the calanoid copepod *Eurytemora* sp. in the Humber Estuary. *Marine Biology*, **73**, 139–149.

Bodungen, B. von. (1986). Phytoplankton growth and krill grazing during spring in the Bransfield Strait, Antarctica - Implications for sediment trap collection. *Polar Biology*, **6**, 153–160.

Bodungen, B. von, Brockel, K. von, Smetacek, V. & Zeitzschel, B. (1981). Growth and sedimentation of the phytoplankton spring bloom in the Bornholm Sea (Baltic Sea). *Kieler Meeresforschungen Sondheim*, **5**, 49–60.

Bodungen, B. von, Smetacek, V. S., Tilzer, M. M. & Zietzchel, B. (1986). Primary production and sedimentation during the spring in the Antarctic Peninsula region. *Deep-Sea Research*, **33**, 177–194.

Bodungen, B. von, Fischer, G., Nothig, E-M. & Wefer, G. (1987). Sedimentation of krill faeces during spring development of phytoplankton in the Bransfield Strait, Antarctica. In *Particle Flux in the Ocean*, ed. E.T. Degens, S. Honjo & E. Izdar, Mitteilungen aus dem Geologisch-Palaeontologischen Institut der Universitat Hamburg, SCOPE UNEP, Sonderband, **62**, 243–247.

Bodungen, B. von, Nothig, E.-M. & Sui, Q. (1988). New production of phytoplankton and sedimentation during summer 1985 in the South Eastern Weddell Sea. *Comparative Biochemistry & Physiology*, **90B**, 475–487.

Boesch, D. F. (1972). Species diversity of the macrobenthos in the Virginia area. *Chesapeake Science*, **13**, 206–211.

Bogdanov, M. A., Solyankin, E. V. & Radionev, S. N. (1980). The distribution of mingled water and secondary frontal zone in the Sea of Scotia and the distribution of krill swarms. In *Biological Resources of Antarctic Krill*, pp. 238–241. Moscow: VIRNO. (In Russian.)

Bolter, M. (1981). DOC-turnover and microbial biomass production. *Kieler Meeresforschungen Sondheim*, **5**, 304–310.

Bolter, M. & Dawson, R. (1982). Heterotrophic utilization of biochemical compounds in Antarctic waters. *Netherlands Journal of Sea Research*, **16**, 315–332.

Boltovoskoy, D., Alder, V. A. & Spinelli, F. (1989). Summer Weddell Sea microplankton: assemblage structure, distribution and abundance with special emphasis on the tintinnina. *Polar Biology*, **9**, 447–456.

Bonner, W. N. (1958). Notes on the southern fur seal in South Georgia. *Proceedings of the Zoological Society, London*, **130**, 241–252.

Bonner, W. N. (1964). Population increase in the fur seal *Arctocephalus tropicalis gazella* at South Georgia. In *Biologie Antarctique*, ed. R. Carrick, M.W. Holdgate & J. Prevost, pp. 438–443. Paris: Herman.

Bonner, W. N. (1968). The fur seal of South Georgia. *Scientific Report British Antarctic Survey*, **56**, 1–81.

Bonner, W. N. (1976). The status of the Antarctic fur seal *Arctocephalus gazella*. FAO Advisory Committee on Marine Resources Research, Scientific Consultation on Marine Mammals. ACMRR/MM/SC/50.

Bonner, W. N. (1981). Southern fur seals. *Arctocephalus* (Geoffrey Saint-Hilaire and Cuvier, 1926). In *Handbook of Marine Mammals*, Vol. 1., ed. S. H. Ridgway & R. J. Harrison, pp. 161–208. London: Academic Press.

Bonner, W. N. (1984). Conservation and the Antarctic. In *Antarctic Ecology*, vol. 2, ed. R.M. Laws, pp. 821–857. London: Academic Press.

Bonner, W. N. (1985a). Birds and mammals: Antarctic seals. In *Key Environments: Antarctica*, ed. W. N. Bonner & D. W. H. Walton, pp. 203–222. London: Pergamon Press.

Bonner, W. N. (1985b). Impact of fur seals on the terrestrial environment at South Georgia. In *Antarctic Nutrient Cycles and Food Webs*, ed. W.R. Siegfried, P.R. Condy & R.M. Laws, pp. 641–646. Berlin & Heidelberg: Springer-Verlag.

Bonner, W. N. & Laws, R. M. (1964). Seals and sealing. In *Antarctic Research*, ed. R. Priestly, R. J. Adie & G. de Q. Robin, pp. 163–190. London: Butterworth.

Bonner, W. N. & Lewis Smith, R. I. (ed.) (1985). *Conservation Areas in Antarctica*. Cambridge: Scientific Committee on Antarctic Research. 299 pp.

Bonner, W. N., Everson, I. & Prince, P. A. (1978). A shortage of krill *Euphausia superba*, around South Georgia. *International Council for the Exploration of the Sea*, Ser C, CM, 1978, L/22. 4 pp.

Boone, R. J. & Manthey, M. (1983). The anatomical distribution of fluoride within various body segments and organs of Antarctic krill.

Archiv fur Fischereiwissenschaft, **34**, 81–85.

Boronin, A. V. & Frolkina, Zh. A. (1976). Age determination in green notothenia (*Notothenia gibberifrons*) from the Southwest Atlantic. *Trudy Atlantic NIRO,* **70**, 29–37. (In Russian).

Bowen, S. H. (1984). Evidence of a detritus food chain based on the consumption of organic precipitates. *Bulletin of Marine Science,* **35**, 440–448.

Bowman, K. P. (1988) Global trends in total ozone. *Science,* **239**, 48–50.

Boyd, C. M., Heyraud, M. & Boyd, C. N. (1984). Feeding of Antarctic krill, *Euphausia superba. Journal of Crustacean Biology,* **4** (Special Issue No. 1), 123–141.

Boyle, P. R. (ed). (1983). *Cephalopod Life Cycles.*, Vol 1. London: Academic Press. 475 pp.

Boysen-Enney, E., Hagen, W., Hubold, G. & Piatkowski, U. (1991). Zooplankton biomass in the ice-covered Weddell Sea, Antarctica. *Marine Biology,* **111**, 227–235.

Bradfield, P. (1980). The ecology of *Trematomus borchgrevinki* in McMurdo Sound, Antarctica. BSc. (Hons) Project in Zoology, University of Canterbury, Christchurch.

Bradford, J. M. (1978). Sea-ice organisms and their importance in the Antarctic ecosystem. *New Zealand Antarctic Record,* **1**, 43–50.

Brandini, F. P. & Kutner, M. B. B. (1987). Phytoplankton and nutrient distribution off the northern South Shetland Islands (summer 1984-BIOMASS/SIBEX). *La Mer,* **25**, 93–103.

Bratbak, G. & Thingstad, T. F. (1985). Phytoplankton–bacteria interactions: an apparent paradox? Analysis from a model system with both competition and commensalism. *Marine Ecology Progress Series,* **25**, 23–30.

Bregazzi, P. K. (1972). Life cycles and seasonal movements of *Cheriimedon femoratus* (Pfeffer) and *Tryphosella kergueleni* (Miers) (Crustacea:Amphipoda). *British Antarctic Survey Bulletin,* **30**, 1–34.

Brennecke, W. (1921). Die ozeanographischen Arbeiten Den deutschen antarktischen Expedition 1911–1912. *Aus dem Arkiv dem Deuchen Seewarte,* **39**, 1–214.

Brightman, R. I. & Smith, W. O., Jr. (1989). Photosynthesis–irradiance relationships of Antarctic phytoplankton during the austral winter. *Marine Ecology Progress Series,* **53**, 143–151.

Brinton, E. (1984). Observations of plankton organisms obtained by bongo nets during the November–December ice-edge investigations. *Antarctic Journal of the United States,* **19**, 113–114.

Brinton, E. & Antezana, T. (1984). Structure of swarming and dispersed populations of krill (*Euphausia superba*) in Scotia Sea and South Shetland waters during January–March 1981, determined by Bongo nets. *Journal of Crustacea Biology,* **4** (Special Issue No. 1), 45–66.

Brinton, E. & Townsend, A. W. (1984). Regional relationships between development and growth in larvae of Antarctic krill *Euphausia superba*, from field samples. *Journal of Crustacean Biology,* **4** (Special Issue No. 1), 224–246.

Brock, V. E. & Riffenberg, R. H. (1960). Fish schooling: a possible factor in reducing predation. *Journal du Conseil Council International pour l'Exploration de la Mer,* **25**, 307–317.

Brockel, K. von (1981). The importance of nannoplankton within the pelagic Antarctic ecosystem. *Kieler Meeresforshungen Sonderheim,* **5**, 61–67.

Brockel, K. von (1985). Primary production data from the south-eastern Weddell Sea. *Polar Biology,* **4**, 75–80.

Brodie, J. (1965) Oceanography. In *Antarctica,* ed. T. Hatherton, pp. 101–127. London: Mehthuen & Co.

Brodie, P. F. (1975) Cetacean energetics, an overview of intraspecific size variation. *Ecology,* **56**, 152–161.

Broecker, W. S. (1990). Comment on 'Iron deficiency limits phytoplankton growth in Antarctic waters' by John H. Martin *et al. Global Biogeochemical Cycles,* **4**, 3–4.

Brown, K. G. (1957). The leopard seal at Heard Island, 1951–54.

Australian National Antarctic Research Expedition, Interim Report, **16**, 1–34.

Brown, R. G. B. (1980). Seabirds as marine animals. In *Behaviour of Marine Animals. Vol. 4, Marine Birds*, ed. J. Berger *et al.*, pp. 1–39. New York: Plenum Press.

Brown, R. G. B. & Nettleship, D. N. (1981). The biological significance of polynas to Arctic colonial seabirds. *Canadian Wildlife Service Occasional Paper,* **45**, 59–65.

Brown, R. G. B., Cooke, F., Kinner, P. K. & Mills, E. L. (1975). Summer seabird distributions in the Drake Passage, Chilean fjords and off Southern South America. *Ibis,* **117**, 339–356.

Brown, R. N. R. (1913). The seals of the Weddell Sea: notes on their habits and distribution. *Report of the Scientific Results of the Scottish National Antarctic Expedition,* **4**, 185–198.

Brown, S. G. (1962a). The movements of fin and blue whales within the Antarctic zone. *Discovery Reports,* **33**, 1–54.

Brown, S. G. (1962b). A note on the migration of fin whales. *Norsk Hvalfangsttid,* **50**, 13–16.

Brown, S. G. (1971). Whale marking–progress report, 1970. *Report of the International Whaling Commission,* **21**, 51–55.

Brown, S. G. (1977). Some results of sei marking in the southern hemisphere. *Report of the International Whaling Commission, Special Issue,* **1**, 39–43.

Brown, S. G. & Lockyer, G. H. (1984). Whales. In *Antarctic Ecology Vol 2,* ed. R. M.Laws, pp. 717–781. London: Academic Press.

Brownell, R. L., Jr. (1974). Small Odontocetes in the Antarctica. *Antarctic Map Folio Series,* **18**, 13–19. Washington, DC: American Geographical Society.

Bruchhausen, P. M., Raymond, J. A., Jacobs, S. S., DeVries, A. L., Thorndike, E. M. & DeWitt, H. H. (1979). Fish, crustaceans and the sea floor under the Ross Ice Shelf. *Science,* **203**, 449–451.

Bruland, K. W. & Silver, M. W. (1981) Sinking rates of faecal pellets from gelatinous zooplankton (salps, pteropods, doliolids). *Marine Biology,* **63**, 295–300.

Bryden, M. M., Kirkwood, G. P. & Slade, R. W. (1990). Humpback whales, Area V. An increase in numbers off Australia's east coast. In *Antarctic Ecosystems. Ecological Change and Conservation,* ed. K. R. Kerry & G. Hempel, pp. 271–277. Berlin & Heidelberg: Springer-Verlag.

Buchholz, F. (1982), Drach's moult staging system adapted for euphausiids. *Marine Biology,* **66**, 301–305.

Buchholz, F. (1983). Moulting and moult physiology in krill. *Berichte zur Polarforschung,* **4**, 81–88.

Buchholz, F. (1985). Moult and growth in euphausiids. In *Antarctic Nutrient Cycles and Food Webs,* ed. W. R. Siegfried, P. R. Condy & R. M. Laws, pp. 339–345. Berlin & Heidelberg: Springer-Verlag.

Buchholz, F. (1991). Moult cycle and growth of Antarctic krill *Euphausia superba*, in the laboratory. *Marine Ecology Progress Series,* **69**, 217–219.

Buck, K. R. (1981). A study of choanoflagellates (Acanthoecidae) from the Weddell Sea, including a description of *Diaphanoeca multiannulata* n.sp. *Journal of Protozoology,* **28**, 47–54.

Buck, K. R. & Garrison, D. L, (1983). Protists from the ice-edge region of the Weddell Sea. *Deep-Sea Research,* **30**, 1261–1277.

Buck, K. R., Garrison, D. L. & Hopkins, T. L. (1987). Abundance and distribution of tintinnids in an ice edge zone: an AMERIEZ study. *EOS,* **68**, 1773.

Buck, K. R., Bolt, P. A. & Garrison, D. L. (1989). Dinoflagellate cysts from Antarctic sea-ice communities. In *Fourth International Conference on Modern and Fossil Dinoflagellates, Marine Biological Laboratory, Woods Hole, April 16–22, 1989,* p. 27.

Buck, K. R., Bolt, P. A. & Garrison, D. L. (1990). Phagotrophy and fecal pellet production by an athecate dinoflagellate in Antarctic sea ice. *Marine Ecology Progress Series,* **60**, 75–84.

Buckley, J. R., Gammelsrod, T., Johannesson, J. A., Johannesson, O. M. & Roed, L. P. (1979). Upwelling: oceanic structure at the edge of the Arctic ice pack in winter. *Science,* **203**, 165–167.

Budkoviskiy, R. N. & Yaragov, B. A. (1967). Studying the Antarctic krill for the purpose of organizing krill fisheries. In *Soviet Fishery Research on Antarctic Krill*, ed. R. N. Burukovskiy. Washington, DC: US Department of Commerce (TT 67-32683).

Budylenko, G. A. (1978). Distribution and migration of Sei whales in the southern hemisphere. *Report of the International Whaling Commission*, **28**, 373–377.

Budzinski, E., Bykowski, P. & Dutkiewicz, D. (1985). *Possibilities of Processing and Marketing of Products Made from Antarctic Krill*. Rome: FAO Fisheries Technical Paper 268. 46 pp.

Bullivant, J. S. (1969). Bryozoa. *Antarctic Map Folio Series*, **11**, 22–23. Washington, DC: American Geographical Society.

Bunt, J. S. (1960). Introductory studies: hydrology and plankton at Mawson, June 1956 to February, 1957. *ANARE Report*, **56**, 1–135.

Bunt, J. S. (1963) Diatoms in Antarctic sea ice as agents of primary production. *Nature* (London), **199**, 1255–1257.

Bunt, J. S. (1964a). Primary productivity under sea ice in Antarctic waters, 1. Concentrations and photosynthetic activities of Antarctic marine microalgae. *Antarctic Research Series*, **1**, 13–26.

Bunt, J. S. (1964b). Primary productivity under the sea ice in Antarctic waters. Influence of light and other factors on photosynthetic activities of Antarctic marine microalgae. *Antarctic Research Series*, **1**, 27–31.

Bunt, J. S. (1967) Some characteristics of microalgae isolated from Antarctic sea ice. *Antarctic Research Series*, **11**, 1–14.

Bunt, J. S. (1968a). Microalgae of the Antarctic pack ice zone. In *Symposium on Antarctic Oceanography*, ed. R. I. Currie, pp. 198–218. Cambridge: Scott Polar Research Institute.

Bunt, J. S. (1968b). Influence of light and other factors on the photosynthetic activities of Antarctic Marine microalgae. *Antarctic Research Series*, **11**, 27–31.

Bunt, J. S. (1969). Microbiology of sea ice. *Antarctic Journal of the United States*, **4**, 193.

Bunt, J. S. & Lee, C. C. (1970). Seasonal primary production in Antarctic sea ice at McMurdo Sound in 1967. *Journal of Marine Research*, 28, 304–320.

Bunt, J. S. & Wood, E. J. F. (1963) Microalgae and Antarctic sea ice. *Nature* (London), **199**, 1254–1255.

Bunt, J. S., Lee, C. C. & Boggs, W. J., Jr. (1968). Microalgae and Protozoa of Antarctic pack ice. *Antarctic Journal of the United States*, **3**, 87.

Burchett, M. S. (1982). The ecology of some coastal fish populations at South Georgia. *Progress in Underwater Science*, **7**, 15–20.

Burchett, M. S. (1983a). Food and feeding behaviour of *Notothenia rossii* nearshore at South Georgia. *British Antarctic Survey Bulletin*, **61**, 45–51.

Burchett, M. S. (1983b). Age and growth of the Antarctic fish *Notothenia rossii* Fisher (1885) from South Georgia. *British Antarctic Survey Bulletin*, **60**, 45–62

Burchett, M. S. (1983c). Life cycle of *Notothenia rossii* from South Georgia. *British Antarctic Survey Bulletin*, **61**, 71–73.

Burchett, M. S., Sayers, P. J., North, A. W. & White, G. M. (1983). Some biological aspects of the nearshore fish populations at South Georgia. *British Antarctic Survey Bulletin*, **59**, 63–74.

Burchett, M. S., DeVries, A. & Briggs, A. J. (1984). Age determination and growth of *Dissothicus mawsoni* (Norman, 1937) (Pisces, Nototheniidae) from McMurdo Sound (Antarctica). *Cybium*, **8**, 27–31.

Burger, A. E. (1979). Breeding biology, moult and survival of lesser sheathbills *Chionis minor* at Marion Island. *Ardea*, **67**, 1–14.

Burger, A. E. (1985). Terrestrial food webs in the sub-Antarctic: island effects. In *Antarctic Nutrient Cycles and Food Webs*, ed. W. R. Siegfried, P. R. Condy & R. M. Laws, pp. 582–591. Berlin & Heidelberg: Springer-Verlag.

Burger, A. E., Lindeboom, H. J. & Williams, A. J. (1978). Mineral and energy contributions of guano of selected species of seabirds to the Marion Island terrestrial ecosystem. *South African Journal of Antarctic Research*, **8**, 59–70.

Burkhill, P. H. (1982). Ciliates and other microplankton components of a nearshore food web: standing stocks and production processes. *Annales de l'Institut Oceanographique*, **58** (Supplement), 335–349.

Burkholder, P. R. & Mandelli, E. F. (1965). Productivity of microalgae in Antarctic sea ice. *Science*, **149**, 972–874.

Burns, N. M. & Rosa, F. (1980). *In situ* measurement of the settling velocity of organic carbon particles and 10 species of phytoplankton. *Limnology & Oceanography*, **25**, 855–864.

Butterworth, D. S. (1984).. Antarctic ecosystem management. In *Selected Papers Presented to the Scientific Committee of CCAMLR 1982–1984. Part II*, pp. 15–42. Hobart: Commission for the Conservation of Antarctic Marine Living Resources.

Butterworth, D. S. (1986). Antarctic marine ecosystem management. *Polar Record*, **23**, 37–47.

Bykova, V. P. & Radakova, T. N. (1981). Changes in the properties of pre-cooked frozen krill flesh during storage. In *Krill Processing Technology*, ed. V. P. Bykov, pp. 7–16. Moscow: VIRNO. (In Russian with English summary.)

Cadée, G. C., Gonzales, H. & Schnack-Schiel, S. G. (1992). Krill diet affects faecal string settling. *Polar Biology*, **12**, 75–80.

Calhaem, I. & Christoffel, D. A. (1969). Some observations of the feeding habits of a Weddell seal, and measurements of its prey. *New Zealand Journal of Marine and Freshwater Research*, **3**, 181–190.

Car, M. & Codspoti, L. A. (1968). Oceanographic cruise summary, Ross Sea, Antarctica, February 1968. Informal Report No. 68–64, Naval Oceanographic Office, Washington, DC 21 pp.

Carey, A. G., Jr. (1985). Marine ice fauna: Arctic. In *Sea Ice Biota*, ed. R. A. Horner, pp. 173–203. Boca Raton, FL: CRC Press.

Carlucci, A. F. & Cuhel, R. L. (1977). Vitamins in the South Polar Seas: distribution and significance of dissolved and particulate Vitamin B_{12}, Thymine and Biotin in the Southern Indian Ocean. In *Adaptations Within Antarctic Ecosystems*, ed. G. A. Llano, pp. 115–128. Washington DC: Smithsonian Institution.

Carmack, E. C. & Forster, T. D (1975). On the flow of water out of the Weddell Sea. *Deep-Sea Research*, **22**, 711–724.

Caron, D. A. (1987). Grazing of attached bacteria by heterotrophic microflagellates. *Microbial Ecology*, **13**, 203–218.

Caron, D. A., Davis, P. G., Madin, L. P. & Siebruth, J. McN. (1982). Heterotrophic bacteria and bactivorous Protozoa in oceanic macroaggregates. *Science*, **218**, 795–797.

Caron, D. A., Davis, P. G., Madin, L. P. & Siebruth, J. McN. (1986). Enhancement of microbial population in microaggregates (marine snow) from surface waters of the North Atlantic. *Journal of Marine Research*, **44**, 543–565.

Caron, D. A., Madin, L. D. & Cole, J. J. (1989). Composition and degradation of salp fecal pellets: implications for vertical flux in oceanic systems. *Journal of Marine Research*, **47**, 829–850.

Carpenter, E. J.& Capone, D. G. (eds.) (1983). *Nitrogen in the Marine Environment*. New York: Academic Press.

Carrick, R. (1964). Southern seals as subjects of ecological research. In *Biologie Antarctique*, ed. R. Carrick, M. W. Holdgate & J. Prevost, pp. 421–432. Paris: Hermann.

Carrick, R. (1972). Population ecology of the Australian black-backed magpie, royal penguin and silver gull. In *Population Ecology of Migratory Birds: A Symposium*, pp. 41–99. Washington, DC: U.S. Department of the Interior Wildlife Research Report No. 2.

Carrick, R. & Ingham, S. E. (1962) Studies on the southern elephant seal, *Mirounga leonina* (L.). IV. Breeding and development. *CSIRO Wildlife Research*, **7**, 161–197.

Carrick, R. & Ingham, S. E. (1967). Antarctic sea birds as subjects for ecological research. *JARE Scientific Reports (Special Issue)* No. 1, 151–184.

Carrick, R. & Ingham, S. E. (1970). Ecology and population dynamics of Antarctic seabirds. In *Antarctic Ecology*, vol. 1, ed. M. W. Holdgate, pp. 505–525. London: Academic Press.

Carsey, F. D. (1980). Microwave observations of the Weddell Polyna. *Monthly Weather Review*, **108**, 2032–2044.

Casaux, R. J., Mazotte, A. S. & Barrera-Ora, E. R. (1990). Seasonal aspects of the biology and diet of the near-shore nototheniid fish at Potter Cove, South Shetland Islands, Antarctica. *Polar Biology*, **11**, 63–72.

Castellini, M. A., Davis, R. W., Davis, M & Horning, M. (1984). Antarctic marine life under the McMurdo Ice Shelf at White Island: A link between nutrient flux and seal population. *Polar Biology*, **2**, 229–232.

Castellanos, Z. J. A. & Perez, J. C. L. (1963) Algunos aspectos bioescológicos de la zona intercotidal de Carbo Primavera (Costa de Danco, Peninsula Antarctica). *Contribucíon del Instituto Antártico Argentino*, **164**, 1–29.

Castilla, J. C. & Rozbaczylo, N. (1985). Rocky intertidal assemblages and predation on the gastropod *Nacella (Patinigera) concinna* at Robert Island, South Shetlands, Antarctica. *Instituto Antartico Chileno Serie cientifica*, **32**, 65–74.

Catkins, J. & Thordardottiv, T. (1980) The ecological significance of solar UV rediations on aquatic organisms. *Science*, **239**, 48–50.

Cauwet, G. (1981) Non-living particulate matter. In *Marine Organic Chemistry*, ed. E. K. Dursma & R. Dawson, pp. 71–89. Amsterdam: Elsevier.

Cawthron, M. W. (1978). Whale research in New Zealand. *Report of the International Whaling Commission*, **28**, 109–113.

CCAMLR (1988) *Standard Methods for Monitoring Parameters of Predatory Species*. Hobart: Convention on the Conservation of Antarctic Marine Living Resources. 61 pp.

Cerri, R. D. & Fraser, D. F. (1983). Predation and risk in foraging minnows: balancing conflicting demands. *American Naturalist*, **121**, 552–561.

Chang, F. H. (1984). The ultrastructure of *Phaeocystis pouchetii* (Prymnesiophyceae) vegetative colonies with special reference to the production of new gelatinous envelope. *New Zealand Journal of Marine & Freshwater Research*, **18**, 303–308.

Chapman, D. G. (1970). Re-analysis of Antarctic fin whale population data. *Report of the International Whaling Commission*, **20**, 54–59.

Chapman, D. G. (1973). Management of international whaling and North Pacific fur seals: implications for fisheries management. *Journal of the Fisheries Research Board of Canada*, **30**, 2419–2426.

Chapman, D. G. (1988). Whales. *Oceanus*, **31**, 64–70.

Charnov, E. L., Orians, G. H. & Hyatt, K. (1976). The ecological implications of resources depressions. *American Naturalist*, **110**, 247–259.

Chavez, F. P. & Barker, R. T. (1987). An estimate of new production in the equatorial Pacific. *Deep-Sea Research*, **34**, 1229–1243.

Chekunova, V. I. & Naumov, A. G. (1982). Energy metabolism and food requirements of the marbled Notothenia, *Notothenia rossii mammorata* (Nototheniidae). *Journal of Ichthyology*, **22**, 112–121. (Translated from *Vorosy ikhtiologii*.)

Chekunova, V. I. & Rynkova, T. I. (1974). Energy requirements of the Antarctic crustacean *Euphausia superba*. *Oceanology*, **14**, 434–440.

Chittleborough, R. G. (1958). The breeding cycle of the female humpback whale, *Megaptera nodosa* (Bonnaterre). *Australian Journal of Marine & Freshwater Research*, **9**, 1–18.

Chittleborough, R. G. (1959). Determination of age in humpback whale, *Megaptera nodosa* (Bonnaterre). *Australian Journal of Marine & Freshwater Research*, **9**, 1–18.

Chittleborough, R. G. (1960). Marked humpback whale of known age. *Nature* (London), **187**, 164.

Chittleborough, R. G. (1962). Australian catches of humpback whales 1961. *Report of the Division of Fisheries and Oceanography, CSIRO, Australia*, **34**, 1–13.

Chittleborough, R. G. (1965). Dynamics of two populations of humpback whales, *Megaptera novaeangliae* (Borowski). *Australian Journal of Marine and Freshwater Research*, **16**, 33–128.

Choi, C. (1972). Primary production and release of dissolved organic carbon from phytoplankton in the Western North Atlantic. *Deep-Sea Research*, **19**, 731

Chojancki, J. & Wegelenska, T. (1984). Periodicity of composition, abundance, and vertical distribution of summer zooplankton (1977/1978) in Ezcurra Inlet, Admiralty Bay (King George Island, South Shetland). *Journal of Plankton Research*, **6**, 997–1017.

Christians, O. & Leinemann, M. (1980). Utersuchungen uber Flour im Krill. *Informationer fur Fischwirtschaft*, **27**, 254–260.

Christians, O., Leinemann, M. & Mahanty, M. (1981). Neue Erkentnisse uber den Flouridgehalt im krill. *Informationer fur Fischwirtschaft*, **28**, 70–72.

Clarke, A. (1976). Some observations on krill (*Euphausia superba* Dana) maintained in the laboratory. *British Antarctic Survey Bulletin*, **43**, 111–118.

Clarke, A. (1979). On living in cold water: *K*-strategies in Antarctic benthos. *Marine Biology*, **55**, 111–119.

Clarke, A. (1980a). The biochemical composition of krill, *Euphausia superba* Dana, from South Georgia. *Journal of Experimental Marine Biology and Ecology*, **43**, 221–236.

Clarke, A. (1980b). A reappraisal of the concept of metabolic cold adaptation in polar marine invertebrates. *Biological Journal of the Linnean Society*, **14**, 77–92.

Clarke, A. (1983). Life in cold water: the physiological ecology of polar marine ectotherms. *Oceanography and Marine Biology: An Annual Review*, **21**, 341–353.

Clarke, A. (1984). Lipid content and composition of Antarctic krill, *Euphausia superba* Dana. *Journal of Crustacean Biology*, **4**, (Special Issue No. 1), 285–294.

Clarke, A. (1985). Energy flow in the Southern Ocean food web. In *Antarctic Nutrient Cycles and Food Webs*, ed. W. R. Siegfried, P. R. Condy & R. M. Laws, pp. 571–580. Berlin & Heidelberg: Springer-Verlag.

Clarke, A. & Lakhani, K. H. (1979). Measures of biomass, moulting behaviour and the pattern of early growth in *Chorismus Antarcticus* (Pfeffer). *British Antarctic Survey Bulletin*, **47**, 61–88.

Clarke, A. & Morris, D. J. (1983a). Development of an energy budget for *Euphausia superba*. *Berichte zur Polarforschung*, **4**, 102–110.

Clarke, A. & Morris, D. J. (1983b). Towards an energy budget for krill: the physiology and biochemistry of *Euphausia superba* Dana. *Polar Biology*, **2**, 69–86.

Clarke, A. & Prince, P. A. (1980). Chemical composition and calorific value of food fed to Mollymawk chicks *Diomedea melanophris* and *D. crysostoma* at Bird Island, South Georgia. *Ibis*, **122**, 488–494.

Clarke, A., Holmes, L. J. & White, M. G. (1988a) The annual cycle of temperature, chlorophyll and minor nutrients at Signey island, South Orkney Islands. *British Antarctic Survey Bulletin*, **80**, 65–86.

Clarke, A., Quentin, L. B. & Ross, R. M. (1988b) Laboratory and field estimates of faecal pellet production by Antarctic krill *Euphausia superba*. *Marine Biology*, **98**, 557–563.

Clarke, D. B. & Ackley, S. F. (1981a). Physical, chemical and biological properties of winter sea ice in the Weddell Sea *Antarctic Journal of the United States*, **17**, 107–109.

Clarke, D. B. & Ackley, S. F. (1981b) Sea ice structure and biological activity in the Antarctic marginal ice zone. *Journal of Geophysical Research*, **89**, 2087–2095.

Clarke, D. B. & Ackley, S. F. (1984). Sea ice structure and biological activity in the marginal ice zone. *Journal of Geophysical Research*, **89**, 2087–2095.

Clarke, G. L. (1946) Dynamics of production in a marine area. *Ecological Monographs*, **16**, 323–335

Clarke, M. R. (1956). Sperm whales of the Azores. *Discovery Reports*, **28**, 237–198.

Clarke, M. R. (1972). New technique for the study of sperm whale migrations. *Nature* (London), **238**, 405–406.

Clarke, M. R. (1977) Beaks, nets and numbers. *Symposium Zoological Society London*, **38**, 89–126.

Clarke, M. R. (1980a). Squids and whales. *NERC News Journal*, **2**, 4–6.

Clarke, M. R. (1980b). Cephalopoda in the diet of sperm whales of the southern hemisphere and their bearing on sperm whale biology. *Discovery Reports*, **37**, 1–324.

Clarke, M. R. (1983). Cephalopod biomass estimation from predation. *Memoirs of the National Museum of Victoria*, **44**, 95–107.

Clarke, M. R. (1985). Marine habitats: Antarctic cephalopods. In *Key Environments Antarctica*, ed. W. N. Bonner & D. W. H. Walton, pp. 193–200. Oxford: Pergamon Press.

Clarke, M. R. & MacLoed, N. (1982a). Cephalopods in the diet of elephant seals at Signey Island, South Orkney Islands. *British Antarctic Survey Bulletin*, **57**, 27–31.

Clarke, M. R. & MacLoed, N. (1982b). Cephalopod remains in the stomachs of eight Weddell seals. *British Antarctic Survey Bulletin*, **57**, 33–40.

Clarke, M. R., Croxall, J. P. & Prince, P. A. (1981). Cephalopod remains in regurgitations of the wandering albatross at South Georgia. *British Antarctic Survey Scientific Reports*, **75**, 1–74.

Clark, W. G. (1983). Antarctic fin whale, *Balaenoptera physalus*, recruitment rates inferred from cohort analysis. *Report of the International Whaling Commission* (Special Issue).

Clough, J. W. & Hansen, B. L. (1979).The Ross Ice Shelf Project. *Science*, **203**, 433–434.

Clowes, A. J . (1938). Phosphate and silicate in the Southern Ocean. *Discovery Reports*, **19**, 1–120.

Cole, J. F., Findlay, S. & Pace, M. L. (1988). Bacterial production in fresh and salt water systems: a cross-system overview. *Marine Ecology Progress Series*, **43**, 1–10.

Colos, Y. & Slawyk, G. (1986). C-13 and N-14 uptake by marine phytoplankton. 4. Uptake ratios and the contribution of nitrate to the productivity of Antarctic waters (Indian Ocean sector). *Deep-Sea Research*, **33**(8A), 1039–1051.

Comiso, J. & Gordon, A. L. (1987). Recurring polynas over the Cosmonaut Sea and Maud Rise. *Journal of Geophysical Research*, **92**, 2819–2833.

Comiso, J. C. & Sullivan, C. W. (1986) Satellite microwave and in situ observations of Weddell Sea ice cover and its marginal ice zone. *Journal of Geophysical Research*, **91**, 9663–9681.

Comiso, J. C. & Zwally, H. T. (1984). Concentration gradients and growth and decay characteristics of seasonal sea ice cover. *Journal of Geophysical Research*, **89**, 8081–8103.

Comiso, J. C., Maynard, N. G., Smith, W. O.Jr. & Sullivan, C. W. (1990). Satellite ocean colour studies of Antarctic ice edges in summer and autumn. *Journal of Geophysical Research*, **95**, 9481–9496.

Condy, P. R. (1976). Results of the third seal survey in the Haakon VII Sea, Antarctica. *South African Journal of Antarctic Research*, **6**, 2–8.

Condy, P. R. (1977a). Annual cycle of the elephant seal *Mirounga leonina* (Linn.) at Marion Island. *South African Journal of Antarctic Research*, **14**, 95–102.

Condy, P. R. (1977b). Results of the 4th seal survey in the King-Haakon-VII Sea, Antarctica. *South African Journal of Antarctic Research*, **6**, 2–8.

Condy, P. R., van Aarde, R. J. & Bester, M. V. (1978). The seasonal occurrence and behaviour of killer whales *Orcinus orca* at Marion Island. *Journal of Zoology (London)*, **184**, 449–464.

Conroy, J. W. H. (1975). Recent increases in penguin populations in the Antarctic and SubAntarctic. In *The Biology of Penguins*, ed. B. Stonehouse, pp. 321–336. London: Macmillan.

Conroy, J. W. H. & Twelves, E. L. (1972). Diving depths of the Gentoo Penguin (*Pygoscelis papua*) and Blue-eyed Shag (*Phalacrocorax atriceps*) from the South Orkney Islands. *British Antarctic Survey Bulletin*, **30,** 106–108.

Conroy, J. W. H. & White, M. G. (1973). The breeding status of the King Penguin (*Aptenodytes patagonica*). *British Antarctic Survey Bulletin*, **32**, 31–40.

Conroy, J. W. H., Darling, O. W. H. & Smith, H. G. (1975). The annual cycle of the chinstrap penguin (*Pygoscelis antarctica*) on

Signy Island, South Orkney Islands. In *The Biology of Penguins*, ed. B. Stonehouse, pp. 353–362. London: Macmillan.

Cooke, J. G. & Beddington, J. R. (1982). Further development of an assessment technique for male sperm whales based on length data from the catches. *Report of the International Whaling Commisssion*, **32**, 239–241.

Cooke, J. G. & de la Mare, W. K. (1983). The effects of variability in age data on the estimation of biological parameters in minke whales (*Balaenoptera acutorostratus*). *Report of the International Whaling Commission*, **33**, 333–346.

Copping, A. E. & Lorenzen, C. J. (1980). Carbon budget of a marine phytoplankton-herbivore system with carbon-14 as a tracer. *Limnology & Oceanography*, **25**, 873–882.

Corless, J. O. & Snyder, R. A. (1986). A preliminary description of several new ciliates from the Antarctica including *Cohnilembus grassei* n.sp. *Protistologica*, **22**, 39–46.

Corner, R. W. M. (1972). Observations on a small crabeater seal breeding group. *British Antarctic Survey Bulletin*, **30**, 104–106.

Cota, G. F., Kottmeier, S. T., Robinson, D. H., Smith, W. O.Jr. & Sullivan, C. W. (1990). Bacterioplankton in the marginal ice zone of the Weddell Sea: biomass, production and metabolic activities during the austral autumn. *Deep-Sea Research*, **37**, 1145–1167.

Cram, D. L., Agenbag, J. J., Hampton, I. & Robertson, A. A. (1979). SAS *Protea* Cruise, 1978. The general results of the acoustics and remote sensing study, with recommendations for estimating the abundance of krill (*Euphausia superba* Dana). *South African Journal of Antarctic Research*, **9**, 3–13.

Crawford, C. C., Hobbie, J. E. & Webb, K. L. (1974). The utilization of dissolved free amino acids by estuarine microorganisms. *Ecology*, **55**, 551–563.

Croxall, J. P. (1982a). Energy costs of incubation and moult in petrels and penguins. *Journal of Animal Ecology*, 51, 177–194.

Croxall, J. P. (1982b). Aspects of the population demography of Antarctic and sub-Antarctic seabirds. *Comité National Français des Recherches Antarctiques*, **51**, 479–488.

Croxall, J. P. (1984). Seabirds. In *Antarctic Ecology, Vol. 2*, ed. R.M. Laws, pp. 533–616. London: Academic Press.

Croxall, J. P. (1989). Use of indices of predation status and performance in CCAMLR fishery management. *CCAMLR Selected Scientific Papers SC-CCAMLR SSP16*, pp. 333–366.

Croxall, J. P. & Davis, R. W. (1990). Metabolic rate and foraging behaviour of *Pygoscelis* and *Eudyptes* penguins at sea. In *Penguin Biology*, ed. L. S.Davis & J. T. Darby, pp. 207–228. San Diego: Acadamic Press.

Croxall, J. P. & Furse, J. R. (1980). Food of the chinstrap penguins *Pygoscelis antarctica* and macaroni penguins *Eudyptes chrysolophus* at the Elephant Island group, South Shetland Islands. *Ibis*, **122**, 237–245.

Croxall, J. P. & Hiby, L. (1983). Fecundity, survival and site fidelity in Weddell seals, *Leptonychotes weddelli*. *Journal of Applied Ecology*, **20**, 19–32.

Croxall, J. P. & Kirkwood, E. D. (1979). *The Breeding Distribution of Penguins on the Antarctic Peninsula and the Islands of the Scotia Sea*. Cambridge: British Antarctic Survey.

Croxall, J. P. & Prince, P. A. (1979). Antarctic seabird and seal monitoring studies. *Polar Record*, **19**, 537–595.

Croxall, J. P. & Prince, P. A. (1980a). Food, feeding and ecological segregation of seabirds at South Georgia. *Biological Journal of the Linnean Society*, **14**, 103–131.

Croxall, J. P. & Prince, P. A. (1980b). The food of Gentoo Penguins *Pygoscelis papua* and Macaroni Penguins *Eudyptes chrysolophus* at South Georgia. *Ibis*, **122**, 245–253.

Croxall, J. P. & Prince, P. A. (1982). Calorific value of squid (Mollusca: Cephalopoda). *British Antarctic Survey Bulletin*, **55**, 27–31.

Croxall, J. P. & Prince, P. A. (1983). Antarctic penguins and Albatrosses, *Oceanus*, **26**, 18–27.

Croxall, J. P., Prince, P. A., Hunter, I., McInnes, S. J. & Copestake, P.G. (1984a). The seabirds of the Antarctic Peninsula, islands of the Scotia Sea, and Antarctic Continent between 80°W and 20°W: their status and conservation. In *The Status and Conservation of the World's Seabirds*, pp. 637–660. Technical Publication No. 2: International Council for Bird Preservation.

Croxall, J. P., Ricketts, C. & Prince, P. A. (1984b). Impact of seabirds on marine resources, especially krill, of South Georgia waters. In *Seabird Energetics*, ed. G. C. Waters & H. Rahn, pp. 285–315. New York: Plenum Press.

Croxall, J. P., Prince, P. A. & Ricketts, C. (1985). Relationships between prey life-cycles and the extent, nature and timing of seal and seabird predation in the Scotia Sea. In *Antarctic Nutrient Cycles and Food Webs*, ed. W. R. Siegfried, P. R. Condy & R. M. Laws, pp. 516–535. Berlin & Heidelberg: Springer-Verlag.

Croxall, J. P., McCann, T. S., Prince, P. A. & Rothery, P. (1988a) Reproductive performance of seabirds and seals at South Georgia and Signey Island, South Orkney Islands, 1976–1987: Some implications for southern Ocean monitoring studies. In *Antarctic Ocean and Resources Variability*, ed. D. Sahrhage, pp. 261–285. Berlin Heidelberg: Springer-Verlag.

Croxall, J. P., Davis, R. W. & O'Connell, M. J. (1988b). Diving patterns in relation to diet of gentoo and macaroni penguins at South Georgia. *Condor*, **90**, 157–167.

Csirke, J. (1987) The Patagonian fishery resources and the offshore fisheries in the South-west Atlantic. *FAO Fisheries Technical Paper*, 286. 75 pp.

Culik, B. (1987). Fluoride turnover in Adélie penguins (*Pygoscelis adeliae*) and other bird species. *Polar Biology*, **7**, 179–187.

Currie, R. (1964). Environmental features in the ecology of Antarctic seas. In *Biologie Antarctique*, ed. M.W. Holdgate & J. Prevost, pp. 87–94. Paris: Herman.

Cushing, D. H. (1981). Temporal variation in production systems.In *Analysis of Marine Ecosystems*, ed. A. R. Longhurst, pp. 443–471. London: Academic Press.

Dagg, M. J., Vidal, J., Whitledge, T. E., Iverson, R. L. & Goering, J. J. (1982). The feeding, respiration and excretion of zooplankton in the Bering Sea during a spring bloom. *Deep-Sea Research*, **29**, 45–63.

Daly, K. L. (1990). Overwintering development, growth and feeding of larval *Euphausia superba* in the Antarctic marginal zone. *Limnology & Oceanography*, **35**, 1564–1576.

Daly, K. L. & Macaulay, M. C. (1988). Abundance and distribution of krill in the ice edge zone of the Weddell Sea, austral spring, 1983. *Deep-Sea Research*, **35**, 21–41.

Daniels, R. A.(1979). Nesting behaviour of *Harpagifer bispinis* in Arthur Harbour, Antarctic Peninsula. *Journal of Fisheries Biology*, **12**, 465–472.

Daniels, R. A. (1982). Feeding ecology of some fishes of the Antarctic Peninsula. *Fishery Bulletin, U.S. National Marine Fisheries Service*, **80**, 575–588.

Darnell, R. M. (1967a) The organic detritus problem. In *Estuaries*, ed. G. H. Lauff, pp. 374–375. Washington, DC: Publication No. 83 American Association for the Advancement of Science.

Darnell, R. M. (1967b) Organic detritus in relation to the estuarine system. In *Estuaries*, ed. G. H. Lauff, pp. 376–379. Washington, DC: Publication No. 83 American Association for the Advancement of Science.

David, P. M. (1955). The distribution of *Sagitta gazellae* Ritter–Zahoney. *Discovery Reports*, **27**, 235–278.

David, P. M. (1958). The distribution of chaetognaths in the Southern Ocean. *Discovery Reports*, **29**, 199–228.

David, P. M. (1965). The chaetognatha of the Southern Ocean. In *Biogeography and Ecology of Antarctica*, ed. J. van Meighem & P. van Oye, pp. 296–323. The Hague: Dr W. Junk Publishers.

Davidson, A. T. & Marchant, H. J. (1987). Binding of manganese by Antarctic *Phaeocystis pouchetii* and the role of bacteria in its release. *Marine Biology*, **95**, 481–487.

Davies, A. G. (1990) Taking a cool look at iron. *Nature* (London), **345**, 114–115.

Davies, J. L. (1960). The southern form of the pilot whale. *Journal of Mammology*, **41**, 29–34.

Davis, P. G. & Siebruth, J. McN. (1984). Estuarine and microflagellate predation of actively growing bacteria: estimates by frequency of dividing-divided bacteria. *Marine Ecology Progress Series*, **19**, 237–246.

Davis, R., Castellini, M., Horning, M., Davis, M., Kooyman, G. & Mane, R. (1982). Winter ecology of Weddell seals at White Island. *Antarctic Journal of the United States*, **17**, 183–184.

Davis, R. W. & Kooyman, G. L. (1984). Free-ranging energetics of penguins. In *Seabird Energetics*, ed. G. C. Whittlow & H. Rahn, pp. 245–248. New York: Plenum Press.

Davis, R. W., Kooyman, G. L. & Croxall, J. P. (1983). Water flux and estimated metabolism of free-ranging gentoo and macaroni penguins at South Georgia. *Polar Biology*, 41–46.

Dawbin, W. H. (1966). The seasonal migratory cycle of humpback whales. In *Whales, Dolphins and Porpoises*, ed. K. S. Norris, pp. 145–170. Berkeley, Los Angeles: University of California Press.

Dayton, P. K. (1972). Towards an understanding of community resilience and the potential effects of enrichments to the benthos at McMurdo Sound, Antarctica. In *Proceedings of the Colloquium on Conservation Problems in Antarctica*, ed. B. C. Parker, pp. 81–96. Lawrence, K S: Allan Press.

Dayton, P. K. (1979). Observations on the growth, dispersal and population dynamics of some sponges in McMurdo Sound, Antarctica. In *Biologie des Spongaires*, Vol. 291, Paris: ed. C. Levi & N. Boury-Esnaut, pp. 271–282. Colloques Internationaux du Centre National de la Recherche Scientifique.

Dayton, P. K. (1990). Polar benthos. In *Polar Oceanography Part B: Chemistry, Biology and Geology*, ed. W. O. Smith, Jr., pp. 631–685. San Diego: Academic Press.

Dayton, P. K. & Hessler, R. R. (1972). Role of biological disturbance in maintaining diversity in the deep sea. *Deep-Sea Research*, **19**, 199–208.

Dayton, P. K. & Martin, S. (1971). Observations on ice stalactites in McMurdo Sound, Antarctica. *Journal of Geophysical Research*, **76**, 1579.

Dayton, P. K. & Oliver, J. S. (1977). Antarctic soft-bottom benthos in oligotrophic and eutrophic environments. *Science*, **1977**, 55–58.

Dayton, P. K., Robilliard, G. A. & DeVries, A. L. (1969). Anchor ice formation in McMurdo Sound, Antarctica, and its biological significance. *Science*, **163**, 273–275.

Dayton, P. K., Robilliard, G. A. & Paine, R. T. (1970). Benthic faunal zonation as a result of anchor ice formation at McMurdo Sound, Antarctica. In *Antarctic Ecology*, Vol. I, ed. M. W. Holdgate, pp. 244–258. London: Academic Press.

Dayton, P. K., Robilliard, G. A., Paine, R. T. & Dayton, L. B. (1974). Biological accommodation in the benthic community at McMurdo Sound, Antarctica. *Ecological Monographs*, **44**, 105–128.

Dayton, P. K., Watson, D., Palmisano, A., Barry, J. P., Oliver, J. S. & Rivera, D. (1986). Distribution patterns of benthic microalgal standing stock at McMurdo Sound, Antarctica. *Polar Biology*, **6**, 207–213.

Deacon, G. E .R. (1937). A general account of the hydrology of the Southern Ocean. *Discovery Reports*, **15**, 125–152.

Deacon, G. E. R. (1963). The Southern Ocean. In *The Sea, Volume 2, The Composition of Sea-Water, Comparative and Descriptive Oceanography*, ed. M. N. Hill, pp. 281–296. New York: Interscience Publishers.

Deacon, G. E. R. (1964a). The Southern ocean. In *Antarctic Research*, ed. R. Priestley *et al.*, pp. 292–307. Paris: Hermann.

Deacon, G. E. R. (1964b). Antarctic oceanography: the physical environment. In *Biologie Antarctique*, ed. R. Carrick, M. W. Holdgate & J. Prevost, pp. 81–86. Paris: Hermann.

Deacon, G. E. R. (1977). Antarctic Ocean. *Interdisciplinary Science*

Reviews, **2**, 109–123.

Deacon, G. E. R. (1979) The Weddell Gyre. *Deep-Sea Research,* **26**, 981–998.

Deacon, G. E. R. (1982). Physical and biological zonation in the Southern Ocean. *Deep-Sea Research,* **29**, 1–15.

Deacon, G. E. R. (1983). Kerguelen, Antarctic and SubAntarctic. *Deep-Sea Research,* **30**, 77–81.

Deacon, G. E. R. (1984a). Water movements and Antarctic krill. *Journal of Crustacean Biology,* **4** (Special Issue No. 1), 13–15.

Deacon, G. E. R. (1984b). *The Antarctic Circumpolar Ocean.* Cambridge: Cambridge University Press.

Deacon, G. E. R. & Moorey, J. A. (1975). The boundary region between currents from the Weddell Sea and Drake Passage. *Deep-Sea Research,* **28A**, 265–268.

Dearborn, J. H. (1965a). Reproduction in the Nototheniid fish *Trematomus bernacchii* Boulenger at McMurdo Sound, Antarctica. *Copeia,* **3**, 302–308.

Dearborn, J. H. (1965b). Food of Weddell seals at McMurdo Sound, Antarctica. *Journal of Mammology,* **106**, 37–43.

Dearborn, J. H. (1967). Food and reproduction of *Glyptonotus Antarcticus* (Crustacea: Isopoda) at McMurdo Sound, Antarctica. *Transactions of the Royal Society of New Zealand,* **8**, 163–168.

de Baar, H. J. W., Burma, A. G. J., Jacques, G., Nolting, R. F. & Treguer, P. J. (1989). Trace metals–iron and manganese effects on phytoplankton growth. *Beriche zur Polarforschung,* **65**, 34–43.

de Baar, H. J. W., Burma, A. G. J., Nolting, R. F., Cadee, G. C., Jacques, G. & Treguer, P. J. (1990). On iron limitation of the Southern Ocean: experimental observations in the Weddell Sea. *Marine Ecology Progress Series,* **65**, 105–122.

De Broyer, C. (1977). Analysis of gigantism and dwarfness of Antarctic and Sub-Antarctic Gammaridean Amphipoda. In *Adaptations Within Antarctic Ecosystems,* ed. G. Llano, pp. 327–334. Washington, DC: Smithsonian Institution.

Decho, A. W. (1990). Microbial exopolymer secretions in ocean environments: their role(s) in food webs and marine processes. *Oceanography and Marine Biology: An Annual Review,* **28**, 73–153.

Deflande, G. (1960). Sur la presence de *Pavicorbicula* n.g. *socialis* dans le plankton de l'Antarctique (Terre Adélie). *Revue Algologique,* **5**, 183–189.

Deflande, G. & Deflande-Rigand, M. (1970). Nanofossils siliceux. I. Archaeomonadacae. *Fichier Micropaleontology,* **19**, 4173–4400.

Delepine, R. (1966). La vegetation marine dans l'Antarctique de l'Ouest comparee a cell des Isles Australes Francaises. Consequences biogeographiques. *Compte rendu sommaire des seances. Societie de Biogeography, Paris,* **374**, 52–68.

Delepine, R. & Hureau, J. C. (1968). Comparative study of the vertical distribution of marine vegetation of Archipel de Kerguelen and Isles Crozet. In *Symposium on Antarctic Oceanography,* pp. 164–165. Cambridge: Scott Polar Research Institute.

Delepine, R., Lamb, I. M. & Zimmerman, M. H. (1966). Preliminary report on the marine vegetation of the Antarctic Peninsula. In *Proceedings of the 5th International Seaweed Symposium, Halifax, 1965,* pp. 107–116. London: Pergamon Press.

Dell, R. K. (1964). Zoogeography of Antarctic benthic Mollusca. In *Biologie Antarctique,* ed. R. Carrick, M. W. Holdgate & J. Prevost, pp. 259–269. Paris: Hermann.

Dell, R. K. (1965). Marine biology. In *Antarctica,* ed. T. Hatherton, pp. 129–152. Wellington: A. H. & A. W. Reed.

Dell, R. K. (1972). Antarctic benthos. *Advances in Marine Biology,* **10**, 1–216.

Dell, R. K. & Fleming, C. A. (1975). Oligocene–Miocene bivalve Mollusca and other macrofossils from sites 270 and 272 (Ross Sea), DSDP, Leg 8. *Initial Reports of the Deep Sea Drilling Project,* **28**, 93–700.

DeMaster, D. (1981). The supply and accumulation of silica in the marine environment. *Geochemica et Cosmochemica Acta,* **45**, 1714–1732.

Demers, S., Legendre, L., Therriault, J. C. & Ingram, R. G. (1986) Biological production at the ice–water ergocline. In *Marine Interfaces Ecohydrodynamics,* ed. J. C. J.Nihoul, pp. 31–54. Elsevier Oceanography Series, Vol. 42.

Denham, K. L. & Powell, T. M. (1984). Effects of physical processes on planktonic ecosystems in the coastal oceans. *Oceanography and Marine Biology: An Annual Review,* **22**, 125–168.

Denys, C. J. & McWhinnie, M. A. (1982). Fecundity and ovarian cycles of the Antarctic krill *Euphausia superba* (Crustacea, Euphausiacea). *Canadian Journal of Zoology,* **60**, 2414–2423.

Desbruyeres, D. (1977). Benthic bionomy of the continental shelf of the Kerguelen Archipelago, Macrofauna. 2. Diversity of benthic annelid population in a Fjord close to the Morbihan Gulf. In *Adaptations Within Antarctic Ecosystems,* ed. G. Llano, pp. 227–238. Washington, DC: Smithsonian Institution.

Desbruyeres, D. & Guille, A. (1973). La Faune benthic de I'Archipel de Kerguelen. Première donnes quantitatives. *Comptes rendus de l'Academie des Sciences, Paris,* **276**, 633–636.

Desperin, B. (1972). Note préliminaire sur la machot *Pygoscelis papua* de l'îsle de la Possession (archipel Crozet). *Oiseau,* **42**, 69–83.

De Villiers, A. F. (1976). Littoral ecology of Marion and Prince Edward Islands (Southern Ocean). *South African Journal of Antarctic Research,* Supplement, **1**, 1–40.

DeVries, A. L. (1974). Survival at freezing temperatures. In *Biochemical and Biophysical Perspectives in Marine Biology,* Vol. 1, ed. D. C.Malins & J. R. Sargent, pp. 289–330. London: Academic Press.

DeVries, A. L. (1977). The physiology of cold adaptations in polar marine poikilotherms. In *Polar Oceans,* ed. J. M. Dunbar, pp. 409–420. Calgary: Arctic Institute of North America.

DeVries, A. L. (1978). The physiology and biochemistry of low temperature adaptations in polar marine ecosystems. In *Polar Research. To the Present and the Future,* ed. M.A. McWhinnie, pp. 175–202. AAAS Selected Symposium No. 7. Boulder, CO: Westview Press.

DeVries, A. L. (1983). Antifreeze peptides and glycopeptides in cold-water fishes. *Annual Review of Physiology,* **45**, 245–260.

DeVries, A. L. (1988). The role of antifreeze glycoproteins and peptides in the freezing avoidance of Antarctic fishes. *Comparative Biochemistry & Physiology,* **90B**, 611–612.

DeVries, A. L. & Eastman, J. T. (1978). Lipid sacs as a buoyancy adaptation in an Antarctic fish. *Nature* (London), **271**, 252–253.

DeWitt, H. H. (1970). The character of the midwater fish fauna of the Ross Sea, Antarctica. In *Antarctic Ecology,* Vol. 1, ed. M. W. Holdgate, pp. 305–314. London: Academic Press.

DeWitt, H. H. (1971). Coastal and deep-water benthic fishes of the Antarctic. *Antarctic Map Folio Series,* Vol. 15. 10 pp. Washington, DC: American Geographical Society.

DeWitt, H. H. & Hopkins, T. L. (1977). Aspects of the diet of the Antarctic silverfish, *Pleurogramma Antarcticum.* In *Adaptations Within Antarctic Ecosystems,* ed. G. A. Llano, pp. 557–567. Washington, DC: Smithsonian Institution.

DeWitt, H. H. & Tyler, J. C. (1960). Fishes of the Stanford Antarctic Biological Research Programme, 1958–1959. *Stanford Ichthyological Bulletin,* **7**, 162–169.

Dickie, L. M. (1975). Problems in predation. *Oceanus,* **18**, 30–35.

Dickie, L. M. (1979). Perspectives on fisheries biology and implications for management. *Journal of the Fisheries Research Board of Canada,* **36**, 838–844.

Dickinson, A. B. (1967). Tagging elephant seals for life-history studies. *Polar Record,* **13**, 443–446.

Dieckmann, G., Reichardt, W. & Zielinski, K. (1985). Growth and production of the seaweed, *Himanothallus grandifolius* at King George Island. In *Antarctic Nutrient Cycles and Food Webs,* ed. W. R. Siegfried, P. R. Condy & R. M. Laws, pp. 105–108. Berlin & Heidelberg: Springer-Verlag.

Divorky, G. J. (1977). Sea ice as a factor in seabird distribution and ecology in the Beaufort, Chuchi and Bering Seas. In *Conservation of Marine Birds of Northern North America*, ed. J. C. Bartonek & D. N. Nettleship, pp. 9–17. Washington, DC: US Fish and Wildlife Service, Wildlife Research Report No. 11.

Doi, T. (1979). Ecosystem network analysis relevant to krill in Antarctica. In *Tokai Regional Fisheries Research Laboratory, Tokyo*, pp. 23–32. (In Japanese.)

Doi, T., Ohsumi, S. & Nemoto, T. (1967). Population assessment of sei whales in the Antarctic. *Norsk Hvafangsttid*, **56**, 25–41.

Doidge, D. W. & Croxall, J. P. (1983). Breeding density, pup mortality and mother–pup behaviour in Antarctic fur seals at South Georgia. In *Proceedings of the Fourth Biennial Conference on the Biology of Marine Mammals, San Francisco, December 14–18, 1981.*

Doidge, D. W. & Croxall, J. P. (1985). Diet and energy budget of the Antarctic fur seal *Arctocephalus gazella* at South Georgia. In *Antarctic Nutrient Cycles and Food Webs*, ed. W. R. Siegfried, P. R. Condy & R. M. Laws, pp. 543–550. Berlin & Heidelberg: Springer-Verlag.

Doidge, D. W., McCann, T. S. & Croxall, J. P. (1986). Attendance behaviour of Antarctic Fur seal *Arctocephalus gazella*. In *Fur Seals: Maternal Strategies at Land and at Sea*, ed. R. L. Gentry & G. L. Kooyman, pp. 102–114. Princeton: Princeton University Press.

Dolzhenkov, V. N. (1973). Peculiarities of the distribution of *Euphausia superba* Dana in the Western part of the Pacific sector of Antarctica. *Abstracts of Papers, All-Union Conference on Macroplankton*, pp. 10–12. Moscow: All-Union Research Institute of Marine Fisheries and Oceanography. (In Russian.)

Donnelly, B. G. (1969). Further observations on the southern right whale, *Eubalaena australis*, in South African waters. *Journal of Reproduction & Fertility (Supplement)*, **6**, 347–352.

Doroshenko, N. V. (1979). Populations of minke whales in the southern hemisphere. *Report of the International Whaling Commission*, **29**, 361–364.

Douglas, D. P., Novitzky, J. A. & Fournier, R. O. (1987). Micro-autoradiography-based enumeration of bacteria with estimates of thymidine-specific growth and reproduction rates. *Marine Ecology Progress Series*, **36**, 91–99.

Dring, M. J. & Jewson, D. H. (1979). What does ^{14}C-uptake by phytoplankton really measure? A fresh approach using a theoretical model. *British Phycological Journal*, **14**, 122–123.

Droop, M. R. (1974). Heterotrophy of carbon. In *Physiology and Biochemistry of Algae*, ed. W. D. P. Stewart, pp. 530–539. Berkeley: University of California Press.

Ducklow, H. (1983). Production and fate of bacteria in oceans. *Bioscience*, **33**, 494–501.

Dugdale, R. C. & Goering, J. J. (1967). Uptake of new and regenerated forms of nitrogen in primary productivity. *Limnology & Oceanography*, **12**, 196–206.

Dugdale, R. C. & Wilkerson, F. P. (1990). Iron addition experiments in the Antarctic: a reanalysis. *Global Biogeochemical Cycles*, **4**, 13–19.

Duhamel, G. (1982). Biology and population dynamics of *Notothenia rossii rossii* from the Kerguelen Islands (Indian Sector of the Southern Ocean). *Polar Biology*, **1**, 141–151.

Duhamel, G. & Hureau, J-C. (1981). La situation de la pêche aux îsles Kerguelen en 1981. *La Peche Maritime*, **5**, 1–8.

Duhamel, G. & Hureau, J-C. (1985). The role of zooplankton in the diet of certain sub-Antarctic marine fishes. In *Antarctic Nutrient Cycles and Food Webs*, ed. W. R. Siegfried, P. R. Condy & R. M. Laws, pp. 421–429. Berlin & Heidelberg: Springer-Verlag.

Duhamel, G. & Hureau, J-C. (1990). Changes in fish populations and fisheries around the Kerguelen islands during the last decade. In *Antarctic Ecosystems: Ecological Change and Conservation*, ed. K. R. Kerry & G. Hempel, pp. 323–333. Berlin & Heidelberg: Springer-Verlag.

Duhamel, G. & Pletikowsic, M. (1983). Données biologiques sur les Nototheniidae de Isles Crozets. *Cybium*, **7**, 43–57.

Dunbar, M. J. (1981). Physical causes and biological significance of polynas and other open water in sea ice. In *Polynas and the Canadian Arctic*, ed. I. Stirling & H. Cleater, pp. 29–43. Canadian Wildlife Service Occasional Paper No. 45.

Dunbar, R. B. (1983). Sediment trap experiments on the Antarctic continental margin. *Antarctic Journal of the United States*, **19**, 70–71.

Dunbar, R. B., Anderson, J. B. & Domack, E. W. (1985). Oceanographic influences on sedimentation along the Antarctic continental shelf. In *Oceanology of the Antarctic Continental Shelf*, ed. S.S. Jacobs, pp. 291–312. Washington, DC: Antarctic Research Series No. 43, American Geophysical Union.

Dungan, M. L., Miller, T. E. & Thompson, D. A. (1982). Catastrophic decline of a top carnivore in the Gulf of California rocky intertidal zone. *Science* **215**, 989–991.

Dunlop, W. C., Williams, D. McB., Chalker, B. E. & Banaszak, A. (1989). Biochemical photoadaptation in vision: UV-absorbing pigments in fish eye tissues. *Comparative Biochemistry & Physiology*, **93B**, 601–607.

Durante, W. E. & Moreno, C. A. (1985). Specialized diet of *Hapagifer bispinis*. Its effect on the diversity of Antarctic intertidal amphipods. *Hydrobiologica*, **80**, 241–250.

Eastman, J. T. (1980). Evolutionary divergence in McMurdo Sound fishes. *Antarctic Journal of the United States*, **15**, 151–153.

Eastman, J. T. (1985a). The evolution of neutrally buoyant notothenoid fishes: Their specializations and potential interactions in the Antarctic food web. In *Antarctic Nutrient Cycles and Food Webs*, ed. W. R. Siegfried, P. R. Condy & R. M. Laws, pp. 430–436. Berlin & Heidelberg: Springer-Verlag.

Eastman, J. T. (1985b). *Pleurogramma antarcticum* (Pisces, Nototheniidae) as food for other fishes in McMurdo Sound. *Polar Biology*, **4**, 155–160.

Eastman, J. T. (1988). Lipid storage systems and the biology of two neutrally buoyant Antarctic notothenioid fishes. *Comparative Biochemistry & Physiology*, **90B**, 529–537.

Eastman, J. T. (1991). Evolution and diversification of Antarctic notothenioid fishes. *American Zoologist*, **31**, 106–109.

Eastman, J. T. & DeVries, A. L. (1978). Lipid sacs as a buoyancy adaptation in Antarctic fish. *Nature* (London), **271**, 352–353.

Eastman, J. T. & DeVries, A. L. (1981). Buoyancy adaptations in a swimbladderless Antarctic fish. *Journal of Morphology*, **167**, 91–102.

Eastman, J. T. & DeVries, A. L. (1982). Buoyancy studies of notothenioid fishes in McMurdo Sound, Antarctica. *Copeia*, **2**, 385–393.

Eastman, J. T. & DeVries, A. L. (1985) Adaptations for cryopelagic life in the Antarctic notothenioid fish *Pagothenia borchgrevinki*. *Polar Biology*, **4**, 45–52.

Eastman, J. T. & DeVries, A. L. (1986). Antarctic fishes. *Scientific American*, **254**, 106–114.

Eberhart, L. L. (1977). Optimal policies for conservation of large mammals. *Environmental Conservation*, **4**, 205–212.

Eberhart, L. L. & Siniff, D. B. (1977). Population dynamics and marine management policies. *Journal of the Fisheries Research Board of Canada*, **34**, 183–190.

Eberlein, K., Leal, M. T., Hammer, K. D. & Hickel, W. (1985). Dissolved organic substances during a *Phaeocystis* bloom in the German Bight (North Sea). *Marine Biology*, **89**, 311–316.

Eddie, G. C. (1977). *The Harvesting of Krill*. Rome: FAO, GLO/SO/77/2, Southern Ocean Fisheries Survey Programme. 72 pp.

Edwards, D. M. & Heap, J. A. (1981). Convention on the Conservation of Antarctic Marine Living Resources: a commentary. *Polar Record*, **20**, 353–362.

Edwards, R. & Hennemuth, R. (1975). Maximum yield: assessment and attainment. *Oceanus*, **18**, 3–9.

Efremenko, V. N. (1983). Atlas of the fish larvae of the Southern Ocean. *Cybium*, **7**, 1–75.

Ehrenberg, C. G. (1844). Einige vorlanffge Desultale der Untersuchungen der von der Sudpoleise des Capitain Ross, so wie von den Herren Schayer und Darwin zugehommenen Materialen. *Meber Preussiche Academie der Wissenschaften*, pp. 182–207.

Ehrenberg, C. G. (1853). Uber neue Anschauungen des Kleinsten nördlicher Polarlebens. *Monaistker der Berlin Akademie*, **1853**, 522–529.

Eicken, H. *et al.* (1987). The under-ice water layer. In *The Winter Expedition of the RV 'Polarstern' to the Antarctica (SNT V/1–3)*. *Berichte zur Polarforschung*, **39**, 182–189.

Ekman, V. K. (1928). A survey of some theoretical investigations in ocean currents. *Journal du Conseil, Conseil Permanent International pour l'Exploration de la Mer*, **3**, 295–297.

Ekman, V. K. (1953). *Zoogeography of the Sea*. London: Sidgwick & Jackson. 417 pp.

Eldred, G. E., Miller, G. V., Stark, W. S. & Feeney-Burns, L. (1982) Lipofuscin: resolution of discrepant fluorescence data. *Science*, **216**, 757–759.

Elizarov, A. A. (1971). Peculiarities of water dynamics in places of krill concentrations (*Euphausia superba* Dana). *Trudy Vsesoiuznogo Naucho-issledovatel'skii Morskogo Rybnogo Khoziaistva i Okeanogrraphii*, **79**, 31–40. (In Russian with English summary.)

Elliot, D. H. (1985). Physical geography: geological evolution. In *Antarctica (IUCN Key Environment Series)*, ed. W. N. Bonner & D. W. H. Walton, pp. 39–61. Oxford: Pergamon Press.

El-Sayed, S. Z. (1967). Primary productivity of the Antarctic and SubAntarctic. In *Biology of the Antarctic Seas II*, ed. W. Schmidt & G. Llano, pp. 15–47. Washington, DC: American Geophysical Union.

El-Sayed, S. Z. (1968a). Prospects of primary productivity studies in Antarctic waters. In *Symposium on Antarctic Oceanography, Santiago, Chile, 1966*, ed. R. I. Currie, pp. 227–239. Cambridge: Scott Polar Research Institute/SCAR.

El-Sayed, S. Z. (1968b). On the productivity of the South-west Atlantic Ocean and the waters west of the Antarctic Peninsula. In *Biology of the Antarctic Seas III*, ed. W. Schmidt & G. Llano, pp. 15–47. Washington, DC:American Geophysical Union.

El-Sayed, S. Z. (1968c). Primary productivity of the Antarctic and sub-Antarctic. In *Antarctic Map Folio Series*, Folio 10, ed. V. Bushnell, pp. 1–6. New York: American Geographical Society.

El-Sayed, S. Z. (1970a). On the productivity of the Southern Ocean. In *Antarctic Ecology*, Vol. 1, ed. M. W. Holdgate, pp. 119–135. London: Academic Press.

El-Sayed, S. Z. (1970b). Phytoplankton production in the South Pacific sector of Antarctica. In *Scientific Exploration of the South Pacific*, ed. W. S. Worster, pp. 193–210. Washington, DC: National Academy of Sciences.

El-Sayed, S. Z. (1971a). Biological aspects of the pack ice ecosystem. In *Symposium on Antarctic Ice and Water Masses, Tokyo, Japan, Sept. 19, 1970*, pp. 35–54. Cambridge: Scientific Committee on Antarctic Research.

El-Sayed, S. Z. (1971b). Observations on a phytoplankton bloom in the Weddell Sea. In *Biology of the Antarctic Seas IV* ed. G. Llano & I. E. Wallen, pp. 301–312. Washington, DC: American Geophysical Union.

El-Sayed, S. Z. (1971c) Dynamics of trophic relationships in the Southern Ocean. In *Research in the Antarctic*, ed. L. O. Quam, pp. 73–91. Washington, DC: American Association for the Advancement of Science.

El-Sayed, S. Z. ed. (1977) *Biological Investigations of Marine Antarctic Systems and Stocks Volume 1: Research Proposals*. Cambridge: Scientific Committee on Antarctic Research. 79 pp.

El-Sayed, S. Z. (1978). Primary productivity and estimates of potential yields on the Southern Ocean. In *Polar Research. To the Present and the Future*, ed. M. A. McWhinnie, pp. 141–160. AAAS Selected Symposia 7.

El-Sayed, S. Z. (1981). *Biological Investigations of Antarctic Systems and Stocks (BIOMASS). II. Selected Contributions to the Woods Hole Conference on Living Resources of the Southern Ocean*. Cambridge: Scott Polar Research Institute/SCAR.

El-Sayed, S. Z. (1984) Productivity of Antarctic waters: a reappraisal. In *Marine Phytoplankton and Productivity*, ed. O. Holm-Hansen, L. Bolis & R. Gilles, pp. 19–34. Berlin & Heidelberg: Springer-Verlag.

El-Sayed, S. Z. (1985). Plankton of the Antarctic seas. In *Key Environments Antarctica*, ed. W. N. Bonner & D. W. H. Walton, pp. 135–153. Oxford: Pergamon Press.

El-Sayed, S. Z. (1987). Biological productivity of Antarctic waters: present paradoxes and emerging paradigms. In *Antarctic Aquatic Biology. BIOMASS Scientific Series 7*, ed. S. Z. El-Sayed & A. P. Tomo, pp. 1–22. Cambridge: Scott Polar Research Institute/(SCAR).

El-Sayed, S. Z. (1988a). Seasonal and interannual variabilities in Antarctic phytoplankton with reference to krill distribution. In *Antarctic Ocean and Resources Variability*, ed. D. Sahrhage, pp. 101–119. Berlin & Heidelberg: Springer-Verlag.

El-Sayed, S. Z. (1988b). Productivity of the Southern Ocean: a closer look. *Comparative Biochemistry & Physiology*, **90B**, 489–98.

El-Sayed, S. Z. & Jitts, H. R. (1973). Phytoplankton production in the southeastern Indian Ocean. In *Biology of the Indian Ocean*, ed. B. Zeitzschel, pp. 131–142. London: Chapman & Hall.

El-Sayed, S. Z. & McWhinnie, M. A. (1979). Protein of the last frontier. *Oceanus*, **22**, 13–20.

El-Sayed, S. Z. & Mandelli, E. F. (1965). Primary production and standing crop of phytoplankton in the Weddell Sea and Drake Passage. In *Biology of the Antarctic Seas II*, ed. G. Llano, pp. 87–106. Washington, DC: American Geophysical Society.

El-Sayed, S. Z. & Taguchi, S. (1981). Primary production and standing crop of phytoplankton along the ice-edge in the Weddell Sea. *Deep-Sea Research*, **28**, 1017–1032.

El-Sayed, S. Z. & Turner, J. T. (1977) Productivity of the Antarctic and tropical–subtropical regions: a comparative study. In *Polar Oceans*, ed. M. J. Dunbar, pp. 463–504. Calgary: Arctic Institute of North America.

El-Sayed, S. Z. & Weber, L. H. (1982). Spatial and temporal variations in phytoplankton biomass and primary productivity in the southwest Atlantic and Scotia Sea. *Polar Biology*, **1**, 83–90.

El-Sayed, S. Z. & Weber, L. H. (1986). Size fractionation of Atlantic phytoplankton. *Antarctic Journal of the United States*, **19**, 141–143.

El-Sayed, S. Z., Stockwell, P. A., Reheim, H. A., Taguchi, S. & Meyer, M. A. (1979). On the productivity of the southwestern Indian Ocean. *CNFRA*, 44, 1–43.

El-Sayed, S. Z., Holm-Hansen, O. & Biggs, D. C. (1983). Phytoplankton standing crop, primary productivity, and near-surface nitrogenous nutrient fields of the Ross Sea, Antarctica. *Deep-Sea Research*, **30**, 871–886.

El-Sayed, S. Z., Stephens, F. C., Bidigare, R. R. & Ondrusek, M. E. (1990a). Effects of ultraviolet radiation on Antarctic marine phytoplankton. In *Antarctic Ecosystems: Ecological Change and Conservation*, ed. K. R. Kerry & G. Hempel, pp. 379–385. Berlin & Heidelberg: Springer-Verlag.

El-Sayed, S. Z., Stephens, F. C., Bidigare, R. R. & Ondrusek, M. E. (1990b). Potential effects of solar ultraviolet radiation on Antarctic phytoplankton. In *Effects of Solar Ultraviolet Radiation on Biochemical Dynamics in Aquatic Environments*, ed. N. V. Blough & R. G. Zepp, pp. 141–142. Woods Hole Oceanographic Institution Technical Report WHOI-90-09.

Emison, W. B. (1968). Feeding preferences of the Adélie penguin at Cape Crozier, Ross Island. In *Antarctic Bird Studies (Antarctic Research Series No. 12)*, ed. O. L. Austin, pp. 191–212. Washington, DC: American Geophysical Society.

Eppley, R. W. (1972). Temperature and phytoplankton growth in the sea. *Fishery Bulletin of the National Oceanic and Atmospheric Administration*, **70**, 1063–1085.

Eppley, R. W. (1980). Estimating phytoplankton growth rates in oligotrophic oceans. In *Primary Productivity in the Sea*, ed. P. K. Falkowski, pp. 231–242. New York: Plenum Press.

Eppley, R. W., Horrigan, S. G., Fuhrman, J. A., Brooks, E. R., Price, C. & Sellner, K. (1981). Origins of dissolved organic matter in Southern California coastal waters: Experiments on the role of zooplankton. *Marine Ecology Progress Series*, **6**, 149–159.

Erickson, A. W. (1984). Aerial census of seals, whales and penguins in pack the pack ice of the northwestern Weddell Sea, November 1983. *Antarctic Journal of the United States*, **19**, 121–124.

Erickson, A. W. & Hofman, R. J. (1974). Antarctic seals. *Antarctic Map Folio Series*, Vol. 18, pp. 4–12. Washington, DC: American Geographical Society.

Erickson, A. W., Siniff, D. B., Cline, D. R. & Hofman, R. J. (1971). Distributional ecology of Antarctic seals. In *Symposium on Antarctic Ice and Water Masses*, ed. G. Deacon, pp. 55–76. Cambridge: Scientific Committee on Antarctic Research.

Estep, K. W., Davis, P. G., Keller, M. D. & Siebruth, J. McN. (1986a). How important are oceanic algal nanoflagellates in bactivory? *Limnology & Oceanography*, **31**, 646–650.

Estep, K. W., Nejstgaard, J. C., Skjoldal, R. H. & Rey, F. (1986b). Predation by copepods upon natural populations of *Phaeocystis pouchettii* as a function of the physiological state of the prey. *Marine Ecology Progress Series*, **67**, 235–249.

Estep, K. W., Nejsgaard, J. C., Skjoldal, R. H. & Rey, F. (1990). Predation by copepods on natural populations of *Phaeocystis pouchet* as a function of the physiological state of the prey. *Marine Ecology Progress Series*, **67**, 235–249.

Estrada, M. & Delgado, M. (1990). Summer phytoplankton distribution in the Weddell Sea. *Polar Biology*, **10**, 441–449.

Ettershank, G. (1982). A new look at the age structure of the Antarctic krill, *Euphausia superba*. *Biomass Newsletter*, **4**, 5, 9.

Ettershank, G. (1983). Age structure and cyclical annual size changes in Antarctic krill (*Euphausia superba*). *Polar Biology*, **2**, 189–193.

Ettershank, G. (1984). A new approach to the assessment of longevity in the Antarctic krill *Euphausia superba*. *Journal of Crustacean Biology*, **4** (Special issue No. 1), 295–305.

Ettershank, G., MacDonald, I. & Croft, R. (1982). The estimation of age in the fleshfly *Sarcophaga bullata* using the age pigment lipofuscin. *Australian Journal of Zoology*, **31**, 131–138.

Evans, R. H. (1965). Current observations and lead line soundings McMurdo Sound, Antarctica. US Naval Oceanographic Office. IMR No. 0-18-65. (Unpublished manuscript.)

Everitt, D. A. & Thomas, D. P. (1986). Observations on the seasonal change in diatoms at inshore localities near Davis Station, East Antarctica. *Hydrobiologica*, **139**, 3–12.

Everson, I. (1970a). The population dynamics and energy budget of *Notothenia neglecta* Nybelin at Signey Island, South Orkney Islands. *British Antarctic Survey Bulletin*, **24**, 25–50.

Everson, I. (1970b). Reproduction in *Notothenia neglecta* Nybelin. *British Antarctic Survey Bulletin*, **23**, 81–92.

Everson, I. (1976). Antarctic krill: a reappraisal of its distribution. *Polar Record*, **18**, 15–23.

Everson, I. (1977a). Antarctic marine secondary production and the phenomenon of cold adaptation. *Philosophical Transactions of the Royal Society, Series B*, **279**, 55–66.

Everson, I. (1977b). *The Living Resources of the Southern Ocean*. Rome: FAO, Southern Ocean Fisheries Survey Programme, GLO/SO/77/1. 156 pp.

Everson, I. (1978). Antarctic fisheries. *Polar Record*, **19**, 233–251.

Everson, I. (1981). Antarctic krill. In *Biological Investigations of Marine Antarctic Systems and Stocks. Vol. II: Selected Contributions to the Woods Hole Conference on the Living Resources of the Southern Ocean*. ed. S. Z. El-Sayed, pp. 31–46. Cambridge: Scott Polar Research Institute/SCAR.

Everson, I. (1982). Diurnal variations in mean volume backscattering strength of an Antarctic krill (*Euphausia superba*) patch. *Journal of Plankton Research*, **4**, 155–162.

Everson, I. (1983). Estimation of krill abundance. *Berichte zur Polarforschungen*, **4**, 156–168.

Everson, I. (1984a). Zooplankton. In *Antarctic Ecology*, Vol 2, ed. R. M. Laws, pp. 463–490. London: Academic Press.

Everson, I. (1984b). Fish biology. In *Antarctic Ecology*, Vol. 2, ed. R. M. Laws, pp. 491–532. London: Academic Press.

Everson, I. (1984c). Marine interactions. In *Antarctic Ecology*, Vol. 2, ed. R. M. Laws, pp. 783–819. London: Academic Press.

Everson, I. (1988) Can we satisfactorily estimate krill abundance? In *Antarctic Ocean and Resources Variability*, ed. D. Sahrhage, pp. 199–288. Berlin & Heidelberg: Springer-Verlag.

Everson, I. & Goss, C. (1991). Krill fishing activity in the southwest Atlantic. *Antarctic Science*, **3**, 351–358.

Everson, I. & Ralph, R. (1970). Respiratory metabolism of *Chaenocephalus aceratus*. In *Antarctic Ecology*, Vol. I, ed. M. W. Holdgate, pp. 315–319. London: Academic Press.

Everson, I. & Ward, P. (1980). Aspects of Scotia Sea zooplankton. *Biological Journal of the Linnean Society*, **14**, 93–101.

Falkowski, P. G. (1983). Light–shade adaptation and vertical mixing of marine phytoplankton: a comparative field study. *Journal of Marine Research*, **41**, 215–237.

Falkowski, P. G. & Wirick, C. D. (1981). A simulation model of the effects of vertical mixing on primary production. *Marine Biology*, **65**, 69–75.

FAO. (1976). *Yearbook of Fishery Statistics*. Rome: FAO.

FAO. (1981). *Mammals of the Sea, Vol 3. FAO Fisheries Series No. 5.* Rome: Food and Agricultural Organization of the United Nations.

FAO (1985). *Southern Ocean CCAMLR Convention Area. Fishing Areas 48, 58 and 88. FAO Species Identification Sheets for Fishery Purposes*, Vol. II, pp. 233–471. Rome: FAO, CCAMLR.

Fay, R. R. (1973). Significance of nanoplankton in primary production of the Ross Sea, Antarctica, during the 1972 austral summer. PhD thesis, Texas A&M University, College Station, Texas. 184 pp.

Fell, H. B. & Dawsey, S. (1969) Asteroidea. *Antarctic Map Folio Series*, Vol. 11, p. 41. Washington, DC: American Geographical Society.

Fell, H. B., Holzinger, T. & Sherraden, M. (1969) Ophiuroidea. *Antarctic Map Folio Series*, Vol. 11, pp. 42–43. Washington, DC: American Geographical Society.

Fenchel, T. (1982a). Ecology of heterotrophic microflagellates. I. Some important forms and their functional morphology. *Marine Ecology Progress Series*, **8**, 211–223.

Fenchel, T. (1982b). Ecology of heterotrophic flagellates. II. Bioenergetics and growth. *Marine Ecology Progress Series*, **9**, 25–33.

Fenchel, T. (1982c). The ecology of heterotrophic flagellates. IV. Quantitative occurrence and importance as consumers of bacteria. *Marine Ecology Progress Series*, **9**, 35–42.

Fenchel, T. (1988). Marine plankton food chains. *Annual Review of Ecology & Systematics*, **19**, 19–38.

Fenchel, T. & Harrison, D. (1976). The significance of bacterial grazing and mineral cycling for the decomposition of particulate detritus. In *The Role of Terrestrial and Aquatic Organisms in Decomposition Processes*, ed. J. M. Anderson & A. Macfadyen, pp. 285–299. Oxford: Blackwell.

Fenchel, T. & Lee, C. C. (1972). Studies on ciliates associated with sea ice from Antarctica. I. The nature of the fauna. *Archiv fur Protistenkunde*, **114**, 231–236.

Ferguson, R. L. & Rublee, P. (1976). Contributions of bacteria to the standing crop of phytoplankton. *Limnology & Oceanography*, **21**, 141–145.

Fevolden, S. E. (1979). Investigations of krill (Euphausiacea) sampled during the Norwegian Antarctic Research Expedition. *Sarsia*, **64**, 189–198.

Fevolden, S. E. (1986). Genetic variation of *Euphausia superba* in the Antarctic Peninsula waters. *Sarsia*, **66**, 167–181.

Fevolden, S. E. & Ayala, F. J. (1981). Enzyme polymorphism in Antarctic krill (Euphausiacea): genetic variation between populations and species. *Sarsia*, **66**, 167–181.

Fevolden, S. E. & Schneppenheim, R. (1988). Genetic structure of *Euphausia superba* Dana in the Atlantic sector of the Southern Ocean as demonstrated by different electrophoretic techniques. *Polar Biology*, **9**, 1–8.

Filipova, J. A. (1972). New data on the squids (Cephalopoda, Oegosida) from the Scotia Sea (Antarctica). *Malacologia*, **11**, 391–406.

Fischer, G., Futterer, D., Gersonde, R., Honjo, S., Osterman, D. & Wefer, G. (1988). Seasonal variability of particle flux in the Weddel Sea and its relation to ice cover. *Nature* (London), **335**, 426–428.

Fischer, W. & Mohr, H. (1978). Verhaltensbeobachungen an Krill (*Euphausia superba* Dana). *Archiv fur Fischereiwissenschaft*, **29**, 71–79.

Fogg, G. E. (1966). The extracellular products of algae. *Oceanography & Marine Biology; An Annual Review*, **4**, 195–212.

Fogg, G. E. (1977). Aquatic primary production in Antarctica. *Philosophical Transactions of the Royal Society, London, Series B*, **279**, 27–38.

Fogg, G. E. (1982). Nitrogen cycling in sea waters. *Philosophical Transactions of the Royal Society, London, Series B*, **296**, 511–520.

Fogg, G. E., Nalewajko, C. & Watt, W. D. (1965). Extracellular products of phytoplankton photosynthesis. *Proceedings of the Royal Society, London, Series B*, **162**, 517–534.

Foldvik, A. & Gammelsrød, T. (1988). Notes on Southern Ocean sea-ice and bottom water formation. *Palaeogeography, Palaeoclimatology, Palaeoecology*, **67**, 3–17.

Forster, B. A. (1987). Composition and abundance of zooplankton under the spring sea-ice of McMurdo Sound, Antarctica. *Polar Biology*, **8**, 41–48.

Forster, B. A., Cargill, J. M. & Montgomery, J. C. (1987). Planktivory in *Pagothenia borchgrevinki* (Pisces: Nototheniidae) in McMurdo Sound, Antarctica. *Polar Biology*, **8**, 49–54.

Forster, T. D. (1978) The temperature and salinity fields under the Ross Ice Shelf, Antarctica. *Antarctic Journal of the United States*, **13**, 81–82.

Forster, T. D. (1981). The physical oceanography of the Southern Ocean. *BIOMASS Scientific Series*, **2**, 9–22.

Forster, T. D. (1984). The marine environment. In *Antarctic Ecology, Vol. 2*, ed. R. M. Laws, pp. 345–371.

Forster, T. D. & Carmack, E. C. (1976). Frontal zone mixing and Antarctic bottom water formation in the southern Weddell Sea. *Deep-Sea Research*, **23**, 301–317.

Forster, T. D. & Middleton, J. H. (1984). The oceanographic structure of the eastern Scotia Sea. I. Physical oceanography. *Deep-Sea Research*, **31**, 529–550.

Fowler, C. W. (1980). Indices of population status. In *A Search for Management Criteria*, ed. C. W. Fowler, W. T. Bunderson, M. B. Cherry, R. J. Reyl & B. B. Steele, pp. 283–295. Washington, DC: United States Marine Mammal Commission.

Fowler, C. W. & Smith, T. D. (1981). *Dynamics of Large Mammal Populations*. New York: John Wiley.

Fowler, S. W. & Knauer, G. A. (1986). Role of large particles in the transport of elements and organic compounds through the oceanic water column. *Progress in Oceanography*, **16**, 147–194.

Foxton, P. (1956). The distribution of the standing crop of zooplankton in the Southern Ocean. *Discovery Reports*, **28**, 191–236.

Foxton, P. (1964). Seasonal variation in the plankton of Antarctic waters. In *Biologie Antarctique*, ed. R. Carrick, M. W. Holdgate & J. Prevost, pp. 311–318. Paris: Herman.

Foxton, P. (1966). The distribution and life-history of *Salpa thompsoni* Foxton with observations on a related species *Salpa gerlachi* Foxton. *Discovery Reports*, **34**, 1–116.

Foxton, P. & Roe, H. S. J. (1974). Observations on the nocturnal feeding of some mesopelagic decapod crustaceans. *Marine Biology*,

28, 37.

Fradet, G. (1985) Evaluation of chitosan as a new hemostatic agent. In *Proceedings of the Third International Conference on Chitin/Chitosan. Seregallia, Italy.*

Frakes, L. & Kemp, E. M. (1972). Influence of continental positions on early tertiary climates. *Nature* (London), **240**, 97–100.

Franz, G., Hagen, W., Hempel, I., Marschall, H-P., Marschall, S. & Mizdalski, E. (1987). Die Winter-Expeditioon mit FS 'Polarstern' in die Antarctkis (ANT V/1–3). *Berichte zur Polarforschung*, **39**, 197–204.

Fraser, F. C. (1936). On the development and distribution of young stages of krill *Euphausia superba. Discovery Reports*, **14**, 3–190.

Fraser, W. R. & Ainley, D. G. (1986). Ice edges and seabird occurrence in Antarctica. *Bioscience*, **36**, 258–263.

Freyer, G. (1957). The food of some fresh-water cyclopoid copepods and its ecological significance. *Journal of Animal Ecology*, **26**, 263–286.

Freytag, C. E. (1977). Beiträge zur Biologie von *Notothenia rossii mamorata* Fischer. MS thesis, University of Keil. 72 pp.

Frost, B. W., Landry, M. R. & Hassel, R. D. (1983). Feeding behaviour of large calanoid copepods *Neoclanus cristatus* and *N. plumchrus* from the subarctic Pacific Ocean. *Deep-Sea Research*, **30**, 1–13.

Frost, G. W. & McCrone, L. E. (1979). Vertical distribution and abundance of some mesopelagic fishes in the eastern Subarctic Pacific Ocean in summer. *Fishery Bulletin*, **76**, 751–770.

Fry, W. G. (1964). The pycnogonid fauna of the Antarctic continental shelf. In *Biologie Antarctique*, ed. R. Carrick, M. W. Holdgate & J. Prevost, pp. 263–270. Paris: Herman.

Fryxell, G. A. (1989). Marine phytoplankton at the Weddell Sea ice edge: seasonal changes at the specific level. *Polar Biology*, **10**, 1–18.

Fryxell, G. A. & Hasle, G. R. (1979). The genus *Thalassiosira*: *T. trifulta* sp. nov., and other species with tricolumnar support on strutted processes. *Beihefte zur Nova Hedwigia*, **64**, 13–32.

Fryxell, G. A. & Kendrick, G. A. (1988). Austral spring microalgae across the Weddell Sea ice edge: spatial relationships found along a northernward transect during AMERIEZ 83. *Deep-Sea Research*, **35**, 1–20.

Fryxell, G. A., Villareal, T. A. & Hoban, M. A. (1979). *Thalassiosira scotia* sp. nov.: observations on a phytoplankton increase in early austral spring north of the Scotia Ridge. *Journal of Plankton Research*, **1**, 335–370.

Fryxell, G. A., Theriot, E. C. & Buck, K. B. (1984). Phytoplankton, ice algae and choanoflagellates from AMERIEZ, the Southern Atlantic and Indian Oceans. *Antarctic Journal of the United States*, **19**, 107–109.

Fuhrman, J. A. (1987). Close coupling between release and uptake of dissolved free amino acids in seawater studied by an isotope dilution approach. *Marine Ecology Progress Series*, **37**, 45–55.

Fuhrman, J. A. & Azam, F. (1980). Bacterioplankton secondary production estimates for coastal waters of British Columbia, Antarctica and California. *Applied Environmental Microbiology*, **39**, 1085–1095.

Fuhrman, J. A. & Azam, F. (1982). Thymidine incorporation as a measure of heterotrophic bacterioplankton in marine surface waters: evaluation and field results. *Marine Biology*, **66**, 109–120.

Fuhrman, J. A. & McManus, G. B. (1984). Do bacteria-sized eucaryotes consume significant bacterial production? *Science*, **224**, 1257–1260.

Fukami, K., Simidu, U. & Taga, N. (1985a). Microbial decomposition of phyto- and zooplankton in sea water. 1. Changes in organic matter. *Marine Ecology Progress Series*, **21**, 1–5.

Fukami, K., Simidu, U. & Taga, N. (1985b). Microbial decomposition of phyto- and zooplankton in sea water. 2. Changes in the bacterial community. *Marine Ecology Progress Series*, **21**, 7–13.

Fukuchi, M. (1977). Chlorophyll-a content in the surface waters along the course of the *Fuji* to and from Antarctica in 1976–77. *Antarctic Record*, **60**, 57–69.

Fukuchi, M. (1980). Phytoplankton chlorophyll stocks in the Antarctic Ocean. *Journal of the Oceanographical Society of Japan*, **36**, 73–84.

Fukuchi, M. & Sasaki, H. (1981). Phytoplankton and zooplankton stocks and downward flux of particulate matter around the fast ice edge of Lutzow-Holm Bay, Antarctica. *Memoirs of the National Institute of Polar Research*, **34**, 52–59.

Fukuchi, M. & Tamura, S. (1982). Chlorophyll *a* distribution in the Indian sector of the Antarctic Ocean in 1978–1979. *Antarctic Record*, **74**, 143–162.

Fukuchi, M. & Tanimura, A. (1981). A preliminary note on the occurrence of copepods under the sea ice near Syowa Station, Antarctica. *Memoirs National Institute of Polar Research, Special Issue*, **32**, 51–59.

Fukuchi, M., Tanimura, A. & Ohtsuka, H. (1984). Seasonal change of chlorophyll *a* under fast ice in Lutzow-Holm Bay, Antarctica. *Memoirs National Institute of Polar Research, Special Issue*, **32**, 51–59.

Fukuchi, M., Tanimura, A. & Ohtsuka, H. (1985a). Marine biological and oceanographical investigations in Lutzoe-Holm Bay, Antarctica. In *Antarctic Nutrient Cycles and Food Webs*, ed. W. R. Siegfried, P. R. Condy & R. M. Laws, pp. 52–59. Berlin & Heidelberg: Springer-Verlag.

Fukuchi, M., Tanimura, A. and Ohtsuka, N. (1985b). Zooplankton community conditions under the sea ice near Syowa Station, Antarctica. *Bulletin of Marine Science*, **37**, 518–528.

Fukuchi, M., Fukuda, Y, Ohno, M & Hattori, H. (1986). Surface phytoplankton chlorophyll distribution continuously observed in the JARE-26 cruise (1984/85) to Syowa Station, Antarctica (SIBEX II). *Memoirs National Institute of Polar Research, Special Issue*, **44**, 15–23.

Fukuchi, M., Hattori, H., Sasaki, H. & Hoshiai, T. (1988). A phytoplankton bloom and associated processes observed with a long-term moored system in Antarctic waters. *Marine Ecology Progress Series*, **45**, 279–288.

Fukuda, Y., Ohno, M. & Fukuchi, M. (1985). Surface chlorophyll *a* distribution in the marginal ice zone in Antarctica in 1984/85. *Memoirs National Institute of Polar Research*, **44**, 15–23.

Fukuda, Y., Ohno, M. & Fukuchi, M. (1986). Surface chlorophyll *a* distribution in marginal ice zone in Antarctica, 1984/85. *Memoirs National Institute of Polar Research, Special Issue*, **44**, 24–33.

Fukui, F., Otomo, K. & Okabe, S. (1986). Nutrient depression in a blooming area of Prydz Bay, Antarctica. *Memoirs National Institute of Polar Research*, **44**, 43–54.

Furness, R. W. (1982). Estimating the food requirements of seabird and seal populations and their interactions with commercial fisheries and fish stocks. In *Proceedings of the Symposium on Sea and Shore Birds, African Seabird Group, Capetown*, ed. J. Cooper, pp.1–14.

Gain, L. (1912). La flore algologique des regios antarctiques et subantarctiques. *Seconde Expedition Antarctiques Française*. Paris: Science naturelle Documentation Scientifique. 218 pp.

Gallardo, V. A. & Castilla, J. G. (1968). Mass mortality in the benthic infauna of Port Forster resulting from the eruptions in Deception Island, South Shetland, Islands. *Publication Instituto Antarctico Chileno*, **16**, 1–13.

Gallardo, V. A. & Castilla, J. G. (1969). Quantitative benthic survey of the infauna of Chile bay (Greenwich Island, South Shetland Islands). *Gayana (Zoology)*, **16**, 1–16.

Gallardo, V. A. & Castilla, J. G. (1970). Quantitative observations on the benthic macrofauna of Port Forster (Deception Island) and Chile Bay (Greenwich Island). In *Antarctic Ecology*, Vol. 1, ed. M. W. Holdgate, pp. 242–243. London: Academic Press.

Gallardo, V. A., Castilla, J. C., Retamal, M., Yanez, A., Moyana, H. I. & Hermosilla, J. G. (1977). Quantitative studies on the soft bottom

macrobenthic communities of shallow Antarctic bays. In *Adaptations Within Antarctic Ecosystems*, ed. G. Llano, pp. 361–387. Washington, DC: Smithsonian Institution.

Gambell, R. (1968). Seasonal cycles and reproduction in sei whales of the southern hemisphere. *Discovery Reports*, **35**, 31–134.

Gambell, R. (1972). Sperm whales off Durham. *Discovery Reports*, **35**, 119–358.

Gambell, R. (1973). Some effects of exploitation on reproduction in whales. *Journal of Reproduction & Fertility, (Supplement)*, **19**, 533–553.

Gambell, R. (1975). Variations in reproductive parameters associated with whale stock size. *Report of the International Whaling Commission*, **25**, 182–189.

Gambell, R. (1976a). World whale stocks. *Mammal Review*, **6**, 41–53.

Gambell, R. (1976b). Population biology and the management of whales. In *Applied Biology*, Vol. I, ed. T.H. Coaker, pp. 247–343. London: Academic Press.

Gambell, R. (1977). Dentinal layer formation in sperm whale teeth. In *A Voyage of Discovery*, ed. M. Angel, pp. 583–590. Oxford: Pergamon Press.

Gambell, R. (1985). Birds and mammals: Antarctic whales. In *Key Environments Antarctica*, ed. W.N. Bonner & D.W.H. Walton, pp. 223–241. Oxford: Pergamon Press.

Gambell, R. (1989). How many great whales in the Antarctic. *BIOMASS Newsletter*, **10**(2), 4.

Gamble, J. C. (1978). Copepod grazing during a declining spring phytoplankton bloom in the North Sea. *Marine Biology*, **49**, 303–315.

Garrison, D. L. (1984). Marine planktonic diatoms. In *Significance of Plantonic Life Cycles in Population Survival*, ed. K. A. Steidinger & L. M. Walker, pp. 1–17. Boca Raton, FL: CRC Press.

Garrison, D. L. (1991). Antarctic sea ice biota. *American Zoologist*, **31**, 17–33.

Garrison, D. L. & Buck, K. R. (1982). Sea ice algae in the Weddell Sea. I. Biomass distribution and physical environment. *EOS*, **63**, 47.

Garrison, D. L. & Buck, K. R. (1985a). Microheterotrophs in the ice edge zone: an AMERIEZ study. *Antarctic Journal of the United States*, **19**, 136–137.

Garrison, D. L. & Buck, K. R. (1985b). Sea-ice algal communities in the Weddell Sea: species composition in ice and plankton assemblages. In *Marine Biology of Polar Regions and Effects of Stress on Marine Organisms*, ed. J.S. Gray & M.E. Christiansen, pp. 103–121. New York: John Wiley & Sons.

Garrison, D. L. & Buck, K. R. (1986). Organism losses during ice melting: a serious bias in sea ice community studies. *Polar Biology*, **6**, 237–239..

Garrison, D. L. & Buck, K. R. (1989a). The biota of the Antarctic pack ice in the Weddell Sea and Antarctic Peninsula regions. *Polar Biology*, **10**, 211–219

Garrison, D. L. & Buck, K. R. (1989b). Protozooplankton in the Weddell Sea, Antarctica: abundance and distribution in the ice-edge zone. *Polar Biology*, **9**, 341–351.

Garrison, D. L., Ackley, S. F. & Buck, K. R. (1983). A physical mechanism for establishing ice algal populations in frazil ice. *Nature* (London), **306**, 363–365.

Garrison, D. L. & Van Scoy, K. (1985). Wilkes Land Expedition 1985: biological observations in the ice-edge zone. *Antarctic Journal of the United States*, **19**, 123–124.

Garrison, D. L., Buck, K. R. & Silver, M. W. (1984). Microheterotrophs in the ice-edge zone. *Antarctic Journal of the United States*, **19**, 109–111.

Garrison, D. L., Sullivan, C. W. & Ackley, S. F. (1986). Sea ice microbial communities in Antarctica. *Bioscience*, **36**, 243–249.

Garrison, D. L., Buck, K. R. & Fryxell, G. A., (1987). Algal assemblages in Antarctic pack ice and in ice-edge plankton. *Journal of Phycology*, **23**, 564–572.

Gaskin, D. E. (1976). The evolution, zoogeography and ecology of

Cetacea. *Oceanography and Marine Biology Annual Review*, **14**, 247–236.

Gaskin, D. E. (1982). *The Ecology of Whales and Dolphins*. London: Heineman. 459 pp.

Geesey, G. G. (1982). Microbial exopolymers: ecological and economic considerations. *American Society of Microbiology News*, **48**, 9–14.

George, R. Y. (1979). Behavioural and metabolic adaptations of polar and deep-sea crustaceans: a hypothesis concerning physiological basis for evolution of cold-adapted crustaceans. *Bulletin of the Biological Society of Washington*, **3**, 283–296.

George, R. Y. (ed.) (1984a) Biology of Antarctic krill *Euphausia superba*. *Journal of Crustacean Biology,* **4**, (Special Issue No.1), 337 pp.

George, R. Y. (1984b). Ontogenetic adaptations in growth and respiration of *Euphausia superba* in relation to temperature and pressure. *Journal of Crustacean Biology,* **4**, (Special Issue No. 1), 252–262.

Geraci, J. R. (1975). Pinniped nutrition. *Rapports et Procès-Verbaux des Renunions Conseil International Pour l'Exploration de la Mer*, **169**, 312–323.

Gersonde, R. & Wefer, G. (1987). Sedimentation of biogenic siliceous particles in Antarctic waters (Atlantic Sector). *Marine Micropaleontology*, **11**, 311–332.

Gibson, J. A. E., Garrick, R. C. & Burton, H. R. (1990). Seasonal fluctuation of bacterial numbers near the Atarctic continent. In *Proceedings of the NIPR Symposium on Polar Biology*, Vol. 3, pp. 16–22.

Gieskes, W. W. C. & Elbrachter, M. (1986). Abundance of nanoplankton-size chlorophyll-containing particles caused by diatom disruption in surface waters of the Southern Ocean (Antarctic Peninsula region). *Netherlands Journal of Sea Research*, **20**, 291–303.

Gieskes, W. W. C., Kraay, G. W. & Baars, M. A. (1979). Current ^{14}C methods for measuring primary production: gross underestimates in oceanic waters. *Netherlands Journal of Sea Research*, **13**, 58–78.

Gilbert, J. R. & Erikson, A. W. (1977). Status of seals in pack ice of the Pacific sector of the Southern Ocean. In *Adaptations Within Antarctic Ecosystems*, ed. G. Llano, pp. 703–738. Washington, DC: Smithsonian Institution.

Gilbert, N. S. (1991a). Microphytobenthic seasonality in near-shore marine sediments at Signy Island, South Orkney Islands, Antarctica. *Estuarine Coastal & Shelf Science*, **33**, 89–104.

Gilbert, N. S. (1991b). Primary production by benthic microalgae in nearshore marine sediments of Signy Island, Antarctica. *Polar Biology*, **11**, 339–346.

Gilbert, P. M., Biggs, D. C. & McCarthy, J. J. (1982). Utilization of ammonium and nitrate during austral summer in the Scotia Sea. *Deep-Sea Research*, **29**, 837–850.

Gill, A. E. (1973). Circulation and bottom water formation in the Weddell Sea. *Deep-Sea Research*, **20**, 111–140.

Gillespie, P. A., Morita, R. Y. & Jones, L. P. (1976). The heterotrophic activity for amino acids, glucose and acetate in Antarctic waters. *Journal of the Oceanographic Society of Japan*, **32**, 74–82.

Gilmour, A. E. (1975). McMurdo Sound hydrological observations 1972–73. *New Zealand Journal of Marine and Freshwater Research*, **9**, 75–96.

Gilmour, A. E. (1979) Ross Ice Shelf sea temperatures. *Science*, **203**, 438–439.

Gilmour, A. E., MacDonald, W. J. P. & Van der Hoeven, F. G. (1960). Ocean currents in McMurdo Sound. *Nature* (London), **4740**, 867.

Gilmour, A. E., MacDonald, W. J. D. & van der Hoeven, F. G. (1962). Winter measurements of sea currents in McMurdo Sound. *New Zealand Journal of Marine and Freshwater Research*, **5**, 778–789.

Gleitz, M. & Kirst, G. O. (1991). Photosynthesisirradiance relationships and carbon metabolism of different ice algal assemblages collected from the Weddell Sea pack ice during austral spring. *Polar Biology*, **11**, 385–392.

Glover, H. E., Smith, A. E. & Shapiro, L. (1985). Diurnal variations in photosynthetic rates: comparison of ultraphytoplankton with larger phytoplankton size fractions. *Journal of Plankton Research*, **7**, 519–535.

Goldman, J. C. (1984a). Oceanic nutrient cycles. In *Flow of Energy and Materials in Marine Ecosystems: Theory and Practice*, ed. M. J. R. Fasham, pp. 130–170. New York: Plenum Press.

Goldman, J. C. (1984b). Conceptual role for microaggregates in pelagic waters. *Bulletin of Marine Science*, **35**, 462–476.

Goldman, J. C. & Caron, D. A. (1985). Experimental studies on an omnivorous microflagellate: implications for grazing and nutrient regeneration in the marine microbial food chain. *Deep-Sea Research*, **32**, 899–915.

Gonzales, H. E. (1992). The distribution and abundance of krill faecal material and oval pellets in the Scotia and Weddell Seas, Antarctica. *Polar Biology*, **12**, 81–91.

Goodall, R. N. P. (1978). Report on the small crustaceans stranded on the coast of Tierra del Fuego. *Scientific Report of the Whales Research Institute (Tokyo)*, **30**, 197–223.

Goodall, R. N. P. & Galeazzi, A.R. (1985). A review of the food habits of the small cetaceans of the Atlantic and Sub-Antarctic. In *Antarctic Nutrient Cycles and Food Webs*, ed. W. R. Siegfried, P. R. Condy & R. M. Laws, pp. 566–572. Berlin & Heidelberg: Springer-Verlag.

Gordon, A. L. (1967). Structure of Antarctic waters between 20˚W and 170˚W. *Antarctic Map Folio Series*, 1, 10 pp. Washington, DC: American Geographical Society.

Gordon, A. L. (1969). Physical oceanography on *Eltanin* cruises. *Antarctic Journal of the United States*, **4**, 183–184.

Gordon, A. L. (1981). Seasonality of the Southern Ocean sea ice. *Journal of Geophysical Research*, **86**, 4193–4197.

Gordon, A. L. (1982). Weddell Deep Water variability. *Journal of Marine Research (Supplement)*, **40**, 199–127.

Gordon, A. L. (1983). Polar oceanography. *Reviews of Geophysics and Space Physics*, **21**, 1124–1131.

Gordon, A. L. (1988). Spatial and temporal variability within the Southern Ocean. In *Antarctic Ocean and Resources Variability*, ed. D. Sahrhage, pp. 41–56. Berlin & Heidelberg: Springer-Verlag.

Gordon, A. L. & Goldberg, R. D. (1970). Circumpolar characteristics of Antarctic waters. *Antarctic Map Folio Series*, **13**, 1–19. Washington, DC: American Geographical Society.

Gordon, A. L. & Huber, B. A. (1982). Physical oceanography program in the US–USSR Weddell Sea Polyna Expedition–1981. *Antarctic Journal of the United States*, **17**, 150–152.

Gordon, A. L. & Molinelli, E. M. (1982). *The Southern Ocean Atlas: Thermohaline and Chemical Distributions and the Atlas Data Set*. New York: Columbia University Press.

Gordon, A. L. & Owens, W. B. (1987) Polar oceans. *Geophysical Reviews*, **25**, 227–233.

Gordon, A. L., Georgie, D. T. & Taylor, H. W. (1977a) Antarctic Polar Front Zone in the Western Scotia Sea: summer 1975. *Journal of Physical Oceanography*, **7**, 309–328.

Gordon, A. L., Taylor, H. W. & Georgie, D. T. (1977b) Antarctic oceanographic zonation. In *Polar Oceans*, ed. M. J. Dunbar. pp. 45–76. Calgary, Alberta' Arctic Institute of North America.

Gordon, A. L., Molinelli, E & Baker, T. (1978). Large scale relative dynamic topography of the Southern ocean. *Journal of Geophysical Research*, **83**, 3023–3032.

Gordon, A. L., Martinson, D. G. & Taylor, H. W. (1981). The wind-driven circulation in the Weddell–Enderby Basin. *Deep-Sea Research*, **28A**, 151–163.

Gorelova, T. A. & Gerasimchuk, V. V. (1981). Data on nutrition and daily consumption of juvenile *Pleurogramma antarcticum* Boulenger. In *Fishes of the Ocean*, ed. N. V. Pavin, pp. 103–109. Moscow: Academy of Sciences, USSR.

Gosselin, M., Legendre, L., Demers, S. & Ingram, R. G. (1985).

Responses of sea-ice microalgae to climatic and fortnightly tidal energy inputs (Manitounuk Sound, Hudson Bay). *Canadian Journal of Fisheries and Aquatic Science*, **42**, 999–1006.

Gowing, M. M. (1989) Abundance and feeding ecology of Antarctic phaedarian radiolarians. *Marine Biology*, **103**, 107–118.

Gowing, M. M. & Silver, M. W. 1985) Minipellets: a new and abundant size class of marine faecal pellets. *Journal of Marine Research*, **43**, 395–418.

Gran, H. H. (1932). Phytoplankton: methods and problems. *Journal du Conseil, Conseil Permanent Internationale pour l'Exploration de la Mer*, **8**, 343–358.

Grantham, G. J. (1977). *The Utilization of Krill*. Southern Ocean Fisheries Programme. Rome: FAO, GLO/So/77/3. 61 pp.

Grassle, J. F. & Sanders, H. L. (1973). Life histories and the role of disturbance. *Deep-Sea Research*, **20**, 643–659.

Green, B. & Gales, R. P. (1990). Water, sodium and energy turnover in free-living penguins. In *Penguin Biology*, ed. L. S. Davis & J. T. Darby, pp. 245–268. San Diego: Academic Press.

Green, K., Burton, H. R. & Williams, R. (1989). Diet of Antarctic fur seals *Arctocephalus gazella* (Peters) during the breeding season at Heard Island. *Antarctic Science*, **1**, 317–324.

Green, K. A. (1975). Simulation of the pelagic ecosystem of the Ross Sea, Antarctica: A time varying compartmental model. PhD Dissertation, Texas A&M University, College Station, 157 pp.

Green, K. A. (1977). Role of krill in the Antarctic marine ecosystem. *Final Report to the Department of State, Division of Ocean Affairs, Contract 1722–720248*. 31 pp.

Green-Hammond, K. A. (1981a). Requirements for effective implementation of the Convention on the Conservation of Antarctic Marine Living Resources. *Report to the US Marine Mammal Commission*. No MMC/81/04.

Green-Hammond, K. A. (1981b). 3. Modelling of Antarctic ecosystems. In *Biological Investigations of Antarctic Systems and Stocks*, Vol. II, ed. S. Z. El-Sayed, pp. 22–45. Cambridge: SCAR, SCOR.

Green-Hammond, K. A., Ainley, D. G., Siniff, D. B. & Urquart, N. S. (1983). Selection criteria and monitoring requirements for indirect indicators of changes in the availability of Antarctic krill applied to some pinniped and seabird information. *Report to the US Mammal Commission*. 37 pp.

Grinley, J. R. & David, P. (1985). Nutrient upwelling and its effect in the lee of Marion Island. In *Antarctic Nutrient Cycles and Food Webs*, ed. W. R. Siegfried, P. R. Condy & R. M. Laws, pp. 46–51. Berlin & Heidelberg: Springer-Verlag.

Grinley, J. R. & Lane, S. B. (1979). Zooplankton around Marion and Prince Edward Islands. *CNFRA*, **44**, 111–125.

Groscolas, R. & Clement, C. (1976). Utilization des resérves énergétiques au cours du jeûne de la reproduction chez le manchot empereur *Aptenodytes forsteri*. *Comptes rendu Academie des Sciences (Paris) Series D*, **282**, 297–300.

Grossi, S. McG. (1985). Response of a sea ice microalgal community to a gradient in under ice irradiance. PhD Dissertation, University of Southern California, Los Angeles.

Grossi, S. McG. & Sullivan, C. W. (1985). Sea ice microbial communities. 5. The vertical zonation of diatoms in an Antarctic fast ice community. *Journal of Phycology*, **21**, 401–409.

Grossi, S. McG., Kottmeier, S. T. & Sullivan, C. W. (1984). Sea ice microbial communities. III. Seasonal abundance of microalgae and associated bacteria, McMurdo Sound, Antarctica. *Microbial Ecology*, **10**, 231–242.

Grossi, S. McG., Kottmeier, S. T., Moe, R. L., Taylor, G. T. & Sullivan, C. W. (1987) Sea ice microbial communities. VI. Growth and primary production in bottom ice under graded snow cover. *Marine Ecology Progress Series*, **35**, 153–164.

Grua, P. (1971). Introduction ecologique. Invertebres de l'infralittoral rocheau dan L'Archipel de Kerguelen. *CINFRA*, **30**, 1–66.

Gruzov, E. N. (1977). Seasonal alterations in coastal communities in the Davis Sea. In *Adaptations Within Antarctic Ecosystems*, ed. G. Llano, pp. 263–278. Washington, DC: Smithsonian Institution.

Gruzov, E. N. & Pushkin, A. F. (1970). Bottom commumnities of the upper sublittoral of Enderby Land and the South Shetland Islands. In *Antarctic Ecology*, Vol. 1, ed. M.W. Holdgate, pp. 235–238. London: Academic Press.

Gruzov, E. N., Propp, M.V. & Pushkin, A.F. (1967). Biological association of coastal areas of the Davis Sea, based on the observations of divers (in Russian). *Soviet Antarctic Expedition Information Bulletin*, **6**, 523–533. (English translation).

Gubsch, G. (1979). Investigations on krill *Euphausia superba* Dana off South Shetland Islands. *ICES, C.M., 1979/L*, 34.

Gubsch, G. (1982). Zur Verbreitung und Biologie der Eisfische (Chaenichtyidae) in atlantischen Sektor der Antarktis. *Fischereiforsch*, **20**, 39–47.

Guillard, R. R. L. & Kilham, P. (1977). The ecology of marine planktonic diatoms. In *The Biology of Diatoms*, ed. D. Werner, pp. 372–469. Berkeley: University of California Press.

Gulland, J. A. (1970). The development of the resources of the Antarctic seas. In *Antarctic Ecology*, Vol. 1, ed. M. W. Holdgate, pp. 217–223. London: Academic Press.

Gulland, J. A. (1972). The conservation of Antarctic whales. *Biological Conservation*, **4**, 335–344.

Gulland, J. A. (1976). Antarctic baleen whales: history and prospects. *Polar Record*, **18**, 5–13.

Gulland, J. A. (1983a). The development of fisheries and stock assessment of resources in the Southern Ocean. *Memoirs of the National Institute of Polar Research. Special Issue*, **27**, 233–246.

Gulland, J. A. (1983b). Fish stock assessment: a manual of basic methods. *FAO/Wiley Series on Food and Agriculture*, Vol. 1. Chichester: John Wiley & Sons.

Gulland, J. A. (1985). Comments and questions on ecosystem management. In *Selected Papers Presented to the Scientific Committee of CCAMLR, Part II*, pp. 179–201. Hobart: Convention on the Conservation of Antarctic Marine Living Resources.

Gulland, J. A. (1986). Antarctic treaty system as a resource management mechanism: living resources. In *Antarctic Treaty System*, pp. 221–234. Washington, DC : National Academy of Sciences.

Gulland, J. A. (1987). Management and uncertainty: the example of South Georgia. *Scientific Committee for the Conservation of Antarctic Marine Living Resources, Selected Scientific Papers 1986*, pp. 341–353. Hobart: Convention on the Conservation of Antarctic Marine Living Resources.

Gunther, E. R. (1949). The habits of fin whales. *Discovery Reports*, **25**, 113–142.

Guzman, O. (1983). Distribution and abundance of Antarctic krill (*Euphausia superba*) in the Bransfield Strait. *Berichte zur Polarforschung*, **4**, 169–190.

Guzman, O. & Marin, B. (1983). Hydroacoustic and photographic techniques applied to study the behaviour of krill (*Euphausia superba*) *Memoirs National Institute of Polar Research, Special Issue*, **17**, 129–152.

Hagen, W. (1985). On distribution and population structure of Antarctic Chaetognatha. *Meeresforschung*, **30**, 280–291.

Hagen, W. (1988). On the significance of lipids in Antarctic zooplankton. *Berichte zur Polarforschung*, **49**, 1–129.

Hails, C. J. & Bryant, D. M. (1979). Reproductive energetics of a free-living bird. *Journal of Animal Ecology*, **48**, 471–482.

Hallegraeff, G. M. (1981). Seasonal study of phytoplankton pigments and species composition at a coastal station off Sydney: importance of diatoms and nanoplankton. *Marine Biology*, **61**, 107–118.

Hamada, E., Numanami, H., Naito, Y. & Taniguchi, A. (1986). Observation of the marine benthic organisms at Syowa Station in Antarctica using a remotely operated vehicle. *Memoirs National Institute of Polar Research, Special Issue*, **40**, 289–298.

Hamilton, J. E. (1939). The leopard seal *Hydrurga leptonyx* (de

Blainville). *Discovery Reports*, **18**, 239–264.

Hamner, W. M. (1984). Aspects of schooling in *Euphausia superba*. *Journal of Crustacean Biology*, **4** (Special Issue No. 1), 67–74.

Hamner, W. M., Hamner, P. R., Stroud, S. W. & Gilmer, R. W. (1983). Behaviour of Antarctic krill, *Euphausia superba*: chemoreception, feeding, schooling and moulting. *Science*, **220**, 433–435.

Hamner, W. M., Hamner, P. R., Obst, B. S. & Carleton, J. H. (1989). Field observations on the ontogeny of schooling of *Euphausia superba* furcilae and its relationship to ice in Antarctic waters. *Limnology & Oceanography*, **34**, 451–456.

Hampton, I. (1983). Preliminary report of the FIBEX acoustic work to estimate the abundance of *Euphausia superba*. *Memoirs of the National Institute of Polar Research, Special Issue*, **27**, 165–175.

Hampton, I. (1985). Abundance, distribution and behaviour of *Euphausia superba* in the Southern Ocean between 15° and 30° during FIBEX. In *Antarctic Nutrient Cycles and Food Webs*, ed. W. R. Siegfried, P. R. Condy & R. M. Laws, pp. 294–303. Berlin Heidelberg: Springer-Verlag.

Hanks, J. (1981). Characteristics of population conditions. In *Dynamics of Large Mammal Populations*, ed. C. W. Fowler & T. D. Smith, pp. 47–73. New York: John Wiley & Sons.

Hannah, F. J. & Boney, A. D. (1983). Nanoplankton in the Firth of Clyde, Scotland: seasonal abundance, carbon fixation and species composition. *Journal of Experimental Marine Biology & Ecology*, **67**, 105–118.

Hanson, R. B. & Lowery, H. K. (1985). Spatial distribution, structure, biomass and physiology of microbial assemblages across the Southern Ocean frontal zones during the late Austral Winter. *Applied & Environmental Microbiology*, **49**, 1029–1039.

Hanson, R. B., Lowrey, H. K., Shafer, D., Sorocco, R. & Pope, D. H. (1983a). Microbes in Antarctic waters of the Drake Passage: vertical patterns of substrate uptake, productivity and biomass in January 1980. *Polar Biology* , **2**, 179–188.

Hanson, R. B., Shafer, D., Pole, D. H. & Lowery, H. K. (1983b). Bacterioplankton in Antarctic Ocean waters during the late austral winter: abundance, frequency of dividing cells, and estimates of production. *Applied & Environmental Microbiology*, **45**, 1622–1632.

Hara, S., Tanoue, E., Zenimoto, M., Komaki, Y. & Takaski, E. (1986). Heterotrophic protists along a transect of 75° E in the Southern Ocean. *Memoirs National Institute of Polar Research (Special Issue)*, **40**, 69–80.

Harbison, G. R. & McAllister, V. L. (1979). The filter-feeding rates and particle retention efficiencies of three species of *Cyclosalpa* (Tunicata. Thaloacea). *Limnology & Oceanography*, **24**, 875–892.

Hardy, A. C. (1967). *Great Waters*. London: Collins.

Hardy, A. C. & Gunther, E. R. (1936). The plankton of the South Georgia whaling grounds and adjacent waters, 1926–1927. *Discovery Reports*, **11**, 1–456.

Hardy, P. (1972). Biomass estimates for some shallow-water infaunal communities at Signey Island, South Orkney Islands. *British Antarctic Survey Bulletin*, **31**, 93–106.

Hargraves, B. T. (1975). The importance of total and mixed-layer depth in the supply of organic material to bottom consumers. *Symposia Biologica Hungarica*, **15**, 157–165.

Harm, W. (1980). *Biological Effects of Ultraviolet Radiation. IUPAB Biophysics Series I*. Cambridge: Cambridge University Press. 216 pp.

Harper, P. C. (1972). The field identification and distribution of the thin-billed prion (*Pachyptila belcheri*) and the Antarctic prion (*Pachyptila desolata*). *Notornis*, **19**, 140–175.

Harper, P. C., Knox, G. A., Spurr, E. B., Taylor, R. H., Wilson, G. B. & Young, E. C. (1984). The status and conservation of birds in the Ross Sea sector of Antarctica. In *The Status and Conservation of the World's Seabirds*, pp. 593–608. International Council for Bird

Preservation Technical Publication No. 2.

Harrington, S. A. & Ikeda, T. (1986). Laboratory observations of spawning, brood size and egg hatchability of the Antarctic krill *Euphausia superba* from Prydz Bay, Antarctica. *Marine Biology*, **92**, 231–235.

Harris, G. P. (1980). The measurement of photosynthesis in natural populations of phytoplankton. In *The Physiological Ecology of Phytoplankton*, ed. J. Morris, pp. 129–187. Berkeley & Los Angeles: University of California Press.

Harris, R. P. (1982). Comparison of the feeding behaviour of *Calanus* and *Pseudocalanus* in experimentally manipulated enclosed systems. *Journal of the Marine Biological Association, UK* , **62**, 71–91.

Harrison, R. J. (1969). Reproduction and reproductive organs. In *Biology of Marine Mammals*, ed. T. H. Anderson, pp. 253–348. London & New York: Academic Press.

Harrison, R. J., Matthews, L. H. & Roberts, J. M. (1952). Reproduction in some Pinnipedia. *Transactions of the Zoological Society of London*, **27**, 437–541.

Harrison, W. G. (1986). Respiration and its size-dependence in microplankton populations from the surface waters of the Canadian Arctic. *Polar Biology*, **6**, 145–152.

Harrison, W. G. & Platt, T. (1986). Photosynthesis-irradiance relationships in polar and temperate phytoplankton populations. *Polar Biology*, **5**, 153–164.

Harrison, W. G., Platt, T. & Irwin, B. (1982). Primary production and nutrient assimilation by natural phytoplankton populations of the Eastern Canadian Arctic. *Canadian Journal of Fisheries and Aquatic Sciences*, **39**, 335–345.

Hart, T. J. (1934). On the phytoplankton of the southwest Atlantic and the Bellingshausen Sea. *Discovery Reports*, **8**, 1–268.

Hart, T. J. (1942). Phytoplankton periodicity in Antarctic surface waters. *Discovery Reports*, **21**, 261–356.

Hartman, O. (1967). Larval development of benthic invertebrates in Antarctic seas: early development of *Nothria notialis* (Monro). and *Paronuphis antarctica* (Monro) in Bransfield Strait, Antarctica Peninsula. *JARE Scientific Reports, Special Issue*, **1**, 205–208.

Hasle, G. R. (1964). *Nitzschia* and *Fragilariopsis* species studied in the light and electron microscopes. I. Some marine species of the groups *Nitzschiella* and *Lanceolata*. *Skrifter av det norske Vidensk-Akademii Oslo: Matematish-Natarviden Shalelig Klasse*, **16**, 1–48.

Hasle, G. R. (1965). *Nitzschia* and *Fragilariopsis* species studied in the light and electron microscopes. III. The genus *Fragilariopsis*. *Skrifter av det norske Vidensk–Akademii Oslo: Matematish–Natarviden Shalelig Klasse*, **21**, 1–49.

Hasle, G. R. (1969). An analysis of the phytoplankton of the Pacific Southern Ocean: abundance, composition, and distribution during the Brategg Expedition, 1947–48. *Hvalradets Skrifter*, **52**, 1–168.

Hay, C. H., Adams, N. & Parsons, N. M. (1985). Marine algae of the subAntarctic islands of New Zealand. *National Museum of New Zealand Miscellaneous Series* No 11. 69 pp.

Hayes, P. K., Whitaker, T. M. & Fogg, G. E. (1984). Distribution and nutrient status of phytoplankton in the Southern Ocean between 20 and 70 Deg W. *Polar Biology*, **3**, 153–165.

Hays, J. D. (1969). Climatic record of Late Cenozoic Antarctic Ocean sediments related to the record of world climate. In *Paleoecology of Africa and the Surrounding Islands and Antarctica*, ed. E. M. van Zinderen Bakker, pp. 139–164. Capetown: A. A. Balkema.

Heath, G. R. (1969). Mineralogy of Cenozoic deep-sea sediments from the equatorial Pacific Ocean. *Geological Society of America Bulletin*, **80**, 1997–2018.

Heath, G. R. (1974). Dissolved silica and deep-sea sediments. In *Studies in Paleo-oceanography*, ed. W. W. Hay, pp. 77–93. Society of Econonomic Paleontology and Mineralogy, Special Publication 20.

Heath, R. A. (1971). Circulation and hydrology under the seasonal ice in McMurdo Sound, Antarctica. *New Zealand Journal of Marine &*

Freshwater Research, **5**, 179–515.

Heath, R. A. (1977). Circulation across the ice shelf edge in McMurdo Sound, Antarctica. In *Polar Oceans*, ed. M. J. Dunbar, pp. 129–149. Calgary: Arctic Institute of North America.

Hedgpeth, J. W. (1969). Introduction to Antarctic zoogeography. *Antarctic Map Folio Series*, Vol. 11, pp. 1–9. Washington, DC : American Geographical Society.

Hedgpeth, J. W. (1970). Marine biogeography of the Antarctic regions. In *Antarctic Ecology* Vol. 1, ed. M. W. Holdgate, pp. 97–104. London: Academic Press.

Hedgpeth, J. W. (1971). Perspectives of benthic ecology in Antarctica. In *Research in Antarctica*, ed. L. O. Quasim, pp. 93–136. Washington, DC: American Association for the Advancement of Science Publication No. 93.

Hedgpeth, J. W. (1977). The Antarctic marine ecosystem. in *Adaptations Within Antarctic Ecosystems*, ed. G. A. Llano, pp. 3–10. Washington, DC : Smithsonian Institution.

Heinbokel, J.F. & Beers, J.R. (1979). Studies on the functional role of tintinnids in the Southern California Bight III. Grazing impact on natural assemblages. *Marine Biology*, **52**, 23–32.

Heinbokel, J. F. & Coats, D. W. (1984). Reproductive dynamics of ciliates in the ice-edge zone. *Antarctic Journal of the United States*, **19**, 111–113.

Heinbokel. J. F. & Coats, D. W. (1985). Ciliates and nanoplankton in Arthur Harbor, December 1984 and January 1985. *Antarctic Journal of the United States*, **19**, 135–136.

Heinbokel, J. F. & Coats, D. W. (1986). Patterns of tintinnine abundance and reproduction near the edge of the seasonal pack ice in the Weddell Sea, November 1983. *Marine Ecology Progress Series*, **33**, 71–80.

Heine, A. J. (1960). Seals at White Island. *Antarctic*, **2**, 272–273.

Heinle, D. R. & Flemer, D. A. (1975). Carbon requirements of a population of the estuarine copepod *Eurytemora affinis*. *Marine Biology*, **31**, 235–247.

Heinle, D. R., Harris, R. P., Ustach, J. F. & Flemer, D. A. (1977). Detritus as a food for estuarine copepods. *Marine Biology*, **40**, 341–353.

Hellebust, J. A. (1974). Extracellular products. In *Algal Physiology and Biochemistry*, ed. W. D. P. Stewart, p. 838. Berkeley: University of California Press.

Hellebust, J. A. & Lewin, J. (1977). Heterotrophic nutrition. In *The Biology of Diatoms*, ed. D. Werner, pp. 169–198. Los Angeles: Universiy of California Press.

Hellmer, H. H., Bersch, M., Augstein, E. & Grabemann, I. (1985). The Southern Ocean: A survey of oceanographic and marine meterological research work. *Berichte zur Polarforschung*, **26**, 1–115.

Hemmingsen, E. A. & Douglas, E. L. (1970). Respiratory characteristics of the haemoglobin-free fish *Chaenocephalus aceratus*. *Comparative Biochemistry & Physiology*, **29**, 467–470.

Hempel, G. (1970). Antarctica. In *Fish Resources of the Ocean*, ed. J. A. Gulland, pp. 197–203. Rome: FAP.

Hempel, G. (1985a). On the biology of Polar Seas, particularly the Southern Ocean. In *Marine Biology of Polar Regions and Effects of Stress on Marine Organisms*, ed. J. S. Gray & M. E. Christiansen, pp. 3–33. Chichester: John Wiley & Sons.

Hempel, G. (1985b). Antarctic marine food webs. In *Antarctic Nutrient Cycles and Food Webs*, ed. W. R. Siegfried, P. R. Condy & R. M. Laws, pp. 266–270. Berlin & Heidelberg: Springer-Verlag.

Hempel, G. (1987). The krill-dominated pelagic system of the Southern Ocean. *Environmental International*, **13**, 33–36.

Hempel, G. (1988). Antarctic marine research in winter: the Weddell Sea Project 1986. *Polar Record*, **24**, 43–48.

Hempel, G. & Manthey, M. (1981). On the fluoride content of larval krill. *Meeresforschung Report, Marine Research*, **29**, 60–63.

Hempel, I. (1978). Vertical distribution of eggs and nauplii of krill (*Euphausia superba*) south of Elephant Island. *Meeresforschung*,

29, 53–59.

Hempel, I. (1983). Studies on eggs and larvae of *Euphausia superba* and *Euphausia crystallorophias* in the Atlantic Sector of the Southern Ocean. *Berichte zur Polarforschung*, **4**, 30–46.

Hempel, I. (1985a). Vertical distribution of larvae of Antarctic krill, *Euphausia superba*. In *Antarctic Nutrient Cycles and Food Webs*, ed. W. R. Siegfried, P. R. Condy & R. M. Laws, pp. 308–310. Berlin & Heidelberg: Springer-Verlag.

Hempel, I. (1985b). Variation in geographical distribution and abundance of larvae of Antarctic krill, *Euphausia superba*, in the Southern Atlantic Ocean. In *Antarctic Nutrient Cycles and Food Webs*, ed. W. R. Siegfried, P. R. Condy & R. M. Laws, pp. 304–307. Berlin & Heidelberg: Springer-Verlag.

Hempel, I. & Hempel, G. (1978). Larval krill (*Euphausia superba*) in the plankton and nekton samples of the German Antarctic Expedition 1975/76. *Meeresforschung*, **26**, 206–216.

Hempel, I. & Hempel, G. (1986). Field observations on the developmental ascent of larval *Euphausia superba* (Crustacea). *Polar Biology*, **6**, 121–126.

Hempel, I., Hempel, G. & Baker, A. deC. (1979). Early life history stages of krill (*Euphausia superba*) in Bransfield Strait and Weddell Sea. *Meeresforschung*, **27**, 267–281.

Herndl, G. J. & Peduzzi, P. (1988). The ecology of amorphous aggregations (marine snow) in the Northern Adriatic Sea. 1. General considerations. *Marine Ecology*, **9**, 79–90.

Hewes, C. P., Holm-Hansen, O. & Sakshaug, E. (1983). Nanoplankton and microplankton studies during the Circumnavigation Cruise. *Antarctic Journal of the United States*, **18**, 169–171.

Hewes, C. D., Holm-Hansen, O. & Sakshaug, E. (1985). Alternate carbon pathways at the lower trophic levels in the Antarctic food web. In *Antarctic Nutrient Cycles and Food Webs*, ed. W. R. Siegfried, P. R. Condy & R. M. Laws, pp. 277–283. Berlin & Heidelberg: Springer-Verlag.

Hewes, C. D., Sakshaug, E., Reid, F. M. H. & Holm-Hansen, O. (1990). Microbial autotrophic and heterotrophic eucaryotes in Antarctic waters: relationships between biomass and chlorophyll, adenosine triphosphate and particulate organic carbon. *Marine Ecology Progress Series*, **63**, 27–35.

Heyerdahl, E. F. (1932). *Hvalindustrien Kommander Chr.* Christensens Hvalfangstrumuseum, Sandjeford. Publication No. 7. 160 pp.

Heywood, R. B. & Light, J. J. (1975). First direct evidence of life under the Antarctic Ice Shelf. *Nature* (London), **254**, 591–593.

Heywood, R. B. & Priddle, J. (1987). Retention of phytoplankton by an eddy. *Continental Shelf Research*, **7**, 937–955

Heywood, R. B. & Whitaker, T. M. (1984). The Antarctic marine flora. In *Antarctic Ecology,* Vol. 2, ed. R. M. Laws, pp. 373–419. London: Academic Press.

Heywood, R. B., Everson, I. & Priddle, J. (1985). The absence of krill from the South Georgia zone, winter 1983. *Deep-Sea Research*, **32**, 369–378.

Hicks, G. R. F. (1974). Variation in zooplankton biomass with hydrological regime beneath the seasonal ice, McMurdo Sound, Antarctica. *New Zealand Journal of Marine & Freshwater Research*, **8**, 67–77.

Hill, K. T. & Radthe, R. L. (1988). Gerontological studies on the damsel fish *Dascyllus albisella*. *Bulletin of Marine Science*, **42**, 424–434.

Hill, K. T. & Womersley, C. (1991). Critical aspects of fluorescent age-pigment methodologies: modification for accurate analysis and age assessments in aquatic organisms. *Marine Biology*, **109**, 1–11.

Hinton, M. A. C. (1925). *Report of Papers Left by the Late Major Barrett-Hamilton, Relating to the Whales of South Georgia*. Crown Agents for the Colonies, London, pp. 57–209.

Hitchcock, G. L. (1978). Labelling patterns of carbon-14 net phytoplankton during a winter–spring bloom. *Journal of Experimental Marine Biology and Ecology*, **31**, 141–153.

Hobbie, J.E., Holm-Hansen, O., Packard, T.T., Pomeroy, L.R., Sheldon, R.W., Thomas, J.P. & Wiebe, W.J. (1972). A study of the distribution of activity of microorganisms in ocean water. *Limnology & Oceanography*, **17**, 544–555.

Hobson, L. A., Menzel, D. W. & Barber, R. T. (1973). Primary productivity and sizes of parts of organic carbon in the mixed layers of the ocean. *Marine Biology*, **19**, 298–306.

Hodgson, R. E., Azam, F., Carlucci, A. F., Fuhrman, J. A., Karl, D. M. & Holm-Hansen, O. (1981). Microbial uptake of dissolved organic matter in McMurdo Sound, Antarctica. *Marine Biology*, **71**, 89–94.

Hoepffner, N. (1984). Strategies d'adaption photosynthetiques chez les diatomees de l'Ocean Antarctique: variations du nombre et de la tailles des unites photosynthetiques. *Journal of Plankton Research*, **6**, 881–895.

Hofman, R., Erickson, A. & Siniff, D. (1973). The Ross Seal (*Ommatophoca rossii*). *International Union for the Conservation of Nature and Natural Resources Publication New Series Supplementary Paper No. 39*, 129–139.

Hofman, R., Reichle, R., Siniff, D. B. & Muller-Schwarze, D. (1977). The leopard seal (*Hydrurga leptonyx*) at Palmer Station, Antarctica. In *Adaptations Within Antarctic Ecosystems*, ed. G. A. Llano, pp. 769–782. Washington, DC: Smithsonian Institution

Holden, M. J. (1978). Long-term changes in landings of fish from the North Sea. *Rapports et Proces-Verbaux des Renunions Conseil Permanent International de la Mer*, **172**, 11–26.

Holdgate, M. W. (1967). The Antarctic ecosystem. *Philosophical Transactions of the Royal Society, London, Series* B, **152**, 363–383.

Holdgate, M. W. (1970). Conservation in the Antarctic. In *Antarctic Ecology*, Vol. 1, ed. M. W. Holdgate, pp. 924–935. London: Academic Press.

Holeton, G. F. (1970). Oxygen uptake and circulation by a haemoglobinless Antarctic fish (*Chaenocephalus aceratus* Lonnberg) compared with three red-blooded Antarctic fish. *Comparative Biochemistry & Physiology*, **34**, 447–471.

Holeton, G. F. (1974). Metabolic cold adaptation of polar fish: fact or artefact? *Physiological Zoology*, **47**, 137–152.

Holm-Hansen, O. (1981). Microbial uptake of dissolved organic matter in McMurdo Sound, Antarctica. *Marine Biology*, **61**, 89–94.

Holm-Hansen, O. (1985). Nutrient cycles in Antarctic marine ecosystems. In *Antarctic Nutrient Cycles and Food Webs*, ed. W. R. Siegfried, P. R. Condy & R. M. Laws, pp. 6–10. Berlin & Heidelberg: Springer-Verlag.

Holm-Hansen, O. & Forster, T. D. (1981). A multidisciplinary study of the eastern Scotia Sea. *Antarctic Journal of the United States*, **16**, 159–160.

Holm-Hansen, O. & Huntley, M. (1984). Feeding requirements of krill in relation to food sources. *Journal of Crustacean Biology*, **4** (Special Issue No. 1), 156–173.

Holm-Hansen, O. & Mitchell, B. G. (1991). Spatial and temporal distribution of phytoplankton and primary production in the western Bransfield Strait. *Deep-Sea Research*, **38**, 961–980.

Holm-Hansen, O., El-Sayed, S. Z., Franceschini, G. A., Cuhel, G. A. & Cuhel, R. L. (1977). Primary production and the factors controlling phytoplankton growth in the southern Ocean. In *Adaptations Within Antarctic Ecosystems*, ed. G. A. Llano, pp. 11–73. Washington, DC: Smithsonian Institution.

Holm-Hansen, O., Azam, F., Campbell, L., Carlucci, A. F. & Karl, D. M. (1978). Microbial life beneath the Ross Ice Shelf. *Antarctic Journal of the United States*, **13**, 129–130.

Holm-Hansen, O., Neori, A. & Koike, I. (1982). Phytoplankton distribution, biomass, and activity in the southwest Ross sea. *Antarctic Journal of the United States*, **17**, 150–152.

Holm-Hansen, O., Mitchell, B. G., Hewes, C. D. & Karl, D. M. (1989). Phytoplankton blooms in the vicinity of Palmer station, Antarctica. *Polar Biology*, **10**, 49–57.

Holt, S. (1978). Marine fisheries. In *Ocean Yearbook*, Vol. 1, ed. E. M. Borgeze & N. Ginsberg, pp. 38–83. Chicago: Chicago University Press.

Honjo, S. & Roman, M. R. (1978). Marine copepod fecal pellets: Production, preservation and sedimentation. *Journal of Marine Research*, **36**, 45–57.

Hooker, J. D. (1847). Diatomaceae. *The Botany of the Antarctic Voyage of H. M. discovery ships 'Erebus' and 'Terror', years 1839–1843*, Vol. LVI. London.

Hopkins, T. L. (1971). Zooplankton standing crop in the Pacific sector of the Antarctic. In *Biology of the Antarctic Seas VI*, (Antarctic Research Series, Vol. 17), ed. G. A. Llano & I. E. Wallen, pp. 347–362. Washington, DC: American Geophysical Union.

Hopkins, T. L. (1985a). The zooplankton community of Croker Passage, Antarctic Peninsula. *Polar Biology*, **4**, 161–170.

Hopkins, T. L. (1985b). Food webs of an Antarctic midwater ecosystem. *Marine Biology*, **89**, 197–212.

Hopkins, T. L. (1987). Midwater food web in McMurdo Sound, Ross Sea, Antarctica. *Marine Biology*, **96**, 93–106.

Hopkins, T. L. & Lancraft, T. M. (1984). The composition and standing stock of mesopelagic micronekton at 27° N 86° W in the eastern Gulf of Mexico. *Contributions to Marine Science of the University of Texas*, **27**, 152.

Hopkins, T. L. & Torres, J. J. (1989). Midwater food web in the vicinity of a marginal ice zone in the western Weddell Sea. *Deep-Sea Research*, **36**, 543–560.

Hoppe, H-G. (1981). Blue-green algae agglomeration in surface waters: a microbiotope of high bacterial activity. *Kieler Meeresforschung*, **5**, 291–303.

Hoppe, H-G. (1984). Attachment of bacteria: advantage or disadvantage for survival in the aquatic environment. In *Microbial Adhesion and Aggregation*, ed. K. C. Marshall, pp. 383–301. Berlin & Heidelberg: Springer-Verlag.

Horne, A. J., Fogg, E. G. & Eagle, D. J. (1969). Studies *in situ* of primary production of an area of inshore Antarctic sea. *Journal of the Marine Biological Association, UK* , **49**, 393–405.

Horner, R. A. (1985a). Ecology of sea ice microalgae. In *Sea Ice Biota*, ed. R. A. Horner, pp. 83–103. Boca Raton, FL: CRC Press.

Horner, R. A. (1985b). Taxonomy of sea ice microalgae. In *Sea Ice Biota*, ed. R. A. Horner, pp. 147–157. Boca Raton, FL: CRC Press.

Horner, R.A. (1990). Ice-associated diatoms. In *Polar Marine Diatoms*, ed. L. K. Medlin & J. Priddle, pp. 9–14. Cambridge, UK: British Antarctic Survey, Natural Environment Research Council.

Horner, R. A. & Schrader, G. C. (1982). Relative contributions of ice algae, phytoplankton and benthic microalgae to primary production in nearshore regions of the Beaufort Sea. *Arctic*, **35**, 485–503.

Horner, R. A., Syversten, E. E., Thomas, D. P. & Lange, C. (1988). proposed terminology and reporting units for sea ice algal assemblages. *Polar Biology*, **8**, 249–253.

Horwood, J. W. (1981). On the joint exploitatioin of krill and whales. In *Mammals in the Seas, Volume III*, pp. 355–383. Rome: FAO Fisheries Series No. 5.

Hosaka, N. & Nemoto, T. (1986). Size structure of phytoplankton carbon and primary production in the Southern Oocean south of Australia during the summer of 1983–1984. *Memoirs National Institute of Polar Research, Special Issue*, **40**, 15–24.

Hoshiai, T. (1969). Seasonal variation of chlorophyll *a* and hydrological conditions under sea ice at Syowa Station, Antarctica. *Antarctic Record*, **35**, 52–67.

Hoshiai, T. (1972). Diatom distribution in sea ice near McMurdo Station and Syowa Station. *Antarctic Journal of the United States*, **7**, 85–87.

Hoshiai, T. (1977). Seasonal change of ice communities in the sea ice near Syowa Station, Antarctica. In *Polar Oceans*, ed. M. J. Dunbar, pp. 307–317. Calgary: Arctic Institute of North America.

Hoshiai, T. (1979). Feeding behaviour of *Notothenia rossii mamorata* Fischer at South Georgia. *Antarctic Record*, **66**, 25–36.

Hoshiai, T. (1981a). Proliferation of ice algae in the Syowa Station area, Antarctica. *Memoirs National Institute of Polar Research*, **35**, 1–12.

Hoshiai, T. (1981b). Solar radiations and stability of the undersurface of sea ice governing ice algal proliferation. *Antarctic Record*, **73**, 23–29.

Hoshiai, T. (1985). Autumn proliferation of ice algae in Antarctic sea ice. In *Antarctic Nutrient Cycles and Food Webs*, ed. W. R. Siegfried, P. R. Condy & R. M. Laws, pp. 89–92. Berlin & Heidelberg: Springer-Verlag.

Hoshiai, T. & Kato, M. (1961). Ecological notes on the diatom community of the sea ice in Antarctica. *Bulletin Marine Biological Station Asamushi, Tokoku University*, **10**, 221.

Hoshiai, T. & Tanimura, A. (1981). Copepods in the stomach of a Nototheneiid fish, *Trematomus borchgrevinki* at Syowa Station, Antarctica. *Memoirs National Institute of Polar Research*, **34**, 44–88.

Hoshiai, T. & Tanimura, A. (1986). Sea ice meiofauna at Syowa Station. *Memoirs National Institute of Polar Research, Special Issue*, **44**, 118–124.

Hoshiai, T., Tanimura, A. & Watanabe, K. (1987). Ice algae as food of an ice-associated copepod, *Paralabidocera antarctica* (I. C. Thompson). *Proceedings of the NIPR Symposium on Polar Biology*, **1**, 105–111.

Hoshiai, T., Tanimura, A., Fukuchi, M. & Watanabe, K. (1989). Feeding by the nototheniid fish *Pagothenia borchgrevinki* on the ice-associated copepod, *Paralabidocera antarctica*. *Proceedings of the NIPR Symposium on Polar Biology*, **2**, 61–64.

Hough, J. L. (1956). Sediment distribution in the Southern Oceans around Antarctica. *Journal of Sedimentary Pterology*, **26**, 301–305.

Hubold, G. (1985a). The early life-history of the high-Antarctic silverfish, *Pleurogramma antarcticum*. In *Antarctic Nutrient Cycles and Food Webs*, ed. W. R. Siegfried, P. R. Condy & R. M. Laws, pp. 445–451. Berlin & Heidelberg: Springer-Verlag.

Hubold, G. (1985b). Stomach contents of the Antarctic silverfish *Pleurogramma antarcticum* from the Southern and Eastern Weddell Sea. *Polar Biology*, **5**, 43–48.

Hubold, G. & Ekau, W. (1987). Midwater fish fauna of the Weddell Sea Antarctica. In *Proceedings of the 5th European Ichthyological Congress*, ed. S. O. Kullander & B. Fernholm, pp. 391–396. Stockholm: Swedish Museum of Natural History.

Hubold, G. & Ekau, W. (1990). Feeding patterns of post-larval juvenile Notothenioids in the southern Weddell Sea (Antarctica). *Polar Biology*, **10**, 255–260.

Hudson, R. (1966). Adult survival estimates for two Antarctic petrels. *British Antarctic Survey Bulletin*, **8**, 63–73.

Huey, L. M. (1930). Capture of an elephant seal off San Diego, California, with notes on stomach contents. *Journal of Mammology*, **11**, 229–231.

Hunt, F. (1973). Observations on the seals of Elephant Island, South Shetland Islands, 1970–7!. *British Antarctic Survey Bulletin*, **36**, 99–104.

Hunter, S. (1983). The food and feeding ecology of the giant petrels *Macronectes halli* and *M. giganteus* at South Georgia. *Journal of Zoology (London)*, **200**, 521–538.

Hunter, S. (1985). Breeding biology and population dynamics of giant petrels *Macronectes halli* and *M. giganteus* at South Georgia. *Journal of Zoology (London)*, **200**, 321–358.

Huntley, M. E. & Escritor, F. (1991). Dynamics of *Calanoides acutus* (Copepoda: Calanoida) in Antarctic coastal waters. *Deep-Sea Research*, **38**, 1145–1167.

Huntley, M. E., Tandy, K. S. & Eilertsen, H. C. (1987). On the trophic fate of *Phaeocystis pouchetii*. II. Grazing rates of *Calanus hyperboreus* feeding on diatoms and different size categories of *P. pouchetii*. *Journal of Experimental Marine Biology and Ecology*, **110**, 197–212.

Huntley, M. E., Sykes, P. F. & Marin, V. (1989). Biometry and trophodynamics of *Salpa thompsoni* (Tunicata: Thaliacea) near the Antarctic Peninsula in austral summer 1983–1984. *Polar Biology*, **10**, 59–70.

Hureau, J-C. (1966). Biologie comparée de quelques poissons antarctiques (Nototheniidae). *Bulletin de l'Institut Oceanographique*, **68**, 1–224.

Hureau, J-C. (1970). La faune ichthyologique du secteur indien de l'océan antarctique et estimation du stock de poissons autour des îsles Kerguelen. *Memoires du Museum national d'histoire naturelle*, **43**, 235–247.

Hureau, J. -C. (1979). La faune ichthyologique du secteur indien de l'ocean Antarctique et estimation du stock de poissons autour des iles Kerguelen. *Memoires du Museum national d'histoire naturalle*, **43**, 235–247.

Hustedt, F. (1958). Diatomeen aus der antarktis und dem Sudatlarktik Deutsche Antarktische Expedition 1938–39. *Wissenschaftliche Ergbnisse*, **2**, 103–1911.

Ichihara, T. (1966a). The pigmy blue whale, *Balaenoptera musculus brevicauda*, a new subspecies from the Antarctic. In *Whales, Dolphins and Porpoises*, ed. K. S. Norris, pp. 79–113. Berkeley & Los Angeles: University of California Press.

Ichihara. T. (1966b). Criteria for determining age of the fin whale with reference to ear plug and baleen plate. *Scientific Report of the Whales Research Institute (Tokyo)*, **20**, 17–82.

Ichii, T. & Kato, H. (1991). Food and daily food consumption of southern minke whales in the Antarctic. *Polar Biology*, **11**, 479–487.

Idyll, C. P. (1973). The anchovy crisis. *Scientific American*, **288**, 22–29.

Ikeda, T. (1970). Relationship between respiration and body size in marine plankton animals as a function of the temperature of the habitat. *Bulletin of the Hokkaido University Faculty of Fisheries*, **21**, 91–112.

Ikeda, T. (1984a). Development of the Antarctic krill (*Euphausia superba*) observed in the laboratory. *Journal of Experimental Marine Biology and Ecology*, **75**, 107–117.

Ikeda, T. (1984b). Sequences in metabolic rates and elemental composition (C, N, P) during the development of *Euphausia superba* Dana and estimated food requirements during its life span. *Journal of Crustacean Biology, 4, (Special Issue 1)* 273–284.

Ikeda, T. (1985). Life history of Antarctic krill *Euphausia superba*: A new look from an experimental approach. *Bulletin of Marine Science*, **37**, 599–608.

Ikeda, T. & Bruce, B. (1986). Metabolic activity and elemental composition of krill and other zooplankton from Prydz Bay, Antarctica, during early summer (November–December). *Marine Biology*, **92**, 545–555.

Ikeda, T. & Dixon, P. (1982a). Observations on the moulting in Antarctic krill (*Euphausia superba* Dana). *Australian Journal of Marine & Freshwater Research*, **33**, 71–76.

Ikeda, T. & Dixon, P. (1982b). Body shrinkage as a possible overwintering mechanism of the Antarctic krill *Euphausia superba* Dana. *Journal of Experimental Marine Biology & Ecology*, **62**, 143–151.

Ikeda, T., Dixon, P. & Kirkwood, J. (1985). Laboratory observations of moulting, growth and maturation in Antarctic krill (*Euphausia superba* Dana). *Polar Biology*, **4**, 1–8.

Imber, M. J. (1976). Breeding biology of the Grey-faced petrel *Pterodroma macroptera gouldi*. *Ibis*, **118**, 51–64.

Ingham, S. E. (1960). The status of seals (Pinnipedia) at Australian Antarctic Stations. *Mammalia*, **24**, 422–430.

Ingham, S. E. (1967). Branding elephant seals for life history studies. *Polar Record*, **13**, 447–449.

International Whaling Commission (IWC) (1976). *Report of the International Whaling Commission 26.*

International Whaling Commission (IWC) (1978). *Report of the International Whaling Commission 28.*

International Whaling Commission (IWC) (1979). Report of a Special

Meeting on Southern Hemisphere Minke Whales, Seattle, May 1978. *Report of the International Whaling Commission 29.*

International Whaling Commission (IWC) (1982). *Report of the International Whaling Commission 32.*

International Whaling Commisssion (IWC) (1990). Report of the Scientific Committee. *Report of the International Whaling Commission, 40.*

Irwin, B. D. (1990). Primary production of ice algae on a seasonally-ice-covered continental shelf. *Polar Biology, 10,* 247–254.

Ishii, H., Omori, M., Maeda, M. & Watanabe, Y. (1987). Metabolic rates and elemental composition of Antarctic krill, *Euphausia superba* Dana. *Polar Biology, 7,* 378–382.

Ivanov, A. I. (1964). Characteristics of the phytoplankton in Antarctic waters at the whaling grounds of the flotilla Slava in 1957–58. *Soviet Antarctic Information Bulletin, 1,* 314.

Ivanov, B. G. (1970). On the biology of the Antarctic krill *Euphausia superba. Marine Biology, 7,* 340–351.

Ivashin, M. V. & Mikhalev, Y. A. (1978). To the problem of the prenatal growth of minke whales *Balaenoptera acutirostrata* of the southern hemisphere and of the biology of their reproduction. *Report of the International Whaling Commission, 28,* 201–205.

Iwanami, K., Futatsumachi, S. & Taniguchi, A. (1986). Short-term variation of chemical property of water and microplankton community in the coastal area near Syowa Station, Antarctica, in midsummer of 1984. 1. Chemical property including chlorophyll a. *Memoirs National Institute of Polar Research, Special Issue, 40,* 1–14.

Jackson, L. T., Linick, T. W., Michel, R. L. & Williams, P. M. (1978). Tritium and carbon-14 distributions in McMurdo Sound, 1977. *Antarctic Journal of the United States, 13,* 71–73.

Jacobs, S. S. (1977). Ross Ice Shelf Project: physical oceanography. *Antarctic Journal of the United States, 12,* 43–46.

Jacobs, S. S., Amos, A. F. & Bruckhausen, P. M. (1970). Ross Sea oceanography and Antarctic bottom water formation. *Deep-Sea Research, 17,* 935–962.

Jacobs, S. S., Bruckhausen, P. M. & Ardai, J. L. (1978). Physical oceanography of the Ross Sea. *Antarctic Journal of the United States, 13,* 83–85.

Jacobs, S. S., Gordon, A. L. & Ardai, J. L. (1979). Circulation and melting beneath the Ross Ice Shelf. *Science, 203,* 439–443.

Jacobs, S. S., Fairbanks, R. & Horibe, Y. (1985). Origin and evolution of water masses near the Antarctic continental margin: Evidence from $H^{18}O/H_2^{16}O$ ratios in seawater. In Oceanology of the Antarctic Shelf. *Antarctic Research Series, 43,* 59–85

Jacobsen, D. J. & Anderson, D. M. (1986). Thecate heterotrophic dinoflagellates: feeding behaviour and mechanisms. *Journal of Phycology, 22,* 249–258.

Jacobsen, T. R. & Azam, F. (1984). Role of bacteria in copepod faecal pellet decomposition and colonization, growth rates and mineralization. *Bulletin of Marine Science, 35,* 495–502.

Jacques, G. (1983). Some ecophysiological aspects of the Antarctic phytoplankton. *Polar Biology, 2,* 27–33.

Jacques, G. (1989). Primary production in the open Antarctic ocean during the austral summer. A review. *Vie et Milieu, 39,* 1–17.

Jacques, G. & Hoepffner, N. (1984). Sinking rates of subAntarctic phytoplankton. *Compte rendu Academie Sciences, Paris, 299* (Serie III), *14,* 581–585.

Jacques, G. & Minas, M. (1981). Production primaire dans le secteur indien de l'Ocean Antarctique en fin d'ete. *Oceanologica Acta, 4,* 33–41.

Jacques, G. & Panouse, M. (1991). Biomass and composition of size fractionated phytoplankton in the Weddell Sea Confluence area. *Polar Biology, 11,* 315–328.

Jacques, G. & Treguer, P. (1986). *Les Ecosystems Pelagiques Marins.* Collectios Ecologiques, Vol. 19. Paris: Masson.

Jagger, J. (1985). *Solar-UV Actions on Living Cells.* New York: Praeger Publishing. 202 pp.

Jaka, T. H., Christou, L. & Cook, B. J. (1984). A data bank of mean monthly and annual surface temperature for Antarctica, the Southern Ocean and South Pacific. *ANARE Research Notes, 22,* 1–99.

Jaka, T. H., Christou, L. & Cook, B. J. (1985). Updating the sea ice and climate monitoring programmes. *ANARE Research Notes, 28,* 59–62.

Jakubowski, M. & Byczkowska-Smyk, W. (1970). Respiratory surfaces of white-blooded fish *Chaenichthys rugosus* Regan (Perciformes). *Polskie Archiwum Hydrobiologii, 17,* 273–281.

Jaragov, A. (1969). On the physico-geographical conditions of the krill habotat. *Trudy Vsesoiuznogo Naucho-issledovatel'skii Instituta Morskogo Rybnogo Khoziaistva i Okeanographii, 61.* 85–101. (In Russian.)

Jazdzewski, K., Porebski, J., Rakusa-Suszczewaki, S., Witek, Z. & Wolnomeijski, N. (1978). Biological studies on krill near South Shetland Islands, Scotia Sea and South Georgia in the summer 1978. *Polskie Archiwum Hydrobiologii, 25,* 607–631.

Jazdzewski, K., Jurasz, W., Kittel, W., Presler, E., Presler, P. & Sicinski, J. (1986). Abundance and biomass estimates of the benthic fauna in Admiralty Bay, King George Island, South Shetland Islands. *Polar Biology, 6,* 5–16.

Jenkins, D. G. (1974). Initiation of the protocircum-Antarctic current. *Nature (*London), *252,* 371–373.

Jennings, J. C. Jr., Gordon, L. I. & Nelson, D. M. (1984). Nutrient depletion indicates high primary productivity in the Weddell Sea. *Nature (*London), *309,* 51–54.

Jewell, P. A. & Holt, S. (ed). *Problems of Management of Locally Abundant Wild Animals.* London: Academic Press.

Johannes, R. E. (1965). Influence of marine protozoa on nutrient regeneration. *Limnology & Oceanography, 24,* 928–935.

Johanssen, O. O., Johanssen, J. A., Morison, J., Farrelly, B. A. & Svendsen, E. A. S. (1983). Oceanographic conditions in the marginal ice zone north of Svalbard in early fall 1979 with an emphasis on mesoscale processes. *Journal of Geophysical Research, 88,* 2755–2769.

John, D. D. (1936). The southern species of the genus *Euphausia. Discovery Reports, 14,* 193–324.

John, D. D. (1938). Crinoidea. *Discovery Reports, 18,* 121–222.

John, D. D. (1939). Crinoidea. *British, Australian and New Zealand Antarctic Research Expedition 1901–1904, Report (B), 4,* 189–212.

Johnson, T. O. & Smith, W. O. Jr. (1986). Sinking rates of phytoplankton assemblages in the Weddell Sea marginal ice zone. *Marine Ecology Progress Series, 33,* 131–137.

Johnston, I. A. & Walesby, N. J. (1977). Molecular mechanisms of temperature adaptation in fish myofibrillar adenosine triphosphate. *Journal of Comparative Physiology, 119,* 195–206.

Johnstone, G. W. (1977). Comparative feeding ecology of the giant petrels *Macronectes giganteus* (Gremlin). and *M. halli* (Mathews). In *Adaptations Within Antarctic Ecosystems,* ed. G. A. Llano, pp. 647–668. Washington, DC: Smithsonian Institution.

Johnstone, G. W. (1979). Agonistic behaviour of the giant petrels *Macronectes giganteus* and *M. halli* feeding at seal carcasses. *Emu, 79,* 129–132.

Joint, I. R. & Morris, R. J. (1982). The role of bacteria in the turnover of organic matter in the sea. *Oceanography & Marine Biology. An Annual Review, 20,* 65–118.

Jouventin, P. (1975). Mortality parameters in emperor penguins. In *The Biology of Penguins,* ed. B. Stonehouse, pp. 435–446. London: MacMillan.

Jouventin, P. & Mougin, J-L. (1981). Les strategies adaptatives des oiseau de mer. *Terre et la Vie, Revue d'Ecologie, 35,* 217–272.

Jouventin, P., Stahl, J. C., Weimerskirch, H. & Mougin, J. L. (1984). The seabirds of the French SubAntarctic Islands and Adélie land: their status and conservation. *The Status and Conservation of the Worlds Seabirds. International Council for Bird Preservation Technical Publication, 2,* 609–626.

Joyce, T. M. & Patterson, S. L. (1977). Cyclonic ring formation at the Antarctic Polar Front in the Drake Passage. *Nature* (London), **256**, 131–133.

Joyce, T. M., Zenk, W. & Toole, J. M. (1978). The anatomy of the Antarctic Front in the Drake Passage. *Journal of Geophysical Research*, **83**, 6093–6113.

Joyner, T., Mahnken, C. V. W. & Clark, A. R. (1974). Salmon future harvest from the Antarctic Ocean. *Marine Fisheries Review*, **35**, 20–28.

Kalinowski, J. & Witek, Z. (1980). Diurnal vertical distribution of krill aggregations in the western Antarctic. *Polish Polar Research*, **1**, 127–146.

Kalinowski, J. & Witek, Z. (1982). Forms of Antarctic krill aggregations. *ICES Biological Oceanography Committee C. M. 1982/L: 60*. 9 pp.

Kalinowski, J. & Witek, Z. (1983). Elementy biologii formy grupowego wgstepowania i Zasoby Antarktycznego kryla *Euphausia superba* Dana (Some aspects of biology, forms of aggregation and stocks of Antarctic krill, *Euphausia superba* Dana). Joint Ph. D. Thesis, Sea Fisheries Institute, Godynia, Poland. 207 pp. (In Polish.)

Kalinowski, J. & Witek, Z. (1985). Scheme for classifying aggregations of Antarctic krill. *BIOMASS Handbook No. 27* 9 pp.

Kampa, E. M. & Boden, B. P. (1954). Submarine illumination and twilight movements of a sonic sattering layer. *Nature* (London), **174**, 869.

Kanda, K., Takagi, K. & Seki, Y. (1982). Movement of the larger swarms of Antarctic krill, *Euphausia superba*, populations off Enderby Land during the 1976–77 season. *Journal of the Tokyo University of Fisheries*, **68**, 25–42.

Kane, J. E. (1966). The distribution of *Parathemisto gaudichaudii* (Guer) with observations on its life history on the 0° to 20° E Sector of the Southern Ocean. *Discovery Reports*, **34**, 163–198.

Karanas, J. J., Van Dyke, H. & Worrest, R. C. (1979). Mid ultraviolet (UV-B) sensitivity of *Acartia clausii* Giesbrecht (Copepoda) *Limnology & Oceanography*, **24**, 1004–1116.

Karentz, D. (1990). Ecological considerations of the Antarctic ozone hole on the marine environment. In *Effects of Solar Ultraviolet Radiation on Biogeochemical Dynamics in Aquatic Environments*, ed. N. V. Brough & D. G. Zepp, pp. 137–140. Woods Hole Oceanographic Institution Technical Paper WHOI-90-09.

Karentz, D. (1991). Ecological considerations of Antarctic ozone depletion. *Antarctic Science*, **3**, 3–11.

Karentz, D., Cleaver, J. E. & Mitchell, D. L. (1991a). Cell survival characteristics and molecular responses of Antarctic phytoplankton to ultraviolet-B radiation exposure. *Journal of Phycology*, **27**, 326–341.

Karentz, D., McEuen, F. S. & Land, M. C. (1991b). Survey of mycosporine-like amino acid components in Antarctic marine organisms: potential protection from ultra-violet exposure. *Marine Biology*, **108**, 157–166.

Karl, D. M. & Novitsky, J. A. (1988). Dynamics of microbial growth in surface layers of a coastal marine sediment ecosystem. *Marine Ecology Progress Series*, **50**, 169–176.

Karl, D. M., Holm-Hansen, O., Taylor, G. T., Tein, G. & Bird, D. F. (1991a). Microbial biomass and productivity in the western Bransfield Strait, Antarctica during the 1986–87 austral summer. *Deep-Sea Research*, **38**, 1029–1055.

Karl, D. M., Tilbrook, B. D. & Tein, G. (1991b). Seasonal coupling of organic matter and particle flux in the western Bransfield Strait, Antarctica. *Deep-Sea Research*, **38**, 1097–1126.

Karpov, K. A. & Cailliet, G. M. (1978). Feeding dynamics of *Loligo opalescens. Fisheries Bulletin (California Department of Fish and Game)*, **169**, 45–66.

Kasahara, H. (1967). Prospects of fish production from the sea. *Proceedings of the International Conference on Nutrition*, **7**, 958–964.

Kasamatsu, F. & Ohsumi, S. (1981). Distribution pattern of minke whales in the Antarctic with special reference to the sex ratios of the catch. *Report of the International Whaling Commission*, **31**, 345–348.

Kato, M. (1983). Some considerations of the age at sexual maturity of Antarctic minke whales. *Report of the International Whaling Commission*, **33**, 393–399.

Kato, M., Murano, M. & Segawa, S. (1979). Estimates of the filtration rate of Antarctic krill under laboratory conditions. *Transactions of the Tokyo University of Fisheries*, **3**, 107–112.

Kato, M., Segawa, S., Tanoue, E. & Marano, M. (1982). Filtering and ingestion rates of the Antarctic krill, *Euphausia superba* Dana. *Transactions of the Tokyo University of Fisheries*, **5**, 167–175.

Kaufman, G. W., Siniff, D. B. & Reichle, R. (1975). Colony behaviour of Weddell Seals *Leptonychotes weddelli* at Hutton Cliffs, Antarctica. *Rapports et Proces-Verbaux des Renunions Conseil International Pour l'Exploration de la Mer*, **169**, 228–246.

Kawaguchi, K., Ishikawa, S. & Matsuda, O. (1986). Overwintering strategy of Antarctic krill (*Euphausia superba* Dana) under the coastal fast ice off Ongul Islands in Lutzholm Bay, Antarctica. *Memoirs National Institute of Polar Research, Special Issue*, **44**, 67–85.

Kawakami, T. & Doi, T. (1979). Natural mortality of krill and density of swarms. In *Comprehensive Report on the Population of Krill* Euphausia superba *in the Antarctic*, ed. T. Doi, pp. 19–21. Tokai Regional Fisheries Research Laboratory.

Kawamura, A. (1974). Food and feeding ecology in the southern sei whale. *Scientific Report of the Whales Research Institute (Tokyo)*, **22**, 127–152.

Kawamura, A. (1975). A consideration of an available source of energy and its cost for locomotion in fin whales with special reference to seasonal migrations. *Scientific Reports of the Whales Research Institute (Tokyo)*, **27**, 61–79.

Kawamura, A. (1978). An interim consideration on a possible interspecific relation in the southern baleen whales from the viewpoint of their food habits. *Report of the International Whaling Commisssion*, **28**, 411–420.

Kawamura, A. (1981). Food habits of *Euphausia superba* and the diatom community. *BIOMASS Scientific Sereis*, **2**, 65–68.

Keen, M. (1958). *Sea Shells of Tropical West America: Marine Molluscs from Lower California to Columbia*. Stanford: Stanford University Press. 624 pp.

Kellerman, A. (1986). Zur Biologie der Jugendstadien der Notothenioidei (Pisces) an der Antartischen Halbinsel. *Berichte zur Polarforschung*, **31**, 1–155.

Kellerman, A. (1987). Food and feeding ecology of postlarval and juvenile *Pleurogramma antarcticum* (Pisces: Notothenioidei) in the seasonal pack ice zone off the Antarctic Peninsula. *Polar Biology*, **7**, 307–315.

Kellerman, A. (1990a). Catalogue of early life stages of Antarctic notothenioid fishes. *Berichte zur Polarforschung*, **67**, 45–136.

Kellerman, A. (1990b). Food and feeding dynamics of the larval Antarctic fish *Nototheniops larseni*. *Marine Biology*, **106**, 159–167.

Kellerman, A. & Kock, K-H. (1984). The distribution of postlarval and juvenile notothenioida (Pisces, Perciformes) in the southern Scotia Sea (57–64° S/48–56° W) during FIBEX 1981. *Meeresforschung*, **30**, 82–93.

Kemp. E.M. (1978). Tertiary climate evolution and vegetation history in the southeast Indian ocean region. *Palaeogeography, Palaeoclimatology, Palaeoecology*, **24**, 169–200.

Kennett, J. P. (1968). The fauna of the Ross Sea. Part 6. Ecology and distribution of the Foraminifera. *New Zealand Oceanographic Institute Memoir*, **46**, 1–46.

Kennett, J. P. (1977). Cenozoic evolution of Antarctic glaciation, the circum-Antarctic Ocean, and their impact on global paleoceanography. *Journal of Geophysical Research*, **82**, 3483–3859.

Kennett, J. P. (1983). Paleo-oceanography: global ocean evolution.

Reviews of Geophysics & Space Research, **21**, 1258–1274.

Kennett, J. P., Houtz, R. E., Andrews, P. B., Edwards, A. R., Gostin, V. A., Hajos, M., Hampton, M., Jenkins, D. G., Margolis, S. V., Overshine, A. T. & Perch-Nielsen, K. (1975). Cenozoic paleoceanography in the southwest Pacific ocean, Antarctic glaciation, and the development of the circum-Antarctic current. *Initial Reports of the Deep Sea Drilling Project*, **29**, 1155–1169.

Kenny, R. & Haysom, N. (1962). Ecology of the rocky shores organisms at Macquarie Island. *Pacific Science*, **16**, 245–263.

Keyes, M. C. (1968). The nutrition of pinnipeds. In *The Behaviour and Physiology of Pinnipeds*, ed. R. J. Harrison, R.C. Hubbard, C.E. Petersen, & R.J. Schusterman, pp. 359–395. New York: Appleton-Century-Crofts.

Keys, J. R. (1984) *Antarctic Marine Environments and Offshore Oil.* Wellington: Commission for the Environment, New Zealand Government.

Keysner, E. E., Tot, V. S. & Shilov, V. N. (1974). Characteristics of the behaviour and biological cycles of the marbled notothenia (*Notothenia rossii*) in relation to bottom topography, bottom materials and currents. *Journal of Ichthyology*, **14**, 610–613.

Khailov, K. M. & Burkalova, Z. D. (1976). Release of dissolved organic matter by marine seaweeds and distribution of their total organic production to inshore communities. *Limnology & Oceanography*, **14**, 521–527.

Kikuno, T. (1981). Spawning behaviour and early development of the Antarctic krill *Euphausia superba* Dana, observed on board R. V. *Kaiyo Maru* in 1979/80. *Antarctic Record, Tokyo*, **73**, 97–102.

Killworth, P. D. (1974). A baroclinic model of motions on Antarctic continental shelves. *Deep-Sea Research*, **21**, 815–837.

Kils, U. (1979a). Schwimmverhalten, Schwimmleistung, und Eregiebilanz des Antarktischen Krills *Euphausia superba. Berichte aus dem Institut fur Meereskunde an der Christian-Albrechts-Universitat, Keil*, **65**, 1–71.

Kils, U. (1979b). Swimming speed and escape response of Antarctic krill, *Euphausia superba. Meeresforschung*, **27**, 246–266.

Kils, U. (1979c). Performance of Antarctic krill *Euphausia superba* at different levels of oxygen saturation. *Meeresforschung*, **27**, 35–47.

Kils, U. (1981). *Swimming Behaviour, Swimming Performance and Energy Balance of Antarctic Krill,* Euphausia superba. *Biomass Scientific Series* No. 3. 121 pp. Cambridge: SCAR and SCOR, Scott Polar Research Institute.

Kils, U. (1983). Swimming and feeding of Antarctic krill *Euphausia superba*–some outstanding energetics and dynamics–some unique morphological details. *Berichte zur Polarforschung*, **4**, 130–155.

Kinder, T. H., Hunt, G. L., Jr., Schneider, D. & Schumacker, J. D. (1983). Correlations between seabirds and oceanic fronts around the Pribolof Islands, Alaska. *Estuarine Coastal & Shelf Science*, **16**, 309–319.

King, J. E. (1957). On a pup of the crabeater seal *Lobodon carcinophagus. Annals & Magazine of Natural History*, Series **12**, 619–624.

King, J. E. (1961). The feeding mechanism and jaws of the crabeater seal (*Lobodon carcinpohagus*). *Mammalia*, **25**, 462–466.

King, J. E. (1964). *Seals of the World.* London: British Museum (Natural History).

King, J. E. (1969). Some aspects of the anatomy of the Ross seal, *Ommatophoca rossii* (Pinnipedia: Phocidae). *British Antarctic Survey Scientific Reports*, **63**, 1–54.

Kirkwood, G. P. (1981). Estimating population sizes from relative abundance data: a simulation study. *Report of the International Whaling Commission*, **31**, 729–735.

Klages, N. (1989). Food and feeding ecology of emperor penguins in the eastern Weddell Sea. *Polar Biology*, **9**, 385–390.

Klinch, J. M. & Hofman, E. E. (1986). Deep-flow variability in the Drake Passage. *Journal of Physical Oceanography*, **16**, 1281–1292.

Klindt, H. (1986). Acoustic estimates of the distribution and stock size of krill around Elephant Island during SIBEX I and II in 1983, 1984

and 1985. *Archiv fur Fischereiwissenschaft*, **37**, 107–127.

Knauer, G. A., Hebel, D. & Cipriano, F. (1982). Marine snow: major site of primary production in coastal waters. *Nature* (London), **33**, 630–631.

Knox, G. A. (1960). Littoral ecology and biogeography of the Southern Ocean. *Proceedings of the Royal Society of London, Series B, Biological Sciences*, **152**, 577–625.

Knox, G. A. (1963). The biogeography and intertidal ecology of Australasian coasts. *Oceanography and Marine Biology: An Annual Review*, **1**, 341–404.

Knox, G. A. (1970). Antarctic marine ecosystems. In *Antarctic Ecology*, Vol 1, ed. M. W. Holdgate, pp. 69–96. London: Academic Press.

Knox, G. A. (1975). The marine benthic ecology and biogeography. In *Biogeography and Ecology of New Zealand Shores*, ed. G. Kuschel, pp. 353–403. The Hague: Dr. W. Junk Publishers.

Knox, G. A. (1978). The Southern Ocean. *New Zealand Environment*, **22**, 25–29.

Knox, G. A. (1979). Distribution patterns of the Southern Hemisphere marine biota: some comments on their origin and evolution. In *Proceedings International Symposium on Marine Biogeography and Evolution in the Southern Hemisphere, Auckland, July, 1978*, pp. 43–52.

Knox, G. A. (1980). Plate tectonics and the evolution of intertidal and shallow-water benthic biotic distribution patterns of the Southwest Pacific. *Palaeogeography, Palaeoclimatology, Palaeoecology*, **31**, 267–297.

Knox, G. A. (1983). The living resources of the Southern Ocean: a scientific overview. In *Antarctic Resources Policy: Scientific, Legal and Political Issues*, ed. F. O. Vicuna, pp. 21–60. Cambridge: Cambridge University Press.

Knox, G. A. (1984). The key role of krill in the ecosystem of the southern ocean with special reference to the Convention on the Conservation of Antarctic Marine Living Resource. *Ocean Management*, **9**, 113–156.

Knox, G. A. (1986). Recent New Zealand marine research in the Ross Sea Sector of Antarctica. *Memoirs National Institute of Polar Research, Special Issue*, **40**, 345–363.

Knox, G A. (1988). University of Canterbury Antarctic Research Unit. *New Zealand Antarctic Record*, **8** (2), 33–49.

Knox, G. A. (1990). Primary production and consumption in McMurdo Sound, Antarctica. In *Antarctic Ecosystems: Ecological Change and Conservation*, ed. K. R. Kerry & G. Hempel, pp. 115–128. Berlin & Heidelberg: Springer-Verlag.

Knox, G. A. & Lowry, J. K. (1977). A comparison between the benthos of the Southern Ocean and the North Polar Ocean, with special reference to the Amphipoda and Polychaeta. In *Polar Oceans*, ed. M. J. Dunbar, pp. 423–462. Calgary: Arctic Institute of North America.

Knox, G. A., Waghorn, E. H. & Ensor, P. H. (in press) The summer plankton beneath the McMurdo ice Shelf at White island, McMurdo Sound, Antarctica. *Polar Biology.*

Kobori, H., Sullivan, C. W. & Shizuya, H. S. (1984). Bacterial plasmids in Antarctic microalgal assemblages. *Applied & Environmental Microbiology*, **48**, 515–518.

Kock, K-H. (1975). Verbreitung und biologie der Wichtigsten nutzfischarten der Antarktis. *Mittelungen Institut fur Seefischerei Hamburg*, **16**, 1–75.

Kock, K-H. (1979). On the fecundity of *Champsocephalus gunnari* Lonnberg 1906 and *Chaenocephalus aceratus* Lonnberg 1906 (Pisces, Channichthyidae) off South Georgia Island. *Meeresforschung*, **27**, 177–185.

Kock, K-H. (1980). Graphical analysis of length frequency distribution of *Champsocephalus gunnari* Lonnberg (Channichthyidae). from South Georgia. *Cybium*, **4**, 33–42.

Kock, K-H. (1981). Fischereibiologische Untersuchungen an drei antarktischen Fischarten: *Champsocephalus gunnari* Lonnberg

1905, *Chaenocephalus aceratus* Lonnberg 1906, and *Pseudochaenichthys georgianus* Norman 1937 (Notothenioidei, Channichthyidae). *Mitteilungen aus dem Institut fur Seefisherei der Brundeforschungsanstalt fur Fischerei, Hamburg*, **32**, 1–227.

Kock, K.-H. (1982). Fischerbiologische Unterscheungen bei Elephant Island im März 1981. *Archiv fur Fischeriewissenschaft*, **33**, 127–142.

Kock, K.-H. (1984). Marine habitats: fish. In *Key Environments – Antarctica*, ed. W. N. Bonner & D. W. H. Walton, pp. 17–192. Oxford: Pergamon Press.

Kock, K.-H. (1985). Krill consumption by Antarctic notothenioid fish. In *Antarctic Nutrient Cycles and Food Webs*, ed. W. R. Siegfried, P. R. Condy & R. M. Laws, pp. 437–444. Berlin Heidelberg: Springer-Verlag.

Kock, K.-H. (1987). Marine consumers: Fish and squid. *Environment International*, **13**, 37–45.

Kock, K.-H. & Kellerman, A. (1991). Reproduction in Antarctic notothenioid fish. *Antarctic Science*, **3**, 125–150.

Kock, K.-H. & Koster, F. W. (1990). The state of exploited fish stocks in the Atlantic sector of the Southern Ocean. In *Antarctic Ecosystems: Ecological Change and Conservation*, ed. K. R. Kerry & G. Hempel, pp. 308–322. Berlin & Heidelberg: Springer-Verlag.

Kock, K.-H. & Stein, M. (1978). Krill and hydrographic conditions off the Antarctic Peninsula. *Meeresforschung*, **26**, 79–95.

Kock, K.-H., Duhamel, G. & Hureau, J-C. (1985). Review of the *Biology and Present Status of Exploited Antarctic Fish Stocks*. *Biomass Scientific Series No. 7*. Cambridge: SCAR, Scott Polar Research Institute.

Kogure, K., Fukami, K., Simidu, U. & Taga, N. (1986). Abundance and production of bacterioplankton in the Antarctic. *Memoirs National Institute of Polar Research, Special Issue*, **40**, 414–422.

Koike, I., Ronner, U. & Holm-Hansen, O. (1981). Microbial nitrogen metabolism in the Scotia Sea. *Antarctic Journal of the United States*, **16**, 165–166.

Koike, I., Holm-Hansen, O & Biggs, D. C. (1986). Inorganic nitrogen metabolism by Antarctic phytoplankton with special reference to ammonia cycling. *Marine Ecology Progress Series*, **30**, 105–116.

Koltun, V. M. (1969). Porifera. *Antarctic Map Folio Series* (American Geographical Society), **11**, 13–14.

Komaki, Y. (1966). Technical notes on keeping euphausiids alive in the laboratory with a review of experimental studies on euphausiids. *Information Bulletin Plankton Society of Japan*, **13**, 95–106.

Kompowski, A. (1980a). On feeding of *Champsocephalus gunnari* Lonnberg, 1905 (Pisces, Chaenichthyidae) off South Georgia and Kerguelen islands. *Acta Ichthyologica et Piscatoria*, **10**, 25–43.

Kompowski, A. (1980b). Studies on juvenile *Chaenocephalus aceratus* Lonnberg, 1906 (Pisces, Chaenichthyidae) off South Georgia. *Acta Ichthyologica et Piscatoria*, **10**, 45–53.

Konopka, A. (1983). The effect of nutrient limitation and its interaction with light upon the products of photosynthesis in *Merismopedia tenuissima* (Cyanophyceae). *Journal of Phycology*, **19**, 403–409.

Kooyman, G. L. (1963). Erythrocytes analysis of some Antarctic fishes. *Copea*, **2**, 457–458.

Kooyman, G. L. (1975). The physiology of diving in penguins. In *The Biology of Penguins*, ed. B. Stonehouse, pp. 115–137. London: Macmillan.

Kooyman, G. L. (1981a). Crabeater Seal – *Lobodon carcinophagus* (Hombron & Jacquinot, 1842). In *Handbook of Marine Mammals Vol. 2 Seals*, ed. S. H. Ridgeway & R. J. Harrison, pp. 221–235. London & New York: Academic Press.

Kooyman, G. L. (1981b). Leopard seal – *Hydrurga leptonyx* Blainville, 1820. In *Handbook of Marine Mammals. Vol. 2. Seals*, ed. S. H. Ridgeway & R. J. Harrison, pp. 261–274. London & New York: Academic Press.

Kooyman, G. L. (1981c). Weddell Seal–*Leptonychotes weddelli* Lesson, 1826. In *Handbook of Marine Nammals. Vol. 2. Seals*, ed. S. H. Ridgeway & R. J. Harrison, pp. 275–296. London & New York: Academic Press.

Kooyman, G. L. (1981d). *Weddell Seal: Consumate Diver*. New York: Cambridge University Press. 135 pp.

Kooyman, G. L. & Davis, R. W. (1980). Feeding behaviour of female Antarctic fur seals, *Arctocephalus gazella*. *Antarctic Journal of the United States*, **15**, 159.

Kooyman, G. L., Drabek, C. M., Elsner, R & Campbell, W. B. (1971). Diving behaviour of the Emperor Penguin. *Auk*, **88**, 775–795.

Kooyman, G. L., Keren, D. H., Campbell, W. B. & Wright, J. J. (1973). Pulmonary gas exchange in freely diving Weddell seals, *Leptonychotes weddelli*. *Respiratory Physiology*, **17**, 283–290.

Kooyman, G. L., Gentry, R. L., Bergman, W. P. & Hammel, H. T. (1976). Heat loss in penguins during immersion and compression. *Comparative Biochemistry & Physiology*, **54A**, 75–80.

Kooyman, G. L., Davis, R. W., Croxall, J. P. & Costa, D. P. (1982). Diving depths and energy requirements of King Penguins. *Science*, **217**, 726–727.

Kooyman, G. L., Davis, R. W. & Croxall, J. P. (1986). Diving behaviour of Antarctic fur seals. In *Fur Seals: Maternal Strategies on Land and at Sea*, ed. R. L. Gentry & G. L. Kooyman, pp. 1165–125. Princetown: Princetown University Press.

Kopczynska, E. E., Weber, L. H. & El-Sayed, S. Z. (1986). Phytoplankton species composition in the Indian sector of the Antarctic Ocean. *Polar Biology*, **6**, 161–169.

Koralbel'nikov, L. V. (1956). Quoted in Berzin (1972).

Kosahi, S., Takahashi, M., Yamaguchi, Y. & Aruya, Y. (1985). Size characteristics of chlorophyll particles in the southern Ocean. *Transactions of the Tokyo University of Fisheries*, **6**, 85–97.

Kott, P. (1969a). Antarctic Ascidacea. *Antarctic Research Series*, **13**, 1–239.

Kott, P. (1969b). Ascidacea. *Antarctic Map Folio Series* (American Geographical Society), **13**, 1–9.

Kott, P. (1971). Antarctic Ascidacea II. *Antarctic Research Series*, **17**, 18–82.

Kottmeier, S. T. & Sullivan, C. W. (1987). Late winter primary production and bacterial production in sea ice and seawater west of the Antarctic Peninsula. *Marine Ecology Progress Series*, **36**, 287–298.

Kottmeier, S. T. & Sullivan, C. W. (1988). Sea ice microbial communities (SIMCO). IX. Effects of temperature and salinity on rates of metabolism and growth of autotrophs and heterotrophs. *Polar Biology*, **8**, 293–304.

Kottmeier, S. T. & Sullivan, C. W. (1990). Bacterial biomass and production in pack ice of Antarctic marginal ice zones. *Deep-Sea Research*, **37**, 1311–1330.

Kottmeier, S. T., Musat, A. M., Craft, L. L., Kastendiek, J. E. & Sullivan, C. W. (1984). Ecology of sea ice microbial communities in McMurdo Sound. *Antarctic Journal of the United States*, **19**, 129–131.

Kottmeier, S. T., Miller, M. A., Lizotte, M. P., Craft, L. L. & Sullivan, C. W. (1986). Ecology of sea ice microbial communities during the 1984 winter–summer transition in McMurdo Sound, Antarctica. *Antarctic Journal of the United States*, **20**, 128–130.

Kottmeier, S. T., Grossi, S. McG. & Sullivan, C. W. (1987). Sea ice microbial communities. VIII. Bacterial production in annual sea ice of McMurdo Sound, Antarctica. *Marine Ecology Progress Series*, **35**, 175–186.

Kozlov, A. N. & Tarverdiyera, M. I. (1989). Feeding of different species of Myctophidae in different parts of the Southern Ocean. *Journal of Ichthyology*, **29**, 160–167. (Translated from Voprosy ikhtiologii).

Krebs, W. M. (1983). Ecology of neretic diatoms, Arthur Harbor, Antarctica. *Micropalaeontology*, **29**, 267–297.

Krebs, W. M., Lipps, J. H. & Burckle, L. H. (1987). Ice diatom floras, Arthur Harbour, Antarctica. *Polar Biology*, **7**, 163–171.

Krempin, D. M. (1985). The role of bacterioplankton as producers in two high-productivity marine ecosystems. Ph. D. dissertation, University of Southern California, Los Angeles. 212 pp.

Kriss, A. Ye. (1973). Quantitative distribution of saprophytic bacteria between New Zealand and Antarctica. *Mikrobiologiya*, **42**, 913–917.

Kristensen, T. K. (1980). Periodic growth rings in cephalopod statoliths. *Dana*, **1**, 39–51.

Kuhl, S. & Schneppenheim, R. (1986). Electrophoretic investigation of genetic variation in two krill species *Euphausia superba* and *E. crystallorophias* (Euphausiidae). *Polar Biology*, **6**, 17–23.

Kundo, K. & Fukuchi, M. (1982). Vertical distribution of chlorophyll *a* in the Indian sector of the Antarctic Ocean in 1972–1973. *Antarctic Record*, **74**, 127–142.

Kuramoto, S. & Koyama, K. (1982). Preliminary report of the oceanographic observations on the 22nd Japanese Antarctic Research Expedition (1980–1981). *Memoirs National Institute of Polar Research, Special Issue*, **23**, 5–12.

Kurodo, N. H. (1967). Morpho-anatomical analysis of parallel evolution between diving petrel and ancient auk, with comparative osteological data of other species. *Miscellaneous Reports of the Yamishina Institute of Ornithology & Zoology*, **5**, 111–137.

Kussakin, O. G. (1967). Fauna of Isopoda and Tanaidacea in the coastal zones of Antarctic and SubAntarctic waters. Biological zones of the Antarctic and SubAntarctic waters. In *Biological Reports of the Soviet Antarctic Expeditions (1955–1958)*, pp. 220–239. Akidemiya nauk SSSR Zoologoscheskii Institut Issledovaniya a Fauny morei.

Laevastu, T. & Favourite, F. (1981). Holistic simulation models of shelf-seas ecosystems. In *Analysis of Marine Ecosystems*, ed. A. R. Longhurst, pp. 701–725. London & New York: Academic Press.

Laevastu, T. & Larkin, H. H. (1981). *Marine Fisheries Ecosystem–Its Quantitative Evaluation and Management*. Farnham, Surrey: Fishing News Books.

Lampitt, R. S., Noji, T. & Bodungen, B. von (1990). What happens to zooplankton faecal pellets? Implication for material flux. *Marine Biology*, **104**, 15–23.

Lancelot, C. (1984). Metabolic changes in *Phaeocystis pouchetii* (Hariot) Langerheim during the spring bloom in Belgian coastal waters. *Estuarine Coastal Shelf Science*, **18**, 593–600.

Lancelot, C. & Mathut, S. (1985). Biochemical fractionation of primary production by phytoplankton in Belgium coastal waters during short- and long-term incubations with ^{14}C-bicarbonate. II. *Phaeocystis pouchetii* colonial population. *Marine Biology*, **65**, 13–16.

Lancraft, T. M., Torres, J. J. & Hopkins, T. L. (1989). Micronekton and macrozooplankton in the open waters near Antarctic ice edge zones (AMERIEZ 1983 and 1986). *Polar Biology*, **9**, 225–233.

Lande, R. & Wood, A. M. (1987). Suspension times of particles in the upper ocean. *Deep-Sea Research*, **34**, 61–72.

Larrian, E. (1981). Consecuencia en la biota bentonica de las erupcionesd volcanicas en Isla Deception (62° 57′ S, 60° 29′ S, 59° 04′ W) y su comparacion con Bahia Chile (62° 29′ S, 59° 04′ W), Antarctica. *Memoir Biologie Marine, Universidad de Conception*. 150 pp.

Lasker, R. (1966). Feeding, growth, respiration and carbon utilization of a euphausiid crustacean. *Journal of the Fisheries Research Board of Canada*, **23**, 1291–1317.

Lasker, R. (1975). Field criteria for survival of anchovey larvae: the relation between the inshore chlorophyll layers and successful first feeding. *US Fisheries Bulletin*, **71**, 453–462.

Lasker, R. (1980). Factors contributing to variable recruitment of the northern anchovey (*Eugraulis mordax*) in the Californian current: contrasting years 1975 through 1978. In *Proceedings of the 2nd Symposium on the Early Life History of Fish*. ICES/EHL Symposium/PE, 11.

Latogurskij, V. L. (1972). *Euphausia superba* Dana as a food item of

Notothenia rossii mamorata. *Trudy Atlantic NIRO*, **42**, 167–169. (In Russian.)

Lavigne, D. M., Barchard, W., Innes, S. & Øritzland, N. A. (1982). Pinniped energetics. *FAO Fish Series* (5) **4**, 191–235.

Lavigne, D. M., Innes, S., Worthy, G. A. J., Kovaks, K. M., Schmitz, O. J. & Hickie, J. P. (1986). Metabolic rates of seals and whales. *Canadian Journal of Zoology*, **64**, 279–284.

Laws, R. M. (1956). The elephant seal (*Mirounga leonina* Linn.) II. General, social and reproductive behaviour. *Falkland Islands Dependency Survey, Scientific Reports*, **15**, 1–66.

Laws, R. M. (1959). The foetal growth rates of whales with special reference to the fin whale, *Balaenoptera physalus* Linn. *Discovery Reports*, **29**, 281–308.

Laws, R. M. (1960a). Problems of whale conservation. *Transactions of the North American Wildlife Conference*, **25**, 304–319.

Laws, R. M. (1960b). The Southern Elephant Seal (*Mirounga leonina* Linn.) at South Georgia. *Norsk Hvalfangst-Tidende*, **49**, 446–476.

Laws, R. M. (1961). Reproduction, growth and age of Southern Hemisphere fin whales. *Discovery Reports*, **31**, 327–485.

Laws, R. M. (1964). Comparative biology of Antarctic seals. In *Biologie antarctique*, ed. R. Carrick, M. W. Holdgate & J. Prevost, pp. 445–454. Paris: Hermann.

Laws, R. M. (1973). Population increase of fur seals at South Georgia. *Polar Record*, **16**, 856–858.

Laws, R. M. (1977a). Seals and whales of the Southern Ocean. *Philosophical Transactions of the Royal Society, London, Series B*, **279**, 81–96.

Laws, R. M. (1977b). The significance of vertebrates in the Antarctic marine ecosystem. In *Adaptations Within Antarctic Ecosystems*, ed. G. A. Llano, pp. 411–438. Washington, DC: Smithsonian Institution.

Laws, R. M. (1979). Monitoring whale and seal populations. In *Monitoring the Marine Environment*, ed. D. Nichols, pp. 115–140. Symposium of the Institute of Biology No. 7.

Laws, R. M. (1981). Seal surveys, South Orkney Islands, 1971 and 1974. *British Antarctic Survey Bulletin*, **54**, 136–139.

Laws, R. M. (1984a). Seals. In *Antarctic Ecology* Vol. 2, ed. R. M. Laws, pp. 621–715. London : Academic Press.

Laws, R. M. (1984b). Decade of research on Antarctic and SubAntarctic seals. *South African Journal of Science*, **80**, 25–35.

Laws, R. M. (1985). The ecology of the Southern Ocean. *American Scientist*, **73**, 26–40.

Laws, R. M. & Purves, P. E. (1956). The ear plug of Mysticeti as an indicator of age, with special reference to the North Atlantic fin whale. *Norsk Hvalgangsttid*, **45**, 414–425.

LeBlond, P. H. (1982). Satellite observations of the Labrador Current undulations. *Atmosphere & Ocean*, **20**, 129–142.

Leford-Hoffman, P. A., DeMaster, D. J. & Nittrouer, C. A. (1986). Biogenic-silica accumulation in the Ross Sea and the importance of the Antarctic continental shelf deposits in the marine silica budget. *Geochemica et Cosmochemica Acta*, **50**, 2099–2110.

Legecis, R. (1977). Oceanic polar front in the Drake Passage: satellite observations during 1976. *Deep-Sea Research*, **24**, 701–704.

Legendre, L., Ingram, R. G. & Poulin, M. (1981). Physical control of phytoplankton under sea ice (Monitounuk Sound, Hudson Bay). *Canadian Journal of Fisheries and Aquatic Sciences*, **38**, 1385–1392.

Le Jehan, S. & Treguer, P. (1985). The distribution of inorganic nitrogen, phosphorus, silicon and dissolved organic matter in surface and deep waters of the Southern Ocean. In *Antarctic Nutrient Cycles and Food Webs*, ed. W. R. Siegfried, P. R. Condy & R. M. Laws, pp. 22–29. Berlin & Heidelberg: Springer-Verlag.

Le Maho, Y., Delclitte, P. & Chatonnet, J. (1976). Thermoregulation in fasting emperor penguins. *American Journal of Physiology*, **231**, 913–922.

Lessard. E. J. & Swift, E. (1985). Species-specific grazing rates of heterotrophic dinoflagellates in oceanic waters measured with dual-label radioisotope technique. *Marine Biology*, **87**, 289–296.

Lessard, E. J., Voytek, M. & Rivkin, R. (1987). The heterotrophic based nutrition of microzooplankton and macrozooplankton in McMurdo Sound Antarctica. *EOS*, **68**, 1773.

Leventer, A. (1991). Sediment trap diatom assemblages from the northern Antarctic Peninsula. *Deep-Sea Research*, **38**, 1127–1143

Leventer, A. & Dunbar, R. B. (1987). Diatom flux in McMurdo Sound, Antarctica. *Marine Micropaleontology*, **12**, 49–64.

Levin, S. A., Marin, A. & Powell, T. M. (1988). Patterns and processes in the distribution and dynamics of Antarctic krill. In *Selected Scientific Papers. Part I. SC-CCAMLR-SS P/5*, pp. 281–300. Hobart: Commission on the Conservation of Antarctic Marine Living Resources.

Lewis, E. L. & Perkin, R. G. (1985). Oceanographic investigations in McMurdo Sound. *Antarctic Research Series*, **43**, 145–166.

Lewis, E. L. & Weeks, W. F. (1971). Sea ice: some polar contrasts. In *Symposium on Antarctic Ice and Water Masses*, ed. G. Deacon, pp. 23–33. Tokyo: Scientific Committee on Antarctic Research.

Lewis, M. R., Horne, E. P. W., Cullen, J. J., Oakey, N. S. & Platt, T. (1984). Turbulent motions may control phytoplankton photosynthesis in the upper ocean. *Nature* (London), **311**, 49–50.

Li, W. K. W. (1986). Experimental approaches to field measurements: methods and interpretations. *Canadian Journal of Fisheries and Aquatic Sciences*, **214**, 251–286.

Li, W. K. W., Subba Rao, D. V., Harrison, W. G., Smith, J. G., Cullen, J. J., Irwin, B. & Platt, T. (1983). Autotrophic picoplankton in the tropical ocean. *Science*, **219**, 292–295.

Liebezeit, G. (1985). Residual amino acid fluxes in the upper water column of the Bransfield Strait. *Oceanology Acta*, **8**, 59–65.

Liebezeit, G. & Bodungen, B. von (1987). Biogenic fluxes in the Bransfield Strait: planktonic versus microalgal sources. *Marine Ecology Progress Series*, **36**, 23–32.

Liebezeit, G. and Bolter, M. (1986). Distribution of particulate amino acids in the Bransfield Strait. *Polar Biology*, **2**, 225–228.

Ligowski, R. (1982). Phytogenic food of *Euphausia superba* Dana caught in the Drake Passage and Bransfield Strait, February–March 1981 (BIOMASS-FIBEX). *Polish Polar Research*, **3**, 281–288.

Lillo, S. & Guzman, O. (1982). Study of the abundance, distribution and behaviour of krill at the Bransfield Strait and Drake Passage by means of hydroacoustic techniques. *Instituto Antarctica Chileno (INACH). Scientific Series*, **28**, 17–45.

Lin, Y., Raymond, J. A. & DeVries, A. L. (1976). Compartmentalization of NaCl in frozen solutions of antifreeze glycoproteins. *Cryobiology*, **13**, 334–340.

Lindeman, R. l. (1942). The trophic-dynamic aspect of ecology. *Ecology*, **23**, 399–418.

Lindsay, A. A. (1937). The Weddell seal in the Bay of Whales, Antarctica. *Journal of Mammalogy*, **18**, 127–144.

Linkowski, T. B. & Rembiszewski, J. M. (1978). Ichthyological observations off the South Georgia coasts. *Polski Archiwum Hydrobiologii*, **25**, 697–704.

Linkowski, T.B., Presler, P. & Zubowski, C. (1983). Food habits of Nototheniid fishes (Nototheniidae) in Admiralty Bay (King George Island, South Shetland Islands). *Polish Polar Research*, **4**, 79–95.

Linley, E. A. S. & Newell, R. C. (1984). Estimates of bacterial growth yields based on plant detritus. *Bulletin of Marine Science*, **35**, 409–425.

Lipps, J. H., Krebs, W. N. & Temnikow, N. K. (1977). Macrobiota under Antarctic ice shelves. *Nature (London)*, **265**, 232–233.

Lipps, J. H., DeLaca, J. F., Showers, W., Roman, T. E., Clough, J., Raymond, J., Bradford, J. and DeVries, A. (1978). Benthic marine biology. Ross Ice Shelf project. *Antarctic Journal of the United States*, **13**, 134–141.

Lipps, J. H., Roman, T. E. & DeLaca, T. E. (1979). Life below the Ross Ice Shelf, Antarctica. *Science*, **203**, 447–449.

Lipski, M. (1985). Chlorophyll *a* in the Bransfield Strait and the southern part of the Drake Passage during BIOMASS-SIBEX (December 1983–January 1984). *Polish Polar Research*, **6**, 21–30.

Lishman, G. S. (1985). The food and feeding ecology of Adélie Penguins (*Pygoscelis adelie*) and Chinstrap Penguins (*P. antarctica*) at Signey Island, South Orkney Islands. *Journal of Zoology, London, A*, **205**, 245–263.

Lishman, G. S. & Croxall, J. P. (1983). Diving depths of the Chinstrap Penguin. *British Antarctic Survey Bulletin*, **61**, 21–25.

Lisitzin, A. P. (1972). *Sedimentation in the World Ocean*. Society for Economic Paleontology and Mineralogy, Special Publication 17. 218 pp.

Lisovenko, L. A. & Svetlov, M. F. (1980). Some data on the biology of *Paraliparis* (Family Liparidae) for the South Shetlands. *Journal of Ichthyology*, **20**, 131–135.

Littlepage, J. L. (1964). Seasonal variation in lipid content of two Antarctic marine crustacea. In *Biologie Antarctique*, ed. R. Carrick, M. W. Holdgate & J. Prevost, pp. 163–470. Paris: Hermann.

Littlepage, J. L. (1965). Oceanographic investigations in McMurdo Sound. *Antarctic Research Series*, **5**, 1–37.

Littlepage, J. L. & Pearse, J. C. (1962). Biological and oceanographic observations under an Antarctic ice shelf. *Science*, **137**, 679–680.

Lizotte, M. P. & Sullivan, C. W. (1991a). Photosynthesis–irradiance relationships in microalgae associated with Antarctic pack ice: evidence for in situ activity. *Marine Ecology Progress Series*, **71**, 175–184.

Lizotte, M. P. & Sullivan, C. W. (1991b). Rates of photoadaptation in sea ice diatoms from McMurdo Sound, Antarctica. *Journal of Phycology*, **27**, 367–373.

Lockyer, C. (1972). The age of sexual maturity of the southern fin whale (*Balaenoptera physalus*). using annual layer counts in the ear plug. *Journal du Conseil. Conseil Permanent International pour l'Exploration de la Mer*, **34**, 276–294.

Lockyer, C. (1973). Wet weight, volume and length correlation in Antarctic krill, *Euphausia superba*. *Discovery Reports*, **36**, 152–155.

Lockyer, C. (1974). Investigation of the ear plug of the southern sei whale *Balaenoptera borealis*, as a valid means of determining age. *Journal du Conseil. Conseil Permanent International pour l'Explotation de la Mer*, **36**, 71–81.

Lockyer, C. (1975). Estimates of growth and energy budget for the sperm whale *Physeter catadon*. *United Nations Scientific Consultation on Marine Mammals, Bergen, Norway, 31 August–9 September, 1976*. Rome: FAO of the UN ACMRR/MM/SC/38.

Lockyer, C. (1976). Growth and energy budgets of large baleen whales from the Southern Hemisphere. *United Nations Scientific Consultation on Marine Mammals, Bergen, Norway, 31 August–9 September, 1976*. Rome: FAO of the UN ACMRR/MM/SC/41.

Lockyer, C. (1977a). A preliminary study of variations in age of sexual maturity of the fin whale with year class in six areas of the Southern Hemisphere. *Report of the International Whaling Commission, Special Issue*, **1**, 63–70.

Lockyer, C. (1977b). Observations on the diving behaviour of the sperm whale *Physeter catadon*. In *A Voyage of Discovery*, ed. M. Angel, pp. 591–609. Oxford: Pergamon Press.

Lockyer, C. (1978). A theoretical approach to the balance between growth and food consumption in fin an sei whales with special reference to the female reproductive cycle. *Report of the International Whaling Commission*, **28**, 243–249.

Lockyer, C. (1979). Changes in a growth parameter associated with exploitation of southern fin and sei whales. *Report of the International Whaling Commission*, **29**, 191–196.

Lockyer, C. (1981a). Growth and energy budgets of large baleen whales from the Southern Hemisphere. In *Mammals of the Sea*, pp. 379–487. Rome: FAO Fisheries Series No. 5, Vol. 3.

Lockyer, C. (1981b). Estimates of the growth and energy budget for the sperm whale *Physeter catadon*. In *Mammals of the Sea*, pp. 489–504. Rome: FAO Fisheries Series No. 5, Vol. 3,

Lockyer, C. (1984). Review of baleen whale reproduction and implications for management. *Report of the International Whaling Commission, Special Issue*, 6.

Lockyer, C. & Brown, S. G. (1981). The migration of whales. In *Animal Migration*, ed. D. G. Ainley, pp. 105–137. Cambridge: Cambridge University Press, Society for Experimental Biology, Seminar Series 13.

Lomakina, N. B. (1964). The euphausiid fauna of the Antarctic and notal regions In *Biological Results of the Soviet Antarctic Expedition (1955–1958)*, pp. 245–334. Moscow, Leningrad: Nauka. (In Russian.)

Longhurst, A. R. (1976). Vertical migration. In *The Ecology of the Seas*, ed. D. H. Cushing & J. J. Walsh, pp. 116–137. Oxford: Blackwell Scientific Publications.

Longhurst, A. R. (1981). Significance of spatial variability. In *Analysis of Marine Systems*, ed. A. R. Longhurst, pp. 415–441. New York: Academic Press.

Lowry, J. K. (1969). The soft bottom macrobenthic community of Arthur Harbor, Antarctica. Masters thesis, College of William and Mary, Williamsberg, Virginia.

Lowry, J. K. (1975). Soft bottom macrobenthic community of Arthur Harbor, Antarctica. *Antarctic Research Series*, **23**, 1–19.

Lowry, J. K. (1976). Studies on the macrobenthos of the Southern Ocean. Ph. D. thesis in zoology, University of Canterbury, Christchurch.

Lubimova, T. G. (1982). Zonation of the oceanographic structure and biological resources of the Southern Ocean. In *Tesisy Vesesoyaz konf po teorii formiarovaniya chiselnnosti i ratsionalonogo ispolzovaniya stad promyslovykh ryb* , pp. 205–207. Moscow; VIRNO. (In Russian.)

Lubimova, T. G. (1983). Ecological basis of exploitation of the resources of Antarctic krill. *Memoirs of the National Institute of Polar Research, Special Issue*, **27**, 211–219.

Lubimova, T. G. & Shust, K. V. (1980). Quantitative study of Antarctic krill consumed by principal groups of species. In *Biological Resources of Antarctic Krill*, ed. T. G. Lubimova, pp. 203–224. Moscow: VIRNO.

Lubimova, T. G, Naumov, A. G. & Lagunov, L. L. (1973). Prospects of the utilization of krill and other unconvential resources of the world ocean. *Journal of the Fisheries Research Board of Canada*, 30, 2196–2201.

Lubimova, T. G., Makarov, R. R. & Kamenskaia, E. A. (ed.).(1980). *Antarctic Krill: The Distribution Pattern and Environment* (Antarkticheskii krill Osobemmosti vaspredeleniia i sreda).Moscow: Legkaia i Pischevaia Promyschlenost. In Russian, with English summary.

Lubimova, T. G., Makarov, R. R., Maselenikov, V. V., Shevtsov, W. & Shust, K. V. (1984). The ecological pecularities, stocks and the role of *E. superba* in the trophic structure of the Antarctic ecosystem. In *Selected Papers Presented to the Scientific Committee of CCAMLR, 1981–1984, Part II.*, pp. 391–505. Hobart: CCAMLR.

Lutjeharms, J. R. E., Walter, N. M. & Allanson, B. R. (1985). Oceanic frontal systems and biological enhancement. In *Antarctic Nutrient Cycles and Food Webs*, ed. W. R. Siegfried, P. R. Condy & R. M. Laws, pp. 11–21. Berlin & Heidelberg: Springer-Verlag.

Luxmore, R. A. (1982). Moulting and growth in serolid isopods. *Journal of Experimental Marine Biology and Ecology*, **56**, 63–85.

Lythgoe, J. M. & Dartnall, H. J. A. (1970). A deep sea rhodopsin in a mammal. *Nature* (London), **227**, 955–956.

Macauley, M. C., English, T. S. & Mathisen, O. A. (1984). Acoustic characterization of swarms of Antarctic krill (*Euphausia superba*) from Elephant Island and Bransfield Strait. *Journal of Crustacean Biology* , **4**, (Special Issue No. 1) 16–44.

McAlister, W.B., Sayer, G.A. & Perez, M.S. (1976). Preliminary estimates of pinniped-finfish relationship in the Bering Sea. *Background Paper 19th Meeting Fur Seal Commission, Moscow,*

1976. Seattle: US Dept. of Commerce, NOAA, NMFS.

Mackintosh, N. A. (1934). Distribution of the macroplankton of the Atlantic sector of the Antarctic. *Discovery Reports*, **9**, 65–160.

Mackintosh, N. A. (1937). The seasonal circulation of the Antarctic macroplankton. *Discovery Reports*, **16**, 365–412.

Mackintosh, N. A. (1942). The southern stocks of whalebone whales. *Discovery Reports*, **22**, 197–200.

Mackintosh, N. A. (1965). *The Stocks of Whales.* London: Fishing News Books.

Mackintosh, N. A. (1967). Maintenance of living *Euphausia superba* and frequency of moults. *Norsk Hvalfangst-Tidende*, **5**, 97–102.

Mackintosh, N. A. (1970). Whales and krill in the twentieth century. In *Antarctic Ecology*, Vol. 1., ed. M. Holdgate. pp. 195–212. London: Academic Press.

Mackintosh, N. A. (1972). Life cycle of krill in relation to ice and water conditions. *Discovery Reports*, **36**, 1–94.

Mackintosh, N. A. (1973). Distribution of post-larval krill in the Antarctic. *Discovery Reports*, **36**, 95–156.

Mackintosh, N. A. (1974). Sizes of krill eaten by whales in the Antarctic. *Discovery Reports*, **36**, 157–178.

Mackintosh, N. A. & Brown, S. G. (1953). Preliminary estimates of the southern populations of the larger baleen whales. *Norsk Hvalfangsttid*, **45**, 469–480.

Mackintosh, N. A. & Wheeler, J. F. (1929). Southern blue and fin whales. *Discovery Reports*, **1**, 257–540.

McCann, T. S. (1980a). Population structure and social organization of Southern Elephant Seals, *Mirounga leonina* (L.). *Biological Journal of the Linnean Society*, **14**, 133–150.

McCann, T. S. (1980b). Territoriality and breeding behaviour of adult male Antarctic fur seals, *Arctocephalus gazella*. *Journal of Zoology* (London), **192**, 295–310.

McCann, T. S. (1981a). Aggression and sexual activity of male southern elephant seals, *Mirounga leonina*. *Journal of Zoology* (London), **195**, 295–310.

McCann, T. S. (1981b). The social organization and behaviour of the southern elephant seal, *Mirounga leonina* (L.). Ph. D. thesis, University of London.

McCann, T. S. (1983). Population size and demography of the southern elephant seal. In *Sea Mammals of Southern Latitudes*, ed. M. M. Bryden & J. Ling, pp. 1–19. Adelaide: South Australia Museum.

McCarthy, J. J. & Goldman, J. C. (1979). Nitrogenous nutrition of marine phytoplankton in nutrient depleted waters. *Science*, **203**, 670–672.

McClatchie, S. (1988). Food-limited growth of *Euphausia superba* in Admiralty Bay, South Shetland Islands, Antarctica. *Continental Shelf Research*, **8**, 329–345.

McClatchie, S. & Boyd, C. M. (1983). A morphological study of sieve efficiencies and mandibular surfaces in the Antarctic krill *Euphausia superba*. *Canadian Journal of Fisheries and Aquatic Sciences*, **40**, 995–967.

McConville M. J. (1985). Chemical composition and biochemistry of sea ice microalgae. In *Sea Ice Biota*, ed. R. A. Horner, pp. 105–129. Boca Raton, FL: CRC Press.

McConville, M. J. & Wetherbee, R. (1983). The bottom-ice microalgal community from the annual ice in the inshore waters of East Antarctica. *Journal of Phycology*, **19**, 431–439.

McConville, M. J., Mitchell, C. & Wetherbee, R. (1985). Productivity and patterns of carbon assimilation in a microalgal community from annual sea ice, East Antarctica. *Polar Biology*, **4**, 135–141.

MacDonald, C. M. & Schneppenheim, R. (1983). Breeding structure and stock identity in the Antarctic krill *Euphausia superba*. *Berichte zur Polarforschung*, **4**, 240–245.

MacDonald, C. M., Williams, R. & Adams, M. (1986). Genetic variation and population structure of krill (*Euphausia superba* Dana) from the Prydz Bay region of Antarctic waters. *Polar Biology*, **6**, 233–236.

Macdonald, J. A. & Montgomery, J. C. (1990). Animal adaptations to the Antarctic environment. In *Antarctica: The Ross Sea Region*, ed. T. Hatherton, pp. 220–239. Wellington: DSIR Publishing.

Macdonald, J. A., Montgomery, J. C. & Wells, R. M. G. (1987). Comparative physiology of Antarctic fishes. *Advances in Marine Biology*, **24**, 321–388.

McElroy, J. K. (1980a). The economics of harvesting krill. In *The Management of the Southern Ocean*, ed. B. Mitchell & R. Sandbrook, pp. 81–103. London: International Institute for Environment and Development.

McElroy, J. K. (1980b). The potential of krill as a commercial catch. In *The Management of the Southern Ocean*, ed. B. Mitchell & R. Sandbrook, pp. 60–80. London: International Institute for Environment and Development.

McElroy, J. K. (1980c). Economic evaluation of krill fishing systems. In *Advances in Fish Science and Technology*, ed. J. J. Connell, pp. 314–321. Farnham, Surrey: Fishing News Books.

McHugh, J. L. (1974). The role and history of the whaling commission. In *The Whale Problem: A Status Report*, ed. W. E. Schevill, pp. 322–336. Harvard: Harvard University Press.

McRoy, C. P. & Goering, J. J. (1974). The influence of ice on the primary productivity of the Bering Sea. In *Oceanography of the Bering Sea*, ed. D. W. Hand, pp. 403–421. Fairbanks, A.K.: Institute of Marine Science, University of Alaska.

McSweeny, E. S. (1978). Systematics and morphology of the Antarctic cranchiid squid *Galiteuthis glacialis* (Chun.). *Biology of the Antarctic Sea VII, Antarctic Research Series*, **27**, 1–39.

McWhinnie, M. A. (1964). Temperature responses and tissue respiration in Antarctic crustaceans with particular reference to *Euphausia superba*. *Antarctic Research Series*, **1**, 36–71.

McWhinnie, M. A. & Denys, C. (1978a). Biological studies of Antarctic krill, austral summer 1977–78. *Antarctic Journal of the United States*, **13**, 133–137.

McWhinnie, M. A. & Denys, C. (1978b). *Antarctic Marine Living Resources with Special Reference to Krill* Euphausia superba: *Assessment of Adequacy of Present Knowledge*. National Science Foundation, Washington, DC: Report No. NSF/RA 780489.

McWhinnie, M. A., Denys, C., Parkin, R. & Parkin, K. (1979). Biological investigations of *Euphausia superba* Dana. *Antarctic Journal of the United States*, **14**, 163–164.

Madin, L. P. (1982). Production, composition and sedimentation of salp faecal pellets in oceanic waters. *Marine Biology*, **63**, 217–226.

Mague, T. H., Friberg, E., Hughes, D. H. & Morris, I. (1979). Extracellular release of carbon by marine phytoplankton: a physiological approach. *Limnology & Oceanography*, **25**, 262–279.

Maher, W. J. (1962). Breeding biology of the snow petrel near Cape Hallett, Antarctica. *Condor*, **64**, 488–499.

Makarov, R. R. (1972). Life cycle and dispersion of *Euphausia superba* Dana. *Trudy VNIRO*, **77**, 85–92. (In Russian).

Makarov, R. R. (1973). Some peculiarities of the reproduction of *Euphausia superba* Dana (Crustacea: Euphausiacea) *Abstracts of Papers All-Union Conference on Macroplankton*, pp. 34–35. Moscow: All-Union Research Institute of Marine Fisheries and Oceanography. (In Russian.)

Makarov, R. R. (1975). A study of the repeated maturation of females in euphausiids (Eucarida: Euphausiacea). *Journal of Zoology*, **54**, 670–681.

Makarov, R. R. (1978). Vertical distribution of euphausiid eggs and larvae of the northeastern coast of South Georgia Island. *Oceanology*, **15**, 708–711.

Makarov, R. R. (1979a). Spawning times of Antarctic euphausiids *Biologii Morya, Vladivostok*, **3**, 30–38. (In Russian.)

Makarov, R. R. (1979b). Larval distribution and reproductive ecology of *Thysanoessa macrura* (Crustacea: Euphausiacea). *Marine Biology*, **52**, 377–386.

Makarov, R. R. (1979c). Size composition and conditions of existance of *Euphausia superba* Dana (Crustacea: Euphausiacea) in the eastern part of the Pacific sector of the Southern Ocean. *Oceanology*, **19**, 582–585.

Makarov, R. R. (1983a). Geographical aspects in the investigation of the life history of *Euphausia superba* Dana. *Berichte zur Polarforschung*, **4**, 47–57.

Makarov, R. R. (1983b). Some problems in the investigation of larval Euphausiids in Antarctica. *Berichte zur Polarforschung*, **4**, 58–69.

Makarov, R. R. & Shevtsov, V. V. (1972). Some problems in the distribution and biology of Antarctic krill. *Jerusalem Israel Program for Scientific Translations, (1972) TT 72-50077*. 9 pp.

Makarov, R. R. & Solyankin, E. V. (1982). Living conditions and structure of the population of *Euphausia superba* in the Lasarev Sea area. Tez dolkl III Veses Korf 'Prolemy natsional' nogo ispol 'zovaniya promyslovykh bespozvonochnykh, pp. 61–66. Karlingrad: Atlant NIRO. (In Russian.)

Makarov, R. R., Naumov, A. G. & Shevstov, V. V. (1970). The biology and distribution of Antarctic krill. In *Antarctic Ecology*, Vol. 1, ed. M. W. Holdgate, pp. 173–176. London & New York: Academic Press.

Maksimov, I.V. (1966). *Atlas of Antarctica*, Vol. 1. Moscow.

Malone, T. C. (1980). Algal size. In *The Physiological Ecology of Phytoplankton*, ed. I. Morris, pp. 433–463. London: Blackwell Scientific Publications.

Mandelli. E. F. & Burkholder, P. R. (1966). Primary productivity in the Gerlache and Bransfield Straits of Antarctica. *Journal of Marine Research*, **24**, 15–27.

Mansfield, A. W. (1958). The breeding behaviour and reproductive cycle of the Weddell seal (*Leptonychotes weddelli* Leeson). *Falkland Islands Dependency Survey, Scientific Reports*, **18**, 1–41.

Marchant, H. J. (1985). Choanoflagellates in the Antarctic marine food chain. In *Antarctic Nutrient Cycles and Food Webs*, ed. W. R. Siegfried, P. R. Condy & R. M. Laws, pp. 271–276. Berlin & Heidelberg: Springer–Verlag.

Marchant, H. J. & McEldowney, A. (1986). Nanoplankton siliceous cysts from Antarctica are algae. *Marine Biology*, **92**, 53–57.

Marchant, H. J. & Perrin, R. A. (1990). Seasonal variation in abundance and species composition of choanoflagellates (Acanthoecidae) at Antarctic coastal sites. *Polar Biology*, **10**, 499–505.

Marchant, H. J., Davidson, A. T. & Wright, S. W. (1987). The distribution and abundance of chroococcid Cyanobacteria in the Southern Ocean. *Proceedings of the National Institute of Polar Research Symposium on Polar Biology*, **1**, 1–9.

Marchant, H. J., Davidson, A. T. & Kelly, G. J. (1991). UV-B protecting compounds in the marine alga *Phaeocystis pouchetii* from Antarctica. *Marine Biology*, **109**, 391–395.

Margolis, S. V. & Kennett, J. P. (1970). Antarctic glaciation during the Tertiary recorded in sub-Antarctic deep-sea cores. *Science*, **170**, 1985–1987.

Marin, V. (1988a). Independent life cycles: an alternative to the asynchronism hypothesis for Antarctic calanoid copepods. *Hydrobiologica*, **167/168**, 161–168.

Marin, V. (1988b). Quantitative models of the life cycles of *Calanoides acutus, Calanus propinquus* and *Rhincalanus gigas*. *Polar Biology*, **8**, 439–446.

Marlow, R. J. (1967). Mating behaviour of the leopard seal *Hydrunga leptonyx* in captivity. *Australian Journal of Zoology*, **15**, 1–5.

Marr, J. S. (1962). The natural history and geography of the Antarctic krill *Euphausia superba*. *Discovery Reports*, **32**, 33–464.

Marra, J. (1980). Vertical mixing and primary production. In *Primary Productivity in the Sea*, ed. P. G. Falkowski, pp. 121–137. New York: Plenum Press.

Marschall, H-P. (1983). Sinking speed of krill eggs and timing of early life history stages. *Berichte zur Polarforschung*, **4**, 70–73.

Marschall, H-P. (1985). Structural and functional analysis of the feeding appendages of krill larvae. In *Antarctic Nutrient Cycles and Food Webs*, ed. W. R. Siegfried, P. R. Condy & R. M. Laws, pp.

346–354. Berlin & Heidelberg: Springer-Verlag.

Marschall, H-P. (1988). Overwintering strategy of the Antarctic krill under the pack-ice of the Weddell Sea. *Polar Biology*, **9**, 129–135.

Marshall, N. B. (1953). Egg size in Arctic, Antarctic and deep-sea fishes. *Evolution*, **7**, 328–341.

Marshall, P.F. (1957). Primary production in the Arctic. *Journal du Conseil pour l'Exploration de la Mer*, **23**, 173–177.

Marshall, N. B. (1964). Fish. In *Antarctic Research*, ed. R. Priestly, R. J. Adie & G. de Q. Robin, pp. 206–218. London: Butterworths.

Marshall, S. M. & Orr, A. P. (1955). On the biology of *Calanus finmarchicus*. VIII. Food uptake, assimilation and excretion in adult stage V. *Journal of the Marine Biological Association, UK*, **34**, 495–529.

Martin, D., Kauffman, P. & Parkinson, C. (1983). The movement and decay of ice bands in the Bering Sea. *Journal of Geophysical Research*, **88**, 2803–2812.

Martin, J. H., Knauer, G. A., Karl, P. M. & Broenkow, W. W. (1987). VERTEX: carbon cycling in the norteast Pacific. *Deep-Sea Research*, **34**, 267–285.

Martin, J. H., Fitzwater, S. E. & Gordon, R. M. (1990a). Iron deficiency limits phytoplankton growth in Antarctic waters. *Global Biogeochemical Cycles*, **4**, 5–12.

Martin, J. H., Gordon, R. M. & Fitzwater, S. E. (1990b). Iron in Antarctic waters. *Nature* (London), **345**, 156–158.

Masaki, Y. (1977). Yearly changes in the biological parameters of the Antarctic sei whale. *Report of the International Whaling Commission*, **27**, 421–429.

Masaki, Y. (1979). Yearly changes of the biological parameters for the Antarctic minke whale. *Report of the International Whaling Commission*, **29**, 375–395.

Maslennikov, V. V. (1972). On the effect of water dynamics on the distribution of *Euphausia superba* Dana in the area of South Georgia. *Trudy Vesesoiuznogo Naucho-issledovatel'skii institita Morskogo Rybngo Khoziaiska i Okeanographii*, **75**, 107–117.

Maslennikov, V. V. (1979). Long-term variability in hydrometeorological characteristics of the Southwest Antarctic Atlantic Ocean. *Trudy VIRNO*, **136**, 50–56.

Maslennikov, V. V. (1980). Modern concepts of large-scale circulation of Atlantic water and routes of mass drift of *Euphausia superba* In *Biological Resources of Antarctic Krill*, ed. T.G. Lubimova, pp. 8–27. Moscow: VIRNO. (In Russian.)

Maslennikov, V. V. & Solyankin, E. V. (1988). Patterns of fluctuations in the hydrological conditions of the Antarctic and their effect on the distribution of krill. In *Antarctic Ocean and Resources Variability*, ed. D. Sahrage, pp. 209–213. Berlin & Heidelberg: Springer-Verlag.

Massalaski. A. & Leppard, G. G. (1979). Morphological examination of fibrillar colloids associated with algae and bacteria in lakes. *Journal of the Fisheries Research Board of Canada*, **36**, 922–938.

Mathisen, O. A. & Macaulay, M. C. (1983). The morphological features of a super swarm of krill. *Memoirs of the National Institute of Polar Research, Special Issue*, **27**, 153–164.

Matsuda, O., Ishikawa, S. & Kawaguchi, K. (1987). Seasonal variation of downward flux of particulate organic matter under the Antarctic fast ice. *Proceedings of the NIPR Symposium on Polar Biology*, **1**, 23–34.

Matsuda, O., Ishikawa, S. & Kawaguchi, K. (1990). Fine-scale observation on salinity stratification in an ice hole during the melting season. *Antarctic Record*, **34**, 357–362.

Matthews, L. H. (1929). The natural history of the elephant seal. *Discovery Reports*, **1**, 233–256.

Matthews, L. H. (1931). *South Georgia. The British Empire's SubAntarctic Outpost*. 36 pp. London: Simpkin Marshall.

Matthews, L. H. (1937). The humpback whale, *Megaptera nodosa*. *Discovery Reports*, **17**, 7–92.

Mauchline, J. (1977). Growth and moulting of Crustacea, especially euphausiids. In *Oceanic Sound Scattering Prediction*, ed. N. R.

Andersen & B. J. Zahuranec, pp. 401–422. New York: Plenum Press.

Mauchline, J. (1979). Antarctic krill biology. *BIOMASS Report Series*, **10**, 1–52.

Mauchline, J. (1980a). The biology of mysids and euohausiids. *Advances in Marine Biology*, **18**, 373–595.

Mauchline, J. (1980b). Studies of patches of krill, *Euphausia superba* Dana. *BIOMASS Handbook No. 6*. 36 pp.

Mauchline, J. & Fisher, L. R. (1969). The biology of euphausiids. *Advances in Marine Biology*, **7**, 1–454.

Maxwell, J. G. H. (1977). Aspects of the biology and ecology of selected Antarctic invertebrates. Ph. D. Thesis, University of Aberdeen.

Maxwell, J. G. H. & Ralph, R. (1985). Non-cold-adapted metabolism in the Decapod *Chlorismus antarcticus* and other sub-Antarctic marine crustaceans. In *Antarctic Nutrient Cycles and Food Webs*, ed. W. R. Siegfried, P. R. Condy & R. M. Laws, pp. 397–406. Berlin & Heidelberg: Springer-Verlag.

May, R. M. (1979). Ecological interactions in the Southern Ocean. *Nature* (London), **227**, 86–89.

May, R. M., Beddington, J. R., Clark, C. W., Holt, S. J. & Laws, R. M. (1979). Management of multispecies fisheries. *Science*, **205**, 267–277.

Maykut, G. A. (1985). The ice environment. In *Sea Ice Biota*, ed. R. A. Horner, pp. 21–82. Boca Raton, Florida: CRC Press.

Maykut, G. A. & Grenfell, T. C. (1975). The spectral distribution of light beneath first-year sea ice in the Arctic Ocean. *Limnology & Oceanography*, **20**, 534–563.

Maynard, S. D., Riggs, F. V. & Walters, J. F. (1973). Mesopelagic micronekton in Hawaiian waters: Faunal composition, standing stock and diel vertical migration. *Fishery Bulletin*, **73**, 726–736.

Mayzand, P., Faber-Lorda, J. & Corre, M. C. (1985). Aspects of nutritional metabolism of two Antarctic Euphausiids: *Euphausia superba* and *Thysanoessa macrura*. In *Antarctic Nutrient Cycles and Food Webs*, ed. W. R. Siegfried, P. R. Condy & R. M. Laws. pp. 330–338. Berlin & Heidelbetg: Springer-Verlag.

Medlin, L. K. & Priddle, J. (ed.) (1990). *Polar Marine Diatoms*. Cambridge: British Antarctic Survey, Natural Research Council. 214 pp.

Meguro, H. (1962). Plankton ice in the Antarctic Ocean. *Antarctic Record*, **14**, 1192–1199.

Meguro, H., Kuniyuki, I & Fukushima, H. (1967). Ice flora (bottom type): a mechanism of primary production in the polar seas and growth of diatoms in sea ice. *Arctic*, **20**, 114–133.

Meissner, E. E., Tom, V. S., & Silon, V. N. (1974). Characteristics of the behaviour and biological cycles of the marbled Notothenia, *Notothenia rossii*, in relation to bottom topography, bottom materials and currents. *Journal of Ichthyology*, **14**, 706–708.

Menge, B. A. & Sutherland, J. P. (1976). Species diversity gradients: a synthesis of the roles of predation, competition, and temporal heterogeneity. *American Naturalist*, **110**, 351–369.

Meyer, M. A. (1981). The grazing of *Euphausia superba* Dana on natural phytoplankton populations. M. Sc. thesis, Texas A&M University, College Station, Texas. 97 pp.

Meyer, M. A. & El-Sayed, S. Z. (1983). Grazing of *Euphausia superba* on natural populations. *Polar Biology*, **1**, 193–197.

Mezykowski, T. & Rakusa-Suszczewski, S. (1979). The circadian rhythm in *Euphausia superba* Dana and its carbohydrate metabolism. *Meeresforschung*, **27**, 124–129.

Michel, R. L., Linck, T. W. & Williams, P. M. (1989). Tritium and carbon–14 distributions in sea water from under the Ross Ice Shelf Project Hole. *Science*, **203**, 445–446.

Mileikovsky, S. A. (1971). Types of larval development in marine bottom invertebrates, their distribution and ecological significance: a re-evaluation. *Marine Biology*, **10**, 193–213.

Miller, D. G. M. (1982). Canabalism in *Euphausia superba* Dana. *South African Journal of Antarctic Research*, **12**, 50.

Miller, D. G. M. (1985). The South African SIBEX I Cruise to the Prydz Bay region, 1984: IX Krill (*Euphausia superba* Dana). *South African Journal of Antarctic Research*, **15**, 33–41.

Miller, D. G. M. (1986a). Results from biological investigations of krill (*Euphausia superba* Dana) in the Southern Ocean during SIBEX I. *Memoirs National Institute of Polar Research, Special Issue*, **40**, 117–139.

Miller, D. G. M. (1986b). Modelling and decision making as part of the CCAMLR management regime. (SC-CCAMLR-V/BG/17). In *Selected Scientific Papers 1986*, pp. 295–322. Hobart: Commission for the Conservation of Antarctic Marine Living Resources.

Miller, D. G. M. & Hampton, I. (1989). *Biology and Ecology of the Antarctic Krill* (Euphausia superba *Dana): A Review*. BIOMASS Scientific Series No. 9. 166 pp.

Miller, D. G. M., Hampton, I., Henry, J., Abrams, R. W, & Cooper, J. (1985). The relationship between krill food requirements and phytoplankton production in a sector of the Southern Indian Ocean. In *Antarctic Nutrient Cycles and Food Webs*, ed. W. R. Siegfried, P. R. Condy & R. M. Laws, pp. 362–371. Berlin & Heidelberg: Springer-Verlag.

Miller, K. A. & Pearse, J. S. (1991). Ecological studies of seaweeds in McMurdo Sound, Antarctica. *American Zoologist*, **31**, 35–48.

Miller, M. A., Krempin, D. W., Manahan, D. T. & Sullivan, C. W. (1984). Growth Rates, distribution and abundance of bacteria in the ice-edge zone of the Weddell and Scotia Seas, Antarctica. *Antarctic Journal of the United States*, **19**, 103–105.

Mitchell, B. & Sandbrook, R. (1980). *The Management of the Southern Ocean*. London: Institute for Environment and Development. 162 pp.

Mitchell. B. G. & Holm-Hansen, O. (1991). Observations and modelling of the Antarctic phytoplankton standing crop in relation to mixing depth. *Deep-Sea Research*, **38**, 981–1007.

Mitchell, B. G., Vernet, M. & Holm-Hansen, O. (1989). Ultraviolet light attenuation in Antarctic waters in relation to particulate absorption and photosynthesis. *Antarctic Journal of the United States*, **24**, 179–181.

Mitchell, B. G., Vernet, M. & Holm-Hansen, O. (1990). Ultraviolet radiation in Antarctic waters: particulate absorption and photosynthesis. In *Effects of Solar Ultraviolet Radiation on Biochemical Dynamics in Aquatic Environments*, ed. N. V. Blough & R. G. Zepp, pp. 135–136. Woods Hole Oceanographic Institution Technical Report WHOI–90–09.

Mitchell, E. (1975). Trophic relationships and competition for food in northwest Antarctic whales. In *Proceedings of the Canadian Zoologists Animal Meeting*, ed. M. D. B. Burt, pp. 123–133.

Mitchell, J. G. & Silver, M. W. (1982). Modern archaeomonads indicate sea-ice environments. *Nature* (London), 196, 437.

Mitskevich, I. N. & Kriss, A. Ye. (1973). Total numbers and production of microorganisms in the waters of the Southern Ocean. *Microbiologiya*, 44, 135–140.

Mitskevitch, L. G. & Mosolov, V. V. (1981). A study of proteolytic enzymes of krill. In *Krill Processing Technology*, ed. V. P. Bykov, pp. 21–24. Moscow: VIRNO. (In Russian with English summary.)

Mizroch, S. A. (1980). Some notes on southern hemisphere baleen whale pregnancy trend rates. *Report of the International Whaling Commission*, 30, 361–374.

Mizroch, S. A. (1981a). Further notes on southern hemisphere baleen whale pregnancy rates. *Report of the International Whaling Commission*, 31, 629–633.

Mizroch, S. A. (1981b). Analysis of some biological parameters of the Antarctic fin whale (*Balaenoptera physalus*). *Report of the International Whaling Commission*, 31, 425–434.

Mizroch, S. A. (1983). Reproductive rates in southern hemisphere baleen whales. M. A. thesis, University of Washington. 103 pp.

Mizroch, S. A., Rice, D. W. & Bengtson, J. L. (1986). *Prodomus of an Atlas of Balaenopterid Whale Distribution in the Southern Ocean Based on Pelagic Catch Data*. Seattle Washington: US National Marine Fisheries Service, National Marine Laboratory.

Moebus, K. & Johnson, K. M. (1974). Exudation of dissolved organic carbon by brown algae. *Marine Biology*, **26**, 117–126.

Mohr, H. (1976). Tageszeitlich dedingte Rhyth mik im Verhalten von halbwuchsigen Krill (*Euphausia superba*). *Informationen fur die Fischwirtschaft* , **23**, 132–134.

Moiseev, P. A. (1970). Some aspects of commercial use of krill resources of the Antarctic seas. In *Antarctic Ecology,* Vol. I, ed. M. W. Holdgate, pp. 213–217. London: Academic Press.

Montague, T. L. (1984). Food of Antarctic petrels (*Thalassoica Antarctica*). *Emu*, **84**, 144–245.

Moreno, C. A. (1980). Observations on food and reproduction in *Trematomus bernacchii* (Pisces: Nototheniidae) from Palmer Archipelago, Antarctica. *Copeia*, **1**, 171–173.

Moreno, C. A. & Osorio, H. H. (1977). Bathymetric food habits in the Antarctic fish, *Notothenia gibberifrons* Lonnberg (Pisces: Nototheniidae). *Hydrobologica*, **55**, 139–144.

Moreno, C. A. & Zamorano, J. H. (1980). Selection del los alimentos en *Notothenia coriiceps neglecta* del cinturon demacroalgas de Bahia South Antarctica. *Series Ciencias Instituto Antarctico Chileno*, **25/26**, 33–34.

Morita, R. Y. (1975). Psychrophilic bacteria. *Bacteriological Reviews*, **39**, 144–167.

Morita, R. Y., Griffith, R. P. & Hayasaka, S. S. (1977). Heterotrophic activity of microorganisms in Antarctic waters. In *Adaptations Within Antarctic Ecosystems*, ed. G. A. Llano, pp. 91–113. Washington, DC: Smithsonian Institution.

Morris, D. J. (1984). Filtration rates of *Euphausia superba* Dana: under- or overestimates? *Journal of Crustacean Biology*, **4** (Special Issue No. 1), 185–197.

Morris D. J. (1985). Integrated model of moulting and feeding of Antarctic krill *Euphausia superba* off South Georgia. *Marine Ecology Progress Series*, **22**, 207–217.

Morris, D. J. & Keck, A. (1984). The time course of the moult cycle and growth of *Euphausia superba* in the laboratory. A preliminary study. *Meeresforschung*, **30**, 94–100.

Morris, D. J. & Priddle, J. (1984). Observations on feeding and moulting of the Antarctic krill, *Euphausia superba* Dana. *British Antarctic Survey Bulletin*, **65**, 57–63.

Morris, D. J. & Ricketts, C. (1984). Feeding of krill round South Georgia. I. A model of feeding activity in relation to depth and time of day. *Marine Ecology Progress Series*, **16**, 1–7.

Morris, D. J., Ward, P. & Clarke, A. (1983). Aspects of the feeding in Antarctic krill, *Euphausia superba*. *Polar Biology*, **2**, 21–26.

Morris, D. J., Everson, I., Ricketts, C. & Ward, P. (1984). Feeding of krill round South Georgia. I. A model of feeding activity in relation to depth and time of day. *Marine Ecology Progress Series*, **20**, 203–206.

Morris, D. J., Watkins, J., Ricketts, C., Buchholz, F. & Priddle, J. (1988). An assessment of the merits of length and weight measurements of Antarctic krill, *Euphausia superba*. *British Antarctic Survey Bulletin*. **79**, 27–50.

Mortensen, T. (1936). Echinoidea and Ophiuriodea. *Discovery Reports*, **12**, 199–348.

Mougin, J-L. (1975). Écologie comparée des Procelariidae Antarctique et Sub-antarctiques. *Comité National Français des Reserches Antarctiques*, **36**, 1–195.

Mougin. J-L. & Prévost, J. (1980). Evolution annuelle des effectifs de des biomasses des oiseaux Antarctiques. *Revue d'Ecology la Terre et la Vie*, **34**, 101–133.

Muench, R. D. (1983). Mesoscale oceanographic features associated with the central Bering Sea ice edge: February–March 1981. *Journal of Geophysical Research*, **88**, 2715–2722.

Muench, R. D. & Charnell, R. L. (1977). Observations on medium-scale features along the seasonal ice edge in the Bering Sea. *Journal of Physical Oceanography*, **7**, 602–606.

Muench, R. D., LeBond, P. H. & Hachmeister, L. E. (1983). On some possible interactions between internal waves and sea ice in the marginal ice zone. *Journal of Geophysical Research*, **88**, 2819–2826.

Mujica, A. & Asencio, V. (1983). Distribution and abundance of krill larvae (*Euphausia superba* Dana). *Berichte zur Polarforschung*, **4**, 21–29.

Mujica, A. & Asencio, V. (1985). Fish larvae, euphausiids and zooplankton in the Bransfield Strait (SIBEX–Phase I, 1984). *Series Cientifica INACH*, **33**, 131–154.

Muller-Karger, F. & Alexander, V. (1987). Nitrogen dynamics in a marginal sea-ice zone. *Continental Shelf Research*, **33**, 1389–1412.

Muller-Schwarze, D. & Muller-Schwarze, C. (1975). Relations between leopard seals and Adélie penguins. *Rapports et Proces-Verbaux des Reunions Conseil International Pour l'Exploration de la Mer*, **169**, 394–404.

Muller-Schwarze, D. & Muller-Schwarze, C. (1977). Interactions between south polar skuas and Adélie penguins. In *Adaptations Within Antarctic Ecosystems*, ed. G. A. Llano, pp. 619–646. Washington, DC: Smithsonian Institution.

Mullin, M. M. (1983). *In situ* measurement of filtering rates of the salp, *Thalia democratica*, on phytoplankton and bacteria. *Journal of Plankton Research*, **5**, 279–288.

Mullin, M. M. & Brooks, R.E. (1989). Extractable lipofuscin in larval *Fisheries Bulletin of the United States*, **40**, 407–415.

Mullins, B. W. & Priddle J. (1987). Relationships between bacteria and phytoplankton in the Bransfield Strait and Southern Drake Passage. *British Antarctic Survey Bulletin*, **76**, 51–64.

Mumm, N. (1987). Zur Ernahrungsphyiologies des Krill (*Euphausia superba*) im Winter Untersuchungen anhand der Verdauungstenzyme Amylase und Trypsin. Diplomarbeil Universtat Keil. 97 pp.

Murano, M., Segawa, S & Kato, M. (1979). Moulting and growth of the Antarctic krill in the laboratory. *Transactions Tokyo University of Fisheries*, **3**, 99–106.

Murphy, E. J., Morris, D. J., Watkins, J. L. & Priddle, J. (1988). Scales of interaction between Antarctic krill and the environment. In *Antarctic Ocean and Resources Variability*, ed. D. Sahrhage, pp. 120–130. Berlin & Heidelberg: Springer-Verlag.

Murphy, G. I. (1977). Clupeoids. In *Fish Population Dynamics*, ed. J. A. Gulland, pp. 283–301. London: John Wiley.

Murphy, R. C. (1914). Notes on the sea elephant, *Mirounga leonina* Linne. *Bulletin of the American Museum of Natural History*, **33**, 63–79.

Murrish, D. E. (1973). Respiratory heat loss and water exchange in penguins. *Respiratory Physiology*, **19**, 262–270.

Muzzarelli, R. A. A. (1977). *Chitin*. Oxford: Pergamon Press.

Nachtwey, D. S. (1975). Potential effects on aquatic ecosystems of increased UV-B radiation. In *Fourth Conference on CIAP, February 1975*. Washington, DC, US Department of Transportation.

Nagata, Y., Michada, Y. & Umimura, Y. (1988). Variation in the positions and structures of oceanic fronts in the Indian ocean for the period from 1965 to 1987. In *Antarctic Ocean and Resources Variability*, ed. D. Sahrhage, pp. 92–98. Berlin & Heidelberg: Springer-Verlag.

Naito, Y. & Iwami, T. (1982). Fish fauna in the northeastern parts of Lutz-Holm Bay with some notes on stomach contents. *Memoirs National Institute of Polar Research, Special Issue*, **32**, 64–72.

Naito, Y., Taniguchi, A. & Hamada, E. (1986). Some observations on swarms and mating behaviour of Antarctic krill (*Euphausia superba* Dana). *Memoirs National Institute of Polar Research, Special Issue*, **40**, 153–161.

Nakamura, S. (1973). Report on a survey of the new fishing ground for krill. *Report of the Japanese Marine Fisheries Resources Research Centre*, **9**, 9–14.

Nakamura, S. (1974). Development of *Euphausia* as a valuable protein for humans. Unpublished note, FAO Internal Consultation on Krill, Rome.

Nakamura, M., Kadota, S. & Fukuchi, M. (1982). Epipelagic copepods of Calanoidea in the Indian Sector of the Antarctic Ocean. *Memoirs National Institute of Polar Research Special Issue*, **22**, 28–31.

Nast, F. (1978). The vertical distribution of larval and adult krill (*Euphausia superba* Dana) on a time station south of Elephant Island, South Shetlands. *Meeresforschung*, **27**, 103–118.

Nast, F. (1982). The assessment of krill (*Euphausia superba* Dana) biomass from a net sampling programme. *Meeresforschungen*, **29**, 154–159.

Nast, F. (1986). Changes in krill abundance and in other zooplankton relative to the Weddell Scotia Confluence around Elephant Island in November, 1983, November, 1984 and March, 1985. *Archiv fur Fischereiwissenschaft*, **37**, 73–94.

Nast, F. & Gieskes, W. (1986). Phytoplankton observations relative to krill abundance round Elephant Island in November 1983. *Archiv fur Fischereiwissenschaft*, **37**, 95–106.

Nasu, K. (1974). Hydrography in relation to the distribution of euphausiids in the Antarctic Ocean. *Bulletin of the Japanese Society of Fisheries & Oceanography*, **24**, 35–38.

Nasu, K. (1983). On the geographic boundary of Antarctic krill distribution. *Berichte zur Polarforschung*, **4**, 216–222.

National Academy of Sciences (1981). *An Evaluation of Antarctic Marine Ecosystem Research*. Washington, DC, National Academy Press. 99 pp.

Naumov, A. G. (1962). Some features of the distribution and biology of *Euphausia superba* Dana. *Information Bulletin Soviet Antarctic Expedition*, **39**, 191–193.

Naumov, A. G. & Chekunova, V. I. (1980). Energy requirements of pinnipeds (Pinnipedia). *Oceanology (Moscow)*, **20**, 348–350.

Naumov, A. G. & Permitin, Yu. Ye. (1973). Trophic relationships of *Euphausia superba* Dana and fish of the Southern Ocean (Scotia Sea) *Trudy VIRNO*, **93**, 216–229. (In Russian.)

Nelson, D. M. (1989). Particulate matter and nutrient distributions in the ice-edge zone of the Weddell Sea: relationship to hydrography during the late summer. *Deep-Sea Research*, **36**, 191–209.

Nelson, D. M. & Gordon, L. I. (1982). Production and dissolution of biogenic silica in the Southern Ocean. *Geochemica et Cosmochemica Acta*, **46**, 491–501.

Nelson, D. M. & Smith, W. O., Jr. (1986). Phytoplankton bloom dynamics of the western Ross Sea ice edge. II. Mesoscale cycling of nitrogen and silica. *Deep-Sea Research*, **33**, 1389–1412.

Nelson, D. M., Goering, J. J. & Boisseau, D. (1981). Consumption and regeneration of silicic acid in three coastal upwelling systems. In *Coastal Upwelling*, ed. F. A. Richards, pp. 242–256. Washington, DC: American Geophysical Union.

Nelson, D. M., Smith, W. O., Jr., Gordon, L. I. & Huber, B. A. (1987). Spring distributions of density, nutrients and phytoplankton biomass in the ice edge zone of the Weddell Sea. *Journal of Geophysical Research*, **92**, 7181–7190.

Nelson, D. M., Smith, W.O., Jr., Muench, R. D., Gordon, L. I., Sullivan, C. W. & Husby, D. M. (1989). Particulate matter and nutrient distributions in the ice-edge zone of the Weddell Sea. Relationship to hydrography during the late summer. *Deep-Sea Research*, **36**, 191–209.

Nemoto, T. (1959). Food of baleen whales with reference to whale movements. *Scientific Reports of the Whales Research Institute (Tokyo)*, **14**, 149–290.

Nemoto, T. (1966). Feeding of baleen whales and the value of krill as a marine resource in Antarctica. In *Symposium on Antarctic Oceanography, Santiago Chile, 1966*, ed. R. I. Currie, pp. 240–253. Cambridge: Scott Polar Research Institute.

Nemoto, T. (1970). Feeding patterns of baleen whales in the ocean. In *Marine Food Chains*, ed. J. H. Steele, pp. 241–252. Berkeley: University of California Press.

Nemoto, T. (1972). History of research into food and feeding of euphausiids. *Proceedings of the Royal Society of Edinburgh, B*

(Biology), **73**, 259–265.

Nemoto, T. & Harrison, G. (1981). High latitude ecosystems. In *Analysis of Marine Ecosystems*, ed. A. R. Longhurst. pp. 95–126. London & New York: Academic Press.

Nemoto, T. & Nasu, K. (1975). Present status of exploitation of krill in the Antarctic. In *Oceanology International 75*, pp. 353–360. London: BPS Exhibitions.

Nemoto, T., Doi, T. & Nasu, K. (1981). Biological characteristics of krill caught in the Southern Ocean. In *Biological Investigations of Marine Antarctic Systems and Stocks,* Vol. II, ed. S.Z. El-Sayed, pp. 46–63. Cambridge: SCAR and SCOR, Scott Polar Research Institute.

Nemoto, T., Okiyama, M. & Takahasi, M. (1985). Aspects of the roles of squid in food chains of marine Antarctic ecosystems. In *Antarctic Nutrient Cycles and Food Webs*, ed. W. R. Siegfried, P. R. Condy & R. M. Laws, pp. 415–420. Berlin & Heidelberg: Springer-Verlag.

Neori, A. & Holm-Hansen, O. (1982). Effect of temperature on rate of photosynthesis in Antarctic phytoplankton. *Polar Biology*, **1**, 33–38.

Nettleship, D. N., Sanger, G. A. & Springer, P. F. (1984). *Marine Birds: Their Feeding Ecology and Commercial Fisheries Relationships*. Ottawa: Canadian Fisheries and Wildlife Service Special Publication.

Neushul, M. (1968). Benthic marine algae *American Geographical Society. Antarctic Map Folio Series,* Vol. 10, pp. 9–10. American Geographical Society.

Newell, R, C. (1979). *The Biology of Intertidal Animals*, 3rd edn. Faversham, Kent: Marine Ecological Surveys. 781 pp.

Newell, R. C. & Linley, E. A. S. (1984). Significance of microheterotrophs in the decomposition of phytoplankton: estimates of carbon and nitrogen flow based on the biomass of plankton communities. *Marine Ecology Progress Series*, **16**, 105–119.

Newell, R. C., Lucas, M. I. & Linley, E. A. S. (1981). Rate of degradation and efficiency of conversion of phytoplankton debris by marine microorganisms. *Marine Ecology Progress Series*, **6**, 123–136.

Nicol, D. (1964a). Lack of shell-attached pelecypods in Arctic and Antarctic waters. *Nautilis*, **77**, 92–93.

Nicol, D. (1964b). An essay on size in marine pelecypods. *Journal of Paleontology*, **38**, 948–974.

Nicol, D. (1967). Some characteristics of cold-water marine pelecypods. *Journal of Paleontology*, **41**, 1330–1340.

Nicol, S. (1987). Some limitations on the use of lipofuscin aging technique. *Marine Biology*, **93**, 609–614.

Nicol, S. (1990). Age-old problem of krill longevity. *Bioscience*, **40**, 833–836.

Nicol, S. & Stolf, M. (1989). Sinking rates of cast exoskeletons of Antarctic krill (*Euphausia superba*). and their role in the vertical flux of particulate matter and fluoride in the Southern Ocean. *Deep-Sea Research*, 36, 1753–1762.

Nicol, S., James, A. & Pitcher, G. (1987). A first record of daytime surface swarming by *Euphausia lucens* in the southern Benguela region. *Marine Biology*, **94**, 7–10.

Niebauer, H. J. (1980). Sea ice and temperature variability in the eastern Bering Sea and relation to atmospheric fluctuations. *Journal of Geophysical Research*, **85**, 7509–7515.

Nishida, S. (1986). Nanoplankton flora in the Southern Ocean, with special reference to siliceous varieties. *Memoirs National Institute of Polar Research, Special Issue*, **40**, 56–68.

Nishiwaki, M. (1957). Age characteristics of ear plugs in whales. *Scientific Report of the Whales Research Institute (Tokyo)*, **12**, 23–32.

Nishiwaki, M. (1977). Distribution of toothed whales in the Antarctic Ocean. In *Adaptations Within Antarctic Ecosystems*, ed. G. A. Llano, pp. 783–791. Washington, DC: Smithsonian Institution.

Nishiwaki, M., Ichihara, T. & Ohsumi, S. (1958). Age studies of the fin whale based on the ear plug. *Scientific Report of the Whales Research Institute (Tokyo)*, **13**, 155–169.

Noji, T. T., Estep, K. W., MacIntyre, F. & Norrbin, F. (1991). Image

analysis of faecal material grazed upon by three species of copepods. Evidence for coprohexy, coprophagy and coprochaly. *Journal of the Marine Biological Association, UK*, **71**, 465–486.

Norman, J. R. (1937). B. A. N. Z. Antarctic Research Expedition 1929–1931 under the command of Douglas Mawson, Kt OBE, BE, D. Sc., FRS. Fishes. *Report B. A. N. Z. Antarctic Research Expedition, Series B*, **1**, 49–88.

Norris, K. S. & Mohl, B. (1981). Do Odontocetes debilitate their prey acoustically? In *Fourth Biennial Conference on the Biology of Marine Animals, San Francisco, California, 14–18 December 1981*.

North, A. W. & Ward, D. (1989). Initial feeding of fish larvae during winter at South Georgia. *Cybium*, **13**, 357–364.

North, A. W. & White, M. G. (1982). Key to fish postlarvae from the Scotia Sea. *Cybium*, **6**, 13–32.

North, A. W. & White, M. G. (1987). Reproductive strategies of Antarctic fish. In *Proceedings of the Vth Congress of the European Ichthyological Society 1985, Stockholm*, pp. 381–390.

North, A. W., Croxall, J. D. & Doidge, D. W. (1983). Fish prey of the Antarctic fur seal *Arctocephalus gazella* at South Georgia. *British Antarctic Survey Bulletin*, **61**, 27–37.

Norton, O. I. & Slater, J. G. (1979). A model for the evolution of the Indian Ocean and the breakup of Gondwanaland. *Journal of Geophysical Research*, **84**, 6802–6830.

Nothig, E-M. (1988). Untersuchungen zur Okologie des Phutoplanktons in sudostlichen Weddellmeer in Januar/Februar 1985 (Antarktis III/3). *Polarforschung*, **53**, 1–119.

Nothig, E-M. & Bodungen, B. von (1989). Occurrence and vertical flux of faecal pellets of probably protozoan origin in the southeastern Weddell Sea (Antarctica). *Marine Ecology Progress Series*, **56**, 281–289.

Nothig, E-M., Bodungen, B. von & Sui, Q. (1991). Phyto- and protozooplankton biomass during austral summer in surface waters of the Weddell Sea and vicinity. *Polar Biology*, **11**, 293–304.

Novitsky, J. A. (1987). Microbial growth rates and biomass production in a marine sediment: evidence for a very active but mostly nongrowing community. *Applied Environmental Microbiology*, **53**, 2368–2372.

Nowlin, W. D., Jr., Whitworth, T. III. & Pillsbury, R. D. (1977). Structure and transport of the Antarctic Circumpolar Current at Drake Passage from short-term measurements. *Journal of Physical Oceanography*, **7**, 788–802.

Nybelin, O. (1947). Antarctic fishes. *The Scientific Results of the Norwegian Antarctic Expedition, 1927–1928*, **26**, 1–76.

O'Brien, D. P. (1985). Direct observations of the behaviour of *Euphausia superba* and *Euphausia crystallorophias* (Crustacea: Euphausiacea) under the pack ice during the Antarctic spring of 1985. *Journal of Crustacean Biology*, **7**, 437–448.

O'Brien, D. P. (1987). Description of escape responses of krill (Crustacea: Euphausiacea), with particular reference to swarming behaviour and the size and proximity of the predator. *Journal of Crustacean Biology*, **7**, 449–457.

Obst, B. S. (1985). Densities of Antarctica seabirds at sea and the presence of krill *Euphausia superba*. *Auk*, **102**, 540–549.

Oelenschlager, J. & Manthey, M. (1982). Fluoride content of Antarctic marine animals caught off Elephant Island. *Polar Biology*, **1**, 125–137.

Oelke, H. (1975). Breeding behaviour and success in a colony of Adélie penguins, *Pygoscelis adeliae*, at Cape Crosier, Antarctica. In *The Biology of Penguins*, ed. B. Stonehouse, pp. 363–395. London: Macmillan.

Offredo, C. & Ridoux, V. (1986). The diet of Emperor Penguins *Aptenodytes forsteri* in Adélie Land, Antarctica. *Ibis*, **128**, 409–413.

Offredo, C., Ridoux, V. & Clarke, M. R. (1985). Cephalopods in the diets of Emperor Penguins and Adélie Penguins in Adélie Land, Antarctica. *Marine Biology*, **86**, 199–202.

Ohno, M., Fukada, Y. & Fukuchi, M. (1987). Vertical distribution and standing stocks of chlorophyll *a* in the coastal waters of the

Antarctic Ocean. *Antarctic Record*, **31**, 93–108.

Ohsumi, S. (1964). Examination on age determination of the fin whale. *Scientific Report of the Whales Research Institute (Tokyo)*, **18**, 49–88.

Ohsumi, S. (1971). Some investigations of the school structure of the sperm whale. *Scientific Report of the Whales Research Institute (Tokyo)*, **23**, 1–25.

Ohsumi, S. (1972). Examination of the recruitment rate of Antarctic fin whale stock by use of mathematical models. *Report of the International Whaling Commission*, **22**, 69–90.

Ohsumi, S. (1976). An attempt to standardize fishing efforts as applied to stock assessment of the minke whale in Antarctic Area IV. *Report of the International Whaling Commission*, **26**, 404–408.

Ohsumi, S. (1979). Feeding habits of the minke whale in the Antarctic. *Report of the International Whaling Commission*, **29**, 473–476.

Ohsumi, S & Masaki, Y. (1975). Biological parameters of the Antarctic minke whale at the virginal population level. *Journal of the Fisheries Research Board of Canada*, **32**, 995–1004.

Ohsumi, S. & Nasu, K. (1970). Range and habitat of the female sperm whale with reference to the oceanographic structure. International Whaling Commission. Paper Sp/7 to Special Meeting on Sperm Whale Biology and Stock Assessments, 1970 (Honolulu).

Ohsumi, S., Masaki, Y & Kawamura, A. (1970). Stock of Antarctic minke whale. *Scientific Report of the Whales Research Institute (Tokyo)*, **20**, 1–16.

Okutani, T. & Clarke, M. R. (1985). *Identification Key and Species Description for Antarctic Squids*. BIOMASS Handbook No. 21. 57 pp.

Oliver, J. S. & Slattery, P. N. (1985). Effects of crustacean predators on species composition and population structure of soft-bodied infauna from McMurdo Sound, Antarctica. *Ophelia*, **24**, 155–175.

Oliver, J. S., Oakden, J. M. & Slattery, P. S. (1982). Phoxocephalid amphipod crustaceans as predators on larvae and juveniles in marine soft bottom communities. *Marine Ecology Progress Series*. **7**, 179–184.

Oliver, J. S., Slattery, P. N., O'Connor, E. F. & Lowry, L. F. (1983). Walrus *Obobenus rosmarus* feeding in the Bering Sea: a benthic perspective. *Fishery Bulletin*, **81**, 501–512.

Olsen, S. (1954). South Georgia cod, *Notothenia rossii mamorata* Fischer. *Norsk Hvalfangstid*, **43**, 373–382.

Olsen, S. (1955). A contribution to the systematics and biology of Chaenichthyid fishes from South Georgia. *Nytt Magasin for Zoologi, Oslo*, **3**, 79–93.

Olson, R. J. (1980). Nitrate and ammonium uptake on Antarctic waters. *Limnology & Oceanography*, **25**, 1064–1074.

Ommaney, F. D. (1936). *Rhincalanus gigas* (Brady), a copepod of the southern macrozooplankton. *Discovery Reports*, **13**, 277–384.

Omori, M. (1974). The biology of pelagic shrimps in the ocean. *Advances in Marine Biology*, **12**, 233–324.

Omori, M. (1978). Zooplankton fisheries of the world: a review. *Marine Biology*, **48**, 199–205.

Omori, M. & Ikeda, T. (1984). *Methods in Zooplankton Ecology*. New York: John Wiley. 322 pp.

Omura, H. (1973). A review of pelagic whaling operations in the Antarctic based on the effort and catch data in 10 squares of latitude and longitude. *Scientific Report of the Whales Research Institute, Tokyo*, **25**, 105–203.

Omura, H., Ohsumi, S., Nemoto, T., Nasu, K. and Kasuya, T. (1969). Black right whales in the North Pacific. *Scientific Reports of the Whales Research Institute (Tokyo)*, **21**, 1–78.

Oresland, V. (1990). Feeding and predation impact of the chaetognath *Eukrohnia hamata* in Gerlache Starait, Antarctica. *Marine Ecology Progress Series*, **63**, 201–209.

Øritzland. T. (1970a). Biology and population dynamics of Antarctic seals. In *Antarctic Ecology*, Vol. 1, ed. M. W. Holdgate, pp. 361–366. London & New York: Academic Press.

Øritzland. T. (1970b). Sealing and seal research in the South-west Atlantic pack ice, September–October, 1964. In *Antarctic Ecology*, Vol. 1, ed. M. W. Holdgate, pp. 367–376. London & New York: Academic Press.

Øritzland, T. (1977). Food consumption of seals in the Antarctic pack ice. In *Adaptations Within Antarctic Ecosystems*, ed. G. A. Llano, pp. 749–768. Washington, DC: Smithsonian Institution.

Ostapoff, F. (1965). Antarctic oceanography. In *Biogeography and Ecology in Antarctica*, ed. J. Van Meigham & P. van Oye, pp. 97–126. The Hague: Dr. W. Junk Publishers.

Ottestad, P. (1932). On the biology of some Southern Copepoda. *Havralradets Skrifter*, **5**, 1–61.

Overland, J. E., Reynolds, R. M. & Pearse, C. H. (1983). A model of the atmospheric boundary layer over the marginal ice zone. *Journal of Geophysical Research*, **88**, 2836–2840.

Pace, M. L., Glasser, J. E. & Pomeroy, L. R. (1984). A simulation analysis of continental shelf food webs. *Marine Biology*, **82**, 47–63.

Paerl, H. W. (1974). Bacterial uptake of dissolved organic matter in relation to detrital aggregation in marine and freshwater systems. *Limnology & Oceanography*, **19**, 966–972.

Paine, R. T. (1966). Food web complexity and species diversity. *American Naturalist*, **100**, 65–75.

Painting, S. J., Lucas, M. I. & Stenton-Doseyt, J. M. E. (1985). South African SIBEX I criuse to the Prydz Bay region, 1984: 10. Biomass and production of bacterioplankton, detritus and bacterial relationships. *South African Journal of Antarctic Research*, **15**, 42–52.

Palmisano, A. C. (1986). Changes in photosynthetic metabolism of sea-ice microalgae during a spring bloom in McMurdo Sound. *Antarctic Journal of the United States*, **21**, 176–177.

Palmisano, A. C. & Sullivan, C. W. (1982). Physiology of sea ice diatoms. I. Response of three diatoms to a simulated summer-winter transition. *Journal of Phycology*, **18**, 489–498.

Palmisano, A. C. & Sullivan, C. W. (1983a). Sea ice microbial communities (SIMCO) I. Distribution, abundance and primary production of ice microalgae in McMurdo Sound, Antarctica in 1980. *Polar Biology*, **2**, 171–177.

Palmisano, A. C. & Sullivan, C. W. (1983b). Physiology of sea ice diatoms. II. Dark survival of three ice diatoms. *Canadian Journal of Microbiology*, **29**, 157–160.

Palmisano, A. C. & Sullivan, C. W. (1985a). Pathways of photosynthetic carbon assimilation in sea-ice microalgae from McMurdo Sound, Antarctica. *Limnology & Oceanography*, **30**, 674–678.

Palmisano, A. C. & Sullivan, C. W. (1985b). Growth, metabolism, and dark survival in sea ice algae. In *Sea Ice Algae*, ed. R. A. Horner, pp. 131–146. Boca Raton, FL: CRC Press.

Palmisano, A. C. & Sullivan, C. W. (1985c). Physiological response of micro–algae in the ice-platelet layer to low-light conditions. In *Antarctic Nutrient Cycles and Food Webs*, ed. W. R. Siefried, P. R. Condy & R. M. Laws, pp. 84–88. Berlin & Heidelberg: Springer-Verlag.

Palmisano, A. C., SooHoo, J. B. & Sullivan, C. W. (1984). Photoadaptation in sea-ice microalga in McMurdo Sound. *Antarctic Journal of the United States*, **19**, 131–132.

Palmisano, A. C., Kottmeier, S. T., Moe, R. L. & Sullivan, C. W. (1985a). Sea ice microbial communities. VI. The effect of light perturbation on microalgae at the ice–seawater interface in McMurdo Sound, Antarctica. *Marine Ecology Progress Series*, **21**, 37–45.

Palmisano, A. C., SooHoo, J. B. & Sullivan, C. W. (1985b). Photosynthesis–irradiance relationship in sea ice microalgae from McMurdo Sound, Antarctica. *Journal of Phycology*, **21**, 341–346.

Palmisano, A. C., SooHoo, J. B., SooHoo, S. L., Craft, L. L. & Sullivan, C. W. (1985c). Photoadaptive strategies in a natural population of *Phaeocystis pouchetii* in McMurdo Sound. *Antarctic Journal of the United States*, **20**, 132–133.

Palmisano, A. C., SooHoo, J. B., White, D. C., Smith, G. A. &

Stanton, G. R. (1985d). Shade adapted benthic diatoms beneath Antarctic sea ice. *Journal of Phycology*, **21**, 664–667.

Palmisano, A. C., SooHoo, J. B. & Sullivan, C. W. (1987a). Effects of four environmental variables on photosynthesis–irradiance relationships in Antarctic sea-ice microalgae. *Marine Biology*, **94**, 299–306.

Palmisano, A. C., SooHoo, J. B., Moe, R. L. & Sullivan, C. W. (1987b). Sea ice microbial communities. VII. Changes in under-ice spectral irradiance during the development of Antarctic sea ice microalgal communities. *Marine Ecology Progress Series*, **35**, 165–173.

Palmisano, A. C., Lizotte, M. P., Smith, G. A., Nichols, P. D., White, D.S. & Sullivan, C, W, (1988). Changes in photosynthetic carbon assimilation in Antarctic sea-ice diatoms during a spring bloom: variation in the synthesis of lipid classes. *Journal of Experimental Marine Biology & Ecology*, **116**, 1–13.

Palmisano, A.C., SooHoo, J.B., SooHoo, S.L., Kottmeier, S.T., Craft, L.L. & Sullivan, C.W. (1986). Photoadaptation in *Phaeocystis pouchettii* advected beneath the annual sea ice in McMurdo Sound, Antarctica. *Journal of Plankton Reserach*, **8**, 891–906.

Papenfuss, G. F. (1964). Problems in the taxonomy and geographical distribution of Antarctic marine algae. In *Biologie Antarctique*, ed. R. Carrick, M. W. Holdgate & J. Prevost, pp. 155–160. Paris: Hermann.

Paranjape, M. A. (1967). Moulting and respiration of euphausiids. *Journal of the Fisheries Research Board of Canada*, **24**, 1229–1240.

Parke, M., Green, J. C. & Martin, I. (1971). Observations on the fine structure of zooids of the genus *Phaeocystis* (Haptophyceae). *Journal of the Marine Biological Association, UK*, **51**, 927–941.

Parmelee, D. F. (1976). Banded south polar skua found in Greenland. *Antarctic Journal of the United States*, **11**, 111.

Parsons, T. R., LeBrasseur, R. J. & Fulton, J. P. (1967). Some observations on the dependence of zooplankton grazing on cell size and concentration of phytoplankton blooms. *Journal of the Oceanographic Society of Japan*, **23**, 10–17.

Parsons, T. R., Takahashi, M. & Hargraves, B. (1977). *Biological Oceanographic Processes*. Elmsford, New York: Pergamon Press.

Paterson, R. & Paterson, P. (1989). The status of the recovering stock of humpback whales in east Australian waters. *Biological Conservation*, **47**, 33–48.

Patterson, S. L. & Sievers, H. A. (1980). The Weddell-Scotia Confluence. *Journal of Physical Oceanography*, **10**, 1548–1610.

Pavlov, V. Ya. (1969). The feeding of krill and some features of its behaviour. *Trudy*, **66**, 207–222. (MAAF Translation No. NS94.)

Pavlov, V. Ya. (1974). O cheraktere srjazi mez uptianiem i nekotorymi osobennosyjami povedeniya *Euphausia superba* Dana. *Trudy Vsesoiuznogo Naucho–issledovatel'skii Instituta Morskogo Rybnogo Khoziaiskia i Okeanographii*, **99**, 104–116.

Pavlov. V. Ya. (1977). On the quantitative composition of food for *Euphausia superba* Dana. *Trudy Vsesoiuznogo Naucho-issledovatel'skii Instituta Morskogo Rybnogo Khoziaiskia i Okeanographii*, **86**, 42–54. (Translation Series Fisheries Research Board of Canada (1953), 1974.)

Pawson, D. L. (1969a). Holothuroidea. *Antarctic Map Folio Series*, Vol. II, pp. 36–38. Washington, DC: American Geographical Society.

Pawson, D. L. (1969b). Echinoidea. *Antarctic Map Folio Series,* Vol. II, 38–41. Washington, DC: American Geographical Society.

Payne, M. R. (1977). Growth of a fur seal population. *Philosophical Transactions of the Royal Society London Series B, Biological Sciences*, **279**, 67–79.

Payne, M. R. (1978). Population size and age determination in the Antarctic fur seal *Arctocephalus gazella*. *Mammal Review*, **8**, 67–73.

Payne, M. R. (1979). Growth of the Antarctic fur seal *Arctocephalus gazella*. *Journal of Zoology (London)*, **187**, 1–20.

Pearcy. W. G. (1976). Seasonal and inshore/offshoe variation in the standing stock of micronekton and macrozooplankton off Oregon. *Fisheries Bulletin, U.S.*, **74**, 70–80.

Pearse, J. S. (1965). Reproductive periodicities of *Odonaster validus* Koehler, a common Antarctic asteroid. *Antarctic Research Series*, II, 35–39.

Pearse, J. S. (1969). Antarctic asteroid *Odonaster validus*: constancy of reproductive periodicities. *Marine Biology*, **3**, 110–116.

Pearse, J. S. & Giese, C. (1966). Food, reproduction and organic constitution of the common Antarctic echinoid *Sterechinus neumayeri* (Meissner). *Biological Bulletin*, **130**, 387–401.

Peng, T. H. & Broecker, W. S. (1991). Dynamical limitations on the Antarctic fertilization strategy. *Nature (London)*, **349**, 227–229.

Penny, R. L. & Lowry, G. (1967). Leopard seal predation on Adélie pengiuns. *Ecology*, **48**, 878–882.

Permitin, Yu. E. (1970). The consumption of krill by Antarctic fish. In *Antarctic Ecology,* Vol. I, ed. M. W. Holdgate, pp. 177–182. London: Academic Press.

Permitin, Yu. E. (1973). Fecundity and reproductive biology of icefish (Channichthyidae), fish of the family Muraenolepidae and dragonfish (Bathydraconidae). of the Scotia Sea (Antarctica). *Journal of Ichthyology*, **13**, 204–215.

Permitin, Yu. E. (1977). Species composition and zoogeographical analysis of bottom fish of the Scotia Sea. *Voprosy Ikhtiologii*, **17**, 843–861.

Permitin, Yu. E. & Sil'yanova, Z. S. (1971). New data on the reproductive biology and fecundity of fishes of the genus *Notothenia* (Richardson) in the Scotia Sea (Antarctica). *Journal of Ichthyology*, **11**, 693–705.

Permitin, Yu. E. & Tarverdiyera, M. I. (1972). The food of some Antarctic fish in the South Georgia area. *Journal of Ichthyology*, **12**, 104–114.

Permitin, Yu. E. & Tarverdiyera, M. I. (1978). Feeding of fishes of the families Nototheniidae and Chaenichthyidae in the South Orkney Islands. *Biologiya Morya*, **2**, 75–81 (in Russian.)

Perrin, R. A., Lu, P. & Marchant, J. (1987). Seasonal variation in marine phytoplankton and ice algae at a shallow coastal site. *Hydrobiologia*, **146**, 33–46.

Peterson, B. J. (1980). Aquatic primary productivity and the $^{14}CO_2$ method: a history of the productivity problem. *Annual Review of Ecology and Systematics*, **11**, 369–385.

Peterson, P. H. (1979). predation, competitive exclusion, and diversity in soft-sediment benthic communities of estuaties and lagoons. In *Ecological Processes in Coastal Marine Systems*, ed. R. J. Livingston, pp. 223–264. New York & London: Plenum Press.

Piakowski, U. (1985a). Map of the geographical distribution of macrozooplankton in the Atlantic sector of the Southern Ocean. *Breichte fur Polarforschung*, **30**, 264–279.

Piakowski, U. (1985b). Distribution, abundance and diurnal migration of macrozooplankton in Antarctic surface waters. *Meeresforschung*, **20**, 264–279.

Picken, G. B. (1980). Reproductive adaptations of Antarctic benthic invertebrates. *Biological Journal of the Linnean Society*, **14**, 67–75.

Picken, G. B. (1985a). Marine habitats: benthos. In *Key Environments: Antarctica*, ed. W. N. Bonner & D. W. H. Walton, pp. 154–172. Oxford: Pergamon Press.

Picken, G. B. (1985b). Benthic research in Antarctica. In *Marine Biology of Polar Regions and the Effect of Stress on Marine Organisms*, ed. J. S. Grey & M. E. Christiansen, pp. 167–184. London: John Wiley.

Pingnee, R. D. (1978). Cyclonic eddies and cross frontal mixing. *Journal of the Marine Biological Association, UK*, **58**, 955–963.

Platt, H. M. (1980). Ecology of King Edward Cove, South Georgia. I. Macrobenthos and the benthic environment. *Bulletin British Antarctic Survey*, **49**, 231–238.

Platt, T. & Harrison, W. G. (1985). Biogenic fluxes of carbon and oxygen in the ocean. *Nature* (London), **318**, 55–58.

Platt, T., Sabba Rao, D. V. & Irwin, B. (1983). Photosynthesis of picoplankton in the oligotrophic ocean. *Nature (London)*, **300**, 702–704.

Platt, T., Harrison, W. G., Lewis, M. R., Li, W. K. W., Sathyendranath, S., Smith, R. E. & Vezina, A. F. (1989). Biological production of the oceans: the case for consensus. *Marine Ecology Progress Series*, **52**, 77–88.

Plotz, J. (1986). Summer diet of Weddell Seals (*Leptonychotes weddelli*) in the eastern and southern Weddell Sea, Antarctica. *Polar Biology*, 6, 97–102.

Pocklington, R. (1979). An oceanographic interpretation of seabird distributions in the Indian Ocean. *Marine Biology*, **51**, 9–21.

Poleck, T. P. & Denys, C. J. (1982). Effects of temperature on the moulting, growth and maturation of the Antarctic krill *Euphausia superba* (Crustacea: Euphausiacea) under laboratory conditions. *Marine Biology*, **70**, 255–265.

Pollard, P. C. & Moriarty, D. J. W. (1984). Validity of titriated thymidine method for estimating bacterial growth rates: measurement of isotope dilution during DNA synthesis. *Applied & Environmental Microbiology*, **48**, 1076–1083.

Pomeroy, L. R. (1974). The ocean's food web: a changing paradigm. *Bioscience*, **24**, 499–504.

Pomeroy, L. R. (1979). Secondary production mechanisms of continental shelf communities. In *Ecological Processes in Coastal and Marine Systems*, ed. P. J. Livingston, pp. 163–186. New York: Plenum Press.

Pomeroy, L. R. (1980). Detritus and its role as a food resource. In *Fundamentals of Aquatic Systems*, ed. R. K. S. Barnes & K. H. Mann, pp. 84–102. Oxford: Blackwell.

Pomeroy, L. R. & Deibel, D. (1980). Aggregation of organic matter by pelagic tunicates. *Limnology & Oceanography*, **25**, 643–652.

Pomeroy, L. R. & Deibel, D. (1986). Temperature regulation of bacterial activity during the spring bloom in Newfoundland coastal waters. *Science*, **233**, 359–361.

Pomeroy, L. R., Darley, W. M., Dunn, E. L., Gallagher, J. L. K., Haines, E. B. & Whitney, D. M. (1981). Primary production. In *The Ecology of a Salt Marsh*, ed. L. R. Pomeroy & R. G. Wiegert, pp. 39–67. New York: Springer-Verlag.

Pomeroy, L. R., Hanson, R. B., McGillivary, P. A., Sherr, B. F., Kirchmann, D. & Diebel, D. (1984). Microbiology and chemistry of fecal pellets of pelagic tunicates: rates and fates. *Bulletin of Marine Science*, **35**, 426–439.

Porter, K. G., Sherr, E. B., Sherr, B. F., Pace, M. & Sanders, R. W. (1985). Protozoa in planktonic food webs. *Journal of Protozoology*, **32**, 409–415.

Poulet, S. A. (1978). Comparison between five coexisting species of copepods feeding on naturally occurring particulate matter. *Limnology & Oceanography*, **23**, 1126–1143.

Poulet, S. A. & Chanut, J. P. (1975). Nonselective feeding of *Pseudocalanus*. *Journal of the Fisheries Research Board of Canada*, **32**, 706–713.

Powell, A. W. B. (1965). Mollusca of Antarctic and SubAntarctic seas. In *Biogeography and Ecology in Antarctica*, ed. J. Von Mieghan & p. Van Oye, pp. 333–380. The Hague: Dr. W. Junk Publishers.

Powell, W. M. & Clarke, G. L. (1936). The reflection and absorption of daylight at the surface of the ocean. *Journal of the Optical Society of America*, **26**, 111–120.

Presler, P. (1986). Necrophagus invertebrates of Admiralty Bay of King George Island (South Shetland Islands). *Polish Polar Research*, **7**, 25–61.

Preslin, B. B. & Alldredge, A. L. (1983). Primary production of marine snow during and after an upwelling event. *Limnology & Oceanograhy*, **28**, 1156–1167.

Preslin, B. B. & Ley, A. C. (1980). Photosynthesis and chlorophyll *a* fluorescence rhythms in marine phytoplankton. *Marine Biology*, **55**, 295–307

Prévost, J. (1961). *Ecology du Manchot Empereur*. Paris: Hermann.

Prévost, J. (1981). Population, biomass and energy requirements of

Antarctic birds. In *Biological Investigation of Antarctic Systems and Stocks (BIOMASS Volume II)*, ed. S. Z. El-Sayed, pp. 125–139. Cambridge: SCAR.

Prévost, J. & Mougin, J-L. (1970). *Guide des Oiseaux et Mammifères des Terres Australes et Antarctiques Françaises*. Neûchatel: Delachaux et Niestle.

Price, H. J. (1989). Swimming behaviour of krill in relation to algal patches: a mesocosm study. *Limnology & Oceanography*, **34**, 649–659.

Price, H. J., Boyd, K. R. & Boyd, C. M. (1988). Omnivorous feeding behaviour of the Antarctic krill *Euphausia superba*. *Marine Biology*, **97**, 67–77.

Priddle, J. (1990). Antarctic planktonic ecosystem. In *Polar Marine Diatoms*, ed. B. W. Mullins & J. Priddle, pp. 25–34. Cambridge: British Antarctic Survey, Natural Environment Research Council.

Priddle, J., Hawes, I, & Ellis-Evans, J. C. (1986a). Antarctic aquatic ecosystems as habitats for phytoplankton. *Biological Reviews*, **61**, 199–238.

Priddle, J., Heywood, R. B. & Theriot, E. (1986b). Some environmental factors influencing phytoplankton production in the Southern Ocean round South Georgia. *Polar Biology*, **5**, 65–79.

Priddle. J., Croxall, J. P., Everson, I., Heywood, R. B., Prince, P. A. & Sear, C. B. (1988). Large-scale fluctuations in distribution and abundance of krill: A discussion of possible causes. In *Antarctic Ocean and Resources Variability*, ed. D. Sahrhage, pp. 169–182. Berlin Heidelberg: Springer-Verlag.

Prince, P. A. (1980a). The food and feeding ecology of blue petrel (*Halobaena caerula*) and dove prion (*Pachyptila desolata*). *Journal of Zoology (London)*, **190**, 59–76.

Prince, P. A. (1980b). The food and feeding ecology of grey-headed albatross *Diomedea chrysostoma* and black-browed albatross *D. melanophris*. *Ibis*, **122**, 746–788.

Prince, P. A. (1985). Population and energetic aspects of the relationship between Blackbrowed and Greyheaded Albatrosses and the Southern Ocean marine environment. In *Antarctic Nutrient Cycles and Food Webs*, ed. W. R. Siegfried, P. R. Condy & R. M. Laws, pp. 473–477. Berlin & Heidelberg: Springer-Verlag.

Prince, P. A. & Payne, M. R. (1979). Current status of birds at South Georgia. *Bulletin British Antarctic Survey*, **48**, 103–108.

Priscu, J. C., Priscu, L. R., Palmisano, A, C, & Sullivan, C. W. (1987). The effect of temperature on inorganic nitrogen and carbon metabolism in sea-ice microalgae. *Antarctic Journal of the United States*, **20**(5), 196–198.

Probyn, T. A. & Painting, S. J. (1985). Nitrogen uptake by size-fractionated phytoplankton populations in Antarctic surface waters. *Limnology & Oceanography*, **30**, 1327–1332.

Propp, M. V. (1970). The study of the bottom fauna at Halswell Islands by scuba diving. In *Antarctic Ecology,* Vol. I, ed. M. W. Holdgate, pp. 239–241. London: Academic Press.

Prutko, V. G. (1979). On the occurrence of the opah *Lampris guttatus* (Osteichthyes, Lampridae) in the southern part of the Indian Ocean. *Journal of Ichthyology*, **19**, 140–141.

Purves, P. E. (1955). The wax plug in the external auditory meatus of the Mysticeti. *Discovery Reports*, **27**, 293–302.

Pyke, G. H., Pulliam, H. R. & Charnov, E. L. (1977). Optimal foraging: A selective review of theory and tests. *Quarterly Review of Biology*, **52**, 137–154.

Quentin, L. B. & Ross, R. M. (1984). School composition of the Antarctic krill *Euphausia superba* in the waters west of the Antarctic Peninsula in the Austral summer of 1982. *Journal of Crustacean Biology*, **4** (Special Issue No. 1), 96–106.

Quentin, L. B. & Ross, R. M. (1985). Feeding by Antarctic krill, *Euphausia superba*: does size matter? In *Antarctic Nutrient Cycles and Food Webs*, ed. W. R. Siegfried, P. R. Condy & R. M. Laws, pp. 372–377. Berlin & Heidelberg: Springer-Verlag.

Quentin, L. B. & Ross, R. M. (1991). Behavioural and physiological characteristics of the Antarctic krill *Euphausia superba*. *American*

Zoologist, **31**, 49–63.

Racovitza, E. G. (1900). La vie des animaux dt des plantes dans l'Antique. *Bulletin du Societe Royale Belgique de Geographie (Brussels)*, **24**, 177–230.

Radok, U., Streten, N. & Weller, G. E. (1975). Atmosphere and ice. *Oceanus*, **18**, 16–27.

Ragulin, A. G. (1969). Underwater observations of krill. *Trudy Vsesoiuznogo Naucho-issledovatel'skii Instituta Morskogo Rybnogo Khoziaiskia i Okeanographii (Trudy VINRO)*, **66**, 231–234 (MAAF Translation No. NS 92.)

Rakusa-Suszczewski, S. (1978). Environmental conditions within krill swarms. *Polskie Archiwum Hydrobiologii*, **25**, 585–587.

Rakusa-Suszczewski, S. (1982). Feeding of *Euphausia superba* Dana under natural conditions. *Polish Polar Research*, **3**, 289–297.

Rakusa-Suszczewski, S. (1983). The relationship between the distribution of plankton biomass and plankton communities in the Drake Passage and Bransfield Strait (BIOMASS-FIBEZ, February–March 1981). *Memoirs National Institute of Polar Research, Special Issue*, **27**, 77–83.

Rakusa-Suszczewski, S. & Klekowski, R. Z. (1973). Biology and respiration of the Antarctic amphipod (*Paramoea walkeri* Stebbing) in the summer. *Poliski Archiwum Hydrobiologii*, **20**, 475–488.

Rakusa-Suszczewski, S. & Opalinski, K. W. (1978). Oxygen consumption in *Euphausia superba*. *Poliski Archiwum Hydrobiologii*, **25**, 633–642.

Ralph, R. & Maxwell, J. G. H. (1977a). Growth of two Antarctic lamellibranchs: *Adamussium colbecki* and *Laternula elliptica*. *Marine Biology*, **42**, 171–175.

Ralph, R. & Maxwell, J. G. H. (1977b). The oxygen consumption of the Antarctic limpet *Nacella (Patinigera) concinna*. *British Antarctic Survey Bulletin*, **45**, 19–23.

Ralph, R. & Maxwell, J. G. H. (1977c). The oxygen consumption of the Antarctic lamellibranch *Gaimardia trapesina* in relation to cold adaptation in polar invertebrates. *British Antarctic Survey Bulletin*, **45**, 41–46.

Rassoulzadegan, F. & Sheldon, R. W. (1986). Predator–prey interactions of nanozooplankton and bacterial in an oligotrophic marine environment. *Limnology & Oceanography*, **31**, 1010–1021.

Rassoulzadegan, F., Laval-Pueto, M. & Sheldon, R. W. (1988). Partition of the food ration of marine ciliates between picoplankton and nanoplankton. *Hydrobiologia*, **159**, 75–88.

Rawlence, D. J., Ensor, P. H. & Knox, G. A. (1987). Summer tide-crack phytoplankton at White Island, McMurdo Sound, Antarctica. *New Zealand Journal of Marine & Freshwater Research*, **21**, 91–97.

Ray, G. C. (1970). Population ecology of Antarctic seals. In *Antarctic Ecology*, Vol. I, ed. M. W. Holdgate, pp. 398–414. London: Academic Press.

Ray, G. C. (1981). Ross seal. In *Handbook of Marine Mammals*, ed. S. H. Ridgway & R. J. Harrison, pp. 237–260. London: Academic Press.

Raymond, J. A. (1975). Fishing for Antarctica's largest fish the Antarctic cod. *Marine Technology Society Journal*, **19**, 32–35.

Raytheon Service Company (1983). Report on the McMurdo Sound Water Quality Study Unpublished report to the U. S. Office of Polar Programs.

Reeburg, W. S. (1984). Fluxes associated with brine motion in growing sea ice. *Polar Biology*, **3**, 29–33.

Regan, C. T. (1914). Fishes. *British Antarctic ("Terra Nova"). Expedition 1910, Natural History Report, Zoology*, **1**, 1–54.

Reichardt, W. (1987). Burial of Antarctic macroalgal debris in bioturbated deep-sea sediments. *Deep-Sea Research*, **34**, 1761–1770.

Reid, F. M. H. (1983). Biomass estimation of components of marine nanoplankton and picoplankton by the Utermohl settling technique. *Journal of Plankton Research*, **5**, 235–252.

Reid, F. M. H., Fuglister, E. & Jordan, J. B. (1970). Phytoplankton taxonomy and standing crop. In *The Ecology of Plankton off La Jolla, California, in the Period April Through September, 1967*, ed. J.D.H. Strickland, pp. 57–66. Berkely, CA: University of California Press.

Rembiszewski, J. M., Krzeptowski, M. & Linkowski, T. (1978). Fishes (Pisces) as a by-catch in fisheries of krill *Euphausia superba* Dana (Euphausia, Crustacea). *Poliski Archiwum Hydrobiologii*, **25**, 677–695.

Repenning, C.A., Peterson, R.S. & Hubbs, C.L. (1971). Contributions to the systematics of southern fur seals, with a particular reference to Juan Fernandez and Guadelupe species. In *Antarctic Pinnepedia*, ed. W.H. Burt. *Antarctic Research Series* **18**, pp. 1–34. Washington DC: American Geophysical Society.

Retamal, M. A., Quintana, R. & Neira, F. (1982). Ánálysis cauliy cuantitatiro de las communidades benthónicas en Bahis Foster Isla Deception) (XXXV Expedition Antarctica Chilena, enero 1981). *Publication Instituto Antarctico Chileno Series Cientifica*, **29**, 5–15.

Ribec, C. A., Ainley, D. G. & Fraser, W. R. (1991). Habitat selection by marine mammals in the marginal ice zone. *Antarctic Science*, **3**, 181–186.

Richardson, M. D. (1972). Benthic studies in the Antarctic. *Antarctic Journal of the United States*, **7**, 185–186.

Richardson, M. D. (1975). The dietary composition of some Antarctic fish. *British Antarctic Survey Bulletin*, **41/42**, 113–120.

Richardson, M. D. (1979). The distribution of Antarctic marine macroalgae related to depth and substrate. *British Antarctic Survey Bulletin*, **49**, 1–12.

Richardson, M. D. & Hedgpeth, J. W. (1977). Antarctic soft-bottom macrobenthic community adaptation to a cold, stable, highly productive, glacially affect environment. In *Adaptations Within Antarctic Ecosystems*, ed. S. Llano, pp. 181–196. Washington, DC: Smithsonian Institution.

Richdale, L. E. (1963). Biology of the sooty shearwater *Puffinus griseus*. *Proceedings of the Zoological Society of London*, **141**, 1–117.

Ricker, W. E. (1968). *Methods for Assessment of Fish Production in Fresh Waters*. IGP Handbook No. 3. 313 pp.

Ridgeway, S. H. & Harrison, R. J. (1981). *Handbook of Marine Mammals*. London: Academic Press. Vol. 1, 233 pp.; Vol. 2, 359 pp.

Ridoux, V. & Offredo, C. (1989). The diets of five summer breeding seabirds in Adélie Land, Antarctica. *Polar Biology*, **9**, 137–145.

Riebesell, U. (1989). Comparison of sinking and sedimentation rate measurements in a diatom winter/spring bloom. *Marine Ecology Progress Series*, **54**, 109–119.

Riebesell, U., Schloss, I. & Smetacek, V. (1991). Aggregation of algae released from melting sea ice: implications for seeding and sedimentation. *Polar Biology*, **11**, 239–248.

Riley, G. A. (1963). Theory of food chain relations in the Ocean. In *The Sea*, Vol. 2, ed. M. N. Hill, pp. 438–463. New York: Wiley Interscience.

Rivkin, R. B. (1991). Seasonal pattern of planktonic production in McMurdo Sound, Antarctica. *American Zoologist*, **31**, 5–16.

Rivkin, R. B. & Putt, M. (1987). Heterotrophy and photoheterotrophy by Antarctic microalgae: light-dependent incorporation of amino acids and glucose. *Journal of Phycology*, **23**, 442–452.

Roberts, B. B. (1940). Life cycle of Wilson's petrel *Oceanites oceanicus* (Kuhl.). *British Grahamland Expedition 1934–47 Scientific Reports*, **1**, 141–194.

Roberts, L. (1989). Does the ozone hole threaten Antarctic life. *Science*, **244**, 288–289.

Robertson, A. I. (1979). On the relationship between annual production:biomass ratios and life spans of marine invertebrates. *Oecologia*, **38**, 193–202.

Robin, G. deQ. (1988). Antarctic ice sheet, its history and response to sea-level and climate changes over the past 100 million years. *Palaeogeography, Palaeoclimatology, Palaeoecology*, **67**, 31–50.

Rodhouse, P. G. (1990). Cephalopod fauna of the South Scotia Sea at

South Georgia: Potential for commercial exploitation and possible consequences. In *Antarctic Ecosystems: Ecological Change and Conservation*, ed. K. R. Kerry & G. Hempel, pp. 289–298. Berlin & Heidelberg: Springer-Verlag.

Rodman, M. R. & Gordon, A. L. (1982). South ocean bottom water of the Australian-New Zealand sector. *Journal of Geophysical Research*, **87**, 5711–5788.

Roe, H. S. J. (1967). Seasonal formation of laminae in the ear plug of the fin whale. *Discovery Reports*, **35**, 1–30.

Røed, L. P. & O'Brien, J. J. (1983). A coupled ice-ocean model of upwelling in the marginal ice zone. *Journal of Geophysical Research*, **88**, 2863–2872.

Rogers, J. C. & VanLoon, H. (1979). Spatial variability of sea level pressure and 500 mb height anomalies over the Southern hemisphere. *Monthly Weather Review*, **110**, 1375–1392.

Roman, M. R. (1984a). Utilization of detritus by the copepod *Acartia tonsus*. *Limnology & Oceanography*, **29**, 949–959.

Roman, M. R. (1984b). Ingestion of detritus and microheterotrophs by pelagic marine zooplankton. *Bulletin of Marine Science*, **35**, 177–494.

Ronan, T. E., Jr., Lipps, J. A. & Delaca, T. E. (1978). Sediments and life under the Ross Ice Shelf. *Antarctic Journal of the United States*, **13**, 141–142.

Rönner, U., Sorenson, F. & Holm-Hansen, O. (1983). Nitrogen assimilation by phytoplankton in the Scotia Sea. *Polar Biology*, **2**, 137–147.

Roper, C. E. F. (1969). *Systematics and Zoogeography of the Worldwide Bathypelagic Squid Bathyteuthis (Cephalopoda: Oregopsida). US National Museum Bulletin 291*. Washington, DC: Smithsonian Institution Press. 211 pp.

Roper, C. E. F. (1981). Cephalopods of the southern ocean region: potential resources and bibliography. In *BIOMASS,* Vol. II, ed. S. Z. El-Sayed, pp. 99–105. Cambridge: SCAR, SCOR, Scott Polar Research Institute.

Rosenberg, A. A., Beddington, J. R. & Basson, M. (1986). Growth and longevity of krill during the first decade of pelagic whaling. *Nature* (London), **324**, 152–154.

Ross, R. M. (1982). Energetics of *Euphausia pacifica*. 2. Complete carbon and nitrogen budgets at 8° and 12°C throughout the life-span. *Marine Biology*, **68**, 15–23.

Ross, R. M. & Quentin, L. B. (1983a). *Euphausia superba*: fecundity and the physiological ecology of its eggs and larvae. *Antarctic Journal of the United States*, **17**, 166–177.

Ross, R. M. & Quentin, L. B. (1983b). Spawning frequency and fecundity of the Antarctic krill *Euphausia superba*. *Marine Biology*, **77**, 201–205.

Ross, R. M. & Quentin, L. B. (1986). How productive are Antarctic krill. *Bioscience*, **36**, 264–269.

Ross, R. M., Quentin, L. B. & Amsler, M. O. (1985). *Euphausia superba*: a preliminary report on three areas of investigation. *Antarctic Journal of the United States*, **19**(5), 153–155.

Rounsevell, D. E. & Brothers, N. P. (1984). The status and conservation of seabirds at Macquarie Island. In *Status and Conservation of the Worlds Seabirds*, pp. 587–592. International Council for Bird Preservation, Technical Publication No. 2.

Rounsevell, D. E. & Eberhard, I. (1980). Leopard seals, *Hydrurga leptonyx* (Pinnipedia) at Macquarie Island. *Australian Journal of Marine & Freshwater Research*, **7**, 403–415.

Rowedder, U. (1979). Some aspects of the biology of *Electrona antarctica* (Gunther 1878). (Family Myctophidae). *Meeresforschung*, **4**, 244–251.

Rudd, J. T. (1932). On the biology of the Euphausiidae. *Hvalradets Skrifter*, **2**, 1–105.

Rudd, J. T. (1954). Vertebrates without erythrocytes and blood pigments. *Nature* (London), **173**, 848–850.

Rudd, J. T. (1965). The ice fish. *Scientific American*, **213**, 108–114.

Russek, Z., Kaspryzk, Z. & Szostak, S. (1981). Preliminary economic evaluation of commercial krill catches. *Stud. Mater. Morsk. Inst. Ryb., Gdynia*, **42**, 100 pp. (in Polish with English summary).

Ryther, J. H. (1969). Photosynthesis and fish production in the sea. *Science*, **166**, 72–76.

Sabourenkov, E. N. (1990). Mesopelagic fish of the Southern Ocean: Summary results of recent Soviet studies. In *Selected Scientific Papers, Scientific Committee of CCAMLR*, pp. 433–458. Hobart: Convention on the Conservation of Antarctic Marine Living Resaources.

Sadlier, R. M. F. S. & Lay, K. M. (1990). Foraging movements of Adélie penguins (*Pygoscelis adeliae*) in McMurdo Sound. In *Penguin Biology*, ed. L. S. Davis & J. T. Darby, pp. 157–179. London: Academic Press.

Sahrhage, D. (1978). Length-weight correlation in Antarctic krill *Euphausia superba*. *Meeresforschung*, **26**, 47–49.

Sahrhage, D. (ed.) (1988a). *Antarctic Ocean and Resources Variability*. Berlin & Heidelberg: Springer-Verlag. 304 pp.

Sahrhage, D. (1988b). Some indications for environmental and krill resources variability in the Southern Ocean. In *Antarctic Ocean and Resources Variability*, ed. D. Sahrhage, pp. 33–40. Berlin & Heidelberg: Springer-Verlag.

Saijo, Y. & Kawashi, T. (1964). Primary production in the Antarctic Ocean. *Journal of the Oceanographic Society of Japan*, **19**, 190–196.

Sakshaug, E. & Holm-Hansen, O. (1984). Factors governing pelagic production in polar oceans. In *Marine Phytoplankton and Productivity*, ed. O. Holm-Hansen, O. L. Bolis & R. Gilles, pp. 1–18. Berlin & Heidelberg: Springer-Verlag.

Sakshaug, E, & Holm-Hansen, O. (1986). Photoadaptation in Antarctic phytoplankton: variations in growth rate, chemical composition, and *P* vs *I* curves. *Journal of Plankton Research*, **8**, 549–573.

Sakshaung, E. & Skjoldal, H. R. (1989). Life at the ice edge. *Ambio*, **18**, 60–67.

Samyshev, E. Z. (1986). Bacterioplankton of Antarctic coastal waters: concentration, production and bacterial destruction. *Oceanology*, **26**, 508–512.

Sanders, H.L. (1969). Benthic marine diversity and the stability-time hypothesis: diversity and stability in ecological systems. *Brookhaven Symposium in Biology*, **22**, 71–81.

Sanders, H. L. (1979). Evolutionary ecology and life-history patterns in the deep sea. *Sarsia*, **64**, 1–7.

Sargent, J. R. (1976). The structure, metabolism and function of lipids in marine organisms. In *Biochemical and Biophysical Perspectives in Marine Biology,* Vol. 3, ed. D. C. Molins & J. R. Sergent, pp. 249–212. London & New York: Academic Press.

Sasaki, H. (1984). Distribution of nano- and microplankton in the Indian Sector of the Southern Ocean. *Memoirs National Institute of Polar Research, Special Issue*, **2**, 38–50.

Sasaki, H. & Hoshiai, T. (1986). Sedimentation of microalgae under Antarctic fast ice in summer. *Memoirs National Institute of Polar Research, Special Issue*, **40**, 45–55.

Sasaki, H. & Watanabe, K. (1984). Underwater observations of ice-algae in Lutzow-Holm Bay, Antarctica. *Antarctica Record*, **81**, 1–8.

Sato, T. & Hatanaka, H. (1983). A review of assessment of Japanese distant-water fisheries for cephalopods. In *Advances in Assessment of World Cephalopod Resources*, ed. J. F. Caddy, pp. 145–180. Rome: FAO Fisheries Technical Paper No. 231.

Satoh, H., Fukami, K., Watanabe, K, & Takahashi, E. (1989). Seasonal changes in heterotrophic bacteria under fast ice near Syowa Station, Antarctica. *Canadian Journal of Microbiology*, **35**, 329–333.

Satoh, H., Watanabe, K., Kanda, H. & Takahashi, E. (1986). Seasonal changes of chlorophyll *a* standing stocks and oceanographic conditions under fast ice near Syowa Station, Antarctica. *Antarctic Record*, **30**, 19–32.

SCAR (1989). *Waste Disposal in Antarctica. Report of the SCAR Panel of Experts on Waste Disposal*. Cambridge: Scientific Committee on Antarctic Research. 53 pp.

SCAR/SCOR (1979). *Antarctic Bird Biology.* SCAR Working Group on Biology. BIOMASS Report Series No. 8. 21 pp.

SCAR/SCOR (1983a). *Meeting of the BIOMASS Working Group on Bird Ecology.* Group of Specialists on Southern Ocean Ecosystems and Their Living Resources. BIOMASS Report Series No 33 pp.

SCAR/SCOR (1983b). *Meeting of the SCAR Group of Specialists on Southern Ocean Ecosystems and Their Living Resources.* BIOMASS Report Series No. 35. 41 pp.

SCAR/SCOR (1983c). *First Meeting of the ad hoc Group on Squid Biology.* BIOMASS Report Series No. 33. 81 pp.

SCAR/SCOR (1988). *Proposal for a Scar Multidisciplinary Program for the Antarctic Sea Ice Zone (ASIZ).* (mimeo.) 33 pp., plus 33 figs.

SCAR/SCOR (1990). *Report of the SCAR/SCOR Workshop on the Ecology of the Antarctic Sea Ice Zone, 18–21 May, 1990, Trondheim, Norway.* (mimeo.) 26 pp.

SC-CCAMLR (1985). *Report of the Fourth Meeting of the Scientific Committee. SC-CCAMLR-V, Annex 6*, pp. 145–190. Hobart: Convention on the Conservation of Antarctic Marine Living Resources.

SC-CCAMLR (1990a). *Report of the Ninth Meeting of the Scientific Committee. Hobart, Australia 22–26 October, 1990*, pp. 1–65. Hobart: Commission on the Conservation of Antarctic Marine Living Resources.

SC-CCAMLR (1990b). Fish stock assessment – Report of the Working Group. In *Report of the Ninth Meeting of the Scientific Committee, Annex 6*, pp. 281–336. Hobart: Commission for the Conservation of Antarctic Marine Living Resources.

Scheffer, V. B. (1958). *Seals, Sea Lions and Walruses: A Review of the Pinnepedia.* Stanford: Stanford University Press.

Schlosser, P. (1986). Helium: a new tracer in Antarctic oceanography. *Nature* (London), **321**, 195–196.

Schnack, S. B. (1983a). Feeding of two Antarctic copepod species (*Calanus propinquus* and *Metridia gerlachei*) on a mixture of centric diatoms. *Polar Biology*, **2**, 63–68.

Schnack, S. B. (ed.). (1983b). On the biology of Krill *Euphausia superba.* In *Proceedings of the Seminar and Report of the Krill Ecology Group, Bremerhaven, 12–16 May 1983. Berichte zur Polarforschung*, Vol. 4. 303 pp.

Schnack, S. B. (1985a). A note on the sedimentation of particulate matter in Antarctic waters during summer. *Meeresforschungsergebnisse*, **30**, 306–315.

Schnack, S. B. (1985b). Feeding of *Euphausia superba* and copepod species in response to varying concentrations of phytoplankton. In *Antarctic Nutrient Cycles and Food Webs*, ed. W. R. Siegfried, P. R. Condy & R. M. Laws, pp. 311–323. Berlin & Heidelberg: Springer-Verlag.

Schnack, S. B., Smetacek, V. & Bodungen, B. von. (1985). Utilization of phytoplankton by copepods in Antarctic waters during spring. In *Marine Biology of Polar Regions and Effects of Stress on Marine Organisms*, ed. J. S. Gray & M. E. Christiansen, pp. 65–81. Chichester, U K: John Wiley.

Schneppenheim, R. (1990). Concentration of fluoride in Antarctic animals. *Meeresforschung/Report Marine Research*, **28**, 179–182.

Schneppenheim, R. & MacDonald, C. M. (1984). Genetic variation and population structure of krill (*Euphausia superba*) In the Atlantic sector of Antarctic waters and off the Antarctic Peninsula. *Polar Biology*, **3**, 19–28.

Sciermammano, F., Jr. (1989). Observations of Antarctic Polar Front motions in a deep water expression. *Journal of Physical Oceanography*, **9**, 221–126.

Scolaro, J. A. (1976). Censo de elefantes marinos (*Mirounga leonina* L.). en el territorio continental Argentino. *Commission Nacional de Estudios Geo-Heliofisicos, Centro Nacional Patagonica, Informes Tecnicos*, **1. 4. 1**, 1–12.

Segawa, S, Kato, M. & Murano, M. (1983). Growth, moult and filtering rate of krill in laboratory conditions. *Memoirs National Institute of Polar Research, Special Issue*, **27**, 93–103.

Sergeant, D. E. (1962). The biology of the pilot or pothead whale *Globiceohala melaena* (Traill) in Newfoundland waters. *Bulletin Fisheries Research Board of Canada*, **132**, 1–84.

Sergeant, D. E. (1969). Feeding rates of cetacea. *Fiskeridirektorastets Skrifter Serie Havunderøskelser*, **15**, 246–258.

Sergeant, D. E. (1973). Feeding, growth and productivity of northwest Atlantic harp seals (*Pagophilus groenlandicus*). *Journal of the Fisheries Research Board of Canada*, **30**, 17–29.

Servais, P., Billen, G. & Vives Rojo, J. (1985). Rate of bacterial mortality in aquatic environments. *Applied & Environmental Microbiology*, **40**, 1440–1455.

Seventy, D. L. (1957). The banding of *Puffinus tenuirostris* (Temminck). *CSIRO Wildlife Research*, **2**, 51–59.

Shackleton, N. J. & Kennett, J. P. (1975). 17. Paleotemperature history of the Cenozoic and the initiation of Antarctic glaciation: oxygen and carbon isotope analysis in DSDP sites 277, 279, and 281. *Initial Reports of the Deep Sea Drilling Project*, **29**, 743–755.

Sheldon, R. W., Prakash, A. & Sutcliffe, W. H., Jr (1972). Size distribution of particles in the ocean. *Limnology & Oceanography*, **17**, 327–340.

Shevchenko, V. (1976). The nature of interrelationships between killer whales and other cetaceans. Fisheries and Marine Series Translation Series No. 3839 of Kharakter vzaimootnoshenii kasahiki i drugikh kitoobraznykh. *Morsk Mleikopitayushchie Chast*, **23**, 174–175, 1975.

Sherman, K. & Ryan, A. F. (1988). Antarctic marine living resources. *Oceanus*, **31**, 59–63.

Sherman, K., Jones, C., Sullivan, L., Smith, W., Berrien, P. & Ejsymont, L. (1981). Congruent shifts in sand eel abundance in western and eastern North Atlantic ecosystems. *Nature* (London), **291**, 486–489.

Sherr, B. F. & Sherr, E. B. (1984). Role of heterotrophic protozoa in carbon and energy flow in aquatic systems. In *Current Perspectives in Microbial Ecology*, ed. M. J. Klug & C. A. Reddy, pp. 412–423. Washington, DC: American Society for Microbiology.

Sherr, B. F., Sherr, E. B. & Berman, T. (1983). Grazing, growth and ammonium excretion rates of a heterotrophic microflagellate fed with four species of bacteria. *Applied & Environmental Microbiology*, **45**, 1196–1201.

Sherr, E. B. & Sherr, B. F. (1983). Double staining epifluorescence technique to assess frequency of dividing cells in natural populations of heterotrophic microprotozoa. *Applied & Environmental Microbiology*, **46**, 1388–1393.

Sherr, E. B. & Sherr, B. F. (1987). High rates of consumption of bacteria by pelagic ciliates. *Nature* (London), **325**, 710–711.

Sherr, E. B., Sherr, B. F., Fallon, R. D. & Newell, S. Y. (1986). Small aloricate ciliates as a major component of the marine heterotrophic nanoplankton. *Limnology & Oceanography*, **31**, 177–183.

Sherr, E. B., Rassoulzadegan, F. & Sherr, B. F. (1989). Bactivory by pelagic choreotrichous ciliates in coastal waters of the NW Mediterranean Sea. *Marine Ecology Progress Series*, **55**, 235–240.

Shimadzu, Y. (1984a). A brief summary of Japanese fishing activity in relation to Antarctic krill, 1972/73–1982/83. In *Selected Papers Presented to the Scientific Committee of CCAMLR, 1982–1984, Part I*, pp. 439–452. Hobart: Convention on the Conservation of Antarctic Marine Living Resources.

Shimadzu, Y. (1984b). A review of Antarctic ecosystem models. In *Selected Papers Presented to the Scientific Committee of CCAMLR, 1982–1984, Part II*, pp. 221–246. Hobart: Convention on the Conservation of Antarctic Marine Living Resources.

SHMIREP (1990). *Report of the Subcommittee on Southern Hemisphere Minke Whales.* Cambridge: International Whaling Commission.

Showers, W. J., Jr., Daniels, R. A. & Laine, D. (1977). Marine biology at Palmer Station, 1975 austral winter. *Antarctic Journal of the United States*, **12**, 22–25.

Shulenberger, E., Wormuth, J. H. & Loeb, V. J. (1984). A large swarm of *Euphausia superba*: overview of patch structure and composition. *Journal of Crustacean Biology*, **4** (Special Issue No. 1), 75–95.

Shust, K. V. (1969). Visual observations on Antarctic krill made on board the factory ship *Akademik Knipovich. Trudy Vsesoiuznogo Naucho-issledovatel'skii Instituta Morskogo Rybnogo Khoziaiskia Okaenographii (Trudy VNIRO)*, **66**, 223–230. (MAAF Translation No. RTS 5588.)

Shust, K. V. (1978). Brief communications on the distribution and biology of members of the genus *Micromesistius* (Family Gadidae) *Journal of Ichthyology*, **18**, 490–492.

Sicrachi, M. E. & Siebruth, J. M. (1986). Sunlight induced decay of planktonic marine bacteria in filtered seawater. *Marine Ecology Progress Series*, **33**, 19–27.

Siebruth, J. McN. (1967). Microbiology of Antarctica. In *Biogeography and Ecology of Antarctica*, ed. J. van Miegham & P. van Oye, pp. 267–295. The Hague: Dr W. Junk Publishers.

Siebruth, J. McN. (1969). Studies on algal substances in the sea. III. Glebstoff (humic material) in terrestrial and marine waters. *Journal of Experimental Marine Biology and Ecology* , **2**, 174–184.

Siebruth, J. McN. (1979). *Sea Microbes*. New York: Oxford University Press.

Siebruth, J. McN. (1984). Grazing of bacteria by protozooplankton in pelagic marine waters. In *Heterotrophic Activity in the Sea*, ed. J. Hobbie & A. J. LeB. Williams, pp. 405–444. New York: Plenum Press.

Siebruth, J. McN. & Davis, P. G. (1982). The role of heterotrophic nanoplankton in the grazing of planktonic bacteria in the Sargasso and Caribbean Seas. *Annales de l'Institut Oceanographique, Paris*, **58**, 285–296.

Siebruth, J. McN., Smetacek, V. & Lenza, J. (1978). Pelagic ecosystem structure: heterotrophic compartments and their relationship to plankton site functions. *Limnology & Oceanogrpahy*, **23**, 1256–1263.

Siegel, V. (1982). Relationships of various length measurements of *Euphausia superba* Dana. *Meeresforschung*, **29**, 114–117.

Siegel, V. (1985). On the fecundity of the Antarctic krill *Euphausia superba* (Euphausiacea). *Archiv fur Fischereiwissenschaft*, **36**, 185–193.

Siegel, V. (1986a). Structure and composition of the Antarctic krill stock in the Bransfield Strait (Antarctic Peninsula) during the Second International BIOMASS Experiment (SIBEX). *Archiv fur Fischereiwissenschaft*, **37**, 51–72.

Siegel, V. (1986b). Unterschungen zur Biologie des Antarkischen Krill, *Euphausia superba*, im Bereich der Bransfield Strabe und angrenzender Gebiete. *Mitteilungen Institut fur Seefischerei, Hamburg*, **38**, 1–244.

Siegel, V. (1987). Age and growth of Antarctic Euphausiacea (Crustacea) under natural conditions. *Marine Biology*, **96**, 483–495.

Siegel, V. (1989). Winter and spring distribution and status of the krill stock in Antarctic Peninsula waters. *Archiv fur Fischereiwissenschaft*, **39**, 45–72.

Siegfried, W. R. (1985). Birds and mammals: oceanic birds of the Antarctic. In *Key Environments: Antarctica*, ed. W. N. Bonner & D. W. H. Walton, pp. 242–265. Oxford & New York: Pergamon Press.

Siegfried, W. R. & Croxall, J. P. (1983). Progress and prospects of ornithological research within BIOMASS. *Memoirs National Institute of Polar Research, Special Issue*, **27**, 193–199.

Siegfried, W. R., Williams, A. J., Burger, A. E. & Berruti, A. (1978). Mineral and energy contributions of eggs of selected seabirds to the Marion Island terrestrial ecosystem. *South African Journal of Antarctic Research*, **8**, 75–87.

Siegfried, W. R., Condy, P. R. & Laws, R. M. (ed.). (1985). *Antarctic Nutrient Cycles and Food Webs. Symposium on Antarctic Biology, Wilderness, South Africa, 12–16* September 1983. Berlin & Heidelberg: Springer-Verlag. 700 pp.

Sievers, H. A. & Nowlin, W. D., Jr. (1988). Upper ocean characteristics in Drake Passage and adjourning areas of the Southern Ocean, 39° W – 95° W. In *Antarctic Ocean and Resources Variability*, ed. D. Sahrhage, pp. 57–80. Berlin & Heidelberg: Springer-Verlag.

Silver, M. W. & Alldredge, A. L. (1981). Bathypelagic marine snow: deep sea algal and detrital community. *Journal of Marine Research*, **39**, 501–530.

Silver, M. W., Mitchell, J. G. & Ringo, D. L. (1980). Siliceous nanoplankton. II. Newly discovered cysts and abundant choanoflagellates in the Weddell Sea, Antarctica. *Marine Biology*, **58**, 211–217.

Silver, M. W., Gowing, M. M., Brownlee, D. C. & Corless, J. O. (1984). Ciliated protozoa associated with oceanic sinking debris. *Nature* (London), **309**, 246–248.

Simpson, R. D. (1976a). The shore environment of Macquarie Island. *A. N. A. R. E. Report, Series B*, (1), **125**, 1–41.

Simpson, R. D. (1976b). Physical and biotic factors limiting the distribution and abundance of littoral molluscs on Macquarie Island (sub-Antarctic). *Journal of Experimental Marine Biology & Ecology*, **21**, 11–19.

Simpson, R. D. (1977). The reproduction of some littoral molluscs from Macquarie Island. *Marine Biology*, **44**, 125–142.

Siniff, D. B. (1982). Seal population dynamics and ecology. *Journal of the Royal Society of New Zealand*, **11**, 317–327.

Siniff, D. B. (1991). An overview of the ecology of Antarctic seals. *American Zoologist*, **31**, 143–149.

Siniff, D. B. & Bengtson, J. L. (1977). Observations and hypotheses concerning the interactions among crabeater seals, leopard seals, and killer whales. *Journal of Mammology*, **58**, 414–416.

Siniff, D. B. & Stone, S. (1985). The role of the leopard seal in the tropho-dynamics of the Antarctic marine ecosystem. In *Antarctic Nutrient Cycles and Food Webs*, ed. W. R. Siegfried, P. R. Condy & R. M. Laws, pp. 555–560. Berlin & Heidelberg: Springer-Verlag.

Siniff, D. B., Cline, D. R. & Erickson, A. W. (1970). Population densities of seals in the Weddell Sea, Antarctica in 1968. In *Antarctic Ecology*, Vol. I, ed. W. M. Holdgate, pp. 377–394. London & New York: Academic Press.

Siniff, D. B., Tester, J. R. & Kuechle, V. B. (1971). Some observations on the activity patterns of Weddell seals as recorded by telemetry. In *Antarctic Pinnipedia, Antarctic Research Series*, Vol. 18, ed. W. H. Burt, 173–180. Washington, DC: American Geophysical Union.

Siniff, D. B., Stirling, I., Bengtson, J. L. & Reichle, R. A. (1977a). Biota of the Antarctic pack ice: R/V *Hero* Cruise 1976–77. *Antarctic Journal of the United States*, **15**, 160.

Siniff, D. B., DeMaster, D. P., Hofman, R. J. & Eberhart, L. L. (1977b). An analysis of the dynamics of a Weddell seal population. *Ecological Monographs*, **47**, 319–335.

Siniff, D. B., Stirling, I., Bengtson, J. L. & Reichle, R. A. (1979). Social and reproductive behaviour of crabeater seals (*Lobodon carcinophagus*) during austral spring. *Canadian Journal of Zoology*, 57, 2243–2255.

Siniff, D. B., Stone, S., Reichle, D. & Smith, T. (1980). Aspects of leopard seals (*Hydrurga leptonyx*) in the Antarctic Peninsula pack ice. *Antarctic Journal of the United States*, 15, 160.

Sissenwine, M. P. (1985). Modelling: the application of a research tool to Antarctic marine living resources. In *Selected Papers Presented to the Scientific Committee of CCAMLR. Part II.*, pp. 369–390. Hobart: Convention on the Conservation of Antarctic Marine Living Resources.

Skottsberg, C. (1907). Zur Kenntnis der Subantarktischen und Antarktischen Meeresalgen. I. Phaephyceae. *Wissenschaftliche Ergbnisse der Schwedischen Sudpolarexpedition, 1901–03*, **IV**, 6.

Skottsberg, C. J. F. (1941). Communities of marine algae in Aubabtarctic and Antarctic waters. *Konglia svenska Veteetenskapsa Kademions Handlinger*, **19**(4), 1–92.

Skottsberg, C. J. F. (1964). Antarctic phycology. In *Biologie*

Antarctique, ed. R. Carrick, M. W. Holdgate & J. Prevost, pp. 147–154. Paris: Hermann.

Slawyk, G. (1979). ^{13}C and ^{15}N uptake by phytoplankton in the Antarctic upwelling area: results from the *Antiopd 1* cruise in the Indian Ocean sector. *Australian Journal of Marine & Freshwater Research*, **30**, 431–448.

Slijper, E. J. (1962). *Whales*. London: Hutchinson.

Slosarczyk, W. (1983). Juvenile *Trematomus bernacchii* (Boulenger, 1982) and *Pagothenia brachysoma* (Proppenheim, 1962). (Pisces, Nototheniidae) in krill concentrations off Balleney Island (Antarctica). *Polish Polar Research*, **4**, 57–69.

Slosarczyk, W. & Rembiszewski, J. M. (1982). The occurrence of juvenile Notothenioidea (Pisces) within krill concentrations in the region of the Bransfield Strait and the southern Drake Passage. *Polish Polar Research*, **4**, 299–312.

Small, L. F., Fowler, S. W. & Unlu, M. Y. (1979). Sinking rates of natural copepod faecal pellets. *Marine Biology*, **51**, 223–241.

Smayda, T. J. & Bienfang, P. K. (1983). Suspension properties of various phyletic groups of phytoplankton and Tintinnids in an oligotrophic, subtropical system. *Marine Ecology*, **4**, 289–300.

Smayda, T. J. & Boleyn, B. J. (1965). Experimental observations on the fluctuation of marine diatoms. I. *Thalassosira* cf. *nana*, *Thalassosira rotula* and *Nitzschia seriata*. *Limnology and Oceanography*, **10**, 449–509.

Smetacek, V. S. (1980). Annual cycle of sedimentation in relation to plankton ecology in the western Keil Bight. *Ophelia, Supplement*, **1**, 65–67.

Smetacek, V. S. (1981). The annual cycle of protozooplankton in the Keil Bight. *Marine Biology*, **63**, 1–11.

Smetacek, V. S., Scharek, R. & Nothig, E-M. (1990). Seasonal and regional variation in the pelagial and its relationship to the life history cycle of krill. In *Antarctic Ecosystems. Ecological Change and Conservation*, ed. K. R. Kerry & G. Hempel, pp. 103–114. Berlin & Heidelberg: Springer-Verlag.

Smith, E. A. & Burton, R. W. (1970). Weddell seals of Signey Island. In *Antarctic Ecology*, Vol. I, ed. M. W. Holdgate, pp. 415–428. London: Academic Press.

Smith, G. A., Nichols, P. D. & White, D. C. (1986). Fatty acid composition and microbial activity of benthic marine sediment from McMurdo Sound, Antarctica. *FEMS Microbial Ecology*, **38**, 219–231.

Smith, G. A., Nichols, P. D. & White, D. C. (1988). Benthic nearshore microbial communities of McMurdo Sound. Paper presented at the Fifth SCAR Symposium on Antarctic Biology, Hobart, Australia, 29 August – 3 September, 1988.

Smith, G. A., Davis, J. D., Muscat, A. M., Moe, R. L. & White, D. C. (1989). Lipid composition and metabolic activities of benthic near-shore microbial communities of Arthur Harbour, Antarctic Peninsula: comparisons with McMurdo Sound. *Polar Biology*, **9**, 517–524.

Smith, J. M. B. & Simpson, R. D. (1970). Biotic zonation on rocky shores of Heard Island. *Polar Biology*, **4**, 89–94.

Smith, M. A. K. & Haschemeyer, A. E. V. (1980). Protein metabolism and cold adaptation in Antarctic fishes. *Physiological Zoology*, **53**, 373–382.

Smith, M. A. K., Mathews, R. W., Hudson, A. P. & Haschemeyer, A. E. V. (1980). Protein metabolism of tropical reef and pelagic fish. *Comparative Biochemistry & Physiology*, **65B**, 415–418.

Smith, M. S. R. (1965). Seasonal movements of the Weddell seal in McMurdo Sound, Antarctica. *Journal of Wildlife Management*, **29**, 464–470.

Smith, N. R., Dong, Z., Kerry, K. R. & Wright, S. (1984). Water circulation in the region of Prydz Bay, Antarctica. *Deep-Sea Research*, **31**, 1121–1147.

Smith, P. E. (1978). Biological effects of ocean variability: Time and space scales of biological response. Rapports et Procès-Verbaux des Reuniones Conseil Permanent International pour Exploration de la Mer, **173**, 117–127.

Smith, R. C. & Baker, K. S. (1982). Assessment of the influence of enhanced UV-B on marine primary productivity. In *The Role of Ultraviolet Radiation in Marine Ecosystems*, ed. J. Catkins, pp. 509–537. New York: Plenum Press.

Smith, R. C., Baker, R. S., Holm-Hansen, O. & Olsen, R. (1980). Photoinhibition of photosynthesis in natural waters. *Photochemistry & Photobiology*, **31**, 385–592.

Smith, R.C., *et al.* (1992). Ozone depletion: ultraviolet radiation and phytoplankton biology in Antarctic waters. *Science*, **255**, 952–959.

Smith, R.E.H., Geider, R.J. & Platt, T. (1984). Microplankton productivity in the oligotrophic ocean. *Nature* (London), **311**, 252–254.

Smith, V. R. (1977). A quantitative description of energy flow and nutrient cycling in the Marion Island terrestial ecosystem. *Polar Record*, **18**, 361–370.

Smith, V. R. (1978). Animal-plant-soil nutrient relationships on Marion Island (subAntarctic). *Oecologia*, **32**, 239–253.

Smith, W. O., Jr, (1987). Phytoplankton dynamics in marginal ice zones. *Oceanography & Marine Biology. Annual Review*, **25**, 11–38.

Smith, W. O., Jr & Kettner, G. (1989). Inorganic nitrogen uptake by phytoplankton in the marginal ice zone of the Fram Strait. *Rapports et Procès-Verbaux des Reuniones Conseil Permanent International pour l'Exploration de la Mer*, **188**, 90–97.

Smith, W. O., Jr & Nelson, D. M. (1985a). Phytoplankton biomass near a receding ice-edge in the Ross Sea. In *Antarctic Nutrient Cycles and Food Webs*, ed. W. R. Siegfried, P. R. Condy & R. M. Laws, pp. 70–77. Berlin & Heidelberg: Springer-Verlag.

Smith, W. O., Jr. & Nelson, D. M. (1985b). Phytoplankton bloom produced by a receding ice edge in the Ross Sea: spatial coherence with the density field. *Science*, **227**, 163–166.

Smith, W. O., Jr. & Nelson, D. M. (1986). The importance of ice edge phytoplankton production in the Southern Ocean. *Bioscience*, **36**, 251–257.

Smith, W. O., Jr. & Nelson, D. M. (1990). Phytoplankton growth and new production in the Weddell Sea marginal ice zone during austral spring and autumn. *Limnology & Oceanography*, **35**, 809–921.

Smith, W. O., Jr. & Sakshaug, E. (1990). Polar phytoplankton. In *Polar Oceanography Part B. Chemistry, Biology and Geology*, ed. W. O. Smith Jr., pp. 477–525. San Diego: Academic Press.

Smith, W. O., Jr, Baummann, M. E., Wilson, D. L. & Aletsee, L. (1987). Phytoplankton biomass and productivity in the marginal ice zone of the Fram Strait during summer 1984. *Journal of Geophysical Research*, **92**, 6777–6786.

Smith, W. O., Jr, Keene, N. K., & Comiso, J. C. (1988). Interannual variability in estimated primary productivity of the Antarctic marginal ice zone. In *Antarctic Ocean and Resources Variability*, ed. D. Sahrhage, pp. 131–139. Berlin & Heidelberg: Springer-Verlag.

Soevik, T. & Braekhan, O. R. (1979). Fluoride in Antarctic krill (*Euphausia superba*) and the Atlantic krill (*Megayctiphanes norvegica*). *Journal of the Fisheries Research Board of Canada*, **36**, 1414–1416.

Solyanik, G. A. (1963). An interesting ichthyological find. *Soviet Antarctic Expedition Information Bulletin*, No. 42.

Solyanik, G. A. (1964). Experiment in marking seals from small ships. *Soviet Antarctic Expedition Information Bulletin*, **5**, 212.

Solyanik, G. A. (1965). Distribution and nutrition of bathypelagic fish *Notolepis coatsi* (Paralepidae Family) *Antarctic Expedition Information Bulletin*, **5**, 365–366.

Solyanik, G. A. (1967). The food of the Antarctic fish (*Electrona Antarctica* Gunth.). *Soviet Antarctic Expedition Information Bulletin*, **6**, 443.

Somero, G. N. (1969). Enzyme mechanisms of temperature compensation: immediate and evolutionary effects of temperature on enzymes of aquatic poikilotherms. *American Naturalist*, **103**, 517–530.

Somero, G. N., Giese, A. C. & Wohlschlag, D. E. (1968). Cold adaption in the Antarctic fish *Trematomus bernacchii*. *Comparative Biochemistry & Physiology*, **26**, 223–233.

Sommer, U. (1989). Maximal growth rates of Antarctic phytoplankton: only weak dependence on cell size. *Limnology & Oceanography*, **34**, 1109–1112.

Sommerville, M. & Billen, G. (1983). A method of determining exoproteolytic activity in natural waters. *Limnology & Oceanography*, **28**, 190–193.

Sondergaard, M. (1989). Release of extracellular organic carbon by phytoplankton: present knowledge and current research. In *Proceedings of Seminar on Phycology and Water Quality to Mark the Retirement of Vivienne Cassie-Cooper*. DSIR Botany Division b, Christchurch, New Zealand Newsletter Supplement No. 6, p. 12.

SooHoo, J. B., Palmisano, A. C., Lizotte, M. P., Kottmeier, S. T., SooHoo, S. L. & Sullivan, C. W. (1987). Spectral light absorption and quantum yield of photosynthesis in sea ice microalgae and a bloom of *Phaeocystis pouchetii* from McMurdo Sound, Antarctica. *Marine Ecology Progress Series*, **39**, 175–189.

Soot-Ryen, T. (1951). Antarctic Pelecypods. *Scientific Research Norwegian Antarctic Expedition 1927–1928*, **3**, 1–46.

Sorokin, Yu. I. (1971). On the role of bacteria in the productivity of tropical oceanic waters. *Internationale Revue der Gesamte Hydrobiologie und Hydrographie*, **56**, 1–48.

Sorokin, Yu. I. (1981). Microheterotrophic organisms in marine ecosystems. In *Analysis of Marine Ecosystems*, ed. A. R. Longhurst, pp. 293–342. New York: Academic Press.

Sorokin, Yu. I. (1982). The role of microheterotrophs in the functioning of marine ecosystems. *Uspekhi Sovremennoi Biologii*, **93**, 236–252.

Sorokin, Yu. I. & Federov, V. K. (1978). Classification of bacterioplankton in Antarctic waters. *Trudy IOAN SSSR*, **112**, 69–75.

Sorokin, Yu. I. & Kogelschatz, J. E. (1979). Analysis of heterotrophic microplankton in an upwelling area. *Hydrobiologia*, **66**, 195–208.

Sorokin, Yu. I. & Mikleev, V. N. (1979). On the characteristics of Peruvian upwelling system. *Hydrobiologica*, **62**, 165–189.

Sosinski, J. & Kuranty, J. (1979). Morze Scotia-nowy nejon Polowow ryb Polskiego Rybolowstwa. *Technikai Gospodarka Morska*, **29**, 12–15.

Sosinski, J. & Sikora, K. (1977). Wyniki baden ichtiologicznych prowadzonych na MT *Gemini* w czasie II. Polskiej Ekspedycji Antarkycznei. *Biuletyn Morskiego Institutu Rybackiago*, **43**, 23–29.

Soutar, A. & Isaacs, J. D. (1974). Abundance of pelagic fish during the 19th and 20th centuries as recorded in anaerobic sediments off California. *Fisheries Bulletin, NOAA. US Department of Commerce*, **72**, 257–275.

South, G. R. (1979). Biogeography of benthic marine algae of the Southern Oceans. In *Proceedings of the International Symposium on Marine Biogeography and Evolution in the Southern Hemisphere,* Vol. I, pp. 85–108. Wellington: NZ DSIR Information Series 137.

Southern Ocean Convention Workshop (1980). *Southern Ocean Convention Workshop on the Management of Antarctic Marine Living Resources 1980: Report and Recommendations*. Washington, DC: The Centre for Environmental Education – The Whale Protection Fund. 36 pp.

Spies, A. (1987). Growth rates of Antarctic marine phytoplankton in the Weddell Sea. *Marine Ecology Progress Series*, **41**, 267–274.

Spindler, M. & Dieckmann, G. S. (1986). Distribution and abundance of the plantic Foraminifera *Neogloboquadrina pachyderma* in sea ice of the Weddell Sea (Antarctica). *Polar Biology*, **5**, 185–191.

Spiridonov, V. A., Gruzov, E. N. & Pushkin, A. F. (1985). Issledovaniia stai antarkicheskoi *Euphausia superba* (Crustacea: Euphausiacea) pod l'dom. (Investigations of schools of Antarctic *Euphausia superba* under the ice. *Zoologicheskii Zhurnal*, **64**, 1655–1660.

Spurr, E. B. (1975). The breeding of the Adélie penguin *Pygoscelis adeliae* at Cape Bird. *Ibis*, **117**, 324–338.

Squire, V. A. (1987). The physical oceanography and sea ice characteristics of the Southern Ocean. In *Primer Symposium Espanol de Estudios Antarcticos, Pama de Mallorca, 30 June-July 1985*, pp. 201–226

Squires, H. J. (1957). Squid *Illex illecebrosus* (Le Sueur) in the Newfoundland fishery area. *Journal of the Fisheries Research Board of Canada*, **14**, 693–728.

Stahl, J. C., Jouventin, P., Mougin, J. L., Roux, J. P. & Weimerskirch, H. (1985). The foraging zones of seabirds in the Crozet Islands sector of the Southern Ocean. In *Antarctic Nutrient Cycles and Food Webs*, ed. W. R. Siegfried, P. R. Condy & R. M. Laws, pp. 479–486. Berlin & Heidelberg: Springer-Verlag.

Stasenko, V. D. (1967). Determining the national krill fishing methods and the commercial effectiveness of the chosen fishing gear. In *Soviet Fishery Research on Antarctic krill*, ed. A.V. Burikovski, pp. 61–78. Washington, DC: US Department of Commerce. (Translated from Russian.)

Steele, J. H. (1974). *The Structure of Marine Ecosystems*. Cambridge, MA: Harvard University Press.

Steeman-Nielsen, E. (1952). The use of radio-active carbon for measuring organic production in the sea. *Journal du Conseil International pour l'Exploration de la Mer*, **18**, 287–295.

Steen, J. B. & Berg, T. (1966). The gills of two species of haemoglobin-free fishes compared to those of other teleosts – with a note on severe anaemia in an eel. *Comparative Biochemistry & Physiology*, **18,** 517–526.

Stein, M. (1988). Variation of geostropic circulation off the Antarctic Peninsula and in the southwest Scotia Sea. In *Antarctic Ocean and Resources Variability*, ed. D. Sahrhage, pp. 81–91. Berlin & Heidelberg: Springer-Verlag.

Stepnik, R. (1982). All-year population studies of Euphausiacea (Crustacea) in Admiralty Bay (King George Island, South Shetland Islands, Antarctica). *Polish Polar Research*, **31**, 53–72.

Steyeart, J. (1973). Distribution of planktonic diatoms along an African-Antarctic transect. *Investigacion Pesquera*, **37**, 295–328.

Stirling, I. (1965). The seals at White Island: A hypothesis on their origin. *Antarctica*, **4**, 310–313.

Stirling, I. (1969a). Ecology of the Weddell Seal in McMurdo Sound, Antarctica. *Ecology*, **50**, 573–586.

Stirling, I. (1969b). Tooth wear as a mortality factor in the Weddell seal *Leptonychotes weddelli*. *Journal of Mammology*, **50**, 559–565.

Stirling, I. (1969c). Distribution and abundance of the Weddell seal in the western Ross Sea, Antarctica. *New Zealand Journal of Marine and Freshwater Research*, **3**, 191–200.

Stirling, I. (1971a). Population dynamics of the Weddell seal (*Leptonychotes wedelli*) in McMurdo Sound. In *Antarctic Pinnipedia. Antarctic Research Series*, Vol. 18, ed. W. H. Burt, pp. 141–161. Washington, DC: American Geophysical Union.

Stirling, I. (1971b). Population aspects of Weddell seal harvesting at McMurdo Sound, Antarctica. *Polar Record*, **15**, 653–667.

Stirling, I (1972). Regulation of numbers of an apparently isolated population of Weddell seals (*Leptonychnotes weddelli*). *Journal of Mammology*, **53**, 107–115.

Stirling, I. (1975). Factors affecting the evolution of social behaviour in the pinnipedia. *Rapports et Procès-Verbaux des Reunios Conseil Permanent International pour l'Exploration de la Mer*, **169**, 205–212.

Stirling, I. (1980). The biological significance of polynas in the Canadian Arctic. *Arctic*, **33**, 303–315.

Stirling, I & Cleator, H. (eds) (1981). *Polynas in the Canadian Arctic*. Ottawa: Canadian Wildlife Service Occasional Paper No. 45. 70 pp.

Stockner, J. G. (1988). Phototrophic picoplankton: an overview from marine and freshwater ecosystems. *Limnology & Oceanography*, **33**, 765–775.

Stockner, J. G. & Anita, N. J. (1986). Algal picoplankton from marine and freshwater ecosystems: a multidisciplinary perspective. *Canadian Journal of Fisheries and Aquatic Sciences*, **43**, 2472–2503.

Stoeckner, D. K., Michaels, A. E. & Davis, L. H. (1987). Large proportion of marine planktonic ciliates found to contain functional chloroplasts. *Nature (London)*, **326**, 790–792.

Stoeckner, D. K., Silver, M. W., Michaels, A. E. & Davis, L. H. (1988). Obligate mixotrophy in *Labaea strobila,* a ciliate which retains chloroplasts. *Marine Biology*, **99**, 415–423.

Stone, H. S. & Siniff, D. B. (1983). Leopard seal feeding and food consumption in Antarctic spring and summer. In *Proceedings of the Fourth Biennial Conference on Biology of Marine Mammals, December 14–18*, pp. 14–18.

Stonehouse, B. (1963). Observations on Adélie penguins at Cape Royds, Antarctica. *Proceedings of the 13th International Ornithological Congress*, pp. 766–779.

Stonehouse, B. (1964). Bird life. In *Antarctic Research*, ed. R. J. Adie & G. deQ. Robin, pp. 219–239. London: Butterworths.

Stonehouse, B. (1967). The general ecology and thermal balance of penguins. *Advances in Ecological Research*, **4**, 131–196.

Stonehouse, B. (1970). Adaptation in polar and subpolar penguins. In *Antarctic Ecology,* Vol. I, ed. M. W. Holdgate, pp. 526–541. London: Academic Press.

Stonehouse, B. (1982). La zonation ecologique sur les hautes latitudes australes. *CNFRA*, **51**, 531–536.

Stonehouse, B. (1985). Birds and mammals – penguins. In *Key Environments ... Antarctica*, ed. W. N. Bonner, pp. 266–292. Oxford: Pregamon Press.

Stout, W. E. & Shabica, S. V. (1970). Marine ecological studies at Palmer Station and vicinity. *Antarctic Journal of the United States*, **5**, 134–135.

Strange, I. J. (1980). The thin-billed prion, *Pachyptila belcheri*, at New Island, Falkland Islands. *Gerfaut*, **70**, 411–445.

Stretch, T. J., Hamner, P. P., Hamner, W. M., Michel, W. C., Cook, J. & Sullivan, C. W. (1988). Foraging behaviour of Antarctic krill *Euphausia superba* on sea-ice microalgae. *Marine Ecology Progress Series*, **44**, 131–139.

Studentsky, S. (1967). Foreword. In *Soviet Research on Antarctic Krill*, ed. R. N. Burkovskii, pp. 2–4. Washington, DC: Clearing House for Federal Scientific and Technical Information, Translation No. TT 367–32683.

Sullivan, C. W. (1985). Sea ice bacteria: reciprocal interactions of the organisms and their environment. In *Sea Ice Biota*, ed. R. A. Horner, pp. 159–171. Boca Raton, FL: CRC Press.

Sullivan, C. W. & Palmisano, A. C. (1981). Sea-ice microbial commumities in McMurdo Sound. *Antarctic Journal of the United States*, **16**, 126–127.

Sullivan, C. W. & Palmisano, A. C. (1984). Sea ice microbial communities: Distribution, abundance and diversity of ice bacteria in McMurdo Sound, Antarctica in 1980. *Applied & Environmental Microbiology*, **April 1984**, 788–795.

Sullivan, C. W., Palmisano, A. C., Kottmeier, S. & Moe, R. (1982). Development of the sea ice microbial community in McMurdo Sound. *Antarctic Journal of the United States*, **18**(5), 155–157.

Sullivan, C. W., Palmisano, A. C. & Soohoo, J. B. (1984). Influence of sea ice and sea ice biota on downwelling irradiance and spectral composition of light in McMurdo Sound. *International Society for Optical Engineering Proceedings, 489, Ocean Optics*, **7**, 159–165.

Sullivan, C. W., Palmisano, A. C., Kottmeier, S., Grossi, S. McG. & Moe, R. (1985). The influence of light on growth and development of the sea-ice microbial community of McMurdo Sound. In *Antarctic Nutrient Cycles and Food Webs*, ed. W. R. Siegfried, P. R. Condy & R. M. Laws, pp. 78–83. Berlin Heidelberg: Springer-Verlag.

Sullivan, C. W., McClain, C. R., Comiso, J. C. & Smith, W. O., Jr. (1988). Phytoplankton standing crops with an Antarctic ice edge assessed by satellite remote sensing. *Journal of Geophysical Research*, **93**, 12487–12498.

Sullivan, C. W., Cota, G. F., Krempin, D. W. & Smith, W.O., Jr. (1990). Distribution and activity of bacterioplankton in the marginal ice zone of the Weddell–Scotia Sea during austral spring. *Marine Ecology Progress Series*, **63**, 239–252.

Suskin, V. A. (1985). Planktonnye soobshcjestva antarkticheskoi chasti Atlantiki. In *Biologicheskie Osnovy Promyslovogo Osvoeniia Otkrytykh Rainov Okeana*, ed. M. E. Vinogradov & M. V. Flint, pp. 29–39. Moscow: Nauka.

Sverdrup, H. U. (1953). On conditions for the vernal blooming of phytoplankton. *Journal du Conseil, Conseil Permanent International pour l'Exploration de la Mer*, **18**, 287–295.

Sverdrup, H. E., Johnson, M. W. & Fleming, R. H. (1942). *The Oceans: Their Physics, Chemistry and General Biology*. Englewood Cliffs, NJ: Prentice-Hall.

Svetlov, M. F. (1978). The porbeagle *Lamma nasus* in Atlantic waters. *Journal of Ichthyology*, **18**, 850–851.

Swithinbank, C., McClain, P. & Little, P. (1977). Drift tracks of Antarctic icebergs. *Polar Record*, **18**, 495–501.

Taguchi, S. & Fukuchi, M. (1975). Filtration rate of zooplankton community during spring bloom in Akkeshi Bay. *Journal of Experimental Marine Biology & Ecology*, **19**, 145–164.

Takahashi, E. (1981). Loricate and scale-bearing protists from Lutzow-Holm Bay, Antarctica. I. Species of Acanthoecidae and Centrohelida found at a site selected on fast ice. *Antarctic Record*, **73**, 1–22.

Takahashi, E. (1987). Loricate and scale-bearing protists from Lutzow-Holm Bay, Antarctica. II. Four marine species of *Paraphysomonas* (Chrysophyceae) including two new species from the fast-ice covered coastal area. *Japanese Journal of Phycology*, **35**, 155–166.

Takahashi, M. (1983). Trophic ecology of demersal fish community north of the South Shetland Islands with note on the ecological role of krill. *Memoirs National Institute of Polar Research, Special Issue*, **27**, 183–192.

Takahashi, M. & Bienfang, P. K. (1983). Size structure of phytoplankton in subtropical waters. *Marine Biology*, **76**, 203–211.

Takahashi, M. & Nemoto, T. (1984). Food of some Antarctic fish in the Western Ross Sea in the summer of 1979. *Polar Biology*, **3**, 237–239.

Taljaard, J. J., *et al.* (1969, 1971). *Climate of the Upper Air. Part 1. Southern Hemisphere*. Washington: US National Center for Atmospheric Research.

Tande, K. S. & Bamstedt, U. (1987). On the trophic fate of *Phaeocystis pouchetii*. I. Copepod feeding rates on solitary cells and colonies of *P. pouchetii*. *Sarsia*, **72**, 313–320.

Taniguchi, A., Hamada, E., Okazaki, M. & Naito, Y. (1986). Distribution of phytoplankton chlorophyll continuously recorded in JARE-25 cruise to Syowa Station, Antarctica (SIBEX I). *Proceedings of the Eighth Symposium on Polar Biology, 1985. Memoirs National Institute of Polar Research, Special Issue*, **44**, 3–14.

Tanimura, A. (1981). Distribution of chlorophyll *a* along the course of the *Fuji* to and from Antarctica in 1979–1980. *Antarctic Record*, **72**, 35–48.

Tanimura, A., Minoda, T., Fukuchi, M., Hoshiai, T. & Oktsuka, H. (1984). Swarm of *Paralabidocera antarctica* (Calanoida, Copepoda) under sea ice near Syowa Station, Antarctica. *Antarctic Record*, **82**, 12–19.

Tanimura, A., Fukuchi, M. & Hoshiai, T. (1986). Seasonal changes in the abundance and species composition of copepods in the ice-covered sea near Syowa Station, Antarctica. *Memoirs National Institute of Polar Research, Special Issue*, **40**, 212–220.

Tanoue, E. (1985). Organic chemical composition of fecal pellet of the krill *Euphausia superba* Dana. I. Lipid composition. *Tokyo University of Fisheries Transactions*, **6**, 125–134.

Tanoue, E. & Handa, N. (1980). Vertical transport of organic materials in the northern Pacific as determined by sediment trap experiment. Part 1. Fatty acid composition. *Journal of the Oceanographic*

Society of Japan, **36**, 231–235.

Tanoue, E. & Hara, S. (1986). Ecological implications of fecal pellets produced by the Antarctic krill *Euphausia superba* in the Antarctic Ocean. *Marine Biology*, **91**, 359–369.

Tanoue, E., Handa, N. & Sakugawa, H. (1982). Difference of the chemical composition of organic matter between fecal pellet of *Euphausia superba* and its feed *Dunaliella tertiolecta*. *Tokyo University of Fisheries Transactions*, **5**, 189–196.

Tanoue, E., Zenimoto, M., Komaki, Y. & Handa, N. (1986). Distribution of particulate inorganic materials in the Pacific and Indian sectors of the Antarctic Ocean in the austral summer. *Memoirs National Institute of Polar Research, Special Issue*, **40**, 380–394.

Targett, T. (1981). Trophic ecology and structure of coastal Antarctic fish communities. *Marine Ecology Progress Series*, **4**, 243–263.

Tarpy, C. (1979). Killer whale attack. *National Geographic Magazine*, **155**, 542–545.

Tarverdiyera, M. I. (1982). The food consumption, daily ration and feeding habits of the ice fish *Champsocephalus gunnari* Lonnberg of the South Orkneys. In *Characteristics of the Pelagic Community from the Sea of Scotia and Adjacent Waters*, pp. 69–76. Moscow: Trudy VIRNO.

Tarverdiyera, M. I. & Pinskaya, I. A. (1980). The feeding of fishes of the families Nototheniidae and Channichthyidae on the shelves of the Antarctic Peninsula and the South Shetland Islands. *Journal of Ichthyology*, **20**, 50–60.

Taylor, G. T. (1982). The role of pelagic heterotrophic protozoa in nutrient cycling: a review. *Annales de l'Institut Oceanographique*, **58**, 227–241.

Taylor, G. T., Iturriaga, R. & Sullivan, C. W. (1985). Interactions of bactivorous grazers and heterotrophic bacteria with dissolved organic matter. *Marine Ecology Progress Series*, **23**, 129–141.

Taylor, R. H., Wilson, P. R. & Thomas, B. W. (1990). Status and trends of Adélie penguin populations in the Ross Sea Region. *Polar Record*, **26**, 293–304.

Taylor, R. H. (1962). The Adélie penguin *Pygoscelis adeliae* at Cape Royds. *Ibis*, **104**, 176–204.

Tayor, R. J. F. (1957). An unusual record of three species of whale being restricted to pools in Antarctic sea ice. *Journal of Zoology*, **129**, 325–331.

Tchernia, P. (1974). Étude de la derive antarctique Est-Quest au moyen d'icebergs suivi par la satellite. *Comptes Rendus Academie des Sciences (Paris)*, **278**, 667–670.

Tchernia, P. (1980). *Descriptive Physical Oceanography*. Oxford: Pergamon Press. 253 pp.

Tchernia, P. & Jeannin, P. F. (1984). Circulation in Antarctic waters as revealed by iceberg tracks 1972–83. *Polar Record*, **22**, 263–269.

Tenaza, R. (1971). Behaviour and nesting success relative to nest location in Adélie penguin (*Pygoscelis adeliae*). *Condor*, **73**, 81–92.

Terazaki, M. (1989). Distribution of chaetognaths in the Australian sector of the southern ocean during BIOMASS SIBEX Cruise (KH-83–4). *Proceedings of the National Institute of Polar Research Symposium on Polar Biology*, **2**, 51–60.

Terazaki, M. & Wada, M. (1986). Euphausiids collected from the Australian Sector of the Southern Ocean during BIOMASS SIBEX Cruise (KH-83-4). *Memoirs National Institute of Polar Research, Special Issue*, **40**, 97–109.

Testa, J. W. (1987). Long-term reproductive patterns and sighting bias in Weddell seals (*Leptonychotes weddelli*). *Canadian Journal of Zoology*, **65**, 1991–1999

Testa, J. W. & Siniff, D. B. (1987). Population dynamics of Weddell seals (*Leptonychotes weddelli*) in McMurdo Sound. *Ecological Monographs*, **57**, 149–165.

Testa, J. W., Siniff, D. B., Ross, M. J. & Winter, J. D. (1985). Dynamics of Weddell seal–Antarctic cod interactions in McMurdo Sound, Antarctica. In *Antarctic Nutrient Cycles and Food Webs*, ed. W. R. Siegfried, P. R. Condy & R. M. Laws, pp. 561–565. Berlin &

Heidelberg: Springer-Verlag.

Thomas, G. (1982). The food and feeding ecology of the light-mantled sooty albatross at South Georgia. *Emu*, **82**, 92–100.

Thomas, J. A. & DeMaster, D. P. (1983). Parameters affecting survival of Weddell seal pups (*Leptonychotes weddelli*) to weaning. *Canadian Journal of Zoology*, **61**, 2078–2083.

Thomas, P. B. & Green, K. (1988). Distribution of *Euphausia crystallorophias* within Prydz Bay and its importance to inshore the marine ecosystem. *Polar Biology*, **8**, 327–331.

Thomas, P. B. & Jiang, J. (1986). Epiphytic diatoms of the inshore marine areas near Davis Station. *Hydrobiologia*, **140**, 193–198.

Thorson, G. (1950). Reproductive and larval ecology of marine bottom invertebrates. *Biological Reviews*, **25**, 1–45.

Throndsen, J. (1973). Motility in some marine nanoplankton flagellates. *Norwegian Journal of Zoology*, **21**, 193–200.

Thurston, M. H. (1972). The crustacean amphipoda of Signey Island, South Orkney Islands. *British Antarctic Survey Scientific Report No. 71*. 127 pp.

Tickell, W. L. N. (1967). Movements of the black-browed and grey-headed albatrosses in the South Atlantic. *Emu*, **66**, 357–367.

Tickell, W. L. N. (1968). The biology of the great albatrosses *Diomedea exulans* and *Diomedea epomophora*. In *Antarctic Bird Studies*, ed. O. L. Austin, Jr., *Antarctic Research Series* Vol. 12. pp. 1–55.

Tikhomirov, E. A. (1975). Biology of the ice forms of seals in the Pacific section of the Antarctic. *Rapports Procès-Verboux des Renunions Conceil International Pour l'Exploration de la Mer*, **169**, 409–412.

Tilzer, M. M. & Dubinsky, Z. (1987). Effects of temperature and day length on the mass balance of Antarctic phytoplankton. *Polar Biology*, **7**, 35–42.

Tilzer, M. M., Bodungen, B. von & Smetacek, V. (1985). Light-dependence of photosynthesis in the Antarctic Ocean: Implications for regulatory productivity. In *Antarctic Nutrient Cycles and Food Webs*, ed. W. R. Siegfried, P. R. Condy & R. M. Laws, pp. 60–69. Berlin & Heidelberg: Springer-Verlag.

Tilzer, M. M., Elbracher, M., Geiskes, W. W. & Beeze, B. (1986). Light-temperature interactions in the control of photosynthesis in Antarctic phytoplankton. *Polar Biology*, **5**, 105–111.

Tomlin, A. G. (1967). *Cetacea, Mammals of the USSR and Adjacent Countries*. (Israel Program for Scientific Translations, Jerusalem).

Torres, J. J, Lancraft, T. M., Weigle, B. L. & Hopkins, T. L. (1984). Distribution and abundance of fishes and salps in relation to the marginal ice zone of the Scotia Sea, November and December, 1983. *Antarctic Journal of the United States*, **19**(5), 117–119.

Torres, J. J., Hopkins, T. L., Lancraft, T. M. & Donnelly, J. (1989). AMERIEZ 1988: aspects of the ecology and physiology of zooplankton and micronekton in the vicinity of the winter ice edge. *Antarctic Journal of the United States* **24**, 163–164.

Townsend, C. H. (1935). The distribution of certain whales as shown by logbook records of American whale ships. *Zoologica (New York)*, **19**, 1–50.

Tranter, D. J. (1982). Interlinking of physical and biological processes in the Antarctic Ocean. *Oceanography & Marine Biology Annual Reviews*, **20**, 11–35.

Treshnikov, A. F. (1964). Surface water circulation in the Antarctic Ocean. *Information Bulletin Soviet Antarctic Expedition*, **45**, 81–83.

Treshnikov, A. F., Alekseyev, G. V., Sarukanyan. E. I. & Smirnov, N. P. (1978). Water circulation in the Southern Ocean. *Trudy Arktichskii Naucho-issle-dovatel'skii Institut*, 345, 24–28. (English translation Scipton Publishing Co., Washington, DC , pp. 21–35.)

Tressler, W. L. & Ommundsen, A. M. (1962). *Seasonal Oceanographic Studies in McMurdo Sound, Antarctica*. US Navy Hydrographic Office Technical Report 125. 141 pp.

Trillmich, F. (1978). Feeding territories and breeding success of south polar skuas. *Auk*, **95**, 23–33.

Trimble, A. M. & Harris, G. P. (1984). Phytoplankton population dynamics of a small reservoir: use of sediment traps to quantify the loss of diatoms and recruitment of summer bloom-forming blue-green algae. *Journal of Plankton Research*, **6**, 897–917.

Trivelpiece, W. Z. & Volkman, N. J. (1982). Feeding strategies of synpatric polar (*Catharacta maccormicki*) and brown skuas (*C. longbergi*). *Ibis*, **124**, 50–54.

Trivelpiece, W. Z., Butler, R. G. & Volkman, N. J. (1980). Feeding territories of brown skuas (*Catharacta lonnbergi*). *Auk*, **97**, 669–676.

Trivelpiece, W. Z., Bengtson, J. L., Trivelpiece, S. G. & Volkman, N. J. (1986). Foraging behaviour of gentoo and chinstrap penguins as determined by radiotelemetry techniques. *Auk*, **103**, 771–781.

Trivelpiece, W. Z., Trivelpiece, S. G., Guepel, G. R., Kjelmyr, J. & Volkman, N. J. (1990). Adélie and chinstrap penguins: their potential as monitors of Southern Ocean marine ecosystems. In *Antarctic Ecosystems, Ecological Change and Conservation*, ed. K. R. Kerry & G. Hempel, pp. 191–202. Berlin & Heidelberg: Springer-Verlag.

Truesdale, R. S. & Kellog, T. B. (1979). Ross Sea diatoms: modern assemblage distributions and their relationship to ecologic, oceanographic, and sedimentary conditions. *Marine Micropaleontology*, **4**, 13–31.

Tucker, M. J. & Burton, H. R. (1990). Seasonal and spatial variations in the zooplankton community of an eastern Antarctic coastal location. *Polar Biology*, **10**, 571–579.

Turbott, E. G. (1952). Seals of the southern ocean. In *Antarctica Today*, ed. F. A. Simpson, pp. 195–215. Wellington: Reed.

Turner, J. T. (1977). Sinking rates of fecal pellets from marine copepod *Pontella meadii*. *Marine Biology*, **40**, 249–259.

Twelves, E. L. (1972). Blood volumes of two Antarctic fishes. *British Antarctic Survey Bulletin*, **31**, 85–92.

Tyler, J. C. (1960). Erythrocyte counts and haemoglobin determinations for two Antarctic Nototheniid fishes. *Stanford Ichthylolgical Bulletin*, **7**, 199–201.

Uribe, E. (1982). Influence of the phytoplankton and primary production of the Antarctic waters in relationships with the distribution and behaviour of krill. *Instituto Antarctico Chileno, Scientific Series*, **28**, 147–163.

Uschakov, P. V. (1963). Quelques particularités de al bionomie benthique de l'Antarctique de l'est. *Cashiers de Biologie Marine*, **4**, 81–89.

van Aarde, R. J. & Pascel, M. (1980). Marking southern elephant seals on Isles Kerguelen. *Polar Record*, **20**, 62–65.

Van Andel, T. H. & Moore, T. C., Jr. (1974). Cenozoic calcium carbonate distribution and calcite compensation depth in the central equatorial Pacific Ocean. *Geology*, **2**, 87–92.

Vanhoeffen, E. (1902). Van der deutschen Sudpolar expedition Fischereiversuche. *Petermans geographische Mitteilungen Erganzungschaft*, **47**, 19–20.

van Loon, H. & Shea, D. J. (1987). The Southern Oscillation. Part VI. Anomalies of sea level pressure on the southern Hemisphere and on Pacific sea surface temperature during the development of warm event. *Monthly Weather Review* **115**, 370–379.

Vaqué, D., Duarte, C. M. & Marrasé, C. (1989). Phytoplankton colonization by bacteria encounter probability as a limiting factor. *Marine Ecology Progress Series*, **54**, 137–140.

Vargo, G. A., Fanning, K., Heil, C. & Bell, L. (1986) Growth rates and the salinity response on an Antarctic ice microflora community. *Polar Biology*, **5**, 241–247.

Veit, R. R. & Braun, B. M. (1984). Hydrographic fronts and marine bird distribution in the Antarctic and sub-Antarctic. *Antarctic Journal of the United States*, **19**(5), 165–167.

Veldhuis, M. J. W. & Admiraal, W. (1985). Transfer of photosynthetic products in gelatinous colonies of *Phaeocystis pouchetii* (Haptophyceae) and its effect on the measurement of excretion rate. *Marine Ecology Progress Series*, **26**, 301–304.

Verity, P. G. (1986). Grazing of phytotrophic nanoplankton by microzooplankton in Narragansett Bay. *Marine Ecology Progress Series*, **29**, 105–115.

Vernet, M., Mitchell, B. G. & Holm-Hansen, O. (1989). UV radiation in Antarctic waters: response of phytoplankton pigments. *Antarctic Journal of the United States*, **23**, 181–183.

Vervoort, W. (1957). Copepods from Antarctic and sub-Antarctic plankton samples. *Report of the B.A.N.Z. Antarctic Research Expedition*, **3**, 1–150.

Vincent, W. F. (1988). *Microbial Ecosystems of Antarctica*. Cambridge: Cambridge University Press. 304 pp.

Vinogradov, M. E. & Naumov, A. G. (1958). Quantitative distribution of plankton in Antarctic waters of the Indian and Pacific oceans. *Information Bulletin Soviet Antarctic Expedition*, **1**, 110–112.

Voisin, J-F. (1972). Notes on the behaviour of the killer whale, *Orcinus orca* (L.). *Nytt Magasin for Zoology*, **20**, 93–96.

Voisin, J-F. (1976). On the behaviour of the killer whale, *Orcinus orca* (L.). *Nytt Magasin for Zoology*, **24**, 69–71.

Volkman, N. J. & Trivelpiece, W. (1981). Nest-site selection among Adélie, chinstrap and gentoo penguins in mixed species rookeries. *Wilson Bulletin*, **93**, 243–248.

Volkman, N. J., Presler, P. & Trivelpiece, W. (1980). Diets of pygoscelid penguins at King George Island, Antarctica. *Condor*, **82**, 373–378.

Volkovinskii, V.V. (1966). Studies on primary production in the waters of the Southern Ocean. *Abstracts of Papers Presented at the Second International Oceanology Congress (Moscow), 1966.* pp. 386–387.

Voous, K. H. (1965). Antarctic birds. In *Biogeography and Ecology in Antarctica*, ed. J. van Meighem & P. van Oye, pp. 649–689. The Hague: Dr W. Junk Publishers.

Voronina, N. M. (1966). Distribution of zooplankton biomass in the Southern Ocean. *Oceanology*, **6**, 836–846.

Voronina, N. M. (1968). The distribution of zooplankton in the Southern Ocean and its dependence on the circulation of water. *Sarsia*, **34**, 264–277.

Voronina, N. M. (1969). Plankton of the Southern Ocean. In *Atlas of the Antarctica*, Vol. 2, pp. 496–505. Leningrad: Gidrometizdat..

Voronina, N. M. (1970). Seasonal cycles of some common Antarctic copepod species. In *Antarctic Ecology*, Vol. 1, ed. M. W. Holdgate, pp. 161–172. London & New York: Academic Press.

Voronina, N. M. (1971). Annual cycle of Antarctic plankton (in Russian). In *Fundamentals of the Biological productivity of the Ocean and Its Exploitation*, ed. V. Beklemishev, pp. 64–71. Moscow: Nauka.

Voronina, N. M. (1972). Vertical structure of a pelagic community in the Antarctica. *Oceanology (Okeanologiya)*, **12**, 415–420.

Voronina, N. M. (1974). An attempt at a functional analysis of the distributional range of *Euphausia superba*. *Marine Biology*, **24**, 347–352.

Voronina, N. M. (1978). Variability of ecosystems. In *Advances in Oceanography*, ed. H. Charnock & G. E. R. Deacon, pp. 221–243. New York: Plenum Press.

Voronina, N.M. (1984). *Pelagic Ecosystems of the Southern Ocean.* (*Ekosistemy pelagiali Iuzhnoga okeana.*) Moscow: Nuaka. 206 pp. (In Russian.)

Voronina, N. M., Memshutkin, V. V. & Tsetlin, V. B. (1979). Mathematical simulation of the space-time distribution and age structure of a population of Antarctic copepods. *Oceanology (Okeanologiya)*, **19**, 122–131.

Voronina, N. M., Memshutkin, V. V. & Tseytlin, V. B. (1980a). Production of an abundant species of copepod, *Calanus acutus*. *Oceanology (Okeanologiya)*, **20**, 137–141.

Voronina, N. M., Memshutkin, V. V. & Tseytlin, V. B. (1980b). Model investigations of an annual cycle of the abundant species *Rhincalanus gigas* and an estimate of its production in the Antarctica. *Oceanology (Okeanologiya)*, **20**, 709–713.

Voronina, N. M., Memshutkin, V. V & Tsetlin, V. B. (1981). Secondary production in the pelagic layer of the Antarctica. *Oceanology (Okeanologiya)*, **20**, 714–715.

Vosjan, J. H., Dohler, G. & Nieuwland, G. (1990). Effect of UV-B irradiance on the ATP content of microorganisms of the Weddell Sea (Antarctica). *Netherlands Journal of Sea Research*, **25**, 391–393.

Voss, G. L. (1973). Cephalopod resources of the world. *FAO Fisheries Circular*, **149**, 75.

Voytek, M. A. (1990). Addressing the biological effects of decreased ozone on the Antarctic environment. *Ambio*, **19**, 52–61.

Wadhams, P. (1983). A mechanisms for the formation of ice edge bands. *Journal of Geophysical Research*, **88**, 2813–2818.

Wadhams, P. & Squire, V. (1983). An ice-water vortex at the edge of the East Greenland Current. *Journal of Geophysical Research*, **88**, 2770–2780.

Waghorn, E. J. (1979). Two species of copepoda from White Island, Antarctica. *New Zealand Journal of Marine & Freshwater Research*, **13**, 459–470.

Waghorn, E. J. & Knox, G. A. (1989). Summer tide-crack zooplankton at White Island, McMurdo Sound, Antarctica. *New Zealand Journal of Marine & Freshwater Research*,

Wakatsuchi, M. (1982). Seasonal variations in water structure under the fast ice near Syowa Station. *Antarctic Record*, **74**, 85–105.

Walsh, J. J. (1971). Relative importance of habitat variables in predicting the distribution of phytoplankton at the ecotone of the Antarctic upwelling ecosystem. *Ecological Monographs*, **41**, 291–309.

Walsh, J. J. (1978). The biological consequences of interaction of the climatic El Nino and event scales of variability in eastern tropical Pacific. *Rapports et Procès-Verbaux des Renunions Conseil Permanent International pour l'Exploration de la Mer*, **173**, 182–192.

Walton, D. W. H. (1977). Radiation and soil temperature 1972–74 Signey Island terrestrial reference site. *British Antarctic Survey Data*, 1, 1–51.

Warham, J. (1963). The rockhopper penguin, *Eudyptes chrysocome*, at Macquarie Island. *Auk*, **80**, 229–256

Warham, J. (1971). Aspects of the breeding behaviour in the royal penguin (*Eudyptes chrysolophus schlegeli*). *Notornis*, **18**, 91–115.

Warham, J. (1972). Aspects of the biology of the erect-crested penguin, *Eudyptes sclateri*. *Ardea*, **60**, 145184.

Warham, J. (1974). The breeding biology and behaviour of the Snares crested penguin. *Journal of the Royal Society of New Zealand*, **4**, 63–108.

Wassman, P., Vernet, M, Mitchell, B. G. & Rey, F. (1990). Mass sedimentation of *Phaeocystis pouchetii* in the Barents Sea. *Marine Ecology Progress Series*, **66**, 183–195.

Watanabe, K. (1982). Centric diatom communities found in Antarctic sea ice. *Antarctic Record*, **74**, 119–126.

Watanabe, K. (1988). Sub-ice microalgal strands in the Antarctic coastal fast ice near Syowa Station. *Japanese Journal of Phycology*, **36**, 221–229.

Watanabe, K. & Nakajima, Y. (1982). Vertical distribution of chlorophyll *a* along 45° E in the southern ocean, 1981. *Memoirs National Institute of Polar Research, Special Issue*, **23**, 73–86.

Watanabe, K. & Satoh, H. (1987). Seasonal variations of ice algal standing crop near Syowa Station, East Antarctica in 1984/84. *Bulletin of the Plankton Society of Japan*, **34**, 143–164.

Watanabe, K., Nakajima, Y & Naito, Y. (1982). Higashi Onguru-to engan de no hyoka sensui chosa hokoku (SCUBA ice diving along the coast of East Ongul Island, Antarctica). *Nankyoku Shiryo (Antarctic Record)*, **75**, 75–92.

Watanabe, K., Satoh, H. & Hoshiai, T. (1990). Seasonal variation in ice algal assemblages in the fist ice near Syowa Station in 1983/84. In *Antarctic Ecosystem: Ecological Change and Conservation*, ed. K. R. Kerry & G. Hempel, pp. 136–142. Berlin & Heidelberg: Springer-Verlag.

Waters, T. F. (1969). The turnover ratio in production ecology of freshwater invertebrates. *American Naturalist*, **103**, 173–185.

Watkins, J. L. (1986). Variations in the size of Antarctic krill, *Euphausia superba* Dana, in small swarms. *Marine Ecology Progress Series*, **31**, 67–73.

Watkins, J. L., Morris, D. J., Rickets, C. & Priddle, J. (1986). Differences between swarms of Antarctic krill and some implications for sampling krill populations. *Marine Biology*, **93**, 137–146.

Watson, G. E., Angle, G. E., Phillip, J., Harper, P. C., Bridge, M. A., Schlatter, R. P., Tickell, W. L. W., Boyd, J. C. & Boyd, M. M. (1971). *Antarctic Map Folio Series*, 14, 1–18. Washington, DC: American Geographical Society.

Watson, G. E., Angle, J. P. & Harper, P. C. (1975). Birds of the Antarctic and SubAntarctic. *Antarctic Research Series*, **12**, 1–350.

Weber, L. H. (1984). Spatial variability of phytoplankton in relation to the distributional patterns of krill (*Euphausia superba*). PhD thesis, Texas A&M University, College Station, Texas.

Weber, L. H. & El-Sayed, S. Z. (1985a). Spatial variability of phytoplankton and the distributions and abundance of krill in the Indian Sector of the Southern Ocean. In *Antarctic Nutrient Cycles and Food Webs*, ed. W. R. Siegfried, P. R. Condy & R. M. Laws, pp. 285–293. Berlin & Heidelberg: Springer-Verlag.

Weber, L. H. & El-Sayed, S. Z. (1985b). Phytoplankton studies in relation to krill investigations. Phytoplankton data from the February–April 1980 cruise of R.S.S.A. *Agulhas*. Technical Report, Texas A&M University, College Station, Texas.

Weber, L. H. & El-Sayed, S. Z. (1986a). Size fractionated phytoplankton standing crop and primary productivity in the west Indian sector of the Southern Ocean (R. S. S. A. *Agulhas* Cruise; February–March 1985). Technical Report, Texas A&M University, College Station, Texas.

Weber, L. H. & El-Sayed, S. Z. (1986b). Phytoplankton data from the November–December 1984 cruise of the *Polarstern* to the BransfieldStrait/Elephant Island region of the Southern Ocean. Technical Report, Texas A&M University, College Station, Texas.

Weber, L. H. & El-Sayed, S. Z. (1987). Contribution of net-, nano- and picoplankton to the phytoplankton standing crop and primary productivity of the Southern Ocean. *Journal of Plankton Research*, **9**, 973–994.

Weber, L. H., El-Sayed, S. Z. & Hampton, I. (1986). Variance spectre of phytoplankton, krill and water temperature in the Atlantic Ocean south of Africa. *Deep-Sea Research*, **33**, 1327–1343.

Weeks, W. F. & Ackley, S. F. (1982). The growth, structure, and properties of sea ice. CCREL Monograph 82–1. Hanover, NH: United States Army Cold Regions Research and Engineering Laboratory.

Weeks, W. F. & Lee, O. S. (1962). The salinity distribution in young sea ice. *Arctic*, **15**, 92–109.

Wefer, G., Suess, E., Balzer, W., Liebezeit, G., Miller, P. J., Ungerer, A. & Zenk, W. (1982). Flux of biogenic components from sediment trap deployment in circumpolar waters of the Drake Passage. *Nature* (London), **199**, 145–147.

Wefer, G., Fischer, G., Fuetterer, D. & Gersonde, R. (1988). Seasonal particle flux in the Bransfield Strait, Antarctica. *Deep–Sea Research*, **35**, 891–898.

Weimerskirch, H. (1982). La stratégie de reproduction de l'albatros fuligineux à dos sombre. *Comité National Français des Recherches Antarctique*, **51**, 437–447.

Wetzel, R. G. (1984). Detrital dissolved and particulate organic carbon functions in aquatic systems. *Bulletin of Marine Science*, **35**, 503–509.

Whitaker, T. M. (1977a). Sea ice habitats of Signy Island (South Orkneys) and their primary productivity. In *Adaptations Within Antarctic Ecosystems*, ed. G. A. Llano, pp. 75–82. Washington, DC:

428   *References*

Smithsonian Institution.

Whitaker, T. M. (1977b). Plant production in inshore waters of Signy Island, Antarctica. PhD thesis, University of London.

Whitaker, T. M. (1982). Primary production of phytoplankton off Signy Island, South Orkneys, the Antarctic. *Proceedings of the Royal Society of London, series B,* **214**, 169–189.

White, D. C., Smith, G. A. & Stanton, G. R. (1984). Biomass community structure, and metabolic activity of the microbiota in benthic marine sediments and sponge spicule mats. *Antarctic Journal of the United States*, 19, 125–126.

White, D. C., Smith, G. A., Nichols, P. D., Stanton, G. R. & Palmisano, A. (1985). Lipid composition and microbial activity of selected recent Antarctic benthic marine sediments and organisms: a mechanism for monitoring and comparing microbial populations. *Antarctic Journal of the United States*, 19, 130–132.

White, M. G. (1975). Oxygen consumption and nitrogen excretion by the giant Antarctic isopod *Glyptonotus antarcticus* Eights in relation to cold-adapted metabolism in marine polar poikilotherms. *Proceedings of the 9th European Marine Biology Symposium*, pp. 707–724.

White, M. G. (1977). Ecological adaptations by Antarctic poikilotherms to the polar marine environment. In *Adaptations Within Antarctic Ecosystems*, ed. G. A. Llano, pp. 197–108. Washington, DC: Smithsonian Institution.

White, M. G. (1984). Marine benthos. In *Antarctic Ecology,* Vol. 2, ed. R. M. Laws, pp. 421–461. London: Academic Press.

White, M. G. & Conroy, J. W. H. (1975). Aspects of competition between pygoscelid penguins at Signey Island, South Orkney Islands. *Ibis*, **117**, 371–373.

White, M. G. & Robins, M. W. (1972). Biomass estimates from Borge Bay, South Orkney Islands. *Bulletin British Antarctic Survey*, 31, 45–50.

White, M. G., North, A. W., Twelves, E. L. & Jones, S. (1982). Early development of *Notothenia neglecta* from the Scotia Sea, Antarctica. *Cybium*, **6**, 43–51.

Whitehead, M. D., Johnstone, G. W. & Burton, H. R. (1990). Annual fluctuations in productivity and breeding success of Adélie penguins and fulmarine petrels in Prydz Bay, East Antarctica. In *Antarctic Ecosystems. Ecological Change and Conservation*, ed. K. R. Kerry & G. Hempel, pp. 214–223. Berlin & Heidelberg, Springer-Verlag.

Wiebe, W. J. & Pomeroy, L. R. (1972). Microorganisms and their association with aggregates and detritus in the sea: a microscopic study. *Memories de l'Institut Italiano di Idriobiologia*, **24**(Supplement), 325–352. ʻ

Wigley, R. L. & McIntyre, A. D. (1964). Some quantitative comparisons of offshore meiobenthos and macrobenthos south of Martha's Vineyard. *Limnology & Oceanography*, **9**, 485–493.

Williams, A. J. (1984). The status and conservation of sea birds on some islands in the African sector of the Southern Ocean. In *The Status and Conservation of the World's Seabirds*, Technical Publication, No. 2, 627–636. The International Council for Bird Preservation.

Williams, A. J. & Siegfried, W. R. (1980). Foraging ranges if krill-eating penguins. *Polar Record*, **20**, 159–162.

Williams, A. J., Siegfried, W. R., Burger, A. E. & Berruti, A. (1977). Body composition and energy metabolism of moulting eudyptid penguins. *Comparative Biochemistry & Physiology*, **56A**, 27–30.

Williams, A. J., Burger, & Berruti, A. (1978). Mineral and energy contributions of carcasses of selected species of seabirds to Marion Island terrestrial ecosystem. *South African Journal of Antarctic Research*, **8**, 53–58.

Williams, A. J., Siegfried, W. R., Burger, A. E. & Berruti, A. (1979). The Prince Edward Islands: a sanctuary for seabirds in the Southern Ocean. *Biological Conservation*, **15**, 59–71.

Williams, P. J. LeB. (1975). Biological and chemical aspects of dissolved organic compounds in sea water. In *Chemical Oceanography,* Vol. 2, (2nd edn.), ed. J. P. Riley & G. Shirrow, pp. 301–363. London: Academic Press.

Williams, P. J. leB. (1981). Incorporation of microheterotrophic processes into classical paradigm of the plankton food web. *Kieler Meeresforschung Sonderheft*, **5**, 1–28.

Williams, P. J. leB., Berman, T. & Holm-Hansen, O. (1976). Amino acid uptake and respiration by marine heterotrophs. *Marine Biology*, **35**, 41–47.

Williams, R. (1983). The inshore fishes of Heard and Macquarie Islands, Southern Indian Ocean. *Journal of Fisheries Biology*, **23**, 283–292.

Williams, R. (1985a). Potential impact of a krill fishery upon pelagic fish in the Prydz Bay area of Antarctica. *Polar Biology*, **5**, 1–4.

Williams, R. (1985b). Trophic relationships between pelagic fish and euphausiids in Antarctic waters. In *Nutrient Cycles and Food Webs*, ed. W. R. Siegfried, P. R. Condy & R. M. Laws, pp. 452–459. Berlin & Heidelberg: Springer-Verlag.

Williamson, G. R. (1975). Minke whales off Brazil. *Scientific Reports of the Whales Research Institute (Tokyo)*, **27**, 37–59.

Wilson, D. L., Smith, W.O., Jr. & Nelson, D. M. (1986). Phytoplankton bloom dynamics of the western Ross Sea ice edge. I. Primary productivity and species-specific production. *Deep-Sea Research*, **33**, 1375–1387.

Wilson, E. A. *(1907). Stenorhincus leptonyx*, the sea leopard. *National Antarctic Expedition, 1901–1904. Natural History, Zoology*, **2**, 26–30.

Wilson, E. O. & Bossert, W. H. (1971). *A Primer of Population Biology*. Sunderland: Sinauer Associates.

Wilson, G. J. (1983). Distribution and abundance of Antarctic and sub-Antarctic penguins: a synthesis of current knowledge. BIOMASS Scientific Series No. 4. 46 pp.

Wilson, K. J. (1990). Fluctuations in populations of Adélie penguins at Cape Bird, Antarctica. *Polar Record*, 26, 305–308.

Wilson, R. P. (1989). Preliminary assessment of depth utilization by Adélie and Gentoo Penguins at Esperanza, Antarctica. *Cormorant*, **17**, 1–8.

Wilson, R. P., Culik, B. M., Adelung, D., Spairani, H. J. & Coria, N. R. (1991). Depth utilization by breeding penguins, *Pygoscelis adeliae*, at Esperanza Bay, Antarctica. *Marine Biology*, **109**, 181–189.

Witek, Z., Koronkeiwicz, A. & Soszka, G. J. (1980). Certain aspects of the early life history of krill, *Euphausia superba* Dana (Crustacea). *Polish Polar Research*, **1**, 97–115.

Witek, Z., Grelowski, A. & Wolnomiejski, N. (1981). Studies in aggregations of krill (*Euphausia superba*). *Meresforschung*, **28**, 228–243.

Witek, Z., Grelowski, A. & Kalinowsky, J. (1982a). Formation of Antarctic krill concentrations in relation to hydrodynamic processes and social behaviour. *ICES CM 1982/L*, 59.

Witek, Z., Pastuzak, M. & Grelowski, A. (1982b). Net-phytoplankton abundance in western Antarctic and its relationship to environmental conditions. *Meeresforschung*, **29**, 166–180.

Witek, Z., Kittel, W., Czkieta, H., Zmijewoska, M. I. & Presler, E. (1985). Macrozooplankton in the Southern Drake Passage and the Bransfield Strait during BIOMASS-SIBEX (December 1983–January 1984). *Polish Polar Research*, **6**, 95–115.

Witek, Z., Kalinowski, J. & Grelowski, A. (1988). Formation of Antarctic krill concentrations in relation to hydrodynamic processes and social behaviour. In *Antarctic Ocean and Resources Variability*, ed. D. Saharhage, pp. 237–244. Berlin Heidelberg: Springer-Verlag.

Wohlschlag, D. E. (1964). Respiratory metabolism and ecological characteristics of some fishes in McMurdo sound, Antarctica. *Antarctic Research Series*, **1**, 33–62.

Wolnomiejski, N., Chlapowski, K., Porebski, J. & Gorbacik-Wesolowka, A. (1978). Obserwacje nad ekologia antarktyczrego kryala (*Euphausia superba* Dana) *Studi i Materialy MIR, Gdynia, A23*. 9 pp. (In Polish).

Wood, W. F. (1987). Effect of solar ultra-violet radiation on the kelp

Ecklonia radiata. Marine Biology, **96**, 143–150.

Woodley, J.D. *et al.* (1991). Hurricane Allen's impact on Jamaican coral reefs. *Science*, **214**, 749–755.

Wormuth, J. H. (1987). Interannual variability in Antarctic zooplankton populations round the tip of the Antarctic Peninsula (abstract). *Intergovernmental Oceanographic Commisssion Report*, **50**, 10.

Worrest, R. C. (1982). Review of the literature concerning the impact of UV-B radiation upon marine organisms. In The *Role of Solar Ultraviolet Radiation in Marine Ecosystems*, ed. J. Calkins, pp. 429–457. New York: Plenum Press.

Worrest, R. C. (1983). Impact of solar ultraviolet-B radiation (290–320 nm) upon marine microalgae. *Physiologia Plantarum*, **58**, 428–434.

Worrest, R. C., Van Dyke, H. & Thompson, B. E. (1978). Impact of enhanced solar ultraviolet radiation upon a marine community. *Photochemistry & Photobiology*, **27**, 471–478.

Worrest, R. C., Wolniaowski, K. U., Scott, J. D., Brooker, D. L., Thompson, B. E. & Van Dyke, H. (1981). Sensitivity of marine phytoplankton to UV-B radiation: impact upon a model ecosystem. *Photochemistry Photobiology*, **33**, 223–227.

Wright, R. T. & Coffin, R. B. (1984). Measuring microzooplankton grazing on planktonic marine bacteria by its impact on bacterial production. *Microbial Ecology*, **10**, 137–149.

Wyanski, D. M. & Targett, T. E. (1981). Feeding biology of fishes in the endemic Antarctic Harpagiferidae. *Copeia*, **3**, 686–693.

Yamaguchi, Y. & Shibata, Y. (1982). Standing stock and distribution of phytoplankton chlorophyll in the Southern Ocean south of Australia. *Transactions of the Tokyo University of Fisheries*, **5**, 111–128.

Yamanaka, I. (1983). Interaction among krill, whales and other mammals in the Antarctic ecosystem. *Memoirs National Institute of Polar Research, Special Issue*, **27**, 220–232.

Yeates, G. W. (1968). Studies on the Adélie Penguin at Cape Royds 1964–65 and 1965–66. *New Zealand Journal of Marine & Freshwater Research*, **2**, 472–496.

Yeates, G. W. (1975). Microclimate, climate and breeding success in Antarctic penguins. In *The Biology of Penguins*, ed. B. Stonehouse, pp. 397–409. London: MacMillan.

Yentsch, C. S. & Yentsch, C. M. (1982). The attenuation of light by marine phytoplankton with special reference to the absorption of near UV radiation. In *The Role of Ultraviolet Radiation in Marine Ecosystems*, ed. J. Catkins, pp. 691–706. New York: Plenum Press.

Young, E. C. (1963a). The breeding behaviour of the South Polar Skua *Catharacta maccormicki. Ibis*, **105**, 205–233.

Young, E. C. (1963b). Feeding habits of the South Polar Skua *Catharacta maccormicki. Ibis*, **105**, 301–318.

Young, E. C. (1980). The present status of Antarctic Ornithology. *Bulletin of the British Ornithological Council*, **100**, 102–115.

Yukhov, V. L. (1971). The range of *Dissostichus mawsoni* Norman and some features of its biology. *Journal of Ichthyology*, **11**, 8–18.

Zacharov. G. P. & Frolkina, Z. A. (1976). Some data on the distribution and biology of Patagonian toothfish (*Dissostichus eleganoides* Smitt) occurring in the southwest Atlantic *Trudy Atlantic VIRO*, **65**, 143–150. (In Russian).

Zaneveld, J. S. (1966a). The occurrence of benthic marine algae under shore-fast ice in the western Ross Sea, Antarctica. *Proceedings of the 5th International Seaweed Symposium, Halifax, 1965*, pp. 217–231. London: Pergamon Press.

Zaneveld, J. S. (1966b). Vertical zonation of Antarctic and sub-Antarctic benthic marine algae. *Antarctic Journal of the United States*, **1**, 211–213.

Zaneveld, J. S. (1968). Benthic marine algae. Ross Island. *Antarctic Map Folio Series*, Vol. 10, pp. 10–12. American Geographical Society.

Zdanowski, K.M. (1985). Distribution of bacteria, organic carbon and amino acids in the southern part of the Drake Passage and Bransfield Strait during BIOMASS-SIBEX (December 1983–January 1984). *Polish Polar Research*, **6**, 43–63.

Zemsky, V. A. (1962). *Whales of the Antarctic*. Karlingrad. (In Russian.)

Zenkovich, B. A. (1969). Whales and plankton. In *Food and Feeding Behaviour of Whales*, ed. V. A. Asenev, B. A. Zenkovich & K. K. Chalskii, pp. 150–152. Moskova: Izdatel'stro Nauka. (In Russian.)

Zenkovich, B. A. (1970). Whales and plankton in Antarctic waters. In *Antarctic Ecology,* Vol. 1, ed. M. W. Holdgate, pp. 183–185. London: Academic Press.

Zink, M. (1981). Observations of seabirds during a cruise from Ross Island to Anvers Island, Antarctica. *Wilson Bulletin*, **93**, 1–20.

Zinova, A. D. (1958). Composition and character of the algal flora near the shores of the Antarctic Continent in the vicinity of Kerguelen and Macquarie Islands. *Information Bulletin Soviet Antarctic Expedition*, **3**, 47–49.

Zölzer, F. & Kiefer, J. (1989). Zelluläre Wirkungen der ultravioletten Komponente des Sonnenlichts. *Naturwissenschaften*, **76**, 489–495.

Zumberge, J. H. & Swithinbank, C. (1962). The dynamics of ice shelves. *Antarctic Research, Geophysical Monographs*, **7**, 197–218.

Zurr, R. (1977). The age and growth of *Trematomus bernacchi* and *Trematomus centronotus* at White Island, Antarctica. B. Sc. (Hons) thesis in Zoology, University of Canterbury, Christchurch, New Zealand.

Zvereva, Zh. A. ed. (1975). Seasonal changes of Antarctic plankton in the Molodozhnaya and Mirny region. Geographical and seasonal variations of marine plankton. *Exploration of Marine Fauna*, **12**. (Jerusalem, IPST. pp. 248–262).

Zwally, H. T., Comiso, J. C., Parkinson, C. L., Campbell, W. J., Carsey, F. D. & Gloersen, P. (1983a). *Antarctic Sea Ice, 1973–1976: satellite Passive-microwave Observations*. NASA Special Publication SP 459. 206 pp.

Zwally, H. J., Parkinson, C. L. & Comiso, J. C. (1983b). Variability of Antarctic sea ice and changes in carbon dioxide. *Science*, **220**, 1005–1012.

Index

Individual organisms are listed under vernacular and/or scientific names as used in the text; see both.